Music

The systematic academic study of music gave rise to works of description, analysis and criticism, by composers and performers, philosophers and anthropologists, historians and teachers, and by a new kind of scholar - the musicologist. This series makes available a range of significant works encompassing all aspects of the developing discipline.

A Dictionary of Musical Terms

This illustrated dictionary, written by the prolific Victorian composer Sir John Stainer (1840-1901) – best remembered today for his oratorio The Crucifixion – and W.A. Barrett, was first published by Novello in 1876. It provides definitions for 'the chief musical terms met with in scientific, theoretical, and practical treatises, and in the more common annotated programmes and newspaper criticisms', ranging from short explanations of the Italian words for tempi, through descriptions of ancient instruments to expansive articles on such topics as acoustics, copyright, hymn tunes, the larynx and temperament. That it subsequently ran to several further editions suggests that it provided welcome guidance for the concert-going public in the nineteenth century.

Cambridge University Press has long been a pioneer in the reissuing of out-of-print titles from its own backlist, producing digital reprints of books that are still sought after by scholars and students but could not be reprinted economically using traditional technology. The Cambridge Library Collection extends this activity to a wider range of books which are still of importance to researchers and professionals, either for the source material they contain, or as landmarks in the history of their academic discipline.

Drawing from the world-renowned collections in the Cambridge University Library, and guided by the advice of experts in each subject area, Cambridge University Press is using state-of-the-art scanning machines in its own Printing House to capture the content of each book selected for inclusion. The files are processed to give a consistently clear, crisp image, and the books finished to the high quality standard for which the Press is recognised around the world. The latest print-on-demand technology ensures that the books will remain available indefinitely, and that orders for single or multiple copies can quickly be supplied.

The Cambridge Library Collection will bring back to life books of enduring scholarly value across a wide range of disciplines in the humanities and social sciences and in science and technology.

A Dictionary of
Musical Terms

EDITED BY JOHN STAINER
AND WILLIAM BARRETT

CAMBRIDGE
UNIVERSITY PRESS

CAMBRIDGE UNIVERSITY PRESS

Cambridge New York Melbourne Madrid Cape Town Singapore São Paolo Delhi

Published in the United States of America by Cambridge University Press, New York

www.cambridge.org
Information on this title: www.cambridge.org/9781108000918

This edition first published 1876
This digitally printed version 2009

ISBN 978-1-108-00091-8

A DICTIONARY

OF

MUSICAL TERMS

EDITED BY

J. STAINER, M.A., Mus. Doc.,

MAGD. COLL., OXFORD,

AND

W. A. BARRETT, Mus. Bac.,

S. MARY'S HALL, OXFORD.

LONDON:

NOVELLO, EWER AND CO.,

1, BERNERS STREET (W.), AND 35, POULTRY (E.C.)

PREFACE.

IN a work of reference of this kind it is always difficult to find any definite principle by which to include or exclude the words to be explained. On the one hand, if all words—however rare their use in music—were to be given, the bulk of the book would be inconveniently large: on the other hand, words seldom met with are from that very fact often more in need of explanation.

The Editors hope, that from practical experience and knowledge, they have succeeded in collecting the chief musical terms met with in scientific, theoretical, and practical treatises, and in the more common annotated programmes and newspaper criticisms. That every subject should be treated in an exhaustive manner would be, of course, impossible; but the Editors have endeavoured to give sufficiently true outlines of matters of fact to inform the amateur correctly, and intimate to the musical student the results to which his own reading will probably tend.

The Editors are largely indebted to the following gentlemen who have contributed important articles, or have in other ways rendered them valuable assistance :—

R. H. M. Bosanquet, Esq., M.A., Fellow of St. John's College, Oxford, author of the article " TEMPERAMENT."

J. Bulley, Esq., M.A., of the Middle Temple, Barrister-at-Law, author of the articles " LICENSING " and " COPYRIGHT."

F.. Champneys, Esq., M.A., M.B. (Oxon), M.R.C.P., F.L.S., Medical Registrar of St. Bartholomew's Hospital; late Radcliffe Travelling Fellow of the University of Oxford, author of the articles " EAR," " LARYNX," and " LARYNGOSCOPE ;" and for his explanation of the formation of the hand given in the article " FINGERING."

W. Chappell, Esq., F.S.A., author of the articles " BALLAD " (Old English), " GREEK MUSIC " (Ancient Systems of), and " NOTATION " (Early Systems of).

A. E. Donkin, Esq., M.A., F.R.A.S., Fellow of Exeter College, Oxford, author of the article " ACOUSTICS."

A. J. Ellis, Esq., B.A., F.R.S., F.S.A., F.C.P.S., F.C.P., formerly Scholar of Trinity College, Cambridge, author of the article " DUODENE."

Henry Gadsby, Esq., for his account of Sonata Form in the article " FORM."

Rev. T. Helmore, M.A., Chaplain-in-Ordinary to the Queen, author of the article " PLAIN SONG."

John Hullah, Esq., Government Inspector of Training Schools, for extracts from a paper read before the Musical Association on "NOMENCLATURE."

W. G. McNaught, Esq., author of the article "TONIC SOL-FA."

W. H. Monk, Esq., Professor of Vocal Music, King's College, London, author of the article "HYMN TUNES."

Also to—

Messrs. Broadwood, for permission to publish diagrams of their pianoforte action.

Messrs. Cassell, for permission to quote from Musical Articles in the "Bible Educator."

Messrs. Chappell, for permission to quote from "Popular Music in the Olden Time."

Messrs. Erard, for permission to reproduce their diagrams of pianoforte action.

A. J. Hipkins, Esq., for valuable information on the subject of Tuning-Forks and Pitch.

W. H. Husk, Esq., for an important list of early printed music, and other assistance.

Messrs. Murray, for permission to quote music from Lane's "Modern Egyptians."

Sacred Harmonic Society, for offering special facilities for the use of their valuable library.

Rev. J. Troutbeck, M.A., Chaplain-in-Ordinary to the Queen, for permission to reprint diagrams from Troutbeck and Dale's "Music Primer."

Henry Willis, Esq., for diagrams and explanations of his Pneumatic Bellows.

DICTIONARY

OF

MUSICAL TERMS.

A. (1) The note called *Proslambanomenos* in the greater perfect system of the Greeks. The letter-name of *Mese*, the highest note of the middle tetrachord; and of *Nete*, the highest note of the upper tetrachord. [Greek Music.]

— (2) The first note of (1) the Hypo-Dorian mode, or church-scale, commencing four notes below the Dorian; (2) the Hyper-Phrygian mode, or church-scale, commencing four notes above the Phrygian; (3) the Eolian mode. [Greek Music.]

— (3) The next note above Gamma Ut, in the Grave Hexachord of the Guidonian system, where it is *A re.* Also, the first note of the acute and super-acute Hexachords, in which it is *a la mi re.* [Notation.]

— (4) The normal minor scale of modern music, so-called because it is the relative minor of C. It is sometimes also named the *natural* minor scale, because no sharps or flats are required in its signature.

— (5) The normal sound (*Ger.Normalton*), because the instruments of an orchestra tune to this note, as given by the Oboe or Organ.

— (6) The key-note of the major scale, which has three sharps for its signature.

— (7) The name given to a string tuned to the sound A. The A-string of a violin is its *second* string; of a viola, its *first* string; of a violoncello, its *first* string; but on this instrument it is one octave lower in pitch than the A-string of a violin or viola; of a Double-Bass, its *third* string, which is two octaves lower in pitch than the first string of a violoncello; of a guitar, its *sixth* string. The string tuned highest in pitch is called the first string of an instrument; the next below it, the second; and so on.

— (8) The actual sound ♯ is in some systems represented by A (capital letter), while AA represents the note one octave below that sound, and AAA the note two octaves below

it. Proceeding upwards, the note one octave above A is represented by a (italic); that two octaves above it by *a* (once underlined); that three octaves above it, by *a* (twice underlined), and so on. [Pitch.]

A. (*It.*) At, by, in, for, to, with, towards, &c.; *a prima vista,* at first sight; *a battuta,* lit. by the beat, in strict time; *a tempo,* in time, &c. &c.; *q.v. sub vocibus.*

A. (*Fr.*) For, by, on; *à deux mains,* for two hands, &c.; *q.v. sub vocibus.*

Abacus (*Lat.*) ἄβαξ (*Gk.*) Any square tablet; hence, a board on which calculations were made; hence, in music, a diagram of the notes with their names.

A ballata (*It.*) (1) In the ballad style. Applied to any song, duet, or chorus, constructed in the ballad or narrative form. Also to a song with a refrain in chorus, as is found in many old and modern English songs; for example, the song of which a portion runs:

> "Ich have house and land in Kent,
> And if you love me, love me now;
> Two pence half penny is my rent,
> Ich cannot come everich day to woo."

Chorus.

> " Two pence half penny is his rent,
> He cannot come everich day to woo "

—is a song, *a ballata.*

(2) The term is also used to describe a vocal piece, that may be danced to. [Ballad.]

Abbandonamente (*It.*) With self-abandonment, despondingly.

Abbandonarsi (*It.*) To abandon oneself (to the influence of the music).

Abbandono, con (*It.*) With self-abandonment, passionately.

Abbassamento (*It.*) A lowering. *Abbassamento di mano,* a lowering of the hand; *abbassamento di voce,* a lowering of the voice.

A battuta (*It.*) In strict time. This term is usually employed when a break in the time of

A

a movement has occurred, and it is desirable to resume the original pace "by the beat."

WEBER.

-die angst die je-de Hoffnung raubt.

Abbelire (*It.*) To overload a plain melody with ornaments.

Abbelitura (*It.*) Ornament, embellishment.

Abblasen (*Ger.*) To sound a trumpet call.

Abbreviare (*It.*) To shorten.

Abbreviation. A system frequently employed in music, by which a portion of a technical term is made to stand for the whole. The following is a list of the abbreviations in most common use; the explanation of each term may be found on reference to the words themselves in their proper places:

Accel. ... / Accel⁰ ... }	Accelerando
Acc. ... / Accom... / Accomp. }	Accompaniment
Accres......	Accresciamento
Adg⁰ or ad⁰.	Adagio
Ad l ...... / Ad lib ... }	Ad libitum
Affett⁰ ...	Affettuoso
Affrett⁰ ...	Affrettando
Ag⁰ ...... / Agit⁰ ... }	Agitato
All⁰	Allegro
Allgtt⁰ ...	Allegretto
All' ott... / All' 8ᵛᵃ... }	All' ottava
Al seg	Al segno
And⁰⁰	Andantino
And⁰ᵉ	Andante
Anim⁰	Animato
Arc ...... {	Coll Arco, or Arcato
Arp⁰......	Arpeggio
Ard⁰......	Ardito
A t. ...... / A tem ... / A temp .. }	A tempo
Aug ...... {	By Augmentation.
B .... {	Bass (voice) / Bassoon / Contre Bass
B C........	Basso continuo
Brill........	Brillante
C.B.	Col Basso
C.D.	Colla destra
C.S.	Colla sinistra
Cad	Cadence
Cal	Calando
Can	Cantoris
Cant	Canto

Cantab ...	Cantabile
Cello	Violoncello
Cemb	Cembalo
Ch.	Choir organ
Chal	Chalameau
Clar	Clarinet
Clar⁰ᵗᵗᵒ ...	Clarinetto
Clar	Clarino
Co. So. ...	Come Sopra
Col C. ...	Col Canto
Col ott⁸ ...	Coll' ottava
Col Vo. ...	Colla voce
Con. esp. {	Con espressione
Cor.	Cornet or horn
Cres⁰ ... / Cresc ... }	Crescendo
C.S.	Colla Sinistra
C. 8ᵛᵃ	Coll' ottava
C⁰ 1ᵐᵒ	Canto primo
Co. 1ᵐᵒ ...	Come primo
C⁰ᵗᵉ	Concerto
D. ...... {	Destra, droite, right
D.C.	Da Capo
Dec	Decani
Decres ...	Decrescendo
Delic	Delicamente
Dest	Destra
Diap	Diapasons
Dim	By Diminution
Dim	Diminuendo.
Div	Divisi
Dol	Dolce
Dolcis ...	Dolcissimo
Dopp. ped..	Doppio pedale
D.S.	Dal segno
Energ	Energicamente
Espr ... / Espres ... }	Espressivo
F. or for ...	Forte

Fag	Fagotto
Falset	Falsetto
Ff. or Fff...	Fortissimo
Fl.	Flauto
F.O. ... / F. Org. .. }	Full Organ
Fz. ... / Forz. ... }	Forzando
G	Gauche
G. O. ... / G. Org. ... / Gt. ...... }	Great Organ
Grand⁰ ...	Grandioso
Graz⁰ ...	Grazioso
Gr.	Grand
Hauptw. } / Hptw. ... / H.P ... }	Hauptwerk
Haut.	Hautboy
H.C.	Haute Contre
Intro.	Introduction
Inv	Inversion
L	Left
Leg	Legato
Legg⁰	Leggiero
L.H..........	Left hand
Lo.	Loco
Luo.	Luogo
Lusing. ...	Lusingando
M. ...... } / Main. ... / Mano. ... }	Manual
Maest⁰ ...	Maestoso
Magg	Maggiore
Man.........	Manuals
Manc ... / Man⁰⁰ ... }	Mancando
Marc.	Marcato
M.D...... {	Mano Diritta / Main Droite / Manu Dextrâ
M.G......	Main Gauche
M.M. ... {	Maelzel's Metronome
M.M. = 92 ... {	The beat of a crotchet is equal to the pulse of the pendulum of the Metronome said to be Maelzel's, with the weight set at 92.
M.P.	Mezzo piano
MS. ... {	Manuscript or Mano Sinistra
Mus. Bac {	Bachelor of Music
Men.	Meno
Mez.	Mezzo
M.V.	Mezzo voce
Mf. or Mff..	Mezzo forte
Modto. ...	Moderato
Mus. Doc..	Doctor of Music
Ob. ...... {	Oboe, or Hautbois

Obb.	Obbligato
Oberst. ...	Oberstimme
Oberw. .. / Obw. .. }	Oberwerk
Oh. ped. ...	Ohne pedal
Org.	Organ
8ᵛᵃ ...... / 8ᵃ ...... }	Ottava
8ᵛᵃ alta ...	Ottava alta
8ᵛᵃ bas. ...	Ottava bassa
P.	Piano
Ped.........	Pedal
Perd.	Perdendosi
P.F.	Piu forte
Piang.	Piangendo
Pianiss. ...	Pianissimo
Pizz.	Pizzicato
Pmo. ... / PP. ... }	Pianissimo
PPP. ... / PPPP.... }	Pianississimo
1ᵐᵃ.........	Prima
1ᵐᵒ.........	Primo
4ᵗᵗᵉ	Quartet
5ᵗᵗᵉ	Quintet
Rall.	Rallentando
Raddol. ...	Raddolcendo
Recit.	Recitative
Rf., rfz., / or rinf. }	Rinforzando
R.H.	Right hand
Ritar.	Ritardando
Riten.	Ritenuto
S.	Senza
ꭗ	A Sign
Scherz. ...	Scherzando
2ᵈᵃ	Seconda
2ᵈᵒ	Secondo
Seg.	Segue
Sem. ... / Semp. ... }	Sempre
7ᵗᵗ	Septet
6ᵗᵗ	Sestet
Sfz.	Sforzando
Smorz. ...	Smorzando
Sinf.	Sinfonia
S. Int.... {	Senza interruzione
S.S. ... / S. Sord . }	Senza Sordini
Sos. ...... / Sos⁴ ... }	Sostenuto
Spir	Spiritoso
S.T.	Senza Tempo
Stacc.	Staccato
St. Diap. {	Stopped Diapason
String......	Stringendo
Sw.	Swell organ
Sym.	Symphony
T. ...... {	Tenor, tutti, tempo, tendre
T.C..........	Tre corde
Tem.	Tempo
Tem. 1⁰ ...	Tempo primo
Ten.	Tenuto
Timb.	Timballes
Timp.	Timpani
Tr.	Trillo

(2)

Trem.	......Tremolando	V.	.........Volti
3º	.........Trio	Va.	.........Viola
Tromb.	...Trombi	Var.	......Variation
Tromb.	...Tromboni	Vcllo	......Violoncello
T.S.	......Tasto solo	Viv.	......Vivace
		Vo.	...
U.	........Una	Vno.	... } Violino
U.C.	......Una corda	Violº	...
Unis.	......Unisoni	V.S.	......Volti Subito
		Vⁿⁱ	...... } Violini
V.	.........Voce	V.V.	...

There are other abbreviations employed in manuscript or printed music, the chief of which are as follows:

In time, a dash with a figure above signifies the length of the pause in bars, *e.g.*:

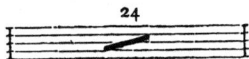

In notes, the trouble of writing a passage in full is saved by the use of abbreviations, *e.g.*:

Repetition phrases are thus shortened:

Abbreviations, by signs, of musical graces:

Abbreviature (*It.*). Abbreviations.
Abbreviazione (*It.*) An abbreviation.

Abcidiren (*Ger.*) (1) To use a system of solmisation. A series of exercises in which the names of the notes are used instead of words. (2) A method of instruction for sight singing.

Abellare (*It.*) To decorate, ornament, or embellish.

Abellimento (*It.*) A decoration, ornament, or embellishment.

Abendglocke (*Ger.*) The Curfew, evening bell.

A bene placito (*It.*) At pleasure. The singer or performer may alter the time, introduce ornaments, cadenzas, &c., according to fancy, or may use certain instruments specified, or not, without detriment to the effect required. [Chamber Music.]

Abenteuerlich (*Ger.*) Strange and uncouth. The music of the new German school is so called by the unthinking.

Abgestossen (*Ger.*) Struck off. Staccato.

AbgeleiteterAkkord (*Ger.*) An inversion of a chord.

Ab initio (*Lat.*) From the beginning. [Da capo.]

Abkürzungen (*Ger.*) Abbreviations.

Abréger (*Fr.*) To shorten, curtail, abridge.

Abrégé (*Fr.*) Shortened.

Abreissung (*Ger.*) A sudden pause.

Abrupt cadence. An interrupted cadence. [Cadence.]

Abrupt modulation. A sudden change of key for which no preparation has been made. [Modulation.]

Absatz (*Ger.*) Cadence. [Cadence.]

Abschnitt (*Ger.*) Section. [Phrase.]

Absetzen (*Ger.*) } To render music 'stac-
Abstossen (*Ger.*) } cato.'

Abub. [Ambubajæ.]

Abwechselnd (Ger.) Alternating, *mit abwechselnden Manualen*, alternately from the great to the choir organ.

Académie de Musique (*Fr.*) An academy of music.

Académie Royale de Musique (*Fr.*) The opera house in Paris.

Académie Spirituelle (*Fr.*) A concert or performance of sacred music.

Academy of Music. A name given to an organised society of performers and teachers of music; originally applied to the Royal Academy of Music, founded 1824 in London.

A cappella, or, Alla cappella (*It.*) (1) In the church style, vocal pieces unaccompanied, especially those of the Italian school, because the music sung in the Sistine Chapel was never accompanied by instruments. [School.]

(2) Church music in a duple time (two or four minims in each bar), this being for a long period considered more ecclesiastical than triple measure.

A capriccio (*It.*) At will, according to individual fancy.

Acathistus. A hymn of praise, sung in the Greek Church in honour of the Blessed Virgin, upon the Saturday in the fifth week in Lent, by the whole congregation standing.

Accarezzevole (*It.*) (Lit. flatteringly.) Agreeable, pleasing; used occasionally to describe the anticipation of notes.

Accarezzevolmente (*It.*) In a caressing style.

Accelerando or accellerato (*It.*) Gradually increasing the pace.

Accent (*Fr.*) A sign used in old French music for the Harpsichord:

The custom of employing a variety of ornaments in harpsichord music, arose from the fact that the instrument was not capable of sustaining tone without the use of repeated touches.

Accent.—In its ancient and widest sense, a sign placed over a syllable to indicate the elevation of the voice when pronouncing it. Hence, the term came to imply a raising upwards of the voice in the scale series from the monotone or note of recitation, to a sound of higher pitch. By using various forms of accents, different elevations of the voice were obtained, until a rude sort of chant resulted. The most ancient known accents, those of the Hebrews as found in the Pentateuch, Psalms, and Book of Job, were interpreted only by tradition, not according to definite rule. Unfortunately therefore in comparing the musical rendering of them as taken down in modern notation by authors in various parts of Europe, it will be found that their original force is now quite unknown, and that the various "foliations" which are supposed to represent their meaning, are the growth of many surrounding musical or other indirect influences.

2. In early Greek Church music, the accents had to a great extent, a plain and definite intention, and as they were fixed and adapted to various poems by John of Damascus in the 8th century, and their use has been kept up in its purity to this day in Byzantine music, a very good insight into early forms and principles of notation can be obtained. [Greek Church music.]

3. In mediæval music the term *accent* was also applied to musical notation, the first two and most common of the signs being the *accentus acutus*, and *accentus gravis*. Afterwards the term came to signify the system generally, and so became synonymous with *neuma*, under which head information as to

mediæval notation will be found. [Neuma.] [Old systems of *notation*.]

4. In plain song, the term accent, or *accentus ecclesiasticus*, was used to designate that system of movement of the voice, by learning the principles of which (*modus legendi choraliter*), a chanter could read collects, epistles, gospels, &c., from an un-noted book. Hence, it resolved itself into a series of rules relating to the inflexions or intonations of the voice on reaching a comma, semicolon, colon, full stop, and also a note of interrogation. But perfect uniformity is not to be found in these regulations regarding the *puncta*. According to its position in the sentence, or the interval covered by the movement of the voice, accent was said to be (1) immutabilis, (2) medius, (3) gravis, (4) acutus, (5) moderatus, (6) interrogativus, (7) finalis. The following are examples of these different species:

immutabilis.

Lec-ti-o E-pi-sto-læ Sanc-ti Pau-li

medius.

et o-pe-ra-tur vir-tu-tes in vo-bis:

gravis.

Be-ne-fi-cen-tur in Te om-nes gen-tes.

acutus.

Cum Spi-ri-tu cœ-pe-ri-tis nunc,

moderatus.

cum fi-de-li, ex o-pe-ri-bus le-gis,

interrogativus.

an ex au-di-tu fi-de-i?

finalis.

A-ni-ma me-a ad Te De-us.

But according to some authors, the epistle should be on monotone, except at a point of interrogation, *e.g.*:

Lec-ti-o li-bri Sa-pi-en-ti-æ

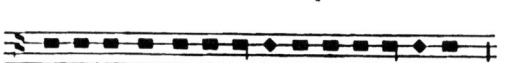
Be-a-tus vir qui in-ventus est si-ne ma-cu-lâ, &c.

Quis est hic et lau-da-bi-mus e-um?

But in some countries, the epistle is chanted with the greatest elaboration, the note above the reciting note being introduced before the full stop, and the whole of an interrogative sentence being recited on a note below the *ut*. But as these uses differ not only in various places, but according to the Church seasons, an exhaustive account is impossible.

In chanting the gospel, an *accentus medius* takes place at the fourth syllable from a full stop, or thereabouts, and also the *accentus interrogativus*.

Se - quen - ti - a Sanc - ti Ev - an - ge - li - i

se - cun - dum Mat - thæ - um, &c. In il - lo

tem - po - re dix - it Si - mon Pe - trus ad Je - sum, &c.

quid er - go e - rit no - bis? &c. Et vi - tam

e - ter - nam pos - si - de - bit.

In the chanting of collects, a fall from Ut to La, or from Fa to Re takes place at a *punctum principale*, and from Ut to Si, or Fa to Mi once only at a *semipunctum*.

The accentus ecclesiasticus of lections and prayers must not be confused with those inflexions which tradition assigns to other parts of the service, such as confessions, proper prefaces, and lections of the Passion; all of which are to be found noted in authorised books. It should be remarked that the Belgian and French uses often differ much from that of the Romans, although uniformity in such things is without doubt desirable.

5. In modern music, accent is the stress which recurs at regular intervals of time. By the proper grouping of a series of accents, rhythm is produced. When music was indissoluble from poetry, a sign for marking accent was not needed, but it is necessary to point out in order to avoid confusion, that our word accent corresponds more to the ancient *ictus* than to *arsis*. For although the latter represented a raising of the voice, it did not necessarily occur on a long syllable, whereas it is considered a fault in modern music, if a short syllable occurs on an accented note. The position of the accent is plainly and simply indicated by upright strokes called bars [Bar], it being understood that the first note inside a bar is without exception accented. The measurement of the whole duration of

the notes between these accents, is recorded at the commencement of a movement, and constitutes what is called the time-signature. In bars containing more than one group of notes, as is the case in compound times, other accents occur on the first note of each group, but they are not so strong as that falling on the first note of the first group. The latter therefore is called the primary or principal accent; the former secondary or subordinate. Besides these normal positions of accents, there are others which can be produced at any point by the use of a sign > or *sf*. An accent can also be displaced for a time from its usual seat by binding an unaccented chord to a like chord at a point of accent, and so preventing its repercussion; or, by both combined.

Beethoven's Sym., No. 3.

The throwing of the accent on to an unaccented part of the bar is called syncopation. A similar effect can be produced by a process the converse of the above, that is by making rests fall where an ictus is expected, *e.g.*:

Beethoven's Sym. No. 3.

This intentional upsetting of our accepted notions of the expected position of accent is capable of a most remarkable and powerful effect. Heard by a musician just two centuries ago, its effect would probably not have been so striking, as he would have supposed the writer to have changed from triple to duple time, a constant habit in those days. Such accents are sometimes called *cross*, or *false*.

Accentuare (*It.*) To accent.

Accentuation. The act of accenting, or giving to certain notes their due emphasis.

Accessory stops and movements. Stops and movements acting only on the mechanism of an organ, not having pipes in connection with them, as, Couplers, Tremolo, Signal to the blowers; Composition pedals, &c.

Acciaccatura (*It.*) A short appogiatura, *e.g.*:

lightly yet clearly to be sung, or played.

Accidentals. Sharps, flats, or naturals, introduced into a piece of music, beyond those already in the signature.

A cinque (*It*). In five parts.

Accollade (*Fr.*) A brace, uniting several staves, as in pianoforte or organ music, or in a score.

Accommodare (*It.*) To tune an instrument in agreement with another.

Accompagnamento (*It.*) } [Accompani-
Accompagnement (*Fr.*) } ment.]

Accompaniment *ad libitum*. *Accompaniment at will*. That is, one which can be played or omitted without injury to the harmonic construction of a composition, c.f. *obbligato*.

Accompaniment *obbligato*. [Obbligato.]

Accompaniment. A separate part or parts, for voices or instruments, added to a solo or concerted piece. Accompaniment may consist of a single simple instrument, such as a violin or flute, or a single compound instrument as an organ or pianoforte, a combination of selected orchestral instruments, or a whole band, or of voices in harmony. Accompaniments are those portions of a composition which are independent of the principal parts, and which are added to support, or to produce such effects as would be otherwise unattainable. Accompaniment should always be subservient to the chief part. so as not to overload or obscure it, and should be so constructed, that the voice or voices or solo instruments should be made to appear to the most favourable advantage. In the earliest records we possess, it is found that some sort of accompaniment was generally employed either to assist the voice, or mark the time or rhythm of the songs sung: of these many examples could be quoted if it were necessary. In the Bible, instances are mentioned in which singing is accompanied by musical instruments; but of the nature of these accompaniments we can form no definite idea, beyond the fact that, from a comparative knowledge of the instruments spoken of, it is presumed that little, if any

attempt was made to gain independent effects. The ancient Greek dance, and the poetry of the tragedy, was always accompanied, at first with the lyre, afterwards with the flute.

Donaldson, in his "Theatre of the Greeks," says, that the Ancient Dorian Choral song, the Pœan, was originally accompanied with the Harp (φόρμιγξ.)

According to modern views, an accompaniment implies some construction in harmony, but the ambiguity with which the terms melody and harmony are employed by the ancient Greek and Latin, as well as by the more modern writers, has given rise to a doubt as to whether they had any knowledge of the art of combining certain concords according to such rules as we now possess. The science of harmony is of relatively modern growth, and the art of employing instruments in combination, as accompaniments to vocal music, is more recent than the growth of harmony.

It has been stated that dancing is of greater antiquity than singing, and that singing was generally the usual accompaniment to dancing. The same root supplying many words referring alike to dancing, singing, and playing, suggests a common origin for dancing and its accompaniment. Most of the words of ancient ballads are set to tunes that were danced to, and the practice is still observed of arranging words to melodies, that were originally intended to accompany the dance. So that the "new" idea of singing waltzes or other dance measures, is but a revival of the ancient practice. Nothing seems more natural than that those not actually engaged in dancing, but as interested spectators, upon the recurrence of a musical phrase should accompany it with the voice. This would form such a burden or chorus as that alluded to by Shakespeare :

"Foot it featly here and there,
 And let the rest the burden bear."

Some simple instrument would be employed to play the tune, either with or without some means of marking the time or rhythm; a combination like that of the pipe and tabour, would form an adequate accompaniment to the dance, as the burden would to the song. As most of the mediæval learning and accomplishments came through the Church, it is very reasonable to assume that the methods of the Church would be reflected in the practices of every-day life. And as it is known that the organs employed in the service were so constructed as to be adapted only for the purposes of melody, it is scarcely probable that harmony should have been in use as an accompaniment to secular songs and tunes. Although instruments were employed as accompaniments to the voice, there is no reason for supposing that they were not at times engaged in the performance of purely instrumental pieces, but on the contrary, the numerous instances in which musical instruments are mentioned in ancient English poetry, show that the performers were not only accustomed to accompany singing with their several instruments, but they also imply that they were able to play independent pieces. [Mediæval musical instruments.]

In some instances we find that the accompanist was distinct from the singer, for example: " In Alwyni episcopi . . . et durante pietancia in aula conventus, sex ministralli, cum quatuor citharisatoribus, faciebant ministralcias suas." Regis. Prior: S. Swithini Winton (c. 1374). It cannot be ascertained whether the harpers did any more than play the same melody to which the poems were recited, or by the constant repetition of certain notes serve any other purpose but that of maintaining the pitch or rhythm.

The following quotation from David Lyndsay's poem, " The Dreme," 1579, implies the performance of a purely instrumental piece:

" Thay beir ane ald stok-image throu the toun,
With talbrone, trumpet, shalme, and clarione."

Whether this combination produced concord, or unison, it is impossible now to decide, for, as before stated, the loose manner with which the terms melody and harmony are employed helps to confuse, rather than to make clear all conjecture. For example:

" And all above there lay a gay sautrie,
On which he made on nightis melodye." *Chaucer.*

Again, in the " Lyfe of Saint Werburge," printed by Pynson in 1521, we read :

" Certayne at each course of service in the Hall
Trumpettes blewe up, shalmes, and claryouns
Shewynge theyr melody, with toynes musycall "

and again in the same poem :

" A singuler Mynstrell, all other ferre passynge
Toyned his instrument in pleasaunt armony."

In the two first quoted examples, that which is called melody might well be harmony, and in the third, that which is called harmony might well be melody.

In nearly every list of instruments of minstrelsy, there are one or two pulsatile instruments spoken of — " Tymphans, tabours, nacaires," whose use was to mark the rhythm, sung, played, or danced to ; but where these regular instruments were wanting, the clapping of hands, the beating of a stick upon a shovel, or the clashing of two sticks together, or the " ancient natural instruments of our islands," as Dr. Burney calls the tongs, marrow-bones and cleavers, salt-box and rolling-pin, with the hurdy-gurdy, were employed as accompaniments to rustic songs or dances. These " natural instruments" required little skill to use, beyond a correct sense of rhythm, though there are instances on record where some degree of science was brought to bear in their employment. The butchers of Clare Market, in the parish of St. Clement Danes in London, were at one time noted for their aptitude in playing tunes with marrow-bones upon cleavers of various sizes capable of sounding a scale of notes, in a manner somewhat similar to the hand-bell ringing in the North of England, but their performances were ultimately made independent, and therefore could scarcely be considered as accompaniments. Addison's description of a Burlesque musician, and his cultivation of strange instruments for accompaniment, may be read with interest in reference to this subject (Spectator, No. 570.) Skelton, in his description of RIOT, speaks of one, who

" Counter he coulde, O LUX, upon a potte,"

probably meaning that while he sang the melody of the ancient hymn, " O Lux, beata Trinitas," he would beat upon the vessel he had been drinking out of, a part, in derisive imitation of the florid counterpoint sung by the monks during service. The poets and authors of the middle ages give no lucid information concerning the abilities of the musicians of their times, probably on the presumption, that because the method of their performances was well known and understood by every one, no particular description was needed. All our knowledge on the subject is derived from inference, and so it is assumed that the minstrels and later musicians, previously to the 16th century, had little, if any, knowledge of harmony; or if they had, they probably left the practice of it to the Church.

There is a further reason for supposing that the ancient minstrels accompanied their songs by playing the same melody which was sung, in the character of the majority of the instruments alluded to in old writings :—

" Harpys, fythales, and eke rotys
Lutys, ribibles, and geternes,
Orguys, cytolis, monacordys
 . . . . trumpes, and trumpettes
Lowde shaluys, and doncettes."

The drone of the bagpipe and the fundamental sound of the drum might suggest the formation of harmony; the character and construction of the earliest piece of harmony we possess, " Sumer is icumen in" offering curious confirmation of this notion.

All writers are agreed as to this being the oldest song with musical notes extant. Warton believed it to belong to the 15th century, but Sir Frederick Madden showed it to be at least two hundred years older; and judging by the character in which it is written, and other evidence, fixed its date at about the year 1250. It is among the Harleian MSS. in the British Museum, The piece is arranged as a continuous melody; but by commencing that melody at certain indicated places, it forms a canon in the unison in four parts, with a "pes," a foot, or burden for two other parts.

The first attempts at accompaniment in harmony were arranged for the voice, in a manner that to our ears would be simply barbarous [Diaphony], [Descant], [Fa burden]. It was only by slow degrees that it was discovered that certain instruments were capable of producing complicated sounds forming harmony, and were therefore especially valuable for accompaniment. The chief among these instruments was the Lute, which appears to have been a favourite instrument in Chaucer's time, and to have continued in favour in one form or another, until the virginals and spinetts, being of more convenient form and less trouble to keep in order, completely superseded it. [Tablature.]

The opportunity the virginals and spinetts gave for the employment of both hands, tended considerably towards the improvement of accompaniments, as well as developing the power of execution for solo purposes. "Consorts of viols" were at first used only "for Cantilenas and tunes for dancing," though compositions were occasionally so arranged as "to be apt for viols or voyces," and when instruments were employed with voices they generally played the same notes as the voices, a practice observed until the time of Handel. No doubt an organist accompanying some of the services and anthems in Church, occasionally indulged in a little license in the matter of fingering, and introduced flourishes and cadences according to fancy, while the choir were singing the plain vocal harmonies. A copy of a portion of Gibbons's service in F [1583-1624] found among the old music in Magdalen College, Oxford, in which such variations are written down, is still preserved. Although the MS. belongs to the middle of the 17th century, there is no doubt but that it records a continuation of a custom of long standing. The character of this accompaniment may be seen by the following quotation:

A comparison of the vocal with the organ score, here shows that the ornaments introduced are such as involve little, if any departure from the rules of harmony, while they impart a distinct character to the accompaniment, such a character as most of the spinett or harpsichord music of the period possessed. The peculiarity of all old key-board stringed instruments, their feebleness of tone and their lack of sustaining power, probably suggested to the skilful player the necessity of breaking up the accompaniments to vocal music, ornaments and graces being considered perfectly legitimate so long as they did not interfere with the essential notes of the harmony as represented by the figured bass. But as in many cases it was doubtless deemed unwise to attempt display in the accompaniments during the singing, therefore all exhibition of skill on the part of the accompanist was reserved for the *ritornelli*, with which songs of the 17th century abound.

It was Monteverde [1568-1643] who, among other of his art-benefiting inventions, conceived the idea of constructing independent accompaniments for instruments, breaking up long notes into effective repetitions, and so imparting novel rhythms and striking instrumental figures. From his conception arose the Italian school of accompaniment—a school which influenced all musical teaching for more than a hundred years, and only decayed with the growth of a distinct style of instrumentation, the result of Italian ideas implanted in the German mind, after which the Symphony and Sonata, retaining names derived from their connection with vocal music, became independent and distinct, and accompaniment once more was lifeless and uninteresting, a mere adventitious aid. Indifference with regard to the part accompaniment should play, marked most of the music produced for a long period, but the power of the genius of Mendelssohn aroused new thoughts and new deeds, and care as great as that involved in the production of a vocal piece was employed in accompaniments, with true artistic effect. The followers of Wagner, in imitation of him, are striving to impart a new form to accompaniment, by giving to every instrument employed, a certain amount of independent work to do—a practice at once laudable and ingenious, but neither novel nor needful. It is laudable, for the reason that it is as well to interest the performer; it is ingenious, as no common amount of thought is involved in its production; it is not novel, for it was the practice of the Italian writers, and it is not needful, as accompaniment should always be subservient to the thing accompanied.

Purcell was among the first of the musicians in England who attempted to give colour to the accompaniments in the scores of his operas, but only occasionally introduced variety in the organ parts of his Anthems. The works of the musicians of the latter portion of the 17th and the commencement of the 18th centuries, show a desire to depart from the habitual rule, by giving independent melodies to the accompanying parts, specimens of which may be traced in Blow's Amphion, and contemporary works. The scores of J. S. Bach's "Passions" and other of his compositions, contain some excellent specimens of free instrumental parts in the accompaniments, and many of Handel's *obbligati* foreshadow the true use of orchestral colouring, a shadow to which substance was given by Haydn, Mozart, and Beethoven.

The influence of conventionality may be observed in accompaniments from the earliest period to the present day. Because it was the practice in olden time to accompany recitative upon the "cembalo," composers rarely thought of setting down more than a figured bass to these parts of their scores, excepting when the recitative took something of the form of the "soliloquæ;" and because the "maestro di cembalo" became an obsolete office in the orchestra, as soon as conductors considered it to be undignified to do other than direct with the bâton, it was necessary that some mode of accompanying recitative should be devised, and the figured bass was interpreted by a violoncello and double bass. Trumpets and drums were generally employed together, as much for rhythmical, as for any other purpose; and many other instances of the thoughtless practice of taking things for granted, and doing that which was held to be correct, because it was the custom, are to be found in well-known works of the lesser lights in music, the great thinkers constantly despising ordinary forms, and inventing new ones, which in their turn became models for imitation, and therefore standards of conventionality.

The bagpipe, fiddle, lute, cittern, virginals, spinett, harpsichord, pianoforte, harp, and guitar have each had their turns of favour and appreciation at several times.

The use of the guitar for an accompaniment became exceedingly popular during the latter part of the last century, to the injury of the makers of pianofortes, until Kirkman gave away a number of cheap guitars to milliners' apprentice girls, and so made the instrument unfashionable. The portability of both harp and guitar rendered them useful for the purposes of accompaniment, more especially at a time when the pianoforte was less frequently found in dwelling-houses than it is now; but improved mechanism and tone, together with smallness of cost, have made the pianoforte the most available accompanying instrument in private as well as in public; and the fact that one is to be found in nearly every house has contributed greatly towards the neglect of more portable means of accompanying songs and other household music.

Accompanist. The player who accompanies. The qualities necessary to form a good accompanist are, (1) that he possess a knowledge of reading music at sight, and of harmony; (2) that he should be acquainted with the style of the music performed; (3) that he should know the characteristics of those performers whom he is called upon to accompany; (4) that while playing with firmness and decision, he should not attempt to lead.

Accoppiato (*It.*) Joined or connected.

Accord (*Fr.*) (1) The series of notes to which an instrument is tuned, *e.g.*, *Accord du Violon*,

hence, *Accord à l'ouvert*, open strings, *q.v.*

(2) A chord. Concord, hence, *D'accord*, in tune.

Accord de sixte Ajoutée (*Fr.*) The chord of the Added Sixth. [Added Sixth.]

Accordamento (*It.*) } Agreement in tune.
Accordanza (*It.*) }

Accordando (*It.*) Tuning.

Accordare (*It.*) To tune.

Accordato (*It.*) Tuned.

Accordatura (*It.*) [Accord.]

Accorder (*Fr.*) To tune an instrument.

Accordeur (*Fr.*) A tuner.

Accordion. A simple musical instrument, of oblong form, invented by Damian, of Vienna, in 1829. The tone is produced by the inspiration and respiration of a pair of bellows acting upon metallic reeds or tongues. [Free reed.]

The first instruments had only four buttons, or keys, each of which acted on two reeds, making the compass one octave of diatonic scale, but with a separate arrangement, by which these notes might be accompanied with a tonic and dominant harmony. At first it was used only as a toy, but the introduction of a chromatic scale made the Accordion more capable of producing a varied melody and harmony, although the awkwardness of the form was always a hindrance to its use. The German Accordion or Concertina (*q.v.*) of hexagonal form made the principle of the accordion more acceptable. The English concertina (*q.v.*) and the harmonium (*q.v.*) are superior instruments constructed upon similar principles.

Accordo (*It.*) Concord, agreement, harmony.

Accordoir (*Fr.*) A tuning key or hammer.

Accresciuto (*It.*) Increased. Augmented as applied to intervals.

Acetabulum. An ancient instrument, originally made of earthenware, afterwards of metal, which, when struck with a rod, produced a sweet sound. [See an allusion to it in Boet. de Inst. Mus., Lib. i. cap. xi.]

Achromatic. Not chromatic.

Achtel (*Ger.*) A quaver ♪. The eighth part of a semibreve.

Achtelpause. A quaver rest 𝄾.

A chula (*Port.*) A dance similar to the Fandango, *q.v.*

Acoustics. The science which treats of the nature and laws of sound.

2. The sensation of sound consists in the communication of a vibratory motion to the tympanic membrane of the ear, through slight and rapid changes in the pressure of the air on its outer surface.

3. The mode of propagation of sound in air may be explained in the following manner. Suppose a small particle of fulminating silver to be exploded in free air; the air particles immediately contiguous are driven outwards in all directions by the explosion, their motion is almost instantaneously communicated to the adjacent ones, those first agitated coming at the same time to rest; the adjacent ones pass on the impulse in the same way to those at a greater distance, and so on; thus the explosion gives rise to what may be looked on as a rapidly expanding shell of constant thickness, containing at any instant between its exterior and interior surfaces a stratum of agitated air particles each one of which performs a single vibration to and fro during the passage of the shell over it; in other words the exterior and interior surfaces of the shell are at any time the *loci* of all those points at which the particles at that instant come under the influence of the impulse, and are left at rest by it respectively, so that its thickness depends both on the rapidity of their vibration and the rate at which they pass on the impulse, one to another.* Let us suppose now that immediately after the first explosion a second were to take place; then, in exactly the same way there would be a second pulse propagated in all directions. If a series of explosions at regular intervals were to take place, there would be a regular series of these expanding shells; and if the intervals were sufficiently small, the alternate changes of pressure, due to the successive collisions of the air particles against the tympanic membrane of an ear in the neighbourhood of the explosions would convey to the brain a sensation of a continuous note. Exactly the same thing occurs if, for a series of explosions, are substituted the vibrations of an elastic body; and it is, in general, by the latter means that all sounds, and especially musical ones, are produced. The motion of a sound wave must not be confounded with the motion of the particles which transmit the wave. In the passage of a single wave each particle over which it passes makes only a small excursion to and fro, the semi-length of which is called the *amplitude* of the vibration, the time occupied during one vibration being called its *period*.

4. The intensity of a sound is proportional to the square of the maximum velocity of the vibrating particles. It also approximately varies inversely as the square of the distance from the origin of the sound; for, supposing the latter to be produced at a uniform loudness, the same amount of energy has to be communicated to the particles contained within the external and internal surfaces of shells of the same thickness but of different *radii*. For

* The word vibration must be taken in its full sense, viz.: as meaning the whole motion of the particle during the time that elapses from the instant it sets off from its original position to the instant when it next regains that position, and is ready to start again over the same path.

example, if we take a shell of air whose internal radius is one foot, one of the same thickness whose radius is two feet will contain four times the quantity of matter; one whose radius is three feet, nine times the quantity, and so on. Thus the amount of matter over which a given quantity of energy has to be distributed augments as the square of the distance from the origin of sound, and therefore the amount of energy, or, what comes to the same thing, the intensity of the sound, diminishes in the same ratio.

5. At a temperature of *zero Centigrade* sound is propagated at the rate of about 1090 feet per second, and this speed augments about two feet per second for every additional degree of temperature; thus at 15° C. the rate of propagation would be about 1120 feet per second. The velocity of sound in air depends on the elasticity of the air in relation to its density. It is also directly proportional to the square root of the elasticity, and inversely proportional to the square root of the density. Now for a constant temperature the elasticity varies as the density, hence in this case they neutralise one another, and the velocity of the sound is independent of the density of the air.

6. One sound differs from another not only in quantity, but also in quality and pitch. * The pitch of a sound depends on the number of vibrations per second by which it is caused: the greater this number is the higher is the sound, and *vice versâ;* thus pitch is a more or less relative term, and it is therefore necessary to have some standard to which different sounds may be referred. This standard is so chosen that the middle C of the pianoforte shall be produced by 264 vibrations per second.†

7. Knowing the velocity of sound in air we can estimate the different wave lengths corresponding to notes of different pitch in the following manner. The wave length is the distance through which the sound travels while any particle over which it passes describes a complete vibration; hence, if we know the number of vibrations the particle performs per second, the required wave length will be found by dividing the number of feet over which the sound travels per second, by that number. Now, by means of an instrument invented by Cagniard de la Tour, and by him named the *syren*, the number of vibrations corresponding to a note

of any given pitch can be determined very exactly. For a detailed account of this instrument and of its improvements by Helmholtz, the reader is referred to Tyndall's Lectures on Sound, p. 64; but to describe it shortly it may be said in its original form to consist of two equal discs, one forming the top of a hollow fixed cylinder into which air can be driven, the other capable of revolving concentrically upon it with the smallest possible amount of friction. A circle of small holes equidistant from each other is bored upon each disc and concentric with it; those in the upper disc being inclined slantwise to its plane, those in the lower being slantwise also but in the opposite direction; there are also arrangements both for driving a constant supply of air into the hollow cylinder, and for registering the number of revolutions the upper disc performs in a minute; thus, when the upper disc is so turned that its holes coincide with those of the lower, and air is forced into the cylinder, it will pass out through the perforations, and by reason of their obliquity will cause the moveable disc to revolve with a rapidity corresponding to the pressure; and each time that the holes of the former coincide with those of the latter a number of little puffs of air get through simultaneously, giving rise to an agitation in the surrounding atmosphere which spreads round in all directions in the way before described, and if the pressure of the air in the cylinder is sufficient, the series of impulses thus given will link themselves together, forming a continuous note.‡

Hence, to determine the number of vibrations per second, corresponding to a sound of given pitch, we have only to maintain such a pressure of air in the syren as will cause it to produce the same sound for the space of a minute, and note the number of revolutions registered in that time. Now, for every revolution of the upper disc, the same number of sound waves are propagated around as there are perforations, hence the whole number propagated in a second will be the product of the number of holes and number of revolutions per minute divided by 60; and this result will evidently be the required number of vibrations per second caused by the given sound.

To apply this to find the wave length corresponding to the note given by the open C string of the violoncello, we should adjust the

‡ It should be remarked that the pitch of the sound would be exactly the same if there were only one perforation in the revolving disc, the number of holes merely serving to increase its intensity; if the number of holes in the revolving disc is less than the number in the lower one, those of the former must be situated so as all to coincide simultaneously with an equal number of the latter.

supply of air to the syren till it gives a note of the same pitch. Supposing the number of holes in each disc to be 18, the number of revolutions per minute would be found to be 220. Hence the number of vibrations per second of the string, and therefore of the surrounding particles of air, would be $\frac{220 \times 18}{60}=66$. Supposing the temperature were 16° C the velocity of sound would be about 1122 feet per second, and the quotient obtained by dividing this number by 66 gives the wave length corresponding to that number of vibrations per second; that is, just 17 feet; the sound then will travel through this distance during the time the string takes to perform one complete vibration.

8. If the number of vibrations per second be increased, the pitch of the sound caused by them is raised, and *vice versâ*, as can easily be illustrated by driving more or less air into the syren, and observing the sound it produces. Dr. Wollaston has shown (Phil. Trans. 1820, p. 336) that if the number be increased, beyond a certain limit the sound becomes inaudible, although this limit is not the same for all ears, some persons being perfectly sensible of sounds inaudible to others. In general it is probable that no sound is heard when the number of vibrations per second exceeds 40,000; while on the other hand the perception of pitch appears to begin when the number of vibrations is somewhere between 8 and 32, the wave length being in the former case about 0·03 of an inch—in the latter ranging from 140 feet to 35 feet.

9. Sounds are primarily divided into two classes, musical and unmusical; the former being defined as those produced by regular or periodic vibrations, the latter by such as are irregular or non-periodic. These definitions require some explanation, since, by sounding together a sufficient number of notes sufficiently near in pitch, it is plain that we could produce as unmusical a sound as we pleased, although the components would be themselves due to periodic vibrations, and would be therefore musical. The answer to this is found in the fact that when two or more sets of sound waves impinge on the ear at the same instant, since each one cannot impress its own particular vibration on the tympanum contemporaneously with those of the others, the motion of the latter membrane must be in some way the *sum* of all the different motions which the different sets of waves would have separately caused it to follow; and this is what in fact does happen, *i.e.*, the vibrations due to each set combine and throw the tympanum into a complicated state of vibration, causing the sensation of the consonance or combination of the different sounds from which the sets of sound waves proceed.

Now the unassisted ear is only able to distinguish the separate notes out of a number sounded at once up to a certain point; beyond this it fails to distinguish them individually, and is conscious only of a confused mixture of sounds which approaches the more nearly to the character of noise the more components there are, or the nearer they lie to one another. A noise, then, may be defined as a sound so complicated that the ear is unable to resolve or analyse it into its original constituents.

10. As the character of a sound depends upon that of the vibrations by which it is caused, it is important to know of what kind the latter must be in order that they may give the sensation of a perfectly simple tone, *i.e.*, one which the ear cannot resolve into any others. Such a vibration is perhaps best realised by comparison with that of the pendulum of a clock when it is swinging only a little to and fro. Under these circumstances it is performing what are called harmonic vibrations, and when the air particles in the neighbourhood of the ear are caused by any means to vibrate according to the same law as that which the pendulum follows, and also with sufficient rapidity, a perfectly simple tone is the result. Such a tone is, however, rarely heard except when produced by means specially contrived for the purpose. If a note on the pianoforte is struck, the impact of the hammer on the string throws it into a state of vibration which, though periodic, is not really harmonic; consequently we do not hear a perfectly simple tone, but one which is in reality a mixture of several higher simple tones with that one which corresponds to the actual length of the string. The former are, however, generally faint, and become associated by habit with the latter, appearing to form with it a single note of determinate pitch. These higher tones are the *harmonics* of the string, and are produced by vibrations whose numbers per second are respectively twice, three times, four times, &c., as great as those of the fundamental tone of the string (§ 13). The same may be said of the notes of all instruments, including the human voice, which are usually employed for the production of musical sounds.

11. Since the consonance of two or more such simple tones always gives a more or less musical sound, and since also the ear is always more or less capable of resolving the latter into its components, the question naturally arises whether all sounds are not, theoretically at least, resolvable into simple tones. The answer to this is contained in a celebrated theorem due to the French mathematician Fourier. He has shown that any periodic vibration is the result of combining together a certain number of simple harmonic

vibrations whose periods are aliquot parts of that of the former; and we have conclusive reasons for supposing that, in the same way as a compound periodic vibration gives rise to a compound sound (§ 9), so the simple tones into which the ear resolves the latter are respectively due to the simple harmonic vibrations which, as the above mentioned theorem proves, make up the former.*

12. The theorem of Fourier referred to in the preceding article is of such great importance in all questions connected with acoustics that a few words illustrative of it may not be out of place.†

If a peg is fixed into the rim of a wheel capable of revolving about a fixed centre, and at right angles to the plane of the wheel, and if the latter is caused to rotate uniformly and is looked at edgeways the peg will appear to move up and down in a straight line, its velocity being the greatest at the middle of its course, and diminishing as it approaches each end. Under these circumstances the peg appears to perform harmonic vibrations.

Now suppose a second wheel, also furnished with a peg in its rim, is made to revolve about the peg of the first as an axis. If the latter is at rest the peg of the second will appear, looked at as above, to perform harmonic vibrations; but if the former is also caused to revolve these vibrations are no longer harmonic, but are the result of adding together the separate harmonic vibrations of the two pegs, in other words of *superposing* the harmonic vibrations which the second peg performs if the first wheel is at rest, upon those which the first peg performs when it is itself in motion. Now it is evident that by continuing this process indefinitely, and by giving the wheels different *radii*, and different uniform velocities of rotation, the final motion of the last peg looked at sideways as before, would be an exceedingly complicated one, and that an infinite number of different vibrations could be produced by varying the number, position at starting, *radii*, and velocities of the wheels, though it could not be assumed without proof that *every possible variety* could be so produced. This however is what Fourier's theorem asserts, provided that the velocities of rotation of the several wheels of the series

are in the proportion of 1, 2, 3, 4, &c. ‡ In other words, every periodic vibration is the resultant of a certain number of harmonic vibrations whose periods are one-half, one-third, one-fourth, &c., &c., that of the former.

13. A harmonic scale is formed by taking a series of notes produced by vibrations whose numbers in a given time are respectively as 1, 2, 3, 4, &c.

If we take as fundamental tone the open C string of the violoncello, the series of tones which with it form a harmonic scale will be as follows:—

The notes marked with an asterisk do not exactly represent the corresponding tones; but are the nearest representatives which the modern notation supplies. All the notes of the harmonic scale can theoretically be produced by either a single string, or by a simple tube used as a trumpet. If we lightly touch the string of a violin, without causing it to come in contact with the finger board, at any one of a series of points dividing it into a number of equal parts, and excite it by means of a bow, it no longer vibrates as a whole, but separates into the number of equal vibrating segments which is the least possible consistent with that point forming one of their points of division; the latter remain stationary, or very nearly so, and are called nodes, their number being evidently just one less than that of the segments. It is plain that if the point of application of the bow be one of a series of nodes, no sound will be produced, provided, of course, the finger remains on any other of the same series, and this may serve to explain why it is sometimes difficult to bring out the higher harmonics of a violin, as the bow may, unconsciously to the performer, be passing exactly over one of the corresponding nodes. The first harmonic, as it is called, of the open string is produced by touching it while in a state of vibration at its middle point, and thereby dividing it into two equal portions, both of which vibrate twice as fast as the whole, and accordingly give the octave. The second harmonic, or the twelfth of the fundamental, corresponds to a division of the string into three equal portions, and so on. And generally, in order to produce the nth harmonic the finger should touch the string at any one of the series of points which divide it into n equal portions. § In

---

* A periodic vibration is any movement which recurs after equal intervals or periods of time, such as that of a uniformly working punching machine, or of the hammer of a clock bell when it is striking, and so on. It should be observed that though all harmonic vibrations are periodic, it is by no means the case that all periodic vibrations are harmonic. See foot note to § 2.

† For a complete discussion and demonstration of the theorem, the reader is referred to the work on Acoustics by the late Professor Donkin, published in the Clarendon Press series.

‡ The *order* in which the wheels are arranged with respect to their velocities is quite arbitrary.

§ That is supposing n to be a prime number (*i.e.* having no divisors). If such is not the case, it is plain that some points of the series when touched would give harmonics of lower pitch.

practice, however, the finger should always touch the string at the point of division adjacent to either end.

14. The harmonics of a simple tube used as a trumpet are the same as those of a vibrating string, *viz.*, the octave, twelfth, fifteenth, &c., and are produced by modifications of the breath and lips; but there is a great difference between the nature of the vibrations which produce sound, in the case of strings and pipes. In the former case the vibrations are executed at right angles to the length of the string, that is, are *lateral*, while in the latter they are in the direction of the pipe, or *longitudinal*, and are the vibrations of the air itself within it.

15. When an open organ pipe is sounding its fundamental tone, the particles of the column of air within it are all, more or less, in a state of vibration parallel to the length of the pipe, of which the intensity is at its maximum at the two ends, growing less and less towards the middle, where there is a node, that is, a point of no disturbance. The harmonics of an open pipe follow the same law as those of a simple trumpet, or vibrating string.

The fundamental note of a stopped organ pipe is an octave below the fundamental note of an open one of the same length. When it is sounding this note there is no node, and the first harmonic is a fifth above the octave, the second a major sixth above the first, the third a diminished fifth above the second, and so on. Or, more simply, the successive tones of the harmonic scale of an open pipe are produced by vibrations which are as 1, 2, 3, 4, &c., those of a stopped pipe by vibrations which are as 1, 3, 5, 7, &c.

16. It was stated (§ 10) that the sound of a vibrating string was in general compounded of a number of simple tones, and a well trained ear can detect a considerable number of them. If it were not for these harmonic components the tones of strings, pipes, of the human voice, or in short, of every instrument most generally used for the production of sound, would be flat and uninteresting like pure water. Each harmonic component is by itself a simple tone, and is due to the vibration of the corresponding segment of the string superposed upon that of the whole. The same statement applies, *mutatis mutandis* to pipes, whether open or stopped. That the harmonics of different instruments greatly influence their several characters is observable in the difference of the tones of a flute, and clarinet. A flute is an open pipe. a clarinet a stopped one; in the former, therefore, the harmonics follow the order of the natural numbers 1, 2, 3, 4, and in the latter the order 1, 3, 5, 7; —the

intermediate notes being supplied by opening the lateral orifices of the instrument.

17. When two simple tones, that is (as explained above), notes deprived of all the harmonic components which under ordinary circumstances accompany them, are sounded together very nearly in unison, there are heard what are called *beats* succeeding one another at regular intervals, their rapidity depending inversely on the smallness of the interval between the two tones. Their origin may be explained thus: Suppose the tones to be produced by vibrations numbering 500 and 501 per second respectively, then every 500th sound wave of the former will strike on the tympanum at exactly the same instant as every 501st of the latter and will reinforce it; while at the 250th of the first the corresponding wave of the other will be just half a period in front of it. Now a sound wave consists of a condensed and rarified stratum of air particles, and therefore the condensed portion of one wave here coincides with the rarified portion of the other and neutralises it. Thus there will be an alternate reinforcement and diminution of sound, every second, from the maximum intensity when both waves impinge on the tympanum at the same instant to the minimum when they counteract each other as much as possible and *vice versâ*.

In the above case it was supposed that the number of vibrations of one tone were only *one* more per second than those of the other; but if the difference of the numbers had been *two*, for instance, then in one second the first tone would have gained two vibrations on the other, and there would have been two beats; and in general the number of beats per second is always equal to the difference between the two rates of vibrations per second.

18. In the preceding section, the cause of beats due to two simple tones of nearly the same pitch was explained, and it was seen that the number of beats per second was always equal to the difference of the numbers of vibrations per second of each tone; so that as the interval between them increased so would the number of beats increase in a given time. Hence it is obvious that if the interval became sufficiently large, the beats would succeed each other so rapidly as to become undistinguished. For instance, in the case of the fifth whose lower and upper tones are produced by vibrations numbering 264 and 396 per second respectively, the number of beats per second would be 132 and would therefore be undistinguishable—and still more so supposing the upper tone to have 397 or more vibrations per second; but, on the other hand it is a well-known fact, that if an imperfect fifth, octave, or any other tolerably simple interval is played on a violin or violoncello,

the beats are most distinctly heard succeeding each other at perceptible intervals—whereas according to what was said above they should occur so rapidly as not to be heard at all. Two explanations of this phenomenon have been given, of which by far the most simple is due to Helmholtz—and which here follows. It appears that when the tones are simple and at a sufficiently large interval the beats should occur too rapidly to be heard, whereas when the interval is played on a violin they are easily distinguishable. The reason of this fact is that in the latter case the tones are no longer simple but compound—and the beats which are heard are not due to the fundamental tones themselves but arise from two of their harmonic components which are nearly in unison. Suppose the ratio of the interval between the fundamental tones to be $\frac{m}{n}$, that is, let $\frac{m}{n}$ be the fraction, reduced to its lowest terms, which is formed by putting in the numerator the number of vibrations per second of the upper tone, and in the denominator those of the lower. Then it is plain that the nth harmonic component of the tone m, will be of the same pitch as the mth harmonic component of the tone n; for they will each have exactly mn vibrations per second. Now let $\frac{M}{N}$ be the ratio, expressed in the same way, of another interval, nearly, but not quite, equal to $\frac{m}{n}$; then the nth harmonic component of M will have Mn vibrations per second, while the mth component of N will have Nm. Now since $\frac{M}{N}$ is nearly equal to $\frac{m}{n}$, the difference between Mn and Nm will be a small number; and when the two notes are sounded together the number of beats per second will be equal to that difference.

For example, let $\frac{m}{n}$ be the ratio of a fifth, that is the fraction $\frac{3}{2}$, and let $\frac{M}{N}$ represent very nearly the same interval, say $\frac{397}{264}$; then the difference between Mn and Nm, or 794 and 792, is 2; hence if two strings tuned apart at an interval represented by $\frac{397}{264}$ are sounded simultaneously there will be two beats heard per second.

19. When the vibrations of the air due to a number of different sounds which co-exist at the same time are infinitely small, they are merely superposed one on another, so that each separate sound passes through the air as if it alone were present; and this law of superposition holds, though only approximately, until the vibrations have increased up to a certain limit, beyond which it is no longer true. Vibrations which give rise to a large amount of disturbance produce secondary waves; and it is to these that the phenomena of resultant tones are due.

Thus if two notes a fifth apart, for instance, are forcibly sounded together, a third tone is heard an octave below the lower of the two, and this ceases to be perceptible when the loudness of the concord diminishes. In general the resultant tone of any combination of two notes is produced by a number of vibrations per second equal to the difference of the numbers per second of the notes. This fact formerly led to the supposition that the resultant tone was produced by the beats due to the consonance, which, when they occurred with sufficient rapidity, linked themselves together so as to form a continuous musical note. If this were so it is clear that the resultant ought to be heard when the original notes are sounded gently as well as forcibly; and it was the failure of this condition that led Helmholtz to the re-investigation of their origin. These resultant tones have been named by him *difference tones;* he has also discovered the existence of resultant tones formed by the sum of the numbers of vibrations of the primaries. These *summation tones* as they are called cannot be explained on the old theory.

20. The theory of beats explains the law that the smaller the two numbers are, which express the ratio of their vibrations, the smoother is the combination of any two tones. When two simple tones are sounded together whose rates of vibration per second differ by more than 132, the beats, according to Helmholtz, totally disappear. As the difference grows less the beats become more and more audible, the interval meanwhile growing proportionately dissonant, till they number 33 per second, at which point the dissonance of the interval is at its maximum.

This, however, depends upon the position of the interval as regards its pitch. For it should be remembered that though the *ratio* of any given interval remains the same whatever the absolute pitch of its tones may be, yet the difference of the actual numbers of their vibrations, and therefore the number of beats due to their consonance, alters with it. And *vice versâ*, if the difference of the number of vibrations remains constant, the interval must diminish as its pitch rises. For instance, either of the following combinations

would give rise to 33 beats per second, since the numbers of vibrations of their tones per second, are 99-66, and 528-495, respectively. Now it is obvious that in the latter case the dissonance would be far greater than in the former.

The above explanation of the cause of dissonance is also due to Helmholtz, and completely solves a question which had remained unanswered since the time of Pythagoras, although that philosopher made the important discovery that the simpler the ratio of the two parts into which a vibrating string was divided, the more perfect was the consonance of the two sounds.

21. The sound of the piano, violin, &c., is only in a small measure due to the actual vibration of the strings themselves. The latter communicate their own motion to the sound board of the piano, and to the front, back, and enclosed air of the violin. In the latter instrument communication is made to the surrounding air from that within it by means of the f holes.

If a string were merely stretched between two pegs firmly fixed in a stone wall and caused to vibrate, scarcely any sound would be heard at all, owing to the mass and rigidity of the wall, which would refuse to be thrown into vibration by so small an amount of energy as that which the string would possess. On the other hand, the sound board of a piano readily answers to the vibrations imposed on it when the string is struck, and having a large surface in contact with the air, every point of which originates a system of waves, it causes a full and powerful sound.

22. The vibrations of straight rods may be either longitudinal or transversal. The former have not been generally employed for the production of musical sounds; the latter are such as take place when a tuning fork is struck, or when a musical box or triangle is played. In the case of a curved rod the vibrations are more complicated, but there is one interesting case, namely, that in which the curved rod takes the form of a circular ring. In this case the fundamental tone is obtained by suspending it horizontally by four strings attached at equidistant points in the circumference, and by lightly tapping it midway between any two. If the number of vibrations then given be $2n$ per second, those of the successive harmonics are proportional to $3n\sqrt{6}$, $4n\sqrt{13}$, $5n\sqrt{22}$, &c.

23. The nature of the vibrations of a bell may be partly inferred from those of a ring, as the bell may be considered as consisting of a connected series of rings of different diameters all vibrating simultaneously; thus the fundamental tone of a bell would cause it to divide itself longitudinally into four equal segments, corresponding to the four quadrants into which the suspended ring divides. The period of its vibrations could not, however, be similarly inferred.

24. The vibration of plates is not, musically speaking, a subject of much interest, as the only instruments which depend upon it directly for the production of their sounds, are gongs and cymbals, and the same may be said of membranes. Chladni was the first to show the positions of the lines of nodes on a plate, by clamping it horizontally in a vice, and causing it to vibrate by passing a violin bow over one edge, having previously sprinkled it with a little sand. The lines of nodes being those parts of the plate which, like the nodes of a string (§ 13), are not thrown into vibration, remain covered with the sand which collects there from the vibrating portions, and in this way very curious and interesting figures are produced.

Act (Acte, *Fr.*; Akt, *Ger.*; Atto, *It.*) A distinct division in the plot or design of a drama or opera, forming an incident complete in itself, but bearing reference to the general idea of the whole. Every dramatic plot naturally divides itself into three portions: the exposition, the development, and the conclusion; and this division would seem to point to the separation of a dramatic design into three acts, but where the piece is in four, five, or more acts, it will be found on examination that the tripartite division is essentially the same, greater prominence or care in detail being given to one or more of the sections. Thus the exposition may be spread over two or three acts, the development over one or two, and the conclusion or unravelling, reserved for the final act.

The classical trilogies—groups of three tragedies—were most frequently united by a common idea, each forming a complete incident, connected by a bond of sympathy, sentiment, or subject with the grand design.

Bartholomé Torres Naharro, of Torre in Spain, who wrote at the commencement of the 16th century, is said to have been the first who suggested the division of plots into acts, or *jornados*, although Cervantes claims the invention for himself. It is certain that Naharro's printed dramas are not so divided.

Donaldson, in speaking of the Æschylean Trilogy (the Agamemnon, Choephorœ, and the Eumenides), says, that the three plays mutually cohere, is plain; and as they were actually brought on the stage in sequence, they may be regarded as so many acts of one grand heroic drama. This is mentioned, in order to vindicate the practice of Shakspeare and other modern dramatists, in compressing into one drama an extensive cycle of human destinies; because the very objection that has been made to the practice is the alleged example of the ancients to the contrary.

Wagner's *Nibelungen* trilogy, though stated to be "new from end to end" in idea and design, bears a close affinity to the ancient Greek drama. For the subject is mythical and "the mythical subject has a plastic unity; it is perfectly simple and easily comprehensible, and it does not stand in need of the numberless small details, which a modern playwright is obliged to introduce to make some historical occurrence intelligible. It is divided into a few important and decisive scenes, in each of which the action arises spontaneously from out of the emotions of the actors; which emotions, by reason of the small number of such scenes, can be presented in a most complete and exhaustive manner." In many modern operas, the division of the work into acts is made, less with reference to dramatic principles, than to the requirements of the stage-manager.

Act Music in Oxford. Cantatas composed by the Professor of music, to words written by the Professor of poetry, and performed at grand commemorations in the University.

Act tunes. [Playhouse tunes.]

Acte de Cadence (*Fr.*) Certain chords by means of which the final cadence is introduced.

Action. The mechanism of an organ or pianoforte, or other compound instruments.

Acuta. The accent attached to certain letters in the Greek system of musical notation, thus, M´

Acuta. An organ stop. [Sharp mixture.]

Acutæ claves, acuta loca, acutæ voces. Those keys, places, and sounds, which lie between 'alamire acutum' and 'alamire superacutum' of the Hexachords, that is between little a

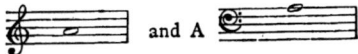

 and A

Acute. High as to pitch; opposed to grave.

Adagietto (*It.*) A diminutive of Adagio.

Adagio (*It.*) Slowly; also a name given to a movement written in that time.

Adagio assai
——— **di molto** } Very slowly.
——— **cantabile.** Very slow, and sustained, as if being sung.
——— **patetico.** Slow and with pathos.
——— **pesante.** Slow and weighty.
——— **sostenuto.** Slow and sustained.

Adagiosissimo (*It.*) (superlative of Adagio). More than usually slow, very slow indeed.

Added Sixth, Chord of the. This dissonant combination of sounds is so called because it has the appearance of a common chord of the Subdominant of the key in which it occurs, with the addition of a sixth from the bass note, *e.g.*:

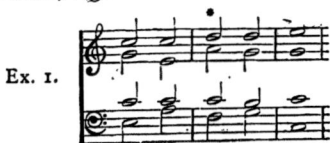

Ex. I.

The above example being in the key of C, the Subdominant of the scale is F, and a common chord of F consists of F, A, and C, to which is found added at * the sixth of the bass note: namely, D. Although as a mere name, the expression *added sixth* may not be without value, it is by many authors considered very doubtful whether the notes, F, A, C are really the constituents of a Subdominant common chord; and the fact that the apparent fifth of this chord (C) is nearly always treated as a discord, and made to descend, is rightly cited as the cause of their doubt.

This naturally leads to the second explanation of the chord, which is, that it is an inversion of the chord of the seventh on the super-tonic, *e.g.*:

Ex. 2.

Seventh on Supertonic. 1st Inversion.

But, the system of constructing chords on every degree of the scale, though once much adopted, is daily losing ground; and justly, because by it, the particular progression of each component note of a chord, either has to be ignored, or else treated of with an amount of detail which is puzzling to the student, owing to the impossibility of laying down several laws as to the usual progression of stated intervals.

A third explanation is, that it is a *dominant* chord—consisting of the fifth, seventh, ninth, and eleventh from that root, *e.g.*:

Ex. 3.

The objection to this is, that the bass note of the chord (F), in nine cases out of every ten, *ascends* in the resolution, as seen in Ex. I. But, on the other hand, it will be found that the ninth (A), and the eleventh (C), descend properly, and it is a fact well known to careful analysts of harmony, that when several discords are heard simultaneously, the *regular* resolution of part of them often completely satisfies the ear; and also, that when the root or generator of a chord is omitted, there is more license in its treatment.

A fourth explanation has been offered: it is to the effect that the chord contains two minor sevenths, namely, F and C, derived from two roots, G and D respectively:

Ex. 4.

If both sevenths were properly resolved, consecutive fifths would ensue, therefore one (and generally the lower one) is made to ascend, on the principle just mentioned above. It is also urged that the lower seventh, F, is practically resolved, if the progression be followed to the cadence in C. In favour of this view, it is also stated that chords built upon the dominant of a scale *and* its fifth are not uncommon, as for instance chords of the augmented sixth, &c. Whatever explanation be accepted, it is manifest that as this chord is made up of four notes, it can occur in as many positions, each note forming it being in turn placed in the bass, *e.g.*:

Ex. 5.

It is *resolved* generally as in the above example, but many other resolutions are occasionally met with, *e.g.*:

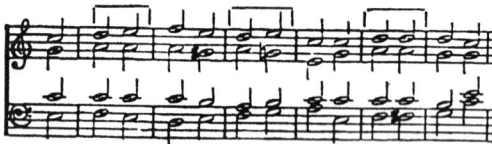

When the other positions of the chord are used, greater scope for varied resolution will be found.

The chord of the Added Sixth is also to be found in the minor series of chords amongst those authors who accept, though perhaps under protest, the exigencies of the tempered scale, *e.g.*:

From this source a vast number of resolutions of the chord of the Added Sixth will be attainable, the tracing of which in the works of great masters will be found as instructive as interesting.

Additato (*It.*) Fingered, having signs pointing out what fingers are to be used for certain passages. [Fingering.]

Addition. The old name for a dot or point.

Additional accompaniments. Parts not in an original score, but added by another hand. Such additions may be made for the following reasons: 1, because the author accidentally left his score in an incomplete state: 2, for the supposed purpose of beautifying the original, by supplying parts for instruments either unknown or imperfectly known in the author's time: 3, to enable modern performers to play such parts as were intended for instruments now obsolete, or those of a similar tone now in use: 4, in order to compensate for the altered constitution of the orchestra, in which the number of stringed instruments is now larger in proportion to the number of reed wind-instruments, than formerly: 5, that, when for the sake of adding to the power or volume of tone other instruments must be added, they should be of varied qualities of tone instead of a mere numerical reinforcement of those already used in the original.

Additional keys. Keys added to enlarge the compass of any instrument.

Addolorato (*It.*) In an afflicted manner, sorrowfully.

A demi jeu (*Fr.*) With half the power of the instrument.

A demi voix (*Fr.*) At half voice. [Mezzo voce.]

A deux (*Fr.*)
A due (*It.*) For two voices or instruments. When the parts of two instruments are written on one line the portion to which this term is prefixed is intended to be performed by both in unison; the opposite term is *divisi q.v.*

A deux temps (*Fr.*) In common time of two in a bar.

A deux valse (*Fr.*) [Valse.]

Adirato (*It.*) In an angry manner.

Adiaphonon. An instrument of the Pianoforte class, not liable to get out of tune. Invented by Schuster of Vienna in 1820.

Adjunct notes. Short notes, not essential to the harmony, occurring on unaccented parts of a bar. [*c.f.* Auxiliary notes. Passing notes.]

Ad libitum (*Lat.*) At will. (1) In passages so marked, the time may be altered at the will of the performer.

(2) A cadenza *ad libitum* is a cadenza, the construction of which is left to the performer.

(3) Accompaniments *ad libitum* are additions to a piece, which may be performed, or not, at discretion.

(4) The word is also used to indicate the point at which a cadenza may be introduced in a concerto.

Adornamento (*It.*) An ornament, or grace.

Ad placitum (*Lat.*) At pleasure. A free part. A part added to a strict Canon, which does not come under the laws which govern that class of composition.

A due corde (*It.*) On two strings. [Adeux.]

—— **stromenti** (*It.*) For two instruments.

A due voci (*It.*) For two voices.

A dur (*Ger.*) The key requiring three sharps to complete the major scale. The key of A major.

Ad videndum (*Lat.*) A species of counterpoint, which was written down or noted, as opposed to that which was *alla mente* or improvised.

Æolian harp. [Eolian.]

Æolian mode. [Eolian.]

Æolian piano. A piano having wooden bars, instead of strings, which, when struck by the hammers, produced a tone of peculiar quality.

Æolodicon. Æolodion. A musical instrument, the sounds of which are produced by the striking of steel springs by hammers set in motion by an ordinary key-board.

Æolomelodicon, called also a Choraleon; an Æolodicon having brass tubes over the metal springs, for the purpose of giving more power to the tone.

Æolopantalon, a pianoforte in connection with the Æolodicon.

Æquisonæ voces (*Lat.*) Equal sounds, but not unison; that is, such a consonant combination as, a note and its octave; or a note and its super-octave.

AEVIA. The vowels in the word Alleluia, used in mediæval "prick song" as an abbreviation for that word, especially in Antiphons.

No-tum fe-cit Do-mi-nus, AEVIA.

Sa-lu-ta-re Su-um. AEVIA.

c.f. EVOVÆ.

Affabile (*It.*) In a pleasing kindly manner.

Affannato (*It.*) In a distressed manner.

Affannosamente (*It.*) Restlessly.

Affannoso (*It.*) Mournfully.

Affetto, con (*It.*) With affection.

Affettuosamente (*It.*) Affectionately.

Affettuoso (*It.*) Affectionately.

Affinity. Connection by relation. Keys of affinity. [Relative Keys.]

Afflitto, *or* con **afflizione** (*It.*) Aflictedly, with sadness.

Affrettando (*It.*)
Affrettate (*It.*) } Hastening the time.
Affrettore (*It.*)

A fofa (*Port.*) A dance, like the Fandango, *q.v.*

Agevole (*It.*) } With facility and light-
Agevolezza (*It.*) } ness.

Aggraver la fugue (*Fr.*) To augment the subject in a fugue.

Agilità, con (*It.*) With sprightliness.

Agilité (*Fr.*) Lightness and freedom in playing or singing.

Agilmente (*It.*) } Cheerfully, in a lively
Agilmento (*It.*) } manner.

Agitamento (*It.*) Restlessness.

Agitato (*It.*) An agitated or restless style of playing or singing, in which the time and expression is broken and hurried.

Agitazione, con. (*It.*) With agitation.

Agnus Dei (*Lat.*) [Mass.]

Agoge (*Gk.*), ἀγωγή. (*Lat.* ductus; *It.* conducimento.) The name of one of the subdivisions of Melopœia *q.v.* among the Greeks. The order in which successive notes of the scale followed each other, with regard to their pitch, in a melody. It is thus defined by Aristoxenus: ἀγωγὴ μὲν οὖν, ἐστὶν ἡ διὰ τῶν ἑξῆς φθόγγων ὁδὸς τοῦ μέλους. There were three kinds of Agoge: 1st, εὐθεῖα (ductus rectus), when the melody proceeded from a grave to a higher sound by single degrees, εὐθεῖα μὲν καλεῖται ἡ ἀπὸ βαρύτητος εἰς ὀξύτητα (Aristides, Quin); 2nd, ἀνακάμπτουσα (ductus revertens), when a higher sound was followed by a lower; 3rd, περιφερής (ductus circumcurrens), when a modulation was introduced in an ascending, and afterwards, descending succession of notes, by making one of the notes, which was flattened in ascending, sharp on descending; or, *vice versâ, e.g.*:

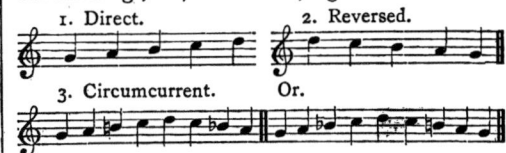

1. Direct.   2. Reversed.

3. Circumcurrent.   Or.

Agoge rhythmica. The succession of melodic sounds viewed with regard to their *accent*, and *rhythm*.

A grand chœur (*Fr.*) Full chorus. Applied to compositions written for the full choir in opposition to the *petit chœur*, which originally consisted of three parts only.

Agrémens (*Fr.*) Turns, graces, and embellishments in Harpsichord music.

Aigu (*Fr.*) Acute, high.

Air. In its modern sense, a tune, or the tune. The word air was formerly used to describe dance tunes, as "Court Ayres, Pavins, Corants and Sarabands," also melodies for instruments; for before the invention of the Sonata, the music for concerts (*concertos*) of violins, consisted altogether of *airs* in three and sometimes four parts. The word air (*aria*), first used by Italian writers in the 16th century, was, when translated into English, represented by the word "fancy." Lord Bacon in his essay on "Beauty," uses the word *air*, and perhaps unintentionally describes its character thus—"the sweetest airs in music are made by a kind of felicity, and not by rule." The air was formerly assigned to the middle voice part or *medius*, corresponding to our tenor. The practice of giving the air to the soprano, or upper part, arose from the custom of the Italian theatres, where the "musico," while being supposed to sing the air in the tenor, really sang it in the soprano range. It was afterwards adopted by the composers of instrumental music, and the habit of giving the principal melody to the highest voice or instrument has continued until now. [Ballad.] [Sonata.] [Song.]

Ais (*Ger.*) A sharp.

Akkord (*Ger.*) A chord, as *Nonen-akkord*, chord of the ninth, &c.

A la, Al, All', Alla (*It.* and *Fr.*) Like, in, at, &c.

A la même (*Fr.*) In the original time.

A la mi re. The name of the note *a* in the acute and super-acute hexachords of the Guidonian system. [Notation.]

Alamoth (*Heb.*) This word occurs in Ps. lxviii. 25. "First go the *sharim* (singers), then follow the *neginim* (kinnors), in the midst are *alamoth* (damsels playing on the timbrels)." Gesenius and others understand the word to signify treble music, "vox clara et acuta, quasi virginum." But, on the other hand, in 1 Chron. xv. 20 the names of *men* are given as players of "nebels on alamoth." It is one of the many obscure musical terms which are met with in the Bible. It however seems to have been associated with *nebels*, much as the expression *sheminith* is with *kinnors*, and may therefore be supposed to refer to the pitch or method of playing on those instruments.

Alarum, All'armi (*It.*) A call to arms.

"Alarums sounded, and ordnance shot off"
(*Shakspeare.*)

Originally a general shout; afterwards, a recognised signal by trumpets and drums.

Alberti Bass. A bass consisting of *arpeggios* or *broken harmony*, e.g. :

so-called after its reputed inventor, Domenico Alberti, who died in 1739.

Alcuna licenza, con (*It.*) With a little license; that is, the power of altering the time at will.

Aliquot tones. Overtones or harmonics. [Acoustics, § 9.]

A livre ouvert (*Fr.*) At sight.

Alla breve (*It.*) A direction that the notes are to be made shorter; that is, the pace taken quicker than usual. It is generally found attached to movements having four or eight minims in a bar, and is expressed in the signature by ₵. The following unusual sign for *alla breve* is found in the signature of one of the exercises "pour le Clavecin," by J. S. Bach, as published about 1760 :

[Time.]

Alla caccia (*It.*) In the hunting style.

—— **camera** (*It.*) In the style of chamber music, *q.v.*

—— **cappella** (*It.*) [A Cappella.]

—— **diritta.** By direct intervals.

—— **hanacca.** In the style of the *hanaise*, a sort of polka, or polacca polonaise.

—— **marcia.** In the style of a March.

Alla mente (*It.*) A barbarous species of counterpoint in thirds and fifths, improvised upon the plain song, called in France "Chant sur le livre," and in England "Fa burden." This peculiar harmony is said to have had its rise in the 12th century, but it is probably older, as Hucbald, who was living about the year 880, describes it, as also did Odo, Abbot of Cluny, in his Enchiridion [c. 920.] While the use of this hideous harmony was encouraged by the church, musicians of feeling never failed to protest against it, therefore we find after Hucbald, Odo, and Franco of Cologne—Johannis de Muris, and others complaining of its use, and suggesting various measures for its reform, and by degrees paving the way to the modern system of counterpoint. The decree of the Pope John XXII, dated at Avignon 1322, had some effect in checking its use, but did not entirely suppress it, as it was sung as late as the middle of the 15th century.

Alla militare. (*It.*) In a military manner.

—— **moderno** (*It.*) In the modern method.

All' antico (*It.*) In the old style.

Alla polacca (*It.*) Like a polonaise.

—— **quinta** (*It.*) At the fifth.

—— **rovescio** (*It.*) By contrary motion. [Rovescio.]

—— **siciliana** (*It.*) A species of melody in $\frac{6}{8}$, $\frac{12}{8}$, or $\frac{6}{4}$, having the longest note at the accented pulse. Handel's Pastoral Symphony is *alla siciliana*.

Alla stretta (*It.*) Bringing closer and closer, alike as to subject and movement.

Alla zoppa (*It.*) Lamely, halting, against time, syncopation.

Allegramente (*It.*) Joyfully.

Allegretto (*It.*) (Diminutive of *allegro*.) (1) Slower than allegro. (2) A movement in this time.

Allegrettino (*It.*) (Diminutive of allegretto.) (1) Not so fast as *allegretto*. (2) A short allegretto movement.

Allegro (*It.*) (*Lit.* joyful.) Quick, lively. The word is occasionally employed to describe a whole movement of a quartett, sonata, or symphony. In music it is sometimes qualified as :—

Allegro agitato	(*It.*)	Quick and in an excited manner.
„ assai	„	(*Lit.*) Fast enough. A quicker motion than simple allegro.
„ commodo or comodo	„	An easy, graceful allegro.
„ con brio	„	Quickly and with spirit.
„ con fuoco	„	Rapidly and with fire.
„ con moto	„	With sustained joyfulness.
„ con spirito	„	Joyfully and with spirit.
„ di bravura	„	A movement full of executive difficulties intended to exhibit the capacity of the singer or player.
„ di molto	„	Exceedingly quick.
„ furioso	„	Rapidly and with fury.
„ giusto	„	In quick but steady time.
„ ma grazi-osa	„	Lively and with graceful motion.
„ ma non presto	„	Rapidly, but not too fast.
„ ma non tanto	„	Quickly, but not too much so.
„ ma non troppo	„	Lively, but not too fast.
„ moderato	„	Moderately quick.
„ molto	„	Very quick.
„ risoluto	„	Lively and with firmness and decision.
„ veloce	„	Lively and with speed.
„ vivace	„	Lively and brisk.
„ vivo	„	Quick and lively.

Allein (*Ger.*) Alone, as *Sanfte Stimmen allein*, soft stops only.

Alleluia. Latin for Hallelujah. (*Heb.*) Praise ye the Lord. An invitation to praise, used in every Christian community with varying regularity. St. Augustine says that the African Church used it between the feasts of Easter and Pentecost, and it is at that time that its use is more prevalent in the ritual of the Eastern and Western churches than at other seasons of the Christian year. In the Roman Catholic Church it is not employed from Septuagesima to Easter, but in the Anglican Church it is said twice at least every day throughout the whole year, the English form, "Praise ye the Lord," being substituted in the present Prayer-book for the ancient Hebrew word which was inserted in the first Prayer-book of Edward VI. The word Hallelujah being a short, musical, and rhythmical word, is frequently used by many anthem-writers—apparently without a just understanding of its meaning—to eke out an idea in music; but at other times the word has been set to music with sublime effect, as by Beethoven in his " Mount of Olives," and by Handel in his " Messiah." Carl Engel, in " The Music of the Most Ancient Nations," gives examples of melodies sung by the Copts, and the women of Syria, Arabia, and Persia, to the word.

Allemande (*Fr.*) Alemain, Allemaigne, Almain, a dance in duple time, said to have been invented by the French in the reign of Louis XIV. as a symbolical allusion to the newly-acquired German provinces. It was revived and frequently performed at the theatres during the time of the First Napoleon, during whose rule it became exceedingly popular. The measure was slow, and the steps were made in a rapid sliding manner as in the modern waltz, but there was no turning, only a peculiar entwining and unloosening of the arms of the dancers in the various steps. It is said by some that the Allemande was invented in the lesser provinces of Germany or Switzerland. Scarlatti, Corelli, Bach, Handel, and other composers of the period they represent, incorporated the measure of this dance in their Suites, Sonatas, and Lessons, in which it was written in common time of four crotchets in a bar.

The tradition concerning the origin of its invention, mentioned above, is very picturesque, but it is not founded in fact. Louis XIV. took Strasbourg by surprise in the time of peace, in the year 1681, and the treaty of Ryswick which confirmed his possession was not made until 1697. It is quite possible to believe that the fulsome flattery of his flippant court would magnify an act of rapine into a worthy victory, and that empty-headed adulators would find heels light enough to dance their joy at the same; but unfortunately for the story, there were Allemandes in existence before the time of the illegal seizure. In England, Almaines as musical compositions were published in 1662, in a book called " Courtly Masquing Ayres," and there were those by Lully, issued in France, bearing date 1670; the subjoined one, by Dumont, is even earlier, as it is to be found in " Meslanges à 2, 3, 4 et 5 parties, avec la basse continue, contenante plusiers chansons, motets, Magnificat, prèludes et ALLEMANDES pour l'orgue et pour les violes; livre 1ᵐᵉʳ; Paris, Robert Ballard, 1649." It is not even possible to refer the origin of the dance to the recovery of the towns in the Low Countries, as Turenne did not win them until six years after Dumont's publication.

The mention of the word as a dance is to be found in earlier writings than either of the above-mentioned, for there is a passage in Ben Jonson's play, "The Devil is an Ass," first acted in 1610, which proves the dance to have been known in his time:

" He may, perchance, in tail of a sheriff's dinner,
Skip with a rhyme on the table, from New-nothing,
And take his *Almain*-leap into a custard,
Shall make my lady mayoress and her sisters
Laugh all their hoods over their shoulders."

The old Almains probably had leaping steps, as the foregoing passage, and another from George Chapman's "Alphonsus, Emperor of Germany," would imply:

" We Germans have no changes in our dances,
An Almain and an Up-Spring—that is all."

This play was printed in 1599.

ALLEMANDE.

HENRI DUMONT, 1610-1684.

Allentamento *(It.)*
Allentato *(It.)* } Yielding, slackening the time, giving way.

All' improvista *(It.)* Without preparation, extemporaneously.

Al loco *(It.)* (*Lit. in the place.*) (1) A term which is used to counter-order a previous direction to play an octave higher or lower.

(2) A direction to a violinist to return from a shift to his previous position. [Shift.]

Allonger l'archet *(Fr.)* To prolong the stroke of the bow.

All' ottava *(It.)* At the octave, a direction to play an octave higher, or lower, than is written.

All' unisono *(It.)* In unison or octaves.

Alphorn. Alpine horn. A long tube of fir-wood played by the herdsmen of the Alps. It has the same natural series of sounds as a trumpet, but does not possess any means of reducing the tenth harmonic to the ordinary pitch of our scale. [Ranz des Vaches.]

Al piacere *(It.)* At pleasure.

Al rigore di tempo *(It.)*
Al rigore del tempo *(It.)* } In strict time.

Al riverso *(It.)*
Al rovescio *(It.)* { By contrary motion, that is, answering an ascending interval by one descending a like distance, *e.g.*:

HANDEL.

Egypt was glad.

Answers *al rovescio* are found in Imitation, Fugue, and Canon.

Al segno *(It.)* To the sign. *D'al segno* *(It.)* from the sign 𝄋. Directions that the performer must return to that portion of the piece marked with the sign 𝄋, and conclude with the first double bar which follows, or go on to the word *Fine*, or to the pause ⌒.

Alt *(Ger.)* Alto voice, part, or instrument.

Alta *(It.)* High or higher. As 8*va alta*, an octave higher.

Alterata *(Lat.)* A name given to those scales into which notes were introduced foreign to the old church modes.

Alteratio *(Lat.)* In mediæval music, the doubling of the value of a note. " Alteratio est proprii valoris alicujus notæ duplicatio" (Tinctor). This *alteratio* only took place when a note was in a certain relation to those near it; *e.g.*, if two longs preceded a maxim "in modo majori perfecto" [Modus] the latter of them underwent *alteration :* and if two breves "in modo minore perfecto" preceded a long, the latter underwent alteration; and so on. A perusal of the eight general, and four particular rules which governed *alteration,* will cause the reader to be thankful that modern music has been relieved of such complications.

Alterato *(It.)* } Altered, augmented (with
Alteré *(Fr.)* } reference to intervals).
Alternamente *(It.)* }
Alternando *(It.)* } Changing by turns.
Alternativo *(It.)* }
Altgeige *(Ger.)* The tenor violin, the viola. [Viola.]
Altieramente *(It.)* Proudly, grandly, haughtily.
Altisono *(It.)* Sonorous, ringing.
Altissimo *(It.)* The highest.
Altista *(It.)* A name formerly given to an alto singer.
Alto-basso *(It.)* An ancient Venetian stringed instrument, a Hackbret, *q.v.* It was formed of a square box of pine-wood, supported on legs and strung with catgut. The player struck the strings with a sort of bow, which was held in the left hand, the right hand being engaged in holding a sort of flute or flageolet with which a melody was performed. The instrument was only used by the lower class of people, and is now obsolete.
Alto clef. The C clef, placed upon the third line of the stave, in order that the notes proper to the Alto voice may be conveniently represented :

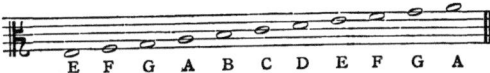

E F G A B C D E F G A

The Alto clef is also used for the Tenor violin or viola. [Clef.]
Alto viola *(It.)* The tenor instrument of the violin family, called Alto, Tenor, or Viola. *(Ger.)* Bratsche or Altgeige. [Viola.]
Alto voice. Called also counter-tenor, when used by men, and counter-alto or contralto, when used by women. It is the deepest tone of voice among women and boys, to whom it may be said to be natural, and it is called the highest voice among men for lack of a better term to describe it. Properly speaking, the tenor voice is the highest man's voice, the alto or counter-tenor voice being entirely an artificial production, and

simply a development of the *falsetto*. The register usually written for this voice lies between tenor G and treble C,

As the best notes of the alto voice are within the octave from B flat, those notes are most generally employed, for the higher notes are harsh and discordant, and the lower of small musical quality, and therefore ineffective. The alto voice in man is mostly formed upon an indifferent bass voice, and there is always a break between the chest and the head voice; this break varies between

C and E and the careful union of the chest and head qualities of voice, and the judicious employment of the "*mezza voce*" are characteristic of every good alto singer. The alto voice is almost peculiar to English singers, not one of the continental nations possessing the capability of producing the quality or of appreciating it when produced; the consequence is, that there is no music written for this voice by any but English composers, and the majority of writers of the present day forming their style upon the foreign model, neglect and ignore the voice, disregarding its claim to usefulness, in places and at times, when and where female voices are unavailable. The value of the voice, its flexibility, sympathetic quality, and harmonious power, when carefully cultivated, are well displayed in cathedral music, and glee singing: a great number of melodious compositions by the most noted English writers, depend upon the alto voice for their proper effect. Many of the songs in Handel's oratorios were assigned to this voice, which are now, in consequence of the heightened pitch at present employed, sung by females: for instance, the part of Solomon in the oratorio of that name; of Barak and Sisera in the oratorio of " Deborah;" and of Daniel in "Belshazzar;" are each given to an alto voice. As this practice is of quite recent growth, it is but reasonable to conclude that Handel intended the music of the wisest king, and that of the two brave warriors to be sung by men altos, rather than by women, for the sake of appearance, if for no more powerful reason. The fact before alluded to, of the non-recognition of the voice by foreigners, has given an advantage to English musical literature not enjoyed by any other people, in the cultivation and sole possession of the Glee and the Anthem.

As many of the principal effects are obtained in these two species of composition through the medium of the alto voice, if only for the sake of the performance of the many noble specimens of art in these two styles, the alto voice will always be cultivated in England until such time as the Glee and Anthem cease to exist. The cultivation of the Part-song has almost superseded the use of the alto voice in modern music, for the upper part in this class of composition is given to tenor voices, and the difficulty in producing the notes of the higher register so far influences the character of the music written, that many of the part-songs for male voices are of a bold, boisterous style, entirely different to that of the glee, which by reason of the peculiarity of the alto voice is of a more quiet character, depending in a great measure for its effect upon delicate and expressive singing. Many composers of eminence have completely ignored the alto voice, whether male or female, a quantity of music for Church use being written for treble, tenor, and bass, as by Cherubini and others.

In quality and power of expression the female alto voice is peculiar, and unlike any other voice. Its character is grave, tender, spiritual, and moving, and is admirably adapted to express emotions of dignity, grandeur, and piety. The male alto being an artificial voice, its usefulness is of limited duration, for when the singer is past fifty years of age the voice becomes harsh, reedy, nasal, and the break is painfully apparent.

Altra, *fem. (It.)* ⎫
Altri, *pl.* *(It.)* ⎬ Other, another, others.
Altro, *mas. (It.)* ⎭

Altschlüssel *(Ger.)* Alto clef.

Altviole *(Ger.)* [Alto Viola.]

Alzamento di mano *(It.)* Raising the hand in conducting.

Alzando *(It.)* Lifting up, raising, elevating.

Altzeichen *(Ger.)* The alto clef,

Amabile *(It.)* Lovely, gentle, tender.

Amabilità, con *(It.)* With gentleness, tenderness.

Amarevole *(It.)* Sad, bitter.

Amarezza, con *(It.)* With sadness.

Amarissimamente *(It.)* ⎫
Amarissimo *(It.)* ⎬ Very bitterly.
In a mournful, sorrowful style.

Amateur *(Fr.)* A lover of music; one who pursues the practice of any art for pure love, in distinction to one who is engaged in its employment for pay.

Ambira *(Afr.)* A kind of drum or pulsatile instrument, made of wood, in cylindrical form, upon which a series of tongues of iron, cane, or wood are so arranged that they may be made to vibrate upon pressure. The Ambira is used by the negroes of Senegambia and Guinea.

Ambitus *(Lat.)* (*lit.* circuit.) The *compass* of an ancient church tone. The word is,

however, used sometimes in a more extended sense than our word *compass*, as it is made to signify the proper steps which lie between the extreme limits of the tone—"Toni debitus ascensus et descensus." The rules (regulæ) which govern the *ambitus* depend upon the position of the *final* of the tone, and although much elaborated in mediæval treatises, their force seems to be that the proper *ambitus* should (regulariter) not exceed the octave (diapason) included between the highest note of the mode above the final and the lowest below it, except " by licence" (licentialiter). These dispensations only allow the introduction of three notes outside the *ambitus* in each direction, an authentic mode being allowed a descent to the lowest note of its corresponding plagal tone; a plagal tone being allowed to ascend to the highest note of its corresponding authentic. This fact, simple enough in itself, is cleverly put into a shape as unintelligible as possible in the following lines, framed for the supposed assistance of the student :

" Undenis gradibus vult juste vadere prothus.
Per sex et quinas claves vult deuterus ire.
Octo tribus gradibus vult juste cepere tritus.
Per sex quinque gradus juste capit ire tetrardus."

Ambo *or* **Ambon** *(Gk.,* ἄμβων from ἀναβαίνω.) A desk or pulpit. The raised platform in Eastern churches, on which the singers mounted when they sang. A canon of the Council of Laodicea (A.D. 360-370) decreed that no one should sing in the church besides the regular singers (πλὴν τῶν κανονικῶν ψαλτῶν), who ascended the *ambo* and sang from the parchment (ἀπο διφθέρας). This early attempt to bring about the separate performance of trained choir-singers did not obtain any favour in the Western churches of that period, and with the introduction of congregational song, the *ambo* became disused.

Ambrosian Chant. The system of church-song introduced by Ambrose, Bishop of Milan, in the fourth century. It formed the basis of the Gregorian system. [Plain Song.]

Ambrosian Hymn. The " Te Deum" so-called, because, by some, its authorship is attributed to Bishop Ambrose.

Ambrosian Te Deum. A musical setting of the Te Deum in plain-song, called after Bishop Ambrose because of its antiquity and the possibility of its having been the first setting of the Hymn after the introduction of properly-regulated song into Christian worship. Marbecke, who adapted it to English words, chose a simple setting, and a comparison between his version and others will be found interesting. Meibomius (in his well-known work, Ant. Mus. Auct. Septem. 1652), published it with Greek notation, as an exponent of his own principles, not as a copy of any authorized edition. [Plain Song.]

Ambubajæ (*Lat.*) Companies of immoral Syrian women, who attended festivals and gatherings among the Romans as minstrels. Their instruments were called *abub*, or *ambub*, whence their name.

Ambulant (*Fr.*) Wandering. Applied to strolling musicians.

Ame (*Fr.*) The sound-post of a violin, or other stringed instrument of its kind.

American Organ. An instrument having one or more manuals, and registers which control series of free reeds. It is, in its principles of construction, diametrically opposed to the Harmonium, for whereas in this, air is forced through the reeds from a bellows, — in the American Organ the action of the treadle exerts *suction*. When it is required to shut off a row of reeds, the putting in of the stop-handle places a thick air-tight covering of *felt* over the outside of the row of reeds, so that the air cannot be sucked through them,—the drawing of the stop, by removing this obstruction, allows the free passage of the air through the reeds. In short, in the Harmonium, air is blown from the bellows through the reeds; in the American Organ, air is sucked through the reeds into the bellows. There are, however, other differences. The reeds of the American Organ are thinner than those of the Harmonium, and are slightly curved in shape, by which greater quickness of *speech* is insured. A very beautiful *undulating* tone is obtained by setting in motion a rotating *fan*, immediately above one of the rows of vibrators. This, by producing a variable pressure of air just outside the reeds, affects also their vibration as they draw it in. The mechanism which sets the fan in motion is called the *Vox Humana* stop. When there is an *Expression* stop it gives the player some control over the pressure of suction, and thus it is the converse of the stop of the same name in the Harmonium; but the effects which can be produced by its use are more striking in the latter instrument. The tone of American Organs is extremely melodious and sweet, but it does not *travel* well. For chamber music these instruments are eminently qualified, not only because of the character of their tone, but because they possess the enormous advantage of remaining for a longer period and under varying circumstances—*in tune.*

A mezza aria (*It.*) A compromise between Air and recitative. [Aria parlante:]

A mezza voce (*It.*) With half the strength of the voice. (2) The quality between the chest and head voice. (3) The subdued tone of instruments.

A moll (*Ger.*) A minor, the tonality of the relative minor to the key of C.

A monocorde (*Fr.*) On one string.

Amore, con (*It.*) With love, affection, tenderness, ardour.

Amorevole (*It.*) Affectionately.

Amorevolmente (*It.*) Tenderly.

A Moresco (*It.*) In the Moorish style.

Amorosamente (*It.*) Lovingly.

Amoroso (*It.*) In a loving style.

Amor-schall. A horn of peculiar construction invented in the year 1760, by Kölbel, one of the musicians of the Emperor of Russia. It was intended as an improvement upon the ordinary French horn, but the introduction of the cylinder and valve system led to the disuse of the Amor-schall. A duet for these instruments was composed by Cherubini, and dedicated to Lord Cowper.

Amphibrachys. A foot consisting of a long between two short syllables, ˘ ¯ ˘. [Metre.]

Amphimacer. A foot consisting of a short between two long syllables, ¯ ˘ ¯. [Metre.]

Amplitude of vibration. The distance from the point of rest of a particle, to either end of its journey, when a sound-wave passes over it. [Acoustics, §3.]

Ampollosamente (*It.*) ⎱ In a bombastic,
Ampolloso (*It.*) ⎰ inflated style.

Ampoulé (*Fr.*) Bombastic.

Amusement (*Fr.*) A short and lively piece of music. (*It.*) *Divertimento.*

Anabasis (*Gk.*), ἀνάβασις, a succession of ascending sounds.

Anabathmi (*Gk.*), ἀναβαθμοὶ, the name given to certain antiphons in the Greek Church; so called because their words were selected from the Psalms called in the Septuagint ῷδαὶ τῶν ἀναβαθμῶν (Ps. 120-134 in Eng. version), "Songs of degrees," the *gradual* Psalms of the Roman use.

Anakampsis (*Gk.*), ἀνάκαμψις, a succession of descending sounds.

Anakamptos. [Anakampsis.]

Anakara (*Gk.*) The ancient kettledrum. A larger sort was used for battle purposes, and there was a smaller drum which a woman could hold with one hand and beat with the other. [Drum.] [Nacchera.]

Anakarista (*Gk.*) A drum player.

Anapæst. A foot consisting of a long preceded by two short syllables, ˘ ˘ ¯. [Metre.]

Anaploke (*Gr.*) ἀναπλοκή. A combination of notes ascending the scale; opposed to καταπλοκή, a descending series of combined sounds.

Anche (*Fr.*) The reed in the mouth-piece of a hautboy, bassoon, &c., the name also applied to a reed in an organ. [Reed.]

Ancia (*It.*) [Anche.]

Ancora (*It.*) Again, once more, encore.

Ancor piu mosso (*It.*) Still quicker, more motion yet.

Andacht (*Ger.*) Devotion.

Andächtig (*Ger.*) Devotionally, devoutly.

Andamento (*It.*) (1) An accessory idea, or episode ; an accessory part, in a Fugue. (2) In the style of an Andante.

Andante (*It.*) Walking. In the early part of the last century, music so marked was understood to be of a grand yet cheerful style, but in the present day it implies a movement which is slow, graceful, distinct and peaceful. The word is sometimes used as a substantive, in speaking of that portion of a symphony or sonata so marked. The many modifications both of pace and style are expressed as below :

Andante affettuoso, in an easy, pathetic style.

Andante cantabile, in a singing style.

Andante con moto, an uninterrupted andante.

Andante grazioso, in graceful motion.

Andante maestoso, with majesty.

Andante non troppo, moderately, but not too slow.

Andante pastorale, graceful, and with pastoral simplicity.

Andantemente (*It.*) Easily, fluently, without interruption, in the manner of an Andante.

Andantino (*It.*) A diminutive of Andante, unfortunately interpreted in two directly opposite ways. By some it is understood to mean, *not so slow* as andante : by others, *rather slower* than andante. This difference of opinion results from the ambiguity of an expression which literally means "rather going."

Andante sostenuto, moderately, and very smoothly.

Andar diritto (*It.*, Go straight on.

Andare in tempo (*It.*) To go in time. Keep the time.

Anelantemente (*It.*) Ardently, eagerly, pantingly.

Anelanza
Anelito (*It.*) } Shortness of breath.

Anemochord. A variety of the Eolian harp, made by Jacob Schnell, in Paris, 1789. [Eolian harp.]

Anemometer. [Wind-gauge.]

Anesis (*Gk.*) ἄνεσις, from ἀνίημι, to loosen. (1) The progression from a high sound to one lower in pitch. (2) The tuning of strings to a lower pitch (ἄνεσις χορδῶν.)

Anfangs-ritornel (*Ger.*) Introductory symphony. [Symphony, § 4.]

Anfangs-grunde (*Ger.*) Rudiments, principles, beginnings.

Angelica (*Ger.*)
Angelique (*Fr.*) } [Vox angelica.]

Angenehm (*Ger.*) Pleasing, agreeable.

Anglaise (*Fr.*) } The English contra danse.
Anglico (*It.*) } [Country dance.]

Anglican Chant. [Chant.]

Angore (*It.*) Anguish, grief, distress, passion.

Angosciamente (*It.*) } Sorrowfully,
Angosciamento (*It.*) } anxiously.

Angosciosissamente (*It.*) With extreme sorrow.

Angoscioso (*It.*) Anxious, painful.

Anhaltende Cadenz (*Ger.*) A lengthened cadence, an organ or pedal point.

Anhang (*Ger.*) [Coda.]

Anima, con (*It.*) With animation, spirit.

Animato (*It.*) Lively.

Animazione (*It.*) Liveliness, animation.

Animo, con (*It.*) With courage, spirit, dash, and fire.

Animo Corde (*It.*) [Anemochord.]

Animosamente (*It.*) Spiritedly, energetically.

Animosissamente (*It.*) }
Animosissimo (*It.*) } Exceedingly bold, energetic, and spirited.

Animoso (*It.*) Lively, energetic.

Anklang (*Ger.*) Tune, harmony, accord.

Anklingeln (*Ger.*) To sound or ring a bell.

Anklingen (*Ger.*) To accord in sound, to be in tune.

Anlage (*Ger.*) Indication of talent : the sketch of a musical thought ; also the plan or design of a composition.

Anlaufen (*Ger.*) To increase or swell in sound.

Anleitung (*Ger.*) Instruction, guidance, direction, preface.

Anmuth (*Ger.*) Charm, sweetness, grace, agreeableness.

Anonner (*Fr.*) To stutter, to hesitate. To stumble in performing, to play in an unskilful style.

Anpfeifen (*Ger.*) To whistle at, to hiss at ; in music, to condemn. [Fiasco.]

Ansatz (*Ger.*) (1) Attack, *q.v.* (2) The adjustment of the mouth to the position required for the production of the voice in singing. (3) The adjustment of the lips necessary for the proper production of the tone of wind instruments, as in French, "embouchure," and in English, "lipping," *q.v.*

Anschlag (*Ger.*) (1) Touch, or the production of tone upon such keyed instruments as the organ, pianoforte, or harmonium. (2) The clash of a discord before resolution. [Percussion.]

Ansingen (*Ger.*) To welcome with song.

Ansprechen (*Ger.*) } To sound, to sing, to
Anstimmen (*Ger.*) } give out tone.

Anstimmung (*Ger.*) Intonation, sounding, singing.

Antecedent. (1) A phrase or point proposed for Imitation. (2) Any passage which is answered. (3) The subject of a Fugue.

Anthem.—A composition for voices, with or without organ or other instrumental accompaniment, enjoined by the Ritual of the Anglican Church to be sung at Morning and Evening service, "in choirs and places where they sing." The words are generally selected from the Psalms, or other portions of the Bible, but paraphrases of Scripture, and words in prose and metre, of less authority, are sometimes used. It is the one ornament of the Service, reserved for the Choir, in which the congregation takes no part.

2. Anthems may be divided into various kinds, according to the character of the words; but with this division it is not our province to deal. The form of the music suggests four divisions, namely: the Full, the Full with verses, the Verse, and the Solo. When Anthems were accompanied with instruments other than the organ, they were formerly called Instrumental Anthems.

3. A Full Anthem, which is the earliest model, consists entirely of chorus, with or without Organ accompaniment. A Full and Verse Anthem is one in which certain parts are assigned to voices *soli*, with choruses to commence and conclude. A Verse Anthem is one that *begins* with portions intended to be sung by a single voice to a part, the word *verse* probably meaning a turn of thought to be forcibly or clearly expressed, a change of treatment or sentiment properly echoed in the style of the music. The words of the *verse* are often chosen from portions of Scripture other than the main body of the Anthem, by way of gloss. The chief voices on one side, Decani or Cantoris, usually sing the Verse, and the whole choir, both sides, the chorus or Full part. The character of the Solo Anthem is sufficiently obvious, through its title; in every case there is, however, a concluding chorus, even if it be only the word *Amen* once sung. An Instrumental Anthem may partake of either or all the characteristics of the Anthems above described. At the end of the 17th and beginning of the 18th centuries the Instrumental Anthem was in frequent use at the Chapel Royal, St. James's; and, until thirty years ago, the whole of the music sung at the Festival of the Sons of the Clergy, at St. Paul's Cathedral, was regularly given with the accompaniment of a full orchestra. This custom was revived on the like occasion in 1873 with fine effect.

The Anthem is especially an English production, a development of the Motett; but the *Antifona* of the Italians, the *Antienne* of the French, and the *Wechselgesang* of the Germans, preserve to this day the character of the same prototype. The Antiphon was a special selection of words intended to be suitable to the service for the day, and was invariable, but the words of the Anthem in the Anglican Church were chosen by the composer, with or without reference to any particular Season, the early composers very rarely mentioning the special season for which they intend their music. The ignorance of Præcentors and other rulers of the choir, or their partiality for some one class of composition has often led them into having Anthems performed that are ludicrously inappropriate to the Season.

4. The history of the Anthem may be comprised within a period of little more than three centuries, and falls into three divisions, namely: the Motett period, the Verse period, and the Modern period. The Motett period lasted from the time of the Reformation to the death of Henry Lawes, say from 1550 to 1650. During the troublous times of the Commonwealth, the Anthem, in common with nearly all other Church music, excepting hymn tunes, had little or no life or character. The Verse period existed from 1670 to about 1777, the time of the death of the elder Hayes. To this succeeded another lapse of more than forty years, during which time Church needs in this matter were supplied by a series of adaptations from Oratorios and Masses, which were greatly favoured,—even Madrigals were laid under forced contribution. The absence of proper encouragement to original composers prevented many able writers, the elder Samuel Wesley among others, from employing their talents towards relieving the want of the Church. That Wesley was a writer of no mean order of genius the existence of his Latin Motetts "Omnia Vanitas," "In Exitu Israel," "Exultate Deo," sufficiently proves.

The modern period commenced with Thomas Attwood, and was continued by the younger Samuel Sebastian Wesley, and John Goss. The earliest composers of music for the Reformed Church have left no examples of either solo or verse Anthems, their contributions to this order of music being similar in character and construction with the Motett of the Italian Church. The greater portion of the Anthems, by the early English writers, were adaptations of English words to music formerly set to Latin words, a proceeding both useful and needful in the shifting period immediately succeeding the Reformation. The first music set to English words for the service of the Church—exclusive of Marbecke's plain-song—was the work of Thomas Tallis, organist to the Court, in the reigns of Henry VIII., Edward VI., Queens Mary and Elizabeth; and much of his music, which is still extant, is a mere collection of dry contrapuntal exercises without much attempt at musical or religious expression, although some of it exhibits great originality and an agreement with the character of the words. The next writer of importance was William Byrde (1543-1623.) His Anthems, set to Latin words, and first published in 1589 under the title of "Cantiones Sacræ," were afterwards adapted, probably by himself, to English words of like character. One of them, still frequently in use, "Bow Thine ear," or "Be not wroth, very sore," for there are two versions of the same composition, was originally sung to the words, "Civitas sancti Tui," the second part of the Motett, "Ne irascaris;" and the music beautifully expresses the sentiment of the text. It is only occasionally that such a happy combination is found in the works of Anthem writers up to the period of the restoration of Charles II.; for, although the compositions of Tye, Tallis, Farrant, Allison, Morley, Hooper, Byrde, Bull, and Gibbons, are models of constructive skill, there is little that could be fairly called musical expression to be found in any one of them. Neither was there any distinction of style between sacred and secular music at this period. For example, the madrigal by Gibbons, "The Silver Swan," and his Anthem, "Hosanna," might change places, so that the madrigal might be made an anthem, and the anthem a madrigal, without any violation of character, and yet each would be counted a noble specimen of its class. It was not until men's manners and modes of thought had undergone the change brought about by the emancipation necessarily succeeding a reformation in religion, that a special and marked difference was made between the style of music used for the Church and that for secular purposes. For nearly twenty years, that is, from the death of Lawes in 1645, to the time when Pelham Humphreys was writing. Church music was represented by such writers as Child and Rogers, the best of whose compositions are but pale reflections of old styles. The pause in church matters, during the Commonwealth, had its bad effect upon Church music, until the new interest aroused by the works of foreign writers produced fresh vitality. When Humphreys began to supply the want in Church music caused by the revival of the service according to the Ritual of the Prayer-book, some degree of difficulty arose, for it was impossible to pursue the practice formerly in vogue, of making little, if any, difference in the style of sacred and secular music, for secular music had now assumed a character unfitted for the dignity and solemnity of Divine worship. To meet this difficulty a sort of compromise was effected; the secular style of a preceding generation was adopted as the prevailing standard character for Church music, a practice which has continued in use to this day. Now, as then, recently acquired ideas were used in combination with old fashioned notions, and at the period of the history of the Anthem, now being treated of, the novelty introduced was the Verse, the effect of French and Italian influence upon English music. The best Verse and Solo Anthems are those by Humphreys, Purcell, Wise, Weldon, Blow, Croft, and Greene; and, with the last named writer, the verse Anthem proper culminated, and then decayed, for the poor productions of Nares, Kent, Pring, and others, although popular in their day, simply lumber the shelves upon which they are placed. Boyce and the elder Hayes were more successful in their Full, than in their Verse Anthems, some of which are models of beauty and effective writing. It is a singular fact that for many years there was a hiatus in the supply of original Anthems, the exigencies of the Church service being supplied by a series of bad arrangements, for, counting the single contributions furnished by men of genius like Battishill, who were living between the time of Boyce and Wesley, the majority of these contributions were the weak repetition of themes that had been better treated before. Thomas Attwood, a pupil of Mozart, and organist at St. Paul's Cathedral, was the first who made the laudable endeavour to supersede bad arrangements by attempting to give some adequate and connected expression to the words set as Anthems; and, although his works are to a great extent valueless as Church music, his intention should be mentioned with respect, especially as his writings and mode of thought aroused the emulation of a worthy series of followers.

It is interesting in reviewing the history of the Anthem to notice to what an extent organ accompaniment has developed and expanded. The Anthems of the first period are as effective without organ support as with it, and in those choirs in which an unaccompanied service is sometimes performed, they form the repertory from which selections are made. The organ part to Anthems of the second period is almost indispensable, by reason of the frequency with which *ritornelli*, and solos and duets are introduced. In the Anthems of the more modern period the organ is exalted almost to the dignity of a solo instrument, many Anthems being written less for vocal than for instrumental effect. The variety of stops, improved mechanism of the organ, and the advanced skill of cathedral organists form a combination too tempting to the composer, who is, in most cases, himself an organist. The tendency of most of the music written for the organ is to treat it as an imitation of an orchestra; this improper use of the instrument is influencing the character of the Anthems of the present day; and, unless composers are wise in time, the Church music of the latter part of the 19th, will be as feeble and as useless to future generations as that of the latter part of the 18th century.

5. The first published collection of Anthems in score was that made in 1724 by Dr. W. Croft, of his own compositions, the only piece of Church music' which had been previously issued in this style, being a service by Henry Purcell. The old practice of printing each part separately not only led to the loss of the several parts, but also increased the difficulty of a correct understanding of the effect, for want of a score. Of Barnard's Church music, printed in this manner, no perfect copy is known to exist, as even the parts intended for the several voices on the Decani and Cantoris sides of the choir were published in separate and distinct books.

6. Many suggestions have been made as to the derivation of the word Anthem, of which the following are the chief:—

(a). From the word Antiphon, it being understood that the Anthem was the successor of the more ancient Antiphon. If it was the intention of the framers of the Prayer-book to continue the use of the Antiphon it would probably have been expressed, and a table of the Antiphons proper to the Church Seasons would have been compiled and inserted among the directions for order of the service, in like manner with the table of lessons and the division of the Psalms. If, however, this direction was omitted, the tradition of their retention would doubtless remain, and so it would be found that the early Anthem writers would have been saved the trouble of making their own selection of words, and' would have set to music the words of the Antiphons, all of which were taken from Scripture, and therefore in conformity with the principle of the Reformation; but this was not done, as a reference to the Anthems in Barnard's Collections, and to the words in Clifford's Anthem-book, sufficiently shows.

(b). From ἀντίφωνος, or according to some, the mediæval ἀνθυμνὸς, on the supposition that the Anthems or Antiphons were sung from side to side of the church. The choir being still divided according to ancient custom, the practice of antiphonal singing is apparently maintained, if by such a term alternation is implied. But Antiphony means classically, singing at the octave, and anthem singing is the reverse of such antiphonal singing.

Durandus gives another meaning to the word, when he says, that the sentences which precede the Psalms and Canticles are called Antiphons "non quia alternatim a diversis choris cantentur; sed quia sicut claves et indices, ad quorum modulationem ac sonum, sequens canticum psalmusque alternatim cantatur. Tonus enim totius psalmi ex tono antiphonæ sumitur"—"not because they are sung by two choirs alternately, but because they are as keys and indices to the tone and mode, to which the Canticle or Psalm following ought to be chanted antiphonally. For the tone of the whole Psalm is taken from that of the Antiphon." When the Præcentor of ancient times started the Tone for the psalms some sort of antiphonal singing was practised between him and the Choir, in singing the Antiphons; and the connection of the word Anthem with *responds* and *invitatories* in the preface to the Prayer-book, would seem to imply alternate singing. The word Anthem is used three times in the Prayer-book, to the Venite, to the portions of Scripture appointed to be sung in place of the Venite on Easter-day, and in the Rubric after the third Collect. In two out of these three cases the word is used in the same sense as the old Antiphon. An antiphonal character (in the sense of alternating) is implied by the use of the words in the Office for the Communion of the Sick in the Liturgy of King Edward VI., A.D. 1549, but as the office does not comprise singing, it may be inferred that the words Anthem and Antiphon in this case refer to other than a musical meaning. It may be here mentioned that the word Anthem was at one time applied to texts of Scripture—Bishop Scory's text for his sermons preached at St. Paul's Cross, being called his Anthem—and also to secular compositions as well as sacred. In the Prioress's Tale, of Chaucer, the words—

"—— bad me for to synge
This antym veraily in my deying,"

refer to the ancient Hymn, "Alma redemptoris." Shakspeare makes Falstaff use the word with a very different application; and the "Boar's Head Carol" annually sung at Queen's College in Oxford, was until recently, called an Anthem in the printed copies.

(c). A derivation from the word ἀνάθεμα has been suggested, under the impression that an Anthem is an invocation; and it is curious to note in confirmation of this conjecture, that in the original edition published in 1663, of Clifford's words of Anthems, the first book of its kind ever issued, the majority of the selected verses set as Anthems—144 out of 167 —are of an invocatory character.

(d). Lastly, the word has been derived from ανθημα (a flower), from whence the word anthology. The ancient and still existing name for the book containing the words and notes of the anthems or antiphons, is Anthologium or Antiphonarium, probably from the idea that a collection of such words might reasonably be considered as a series of choice flowers from Holy writ, as the Anthem was formerly held to be the flower of the service, by those who attended church for the sake of listening to it only, and who left in an unseemly manner at its close,—a vicious habit which is scarcely yet extinct.

Anthema (*Gk.*) ἄνθεμα, short poetic form of ἀνάθημα, literally anything set up (ἀνατίθημι), hence ornaments or apparatus of a feast; hence *music and dancing*.

Anthologium (*Gk.*) A collection of antiphons set to music. A term used in imitation of the word ἀνθολογίαι, collections of small Greek poems, selected and made up, as it were, into a nosegay, from ἄνθος, a flower, λέγω, to pick. [Antiphonarium.]

Anthropoglossa (*Gk.*) [Vox Humana.]

Antibacchius. A foot consisting of two long syllables, followed by one short, ˉ ˉ ˘

Anticipation. The introduction of notes before the time in which they are naturally expected in the harmony, *e.g.*:

Antico (*It.*) Ancient.

Antienne (*Fr.*)
Antifona (*It.*) } [Anthem.]

Antifonario (*It.*)
Antiphonaire (*Fr.*) } [Antiphonary.]

Antiphon. (1) In ancient Greek music antiphony (ἀντιφωνή, or ἀντίφωνοι) meant "sounds in octaves" as being responsive to, or over against each other. The relation between sounds at the interval of an octave was thus implied by ἀντιφωνή, while the actual interval of an octave was called *diapason*.

(2) From the above meaning of the word it came in time to be applied to the alternate singing of choirs, as being similar in some respects to the ἐπίρρημα and ἀντεπίρρημα of the old Tragedy. The word Antiphony is the more appropriate for recitation *alternatim* if it be remembered that in the earliest public services of Christianity a choir of women and children was often responded to by a choir of

men: δύο γίνονται τὸ πρῶτον χοροί, ὁ μὲν ἀνδρῶν, ὁ δὲ γυναικῶν (Philo de Vita, cont.). The custom of antiphonal singing seems to have been first introduced at Antioch by Diodorus and Flavian: οὗτοι πρῶτοι διχῇ διελόντες τοὺς τῶν ψαλλόντων χοροὺς ἐκ παραδοχῆς ἄδειν τὴν Δαυιδικὴν ἐδίδαξαν μελῳδίαν· καὶ τοῦτο ἐν Ἀντιοχίᾳ πρῶτον ἀρξάμενον παντόσε διέδραμε καὶ κατέλαβε τῆς οἰκουμένης τέρματα (Theod. Hist. Eccl.). Afterwards, through the musical ability of Ambrose, the same system of psalmsinging became general in the Western church. Although Christian authors give accounts of antiphonal singing as something new, there can be no doubt of its great antiquity. There are sufficient allusions to it in the Old Testament to show that it was well known to the Jews; and the very structure of many of the Psalms implies its existence. In our own times, the choirs of cathedrals and churches are usually (when seated in the chancel,—not in a west gallery) divided into two sides, one called Decani, from the fact that it is on the Dean's side of the choir (south); the other, Cantoris, because it is placed on the Precentor's or Succentor's side (north). The Psalms are sung by alternate verses, from side to side, both sides joining in the Gloria Patri. In some foreign churches, the Antiphony consists of the chanting of one verse by a single voice, the next being sung by the full choir, in response. This is not a correct system, ritualistically speaking, although, in the Church of England, in those rare places where they do *not* sing, the minister and congregation go through an exactly similar process. The Antiphony, which was once common in this country, between the minister and parish-clerk, who rivalled each other in the uncommon phases of meaning which their particular method of "saying" the Psalms often rendered prominent, is now happily almost obsolete. Miraculous stories of the introduction of responsive choir-singing are not wanting. Socrates, in his ecclesiastical history (Book vi. chap. viii), says: "Ignatius, third Bishop of Antioch in Syria from the Apostle Peter, who had also conversed familiarly with the Apostles themselves, saw a vision of angels hymning in alternate chants the Holy Trinity; after which he introduced the mode of singing he had observed in the vision into the Antiochian Churches, whence it was transmitted by tradition to all the other churches."

(3) A short sentence, generally from Holy Scripture, sung before and after the Psalms for the day, or the Canticles, selected for its appropriateness to the Church season in which it is sung. As an example, one of the Antiphons used on the fourth Sunday in Advent is here given:

Ca-ni-te tu - ba in Si - on, qui-a pro-pe est

di- es Do -mi-ni: ec-ce ve - ni-et ad Sal-van-dum nos

(Then follows Ps. cx. to Tone I.). "Dixit Dominus."
Al- le -lu - ia, Al-le -lu - ia.

The use of the Antiphon in this manner, has no doubt grown out of the frequent recurrence of Alleluia, and other devout exclamations as found in the Psalms, which have ever been used in the Church as "Responsoria." The Gallican "Liturgy," which may with probability be ascribed to the second century, commences with an Antiphon. But the word Antiphon is used in many other senses, sometimes even given to a complete set of Versicles and Responses; thus Augustine and his followers are said to have entered Canterbury singing as an Anthem (Antiphona) one of the Litanies. Certain of the hymns sung at the end of Compline are also called Antiphons.

(4) The greater Antiphons (Antiphonæ majores) are sung on the eight days preceding Christmas-day, before the Magnificat. The first of them commences with the words, "O Sapientia," which is still found in the calendar of the English Prayer-book, on December 16th. It will be found interesting to compare the text of these greater Antiphons as found in the Sarum use, and in the Vesperal now issued from Mechlin.

(5) In the early Greek Church, in the services of which, hymns and canticles of all kinds were sung by two alternating choirs, the word Antiphon was specially applied to the three canticles which preceded the lesser Introit.

(6) Antiphona (*Lat.*) An Anthem. The English word is supposed to have been corrupted from the Latin. But several other explanations, which have been brought forward from time to time, will be found *sub voce.* [Anthem.]

Antiphonarium (*Lat.*)
Antiphonaire. Anti- } [Antiphonary.]
phonier (*Fr.*)
Antiphonary. } A service book of the
Antiphoner. } Roman Church, which contained originally the *antiphons* sung in the services of the Hours, properly arranged and *noted,* to which, from time to time, other portions of music and words were added, such as Invitatories, Hymns, Responses, &c. The advantage, perhaps necessity, of referring to ancient copies of service-books for the true restoration of plain-song, which has ever had a tendency to vary in its character

by unauthorized additions, or *foliations*, was felt as much one thousand years ago as it is now. For we read that the good lessons in plain-chant given to the French clergy, when Pope Stephen II. was the guest of Pepin, King of France, were soon forgotten; and that in the time of his son, Charlemagne, the church-song had become exceedingly corrupt. Charlemagne, for the purpose of remedying this, obtained the services and help of Theodore and Benoît, who carried with them from Rome a copy of the *Antiphoner* of Gregory, which the Pope himself (Adrian) had *noted.* Other accounts are to be found of these reformations of plain-chant, all of which however point to the importance of the preservation of, and reference to, old antiphoners. And later on, in the 12th century, we find St. Bernard the Abbot making efforts to stem the tide of innovations, by publishing his tract—"De Cantu seu correctione Antiphonarii"—in which he says, "take the antiphonary used at Rheims, and compare it with that of Beauvais, or Amiens, or Soissons, which are almost at your doors, and see if they are the same, or even like each other."

The number of service-books seems to have rapidly increased; for, by the constitutions of Archbishop Winchelsey (A.D. 1305) it was required that every church in the province of Canterbury should be provided with a Legend, an Antiphonary, a Grail, a Psalter, a Troper, an Ordinal, a Missal, and a Manual. In 1549, when all such books were abolished to make way for the "Booke of Common Praier," they appear to have been still more numerous: being described as "Antiphoners, Missals, Grayles, Processionals, Manuals, Legends, Pies, Portuasses, Primers in Latin or English, Couchers, Journals, and Ordinals." The Grayle, or Gradual, contained tracts, sequences, hallelujahs, creeds, offertories, the sanctus, and the office of sprinkling with holy water. Legends, or Lectionaries, contained the Lessons, which were not in the Antiphonary. It is unnecessary here to enter into an explanation of all these terms; suffice it to say, that the copying of choir-books was a matter of great labour, and that the books themselves were in consequence very costly. It is related by Spelman that two antiphonaries cost the Monastery of Crabhuse, in Norfolk, twenty-six marks in the year 1424; and it is also related that a common Missal cost five marks—a year's income of a cleric at that time. Upon the dissolution of monasteries, valuable books of this sort were dispersed throughout the country, and, from carelessness or wanton waste, destroyed in large numbers.

Antispastus. A foot, consisting of two long between two short syllables, ⌣ − − ⌣

Antistrophe. [Strophe.]

Anwachsend (*Ger.*) Swelling, crescendo.

Aperto (*It.*) Open. The use of the damper-pedal in pianoforte music.

Appelregal (*Ger.*) A reed stop in the organ now no longer made ; the pipes, which were small, had a round hollow nob at the top like an apple, whence the name.

Antode(*Gk.*) ἀντῳδή. Responsive singing.

Aoidoi (*Gk.*). plural of ἀοιδός. Minstrels, bards. (*Lat.*) *Vates.* [Bard.]

A piacere (*It.*) ⎱ (1)At pleasure. Not
A piacimento (*It.*) ⎰ strictly in time, ad libitum. (2) The introduction of a cadenza.

Aplomb (*Fr.*) Steadiness, self-possession.

A poco a poco (*It.*) More and more. By degrees. Applied to the increase of time or expression.

A poco piu lento (*It.*) A little slower.

A poco piu mosso (*It.*) Somewhat faster.

Apollo-lyra. [Psalmmelodicon.]

Apollonicon. An organ. invented in 1800 by John Henry Völler, of Hesse Darmstadt, and manufactured in London by Messrs. Flight and Robson in 1828; it consisted of about 1900 pipes, with six sets of keys, so that half a dozen performers might play simultaneously. The action was so arranged, that it might be performed upon by six players in the ordinary manner, or the various effects might be elicited by the revolution of certain cylinders which set the wind in motion, and regulated the stops according to the character of the music played. An imitation of an orchestra, with the usual instruments, including kettle-drums, was the object sought to be gained by the invention.

Apolutikion (*Gk.*) ἀπολυτίκιον. A hymn sung at the close of Vespers in certain seasons of the Greek Church. The word is probably derived from the opening sentence of the Nunc Dimittis, " νῦν ἀπολύεις τὸν δοῦλόν σου," and signifies a hymn of dismissal.

Apopemptic Song. An ancient farewell or parting hymn usually sung to a stranger about to return to his own land. Apopemtic strains were sung to the gods on certain days on which it was believed that the several deities returned to their original countries.

Apotome (*Gk.*) Ἀποτομή. A major semitone. " Major pars toni : quæ semitonium majus vulgariter dicitur" (Tinctor.) "Id quod vere semitonium nuncupatur. pars toni minor est quam dimidia. Reliqua igitur pars. quæ major est. apotome nuncupatur a Græcis, a nobis vero potest vocari *decisio*." (Boethius De Inst. Mus., Lib. ii., cap. 29 et 30.)

Appassionato (*It.*) With feeling, passion, or affection.

Appassionamento (*It.*) With passion, love.

Appassionatamente (*It.*) Passionately.

Appenato (*It.*) With an expression of suffering, with bitterness or grief.

Applause. Praise or approbation expressed by clapping the hands, stamping the feet or the utterance of certain cries, as *bravo, encore.* In the ancient Greek theatre, Donaldson says, that "the conduct of the audience was much the same as that of the spectators in our own theatres, and they seem to have had little scruple in expressing their approbation or disapprobation, as well to the poet as to the actors. Their mode of doing this was sometimes very violent, and even in the time of Machon it was customary to pelt a bad performer with stones."

Hissing, as an expression of disapproval or contempt, is of very ancient use, and it was the custom to augment the power of the hiss, by blowing through reeds and whistles, a custom not altogether unrepresented in later times, when cat-calls, introduced into an English theatre, gave Addison a subject for an amusing paper (No. 361) in the Spectator. The hollow pipe of a key serves the purpose of the ancient *calamus* or *fistula*, in modern Italy, and the frequency with which indifferent operas are received " colla chiave," proves that the spirit of old times still lives and is active. [Fiasco.]

History shows us that applause was not confined to secular performances, but was allowed and even looked for in churches as well as theatres. Hone, in his " Ancient Mysteries described," quotes the following passage relative to this custom : Jerome desired Gregory Nazianzen to explain to him what was meant by *the second Sabbath after the first*, in St. Luke vi. 1. Gregory answered, " I will teach you that at Church, where, *when all the people shall applaud me*, you will be forced to know, what you do not know; for if you only keep silence, you will be looked upon as a fool."

At one time encores were not permitted in France, neither were calls allowed for the author of a piece which had given pleasure. When reforms were taking place, opportunities were found to break through this rule, Jean Baptiste Lemoine or Moyne, in 1789, being the first composer called upon the stage in France after the performance of his opera, "Nephté." A few years later in Italy, Paisiello was the means of removing the prohibition on the audience from applauding at all in San Carlo, for he induced the King to set the example of the change, by applauding an aria sung by Carlo Raino, in the opera "Papirius," produced in the year 1805.

It has been happily said that " Il piu grand 'omaggia alla musica sta nel silenzio," and, influenced by some such principle, the better sort among a mixed audience refrain from indiscriminate applause, encores intended as compliments often becoming an oppressive tax, levied by the unthinking, or those who care little for true art. The general opinion of the reasonable on this subject, is expressed in the following epigram:—

> " The ' sovereign people ' rule all things,
>   So levellers would say;
> But all ' encores ' in concert-rooms,
>   The ' shilling people ' sway."

[Claque.]

Applicatur (*Ger.*) (1) The art of using the fingers freely upon a musical instrument of any kind, (2) shifting *q.v.* and recovering the original position.

Appoggiando (*It.*) Drawing out, lengthening, leaning upon.

Appoggiato (*It.*) Supported. Appoggiato notes are those notes which suspend the resolution, or that supply gaps in passages of intervals. See also PASSING NOTE, SUSPENSION, and SYNCOPATION.

Appoggiatura (*It.*) A note leant upon in singing or playing, applied to beats and grace notes, *q.v.*

Apprestare (*It.*) To make ready, to prepare for playing, to set in tune.

A première vue (*Fr.*) } At first sight.
A prima vista (*It.*) }

A punta d'arco (*It.*) With the end of the bow near the point.

A punto (*It.*) In exact time, precise, strict, accurate.

Apycni (*Gk.*) (ἄπυκνοι). The notes Proslambanomenos (προσλαμβανόμενος), nete synemmenon (νήτη συνημμένων), and nete hyperboleon (νήτη ὑπερβολαίων) of the Greek system of music. The notes are so named because of their remoteness from each other (from ἄπυκνος, not close, not dense).

A quattro mani (*It.*) *À quatre mains* (*Fr.*) For four hands on one instrument, that is, as a duet for two performers on the pianoforte or organ.

A quattro parti (*It.*) } *A quatre seuls* (*Fr.*)
A quattro, soli (*It.*) } For four soloists.

A quattro voci (*It.*) *A quatre voix* (*Fr.*) For four voices in harmony.

Arbitrio (*It.*) Will, pleasure, *a suo arbitrio*, at his pleasure.

Arcato (*It.*) With the bow, as opposed to *pizzicato*, plucked with the finger. *Coll' arco* is a direction to the same effect.

Arched viall. An instrument somewhat in fashion like a hurdy-gurdy, invented about A.D. 1664, and thus described by Pepys in his Diary, under the date October 5th, in that year: "To the Musique meeting at the Post Office, where I was once before. And thither anon came all the Gresham College, and a great deal of noble company; and the

new instrument was brought, called the Arched Viall, where being tuned with Lutestrings, and played on with kees like an organ, a piece of parchment is always kept moving; and the strings, which by the kees are pressed down upon it, are grated in imitation of a bow, by the parchment; and so it is intended to resemble several vyalls played on with one bow, but so basely and so harshly, that it will never do. But after three hours' stay it could not be fixed in tune; and so they were fain to go to some other music of instruments." Pepys had probably no design in writing the word viall in the manner in which he has done; but, in doing so, he has intimated a connection with ancient vielle or hurdy-gurdy, which the Arched viall somewhat resembled; the parchment was doubtless "always kept moving" by means of a wheel.

Archeggiamento (*It.*) (1) The same as *arcato*, or *coll' arco*. (2) The use of the bow.

Archet (*Fr.*) Arco (*It.*) The bow with which stringed instruments are played. [Bow.]

Archicembalo (*It.*) Archicembalo (*Lat.*) A cembalo with an enharmonic scale, supposed to have been invented about the year 1537 in Italy, described by Salinas as having each tone divided into parts, of which three were given to the greater semi-tone and two to the less, the whole octave being divided into thirty-one parts.

Archlute, arciliuto (*It.*) Archiluth (*Fr.*) [Theorbo.]

Arco (*It.*) The bow. *Coll' arco*, with the bow, as opposed to *Pizzicato*, pinched by the finger.

Ardente (*It.*) (*Fr.*) Ardently, with fire.

Arditezza, con (*It.*) With boldness, energy.

Ardito (*It.*) Bold and energetic.

Aretinian syllables. The names Ut, Re, Mi, Fa, Sol, La, given to the Hexachord by Guido d'Arezzo (Guido Aretinus). These syllables happen to occur in consecutive notes of the scale, in an ancient hymn to S. John Baptist.

UT que-ant la-xis RE-so-na-re fi-bris,

MI-ra ge-sto-rum FA-mu-li tu-or-um,

SOL-ve pol-lu-ti LA-bi-i re-a-tum.

Sanc-te Jo-an-nes.

From the system of over-lapping Hexachords, arise the compound names of notes such as E-la-mi, A-la-mi-re, &c., which are explained under Notation.

Arghool. A simply constructed wind instrument, now used in Egypt. It is made of common cane, and is played by mouth-pieces containing reeds. There are two species of *arghool*; the first (Fig. 1) consists of two tubes both pierced with holes, so that the performer may play in thirds and sixths; the second (Fig. 2) consists also of two tubes, but one only is pierced with holes, the other being longer and used as a *drone*. The pitch of the drone can be altered by the addition of extra pieces, which are attached to the instrument, as are also the mouth-pieces, by waxed thread.

Fig. 1.

Fig. 2.

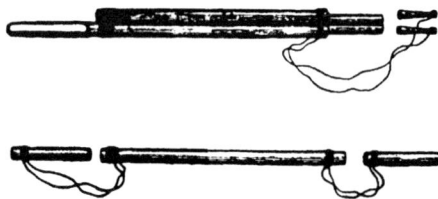

Aria (*It.*) An air, tune, song, or melody in rhythmical proportion, now understood to mean a movement for a single voice or instrument, with an accompaniment. [Air.]

Aria d'abilita (*It.*) A song of difficult execution, requiring great skill in its proper and satisfactory performance.

Aria buffa (*It.*) A song with some degree of humour in the words, or in the treatment of the music.

Aria cantabile (*It.*) An air in a graceful, flowing style, capable of much musical expression.

Aria concertante (*It.*) An air in the concert style, that is a melody for a single voice, accompanied by instruments having *obbligato* or solo passages assigned to them.

Aria di bravura (*It.*) A melody with florid, bold, and energetic passages and phrases for the voice. An *aria di bravura* is more or less an *aria d'abilita*.

Aria fugata (*It.*) A song or air, in which the accompaniment is written in fugal style, or in imitation. The difficulty of expressing dramatic emotions in this species of composition led to its ultimate disuse, though at one time it was greatly in favour. The subjoined specimen, perhaps one of the most expressive of its class, is said to be the work

of Bononcini, usually called the rival of Handel, but it may be the production of either of the other writers concerned in the opera of Thomyris, from whence it was taken. This opera, produced under the direction of Heidegger, at the "King's Theater, in yᵉ Haymarket" in 1709, was a pasticcio of melodies and compositions selected from the works of Albinoni, Gasparini, Steffano, Scarlatti, and Bononcini. The opera was called English, though the singers delivered some portions in Italian, and others in English. The libretto of the opera was by no means of a high poetical order.

"Aria fugata" out of the Opera of Thomyris.

Free - dom, thou greatest bles - sing. thou greatest

blessing, why have I lost my joys, ...

Pi - ning,

pp

no rest pos- ses -sing, no rest pos - ses- sing, Grief

all my hours employs, grief all my hours employs.

Thy

loss now to my eyes a flood of tears will cost, Oh ..

.. why do we not prize our trea sure till 'tis lost.

Aria parlante (*It.*) (1) Vocal music suitable to, and designed for, a proper declamation of the words.

(2) A style of song-writing invented towards the close of the 16th century by those Florentine dilettanti who, imbued with the spirit of Renaissance which had already revolutionized other arts, turned their attention to the necessity of ridding music of cold formalities and restoring it to its proper function, which indeed it held among the Greeks, of being a just vehicle of the ever-varying emotions which poetry calls forth. Monteverde, Peri, Corsi, and Caccini, were the musicians who made the first attempts at *aria parlante*, several operas being composed by them individually or in combination, to words by Rinuccini, in which the *aria parlante* occupied an important position. The *aria parlante* was not a *recitative*, but was sung in strict time. The latter, however, very soon grew out of the former, and assumed a separate existence in the works of Carissimi.

In the preface to the first Opera printed with the music, "Le Musiche de Jacopo Peri, Nobil Fiorentino, sopra L'Euridice de Signor Ottavio Rinuccini, Rappresentate nello Sponsalizio della Christianissima Maria Medici, Regina di Francia e di Navarra. In Venetia, MDCVIII," the author states that the groundwork of the imitation proposed "usassero un armonia, che avanzado quella del parlare ordinario."

The character of this harmony, which was intended to be a medium between common speech and singing, will be seen in the following Aria parlante for Pluto, in answer to Orpheus seeking Euridice :

PLUTONE.

On - de co - tan - to ar - di - re Chi

- nan - ti al di fa - ta - le, Scend' a miei

bas - si reg - ni un huó mor - ta - le.

[Opera.] [Recitative.]

Aria Tedesca (*It.*) An air in the German style—that is to say, in which the accompaniment is inseparable from the melody.

Arie aggiunte (*It.*) Supplementary songs introduced into a work after the first performance or representation.

Arietta (*It.*) The diminutive of aria; a short air or melody.

Ariette (*Fr.*) [Arietta.]

Arioso (*It.*) In the style of an air. (1) A direction that the music to which it refers is to be performed tunefully, sweetly.

(2) An intimation that recitative form has more or less been incorporated into, or perhaps superseded by, a smooth and melodious treatment of the words. The *Arioso* is found in its perfection in the works of Mendelssohn, but examples of it are not wanting in older writers, although they are simply called recitative, *e.g.*, "Behold and see" ("Messiah") and in Nos. 17 and 74 of Bach's Passion (St. Matthew).

Aristoxenians. The followers of the musical system of Aristoxenus. *c.f.* Pythagoreans.

Armer la clef (*Fr.*) To indicate the key by the number of sharps or flats in the signature.

Armoneggiare (*It.*) To harmonise, to sound in chords.

Armonia (*It.*) [Harmony.]

Armonista (*It.*) A harmonist.

Armonica (*It.*) Harmonica, Armonicon, Harmonicon. (1) The musical glasses, a series of glass cups of various sizes and thicknesses, capable of producing the different notes of the diatonic scale by friction upon the edges. The name armonica was given to this instrument by Benjamin Franklin, to whom also the credit of the invention is sometimes given, but the idea was suggested by a Mr. Pickeridge, an Irish gentleman, and first carried out by M. Delaval, and was in use long before the name *armonica* was given to it by Franklin.

(2) An instrument now used by children, consisting of a flat oblong box, containing free reeds so arranged that when applied to the mouth, inspiration and respiration through the orifices in the side, produce different sounds of the scale, in a series. [Cheng.] [Harmonium.]

Arpa (*It.*) [Harp.]

Arpa doppia (*It.*) A double harp. [Harp.]

Arpanetta *or* **arpanella** (*It.*) A small harp.

Arpége (*Fr.*) [Arpeggio.]

Arpeggiando (*It.*) Playing arpeggio, *q.v.*

Arpeggiare (*It.*)⎫ To strike the notes of a chord in succession in
Arpeggiato (*It.*)⎬ the manner of harp playing.

Arpeggiatura (*It.*) [Arpeggio.]

Arpeggio (*It.*) In the style of a harp. A term applied to the notes of a chord when they are struck consecutively, instead of simultaneously.

Una corda.

In pianoforte music a waved line is written beside a chord intended to be played *arpeggio* :

Arrangement. A selection or adaptation of the parts of a composition, to fit them for performance by other voices or instruments than those originally designed.

There are very few examples existing of acknowledged arrangements in the earliest musical publications: for few ever thought of tampering with an author's compositions so far as to divert them from their original intentions. The adaptation of new words,

although it occasionally involved a slight alteration in the time-value of some of the notes, was a matter of small importance ; and the musician who undertook such a matter rarely gave himself the credit of having done so clever a thing as modern arrangers would have us believe such an alteration to be. Thus Nicolas Yonge, in his collection of Madrigals, "Musica Transalpina," London 1588, leaves it to the judgment of the reader to infer the part he took in giving his book to the world, calling his work "Madrigales translated of four, fiue, and sixe parts, chosen out of diuers excellent Authors, vvith the first and second part of La Verginella, made by Maister Byrd, out of two Stanz's of Ariosto, and brought to Speak English with the rest. Published by N. Yonge in favour of such as take pleasure in Musick of voices." For a somewhat lengthened period arrangements were described as "brought to light," "framed," "figured," "fitted," "made proper," and "newly set forth," for example : "Lessons for Consort, made by sundry excellent authors, and set to sixe severall instruments, Namely, the Treble Lute, Treble Violl, Base Violl, Bandora, Citterne, and the Flute. Now newly *set forth* by Philip Rossetor, 1609."

Richard Alison, in his book "An Howres Recreation in Musicke, apt for Instruments and Voyces" (1606), describes his arrangement as "*Framed* for the delight of gentlemen and others which are well affected to that qualitie." A Dutch edition of Gastoldi's ballets for "5 en 6 stemmen, te singen of speelen," 1648, is "gestelt"—that is, arranged or accommodated — "of 3 en 4 stimmen," and this is perhaps one of the earliest instances of an alteration of an original design. Arrangements such as these could only be called into existence by the desire to possess condensations of larger works.

The "Modulorum Hortus ab excellentissimæ Musicæ auctoribus" is described as being merely collected by R. Floridus, Rome, 1647,—"in lucem curavit edendam." A few years later arrangements are described as "transpositions." Thus, in the Mercurius Musicus for 1699, the "New teaching songs, compos'd . . . . With a Thorow Bass for the Harpsichord or Spinett," we have the further intimation of "The songs being *Transpos'd* for the Flute at the end of the Book." In the "Orpheus Britannicus, a collection of all the choicest songs for One, Two, and Three Voices, composed by Mr. Henry Purcell ; together with such Symphonies for Violins or Flutes as were by him designed for any of them, and a Thorow-bass to each song, figur'd for the Organ, Harpsichord, or Theorbo Lute (1698-1702) ; also, in "Suits of the most Celebrated Lessons for Viols, collected and *fitted* to the Harpsichord or Spinett, by William Babell (1702) ;" and in "A choice Collection of Lessons, being excellently *Sett* to the Harpsichord, viz. Old Simon the King, Moteley's Maggot, Mortlack's Grounds, and several others (by Blow and Purcell) 1705." In "A Collection of the Newest Minuets, Rigadoons, and French dances perform'd att Court and Publick entertainments," 1716. The tunes are made "*proper* for the Violin, Hoboy, or Flute," and in "Six Setts of Choice Opera Songs or Arietts, with their Symphonys *fitted* for two Flutes. The Second Parts being compleat and airy as the first, not thin and heavy as Second Trebles usually are ;" in both parts their proper Variations for the Humour of the Flute (1712.)

A little later in date, we find, "Song in the Opera of Flora, with the Humorous Scenes of Hob, designed by yᵉ celebrated Mr. Gravelot, and engrav'd by G. Bickham, Junr. The Musick proper for yᵉ Violin, German and Common Flute, Harpsichord, or Spinet, with a New Base, and thoro' Base to each Song" (1737). The business of arrangement, that is to say, of altering music intended for one purpose, so that it might serve another—more or less hinted at in the preceding collections—arose with the popularity of Handel's works ; thus, copies of "favourite Choruses" out of Mr. Handel's celebrated oratorios "adapted for the Harpsichord or organ and a single voice," began to appear soon after his death. Such "arrangements" being part and parcel of the system of piracy which was most ingeniously and unblushingly carried on during the last century. A chorus arranged for a single voice ceasing of course to be a chorus ; but, as a double security, many of these pieces were made cleverly incorrect. Thus Pitt, organist of Worcester, evaded all copyright that might have existed by arranging. his "Church music" from the sacred works of Handel, by a system of dove-tailing and occasional alteration of key.

"The beauties of Handel, consisting of his most favourite Songs, Duets, and Trios ; arranged with a separate accompaniment for the pianoforte, and figured from the MS. scores of the author, by Jos. Corfe" (c. 1782) is perhaps one of the earliest collections of confessedly "arranged" music. In 1795, J. W. Holder, Mus. Doc., Oxon, one of the most talented pianoforte players of his time, published an arrangement of the choruses of Handel for four hands, which were the standard pieces of their kind for many years, being frequently played by two performers on one organ also. Giambattista Cimador (1750-1810) was probably the first who was employed by the publishers of London on purpose to make arrangements of large works for the piano-

forte, or small bands, his arrangement of Twelve Symphonies by Mozart, as sestetts with a seventh part, *ad libitum*, being considered at the time they were made as of more than ordinary excellence. These were undertaken by Cimador out of pure love for Mozart's works, and a desire to communicate that love to the musicians of his time who thought "Mozart's symphonies too arduous and difficult."

About the same time J. S. C. Possin (1755-1822), a musician of such singular modesty that he never would have his name printed with his works, arranged for Salomon the twelve symphonies of Haydn, known as the "Salomon set," for the pianoforte, in "an admirable manner ;" indeed, says his biographer, "they were the first adaptations of orchestra music worthy of notice." From that time to the present "adaptations, arrangements, and transcriptions," have been issued in unlimited quantities, of more or less value.

Arranger (*Fr.*) To arrange a piece of music. [Arrangement.]

Arrangiren (*Ger.*) To arrange a piece of music. [Arrangement.]

Arsis (*Gk.*) ἄρσις (from αἴρω), a raising, an elevation, as opposed to thesis (θέσις, from τίθημι), a depression or lowering.

There are two kinds of Arsis. (1) of accent ; (2) of metre.

The former of these does not perhaps call for special attention from musicians, unless it be looked upon as a subject into which their educated *ear* qualifies them to enter; or unless it be considered (as it undoubtedly was by the Greeks) as an essential part of the education of those who attempt to set *words* to *music*. The latter has been explained from two opposite points of view, both of which, however, are closely connected with the former,—a slight sketch of the whole subject is therefore subjoined :

(1) Though not accepted without dispute, the following facts seem generally to be admitted ; first, that in speaking, the voice is constantly varying slightly in pitch, that is, is not absolutely on *monotone;* next, that the component syllables of polysyllabic words are not exactly of the same duration; lastly, that there is an emphasis on particular syllables, which is independent alike of the raising or depression of voice, and of the length of time during which any syllable is held.

The elevation, or pitch of the voice is classically termed Accent (from *ad* and *cantus*, just as προσῳδία is from πρὸς and ᾠδή) ; the duration of syllables is called Quantity ; and the metrical emphasis is called Ictus.

Accent is of two kinds, vocabular and

oratorical. The former is that method of pronunciation which a word receives if it stands alone in a vocabulary or dictionary; the latter that which it receives in consideration of its position in a sentence, words being of course influenced by the meaning to be expressed in a sentence of prose, or by their metrical position in verse.

There can be no doubt that a nice ear and appreciation of pitch is required before accent and quantity can be distinguished from each other in modern languages. With regard to ancient languages the same difficulty does not exist, because, putting aside the question of the correctness of our pronunciation of them, quantity is governed by either known laws of syllabic structure and position, or by the actual shape of the letters. Hence, many have thought that *quantity* does not exist in modern languages, and all that we possess is accent (elevation of the voice) and emphasis, and that these two always coincide, and are commonly included in the one term *accent*. But as a matter of fact, the pitch of voice is in modern languages quite independent of quantity, *e.g.*, *precarious, request*, &c., in which the voice is high for the short syllable, drops in pitch for the long, yet no one can doubt that there are long syllables in these words, just as much as in such others, as *probable, symmetry, pendant*, &c. The pronunciation of English in the common conversation will give but a very slight clue to the intricacies of our language in this respect. For, in addition to the acute accent already spoken of, we certainly have a *flat* accent corresponding to the Greek `, *e.g.*, cumbersòme, where the voice drops a little below what might be termed its key-note. We have also the up-and-down slide indicated by the Greek circumflex, *e.g.*, feârful, loâthsome. But with us these are always oratorical, never vocabular.

Having said thus much as to elevation and depression of the voice, it is now time to show how *arsis* is used as a musical term. According to Scaliger, when the voice is raised on a syllable it is called *arsis*, when it returns to its original position it is called *thesis*. Priscian (see Foster on Accent, p. 81, note) not only says the same thing, but gives as an example the word *natura*, pointing out that there is an *arsis* at the syllable *tu*, and thesis on *ra*. In this sense *arsis* is evidently the accent, or elevation of the voice, which has been already spoken of.

(2) But *arsis* and *thesis* are not only applied to the elevation and depression of voice, but also to the *strong* and *weak* parts of metrical scansion. But unfortunately, scholars have used these terms in two ways. For instance, Tate says (see Donaldson, Theatre of the

Greeks, p. 371), "those syllables which have the metrical *ictus* are said to be in *arsi;* those which have it not, in *thesi* . . . . . the latter is sometimes called the *debilis positio*." In this he follows Bentley, who makes *ictus* (or *percussio*), *elevatio*, and *arsis* synonymous.

To this other scholars object, and say truly that a syllable often is in *arsi* as regards *metre*, when it is in *thesi* as regards accent (elevation of voice). Also, Victorinus says distinctly that "*arsis* and *thesis*, as used by the Greeks, refer to the movement of the foot (significant pedis motum), and that the former is 'the elevation of the foot' *without sound*, the latter the 'lowering of the foot' to the ground, *with a sound*, the *sounds* marking the metrical ictus. To this Foster (on Accent, p. 166) agrees. With these authors, therefore, *ictus* and *thesis* are synonymous.

Hence, musicians who agree with the former of these opinions and make *arsis* and *ictus* synonymous are justified in saying that there is an *arsis* on the down-beat of every bar, and its up-beats are in *thesi*, for if *thesis* is *debilis positio*, it would be absurd to say that this occurs on the down-beat, except in some rare cases of syncopation.

Those musicians, on the other hand, who believe that *ictus* and *thesis* coincide, because the *thesis* of the foot marked the *ictus* of the metre, have a perfect right to say that the down-beat of a bar is in *thesi*, and an up-beat in *arsi*.

Inasmuch as the confusion among musicians in using these terms has resulted from the disagreement of scholars as to their proper application, it is much to be hoped that they will be allowed to sink into disuse. The expressions, *strong position* and *weak position* of the bar, imply all that is understood by *arsis* and *thesis*, without the risk, by their use, of calling forth absolutely contradictory opinions as to their meaning.

Art (*Ger.*) Species, kind, sort, as *auf polnische Art*, a sort of *polonaise*, &c.

Articulation. (1) In singing, the art of distinct pronunciation. (2) In instrumental music, the art of producing proper tone by a right adjustment of the fingers, or the lips. The latter application of the term is less commonly met with than the former.

Artist. One who possesses in a high degree that appreciation of the beautiful and that refined temperament, which, when duly trained and educated, become active faculties, and render their owner an able and influential exponent of Art.

As (*Ger.*) A♭.

Asamentata, Assamenta, or **Axamenta** (*Lat.*) The songs or hymns sung by the Salii, *q.v.*

As dur (*Ger.*) The key of A flat major.

(38)

Ashantee Trumpet. An instrument formed of the tusk of an elephant carefully hollowed. Its peculiarity consists in the fact that the embouchure is not at the end, but in the side, a short distance from it.

As moll (*Ger.*) The key of A flat minor.

Asor. [Azor.]

Asosra (*Heb.*) [Chatzozerah.]

Ascaules (*Gk.*) ἀσκαύλης, a player on the ascaulos.

Ascaulos (*Gk.*) ἄσκαυλος, a bagpipe, from ἀσκός, a leathern bag, and αὐλός, a pipe. [Bagpipe.]

Aspiration (*Fr.*) (1) The sign ′ for shortening the duration of a note. [Spiccato.]

(2) A former name for an appoggiatura.

Aspirare (*It.*) To take breath audibly, bad management of the breath in singing.

Asprezza (*It.*) Harshness, severity.

Assai (*It.*) Enough, sufficient.

Assemblage (*Fr.*) (1) A series of rapid passages executed on wind instruments. (2) double tongueing on the flute or cornet.

Assez (*Fr.*) Enough, very, as, *assez lent*, rather slow.

Assonance. Agreement of tone, consonance.

A string. [A §7.]

A suo arbitrio (*It.*) At his judgment, or pleasure.

A suo commodo (*It.*) At his leisure.

A suo bene placito (*It.*) At his pleasure.

A suo luogo (*It.*) At his position or place.

Atabal. A Moorish tambour.

A table sec (*Fr.*) The performance of vocal exercises without the accompaniment of an instrument. *Sec.* lit. *dry*, *c.f.* Lat. *assa vox*, an unaccompanied voice, and *assæ tibiæ*, flutes used without a voice accompaniment.

A tempo (*It.*) In time. [A battuta.]

A tempo commodo (*It.*) In a convenient, easy, moderate time.

A tempo di Gavotta (*It.*) In the time of the Gavotte, *q.v.*

A tempo di Minuetto (*It.*) In the time of the Minuet, *q.v.*

A tempo giusto (*It.*) At a just pace. (1) In general, an indication that the movement should be taken at a moderate tempo. (2) A direction (in older writers) to return to strict time after irregular declamation.

A tempo ordinario (*It.*) At an ordinary pace.

A tempo primo (*It.*) In the time first given.

A tempo rubato (*It.*) Robbed time; time made slightly irregular for the sake of expression.

A tre (*It.*) For three voices, instruments, or parts.

A tre mani (*It.*) For three hands upon an organ or pianoforte.

A tre parti (*It.*) For three parts.

A tre soli (*It.*) For three principals, either vocal or instrumental performers.

A tre stromente (*It.*) For three instruments.

A tre voci (*It.*) For three voices, or parts.

Attacca (*It.*) Commence at once, without a pause.

Attacca subito (*It.*) [Attacca.]

Attaccato subito (*It.*) To be begun at once.

Attack. (1) A vigorous entry of voices or instruments at a leading point. (2) A courageous rendering.

Attacco (*It.*) (Lit. sticking, cleaving to.) A term given to a short and well-defined theme, or passage, in fugal imitation.

Attendant Keys. Relative keys, keys of affinity. Attendant keys in a scale are the relative minor or major, the dominant and subdominant, and their relative minors or majors. [Relative Keys.]

Atto [*It.*] An act in an opera. [Act.]

Attore or **Attrice** (*It*). An actor or actress, the chief singers in an opera.

Aubade (*Fr.*) (1) An open air morning concert, the antithesis of a serenade. (2) The word is derived from *aube*, day-break, and was similar in character to the English "Hunts up" (*q.v.*) Sometimes unmusical noises were made for an aubade, and so the word came to be employed as a term for an insult. The *Aubades de Calène* occupied in France the position of the Waits (*q.v.*) in England, as they were performed in the evening for a month or so before Christmas. Although doubtless of religious origin, the performers gradually introduced secular melodies. The players, like the Waits, were officially licensed. The word *Calène* is a French provincial form of the word Calendes, Christmas Day being formerly called "le jour des Calendes."

Audace, con (*It*). With vigour, boldness.

Auditory nerve. [Ear.]

Auferions (*Old Eng*.) Wire strings.

Aufgeweckt (*Ger*.) Brisk, lively, sprightly, cheerful.

Aufgewecktheit (*Ger*.) Sprightliness, liveliness.

Aufhalten (*Ger*.) To stop, to keep back, retard.

Aufhaltung (*Ger*.) Suspension. [Harmony.]

Auflösung (*Ger*.) Resolution of a discord.

Aufschlag (*Ger*.) Unaccented beat.

Aufstrich (*Ger*). An up bow in violin playing.

Auftakt (*Ger*.) The unaccented part of a bar.

Augmentatio (*Med. Lat*.) The lengthening of a note by the addition of half its length, thus corresponding to the use of the modern dot.

Augmentation. The introduction of the subject of a fugue or canon, in the course of its progress, in notes of longer duration than those in which it was first proposed. [Fugue.]

Augmented interval. [Interval.]

Augmented subject. [Augmentation.]

Auletes (*Gk*.) Αὐλητης. A player on the Aulos or Flute. [Aulos.]

Auletrides (*Gk*.) Plural of αὐλητρίς. Female players on the Aulos or Flute, *q.v.*

Aulæum (*Lat*.), αὐλαία (*Gk*.) The curtain of a theatre.

Aulos (*Gk*.) αὐλός, derived from ἄημι, to blow, as *flute* is from the Lat. *flo*. The most important wind instrument of the Greeks. The aulos was sometimes double, the two tubes being called *dextra* and *sinistra*, and sometimes *male* and *female*. Though generally rendered *flute*, there is much reason for supposing that it was a reed-instrument, or, at the least, that the term, used generally, included instruments of the *oboe* family. The fact that the two tubes were often of different lengths (*impares*) has been explained by saying that they were tuned in different modes. But it is far more probable that they were constructed like the *arghool*, and that the longer tube gave out a drone. The double flute was not unknown to the ancient Egyptians and Assyrians, as shown in figs. 1 and 2, but they were divergent, or perhaps actually separate from each other. Fig. 3 represents two ancient Greek flutes, preserved in the British Museum.

Fig. 1.

Fig. 2.

Fig. 3.

A una corda (*It*.) With, or on, one string. A direction (1) in pianoforte music, to use the soft pedal. (2) In music for stringed instruments to play the passage so marked on one string only, by the shift. [Shift.]

Ausarbeitung (*Ger*.) The working out of a theme, the climax of a composition.

Ausdruck (*Ger*.) Expression, *q.v.*

Ausführung (*Ger*.) (1) Performance or execution. (2) The working out of a subject in composition.

Aushaltung (*Ger*.) The time a note occupies in sounding, the duration of sound, sustaining a sound.

Aushaltungs-zeichen (*Ger*.) A pause ⌢

Äussere Stimmen (*Ger*.) [Extreme parts.]

Ausweichung (*Ger.*) Change, modulation.

Authentic cadence. A final close, in which the common chord of the Tonic is immediately preceded by the common chord of the dominant. [Cadence.]

Authentic mode. The name given to those modes on which were afterwards constructed other modes called Plagal, by an alteration of the pitch to a fourth below. [Plain Song.]

Authentic part of the Scale, in Counterpoint and Fugue, is that which lies between a note and its Dominant, whilst that which lies between the Dominant and its superior Tonic is termed Plagal. The terms are used chiefly in connection with Subject and Answer. [Fugue.]

Autos Sacramentales (*Sp.*) One of the early forms of Spanish drama, similar in some respects to the mysteries and moralities in England, but in which music and dancing formed an important part. The *Autos* had reference to the adminstration of the Sacraments according to the ideas received by the people.

Auxiliary Notes. Notes not essential to the harmony, introduced for the sake of breaking monotony, or of giving freedom of motion to one or more of the parts. They may occur on either the accented or the unaccented part of the bar, and if introduced below the melody should be only a semitone from the proper note of that melody, but if above they may be either a tone or a semitone as the position in the scale would warrant, or taste suggest.

BEETHOVEN. No. 4 Symphony.

Examples of extended auxiliary notes, and of auxiliary notes, on the accented part of the bar.

VERDI. Coro " Vedi le fosche" (Trovatore).

ROSSINI. " Guillaume Tell " Overture.

AUBER. Coro " En bons militaires buvons" (Fra Diavolo).

Auxiliary Scales. The scales of relative or attendant keys, *q.v.*

Ave Maria (*Lat.*) (Hail ! Mary.) The angel's salutation of the Blessed Virgin Mary, used in the Roman Catholic Church as an Antiphon.

Avena (*Lat.*), lit. *oats.* An oaten pipe, hence (1) any simple reed used as a shepherd's pipe—"est modulatus avena Carmen," Tibull, 2, 1, 53. (2) The syrinx or pan-pipes, reeds joined together with wax—"pastor junctis pice cantat avenis," Ovid, Tristia 5, 10, 25. [Pan-pipes.]

A vista (*It.*) For *a prima vista*, at first sight.

Away. A direction in Mace's Musicks Monument, published in 1676, signifying a return to the original time.

Azione Sacra (*It.*) Sacred dramas. [Autos Sacramentales. Oratorio. Passion Music.]

Azor (*Heb.*) This word which occurs in the Book of Psalms and elsewhere, is variously rendered according to the view which is taken of its association with *nebel*. In Psalm xxxiii., 2, "Sing unto him with a *nebel* and *azor*" some drop the " and " and understand *azor* as qualifying *nebel*, making the compound word to signify a " ten-stringed nebel " (psalterium decem chordarum). Whether the *azor* was a distinct instrument, or not, it is impossible to say, although Engel, Fétis, and some other authors have so considered it, and have ventured to assign to it a definite number of strings.

(41)

B.

B. (1) The name of the note above Pros-lambanos, in the greater perfect system of the Greeks. The first note of the lowest Tetra-chord (Hypaton). [Greek Music.]

(2) The third note of the grave hexachord of the Guidonian system, in which it is B mi. [Notation.]

(3) The seventh note of the normal scale C, the note *Si* [Si], in Tonic Sol-fa system *Te*.

(4) The major scale having five sharps in its signature.

(5) The note B♭ in Germany, where B♮ is known as H, whence the possibility of making the letters B, A, C, H, into a fugue subject,

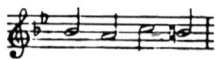

as has been done by Bach, Schumann, Liszt, and others.

(6) In old solmizations this note was called a *Mi*. [Solfeggio.]

There is no *authentic* church-mode com-mencing on this note, owing to the imper-fection of its fifth when unraised by the signature.

B. Abbreviation of *Bass* voice, *Bassoon*, and *Double-bass*.

Baar-pÿp. The name of a stop in some of the Dutch organs; (*lit.*) the Bear-pipe, written also Bär-pfeife and Bären-pfeife, so called from the instrument played as an ac-companiment to dancing bears.

Baas or Base Dance. A dance or slow movement, similar to the Measure, *q.v.*, or the minuet, so called probably in contradistinction to the vaulting dances in which greater agility was displayed.

"And then came downe the l. prince and the lady Cecill, and daunced two baas daunces, and departed up againe; the l. prince to the King, and the lady Cecill to the Queene."—*Wright's Provincial Dictionary.*

Baccalaureus Musicæ (*Lat.*) Bachelor in Music.

Bacchanalian Song. (1) Songs sung in procession during the worship of Bacchus. (2) Any song in praise or defence of wine drinking, of which there are numbers belonging to the 18th century.

Bacchia. Kamschatdale dance, in ⅜ time.

Bacchius. A foot consisting of one short and two long syllables. [Metre.]

Bacciocolo (*It.*) Tuscan musical instru-ment of the guitar kind.

Bachelor of, or in, Music. The first of the degrees in music at the Universities of Oxford, Cambridge, and Dublin. At Cam-bridge the degree is conferred next in seniority to that of Master of Arts. In Oxford and Dublin it is the lowest step in the Scale of Graduates. The hood worn by the Oxford and Dublin Bachelors is of blue silk, trimmed with white fur; at Cambridge the hood is the same as that worn by Masters of Arts. The degree is not conferred by any foreign Uni-versity.

Backfall. A Turn in Lute or Harpsichord music, *written* thus [symbol] *played* [symbol]

Back fall. [Organ, § 10.]

Badinage (*Fr.*) Playfulness.

Bagana. The ten-stringed lyre of the Abyssinians. It has only five different notes, but each note has its octave-string.

Bagatelles (*Fr.*) Sketches, short pieces, trifles.

Bagpipe. The *ascaulus* (ἄσκαυλος) of the Greeks (from ἀσκός, a leathern bag, and ἀυλός, a pipe); the *tibiæ utriculariæ* or *utricularium* of the Romans; *sampogna* or *zampogna* of Italy; the *cornemuse* of France; the *chifonie* or *symphony* of the middle ages; the *sougga-rah* or *zouggarah* of the Arabians. An ancient wind instrument of almost universal adoption, formerly in common use in every part of Europe, but now only found in parts of Italy, Sicily, Calabria, Brittany, Poland, and Scot-land, in form more or less varied; in Ireland the bagpipes under the name of the Union pipes, are yet to be met with, but as a musical instrument among the English it has completely disappeared, in consequence of the advance in musical taste. A form of bagpipe is probably meant by the word *symphonia* (Dan. iii. 15) translated in the Italian version of the Bible *zampogna*. In its general construc-tion the bagpipe consists of a leathern bag fre-quently formed of the whole skin of a kid or other small animal, which contains the wind conveyed from the mouth of the player through a tube, a small valve preventing its rapid escape. The sound comes from three pipes, two of which united are called the *drone*, and are capable of producing only·one note each, the key-note and its fifth. These two notes are heard throughout the performance. The third pipe, the *chanter*, furnished with a reed, is bored with six or eight holes which are stopped by the ends of the fingers of the performer. The scale of some of the Scotch bagpipes, with eight ventages, is in the minor mode with the seventh flat:

in others with six holes, the fourth and seventh are omitted:

that of the Calabrian bagpipe is the diatonic scale:

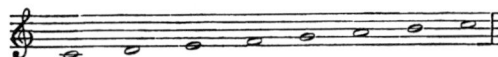

The bagpipe was known to the Anglo-Saxons, and that it was at one time in England a popular instrument, may be inferred from the frequent mention made of it in mediæval times. Strutt quotes a MS. recording many payments made to bagpipers in the reign of Edward III., about 1335, both for their personal performance and as an allowance to enable them to visit the foreign minstrel schools. The same authority also records a payment to another bagpiper in 1494. The manner in which the instrument is mentioned by Chaucer, and other poets, shows it to have been exceedingly popular and of frequent use in England in their days; and a large number of tunes quoted or alluded to in William Chappell's "Popular Music" bear evidence of having been of bagpipe character. There is no proof that the bagpipe is a national Scottish instrument, for its introduction into Scotland only dates from the time it began to be disused in England.

There is a tradition that bagpipes were used at the Battle of Bannockburn, and there is a tune, "Hey taitti, taittie," said to be the identical march played by them. Ritson, in his preface to a collection of Scottish songs, doubts whether the Scots had any martial music, and quotes Froissart's account of each soldier in the army wearing a little horn, on which, at the onset they would make such a horrible noise "as if all the devils in hell had been let loose." He further notes that as these horns are the only instruments mentioned by Barbour the Scottish chronicler, it must remain a moot point whether Bruce's army was ever cheered by the sound of a bagpipe.

The earliest mention of the bagpipe as forming part of the military music of the Scotch was at the Battle of Balrinnes (1594), though the oldest known pibroch is called the "Battle of Harlaw," but it could not be contemporary with the event (1411). There is mention of trumpets and drums in the old ballad relating to the battle, but none of the bagpipe:

> "The armies met, the trumpet sounds,
> The dandring drums alloud did touk."

The Irish or Union pipes are furnished with a pair of bellows (worked with the elbow) with which to inflate the bag. There are three drones, two tuned in unison, and one an octave below; most pipes have a valve by means of which the drone can be silenced, and there is also a contrivance for sounding at will the common chord of the key note in which the pipes are set. The quality of the chanter is more like that of the clarinet than the oboe, and the general tone of the Irish pipes is softer and less piercing than the Scottish bagpipe. The native Irish pipers call the instrument "ullan piobe," the pipes of the elbow. Shakespeare's mention of "woollen pipes" in the "Merchant of Venice," Act. iv. sc. 1:

> "Why he, a harmless necessary cat
> Why he, a *woollen* bagpipe,"

refers probably to the "ullan pipes;" and the word "union," as applied at the present day, may be only a modern substitute for the right word, for it is difficult to see the force of the application of the term "union" to bagpipes, unless the word be a corruption of a proper term.

It is supposed that the bagpipe came originally from the East; it is still to be met with in use among many Eastern nations. In India, China, Persia, and Egypt, it is the subject of frequent mention by many travellers.

Baguettes (*Fr.*) Drumsticks.

Baisser (*Fr.*) To lower.

Balafo. A musical instrument popular among the negroes of Senegambia. It is made of a series of graduated pieces of wood, placed over gourds, which act as resonance-boxes, is struck with hammers, and has a scale of two octaves, sometimes tuned in accordance with the white notes of a pianoforte,

Balalaika (*Russ.*) A Russian instrument, in form like a guitar, but narrower and of less depth; it has two strings. With it the Russian Moujiks accompany their popular songs.

Balancement (*Fr.*) Tremolo.

Balcken or **Balken** (*Ger.*) The bar under the belly of a violin.

Balg (*Ger.*) Bellows, wind-chest.

Balgentreter (*Ger.*) The bellows-treader. In old organs the blower worked the bellows by standing on them in turns.

Ballad. A song designed to suit a popular audience. A varied derivation has been claimed for the term, which doubtless meant originally a dance song. Hence its connection with the Mediæval Latin word *ballare*, (βάλλω, βαλλίζω). As a poem, the ballad has undergone so many transmutations that it is difficult to describe it properly, many pieces to which the term is applied having little or nothing in common with the primitive form, and poems of exactly similar character being described at one time as romances, at another ballads, at another lyric-epics. The Italians—among other writers, Dante—gave the title *ballata* to short lyrical pieces of inartistic construction allied to the sonnet or madrigal. It was against the French equivalent for these *ballate* that Molière wrote. The Spanish romances, erroneously called ballads, belong to epic poetry. The ballad, as we now understand its meaning and application, is confined to the people of Northern Europe, the Germans, following Bürger, the creator of the modern ballad, have given it an artificial character by the introduction of reflections arising out of the incidents. A ballad, properly speaking, is a simple narrative of one or more events, told without gloss, commentary, or deduction, set to a tune sufficiently rhythmical to act as one of the original purposes of a ballad, namely, a dance tune. The old ballad tunes still existing are nearly all of this character. In fact, the majority of the melodies have been recovered from having been preserved in collections of them made by dancing masters at various periods. The title of Ballet or Ballad—says Warton—was often applied to poems of considerable length, of various subjects, sometimes to prose compositions, sometimes to plays or interludes, sometimes to religious verses or discourses.

Ballad (Old English). The English have ever been a ballad-loving people, and although the taste was more widely diffused among all classes in former days than now, yet there is no present sign that it will soon die away. Ballads were embodied into our earliest histories, because the bards or minstrels—called Scopes in the language of the country[*]—were the earliest of our historians. The Scope was both poet and musician. He recorded deeds of ancient valour, and enlarged upon them in order to stimulate the warlike spirit of his hearers. He adopted ancient stories of adventures. and re-applied them to some more recent hero, in order to give greater interest

in them to those who were assembled around him. In the Anglo-Saxon Chronicle we have about a dozen fragments of historical ballads, but these commence only from Athelstan's victory over the Danes. When William of Malmesbury was writing the history of King Edward, son of Alfred the Great, he said: "Thus far I have written from trustworthy testimony—that which follows I have learnt more from old ballads, popular through succeeding times, than from books written expressly for the information of posterity. I have subjoined them, not to defend their veracity, but to put the reader in possession of all I know."[†]

Again, after recounting the pride of King Edgar in having compelled subject kings to be his oarsmen, while he sat at the prow, William says: "For this he is justly blamed by history, but the other imputations which I shall mention hereafter, have rather been cast upon him by ballads."[‡]

It may be asked, "what kind of music had these ballads?" The answer will be that, although we have no existing specimen of ballad music of such early dates, yet we have hymns to Latin words, some of which have more tune in them than would be expected, and that they are our only existing means of forming a judgment. It was not mere natural song with indefinable sounds, but with regulated notes upon the diatonic scale. In the year 951 the double organ at Winchester Cathedral had 400 pipes and required two organists. It was intended to be heard all over Winchester, in honour of Saint Peter, to whom the Cathedral was dedicated. Wolstan, or rather Wulfstan, of Winchester, who describes it fully in his Life of Saint Swithun, was himself the author of a treatise on Harmony (*De tonorum Harmonia*), which was a standard book, and remained in use 200 years after it had been issued. William of Malmesbury, writing after 1100, describes this book as "very useful" (*valde utile*). It is quoted (or else some second treatise on music by the same author) as the *Breviloquium Wolstani*, at the end of the 13th century. We have Winchester hymns with music on four lines and spaces in the time of Ethelred II. (978 to 1016), and even the words of these hymns are not to be found in any foreign collection. They are, however, by no means solitary specimens of English hymnology of the same kind, and as they

---

[*] Anglo-Saxon " Scóp " or " Sceop."

[†] Sequentia magis cantilenis per successiones temporum detritis, quam libris ad instructiones posteriorum elucubratis, didicerim." (*De Gestis Regum Anglorum*, Lib. 2, cap. 6.)

[‡] "Inde merito, jureque, culpant eum literæ; nam ceteras infamias, quas post dicam, magis resperserunt cantilenæ." (*De Gestis Regum Anglor.*, Lib. 2, cap. 8.)

are before the time of Guido d'Arezzo, they must be considered as proofs that the English used lines and spaces before other nations. The only difference between this most ancient English notation on lines and spaces, and that which came into use after Guido's system had been relinquished (for he employed only red and yellow lines for F and C, which was incompatible with the use of four lines and spaces because C was under F), was that the English placed any letter of the scale at the signature, and in the later use of lines and spaces only F, C, or G, were so placed. We have also an extant Kyrie composed by St. Dunstan, which, when rendered into modern notation, will be found a favourable specimen of early music. As to secular music, we find in the *Gesta Herwardi*, or the Life of Hereward, who was son of Leofric, Earl of Mercia, and the Lady Ædiva (the Lady Godiva of popular fable), that he seized the harp and sang " with correct musical intervals " (for that is the meaning of " per discrimina vocum "*), sometimes alone, and at other times in three parts with his companions after the manner of the Gyrwians.† These Gyrwians were the inhabitants of the fenny districts between East Anglia and Mercia, including Peterborough (then called Medeshamstede) in the north, and the Isle of Ely in the south. This was not a district likely to be in advance of the rest of England, and yet, even here, we read of singing in three parts as customary.

When Archbishop Alfric wished to translate the Latin word "Concentor" for his vocabulary of Latin and English words, he rendered it by "mid-singend," which seems sufficiently to express singing in three parts, for there would be no middle in two or four. It might perhaps have been taken to mean " singing all together," or in " chorus," if Alfric had not also given two different translations of " Chorus,"‡ besides others for " Song," " Duet," " Tune for an instrument alone," " Harmony," " Discord,"§ &c., all which, taken together, are sufficient to prove the very early cultivation of music in England.

These notices of early music may not appear, at first sight, to be immediately connected with our text of " Old English Ballads," but the arts of music and poetry were then united, all poetry being intended to be sung; and there is so much new matter to be adduced in the history of music, especially in that of our own country, of which Dr. Burney's account is most inaccurate, that it is difficult to avoid the temptation of referring to the subject. If we desire to prove that music was cultivated by the working classes as well as by those above them, we may quote the fact of the Watermen of London having made a round for three voices, in honour of Sir John Norman, Lord Mayor of London, who, in 1453, commenced the custom, which became afterwards established, of going to Westminster in his barge to be sworn into his office of Lord Mayor, instead of riding both to and fro with a procession on horseback as before. The music of the Round‖ is like the chiming of bells from one church steeple to another, and might be sung by hundreds of men together to the words,

> " Heave and ho, rumbelow,
> Row the boat, Norman, row,
> Row to thy Leman."

The idea of representing the taking charge of the City of London, as a " leman " or " loved one," was quite watermanic.

The people were then fond of singing, and altogether more cheerful than after the advent of that severe puritanism which told them, in the words of Prynne, to " go about chattering like cranes, and cooing like doves for their own *and others'* sins."¶ Solomon thought that there was a time for everything—"a time to dance, a time to sing, and a time to play ; " but these wise-acres did not. They put down the Maypoles and the dances on the village green, and thus reduced the people to drinking and to earnest politics as the only excitements left to them.

The character of " Merry England " will compare favourably with that of " Old England "— for England had not the title of " Old " until a " New England " had been planted in America, and puritanism had become both rampant and dominant at home.

" The merry, free, and frank disposition of the Old English," says Camden, " was thus described by Alfred of Beverley " (who died A.D. 1136): " England, *full of sports*, a free people, delighting in jokes."** In the same

---

* It is a quotation from Virgil's " septem discrimina vocum," and one frequently employed to express the seven intervals of the diatonic scale, viz., A, B, C, D, E, F, G.

† " Multipliciter cum ea [cythara] canendo, et per discrimina vocum, nunc solitarie, et nunc tripliciter cum suis sociis, more Girwiorum, cantavit." (From a photographic copy of the Peterborough Manuscript.)

‡ " Singende heap " and " Hluddra sang."

§ " Sang," " twegra sang," " answege sang," " geð —waere sang," and " ungeswege sang." (*Vocabularies* edited by T. Wright, F.S.A., p. 28, privately printed by Joseph Mayer, Esq., of Liverpool, F.S.A., &c.)

‖ The easy music of this little Round is printed in *Popular Music of the Olden Time*, Vol. II. p. 783.

¶ Prynne was parodying Hezekiah's words when he thought himself dying: " Like a crane or a swallow, so did I chatter: I did mourn as a dove: " but Hezekiah was mourning for his sickness, and not for the sins of others.

** " Anglia, plena jocis, gens libera, et apta jocari."— *Camden's Remaines.*

strain runs William of Malmesbury, referring to the Norfolk and Suffolk men, or East Anglians: "they are a merry, pleasant, jovial race, but apt to carry their jokes to an irritating excess."[*] For a third testimony we may take an extreme part of England : "Merry Michael, the Cornish poet, piped this upon his oaten pipe, for Merry England," says Camden :

"For money, dinners, varied drinks, no land will e'er be found
Like England, famous England, where the fertile soil is crown'd
With countless flocks and herds, and where all social joys abound. "[†]

We know from another source that there was no lack of tunes when the Normans came, for Thomas, the first Norman Archbishop of York (1070), set about collecting those which he heard from the minstrels, and wrote hymns to them.[‡] Richard de Ledrede, a Londoner, who was Bishop of Ossory, from 1318 to 1360, did the same thing ; but carried the tunes to Ireland with him. We know the names of the ballads, because they are written in the Red Book of Ossory over his Latin hymns. Among them are "Sweetest of all, sing!" "How should I with that old man?" "Do, do, nightingale, sing full merry," and "Good day! my leman dear." Thus he anticipated the Rev. Rowland Hill, or whoever else may have said, that "the Devil should not have all the pretty tunes." And yet there was some danger from this appropriation of secular words, lest they might become so fixed in the memory as to crop up unexpectedly and unwittingly. Giraldus Cambrensis relates a case that should have been a warning. It is of a priest in Worcestershire, who had been listening to choral singing and dancing near the church during the night, and who, in pure forgetfulness, sang one of these popular burdens in the morning, instead of greeting the people with "Dominus vobiscum."

As to London, the first good description of the city and of its customs was written in 1174 by Fitz-Stephen (Stephanides), the friend and biographer of Thomas Becket. He says that "in summer evenings the young people danced till dark, to the sound of the harp (or cittern), and that some of the maidens acted as the musicians."[§] Also that, on festival days, the boys of the London schools attached to the three principal churches "contended with each other in verse," and wound up their contests "by recitations of epigrams, *ballads*, and rhymes, in which the foibles and frailties of their fellows were sarcastically exposed, without naming the individuals." At this "the auditors, who were prepared to enter into the jest, shook the assembly with peals of laughter."

These are gayer pictures and of more content, than are common now. Examples might be continued to the extent of a volume, but one more, from Oxford in the reign of Queen Elizabeth, will suffice. It was written by the learned Dr. John Case, whose *Speculum moralium Quæstionum in universam Ethicen Aristotelis*, was the first book printed at the new press at Oxford in 1585. The extract is from *The Praise of Musicke*, printed at Oxford by John Barnes, in the following year: "Every troublesome and laborious occupation hath musick for a solace and recreation, and hence it is that the wayfaring men solace themselves with songs, and ease the wearisomness of their journey ; considering that musicke, as a pleasant companion, is unto them instead of a waggon on the way. And hence it is that manual labourers and mechanical artificers of all sorts keep such a chanting and singing in their shoppes—the tailor on his bulk, the shoemaker at his last, the mason at his wall, the shipboy at his oar, the tinker at his pan, and the tiler on the house-tops." Even the proverbially merry cobler has now almost ceased to sing, and tailors seek only to mend the State. A tuneless tailor, in former days, was such a *rara avis* as to become at once an object of suspicion. "Never trust a tailor that does not sing at his work," says Fletcher, "for his mind is of nothing but filching." The treatment of the poor was perhaps less considerate than now ; but the people having their amusements were certainly more content. The number of ballads left for entry at Stationers' Hall at the end of year 1560 was 796, and only 44 books.

We have still a large number of extant ballads, such as were printed on one side of a sheet of coarse paper, to be sung about the streets and villages in the 16th and 17th centuries. Their tunes are also to be found, being included in early collections of country dances. Ball and ballad are words derived from the same root, and when the people danced country-dances they accompanied them with song. Nearly every old ballad

---

[*] "Gens læta et lepida, facetaque festivitate jocorum ad petulantiam pronior." (*Gesta Reg. Anglor.*, Book 2, cap. 13.·

[†] "Nobilis Anglia pocula, prandia donat, et æra,
Terra juvabilis et sociabilis, agmine plena:
Omnibus utilis, Anglia fertilis est et amœna."—
Camden's Remaines.

[‡] "Si quis in auditu ejus arte jocularia, aliquid vocale, sonaret, statim illud in divinas laudes effigiabat."—W. *Malmesbury.*

[§] "Puellarum cithara choros ducit usque imminente luna, et pede libero pulsatur tellus." (*Descrip. Lond.*, ed. T. Pegge.)

has the name of the tune printed upon it for which it was intended, and it has been owing to this combination of circumstances that so many of our national airs have been recoverable, and that words and tune could be re-fitted together in authentic forms. Mere tradition is the frailest of guides in music, for hardly do any two untaught singers sing an air alike, and they often vary the tune between one stanza and another.

Captain Cox, the Coventry mason, is the first recorded collector of old printed ballads. He is mentioned by Laneham in his letter from Kenilworth in 1575. The next in order of date is the learned Selden. He lent his collection to Samuel Pepys, the amusing diarist, who did not return it. We are, in all probability, indebted to that circumstance for its preservation; for Pepys left his library, including his collection of ballads and those borrowed from Selden, to Magdalene College, Cambridge, where they remain under the strictest custody, owing to the terms of the bequest. Old Pepys took the greatest care to prevent others from indulging in his own little habit of filching.

The united collections of Selden and Pepys (or of Pepys including those ballads that he borrowed from Selden) are bound in five folio volumes containing 1785 ballads, mostly with second parts. Sometimes two ballads were printed upon one page, and these would enlarge the above named number. In addition to the broadsides there are three volumes, lettered " Penny Merriments," which were also collected by Pepys, and which include a large number of "Garlands," that are in themselves collections of ballads, but printed in octavo or other small size, instead of "in broadside," i.e., on one side of a folio page.

A second great collection of broadside ballads is that which is now called the Roxburghe Collection. John, Duke of Roxburghe, was only one of several proprietors through whose hands the collection successively passed; but his name became especially connected with it, owing to the notoriety of the comparatively large price it produced at the sale of his library. The collection had been purchased for the Duke at the auction of Mayor Thomas Pearson's library in 1788 for £36 14s. 6d., and was resold in 1813, with the duke's additions, for £477 15s. It was originally formed by Robert Harley, who was raised to the peerage as Earl of Oxford and Mortimer in 1711, the same whose magnificent collection of manuscripts, known as the Harleian Collection, is one of the wonders of the British Museum.

This collection consists of four volumes, containing 2133 pages of ballads. Sometimes one ballad takes two pages including its second part, and sometimes two ballads are printed on the same page. It was purchased for the British Museum at the sale of the library of the late Benjamin Heywood Bright, M.P., in 1845.

Another important collection of ballads in the British Museum is that formed by Bagford, who was agent in purchasing for Harley, Earl of Oxford. It is bound in three volumes. There are also many minor collections in the same library, and a large number of political ballads and songs among " The King's Pamphlets."

For early date there are no extant collections to compare with those of Mr. Henry Huth, Mr. S. Christie-Miller, and of the Society of Antiquaries of London. These are unrivalled for rarity, but they are not of so large an extent as some others.

The Bodleian Library at Oxford is particularly rich in ballads, and the Public Library at Cambridge particularly poor, if, indeed, it possess any collection at all. Oxford can boast of the Douce collection, which is, perhaps, next in extent to the Roxburghe and Pepys, but rather later, as to average date, than either. It contains 877 ballads bound in 4 vols., the fourth volume being later than the rest. The Bodleian also possesses Anthony Wood's famous collections, both in print and in manuscript, as well as a smaller number of printed ballads collected by Rawlinson. Wood's printed collection is of 279, and the Rawlinson of 218 black-letter ballads, and (as a rough guide to the number of duplicates to be found in the great public libraries) it may be stated that although the Roxburghe Collection contains about ten times the number of the Rawlinson, yet the latter includes 130 ballads, of which no edition whatever is to be found in the Roxburghe. Yet they are generally of coeval dates.

The Cheetham Library, Manchester, possesses an extensive collection of ballads presented by James Orchard Halliwell, F.R.S. Of other collections in private hands, it may be sufficient to name first, that of the late W. Ewing, F.S.A., Scot., which, according to the printed catalogue, contains 408 ballads; a collection at Osterley Park; and a rare collection formed by Mr. J. Payne Collier, and now in the possession of Frederic Ouvry, Esq., Treasurer to the Society of Antiquaries.

There are, no doubt, many more collections in private hands, as well as many ballads scattered in collections of pamphlets, both in public and private libraries; but even in those already named, the number of extant English ballads dating from the reign of Henry VIII. to the year 1700 cannot be computed at less than ten thousand. It would be much larger, if ballads printed with music were taken into account, or even if manuscripts, like the Percy folio, and Wood's collection, were included in the calculation. The tunes for some thousands of them have been traced, and many are printed in the "History of Popular Music of the Olden Time." "In a word," says an old writer, "scarce a cat can look out of a gutter, but up starts a halfpenny chronicler, and presently *a proper new ballad of a strange sight* is indited."

Ballade (*Ger.*) A dance, also a ballad.

Ballata (*It.*) The melody of any song which may furnish a tune for dancing. [Ballet.]

Ballatetta (*It.*) Diminutive of Ballata.

Ballematia.
Ballistia. } Songs in dance-style.

Ballet. A Madrigalian part-song with a *fa la* chorus. The "Ballets" or "fa las" of Giovanni Gastoldi [1532-1598] the reputed originator of this form of vocal music, are in most cases in simple counterpoint — note against note—but the rhythm, strongly marked and well defined, is admirably suited to the purposes of the dance which these vocal harmonies were intended to accompany. There are many examples of Ballets to be found in the writings of the Elizabethan madrigal composers.

Ballet (*Fr.*) A representation in dancing and gesticulation, of some story, without words.

The rise of the Ballet is almost coeval with dancing itself, for it is difficult to believe that any number of dancers could have so disported themselves as to give delight to the spectators, if there had not been some definite and organised arrangement. The dances described as having been led by Miriam, David and Jephtha's daughter, the Emmeloeia, the Pyrrhic dances, the Motions of the Mimes, Minstrels, and Joculators, and the homely dances popular among the peasantry, besides the more stately measures favoured by people of high degree, were all ballets—in which certain motions were made to the sound of music, and whose gestures and actions had meanings and intentions that were commonly understood. When these dances were transferred from home circles to the stage, the gestures and actions made were such that could be readily interpreted by the lookers-on, and even when great skill was acquired by the performers in following ages, the old conventional signs, attitudes, and motions were retained, that all who chose might understand. The first ballets on the stage were those that were introduced into the oratorios, masques, and comedies, each being a development of portions of certain entertainments, from which they arose in common.

The oratorio and the drama arose from the ancient sacred and classical plays and the mediæval mysteries and moralities, and circumstances gave importance to particular parts of those productions, so that from forming a continued or dependent whole, they became detached and separate, and made what seemed in later years distinct things of those that had a common origin. The splendour of the Court Masques, the glory of the unity of the genius of the poet, architect, painter, and musician, are matters of history. Give prominence to the music, let the poetry fade away from inanity, retain the skill and genius of the machinist and scene painter, and you have opera. Let your poet write prose, have as little music as possible, respect the scenic effects and mechanical means, and drama is the result. Dispense with poetry or words of any kind, make music subservient, but do all that can be done with scenery and machinery, and make the dramatis personæ bound, caper, and gesticulate, and ballet is the product.

The Ballet had its origin in the Masques, which were written for and often performed by princes and other distinguished personages. In England, Italy, and France, it arose almost simultaneously out of the remains of the Masque. Count Aglio, at Turin, invented pieces that were at the same time pastoral, mythological, allegorical, and fantastic, in which the princes of the Court took part. In France Louis XIII. danced in a ballet, and his successor, Louis XIV., did the same in his turn, these ballets being portions of spectacles that were operatic, dramatic, and terpsichorean by turns or in combinations. Antoine de la Motte improved the ballet, and made it distinct, and independent of other means for explanation and elucidation; he also encouraged the introduction of female dancers, till then almost unknown in Europe, and from that time the ballet gradually sank from importance and consideration, and became a mere exhibition of artificial agility and natural comeliness. It is not many years since it was a very considerable item in the evening's entertainment at the opera in England, rivalling in spectacular splendour the famous ballets of Milan, the absence of vigour and intellectual power in the operas produced being counterbalanced by the so-called glory of the ballet. But as people began to be alive to the fact that contortions, dislocations, and indecent postures were the reverse of elevating or instructive, and not really amusing, the patronage of the ballet as a distinct entertainment fell away and finally ceased altogether, and an attempt to revive it apart from and out of the course of the situations of an opera, during the season of 1871, met with so little encouragement that it was silently abandoned. The ballet was once a poem and a power: kings did not scorn to exhibit trained and practised personal skill for the edification of their loyal subjects, and the exaltation of the exercise in which they indulged ; but the "improvements" of De la Motte introduced an element which was at once the cause of its glory and of its shame, its culmination and contempt. [Dance.]

Balletto (*It.*) A ballet, a dance.

Ballet-master. One to whom is entrusted the direction of the motions of the ballet, and the order of the performers.

Balli Inglesi (*It.*) English dances.

Balli della Stiria (*It.*) Styrian dances.

Balli Ungaresi (*It.*) Hungarian dances. Dances in the Hungarian style.

Ballo (*It.*) A dance, a ball.

Ballonchio (*It.*) [Passamezzo.]

Ballonzare (*It.*) To dance wildly, recklessly, without rule.

Band (*Ger.*) A part, a volume, any thing sewn together.

Band. Instrumentalists collected together for the performance of music.

(1) Brass Band. A collection of players on brass wind-instruments.

(2) String Band. (*a*) That portion of an orchestra which consists of players on stringed-instruments of the violin family. (*b*) A band consisting only of instruments played with a bow.

(3) Wind Band. *Stromenti di fiato* (*It.*) That portion of an orchestra which consists of players on flutes, oboes, clarinets, bassoons, and horns ; but not on trumpets, trombones, and other loud brass instruments, these being included only under the sign "tutti."

(4) Wood Band. The players on the wood wind-instruments, flutes, oboes, clarinets, bassoons ; but not on the serpent, which is usually classified with brass instruments.

(5) Military Band. A number of musicians belonging to a regiment in the service of the King or Queen of a country. In England, those who perform upon instruments provided by the officers of the corps to which they belong, the military regulations only recognising side drums, fifes, bugles, and trumpets, as necessary ; these are supplemented by clarinets, flutes, cornets, bassoons, horns, trombones, ophicleides, bombardons, triangles, cymbals, big drums, &c., and the combination is known as a military band. The band is conducted by some one skilled in directing and arranging, who is usually a civilian, but the bandsmen over whom he presides are in every other respect the same as private soldiers. Military bands are sometimes used upon the opera stage, for the purpose of gaining an increased effect.

Banda (*It.*) A military band. [Band § 5.]

Bandora (*Fr.*) [Bandore.]

Bandore. An English form of the ancient Greek Pandoura, having twelve strings of steel-wire. The Bandore is said to have been invented by John Rose, of London, in 1561.

Banduira. A form of guitar, strung with wire instead of cat-gut. [Pandoura.]

Banja or **Banjo.** A stringed instrument of supposed African origin, popular with the negroes of America, and one of the most important musical instruments employed by troupes of fictitious negroes. The instrument consists of a handle, which, running the whole length, serves at once as finger-board, as support for the hoop, over which a skin, acting as sounding board, is stretched, and also as a hold for the pegs which tighten and keep the strings in tune. The banjo is strung with five strings, so arranged that they may be *stopped* in the ordinary way to vary the melody or harmony, together with an octave string which is never stopped. The tuning, which may be in any key, is generally according to the following plan :

Octave string.

The character of banjo music is sprightly and well adapted for dancing, for which it is as often used as it is for accompanying the voice.

Bar. A line drawn from the top to the bottom of the stave to denote the division of the time in a piece of music, and the place of the strong accent. Each portion comprised within two of these lines is also called a bar. In mediæval music the bar, also called the *lesser* bar, to distinguish it from the greater or double bar, was often used solely for the purpose of showing the end of a line or sentence of the words, hence it was said "to give time for the whole choir together to draw breath" (Nievers, sur le Chant Gregorien); whereas the two great bars or the double bar is "the most efficacious contrivance that can be thought on to remedy all the cacophonies and contrarieties in the voices of the singers, who without them could not guess when to rest." (*Ibid.*) Mr. Chappell ("Popular Music of the Olden Time") remarks that the Tunes in the "Dancing Master," printed in 1651 in only a single part, have no bars, but that the score of the moral play, "The four elements" (to which Dr. Dibdin has ascribed the date 1510), is barred. He further adds, that so far as he has observed, all music in the ordinary notation, even for one voice or one instrument, was barred after 1660. It is probable, however, that the regular barring of music had its origin in the system of Tablature, in which its efficacy as a means of pointing out the position of *accent* must have been generally observed. But for a considerable period after the introduction of the bar, its use in ecclesiastical music was very irregular, two, four, six, or even eight minims being included in a bar which, by the signature, should contain only four. In modern music-printing and engraving, care is taken that the bars in the separate lines forming a score shall stand exactly over one another. The neglect of this in early publications in score adds greatly to the difficulty of reading them.

Barbet. [Barbiton.]

Barbiton. An ancient Greek instrument said to have been invented by Anacreon; it was in the form of a lyre, and had seven strings. The name was applied to instruments of the violin class in the 16th and 17th centuries.

Barcarole. A simple melody, composed in imitation of the songs of the Venetian gondoliers, many of which are of striking beauty. Apolloni Salvadore, a Venetian barber and fiddler in 1720, is named as the composer of several popular tunes of this class.

Bard. A name given to hereditary poets and minstrels by all the Celtic nations. In their songs and poems the bards recorded the deeds and prowess of the warriors, kings, and people, at festive and social gatherings ; and at religious assemblies they celebrated the acts and fame of the gods and heroes, accompanying their songs with the harp and crowd or crwth. The power, reputation, and influence of the bards were very great, and the favour of kings, princes, and nobles was accorded to them. They, like the Aoidoi of ancient Greece, were the historians, poets, and chroniclers of their time; they incited their armies to courage in the hour of battle, and by their heroic strains roused the fury and valour of the warriors. In time of peace they were ambassadors, heralds, and the depositaries of all historical tradition, and of much of the learning that was at that time possessed by the community. As an institution they kept longest influence in England, Scotland, and Wales. In the last-named country their privileges were fixed by King Howel Dha, A.D. 940, and a century and a half later Griffith ap Conan revised and reformed the whole system. The Eisteddvodau, as the congregations of Welsh bards are called, were held from time to time until the conquest of Wales by Edward I., in 1284, when the bards were persecuted, and as some authors declare, were put to death. Although the power of the bards was broken, still their Eisteddvodau were encouraged by the rulers of succeeding generations, until the time of Queen Elizabeth, who was the last monarch who made any concessions to the bards of Wales. The preservation of such of their literature that has survived them is owing to several learned societies who have made this object their peculiar study. An Eisteddfod as now understood is a curious compound of heterogeneous matter, for although it is held for the purpose of encouraging national art in music and poetry, its judges appear to be satisfied with the least worthy effusions common to London concert-rooms, provided they are given through the medium of the Cambrian tongue. Little is known of the bards in Scotland beyond the fact that they were similar in constitution to the bards in Ireland, who, like those of Wales, were a hereditary community. The Irish bards were divided into three classes, the Filhedha, the Braitheamain, and the Senachaidhe. The first sang the sacred and heroic songs, and were employed as heralds and counsellors, the second recited and expounded the laws, and the third were the chroniclers and recorders. They were endowed with many privileges and had great influence, and their power over the minds of the people was so strong that severe measures had frequently to be resorted to, to check their sway. In England bardism took a more refined and less exciting form than that which was acceptable to those nations of more strictly Celtic origin. [Minstrels.] [Ballad.]

Bardone. [Viola di Bardone.]

Barem (*Ger.*) An organ-stop, consisting of closed flute-pipes of 8 ft. or 16 ft. pitch, of a soft character of tone.

Barginet, Berginet, Bargaret, or Bergeret. Shepherd's songs, to accompany dances. Songs relating to pastoral matters.

"A bargaret in praising the daisie.
For, as methought, among her notes swete,
She said, ' Si douce est le Margarite.' "
CHAUCER.—*Floure and Leafe.*

Baribasso. A deep bass voice.

Bariolage (*Fr.*) A medley. A cadenza, or series of cadenzas, whose appearance forms a design upon the music paper, "a waistcoat pattern" as it is called by performers.

Baritenor. A deep tenor.

Baritone. A brass instrument. [Metal Wind-Instruments.]

Bariton, or Baryton. [Viola di Bardone.]

Bariton Clarinet. An instrument used in military bands, the tone of which is between the clarinet and bassoon.

Baritone Clef. The F clef placed upon the third line of the stave.

It is not now used, but was frequently employed in vocal music of the 16th and 17th centuries. Purcell's Song, " Let the dreadful engines," was originally written in this clef, and it was also used occasionally for horn parts by Handel, Cooke, and other writers in the 18th century.

Bariton (*Fr.*)
Baritono (*It.*) } The Baritone voice.
Bariton voice. [Barytone.]
Barocco (*It.*)
Barock (*Ger.*) } Unusual, singular, eccentric, whimsical, irregular.
Baroque (*Fr.*) } Applied to a composition with over-chromatic harmonies, or unrhythmical melodic phrasing.
Bärpfeife (*Ger.*) [Baarpÿp.]
Barquade (*Fr.*) An obsolete term for Barcarole, *q.v.*
Barré (*Fr.*) In guitar or lute playing, the pressing of the fore-finger of the left hand across all the strings, so as to alter temporarily the pitch of the instrument, the remaining fingers being at the same time engaged in forming a chord. The first finger, therefore, performs the duties of a capotasto, *q.v.*
Barre de luth (*Fr.*) The bridge of the lute.
Barre de mesure (*Fr.*) [Bar.]
Barre de répétition (*Fr.*) A double bar with points, marking a repeat.

Barrel. A revolving cylinder of wood or metal.

(1) Barrel-organ. An organ in which a wooden cylinder furnished with pegs or staples, when turned round, opens a series of valves to admit a current of air to a set of pipes, producing a tune either in melody or harmony. The barrels are sometimes made moveable, in order to obtain a variety in the tunes, as the capability of a single barrel is necessarily limited. Barrel organs furnished with hymn and psalm tunes, or even voluntaries, were sometimes used in places of worship, but the increased knowledge of music, even in remote places, has led to the introduction of the harmonium, which has superseded the use of barrel organs to a great extent. The tone of barrel organs is incapable of expression or variety, and has consequently been found seriously monotonous. The only advantage belonging to the instrument is its portability, and this renders it available for street musicians, who generally hire one at a small charge, the cost of the instrument (from £20 to £70) being beyond their means. Many of the poor hirers are cruelly used by the Padrone from whom they obtain their instruments. The barrel-organ, as a street entertainment in London, dates from about the year 1790. The stops in a barrel-organ generally consist of a stopped diapason and flute or principal, to which is sometimes added a reed stop of coarse quality. The compass rarely exceeds two octaves and a half.

(2) Barrel of a musical box is constructed in a manner somewhat similar to that of an organ, but is of metal, and instead of opening a series of valves, the pegs and staples set in vibration the teeth of a steel comb, which produce the sounds. [Musical box.]

Barypycni (*med. Lat.*, from *Gk.* βαρὺς *deep*, and πυκνὸς *close*). (1) Lowest strings of tetrachords in the chromatic or enharmonic scale. (2) In ecclesiastical music, those modes which have the *pycnon* or semitone at the bottom of the tetrachord, *e.g.* :

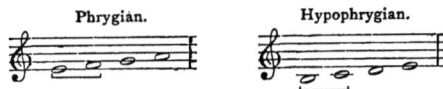

Phrygian.   Hypophrygian.

see mesopycni, oxypycni.

Barytone voice. A voice of fuller quality than a tenor and lighter than a bass, having a compass partly included in both, namely,

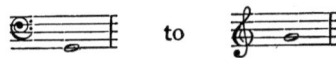

This is the extreme compass, and both limits are rarely reached.

This voice has only been distinguished by name, as being of a separate character, within the present century. Early writers indicate its existence by the use of its special clef. The term Barytone is unmeaning, unless it be looked upon as a corruption of Barytenor, but it is quite possible it was borrowed from the instrument Barytone or Bardone, which occupied a place between the tenor and bass viols. Rousseau calls this voice *Basse-chantante*, or *Basse-taille ;* and Shield, in his " Introduction to Harmony," having used the word Barytone, thinks it necessary to explain in a foot-note that it is " a voice between a tenor and a bass."

Bas-dessus (*Fr.*) Mezzo soprano, or second treble.

Base. Old form of the word Bass.

Bass. Low, as bass trombone, bass viol, bass voice, &c.

Bassa ottava (*It.*) At the lower octave.

Basse (*Fr.*) Bass.

Basse chantante (*Fr.*) A barytone voice.

Basse chiffrée (*Fr.*)
Basse continue (*Fr.*) } A figured bass, a bass part, the accompanying harmonies of which are expressed by numbers.

Basse contrainte (*Fr*). [Ground bass.]

Basse contre (*Fr.*) A deep bass voice, capable of singing below the ordinary bass part.

Basse de cremone (*Fr.*) The bassoon.

Basse de hautbois (*Fr.*) Corno inglese.

Basse d'harmonie (*Fr.*) The ophicleide.

Basse de viole (*Fr.*) The violoncello.

Basse de violon (*Fr.*) Double-bass.

Basse double (*Fr.*) Large double-bass.

Basse figurée (*Fr.*) Figured bass.

Basse fondamentale (*Fr.*) Root-bass or generator. [Harmony.]

Basse recitante (*Fr.*) [Basse chantante.]
Basse taille (*Fr.*) The Barytone voice.
Basset-horn, Corno di Bassetto (*It.*) A transposing instrument of the clarinet order, of a beautiful, soft, and rich quality, invented in Passau about the year 1770, and improved by Lotz of Presburg twelve years later. In form like a long clarinet, with a curved and bell-shaped metal end. The compass extends from F below Gamut to C in Altissimo

With all the intermediate semitones, except the F sharp and A flat in the lower range.

The music is written for it in the bass and treble clefs a fifth higher than the real sound. Mozart has written with brilliant effect for the basset-horn in his "Nozze di Figaro," in "Clemenza di Tito," and in the "Requiem."

Bassetto (*It.*) (1) The diminutive of Basso. A name sometimes given to the tenor violin. (2) A reed stop in the organ of 8 ft. or 16 ft. in length.

Bass Flute. The lowest in pitch of instruments of the flute family, now obsolete.

Its compass was   It was a *flute*

à bec, not a *flauto traverso*; that is, it was blown at the end (like a flageolet), not at a hole in its side. In order to enable the player to reach the remote holes with his fingers, a bent tube turning upwards conveyed the air from his lips to the mouthpiece of the instrument.

Bassgeige (*Ger.*) Bass Fiddle, or Violoncello.

Bass Horn. English Bass Horn, Corno Basso, a kind of serpent. [Serpent.]

Basslaute (*Ger.*) [Bass Lute.]

Bass Lute. [Theorbo.]

Basso (*It.*) A bass singer, also the doublebass, and the bass part.

Basso buffo (*It.*) A comic singer, with a bass voice.

Basso cantante (*It.*) [Basse chantante.]

Basso concertante (*It.*) The principal bass, that which accompanies solos and recitatives.

Basso continuo (*It.*) A bass part figured for the organ or pianoforte.

Basso figurato (*It.*) (1) Basso continuo. (2) A bass part, with running passages.

Basso fondamentale (*It.*) The fundamental ground bass, or root.

Basson (*Fr.*) [Bassoon.]

Basson quinte (*Fr.*) A bassoon, the pitch of which is five notes higher than that of the common bassoon. The part given to it must therefore be written five notes lower than the actual sounds required. Its *written* compass is   sounding

including all the intervening semitones. Its tone is more powerful, but less sympathetic, than that of the *corno inglese.*

Basso numerato (*It.*) A bass, the accompanying harmonies to which, are indicated by numbers.

Bassoon. Basson (*Fr.*) **Fagotto** (*It.*) A reed wind-instrument of deep pitch, with a compass of more than three octaves from low B flat.

This compass includes all the intermediate semitones, with the exception of

which are as yet to be obtained only from instruments of improved construction. Some performers can produce three notes higher than the B flat, but for all common orchestral purposes they are unnecessary. The bassoon ordinarily forms the bass or deepest tone among wood wind-instruments, and is capable of excellent independent effects, among which the grotesque ought not to be forgotten, as in Beethoven's "Pastoral Symphony," and the "Clown's March," in the music to the "Midsummer Night's Dream," by Mendelssohn.

It is customary to write for the Bassoon in the Bass clef, and as the instrument is usually employed in pairs, one stave serves for the two parts. The tenor clef is often employed for the higher notes of the register of the Bassoon, sometimes in a separate stave.

Some writers assert that the Bassoon is the invention of Afranio of Ferrara in 1540, and that he gave it the name Fagotto from its resemblance to a bundle or fagot of sticks (his instrument being made of several pieces laid together), but it was known long before under the name of Buisine, Buzaine, Courtal, Bombard, or Wait.

There is reason to believe that the Bassoon is of Eastern origin, introduced into western Europe in the twelfth century, and that it is an improvement of the drone-pipe of the Bagpipe. The Egyptian word for a pipe of deep tone, and for the drone of the Bagpipe is, according to E. W. Lane ("Modern Egyptians"), *Zummarah-bi-soan*, and the manner in which the word *Buzaine, Buisine,* is used in mediæval MSS., shows a possible connection with this origin. The instrument was introduced into the orchestra about the commencement of the 18th century; for a long time it was employed to strengthen the voice parts only. Handel generally makes it double the bass voice part, or treats it as a bass to the oboe; he has, however, made excellent use of it as a solo instrument in the scene of Saul and the Witch of Endor, in his oratorio of " Saul."

Basso ostinato (*It.*) Ground bass.

Basso ripieno (*It.*) The bass of the full, or chorus parts.

Basspommer (*Ger.*) A deep-toned instrument of the Oboe family, precursor of the Bassoon.

Bass-Posaune (*Ger.*) Bass trombone. [Trombone.]

Bassschlüssel (*Ger.*) The bass clef.

Bass Trumpet. An old instrument, now superseded by the trombone.

Bass Tuba. A brass instrument, a species of bombardon, not capable of such rapid execution as bass ophicleides, but producing a much finer quality of tone. It has the enormous compass of four octaves from

with all the chromatic intervals.

It is sometimes treated as a transposing instrument, in which case it is in E♭ or F, and its part has to be written a minor third, or major fourth higher respectively than the actual sounds given above.

Bass Viol. (1) A familiar name for the violoncello. (2) The largest and deepest in tone among a chest of viols, which had five and sometimes six strings, and a fretted finger-board. The manner of tuning the open strings varied according to the music to be played.

Playford (Introduction to the Skill of Music) mentions three sorts of Bass viols " as there are three manners of ways in playing." "First, a *Bass viol* for consort must be one of the largest size, and the strings proportionable. Secondly, a *Bass viol* for divisions must be of a less size, and the strings according. Thirdly, a *Bass viol* to play *Lyra-way*, that is by *Tablature*, must be somewhat less than the two former, and strung proportionably."

The common *accordatura* of the six-string instrument was as follows:

Bass Voice. The lowest register of the human voice, having a compass ranging between two octaves from lower D:

The whole of the bass voice should be produced from the chest, and the most useful notes, and those generally written are between G and tenor C:

A bass voice rarely reaches full perfection of quality or sonorousness before the possessor is thirty years of age, and a true bass voice has seldom much flexibility.

Batillus. An instrument formerly employed by the Armenians in their Church service to supply the place of bells, which they were forbidden to use. A board struck with a hammer.

Bâton (*Fr.*) (1) A stick used in beating time. (2) The method of a conductor is called his *bâton*. (3) A pause of two or more bars is also so named, *e.g.* a *bâton* of five measures or bars.

Battement (*Fr.*) An ornament in singing, opposed to the Cadence (*Fr.*) *e.g.* :

is called a *cadence*, whereas the following

is a *battement*. [Beat.]

Battere, il (*It.*) The down-stroke in beating time.

Batterie (*Fr.*) A roll upon the side drum.

Battery. An effect in harpsichord music, written and played

Battimento (*It.*) [Battement.]

Battuta (*It.*) (1) In correct time. (2) A bar.

Bau (*Ger.*) The structure of musical instruments.

Bauernleyer (*Ger.*) [Hurdy-gurdy.]

Bauerpfeife (*Ger.*) An organ stop of 8 ft. length of a small scale.

Baxoncillo (*Sp.*) An organ stop like an open diapason.

Bayles (*Sp.*) Comic dancing songs, many of which were written by Quevedo in the Spanish gipsy dialect. [Ballad.]

B. C. Basso Continuo.

B cancellatum (*Lat.*) The cancelled B. The note B♭ as altered by means of a ♮ or ♯ in old music. Up to the middle of the 18th century the ♯ frequently had the force of the ♮ as now used.

B dur (*Ger.*) The key of B♭ major.

B durum (*Lat.*) B natural. [B quadratum.]

Bearings. Those few notes which a tuner accurately tunes or *lays down* before proceeding to adjust the whole compass of the instrument.

Beat. (1) A short shake, or transient grace note, played or sung before the note it is desired to embellish. The beat is always a semitone lower than the ornamented note.

(2) The portion of a bar of music occupied by the movement or supposed movement of the hand in counting time. Thus, a beat in ⁶⁄₈ time is equal to three quavers; a beat in ³⁄₂ time is equal to a minim.

(3) The peculiar "throbbing" heard when sounds not quite identical in pitch are sounded together. [Acoustics, § 14, 15.]

Bebung (*Ger.*) The tremolo stop in an organ.

Bebisation. A series of syllables recommended by Daniel Hitsler, a Fleming, in 1630, as a means of teaching the notes. He proposed to substitute the syllables la, be, ce, de, mi, fe, gi, for ut, re, mi, fa, sol, la, si, already in use.

Becarre (*Fr.*) a natural, ♮.

Bec (*Fr.*) A mouth-piece, *lit.*, a beak.
Becco (*It.*) [Flute à bec.]

Becco polacco (*It.*) A large bag-pipe.

Becken (*Ger.*) A cymbal.

Bedon (*Fr.*) An obsolete term for a drum, or tambour.

Begeisterung (*Ger.*) Spirit, excitement, enthusiasm.

Begleiten (*Ger.*) To accompany.

Begleitende Stimmen (*Ger.*) Accompanying voices or parts.

Begleitete Fuge (*Ger.*) A Fugue with free parts. [Free parts.]

Begleitung (*Ger.*) Accompaniment.

Beitöne (*Ger.*) Aliquot tones. [Harmonics.]

Bell. [Bells.]

Bell. The lower termination of any tubular musical instrument which by the outward turning of the rim assumes the form of a bell. Fr. *Pavillon*, Ger. *Schallstück*.

Bell diapason. An organ stop consisting of open metal pipes with bell mouths. Its tone is more reedy and powerful than that of an ordinary open diapason. Generally of 8ft. length.

Bellezza (*It.*) Beauty of expression and tone in playing and singing.

Bell Gamba. An organ-stop, the pipes of which are conical and surmounted by a bell. It was introduced by **Mr. Hill**, organ-builder, of London. Its tone is remarkably sweet, not unlike that of a stringed instrument, though somewhat more reedy. The pipes speak rapidly.

Bellicosamente (*It.*) Warlike, martial.
Bellicoso (*It.*)

Bell metronome. A metronome in which the recurrence of a set number of beats is marked by the sound of a bell. [Metronome.]

Bell Open Diapason. [Bell Diapason.]

Bellows. In the harmonium, organ, concertina, &c., that contrivance by means of which wind is supplied to the pipes, tongues, or reeds. [Organ.]

Bell Piano. [Glockenspiel.]

Bells. 1. Musical instruments of percussion, consisting of a series of metal basins or cups, the outline of which has from time to time been modified. The materials of which bells are usually made are copper and tin, the proportions varying in several countries and even among the manufacturers.

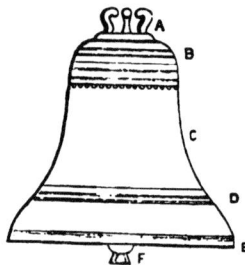

The various parts of the bells are A, the Canons; B, the Shoulder; C, the Waist; the thick part between D and E, the Sound Bow; E, the Rim or lip; F, the Clapper.

The following analyses of English and some foreign bells, will give a correct idea of the composition of the ancient bells.

ENGLISH BELLS.		PARIS BELLS.	
Copper	80·0	Copper	72·9
Tin	10·1	Tin	25·56
Zinc	5·6	Iron	1·54
Lead	4·3		

		SWISS HOUR BELLS.	
		Copper	75·0
ROUEN BELLS.		Tin	25·0
Copper	72·0	Mr. Denison recommends on theoretical grounds the following proportion	
Tin	25·0		
Zinc	1·8	Copper	76·5
Lead	1·2	Tin	23·5

2. The use of bells to call worshippers together is supposed to be of Christian origin, but it is said that the feast of Osiris in Egypt was announced by the ringing of bells. Aaron and the Jewish high priests had bells attached to their vestments, and

Plutarch says that small bells were used in the mysteries of Bacchus, and the priests of Cybele at Athens employed bells in their rites. The Greeks sounded bells in their camps, and the Romans indicated the hours of bathing and business by the tintinnabulum. It is also said, that in some places large gongs were suspended in the air, and as the wind brought them together, so was the character of the sounds made, interpreted as an unfavourable or favourable augury. Trumpets were employed among the Jews to call the faithful to worship (Exodus xx., 13; Numbers x., 2; Joel ii., 15). Plates of iron are still used in the Levant, and a plank of wood is occasionally employed for the same purpose that we use bells in some of the old Wallachian monasteries. In the East the call to prayer is made by the Muëddin of each mosque, who, having ascended the gallery of the mad'neh or minaret, chants the "hadan" or call to prayer, apparently in opposition to the Christian use of bells. [Hadan.]

The introduction of bells into churches is attributed to Paulinus, Bishop of Nola, in Campania, about the year 400, but there is an epistle of that bishop still extant in which he describes his church, but makes no mention of either tower or bells; indeed, it is believed that towers were not constructed until two centuries later. Yet it is not a little remarkable that the general name for bells was Nolæ or Campanæ, and hence the words *knoll* as meaning the sound of a single bell, and *campanile* a bell tower. Sabianus, who was Pope in 604, ordered the bells to ring the *horæ canonicæ* at the proper times during the day, and Benedict, Abbot of Wearmouth, brought his bells from Italy about the year 680. Bells were hung in towers in the East in the 9th, and in Germany in the 11th century. Those that were in use before are supposed to be hand bells; several examples, as old as the 6th century, are still preserved in some parts of Europe and the United Kingdom. St. Patrick's bell, St. Ninian's bell, St. Gall's bell, and others are plates of iron rivetted together. St. Gall's bell (about 646) is still shown in the monastery of the city called by his name in Switzerland. In the 13th century larger bells were cast, but it was not until the end of the 15th century that they began to assume great proportions. St. Dunstan, in the 10th century, seems to have the credit of having established the first foundry in England, Glastonbury, Malmesbury, and other places having been furnished with bells by him. Bells were rung not only to indicate the commencement of certain services, but also were tolled to mark certain stages in those services. Thus we find mention made of the Saints or Sanctus bell, the Compline bell, the Judas bell, the Pardon or *Ave* bell, the Passing bell, the last tolled to warn all "Christen soules" to pray for the parting soul of the dying. Bells, being thus intimately connected with the services of the Church, have been supposed to possess a certain sacred character. They were founded with religious ceremonies, consecrated, baptised, and were anointed with holy oil (see Schiller's "Lay"). St. Colomba, in the 6th century, made use of a bell whose name was "Dia Dioghaltus," or "God's vengeance," to test the truth of assertions made, as it was believed that the wrath of God would speedily overtake any who swore falsely by it. Pious inscriptions are frequent on bells of the middle ages, and inscriptions, not always pious, are found on those of later date. Bells were often rung to allay storms, there being a special endowment belonging to Old St. Paul's, "for ringinge the hallowed belle in great tempestes and lightninges." The curfew bell, still sounded in many parts of England and Scotland, is of more ancient practice than the period usually assigned as its commencement, the reign of William the Norman; and there are many social practices announced by the ringing or tolling of the church bells.

3. Change ringing, or campanology, is frequently practised when there are more than three bells, such changes being known by the names of bob-majors, bob triples, Norwich court bobs, grandsire bob-triples, and caters. The number of changes a set of bells is capable of, may be known by in-multiplying the numbers of the set. Thus, three bells may ring six changes, 1 2 3, 1 3 2, 2 1 3, 2 3 1, 3 2 1, 3 1 2; four bells will give 24 changes; 5 bells, 120 changes; 6 bells, 720 changes; 7 bells, 5,040 changes; 8 bells, 40,320 changes; 9 bells, 362,880 changes; 10 bells, 3,628,800 changes; 11 bells, 39,916,800 changes; 12 bells, 479,001,600 changes. To ring the changes that 12 bells are capable of, would take 91 years at two strokes per second, while a peal of 24 bells can make so many changes that it would occupy 117,000 billions of years to ring them all.

The technical terms for the various peals, on sets of bells of different numbers, are the following:

Rounds	On three bells.	
Changes or singles	„ four	„
Doubles or grandsires	„ five	„
(Bobs) Minor	„ six	„
Triples	„ seven	„
(Bobs) Major	„ eight	„
Caters	„ nine	„
(Bobs) Royal	„ ten	„
Cinques	„ eleven	„
(Bobs) Maximus	„ twelve	„

4. A bell is said to be "set" when she is mouth upwards, at "hand stroke" when the "sallie" or tuft on the rope has to be pulled,

at "back stroke" when the ringer has to pull the end of the rope. A bell is said to be "going up" when she moves her position in the change from "treble" towards that of "tenor," and "down" when she is changing her position from that of "tenor" towards that of "treble." A bell is said to be "behind" when she is the last of the changing bells, and at "lead" when she is the first. Thus the progress from "lead" to behind is said to be "going up," and from behind to lead is called "going down." "Dodging" is moving a place backwards out of the ordinary hunting course. A bell is said to be "hunting up" when she is pulled after the one which previously pulled after her. A bell is said to "make a place" when she strikes two blows in succession at any one place. To "lie a whole pull" is synonymous with "making a place." Two blows at "lead" and "behind" are a part of "hunting," in making these therefore a bell is not said to be "making a place." "Bob" and "singles" are words used to produce a certain series of changes by disturbing the ordinary system of "hunting." The full knowledge of the meaning of these and many other technical terms used in ringing can only be learnt in the belfry. The method of Doubles named after Stedman (1640) is, in principle, as follows: while three of the bells are ringing changes, the other two are dodging behind, but at the completion of each set of six changes one bell comes down from behind to take part in the changes, one, of course, at the same time going up behind to take part in the dodging.

5. Bells are occasionally employed as orchestral instruments—small bells, tuned to a certain scale, being most favoured—as in Victor Masse's "Les noces de Jeannette," a whole peal of small bells being used with great effect. These, as in Mozart's "Magic Flute," are so arranged as to be played with keys, like a pianoforte. [Glockenspiel.]

Auber employs a single bell in the finale to "Fra Diavolo." Rossini has introduced a bell sounding

in the opening of the second act of "William Tell." Donizetti also, in the finale to "Lucia di Lammermoor," has written for a bell tuned to the same note. Meyerbeer, in his "Huguenots," employs a bell in

with clarinets and bassoons. In "Dinorah," in what is popularly known as the "Goat Trio," a bell with the note

is used. Ambroise Thomas has a series of

clever harmonies for the orchestra in his opera "Hamlet," while a deep-toned bell strikes the midnight hour. Flotow, in "Martha," uses a bell, as does Gounod in "Jeanne d'Arc," tuned to the following note:

and there are numerous other instances where bells of all grades of tone have been used with skill and effect.

Bell founding. The shape and proportions of the intended bell having been decided upon according to a certain scale, the first part of the process of casting is commenced, by constructing an inner mould called the *core*, by which the form of the inside of the bell is determined. This *core* has a foundation of rough brickwork or iron, hollow in the centre, afterwards plastered over with loam or soft clay. A guage of wood, called a *crook*, made to revolve or sweep round on a central pivot by the hand of a workman, gives the clay the exact form required. This process will be at once understood on reference to the following diagram. A is the *core*, B the *crook*, which is fastened to C, the *pivot* on which it revolves:

The *core* is hardened by a fire made in its hollow, and when it is sufficiently "set," it is covered with grease and tan, over which is placed a coating of haybands and loam, of the thickness of the intended bell, and upon this the *cope* or outer mould is shaped. When this is dried it is removed, the thickening of haybands and loam which represented the shape of the bell to be cast, is destroyed, and the two moulds, the *core* and the *cope*, are examined and finished.

The *core* is sometimes made on an iron foundation, instead of brickwork, in which case it can be dried in a furnace, instead of by the fire in its hollow. The *cope* having been carefully adjusted over the *core*, the head and the staple to hold the clapper are then fitted on, and the whole mould is firmly imbedded in the earth, leaving only the holes at the top visible.

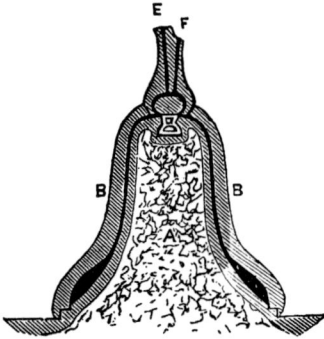

The above diagram shows the position of mould ready for the metal. A is the *core*, B the *cope*, F the channel for the metal to run in, E the hole for the air and gases to escape during the casting, and the thick black line the section of the bell. When the metal is quite ready, the furnace-door is opened, and the molten mass rushes down a channel, previously prepared, into the moulds sunk in the pits, and excepting mishaps, from insecure "bedding," the splitting of the *cope*, or other accidents, the bell is cast, and, when cold, is dug from the pit, the clay mould destroyed, and the bell is ready for the next process, that of tuning. The tuning is effected by means of a lathe and some simple machinery. If the bell requires sharpening, the diameter is lessened in proportion to its substance, if it is too sharp, the sound-bow is thinned by the same means ; but, as a rule, bells are now so accurately cast, that little if any tuning is necessary after the bell leaves the mould. It is stated in "Knight's Encyclopædia, 1854," that the German bell-founders made the various dimensions of the bell to bear certain ratios to each other. The thickest part where the hammer strikes is called the "Sound Bow." If this thickest be called one, then the diameter of the mouth equals 15, the diameter of the top or shoulder 7½, the height equals 12, and the weight of the clapper $\frac{1}{40}$ of the weight of the bell.

Denison recommends that the sound bow of the three or four larger bells of a peal should be of the thickness of a thirteenth of the diameter, and that the smaller bells may gradually increase in thickness up to the twelfth in a peal of six, the eleventh in a peal of eight, and to the tenth in a peal of ten or twelve, greater thickness impeding the freedom of the sound.

The bells of the Cathedral at Exeter, one of the largest peal of bells in England, the greater number of which were cast in 1676, have the following weights, diameters, and tones ;—

WEIGHT.			DIAMETER.		TONE.
Cwt.	qr.	lb.	Ft.	in.	
67	1	20	5	11½	B flat.
46	3	14	5	4½	C.
38	1	16	4	11	D.
30	1	12	4	7	E flat.
21	0	0	4	1	F.
15	0	0	3	10	G.
12	2	0	3	4½	A.
10	1	2	3	1½	B flat.
9	3	20	3	0	C.
8	3	20	2	9½	D.

The relative diameters of a peal of eight tuneable bells should be according to the following proportion : 60, 53½, 48, 45, 40, 36, 32, 30. The relative weights being generally in the proportion, 100, 70·23, 51·2, 42·2, 29·63, 21·6, 15·18, 12·5.

Belly. The upper plate of the resonance-box. In instruments of the Violin and Guitar family the strings are stretched over the belly, and the bridge across which they pass is so placed as to set the belly, and by its means, the air contained in the resonance-box, into vibration. In instruments of the Pianoforte class, the belly is that thin plate of fir-wood which, placed behind the strings, acts as a sound-board. Instead of an upper plate of wood, the guitars of many of the less civilized nations have a stretched parchment. The belly thus formed answers all the purposes of resonance for which it is intended; the Kissar of Nubia, the Banjo of the American negroes, the Nanga or Negro Harp which shares the combined designs of a guitar and harp, may be quoted as examples.

Bemes or Beemes. Saxon Trumpets or Bugles.

"Of brass they broughten beemes and box,
Of horn and bone, in which they blew and pouped,
And therewithal they shriked and they houped ;
It seemed as that the heven shulde falle."
Chaucer. "Nonne preestes tale." See also the "Romaunt of the Rose."

Bémol (*Fr.*) The sign ♭.

Ben (*It.*) Well. *Ben marcato*, well and clearly marked.

Bene (*It.*) Well. Used as an expression of approval during a performance.

Benedictus (*Lat.*) [Mass.]

Bene placito (*It.*) At pleasure, *ad libitum*, e.g., "Bassani's Ballate corrente, Gighe, e Sarabande, a violino, e violone, overo spinetta, con il secondo violino *à bene placito*" (1684).

B quadro (*It.*) The square B or ♮, that is, B durum or *natural*, as opposed to the ♭, soft B, B molle, or rounded b which, in its slightly altered outline, is now known as a flat. That the note B was the first note altered by an accidental, accounts for the fact that signs of ♭ and ♮ are of general application.

Bequadro (*It.*) }
Béquarre (*Fr.*) } The sign ♮.

Berceuse (*Fr.*) A cradle song.

Bergomask. Burgomask. Bergamasca. A lively dance in triple time, for two clumsy performers, in imitation of the dances of the country people of Bergamo, who were considered the least graceful of the Italians.

"Will it please you to see our epilogue, or to hear a Bergomask dance, between two of our company?"
Shakespeare.

Bes (*Ger.*) The note B double flat.

Besaiten (*Ger.*) To string an instrument.

Bewegung (*Ger.*) Motion.

Bhat. A Hindu Bard.

Bianca (*It.*) A minim, ♩. The *white* note, as opposed to the ♪, or black note (*nero*).

Bichord. Having two strings to each note.

Bicinium (*Lat.*) A duet, from *bis* and *cano.* "Cum duo canunt, *bicinium* appellatur; cum multi, *chorus.*"

Bifara (*Lat.*) An organ-stop, with two pipes to each note, producing a tremulant effect. [Vox Angelica.]

Bilancojel. An Indian flute with seven holes, played by a mouthpiece.

Bimmolle (*It.*) a flat, ♭. [See B Quadratum.]

Bina, or Vina. An Indian guitar, with a long finger board, and a gourd attached to each end. Seven strings or wires wound round pegs in the usual way are attached to the finger board, four on the surface, and three at the sides. There are about twenty frets, some standing up as high as an inch from the finger board; these are fastened with wax, and the performer regulates the positions of them at his pleasure. In the performance one gourd is rested on the left shoulder, and the other on the right hip. Its scale consists of a series of small intervals lying between a note and its octave, in the bass-stave.

Binary Form. The form of a movement which is founded on two principal themes or subjects. [Sonata Form.]

Binary Measure. Common time. [Tonic-Sol-fa.]

Bind. (1) A curved line, ⌒, a sign which, when placed over two notes of the same name or same pitch (enharmonically changed), directs that the two are to be sustained as one. It is of frequent occurrence at points of Syncopation and Suspension.

&c.

Enharmonic change, or Modulation.

Suspension.

Syncopation.

When a curved line is placed over two notes, not of the same name or pitch, it is called a *Slur*, and directs that they are to be played smoothly, *e.g.*:

It is to be regretted that the horizontal line introduced by Sir W. S. Bennett as a *Bind*, so that no confusion can exist between the *Bind* and *Slur*, has not been generally adopted, *e.g.*:

(2) A Brace (*Fr., Accolade*) which binds together the separate parts of a score.

Binde (*Ger.*) [Bind.]

Bindebogen (*Ger.*) The bind-bow. [Bind.]

Bindung (*Ger.*) Syncopation, suspension, so called because the notes forming it are *bound*, or at least might be so written.

Bindungszeichen (*Ger.*) A slur or bind.

Birn (*Ger.*) That portion of a clarionet or similar instrument in which the mouth-piece is inserted, so called from its *pear*-like shape.

Bis (*Lat.*) Twice. (1) A direction that the passage over which it is placed shall be twice played or sung. Its use is generally limited to short passages, marks of *repeat* being written for a long repetition. It is placed under or over a slur, *e.g.*:

(2) Again. *Encore.*

Bischero (*It.*) The peg, or pin, with which the strings of an instrument are secured.

Biscroma (*It.*) } A semiquaver, ♪.
Biscrome (*Fr.*) }

Bisdiapason. The interval of a double octave, or fifteenth.

Bissex. A kind of guitar with twelve strings (*Ger.* Zwölfsaiter), invented by Van-hecke in 1770. Of the twelve strings six were over the finger-board, six below, hence the name *twice-six.* Its compass was three and a half octaves.

Bis unca (*Lat.*) A semiquaver ♪, or note with *two hooks*.

Bit. A small piece of tube, generally furnished with two raised *ears.* It is used for supplementing the crook of a trumpet, cornet-a-piston, &c., so as to adapt the instrument to a slight difference of pitch.

Bizzarramente (*It.*) }
Bizzarria (*It.*) } { Fantastically, wonderfully. Singularity, affectation. Odd, droll.
Bizzarro (*It.*) }

Blanche (*Fr.*) A minim ♩ [Bianca.]

Blanche pointée (*Fr.*) A dotted minim.

Blasebalg (*Ger.*) The bellows of an organ. Saxon *bles-belg*, a wind-bag.

Blase-instrument (*Ger.*) Wind instrument. Flute, oboe, bassoon, cornet, trumpet, trombone, &c.

Blase-musik (*Ger.*) Music for wind instruments.

Blatt (*Ger.*) A vibrating tongue or blade. [Reed.]

Blech-instrumente (*Ger.*) [Metal wind instruments.]

B mol (*Fr.*) The note B♭.

B moll (*Ger.*) The key B♭ minor.

B molle (*Lat.*) The note B♭. *c.f.* B quadratum.

Bobibation or Bocedisation. Solfeggi taught by Huberto Walraent at the end of the 16th century for scale practice, which were bo, ce, di, ga, la, mi, ni. [See Bebisation.] Bobisation or Bocedisation, in which the syllables bo, cé, di, ga, lo, ma, ni were substituted for those attributed to Guido, was introduced and taught in many schools in Flanders, and so this peculiar use came to be called Belgian solmisation. Walraent's method was adopted in Italy in 1599 by Henri de la Putte, who wrote an elaborate Latin treatise in defence of it; and a few years later Calwitz, ignoring its invention and taking the credit to himself, introduced it into Germany. In Spain and France the method was proposed by Pietro de Ureno and John Lemaire, but without success. To the last-named musician the addition of the syllable SI for the leading note is attributed. Bobisation was accepted by some musicians and rejected by others, and the result was a petty war, which lasted until the commencement of the 18th century. Hitzler, a few years later, suggested the use of the syllables la, be, ce, de, me, fe, ge—this system he called *bebisation* or *labecedation;* and Graun recommended da, me, ni, po, tu, la, ba, from which his plan was called *damenisation.*

Bob major. Bob maximus, Bobs. [Bells.]

Bocal (*Fr.*) The mouth-piece of the horn, serpent, trombone, &c.

Bocca (*It.*) The mouth. *Con bocca chiusa,* with closed mouth, humming.

Bocca ridente (*It.*) *Smiling mouth,* the position of the mouth needful for the production of pleasing tone.

Bocchino (*It.*) A mouth-piece of wind instruments.

Bockpfeife (*Ger.*) Bagpipe.

Bockstriller (*Ger.*) A goat-like tremolo upon one note, a bad shake. [Vibrato.]

Boden (*Ger.*) [Body.]

Body. The resonance box of a string instrument. That part of a wind instrument which remains after the removal of mouth-piece, crooks, and bell.

Bogen (*Ger.*) Bow.

Bogenclavier (*Ger.*) [Tetrachordon.]

Bogenführung (*Ger.*) The art of playing with a bow upon stringed instruments.

Bogenstrich (*Ger.*) The stroke of the bow.

Bolero (*Sp.*) A Spanish dance in triple measure with strongly-marked accent, also called Cachuca. It is accompanied with singing and castanets, and the performer assumes in the course of the dance all the various feelings supposed to be excited by love, from the greatest shyness to the highest ecstasy. [Chica.]

Bombard. Bombarde (*Fr.*) A reed stop on the organ, usually among the pedal registers, of large scale, rich tone, and often on a heavy pressure of wind.

Bombardino (*It.*) A small bombardo, *q.v.*

Bombardo (*It.*) A mediæval wind instrument, the precursor of the oboe, of which it was no doubt a large and coarse species. The word *Pommer*, applied to these instruments, was a corruption of the Italian name. The *chalameau* or *shawm* (Ger.*Schalmey*) was the smallest of this class, the *bombardone* the largest. Clarinets, oboes, and bassoons, now so clearly defined, grew out of one common parentage. The clarinet has but one vibrating reed ; the oboe and bassoon double vibrating reeds.

Bombardon. A brass instrument, in tone not unlike an ophicleide. It is not capable of rapid execution. The compass is

Music for it is written without transposition, although it is in F.

Bombaulius, βομβαύλιος (*Gk.*) A facetious name for a bag-piper. A pun on the words αὐλητής, a flute-player, and βομβύλιος, a buzzing insect, whence our word, bumble-bee ; *c.f.,* Latin, *Bombus.*

Bombyx (*Gk.*) βόμβυξ. A Greek flute, perhaps so named from its supposed resemblance to the silk-worm. It was probably a reed-instrument of powerful tone. The following illustration is given by Burney from a sarcophagus in the Capitoline Museum, at Rome.

Bones. Four pieces of the ribs of horses or oxen, held in the hands and struck together for the purpose of marking time, in accompaniment to the voice or an instrument. The bones are of ancient use in England, and are alluded to by Shakespeare in the fourth act of "A Midsummer Night's Dream," as forming one means of rustic music. And in figures designed by Inigo Jones for the Court Masques one is represented playing upon knicky-knackers of bone or wood. The word knicky-knackers, by which the bones are known to the country people, may have its origin from the word "nakeres." In Strutt's "Sports and Pastimes," a payment is recorded as being made to Janino le Nakerer, among the minstrels of King Edward II. The nakerer was probably the drummer ; but, as the minstrels frequently indulged in burlesque music, Janino may have been the performer on that primitive or rustic instrument, the bones.

Bon temps de la mesure (*Fr.*) The accented portion of the bar.

Bordone (*It.*) [Bourdon.] [Viola di Bardone.]

Boulou. A harp used by the negroes of Senegambia and Guinea, in shape like the Oriental harp. Its strings are of fibre.

Bourdon (*Fr.*) (1) A drone bass, a burden such as that produced by a bagpipe, or a hurdy-gurdy. [Burden.] (2) An organ stop, consisting of stopped wooden pipes, generally of 16 ft. tone. Sometimes, but rarely, the upper part is of metal. It is found on manuals as a "double" stop, and also on the pedal organ as a soft foundation-stop. It was formerly made of a large scale in England, but from a better knowledge of scientific principles organ builders are now able to produce a strong and pure body of tone from a pipe of moderate scale. As a rule, it is important that it should be free from a preponderance of harmonics or overtones, but sometimes they are purposely produced with the fundamental note, in which case the stop is called *quintaton,* because the first harmonic or over-tone of a stopped pipe is its twelfth, or octave fifth. Hence a Bourdon was sometimes said to be *fifthy.*

Bourrée (*Fr.*) A dance tune in common time, said by Hawkins to come from Auvergne. Other writers give Biscay as its birthplace. The earliest mention of it is probably about 1580. It is still popular with the peasants of Lower Brittany. It often forms one of the movements of the earlier Sonata.

Boutade (*Fr.*) A dance which was supposed to be impromptu.

Bow. An instrument of wood and horsehair, employed to set the strings of the violin, &c., in vibration. The bow, originally curved, as its name implies, has been subject to many changes of shape from time to time, from a large curve to an almost flat form.

Fig. 1.

Fig. 2.

Fig. 3.

Fig. 4.

Fig. 5.

The bow shown in fig. 1 is that still used with the *rebab* of Algeria. Fig. 2 is given by Gerber from a MS. of the 8th or 9th century. The bow now used for the violin is about 29 inches in length (almost straight, but with a slight curve *inwards*, not outwards, as in the older bows), the violoncello bow being a little shorter, fig. 5. Christopher Simpson (1676) says that twenty-seven inches was the length of the bow in his time, the "sonata bow," fig. 3, according to tradition, being only twenty-four inches, the common " fiddle-stick " being still shorter. The form of the bow, which was anciently employed for all stringed instruments of the violin kind, known now as the " Corelli bow," fig. 4, is to a certain extent preserved in the double-bass bow as at present employed in England.

Most of our stringed-instruments can be traced to an Eastern source, but as the earliest figure of the bow is found in MSS. relating to this country, it has been supposed that it is of British origin. There are many representations of it in MSS. as early as the Anglo-Saxon period (see " Sandy's History of the Violin," pp. 52, 53, &c.), and later through successive generations, besides existing specimens of actual ancient bows, all of which partake of the *bowed* character, as seen in fig. 1. The curved bow was still in fashion until the death of Handel, if any trust is to be placed in contemporary pictures and drawings.

The little that is known of the early bows gives the notion that they were incapable of producing anything like delicacy of tone ; and it was not until the early part of the 17th century, when violin-playing began to be cultivated, that we find that any attempt was made to improve either the form of the bow or the means of stretching the horse-hair, so that an even pressure might be obtained. The alteration from the bowed form is said to have been made after a suggestion by Tartini [1692-1770]. There is every reason to believe that the improvement in violin-playing due to him could only be effected by means of a better bow than the clumsy one of his time. The earliest improvement was made when a metal band, with teeth-like edges, was introduced, with the design of regulating the position and tension of the hair at or near the handle. This helped to prevent the hair assuming the cord-like form which players found to be awkward and clumsy. But it was reserved for François Tourte [1747-1833] to devise the plan of keeping " the hair flat by means of a clasp." Tourte also introduced the screw and button for slackening or tightening the hair at pleasure, and was the first to choose Brazil-wood as a material in bow-making. It was the father of Tourte who attempted the first improvements in bow-making, but it was the son above-mentioned who introduced the most valuable inventions. The bows of the younger Tourte are almost as much sought as those of the elder Dodd [1705-1810], who lived to the great age of 105 years, but the works of the last-named are most highly valued. Panormo, Tubbs, and Chanot are counted among the chief of modern bow-makers.

Bow-hand. The term is employed by violinists to describe the power and skill with which a player produces the tone of his instrument.

Bowing. The art of managing the bow, so as not only to bring out the best tone the instrument is capable of, but also so to phrase the passages played that the best possible character may be imparted to the music. The importance both to a violinist, and a composer of music for the violin, of a thorough knowledge of the art of bowing, cannot be overrated. By varying the system of bowing, a simple musical sentence may be changed in its character, almost indefinitely. Formerly, very little attention was paid to this subject, the system of bowing being left very much to the discretion of the players, who only occasionally had such general directions as *legato* or *staccato*. There always, however, existed certain traditional rules, *e.g.* that the down-bow should be used at the first beat of a bar, or where any great emphasis was required (as in some cases of syncopation); also, that where no directions are given, the passage should be *bowed*, that is, the notes should be alternately played by an *up* and *down* bow. But it is evident that in simple music, of triple measure, these rules will clash, for, alternate bowing will lead to the recurrence of an up-bow on every alternate down-beat. Hence, even if an excellent band is playing music up to the date of, and including that by Handel, it must have often been observed that the bowing is far from being uniform. In modern music, every direction is given to the performers which is requisite for the production of absolute uniformity, and more than this, the various effects which are capable of production by the different systems of bowing are used as part of a composer's material. The prominent features in modern bowing are the more frequent antithesis between *legato* and *staccato*, and the use of at least three kinds of the latter. When notes have the ordinary dot placed above them they are *bowed* staccato ; when the dots are under a slur, they are played with *one bow* (that is by the movement of the bow in one direction) the short length of the sounds being brought about by keeping the bow always *lying on the string*, so that any movement of the bow which has produced a sound shall be followed by absolute silence. The third kind of staccato is produced by holding the bow as lightly as possible and allowing it almost to dance upon the string. In this manner rapid passages may be played either by *one* bow up or down, or by an alternate bowing, during which the movement of the bow at right angles to the string is so slight that it seems to rise and fall almost perpendicularly. A favourite division of four rapid notes is to make two legato and the following two staccato. The well-known Var. II. of Beethoven's Sonata for Violin, known as the "Kreutzer," is a good illustration of this:

The effect which results from moving the bow on an unaccented part of the bar is most striking and beautiful, *e.g.* (from the same Sonata):

and in the following (Beethoven Symphony, No. 9):

Groups of three notes are often divided into two legato and one staccato, *e.g.*:

less often into one staccato and two legato, *e.g.*:

Two notes out of eight are often made staccato, *e.g.*:

The above few examples may serve to give some idea of the inexhaustible resources of the art of bowing. It will of course be understood that what is here said of the violin applies equally to the viola and violoncello. But, in consequence of the thickness of the strings, the double-bass is not so capable of rapid contrasts of bowing as the rest of its family. In studies and exercises it is usual now to direct a down-bow by the sign ⌐; and an up-bow by ^. The French terms corresponding to these signs are *tiré* (draw); *poussé* (push), sometimes abbreviated by *p* and *t*.

The quality of tone produced depends not only on the nature and quantity of pressure exercised by the bow upon the strings, but also upon the position of the point of impact. Thus, if played very close to the bridge (*sul' ponticello*), the tone is of peculiar brightness and shrillness; as the bow is used further from the bridge, the tone passes through a stage of great purity and strength, until, at close proximity to the finger-board, it becomes soft and somewhat dull. The practised performer chooses that part of the string capable of producing the tone best suited to the passage he is playing, and he draws it forth with that part of bow most suitable for the purpose. As a general rule, from the heel to about the middle of the bow, is the part naturally used for *forte* or *sforzando* passages; and from the middle to the point for those of a more delicate character. But actual experience is the only method of learning the intricacies and beauties of the art of bowing.

Boyau (*Fr.*) Cat-gut strings.

B quadratum (*Lat.*) B quadrum (*Lat.*) B quarre (*Fr.*)	B natural. The name of B quadratum or B square was given by reason of its shape, which was originally that of a gothic B. [B cancellatum.]

Brabançonne. The Belgian patriotic song first sung at the time of the revolution of 1830. The words were written by an actor named Jenneval, at that time engaged at the theatre at Brussels, the music being set by a singer named Campenhout. Upon the death of Jenneval at Berghem his mother was allowed a pension of 2400 fr. Campenhout was appointed director of the Royal Chapel.

Brace. (1) A mark connecting two or more staves together.

(2) The leather slides upon the cords of a drum, used for raising or lowering the tone by tightening or loosening the head.

Bransle (*Fr.*) Brawl.

Brawl. An old round dance in which the performers joined hands in a circle. A country dance.

"Then first of all he doth demonstrate plain
The motions seven that are in nature found,
Upward and downward, forth, and back again,
To this side, and to that, and turning round;
Whereof a thousand brawls he doth compound,
Which he doth teach unto the multitude,
And ever with a turn they must conclude."
SIR JOHN DAVIES. *Orchestra*, 1607.

The brawl and the bransle were the same dance. Douce gives an account of "le branle du bouquet,' from "Deux dialogues du nouveau langage François, Italianize," Anvers, 1579, in which, kissing the whole of the ladies, by each of the gentlemen in turn, seems to have been one of the chief features in the dance.

The following Braule from Delaborde's specimens (of the 15th or 16th century) shows the rhythm of this dance :

Bratsche (*Ger.*) The Tenor Violin, Alto, or Viola. So called from the *Viola da braccia*, or viola held on the arm, as distinguished from the *viola da gamba*, or viola held between the legs, the precursor of the violoncello. [Viola.]

Brava, *fem.* (*It.*) ⎫
Bravi, *pl.* (*It.*) ⎬ Well, or bravely, done.
Bravo, *mas.* (*It.*) ⎭

Bravura (*It.*) Aria di bravura. An air, distinguished from a simple melody by the introduction of florid passages. [Air.]

Break. (1) The point of junction in the quality of tenor, soprano, and alto voices. A genuine bass voice has no break. The lower range is called *voce di petto*, or chest voice; the upper, *voce di testa*, or head voice; and the place of junction is called the break. A properly-cultivated voice should have the break so under control, that the union of the two qualities should be imperceptible. [Larynx.]

(2) In the clarinet the break in the tone of the instrument occurs between B flat and B natural,

Hence, rapid passages containing frequent transitions from one register to the other are impossible on that instrument. In trumpets and horns, when from imperfect lipping, the note produced is other than the tone intended, such note is called a break. A similar result often occurs in imperfectly-formed or unset voices.

(3) Break, in an organ stop, is the sudden alteration of the proper scale-series of the pipes by returning to those of an octave lower in pitch. A break becomes necessary in the smaller compound stops, for, when proceeding far upwards in pitch, it is found that the pipes would be so small as to be inaudible. As mixtures, sesquialteras, and other stops of the same class, are generally formed of several ranks of high harmonics, breaks in them are frequent. The break generally takes place between C and C♯, or F and F♯; but organ-builders do not act with uniformity, either as to the position of the break, or the exact series of sounds to be produced on the return.

Breast. The voice.

" Trulye two degrees of men, which have the highest offices under the Kinge in all this realme, shall greatly lacke the use of singinge, preachers, and lawyers, because they shall not, withoute this, be able to rule their breastes for everye purpose."—*Ascham's Toxophilite.*

" By my troth, the fool has an excellent breast."— SHAKESPEARE, *Twelfth Night*, ii., 3.

" The better brest, the lesser rest,
To serve the queer, now there, now heer,
For time so spent, I may repent
And sorrowe make."

TUSSER (*Five hundred points of good husbandry*, 1540).

Breve. In Mediæval music, the note equal to half the value of a *long*, and one quarter the double *long* or maxima. Its shape was ■. " Quandocunque punctus quadratus invenitur, qui caret omni tractu *brevis* dicitur" (Franco, of Paris.) Breves like other notes in the early attempts at mensurable music, affected the length of other notes, and were in turn affected by other notes according to their relative position. A *long* " in modo perfecto " was reduced by one third or made imperfect by having a *breve* next to it on either side. A breve " in tempore perfecto " was made imperfect, that is, was reduced from three to two beats, by juxtaposition with a semibreve. A breve was also subject to " alteratio " that is, being made longer when between two longs. When so altered it was called *alterata* or shortly *altera*. All these laws and many others of a like character were drawn up by writers in the fifteenth century, in the dawn of " mensurable " music. Having discovered the utility of showing the relative length of notes by their shape, authors seem to have revelled in constructing new complications. These were gradually dropped by succeeding writers, until the breve became the unit of duration, a position which it held for nearly two centuries. The Semibreve is now our recognized unit, the Breve being a *double* note and of rare occurrence. But these changes have been a slow growth, not sudden alterations of existing opinions or practices.

Brett-geige. Bret-Geige (*Ger.*) A pocket fiddle ; hence, Fr. *pochette*, Ger.*Taschengeige*. It. *sordino*, from the small quantity of tone it is capable of producing. Eng. *kit*.

Bridge. A piece of wood which, on instruments having a resonance-box, performs the double duty of raising the strings above the belly, and of terminating at one end their vibrating portion. In instruments played with the bow, the bridge is arched, in order to allow the bow to impinge upon any one string without touching others. In instruments, such as the guitar and pianoforte, its upper edge runs parallel to the belly. In violins, the material and adjustment of the bridge are of great importance. Some instruments require a bridge made of coarse-grained wood, others of close-grained. It stands on two legs ; that on the right hand should rest on the belly at a short distance behind the sound post. The legs should lie flat on the surface of the belly, in order that the vibrations of the strings should be duly transferred to the resonance-box. The tone of an instrument is largely influenced by the position of the bridge, and only great experience and nice handling can discover where it is best set up.

Brillante (*It.* and *Fr.*) Brilliant, in a showy sparkling style.

Brillenbässe (*Ger.*) "Spectacle basses," music for the drum, so called from its resemblance to a pair of spectacles.

Brindisi (*It.*) A melody in triple time of a florid character, so arranged as to exhibit the change from the chest to the head voice in rapid succession, something similar to the German *jodl. q.v.* The air "Libiamo" in Verdi's "La Traviata," is called a *brindisi*.

Brio, con (*It.*) With spirit, vigour, and force.

Brioso (*It.*) Joyfully, vigorously, forcibly.

Brisé (*Fr.*) [Broken chords, arpeggios.]

Brisk. Lively. A term frequently used by writers of the last century before the general adoption of the term *vivace*.

Broderies (*Fr.*) Ornaments with which it was the fashion in a past age to cover any simple melody; these were generally left to the caprice of the performer, until Rossini set the fashion of writing those ornaments which he wished his music to bear.

Broken cadence. An interrupted cadence.

Broken chords. [Arpeggio.]

Broken music. Probably music played on harps, guitars, or lutes, because the sounds of these instruments cannot be sustained at will. Shakespeare, "Troilus and Cressida," Act iii. sc. 1 :

"Fair prince, here is good broken music."

Also "Henry V," Act. ii. sc. 1 ; "As you like it," Act i. sc. 2.

Brontium (*Gk.*) βροντεῖον. A contrivance for imitating thunder, used in the Greek theatre. Sheets of copper were laid out in the hyposcenium over which were rolled bladders filled with pebbles.

B rotundum (*Lat.*) B flat. See B cancellatum.

Brummeisen or **Maultrommel** (*Ger.*) Jew's-harp. From *Maul*, the mouth. [Jew's-harp.]

Bruscamente (*It.*) Coarsely, roughly, strongly accented.

Buccina. Bucina (*Lat.*) A crooked horn or trumpet, *tuba* being the straight trumpet. It was used as a signal for changing the night-watches, hence the expressions *ad primam bucinam, secundam*, &c., at the first and second watches. Public assemblies were also summoned by it in early Roman times. Poets and sculptors have represented Triton as blowing through a *bucina*, from *bucinum*, a shell called the sea-trumpet.

Buccinator. A muscle situated in the fleshy part of the cheeks. It is so called because, when the cheeks are filled with air, the contraction of the buccinator muscles forces it out. It derives its name from *buccinare*, Lat., to blow a trumpet.

Buccolica (*It.*) ⎫ Rustic, *à la bucolique*,
Bucolique (*Fr.*) ⎬ in a rustic manner.

Büchse (*Ger.*) The boot or foot of an organ pipe.

Buffet (*Fr.*) An organ case. Key-board case.

Buffa (*It.*) *fem.* ⎫ Comic. *Aria buffa*,
Buffo (*It.*) *mas.* ⎬ a humorous melody; *opera buffa*, a comic opera. In mediæval Latin *buffa* meant a slap on the face, and in Italian *buffare* means to blow wind through the mouth ; *c.f.* Scotch *buffie*, puffed.

Buffone (*It.*) A comic singer in the opera.

Buffonescamente (*It.*) In a burlesque or humorous style.

Bugle. (1) A hunting-horn of a straight or curved form. (2) A copper instrument of the horn quality of tone, but of less compass, furnished with keys. The tone is sweet, powerful, and distinct; it has rarely been employed in the orchestra. There are bugle horns in C, B flat, and E flat, each capable of producing its generator and 7 harmonics. The ventil-horn is an improvement upon the bugle. The word Bugle, from the Anglo-Saxon *buge*, to *bend* or *curve*, was anciently applied to many things of a curved shape, thus, the head of a bishop's crozier was called the *bugle*, and the crozier itself the *bugle-rod*. The handle of a kettle, basket handles, and a peculiar sort of elongated glass-bead are each called by the name *bugle*. Some writers derive the word from *bowgle* or *bougle*, a bull, on the ground that the earliest horns were bull's horns, and that the earliest representations of hunting horns are in shape like bull's horn. [Metal wind instruments.]

Buonaccordo (*It.*) A small triangular spinet for the use and amusement of children, the notes of which were made small to suit the length of their span.

Buonamente (*It.*) Justly, truly.

Buona nota (*It.*) Accented note.

Buon gusto (*It.*) In good taste.

Burden. (1) The chorus or refrain of a song. [Ballad.] (2) The drone of the bagpipe. (3) The tune sung as an accompaniment to a dance when there were no instruments.

> " Foot it featly here and there,
>   And let the rest the burden bear."

" Belike it hath some *burden* then "

And clap us into *Light o' love*, that goes without a burden.
Do you sing it, and I'll dance it."—*Shakespeare.*

> " This sompnour bear to him a stiff bordoune
>   Was never trompe of half so gret a soun."
>   *Chaucer.*

Burla (*It.*) A jest.
Burlando. Burlescamente. } [Buffo.]

Burlesca (*It.*) A jest, a movement in a jocular style, *c.f.* scherzo.

Burletta (*It.*) A comic operetta, a farce interspersed with songs.

Busaun. Busain. Buzain A reed-stop on the organ. Generally of 16 ft. length, and on the pedal organ. Its quality of tone is soft. It is not improbable that this word is connected with *bassoon.*

Bussone (*It.*) An obsolete wind-instrument, *c.f.* bassoon.

Button. (1) A small round piece of leather which, when screwed on the tapped wire of a tracker, prevents it from jumping out of place. [Organ.] (2) The keys of the first-made accordions. [Accordion.]

Buxus. Buxea tibia (*Lat.*) A flute made of boxwood.

> " Tympana vos buxusque vocant Berecyntia matris
>   Idææ."—Virg. Æ. ix. 619.

Byssynge songes (*early Eng.*) Lullabyes, cradle songs.

C.

C. (1) The note *Ut* in the Guidonian system and in modern French and Italian nomenclature.

— (2) The letter whose original form was afterwards modified into the C clef.

— (3) The first note of the Hypo-Eolian mode. The first note of the Ionian mode.

— (4) The first, or key note of the modern normal scale, so called because if it be desired to write down the scale now used, C is the only note from which the series can start unless sharps or flats be added.

— (5) A capital letter C signifies the note in the second space of the bass stave (Tenor C). A small *c* signifies the note one octave above this, *middle C*. [Pitch.]

Cabaletta (*Sp.*) (*Lit. a little horse.*) A melody in rondo form, at first sung simply, afterwards with variations, probably so called because accompaniments to cabalettas were in triplet form like the noise made by a horse cantering.

Cabinet d'orgue (*Fr.*) Organ case.

Cabinet Pianoforte. An old-fashioned upright pianoforte, about six feet in height. [Pianoforte.]

Cabiscola (*Lat.*) A corruption of the words caput scholæ. The præcentor in a choir (Præcentor). In Narbonne and many parts of Italy, the office of capischol was held by the Dean.

Caccia (*It.*) Hunting. (1) Music accompanied by horns, or in praise of field sports, is said to be *alla caccia*, in the hunting style.

(2) Instruments used in hunting are called *da caccia*, as *oboe da caccia*, hunting oboe, a large kind of oboe; *corno da caccia*, hunting horn.

Cachuca (*Sp.*) A Spanish dance. [Bolero.]

Cacophony (*Gk.*)
Cacophonie (*Fr.*) } Harsh sounding music —not necessarily incor-
Cacofonia (*It.*) } rect, but often treated as though it were, because of its unusual appeal to imperfect judgment. The word is, however, generally used in a bad sense.

Cadence. (1) A vocal or instrumental shake or trill, run or division, introduced as an ending, or as a means of return to the first subject.

(2) The end of a phrase, formerly called a fall, either in melody or harmony.

" That strain again
It had a dying fall."—*Shakespeare.*

(3) There are four principal forms of cadence in harmony, the whole, or authentic, the half, the interrupted, and the plagal cadence. When the last chord—the major or minor chord of the key note—is preceded by the major chord of the dominant, such cadence is called whole or perfect. If the last chord is the dominant and is preceded by the chord of the tonic, the cadence is called half or imperfect. When the last chord of the phrase is other than the tonic chord and is preceded by that of the dominant, the cadence is said to be interrupted, false, or deceptive. The cadence, called plagal, is that in which the chord of the tonic is preceded by the major or minor chord of the subdominant. The whole cadence is used to conclude most modern music; the half and the interrupted cadence in the progress of a harmonised melody. The plagal cadence was frequently employed as a close by the old contrapuntal writers.

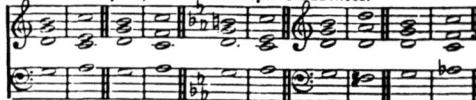
Whole or Perfect Cadences.   Half or Imperfect Cadences.

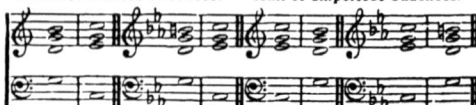
Interrupted, False or Deceptive Cadences.

Plagal Cadences.

By some authors, cadences are divided into two kinds, perfect and imperfect; the authentic and plagal being considered perfect; all other cadences, imperfect. From another point of view cadences have been divided into simple and compound; a cadence being simple when both the penultimate and final chords which form it are plain common chords; and compound when suspensions or other devices are introduced, e.g.:

Simple Cadence.   Compound Cadence.

A series of cadences can be constructed by making any one of the *relative chords* (or its inversions) precede the final tonic chord, a relative chord being a common chord which can be made up out of the notes of any given scale. The relative chords of C are therefore D minor, E minor, F major, G major, A minor, but not B major or minor, as there is no F♯ in the key of C. We shall, therefore, get this series:

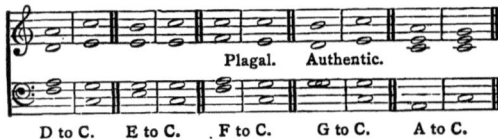

Plagal.   Authentic.

D to C.   E to C.   F to C.   G to C.   A to C.

And from the relative chords of the minor scale:

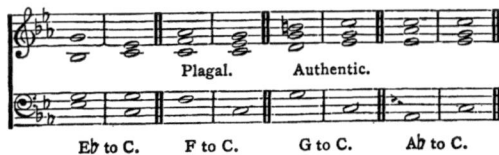

Plagal.   Authentic.

E♭ to C.   F to C.   G to C.   A♭ to C.

It will be observed that there is no relative chord on the second or seventh degree of the minor mode owing to the imperfection of the interval of the fifth. For further information see Stainer's "Theory of Harmony."

Cadence imparfaite (*Fr.*) An imperfect cadence.

Cadence parfaite (*Fr.*) A perfect cadence.

Cadence perlée (*Fr.*) A brilliant cadence.

Cadence rompue (*Fr.*) A broken or interrupted cadence.

Cadenz (*Ger.*) [Cadence.]

Cadenza (*It.*) (1) A passage introduced towards the close of the first or last movement of a concerto, either actually extempore or of an impromptu character. (2) A running passage at the conclusion of a vocal piece. Solo performers in times past were accustomed to display their skill and invention in a final flourish, apparently extempore, but often the result of careful study and preparation. In some cases, however, the attainment of the performer was the object of the display, and hence the added cadenza was often so inappropriate and incongruous, especially in vocal music, that composers felt bound to write down all the ornaments or embellishments they considered their music capable of bearing. Purcell is said to have so acted with regard to many of his songs; and it has been supposed that the runs or divisions so common in music of the 18th century were introduced as concessions to the custom of the time of ornamenting a plain melody. Every performer considered himself at liberty to alter an air to suit his own peculiarities, and singers were estimated according to their vocal agility. An extract from a diary kept at Rome in 1697, by a young Scotch gentleman, speaking of Corelli and his playing, says: "This is his manner in adagios, to which he adds innumerable graces; not crowded in confusion as some do, but gentle, easy and sliding, and suited withal to the composition of the other parts, which no man but he who has taste and knowledge of the composition, can perform." When a great master in art sets the example, followers are always found, and what is pleasing in a man of genius becomes the reverse when imitated. Although cadenzas were fashionable in the time of Handel, instances of fully written examples by him are rare. The conclusion of the duet, "O lovely peace," in "Judas Maccabæus," is one of the few specimens he has left. Many of the songs in his oratorios were constantly so changed by the singers by means of graces, notes, and turns, that their form was completely disguised. But while the custom existed there were not wanting some musicians who constantly protested against what they considered the ill-usage of an author's ideas, forgetting that the composer, probably knowing the bad habit of his singers, had constructed his melodies so that they might not suffer by the overlading of *fioriture*. Rubinelli the singer, on his first appearance in England, was censured for embellishing and changing his airs. On his second appearance in this country, he determined to sing without introducing a single ornament not written, and so fickle was the taste of the time (c. 1780), that when he sang "Return, O God of Hosts," from "Samson," in Westminster Abbey, his hearers thought the song and his style of singing alike insipid.

The omission of ornaments in a musical performance was a matter for surprise a century earlier than that just named. Richard Lygon, in his "History of Barbadoes, 1687," describes his satisfaction at hearing a minstrel sing a song, "savouring much of antiquity — no *graces, double relishes, trillos, grupos,* or *piano-fortes,* but plain as a packstaff; his lute, too, was but of ten strings, so that the rarity of this antique piece pleased me beyond measure."

Cathedral chants, services, and anthems —even psalm and hymn tunes—were written with every possible florid turn, as shown by existing examples of the Church compositions of the latter part of the last century.

The story told of the elder Dubourg and Handel's comment upon his cadenza is well known; and there is another anecdote illustrating the absurdity of a misplaced cadenza, told concerning the trombone player at the first performance of Mendelssohn's "Lobgesang." The composer met the player and asked him if he had looked at his part, as he had given him plenty of important work to do. "O yes, Herr Director, I have studied it carefully." The astonishment of Mendelssohn may be imagined when at the rehearsal he heard the result of the *careful study* of the trombonist in the announcement of the initial phrase of the symphony as follows:

Mendelssohn, in his sweet manner, told the performer that he would rather have the phrase played as he had written it. Other musicians of less agreeable dispositions have sarcastically thanked performers for taking "so much trouble to sing or play notes that were not written;" and it is on record that Beethoven repeatedly quarrelled with vocalists for not adhering to his text, and it is also well known that Rossini wrote every cadenza out in full, "for he thought it better so to do than to trust to the *gaucheries* of conceited vocalists."

In instrumental compositions the habit of leaving a space for the *ad libitum* fancies of the performer opened a door for the admission of eccentricities and absurdities, which the better sort of musicians have sought from time to time to remedy, by the composition of suitable cadenzas as much as possible in accordance with the original composer's design. Clementi wrote cadenzas for the whole of Mozart's concertos, and Dr. Hiller and others have done like things for other works in which spaces have been left.

The cadenza has been made the vehicle for the expression of musical humour, as by Mendelssohn in the Music to "A Midsummer Night's Dream," and of quaintness in instrumentation, as in Beethoven's No. 5 Concerto, and in other works needless to particularise. "It is usual," says Jousse in his "Dictionary of Music," "to commence a cadenza with a plain note or chord sung or held out, so that

the accompanying performers may know when it has been begun; and it is also customary to make a long shake at the end of the cadenza, as a signal that the accompaniment is to be resumed."

Cadenza d'inganno (*It.*) A deceptive cadence.

Cadenza fioritura (*It.*) An ornamental cadence.

Caisse (*Fr.*) A drum.

Caisses claires (*Fr.*) Kettle drums; *grosse caisse* (*Fr.*), big drum.

Caisse roulante (*Fr.*) Side-drum, or snare-drum.

Calamus. (Gk. κάλαμος) A reed-flute. Probably a simple rustic instrument like our oaten-pipe. But some suppose it to have been similar in construction to the *syrinx*, or pan-pipes, and to have been synonymous with *arundo*. From *calamus* is derived the post-classical *calamaulos*, a flute made of reed, whence calamaulis (καλαμαύλης and καλαμαυλήτης) a player on reed-pipes; hence too, *chalameau*, *schalmey*, *shawm*, the precursor of the modern clarinet, one of the registers of which is still said to be of *chalameau* tone.

Calando (*It.*) (*Calare*. To descend, decrease.) A passage marked *calando* is to be sung or played with decreasing volume of tone and slackening pace.

Calandrone (*It.*) (Calandra, a woodlark.) A small reed instrument of the shawm or clarinet character, with two holes, much used by the Italian peasantry.

Calascione. [Colascione.]

Calata (*It.*) An Italian dance in $\frac{2}{4}$ time, of a sprightly character.

Calcando (*It.*) Hurrying, pressing the time.

Calcant (from *Lat.* Calcare.) Treading. The bellows-treader (balge-treter) of the old German organs.

Calcanten-glocke (*Ger.*) Bells sounded by means of pedals.

Call. A military term for the variations of certain musical notes played on a trumpet or bugle, or a special sort of beat upon the drum, each call being the signal for a definite duty.

Call. A toy instrument made by winding a narrow tape round two small oblong pieces of tin, so that one fold of the tape may be set in vibration when blown through. The call is used by men who *work* the drama of "Punch and Judy."

Ça ira (*Fr.*) 'That will do.' The refrain of a song popular during the revolution in France in 1793. The melody to which it was sung was a favourite with the unhappy Queen

Marie Antoinette. The song was called the "Carillon national."

Le refrain.

Ah l. ça ira, ça ira, ça ira,
Le peuple en ce jour sans cesse répète.
Ah l ça ira, ça ira, ça ira,
Malgré les mutins, tout reussira.

Calma, con (*It.*) With calmness.

Calmata (*It.*) Calmed, quieted, appeased.

Calore, con (*It.*) With heat, warmth.

Caloroso (*It.*) Warmly, full of passionate feeling.

Cambiare (*It.*) To turn, change, alter.

Cambiata (*It.*) [Nota cambiata.]

Camera, musica di (*It.*) [Chamber Music.]

Camminando (*It.*) Walking, flowing, *andànte.*

Campana (*It.*) A bell. [Bells.]

Campanella,-o, (*It.*) A small bell.

Campanellino (*It.*). A very small bell.

Campanista (*It.*) A bell-ringer.

Campanology. The knowledge of the construction and use of bells. [Bells.]

Campanetta (*It.*) A set of bells tuned to a scale, and played with hammers or keys. [Glockenspiel.]

Canaries. A dance probably of English invention. The melody was a lively air of two phrases. Purcell introduced a Canaries tune in his opera of "Dioclesian."

The following example (from Delaborde) shows the rhythm of this dance:

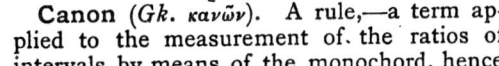

Cancrizans. [Canon Cancrizans.]

Canon (*Gk.* κανών). A rule,—a term applied to the measurement of. the ratios of intervals by means of the monochord, hence the system of Pythagoras was called the *canon* of Pythagoras; that of Euclid, the *canon* of Euclid. Hence, too, the science of calculating musical intervals is called *canonik.* *Sectio canonis* (*Lat.*), a division of a string, or monochord, formed by a moveable bridge or frets.

Canon. Owing to the various forms which canons assume it is almost impossible to give a general definition which will be intelligible. The essence of a canon is this, that the music sung by one part shall, after a short rest, be sung by another part note for note. The simplest form is when there are only two parts, *e.g.*:

The above is called a canon 2 in 1 at the octave, because two parts are singing one thing at that interval. The part which commences is called the *subject*, or *antecedent* (guida); that which follows, the *answer* or *consequent* (consequenza). The above is also an *infinite* canon, because, anyone having such a remarkable desire as to play it for ever, could do so. The pause shows where it may be concluded.

The above (Ex. 2) is also 2 in 1, but at the under-fifth.

Ex. 3 is a canon 2 in 1 at the upper sixth, the upper part being the consequent.

The above example (4) shows a canon 2 in 1 at the octave, with a *free* accompaniment. Any part of a canon which is not an antecedent or consequent is said to be a *free part* (*ad placitum*). It is also *finite* because there is no repeat, the canon being dropped at the close of the theme. The same description will apply to the next example (5).

Ex. 5. *Clarinet.*　　　BEETHOVEN. Symphony, No. 4.

Ex. 6. (Transposed.)
Non no-bis Do-mi-ne, non no --

The above well-known canon by Byrde is 3 in 1, because there is only one theme which all the three parts sing.

Ex. 7.　　　　　J. S. BACH. Mass in B minor.

Do - na no - bis pa - cem pa - -

The above example (7) is a finite canon 4 in 1.

Ex. 8.　　　　　ATTWOOD. Service in F.

Glo - ry be to the Fa - ther, and

The above example (8) shows a canon 4 in 2 because it is in four parts and there are two themes. Enough has been given to show the exact meaning of the numerical descriptions of canons; the first number giving the number of the parts in which it is composed; the second number, the number of themes sung by them, thus 16 in 4 signifies that 16 parts have 4 subjects; 8 in 1 that 8 parts sing in turn the same theme, &c. A canon by *augmentation* is when the consequent is double the length of the antecedent, *e.g.*:

Ex. 9.　　　　　From CHERUBINI.

A canon by diminution is when the consequent is half the value of the antecedent, *e.g.*:

Ex. 10.　　　　　From CHERUBINI.

Fragments of canon by *augmentation* and diminution are not uncommon in fugal writing, *e.g.* :

Ex. 11.   HANDEL.

&c.

A canon by triple or quadruple augmentation is when the three or four parts of which it is composed are each twice the time-value of its predecessor. A canon is said to be *strict* when the consequent follows the antecedent at an exact interval (say a major fifth or fourth, &c.) regardless of key tonality. The canon in Ex. 3 is not therefore strict. If it were so, the consequent must be in the *key* of the sixth above, which would be impossible. A canon by *inversion* is when the consequent follows the *inverted intervals* of the antecedent, *e.g.* :

Ex. 12.   PURCELL.

&c.

The above (Ex. 12) is a canon 4 in 1, because there is only one antecedent. The part appearing like a second antecedent being only the inversion of the first. A canon by *retrogression* is when the parts forming it (generally, only one is antecedent and one consequent) sing each other's notes backwards. An example will be found under "canon cancrizans."

Originally canons were a kind of musical riddle, the antecedent, and the number of parts, only being given ; and the student being required to solve the problem. Thus, Ex. 1 would be put forth:

a 2.

And Ex. 2:

a 2.

"Non nobis Domine" would be given thus :

a 3 Voci.

Non no-bis, &c.

From this method of enunciating canons, the name is probably derived, as the reader had to discover the *rule* or *canon* on which the composition was constructed. A canon written out in full was called *canone aperto*, and one written in riddle-form *canone chiusa*. A canon at the unison becomes a *round*, if the antecedent has a cadence before the entry of the consequent. Thus every round is a canon at the unison, although a canon at the unison is not necessarily a round. [Round.] Some of the early writers have left canons of the greatest ingenuity. Some very good specimens are to be found in Hawkins. It had been well if the labour and perseverance which must have been requisite for their production could have been more profitably directed. The constant study of canon-writing is much to be deprecated, as it checks the inventive faculty, and at most only teaches the student how to force themes into cohesion. It is probable that much of the ugly and crabbed part-writing of the 17th and early part of the 18th century is due to the over estimation of canons. Canonical imitation with free accompaniment is, however, capable of very beautiful effects. Specimens of this style have already been given in Ex. 4 and 5, and the fine example in Mendelssohn's 95th Psalm may be studied with advantage. The highly dramatic effect of the canon in two parts, afterwards breaking into four, at the words, "And the sea was upheaved," in No. 34 of Mendelssohn's "Elijah," is so well-known that it need not be quoted here.

Canone al sospiro (*It.*) A canon, the subject of which is answered at the half-beat :

The answer to any subject is said to be *close* when it enters shortly after the subject. A canon *al sospiro* is therefore the most *close* of all canons, as it is impossible to answer at less time than the beat.

Canone aperto (*It.*) A canon written out in full.

Canon cancrizans. A canon by retrogression. A canon practically consisting of two parts in double counterpoint, that is, parts which are grammatically interchangeable, so constructed that they may read actually backwards, hence probably the derivation of cancrizans, *walking backward like a crab*. The following example will be found to consist only of four bars, at the close of which, having exchanged lines, the parts proceed backwards. A canon cancrizans may of course be accompanied by free parts :

From ANDRÉ's "Lehrbuch der Tonkunst," 1832.

The following is a canon cancrizans with a bass part *per recte et retro* :

Productions of this class are utterly value-less as contributions to art.

Canone chiuso (*It.*) A close canon. [Canon.]

Canone infinito or **perpetuo** (*It.*) Never ending canon. Infinite canon.

Canone sciolto (*It.*) A free canon, not strict.

Canonici. A name given to followers of the Pythagorean system of music, as opposed to Musici, the followers of the Aristoxenian system. [Pythagoreans.]

Cantabile (*It.*) In a singing style.

Cantamento (*It.*) The air or melody of a phrase.

Cantando (*It.*) [Cantabile.]

Cantadour (*Old Fr.*)⎱ A street singer.
Cantambanco (*It.*) ⎰ A mountebank.

Cantante (*It.*) A singer.

Cantare (*It.*) To sing.

Cantare a aria (*It.*) To sing with a certain amount of improvisation. [Penillion singing.]

Cantare a orecchio (*It.*) To sing by ear.

Cantare di maniera (*It.*)⎱ To sing in a
Cantara di manierata(*It.*)⎰ florid or ornamental style.

Cantata (*It.*) A cantata consisted originally of a mixture of recitative and melody, and was given to a single voice, but the introduction of choruses altered the first character of the cantata, and gave rise to some confusion in the manner of describing it. So that it has been variously defined as "an elegant and passionate species of vocal composition for a single voice," "a long vocal composition, the text of which is Italian," "a kind of short oratorio, or opera not intended for the stage," "a short piece of vocal music of a pathetic character," "one of the Psalms or portions of Scripture set to music for voices and instruments," according to the work the describer had in his mind at the time, but a cantata is now understood as a short work in the musical form of an oratorio, but without *dramatis personæ*.

Cantatilla (*It.*) ⎱ The diminutive of Can-
Cantatina ⎰ tata.

Cantatore (*It.*) A male singer.

Cantatrice (*It.*) A female singer.

Cantatorium. A music book.

Cantellerando (*It.*) Singing in a subdued voice, trilling.

Canti carnascialesci (*It.*)⎧ Songs sung
Canti carnivali ⎨ during the
⎩ carnival.

Cantici (*It.*) Another name for the Laudes spirituali, or songs sung in the old Romish church in praise of God, the Blessed Virgin and Saints, and Martyrs.

Canticle (1) A song or hymn in honour of God, or of some special sacred event.

(2) The word is also applied to certain detached psalms and hymns used in the service of the Anglican Church, such as the *Venite exultemus, Te Deum laudamus, Benedicite omnia opera, Benedictus, Jubilate Deo, Magnificat, Cantate Domino, Nunc dimittis, Deus misereatur*, and the verses used instead of the Venite on Easter-day.

Canticum (*Lat.*) (1) A song. (2) A song in the Roman comedy accompanied by music and dancing. Sometimes one person sang the song while another went through the appropriate gesticulation.

Cantilena (*Lat.*) (1) An oft-repeated, old song. (2) In mediæval music, singing exercises, in which were introduced all the intervals of the scale, &c. (3) In old church-song the plain-song or canto-fermo sung in unison by one or more persons to an organ accompaniment. (4) A ballad.

Cantilenare (*It.*) To sing without accompaniment.

Cantilenaccia (*It.*) Bad singing.

Cantillatio (*Lat.*) Declamation in a singing style, applied to a method of reading the Epistles and Gospels in the church. [Accentus Ecclesiasticus.]

Cantino (*It.*) The smallest string upon the violin. The E string. (*Fr.*) *chanterelle*.

Cantique (*Fr.*) A sacred song or melody, a canticle.

Canto (*It.*) The upper voice-part in concerted music, so called because it has the melody or air. [Air.]

Canto a cappella (*It.*) Sacred music; *cantore di cappella*, the præcentor.

Canto armonico (*It.*) A part-song.

Canto cromatico (*It.*) A scale or song in chromatic style.

Canto fermo (*It.*) [Cantus firmus.]

Canto figurato (*It.*) Florid melody, or melody varied. [Cantus figuratus.]

Canto Gregoriano (*It.*) Gregorian chant.

Cantollano (*Sp.*) Plain chant.

Canto plano (*It.*) Plain chant.

Canto primo (*It.*) First soprano.

Canto recitativo (*It.*) Declamatory singing, recitative.

Canto ripieno (*It.*) Additional soprano chorus-parts. [Ripieno.]

Canto secondo (*It.*) Second soprano.

Cantor. [Precentor.]

Cantor choralis (*Lat.*) Chorus master.

Cantore (*It.*) A general name for a singer.

Cantoris (*Lat.*). (From the word Cantor.) The cantoris side in a cathedral choir is the side upon which the Precentor sits, usually the north side, opposite to Decani.

Cantus Ambrosianus (*Lat.*) Ambrosian chant. [Plain-song.]

Cantus coronatus. [Cantus fractus.]

Cantus durus (*Lat.*) Music which modulated into a key having one or more sharps in its scale. Such keys were at one period strictly proscribed by church-musicians.

Cantus ecclesiasticus (*Lat.*) (1) In a general sense, plain-song and other early church-melodies. (2) The method of *singing* as opposed to *saying* Lections, Collects, Gospels, and special offices, such as the Improperia, &c. See Accentus ecclesiasticus under Accent § 4, and " Passion Music."

Cantus figuratus (*Lat.*) Florid church song, that is, in which more than one note of music was sung to a syllable. The purest system of ancient church-song prescribed only one note to each syllable. [Plain song.]

Cantus firmus (*Lat.*) (1) The *tenor* or chief melody, originally sung by the tenor-voices, afterwards transferred to the treble-part, hence called *Canto*. (2) A fragment of plain-song, to which counterpoint has been added. (3) Any subject chosen for contrapuntal treatment, generally a short diatonic passage of semibreves or other long notes.

Cantus fractus (*Lat.*) A broken melody, a term applied to a tune which proceeded either by perfect or imperfect consonances. When accompanied by a Faburden, or Fauxbourdon, it was called Cantus coronatus.

Cantus Gregorianus (*Lat.*) The Gregorian system of church-song. [Plain song.]

Cantus mensurabilis (*Lat.*) Mensurable-song. The very name of this art explains at once its scope and the probable date of its birth. The indissoluble association of music and poetry, or of music, poetry, and dancing, in ancient times, rendered a system of notation, by which the comparative duration of sounds could be exhibited to the eye, unnecessary. If the metre of the poetry were duly appreciated, the length of the musical notes to which the poetry was set would be undoubted. If dancing accompanied the music and poetry, it would be, of course, impossible to sing to any other rhythm than that prescribed by the movement of the feet. As long as music of this kind was unisonous, or, at-most, consisted of a series of chords, the component parts of which were of equal length, no difficulty or doubt as to the length of notes could occur. But when prose-writing was set to music, and still more when, in polyphonous compositions, it was desired that a particular voice should sing two or more notes to one note of another, it became an absolute necessity that the signs used should be so formed as to direct the performer, without a chance of doubt, as to how long he should hold any note with reference to that held in another part. Hence, the formation of Cantus mensurabilis. As to the date of its invention, learned and reliable authors differ much in their opinion. Having been ascribed to Johannes de Muris (circ. 1330) for many centuries by writers who have been but too ready to copy from each other, asking no questions, it seems that the laurel must be taken from his brow, and that the credit is due to authors who lived—some say a few years, others two centuries at least—before him. It is, however, certain that Robert de Handlo wrote on the subject before Johannes de Muris, and equally certain that Robert de Handlo had the benefit of the labours of Franco. But here a new difficulty arises: not only was Franco so common a name that many learned Francos existed at the same date, but at least three of this name were musicians—Franco of Paris, Franco of Cologne, Franco of Liege. Nor is this all—two distinct dates are attributed to the Franco who wrote on Cantus mensurabilis, which differ by about 200 years ! The reader who cares to enter deeply into this question may refer to Fétis, Kiesewetter, Hawkins, Burney, Forkel, and Coussemaker, all of whom have bestowed much thought on the subject; having done so, he will find that he is still in ignorance. The truth is, that mensurable music, like many other highly important ingredients of our intellectual life, was a *growth*, not a sudden invention. There are evidences that in the twelfth century a proportionate subdivision of the length of sounds was reached after, and naturally enough, the first step was, that two sounds might be sung to one, hence the *long* and *short*, or *long* and *breve*, as they were called. The shortest note or *minim* found its way into use, probably, in the thirteenth century, and was in time followed by other subdivisions. Then followed the triple division of notes, a threefold division being called *perfect* on theological grounds; then rapidly followed, in the 14th and 15th centuries, a complication of mensurable signs, which now baffles the most enthusiastic interpreter of music of that period, — the value of notes varying according to their position with regard to other notes; or, according to the position of the tails, if up or down, or on the right or left sides; or, as to the complete blackness or open outline (*evacuatio*) of the notes; or as to the manner in which consecutive sounds to one syllable were written in *continuous lines*, forming *ligatures*. Happily, from the 16th century a genuine taste for part-music led to an unremarked disuse of these utterly useless conceits, a full account of which can only be found in ancient learned treatises, where any one having more taste for music than antiquities, will do well to leave them.

Cantus planus (*Lat.*) Plain song.

Cantus Romanus (*Lat.*) Roman chant or song. (1) The Gregorian system of music. (2) The early attempts at harmonizing a melody known as the *organum*.

Canun or **Kanoon** (*Turkish*). An instrument strung with cat-gut, in form like a dulcimer, with which the women in the harems accompany their singing. The sound is brought out by means of plectra—thimbles made of tortoiseshell pointed with cocoanut wood, and worn upon the ends of the fingers.

Canzona (*It.*) (1) A short song, in which the music is of much more importance than the words. It is one of the ancient forms of measured melody, and when the older writers employed it, it was usually made the vehicle for the display of skill and contrivance in the treatment of the phrases in fugal imitation. A secondary meaning of the word, *scoffing* or *banter*, perhaps accounts for the use of a *form* in which a musical imitation or *mocking* was shown.

(2) In the early part of the last century the word was used to describe an instrumental composition, similar to the sonata as then known.

(3) It was also understood to mean the same as allegro, "for it denotes that the movement of the part to which it is fixed ought to be after a lively, brisk, or gay manner."

CANZONA.*

GIROLAMO FRESCOBALDI (1591—1640).*

Canzonaccia (*It.*) A commonplace song.
Canzoncina (*It.*) A short poem or air.

* From " Il secondo libro di Toccate, Canzone versi d'Hinni Magnificat, Gagliarde, Correnti, et Altri Partite, di Cembalo et Organo." Rome, 1637.

Canzonet, Canzònetta (*It.*) A diminutive of canzona, " denoting a little short song, tune, cantata, or suonata." Originally applied to a short song in parts. Luca Marenzio, Giovanni Ferreti, and Horatio Vecchi are said to have excelled in this species of composition. The title was also employed by poets to describe verses either of a trifling character or subject; and musicians, when they set such words, repeated the poet's title without reference to the musical meaning of the word. Brossard, " Dictionnaire de Musique, 1703," speaks of two sorts of canzonets—the Neapolitan, with two phrases, and the Sicilian, a sort of jig in $\frac{12}{8}$ or $\frac{6}{8}$ time, each in rondo form. Thomas Morley (1597) describes a series of madrigals as " Canzonets, or Little Short Songs to Four Voyces; celected out of the best and approued Italian Authors;" and Haydn's use of the word with reference to his well-known examples will be familiar.

Canzoniere (*It.*) A lyric poem or song.

Caoinan (*Irish.*) A funeral song (Keeners).

Capellmeister (*Ger.*) Maestro di Cappella (*It.*) (1) The musical director of a church or chapel. A post of considerable honour, especially when connected with a royal or ducal chapel. The list of eminent musicians, from Palestrina to Mendelssohn, who have held such offices is very large, and the fact that men of general musical ability have thus been necessarily brought into contact with sacred music, has probably greatly influenced the character of the compositions of the 16th, 17th, and 18th centuries. There is no post in the English Church or at our Court which exactly corresponds to that of Capellmeister, including as it does the duties—as circumstances may require—of conductor, accompanist, choir-trainer, and composer. The *choir-master*—an office lately instituted or revived in this country—is perhaps the nearest approach to the Capellmeister. By the combination, which not unfrequently took place, of the offices of " Composer to his (or her) Majesty " and " Master of the Children of the Royal Chapel," a veritable Capell meister was created. In our cathedrals the precentor and organist practically divide the duties of this post.

(2) The title has sometimes been applied to a conductor of a band or an opera.

Capellmeister Musik (*Ger.*) A term of contempt for music *made* and not inspired.

Capiscolus (Precentor) Cabiscola.

Capistrum (*Lat.*) A muzzle. A sort of bandage wound round the head and face of the ancient trumpeters, to protect the cheeks while playing their instruments, on account of the unusual exertion necessary for the proper production of tone.

Cappella, alla (*It.*) In the ecclesiastical style. In duple time. [A cappella.]

Capo (*It.*) Head, commencement.

Capo, da (*It.*) A direction to return to the first or other indicated movement.

Capo d'opera (*It.*) The principal song or piece in an opera.

Capo tasto (*It.*) (Lit. head-stop.) A mechanical arrangement by which the pitch of the whole of the strings of a guitar is raised at once. The capo tasto, or capodastro as it is sometimes called, is screwed over the strings on to the finger-board and forms a temporary nut, *e.g. con capo tasto sulla 3a Poz.*

Capriccietto (*It.*) A little caprice, or fancy.

Capriccio (*It.*) A freak, whim, fancy. A composition irregular in form.

Caprice (*Fr.*) [Capriccio.]

Capriccioso (*It.*) Whimsical, humorous.

Caractères de musique (*Fr.*) The signs used in music. [Notation.]

Caral (*old Eng.*) Kyrriole (*Ang.-Sax.*) [Carol.]

Carattere (*It.*) Character, dignity, quality.

Carezzando (*It.*) ⎫ Caressingly, singing or
Carezzevole (*It.*) ⎬ playing with a frequent introduction of notes of anticipation or *appogiatura.*

Caricato (*It.*) Loaded, over displayed.

Carillon. A set of bells so arranged as to be played by hand or by machinery. The word has by some authors been connected with (*Fr.*) *clarine*, a little bell, which is probably connected with (*Lat.*) *clarisonus;* but others derive it from the word *quadrille*, or *quadriglio*, on the ground that this dance was popular, and probably "set" to bells, in the 16th century. There can be no doubt as to the antiquity of thus using *small* bells. They were probably graduated in size so as to produce a diatonic scale, and were called a Tintinnabulum.

Fig. 1.

Fig. 2.

Fig. 3.

Fig. 1 is given by M. Coussemaker as being from a MS. probably of the 9th century. Fig. 2 is from an ancient Psalter in the British Museum. Fig. 3 is from a MS. in the Royal Library of Brussels. Five seems to have been the number of bells usually employed in earliest times, but they were afterwards increased to six or seven. It is to the bell-founders of the Low Countries we owe the perfecting of the art of bell-founding and the construction of carillons, during the 15th, 16th, 17th, and 18th centuries. Preeminent among them stands the Van den Gheyn family, whose works are to be found in almost every Belgian belfry. Originally of Mechlin, they afterwards removed to Louvain, where Matthias Van den Gheyn (b. 1721) deservedly attained the highest fame, as organist, composer, carillon-maker, and carilloneur. The brothers Von Aerscholdt, the great bell-founders, now living in Louvain, are lineal descendants of Matthias Van den Gheyn. The finest carillons, namely those at Antwerp, Mechlin, Bruges, Ghent, and Namur, consist of about forty bells, extending from huge specimens of several tons in weight up to little bells weighing only a few pounds.*

* The fine chimes in Mechlin consist of 45 bells, the largest of which weighs between 9 and 10 tons. This rich-toned bell was cast by Aerscholdt in 1844. At Ghent there are 48 bells (44 above and the 4 heaviest in the lower storey), the largest of which was cast by Du Mery, 1744, and weighs about $5\frac{1}{2}$ tons. At Antwerp there are in reality two carillons—one connected to the machinery, and in use, the other disused. That in use consists of 48 bells, the largest of which weighs about 7 tons. At Bruges there are 48 bells, the largest nearly 10 tons. At Namur there are about 50 bells, the largest about 4 tons. Many of the bells in the Belgian chimes are found to be of Dutch make, and (by their inscriptions) have been issued from old foundries in Amsterdam, Rotterdam, Zutphen, and elsewhere.

They are in most cases arranged as follows: the smaller bells are fixed to strong timbers and arranged in rows, according to size, the largest being nearest to the floor—the bells and framework thus representing the outline of a pyramid. Where there are many specially large bells, these are generally placed in a lower storey, not uncommonly below the chiming machinery. To each bell is attached one or more hammers on the outer side, and a clapper in the inside. To the lever-end of the hammers thick wires are attached, which pass down to long iron rods. The lever-end of these rest on the *tambour*, or barrel, on which are arranged projecting staples. When the barrel is turned (which is done by ordinary clockwork) the staple forces up the end of the iron rod, the other end at the same time pulling down the wire and raising the hammer. When the barrel *releases* the iron-rod, it drops suddenly and causes the hammer to strike the bell. Some time is of course required for the raising of the larger hammers, hence the necessity of having several hammers to some of the bells, so that if a quick repetition of the sound is required, one hammer shall be ready to strike while another is being brought into position. There are, therefore, always a larger number of staples on the barrel than there are bells in the carillon. The clapper, before-mentioned as being in every bell, is held by a wire-loop, within an inch or two of the side of the bell; this wire passes down to the *clavier*, or keyboard—a series of small round sticks, arranged in an order similar to that of the black and white keys of a pianoforte, but separated from each other by a sufficient distance to allow each one to be struck with the *fist* without fear of that on either side of it being also struck. The clappers of the heaviest bells are, owing to their weight, generally attached to a pedal-board, and the carilloneur usually guards his hand with a thick glove when playing.

It will be understood from this short description that the mechanism by which these beautiful bells are chimed and played is of the roughest description. Vast improvements have, however, been lately made, chiefly in England; and Messrs. Gillett and Bland have invented an ingenious piece of mechanism, by which the hammers are held up constantly, and only have to be *released* by the action of the barrel. This insures a regularity in the striking which cannot on the old system be attained, and does away with the necessity for multiplying hammers to a single bell.

The higher octaves contain generally a complete *chromatic* scale. But the heavier bells, owing to their great cost and the large amount of room they occupy, are limited to such important fundamental basses as tonic, subdominant, and dominant; or, at most, to the first five degrees of the *diatonic* scale. A short "flourish" is played at the half-quarter, a slightly longer phrase at each quarter, a tune at each half hour and hour. It is to be regretted that we in England are but just beginning to appreciate the beauty of the effect produced by carillon-music. But, on the other hand, nowhere but in England can genuine change-ringing be heard, in which, the tone produced by the bells as they swing completely round is totally different in character from that obtained by the dead stroke of a hammer. But bells can be easily arranged so as to do the double duty of chiming and change-ringing, and it is to be hoped that they will often in future be so arranged.

Carilloneur (*Fr.*) Bell-player. [Carillons.]

Carita, con (*It.*) With tenderness.

Carmagnole. A dance accompanied by singing, named from Carmagnola in Piedmont. Many of the wildest excesses of the French revolution of 1792 were associated with this dance. It was afterwards applied to the bombastic reports of the French successes in battle. The song commenced with "Madame Véto avait promis," and each verse ended with the burden "Dansons la carmagnole, vive le son du canon."

Carol. To sing or warble, to celebrate in song.

Carol. A song of praise, applied to a species of songs sung at Christmas-tide. It originally meant a song accompanied with dancing, in which sense it is frequently used by the old poets (perhaps connected with *choraula*). It appears to have been danced by many performers, by taking hands, forming a ring, and singing as they went round. It will be readily imagined that a dance of this character would lead to a certain wildness if not rudeness of behaviour, so that the warning contained in the following verse addressed to those of gentle blood who indulged in the exercise, might not be altogether unnecessary:

> "Fille quant ferez en karolle
> Dancez gentiment par mesure
> Car, quant fille se desmesure
> Tel la voit qui la tient par folle."

Bishop Taylor says that the oldest carol was that sung by the heavenly host when the birth of the Saviour was announced to the Shepherds on the plains of Bethlehem. It is probable that the practice of singing carols at Christmas-tide arose in imitation of this, as the majority of the carols declared the good tidings of great joy; and the title of Noels, nowells, or novelles, applied to carols, would seem to bear out this idea.

Carol singing is of great antiquity among Christian communities, as the carol by Aurelius Prudentius, of the 4th century, will show.

This poem contains twenty-nine stanzas, commencing:—

> "Quid est quod arctum circulum
> Sol jam recurrens deserit,
> Christusne terris nascitur,
> Qui lucis auget tramitem?"

Carols were both serious and humorous in the 14th and 15th centuries. Mr. Chappell quotes a tune that might be sung to words of either character, but bearing reference to the observances of the season of Christmas. (Popular Music, i. 42.)

In later times carols were written of a more sober character, and we find in 1630 the publication of "Certaine of David's Psalmes intended for Christmas carols fitted to the most sollempne tunes everywhere familiarlie used, by William Slayter, printed by Robert Yong." Upon a copy of the later edition (1642), preserved in the British Museum, a former possessor has written the names of some of these tunes; for example, Psalm 6, to the tune of Jane Shore, Psalm 9 to Bara Forster's Dreame, Psalm 43 to Crimson Velvet, Psalm 47 to Garden Greene, &c. Shakspeare alludes to the Puritan practice of adapting religious words to secular melody in his "Winter's Tale:"

> "There is but one puritan among them and he sings psalms to hornpipes."

After the Restoration, carols of the old kind became again popular, and from that time to the present the singing of carols at Christmas became steadily encouraged.

Warton supposes the religious carol to have been introduced by the Puritans, but this is a mistake, as a reference to Mr. Wright's collection, made for the Percy Society, will show.

The earliest printed collection was made by Wynkyn de Worde, 1521, but all these are of a convivial character.

Many of the old carols had scraps of Latin intermixed with English, as—

> "Puer nobis natus est de Maria Virgine
> Be glad lordynges, be the more or lesse,
> I bring you tydinges of gladnesse
> As Gabriel me bereth witnesse."

Compare also "In dulci jubilo," in which Latin and German were used.

Carola (*It.*) A dance accompanied by singing, which grew into unenviable notoriety during the Republic of 1792 in France. *c.f.* carmagnole.

Cartellone (*It.*) The prospectus of an operatic season.

Carnyx (*Gk.*) An ancient Greek trumpet of a shrill tone, known afterwards to the Celts and Gauls. κάρνυξ (*Gk.*) *c.f. cornu.*

Cassa-grande (*It.*) The big drum.

Cassatio. [Suite.]

Castagnette (*It.*) **Castagnettes** (*Fr.*) **Castañuelas** (*Sp.*) Castanets.

Castanets. A musical instrument of percussion introduced into Spain by the Moors. The castanets were originally dried chestnut husks, from whence their name is derived, but were afterwards made of hard wood, by which means the tone was rendered more defined. The ancient κρόταλον, was a species of castanet (knicky-knackers). [Bones.]

Castrato (*It.*) A male singer with a peculiarity of voice, produced by a natural deprivation procured in early youth for the purpose of preserving the normal tone.

Catch. A species of canon or round for three or four voices, in which the words are so contrived that by the union of the voices a different meaning is given by the singers *catching* at each other's words. Poems of a trivial character, similar in style to nursery-rhyme doggrels, were also called catches. For example, there is a poem by "the learned clarke, Lewis Wager," printed in 1567," beginning:

> "I have a pretty titmouse
> Come pecking on my toe;"

and one of John Lyly's songs from "Endymion," 1591, is distinguished by the title of "a catch." The musical catch originated about the early part of the 17th century, the first collection of catches being made by Ravenscroft in 1609, under the title of "Pammelia, Musicks miscellanie, or mixed varieties of pleasant Roundelays and delightfull Catches of 3, 4, 5, 6, 7, 8, 9, 10 parts in one; none so ordinarie as musicall; none so musicall as not to be all very pleasing and acceptable." These, and others contained in later publications are little else than rounds, without the humour, so called, of the catch as it was afterwards accepted. William Jackson, of Exeter, says that "they are three parts obscenity and one part music. If they are not indecent, they are nothing. There is no particular object in them, but they are a species of musical false wit." Of the few catches which may be yet sung in a mixed company, "Would you know my Celia's charms?" by S. Webbe, and "Have you read Sir John Hawkins's History?" and "Ah! how Sophia," by Callcott, are the most favourable specimens. The words of the first are as follows:

> "Would you know my Celia's charms,
> Which now excite my fierce alarms?
> I'm sure she has fortitude and truth
> To gain the heart of every youth.
>
> She's only thirty lovers now,
> The rest are gone I can't tell how;
> No longer Celia ought to strive,
> For certainly she's fifty-five."

The humour of this catch consists in the emphasis placed upon the words *fortitude*, *thirty*, and *fifty-five*, by which it appears to the hearers that each singer is contending in turn to uphold his notion of the age of the lady. In the second, the words " Burney's History " are made to sound like " burn his history," and in the third, one voice cries, " a house a fire," another, " go fetch the engines," while one apparently indifferent exclaims, " I'm but a lodger," from the following words :

> ' Ah ! how, Sophia, could you leave
> Your lover, and of hope bereave,
> Go fetch the Indian's borrowed plume,
> But richer far than that you bloom.
> I'm but a lodger in her heart,
> Where more than me I fear have part."

There were formerly a number of clubs supported for the purpose of encouraging the production and performance of this species of musical trifle, only one or two of which are at present in existence, a better feeling having diverted the main object of these societies into the encouragement and execution of glees, part-songs, &c. [Round, canon.]

Catena di trilli (*It*). A chain, or succession, of short vocal or instrumental shakes.

Catgut. Boyau (*Fr.*), Minugia (*It.*), Darm (*Ger.*) The name given to the material of which the strings of many musical instruments are formed; it is made from the intestines of the sheep, and sometimes from those of the horse, but never from those of the cat.

Cathedral Music. A term applied to that music which has been composed to suit the form of service used in our cathedrals since the Reformation. It includes settings of canticles and also of anthems. The first writers of this class of music were Marbecke, Tallis, Tye, and Byrd, and the works of the two last named especially illustrate the state of cathedral music at the period in which they lived, for they employed Latin and English words to the same music, so that it might be available whether the service was according to the ancient or reformed usage. The style of the earliest cathedral music was formed on the model of the Italian motets and other sacred compositions, and with the exception of a difference in the words was identical with the secular music of the period.

It was feared that the Commissioners appointed by the Statute 27 Henry VIII. to compile a body of ecclesiastical laws " as should in future be observed throughout the realm," taking into consideration the abuse of music in the Church, would forbid its use altogether. As the King was fond of music they deemed it politic to retain it for the service of the Church, but they implied a return to simple forms, in directing certain parts of the service to be sung by the "ministers and clarkes " in a plain, distinct, and audible manner. The rubric of the First Book of Edward VI. prescribes the saying or *singing* of "mattens and evensong;" and in the minis-

tration of the Communion that the clerks shall sing in English for the office or "Introite as it is called," a psalm appointed for that day. And again it directs that the clerks shall sing one or many of the sentences therein mentioned, according to the length and shortness of the time that the people be offering. In John Marbecke's " Booke of Common Praier noted " 1550, it will be seen that the whole of the service was sung either to some general kind of recitation or intonation with small inflections, to an adaptation of the ancient cantus or *accentus ecclesiasticus*, or to some modification of the old use by Marbecke himself. Queen Elizabeth in her injunctions concerning the clergy and laity of this realm, published in the first year of her reign, 1559, desired the " continuance of syngynge in the Churche " and " that there bee a modeste and destyncte song so used in all parts of the Common Prayers in the Churche, that the same may be as playnely understanded as if it were read without syngynge."

Notwithstanding this injunction the use of singing and of organs in the Church was only maintained by a majority of one in the Lower House of Convocation, a strong objection to Cathedral music existing even in that early period. After Marbecke's book, which has music in one part only, John Day (1560) published a service in four parts, adding five years later, those " offices " which had been omitted in the former collection. These preserved to a certain extent the prescribed or adopted " use " in those parts of the service which were always intended to be performed simply, the publication also indicated the places where a more elaborate musical setting might be allowed, and composers taking advantage of the licence wrote original music for the Venite, Te Deum, Benedictus, Jubilate, Communion Service, the Canticles used at evensong, and "such godly praiers and psalmes in the like form to the honor and praise of God,"—" so they may be songe as anthems." The use of organs and singing in the Church was nevertheless a sore grievance to the Puritans; they did not, however, object to metrical psalms, and employed them whenever and wherever possible; but the cathedrals always objected to their introduction, as not being cathedral music properly so called; it is within the last ten years only that hymns or psalm tunes have been sung in cathedrals as an integral part of the ordinary service. In the time of the Commonwealth metrical psalms were the only things sung in the churches, but they were also sung at other times, and it was not until the Restoration of Charles II. that Cathedral service was resumed, this time in a considerably altered form. The Communion Service or Mass, in times past held to be the most important act of worship, was placed in the back - ground, and was, when celebrated, given without the aid of music. Church composers did not take the trouble to set those parts of the service which were never performed, and consequently there is not a single "Gloria in excelsis" produced by any cathedral writer between 1660 and 1840, other than as an anthem. When so set, it was considered allowable to omit some sentences and add others at discretion, so that it would be scarcely available for the Communion Service. The "Sanctus" was set to music, as it became the habit to sing it in the place of the Introit, a fashion not yet dead in many cathedrals. When the Communion Service was restored to its true importance about twenty-five years since, adaptations of Marbecke's arrangements were freely and properly used, until a new generation of composers employed their talents to supply the deficiency. At the time of the Restoration, the character of cathedral music also underwent a change. The influence of the French school may be traced in the writings of Purcell, Humphries, Blow, Wise, Weldon, and others. It is not a little strange that while most temporary influences can be seen in the various periods of cathedral music, there are few instances of any church composers copying Handel's style, and none in which it was done with success. Dr. Greene, his contemporary, has a special character of his own, Dr. Boyce has also *his* individuality, and the elder Hayes shows no leaning towards the great oratorio writer. Handel's oratorios, though not written for the cathedral, are often laid under contribution, whereas the anthems composed by him for the service of the Church are comparatively neglected and unknown.

At the latter part of the last century and the beginning of the present, cathedral music was at its weakest point; adaptations, arrangements, florid melodies, with paltry accompaniments, chants of a gay and undignified style, and all music used in the service, showing the influence of a general indifference and carelessness, which, to a certain extent, still exists, though happily in no strong degree, for a more reverent feeling abounds and is nourished. Cathedral music, like every other branch of art, should increase and be progressive, should take advantage of every new discovery or admitted truth in music. All styles should be fairly represented, and no one style should be considered as indicative of special doctrinal views. There are few who seriously object to a building in which successive styles are seen, but on the contrary think that all that is good should be retained. The many who have spoken in

music in past ages should have their sayings preserved when they are worthy of being kept, but it would be folly to insist upon the retention of all that could be gathered of the works of a writer, because he has said one happy and lasting thing. It is not given to men to be wise at all times, and the best of cathedral musicians have written unworthy stuff. Taste and good sense, free from prejudice, will guide to a proper and useful selection, so that cathedral music for ordinary purposes may include the thoughts uttered under all influences in many ages.

The small number of voices considered sufficient for the usual services of our cathedrals is a bar to grand effects. This has been felt by composers, who have been compelled so to arrange their music that it may produce adequate effects from the usual small choirs. Probably with a prophetic view of the future augmentation of the musical staff of a cathedral, many modern composers have so constructed their works, that while they are not ineffective with a small body, they are nobly grand when given by increased numbers. So that there is reason to believe that in the days of the future, when cathedral choirs shall be in numbers and skill worthy of the service to which they minister, cathedral composers will be equal to the task of writing music suitable to the time and place. The grand effect produced by a large body of voices in a cathedral during the performance of an oratorio upon the occasion of a festival is never without some influence in turning men's minds to higher things. Music is the handmaid of religion, and there can be no reasonable objection to the introduction of oratorios and other extensive sacred compositions, with all the effects that a trained choir and orchestra can produce, provided always, that such performances are made an integral part of an act of worship. In the metropolis such performances have been given with the most satisfactory results at stated times, and the day may not be very far distant, when they may be made of more frequent occurrence, and so, our cathedrals, by calling into requisition all musical talent, inventive or executive, will become again what they once were, the nurseries and centres of musical culture and knowledge.

Catlings. The smallest sized lute-strings.

Cauda (*Lat.*) The tail of a note.

Cavaletta (*It.*) [Cabaletta.]

Cavaletto (*It.*) (1) A little bridge. (2) The break in the voice.

Cavalquet (*Fr.*) A trumpet-signal to cavalry.

Cavata (*It.*) [Cavatina.]

Cavatina (*It.*) A melody of a more simple form than the *aria*. A song without a second part and a "*Da capo*." The term is, however, applied with less strictness to airs of other kinds. (See " Be thou faithful," in Mendelssohn's " St. Paul," and " Salve dimora," in Gounod's " Faust," &c.)

C.B. Abbreviation for Contra-basso.

C barré (*Fr.*) The term for the time indicator. C with a dash through it.

C clef. The clef showing the position of middle C, in which are written the alto, tenor, and (in old music) other parts.

Soprano Clef. Mezzo-Soprano Clef.   Alto Clef   Tenor Clef.

[Clef.]

C dur (*Ger.*) C major.

Cebell. The name of an air or theme in common time of four bar phrases, forming a subject upon which to execute " divisions " upon the lute or violin. This style of air, although frequently found in books for the violin in the 17th century, is now obsolete; its principal feature was the alternation of grave and acute notes which formed the several strains. The following are examples:

THO. MACE, 1676.

H. PURCELL, b. 1658.

Celere (*It.*) Quick, swift.

Celerita, con (*It.*) With speed, haste. Quickly.

Celeste (*Fr.*) A direction for the use of the soft pedal.

Celeste, voix (*Fr.*) A stop on the organ or harmonium. [Vox Angelica.]

Celeusma (*Gk.*) κέλευσμα, or κέλευμα (from κελεύω, to urge on, to command). The word or sing-song of the κελευστής (fugle-man or leader), by which oarsmen were encouraged to row rhythmically, and by which, to this day, sailors pull uniformly and simultaneously at a rope.

Celli. *Abb.* of violoncelli.

Cello. *Abb.* of violoncello.

Cembalista (*It.*) A pianoforte player.

Cembalo. Clave - cembalo, cimbalo. A harpsichord. [Pianoforte.]

Cembanella (*It.*) [Cennamella.]

Cennamella (*It.*) A pipe, or flute.

Cento (*Lat.*) (In Greek κέντρων.)

Centone (*It.*) Patch-work. A musical work made up of extracts from an author's compositions, as a *cento* was from an author's poems. *c.f.* pasticcio.

Cercar la nota (*It.*) To feel for a note, to reach it by slurring.

Cervalet or **Cervelat** (perhaps *dim.* of cervus, signifying a little stag-horn). An ancient wind-instrument of a small size, from which, by means of a reed, tones similar in character to those of the bassoon could be produced.

Ces (*Ger.*) C flat.

Cetera (*It.*) A citarra or guitar.

Chacona (*Sp.*) ⎫ A slow dance in $\frac{3}{4}$ time,
Ciaconna (*It.*) ⎬ frequently constructed
Chaconne (*Fr.*) ⎭ upon a ground bass, and sometimes formerly introduced as a movement of a sonata. [Chica.]

It is usually stated that the *chaconne* is in the major mode, and that *passacaille* which is somewhat similar to it in rhythm is in the minor. This is not the case, as the following theme on which Bach's celebrated *ciaccona* for violin solo is founded, will show:

Chair organ. A name given to the Prestant or choir-organ, from a notion that it formed the seat of the organist, when placed behind him.

Chalameau (*Fr.*) Stem, or straw-pipe, from the Latin *calamus*, a reed. The lower register of the clarinet and the basset-horn is called the *chalameau* tone, from the obsolete instrument *shawm*, *schalmey*, precursor of the oboe and clarinet.

Chamber music. Kammermusik (*Ger.*) **Musica da camera** (*It.*) Vocal or instrumental compositions suitable for performance in a chamber, as opposed to a concert-room. The performance in private upon single instruments of any class constituted the first chamber music properly so-called. Strictly speaking, any music vocal or instrumental played in private is chamber music; but the term is now applied not only to performances upon a single instrument, with or without accompaniment, but also to any combination of different instruments, with only one player to each part—duets, trios, quartetts, &c., for voices or instruments. It is probable that the first chamber music constructed as such was entirely vocal, and not of much earlier date than the end of the 15th or the beginning of the 16th centuries—the Scolia of the Greeks, the music of the minstrels, and of public and private musicians of later date, including among the former " the waits," " noises," and other private bands, not being of a character that could fairly be called by the title chamber music. Therefore the Madrigal will be regarded as among the first specimens of chamber music. The titles of more than one collection, for example, " Madrigali di Tavolina," " Madrigali di Camera," " Madrigali Concertati," " Madrigali et Arie per sonare et cantare," and so forth, together with the peculiar style in which many of the early books are printed,—two parts on one page intended to be read by two persons seated opposite to each other at the same table—would show conclusively that they were intended as chamber music.

The addition of instrumental accompaniments to madrigals probably arose out of a desire to support the voices and keep them in tune, as well as to give employment to those who could play and not sing, but who were desirous of taking part in that which was going on. This practice—at first a mere conciliation to the instrumentalists — suggested the use of instruments alone for the purposes of concert. Thus we find attached to the early productions, instructions to the effect that they are " apt for Instrumentes and Voyces," as in Alison's " An Howres Recreation in Musicke," or as in Bonaffino's " Madrigali," that they are available " per cantar e sonar nel Clave cimbalo, Chitarrone ò altro simile Instrumento," or as in the later editions of Byrd's Psalmes, Songs, and Sonnets, framed to be " fit for Voyces or Viols." Doubtless from such small beginnings the writers of the time were induced to compose " Consort lessons," " Ayres," " Fancies," " Canzone da Sonare," and the like, often written in six parts, the number of viols in a " chest." These compositions at first differed very little in point of form and treatment from the madrigals from whence they were derived, until the demand arose for pieces of less dignity, in obedience to which demand we find dance tunes, "Almaines, Ayres, Corants, Sarabands, Moriscoes, Jiggs, &c.," hitherto only set for a single instrument, arranged in parts for "Viols or Violins;" and these and other dance-tunes issued in *suites* made into the first sonatas, and the symmetrical shape in which each was necessarily written for the purposes of the dance gave rise to that which is known as Form. The word Sonata, at first applied to pieces for a solo instrument, as well as to those for several, became gradually to be used as a term for compositions of a certain character for a single compound instrument, as the organ, harpsichord, or pianoforte.

The most important era in the history of chamber music was the final quarter of the last and the first of the present centuries; the labours of Boccherini, whose trios, quartetts, and quintetts are form-like, easy, and graceful, as well as those of Fiorillo, Giardini, Pugnani, and Viotti, leading to the foundation of the school in which Pleyel, Haydn, Mozart, and Beethoven were such apt pupils and masters.

Changeable chant. A single or double chant which can be sung either in the major or minor mode without other alteration than the substitution of the minor third and sixth of the scale for those of the corresponding major.

W. TURNER.

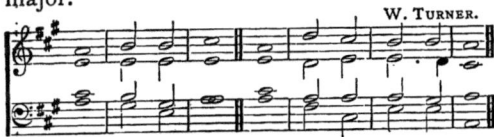

W. TURNER.

Change of voice. [Larynx.]
Change ringing. [Bells.]
Changer de jeu (*Fr.*) To alter the stops on an organ or harmonium.
Changes. The altered melodies produced by varying the sounds of a peal of bells. [Bells.]
Changing notes. Passing notes or discords which occur on the accented parts of a bar.
Chanson (*Fr.*) (1) A song. (2) A national melody. (3) A part-song.
Chansonnette (*Fr.*) A little song.
Chant. A short musical composition to which the Canticles and the prose version of the Psalms are sung, either in unison or in four-part harmony. There are two kinds of chant in common use—the Anglican and the Gregorian.

(1) A Gregorian chant consists of five parts; the intonation; the first reciting note or dominant; the mediation; the second reciting note or dominant; the ending, *e.g.*:

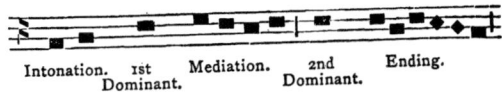

Intonation. 1st Mediation. 2nd Ending.
            Dominant.   Dominant.

The intonation is used generally to every verse of a canticle, but only to the first verse of a psalm, unless a special psalm be used on a solemn occasion, as for instance the Miserere (Psalm li.) during Lent.

With regard to the pointing of the Prayer-book version of the Psalms, several important facts have to be considered. The undoubted object of the chants as originally used in the Roman Church was to enable, as far as possible, a pure *syllabic* recitation of the words, so many of the words of a verse being recited on the dominants as would leave one syllable only to each note of the mediation and ending. As these chants were in use many centuries before the invention of *cantus mensurabilis*, it is quite impossible that they were ever sung rhythmically at the close of each recitation. But there is a growing tendency to treat the Gregorian chants Anglican-wise, and either by accents or bars, to definitely shape out their rhythm. If any proof were wanting of this fact, it is only necessary to give the following:

Ex. 1. *a.*   4th Tone.

b.

The ending of the first of these is evidently intended to be in triple measure, that of the second in duple. But to force the ending into either one of these measures is to wilfully cast aside the invaluable property it possesses of bearing an accent on any note, as the words require. A like desire for modern chant-form has led to the following differences of accent:

Ex. 2. *a.*   From SARGENT'S PSALTER.

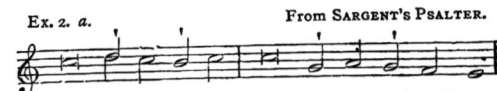

b.   From GRAY.

Ex. 3. *a.*

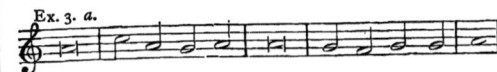

b.

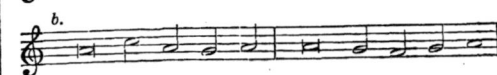

It will be seen from the above, that in proportion to the adoption of strict time in the ending, the true use of chants for syllabic treatment becomes lost. In short, "Gregorians," as used for the most part in England at the present time, are nothing more than ordinary chants, not, however, having an uniform number of bars of music. Hence the same difficulties present themselves which will be explained below in the account of Anglican pointing, e.g.:

Ex. 4. a.

at the presence | of the God of Jacob.

b.

at the presence of the | God of Ja - cob.

It is generally understood that when the number of notes exceeds the number of syllables, the notes not required may be omitted, e.g.:

Ex. 5. From SARGENT.

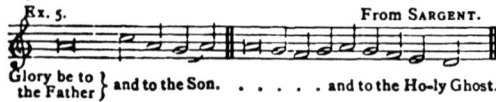

Glory be to } and to the Son. . . . . . and to the Ho-ly Ghost.
the Father }

This is a negative proof of the original syllabic tendency of Gregorian pointing, it being merely a corollary of the law that there should be " one syllable to one note," to say, " if only a few syllables are left, let the notes not wanted be omitted." This rule is now generally neglected; and, even in canticles with such short verses as the Te Deum, the syllables are *slurred* to the superfluous notes, lest the hearers' notion of " the tune " should be disturbed.

In 1843, the Rev. F. Oakeley published his Gregorian Psalter, carrying out, in its integrity, the principle of the syllabic system, e.g.:

Ex. 6. From OAKELEY.

My soul truly waiteth | still up - on God:

for of Him com - eth my sal - va - tion.

Ex. 7. From OAKELEY.

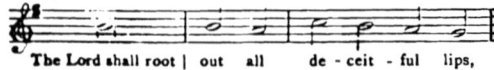

The Lord shall root | out all de - ceit - ful lips,

and the tongue that speak - eth proud things.

Notwithstanding its merits, this Psalter seems not to have been largely used, and where used has been superseded by others in which the tones have been "anglicanized" and made more palatable by the unjustifiable introduction of fixed accent and rhythm.

Another danger which presents itself to the advocates of Gregorian chants is their limited

number. It is out of the question that new Gregorian chants should be "expressly composed" for Psalters, but it is absolutely necessary to provide a variety of chants to avoid the monotony of over-repetition. Hence it is, (1) that *endings* heard on the Continent, whatever be their modern growth or their incompatibility with the Gregorian scale, are greedily seized and made use of in this country; and (2) that *foliations* or the vicious introduction of auxiliary notes, above or below the genuine notes of the chant, are as readily welcomed by Gregorian editors, e.g.:

Ex. 8.

Ex. 9.

Ex. 10.

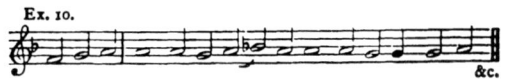

&c.

Ex. 8 is called a form of the 5th tone, No. 9 a form of the 4th.

Ex. 10 shows a foliated form of the mediation of the 1st tone. The division of the plain tones and foliated tones into ferial and festival does credit to the ingenuity, but not to the historical integrity, of Psalm-pointers.

The French and Belgians have ever been celebrated as clever adulterators of plain-song; and as their manuals now form the chief textbooks of English Gregorianizers, it is not difficult to prophecy a general decadence of the art of Gregorian chanting in this country.

(2) An Anglican chant is of two sorts, single and double. A single chant is in two strains, the first of three, and the second of four bars in length:

PELHAM HUMPHREYS.

A double chant has the length of two single ones :*

ROBINSON.

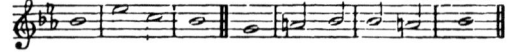

* It has been stated, and the statement is often repeated, that the double chant was suggested by the accidental performance of two single chants in succession by a nameless pupil of Hine, who was organist of Gloucester Cathedral between the years 1710 and 1730. In "Boyce's Cathedral Music," published 1760—1778, is a double-chant by John Robinson, who was organist of Westminster Abbey from 1727 to 1762, dying at the ripe age of eighty; and as there exists a MS. copy of the same chant in the handwriting of Dr. Turner, the father-in-law of Robinson, with the date 1706, in one of the old MS. service-books belonging to St. Paul's Cathedral, there is reason for questioning the story concerning the accepted origin of the double-chant.

The two strains are also called *halves;* one half is sung to that part of a verse of the Prayer-book version of the Psalms on each side of the colon, whether the number of words be many or few, whether the sentence is complete or not ; as :

When the company of the spearmen and multitude of the mighty are scattered abroad among the beasts of the people, so that they humbly bring - - - - - } pieces of silver:

And when he hath scattered the people - - - } that de-light in war;
or,

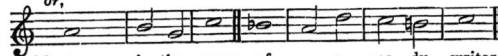

My tongue is the pen: of — a rea-dy writer.

The opening chord of a chant, and also the first chord after each double bar, may be sustained at will, to accommodate the number of syllables contained in each part of the verse. These chords are called *reciting notes,* those which follow are called the *inflections;* or, according to some, the first half of the chant is the *mediation,* and the second the *cadence.* The fitting of the words to the music is called *pointing.* The pointing of the Psalms and Canticles is a matter concerning which there are diversities of opinion. The principal object to be aimed at in pointing is "the apportioning out of the emphasis of the words to be sung, after the manner that an eloquent speaker would recite them ;" but as sentences are capable of as many accents more or less sensible as there are words, the diversity of opinion on the subject is not to be wondered at. The words are divided in the Prayer-book not always in the best manner as regards their complete grammatical sense ; and as it is at present deemed unwise to adopt any plan but the one therein suggested, difference of opinion will exist until a change is made in its system of stops. The varieties of pointing arise from the desire to unite an oratorical with a musical accent ; and the many ways in which this is attempted will be best seen by the following quotations from pointed Psalters in frequent use.

[The lines after each set of words indicate the place of the bar in the chant.]

Psalm cxxxvii.

No. 1. Dr. WESLEY'S PSALTER.

For they that led us
away captive required
of us then a sóng and | melody in our | heaviness.

No. 2. THE CATHEDRAL PSALTER.

For they that led us
away captive required
of us then a song and
mélody | in our | heaviness.

No. 3. THE CONGREGATIONAL PSALTER.

For they that led us
away captive required
of us then a song and
melodý in | our | heaviness.

No. 4. MONK AND OUSELEY'S PSALTER.

For they that led us
away captive required
of us then a song and
melody in our | heavi- | -ness.

The *form* of the chant has been the real cause of the difficulties of pointing. An ordinary melodic sentence consists of two, four, or eight bars, but the chant has first three, then four bars. This peculiarity does not, however, offend the ear so much as the eye, for in reciting, the rhythmical cadence is to a certain extent completed.

Various theories have been put forth to account for the 7-bar or twice 7-bar form of the Anglican Chant, all writers being agreed that a 7-bar phrase is not actually presented to the ear in the process of chanting. The theorists may be divided into two classes—those who would add a bar to the commencement of the chant, that is, to the reciting note ; and those who would add a bar at the half cadence and whole cadence. The following is the method in which the former would write out Robinson's Chant :

Ex. 1.

Those who lean to the latter opinion would write it thus :

Ex. 2

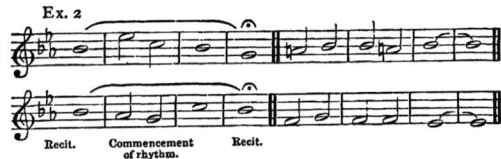

Recit.   Commencement   Recit.
of rhythm.

In opposition to the first view taken, it may be urged that in music the chords of cadence *precede* the final chord, and in Ex. 1, they fall on the final accent, as is shown by doubling the bars, *e.g.* :

Except in rare forms of dance-tunes the above rhythm would be unbearable. In favour of the second form (Ex. 2), it may be stated that in all the best pointed Psalters an accent, a larger fount of type, or a bar, marks the close of the Recitation and commencement of the musical rhythm, and that the syllable or syllables so made prominent only occupy *one* bar of time. In opposition to the second form, it may be remarked that the final bar of both halves of a double chant is not *in practice* held out for the length of two bars. One or the other of these theories may be true, and the reader is left to decide on their respective merits. ·

Certain writers have assumed that the Anglican Chant is a highly tractable collection of sounds, bound by no laws of rhythm ; and acting on this notion, have attempted to *unbar* some modern chants. This view has led to a system of pointing by which as many words as possible are collected on the reciting note, *e.g.* :

Praise Him in the sound of the| trum- | pet, || &c.

Praise Him in the cymbals and | dan- |ces,|| &c.

Praise Him upon the well-tuned| cym -|bals || Praise Him upon the | loud-|cym-|bals|i

The above system (known as the "Sudbury") is said to be smooth, but the number of *slurs* involved would produce this effect, although opposed to the true principles of chanting.

It has been said "that the best practical solution of the difficulty of chanting would be offered by selecting a set of the most appropriate chants, whose melodies, within the range of all voices, would not suffer by being sung by a whole congregation, and to have every word set to a note of relative length, so as to ensure evenness of tone and accuracy of accent." Some of the early church composers have left examples of the Venite set to distinct music, often chant-like, so that the thing here suggested would not be so great a novelty. But it would be difficult to make such a plan general, for, leaving out of the question the additional time such a service would occupy, none but educated choirs could perform it, and the ordinary chant is so easy that there is little if any trouble needed to teach it to unskilful choristers. The chant at present in use might be retained, and if elocution is the main object of chanting, a different system of pointing might be devised, by employing the present authorised division of the verses only when convenient. Alterations might be made in a verse (1) when the sense is incomplete in it, (2) when a verse contains two distinct subjects, (3) when the present colon interrupts the logical sequence, *e.g.*:

(1) Psalm xvii.

8. Keep me as the apple of an eye: hide me under the shadow of thy wings, (9) from the ungodly that trouble me.

(2) Psalm lxxxix.

49. Remember Lord the rebukes that thy servants have : and how I do bear in my bosom the rebukes of many people ; (50) wherewith thine enemies have blasphemed thee, and slandered the footsteps of thine anointed.
Praised be the Lord for evermore : Amen and Amen.

(3) Psalm xiv.

11. Who shall give salvation unto Israel out of Sion ? (:) when the Lord turneth the captivity of his people, then shall Jacob rejoice, and Israel shall be glad.

In some of the numerous editions (issued between the years 1655 and 1730) of Playford's " Introduction to the Skill of Musick," there is an appendix containing the " order of singing the Divine Service in Cathedrals." In these it is said that "the Venite is begun by one of the choir, then sung by sides, observing to make the like break or close in the middle of every verse, according as it is shorter or longer." The use or tune for each day in the week is given to the first verse of the Venite, and these tunes are such as are now called Gregorian. There are two others —" Canterbury tune " and " Imperial tune " —" proper for Choir ; to sing the Psalms, Te Deum, Benedictus, or Jubilate, to the organ or sometime without it." The manner in which the words are disposed will be seen by the following copy of the first-named of these tunes :

O come, let us sing un-to the Lord   Let us heart- i - ly

re- joice in   the strength of our sal - va - ti - on.

Dr. Turner, 1706, gives the pointing of the same verse as follows :

O come, let us sing un - to the Lord: let us

heart- i - ly re-joice in the strength of our sal - va - ti - on.

It will be seen that this chant contains only five complete bars of four crotchets each. The bars in it do not indicate the place of accent, or even the best division of the chant for the purpose of pointing. The earliest printed copy of a now well-known chant by the same author, is given in the following form (from " Fifty double and single chants being the most Favourite as performed at St. Pauls, Westminster, and most of the Cathedrals in England. London : Printed for C. and S. Thompson, at No. 75, St. Paul's Churchyard ").

In the following example (from the "Harmony of Sion") the chant is compressed into four bars.

We praise Thee, O God: we acknowledge Thee to be the Lord.

And Dr. Boyce, in his "Cathedral Music," writes the Venite to the chant ascribed to Tallis thus:

O come, let us sing un - to the Lord,

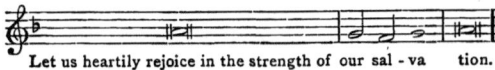

Let us heartily rejoice in the strength of our sal - va - tion.

The method of chanting the Psalms adopted in the present day is for each of the two divisions of the choir to sing a verse alternately. In some places where a double chant is used the whole of the chant is sung to two verses by each side in turn. In one cathedral (Oxford) each side sings one half of a verse only. In consequence of this custom of the alternate chanting of the Psalms, it is supposed that wherever alternate singing is mentioned in ancient records, chanting is meant. The objections entertained against chanting by the followers of Wickliffe, and in later time by those of Calvin, were expressed in violent terms, not altogether necessary to repeat here. It is true these reformers approved of the people joining "with one voice in a plain tune, but not of tossing the Psalms from one side to the other with intermingling of organs." Less moderate in their deeds than in their words, the Puritans, when in power during the Commonwealth, destroyed all organs and every music-book they could lay their hands upon. Metrical psalmody supplied the place of chanting, the Psalms were rarely if ever sung, and so, in contradistinction to Sternhold and Hopkins, or Tate and Brady, were called the "Reading Psalms," a practice continued as lately as the year 1873, when the Psalms for the day sung at the meeting of the Charity Children in St. Paul's Cathedral were so called. Chanting was regarded as essentially Popish, and alternate singing an abomination even among church people. It was never heard in parish churches in the last century, the cathedrals alone retaining the traditional use. By degrees a change was effected; the unclean thing was handled without any alarming effect, and even Dissenters changed their opinions upon the subject. Instead of condemning chanting, they adopted it. Dr. Channing thought it "the most purely Protestant music;" Mr. Newman Hall considered it "a homage to the Bible, calculated to make the Word of God better known, appreciated, and loved;" others would "by no means have it banished;" and the preface to the fourth edition of a little book called "Euphonia" (1870), designed to familiarise Non-conformists with the principles of chanting, states that "the objections entertained by many to the ancient practice of chanting having been much diminished, there is now a growing feeling in favour of singing portions of the Bible in the very words of Scripture, rather than through the medium of metrical versions exclusively." This book, which is historically valuable, contains one hundred portions of Scripture pointed for chanting, together with a selection of familiar, if not good, Anglican chants; the principle guiding the choice being liveliness of melody and general tunefulness. These facts tend to show that the usefulness of chanting is in process of general recognition by "all who profess and call themselves Christians;" that it is no longer held to be the type of a peculiarity of religious opinion; that there is a mutual interchange of means towards a spiritual end; that whereas one side does not disdain to encourage the use of metrical psalmody in its services, the other borrows chanting, defending it as "a simple but impressive mode of worship."

Chants have been found convenient means of rendering hymns of irregular metre, or any hymn of which a simple musical treatment is required.

Chant (*Fr.*) (1) Song, tune. (2) The voice part or melody.

Chantant (*Fr.*) Singing, musical, as *café chantant*, a musical coffee-house.

Chant en ison, or chant égal (*Fr.*) (1) The name of a species of chant, consisting of two sounds only, which was adopted by many of the old religious orders. (2) Monotone.

Chanter. A name given to the singing priest on duty.

Chanter à livre ouvert (*Fr.*) To sing at sight.

Chanterelle (*Fr.*) (1) The first or highest string upon instruments played with a bow. The E string of the violin, and the A of the viola and violoncello. (2) The highest string of a guitar or lute.

Chanterres (*Fr.*) A name given to ballad

or poem singers in mediæval times, originally applied to the Provençal Cantadours.

Chanteur (*Fr.*) A male singer.
Chanteuse (*Fr.*) A female singer.

Chant gregorien (*Fr.*) Plain song.

Chant pastoral (*Fr.*) A shepherd's song, or melody in imitation of one.

Chantries. Endowed foundations in the Romish Church, instituted for the due performances of requiem masses for the repose of the soul of the founder and his family. Chantries were attached to existing parish churches, or more frequently to monastic establishments and cathedrals. At the Reformation the practice of soul-masses and the chantries became disused, and their revenues absorbed.

Chant-royal (*Fr.*) A certain form of early French poetry set to music. Pasquier describes it as a song in honour of God, the Virgin, or the saints, or any other " argument of dignity, especially if coupled with distress." The *chant-royal* was written in heroic stanzas, and closed with a *L'envoy* or stanza containing a dedication, recapitulation, or moral.

Chantry priest. A chaplain or singing parson attached to a chantry. One whose duty it was to sing masses for the speedy deliverance of the soul of a founder or benefactor from purgatory.

Chant sur le livre (*Fr.*) A system of descant by which the part sung by one voice, as written in the open book, could be accompanied by another voice in counterpoint, more or less free, according to the movement of the *canto fermo*, which was sung generally by a bass voice, the *déchant* being taken by a tenor or other high voice. It was necessary that the singer of the *canto fermo* or plainsong should render it *à la rigueur*, that is, should not make those slight changes of the length of the notes which would be justifiable and usual when singing alone; nor could he hold out the rests (*tenere punctum*) as he otherwise would, lest the *déchanteur* should be upset in his calculations. The full rules of this system are to be found in early treatises. It was called in Italy *contrapunto di mente*, or *alla mente*.

Chapeau Chinois (*Fr.*) A set of small bells arranged in the form of a Chinese hat. *Pavillon chinois*.

Characteristischer Ton (*Ger.*) The leading note. (*Fr.*) *sensible*.

Characters. A general name for the signs employed in music, such as brace, bind, bar, sharp, flat, natural, clef, stave, shake, turn, beat, and the signs of words indicating time and expression, *e.g.* < > C C̦, &c.

Characterstücke (*Ger.*) Pieces of music written with the intention of describing certain impressions by means of sound. Beethoven's Pastoral Symphony, Mendelssohn's Reformation Symphony, and the overture and music to " A Midsummer Night's Dream," are specimens of this style of composition.

Charivari (*Fr.*) Mock music, clatter.

Chasse (*Fr.*) Hunting; *à la chasse*, in the hunting style.

Chatzozerah (*Heb.*) The *chatzozerah* is generally thought to have been a straight trumpet, with a bell or " pavillon " as it is termed. Moses received specific directions as to making them. " Make thee two trumpets of silver; of a whole piece shalt thou make them: that thou mayest use them for the calling of the assembly, and for the journeying of the camps." In Ps. xcviii. 6, the *chatzozerah* and *shophar* are brought into juxtaposition : " With *chatzozerah* and sound of *shophar* make a joyful noise before the Lord the King ;" or, as it incorrectly stands in the Prayer-book version, " With trumpets also and shawms, &c." In this passage the Septuagint has it, Ἐν σάλπιγξιν ἐλαταῖς, καὶ φωνῇ σάλπιγγος κερατίνης, " With ductile trumpets, and the sound of horn-trumpets." So, too, the Vulgate: " In tubis ductilibus et voce tubæ corneæ." The word *mikshah*, which is applied to the description of the *chatzozerah* in Num. x. 2, which means " rounded " or " turned," may either apply to a complete twist in the tube of the instrument, or, what is more probable, to the rounded outline of the *bell*. But if the former is the real interpretation of the epithet, it would make it more like a trombone, and similar in form to that depicted on the Arch of Titus. But, on the other hand, the account given by Josephus points out the latter characteristic of shape. He says, " Moses invented a kind of trumpet of silver; in length it was little less than a cubit, and it was somewhat thicker than a pipe; its opening was oblong, so as to permit blowing on it with the mouth; at the lower end it had the form of a bell, like a horn." It seems chiefly to have been brought into use in the Hebrew ritual, but was also occasionally a battle-call, and blown on other warlike occasions.

Check-action. [Pianoforte.]

Check-spring. A small spring added for the assistance of any weakness in the return of action in the mechanism of an organ.

Chef d'attaque (*Fr.*) The leader of an orchestra, or chorus.

Chef d'œuvre (*Fr.*) The master-work of any composer.

Chef d'orchestre (*Fr.*) (1) The leader. (2) Conductor of an orchestra.

Chelidonizing (from the *Gk.* χελιδονίζω, to twitter like a swallow). Singing the swallow-song (χελιδόνισμα), a popular song sung by Rhodian boys in the month Boëdromian, on the return of the swallows, and made into an opportunity of begging. A similar song survives in modern Greece. A *crow* was also carried about by begging boys who sang; whence *Gk.* κορωνίζω. Examples of both songs are given by Athenæus. Pamphilicus of Alexandria, in his chapter on names, calls the men making collections for the crow, *coronistæ*, and their songs, *coronismata*. There was a similar custom in Ireland on St. Stephen's day. A number of young men carried a furze-bush on which a wren was tied, and stopping before the houses of the gentry, repeated the following lines:

"The wren, the wren is the king of all birds,
Was caught on St. Stephen's day in the furze,
Although he's little, his family's great,
Then pray, kind gentle folks, give him a treat."

In England and Scotland there are many customs of a like character, as for example, "going a gooding" on St. Thomas's day; singing the *Hagmena* on the three days preceding Christmas day; the children's May-day march, when they carry garlands of spring-flowers and boughs, and stopping at the doors of people of the better sort, sing a long song, one verse of which runs:

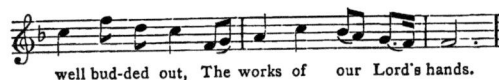

A branch of May we have brought you, And at your door it stands; It is but a sprout, but it's well bud-ded out, The works of our Lord's hands.

Chelys. (*Gk.*) χέλυς, lit. *a tortoise* (*Lat. testudo*). (1) The lyre of Mercury, supposed to have been formed by strings stretched across a tortoiseshell. (2) In the 16th and 17th centuries a bass-viol and division-viol were each called *chelys*.

Cheng. The Chinese organ, which consists of a series of tubes having free reeds. It is held in the hand and blown by the mouth. The introduction of this instrument into Europe led to the invention of the accordion and harmonium. Kratzenstein, an organ-builder of St. Petersburg, having become possessed of one, conceived the idea of applying the principle to organ-stops. The tone of free reeds is enforced by tubes, as in the cheng and in certain organ-stops, but the tubes can be dispensed with, as is the case in a harmonium.

Cherubical hymn. The *ter sanctus*, or *trisagion* in the service of the Holy Communion, "Holy, holy, holy," &c.

Chest of viols. An expression signifying a set of instruments necessary for a "consort of viols." They were six in number, namely two trebles, two tenors, and two basses. A chest of viols, with a harpsichord or organ, with an occasional hautboy or flageolet, formed an ordinary orchestra in the early part of the 17th century.

Chevalet (*Fr.*) The bridge of a stringed instrument.

Cheville (*Fr.*) A peg for a violin, guitar, lute, &c.

Chevroter (*Fr.*) To skip, quiver, to sing with uncertain tone, after the manner of goats. *Alla vibrato.*

Chiara (*It.*) Clear, distinct, pure, *e.g.*, *chiara voce*, clear voice; *chiara quarta*, a perfect fourth.

Chiaramente (*It.*) Clearly, purely, distinctly.

Chiarezza, con (*It.*) With brightness, clearness.

Chiarina (*It.*) A clarion or trumpet.

Chiave (*It.*) (1) Key or clef. (2) A failure. [Fiasco.]

Chica. The name of a dance popular among the Spaniards and the South American settlers descended from them. It is said to have been introduced by the Moors, and to have been the origin of the Fandango, which some writers declare to be the Chica under a more decent form. It is of a similar character with the dance of the Angrismene performed at the festivals of Venus, and still popular among the modern Greeks. The English jig is said to be one form of the Chica. It is not a little singular that the word came into use soon after a free intercourse with Spain was opened. The words Chaconne

(*Fr.*), Ciaccona (*It.*), Cachuca (*Sp.*), Czardasch (*Hungarian*), describe modern modifications of the Chica. [Bolero.] [Country Dance.]

Chiesa (*It.*) Church. *Sonata di Chiesa.* A sacred sonata.

Chiffres (*Fr.*) Figures, *basse chiffrée*, figured bass.

Chime. (1) To play a tune on bells, either by machinery or by hand, by means of hammers, or swinging the clappers, the bell remaining unmoved. It is opposed to *ringing* in which the bells are *raised*, that is, swung round. (2) A carillon.

Chirimia (*Sp.*) An oboe (from Chirimoya, a pear), the portion of the oboe in which the mouth-piece is inserted, called in German *Birn*, a pear.

Chirogymnast. Finger-trainer. A contrivance for strengthening the fingers, consisting of a cross-bar, from which are suspended rings attached to springs. The term is also applied to any apparatus designed for a like object.

Chironomy. *Gk.* χειρονομία. (1) Gesticulation by the use of the hands. (2) Directions given by movements of the hand, especially to a chorus. In the early church of the West such a system was much in vogue; and some have maintained that the signs of sounds, as then written, were merely pictorial representations of the movement of the hand.

Chiroplast. Finger-former. An instrument invented by Logier in 1810, to facilitate the proper method of playing the pianoforte. It consisted of a position-frame, finger-guides, and a wrist-guide. The position-frame consisted of two parallel rails extending from one extremity of the keys to the other, and fastened to the pianoforte. This frame served as a line upon which the finger-guides travelled; these guides were two moveable brass frames, with five divisions for the fingers, and to each guide was attached a brass wire with a regulator, called the wrist-guide, by which the position of the wrist was preserved from inclination outwards. With the instructions for the use of the chiroplast, progressive lessons on the pianoforte were given; and in the success attending the use of the hand-guide, these lessons, which were cleverly designed, had doubtless as much to do with the machine itself, which, however, soon fell into disuse.

Chitarra (*It.*) A guitar.

Chitarra col arco (*It.*) A violin with sides gently curved, as in a guitar; without corners, as in an ordinary violin.

Chitarrina (*It.*) A small Neapolitan guitar.

Chiudendo (*It.*) Closing, ending. The word is generally employed in connection with another, *chiudendo colla prima strofe*, ending with the first verse.

Chiuso (*It.*) Close, hidden, concealed,

e.g., canone chiuso, a close canon, [Canon]; *con bocca chiusa*, with the mouth closed, humming.

Chœur (*Fr.*) [Chorus.]

Choir. (1) A part of the building in a cathedral or collegiate chapel set apart for the performance of the ordinary daily service. The choir is generally situated at the eastern end of the building, and is frequently enclosed by a screen, upon which the organ is placed. (2) The minor canons, choral vicars, and choristers, or other singers taken collectively, are spoken of as the choir. The choral body is usually divided into two sets of voices, the one sitting on the north and the other on the south side of the chancel, and are known by the respective titles of Cantoris and Decani from their nearness to the Cantor (or Precentor) and to the Decanus (or Dean). In most cathedrals and collegiate chapels, the Decani side is held to be the side of honour, the best voices are placed there, and all the "*verses*" or *soli* parts, if not otherwise directed, are sung by that side, which is also considered the "first choir" (*coro primo*) in eight-part music.

Choir-man. An adult member of a choir.

Choir Organ. [Organ, § 1.]

Chor (*Ger.*) Chorus. Choir of a church or concert room.

Choragus. (*Lat.*) (1) The leader of the chorus in the ancient Greek drama. [Chorus.] (2) The title of a musical official at Oxford University, whose duties are described in the Statutes.

Choral. (1) Of, or belonging to the choir, concert, or chorus. Choral service, a service with music. (2) A hymn or psalm tune.

Chorāle (*Ger.*) [Hymn tunes.]

Choraliter (*Ger.*) In a choral form.

Choralmässig (*Ger.*) [Choraliter.]

Choral Music. Vocal music in parts, as opposed to instrumental.

Choral Service. A service of song; a service is said to be *partly* choral, when only canticles, hymns, &c., are sung; *wholly* choral, when in addition to these, the versicles, responses, &c., are sung.

Choral Vicars. [Lay Vicars.]

Chor-amt (*Ger.*) Choral service. Cathedral service.

Choraules (*Gk.* χοραύλης from χορός and αὐλέω.) (1) A player on the flute in the Greek Theatre. (2) One who keeps a chorus and plays in it himself.

Chord. A combination of musical sounds, consonant or dissonant. [Harmony.]

Chord. A string.

Chorda characteristica. A chord of the 7th in which a leading note appears.

Chordæ essentiales (*late Lat.*) The tonic and its 3rd and 5th. The key-chord.

Chordaulodion. A self-acting musical instrument, invented by Kauffmann, of Dresden, in 1812.

Chor-dienst (*Ger.*) [Chor-amt.]

Chordometer. A gauge for measuring the thickness of strings.

Chords étouffés (*Fr.*) (1) Chords played on the pianoforte with the *sordino* pedal held down.. (2) Chords on the harp, lute, guitar, or dulcimer, *damped* by placing the hand gently on the strings.

Choriambus. A metrical foot consisting of two short between two long syllables.

Chorister. A member of a choir whether juvenile or adult. At the present day the *children* of the choir of a church or cathedral, are those usually distinguished by the term, but so recently as the commencement of the present century, all who were engaged in taking part in the musical portion of the service, were called choristers. The word derived from χορός, by metonomy came to signify a band of singers or dancers, or any member of such a band, and hence the term is often applied to a singer in a chorus not necessarily belonging to a church, just as *choir* is applied to the place in which church singers sit, as also to any body of singers of sacred or secular music. For example, *Les enfans de chœur*, children of the choir or chorus; *Dom-chor*, cathedral choir or chorus, and *Coro del chiesa*, church choir or chorus; Choristers, or boy singers, called "clerks of the third form," in some places, are attached to every cathedral in England, and receive advantages of more or less value, in exchange for their services as members of the choir. In addition to necessary instruction in music, they have an education in other matters, varying in many places according to the construction put upon the Statutes by the deans and chapters of the cathedrals. The interpretation of these Statutes has been the subject of grave dispute, as the advantages accruing to the choristers have been from time to time most shamefully ignored. In days past, the children have been shut out from the enjoyment of preferential privileges made concerning them, and their education and moral training has been so little cared for, that many a child who in early years was familiarised with the most sacred matters, has acquired for them the proverbial result of familiarity. A better state of things is now being brought into existence with a result which cannot be considered other than hopeful.

In some places private instructors have been engaged to teach cathedral choristers a few matters besides music; in others they are admitted into the chief grammar schools of the several cities. The course of instruction also varies, for in some cases they are taught the simple elements of reading and writing, in others they learn as much of the higher branches of education as is possible in addition to the duties of their profession. In many instances their musical instructors impart no more than is absolutely needful for the exercise of cathedral duty, and in some music is taught scientifically as well as practically, not only in connection with the immediate work in hand, but also with reference to future use. In very few instances are the boys boarded and lodged within the precincts of the cathedral, or placed under the immediate care of the cathedral authorities out of the hours devoted to duty—a matter of much regret. The organist is sometimes musicmaster of the choristers, sometimes the office is distinct, and is held independently of the organist. In many cathedrals a sum of money as apprentice fee is paid to a chorister on leaving the choir; this is instead of the money at one time set apart for the maintenance of the chorister as a student at the universities. For instance, in the Statutes of Stoke College, in Suffolk, founded by Parker, Archbishop of Canterbury, are these words: "of which said queristers, after their breasts be changed (their voices broken) we will the most apt of wit and capacity be holpen with exhibition of forty shillings, the rest with lesser summe."

In olden times, choristers were privileged to demand a fee from every newly installed officer of the church, and to levy "spur money" from all who attended the service in riding gear. In the former case the fee varied according to the position of the installed officer, and was paid without conditions being imposed in return; in the latter, the wearer of spurs could require the youthful tax-gatherer to repeat his "gamut" perfectly; if he hesitated, he lost his spur-money. The boys of the Chapel Royal were the last to keep up the custom which has now fallen into disuse with many others equally absurd. For example: the choristers in many cathedrals and collegiate establishments were permitted to rule over their superiors for a short period once a year, generally from December 6th, the Feast of St. Nicholas (the patron saint of sailors, parish clerks, thieves, and boys) until Innocents-day, December 28th. From the aptitude acquired in these ludicrous ceremonies, the choristers gained such a skill in acting that they were selected to perform in the mystery plays of old time, and later to represent the masterly conceptions of such writers as Shakespeare, Ben Jonson, and others. It was not alone to the choir boys attached to unimportant establishments that these matters were entrusted, but also to the children of "Powle's churche" and of the "Chapel Royale" of Her Majesty Queen

Elizabeth. The possession of such powers and privileges may have been exceedingly pleasing while it lasted, but the ill sorted union of the theological and the theatrical is happily dissolved, it is hoped for ever.

The life of a chorister in these remote days was, however, not all bliss, as the owner of a good voice would probably find to his cost, more especially if he was not fortunate enough to belong to St. Paul's Cathedral, or the Chapel Royal, for there were officers armed with the awful warrant of the Royal Court, empowering them to roam the country, to visit all churches and cathedrals of the lesser sort in which choral singing was practised, and to select and take away all boys "with good breasts," that is to say, all with voices of more than ordinary excellence, for the service of the privileged choirs. The "placard" or warrant was often used illegally, and children were impressed for choirs other than those above mentioned. There is reason for believing that choristers so gained were in general badly used, if we may trust Thomas Tusser (1523-1580), the author of " Five hundred points of good husbandry," for he speaks of his good fortune in having been assigned to John Redford, organist of St. Paul's, in terms which prove that choristers were not so kindly used in other places. His situation at Wallingford, from whence he was impressed, he laments in the words :

"O shameful time ! for every crime
What toosed ears, like baited beares.
What bobbed lippes, what yerkes, what nips,
What hellish toies !
What robes, how bare, what colledge fare,
What bread, how stale; what penny ale,
Then Wallingford, how wert thou abhor'd
Of silly boies."

In another verse he contrasts his treatment :

" But marke the chance, myself to vance,
By friendships lot to Pauls I got,
So found I grace a certayn space
Still to remaine
With Redford there, the like no where,
For cunning such, and vertue much ;
By whom some part, of musicke art
So did I gain."

On the Continent choristers are attached to many cathedrals, but their duties and education are based upon a different system to that in general use in Great Britain at the present time. Before the time of the dissolution of the monasteries the position of choristers was much the same as that enjoyed abroad by them, and it was no uncommon thing to find " the children of the choir " in after life occupying stations of eminence and trust in both Church and State. The venerable Bede, St. Swithun, St. Hugh of Lincoln, William of Wykeham, William Wainfleet, Erasmus, and his friend, Dean Colet, the founder of St.

Paul's School, and scores of other distinguished men were choristers. The musicians who have gained the first knowledge of their art within the walls of a church are many, and comprise among others the names of Palestrina, Frescobaldi, Orlando di Lasso (impressed from Hainault into Italy as a child), Padre Martini, John Sebastian Bach, Haydn, William Byrd, Tallis, Dr. Bull, Dr. Rogers, Dr. Blow, Elias Ashmole, Henry Purcell, Dr. Croft, Pelham Humphreys, Dr. Greene, Battishill, Dr. Burney, Attwood, and many famous living musicians whose names it is not necessary here to catalogue.

Chorton (*Ger.*) (1) The ancient ecclesiastical pitch in Germany. It was supposed to be higher than that employed for secular music by about a tone. The terms Kammerton and Chorton were used to signify the difference between a high and a low pitch for the same denominated sound. (2) The melody of a hymn or psalm tune.

Chorus. Chor (*Ger.*) Chœur (*Fr.*) Coro (*It.*) (1) A band of singers and dancers employed on certain occasions in the ancient Greek theatres, and other public places. It was the custom for the whole population of a city to meet on stated occasions, and to offer thanksgivings to the gods for any special advantages obtained, by singing hymns accompanied with dances. Donaldson derives the word from χορος, the name of the place where these exercises were performed in Sparta, and shows the connection between the civil and religious ceremonies of the ancient Greeks, saying that music and dancing were the basis of the religious, political, and military organisation of the Dorian States. The choral songs were always written in the Doric dialect, and the choral dances were Dorian also. In course of time, as the fine arts became more cultivated, the duties of the chorus as a branch of worship devolved upon a few, and ultimately upon one, who bore the whole expenses, when paid dancers were employed. This person was called the choragus and it was his business to provide the chorus in all plays, whether tragic or comic. His first duty after collecting his chorus was to find and pay a teacher (χοροδιcάσκαλος) who instructed them in the songs and dances which they had to perform. The choragus was allowed to press children, if their parents did not give them up of their own accord. He lodged and maintained the chorus until the time of performance and provided them with such aliments as conduce to strengthen the voice, he had also to find masks and dresses. The honour was much coveted among the wealthy Athenians. The choragus who exhibited the best theatrical entertainment generally received a tripod as a reward of praise.

The choral dance reached its perfection in the χορὸς κυκλικός at Athens. This chorus consisted of 50 persons. The number of the chorus varied in later times according to the performance. The χορὸς τραγικός consisting of from 12 to 15, the χορὸς κομικός of 24, and the χορός σατυρικός of the same number as the τραγικός. The chorus in the time of the Attic tragedy consisted of a group of persons, male and female, who remained in the theatre as witnesses as well as spectators. When they spoke, it was to offer reflections on the scene passing before them, taking part with or against the *dramatis personæ* by offering advice, comfort, exhortation, or dissuasion. At times the chorus was divided and spoke antiphonally. These divisions moved according to a pre-arranged order, which movement probably originated the naming of the stanzas which were called *strophe, antistrophe,* and *epode.* When not engaged in singing, the chorus grouped itself upon a platform called the Thymele, which was in the centre of the building, and from whence all measurements were made, the semicircle of the amphitheatre being described from it as its centre. Of the exact part music played, whether elaborate compositions were employed or not, little is now known. It is supposed that a simple rhythmical declamation analogous to chanting was used. The accompaniment of flutes in unison was made use of for the choruses. The chorus declined with the ancient tragedy, and the few attempts made by modern writers to revive the manner of the ancients, as in Schiller's "Braut von Messina" have not been successful. The well-known Antigone and Œdipus Colonæus of Mendelssohn can scarcely be regarded as a reproduction of the ancient Greek chorus, owing to the insuperable difficulty of adapting modern instrumentation to the spirit and observances of the older customs.

(2) A musical instrument variously described by different writers. A bagpipe must have been signified when the word was used in the 10th century, as a chorus or corus is described as "pellis simplex cum duobus cicutis." The word is supposed to be connected with *cornemuse,* as it is sometimes written *cormusa* and *corusa.* In the Promptorium Parvulorum, 15th century, the word is used to describe "a crowde, an instrument of musyke;"—the drone of the bagpipe and the unstoppable strings of the "crowde" bearing a sort of burden or chorus to the melody played on the other pipes or strings. Busby in his "Dictionary of Music," 1810, says that the word is the old Scottish name for a trumpet of loud tone.

(3) A personage in some of Shakespeare's plays, who between the acts utters reflections upon scenes that are past, and describes scenes to come.

(4) A composition for a number of singers, with or without accompaniment, intended as the expression of the united sentiments of a multitude. A chorus may be independent and complete in itself, or may be a portion of a large work either sacred or secular. It may contain opposed sentiments interwoven, as in the Kermesse scene in Gounod's "Faust;" in Meyerbeer's "Huguenots," and "L'Etoile du Nord;" Wagner's "Tannhäuser" and "Lohengrin;" according to the purposes of the drama. Choruses with opposed subjects are not infrequent in oratorios, as in Handel's chorus, "Fixed in his everlasting seat," in "Samson." The union of independent themes may be traced by the student with advantage, in the choruses of such compositions as Bach's Passion music, &c. Double, triple, or even quadruple choruses are often found in the works of the old Italian church writers, as well as in the sacred compositions of Bach, Handel, and later musicians.

The choruses in the early Italian operas were devoid of dramatic character, and in fact, were often independent of the action of the opera in which they were inserted. As they contained occasional reflections on passing events they were in some sort connected with the ancient Greek chorus, the stage directions enjoining the dancers to accompany the singing with motions and gestures, also formed another link binding them to their ancient model. The invention of the operatic chorus, or rather the introduction of combined voices as a necessary part of the dramatic action is claimed by the French. Many of the lesser musical dramas, burlettas, interludes, &c., had no choruses properly speaking, a glee or some concerted piece for the principals being all that is found in them. The choruses of Lully are not very dramatic, and those of Rameau are very badly constructed, and often incorrect as to their harmony, so that the improvements introduced by these two masters were not extended to the chorus. Among the followers of Lully, Campra (1660-1744) is the most distinguished; he treated his choruses in a more advanced manner than his model, not only in the development of harmonic effects, but also by the introduction of novel rhythms. Gluck invented *morceaux d'ensemble,* grand indeed, when compared with the choral effects by other composers of his own and preceding times; Spontini added new instrumental colouring; Cherubini employed the graces of form to clothe the musical outlines suggested by his predecessors; Rossini did as little comparatively for the chorus from a dramatic point of view, as Meyerbeer did much. Some of Bellini's choruses are conceived in fine dramatic spirit; Verdi's, though occasionally vulgar in detail, are by no means wanting in general force and appropriateness; the faults they exhibit are due to the influence of the fetters of tradition, and a wearying use of simple tonic and dominant harmonies; Gounod's are often admirable, but as the expression of the voices and opinions of a multitude. Wagner's choruses are nearest the true ideal. In many of the early English operas the chorus is an inconsiderable item. Exception must. however, be made in favour of those by Henry Purcell, whose works of this class exist. while many of the other portions of his operas have fallen out of memory. Neither Lampe, Arne, or Storace paid much attention to the development of chorus, but its improvement in smaller dramatic works is due to Sir Henry Bishop. As conductor of the music at Covent Garden Theatre for many years, he produced a series of compositions of more or less value, some of which live, while the dramas and plays for which they were written have fallen completely into oblivion. His earlier choruses have the *glee* attached, the part for the multitude of voices being as easy as possible. It is presumed that operatic chorus singing was not in its highest state of perfection in the days of Mozart or Beethoven, for neither of these composers has given the chorus much that is difficult or important in their operas—a matter of necessity perhaps, as it was hard to find a body of singers in those days, who would be so far content with the gifts they possessed as to accept an inferior position. Chorus singing was very little cultivated in London so recently as the time when the Sacred Harmonic Society was established, for it was found necessary to invite a contingent of singers from the North of England to take up a residence in the Metropolis, employment being found for them for the hours when their vocal services were not required.

If it is necessary to account for the slow growth of operatic chorus, when compared with the progress made in other portions of the musical drama. a very simple reason can be found, in the fact of the difficulty attending the first performance of a variety of works when the singers have to commit the whole of their parts to memory. Straightforward as many of Handel's choruses are, it was found necessary to make some slight alterations in the choruses of such a work as " Acis and Galatea" when given on the stage. It is not difficult to gain the most sublime effects from chorus singing when the performers have the copies before their eyes. as the performance of oratorios and similar works by large choral societies can sufficiently testify.

In the Oratorio, the chorus is of the greatest importance, and the number of voices to a part is generally larger than it was in the time of Handel, though some writers question the advantage gained by multiplying the forces, as it is supposed by them that a greater number of voices does not necessarily produce a proportionate power of tone, and the difficulty of moving a large body in concert may involve a change of *tempi*, but this need not be the case with a trained body well acquainted with the works performed. It is said that " a chorus of thirty-five voices from the Pope's chapel who sang at the Coronation of Napoleon I., in the Cathedral of Notre-Dame, Paris, produced a far greater and more wonderful effect when they entered singing the *Tu es Petrus*, than another chorus of hundreds of voices, and eighty harps, that had been assembled and trained for the same occasion, in expectation of surpassing all that man could imagine." As the knowledge of music is more general in the present day, this objection cannot with reason be entertained now, otherwise the choruses at the Handel Festivals could not be held to be the most attractive features of such gatherings.

(5) The union of a number of voices for the joint performance of a composition. The whole of the male and female singers other than the principals whether in the oratorio, drama, or at a concert.

(6) The refrain or burden of a song whether sung by one or by many voices. As for example :

<blockquote>

(a) I lov'd a lass, a fair one,
    As fair as e'er was seen;
    She was indeed a rare one,
    Another Sheba Queen.
    But fool, as then I was
    I thought she lov'd me too,
    But now, alas ! she's left me.

Chorus.   Falero, lero, loo.

</blockquote>

GEORGE WITHER.

<blockquote>

(b) Lisette. dont l'empire
    S'étend jusqu'à mon vin,
    J'éprouve la martyre
    D'en demander en vain.

    Pour souffrir qu'à mon âge
    Les coups me soient comptés,
    Ai-je compté, volage,
    Tes infidelités ?

Chœur.   Lisette, ma Lisette,
    Tu m'as trompé toujours,
    Mais vive la grisette
    Je veux, Lisette,
    Boire à nos amours.

</blockquote>

BERANGER.

<blockquote>

(c) Lasst tanzen uns und springen,
    Hier, wo die Blumen stehn;
    Und frohe Lieder singen,
    Im Freien klingt es schön.

Chor.   Und frohe Lieder, &c.

</blockquote>

UHLAND.

(7) The name given to the mixture and compound stops in an organ.

Christe eleison (*Gk.*) A portion of the kyrie in the mass. [Mass.]

Christmas Carol. [Carol.]

Christmas Music. (1) Cantatas, the words of which are suitable to Christmas tide. (2) Music played by waits. [Waits.]

Chroma (*Gk.* χρῶμα, colour or complexion). The name of one of the modifications of the Greek musical scale. The principal chromatic scale of the Greeks was called χρῶμα *τοναἰον*; its chief characteristic is the omission of the 4th and 7th. [Greek Music.]

Chroma duplex (*Lat.*) (1) A semiquaver. (2) A double sharp.

Chromatic. That which includes notes not belonging to a diatonic scale.

(1) A chromatic chord is that which contains a note or notes foreign to diatonic progression, *e.g.*:

(2) Chromatic harmony is that which is made up of chromatic chords.

(3) A chromatic interval is that which is augmented or diminished, *e.g.*:

(4) Chromatic modulation is a passing into an extreme key, by means of chromatic harmony.

(5) A chromatic scale is one which consists of a succession of semitones.

Chromatique (*Fr.*) } Chromatic.
Chromatisch (*Ger.*) }

Chrotta. [Crowd.]

Church modes. [Plain Song.]

Ciaccona (*It.*) [Chaconne.]

Cicogna (*It.*) The mouth piece of a wind instrument; *lit.* a beak.

Cicuta (*Lat.*) A flute or pan-pipes, made from the stalks of the hemlock plant.

Cimbalo (*It.*) (1) Harpsichord. (2) *cimbali*, cymbals. (3) A tambourine.

Cimbel (*Ger.*) A mixture-stop in German organs.

Cimbelstern (*Ger.*) *Lit.* cymbal-star. A mechanical contrivance in some German organs, consisting of star-shaped cymbals attached to a wheel which is set in motion by a pedal.

Cink (*Ger.*) } A small reed stop on foreign
Cinq (*Fr.*) } organs.

Cinque (*It.*) A fifth part in concerted music.

Cinyra. An old term for a harp.

Circular Canon. A canon so constructed that it closes in the key one semitone above

that in which it commences. As, at each repeat, it begins, not at the *original* pitch, but at the pitch at which it closed, it is evident that twelve repetitions would take it through all the known keys.

Circulus (*Lat.*) A circle. One of the time signatures of early music. It was only applied to *tempus perfectum* and *tempus imperfectum*, that is to the division of a breve into semibreves. When the breve was divided into three semibreves (tempus perfectum) a complete circle was placed at the signature " quia forma rotunda perfecta est." When the breve was divided into two semibreves (tempus imperfectum) a broken circle or semicircle was used. This last sign is now corrupted into a C which is erroneously said to stand for *common* time. [Time.]

Cis (*Ger.*) The note C sharp.

Cis-cis (*Ger.*) The note C double sharp.

Cis dur (*Ger.*) The key of C sharp major.

Cis moll (*Ger.*) The key of C sharp minor.

Cistella (*Lat.*) A dulcimer, *lit.* a little box.

Cistre (*Fr.*) [Cittern.]

Cistrum. [Sistrum.]

Citara (*It.*) A cittern. A guitar.

Cithara (*Gk.* κιθάρα). The ancient lute. It probably differed from the lyre in having something behind the upper part of the strings, whereas the lyre-strings were open on both sides. [Guitar.]

Cithara bijuga. A guitar or lute having a *double neck*. Some of the strings passed along the side of the finger-board and could not therefore be stopped, and some of the higher strings were tuned in pairs in unison. Sometimes it was strung with *wire* and played with a plectrum like a cithara; at others, it was strung with cat-gut and played like a lute.

Citharœdus. One who sings whilst playing the cithara, whereas a *citharista* only played.

Citole. An instrument similar in form to the dulcimer. The name is supposed by some to be derived from *cistella* a little box; by others, from *cithara*, a guitar. It is frequently mentioned by early poets, apparently with various meanings. William Guiart (1248) says:—

" Qui le roi de France à celle crée
  Enveloppa si de parolles
  Plus douces que son de citoles."

Chaucer's allusion to it would imply that it was a kind of guitar:—"A citole in hir right hand had sche."

Cittern. An old English name for a guitar strung with wire instead of with gut. It had eight strings tuned to four notes *g*, *b*, *d*, and *e*, or corresponding intervals. The instrument was at one time very popular, a cittern being part of the furniture of a barber's shop, the customers amusing themselves with it while waiting. The music for the cittern was written in Tablature. There were several instruction books for the instrument issued, while it was still in use. The title of the earliest known is " The Cittharn Schoole, by Antony Holborne, Gentleman, and servant to Her Most Excellent Maiestie. Hereunto are added six short Airs, Neapolitan like to three voyces without the Instrument : done by his brother William Holborne. London, 1597." [Guitar.]

Civetteria, con (*It.*) In a coquettish manner.

Clairon (*Fr.*) [Clarion.]

Clang. (1) *Timbre* (*Fr.*) *Klang* (*Ger.*) Quality of tone. (2) The peculiar "ringing" noise or *din* produced by the clash of metals, or the blast of loud wind instruments. Lat. *clangor.* The Gk. κλαγγή is also applied to the *whiz* or *twang* caused by the discharge of an arrow, &c.

Clapper. [Bells.] [Bones.]

Claque (*Fr.*) A body of hired applause-makers, openly employed in France and sometimes secretly resorted to in England. The " claque " in France is divided into several ranks ; *rieurs, pleureurs, chatouilleurs, bisseurs*, and so forth. These officers distributed in several parts of the theatre, laugh, weep, gossip with their neighbours, cry *encore*, &c., under the direction of a fugle-man whose business it is to study the work produced, and after consultation with the author, the performers, and the stage manager, to direct and regulate the reception of certain portions of the entertainment.

Claque-bois (*Fr.*) [Gigelira.]

Clarabella. An organ stop consisting of open wood pipes, invented by Bishop. It is of a soft and sweet quality of tone. It is generally merged into a Stopped diapason below middle C, as the larger pipes do not produce a clear tone. It is usually of 8 ft. pitch.

Clara voce (*It.*) A clear voice.

Claribel Flute. An organ stop of similar construction to the clarabella, but generally of 4 ft. pitch.

Clarichord. A stringed instrument of mediæval times, by some writers presumed to be identical with the clavichord, the precursor of the spinet, harpsichord and pianoforte.

The earliest stringed instrument with a key-board for the fingers, is said to have been invented about the year 1300, in Italy, and to have been called Clavycytherium, the cithara or harp with keys. In the Musurgia of Luscinius, printed in 1536, a picture of this early instrument is given, but as there is no statement that it had been drawn from an existing example, and moreover, as it appeared nearly two centuries and a half after the supposed invention, its likeness is at the least rather doubtful. Trustworthy representations of keyed instruments are very rare before the latter of the above dates, and a consequent amount of confusion exists, as well with regard to forms as to names. In the few early English glossaries extant, no clear or lucid description of the majority of instruments in existence can be obtained, and many modern writers, misled by varied spelling, and the number of different names for the same thing, have exercised their wits in finding a variety of forms, shapes, and uses for that which was after all but of one character, and probably the same thing described variously. To speak of the older names of instruments of the kind now under consideration, the words clavichord, monochord, manichord, clavycymbal, cembalo, clavecin, all have the same meaning, a stringed instrument with keys played by hand. Some writers explain the words clavichord to be so called, because the strings were wrested in tune with a *key* (clavis) ;—this description would also apply to the clarichord, called also claricols, clarigold, &c., for that was kept in tune by a wrest, as William Cornishe in his poem, " A treatise betwene Trouthe and Enformacion." 1500, tells us. He says:

" The clarichorde hath a tunely kinde
As the wyre is wrested hye and lowe
So it tuneth to the players mynde,
For as it wrested so must it nede showe.
Any instrument mystuned shall hurt a trewe song,
Yet blame not the clarichord the wrester doth wrong."

By this it would appear that the clarichord was a kind of harp, tuned as it was required to be used, and it is somewhat singular that as the words clarichord, clarigols, clarigold, &c., are only used in ancient English writings, no form of them being found in old French or Latin, the derivation of the word from an ancient British etymon, such as *clar*, to grip or bend, would be applicable to the harp as an instrument whose strings were plucked or gripped, the modern Irish word for playing on harps is claꞃeoꞃꞃeꞃ (clarediser), and the harp itself is called claꞃꞃcaꞇ (clarscat), gripped or clawed string. The word ꞃcaꞇ might be compared with the German Saite.

Dr. Rimbault, after quoting the definitions of the word clarichord given by a few of the lexicographers of the 17th century, observes that they make " no distinction between the terms clarichord and clavichord, but the one can hardly be a corruption of the other." He adds that the " words suggest a totally different etymology," and he then proposes that it might be from the French word *claire*, denoting a transparent tone; but in the earliest musical dictionaries clarichord is said to be "called also the Dumb spinet, on account of the cords being covered with pieces of cloth." The Clavechord or clavecimbalo is said to signify a harpsichord. In every instance in which the word clarichord is employed before the 16th century it might be fairly be translated harp.

At the marriage of James of Scotland with the Princess Margaret, in the year 1503, "the king began before hyr to play of the clarychordes and after of the lute. And upon the said clarychorde Sir Edward Stanley played a ballade and sange therewith." (Warton, "History of English Poetry.") It is quite possible that the similarity of the two letters v and r in ancient MSS. might have led the transcribers to mistake one for the other, and by writing clarichord or clavichord indiscriminately they might innocently cause controversy. All modern authorities on the subject declare that the words are of separate and distinct origin. [Pianoforte.]

Clarin (*Ger.*) A species of trumpet, a clarion, also an organ reed stop of 4 ft. pitch. *Clarin-blasen*, the sound of a trumpet. Sometimes the word is applied to the soft tones produced on this instrument.

Clarinet
Clarinette (*Fr.*) } An important wind instrument said to have
Clarinetto (*It.*) } been invented by John Christopher Denner, who was born in Leipsic, in 1654, but it was in reality only a modification and improvement of the more ancient *shawm* or *chalameau*. Most authors relate that Denner invented the instrument in 1659, at which date he was four years old; but it was made by him after his residence in Nuremberg, in 1690. The name clarinet, or *clarionet* was probably attached to it on account of its pure and brilliant tone not unlike that of the clarion or trumpet. In modern instruments of this class, the tone has been rendered far purer and sweeter than that originally produced. The difference between the tone of the hautboy and that of the clarinet, is due to the circumstance that the one has a double, and the other a single reed. The difference in the nature of the scale arises from the fact that the hautboy is conical, while the clarinet is a cylinder, the series of harmonics in the hautboy following each other in the ratio 1, 2, 3, 4, &c., those of the clarinet 1, 3, 5, 7, &c., hence, that whereas the first *overtone* of the former is its octave, the first *overtone* of the latter is its twelfth. On this fact depends the difficulty of making shakes and of playing rapid passages on certain parts of the clarinet. All sudden changes from the end of the first range of twelve notes to the commencement of the second series, are difficult, some impossible.

The compass of the instrument is about three octaves and a half from tenor E, including all the intermediate semitones. The clarinet being of the nature of a stopped pipe, as to its harmonics, can be played from its lowest note E up to twelve notes higher without a break by means of its keys. At this point the player has to increase the pressure of wind, and commence a new series of sounds, the transition between these two registers forming the chief difficulty in "clarinet blowing." The registers are four in number, and are as follows:

1. The low includes all notes between

2. The second between

3. The third between

4. The fourth comprises all remaining notes from

The first two registers are called the "chalameau part," and when this is employed for any continued time it is written an octave higher, with the direction "chal, or chalameau" to the player. There are three lengths of tubing employed for the clarinet, by which means the instrument may be made to sound three different scales according as the tube is short or long. The longer tube is used for the A clarinet, a medium for the B flat, and the shorter for the C.

As the fingering is in each case the same in each instrument it has been found convenient to adopt C as the normal scale, so that a piece of music apparently the same to the eye is different to the ear, according to the clarinet employed. Thus the passage written as follows:

When played upon a C clarinet would sound as it stands, upon an A clarinet would sound:

And upon a B flat clarinet, as:

It is, however, easy to make each instrument give out the same notes by employing a change in the signature, thus the passage for the A clarinet should be written:

And for the B flat clarinet:

when they will each give the sounds as written in No. 1.

The kind of clarinet required is usually stated at the commencement, as clarinet in A, B flat, or C, and whenever a change is needed during the progress of a piece, the same is indicated during a period of rest for the instrument, by the words change to A, B, or C, as the case may be.

The advantage of a change of clarinet is that complicated scales upon one instrument become easy upon another. For instance the scale of F sharp major which is very difficult on a C clarinet, when played upon an A clarinet is fingered as A major, the real sounds produced being those of the scale of F sharp major. Similarly the scale of D flat major would become the scale of E flat major on a B flat clarinet. This accounts for the fact that the clarinet part in a full score is sometimes in a flat key while the movement is in a sharp key. For example a piece in the key of E minor (one sharp) not uncommonly has a part for an A clarinet written, of course, in G minor with two flats.

The favourite (because easy) keys of the clarinet are the keys of C, F, and G, B flat, E flat, A flat and D with their relative minors. Hence the skill of the composer is shown in writing for that clarinet capable of producing the best effects in certain keys.

Clarinets are usually employed in pairs, and the parts are ordinarily written on one stave. They, in conjunction with the two bassoons similarly written, form a grand basis or support for all the other wind instruments. The small E flat clarinet (playing a minor third above the notes actually written) is used in military bands. Its tone is shrill and piercing. The introduction of the clarinet as a regular instrument in the orchestra of the opera is due to J. Christian Bach, who wrote special parts for a pair of clarinets in his opera "Orione, ossia Diana vendicata," which was produced in London in 1763.

Clarinettista (*It.*) **Clarinettiste** (*Fr.*) A performer on the clarinet.

Clarinetto (*It.*) [Clarinet.]

Clarino (*It.*) (1) A trumpet. (2) An organ stop, consisting of reed pipes, generally of 4-ft. pitch.

Clausula (*Lat.*) A close or cadence, *e.g.*:

clausula falsa, a false cadence; *clausula finalis*, a final cadence, &c.

Clavecin (*Fr.*) (1) A harpsichord. (2) The keys by means of which the *carilloneur* plays upon the bells. [Pianoforte.]

Claviatur (*Ger.*) (1) The key board of an organ or pianoforte. (2) Fingering.

Clavi-cembalum (*Lat.*) Clavicembalo (*It.*) [Pianoforte.]

Clavichord. [Clarichord.]

Clavicylinder. An instrument in the form of tubes or cylinders of glass, invented by Chladni. There was another instrument with the same name made of plates of glass of graduated lengths, the tone of which was produced by hammers set in motion by a key-board.

Clavicytherium. [Clarichord.]

Claviglissando. An instrument with a key-board, invented by C. W. Le Jeune, which is intended to combine the properties of the violin and harmonium—of the violin in obtaining a slide or portamento, and the harmonium in the capability of imitating the tones of various wind instruments.

Clavier (*Ger.*) (1) The pianoforte. (2) A
Clavier (*Fr.*) row of keys on an organ.

Clavierauszug (*Ger.*) A pianoforte score, as opposed to *Partitur*, a full score.

Clef (*Lat. clavis.*) The sign placed at the commencement of a staff or stave, showing the absolute pitch, the lines without it showing only the *relative* distances of sounds. When it was found that *neumes* could be better interpreted by the use of lines, a red and a yellow line were used, it being understood that the former bore the note F, the latter C. It is easy to see, that the fact having been once established that lines could represent notes, it would be found much easier to attach the letter itself to the commencement of the lines, than to *colour* the line. The coloured lines were invented by Guido, but Walter Odington (13th century) used one of the letters of the musical notes as a clef to his stave of four lines. At this period, it was not usual to employ leger lines, but if the voice exceeded in compass beyond the limit of the stave, the position of the clef was altered; a practice still retained in plain-song books. [Notation.] The letters C and F were most commonly used in all ecclesiastical music up to the time of Palestrina, after which other clefs were introduced.

There were five sorts of clefs in use in the 16th century, namely, the gamut Γ, from the Greek gamma, the F, C, g and d clefs. These were ultimately reduced to three, the gamut and the d clefs being found to be unnecessary. The position of the clefs was held to represent a certain pitch, and as it was supposed that the scale was incapable of extension beyond the notes indicated by the clefs gamut and d, their places marked the boundary of ecclesiastical compass. The other clefs might be made moveable if needed, for reasons already intimated, but whatever the number of lines above or below the clefs, each clef represented a particular sound. Thus, the F clefs indicated F *finale*, the C clef, *acutum*, and the G clef, G *superacutum*, &c. Many of the musical treatises of the 16th century contain a chapter "De Clavibus signatis," which is interesting as showing the form of the clefs as then employed.

All the writers of these tracts distinguish between the clefs proper to plain-song, and those employed for figurate or mensurable music. In the following copies of these arrangements of clefs, those for plain-song are on the left, and those for figurate music on the right. No. 1, from Finck's "Practica Musica," 1556:

Signa
clavium
in utroque
cantu.

Et ponuntur omnes in lineali situ, quædam tamen sunt magis familiares, utpote F et C, g rariuscule. Γ vero et dd rarissime utimur. Unde, Linea signatas sustentat scilicet omnes. Et distant inter se mutuo per diapentem. F tamen γάμμα distinguat septima quamvis.

No. 2, from "Erotemata Musices Practicæ," by Ambrosius Wilphlingsederus, 1563:

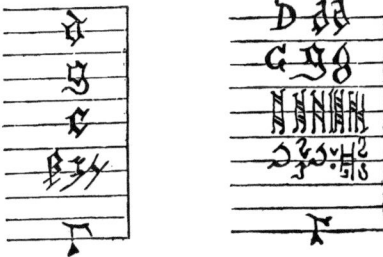

In chorali cantu simpliciter
prescribuntur ita.

In mensurali vero hoc modo.

No. 3, from "Erotemata Musicæ," by Lucas Lossius, 1570:

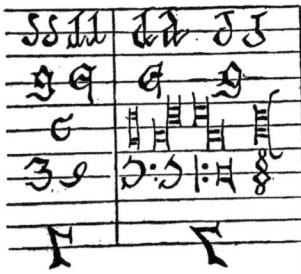

In cantu chorali.

In cantu figurali.

In later times three clefs F, C and G were

found sufficient for all purposes. The C clef appears upon all lines but the fifth.

The first is called the *Soprano*, and is most frequently found in ecclesiastical music, though it not uncommonly indicates the treble voice part in modern full scores. The second is called the *Mezzo Soprano*, and is assigned to second treble, and sometimes alto voices, and in music of the early part of the 18th century is often used for the tenor violin. The third is the *Alto*, and the fourth the *Tenor* clef; the former being used for alto voices, violas, and the highest trombone, the latter by tenor voices, trombones and the upper register of the bassoon and violoncello. The F clef is placed upon the fourth line of the stave and is used for all bass voices and instruments. When it is found upon the third line as in some old music it is called the baritone clef:

The following quotations from music books of various dates will show the forms through which the several clefs have passed. The "Compendium Musicæ," by Lampardius, 1537, is supposed to be the earliest printed book in which the G clef is used in a shape nearly similar to that now employed:

In Lully's and other French scores it is sometimes placed upon the *first* line:

In this position it was called the "French violin clef;" and in an earlier work by Christopher Demantius, "Isagoge Artis Musicæ," 1656, it appears upon the third line:

In "Ayres and Dialogues for one, two, and three voyces," by Henry Lawes, 1653, the forms of the clefs are as follows:

In Christopher Simpson's "Compendium of

Practical Musick," 1678, the clefs are in this shape :

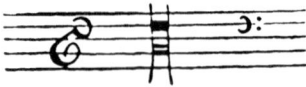

Playford's Psalms, third edition, 1697, the following are the forms :

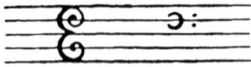

Matthew Wilkins's "Book of Psalmody," 1699:

Dr. Croft's "Thirty Select Anthems," 1724:

Godfrey Keller's "Rules for playing a thorow-bass," 1731:

Emanuel Bach's "Sechs leichte Clavier Sonaten," 1766 :

Malcolm, "A Treatise of Music," 1779 :

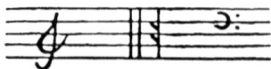

Shield's "Introduction to Harmony," 1800 :

In many modern French music books the F clef is written thus :

In this a resemblance to the letter F, the ancient clef sign for this pitch, may be traced. Many writers have maintained that clefs create difficulties in the way of a "right understanding of music," and have therefore suggested their removal or the substitution of simpler signs.

Thomas Salmon, 1676, proposed the use of the letter T, for the treble clef, M for the mean or C clef, and B for the bass clef. His proposal led him into a controversy with Matthew Locke, which was maintained on both sides in language not very creditable to either. Francis Delafond, in 1725, suggested the use of one clef only, the F, or bass clef. A century later, Miss Glover, in a pamphlet explaining her views on what she called the Tetrachordal System, proposed to abolish all clefs, a proposition which has since been carried out in the Tonic-Sol-fa method of teaching singing. The use of the treble clef for all purposes has also been recently advocated, but with little success.

Clivus (*Lat.*) [Neumes.]

Clocca (*Med. Lat.*) A bell. Irish *clog*, a small bell. Fr. *cloche*. Ger. *Glocke*.

Cloche (*Fr.*) A bell.

Clochettes (*Fr.*) Hand-bells.

Clock, to. To set a bell in vibration, by attaching a rope to the clapper, and swinging it to and fro till it strikes the side of the bell which remains stationary. It is an undesirable practice, as many valuable bells have in this manner been cracked.

Clokerre (*Old Eng.*) *Clocherre* (*Old Fr.*) A belfry. In low Latin, *clocherium*.

Close harmony. Harmony produced by drawing the parts which form it closely together.

Close play. A direction in lute playing. The following explanation of the term is from Barley's Lute book : " Thou shalt not neede but to remoove those fingers which thou shalt be forced, which manner of handling we call *close* or *covert* play." It would appear to correspond to the *smooth style* sometimes adopted on the organ or other keyed instruments.

Clynke-bell. [Chimes.]

C moll (*Ger.*) C minor.

Coalottino. [Concertino.]

Coda (*It.*) (1) The tail of a note. (2) The bars occasionally added to a contrapuntal movement after the close or finish of the *canto fermo*. (3) The few chords or bars attached to an infinite canon in order to render it finite ; or a few chords *not in canon*, added to a finite canon for the sake of obtaining a more harmonious conclusion. (4) An adjunct to the ordinary close of a sonata, or symphony, &c., for the purpose of enforcing the *final* character of the movement.

Codetta (*It.*) *dim.* of coda. A short coda.

Codon (*Gk. κώδων.*) (1) A small bell, such as those attached to the trappings of horses. (2) A crier's bell. (3) The bell of a trumpet (Fr. *pavillon*). (4) A trumpet with a bell-mouth.

Cogli stromenti (*It.*) With the instruments.

Coi (*It.*) With; *e.g. coi bassi,* with the basses; *coi violini,* with the violins.

Col (*It.*) With ; *e.g.* :

Col arco, with the bow.
Col basso, with the bass.
Col canto, with the melody.
Colla destra, with the right hand.
Coll' arco, with the bow.
Colla parte, with the principal part.
Colla punta dell' arco, with the point of the bow.
Colla sinistra, with the left hand.
Colla voce, with the voice.

College of Organists. A modern institution established in London, for the purpose of strengthening and improving the position of organ players, granting diplomas, and of providing suitable performers for the service of the church.

College youths. A London Society of bell ringers, formerly confined to members of the universities.

Col legno (*It.*) With the wood. A direction to strike the strings of a violin with the back or wood of the bow.

Collet de violon (*Fr.*) The neck of a violin.

Collinet (*Fr.*) [Flageolet.]

Colophony. Colofonia (*It.*) Colophonium (*Lat.*) Colophonie (*Fr.*) Resin. The gum used for making the hair of bows rough, so as to set the strings freely into vibration. So called from Colophon in Greece (κολοφωνία, and ῥητίνη, gum.)

Color (*Lat.*) Colour. A term variously employed in mediæval treatises on music to represent : a repetition of a sound in part music (repititio ejusdem vocis); purity of tone (pulchritudo soni) ; a movement of the voice from the part (florificatio vocis) ; an alteration of rhythm by different voices (idem sonus repetitus in tempore diverso a diversis vocibus) ; a discord purposely introduced for the sake of variety (aliquando unus eorum ponitur in discordantiam propter *colorem* musicæ). Some have gathered from the definition— " Repetitio diversæ vocis est idem sonus repetitus in tempore diverso a diversis vocibus," that a musical *canon* is meant to be described. (2) The coloured lines first used for the purpose of rendering *neumes* more intelligible. " Quamvis perfecta sit positura neumarum, cæca omnino est et nihil valet sine adjunctione literarum vel *colorum* " (Guido). [See Clef and Notation.]

Coloratura (*It.*) Divisions, runs, trills, cadenzas, and other florid passages in vocal music.

Coloscione or **Colachon.** A species of guitar, called also Bichordon or Trichordon, according as it was strung.

Come (*It.*) As, like ; *e.g.* :
Come prima. As at first. *Come sta,* as it stands.

Comes (*Lat.*) The answer to the *Dux* or subject. [Fugue.]

Comic opera. An opera in which the incidents are of a humorous description. The comic opera is of Italian origin and French development, each subject treated by musicians of other nations owing its rise either to some one or other theme already taken by French composers of comic operas, or from the vaudevilles which preceded, and formed the pattern of, the comic operas. Boieldieu, Herold, Auber, Adam, Thomas, Offenbach, Lecocq, are the most successful representatives of the modern school of comic opera writers. [Vaudeville, Opera, &c.]

Comic song. A song developing in humorous verse some ludicrous idea or incident set to a tune already popular, or with a melody easy to be caught up by the hearers, in order that they may be ready when called upon to join in the chorus which usually accompanies such songs. Songs of a humorous description are of high antiquity, but as their humour is generally of a bad character, specimens of this class of literature are not fitted either for general or for particular readers. The ballads and stories which would please an audience of a past age and which have found their way into many collections of ancient songs, are scarcely respectable even for their antiquity.

Comma. The small interval between a major and a minor tone, that is between a tone whose ratio is 8 : 9 and one whose ratio is 9 : 10. The ratio of a comma is therefore 80 : 81. A Pythagorean comma is the difference between the note produced by taking 7 octaves upwards and 12 fifths.

Common chord. A note accompanied by its major or minor 3rd and perfect 5th. [Harmony.] In thorough bass, the figure 3, a sharp, flat or natural, as the case may be, or the absence of any letter, character, or figure, denotes the common chord of the bass note. When there is more than one chord on the same bass note, the common chord is figured $\frac{5}{3}$.

Common or Duple time. Time with two beats in a bar or any multiple of two beats in a bar. The beats may be of the value of any note or rest or compound of notes and rests, providing the sum required by the time sign be exactly contained in each bar. Common time is of two kinds, simple and compound. Simple common time is that which includes four beats in a bar, or any division of that number, or square of the number or its divisions. The signs used to express simple common time are the following: $\frac{2}{1}, \frac{2}{2}, \frac{2}{4}, \frac{4}{4}, \frac{4}{8}$, and the characters C and ₵. In these signs the upper figure denotes the quantity of notes required in the bar, and the lower figure the quality of the notes, 1 signifying a semibreve, 2 a minim, 4 a crotchet, 8 a quaver, and so on, each figure showing the relative proportionate value to the semibreve which is now reckoned as the time-standard. The sign (C) is called the sign of alla capella time, and is usually followed by four minims in a bar, played or sung in slow time; the sign (₵) is called the sign of alla breve time, and has also four or eight minims in a bar played or sung in a shorter time, as its title implies. The use of words directing the pace in which pieces of music are intended to be taken, has created a certain amount of confusion in the use and meaning of all the time signs descriptive of form in a bar [Expression, Time]. Compound common-time is expressed by the signs $\frac{6}{4}$, $\frac{6}{8}$, $\frac{12}{8}$, such signs meaning two or four beats of three crotchets or quavers to each beat.

In mediæval music a circle O was used to indicate what was called perfect time (tempus perfectum), a portion of the circle being omitted C showed that the time was imperfect, a line through the latter sign ₵ meant a more rapid pace than that required when the C alone was used. When these signs were reversed they implied that the music was to be taken faster than if they were in their ordinary places. Thus the degree of rapidity would be shown by the time signs arranged as follows : O C Ɔ ₵ Ɔ̸

Commodamente (*It.*) *lit.* in a convenient manner. Easily, quietly.

Commodo (*It.*) Easily, at will, without haste.

Compagnia del gonfalone (*It.*) An ancient society of mystery or miracle play actors established at Rome, in 1264, who illustrated their dramatic performances of sacred subjects with music. They took their name from the banner (gonfalone) which they bore. Their performances are supposed by some writers to have suggested the Oratorio.

Company of Musicians. One of the chartered companies of the City of London, which, like the majority of such companies, has become by time perverted from the original purpose of its foundation. The charter was granted by King Charles I., in 1636, to divers musicians under the style and title of the Marshal, Wardens, and Commonality of the Art and Science of Music, in Westminster, in the County of Middlesex. This charter was confirmed by letters patent from King Charles II.

Compass. The whole range of sounds capable of being produced by a voice or instrument.

Compiacevole (*It.*) Pleasant, agreeable, charming.

Complement. The interval which must be added to any other interval, so that the whole shall be equal to an octave; *e.g.*, the complement of a 3rd is a 6th; that of a 4th, a 5th; of a 5th, a 4th; and so on. It will be seen that the intervals are always considered as overlapping.

Compline (from the Lat. completorium). The short evening service which *completes* the day-hours.

Composer. (1) An author of music. One who " finds out musical tunes." (2) An inventor and arranger of a series of changes in bell ringing.

Composition. (1) A piece of music, for voices or instruments, or a combination of both effects, constructed according to the rules of art. (2) The art of composing music, guided by scientific rules. (3) In an organ, the particular combination of sounds which form a compound stop. (4) A mechanical arrangement on the organ by which certain combinations of stops may be employed or not, at the wish of the performer, upon his opening or closing a valve, or by using a pedal which acts upon the sliders.

Composizione (*It.*) A composition.

Composizione di Tavolino (*It.*) Table music. Convivial compositions, *c.f.* Ger. *Lieder-tafel*. [Chamber music.]

Compound intervals. Intervals greater than an octave, as opposed to *simple* intervals which are less than an octave.

Compound Stops. Organ stops having more than one rank of pipes.

Compound Times. Times in which the bar is divided into two or more *groups* of notes, *e.g.*, $\frac{6}{8}$ which consists of two groups of three notes; $\frac{9}{8}$ which consists of three groups of three, &c. Compound Times are classified as duple or triple, according to the number of groups in each bar, not according to the number of notes in each group; *e.g.*, $\frac{6}{8}$ is a duple time; $\frac{9}{8}$ a triple time; $\frac{12}{8}$ (four groups of three) a duple time, &c. The principal accent falls on the first note in each bar, and a subordinate accent on the first note of each group.

Comus (*Gk.* κῶμος). A revel, carousal, merry making with music and dancing. The revellers paraded the street crowned, carrying torches, and sang verses in praise of the gods or the victors in the games.

Comus. (*Gk.* κομμός). A mournful song sung in alternate verses by an actor and a chorus in the Attic drama.

Con (*It.*) With; *e.g. con amore*, with affection ; *con moto*, with spirited movement; *con sordini*, with the mutes on, &c. (See the words to which it is prefixed.)

Concento (*It.*) Harmony.

Concentus (*Lat.*) (concinno). Musical

harmony, Part music; *e.g., concentus vocis Lyrœque.* Consonance; *e.g., concentus tubarum ac cornuum.*

Concert. (1) A performance of music in which several executants are employed. Concerts of music, to which the general public is admitted by payment, are of comparatively recent origin in the history of music. Public musical performances, more or less connected with state or religion, were anciently given from time to time, on occasions of importance. Kings, nobles, and civic officials, employed musicians in their trains, but their performances could scarcely be considered in the light of concerts. Organized bands of musicians who performed in the houses of the great and wealthy; "waits" and "noises" are frequently mentioned in old records, but concerts of music in hired houses, assembly rooms of taverns, &c., apart and distinct from the "entertainment" ordinarily provided at hostelries are rare before the time of Charles II. Pepys, in his Diary, speaks of "musick meetings" and "concerts," but they were private affairs, and therefore not within the meaning of the term as now understood. The first public concert in England was given at Oxford, in the year 1670, the first in London two years later. After which a periodical concert was established in Aylesbury Street, Clerkenwell, over the shop of Thomas Britton, the musical small-coalman. Before this time musicians roved from tavern to tavern, instruments in hand, waiting the pleasure of the guests "if they were willing to heare any musick." These bands of fiddlers played by the hour together such popular tunes as were best calculated to delight audiences gathered *impromptu*. But from all that can be learned, their performance was not scientific; "for the most part it was that of violins, hautboys, and trumpets, without any diversity of parts, and consequently in the unison."

The advertisement of the first London concert is still extant, and runs as follows :—

"These are to give notice, that at Mr. John Banister's house (now called the Musick School) over against the George Tavern, in White Fryers, this present Monday, will be music performed by excellent masters, beginning precisely at 4 of the clock in the afternoon, and every afternoon for the future, precisely at the same hour. *London Gazette*, Dec. 30th, 1672." From this time forward concerts of all kinds, vocal and instrumental, given not only "by excellent masters" but also by those who cannot with justice be called either "masters" or "excellent," become common enough. It would be both tedious and unnecessary to trace the history of concerts step by step, neither is it to the present pur-

pose to describe in detail the several sorts of concerts which have taken place since that given "over against the George Tavern." It may not, however, be uninteresting to state that the word has been applied to the performance of oratorios in church as the following quotation will show :

"The Oratorios for the opening of the elegant Organ now erected in the Minster, at Beverley, will be on the 20th, 21st, and 22nd of September, 1769, viz :

"On Wednesday the 20th, the Sacred Oratorio of the Messiah.

"On Thursday, the 21st, the Oratorio of Judas Maccabæus.

"On Friday the 22nd, the Oratorio of Samson; and that being the Anniversary of the King's Coronation, the Performance will conclude with Mr. Handel's grand Coronation Anthem.

"The first violin by Mr. Giardini. The principal voices by Mrs. Hudson, of York, Miss Radcliffe, Mr. Norris, and Mr. Matthews, both of Oxford. The remainder of the band will be numerous, and will consist of the best performers, vocal and instrumental, that can be procured.

"Tickets for the Great Aisle at 5s. each. Galleries at 2s. 6d. each, to be had of Mr. Hawdon, organist, of Mr. Norris, at the Bell, and of Mrs. Todd, at the Tyger, in Beverley; of Mr. Forster, carver, in Salthouse Lane, and of Mr. Ferraby, Bookseller, in the Butchery, in Hull. Of whom may be had Books of the Oratorios, with Mr. Handell's Alterations and Additions, as they will be performed at Beverley. Price 4d. each. The North doors will be open'd at Ten in the Morning, and the Concert to begin at Eleven. The Great Aisle will be fill'd with Benches, And to add to the solemnity of the performance, the singers will be dress'd in surplices.

"All tickets transferable. No Money taken at the Door.

"A Concerto upon the Organ each Day. And Mr. Giardini will oblige the company with a Solo.

☞"An Assembly on Wednesday and Friday."

Concertante (*It.*) (1) A composition suitable for performance at a concert. (2) A composition in which several of the parts are in turn brought into prominence.

Concerted music. Music for two or more performers, either vocal or instrumental, as opposed to a vocal or instrumental solo, with or without accompaniment by a single instrument.

Concertina (*Eng.*) A portable musical instrument of hexagonal form, invented by Professor Wheatstone, consisting of a series of vibrating metal reeds acted upon and set in motion by the current of air, caused by a bellows placed in the body of the instrument connecting the two ends in which the metal tongues or springs are fixed and worked by the player, both hands being in such a position that the wrists move the bellows while the fingers are free to press the stops or keys which cause it to sound. The compass of the concertina is of three and a half octaves with intermediate semitones from fiddle G :

Each note in this scale is double, that is to say, is capable of being produced by the inspiration or respiration of the bellows. [Accordion.]

Concertina (*Ger.*) An instrument of shape similar to the English concertina, but of less finished appearance and more limited compass. The bellows excites the vibration of the free metallic reeds as in the English concertina, but the scale instead of being double is single, that is, the respiratory note is different to the inspiratory note, and has only those chromatic notes necessary for the modulation of melody into the tonic or dominant of the scale in which the instrument is tuned. There is also an escape valve to allow the passage of superfluous air, a contrivance not necessary on the English concertina, where the notes are of double sound. The German concertina is capable of being performed only in the one key in which it is tuned, the English concertina can be played in any key.

Concertino (*It.*) (1) The principal instrument in a concerto as *violino concertino*. (2) The diminutive of concerto.

Concerto (*It.*) (1) A concert. (2) A composition for the display of the qualities of some especial instrument, accompanied by others of a similar or dissimilar character. A concerto may be for a solo violin, or violoncello with an accompaniment for strings, or wind; or it may be for a pianoforte, violin, or any wind instrument, and a full band. Those for pianoforte, violin, or organ, are generally made of more classical character than those for any wind instrument, as in many cases the last named are constructed by the performers themselves with the object of exhibiting their own accomplishments, and their artistic taste. In a work by Scipio Bargaglia, published in Venice, 1587, "Trattimenti ossia divertimenti da Sonare," the word concerto is applied to a piece for a solo instrument with accompaniment, probably for the first time. The concerto is usually constructed in symphonic form, but without a minuet or scherzo. Though the early concertos show some deviation from the plan now accepted, they were, however,

designed according to rules or plans, accepted or allowed from time to time. The concertos of Corelli, Torelli, Bach, Tartini, and writers of the periods in which those masters lived are only different from their suites in that a solo instrument has the accompaniment of other instruments.

Torelli (1683-1708) was the first writer who suggested an extension of the number of instruments employed in a concerto, and by this means pointed the way to the symphony. He called this sort of composition "Concerto Grosso." In his plan he gives certain phrases to one or more solo instruments which are repeated by the full band employed. Handel constructed his "Concerti Grossi" on the same model. Vivaldi (1690-1743) further developed the idea; Gossec, Haydn, and Mozart settled the form as it stands at present, and Beethoven, Weber, and Mendelssohn have left noble examples of their musical powers in their works of this class.

Concerto spirituale (*It.*) Concert spirituel (*Fr.*) A concert formed of a miscellaneous selection of vocal and instrumental pieces with words of a sacred character. The concerts spirituels in Paris were founded in the year 1725.

Concertmeister (*Ger.*) The leader of the band, the conductor.

Concert-spieler (*Ger.*) A performer; a solo-player; the player of a concerto.

Concert-stück (*Ger.*) A concert piece, a concerto.

Concha (*Lat.*) A trumpet in the conventional form of a shell fish; Triton's horn; a conch.

Concitato (*It.*) Moved, disturbed, agitated.

Concord. [Harmony.]

Conductor. (1) A director or leader of an orchestra or chorus. It is supposed that a leader or a fugleman was employed by the Assyrians, to regulate the rhythm of the songs or dances; he was armed with two sticks, one of which he beat against the other, and so marked the time or accent.

Among the Greeks the Coryphœus or exarchus led the dance, and in everything requiring united action, a leader or conductor by his voice or certain understood gestures secured the desired result. The word in connection with music has several applications. It signifies one who directs with a bâton the performance of a band of players. It is also applied to one who accompanies vocal or instrumental pieces on the pianoforte. A conductor, as an independent time beater, was not known until the end of the last century. The player who sat at the harpsichord gave the time to the leader of the band, who, directing his subordinates, was called conductor. [Orchestra.]

(2) The inventor or leader of a chime, or

change in bell ringing, is also known as the conductor or composer.

Conductus (*Lat.*) The name given to a certain vocal composition in parts, in the 13th and 14th centuries. It has been variously described as a composition having descant on an *original* melody (qui vult facere conductum, primum cantum debet invenire pulchriorem quam potest, &c., *Franco of Cologne*); on an original or borrowed theme (conducti sunt compositi explicabilibus canticis decoris cognitis vel inventis, &c., *Walter Odington*). The definition of John of Garland points to an elaborate construction: "conductus autem est super unum metrum, multiplex consonans cantus qui etiam secundarias recipit consonantias." . . . "In florificatione vocis fit color ut commixtio in conductis simplicibus." Conducti were sometimes sung without words. They were called simple, double, triple, or quadruple, but the real distinction between the different kinds cannot be clearly learnt from the old treatises. All the information which can be brought together will be found in Coussemaker's *L'Art harmonique aux XIIe et XIIIe siècles.*

Cone Gamba. [Bell Gamba.]

Confrérie de St. Julien. A Society of Musicians in France, at one period possessing great power. At the end of the 13th century, the troubadours ceased to exist, the "courts of love" were closed, the sentiment of the troubadour poetry was no longer enjoyed, and the excesses of the singers and poets were the things for which they were best or worst remembered. Their followers, no longer having poetry as a veil and excuse for their peculiarities, became disreputable, and led a wandering, careless, and shifty life; the sins of their masters were visited upon their devoted heads, and they became Ishmaelites against whom every man's hand was raised, and who had inclination but not power to lift hand against every man. They were no longer welcome for their skill at all times as heretofore. They were no longer free to enter the houses of the great and wealthy "without leave and license previously had and obtained," as they had been when in attendance upon some poet prince or troubadour sovereign. It was, however, necessary that they should live, and those that did not become openly dishonest, "robbers on the king's highway with a gallows at the end of it," sought the means of livelihood in another sphere than that to which they had previously been always welcomed in. The love for music still existed among a lower class of people, and these gladly received the musicians and performers "whose strains had made many a gentle heart beat quickly," as a proof of their own elevation of taste in matters of courtesy and refinement. Gathering courage by the patronage bestowed upon them, and deeming it needful to "sort their humours" to those of the people for whose amusement they exercised their calling, they made a change in their programme and spoke out openly that which had hitherto been conveyed only through a delicate innuendo. Their success was complete, and to save the effect of troubles which might arise from an ungodly enterprise, they became apparently religious, placed themselves under the protection of a patron saint, Julien, Archbishop of Toledo, who after having led a life of vicissitude and vagabondage, died in 662, and became the tutelar protector of all vagabonds except thieves—who were committed to the care of St. Nicholas. There was also another Saint who divided the honours of their devotions, Genesius, a comedian, who was martyred for his Christianity at the end of the 4th century. Under the care of these two patrons, the musicians flourished, and in the year 1330, settled themselves in the good city of Paris, and formed themselves into a guild for mutual protection and support. The title by which they were enrolled was that of the "Compagnons, jongleurs, menestreux or menestriers," and this title sufficiently indicated their position of *companions, yokefellows,* and *servants* to the former troubadours. They had sufficient interest left with the friends and connexions of their old masters to obtain "sealed letters" in November 27th, 1331, recognising their position; and they lived together in one street, hence, called *St. Julien des ménétriers.* To this quarter all had to come who desired their services, and as the minstrels became further encouraged and increased in numbers they assumed a line of conduct which caused William de Germont, Prefect of Paris, to place various restrictions upon them, which were continued with additions and modifications by his successors.

By a decree issued in the year 1393, the pain of imprisonment was visited upon all members of the guild who offended by reciting scurrilous and scandalous verses either in the streets or in the houses of those who hired them. This check caused a division of the society, the one part devoting itself to the practice of tumbling and rope-dancing—these were called *baceleurs*—the other carrying on the music-entertaining business—took to viol playing, and marked a certain progress in their art, by the introduction of bass instruments hitherto not used by them. They distinguished themselves by the title of "*Ménestrels joueurs d'instrumens tant haut que bas.*" By this name they were recognised by Charles VI., who gave them letters patent dated April 14th, 1401. Armed with this document they elected a chief called "Roi des ménestrels," and they built and endowed a chapel in the Rue St. Martin, as much to conciliate the ecclesiastical powers, as to mark their attachment to religious forms. They had a monopoly of all music in France, especially in Paris; no one could learn an instrument without employing a member of the confraternity, no one could give a banquet of music without the leave and license of the Confrérie de St. Julien. Even the king, not to speak of the mayor of Paris, was compelled to be indebted to them for the after dinner amusement of his guests, as well as for the means of giving brilliancy to pageants, processions, and other state businesses. The Confrérie were all-important in the matter of vocal and instrumental music; they had the monopoly of the court and municipal music of Paris until the reign of Louis XIV., who in 1658 was weak enough to confirm their charter and privileges. These privileges must have been great, for they allowed the title of musician to be possessed by those who had funds sufficient to purchase fellowship in the guild: musical skill was of no import, for neither city or court cared for the performances of the Confrérie, though they were compelled to pay handsomely for that which they would rather have dispensed with. If the cultivation of true musical science had been the object in the maintenance of the guild, musical composition from the 14th to the 17th centuries would have been less of a puzzle and annoyance than it is: but unfortunately for the body, in course of time, pressure from without was brought to bear, and the whole thing collapsed, though not without a struggle. From the date when attention was drawn to it for its inefficiency and incompetency, to the day when it finally ceased to exist, no less a period than 100 years elapsed. Louis XIV. in 1660 happened to hear a piece of music by a rising composer called Jean Baptiste Lully, and thinking that it was exactly the sort of lullaby or reveillé he should like to hear performed in his own palace, desired to have it executed by his own court band, but, alas! they were musicians only in name, and this little request gave them trouble. But they plucked up courage; the king was informed that they held their places by prescriptive right, and as it had not been the custom for the "Musiciens du Roi," to exercise the art which they professed and were paid for, for many generations, the king's request was unreasonable and unconstitutional. The confraternity would still enjoy their privileges and emoluments and the king must go without his music. This he was not inclined to do: he was therefore pleased to command and ordain that Lully should organise a band. himself at the head, and in order to avoid collision with the patent place-holders and privileged inefficients, this new band of practical musicians, these four and twenty were to be called "Petits violons du Roi," the king's little fiddlers, instead of the king's musicians, a very nice and comforting distinction. By degrees the income arising from the property possessed by the confraternity of St. Julien was applied to a proper purpose, the king's chamber music was executed by legitimate performers, and the perverted association was finally suppressed in 1761, after four hundred years of profitable but comparatively useless existence.

Congregational music. Music in which the people or congregation take part, as opposed to that which is sung by the trained choir alone. The plain-song of the Responses, Creeds, and of the Lord's Prayer; and the melody of psalm and hymn tunes are congregational music, but services and anthems are specially set aside for performance by the choir, acting as it were as the skilled representatives of the listening and meditating people.

Conjunct. (1) One of the Greek systems of music. [Greek Music.] (2) Conjunct motion, a succession of sounds proceeding by single degrees.

Consecutives. A forbidden progression of parallel fifths or octaves, *e.g.*:

Consecutive fifths.   Consecutive octaves.

Consecutives are considered to be *saved*, if they do not occur between the *same two parts*, as shown in the following (Ex. 3), which embodies the harmonic progressions of Ex. 1:

That consecutive fifths are often productive of an ugly and distressing effect, is not to be denied; but their use when not objectionable seems to have been somewhat thoughtlessly forbidden by musical law-givers. The great masters not unfrequently use them with good results, as will be seen by the following examples. (Stainer's "Theory of Harmony.")

BACH. "Motett," No. 2.   HANDEL's "Solomon." "Almighty power."

MENDELSSOHN'S "St. Paul."
"To God on high."

MENDELSSOHN'S "St. Paul."
"To Thee, O Lord."

SPOHR'S "The Last Judgment."
Introduction to Part III.

HAYDN'S Symphony, No. 4.

MOZART's Symphony, No 4.

BEETHOVEN's Pianoforte Sonata, No. 1, Op. 29.

It having been found by experience that the early attempts at harmony known as *diaphony* and *organum*, which consisted entirely of consecutive quarts, quints, and octaves, were remarkably unpleasant and barbarous, it is probable a reaction took place which led to the indiscriminate condemnation of consecutive fifths.

No satisfactory reason has yet been brought forward for the unpleasant effect of consecutive fifths, but it is easy to see why consecutive *octaves* should not be allowed in pure part-writing. If in a duet, or trio, for instance, one part occasionally moves in unison or octaves with another, such a part is for the time *wasted*, and loses its power of forming a distinct melody or adding a real contribution to the harmony. But, on the other hand, any phrase, however short, may be legitimately enforced or strengthened by doubling at the unison or octave. Thus, the bass may be doubled by the left hand or the melody by the right hand, in pianoforte or organ music, and voices may join in unison whenever it is thought desirable. So, too, in writing for a full band, a theme or motive may be enforced by the combination of any instruments, at the unison, octave, or double octave; but, instruments playing in parts are not allowed to combine in such a manner unless for such a purpose.

Consecutives are said to be *hidden* when the progression of two parts gives the impression that they have occurred, although they have not actually been written, *e.g.*:

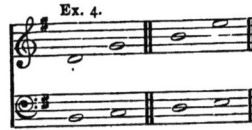

Ex. 4.

Hidden fifths. Hidden octaves.

They are to be discovered by filling up the interval of one of the parts with the intermediate scale-series, *e.g.*:

Ex. 5.

The law against hidden fifths and octaves has never been directed against the movement of inner parts, but only against that of *extreme* parts. But even this has been greatly relaxed in modern music, *e.g.*:

Ex. 6.

Consecutives are said to be "by contrary motion" when the parts forming them proceed in opposite directions, *e.g.*:

SCHUMANN's "Luck of Edenhall."

Consequent. *Consequenza* (*It.*) The answer to a fugue-subject or any subject proposed for imitation. [Dux.] [Guida.]

Conservatorium (*Lat.*) **Conservatorio** (*It.*) **Conservatoire de musique** (*Fr.*) A public music school.

The Italian academies or conservatories are the most ancient, and were formerly attached to hospitals and other benevolent institutions, and were intended for the education of the poor and fatherless, or orphans. Education, board and clothing, were dispensed without cost to both male and female pupils. The conservatorio at Milan was founded in 1808, and the advantages of the instruction of the professors is sought and obtained by many who are not eligible for the foundation, but who can obtain the benefit of a superior musical education at a small cost.

The first school of the kind was established in France, in 1784, with the title of " L'école royale de chant et de déclamation." A national institute was started during the period of the Revolution, to supply the want of musicians in the army; this institute became the present Conservatoire de musique, for the support of which the government is charged with an annual sum of 140,000 francs. Many of the masters have been, and still are, men famed throughout the world for their practical skill and their success in teaching, and the text books used at the conservatoire are among the standard works of reference in their department. There are also establishments of a similar character at Brussels, Cologne, Prague, Warsaw, Vienna and Leipsic, the last named, established under the direction of Mendelssohn, is held to be one of the best in Germany.

Consolante (*It.*) In a consoling, comforting manner.

Consonance. Consonanz (*Ger.*) [Harmony.]

Consonant. Concordant.

Consonant interval. [Interval.]

Con sordini (*It.*) (1) With the mutes on. (2) With the soft pedal at the pianoforte held down.

Consort. (1) A consort of viols was a complete set, the number contained in a chest, usually six. [Chest of Viols.] (2) The sounds produced by the union of instrumental tone.

Consort. (1) To sound together, to form agreeable sounds by combination. (2) To form a concord.

Con stromenti (*It.*) With the instruments.

Continued Bass. [Figured Bass.]

Continuo (*It.*) [Figured Bass.]

Contours. Conteurs (*Fr.*) [Troubadours.]

Contra (*It.*) Against. In compound words this signifies an octave below, *e.g.*: *Contra-gamba*, a 16 ft. gamba; *Contra-basso*, a double bass; *Contra-fagotto* a double bassoon, &c.

Contra-bassist. A double-bass player.

Contra-basso (*It.*) [Double-bass.]

Contra-danza (*It.*) [Country-dance.]

Contra-fagotto (*It*) [Double bassoon.]

Contralto voice. The voice of deepest tone in females. It is of a quality allied to the tenor voice in men, and the usual compass is within two octaves. The best notes of the range are between G or A flat below, and C or D above:

The notes above these are of a somewhat harsh and forced character, those below of little musical value. In most contralto voices there is a break varying between C sharp and A flat in the lower part of the register, and the careful adjustment of the two qualities of tone above or below this break is one of the chief qualities of good contralto singing. [Alto Voice.]

Contraposaune. An organ stop 16 ft. and 32 ft. pitch.

Contrappuntista (*It.*) A writer on, or a composer of counterpoint.

Contrappunto (*It.*) [Counterpoint.]

Contrappunto alla mente (*It.*) Impromptu counterpoint. [Alla Mente.] [Chant sur la livre.]

Contrappunto doppio (*It.*) Double counterpoint. [Counterpoint.]

Contrapuntal. Belonging to counterpoint.

Contrapuntist. A writer on, or a composer of counterpoint.

Contr'arco (*It.*) False or incorrect bowing on the violin, &c.

Contrary motion. Melodies or chords proceeding in opposite directions. [Motion.]

Contrassoggetto (*It.*) [Counter subject.]

Contra tempo (*It.*) Against time. (1) The part progressing slowly while another is moving rapidly:

(2) Syncopation.

Contra-tenor. [Alto.]

Contratöne (*Ger.*) Deep tones of the bass voice.

Contra-violone (*It.*) Double-bass.

Contre-basse (*Fr.*) Double-bass.

Contre-danse (*Fr.*) [Country dance.]

Contrepartie (*Fr.*) Counterpart, opposite. The entry of a second voice with a different melody, making harmony with the first.

Contrepoint (*Fr.*) Counterpoint.

Contrepointiste (*Fr.*) Contrapuntist.

Contre-sujet (*Fr.*) [Counter subject.]

Contre-temps (*Fr.*) Against time. Syncopation.

Conversio (*Lat.*) Inversion.

Convict of music. An institution for musical instruction in Leipsic; from Lat. *convictus (convivere)*, living together, social intercourse. [Conservatorio.]

Coperto (*It.*) Covered, concealed. *Timpani coperti*, muffled drums; *quinti coperti*, concealed fifths, hidden fifths.

Copula (*Lat.*) In mediæval music a free use of slurred running notes in descant.

Copyright is the exclusive right or privilege of printing, or reprinting, publishing, or selling his original work which is allowed by the law to an author. It is doubtful whether this is a right at common law, or whether (which seems the better opinion) it is merely the creature of legislative enactment. (See on this point the cases of Southey *v.* Sherwood,

2 Mer. 435; Tonson *v.* Collins, 1 W. Bl. 301; Miller *v.* Taylor, 4 Burr 2303; Jeffreys *v.* Boosey, 4 H. L. C. 815.) By Statute 8 Anne, c. 19, § 1, a copyright was given to books then printed for 21 years, and to authors and their assignees, an exclusive copyright for 14 years. By § 9 of the same statute, another similar period was given, at the expiration of 14 years, if the author was then living. This Act was extended to the United Kingdom by 41 Geo. III. c. 107. By 54 Geo. III. c. 156, § 4, authors and their assignees had exclusive copyright for 28 years from the day of publication; and, if the authors were living at the expiration of that period, for the residue of their lives. The present law of copyright is to be found in 5 and 6 Vict. c. 45, which amends the general law on the subject, repeals the above-mentioned statutes, and extends the privileged period to the author's life and for 7 years after his death; but if that period falls short of 42 years, then for 42 years from the first day of publication. So that if an author lives for 42 years after publication, the copyright will exist for $42 + 7 = 49$ years. The remedy for unlawfully printing a book within the British Dominion is (1) an action on the case, which must, however, be commenced within one year, or (2) by special injunction in equity to restrain the progress of the injury and to compel an account of the profits which have accrued therefrom. By § 2 of this statute the word "book" includes a sheet of music. Lord Mansfield in construing the previously existing law said, "the words of the Act of Parliament are very large, *books and other writings.*" It is not confined to language or letters. Music is a science; it may be written and the mode of conveying the idea is by signs or marks. A person may use the copy by playing it, but he has no right to rob the author of the profit by multiplying copies of it and disposing of them to his own use. If the narrow construction contended for were to hold, it would equally apply to algebra, mathematics, arithmetic, hieroglyphics. All these are conveyed by signs and figures (Bach *v.* Longman; Cowp. 623), and this is so, even though the music was published on a single sheet of paper (Clementi *v.* Goulding, 11 East 244.) And it has been held that in a declaration for pirating a book, an allegation, that the plaintiff was the author of a book, being a musical composition called A, was supported by showing him to be the author of a musical composition comprised in and only occupying one page of a work with a different title, which contained several other musical compositions (White *v.* Gerrock, 2 B. and A. 298.) It is of course impossible within our necessary limits to discuss all the points of law that have been decided on the subject of

musical copyright; but with regard to *originality* we may mention the case of Lover *v.* Davidson (1 C. B., N. S., 182) in which it was held that one who adapts to an old air words of his own, adding thereto a prelude and accompaniment, also his own, acquires a copyright in the combination, and may, in an action for infringement against one who has pirated the whole, properly describe himself as the proprietor of the entire composition. In this case Samuel Lover had adapted the words of the "Low Back'd Car" to an air previously known as the "Jolly Plough Boy." It is not, however, lawful to publish as quadrilles or waltzes the airs of an opera of which there exists an exclusive copyright (D'Almaine *v.* Boosey, 1 Y. and C. 289.) It may also be noticed that the publication of a piece of music, not for sale or hire, but by the gratuitous distribution of lithographed copies among the members of a musical society is a publication for which a party is liable as for an invasion of the copyright of the proprietor (Novello *v.* Sudlow, 12 C. B. 177.) In order to assign a copyright, it is only necessary to do so by a written instrument, which need not be under seal. But an agreement to execute such an assignment will not operate as an assignment so as to render inoperative a subsequent regular assignment to a third party. By 5 and 6 Vict., c. 45, § 13. copyrights may be registered at Stationers' Hall, on payment of a fee of five shillings. A book of Registry of the proprietorship and assignment of copyrights is there kept, and is open for inspection at reasonable hours, on payment of a fee of one shilling, and certified copies must be given on demand and on payment of a fee of five shillings to the proper officer of the Stationers' Company. These copies so certified are receivable as evidence in all courts and summary proceedings, but they are rebuttable by other evidence. In the case of musical and dramatic compositions they are *prima facie* evidence of the right of representation, but this presumption is similarly rebuttable by evidence of a contrary character.

Cor (*Fr.*) A horn.

Corale (*It.*) Chorale, hymn or psalm tune. [Hymn Tune.]

Cor Anglais (*Fr.*) *Corno Inglese* (*It.*) English horn. A reed instrument of the hautboy character, possessing a compass of like extent but of lower pitch. Its scale is two octaves and a fifth from bass E with the intermediate semitones:

these being the actual sounds produced. The music for the cor Anglais is written in the treble clef, and the instrument transposes the sound a fifth below. Gluck introduced the instrument in his "Orfeo," Meyerbeer has made frequent use of it, and Rossini produces a fine effect in the overture to "William Tell" by means of its tone, but Beethoven only once employed it,—Mozart and Weber never.

Coranach, Coranich, Coronach, Cronach (*Gaelic.*) The word for a funeral song among the Scotch Highlanders; it is said to be derived from *corah-rainach* a crying together. [Keeners.]

Coranto (*It.*) *Courante* (*Fr.*) Current traverse (*Old Eng.*) (1) An Italian form of the country dance. (2) A movement in a suite or sonata of the early writers. The following is given as an early specimen:

GIROLAMO FRESCOBALDI, 1591-1640.

Corda, sopra una (*It.*) *Sur une corde* (*Fr.*) A direction that the passage is to be played on one string. [A una corda.]

Cordatura (*It.*) [Accordatura.]

Cordax (*Lat.*) Κόρδαξ (*Gk.*) An ancient Greek dance of a wanton character, in the old comedy; but sometimes danced off the stage by drunkards.

Corde à jour ⎱ **Corde à vide** ⎰ (*Fr.*) An open string.

Cor de chasse (*Fr.*) A hunting horn.

Corde fausse (*Fr.*) A false string. [String.]

Corde signal (*Fr.*) A bugle.

Cor de vaches (*Fr.*) Cow-horn, used in many places abroad to call the cattle home, and formerly employed in England to rouse the labourers to their work.

" No more shall the horn
Call me up in the morn."

Corifeo (*It.*) [Coryphœus.]

Cormuse. [Bagpipe.]

Cornamusa (*It.*) *Corne muse* (*Fr.*) [Bagpipe.]

Cornare (*It.*) *Corner* (*Fr.*) To sound a horn.

Cornet. *Cornetto* (*It.*) *Zinken* (*Ger.*) An obsolete reed wind-instrument not unlike a hautboy, but larger and of a coarser quality of tone. In this country they were of three kinds, treble, tenor, and bass. The tubes gradually increased in diameter from the mouthpiece to the end, and their outline was gently curved, hence the Italian name *cornetto curvo.* In Germany, as in England, they were once in common use for sacred and secular purposes. They were often made of wood neatly covered with dark leather. [Waits.]

2. A reed stop on the pedals of some German organs, of 4 or 2 feet in length.

3. *Mounted cornet.* A solo stop on old organs, so called because it was placed on a separate sound board, and raised a few feet above the surrounding pipes, for the purpose of giving its tone special prominence. It consisted of several ranks of pipes, generally of five, namely, an open or stopped diapason (usually the latter), a principal, 12th, 15th, and tierce. Thus, if the stop were drawn, and

the finger held on middle C, the following sounds would be heard simultaneously:

Although these would of course combine into one, and not be audible as separate and distinct sounds, yet it may be supposed that such a combination of loud harmonics with a comparatively soft ground-note would produce a most disagreeable and nasal tone. But, notwithstanding its unpleasant *timbre* it was a favourite stop in the last and in the early part of this century, and its general introduction into the best organs gave rise to a vicious and trumpery literature of " cornet voluntaries." The characteristic of these was, that while the left hand held down a soft chord on the choir organ, the right was engaged in *passages, turns, shakes*, and other musical capers, on the cornet stop of the great organ. The usual compass of the stop was from middle C upwards, but sometimes it commenced at tenor C. A large number of cornet stops were removed to make way for the clarabella when first invented by Bishop, and better taste has so far ejected them that a specimen in good playable condition may be looked upon as a curiosity.

4. *Echo cornet.* A stop often found in swell organs. Originally it consisted of the same series of ranks of pipes as the mounted cornet, but was always of a very small scale. But the name is now often applied to any small-scale sesquialtera or mixture enclosed in the swell box.

5. *Cornet-à-pistons.* A modern brass instrument of the trumpet family, but having valves or pistons by means of which a complete chromatic scale can be produced. In proportion to the number of valves introduced into tube-instruments, the quality of their tone is deteriorated, but notwithstanding this loss of purity and brilliancy, the cornet is most useful and valuable for many purposes. It has been brought into discredit by being unwisely used in some orchestras as a substitute for its parent, the trumpet, with the grandeur of which it cannot compete. [Metal Wind-instruments.]

Cornetto (*It.*) [Cornet.]
Corno (*It.*) [Horn.]
Corno alto (*It.*) High horn.
Corno basso (*It.*) Low horn.
Corno di bassetto (*It.*) [Basset-horn.]
Corno di caccia (*It.*) [Caccia.]
Corno Inglese (*It.*) [Cor Anglais.]
Cornopean. [Cornet, § 5.]
Coro (*It.*) [Chorus.]
Cor omnitonique (*Fr.*) A horn on which by the use of valves, a chromatic scale could be played.

Corona (*It.*) A pause.
Coronach. [Coranach.]
Corps de voix (*Fr.*) The quality or the fulness of the voice.
Corrente (*It.*) [Coranto.]
Corrépétiteur (*Fr.*) Correpetitore (*It.*) The instructor of the chorus, one who teaches the choral body to sing their several parts by ear.
Corti's organ. [Ear.]
Coryphæus (*Lat.*) Κορυφαῖος (*Gk.*) (1) A leader or conductor of the dances or chorus. (2) An officer in the University of Oxford, whose duty it is to give instruction in music.
Coryphée (*Fr.*) (1) A leader of the groups of dancers. (2) A female dancer.
Cotillon (*Fr.*) *lit.* under-petticoat. A lively, spirited dance, originally performed by a male and a female, in which the latter alternately attracted and repulsed her partner. It was first called cotillon in the reign of Louis XIV. was expanded in its design by the French in the last century, and arranged for eight persons. It is now danced with any step by an unlimited number of dancers. When it is possible, chairs are placed round the room for the performers. " Each gentleman places his partner on his right hand. There is no rule that any particular figure shall be danced. The selection is left to the determination of the leading couple who commence the figure, which the other couples repeat in succession. In large parties of twenty-four or thirty couples, it is customary for two or more couples to perform the same figure at the same time. The constant variety of the figures enables each gentleman to dance with almost every lady." The figures from which a selection is made are called the pyramid; the two flowers; the great bound and pass-under; the cushion; the round; the basket, ring, and flower; the two lines of six; the coquette; la gracieuse ; the mirror; the handkerchief; the star; the cards; the double moulinet; the deceived lady; the quadrille; the two chairs; the rounds multiplied ; the lancers; the three chairs, &c.: the whole being more or less allied to the old-fashioned country dance. It is not at all improbable that the tune " Petticoat loose " given in the article, " Country dance," furnished the title to the Cotillon.

Couac (*It.*) An onomatopœic word for the sound made by bad blowing on the clarinet, oboe, or bassoon. The quacking sound, the goose note.
Couched harp. [Spinett.]
Coulé (*Fr.*) A glide. (1) Slurred notes. (2) A *slide* in dancing. (3) An ornament in harpsichord music; *e.g.*:

Counterpoint. The term "counterpoint" in its broadest sense may be defined as "the art of adding one or more parts to a given melody;" in its more limited sense as, "the art of harmonising a theme by adding parts which shall be in themselves melodious." The terms subject, melody, canto fermo, and theme, are synonymous. The common definition of counterpoint as the "art of combining melodies" is not strictly logical, unless the word "melody" has a definition not generally accepted; because, distinct melodies are never given to the student to be combined by him unless they have been previously proved capable of combination; and if a composer should attempt to combine two distinct melodies in accordance with the laws of strict counterpoint he will probably find it necessary to eliminate so much of one or both of his subjects that little real musical melody is left. The contrapuntist's notion of a melody is—a succession of sounds which does not infringe certain theoretical laws. No wonder then that authors who have bound themselves by the commands of counterpoint seem to have trodden in one almost identical path and to have added little that is valuable to the literature of counterpoint. Those masters who have exceptionally combined great genius with a deep study of the art of counterpoint, such as Bach, Cherubini, and Mozart, exhibit in their works more than any other authors do, with what beneficial results the laws of counterpoint may be purposely broken, for it cannot be denied that the first fact which startles, and shakes the faith of the student of counterpoint, is that the preaching and practice of contrapuntists are so thoroughly inconsistent. Their books consist of rules, their compositions of exceptions. But it would be dishonest to blink the fact that much good was for a time done by counterpoint, by eliminating crudities in harmony, by introducing an interesting rhythmical correlation of parts, and by opening to ingenious writers a large field for imitative construction of music at a time when the resources of key, modulation, form, and variety of tone in instruments, were greatly limited. Whether a course of study in counterpoint is not more interesting to the lover of musical history than beneficial to the gifted young composer, the reader may perhaps be able to judge for himself after reading the rules of the art and seeing the examples of its scope given below.

Counterpoint is simple or double. There are five species of simple counterpoint.

1, when the added part is note against note of the subject; 2, when the added part is two notes to one of the subject; 3, when the added part is four notes to one of the subject; 4, when the added part is in syncopation to each note of the subject; 5, when the added part is free, or has a florid accompaniment to each note of the subject.

In the first species, note against note, in two parts, the following rules and regulations are to be observed:

1. No discords are allowed.
2. More than three consecutive 3rds or 6ths are forbidden.
3. Consecutive 5ths and 8ths are forbidden.
4. The fourth is to be considered a discord.
5. No augmented or diminished intervals are to be used in the progression of the subject or counterpoint. The major 6th, major 7th, and minor 7th are similarly disallowed.
6. A tritone (or augmented 4th) should be avoided, between the component notes of a chord and that which immediately follows it.
7. False relations are forbidden.
8. Of the three kinds of motion—similar, oblique, and contrary—contrary motion is to be preferred.
9. Hidden fifths and octaves are forbidden.
10. Unison between subject and counterpoint is forbidden.

The first rule requires no explanation. The second is given to insure the independence of the counterpoint, as it is evident that if one part constantly follows another at the interval of the 3rd or 6th, it cannot possibly be said to form a separate melody. The third and fourth rules need no explanation. The fifth rule is saddled with many exceptions, as might be expected; the major 6th and augmented 4th in ascending, and the diminished 7th in descending, are tolerated. The origin of the sixth rule is to be traced in the difficulty of making dominant and subdominant harmony succeed each other with good effect, *e.g.*:

is certainly unpleasant to the ear, whereas

is certainly not so unpleasant, though equally forbidden by strict contrapuntists. The rule against false relations (7) is necessary in two-part writing, as it is impossible to introduce them with good effect. Such progressions as the following are palpably inadmissible:

Rule 8 may be proved necessary on the same grounds as given in explanation of rule 2. Two parts cannot be forming separate *melodies*

when moving in similar motion, much less can they be doing so in oblique motion, in which, one part stands still: therefore, contrary motion is preferable as probably leading to more variety. ' The law against the use of hidden fifths and octaves, includes under it the well-known contrapuntal rule: "do not proceed from an imperfect to a perfect interval by similar motion," the fifth and octave being the only perfect intervals admissible in two-part counterpoint of the first species. The presence of hidden fifths or octaves is discovered by filling up the intervals between the consecutive notes of each part with the intermediate degrees of the scale, thus:

Hidden fifths.   **Hidden octaves.**

or where both parts move by a skip:

The examples given throughout this article are taken from Fux, "Gradus ad Parnassum," 1725, a work from which all later authors have borrowed largely, Cherubini and Ouseley not excepted: it is fair therefore to suppose that these specimens of counterpoint meet with the approval, if not the admiration, of modern expositors of the art.

Counterpoint.

Canto fermo.

The above is said to be "contrapunto sopra il soggetto." The following example has the same subject in the upper part, "contrapunto sotto il soggetto."

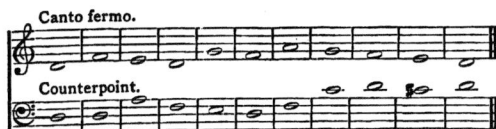

Canto fermo.

Counterpoint.

The second species of simple counterpoint is subject to the following rules and regulations:

1. Of the two notes in the counterpoint, the first must be a concord, the second may be a concord or passing discord.

2. Consecutive fifths or octaves on successive down-beats are forbidden. Some authors however admit the latter of these progressions if the skip to the second note is greater than a third.

3. Scale passages are preferable to broken harmony.

4. The counterpoint may commence on the up-beat of the first bar.

5. The cadence of the subject should be harmonised by contrary motion.

6. The interval of a fourth may occasionally be used on the down-beat.

7. A false relation is not avoided by the introduction of a passing note or passing discord.

A passing discord is a discord having a degree of the scale on each side of it, e.g.:

The first rule therefore forbids a discord to be a skip. The second rule is to prevent the use of such progressions as the following:

The third rule strives to enforce independence of motion in the counterpoint, e.g.:

In this example, the upper part is practically harmonised by the lower one, the first bar representing the chord of C, the next two bars a chord of G. Rules 4, 5, and 6, require no explanation. Rule 7 is to prevent the admission of such passages as the following:

The following are specimens of this species:

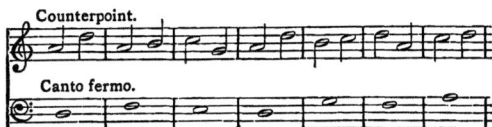

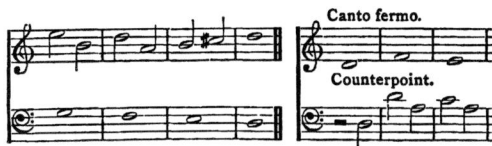

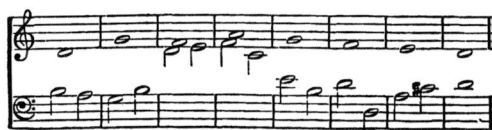

Counterpoint.

Canto fermo.

Canto fermo.

Counterpoint.

If counterpoint in triple time is used, the first minim must be a concord, the other two may be concords or passing discords as may be found desirable.

The third species of counterpoint in two parts in which there are four notes to each note of the canto fermo, is subject to the following rules and regulations:

1. The fourth note must be a concord, the second and fourth may be passing discords.
2. The third note may sometimes be a passing discord, but should be generally a concord.
3. The first bar may commence with a crotchet rest, if the note immediately after the rest is a concord.
4. The cadence should be by contrary motion.
5. There may be unison between counterpoint and subject, provided it does not occur on the first note of the bar.
6. The tritone is to be avoided between any four notes of the counterpoint, unless they occur as an integral part of the scale, that is, having the next note of the scale on each side of them.
7. Octaves and fifths between counterpoint and subject should not occur on successive down beats; or between the third crotchet of one bar, and the first crotchet of the following bar.

The cases in which the third note may be a discord (see 2) are of the following kind:

The sixth rule is to prevent the use of such passages as the following:

It will, however, be noticed that a passage almost similar to the above, occurs in the second of the two models given below from Fux. Rule 7 is constantly broken. Fux himself gives the following as a specimen of a cadence in this species:

The fourth species of counterpoint in two parts, is that in which the counterpoint though containing practically note against note of the subject, has each note bound into the following bar, or, syncopated.

The following rules and regulations are to be observed:

1. That which is incorrect " sine ligatura " is incorrect when " cum ligatura."
2. It is necessary to begin on the up-beat.
3. Syncopations may be concordant or discordant, a concordant syncopation being one that is heard in both bars (half of each) as a concord: a discordant syncopation one that is a concord on the up-beat, but forms a discord on the down-beat.
4. If necessary, the syncopations may be relinquished for the space of two minims.
5. The best cadence is formed by the suspension 7 6 on the supertonic.

Rule 1 is directed against such progressions as the following:

For, tested by the omission of the ligatures, it appears thus:

According to this rule the following passage is correct:

Although it seems to infringe rule 2 of the second species, and rule 7 of the third species, but without ligatures it becomes merely a succession of 6ths:

The following are specimens of counterpoint of this species:

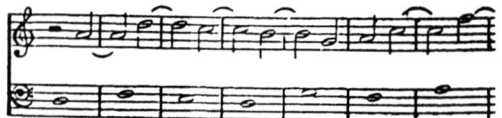

(Transposed.)

When this species is used in triple time the second note of the bar may be a concord or passing discord, the third must be a concord bound into the next bar and forming a syncopated concord or suspended discord.

The fifth species of counterpoint, florid or figurate counterpoint, consists of a mixture of the various kinds just given, and so far as it proceeds in any one species, is subject to the laws and regulations of that species. Shorter notes may occasionally be used. The following are examples:

(Transposed.)

Counterpoint in three parts is, generally speaking, bound by the rules of its corresponding species in two parts. The additional part, however, makes the following rules necessary in the first species, note against note.

1. Every chord should be a common chord, if possible. When not possible the chord $\frac{6}{3}$ may be used.
2. The third of the common chord should not be doubled.

3. The term "chord $\frac{6}{3}$" includes under it the chord $\frac{6}{3}$ on the supertonic, that is, the second inversion of the chord of the minor seventh, the root being omitted. As the old masters did not consider this chord a discord, the seventh of the root (third of the chord) is frequently resolved upwards by them. It will not be necessary to give specimens of counterpoint in every form of which it is capable, one example of each species will suffice, if the reader will remember that the canto fermo may appear in upper, lower, or middle parts. The student of counterpoint should refer to Fux, "Gradus ad Parnassum" Vienna, 1725, or to an English translation called "Practical rules for learning composition," printed by Welcker, Gerrard Street, Soho (at the end of the last century), or to Cherubini's work (Novello, London).

The second species of counterpoint in three parts contains one part having two notes to each note of the subject.

1. A syncopation is allowed to take place immediately before the cadence.
2. The third of the common chord should not be doubled.

The following is a specimen of counterpoint of this species:

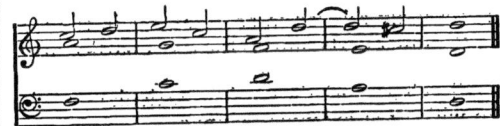

The third species of counterpoint in three parts contains one part having four notes to each note of the subject. A syncopation before the cadence is not permitted in this species:

A mixed kind of counterpoint, containing one part having two notes to each note of the subject, and another having four notes to each note of the subject, may be classified under this species:

(Transposed.)

Canto fermo.

The fourth species of counterpoint in three parts contains one syncopated part:

Counterpoint.

Counterpoint.

Canto fermo.

The fifth species of counterpoint in three parts contains one figurate or florid part. It is unnecessary to give an example of this species.

In counterpoint of four parts, the rules of two-part and three-part counterpoint are necessarily relaxed to some extent in the case of the inner parts, unless the inner parts consist of the canto fermo and the counterpoint specially characteristic of the particular species to which the example belongs.

The following rules and regulations apply to four-part counterpoint generally:

1. In the first species, only common chords should be used, but the chord $\frac{6}{4}$ may occasionally be used.

2. In every species, the different parts should be as much as possible equidistant.

3. Two parts may occasionally cross each other.

4. The laws against hidden fifths and octaves do not bind inner parts, and consecutive fifths by contrary motion are sometimes permitted.

It will be sufficient if two examples of four-part counterpoint are given:

(Second Species.)

(Fourth Species.)

Counterpoint may be in 5, 6, 7, 8 or even 16 parts, but enough has been said to give the reader an insight into its principles.

Counterpoint (Double) has been well described as a " kind of artificial composition where the parts are inverted in such a manner that the uppermost becomes the lowermost, and *vice versa*." Or, in other words " the art of making melodies grammatically convertible at certain intervals."

If the melodies are interchanged at the interval of an octave, the double counterpoint is said to be " at the octave," but if the inverted melody is transposed one note, the other melody remaining untransposed, the double counterpoint is said to be at the 9th. Similarly, the double counterpoint may be at the 10th, 11th, 12th, 13th or 14th. But double counterpoint at some of these intervals imposes such difficulties in the construction of the component melodies, that it is rarely met with. Double counterpoint at the 8th, 10th and 12th, are the kinds most commonly used, and shall be explained in order. It will be seen if the following passage:

be inverted by playing the lowest line an octave higher, and the highest an octave lower, thus:

that the intervals between the two parts have undergone an entire change, with the exception of the octave which has become a unison. Thus the 2nd has become a 7th.

,,	3rd	,,	6th.
,,	4th	,,	5th.
,,	5th	,,	4th.
,,	6th	,,	3rd.
,,	7th	,,	2nd.
,,	8th	,,	1st.

We have above, then, a complete scheme of

the changes intervals undergo by inversion at the octave. It is evident that the following rules must be observed :

1. As the 5th becomes a 4th, and the 4th is a discord, the 5th must be treated as a discord, if used at all. As a discord, it may be prepared, or treated as a passing discord.
2. The octave must be approached by a single degree, not a skip, in strict style.
3. As it is usual to place the upper melody an octave lower, leaving the lower unchanged, the interval of an octave between the two parts must not be exceeded, otherwise the object of inversion will be lost, *e.g.*:

Ex. 1.

will become :

Ex. 2.

In the first and third bars of Ex. 2, no inversion has taken place. If melodies are framed with the intention of altering the pitch of both when inverting them, this rule does not of course hold good, *e.g.*:

4. The melodies should be different in style, and one should commence on the up-beat. The following is an example of double counterpoint at the octave, from Fux :

Inversion (transposed).

If we wish to discover the changes intervals undergo by double counterpoint at the 10th, we can, as before, write them out thus :

1. Consecutive 10ths become consecutive unisons, *e.g.*:

and consecutive 3rds become consecutive octaves ; *e.g.*:

Both consecutive 10ths and 3rds must therefore be avoided.

2. Consecutive sixths become consecutive fifths ; they therefore must be avoided, *e.g.*:

3. The suspension 4 3 becomes a 7th resolved wrongly ; *e.g.* :

4. The interval of a tenth between the upper and lower melodies should not be exceeded, for the reason given in rule 3 of double counterpoint at the octave.

The following example is from Cherubini :

The subject of the above may also be written in the third above and the counterpoint in the octave below, throughout; or again, the counterpoint may be written in the third below, and the subject in the octave below. The following example, from Fux, shows how the same counterpoint may be used at the same time, at the octave and the tenth, each counterpoint being correct when taken separately:

Double counterpoint at the 12th is much less hampered by the change of intervals than many other species.

1. The 6th becomes the 7th, if therefore introduced, it must be as a discord in the lowest part, e g.:

will become when inverted:

or, a sequence of prepared sevenths.
2. The final cadence will require special care in its treatment.
The following is an example of this species:

Interesting examples of combinations of counterpoints at the 10th and 12th are to be found in Fux.

Counterpoints, Triple and Quadruple, as their names show, are the due construction of three or four melodies respectively, in such a manner that they can be interchangeable without involving the infringement of the laws of musical grammar. It will be evident, on consideration, that the octave is the only feasible interval at which counterpoints of this class can be made, unless indeed one or more *free* parts, that is, parts not forming interchangeable melodies, are added. The following is an example of triple counterpoint, written out in full. Of course three sentences at least will be required for the exposition of *triple* counterpoint; four sentences for that of quadruple:

The following example of quadruple counterpoint is from Zimmerman:

It is perhaps necessary to warn the lay reader against the confusion likely to arise between the terms two-part, three-part, four-part, counterpoint; and double, triple, and quadruple counterpoint. The former refers only to the number of parts added to a given subject, and such parts need not necessarily be interchangeable; whereas, the essence of the latter is that in each case all the parts must be capable of substitution one for the other.

Occasionally, specimens of quintuple counterpoint are to be met with, but they may be looked upon more as curiosities than as substantial additions to the musical art.

Counter subject. [Fugue.]

Counter tenor clef. The C clef placed upon the third line of the stave for the use of counter tenor or alto voices, the viola, &c.:

Counter tenor voice. The old name for the alto voice. [Alto voice.]

Country Dance. *Contre-danse (Fr.) Contradanza (It.)* A rustic dance, of English origin, in which performers were arranged face to face, " one set against another," and performed certain prescribed figures. The old method of dancing the " country dance " was to place the ladies and the gentlemen in two parallel lines, the former on the left, the latter on the right, facing their partners. All advance, then retreat, during the first four bars of the music, then cross to opposite places, then advance and retreat, and then re-cross to original places. Each of these movements should occupy the time of four bars of music. The lady who stands at the top, and the gentleman whose place is at the bottom, advance towards each other, *courtesy* and bow, and return to their places. The gentle-man at the top and the lady at the bottom do the same. Then the first named couple advance once more, give right hands and swing quickly round each other back to places. This figure is repeated by the other couple. The lady at the top then advances, gives her *right* hand to her opposite partner, and passes behind the two gentlemen standing in the places next to him: then, through the line and across it, giving her *left* hand this time to her partner, who meets her half way between the two lines, having passed behind the two ladies next to his partner's place. The lady then passes behind the two ladies next in the line, the gentleman moving in the like figure behind the two gentlemen next lowest, and so on, all down the line. At the bottom the lady gives her left hand to her partner, and they *promenade* back to their former places. Then the top couple come forward, *courtesy* and bow, the lady turns to the right, the gentleman to the left, each followed by the rest of her or his line. Top couple meeting at the bottom join hands and raise their arms to form an arch for the other couples to pass under, until all have reached their places except the top couple; these having become the bottom couple, repeat the figure from the beginning until they have worked back to their original places at the top of the lines, and then the dance is ended. Such is a general description of a dance which under various titles has been popular in England for centuries, has been adopted by other nations, and revived from time to time with a few modifications under the several titles applied to it by the people from whom it was last taken. Thus it has been called " contre-danse " and is erroneously said to be French; and when it has been named " coranto " it has been supposed to be Italian.

John Stafford Smith, in his Musica Antiqua, quotes a dance tune which he copied from a MS., now in the Bodleian Library at Oxford, the date of which is probably about the year 1300. The tune is in $\frac{6}{8}$ time, in three sections of nine bars each, and notwithstanding the fact that it has one more bar in each section than the majority of tunes employed as country-dance melodies, can be danced to without difficulty or sense of inconvenience.

Country Dance Tune, about 1300.

It is unnecessary here to enlarge upon the popularity of dancing, throughout all ages; a reference to Strutt's "Sports and Pastimes," and to Chappell's "Popular Music in the Olden Time," will satisfy those who are curious as to details. It may be here stated that the old poets and dramatists, from the time of Chaucer and later, have frequent allusions to the custom, and make mention of many dances by name without giving descriptions, so that it may be inferred that their allusions point to practices in their time so popular that particular description was not deemed needful.

One of the old English names for rustic dances was *hey digyes* or *rounds*.

"While some the rings of bells and some the bagpipes play,
Dance many a merry round, and many a *hy degy*."
DRAYTON'S "Polyalbion," Song xxv.

The "Hay," or "Raye" as it is also called, is probably the same as the "hey digyes." It was danced by many, forming a line or a circle, and the direction was to "wind round *handing* in passing until you come to your places."

"THE HAYE," a Countrie Dance, 1678.

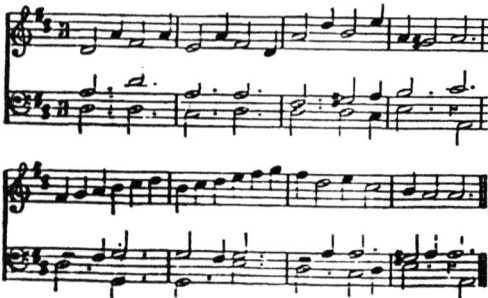

"Dargason" was another name given to the country dance years before the time of the Reformation. Ritson in his Ancient Songs classes it as belonging to a very early period. Mr. Chappell quotes the tune in his "Popular Music," p. 65, and it is of the rhythm common to many country dance tunes:

The same character of tune which suited the country dance was also used for the reel, the round, the morris-dance, the jig, and hornpipe, all of which are offshoots from the one original stem. Those among these dances now performed by one or at most two dancers, were not always so done, the reel was often "four or eight handed or even general," the jig and hornpipe were also dances for many. The two last named probably derived their title from the instruments employed as accompaniments, the usual accompaniment to most country dances was anciently the fiddle, in German *Geige*; or, pipe and tabour. There were many other names given to the country dance in successive ages, and the variety of the titles has led many writers into the belief that there were as many dances as names. The allusions found in the writings of the poets and dramatists have, to a certain extent, increased the confusion in the minds of readers, and commentators not deeming the subject worthy of the consideration it deserves, have often by wrongly directed notes and glosses, made matters in a worse condition than that arising from original error. Sir John Davies (1570-1626) in his poem "Orchestra" is clearer than other authors on the subject. He identifies rounds, corantos, measures, &c., with country dances. His description of a country dance, to be found under "Brawl," is almost the same as that given above, which is the process of performing the country dance to this day. He calls a "measure" "a round dance for ever wheeling," and implies that "as men more civill grew, they did more grave and solemn measures frame" out of the primitive country dance. The "galliard" "a swift and wandering dance with passages uncertain to and fro, yet with a certain answer and consent." The coranto or "current traverses" in which he says of the dancer:

"Everywhere he wantonly must range
And turn with unexpected change"

All these forms are but slight variations of the simple original, and as it is admitted that "no rules have ever been laid down for the composition of a country dance, nor is it indeed confined to any particular measure; so that any common song, or tune, if sufficiently rhythmical may by adoption be made a country dance," the diversities of *tempo* in the several melodies, of the coranto, rondo, galliard, and measure ought not to be taken as a proof of a distinct character of dance.

In the rustic dances the motion was rapid, but when people of less humble condition deigned to adopt them, they varied the figures, made the motion more dignified, and giving a new title to the old diversion, created a certain amount of confusion in the minds of interested posterity. The "stately measure, the graceful minuet, and the courtly quadrille" are each and all country dances, and people of all conditions have indulged in the pastime they offer. Mr. William Chappell ("Popular Music in the Olden Time," p. 626) shows that country dances were popular at court in the reign of Queen Elizabeth, and succeeding reigns. The custom of dancing the ancient English country dance was kept up at court during the reign of George III, as many newspapers and other records show. Thus, in the "Universal Magazine," for June, 1784, we read: "June 4th, the anniversary of the King's birth-day, the drawing-room broke up about half-past five, when their majesties returned to the Queen's palace to dinner; and at about nine in the evening there was a grand ball, which was opened by the Prince of Wales, who walked the first minuets with the Princess Augusta . . . . The country dances began a little before twelve, and continued till past one."

It has been mentioned above that the rhythm of country dance tunes is various, some are in triple and some in duple measure. Among the most popular airs employed for the dance, those called "Sir Roger de Coverley," the "Tank," the "Triumph," "Gee ho, Dobbin," "Merrily danced the Quaker's Wife," "Petticoat Loose," "Gossip

Joan," "The Devil among the Tailors," "Moll in the Wad," and the "Wind that shakes the Barley," are still popular: these are all different in accent and measure, yet all serve the purpose of the dance. It matters not whether the time be $\frac{9}{8}$, $\frac{12}{8}$, $\frac{6}{8}$, or $\frac{4}{4}$; all that is necessary is that the strains should be in four or eight bar phrases to accompany the several movements, and every need is satisfied.

"ROGER DE COVERLEY."

"THE TANK."

"THE TRIUMPH."

"Gee ho, Dobbin."

"Merrily danced the Quaker's Wife."

"Petticoat Loose." (Macfarren's Harmony.)

"Gossip Joan."

"The Devil among the Tailors."

"MOLL IN THE WAD."

"ROLLING IN THE DEW."

the first occupied with the title, as above; the second containing a description "des figures de la contre danse;" the third diagram-plans of the said figures, and the fourth the music, which in the instance quoted above, is as follows:

Country dances when imported into other nations have become as popular as at home. The Italians, in 1740, were said to be "fond to a degree" of them, and about the same period in Paris, "no kind of dance was received with so much favour as they." Dancing masters vied with each other in devising new combinations of figures, and musicians of the common order provided original or borrowed tunes for the dance, many of which were published in single sheets with such titles as "La Nelle. Chartres, countre danse par Mr.——, Mtre. de Danse, prix 4 f. la feuille; à Paris, ches M. de la Chevardiere, Md. de Musique, rue du Roule a la Croix d'or; Mlle. Castagniere, rue des Prouvaires, avec privilege du Roy."

These publications consisted of four pages,

The following diagram from the above work, shows the various figures of another dance, the black marks representing the position of the men; the white marks, that of the women; the arrow-heads, the direction in which they move.

DESCRIPTION DES FIGURES DE LA CONTREDANSE.

1. *La grande chaine, un demi tour.*

2, 3. *La poussette dessus, et dessous, et la pirouette d chaque bout.*

4. *Autre ⅓ tour de chaine, la poussette, et la pirouette au bout.*

5, 6, 7, 8. *Gager d'une place sur le côté; deux se tenant les mains passent en dedans et les deux autres en dehors, continuant d passer de cette maniere 4 fois, jusqu'à ses places, faisant deux balancé d chaque place.*

9. *La chaine des dames sur les côtés.*

10. *Un tour allemande en pirouettant.*

11. *Refaire la chaine des dames.*

12. *Un tour d'allemande.* LA MAIN.

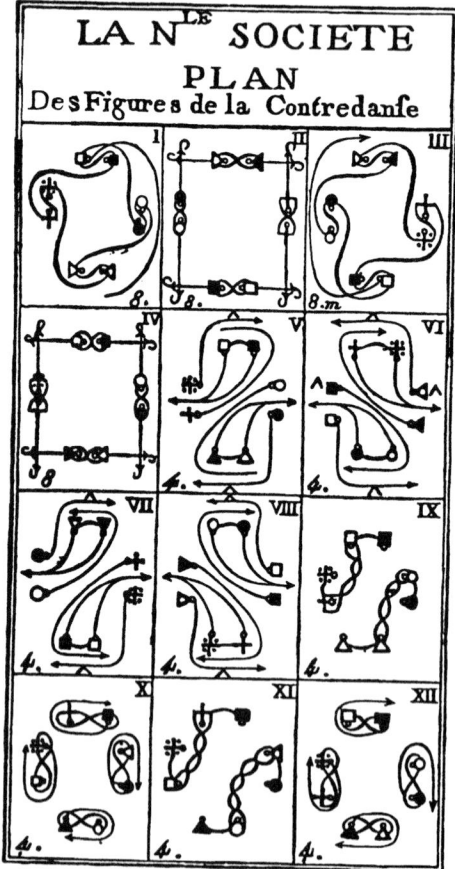

LA N^LLE SOCIETE
PLAN
Des Figures de la Contredanse

The subjoined is the melody to which it was danced:

"LA NOUVELLE SOCIETE," Contre-danse Allemande.

2 fois la rep. du majeur en rondeau, et deux fois chaque rep. du mineur.

Coup d'archet (*Fr.*) Stroke of a bow.

Couper le sujet (*Fr.*) To abbreviate or curtail a musical subject or theme.

Coupler. The mechanism which connects pedals with the manuals; or, different manuals together. [Organ.]

Couplet. (1) Two lines in rhyme, which contain a complete sentence. (2) A verse of a song. (3) Two notes occupying the time of three, *e.g.*:

Courante (*Fr.*) [Coranto.]

Couronne (*Fr.*) The name for the sign of a pause ⌢.

Courtaut, Cortaud, Corthal. An ancient instrument of the bassoon kind. [Bassoon.]

Covered consecutives. Hidden consecutives. [Consecutives.]

Covered strings. Strings of silk, wire, or gut, covered with a fine wire by means of a machine, by a process technically termed string-spinning. Covered strings are used for pianofortes, violins, violoncellos, guitars, &c., the wire covering, by adding weight and strength to the string, makes it slower of vibration, while, on the other hand, it is more elastic than an uncovered string of the same diameter.

Cownterynge yn songe (*Old Eng.*) In Lat. *concentus* or *accentus*, singing an accompaniment to a tune. [Descant.]

Cracovienne. [Polacca.]

Crackle. A direction in lute playing, thus explained by "Maister" Thomas Mace, 1676: "To crackle such three part stops is only to divide each stop, with your thumb and two fingers, so as not to loose time, but give each crotchet its due quantity." [Arpeggio.]

Credo (*Lat.*) One of the movements in a mass. [Mass.]

Crembalum. [Jew's Harp.]

Cremona. (1) A violin made in the town of Cremona. (2) A reed stop in the organ. A corruption of the word Krum or Cromhorn.

Cremorne (*Fr.*) [Krum horn.]

Crepitaculum or **Crepundia** (*Lat.*) An ancient instrument of a character like the castanets, but with sound produced more by friction than striking. [Castanets, Bones, Knicky-knackers.]

Crescendo (*It.*) Increasing, a gradual increase in the force of sound expressed by the sign ⎯⎯◁, or the abbreviation *cres.* The sign was first employed in England by Matthew Locke, in 1676.

Crescendo-zug (*Ger.*) The swell box in the organ. [Organ.]

Creticus (*Lat.*) A metrical foot consisting of one short syllable between two long — ‿ —

Croche (*Fr.*) A quaver, ♪ the *hooked* note. [Nomenclature.]

Croma (*It.*) A quaver ♪

Cromatico (*It.*) Chromatic, as, *fuga cromatica*, a chromatic fugue; *fantasia cromatica*, a chromatic fantasia, &c.

Crom horn. [Krum horn.]

Crooks. Short tubes either straight or curved, adapted for insertion between the mouthpiece and the body of the horn, trumpet, or cornet-à-pistons, for the purpose of altering the key. [Metal wind instruments.]

Crotalum (*Lat.*) κρόταλον (*Gk.*) A rattle, or clapper, used sometimes to mark the rhythm of dancing, in the worship of Cybele. They were generally made of wood, having a loose piece hinged about midway, so that, when shaken in the hand a clattering noise was produced, called by the Greeks πλαταγή.

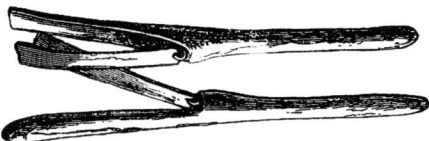

Instruments of this kind were in use among the ancient Egyptians, as the following illustration shows:

Crotchet. A note ♩ one-fourth of the value of a semibreve. [Nomenclature.]

Croupeza, κρούπεζα, κρούπαζα, κρούπανα, κρούπετα (*Gk.* from κρούω, to knock, strike). High wooden shoes worn by flute-players or others, with which the time was marked by striking with the foot; *c.f.* Lat. scrupedæ, women who wore high-heeled boots.

Crowd. Crwth, an ancient instrument, like a violin, with six strings, four of which were played upon by a bow, and the other two played, or plucked with the thumb, as an accompaniment. The neck had a hole, through which the player thrust his hand, so that he could only command the notes lying under his fingers. [Violin.]

Crowle. An early form of the word *corolla* (*Lat.*) a crowd, *q.v.*

C-schlüssel (*Ger.*) The C clef.

Cum sancto (*Lat.*) A portion of the Gloria in the mass. [Mass.]

Cue. A catch word or phrase. The last notes or words of other parts inserted as a guide to singers or players who have to make an entry after rests:

Currende (*Ger.*) Children carol-singers in Germany.

Cushion-dance. An old English round dance, in which each woman selected her partner by placing a cushion before him. Taylor, the Water Poet, calls it a "pretty little provocatory dance," for that reason. There was a dialogue carried on, according to the description given in the "Dancing Master" of 1686; and the note appended to the same description points—perhaps unwittingly—to the probable origin of the dance: "Note. The women are kissed by all the men in the ring at their coming and going out, and likewise the men by all the women." Therefore, it is not at all unlikely that the Cushion-dance was the "Kissing dance." One of the tunes to which it was danced is subjoined, and another melody is printed in Mr. Chappell's "Popular Music," where it is shown that the dance was also called a Galliard. [Cotillon.] [Country Dance.]

CUSHION DANCE.

Custos (*Lat.*) (1) The chief of a college of minor canons. (2) A *direct*, the sign ∿ or ╱, placed at the end of a line or page to show the position of the first note of the line or page following.

Cyclische Formen. Rondoforms. [Form.]

Cymbalista. A cymbal player.

Cymbals. *Cymbalum (Lat.) κύμβαλον (Gk).* Musical instruments of percussion, consisting of two metallic basins, which are set in vibration by being clashed together. The shape of cymbals varies, from that of the actual form of a cup or basin to an almost flat plate. The following illustration shows those used by the Assyrians. It will be remarked that the lower basin is held in a stationary position, while the upper one is dashed on it.

Fig. 1.

The Hebrews had two kinds of cymbals, mentioned by name in Psalm cl. 5, "Praise Him upon the loud cymbals; praise Him upon the high-sounding cymbals." The Arabians have two sorts at the present time, the larger they use in their religious ceremonies, but the smaller are rarely used but for the purpose of accompanying the dance. In India cymbals are used called *talan*, and a smaller sort called *kintal*. An illustration of Indian cymbals is given:

Fig. 2.

The Burmese instruments of this class are of the true basin shape, as shewn in the following:

Fig. 3.

A pair of ancient Egyptian cymbals are in existence; they are about five inches in diameter, and are made of a mixture of copper and silver, and in outline are identical with those now used by modern Egyptians.

As has been the case with other musical instruments, the name cymbal has been applied in various ways. At one period the Italians called a *tambourine* by this name, and at another a *dulcimer*. As the harpsichord was the actual outgrowth of the dulcimer, the harpsichord came to be called *cembalo*, a word still to be found occasionally affixed to the *pianoforte* part of full scores. It is probable that the peculiar clang produced by striking the wire strings of a dulcimer with a wooden hammer gave rise to the association of the name cymbal with dulcimer.

In modern military bands cymbals are used in the ancient manner. One plate is held in each hand of the performer, and the sound is produced by clashing the plates together. In the orchestra of the concert-room, one plate of a cymbal is attached to the upper side of the rim of the big (upright) drum, and the other held in the left hand of the drummer. The tone produced by the beating of these is largely increased in power and depth by the connection with the drum. Very small cymbals were introduced by Berlioz, tuned a fifth apart, as an orchestral instrument, but have not come into common use. Small cymbals are sometimes attached to the fingers and are hence called finger-cymbals:

Fig. 4.

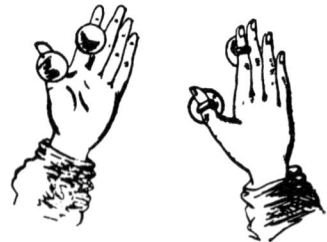

These naturally became associated with castanets; and they have also found their way into the rim of the tambourine, of which instrument they form an important element.

It should be stated that cymbals are not struck together, actually face to face, for by so doing not only would the free vibration of the plates be very much arrested, but they would in all probability be split by the blow. Turkey is still celebrated for its manufacture of cymbals and other instruments of percussion, and exports them in large quantities to all parts of the world. The exact composition of the metal used in Turkey is not known to the manufacturers in other countries.

Cypher-system. [Notation.]

Czakan. A flute made of cane or bamboo.

Czardasch (*Hung.*) [Chica.]

Czimken (*Polish*). A dance similar to the country dance.

D.

D. (1) The first note of the Phrygian, afterwards called Dorian, mode.

(2) The second note of the normal scale C.

(3) The scale having two sharps in its signature.

(4) The name given to a string tuned to D, *e.g.*, the third string of the violin, the second of the viola and of the violoncello.

(5) The name of a clef in old mensurable music, *D excellens*. [Clef.]

(6) *Abb.* for *Discantus, Dessus, Destra*, &c.

Da ballo (*It.*) In dance style.

Da camera (*It.*) For chamber use. In the style of chamber music.

Da cappella (*It.*) In the church style.

Da capo (*It.*) From the beginning. An expression first used by Scarlatti in his "Theodora," signifying that the performer must recommence the piece, and conclude at the double bar marked "Fine."

Da capo al fine (*It.*) From the beginning to the sign *Fine*.

Da capo al segno (*It.*) Repeat from the sign (𝄋) at the beginning.

D'accord (*Fr.*) In tune.

Dach (*Ger.*) Sounding-board. Resonance-body of an instrument.

Da chiesa (*It.*) For the church. In the church style.

Dachschweller (*Ger.*) Swell-box.

Dactyl. A metrical foot, consisting of a long syllable followed by two short syllables.

Dactylion (*G♭.*) An instrument invented by Henri Herz, for strengthening the fingers for pianoforte playing. [*c.f.* Chiroplast.]

Daina or **Dainos.** A term given to some little Lithuanian love-songs.

Daire (*Turkish*). A tambourine.

Da lontano (*It.*) In the distance, *e. g.*, *corni da lontano*, horns heard in the distance.

Dal segno (*It.*) To the sign (𝄋). [Da capo.]

Damenisation. The syllables da, me, ni, po, tu, la, be, which Graun employed for the notes of the scale in his vocal exercises. [Solmization.]

Damp, to. (1) On instruments played by plucking the strings, as the harp, guitar, &c., to check the vibrations by placing the hand lightly on the strings. (2) To apply mechanical dampers.

Damper. (1) Certain moveable pieces of mechanism in a pianoforte, made of wood covered with cloth, which, after the finger has struck the key and left it, immediately check the vibrations of the strings, and prevent that confusion of sound which would result if they were allowed to continue in vibration. (2) The mute of a horn, and other brass wind-instruments.

Dämpfer (*Ger.*) A damper.

Dancing. A graceful movement of the feet or body, intended as an expression of various emotions; with or without the accompaniment of music to regulate its rhythm.

Dancing is mentioned by the earliest writers, both sacred and profane, as a constituent part of religious ceremonies. There are many instances named in the Bible, needless here to particularize, and the ancient Greek poets have abundant allusions to the practice in their writings. Homer mentions dancing and music at social entertainments; Aristotle tells of dancers who were able to express manners, passions, and deeds in rhythmical gestures; Herodotus, Pindar, Athenæus, and others of later date refer to the practice. Donaldson says that all ancient dancing was "either gymnastic or mimetic; it was gymnastic when intended merely as an exercise, it was mimetic when it was designed to express some mental feeling, or to represent by corresponding gestures the words of the accompanying chorus sung."

Athenæus speaks of three divisions of the Greek dance: the Emmeleia (ἐμμέλεια), the Sicinnis (σίκιννις), and the Cordax (κόρδαξ); the first named from the melody played to it, the second from its inventor Sicinnos, and the third probably for the reason hereinafter explained. The Emmeleia, the tragic dance, was a kind of slow dignified movement or ballet. The Sicinnis was of a grotesque character, and was performed with a peculiar shaking of the body and violent motion of the limbs. The Cordax was less decent in style than the last named. It was introduced into comedies, and was performed by actors assuming to be under the influence of wine. In addition to these there were the Pyrrhic or war dances, expressive of the pursuit and encounter of an enemy.

The Roman dances, at first connected with religious observances, became by degrees separated from them, and perhaps degenerated, as it was considered disgraceful for a free citizen to dance, excepting during devotional exercises.

The Almée, or dancing and singing girls of Egypt, the Nautch girls of India, perform, at feasts and solemn occasions, certain dances akin to those which formed part of the ancient observances.

There is ground for the belief that dancing was not discouraged among the early Christians, and there are records showing continuance of the custom among the less orthodox sects at different periods of the history of the Church.

Dancing and pantomimic actions formed part of the amusements sometimes offered by the jongleurs, a body of the minstrel class; their dancing often included acrobatic performances. The common dances, popular among the people in various European countries, vary more in name than in character; and as they are unquestionable legacies of heathen days, have been condemned from time to time by the more serious-minded.

The force and original meaning of dancing is now lost sight of. It is not now regarded in the light of an act of worship, but is encouraged only as a means of social enjoyment. The rude forms of dancing have been softened and polished during successive generations, their character changed, and their identity or connection with their origin disguised under modified motions. Each country in which dancing is practised has considered itself free to change the steps, arrangement, and significance of the dance, or to give preference to one portion of a complicated whole; and such alterations have been accepted as new dances, when they are not really so. The German waltz, the French cancan, the English country-dance, the Spanish bolero, the South American chica, the Italian saltarello, the Hungarian czardasch, are all forms traceable to one source. The allemande, the brawl, the coranto, the fandango, the forlana, the gavotte, the hornpipe, the jota, the kalamaika, the loure, the measure, the minuet, the passecaille, the quadrille, the ringeltanz, the saraband, the tarantella, trenchmore, zapateado, &c., are only different names of the several motions of that called in England the country-dance, with such variations in melody and rhythm as would arise from the use of accompanying musical instruments more or less perfect in their construction, or on account of the speed at which they were danced, by which means a rapid triple measure may be made to seem duple measure. The advancing and retreating in the various figures; the embracing and

unloosing, the stamping, shrieking, and singing in some dances; the "grand chain," or the gallopade which generally marks the concluding figure of a quadrille, are merely mild versions of some of the several peculiarities of the ancient prototype.

The Italians of the 16th century are credited with the distinction of having invented that form of dancing known by the general term of ballet: they arranged the motions and gestures of the body in an expressive pantomime, and reduced the various actions to a series of well-defined and understood rules, so that the performers were able to impart to the spectators a perfect story without the aid of words; but their claim cannot be upheld, as the like thing had been done by the Greeks ages before.

The rhythm of the more important dances will be found described under their respective titles.

Darabooka or **Darabukkeh.** An Arabian drum; the body, to which is attached a handle, is of hollowed wood. There are various kinds of this instrument.

Darmsaiten (*Ger.*) Strings of catgut. [String.]

Dash. (1) A line drawn through a figure in thorough-bass, showing that the interval must be raised one semitone, *e.g.*:

(2) A line drawn through the duple time-sign, *e.g.*, ₵, implying a division either of measurement or of pace.

(3) A short stroke placed above notes or chords, directing that they are to be played *staccato*.

(4) In harpsichord music, a dash passing between two notes, called a slur, or coulé:

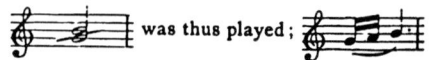

was thus played;

Da teatro (*It.*) In the theatrical style.

Dauer (*Ger.*) Duration or continuance of notes or sound.

Daumen (*Ger.*) The thumb.

D dur (*Ger.*) D major.

Début (*Fr.*) A first appearance.

Débutant, e (*Fr.*) A performer who appears for the first time.

Dec., *abb. of* Decani.

Dec., *abb. of* Decrescendo.

Decachordon (*Gk.*) An instrument with ten strings.

Decani (*Lat.*) A term used in cathedral music, to signify that the part so distinguished is to be sung by the singers on the dean's, or south side of the choir, in contradistinction to "cantoris" the cantor's or præcentor's side. [Cathedral Music.]

Deceptive cadence. [Cadence.]

Décidé (*Fr.*) Firmly, with decision.

Decima (*Lat.*) A 10th, an interval of a 10th; *decima plena de tonis*, a major 10th; *decima non plena de tonis*, a minor 10th; *decima quarta*, a 14th or octave of the 7th; *decima quinta*, a 15th or double octave; *decima tertia*, a 13th or octave of the 6th.

Decimole. [Decuplet.]

Decisio. [Apotome.]

Deciso (*It.*) Determined, decided, with firmness.

Decke (*Ger.*) (1) Cover, an upper or lower plate of a resonance box. (2) The cover of stopped metal organ pipes; *e.g.*, *lieblich gedeckt*, the sweet toned stopped-diapason.

Declamando (*It.*) In a declamatory style.

Declamation. The proper rhetorical rendering of words set to music. [Recitative.]

Décomposé (*Fr.*) Unconnected, incoherent.

Décoration (*Fr.*) Signature of a piece of music.

Decres., *abb.* of Decrescendo.

Decrescendo (*It.*) Decreasing gradually the volume of tone. Indicated in music by the abbreviations Dec., Decres., or the sign

Decuplet. A group of ten notes played in the time of eight or four.

Dedication. An address or inscription to a patron or friend, prefixed to a work.

Dedications frequently form a valuable guide to the historian, as by them it can be ascertained whether the author designed to honour any special individual, or, in the case of early works, whether a production was issued at the "cost and charges" of any particular patron.

Before the time when an author could command a large sale amongst the general public, it was not an uncommon practice to dedicate a book to one who had borne the chief expense in the production, and the ingenuity of the author was exercised in finding expressions sufficiently flattering in return for money expended or presented. The character of these addresses became at one time somewhat fulsome, as may be seen by the following, prefixed to Clifford's "Divine Services and Anthems:" London, 1663; the first book of its kind printed in England:

"To the Reverend Walter Jones, Doctor in Divinity and Sub-Dean of his Majesties Chappel-Royal, &c.:

"Sir,—Under your able patronage I have presumed to shelter this my weak endeavor, which if for no other reason ·than the welmeaning devotion thereof, I was sure would

not be unacceptable or troublesome to you. Be pleased therefore to intermit awhile those seraphical raptures, in the excellency whereof, and your thereto tuned piety, you are so famously happy. And vouchsafe an eare to the mean address of these rudiments (as it were) of Church Musick, which, like other perfections, hath suffer'd meerly through the peoples ignorance. To you therefore more especially doe I dedicate this essay, whose alone competent skill and judgement in the highest mysteries of this divine science, if it shall please you to descend and deign a favourable approbation thereunto, cannot but comand reception from others: since my knowledge at Oxford (improved further at London) of your eminency this way, cannot so far disoblige the world as not to believe you have the supreme mastery in religious musick; by which, as you charm the soul, and all its affections, no doubt you can prevail upon and perswade publick acceptance.

"I submit this piece in this (howsoever rude) manner to your judgement, having attempted, I hope something of tendency to the churches peace and harmony, whereof though I am a smal and an unworthy member, yet a mite even from such is justly expected: For higher works God hath fitted· and ·prepared your most artfull hand, and hath placed you in an orb from whence your melody (as of the spheres) of holiness and constant goodness in and for the church is universally heard with joy and delight. In which happiness, God Almighty long continue you here and late translate you to the angelical choire: So prayes, Reverend Sir, your most devoted and obedient Servant, JAMES CLIFFORD."

Master Thomas Mace, in a more manly mood, dedicated his famous book called "Musick's· Monument" (1676) to a higher power than a sub-dean, on the principle that a man's work should be "dedicated" to God, and only "inscribed" to a fellow-man. His "Epistle Dedicatory" runs as follows:—

"To Thee, One-Only-Oneness, I direct my weak desires, and works; please to protect both them and me; for Thou alone art able (and none but Thee) to make us acceptable unto the world.

"I am not of that Catholic belief
(I mean the Roman's faith) who seek relief
(At th' second hand) from saints; but I thus take
My freedom, and (sans complement) thus make
My seeming bold address: not judging it
A crime with Thee; but rather count it fit;
Part of my duty call'd for, which I owe ꞇ
Unto Thy goodness; therefore thus it show.
I've wondered much to see what great ado
Men make, to dedicate their works, unto
High mortals, who themselves can no way save
From the sland'rous tongues of every envious knave.
Thou (only) art the able-true protector:
Oh be my shield, defender and director,
Then sure we shall be safe.

"Thou know'st (O searcher of all hearts) how I,
With right-downright-sincere-sincerity,
Have longed long to do some little good
(According to the best I understood),
With Thy rich talent, though by me made poor;
For which I grieve, and will do so no more,
By Thy good grace assisting, which I do
Most humbly beg for: Oh adjoyn it to
My longing ardent soul; and have respect
To this my weak endeavour: and accept
(In Thy great mercy) both of it, and me,
Ev'n as we dedicate ourselves to Thee."

This is followed by "An epistle to all divine readers, especially those of the discenting ministry, or clergy, who want not only skill, but good-will to this most excelling-part of divine service, viz., singing of psalms, hymns, and spiritual songs, to the praise of the Almighty, in the publick assemblies of His saints; and yet more particularly to all great and high persons, supervisors, masters, or governors of the Church (if any such should be) wanting skill, or good-will thereunto."

In 1713 Mattheson published a sonata "dedicated to the person who will best perform it," and if it were necessary, many curious instances of remarkable dedications might be quoted to swell the list, but one only must suffice. There is extant a composition by Samuel Wesley, containing a series of intended violations of musical grammar, all of which are duly pointed out, and the whole is dedicated "without permission to William Horsley, Esqre., Mus. Bac., fifth and eighth catcher in ordinary and extraordinary to the Royal Society of Musicians."

Deductio (*Lat.*) The succession of notes as they appear in their proper places in the hexachords, which are in consequence called prima *deductio*, secunda, &c., up to *septima*. [Notation.]

Deficiendo (*It.*) Gradually dying away.

Dégré (*Fr.*) Degree of a scale.

Degree of a scale. A step in the toneladder; it may consist of a semitone, a tone, or (in the minor scale) of an augmented tone.

Degree in music. The rank or title conferred by an University on a candidate who has matriculated, and passed through the necessary examinations. They are of two kinds, Bachelor in (or of) Music, and Doctor of Music. The latter is generally taken by bachelors of several years standing, but in special cases candidates are allowed (by a grace) to accumulate, that is, take both degrees at the same time.

Dehnung (*Ger.*) Expansion, extension.

Dehnungstriche (*Ger.*) A long stroke with the bow.

Délassement (*Fr.*) A light trifling entertainment.

Deliberatamente (*It.*) Deliberately.

Deliberato (*It.*) Deliberate.

Del, della, delle, dello (*It.*) Of the, *e.g.*, *sopra il soggetto della fuga seguente.* On the subject of the fugue which follows, &c.

Delicato, delicatamente (*It.*) Delicately; *delicatissimo*, very delicately; *con delicatezza*, with delicacy.

Délicatesse (*Fr.*) Delicacy of performance.

Delirio, con (*It.*) With excitement, with frenzy.

Delyn *(Welsh)*. The harp.

Démancher (*Fr.*) To cross hands, in pianoforte playing. To shift, in violin playing.

Demande (*Fr.*) The subject, *dux*, or proposition of a fugue.

Demi-baton (*Fr.*) A semi-breve rest.

Demi-cadence (*Fr.*) A half cadence, or the cadence on the dominant. [Cadence.]

Demi-jeu (*Fr.*) Half power. *Mezzo forte*, applied to organ or harmonium playing.

Demi-mesure, demi-pause (*Fr.*) A minim rest.

Demi-quart de soupir (*Fr.*) A demi-semiquaver rest.

Demi-semiquaver. A note of the value of one-fourth of a quaver ♪

Demi-soupir (*Fr.*) A quaver rest.

Demi-ton (*Fr.*) A semitone.

Demoiselle (*Fr.*) A coupler in the organ.

Denis d'or. An instrument having a finger board like a piano, and pedals like an organ, capable of producing a vast number of different qualities of sound. It was invented in 1762 by Procopius Divis, in Moravia.

Derivative. (1) The actual or supposed root or generator, from the harmonics of which a chord is derived. (2) A chord derived from another, that is, in an inverted state. An inversion.

Des (*Ger.*) D flat.

Descant, Discantus (*Lat.*) The addition of a part or parts to a tenor or subject. This art, the forerunner of modern counterpoint and harmony, grew out of the still earlier art of diaphony or the organum, of which it is necessary to give a slight sketch.

Diaphony (διαφωνία) signified in Greek music discordant sounds or dissonance (voces discrepantes vel dissonæ), as opposed to symphony (συμφωνία) consonance. But the term came afterwards to be applied to those first attempts at the harmonic combination of voices, and polyphony, which may be looked upon as the first life-pulse of modern harmony. It is indeed strange that the term *diaphony* should have been selected for these early efforts, for, crude and painful as they are to our ears, they gave undoubted pleasure to those who first listened to them, who speak of their "melodiæ suavitas" and "dulcis concentus;" moreover, diaphony was well known to signify *dissonance*, intervals being divided into symphonic and diaphonic, the former including 4ths, 5ths, and octaves (and their compounds); the latter 2nds, 3rds, 6ths, and 7ths. That they should not have called it "harmony" would not surprise us if they were *only* cognizant of the exact force of the Greek ἁρμονία, but it happens that Isidorus of Seville (in the 6th century), gives the following definition of harmony, "consonantia plurimorum sonorum et coaptatio," a definition which so far diverges from that of the Greek, that it might have included all the efforts of the diaphonists, and indeed might almost pass muster as a definition of *modern* harmony. Why diaphony or the *diaphonia cantilena* was also called *organum* it is difficult to say. A later explanation, namely, that it was because of a supposed similarity to the music of the instrument "organ" is plainly untenable (apte similitudinem exprimat instrumenti, quod organum vocatur)—J. Cotton in Gerbertus Script. II. 263. In time of Charlemagne the art of diaphony must have reached some degree of perfection, as it is certain that Roman *cantors* were called upon to teach certain French chanters the *ars organandi*, and *pueri symphoniaci* were part of the musical staff of Vitalian at the end of the 7th century. The earliest forms of diaphony were of four kinds; when the organum was added to the "principal" or subject *throughout* at the interval (1) of an octave, (2) of a fifth (3) of a fourth, (4) at an octave above *and* below.

These species were combined in three or four-part music, thus presenting to the ear a simple succession of consecutives. It is unnecessary to give examples of each of the above; the following (from Gerbertus) will suffice as illustrations :—

In the above S stands for semitone, T for tone. It is thus rendered by Gerbertus (De Cantu, &c., I. 112.):

Ex. 1.

Tu Pa - tris sem - pi - turn - us es Fi - li - us.

He also gives the following, but in old notes and clefs :

Ex. 2.

Tu Pa-tris sem - pi - turn-us es Fi - li - us.

The next example is from Kiesewetter (Hist. of Modern Music):

Ex 3.

Sit glo - ri - a Do - mi - ni in sæ - cu - la,

læ - ta - bi - tur Do-mi -nus in o - per - i - bus su - is,

In another kind of organum, one voice held on a note like a drone while a second sang the tune.

But the first step towards harmony was to allow the *organizing* voices to have a choice of intervals, instead of compelling them, as seen in the examples above, to move in parallel quarts, quints, and octaves. The following example (No. 4) is from Gerbertus :

Ex. 4.

Te hu - mi - les fa - mu - li mo - du - lis

ve - ne - ran - do pi - is.

In the above it will be observed that several *3rds* are introduced; the admission of this interval (both minor and major) into the list of consonances represents another forward movement in the art of music. But 3rds (and afterwards 6ths) were not allowed to be *perfect*, but classified as *imperfect* consonances, a title which to this day adheres to these beautiful intervals, although their superiority to 4ths and 5ths has compelled modern writers to call a 4th a *discord*, and to forbid consecutive 5ths as an *abomination*. Franco and Garland have a division of intervals which is interesting as marking the transition from the treatment of 3rds and 6ths as discords, and their present position in music. These authors (see Coussemaker, p. 49) classify the unison and octave as perfect consonances; the 4th and 5th as middle consonances; the major and minor third as imperfect consonances.

The next important step in the progress of harmony seems to have been the giving due consideration to what we now term the relative *motion of the parts*. In the early examples (1 to 3) it must have been observed that there is nothing but *similar motion ;* in Ex. 4, *oblique* motion is mixed with *similar ;* and next we find authors boldly laying down the law that when the principal (or melody) ascends, the added organum should descend, and *vice versâ* (ubi in recta modulatione est elevatio, ibi in organica fiat depositio et e converso). This acknowledgment of the beauty and value of *contrary motion* must have given a new impulse to the art. Thus step by step did it grope its way, till in the 11th century important treatises on it were produced, and there can be also traced that sure sign of a healthy circulation of thought, a marked partisanship of different and opposed systems. After this period, instead of the "principal" and its "organum," we begin to read of a "tenor" and its "descant," and by almost imperceptible degrees the old system dies away as the new is grafted and feeds on it. It must not, however, be supposed that the successive changes in diaphony, above sketched, occurred in the exact order in which they are presented to the reader. Systems of art are never of sudden growth, they overlap each other; they perhaps grow side by side for years, perhaps for centuries, until those which have in them the smallest power of development decay, and leave the less-matured but better-constituted systems to survive, with fresh opportunities of thriving.

Descant, Discantus (Lat.), may be said to have come into existence at the end of the 11th or beginning of the 12th century. The word itself is thought by some to be merely a latinized synonym of diaphony; others, among them Franco, considered it to be connected with *de cantu*, something framed on or growing out of a melody. Originally, as had been previously the case with diaphony. it consisted of two parts only, but later in its life developed into motetts and various other forms of composition. The real difference between diaphony and descant seems to have been that the former was rarely, if ever, more complicated than *note against note*, whereas descant made use of the various proportionate value of notes—"Discantus est aliquorum diversorum cantuum consonantia, in quo illi diversi cantus per voces longas, breves, vel

semibreves proportionaliter adæquantur, et in scripto per debitas figuras proportionari ad invicem designantur" (Johan. de Moravia). It also included notes altered semitonally by accidentals, under which circumstances it was called musica ficta vel falsa, feigned or false music. This fact adds interest to a discussion which took place between M. Fetis and M. Coussemaker. The former taxed the latter with having misinterpreted his published specimens of diaphony, because, in it were introduced the tritone and the lesser 5th. M. Coussemaker's answer seems conclusive— it is to the effect that if the parallel motion of diaphony were consistently preserved, either such intervals must occur, or accidentally altered notes, outside the scale, must have been introduced : and such has not been proved to have taken place.

The rules of descant are numerous, and they provided for the regular addition of one part to any other part according to the movement of the tenor. The particular interval by which the *tenor* proceeded, dictated to the *descant* its own progression. It would be useless to give the rules here, as they can only be mastered by the student who carefully reads the many treatises on the subject, so elegantly reprinted by the indefatigable M. Coussemaker (Script. de Musica Medii Ævi). The scope of these rules was from time to time expanded, and in a treatise of the 14th century by Theinred, reprinted by W. Chappell (in the "Choir" newspaper of April 9, 1870), the divergences of the later from the earlier systems are apparent.

At this time, or even earlier, such expressions as *cantus firmus* and *contrapunctus* begin from time to time to be used, giving the first intimation of the art of adding *counterpoint* to a *canto fermo*, which was soon to supersede descant, as descant had superseded diaphony.

Opinions have been divided as to whether descant was merely a form of regulated improvisation, or whether it was a written art. In all probability, it grew from one state into the other. At first, without doubt, its rules were intended to direct a musician how to add "contrapunto alla mente ;" afterwards, when an interesting and successful descant had been framed, and perhaps often repeated, it would indeed be strange if the author had made no attempt to lengthen its existence by committing it to paper ; indeed, one sentence from Johannes de Muris substantiates the fact beyond dispute. He says, "Nihil enim prohibet in duobus cantibus simul esse cantantes plures, tam in tenore quam in discantu." It is inconceivable that a number of voices could be found to add descants *impromptu* without serious discrepancies. Descants were sometimes sung without words.

Descending. Passing from a higher degree of pitch to a lower.

Des dur (*Ger.*) The key of D♭ major.

Des moll (*Ger.*) The key of D♭ minor.

Dessin (*Fr.*) The design or plan of a composition.

Dessus (*Fr.*) One of the old names for the treble or *upper* part in vocal music.

Desto (*It.*) Sprightly.

Destra (*It.*) The right, as *destra mano*, the right hand.

Détaché (*Fr.*) Detached, or staccato notes.

Determinato (*It.*) Resolutely, definitely.

Détonation (*Fr.*) False intonation.

Détonner (*Fr.*) To sing out of tune: to sing harshly or coarsely.

Detto (*It.*) The same; as, *il detto voce*, the same voice.

Deutsche Flöte (*Ger.*) The German flute. [Flute.]

Deutscher Bass (*Ger.*) An instrument of the viol kind, with five or six gut-strings, midway in size between a violoncello and a double-bass.

Deuxième position (*Fr.*) (1) The second position or half-shift on the violin. [Shift.] (2) The second fret on a guitar.

Development of a subject. The elaboration of a given theme according to the rules of art. [Sonata.]

Devoto, Devozione, con (*It.*) With devotion, affection.

Dextra (*Lat.*) The right, *e.g.*, *dextra manu*, with the right hand.

Dextræ tibiæ (*Lat.*) Pipes held in the right hand; generally, the shorter of the *tibiæ impares*. Hence, *tibiæ dextræ* seems to imply a pair of *treble* pipes; *tibiæ sinistræ*, a pair of lower-toned or bass pipes. [Aulos.]

Di (*It.*) By, of, for, with. *Di grado*, by degrees; *stromenti di fiato*, wind instruments; *di chiesa*, for the church; *di bravura*, with *bravura* passages.

Diagonal Bellows. An old form of organ bellows, the construction of which may be thus explained.

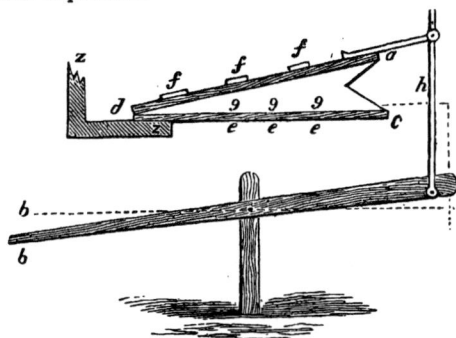

When the bellows are empty, the top (*a*), which is moveable (being hinged at *d*), lies close to the bottom (*c*) which is a fixture, and the handle (*b*) with its levers are in the position described by the dotted lines. Starting thus, if the handle be pressed down, as it leaves the dotted line, the top (*a*) will ascend, and air will enter the bellows through the apertures *e, e, e*. When the handle, having reached its maximum depression, is released, the surface weights (*f, f, f*) exercise their influence to restore the top (*a*) to its horizontal position; but in the mean time, the valves (*g, g, g*) inside the bellows have fallen over the apertures (*e, e, e*), and prevented the egress of the air through them; the air, therefore, is necessarily forced through *z*, the only exit left, into the sound boards below the pipes. It is evident from this, that during the time the handle is being pushed down, no air is being forced into the sound boards, because, the handle while being depressed negatives the effect of the surface weights. Hence, two diagonal bellows, at least, were absolutely necessary in every organ, whilst some had as many as 10, 12, or 14. The organ in St. Paul's Cathedral had originally 4 large diagonal bellows, measuring 8 feet by 4; and that in St. Sulpice, Paris, 14 diagonal bellows. This large number of bellows was sometimes arranged in a row, side by side, sometimes in two rows, one of which was placed over the other. In the latter case, ropes attached to the handles of those in the upper row allowed them to be blown from the same level as those below. Sometimes diagonal bellows were inflated by treadles, so arranged that the blower could easily step from one to another, whence the Ger. "Bälgetreter," "Calcant." One of the chief defects in the diagonal bellows was its inability to supply wind of an uniform pressure. This arose from two causes: the first, because the sides of the folds as they turned inwards, changing from an obtuse to an acute angle, gave more pressure as the top of the bellows gradually fell; the second, because the surface weights would exercise more and more pressure as the top, starting from an inclined plane, approached the horizontal. This defect was in time remedied by attaching to the rod (*h*) or end of the handle (*b*) a spring, whose tension was greatest when the top (*a*) was highest, and when therefore, as explained above, the air was least compressed. [For an account of Horizontal Bellows, see Organ, § 2.]

Dialogue. A duet.

Diana (*It.*), **Diane** (*Fr.*) An aubade, huntsup.

Diapason (*Gk.*) (1) An octave. [Greek music.] (2) The name given in this country to the most important foundation stops of an organ, termed in other countries more properly *Principal*. There are two kinds of diapasons, the open and stopped. Open diapasons on the manuals are nearly always of metal, but on the pedals are often of wood. Stopped diapasons were formerly, in most cases, of wood, but now are frequently made of metal. When two or more open diapasons are on the same manual, they are of different scales. (3) Fixed pitch; *normal diapason*, a recognised standard of pitch. [Pitch.]

Diapason cum diapente. The interval of a 12th.

Diapason cum diatessaron. The interval of an 11th.

Diapente (*Gk.*) The interval of a 5th.

Diapentissare (*med. Lat.*) To descant at the interval of a 5th.

Diaphony. [See under Descant.]

Diaschisma (*Gk.*) διάσχισμα. An approximate half of a *limma*.

Diastema (*Gk.*) διάστημα. An interval.

Diatessaron (*Gk.*) The interval of a fourth.

Diatonic. (1) One of the three *genera* of music among the Greeks, the other two being the chromatic and enharmonic. [Greek Music.] (2) The modern major and minor scales. (3) Chords, intervals, and melodic progressions, &c., belonging to one key-scale. A diatonic chord is one having no note chromatically altered. A diatonic interval is one formed by two notes of a diatonic scale unaltered by accidentals. A diatonic melody is one not including notes belonging to more than one scale. A diatonic modulation is one by which a key is changed to another closely *related* to it.

Diaulion (*Gk.*) διαύλιον. An air played upon the aulos or flute during an interval in the choral song.

Diazeuxis (*Gk.*) διάζευξις. The separation of two tetrachords by a tone: opposed to synaphe (συναφή), or the overlapping of tetrachords. [Greek Music.]

Dichord. (1) An instrument having two strings. (2) An instrument having two strings to each note. [Bichord.]

Di colto (*It.*) Suddenly, at once.

Diecetto (*It.*) A composition for ten instruments.

Diesare (*It.*), **Diéser** (*Fr.*) To sharpen.

Dièse (*Fr.*) A sharp.

Diesis (*Gk.*) δίεσις. Originally the name of a *semitone*, called afterwards a limma. In later writings, applied to a third or quarter of a tone in the enharmonic and chromatic scales. The modern enharmonic diesis is the interval represented by 125 : 128; that is, the difference between three true major thirds and one octave.

Dièze (*Fr.*) A sharp.

Diezeugmenon. [Greek Music.]

Difficile (*It.*) Difficult.

Di gala (*It.*) Merrily, cheerfully.

Digitorium. The name of a small por-

table dumb instrument, invented by M. Marks, for the purpose of strengthening and giving flexibility to the fingers for pianoforte playing. It consists of a key-board with five keys, kept in their places by springs of metal.

Di grado (*It.*) By conjunct intervals.

Dilettante (*It.*) [Amateur.]

Diludium. An interlude.

Diluendo (*It.*) Wasting away, diminishing; *decrescendo*.

Diminished. Made less. (1) Diminished intervals are those made less than minor, *e.g.*: G♯ to F♮ is a diminished 7th, because G to F being a minor 7th, G♯ to F contains one semitone less than the minor interval. Some authors, however, apply this term in a manner liable to lead to much confusion, namely, to a perfect interval when made smaller by *one* semitone, and to an imperfect interval when made less by *two* semitones; thus, according to them, C to G♭ is a diminished 5th, but C to E♭♭ or C♯ to E♭ a diminished 3rd. [Interval.] (2) Diminished subjects or counter-subjects are subjects or counter-subjects introduced with notes half the value of those in which they were first enunciated. (3) A diminished triad is the chord consisting of two thirds on the subtonic, *e.g.*, B, D, F in the key of C.

Diminué (*Fr.*), **Diminuito** (*It.*) Diminished.

Diminuendo (*It.*) Decreasing in power of sound.

Diminution. [Canon.]

Di molto (*It.*) Very much; as, *allegro di molto*, very fast.

Din-din. An Indian instrument of the cymbal class.

Di nuovo (*It.*) Anew, again.

Dioxia. The interval of a 5th. This term was afterwards supersed by *diapente*.

Direct. A sign (w) used at the bottom of a page of music, to indicate the note next to be sung or played:

Directeur (*Fr.*), **Direttore** (*It.*) Director. Manager, guide, conductor of an orchestra.

Direct motion. [Motion.]

Dirge. A solemn piece of music, of a funereal or memorial character, so called from the first word of the Antiphon, "Dirige, Domine Deus meus, in conspectu tuo, viam meam." The office of burial of the dead was called in the Primer (cir. 1400) *Placebo* and *Dirige*, and in the Primer of Henry VIII (1545) is called The Dirige.

Diretta, alla (*It.*) In direct motion.

Dis (*Ger.*) D sharp.

Di salto (*It.*) By a leap, spoken of melody progressing by skips.

Discant. [Descant.]

Discant-Geige (*Ger.*) An old term for the violin.

Discant-Schlüssel (*Ger.*) The soprano clef. Descant clef. [Clef.]

Discord. A chord which when struck or sung requires to be resolved into a concord. [Harmony.]

Discreto, con discrezione (*It.*) Prudently, discreetly, with judgment.

Disdiapason (*Gk.*) An interval of two octaves ; a 15th.

Disinvolto (*It.*) Free, unfettered, naturally.

Disjunct motion. [Motion.]

Dis moll (*Ger.*) D sharp minor.

Disperato, con disperazione (*It.*) Despairing, with desperation.

Dispersed harmony. Harmony in which the notes composing the chord are at wide intervals from each other :

Disposition. Arrangement (1) of the parts of a chord, with regard to the intervals between them ; (2) of the parts of a score, with regard to their relative order ; (3) of voices and instruments with a view to their greatest efficiency or to the convenience of their positions ; (4) of the groups of pipes in an organ, or of the registers or stops bringing them under control.

Dissonance. Discord. [Harmony.]

Dissonare (*It.*) To jar, to make discord.

Distanza (*It.*) Distance, an interval.

Distinto (*It.*) Clear, distinct.

Dithyrambus (*Gk.*) A song in honour of Bacchus, from which arose the first dramatic representations in Athens. The choruses to the early tragedies were in dithyrambic form.

Dito (*It.*) A finger.

Dito grosso (*It.*) The thumb.

Ditone. An interval of two major tones. This interval exceeds the major third, which consists of a major and minor tone, and is discordant.

Ditonus (*Lat.*) [Ditone.]

Ditty. A short, simple air, implying or containing a moral application. The word is said to be derived from the Latin word dictum, and signified a saying or sentence, not always connected with rhythm or music. [Ballad.]

Divertimento (*It.*) A composition of a light, pleasing character, whether vocal or instrumental, written to engage the attention in a cheerful manner.

Divertissement (*Fr.*) [Divertimento.]

Divisi (*It.*) Divided. A direction that instruments playing from one line of music are to separate and play in two parts. The reunion of the parts into unison is directed by the words *a due, e.g.* :

Division. An elaborate variation for voices or instruments upon a simple theme ; a course of notes so connected that they form one series. Divisions for the voice are intended to be sung in one breath to one syllable. The performance of this style of music is called *running* a division :

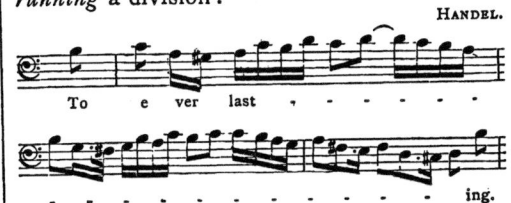

Division viol. A violin with frets upon the finger-board. [Violin.]

Divotamente, divoto (*It.*) *Divozione, con* (*It.*) Devoutly, devotedly, with devotion.

Dixième (*Fr.*) The interval of a 10th.

D moll (*Ger.*) The key of D minor.

Do. The first of the syllables used for the solfeggio of the scale. The note c, to which it is applied, was originally called Ut [Aretinian syllables], and is still called so in France. Its introduction dates from the 17th century. Lorenzo Penna in his "Albori Musicale," 1672, uses *do* for *ut*, and speaks of it as a recent practice. [Solfeggio.] [Notation.]

Doctor of, or in, music. [Bachelor.] [Degree.]

Dodecachordon (*Gk.*) An instrument with twelve strings.

Dodecuplet. A collection or group of twelve notes to be played in the time of eight.

Doigté (*Fr.*) (from Doigter, to finger). Marking by signs or numerals the manner in which a piece of music should be played by the fingers. [Fingering.]

Dolcan. [Dulciana.]

Dolce. A soft-toned 8-ft. organ stop.

Dolce (*It.*) Sweet ; *dolce maniera*, in a sweet style.

Dolcemente, Dolcezza, con (*It.*) With softness and sweetness.

Dolciano, Dolcino (*It.*), *Dulcan* (*Ger.*), *Dulzaginas* (*Sp.*) [Dulciana.]

Dolcissimo (*It.*) With the utmost degree of sweetness.

Dolente, dolentemente, dolentissimo, con dolore, con duolo, doloroso (*It.*) In a plaintive, sorrowful style; with sadness.

Dolzflöte (*Ger.*) The old German flute, with seven ventages and one key.

Domchor (*Ger.*) The choir or body of singers in a cathedral church, usually consisting of boys and men.

Dominant. (1) The fifth degree of the scale. [Harmony.] (2) The reciting note of Gregorian chants. [Chant.]

Dominante (*Fr.*) Dominant.

Donna, prima (*It.*) The principal female singer in an opera.

Doppelbe (*Ger.*) A double flat, ♭♭.

Doppelflöte (*Ger.*) An organ stop, consisting of wood pipes having each two mouths.

Doppelfuge (*Ger.*) A double fugue; a fugue with two subjects. [Fugue.]

Doppelgeige (*Ger.*) One of the names by which the viol d'amour, *q.v.*, is known in Germany.

Doppelgriffe (*Ger.*) Double-stopping on a violin; playing on two strings at once.

Doppelkreuz (*Ger.*) A double sharp ✕.

Doppelschlag (*Ger.*) A double beat or grace note. [Beat.]

Dopio (*It.*) Double, *e.g.*, *doppio movimento*, at double the pace; *doppio pedale*, the pedal part in octaves.

Dopo (*It.*) After.

Dorian mode. [Greek Music.] [Plain Song.]

Dorien (*Fr.*) Dorian.

Dot. (1) A point added to a note, or rest, which lengthens its value by one-half, *e.g.*: ○ . is equal to ♩ ♩ ♩ ; ♩. is equal to ♪ ♪ ♪ When a second dot follows the first (when the note or rest is *doubly dotted*), the second dot adds one-half of the value of the previous dot *e.g.*: ○ . . is equal to ○ ♩ ♪ ; ♩ . . is equal to ♩ ♪ ♬ A dot was called the *point* of addition (punctus), hence a dotted note was called formerly a *pricked note;* this expression must not, however, be connected with *prick-song*, which signifies written music, as opposed to music sung by ear.

(2) When placed over a note, the dot is a direction that the note is to be played or sung *staccato*.

(3) When two or four dots are placed in the spaces of the stave, on either side of a double bar, they are a direction to repeat so much of the music as is enclosed between them.

(4) When placed under a slur, dots are a direction to play *spiccato*, that is, in violin playing, played by the same *bow*, but the bow must remain stationary between each sound. From violin music the term has been trans-

ferred to that for the pianoforte, and sometimes for the voice.

(5) A system of Tablature for wind instruments, the *dot system*. [Tablature.]

(6) Dots were formerly placed over a note to show its subdivision into lesser repeated notes, *e.g.*, would be equal to

Double (*Fr.*) A turn:

Written. *Performed.*

Double. (1) An old term for a variation. In some of Handel's harpsichord lessons, the variations of a theme are marked Double 1, Double 2, &c. A variation on a dance tune is called a double. (2) The repetition of words in singing was also called the "doubles or ingeminations thereof." (3) An artist who understudies a part in an opera, that is, who prepares a part on the chance of the accidental absence of the principal. (4) That which is an octave below the unison in pitch, *e.g.*, *double-bass*, an instrument whose sounds are an octave below those of the violoncello; *double-bassoon*, an instrument similarly sounding an octave below the bassoon; *double-diapason*, an organ stop of 16-ft. pitch.

Double action. [Harp.]

Double backfall. An ornament in old music, *e.g.*:

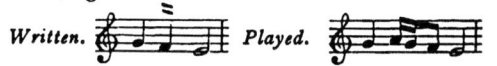

Written. *Played.*

Double bar. A sign formed of two single bars showing (1) the end of a piece, (2) the end of a movement of a work, (3) the end of a portion to be repeated, (4) the commencement of a change of key, (5) the commencement of a change of time, (6) the end of a line of words set to music, as in a hymn tune. [Bar.]

Double-bass. *Violone* (*It.*) *Contre-basse* (*Fr.*) The largest of the stringed instruments played with a bow. The strings are usually tuned a fourth apart to the following notes when three strings are employed:

with the addition of the lower E:

when there are four strings. The compass generally written for the instrument extends to the upper F:

with every intermediate semitone from its lowest note. The actual sounds produced are an octave lower than written, hence the double bass is sometimes called a transposing instrument. The four-stringed double bass is more common abroad than in England, so it is not unusual to find passages written below the lower A, which a three-stringed bass performs on the octave above. Double notes are possible upon the instrument, but are rarely employed as they are ineffective. Continuous rapid passages are best divided between two instruments, but short quick runs are very telling especially when in unison or at the octave with the violoncello. Beethoven in the Pastoral Symphony takes his double bass down to C, an octave below the violoncello:

a passage which is impracticable upon the instrument as now generally constructed.

Beethoven also wrote passages for the instrument which, in his time, were considered too difficult for performance, and it was the custom for the players to "simplify" whenever his works were performed. But the improved skill of the players of the present time has justified the composer's foresight, and all the so-called difficult passages are given with ease and distinctness, even by the least distinguished double-bass player in the orchestra. The bow employed is the only representative now in use of one of the primitive forms, and although it has the advantage of producing a thick, heavy quality of sound in slow movements, it is not always successful in eliciting an even tone in quick passages.

The harmonics on the double bass are of a beautiful flute-like character, and have been made available by solo players in exciting wonder and admiration.

The mute is rarely, if ever, employed, but the *pizzicato* on the instrument has a very fine effect, as in the overture to "Der Freischütz," and elsewhere.

The invention of the double bass is attributed to Gaspar di Salo, 1580; but as the members of the Confrérie de St. Julien were distinguished as players upon "high and low" instruments, it is probable that the reputed invention was after all only an improvement. The introduction of the instrument into the orchestra is due to Michael Monteclarè, about the year 1696. Before this time the Bass-vial or Viola da Gamba was the deepest-toned stringed instrument employed. The "Contra Basso di Viola," mentioned in the score of Jacopo Peri's "Eurydice," is held to have been a larger sort of tenor violin, less in size than a bass-viol, and not a double bass.

Double Bassoon. The deepest-toned instrument of the Bassoon family. It stands in the same relation to the bassoon as a double bass does to the violoncello, that is to say, its sounds are actually an octave below those written. Its compass is

that is to say, from the B♭ below CCC to tenor F. It forms, in the orchestra, a magnificent support to the wind band, but good players are not commonly to be met with, partly because the large size of the instrument renders it very unwieldy, partly on account of the fatigue which the performer necessarily must undergo. The common habit of replacing it by an ophicleide should be discouraged, as the quality of the two instruments differs greatly.

Double beat. An ornament of old music, consisting of a beat repeated.

Double bourdon. An organ stop of 32-ft. tone. On the manuals it rarely goes below middle C; on the pedals it extends of course through the whole compass. It consists of stopped wood-pipes. It is found difficult to produce a pure tone in the longer pipes, as the first harmonic has a strong tendency to assert itself. [Bourdon.]

Double chant. [Chant.]

Double chorus. A chorus for two separate choirs: the several themes may be distinct, or so constructed that united they form one harmony. [Chorus.]

Double counterpoint. [Counterpoint.]

Double croche (*Fr.*) A semiquaver.

Double demisemiquaver. A note whose value is one half of a demisemiquaver.

Double diapason. [Double, § 4.]

Double dièze (*Fr.*) A double sharp.

Double drum. A drum with two heads, used in the bands of foot regiments, and being suspended from the neck of the player is struck with drumsticks held in the right and left hands. [Drum.]

Double flageolet. A flageolet having two tubes and one mouth-piece, admitting of the performance of simple music in thirds and sixths, &c.

Double flat. A sign (♭♭) used in music before a note already flattened in the signature, which depresses the note before which it is placed another half tone. It is contradicted by a natural and a flat.

Double octave. The interval of a 15th.

Double pedal point. A portion of a fugue or melody in which two notes are long sustained, generally the tonic and dominant. [Fugue.] [Sustained note.]

Double quartet. A composition for two sets of four voices or instruments *soli*.

Double reed. (1) The vibrating reed of

instruments of the oboe class. (2) A reed-stop on an organ of 16-ft. pitch.

Double relish. An ornament in old music :

Written.

Played.

Double root. [Sharp sixth.]

Double sharp. A sign (x) used before a note already sharp, to indicate that it is desired to raise the pitch by a semitone. It is contradicted by a natural and a sharp.

Double sonata. A sonata for two solo instruments, as pianoforte and violin, or two pianofortes, &c.

Double stopped diapason. [Bourdon.]

Double-stopping. The stopping of two strings simultaneously with the fingers in violin playing. The practice was first suggested by John Francis Henry Biber in 1681, in a set of solos for a violin and a bass: one of these pieces is written in three staves, two for the violin playing in double-stopping, and the third for the bass. He also in the same work suggests a varied tuning in fourths and fifths for the purpose of making the double-stopping easy.

Double-tongueing. A peculiar action of the tongue against the roof of the mouth used by flute players, to ensure a brilliant and spirited articulation of staccato notes. The term is sometimes applied also to the rapid repetition of notes in cornet playing.

Double travale. A direction in tambourine playing. [Tambourine.]

Down beat. The first beat in each bar is so called, because in counting time the hand or conducting stick is allowed to fall at that place.

Down bow. The bow drawn over the strings from the heel or holding part of the bow to the point; the greatest power of tone in the strings is elicited by the down bow. [Bowing.]

Double trumpet. An organ reed-stop similar in tone and scale to, but an octave lower in pitch than, the 8-ft. trumpet.

Doublette *(Fr.)* A compound organ-stop consisting of two ranks, generally a twelfth and fifteenth.

Doucement *(Fr.)* Softly, sweetly.

Doux *(Fr.)* Soft, sweet.

Douxième *(Fr.)* A twelfth.

Doxology *(Gk.)* The hymn or song of praise—the Gloria Patri—used at the end of the Psalms in the Christian church; also any metrical form of the same.

Doxologia magna *(Lat.)* The version of the angels' hymn, "Gloria in excelsis Deo,"

sung at the celebration of the Holy Eucharist. The greater doxology.

Doxologia parva *(Lat.)* [Doxology.]

Drag. (1) An ornament consisting of descending notes in lute-music ; *strascino, portamento, glissade.* (2) A *rallentando.*

Dramma lyrica, or **per musica** *(It.)* [Opera.]

Drammaticamente *(It.)* } In a dramatic
Drammatico *(It.)* } style.

Dreichörig *(Ger.)* The triple stringed grand pianoforte. A trichord.

Dreiklang *(Ger.)* A chord of three sounds. [Triad.]

Drei-stimmig *(Ger.)* Music in three parts.

Dritta *(It.)* The right hand.

Driving notes. Syncopated notes. Notes driven through the ensuing accent.

Droite *(Fr.)* Right ; as *main droite*, right hand.

Drone. (1) The monotonous bass produced from the larger of the three tubes of bag-pipes. As there are no governing holes in the drone the sound it gives forth serves as a continuous bass to any melody ; the pipe second in size is tuned to give out the fifth above the drone ; and the smaller pipe, called the chanter, has ventages by which the melody is made. [Bagpipes.] (2) The chorus or burden of a song.

Druckbalg *(Ger.)* A reservoir of wind, as in an organ, &c.

Drum. An instrument of percussion, of cylindrical form, having discs of vellum or parchment at each end, so made that the discs can be tightened or slackened at pleasure by means of braces acted upon by sliding knots of leather, or by the later application of screws. There are three kinds of drums : (1) The long drum, with two heads, held laterally and played on both ends with stuffed-nob drumsticks held in the hands of the performer. (2) The side-drum having two heads, the upper one only being played upon by two sticks of wood ; the lower head has occasionally strings of catgut stretched over its surface, and then it is called a *snare* drum. (3) The kettle drum, always employed in pairs.

The drum is a very ancient instrument, of Eastern origin ; it was employed by the Hebrews, Romans, Parthians, and other nations in religious dances, and as signals of war, and was probably first brought to Western Europe by the Crusaders or their followers, the old name for the drum and drummer being almost purely Eastern. [Naker, nakerer.] [Kettledrum.]

Drum-major. The name of an officer in the British army who is responsible for the instruction of drummers in the various roll-calls, and for the invention and construction of new beats, communicated by order of the major of the regiment to the drummers. The office does not appear to be older than the time of Charles II. There was formerly an officer in the Royal Household called the drum-major general, who granted licenses to other than the royal troops for the use of drums in their regiments.

Drum slade. A drummer.

D string. The third open string on violins, the second on tenors, violoncellos, and three-stringed double basses, the fourth on the guitar.

Duan *(Gaelic).* A verse, stanza.

Due, a *(It.)* [Divisi.]

Due corde *(It.)* Two strings. A direction that the same note is to be played simultaneously on two strings of a violin or other instrument of its class. The bow is made to impinge upon two strings, one open, the other stopped to the pitch of the open string.

Duet. A composition for two voices or instruments, or for two performers upon one instrument.

Duetto *(It.)* A duet.

Duettino *(It.)* A little duet.

Due volte *(It.)* Twice.

Dulçaynas *(Sp.)* The name of a larger sort of oboe, or small bassoon, " Se usa un genera de Dulçaynas que parecen nuestras Chirimias."—*Don Quixote.* As it is supposed that the instrument was brought into Spain by the Moors, the word may be derived from the same root as the Egyptian Dalzimr, both instruments being of the oboe or reed kind.

Dulcian, or dulcino *(It.)* The name of a species of small bassoon. [Bassoon.] [Dulciana.] [Dulçaynas.]

Dulciana. A word now applied, in this country, solely to a soft and delicate-toned organ stop, consisting of very *small-scale* flue pipes. Originally, a dulciana (dulcan, dulcian, dolcan, dolcin, or dulzain) was a kind of *hautboy* [Waits], and these terms are still found on some foreign organs as the names of soft *reed-stops*, as at Rotterdam, the Hague, and elsewhere, but in some cases the stop is not actually *reed*, but the pipes by their peculiar shape, narrow at the mouth and widening gradually towards the top, produce a reedy quality of tone. The dulciana stop was introduced into this country, or perhaps invented, by the celebrated organ-builder Snetzler. The first known specimen was included by him in the specification of the organ of St. Margaret's Church, Lynn, in 1754. Stops of this class are universally used, and are of great utility. They are most commonly found on the *Choir* organ.

Dulcimer. One of the most ancient musical instruments, used by various nations in almost all parts of the world, and which, in shape and construction, has probably undergone fewer changes than any other instrument. In its earliest and simplest form, it consisted of a flat piece of wood, on which were fastened two converging strips of wood, across which strings were stretched tuned to the national scale. The only improvements since made on this type are the addition of a series of pegs, or pins, to regulate the tension of the strings; and the use of *two* flat pieces of wood formed into a resonance-box, for the body. The word dulcimer is probably connected with *dolce*, sweet, through the intermediate word *dolcimela;* but the German name, *Hackbret (chopping-board)*, points to the manner in which it is played, the wires being struck by two hammers, one held in each hand of the performer. Perhaps the greatest divergence of form is to be seen in the Japanese *goto, or koto*, an illustration of which is now given :

The next figure shows a dulcimer of Georgia :

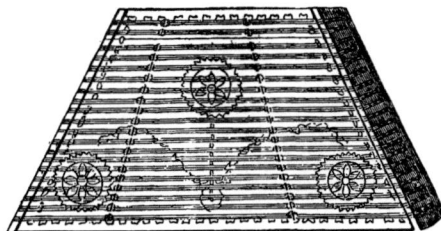

The Italians, who have ever been noteworthy for combining beauty with utility, have not failed to improve upon the original simplicity of the dulcimer, as the following illustration will shew :

The form of the instrument given in the next figure, the dulcimer of Benares, suggests that it is not placed, for use, in the ordinary position :

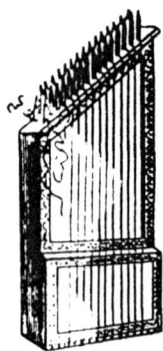

But, the fact which makes the dulcimer of the greatest interest to musicians is, that it is the undoubted forefather of our pianoforte. A modern grand pianoforte is, in reality, nothing more than a huge dulcimer, the wires of which are set in vibration, not by hammers held in the pianist's hands, but by keys: it is a *keyed-dulcimer*.

It is remarkable that in the immediate forerunners of the pianoforte (the spinet, harpsichord, &c.) the strings were plucked, so, the invention of "hammers" which constitutes the real difference between a pianoforte and a harpsichord, was in truth a return to a primitive type.

At one period the dulcimer came to be called in Italy a *cembalo*, possibly from its "ringing" cymbal-like tone, hence the same term was afterwards bestowed upon a *harpsichord (clavi-cembalo)*. In full scores it is not even now an unusual thing to find the pianoforte part marked *cembalo*. The dulcimer is much less commonly met with in England than formerly, but it is still to be heard in some rural districts, as the musical accompaniment of a puppet-show.

The following Swiss dance of the Canton of Appenzell, as arranged for a violin, dulcimer, and bass (from a collection of Swiss songs, &c., Berne, 1826), will give a fair notion of the capabilities of the dulcimer:

Dump or dumpe. The name of an old dance in slow time with a peculiar rhythm. It is doubtful whether it was entirely "dull and heavy," or merely the slowness of the measure that made the title of the dance synonymous with wearisomeness, for Shakespeare makes Peter, in "Romeo and Juliet," say, "O play me some merry dump," which may either have been descriptive of the character of the dance, or it may be a humorous contradiction in terms. Some authors have supposed that the dance is called *dump* from a trick of lute players who struck the open strings with the fist at certain marked intervals of the rhythm.

"MY LADYE CAREY'S DUMPE." (cir. 1600.)

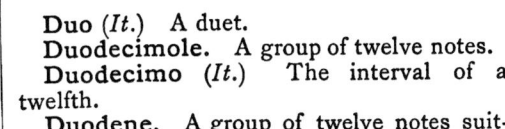

Duo (*It.*) A duet.

Duodecimole. A group of twelve notes.

Duodecimo (*It.*) The interval of a twelfth.

Duodene. A group of twelve notes suitable for playing on ordinary manuals, with definite relations of pitch, arranged for showing relations of harmony and modulation, and for precisely fixing the theoretical intonation of any chords and passages without altering the ordinary musical notation, first introduced by Mr. A. J. Ellis, F.R.S., in the "Proceedings of the Royal Society," vol. xxiii. pp. 3-31, and subsequently more fully explained in an additional appendix (xix.) to his translation of Prof. Helmholtz's treatise "On the Sensations of Tone," 1875. The intention, construction, and notation of duodenes will be best understood from a brief account of their generation.

Let C represent not only a note, but its vibrational number, in Roman letters independently of octave. Italic letters show octaves thus: $C_{,,}$, $C_{,}$, C, c, c', c'', c''', where C is the lowest note on the violoncello. Let the following letters and marks have the values written under them:

D	E	F	G	A	B	$\sharp$	$\flat$	$\dagger$	$\ddagger$
$\frac{9}{8}$C	$\frac{5}{4}$C	$\frac{4}{3}$C	$\frac{3}{2}$C	$\frac{5}{3}$C	$\frac{15}{8}$C	$\frac{135}{128}$	$\frac{128}{135}$	$\frac{81}{80}$	$\frac{80}{81}$

Then $\ddagger$D, read "low D" $= \frac{80}{81} \times \frac{9}{8}C= \frac{10}{9}$C $= \frac{2}{3} \times \frac{5}{3}C= \frac{2}{3}$A; $\dagger$A, read "high A", $= \frac{81}{80}$ $\times \frac{5}{3}$C $= \frac{27}{16}$C $= \frac{3}{2} \times \frac{9}{8}$C $= \frac{3}{2}$D; $\dagger$A$\flat$ read "high A flat"$=\frac{81}{80} \times \frac{128}{135} \times \frac{5}{3}C=\frac{8}{5}C=\frac{4}{5} \times$ 2 C $= \frac{24}{25}$A, and so on. The exact pitch of every note in relation to that of C is therefore given by its symbol.

The marks × quint, + major, − minor, | Greek minor, placed between two symbols, show that they form a Fifth $\frac{3}{2}$, a major Third $\frac{5}{4}$, a minor Third $\frac{6}{5}$, or a Pythagorean minor Third $\frac{32}{27}$, respectively, or their alterations consequent on changing either note by octaves.

†E♭ G An harmonic *cell*, as in the mar-
C E gin. contains C × G vertical, C + E and †E♭ + G horizontal, and C − †E♭, E − G oblique from bottom up to left, and hence all the *elements* of *tertian* harmony (*i.e.*, excluding harmonic Sevenths) and its *triads* C + E − G major, and C − †E♭ + G minor. C is called the First, G the Fifth, E the major Third, and †E♭ the minor Third of the C cell.

†E♭ G An harmonic *heptad*, as in the
†A♭ C E margin, consists of two cells,
F A the Fifth of the lower cell being the First of the upper cell. It contains four *cell triads*, major F + A − C, C + E − G ; minor F−†A♭+†C, C−†E♭+†G ; and two *union* triads, resulting from the union of the two cells into a heptad, major †A♭ + C − †E♭. and minor A − C + E. It has therefore all the six consonant triads containing C, its First, and all the con-dissonant triads containing two notes consonant with C and dissonant with each other (of which the *trine* †A♭ + C + E must be noted), and hence all the elements of chord-relationship.

†B♭ D An harmonic *decad*, as in the
†E♭ G B margin, consists of two hep-
†A♭ C E tads (of C and G) having a
F A common cell (of C), and hence contains three cells, having 3 major and 3 minor cell triads, and 2 major and 2 minor union triads, and hence all the related elements of scalar harmony of Thirds, Fifths and Sevenths. The First of the central cell is called the *tonic* of the decad.

A *trichordal* consists of three cell triads, selected one from each cell in a decad, forming 8 combinations of 7 notes, giving all the scales in use, with their harmonies, named by using *ma*, *mi* (with Italian vowels) for major and minor cell triads, and reading them in order from lowest to highest, thus—

C. *Mamama.*

B−D | F + A − C + E − G + B−D | F + A

C. *Mimima.*

B−D|F−†A♭+C−†E♭+G+B−D|F−†A♭

To show with what note the scale begins, change the *m* of the name of the chord containing it to *p* (for *prima*), or *t* (for *tertia*), or *qu* (for *quinta*), as in C *mapáma* (ordinary major), C *mipíma* and *mapíma* (two ordinary forms of ascending minor), C *mipími* (ordi-

nary descending minor), C *mimipi* (Helmholtz's mode of the minor Sixth). Thus 56 scales, including all the old ecclesiastical modes and their harmonies, may be succinctly described.

†d♭   †f   †a

†g♭	†B♭	D	f♯			
†c♭	†E♭	G	B		‡d♯	
†f♭	†A♭	C	E		‡g♯	
	d♭	F	A		‡c♯	

b♭   ‡d   †f♯

An harmonic *hepta-decad*, as above, where the capital letters indicate the decad of C, and the small letters the newly-added notes, and the oblong contains the *duodene* of C, consists of *seven* decads, having for their tonics the notes of a heptad (of C in the example). It shows six new decads, of each of which the original decad forms the larger part, and hence constitutes the first step in a more general process of modulation, consisting of change into a related decad, and called *decadation*. The heptadecad introduces tetrachordal scales, with chords of the extreme sharp Sixth. The *duodene* represents a decad in the act of changing, by means of the two new notes (d♭ and f♯ in example) called *mutators*, each forming part of two new decads.

A duodene is, therefore, formed on any *root* (as C), by taking the major thirds above and below it (as E and †A♭) to form the *initial trine* (as †A♭ + C + E), and then taking two-fifths above, and one-fifth below each of the notes in that trine. It consists therefore of four trines of major thirds, and three quarternions of fifths, and has three tonics, namely that of †A♭ *mapáma*, that of C decad, and that of E *mipími*. Its notes have a strict relation of pitch, and it contains no interval less than the small semitone or low sharp, $\frac{25}{24}$ (as †A♭ to A). But if the trine above, as †f + †a + c♯ were introduced, two intervals of a comma $\frac{81}{80}$ (as f to †f, and a to †a) and one of a diaskhisma, $\frac{2048}{2025}$ (almost exactly 10-11ths of a comma, as c♯ to d♭), would be introduced, and similarly for a trine below. If we took a quaternion to the right (as ‡c♯ × ‡g♯ × ‡d♯ × a♯), four intervals of a diesis $\frac{128}{125}$ (almost exactly 21-11ths of a comma, as ‡c♯ to d♭) would be introduced. Hence if we write the *duodenal*, that is the symbol of the root of a duodene, at the commencement of any piece of music, we determine the exact pitch which every one of its notes must receive, until we change the duodenal, and thus change the pitch of its notes to a definite amount. If we assume for the root named by the duodenal, the tonic of the decad of the duodene, the change of duodenal points out the actual decadations in the composition, that is, the actual process of the modulation. Thus, to take a simple but crucial example from " God Save the Queen," where the duodenals are written above :—

Observe chords 3, 9, and 13. The duodenal G makes chord 3 from D — †F + †A (in the dominant duodene), because the melody requires the true D in order to sink by a perfect minor Third to B, and the harmony does not treat chord 3 as the dissonance D | F + A. But the duodenal F, makes chord 9 from ‡D — F + A (in the subdominant duodene), because chord 8 contains A, and the change A to †A is unmelodic. But chord 13, in duodene of C, is marked as the dissonance D | F + A, which is duly resolved by the fall of D to C in 14, A being retained from 12. It would of course be possible, and smoother, to use the F duodenal, making chord 13 from ‡ D — F + A. In this way, three theoretical methods of treating the triad on the second of a major scale are accurately shown.

For further details and illustrations, reference must be made to the citations at the commencement of this article.

Duodramma *(It.)* A dramatic piece for two performers only.

Duolo, con *(It.)* With grief, sadness, pathos.

Dur *(Ger.)* Major, as *C dur*, C major.

Dur *(Fr.)* Hard, coarse.

Durate, duramente, duro *(It.)* With harshness, roughly.

Durchführung *(Ger.)* The development of a theme or subject. [Form.]

Durchgehend *(Ger.)* Passing, transient.

Durezza *(It.)* Rigour, harshness.

Dutch concert. A so-called concert in which every man sings his own song at the same time that his neighbour is also singing his, a practice not necessarily so national as convivial. There is another form of Dutch concert, in which each person present sings in turn one verse of any song he pleases, some well-known chorus being used as a burden after each verse. When every person has sung his song, all sing their respective songs simultaneously as a grand *finale*.

Dux *(Lat.)* The proposition, theme, or subject of a fugue, the answer being called *Comes*.

Dystonic *(Ger. from Gk.)* False intonation or discord.

E.

E. (1) The note Hypate in Greek music. [Greek music.]

(2) The key-note of the Church mode called Phrygian.

(3) The note Elami in the system of Hexachords. [Notation.]

(4) The E above tenor C, the octave above it being represented by *e*, the octave below it by EE.

(5) The key having four sharps in its signature.

Ear. The Ear is the organ of hearing, in other words, the organ for the appreciation of sound, *i.e.*, of vibrations of the air or water. All that is necessary to form an ear is a nerve-mass capable of appreciating these vibrations. Its simplest actual expression is a sac, filled with fluids, containing "otoliths" (οὖς, ὠτὸς, an ear, and λίθος, a stone), and supplied with a nerve, a condition best exemplified in the sub-kingdom of Mollusca, represented familiarly by the oysters, the mussels, snails both terrestrial and aquatic, and the octopus. The "otoliths" are masses of carbonate of lime, as may readily be seen by placing one of them dissected out from any of the above mentioned animals (*e.g.* a snail) on a glass slide, covering it with an object glass with sufficient water to fill the interspace between the two, and adding at the side of the covering-glass a drop of any acid (acetic acid, or indeed ordinary vinegar will do very well) while the experimenter observes it through the microscope. Air bubbles—really bubbles of carbonic acid gas—will be seen to pour out from the otolith, and when these have ceased, that body will have entirely disappeared.

It is true that we are suspicious of a specialised organ of hearing even in such animals as possess no specialised nerve system. This is somewhat apparently of a paradox, for it may be asked, How can an animal without nerves feel at all? and is it not highly improbable that if no nerve system exists, any special sense-organ can be developed? The answer to the first of these objections is very plain: all animals, even those who possess no specialised organs whatever manifest the simple phenomena of sensation; all, even the Infusoria and the Amœbæ, of which we hear so much now-a-days, and which are very little more than simple masses of protoplasm, manifest this faculty. Any one who has observed these occupants of almost any drop of water, with a microscope of low power, will have seen enough to convince himself of this. As to the second objection, the fact remains that in some animals which have no undoubted nerves, in some medusæ* or jelly-fish,† we find in the mass forming their body crystals of carbonate of lime, which substance must intensify the vibrations of the water in which they live, and must, when put into a state of motion as a whole, or into one which affects its particles *inter se*, cause by its relative density greater disturbance of the soft matter in which it lies, than would be the case if it were absent.

But leaving this as somewhat problematical, and taking the hearing organ of molluscs as the type, we shall find this type essentially adhered to in the higher animals in spite of endless complications. Let us propound the bold paradox without fear of contradiction, that a man as well as a snail hears in *water*, and that the essential parts of his marvellous hearing apparatus are a sac containing fluid in which are otoliths, and round which are distributed the ultimate filaments of a nerve.

The typical physiology, as well as the typical anatomy of hearing, is very simple. These "ear-stones," by the vibrations conducted to them, are made to rattle in this bag containing fluid, and, by beating against its sides, cause more disturbance to the nerve filaments there distributed than would be caused by the same vibrations if they acted directly on the nerve.

The power of hearing must be very widely if not universally distributed through the animal kingdom, though the hearing organ is not always easy to find. Von Siebold‡ has however discovered this organ in the European field-cricket, situated in the front legs

---

* These medusæ are by some said to possess a ring of nerves, but this is disputed.

† "Gegenbaur, Grundzüge der Vergleichenden Anatomie," p. 129, fig. 15 *e*, and p. 131.

‡ "Lehrbuch von Vergleichender Anatomie," von Siebold und Stannius. Berlin, 1848. Erster Theil, p. 582.

of both sexes. That the lower animals have the power of making music very widely distributed among them is a fact of which any one who reads Mr. Darwin's " Descent of Man," part ii., can very easily convince, himself; the references to this work would be too numerous to give with completeness, and extracts would be impossible, seeing that the subject occupies a considerable portion of the whole work. It is, however, sure that this power is possessed by some spiders (vol. i. p. 339); by many insects, as e.g. of the order Homoptera (p. 350—352), including the Cicados ; of the order Orthoptera (352—360), including crickets and grasshoppers ; of the order Hymenoptera (366), including bees and wasps; of the order Coleoptera (378—385), or beetles ; of the order Lepidoptera (387), or moths and butterflies. All these animals possessing the power of music, which they use principally for attracting the other sex (the male being generally the musician), must possess also organs capable of appreciating such music—auditory organs.

When we reach the sub-kingdom of Vertebrata we find the same type throughout, gradually becoming more complicated as we proceed from the lowest fish to the highest mammal, man ; and it will be convenient to reverse the philosophical order and to describe the human ear first, since after the description of this it will be easy to allude to deficiencies or modifications in the less complicated organs of the lower vertebrata.

The *Human Ear* may be divided into three parts—the external, middle, and internal ear. The two former have the function of conveying vibrations to the latter which appreciates them.

Fig. 1.

LEFT EAR.

(Transverse section).

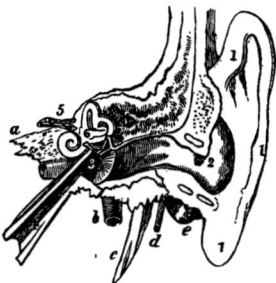

1. Pinna; 2. external auditory meatus or canal; 3. cavity of tympanum and membrane of tympanum (between 3 and 6 chain of small bones) ; 4. eustachian tube; 5. internal auditory canal or meatus giving passage to the auditory and facial nerves ; 6. bony labyrinth (above fenestra ovalis); a. apex of petrous bone; b. internal carotid artery; c. styloid process; d. facial nerve passing to supply muscles of face ; e. mastoid process.

The external ear (see fig. 1.) consists of two parts, the " pinna," or auricle (1), and the external auditory canal or " meatus " (2).

The pinna (1) is that part which is quite external, and which we unscientifically call " the ear," as when we say that a certain person has large or small " ears." It is composed almost entirely of cartilage or gristle, and has complicated foldings, to all of which names have been given, but which it is not our business to give here in detail. The general shape is that of an irregular funnel, having its apex in the auditory canal. The only part of which we shall speak particularly is the " helix," or the margin which is folded in. At the upper and posterior part of this is to be found, in many individuals, a small point or process, generally folded in like the rest of the helix, but sometimes projecting outwards. This is considered by Mr. Darwin to be a strong fact in determining the genealogy of man (" Descent of Man," vol. i. p. 22, fig. 2), for this point is well marked in many of the lower monkeys, as baboons and some species of macacus, and in them is not folded inwards, but stands erect. He thus considers it a reminiscence of some pointed-eared progenitors. He remarks (p. 23, note 26): " This rudiment apparently is somewhat larger in negroes and Australians than in Europeans (see Carl Vogt, " Lectures on Man," Eng. transl., p. 129), these races being confessedly lower and more like the lower animals than Europeans." The pinna is furnished with nine muscles, three of which are called extrinsic and move it as a whole, while the remaining six would, if they contracted, move its parts on one another, and are called intrinsic.

The extrinsic muscles are situated in front, above and behind, and move the pinna therefore forwards, upwards and backwards respectively. The anterior muscle is called the " attrahens aurem," the superior is called the " attollens aurem," and the posterior the " retrahens aurem." These muscles are in man without any function whatever; they do not have any effect on his hearing powers; they are capable of moving the ear only in some individuals, and are only rarely moveable at will. The " retrahens aurem," which is the strongest, is also the most commonly moveable; in some people it is contracted involuntarily in fright, just as in a timid horse who throws back his ears ; it is much more rarely under the control of the will, but is less seldom so than the other muscles. Mr. Darwin (" Descent of Man," vol. i. p. 20) says : " I have seen one man who could draw his ears forwards, and another who could draw them backwards;" but this gives too great an idea of the rarity of such an accom-

K

plishment. A case has been observed in which a boy was able to move his scalp from side to side by alternately contracting the "attollens aurem" of either side, this muscle rising from the "aponeurosis" (or flat tendon) of the "occipito-frontalis" muscle, which has the power of moving the scalp forwards and backwards.

The intrinsic muscles are situated, four on the outer, two on the inner side of the pinna. They have never been known to contract. In some animals, however, they are functional, as any one can see who carefully watches the pinna of the ear of a cat when intent on some sound.

In spite of the complicated structure of the pinna, it is nearly sure that it possesses no effect on our powers of hearing, either by collecting sound to a focus or by conducting it along its substance;[*] that it is in fact of no use as far as hearing is concerned. This is the result of the observations of no less an authority than Mr. Toynbee.[†] It seems also that the nearly precisely similar ears of the orang and chimpanzee are equally functionless ("Descent of Man," vol. i. p. 21).

The external auditory canal (fig. I. 2) is about 1¼ in. long; rather less than the external half is formed of cartilage or gristle, the remainder of bone. Its direction is not directly inwards, but slightly forwards also. It is closed at its inner end by the "membrana tympani" (fig. I. 3), or membrane of the drum. The glands which secrete the wax (ceruminous glands) are situated in the cartilaginous part of the canal, and agree in their structure with the sweat-glands.

Fig. II.

SMALL BONES OF TYMPANUM OR OSSICULA AUDITUS.

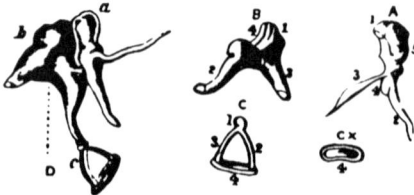

A. Malleus.—1. head; 2. handle; 3. processus gracilis; 4. short process. B. Incus.—1. body; 2. long process with orbicular process; 3. short or posterior process; 4. articular surface receiving head of malleus. C. Stapes.—1. head; 2. posterior leg; 3. anterior leg; 4. base. C*. Base of stapes. D. Bones in natural mutual relations.

The middle ear or tympanum (fig. I. 3) is separated from the external ear by the mem-

* In using a stethoscope, however, we use the conducting power of the cartilage of the ear.
† "The Diseases of the Ear," by J. Toynbee, F.R.S. 1860, p. 12.

brana tympani (fig. III. m, and fig. I. 3), which inclines outwards, making an angle of 45° with the floor. It is a cavity which is not shut off from the air, for the "Eustachian Tube" (fig. I. 4) forms a communication between it and the "pharynx," the upper part of the cavity of the throat.

Fig. III.

OSSICULA AUDITUS AND MEMBRANA TYMPANI IN SITU.

a. Malleus; á. tip of handle of malleus, the letter lies in the cavity of the tympanum; b. incus; c. stapes; m. external auditory canal; m̂. membrane of tympanum; t. line of tension of tensor tympani muscle pulling lower part of malleus inwards; l. line of tension of laxator tympani muscle pulling upper part of malleus inwards; g. slender process of malleus. The axis round which the chain of bones rotates passes through its base.

In the tympanum are situated three small bones (fig. I. 3 to 6, and figs. II. and III.), the Malleus (A), Incus (B), and Stapes (C), the names being derived from their shape. The malleus (hammer) has a round head (1), and a handle (2), and from the base of the head, a thin spike of bone, the "processus gracilis" (3) projects. The Incus (anvil), B, is more like a tooth with two fangs, a long and a short one. The long process (2) carries a knob or tubercle which is originally a separate bone, as it remains in some animals through life. The stapes (stirrup), C, is just like a stirrup. It is very difficult to understand the arrangement of these little bones from description or even from drawings, a model or the actual objects being almost necessary. It may, however, give a general idea of their position to say that the handle of the malleus and the long process of the incus are directed vertically downwards; the slender process of the malleus and the short process of the incus are horizontal, the former being directed forwards, the latter backwards; the stapes is also horizontal, but with its base horizontal and directed inwards. The malleus is anterior in position to the incus. The head of the malleus fits on to the body of the incus (the crown of the tooth), the long process of the incus fits on to the head of the stapes (the part where the stirrup-leather would be attached), and the base of the stapes fits loosely into the "Fenestra Ovalis," an oval window in the bony wall of the internal ear or labyrinth. The whole chain of bones turns round an axis formed by the slender process of the malleus and the short process of the stapes. The handle of the malleus is firmly fixed to the membrana tympani on its inner aspect a little below the middle. There are three muscles in connection with this chain of bones, two are attached to the malleus, one to the stapes. The two attached to the malleus are the tensor and laxator tympani. The former is attached just below, the latter just above the origin of the processus gracilis (see fig. III. *t*, *l*), which, as we observed, is the axis of this chain of bones. The stapedius muscle is attached to the neck of the stapes. These bones are exceedingly important from the point of view of comparative anatomy, since their homologies play very different parts in the lower animals. The homologue of the malleus, for instance, in fish, amphibia, reptiles, and birds, is the " os quadratum " which suspends the lower jaw; and the stapes is in batrachia, reptiles, and birds, the " columella," a long bone, shaped somewhat like a straight post-horn, or stethoscope, which alone discharges the function which these three bones discharge in mammalia. Other interesting points will be related later on in connection with development.

The cavity of the tympanum is practically enlarged by communicating with the " Mastoid Cells," air cavities which occupy the mastoid process of the temporal bone, that process of bone which may be felt behind and below the pinna, and is supposed by phrenologists to be the residence of " Pugnacity," though they have never explained the connection between that propensity and the function which these air-cells really discharge, that of increasing the tympanic cavity.

The internal ear or labyrinth (fig. IV.) is the essential part of the organ. It consists of two parts, a bony cavity enclosed in the thickness of the base of the skull, and a membranous sac within this.

Fig. IV.

RIGHT BONY LABYRINTH

(Smaller figure real size).

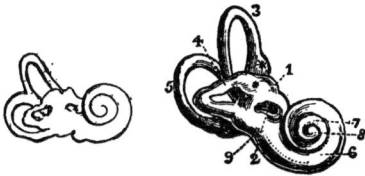

1. Vestibule; 2. fenestra ovalis; 3. superior semicircular canal; 4. horizontal or external semi-circular canal; 5. posterior semi-circular canal; 6. first turn of cochlea; 7. second turn; 8: apex; 9. fenestra rotunda; * ampullæ of semi-circular canals.

The bony labyrinth may be briefly described as a chamber, the " Vestibule " (fig. IV. 1), which sends one prolongation forward (the " cochlea," 6, 7, 8), three others backwards (" semi-circular canals," 3, 4, 5), and has its outer and inner walls perforated, the outer by the fenestra ovalis (2), in which lies the base of the stapes, and by a round hole closed by membrane, and called the fenestra rotunda (9); the inner by a series of holes in a depression called the " Fovea hemispherica," which transmit branches of the auditory nerve from the internal auditory meatus in which lie the auditory and facial nerves. By these two lateral perforations it communicates with the cavity of the tympanum externally, and with that of the cranium internally. Close behind the " Fovea hemispherica " is a small canal, the " Aquæductus Vestibuli," to which reference will be given later, in describing the course of the development of the ear.

The bony semi-circular canals (fig. IV. 3, 4, 5) are three tubes bent so as to form about two-thirds of a circle. They are situated at the upper and back part of the vestibule with which they communicate by five openings, one end of the superior having an opening common also to the posterior semi-circular canal. Each tube at one end has an expansion, called an " Ampulla " (fig. IV.*) These canals are called from their position, superior, posterior, and external. The superior canal is vertical and transverse, the posterior is vertical and longitudinal, and the external is horizontal. The directions of these canals, or the planes in which they lie, will be best understood by placing a book with the two covers at right angles to one another, upright on end on a table, so that one of the covers faces the reader, the other being at right angles to the side of the table at which he is seated. Then the reader will be on the outer or tympanic side, the side of the table opposite to him will be the side of the cranial cavity. The plane of the table will represent the plane of the external or horizontal canal, the plane of the cover opposite to the reader the posterior, and that at right angles to the side of the table at which he is seated the superior canal, which is also the most anteriorly placed of the three. Thus it will be seen that the planes of these three canals are the three planes of a cube, a fact to which allusion will be made hereafter.

* With regard to the terms anterior, posterior, external, and internal, it may be necessary to explain that anterior means on the side towards the face; posterior on the side towards the back of the head, and external and internal remote from or near to an antero-posterior axis drawn from the face to the back of the head.

Fig. v.

VERTICAL SECTION OF COCHLEA, SHOWING ITS THREE
PASSAGES OR SCALÆ.

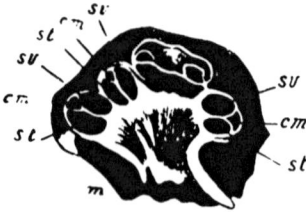

sv. Scala vestibuli; *cm*. canalis membranea, or canalis cochleæ, or ductus cochlearis; *st*. scala tympani; *m*. modiolus.

The cavity of the vestibule is prolonged anteriorly by the cochlea (fig. IV. 6, 7, 8), so-called from its likeness to the shell of a snail. As a whole, it forms a blunt cone with its apex outwards; this cone is formed by a gradually tapering spiral tube, the first curve having its concavity upwards; it is coiled $2\frac{1}{2}$ times round a central column or "Modiolus" (fig. v. *m*), which sends an incomplete partition into the cavity of the tube (fig. VI. 3). This partition is called "Lamina spiralis ossea," and winds in the cavity of the spiral cochlea like the thread of a screw or the staircase in a turret; it is wanting at the apex of the tube. This lamina is completed by two membranes, that nearer the apex of the cochlea called the "Membrane of Reissner" (fig. VI. 1), that nearer the base, the "Membrana basilaris" (fig. VI. *mb*), so that three canals are formed, that on the side of the apex of the cochlea being called the "Scala vestibuli" (fig. v. and VI. *sv*), that next the base called the "Scala tympani" (fig. v. and VI. *st*), and the intermediate one, belonging to the membranous labyrinth (here on the outer wall of the cochlea not lying free), called the "Canalis membranacea, vel Cochleæ," or "Ductus Cochlearis" (fig. v. *cm* VI. *a*). The scala vestibuli and scala tympani communicate at the apex of the cochlea, for the lamina spiralis does not extend quite to the apex, the scala vestibuli communicates below with the cavity of the vestibule as its name implies, the scala tympani would communicate below with the cavity of the tympanum through the fenestra rotunda, but that this is closed by a membrane. Thus it would be possible to get through the fenestra ovalis into the vestibule, thence enter into the semi-circular canals posteriorly, or anteriorly through the scala vestibuli to the apex of the cochlea, there into the scala tympani, through it to the fenestra rotunda, and through it again into

the tympanum. Most books describe the cochlea as divided into two passages, the scala vestibuli and scala tympani, but it is both more accurate and plainer to describe three passages from the first, otherwise it is impossible to account for the canalis membranacea in the description of the membranous labyrinth. The difficulty in understanding this part consists, as will be presently seen, in the fact that whereas all other parts of the membranous labyrinth lie freely in the bony labyrinth, the canalis membranacea is not free at its outer side, the side farthest from the modiolus, but is there attached to the bony labyrinth.

The membranous labyrinth lies, except in one part already alluded to, freely in the cavity of the bony labyrinth, and corresponds almost exactly with it. Between the two is a fluid, the "perilymph," or "liquor Cotunnii;" and within the membranous labyrinth is the "endolymph," another fluid. The membranous labyrinth is the part of the internal ear which is essential to hearing, the bony labyrinth serving to enclose and protect it. The membranous vestibule is divided by a constriction into two halves, which do not communicate. The posterior and larger is called the "common sinus," or "utricle;" with it communicate the membranous semicircular canals, which correspond in arrangement with their bony cases. The anterior and smaller chamber is called the "saccule;" it becomes constricted anteriorly into a narrow canal, called the "canalis reuniens," which opens into the "canalis membranacea" of the cochlea. This latter canal is, as above described, interposed between the scala vestibuli and scala tympani. It ends blindly above at the apex of the cochlea. "Otoliths," or "otoconia" (ear-dust, Gr. οὖς, ὠτὸς, an ear, and κονία, dust), are found in the common sinus or utricle, in the saccule, and in the ampullæ of the semicircular canals; and besides them, the ampullæ are lined with long, stiff, hair-like filaments, called "fila acustica." They are six-sided crystals of carbonate of lime, with pointed ends, and lie in the walls of these parts of the membranous labyrinth. They are occasionally absent. In these parts we also find pigment cells, which seem in some mysterious manner to be essential to the sensitive parts of nearly all the special-sense organs; for they are present in the olfactory region of the nose, as well as in the globe of the eye, and only in the latter is their function known. It is a well known fact, that white cats (cats which have no pigment) are deaf.

Within the canalis membranacea cochleæ, and separated from it by a membrane called the "membrana tectoria," lies an assemblage of structures known as the "organ[*] of Corti," after its describer. This is one of the most beautiful, as well as marvellously complicated, of all the structures in the body.

Fig. VI.

TRANSVERSE SECTION OF ONE COMPLETE PASSAGE OF COCHLEA.

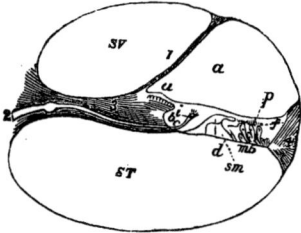

1. membrane of Reissner: 2. auditory nerve; 3. lamina spiralis ossea; 4. spiral ligament; *sv.* scala vestibuli; *st.* scala tympani; *a.* canalis membranacea or ductus cochlearis, or canalis cochleæ; *bc.* sulcus spiralis; *p.* membrana tectoria; *d.* rods of Corti; *f.* cells of Corti and Deiters; *i.* cells of Claudius; *mb.* membrana basilaris; *sm.* scala media.

The organ of Corti, then, has a floor called the "membrana basilaris," attached at the inner side to the lower lip of the free edge of the lamina spiralis ossea, and at the outer side to the circumferential wall of the cochlea. This membrane separates it from the scala tympani. Its roof is a membrane attached on the inner side to the upper lip of the free edge of the lamina spiralis ossea, and at the outer side to the circumferential wall of the cochlea. This membrane separates it from the canalis membranacea vel cochleæ, or ductus cochlearis. The essential part of the organ of Corti is a double series of rods, whose bases are separated by some distance, while their upper ends meet at an angle, the continuous series of rods forming a sort of spiral gabled roof, gradually diminishing as it follows the spiral course of the cochlea. The regularity of their arrangement, seen from above, suggests the key-board of a pianoforte. They have been estimated by Kölliker as about 3,000 in number, and are composed of a dense material. The inner series are more closely set and more numerous than the outer, which they overlap. Both series are enlarged at their bases and heads, especially the latter. The space between their bases and below their junction is called the "scala media" of the cochlea. Thus there are four canals in the cochlea, though this last belongs really to the canalis membranacea. Besides these rods, there are other bodies called "Cells of the organ of Corti." Some are placed between the inner series of rods and the free edge of the lamina spiralis ossea, and are called the "Cells of Claudius." They stand in a single line; their upper ends are provided with stiff bristle-like prolongations, or "cilia." The outer set are like them, but are placed between the outer series of rods and the circumferential wall of the cochlea. They are called the "pedunculated cells of Corti," and are set three deep, their cilia projecting through holes in a membrane extending from the junction of the rods of Corti over the outer cells of the organ of Corti to the circumferential wall of the cochlea, and called by Kölliker the "membrana reticularis." Between the rows of the pedunculated cells of Corti are interposed the "spindle-shaped cells of Deiters," which are fusiform, as their name implies. All of the basilar membrane not otherwise covered, is covered by six-sided cells of epithelium.

The auditory nerve, by which we appreciate sounds, does not rise from the brain, properly so called, but from the medulla oblongata, or that uppermost part of the spinal marrow which is enclosed in the skull, in company with the facial nerve, which supplies all the muscles of the face with motor power. The fibres of the auditory nerve can be traced to the floor of the fourth ventricle, *i.e.,* the expanded upper end of the tube which the spinal marrow really forms; and across this floor, to the fissure or furrow which separates it into two halves. Here they are found to rise from a mass of gray matter, *i.e.,* an assemblage of nerve cells called the "auditory nucleus." Other inconsiderable fibres are added from nerve centres in the neighbourhood, and some fibres are said to be connected with the sensory roots of the fifth or trigeminal nerve, the nerve of facial sensation.[†] It is connected by a small filament with the facial nerve. These two nerves run together along the floor of the cranial cavity outwards and forwards, and leave that cavity by the "internal auditory meatus," a hole in the petrous part of the temporal bone. The facial nerve traverses a canal in that bone, and leaves the bone to emerge by a hole just behind the socket of the lower jaw. While in the temporal bone, it gives off a slender branch called the "chorda tympani," which crosses the membrana tympani and handle of the malleus, and gives a twig to the laxator tympani muscle. It subsequently joins the gustatory nerve, the nerve of taste. Besides this, the facial nerve gives a twig to the stapedius muscle. In the internal auditory meatus, the auditory nerve divides into two portions, both of which contain nerve cells. One division is supplied to the cochlea, the other to the vesti-

---

[*] Zeitschrift für Wissenschaftliche Zoologie, tom. iii.

[†] Hirschfeld and Leveillé, pl. 15, fig. v. 5.

bule. The division which goes to the cochlea pierces the bony wall of the internal auditory meatus, not by one but by many foramina in the centre of the base of the cochlea. The central foramen is larger than the rest, and contains a nerve destined for the last half-turn of the lamina spiralis. The rest of the nerve fibres surround this, and ascending in the substance of the modiolus, they are distributed to the rest of the spiral lamina, piercing its substance, and running outwards to the scala media. These nerves form a continuous spiral ganglion, i.e., a plexus or network of nerve fibres, with the addition of nerve cells near the edge of the spiral lamina. It is probable, but not proven, that their ultimate ends are connected with the organ of Corti.

The vestibular division of the auditory nerve is distributed to the saccule, utricle, and ampullæ of the semi-circular canals, i.e., the parts containing otoliths.

The *development of the Ear* is conducted, in its first stages, like that of the eye or nose. The skin becomes bulged in on the side of the head, and forms a pit which sinks deeper and deeper, while the opening gradually narrows, and at last closes. Thus a closed cavity is formed, and this becomes the membranous labyrinth. Towards it the auditory nerve grows from the developing medulla oblongata. Next a prolongation grows upwards and backwards, persistent in the lower vertebrata but not in mammals, except as the rudiment called the "Aquæductus vestibuli." Next, three portions of the sac get pinched up in an elongated form, these ridges rise higher, and by-and-by the middle or most elevated portion of each becomes separated from the under-lying sac, by its walls coalescing in this part. Thus three tubes are formed open at each end, and one end of each becomes dilated. These are the three membranous semi-circular canals. Another prolongation grows forward and gradually becomes spiral. This is the canalis membranacea cochleæ. The bony case becomes developed round these from cartilage or gristle, from three originally separate pieces called "proötic," "opisthotic," "epiotic" respectively; i.e., anterior, posterior, and superior ear-bones or cartilages. These are separate in cold-blooded vertebrata throughout life. The space between the membranous labyrinth and its bony case is filled up by connective tissue which gradually liquefies and forms the perilymph.

The cavity of the tympanum, the external passage and the eustachian tube are developed out of what is called "the first branchial cleft;" for in the embryo there are formed four arches which lie on the sides of the neck exactly like the arches of the gills of a fish, and between them are similar slits so that the cavity of the gullet here communicates with the outer world. These all close except the first, which remains as the external ear, cavity of the tympanum, and eustachian tube. Some of the clefts however remain occasionally during life. Out of the first arch are developed in order from above downwards, the malleus, a piece of cartilage called "Meckel's cartilage," and the lower jaw, an arrangement persistent in fish; out of the second arch the stapes, stapedius muscle, incus, besides other structures which indirectly suspend the larynx, viz., the styloid process, stylo-hyoid ligament, and part of the hyoid bone. During the whole of fœtal life, according to Kölliker, the tympanic cavity is filled with connective tissue which embeds the little bones, and this only becomes absorbed after the child begins to breathe. The pinna is a lappet developed behind the first branchial cleft.

Propagation of Sound.—In order correctly to understand the sense of hearing we must have acquaintance with the principal laws of acoustics involved. Sound travels through air at about the rate of 1050 ft. a second, in water at about four times this velocity, and in very elastic solid bodies eighteen times as rapidly. In passing from solids to water the velocity is diminished, and from solids to air still more so ; the passage from water to solids is easy, but that from water to air or from air to water, very difficult. Vibrations lose much of their intensity in passing from air to solids. The cases of passage therefore from the medium of least to that of greatest density, i.e., from air to solid, or from the medium of least to that of considerably greater density, i.e., from air to water, are the cases of greatest difficulty in the transmission of vibration. A dry stretched membrane easily receives and transmits vibrations of the air ; and such a membrane placed on the surface of water overcomes in a great degree the difficulty of the passage between air and water. This assistance is enhanced when the membrane is combined with some solid body. Any membrane conducts sounds well when only in water. Sounds, like light, are liable to be reflected whether travelling in water or air.

Certain terms require explanation. Sounds are " communicated " when they are merely conveyed from one sounding body to another, and this can take place in a noise as well as a musical sound. Sounds are "excited"[*] under two circumstances : when the body which is sounding and that to be excited have the same note and the vibration of one produces sym-

---

[*] This property has been utilized in such instruments as the viola d'amore.

pathetic vibration of the other, the bodies are mutually called " reciprocating," while if the vibration of one produces its harmonics in the other, the latter is said, with regard to the exciting body, to be " resonant." According to Helmholtz, "timbre" or "quality" depends on definite combinations of certain secondary sounds or harmonics with a primary or fundamental sound, and such combinations he calls " sound colours."

Hearing.—Sounds may reach the auditory nerve either through the combination of specialized structures lying between the tympanum and the filaments of that nerve, or through the bones of the skull. In the normal state the latter road is so much less efficacious that it may be disregarded ; but when the other route is obstructed or rendered impervious, it then becomes the medium of the communication of sound. That sounds do however reach the auditory nerve in health by this way, anyone may learn by closing his ears and then speaking or singing. Under some circumstances the bones of the skull are the better conductors of the two; a tuning-fork held between the teeth gives a distinctly-audible note long after its vibrations have become inaudible through the air. Sounds are heard under water by this means.

The External Ear.—The *pinna* or *auricle* is said by some authors to help us to hear by reflecting sound into the meatus and by propagating it through its substance to the bony part of the meatus and thence to the membrana tympani. Reflection can only be helped by the large hollow behind the meatus called the concha, and by the point in front of the meatus called the tragus, the concha reflecting the vibrations on to the tragus, and this reflecting them in turn into the meatus. The other parts of the pinna have been supposed to assist sound by conduction, their various folds having the function, according to this view, of receiving vibrations in various planes perpendicularly and thus most favourably for propagation. Another view regards these folds as instrumental in neutralizing conflicting sound waves, that the principal vibrations may be able to enter the meatus without interruption. All these are mere speculations. An animal with moveable ears, such as a horse, turns his ears to the source of sound, but we have no such power, the extrinsic muscles of our ear are generally quite functionless, and never, in any case, possess this power, the only one which would help us to utilize our pinna. Mr. Toynbee believed the pinna to be quite functionless in man (see above).

The *External Meatus* is undoubtedly functional in conducting sounds, its closure will instantly prove this. Its curved course proves that the vibrations must reach the tympanum after manifold reflection from its walls and not directly. It serves to conduct vibrations without dispersion to the tympanic membrane. The column of air which it contains increases the strength of the vibrations which reach it, and by lengthening the tube of the meatus by adding a tube externally, and thus lengthening the column of air, the sounds are much increased in intensity. Its walls must conduct vibration to the membrane of the tympanum, but this function is so inconsiderable that we may practically neglect it.

The *Middle Ear* or *Tympanum.*—The *Membrana Tympani* serves to conduct vibrations received from the external air to the three small bones, the malleus, incus, and stapes, and thus to the internal ear. It is usually in a state of moderate relaxation, and is made more tense by the action of the tensor tympani muscle, and less tense probably by that of the stapedius and perhaps the laxator tympani. The vibrations which it receives are derived from the air in the external meatus, and perhaps also from the bony ring in which it is set.

The state of moderate relaxation which is usual to it, is the most favourable state for vibrating in sympathy with sounds of a wide range. The membrane vibrates reciprocally as a whole if the sound is in unison with the note to which it is (so to say) tuned by the muscles of the small bones, *i.e.* its fundamental ; or in resonance in divisions, if the note sounded is higher than this, one of its harmonics. That it is not always tuned to the very note sounded is obvious, when we consider that this can only be the case when one note only is sounded. It cannot, of course, vibrate reciprocally to a note lower than its fundamental. A membrane has a large power of vibrating sympathetically since its harmonics are very numerous. The effect of increasing the tension of the membrane may be easily tested by closing the nose and mouth and either blowing air out from the lungs or drawing it in. By the former we blow air through the eustachian tube into the cavity of the tympanum, and force the membrane outwards, by the latter we decrease the pressure in the tympanic cavity, and the external air forces the membrane still more inwards than is naturally the case. The result is in either case the same, the sense of hearing is on the whole impaired, though very high sounds are heard better than before. We have stretched the membrane, raised its fundamental note, and diminished its power of vibrating in sympathy with low notes, though we have at the same time increased its range of sympathy upwards. Still it is chiefly improved for *reciprocal* vibrations, for a lax membrane divides itself far more readily into segments which vibrate in sympathy with harmonics, the strength of such vibrations being increased by the number of the segments into which it divides itself.

The tensor tympani (perhaps the laxator tympani, though some deny that this is a muscle at all) and the stapedius are the muscles which regulate the tension of the membrane. These two muscles are generally considered antagonists, and are supplied by different nerves ; the former renders the membrane tenser, the latter, more lax.* They simply tune the drum of the ear, making the membrane tenser for high, laxer for low sounds ; there being practically a degree of tenseness which is most fit for perceiving vibrations of a certain average pitch. For exceedingly loud noises, as explosions, the probability is that the membrane is made tense, since in this state it cannot vibrate so freely. Thus is probably explained the sense of effort which we feel when *expecting* a loud noise which may never occur.

The *ossicula auditus* or small bones of the tympanum, that is, the malleus, incus and stapes, move as one piece, though they are not so tightly joined together but that they can play on one another. It is possible that their particles may also vibrate, but they are not adapted for this, seeing that much vibration must be lost at the joints between them. The direction of the application of the force to the malleus is the same as that in which it acts through the stapes ; a line perpendicular to the membrane is parallel with the long axis of the stapes, or perpendicular to the membrane closing the fenestra ovalis. Each time the membrane of the tympanum is bent inwards the base of the stapes is driven more deeply into the fenestra ovalis. The axis of the chain of bones is described above. Since the tensor tympani is attached to the malleus below, the laxator tympani above this axis, as far as their action on the membrane of the drum is concerned, the malleus is worked by the former muscle as a lever of the third, by the latter as a lever of the first order. These bones are covered with mucous membrane which must insulate them and tend to prevent the propagation of vibrations from them to the air in the tympanum.

The *Eustachian Tube* serves to equalize the pressure on the outer and inner sides of the membrane of the tympanum. It is naturally closed, being only open during swallowing or yawning, when the muscles of

* Some, however, consider both as *tensors* of the membrane

the palate, inserted on opposite sides of the tube are put into action and pull its sides apart, thus temporarily opening it. During a bad cold in the head we often become deaf, especially after blowing the nose. We simply perform the experiment mentioned above of blowing air through the eustachian tube into the tympanum, forcing the membrane outwards, and also rendering it too tense. The eustachian tube, however, is often swollen during a cold, and is pervious only to great pressure of air ; it therefore collapses and imprisons this extra amount of air. Some people know that their best chance of relieving this uncomfortable state is to swallow or yawn, though they do not know the reason. This sometimes opens the eustachian tube, and the much compressed air escapes, the hearing being at once regained. If this does not succeed it is sometimes necessary to pass a catheter, a tube appropriately bent, along the floor of the nose and into the eustachian tube, thus opening it. A very ingenious method was invented by Politzer for this purpose ; the patient, whose eustachian tube is impervious, is given a glass of water, and the surgeon, having closed one of his nostrils with one hand, inserts a tube into the other ; the patient is then told to drink. As he does so, the surgeon blows through the tube, and while the muscles of the palate open, or tend to open the tube, the additional pressure dislodges the plug of mucus or whatever was closing the tube ; it becomes pervious, and hearing is at once restored.

The *air of the tympanic cavity* probably plays little or no part in the production of sound, though some effect must theoretically be produced through it on the membrane closing the fenestra rotunda, and through it in turn on the labyrinth, especially the scala tympani of the cochlea, by means of the perilymph. That this effect must, however, be very small is shown by experiment ; for vibrations are very ill-conducted from the moist side of a membrane to air, and from this air to water through a membrane stretched on its surface, *i.e.* from the inner moist side of the membrana tympani, to the air of the tympanic cavity, and from it to the perilymph by means of the membrane of the fenestra rotunda ; whereas they travel with remarkable intensity between air and water when conducted from the first membrane vibrating in air to the second membrane stretched over water through a chain of insulated solid bodies capable of vibrating as a whole, the last of which communicates with a solid body in close apposition with the second membrane, *i.e.* from the membrana tympani to the membrane of the fenestra ovalis through the ossicula, covered with moist mucous membrane, the last of which, the stapes, has its base in close apposition with the membrane of the fenestra ovalis, being in fact imbedded in it. This is, therefore, the principal route of the vibrations in their passage through the tympanum.

The *membranous labyrinth* is, as above said, the essential part of the auditory apparatus, and hearing remains even if all the structures between it and the external air are disorganized.

As to the special function of its constituent parts, we know nothing certainly; suppositions have been made, but the theories propounded on the question have not advanced beyond the region of hypothesis. The vestibule is probably the most essential part, inasmuch as it is not only the first part of the ear to be developed in man, but is also the first part to appear in the series of vertebrate animals, being present in the lowest fishes, except the amphioxus, which has no distinct organ of hearing.

The *semi-circular canals* are supposed to help us to determine the *direction* of sounds, since they would, if prolonged, intercept vibrations in any direction, being in the three planes of a cube, and this arrangement is found in nearly all cases where they are present at all. But whether they actually fulfil this function is quite unproved. M. Flourens * has experimented on the subject by cutting one or other of these canals, but has not removed the difficulty.

The *otoliths* are supposed to intensify sound by striking against the fine endings of the auditory nerve as they vibrate.

The *cochlea*, by far the most complicated part of the ear, is involved in the same obscurity as regards its functions as the rest of the ear. The complicated structures of the scala media have been supposed merely to deaden vibrations after they have produced their effect on the auditory nerve, thus preventing confusion. But it is by far more likely that they have a higher office to fill, and it is now generally believed that they serve to distinguish pitch. The rods of corti especially seem adapted to this function, arranged as they are in regular graduated

* Solucha. Pflüger's Archiv, vol. viii., quoted in the *London Medical Record*, Feb. 11, 1874. Solucha has made further experiments which make this still more probable. On cutting one or more of these canals the animal executes certain disorderly movements. These are probably due to the fact that the animal has lost proper conceptions as to the position of its head, since somewhat similar movements follow from merely fixing the head unsymmetrically. These canals, probably, possess the function of informing the animal, by a series of unconscious impressions as to the exact position of its head in space, and each canal has an exact relation to a dimension of space.

series, dense as they are in structure, and elaborate as is the distribution of the cochleal nerve in their neighbourhood. They are supposed to vibrate each in sympathy with one note, and to transmit the vibrations to the special twig of the auditory nerve with which each is supposed to be connected. Not only would they thus appreciate pitch, but since "timbre" or "quality" depends on the definite combination of harmonics with a fundamental note (as Helmholtz has shown) they would thus convey what he well calls "sound-colours" to the sensorium, these sound-colours being combinations of a fundamental tone with harmonics, various both in pitch and relative intensity. Dugès, who first propounded the theory that the cochlea was the organ by which we appreciate "pitch," called attention to the concomitant variations in the evolution of the cochlea and the range of the voice in the three classes of mammals, birds and reptiles; the former having the largest, the latter the smallest development of both cochlea and vocal range.

A "musical ear" consists in the power of appreciating and distinguishing aerial vibrations both simple and compound, just as "the good eye for colour" consists in the power of appreciating and distinguishing the simple and compound vibrations of light.

When we hear a sound all that is proven is that particular filaments of the auditory nerve have been excited, not necessarily that there has been any external cause for the sensation. Aural delusions occur, though not so commonly as optical delusions. The singing in the ears which people often hear when they are out of health, overworked, when the blood-vessels of the head are congested, when blood is extravasated, when they are under the influence of a narcotic poison, when they are about to faint; all belong to this category. Many people are painfully conscious, even for many hours after a long railway journey, of the note to which their carriage has been vibrating.

Comparative Anatomy.—The lowest sub-kingdom in which we find any specialised hearing organ is that of the cœlenterata, the familiar representatives of which are the jelly-fish and sea-anemones. In them the ear is simply a sac filled with fluid, in which are crystals of carbonate of lime, the whole called a "lithocyst" or "stone-sac," by which the vibrations are intensified. This is analogous with the primitive auditory vesicle of man.

A similar structure is found in the sub-kingdom "Vermes," or worms, in certain marine worms called "Turbellaria," a familiar representative of which is the worm often seen on the sea-shore and called the "sea-man's bootlace." Many of the higher worms, or annelids, represented by the leech and earthworm, have a pair of such organs in the head, connected by a nerve with the nerve-ring surrounding the gullet.

Arthropoda, the sub-kingdom containing crustacea (crabs, lobsters, shrimps, prawns, and the wood-louse) ; Insecta ; Arachnida (spiders and scorpions) ; and Myriapoda (centipedes), have not all of them distinct hearing organs. In *crustacea* both closed and open hearing organs are found. In the higher crustacea they are found at the base of the inner or smaller pair of antennæ or feelers, and in them they are open. In another creature called Mysis they are placed in the tail, and are composed of an otolithic sac lined with hair-like bodies, reminding us of the human "fila acustica," which are, like them, connected with the endings of a nerve. In those which have open hearing sacs, the particles of sand which are washed in are utilized for otoliths, being fastened in regular order to certain of these hairs. This variety of hearing sacs among crustacea is very instructive ; whether closed or open they are closely connected with the integument, and the fact of their being sometimes open, sometimes closed, reminds us of the gradual development of the human ear, which is at first merely a pit in the integument, and afterwards becomes a closed sac (Gegenbaur, loc. cit. p. 388).

Among *Insects* the power of hearing must be almost universal, since music is so widely distributed among them, but the organs themselves have not been satisfactorily made out in many cases. Some have thought them to be represented by a tight membrane near the base of the feelers, others by the feelers themselves ; among the grasshoppers and crickets by a sac filled with fluid, connected with a nerve, enlarged as it spreads over the sac, the whole sac being placed below a delicate membrane forming the floor of a pit on both sides of the first abdominal ring. In some locusts it is placed on the basal division of the front pair of legs, and is composed of a vibrating membrane like the tympanum, in the neighbourhood of which is an air-chamber connected with one of the tracheæ or air-tubes which pervade the body.*

It may not be uninteresting to insert a detailed description of a very elaborate hearing organ which is found in some orthoptera. The passage is translated from Von Siebold and Stannius, "Lehrbuch der Vergleichenden Anatomie," part i. p. 582 :

"Only in certain orthoptera has a paired organ been successfully discovered which seems provided with the necessary apparatus of a sense of hearing. This organ is represented in the Acrididæ by a depression or pinna surrounded by a horny ring and more or less vaulted over, in the bottom of which a tympaniform membrane is spread out ; on the inner surface of the latter a pair of horn-like appendages rise, between which a vesicle filled with clear fluid, extremely delicate, is fastened as a membranous labyrinth. Connected with this is a special auditory nerve, coming from the third thoracic ganglion, which swells to a ganglion on the tympanic membrane, and ends in the immediate neighbourhood of the labyrinth with a number of little and extremely slender club-shaped rods; loosely surrounded with ganglion cells (? are these endings primitive nerve fibres). The locusts and achetidæ (grasshoppers) possess a similar hearing organ in the 'shins' of both forelegs. Some of the locusts possess on both sides of the 'foreshins,' close under the knee-joint, a depression, while others of this family of the orthoptera are provided on the same spot with two more or less spacious hollows, opening forwards by an aperture (auditory capsules). In these pits and also in the hollows of both anterior tibiæ of the locusts an oval tympanic membrane is fitted. Between the two tympanic membranes the main tracheal stem of the forelegs forms a vesicular swelling, on the superior end of which the auditory nerve rising from the first thoracic ganglion and running down with the main crural nerve swells to a ganglion. From this ganglionic enlargement a band-like nerve mass runs down on the gently excavated anterior side of the tracheal vesicle, upon which nerve mass a linear series of vesicles with watery contents rise which again contain those remarkable club-shaped and slender rods (? primitive nerve fibres). The two great tracheal trunks of the forelegs open with two wide funnel-shaped openings at the posterior edge of the Prothorax, so that here also part of the tracheal system as in acrididæ allows of a comparison with a tuba eustachii. In the achetidæ an opening closed by a silvery membrane (membrana tympani) may be seen on the external side of both forelegs close under the knee-joint, behind which a similar hearing organ is concealed.

"*Note.*—In acheta achatina and italica an equally large tympanic membrane is situated also on the inner side of the forelegs which, in acheta sylvestris, domestica, and campestris is only feebly indicated on this inner side of the tibiæ."

Hearing organs are also found in cockchafers in the root of the posterior wings. In the larva of crabs Heusen has described an ear consisting of an otolithic sac, in the adult the otoliths disappear and the sac is curiously composed of three demi-canals. In the *diptera* or flies they are situated in the rudimentary wings called halteres.

Auditory organs are found in all classes of *molluscs* either connected with the nerve ganglia in the "foot" or motor organ, as in the lower forms (oysters, muscles, snails, and slugs), or with the ganglia below the œsophagus, as in the higher forms. In the cephalopoda (octopus, &c.) they are placed in the mass of gristle which composes the head, and in them the sac is complicated. In all, the type is essentially the same, viz., a membranous sac containing fluid and an otolith or otoliths and supplied by a nerve. In certain mollusca called brachiopoda, hearing organs are found only in the larval state. In all molluscs the otolithic sac seems to be lined

---

* Gegenbaur, loc. cit. p. 389.

with ciliated epithelium, *i.e.*, epithelium which is furnished with eyelash-like hairs which continually lash the fluid in which they live.*

Vertebrate Animals (Fish).—No hearing organ has been found in the lowest fish, the amphioxus or lancelot. In all other fish it is present, and it is very interesting to trace its gradual evolution as we proceed towards the higher representatives. In the myxinoids the vestibule, the only part of the ear constant in fishes, consists of a simple ring-shaped tube lined with cilia, and lies freely at the sides of the head, like the primitive auditory vesicle of the human embryo. In the lamprey the ear consists of a vestibule with two semi-circular canals each of which has an ampulla. In all the higher fishes the labyrinth is enclosed in the bony or cartilaginous skull, and consists of three semi-circular canals, the vestibule being divided into two divisions as in man, with "endolymph" and "otoliths." The otoliths are often very large, as in the cod tribe. In the whiting, for instance, they may easily be found as two porcelain-like bodies, somewhat crescent-shaped and grooved transversely. In the rays the vestibule is prolonged by a tube which opens on the upper flat surface of the head. No fish has an external ear, tympanum, membrana tympani, or cochlea, but the labyrinth is often connected with the air-bladder, either by a tube or by a chain of bones. The air-bladder is thus pressed into the function of assisting the hearing (Weber, "De aure et auditu," p. 1245). In typical fishes we thus get the representatives of the vestibule, saccule and utricle, each with its otolith, and three semi-circular canals of man.

Amphibia.—In those amphibians which retain their gills through life, such as the newt and salamander, we have very little more than we found in fishes. They possess an internal ear only, which consists of a vestibule, three semi-circular canals; and as an addition to the ear of fishes, a "fenestra ovalis," with a small plate closing it, representing the base of the stapes. In one called the axolotl (that animal on which Cortez fed his army) this plate is connected with a little bone, but none of these creatures have a middle or external ear.

In those amphibians which when adult have lost their gills, we find the following additions. The labyrinth or internal ear has an otolithic saccule; in addition to the plate of cartilage closing the fenestra ovalis, which has a small muscle to move it (like the stapedius in man), we find a long thin bone "columella" running through a tympanic

cavity and connected with a third member, a small cartilage which is attached to a tympanic membrane, and has another muscle attached to it (like the tensor tympani in man). In these animals the middle ear or tympanum first appears; this cavity is filled with air and communicates by an eustachian tube with the cavity of the mouth. The tympanic membrane is on the level of the surface of the body—there is no external passage or meatus.

Reptiles.—We divide reptiles into ophidia or serpents, lacertilia or lizards, chelonia, or turtles and tortoises, and crocodilia, crocodiles and alligators.

In serpents we seem to have an ear inferior to that of frogs; they have no eustachian tube, the tympanum does not contain air, but a sort of packing material called cellular or connective tissue, the tympanic membrane, as such, is absent, the tympanum being closed externally by skin. This substitution of cellular tissue for air is very interesting when we remember that in the human embryo the reverse change takes place. With this exception the ear is the same as that of frogs.

In lizards we again find a tympanic membrane and cavity, a eustachian tube, and in some the commencement of an external ear. In the iguana, for instance, there is a slight fold of skin beyond the tympanic membrane, and this is again instructive, for in the human embryo the tympanic membrane is at first on the level of the skin; and the external ear, both the bony and cartilaginous parts of the meatus and the pinna, are subsequent additions.

In turtles and tortoises we find the tympanic cavity divided into two by a bony septum or partition, which, however, is incomplete. The cochlea makes its first appearance as a slight conical bud, as it does in the human embryo, and there is a fenestra rotunda.†

In crocodiles the cochlea becomes bent and divided into two scalæ. The tympanic membrane is placed at the bottom of a deep fissure, and protected by a flap of integument containing cartilage and capable of closing the slit by muscles attached to it; thus we have an external ear. The tympanic cavity communicates with air-cells in many of the bones of the head as in birds. Indeed, to the comparative anatomists to whom the striking difference between feathers and scales is the least difference in the world and quite unim-

---

* Gegenbaur, loc. cit. p. 513.

† There is one lizard of very exceptional structure which possesses a cochlea with an indication of the spiral curve which afterwards produces the form which we find in man. Its name is Hatteria, but it is indeed so full of anomalies that it is best mentioned in a note, and not as a representative of lacertilia.

portant, the crocodile is nothing but a bird with certain practically unimportant distinctions.

The ear of *birds* is composed of an internal ear consisting of a vestibule with a foramen rotundum, and a foramen ovale, a cochlea with an incipient spiral turn, three semi-circular canals, and two cartilaginous bands representing the lamina spiralis ossea; of a middle ear consisting of a cavity, filled with air, communicating with air-cells in most of the bones of the head, provided with a membrana tympani and eustachian tube, and with a columella or stapes. This columella which we have seen from amphibia upwards, is, as we have said, the stapes of man. It is shaped like a long post-horn, or like a stethoscope.

The external ear consists of an external auditory meatus, and an indication of a pinna in the form of a fold of skin just in front of the meatus; this is largest in the owls. In some birds as the bustards the meatus is surrounded by a ring of specialized feathers, which perhaps serve to reflect vibrations towards the tympanum.

The *Ear of Mammals* is in the main so like that of man that it will be sufficient to mention such differences as we find in different classes.

In the internal ear we find that the cochlea has a very variable number of turns. The hedgehog has one-and-a-half turns, the seal two, many ruminants somewhat more, next the camel, horse, and elephant, and many bruta (ant-eaters, sloths, &c.); the bats, apes, and man, two-and-a-half; most carnivora three, the pigs nearly four; the guinea-pig and agouti quite four; and the paca (a rodent) five; marsupials have a very varying number of turns, the kangaroo two-and-a-half (like ruminants which they represent among marsupials), and the opossum nearly five.*

The otoliths are not universally found among mammals. The labyrinth has many variations, for which reference must be made to the larger treatises. The "ossicula auditus" are very variable in shape; in the lowest order of mammals, the monotremata, including the ornithorhynchus (duck-billed platypus), and echidna (Australian ant-eater), the stapes is shaped like that of amphibia, reptiles, and birds; it is a long and thin bone without any division—a "columella," in fact. In cetacea or whales, dolphins and porpoises, the ear is very remarkable; the external auditory meatus is almost obliterated, in one dolphin hardly admitting a pig's bristle. It is probable that the vibrations of sound are communicated in them to the auditory nerve, not by the meatus but by the bones of the head, as in fish, and

in them the tympanic bone, forming the wall of the tympanum and supporting the drum, is very dense and hangs almost independently, reminding one of the large otoliths of fish (Owen), though whether it really fulfils the same office it is difficult to say.

The pinna is absent in most seals, the mole, cetacea, and the ornithorhynchus, in most diving animals it is very small. In some bats it is enormously developed, and has vibratile movements by which it seems to act as a sort of tactile organ "relating to the perception of atmospheric impulses rebounding from surfaces near which the bat approaches in flight."† Spallanzani says that a bat, after being deprived of the power of sight, hearing, and smell, by having the eyes put out, and the ears and nostrils plugged, was still able to avoid obstacles and to pass through openings only just large enough to admit its body.

Some animals have the power of voluntarily closing their external meatus—the elephant and the water shrew, for instance.

Ecbole (*Gk.*) The terms *eclysis* (ἔκλυσις) and *ecbole* (ἐκβολή) refer to the *flattening* and *sharpening* of sounds to adapt them to a change of key-note.

Eccedente (*It.*) Exceeding, *augmented*, a term applied to intervals.

Ecclesiastical modes. [Plain song.]

Echeion. ἠχεῖον (*Gk.*) (1) A hollow vessel, generally of metal (χαλκεῖον) used as a drum or gong. (2) Metallic vases so arranged behind the seats of the ancient theatre as to reinforce the sound of the actors' voices. An account of them is to be found in Vitruvius. (3) The resonance box of a lyre.

Echelle (*Fr.*) A scale, as *échelle chromatique, échelle diatonique*; chromatic scale, diatonic scale.

Echo. A sound produced by reverberation, an imitation of a sound so produced. (1) In old organ music the use of this term signified that a passage so marked was to be played upon the echo-organ, a set of pipes enclosed in a box, by which a soft and distant effect was produced, incapable however of so great expression as that obtained by the use of the *swell*, which is an improvement upon the echo-organ. (2) Echo-stop on a harpsichord was a contrivance for obtaining a soft and distant effect.

Eclisses (*Fr.*) The sides of a lute, guitar or violin.

Eclysis. [Ecbole.]

Ecole (*Fr.*) A school or style of music.

Ecossais (*Fr.*) In the Scotch style.

E dur (*Ger.*) The key of E major, the key having four sharps in its signature.

---

* Gegenbaur, p. 773.

+ Owen, Anat. of Vertebrates, vol. iii. p. 189.

Effect. *Effet (Fr.) Effetto (It.)* The mental impression produced by the performance of music, arising from the genius of the composer in the novel invention of pleasing or striking remedies, or telling harmonies, and the happy fitness of choice of certain passages, vocal or instrumental, in certain understood situations; or the clever interpretation of those passages by the performers.

Eguaglianza *(It.)* Equality, evenness.

Eguale *(It.)* Equal, as *voci eguali*, equal voices.

Egualmente *(It.)* Equally, evenly.

Eighth. The interval of an octave.

Einfach *(Ger.)* Simple; as, *einfache Intervalle*, simple intervals; *einfacher Contrapunkt*, simple counterpoint.

Einfalt *(Ger.)* Simplicity; as, *mit Einfalt und Würde*, with simplicity and dignity.

Eingang *(Ger.)* Introduction, as, *Eingang schlüssel*, introductory key.

Eingestrichen *(Ger.)* Having one stroke, as c', d', &c. [Pitch.]

Einheit *(Ger.)* Unity.

Einleitungs-satz *(Ger.)* An opening phrase, or introduction; an overture.

Einschlafen *(Ger.)* To slacken pace and diminish the power.

Einschlagend *(Ger.) Lit.* striking inwards, as is the case with a *percussion* reed; whereas *aufschlagend* is used with reference to a *free* reed. [Reed.]

Einschnitt *(Ger.)* An incomplete musical sentence or motive.

Eis *(Ger.)* E sharp.

Eisenvioline *(Ger.) Lit.*, iron fiddle. A nail violin, an instrument the sounds of which are produced from pointed pieces of iron. *Ger.,Nagel-geige.*

Eisteddfod *(Welsh).* A congress or session for the election of chief bards, called together for the first time at Caerwys by virtue of a commission granted by Queen Elizabeth, May 26th, 1568. Eisteddvodau have been since held in various places at uncertain intervals, and now (1875) will probably take place annually in localities made known some time before the assembly. The object is the encouragement of native poetry and music.

Eklysis or **Eclysis** *(Gk.)* [See Ecbole.]

Ela. The name given by Guido to the highest note in his scale.

Electric organ. An organ, the key and stop-action of which are connected with the pallets and sliders by the force of an electric current.

Elégant *(Fr.) Elegantemente (It.) Eleganza, con (It.)* Elegantly, with elegance of style.

Elegiac. In the style of an elegy; of a mournful character.

Elegy. ἐλεγεῖον *(Gk.)* (1) A distich consisting of an hexameter and pentameter. (2) A poem in elegiacs. (3) A composition of a mournful and commemorative character.

Elevatio *(Lat.)* (1) Arsis *q.v.* (2) A motett sung at the elevation of the host. (3) The raising of a mode beyond its *ambitus.*

Elevato *(It.)* Raised, exalted.

Elevazione *(It.)* A composition founded upon a special theme, as *Elevazione sopra il Pange lingua.*

Elève *(Fr.)* A pupil.

Eleventh. The interval of an octave and a fourth. A compound fourth.

Embouchure *(Fr.)* The mouth-piece of a wind instrument.

Emmeleia, ἐμμέλεια *(Gk.)* (1) Consonance, concord in musical sounds. (2) A Tragic dance accompanied by music. (3) The music of the Tragic dance.

E moll *(Ger.)* The key of E minor. The relative minor of G major.

Empâter les sons *(Fr.)* To sing legato, or with a *portamento.*

Empfindung *(Ger.)* Emotion, passion, feeling.

Emphasis. Accent. [Arsis.] [Accent.]

Emporté *(Fr.)* Passionate, hurried.

Empressé *(Fr.)* Eager, hurried.

Enarmonico *(It.)* Enharmonic.

Enbadinant *(Fr.)* Scherzando. [Scherzo.]

Encore *(Fr.)* Again, more. A word used in England when a repetition of a piece is desired. It is used both as a noun and as a verb in common writing; as, *an encore, to encore.*

Encœnia. Dedication festivals; in old English, chyrche-holy; Anglo-Sax., cyric-halgung, church hallowing.

Energia, con; energicamente; energico *(It.)* With energy, forcibly.

Enfant de Chœur *(Fr.)* A chorister-boy.

Enfatico *(It.)* With emphasis, earnestly.

Enfler *(Fr.)* To swell, to increase in sound.

Enfasi, con *(It.)* With emphasis.

Enge *(Ger.)* Narrow, close, straight. A term used in reference to the small *scale* of organ pipes, or to the closeness of subject and answer in a *stretto.*

Engel-stimme *(Ger.)* [Vox Angelica.]

Engraving of music. [Printing of music.]

Enharmonic. (1) One of the three genera of Greek music, the other two being the Diatonic and Chromatic. (2) Having intervals less than a semitone, *e.g.*, an enharmonic organ or harmonium is an instrument having more than twelve divisions in the octave, and capable, therefore, of producing two distinct sounds where, on the ordinary instrument, one only exists, as, for instance, G♯ and A♭, &c. An enharmonic *scale* is one containing intervals less than a semitone. (3) An enharmonic modulation is a change as to notation, but not as to sound, *e.g.* :

It is important to notice that an enharmonic modulation is not so termed in strict propriety, because, it is only feasible on an ordinary keyed-instrument by actually ignoring the existence of intervals smaller than a semitone.

Enoplius. ἐνόπλιος (*Gk.*) Warlike music. Music of the war-dance.

Ensemble (*Fr.*) Together. The whole. (1) The general effect of a musical performance. (2) The union of the whole company of performers in a concerted piece.

Entr'acte (*Fr.*) Music played between the acts or divisions of an opera, drama, or other stage performance.

Entrata (*It.*) *Entrée* (*Fr.*) Entry, introduction, or prelude. *Scena d'entrata*, the first *scena* allotted to a vocalist in an opera. (*Fr.*) *scene d'entrée*.

Entrechats (*Fr.*) The peculiar bounds with which a dancer leaps across the stage on entering.

Entremese (*Span.*) A short musical interlude, in one or two scenes, played by a few actors, rarely more than four. Entremeses were mostly of a burlesque character, and when performed between the preludes and the plays, Autos, or Loas, made an interlude of a nature peculiarly acceptable to the Spanish mind. The subjects were chosen from possible events of a droll character in common life, and were mostly written in verse. They cannot be traced to a higher antiquity than the 17th century, and are still popular in remote parts of Spain. When more than ordinary prominence is given to the music, the name Saynetes (the Spanish for dainties) is given to them.

Entremets (*Fr.*) Short dramatic or allegorical entertainments. A remote antiquity is claimed for this species of diversion, which some writers declare to be the origin of the opera and drama. The date of their invention has been fixed at an epoch during the reign of Saint Louis (1226-1270).

The king desired to re-awaken the enthusiasm of his nobles and warriors that they might join him in the endeavour to wrest the Holy Land from the hands of the infidels. He sought the aid of the Duke of Burgundy, who, flattered by the preference shown to him in being selected as the king's agent in the matter, sought every means to carry his wishes into effect. He gave a series of banquets and entertainments to the nobility, who at that time were noted for their luxury, not to say licentiousness; and in the course of these feasts certain allegorical poems, commemorating the deeds of the old warriors and kings, their ancestors, were recited or sung. Appeals were made to the chivalric spirit still supposed to exist in the breast of the scions of a warlike stock, and they were implored to unite in aiding the defenders of their religion in a crusade against the unbelieving occupants of the sacred cities. The stratagem succeeded, the nobles and princes joined with the Duke of Burgundy and bound themselves by oath to follow and support him.

The Entremets thus originated were continued on great occasions, and ultimately became diverted from their primary intention. The performers, *mimes*, *farceurs*, *baladins*, *ménétriers*, &c., as they are variously called, followed the fortunes of their lords, and in course of time invented new *entremets*, no longer confining themselves either to patriotic or religious subjects. These entremets suggested more extended performances, and what can now be gathered of their character has led many, not unreasonably, to assume, that in them was the germ of the modern opera.

In later times when acting was better understood, a further change was made in the style of the subjects selected, and the entremets were almost always of a humorous character, though heroic subjects were sometimes chosen. In 1237, upon the occasion of a marriage, Alberic, in his chronicle, speaks of the entremets then and there performed, and also adds that " Illi qui dicuntur ministrelli in spectaculo vanitatis multa ibi fecerunt, sicut ille qui in equo super cordam in aere equitaret, et sicut illi qui duos boves de scarlate vestitos equitabant cornitantes ad singula fercula quæ apponebantur regi in mensâ." In 1378, at a feast given by Charles V. to his uncle in the castle of St. Germain, two entremets representing the conquest of Jerusalem, by Godfrey de Bouillon, were performed. And at the marriage of Charles IX. in 1572, the entremets were on the subject of the destruction of Troy. Jean Antoine de Baïf in 1573 published " Mimes, entremets, enseignmens et Proverbes," which were simply epigrams, and the change of opinion with regard to the use of the word in De Baïf's mind, shows that even then a gradual alteration in the meaning and force of the entremets was taking place. The word is now employed to signify any small entertainment between two greater ones. *c.f. Entremeses.*

Entusiasmo. Entusiàstico (*It.*) With enthusiasm.

Entwurf (*Ger.*) A sketch.

Eolian Harp. A musical instrument made of a long narrow box of thin even-grained deal, about five or six inches deep, having a circle of small holes drilled in the centre of the upper side. On this side the strings, six or more, are stretched in parallel lines over bridges fixed at each end, the tension being preserved by means of screwpins. The strings must be tuned in unison, and the box placed in a free current of air. A delicate combination of sounds is then produced, somewhat resembling the effect of a full orchestra, without instruments of percussion, when heard at a distance, the sound increasing or decreasing in power with the force of the wind. The usual method of using the instrument is by placing it on the ledge of a half-opened window; but the tone is best produced when the box is made of the exact length of the window opening, and the lower sash of the window closed as far as the box will allow. The Eolian harp is the invention of an Englishman of the name of Pope, and was improved by Kircher, a German (1670). The harmonics heard are due to the overtones of the strings.

> " Behoves no more,
> But sidelong, to the gently waving wind
> To lay the well-tuned instrument reclined;
> From which, with airy flying fingers light,
> Beyond each mortal touch the most refined,
> The God of Winds drew sounds of deep delight."
>
> Thomson's *Castle of Indolence.*

Eolian mode. The fifth of the authentic Gregorian modes. It consists of the natural notes La, Si, Do, Re, Mi, Fa, Sol.

Epicedion. ἐπικήδειον (*Gk.*) A dirge, elegy.

Epigonion (*Gk.*) ἐπιγόνειον. A musical instrument, named after its inventor Epigonus, the date of whose existence is matter of doubt, and the character of the instrument is also somewhat uncertain. It is described as having forty strings, but the method of tuning is absolutely unknown.

Epilenia, ἐπιλήνια (*Gk.*) Vintage songs.

Epinette (*Fr.*) [Spinet.]

Epinicium. ἐπινίκιον (*Gk.*) A song of victory.

Episode. A term in fugue writing, applied to those phrases which are supplemental to the main subjects or their answers. [Fugue]

Epitasis (*Gk.*) ἐπίτασις. (1) The raising of the voice from a low to a higher pitch. (2) The tightening of the strings of an instrument, as opposed to ἄνεσις.

Epithalamium, ἐπιθαλάμιον (*Gk.*) A nuptial song.

Epode, ἐπῳδός (*Gk.*) (1) An after song, the strain of a lyric song after the strophe and antistrophe. (2) A burden or refrain.

E poi (*It.*) And then, after; as, *e poi la coda,* then go to the coda.

Equabilmente (*It.*) Equally, similarly.

Equal voices. A term for an assortment of men's voices or women's voices. Thus, a piece is said to be set for equal voices, when the voices of men only are needed, though the quality of those voices are not equal, the alto voice differing from the tenor as the tenor does from the bass. The like difference in a less marked manner, also exists among women's voices, but when all men's or all women's voices are required, the term equal is applied to each group. The union of the voices of the two sexes is styled "mixed." In its most true sense the term should only be applied to groups of voices of like register and compass.

Equisonans (*Lat.*) The name given to the consonance of the unison and octave.

Equivoca (*Lat.*) Equivocal, or doubtful, *nota equivoca* was, in mediæval music, a note whose value varied according to the length of the notes on either side.

Equivocal or doubtful chords. A name given to combinations of sounds which are common to two or more distinct keys, and which, when heard, make the listener doubtful as to the particular key-tonality into which they are about to be resolved.

The simplest form of chords of this class is to be found in the so-called diminished triad, *e.g.*:

The above chord may be resolved into the keys of C major, C minor, A minor, B minor, or B major (the last two by means of an enharmonic change), thus:

The inversions of this chord give, as might be expected, greater scope for varied progressions than can be obtained from its original position.

The next important doubtful chord is the diminished seventh, but in this case it will be noticed that the numerous resolutions are the result of its possible enharmonic change, whereas, in examples 1, 2, and 3 above, no alteration has been made in the notation of the chord:

If this chord be struck and held down while the eye traces the various changes of notation through which it is capable of passing, it will be found that an impression of an entirely new key is given at each successive change.

Composers have not been slow to avail themselves of the sudden flights into remote keys, which such combinations suggest, *every key* being easily and naturally reached by a judicious treatment of this chord in the position given above or in its other three positions. Another class of chords are used as doubtful chords, though less frequently than those just described, namely, the chords of the extreme sixth (called also sharp or augmented sixth), *e.g.* :

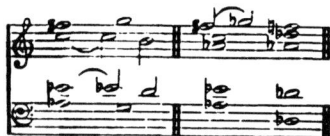

The use of doubtful chords is only to be traced in modern authors; old writers used them rarely, and then only to produce some startling effect, justified by the character of the words in vocal music, or by the professed drift of a piece of orchestral sound-painting.

Erhöhung (*Ger.*) Elevating, enhancing, raising; as. *Erhöhungs-zeichen*, the sign of chromatic elevation. a sharp or natural.

Erniedrigung (*Ger.*) Lowering, depressing, as *Erniedrigungs-zeichen*, the sign for chromatic depression, a flat or natural.

Erst (*Ger.*) First; as, *erster Satz*, first part.

Ersterben (*Ger.*) To die away, *morendo*.

Erweitert (*Ger.*) Extended, augmented, amplified.

Es (*Ger.*) E flat.

Esatto (*It.*) Strict, exact; as, *esatto intonazione*, just intonation.

Es dur (*Ger.*) The key of E flat major.

Esecuzione (*It.*) Execution.

Eses (*Ger.*) E double flat.

Es moll (*Ger.*) The key of E flat minor.

Espace (*Fr.*) A space of the stave.

Espagnuolo, a (*It.*) In the Spanish style.

Espirando (*It.*) Dying away; gasping.

Espressione, con (*It.*) With expression.

Espressivo (*It.*) Expressive.

Essential harmony. Harmony independent of grace, auxiliary, passing, syncopated, anticipating. or pedal notes.

Essential notes. Notes belonging to a key-chord. The essential notes of the chord of F major are F, A, C. [Chordæ essentiales.]

Estinguendo. Estinto (*It.*) Dying away, gradually reducing both power and pace.

Estravaganza (*It.*) A work fanciful and far-fetched in composition or execution.

Estremamente (*It.*) Extremely.

Estro poetico (*It.*) Poetic rage, or fervency.

Etendue (*Fr.*) Extended.

Etouffé (*Fr.*) *Lit.* stifled. *Damped*, by means of pedal, mute, or palm of the hand. [Damp.]

Etouffoirs (*Fr.*) Dampers.

Etude (*Fr.*) A study, exercise, or lesson.

Et vitam. One of the movements of the mass. [Mass.]

Etwas (*Ger.*) Somewhat; as, *etwas langsam*, rather slow, &c.

Euphonia (*Lat.* and *It.*) (1) Sweet sound, *suavitas vocis*. (2) A consonant combination of sounds.

Euphonium. A brass bass instrument, properly belonging to a military band, but frequently introduced into the orchestra as a substitute for the third or bass trombone, to the tone of which the sound of the Euphonium has not the slightest affinity. [Metal wind instruments.]

Euphony. Sweet sound. An agreeable combination of sounds.

Evacuant (*Ger.*) An exhaust-valve, in an organ or other wind instrument.

Evacuatio (*Lat.*) *Lit.* an emptying. In mediæval music, the making of a note in *outline* only, by which its value was reduced by one-third, *e.g.* :

| Semibrevis plena et perfecta. | Semibrevis vacua et imperfecta. |

Other notes were similarly affected by *evacuatio*.

Eveillé (*Fr.*) Sprightly, quick, lively.

Evirato (*It.*) [Castrato.]

Evolutio (*Lat.*) The working out or development of a subject.

Evovae. The vowels of the words "seculorum amen" at the end of the Gloria Patri. Hence used as a name of the *endings* of Gregorian tones, *e.g.*, the following are the evovae of the fourth tones :

Exercise. (1) Preparatory practice in order to obtain skill. (2) A composition intended for the improvement of the singer or player. (3) A composition or thesis, required of candidates for degrees in music in the universities.

Expression. The power or act of rendering music so as to make it the vehicle of deep and pure emotion; the *spirit* of music, as opposed to the mere mechanical production of sound. In rendering works of a high class, a true expression involves the merging of the artist's personality in an enthusiastic effort to carry out to the highest extent, the fullest meaning of the composer. Hence the difficulty of giving a reading of classical works which shall satisfy those critics who have formed their own ideal of the author's conceptions. Compositions of a low order, often achieve great popularity owing to their clever treatment by practised artists, who know how to create an artificial interest in such a work, which its internal merit does not warrant.

Marks of expression are of comparatively modern use. It is said that Locke (c. 1677) was the first Englishman who used signs for *crescendo* and *diminuendo*, but there can be no doubt that an expressive treatment of music has at all times been known and appreciated, although the signs or directions for this expression were unwritten. This remark applies equally to solo and concerted music; in the latter, whether vocal or instrumental, sacred, or secular, the proper treatment of certain passages would, if not traditionally received, be suggested by the leading musicians among the performers. If this be true, directors of modern choirs or orchestras are to some extent justified in adding marks of expression to unmarked works to be performed, it being a fact that, where none exist, singers and players now-a-days sink into an uninteresting dead-level of production.

The absence of such marks gives the greatest latitude to the artist who renders music, and allows him to stamp his reading more with his own individuality than where the expression required is definitely indicated. Thus, some of the old simple songs or tunes depend entirely upon the performer for their true expression; whereas modern music is so full of directions that any intelligent reader may see the drift of the author's meaning. But the fictitious expression obtained only by a strict attention to orders, is vastly different from that true expression which is the offspring of sympathetic genius, which will ever remain the real test of the taste, culture, and ability of an artist.

Expression-stop. In a harmonium the expression stop when drawn, closes the waste-valve of the bellows. Any alteration of the pressure of the feet on the wind-pedals, causes therefore a corresponding alteration of the power of the tone produced. Hence, by a proper sympathy between the pressure of the foot, and the force of sound required, the most delicate contrasts of light and shade can be obtained.

Extempore. Musical improvisation. The art, or rather *gift*, of creating melody and harmony without premeditation. The ancient Greeks were said to have possessed the talent of poetical improvisation; and the gift is found in many races in which the imagination is free and vivid, such as the Arabs, and some tribes of Negroes. Among the former, the extempore effusions relating to small customs and superstitions such as those contained in the Sonnah, among the latter, hymns, religious poems and songs (generally with some rude kind of vocal and instrumental accompaniment), form the themes improvised upon. Some of their songs, originally extempore, afterwards remembered and made traditional, are not without a savage kind of beauty, but like most productions of the class to which they belong, do not appear to produce the effect upon paper it is known they do when sung by an excited body of singers.

In Europe the Italians, above all other nations, cultivate the gift of reciting extempore verses, which are not always mere simple effusions of a few stanzas, but are sometimes marked by extraordinary talent, and are extended to the length of an epic poem. Even tragedies and comedies have been made on the spur of the moment. It is said that the people of Tuscany and of the Venetian territories possess the gift in the strongest degree, and that females as well as males have exhibited powers of this sort.

Petrarch is said to have introduced the custom of singing extempore verses to the lute, and many names of eminent improvisatori are preserved, one of the greatest being Metastasio, who, however, gave up the art at an early period of his long career. Among musicians, the gift of performing extempore upon an instrument is more remarkable than the power of making verses; for it not only requires a special aptitude, but also demands an extensive knowledge of art at ready command. John Stanley, the blind organist, contemporary with Handel, was an extraordinary impromptu player, capable of clothing any suddenly suggested theme with every resource of art. The stories told of J. S. Bach, in this respect, would be incredible, if his works did not show how great and free was his command over the technicalities of composition. The list of eminent musicians who have excelled as extempore performers might be swelled to a large extent, if it were necessary; but it will be sufficient for the present purpose to name only one or two, who may be said to represent the historical sequence of the existence of the faculty of performing at a moment's notice a subject arranged according to any form that might for the time be selected. Mozart possessed the power in no mean degree, for there are records of the fact of his having performed a concerto with only blank sheets of paper before him, he having been either too idle or too busy to write out more than the accompanying parts. Clementi, Moscheles, and Cramer, were famed for this gift, in their day, and the elder Samuel Wesley also was noted for his skill. Secular or trifling melodies have frequently been made themes for improvisation of an amusing or grotesque character.

One of the greatest pleasures Mendelssohn gave to his friends was, that of listening to his extempore playing, and many living musicians of eminence have also displayed their powers as well in public as in private.

It is a singular fact that many performers highly gifted as extempore players, have failed, where it might appear at first sight they were eminently qualified to shine ; a good extempore player often proving an indifferent, if not wholly bad accompanist or composer, and the reverse. The union of the different qualities in one and the same individual is rare.

Extemporize. To play *extempore*.

Extended compass. A range beyond the ordinary limit of a voice or instrument. A pianoforte was formerly said to be of extended compass, when a few notes more than the old five octaves were employed ; now, a pianoforte is not considered of extended compass if it has less than seven octaves.

Extended harmony. [Dispersed harmony.]

Extraneous modulation. A modulation to an extreme or unrelated key. [Modulation.]

Extreme. (1) Outside; as, *extreme parts*, the highest and lowest parts in part-music. (2) Expanded to its furthest limit ; as, *extreme intervals*, intervals greater than major or normal ; *e.g.*, C to G♯ an extreme fifth. Such intervals are called also augmented, superfluous, or sharp. (3) Not closely related ; a modulation into an extreme key is one into any key, other than, its own relative minor, its dominant, and sub-dominant, and their relative minors. (4) An old term for any key having more than three sharps or flats.

Extreme sixth, chord of the. A chord of modern growth, so called because the interval of an extreme or augmented sixth is contained in it, either directly or by inversion. It exists in three principal forms :

Ex. 1. Ex. 2. Ex. 3.

It will be noticed that this chord occurs on the sixth degree of the minor scale, but like many other chords originally formed of notes in the minor scale, it is as frequently resolved into the major key of the tonic, as into the minor; *e.g.*:

Ex. 4. Ex. 5. Ex. 6.

The dominant chord G, B♮, D, which is common to both C major and C minor, forms the connection between the resolutions given in Ex. 1, 2, 3, and those in Ex. 4, 5, and 6.

Various explanations of the origin of this chord have been suggested. Some consider it merely a chord of $\frac{6}{3}$ on the sixth of the minor scale, or the first inversion of the subdominant common chord with the 6th chromatically raised (Ex. 1). Others look upon it as a chord of $\frac{6}{3}$ on the sixth of the major scale, or the first inversion of the subdominant common chord, with the bass-note flattened (Ex. 4). These two opinions obtain favour in proportion to the supposed major or minor tonality of the chord.

Some authors find a much more complicated solution, namely, that it contains the minor ninth of the Dominant, combined with the major 3rd, 7th, and other notes of the fifth above the Dominant. Hence it is called a *double-root-chord*, and $\dfrac{D}{G}$ would be given as its derivative in all the above examples.

This chord, as constructed in Ex. 1 and 4, is sometimes known as the Italian Sixth ; as constructed in Ex. 2 and 5 as the French Sixth ; as constructed in Ex. 3 and 6 as the German Sixth.

The component notes of these are often converted and form different inversions or positions, *e.g.*:

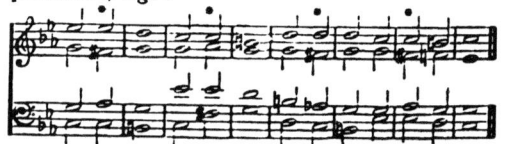

Chords of this kind are occasionally met with in the works of Bach and Handel, but are not of frequent occurrence at that date. Among modern authors, Spohr makes most use of them, and they form an important ingredient of his flowing chromatic progressions.

F.

F. (1) The note called parhypate in the Greater Perfect system of the Greeks. The letter-name of Trite in the upper tetrachord.

(2) The first note of the Eolian mode, or church scale, commencing four notes above the hypo-Eolian. [Greek music.]

(3) The note called "Fa ut" in the hexachord system. [Notation.]

(4) The key-note of the major scale requiring one flat in the signature; and the key-note of the minor scale related to A flat.

Fa. The syllable used in solmisation for F. [Aretinian Syllables.]

Fa bemol (*Fr.*) F flat.

Fablier (*Provençal*). [Troubadour.]

Faburden, Falsobordone (*It.*) *Fauxbourdon* (*Fr.*) One of the early systems of harmonising a given portion of plain-song, or a *canto fermo*. As the word implies, *to faburden* signified originally to hold a *drone* (*bordonizare*). It was afterwards used as a term for a sort of harmony consisting of thirds and sixths added to a canto fermo. It will be remembered that the *organum* was similar in construction, being only *note against note*, but consisted of *fourths, fifths,* and *octaves.* [See Descant.] But when *counterpoint* had superseded both diaphony and descant, the term *faburden* still was retained, and applied to certain species of counterpoint, sometimes (but not always) note against note.

The following examples of Falsobordoni, by Bernabei (middle of 17th century), (from Proske's *Musica Divina*) are specially interesting as showing that composers, even at that time, ventured to alter church song when it suited their convenience. The introduction of the F♯ in the tenor at the close of Ex. 1, to secure a good cadence, disturbs the *mode* of the second tone; and in Ex. 2, the introduction of G♯ is equally fatal to the tonality of the fourth tone.

Ex. 1.

Con – fi – tebor tibi Domine, in toto corde me - o:

in consilio justorum, et congrega - ti - o - ne.

Falsobordone.

Mag-na o-per-a Do-mi-ni, Ex-qui-si-ta in om-nes

vo - lun - ta - tes ej - us.

Ex. 2.

Lau - da - - te pu e - ri Do - mi - num:

lau - da - te no - men Do - mi - ni.

Sit no - men Do - mi - ni be - ne - dic - tum,

Ex hoc nunc et us - que in sæ -cu-lum, in sæ - cu - lum.

Faces d'un accord (*Fr.*) The positions or inversions of a chord.

Fach (*Ger.*) A rank of pipes, as in an organ.

Facile (*Fr.*) Easy.

Facilità (*It.*) *Facilité* (*Fr.*) Facility, readiness of execution.

Facilité (*Fr.*) Made easy. An easy arrangement of a difficult passage.

Facilement (*Fr.*) *Facilmente* (*It.*) Easily, with ease.

Facture (*Fr.*) *Fattura* (*It.*) (1) The construction of a piece of music. (2) The measurement, dimension, or scale of organ pipes.

Fa dièse (*Fr.*) F sharp.

Fagottista (*It.*) A bassoon player.

Fagotto (*It.*) [Bassoon.]

Fagottone (*It.*) A large bassoon [Double bassoon.]

Fall. A cadence.

> " That strain again
> It had a dying fall."—SHAKSPEARE.

Fal las. Short songs with the syllables *fal la* at the end of each line or strain. Morley (c. 1580), who composed some, speaks of them as being a kind of *ballet*. The fal las of Hilton (c. 1600) are held in highest estimation for the freedom of their construction and the beauty of their melodies. Gastoldi is the reputed inventor of fal las.

Falsa musica (*Lat.*) called also *musica ficta*. False or feigned music was that in which notes were altered by the use of accidentals. " Falsa musica est quando de tono facimus semitonium et e converso " (Johannes de Garland).

False cadence. [Cadence.]

False fifth. A fifth altered from its perfect or major state.

False intonation. (1) The production of an unnatural or improper quality of tone. (2) Singing or playing out of tune.

False string. A badly woven string, which produces an uncertain and untrue tone.

Falsetto (*It.*) The artificial or supplementing tones of the voice, higher than the chest or natural voice. Falsetto is present in every voice with more or less power or quality. The similarity of the character of the natural and artificial voice in boys or females renders the two tones less distinct ; but the chest voice and head voice in the man being of two qualities, the falsetto has a special character. The control of the falsetto requires great skill. The voce d'evirato is not falsetto, although high in pitch. [Larynx.]

Falso-bordone (*It.*) [Faburden.]

Fancies. (1) An old name for compositions in an impromptu style ; a fantasy. (2) Short pieces of music without words.

> "And sing those tunes to the over-scutched huswives that he heard the carmen whistle, and sware— they were his *fancies*, or his good-nights."—(SHAKSPEARE.)

Fandango (*Sp.*) A lively Spanish dance in triple time, derived from the Moors. It is a mild form of the Chica, *q.v.* It is danced by two persons, male and female, and accompanied by the sounds of a guitar. The dancers have castanets, which they beat in time to the measure, though sometimes the male dancer beats a tambourine.

Fanfare (*Fr.*) A flourish of trumpets, a call.

Fantaisie (*Fr.*) [Fantasia.]

Fantasia (*It.*) *Fantasie* (*Ger.*) A composition in a style in which form is subservient to fancy. [Form.]

Fantasiren (*Ger.*) To play as fancy directs ; to improvise.

Fantasticamente (*It.*) *Fantastico* (*It.*) *Fantastique* (*Fr.*) Fantastically, in a grotesque manner.

Farandola (*It.*) *Farandoule* (*Fr.*) A dance popular among the peasants of the South of France and the neighbouring part of Italy. It is performed by men and women taking hands, and forming a long line, and winding in and out with a waving motion. The manner of taking hands is peculiar. The men and women are placed alternately, each man's right hand is held by a woman's right hand, and his left by the left hand of another woman, so that along the line, when seen from the front of the row, there is a woman's face and a man's back, and the reverse. The dance is sometimes made the means of fanning popular excitement. A recent traveller, describing his experience of it, says :—" As the night wore on all the roughs in the town turned out, and began dancing the *farandole*—a kind of exciting dance peculiar to the south : men and women, hand in hand, form a long chain, and to a very quick step turn and twist along the various thoroughfares. This dance has the same effect on the fiery Southerners that the scalp dance has on the Red Indians, and makes them quite wild. It was after they had thus worked themselves up to a proper state of excitement that the mob of Avignon massacred Marshal Brune in 1815."

The figures of the *Farandola* by the name of the " Spanish dance," were well known in English ball-rooms thirty years since.

Farsa in musica (*It.*) A musical burletta or farce.

Fascia (*It.*) (1) A bind or tie. (2) The sides of a fiddle.

Fastoso, fastosamente (*It.*) Proudly, haughtily.

Fattura (*It.*) [Facture.]

Fausse corde (*Fr.*) [False string.]

Fausset (*Fr.*) [Falsetto.]

F clef. [Clef.]

F dur. (*Ger.*). The key of F major.

Federclavier (*Ger.*) Spinnet.

Feier (*Ger.*) A festival. *Feierlich*, in a festival style, grandly.

Feld (*Ger.*) (1) The disposition of pipes in an organ. (2) *Feld-flöte*, a rustic flute or pipe. (3) *Feld-musik*, military music. (4) *Feld-ton*, the key of E flat, in which military instruments are often set.

Ferial. Non-festal; as, *ferial use*, music for use on ordinary days.

Fermamente, fermato (*It.*) Firmly, with decision.

Fermata (*It.*) A pause (from *fermare*, to stay, or stop).

Fermo (*It.*) Firm, fast; as, *canto fermo*, the subject or part held firmly, while descant or counterpoint moved about it.

Feroce, con ferocità (*It.*) Wildly, fiercely.

Fertig (*Ger.*) Quick, dexterous.

Fervente, ferventemente (*It.*) Fervently, vehemently.

Fes (*Ger.*) The note F flat.

Fest (*Ger.*) A festival; as, *Festgesang*, a festival cantata.

Fest (*Ger.*) Firm; as, *fester Gesang*, canto fermo. [Fermo.]

Festivamente (*It.*) Solemnly, pleasantly.

Festivita, con (*It.*) With joyfulness.

Festivo (*It.*) Festive, solemn.

Festoso (*It.*) Joyous, gay.

FF. ff., *abb. of fortissimo*. Very loud.

Fiacco (*It.*) Weak, weary, faint.

F holes. The openings in the upper plate of a violin or other instrument having a resonance-body, so called from their common shape *f*.

Fiasco (*It.*) *lit.* a flask or bottle. A term applied to a failure in singing, playing, or representation. The *fistula pastoricia* was blown by the Romans to signify their dissatisfaction, and it is possible that the present use of the term arose from the similarity between the shape of a flageolet (*flaschinei*) and a flask. The Italians now blow some-

times into the pipe of a key, whence the expression *colla chiava*.

Fiato (*It.*) (1) Wind; as, *stromenti di fiato*, wind instruments. (2) Breath, in singing; as in the French *une longue haleine*, a long breath, a long note or passage performed with one respiration.

Ficta musica (*Lat.*) [Falsa.]

Fiddle. [Violin.]

Fidicen (*Lat.*) (From *fides* and *cano*.) A lute or harp player.

Fiedel (*Ger.*) Fiddle.

Fier (*Fr.*) *Fiero* (*It.*) Proud, fierce.

Fieramente, fiero (*It.*) Proudly, fiercely, boldly.

Fife. *Fifre* (*Fr.*), *Querpfeife* (*Ger.*), *Piffera* (*It.*) An ancient musical instrument, the name being cognate with pipe. The compass is two octaves from D:

A combination of fifes and drums is the only music officially allowed in the British army and navy. Although of ancient use in England for military purposes, it was discontinued in the reign of James I., and was not restored until the siege of Maestricht in 1747. The fife in the orchestra is called Flauto piccolo.

Fife. An organ stop. A piccolo, generally of two feet in length.

Fifre. [Fife.]

Fifteenth. The interval of a double octave. Bis-diapason.

Fifteenth. An organ stop of two feet in length on the manuals and four feet on the pedals, consisting of open metal pipes.

Fifth. A diatonic interval of five notes. Its ratio is 2 : 3, the *diapente* of the ancients.

Figura (*Lat.*) A note. *Figura simplex*, a note standing by itself. *Figura ligata*, a ligature, or a single sign expressing more than one note.

Figure. A form of melody or accompaniment maintained throughout the phrase in which it is suggested. In a melody, figure is called sequence. In harmony a figure relates to the rhythmical observance of a certain form in all the accompanying chords to the melody. (2) A musical phrase. (3) A florid melody.

Figurato (*It.*) *Figuré* (*Fr.*) Figured.

Figured Bass. A bass having the accompanying chords suggested by certain numbers above or below the notes. It is at present the most satisfactory system of musical shorthand. The whole of the notes are not always indicated by a corresponding number of figures, because one number generally implies two or more to complete the chord. When there is no figure, it is understood that the common chord of such a note is to be used as its harmony. The following table will show the manner in which figures are used:

The figure 2 implies a 4th and 6th.

" " 3 " 5th perfect, or diminished, according to the position of the note in the key.

The figure 4 implies a 5th, or 5th and 8th.

" " 5 " 3rd and 8th.
" " 6 " 3rd.
" " 7 " 5th and 3rd.
" " 8 " 3rd and 5th.
" " 9 " 3rd and 5th.

A stroke through a figure directs the raising cf the interval by a natural or sharp, as the case may be.

An accidental standing alone implies a corresponding alteration of the 3rd of the chord. Horizontal lines direct the continuance of the harmony of the previous chord. If there are no figures under the previous chord, the line or lines direct the continuance of the common chord of the first note under which they were placed.

Filar la voce (*It.*), *Filer le son* (*Fr.*) To prolong a sound, swelling and diminishing the tone by degrees.

Fin (*Fr.*) The end.

Finale (*It.*) The last movement of a concerted piece, sonata, or symphony; the last piece of an act of an opera; the last piece in a programme.

Fine (*It.*) The end; used to show the end of a piece or movement, after a repeat, or partial repeat.

Finger-board. *Fingerbrett* (*Ger.*) (1) The flat or slightly rounded piece of wood attached to the neck of instruments of the violin and guitar class, on to which the strings are pressed when *stopped* by the fingers. (2) A manual or clavier.

Finger cymbals. [Cymbals.]

Fingering. *Applicatura* (*It.*), *Application* (*Fr.*), *Doigter* (*Fr.*), *Applicatur* (*Ger.*), *Fingersetsung* (*Ger.*) The art of placing and using the fingers properly in performing upon a musical instrument.

(1) When instruments were for the first time constructed so that the leverage of their keys was light and admitted of rapid and ready motion, musicians soon formed rules for the employment of the fingers in such a manner as to give the greatest facility to the player. These rules were properly improved and extended by each master who taught the use of a keyed instrument, and there is reason to suppose that they were kept more or less secret by each teacher, long before it was deemed expedient to set forth the methods in a general publication.

Comparing the earliest published methods of fingering with the musical compositions belonging to the same period, it is difficult to conceive that a clear, distinct, and rapid performance could ever be attained by those methods, for they are of a cramped, stiff and awkward character, while the compositions are of an opposite nature, considering the state of the art at the time.

Such a thing as acquiring a knowledge of a keyed instrument without a master was out of the question, and it is not at all unlikely that this was contemplated by the authors or compilers of the books of instruction.

One of the earliest printed books in which rules for fingering are laid down was Eusebius Ammerbach's "Orgel oder Instrument-Tablatur," Leipsic 1571, where in the fourth chapter a scale is fingered in the following manner:—

Rechte Hand (Right Hand).

1 2 1 2 1 2 1 2   1 2 3 2 1   2 1 2 1

Linke Hand (Left Hand).

3 2 1 0 3 2 1 0   3 2 1 2 1   2 1 2 3

0 stands for the thumb, 1 for the forefinger, 2 for the middle finger, and so on.

The thumb of the right hand was never used in scale passages, that of the left hand only occasionally, the little fingers were only used with the thumbs in spanning chords.

The rules for fingering in striking or playing chords are thus stated: 3rds in either hand were to be struck with the first and third fingers; 4ths, 5ths, and 6ths with the first and fourth; 7ths, octaves, 9ths and 10ths with the thumb and third finger, and only occasionally with the little finger and thumb.

Before saying anything further of other works on the subject, it may be as well to refer to a private MS. book of lessons preserved in the British Museum, and quoted by Stafford Smith in his Musica Antiqua, in which the master has marked the fingering of a passage in a very different manner to that laid down by the German author. It is true that there is a difference of nearly thirty years in the dates between Ammerbach's book and this, but as treatises published later preserve and teach the like awkward system of fingering, a curious confirmation of the conjecture that there was a considerable difference between the theory and the practice cannot fail to strike the thoughtful reader. The MS. referred to bears the date 1599, and the first lesson with the fingering (1 being thumb, 2 forefinger, &c.) is as follows :—

Right Hand.

3 4 3 4 3 3 4 5 4 3 1 3 4 3 4 3 4 5 4 3 2 3 2 1

Now in this fingering all the fingers are brought into play, and though it is somewhat clumsy according to modern views, it is less unhandy than that of Ammerbach, and as we have no ground for assuming that the English teachers had better principles to guide them than their German neighbours, and as it is known moreover, by tradition, that the most skilful players only imparted the secret of their power to favoured pupils, not only at that time but in later years, the assumption is not made without reasonable support.

A modern player would find it a very difficult task to perform the following extract from a " Gagliardo by Orlando Gibbons," printed in " Parthenia," 1611, if he confined himself to the use of three of his fingers in either hand :

or to execute with ease any such a piece as that by Frescobaldi quoted in the article Canzona, belonging to about this period. And yet not only was the peculiarity of fingering as set forth by Ammerbach taught at that time, but was also continued to a later date.

There is a lapse of more than 100 years before the next important book made its appearance, " Das Musikalische Kleeblatt " of Daniel Speer, 1697, in which the improvements suggested are few, the chief of which was the more frequent use of the thumb of the left hand, as will be seen in the following scale fingered according to his directions :

R.H. 1 2 3 2 3 2 3   2 3 2 3 2 3 2 3
L.H. 3 2 1 3 2 1 0   1 0 1 0 1 0 1 0
     2 1 2 1 2 1 2   1 2 1 2 1 2 1
     1 2 3 2 3 2 3   2 3 2 3 1 2 3

That there were differences of opinion on the subject with regard to fingering in the published books of about the same period, is shown by the subjoined quotation from " Kurtzer jedoch gründlicher Wegweiser, vermittelst welches man aus dem Grund die Kunst die Orgel recht zu Schlagen," Augsburg 1698, in which the scale of C is thus

fingered; the thumb being indicated by the circle :

R.H. 1 2 3 2 3 2 3   2 3 2 3 2 3 2
L.H. 2 1 0 3 2 1 0   1 0 1 0 1 0 1
     3 2 1 2 1 2 1 2   1 2 1 2 1 2 1
     0 1 2 3 2 3 2 3   2 3 1 2 3 2 3

The well-known book, published by Walsh, under the title of " The Harpsichord Master, containing Plain and Easy Instructions for Learners on the Harpsichord or Spinnet," 1734, which, passing through many editions, may be fairly considered as correctly representing the method of that period, gives the following directions for fingering :—" Observe in ye fingering of yr right hand, yr thumb is ye 1st, so on to ye 5th, and yr left hand yr little finger is ye 1st, and so on, ye fingers to ascend are ye 3rd and 4th to descend ye 3rd and 2nd."

1 2 3 4 3 4 3 4 3 4 3 4 3 4 5 5 4 3 2 3 2 3 2 3 2 3 2 3 2 1
1 2 3 4 3 4 3 4 3 4 3 4 3 4 5 5 4 3 2 3 2 3 2 3 2 3 2 3 2 1

Mattheson (" Kleine Generalbasschule," 1735) and Maier (" Musiksaal," 1741) agree in their fingering, their method being as follows, little or no advance or alteration having been devised in the meanwhile in other publications.

R.H. 2 3 2 3 2 3 2   3 2 3 2 3 2 3 4
L.H. 2 1 0 1 0 1 0   1 0 1 0 1 0 1 0
     3 2 1 2 1 2 1   2 1 2 1 2 1 0
     2 1 2 1 2 1 2   1 2 1 2 1 2 1

It is stated that J. S. Bach disregarded the ordinary principles taught in instruction books, and employed both thumb and little finger as frequently as the other fingers, whereby a greater power was gained, and the performer was able to move rapidly in extreme keys. Some writers claim the suggestion for the free use of all the fingers, for François Couperin, who, in his work, " L'art de toucher le Clavecin," 1716, describes the method of fingering practised and taught by Bach, and consequently they say that the German is indebted to the Frenchman for his ideas on the subject. But Couperin's fingering is somewhat different from that of Bach, the only similarity in their methods being the constant employment of the thumb.

Couperin, in the work alluded to above, calls the fingers of either hand 1, 2, 3, 4, 5, commencing with the thumb:

Main droite.

1 2 3 4 5

Main gauche.

5 4 3 2 1

And in order to make his fingering acceptable, gives instances of the old style of playing contrasted with his own improvements. In some cases his suggestions are good, in others there is little if any help out of long-standing awkwardness, as the following fingered scale will show:

Progrès d'octaves.

1 2 3 4 3 4 3 4 5 4 3 2 3 2 3 2

His next improved example is better, and more in accordance with modern methods:

"Manière ancienne de faire plusieurs tierces de suite."

4 4 4 4 4 4   4 4 4 4 4 4   3   4 4 4 3 2

2 2 2 2 2 2   2 2 2 2 2 2   2   2 2 2 2 2

"Façon moderne pour couler les mêmes tierces."

2 3 2 3 2 3   2 3 2 3 2 3   1   3 2 1 2

4 5 4 5 4 5   4 5 4 5 4 5   3   5 4 3 3 2

Bach never published his method, but it was made known through Forkel, who acquired it from Emanuel Bach. The peculiar methods of fingering shown in the quotations from the German books seem to have been confined to the country in which they were first given forth, the style adopted in England and France appearing to be borrowed from Italy. Many of the harpsichord instruction books printed in England in the early part of the last century profess to be based upon the "Italian method of fingering," which permitted the constant employment of all the fingers.

The invention of the pianoforte called a new set of instruction book writers into existence, but it required the genius of Cramer, Clementi, and Dussek to liberate learners from the trammels of the harpsichord fingering. Clementi's "Introduction to the Art of Playing on the Pianoforte" was written soon after his return to England, in 1784, and went through many editions. In 1810 he greatly improved the work, and added an appendix to it. Cramer made but few, if any, advances on the method of fingering suggested by Clementi in his "Introduction,"

but Dussek, in his "Book of Instructions," published about 1798, when he began business as a music publisher, laid down a code of rules which have served as the basis of teaching fingering from his time onward.

He recommends the pupil not to play his scales after the old method of fingering, by suffering the fingers to cross each other unnaturally, as in this example, right hand:

+ 1 2 1 2 3 1 2

thereby implying that the old clumsy methods were still taught; but "to set it down as an invariable rule, and without any exception, that whether ascending or descending, the assistance, or rather, the displacing the *thumb* only is sufficient to effect the necessary change of position in the other fingers, the thumb being naturally formed to glide easily under them, without displacing the proper position of the hand."

+ 1 2 + 1 2 3 + 1 2 + 1 2 3 4 3 2 1 + 2 1 + 3 2 1 + 2 1 +
Right Hand.

+ 3 2 1 + 2 1 3 + 2 1 + 2 1 + 1 2 + 1 2 3 + 1 2 + 1 2 3 4
Left Hand.

The free use of all the fingers is now common, and the old rules with regard to the sparing of the thumb so little observed, that there is a tendency to go the opposite extreme in employing it more often than is absolutely necessary. Space cannot here be allowed, or the whole of Dussek's rules for fingering might be reprinted with advantage as a set-off against modern extravagance, but those who have leisure and inclination might study them with profit, for no better code of rules for pianoforte playing have as yet been given to the world.

(2) In violin playing the fingers serve as stops shortening the length of the vibrating portion of the several strings as they are required, a like practice being followed in the performance upon such fingerboard instruments as the lute, mandoline, or guitar, as are plucked with the right hand. Upon the guitar the places of the several degrees are marked on the fingerboard by frets, which, when the string is pressed—always a little behind the one required—serve as a temporary nut.

(3) This is not the place to enter deeply into the anatomy of the hand, which can be found in any text-book on anatomy, and more especially in the elaborate Treatise of Sir Charles Bell. The bones of the hand are joined together by various sorts of joints, some of them fixed, some moveable. The joint by which the thumb joins the bone on which it plays is a remarkable one, admitting of a

most complex series of movements, and since the brain of man is indebted to the hand of man as much as the hand to the brain, each rendering higher development in the other possible, and thus helping to constitute a couple of mutually perfecting factors—by far the greater part of this potentiality on the side of the hand is owing to this articulation of the thumb. The thumb of man is pre-eminent in the animal series.

From a musical point of view another subject is of interest. If we straighten our fingers we shall see that no two of them are of the same length. Now let us bend the fingers on themselves, so as to bring the finger-tips into the middle of the palm, and we shall find that the finger-tips form an almost straight line with one another. The convenience of this to the musician is obvious, in playing keyed instruments such as the pianoforte or organ ; or any wind instrument like the oboe, flute, or clarinet, we have a series of evenly arranged finger-tips ready to the notes. This is a point of what we may call accidental convenience, for the hand of man was not especially adapted for playing instruments. The question now arises how this curious effect is produced, and a few words will explain it. If any one will take the trouble to measure as accurately as he can the length of the first and of the third joint of each finger (the "proximal and distal phalanges") omitting the middle joint, he will find that by subtracting the length of the end (distal) joint which carries the nail from the length of the nearest (proximal) joint which joins the " knuckle," he will get a constant number, in other words, if the proximal phalanx is long, and would carry the finger-tip far beyond the middle of the palm, the distal phalanx is proportionately long and in a bent position of the finger carries the finger-tip proportionately far back towards the palm, or in yet other terms, the number of linear units obtained by subtracting the length of the distal phalanx of each finger from the length of the proximal phalanx of the same finger is constant in all the fingers. This is not *absolutely* correct, for the angles at which the phalanges are bent are not exactly right angles, so that the middle phalanx cannot be quite neglected, but the principle nevertheless we believe to be correct. The muscles which move the fingers and thumb are situated some in the forearm, some in the hand. If any one grasps his forearm, and moves the fingers, he will feel the muscles moving under his grasp. The thumb has the greatest number of muscles attached to it, and therefore takes the precedence in importance; the first or index-finger has a special muscle to extend or straighten it called the extensor indicis or " indicator." This muscle was said

to be absent in all the apes, and there was an old saying, " no ape can point," which was quoted in favour of human superiority—this, however, is not true (Journal of Anat. and Phys., vol. vi. p. 185) ; we trust, notwithstanding, that the pre-eminence of man in the animal kingdom rests on somewhat more important foundations, and need not be ceded, however much apes may point. The little finger has a special muscle to extend or straighten it which the old anatomists called the " auricularis," because it is used to straighten the little finger when the extremity of that member is inserted into the ear. Thus did these ingenious men infuse an element of humour into the driest and apparently least comic of all subjects.

PALM OF HAND. Fig. 1.

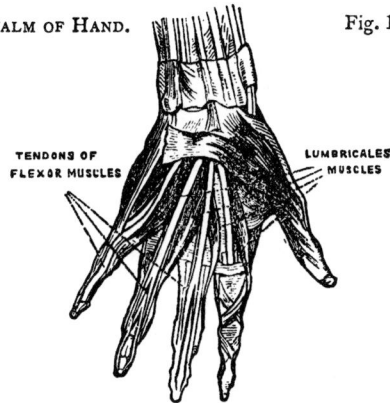

TENDONS OF FLEXOR MUSCLES LUMBRICALES MUSCLES

There are a set of muscles called " lumbricales " (from " lumbricus," a worm, because they are not unlike an earth-worm in size and shape), which are of great importance to musical performers, and in pianoforte players become very largely developed. They are attached to the flexor tendons (which bend the fingers) as they pass along the palm. They help to bend the fingers, but their individual action is somewhat complicated, viz , to bend the finger at the knuckle-joint, but to *straighten* the finger.

But there is one point in the anatomy of the hand which is of great interest to musical performers, especially to pianoforte and organ players. If any one will place the tips of his fingers on a table in a bent position, as if playing the pianoforte, and then try to raise them one at a time, he will find that he can raise his thumb easily, say four or five inches, the forefinger is also very moveable, and can be raised so that the tip is about three inches from the table, the middle finger about two-thirds of that height, and the little finger rather higher. Now let him try to raise the ring finger, keeping the middle and little fingers down, and he will find a peculiar difficulty in doing so. If he is a pianoforte or organ-player he will probably call to mind many exercises which he has toiled at, all of them easy enough but for that unlucky ring finger. In fact, all good writers of exercises have the education of the ring finger very prominently in view. What is the cause of this? It has been asserted popularly that this finger has a tendon too little, but this is just the opposite of the fact.

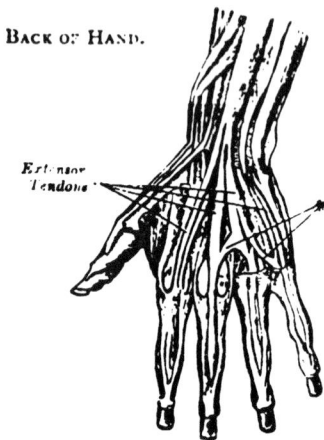

BACK OF HAND. Fig. 2.

Extensor Tendons

If we look at figure 2. we shall see the extensor tendons (the tendons which extend or straighten the fingers) running to the fingers, but, in addition, we shall see that the tendon which goes to the ring-finger gives off a small slip (*) on each side, one of which joins the extensor tendon of the little finger, the other that of the middle finger. Now we observed that none of these three fingers is as moveable as the forefinger. If we observe, also, the direction of these slips we shall see that they do not run straight across from the ring finger to the two on each side, but run at the same time a little towards the fingers. Now if we see what happens when we raise the middle finger alone, we shall observe that the slip will become tight at a certain point, but not until it has passed through a considerable space, the first action being to *relax* the tendinous slip: the same with the little finger. But if we raise the ring finger alone, the slips almost immediately become tight, and prevent its being raised, and the exercises before alluded to have for their purpose the stretching of the tendinous slips, especially in youth, when growth and change are active in the tissues. Now these slips must have some purpose, though it is not at all certain that we know it. It is probable that their purpose is to make the grasp firmer, the three fingers being so associated together that each as it were assists the other, and it is hard to detach one without the rest. They are present in monkeys (see paper before alluded to), and in them would be useful in climbing, in which exercise, strength of grasp is of course of great importance. The forefinger is not included in this association, as its value depends largely on its freedom of independent movement, especially on its capability of being opposed accurately to the thumb.

These slips have an historical interest. Robert Schumann, painfully aware of their presence, and acquainted with the cause of the difficulty connected with the ring finger, tied back that finger for a long time. Not being successful in his operation, he irrecoverably damaged his hand, and injured his pianoforte playing most seriously, and in consequence turned his attention to writing, to which fact we are largely indebted for the number of his masterly compositions. What was a loss to him and to his contemporaries has become a rich gain to posterity. A case is recorded in which an accidental wound to the back of the hand partially divided one of these tendinous slips, and the ring-finger gained a considerably increased degree of motion. The subject of the accident noticed the change on playing the pianoforte after the wound was healed. With regard to the feasibility of this as a definite operation, there is no doubt that if it could be done safely and well, it would be well worth every pianist's while to have these slips divided. But firstly, there is a strong feeling among English surgeons against "improving" nature; and secondly, there would be some risk of inflammation after the operation, which would result in matting the tendons at the back of the hand together, and making matters worse by limiting the freedom of motion still further. Apart from this risk, the operation is simple, easy, and would not be painful.

Fingerleiter. [Chiroplast.]

Fingersatz } (*Ger.*) [Fingering.]
Fingersetzung }

Finite canon. [Canon.]

Finito (*It.*) Finished, ended.

Finto (*It.*) A feint, a term applied to deceptive cadences. [Cadence.]

Fiochetto (*It.*) Slightly hoarse.

Fioco (*It.*) Hoarse.

Fioriscente } (*It.*) Ornamented, florid.
Fiorito }

Fiorituri (*It.*) Ornaments, cadenzas, florid passages in a melody or an accompaniment.

Fis (*Ger.*) F sharp.

Fisfis or fisis (*Ger.*) F double sharp.

Fis dur (*Ger.*) F sharp major.

Fis moll (*Ger.*) F sharp minor.

Fistula (*Lat.*) A pipe. *Fistula dulcis*, a *flûte à bec. Fistula, cui semper decrescit* *arundinis ordo*, pan-pipes. *Fistula eburniola*, the ivory pitch-pipe, from which an orator took the pitch of his voice. *Fistula pastoricia*, the shepherd's pipe, sometimes blown in the theatre as a sign of dissatisfaction. [Flute.]

Fithele (*old Eng.*) The ancient name of the fiddle, probably derived from *fidicula*, a small stringed instrument of the cithara class.

Flageolet. (1) A small pipe with a mouth-piece inserted in a bulb (hence the derivation of the name from the same root from which the word flagon comes), producing a shrill sound, similar, but much softer in quality than that produced from the flauto piccolo. It is an instrument of English invention, and was formerly employed in the orchestra. The obbligato in the song, "O, ruddier than the cherry," in Handel's "Acis and Galatea," is for a flageolet. (2) The tone produced from a violin by lightly pressing the bow near the bridge upon lightly touched strings, is called flageolet or flute tone.

Flageolet tones. The natural harmonics of stringed instruments, so called from their pure flute-like quality of tone. [Harmonics, § 2.]

Flaschinett (*Ger.*) The flageolet.

Flat. (1) The sign ♭, which directs the lowering of the note to which it is prefixed by one semitone. Its shape is derived from the ancient *b*. [B quadratum.] (2) Singing or playing is said to be *flat* when the sounds produced fail to reach the true pitch. (3) Minor; as, a flat 3rd, a flat 5th, &c.

Flatter la corde (*Fr.*) To play expressively upon a stringed instrument with a bow.

Flat tuning. One of the varieties of tuning on the lute; called also French tuning, or French flat tuning, because the French pitch was formerly lower than that used elsewhere. Hence the German term *Franz-ton* for a low pitch.

Flautando, flautato (*It.*) Like a flute; a direction to produce the flageolet tones on the violin, &c. [Flageolet tones.]

Flautino (*It.*) (1) An instrument of the accordion kind. (2) A little flute, piccolo, or flageolet. (3) [Flautando.]

Flauto (*It.*) [Flute.]

Flauto amabile (*It.*), *flute d'amour* (*Fr.*) An organ stop, consisting of sweet-toned closed, or sometimes open, pipes. It is generally of 4 ft. pitch.

Flauto dolce (*It.*) [Flute.]

Flautone (*It.*) [Bass flute.]

Flauto piccolo (*It.*) [Piccolo.]

Flauto traverso (*It.*) The German flute held laterally, flutes having been formerly played with a mouth-piece, whence they were called flutes *à bec*. [Flute.]

Flebile, Flebilmente (*It.*) In a doleful, tearful manner.

Flessibilità (*It.*) [Flexibility.]

Flexibility. The power of free and rapid execution, in vocal or instrumental music.

Fling. A dance performed by Scottish Highlanders to a tune in common time. [Reel.]

F Löcher (*Ger.*) [F holes.]

Florid counterpoint. A counterpoint not confined to any special species, but in which notes of various lengths are used. It is opposed to *strict* counterpoint. [Counterpoint.]

Florid music. Music in which the melody and accompanying parts are of an ornamental and embellished style.

Flöte (*Ger.*) [Flute.]

Flourish. (1) The execution of profuse but unmeaning ornamentation in music. (2) The old English name for a call, fanfare, or prelude for trumpets or other instruments together or alone. (3) The preparatory cadenza for "tuning the voice," in which singers formerly indulged just before commencing their song.

Flüchtig (*Ger.*) Light, rapid.

Flügel (*Ger.*) A grand pianoforte or harpsichord, so called because of the wing-like shape of the top.

Flügel-horn (*Ger.*) A bugle. A valve-horn.

Flute. (1) One of the most widely used of ancient musical instruments, and at this day one of the most important instruments in an orchestra. It has been remarked in speaking of the aulos, that the general idea of a "flute," probably included anciently, not only open tubes, but also instruments having a reed, such for instance, as the oboe. But the word has for many centuries been used only in the former sense.

Of tubes without reeds there are only two kinds—the flute played by a mouth-piece, and that played by placing the lips close against a hole on one side. The former kind was formerly called *flûte à bec;* the latter, *flûte traversiere*, or *flauto traverso*, the cross-flute. The *flageolet*, which still is in use, is a familiar example of a *flûte à bec*, but it is the smallest of its kind, for these instruments were at one time made sufficiently large to be called "tenor" and "bass" flutes; and complete four-part harmony could be obtained from a set [Bass flute]. The larger kinds only exist now as curiosities. The *flûte à bec* was used so commonly in England that it was called on the continent *flûte d'Angleterre*. They came to be called *beak*-flutes, because of the similarity of the mouthpiece, through which the wind is directed against a sharp edge. to the beak of a bird. *Flûtes à bec* were single and double. Such double flutes were familiar both to Egyptians and Assyrians, and illustrations of them will be found on p. 40 (Aulos). The following illustration, from Boissard's Roman Antiquities, is interesting from its great likeness to the modern double-flageolet :

p. 40 (Aulos)

Fig. 1.

The Romans gave various names to their flutes : *calamus* from the material (reed) of which it was made ; *tibia*, because anciently flutes were formed out of a leg-bone, as shown in the following illustration :

Fig. 2.

It is a remarkable fact that flutes of this barbarous construction are to this day used in many parts of Asia. The word *fistula* seems to have been applied both to flageolets and pan's-pipes. Flutes *à bec* have at all times been a favourite object for ornamentation. and the next illustration shows a very beautiful example in carved ivory in the Kensington Museum :

Fig. 3.

The ancients possessed cross-flutes, and it is strange that their real value should have been found out, and their use made general, after so long a period of disuse. that on their re-introduction they were called German flutes as opposed to the old English beak-flute. They were used by the Egyptians, as the following illustration shows :

Fig. 4.

Fétis having obtained the exact measurements of an ancient Egyptian flute preserved in Florence, caused a flute to be made of the like dimensions and shape. The following figure shows it :

Fig. 5.

He found the lowest note it was capable of producing, to be the A below *middle C*. But if Egyptian artists are to be trusted, the flute in Fig. 4 must have been of even graver pitch.

Cross-flutes were known to the Greeks by the name plagiaulos (πλαγίαυλος), and to the Romans as *tibia obliqua*, both of these terms leave no doubt as to their nature. By the Romans the cross-flute was sometimes called also *tibia vasca*, the meaning of which is very doubtful.

It may be necessary to say, that although the *tibiæ* represented flutes of all kinds, yet if a real tibia or shinbone be made into a flute, it is held crossways, and the player blows into a hole in the side.

(2) The "German flute," so popular in England during the last century, has entirely superseded the old English *flûte à bec* in our orchestra, and is now known as *the flute*. Its construction has, from time to time, been improved, until it has now a compass of three octaves.

But as the lowest note is very soft, and three or four of the highest notes are exceedingly shrill, it is safer to consider it as possessing a chromatic scale of about two octaves and a half. Notwithstanding the vast improvements in the key work of flutes (of which, by the way, the ancients seem to have been entirely ignorant), there are shakes on certain notes which are absolutely impossible, and others which are of excessive difficulty, for instance, between C♯ and D♯ a shake is impossible in either octave; and shakes between D and E♭ are almost impossible. The lovely effect of this instrument in an orchestra must be so well known to all as to render it unnecessary to quote special examples of its use.

(3) The piccolo-flute has the same extent of compass as the ordinary flute, but is one octave higher in pitch. When used in an orchestra with moderation and skill, it is capable of producing delightful effects; but, unfortunately, it is so commonly abused that it has got an undeserved bad character. The lower portion of its notes are bright and joyous, but in the upper part of its compass it is so shrill as to only justify its use when rare and special effects are required.

(4) As all open organ pipes of the *flue* class are made on the same principle as the *flûte à bec*, it will be easily understood that *flutes* are one of the most essential class of organ stops. They are of two kinds—open and stopped, and are equally common in metal and wood. The construction of the stopped flute, so far as the mouthpiece (foot) and *lips* are concerned, is identical also with that of the *flûte à bec*, only, of course, its first harmonic will be the twelfth, not the octave, of the primary sound. When organ builders describe some of their flute-stops as *flauto traverso*, or *flûte douce* (another name for the cross-flute), it must be understood that they have only imitated the quality of tone, not the construction of that instrument. By slight modifications of the shape of the different parts of a flute pipe, an almost endless variety of tone may be produced, and organ builders avail themselves of this fact to coin an endless variety of names. If the names so chosen carried with them a hint as to the special construction of each register, it would be unfair to complain of their multiplication; but, with a very few exceptions, this is not the case.

The following are some of the titles appended to flute-stops on English and foreign organs:

(1) Describing their material, as *wood flute, woud,* and *woude-fluit* (in Holland). Metal flute.

(2) Stating whether the pipes are open or closed, as open flute. *Flûte ouverte (Fr.)* Stopped flute. *Gedackt-flöte (Ger.)*

(3) Showing the pitch of the stop, as *bass flute* (16 ft. and 8 ft.) *Flautone* (16 ft.) *Flauto grave* (16 ft.) *Flute principal* (8 ft.) *Flute major* (8 ft.) *Unison flute* (8 ft.) *Flute minor* (4 ft.) *Flûte octaviente* (4 ft.) *Quint flöte* (5⅓ ft.) *Quintaton* (sounding unison and twelfth). Piccolo flute (2 ft.) Flautino (2 ft.) *Klein-flöte* (2 ft.) *Terz-flöte* (1⅗ ft.) *Flute discant. Flûte dessus* (treble flute).

(4) Describing the shape of the pipes, as *Doppel-flöte* (with two mouths). Pyramid flute (having pipes larger at the top than at the mouth). *Flag fluit (Dutch). Flach-flöte (Ger.)* (having flat lips). *Spitz-flöte (Ger.),* and *Flûte pointue (Fr.)* (having pipes smaller at the top than at the mouth). *Rohr-flöte (Ger.),* and *Flûte à cheminée (Fr.)* (having a chimney in the stopper).

(5) Intimating their quality of tone, as full flute. *Hohl-flöte (Ger.),* and *Flûte creuse (Fr.)* (hollow toned). Clear flute. *Hell-flöte (Ger). Lieblich flöte (Ger.)* (lovely toned). *Zart-flöte (Ger.)* (delicately voiced). *Flûte douce (Fr.),* Dulcet. *Flauto dolce (It.)* (sweet-toned). Oboe-flute. Clarinet-flute (slightly reedy in tone). *Sifflöte* (1 ft.) (whistle-flute).

(6) After their supposed nationality, as German flute, *flauto tedesca,* or *allemande. Flûte à bec,* or English flute. *Suabe flute. Schweizer-flöte* (Swiss flute, the German name for what was called in England the *German* flute). *Flauto Francese. Flute Ravena. Czakan flute.*

(7) Implying that the quality of tone is similar to the modern flute, more powerful than the *flûte à bec,* as orchestral flute, *flauto traverso (It.), flûte traversière (Fr.),* and *Travers-flöte, Quer-flöte (Ger.),* (cross-flute), concert flute.

(8) Names which are merely *fancy* titles, as *flute d'amour, jubal flute, portunal flute,* old flute, recorder (flûte à bec), *Wald* and *Bauer-flöte(Ger.)* (pastoral pipe), echo flute (soft toned), *flute tacet, cordedain,* &c.

It would be an advantage alike to organ builders and organists if some definite system of nomenclature of flute stops could be devised and universally adhered to.

Flûte à bec *(Fr.)* [Flute.]

Flûte d'amour *(Fr.)* A low-toned flute, an A flute, sounding a minor third below the notes actually written. It is now obsolete.

Flûte douce *(Fr.)* An organ stop. [Flute.]

Flûte traversière *(Fr.)* The German flute.

Fly. A hinged board which covers the keys of the pianoforte or organ when not in use.

F moll *(Ger.)* The key of F minor.

Foco *(It.)* Fire, spirit.

Focoso *(It.)* With spirit, ardently.

Foglietto *(It.)* A first violin part; the *leader's* part, which contains cues, &c., used by a conductor in the absence of a full score.

Fois *(Fr.)* Time, as *premiere fois,* first time; *derniere fois,* last time (of repeating), &c.

Folia. A Spanish dance, similar to the fandango. The tune of a folia was sometimes written on a ground bass, as was also the Chaconne and Passacaille. [Follia.]

Foliated. A melody or portion of plainsong is said to be *foliated* when slurred notes have been added above or below those of which it originally consisted.

Follia (*Sp.* and *It.*) Variations upon an air or melody, in which the ingenuity was held of more value than beauty. The name "Follias de España" became applied to laborious trifling in other matters besides music.

Fondamentale (*Fr.* and *It.*) Fundamental. *Basse fondamentale, basso fondamentale*, fundamental bass.

Fondamento (*It.*) (1) Fundamental bass. (2) The root or generator of a chord.

Fonds d'orgue (*Fr.*) The foundation stops, the diapasons and 8 ft. flutes on English organs, the *principals* of foreign instruments. In general, all flue stops of 8 ft. pitch, except solo stops of peculiar quality of tone.

Foot. (1) A metrical measure, *pes* (*Lat.*) (2) A drone bass. (3) The chorus of a song. (4) The part of an organ pipe below the mouth. (5) To foot, to dance.

Forlana (*It.*), *fourlane* (*Fr.*) A dance much in favour with the gondoliers of Venice. The tune is a lively measure in 6-8 time, and is similar to the Tarantella, but not so varied in its motions. It is said to have been first danced upon the Frioul, and to take its name from that fact.

La Fourlane Venetienne ou La Barcariuole.

Form. The shape and order in which musical ideas are presented.

This definition is, perhaps, the nearest that can be given of a word of such general meaning. Form has been divided into harmonic and melodic. By harmonic form is meant the key-tonality of chords, such, for instance, as would be illustrated by a comparison of a composition by Palestrina with one by Spohr. But this question of the key relationship of chords is now generally made subordinate to the study of harmony, and is taken from the domain of form. By melodic form is meant the proper grouping of the successive sounds which form a tune. This, again, is made almost foreign to the higher meaning of form, and is held to be subordinate to the laws of rhythm. In its highest sense, form has relation more to the development than to the details of a composition.

In attempting to classify and give names to the portions of music which, by their combination or succession, go to make up a composition or movement, it will be necessary to say at once, that there is no settled or conventional usage of the terms employed, and all that is here done is to bring together those most commonly known, and as to whose meaning but little difference of opinion exists.

The component parts of simple melodic forms may be arranged according to the following order. (*a*) Motive or Theme; (*b*) Section; (*c*) Phrase; (*d*) Sentence; (*e*) Subject.

A theme consists of a note or notes contained in a single bar, whether the time be duple or triple, simple or compound. A single note may form a simple, and two or more a compound motive. Repeated notes belong to the second order:

Simple   Compound

If a theme commences upon any other beat than the first, as much as is necessary to complete the bar, whether of rests or notes, is required to form the theme:

Occasionally a subsidiary theme may be completed upon an incomplete portion of the bar, having been first suggested at the beginning of a bar:

BEETHOVEN.

Two motives form a section:

MOZART.

Sometimes three motives are found in a section:

A simple phrase consists generally of two sections:

MOZART.

BEETHOVEN.

which may sometimes be expanded beyond that limit to five or even more bars, with added motives:

BEETHOVEN.

Phrases of more than four bars may be called compound:

BEETHOVEN.

BEETHOVEN.

A sentence is formed of two phrases whether simple or compound:

BEETHOVEN.

A sentence may be shortened:

BEETHOVEN.

or lengthened:

BEETHOVEN.

Sentences may be said to be compound when two or more are united to form a musical subject. All musical subjects may be analysed by resolving them into their elements, which consist, as shown above, of themes, sections, phrases, sentences, and compound sentences; the union of these, and the connection of the subjects they make up, constitute what is called Form.

The use of the word Subject in the higher development of Form, must not be confused with its special meaning in the art of counterpoint and fugue. Fugue-form will be found treated *sub voce* Fugue.

The study of form is most important to the composer. Without an adherence to its rules compositions are liable to become incoherent, unintelligible, and amorphous, especially in these days, when there is a great tendency, arising from ignorance or mistaken intention, to create music without much or any regard to form; which is as much a necessity to a musical composition, as it is to the design of a picture, a building, or a piece of sculpture. In classical compositions the sonata form is the basis upon which is constructed the Symphony, the Concerto, the Overture and the class of work from which it derives its title.

The sonata may consist of three movements in contrasted tempi and varied forms, but the first movement must be written according to given rules, which will be shown in detail after a general description of the ordinary arrangement of the sonata. Of the three movements the first should be an "allegro," with or without an introduction in slow *tempo*, though sometimes this is dispensed with. It may here be remarked, that whatever key their first movement is written in is the key by which the symphony is known, and all the other movements must be written in keys akin to it, but the last one must be the same as the first. The second movement marked with any *tempo* from andante to adagio, is usually called the "slow movement;" the last movement is usually an allegro, and may be written on the plan of the first movement, or in what is called rondo form. As the symphony is the most important work in which the sonata form is employed, a description of the usual method of constructing it is subjoined, on the principle that the greater includes the lesser. In addition to

(175)

the number of movements in the sonata proper, the symphony has a minuet and trio or a scherzo, movements which are not necessary in the sonata.

The minuet or the scherzo—the latter most usual since Beethoven's day—ordinarily occupies the third place in the order of the movements in the symphony, but occasionally the adagio and scherzo change places, as in Mendelssohn's 3rd Symphony. Sometimes, as in Beethoven's Symphonies, Nos. 7 and 8, an allegretto appears instead of the andante or slow movement, but as there is no fixed rule for the order of the intermediate movements, a composer is at liberty to make such changes as he pleases.

Taking a symphony as a standard, the following is the usual order or form of each movement. The first of these, as has already been said, may begin with an introduction of a slow or moderately slow tempo. This in its design may foreshadow what is to appear in the succeeding allegro. If this is so written, it would give a coherence to the entire first movement; and, on account of the frequently mysterious nature of this kind of instrumental music, coherence and intelligibility is a thing much to be aimed at. The length of the introduction may be left to the discretion of the composer; care being taken to lead well into the allegro or first movement proper. For an admirable example of this sort of treatment, the student is referred to Beethoven's Symphony No. 4. The allegro must contain two principal subjects: varied, and well contrasted, and written so as to give opportunity for good instrumental effect. The first of these is given in the tonic, and when the key of the symphony is well established the composer should prepare the introduction of his second principal theme. The old-fashioned way of doing this, if the symphony were in a major key, was to work up to a major chord on the supertonic of the original scale, sometimes with the 7th added, and by that means to glide into the second subject in the dominant, thus, if the key of symphony were B♭ the movement would eventually arrive at a cadence on the chord of C with major third, the second principal subject being then heard in the key of F, or if the symphony were written in a minor key the composer worked up to a cadence on the dominant of the relative major—thus in a movement in C minor, the second subject always appeared in E♭ major. But the student is warned against blindly following this rule; it should be his aim to make his second theme grow out of the first; thereby avoiding the angularity of what may be termed the cut-and-dried school. The many ways of doing this must be left to the choice, guided by the

ingenuity of the composer, but the chief thing to be borne in mind is to make the subjects melodious, striking, and workable. There may now be introduced one or two subsidiary or episodal subjects, growing out of, and in keeping with either the first or second principal subjects. With this ends what is called the first part of the first movement; a double bar is usually made here, and a repeat marked to the beginning of the allegro. This repeat in the first part of the first movement of a symphony is a *sine quâ non*, as without it the movement loses its distinctive form. The composer must end this portion of the work in the dominant if the key of the symphony is major; or in the relative major if it is written in a minor key. The most interesting part of this portion of a symphony now follows; it is technically known as the "free fantasia." Here the composer's imagination may be employed to its utmost limit; but he must bear in mind only to use material already brought forward in the subjects of the first part of the movement. A disregard of this injunction is the great mistake which composers (especially young ones) make now-a-days, and leads to diffuseness. Again, this portion of the symphony may be spoilt by the composer having to develop subjects which are not clear, well defined, and interesting; therefore to avoid this he should be careful to write subjects in the first part of the movement which will admit of much varied treatment. Having done this, he is at liberty to produce with them any legitimate effects: at the same time he should never allow his music to resemble a vague sort of improvisation, such as is frequently heard in many modern compositions, by so doing, all beauty of form vanishes, and the composer betrays a weakness and want of control over his subjects. These remarks apply with equal force to each portion of the entire work. Not more than a third of the movement should be devoted to the free fantasia; and when it is finished, the first principal subject is re-introduced in the original key, which in due course should be followed by the second principal subject, heard this time in the tonic. Then a coda may follow, after which the movement may come to a close; but it is suggested, for the sake of coherence, that the coda should be formed out of the material already employed, and it should not be too prolonged.

The second, or slow movement, may be similar in form to that of the first, but its character is entirely opposite; and further, no repeat is made at the end of the first part. The prevailing character should be that of pathos and repose; but though the two principal subjects should partake more or less of this, the rhythm of each should be arranged so as to form a striking contrast to the other. In this movement the themes are usually much more elaborately treated than those of the Allegro, and sometimes variations are made upon the first of the principal subjects; examples of this latter style of treatment will be found in the slow movements of Beethoven's Symphonies, Nos. 5 and 9. The key should not be the same as that of the opening Allegro, such an arrangement would very likely produce monotony—the exception to this rule is when the original key is minor, the second movement could then appear in the same key; but it should be in the major mode, or *vice versâ*; any key may be chosen that has some kinship to that of the preceding movement.

If the minuet is selected for the third part, the composer must write it in accordance with the form of the dance of that name. But should the Scherzo be decided upon, he will find he has a much wider field for the expansion of his thoughts. The form of this movement may partake of that of the minuet, only the time should be generally double or three times as fast; it may also be in $\frac{2}{4}$ instead of $\frac{3}{4}$ time. Its character is usually light, fantastic, and even humorous. It is sometimes written with two trios, sometimes without any, as in the case in the Scherzo of Mendelssohn's 3rd Symphony. The key is usually the same as that of the first movement.

The last movement is an Allegro; and is generally somewhat lighter in style than the first movement; though its form may be the same. Rondo form may be adopted for this movement; or it may take the shape of an air with variations, as in the Finale to Beethoven's Symphony, No. 3. It is not necessary to repeat the first part of the finale, if it is written in the form of the first movement; and the free fantasia need not be elaborated to the same extent as in the opening Allegro. The key of the first and last movements must of necessity be the same.

The form of the Concerto is somewhat similar to that of the Symphony; but it differs from it in these respects: (1) The opening movement never appears with an introduction placed before it. (2) The orchestra usually plays both the leading themes in the tonic before they are heard on the solo instrument in the usual symphonic form. (3) The repeat of the first part is not a necessity. (4) The Concerto never contains a Scherzo, and therefore consists but of three movements—the first of which should be an Allegro, the second an Adagio, and the third an Allegro. (5) The movements do not require to be developed at such great length as those of the symphony. (6) A cadenza is usually introduced towards the close of either the first or the third movement, sometimes written by the composer, sometimes left to the performers' improvisation. In all other respects the form of the concerto is identical with that of the symphony.

An improvement in the form of the concerto may yet be made in two particulars. The old plan of beginning the first movement by the orchestra playing the leading subjects in the tonic, before the entrance of the solo instrument, might be dispensed with as unnecessary, because the themes must appear towards the close of the movement in that key. Mendelssohn's Violin Concerto, and that for the Pianoforte in G minor, are examples of the advantage gained by beginning with the solo instrument at once, or after a few bars of orchestral prelude. The other suggestion for improvement is the abolition of all cadenzas, as being redundant. If they are written for the display of the performer's skill, surely the composer should give him sufficient opportunity for this during the movement. If they are to show that the subjects can be treated in a different manner, they should be included in that treatment in the body of either allegro or finale.

The modern overture in strict form should be written in one movement, usually an Allegro, with or without an introduction in a slower *tempo*, and partakes of the nature of the first movement of a symphony, without the repeat of the first part. The subjects of an overture may be lighter in character than those of a symphony; but they must appear in the same order, and be worked out in the same manner; greater importance being given to the coda in the overture than in the symphony. The introduction and allegro must, of course, be in the same key.

The form of the sonata is, as already shown, identical with that of the symphony in all points; the only exception being that a minuet or scherzo is not necessary. The development of the subjects of a sonata ought not to be of the same extent as those of the symphony, concerto, or overture; for the obvious reason that the tone-colour is much less varied; sonatas never being written for more than two instruments. Trios and quartets, &c., for strings and pianofortes, though written in this same form need not be developed to the same extent. Nor should the attempt be made to introduce grand symphonic effects in these works. A warning may be given to composers by pointing out how incomparably finer in effect Mendelssohn's D minor trio is to that of his trio in C minor, for the reason that in the latter work, especially in the last movement, passages are given to the violin and violoncello which never produce the effect they are intended to convey: but nothing of the kind is found in the trio in D minor. Here everything has the character and form of chamber music; and composers should bear in mind not to write symphonic music when they are composing· *musica di camera*; though the form of the work and its movements may be the same as those of a symphony. For a model pianoforte quartet the student is referred to that in G minor, from the pen of Mozart.

The string quartet for two violins, viola, and violoncello, is composed in the same form as the symphony; but also should be written without any striving after symphonic effect or development, care being taken to give each instrument, as much as possible, its equal share of work and independent motion. The quintet, the sestet, septet, and octet should all be written in sonata or symphonic form, each instrument having proper but not obtrusive prominence and independence. The student is reminded that the whole of these remarks are not to be considered absolutely final; since a composer may some day arise, who may alter the present forms of classical instrumental music as much as Haydn and Mozart did in their day. However, as such an one does not exist who has shown us any new form which is better than the old one, the student is exhorted to abide by the rules herein laid down, which are based upon precedent founded by the great masters.

Rondo form differs from sonata or symphonic form, in that the first part is not marked for repeat. The original subject does not modulate, but reappears in its key-chord at the close of the first period, and again after the modulation of the second subject, so that it must be heard three times.

The arrangement of a movement in rondo form is after the following order:

The first subject enters, sometimes without introduction, and remains in its original key. Then follows an episode, modulating into the relative major if the key be minor, or into the dominant if the key be major; after which comes the second subject in the dominant or relative major, as the case may be, followed by a modulation into the original key, to bring back the first subject. This ends the first part, which is not marked for repetition. The second subject, modulating into distant keys, commences the second half. This is followed by the first subject; then an episode, preparing the way for the second subject, and a final episode and coda, generally in the original key, with slight passing modulations. It must be understood that this general outline is sometimes varied by the genius of the

composer; but, as a rule, the order indicated above is followed.

Fortsetzung (*Ger.*) Continuation. Further development or expansion of an idea.

Fort (*Fr.*) *Forte* (*It.*) Loud; expressed in music by the abbreviations *for.* or *f.*

Fortemente (*It.*) Loudly, vigorously, with force.

Forte-piano (*Fr.*, *It.*, and *Ger.*) [Pianoforte.]

Forte possibile (*It.*) As loud as possible.

Fortissimo (*It.*) *Lit.* the loudest. Very loud. The letters *ff* or *ffor* are used as abbreviations of the word.

Forza, con (*It.*) With emphasis.

Forzando (*It.*) *Lit.*, Forcing. Emphasis or musical accent upon specified notes or passages, marked by the signs *sf* or >.

Forzato (*It.*) [Forzando.]

Fourchette tonique (*Fr.*) Tuning-fork.

Fourier's theorem. [Acoustics, § 11.]

Fourniture (*Fr.*) A *mixture* stop on an organ.

Fourth. An interval of four notes.

Fourth flute. [Quart flute.]

Française (*Fr.*) A dance in triple measure, similar in character to the country-dance.

Franchezza (*It.*) *franchise* (*Fr.*) Freedom, confidence.

Franculus (*Lat.*) A mediæval sign or neume for an ascending *brevis plicata*. [Neumes.]

Franz-ton (*Ger.*) French pitch; lower than the recognised concert pitch.

Frasi (*It.*) Phrases.

Freddamente, con freddezza (*It.*) With coldness, indifference.

Fredon (*Fr.*) (1) Vocal ornaments at the will of the performer; a tremolo or quavering upon every note. (2) The *humming* of a tune.

Free chant is a form of recitative music for the Psalms and Canticles, in which a phrase, consisting of two chords only, is applied to each hemistich of the words. The author of the form, Mr. John Crowdy, in his " Free Chant Cadences," claims for it that it removes all difficulties in dividing the words, and enables the unskilled worshipper to join confidently in the chanting, without the assistance of any marks beyond the colons provided for the purpose in the Prayer Book.

Free fugue. A fugue in which the answer and general treatment are not according to strict rules. [Fugue.]

Free parts. Additional parts to a canon or fugue, having independent melodies, in order to strengthen or complete the harmony. [Canon.]

Free reed. [Reed.]

Free style. Composition not absolutely according to the strict rules of counterpoint.

Fregiatura (*It.*) An ornament, embellishment.

French horn. [Horn.]

French sixth. [Extreme sixth.]

French flat-tuning. [Flat-tuning.]

French violin clef. The G clef, placed upon the first line of the stave. [Clef.]

Frets. Small pieces of wood or ivory placed upon the finger-board of certain stringed instruments, to regulate the pitch of the notes produced. By pressing the string down to the finger-board behind a fret, only so much of the string can be set in vibration as lies between the fret and the bridge. Frets are, therefore, nothing more or less than little bridges; hence the word μαγάς came to signify a bridge or a fret. The Egyptian lutes had frets made of camel-gut, tied or glued round the finger-board. All the viols contained in a chest had frets, and some of the early forms of the *violin* were even furnished with them. But not only do they prevent the rapid fingering of difficult passages, but entirely deprive the violin of one of its most charming qualities, that of *slurring* or *portamento*, an attempt to produce which will, on a fretted instrument, result in a well-defined chromatic scale. Another reason for the abandonment of fretted violins was that, in extreme keys, the intervals could not be *tempered*.

Fretta, con (*It.*) With speed, haste, hurry.

Freie Schreibart (*Ger.*) Free writing; composition in a free style.

Frisch (*Ger.*) Lively.

Frölich (*Ger.*) Joyous, cheerful, gay.

Frosch (*Ger.*) The nut of a violin bow, into which the lower end of the hairs is fixed, and which, when moved up or down by means of the screw, tightens or slackens their tension.

Frottola (*It.*) A ballad.

F Schlüssel (*Ger.*) The F or bass clef.

Fuga (*Lat.*) A fugue, *æqualis motus*, a real fugue; *authentica*, a fugue with a subject in the authentic part of the scale; *canonica*, a fugue in canon; *contraria*, a fugue by inversion; *impropria*, or *irregularis*, a free or irregular fugue; *in contrario tempore*, a fugue, the answer of which is differently *accented* to the subject; *libera* or *soluta*, a free or irregular fugue; *per arsin et thesin*, by inversion (1) of rhythm, (2) of interval; *retrograda*, a fugue by contrary motion; *obstinata*, a fugue in which a definite figure is maintained, &c. &c. [Fugue.]

Fuga (*It.*) A fugue, as *fuga doppia*, a double fugue; *fuga ostinata*, a fugue in which a definite figure is maintained; *fuga*

ricercata, a florid fugue, a fugue with florid episodes; *fuga sciolta*, a free fugue.

Fugato (*It.*) In the fugue style; a composition containing fugal imitation, but which is not in strict fugue form.

Fuge (*Ger.*) A fugue.

Fughetta (*It.*) } A short fugue.
Fughette (*Ger.*) }

Fugue. A polyphonic composition constructed on one or more short subjects or themes, which are harmonized according to the laws of counterpoint, and introduced from time to time with various contrapuntal devices; the interest in these frequently heard themes being sustained by diminishing the interval of time at which they follow each other (the *stretto*), and monotony being avoided by the occasional use of episodes, or passages open to free treatment.

So varied are fugues in their character, that it is impossible to give any definition which shall include all kinds, but from what has just been said above, it will be at once seen, that they differ from all other formal or set compositions (the canon only excepted) in that each component part (which might in other works be only a means of harmony) must stand in important relationship to every other part, sometimes even to the extent of being interchangeable with any one of them. The key-relationship, and also the rhythmical form of the sections and phrases of a fugue, have always been modified by contemporary art, and by this means a fugue of an early period may be easily distinguished from one of a later date, until in some modern examples the influence even of the sonata form is plainly discernible. As the growth of the splendid form now known as a fugue has been gradual, having extended over more than three centuries, it is not surprising that the name should, from time to time, have borne various meanings. In old writers it is sometimes used to signify a short theme, the measure or figure of which is to be frequently repeated; at other times, a canon, because herein one part enunciates a subject and then as it were, takes to flight (*fuga*), while the other, or others, pursue it closely note for note. Canons often formed an important ingredient of early fugues.

It is easy to trace the germ of the fugue in the higher developments of counterpoint. When music in two parts was written in conformity with the laws of double counterpoint, each performer found himself setting forth the theme proposed by the other, and the good effect thus produced would naturally suggest a repetition of the theme at other intervals (as in counterpoint), and also in other keys. The two elements of a fugue which separate it from the higher forms of counterpoint are, first, the enunciation of the subject by itself, without harmony ; next the *stretto* or drawing of subjects and answers more closely together. The former is not properly included in counterpoint, as *point* (or note) is no longer *against point* when one part is heard alone ; nor is the latter traceable among the various devices of the art of counterpoint proper.

Fugues have been divided into many classes according to the point from which they have been regarded.

(1) By number of parts ; as, a fugue in two, three, four parts, &c. (*a* 2, *a* 3, *a* 4, &c.)

(2) By number of subjects ; as a *double fugue*, having two subjects ; a *triple* fugue, three subjects, &c.

(3) By the relation of subject and answer ; as a *fugue by inversion*, when the answer moves by the intervals of the *inverted* subject ; by *augmentation* or *diminution*, when the answer has notes of double, or half the length of those of the subject respectively.

(4) By the scale-relation of subject and answer ; as a *tonal fugue*, when the answer is modified according to prescribed rules, so that it shall remain within a given compass, or, within a given key ; a *real fugue* when the answer is at a measured interval to the subject note for note.

(5) By its adhesion to, or neglect of, the laws of fugue form ; as a *free fugue*, a fugue in which *strict* form is occasionally, or for the most part disregarded.

(6) By its scale, or the scale which predominates in it ; as a *Doric fugue*, when the subject, and perhaps also development, is in the Doric mode ; a *diatonic fugue*, in which diatonic harmony prevails ; a *chromatic fugue*, when chromatic passages abound.

The chief elements of a fugue are :—

(1) The subject. *Dux, propositus*, (*Lat.*) *guida*, (*It.*) *antecedent*, &c.

(2) The counter-subject, or, contrapuntal harmonization of the answer by the part which has finished the enunciation of the subject.

(3) The answer. *Comes, Responsio* (*Lat.*); *consequenza* (*It.*) ; *consequent*, &c.

(4) Episodes.

(5) The stretto.

(6) The pedal point—*point d'orgue* (*Fr.*); *Orgel-punkt* (*Ger.*)

The whole of these are bound together into perfect unity, from the fact that the answer is either identical with, or a prescribed imitation of the subject ; the counter-subject or fragments of it are of frequent use as the material of episodes ; the stretto is usually founded on the subject or counter-subject ;

and the pedal point forms the basis of ingenious treatments of the subject or answers, and sometimes even as the basis of the stretto. The first giving out of subjects and answers is called the Exposition ; and when repeated with a different arrangement of the parts, the Counter-exposition.

It can be seen from the above, that handled by a genius, fugue may be infinitely plastic in regard to form. But it must not be forgotten that in its earliest existence it was wretchedly mechanical, as the following directions how to compose a fugue in two parts from Fux (Welcker's English Translation) will prove. " First choose a subject suitable to the key you intend to compose in, and write down your subject in that part wherewith you intend to begin. This done, and having first examined your subject whether it be comformable to your key ; if so, repeat the same notes in the second part, either in the fourth or fifth, and whilst the second part imitates the first wherewith you have begun, put such notes in the first part as will agree with your imitating part according to the directions given in the figurate or florid counterpoint, and after having continued your melody for some bars, regulate the parts thus, that the first cadence may be made in the fifth of the key. Then resume your subject mostly in the same part you have begun with, but by another interval, after having first put a rest of a whole or half bar, which however may be omitted in case there should happen to be a great skip instead of it. After this, endeavour to bring in your second part after some rest, and that before the subject of the first part draws towards a conclusion, and having carried on your subject a little longer, make your second cadence in the third of the key. Lastly, introduce your subject again in either part, and contrive it so that one part may imitate the other sooner than at first, and, if possible, after the first bar, whereupon both parts are to be united, and the fugue finished by a final cadence."

The musical example which he then gives as embodying the result of all this learning, is as follows :

But the art of fugue was not long to remain thus lifeless. The successive improvements made by great masters have exalted it to the highest perfection, and have made it one of the noblest walks of the art of music.

The best way of showing the construction of a fugue will be to describe in detail the nature of the six constituent parts just now enumerated.

(1) The subject should not be very long if it does not contain any modulation, because a lack of interest may result. On the other hand, if it be very short, its treatment in the stretto will be difficult. It generally commences on the tonic or dominant of the scale.

Subjects may be broadly divided into diatonic and chromatic. Of course, a vast number of fugue-subjects lie between these two boundaries, but by a diatonic subject must be understood one on which an author intends to construct a fugue whose interest shall arise from genuine contrapuntal treatment and device, and simple modulations from key to key. By a chromatic subject is meant one which a composer takes with the avowed intention of constructing a fugue whose interest shall result from a complicated interweaving or frequent contrasting of changing key-tonality, with ordinary development of the subjects. The simplest form of diatonic fugue-subject is that which lies in a compass of a fifth, *e.g.* :

Or, when it reaches the compass of the sixth, *e.g.* :

The following is given in order to show a grand subject in this compass, although not strictly worked out :

Diatonic subjects may, however, reach a very extended compass, especially in instrumental music ;

The following is remarkable both for its extended compass and length :

Scale passages, or such as move up or down an octave, have always been largely used as subjects, both in the major, *e.g.* :

And in the minor, *e.g.* :

Sometimes the octave compass of a subject lies between the fifth above and fourth below the tonic, both in the major, *e.g.* :

Ex. 13. HANDEL.

And also in the minor, *e.g.* :

Ex. 14. BACH.

Chromatic subjects are also of varied extent and difficulty. The following, which is capable of much contrapuntal treatment, is commonly met with :

Ex. 15. SALA.

More elaborate chromatic subjects are often found, *e.g.* :

Ex. 16. EBERLIN.

Ex. 17. J. S. BACH.

Sometimes both diatonic and chromatic passages are included in the subject, *c.g.* :

Ex. 18. J. S. BACH.

The interval of a diminished seventh has always been a favourite element of fugue subjects, *e.g.* :

Ex. 19. BACH.

Ex. 20. HANDEL.

Ex. 21. J. S. BACH.

Ex. 22. MOZART.

Ex. 23. J. S. BACH.

Ex. 24. EBERLIN.

Subjects most commonly begin the keynote or its fifth, but there are exceptions to this rule, *e.g.* :

Ex 25. (On the Second of the Scale.) BACH.

Ex 26. (On the Third.) LEUTHARD.

Ex. 27. (On the Fourth.)

Ex 28. (On the Sixth) MATTHESON.

Ex. 29. (On the Seventh.) BACH.

As a rule, the answer enters before the subject is finished, but exceptions are frequent. " He trusted in God " (Handel) may be cited as a well-known case. Sometimes after the subject has finished, a few notes are introduced to link it to the answer. These few notes are called a subject-coda or *codetta*. The name is also applied to the short passage sometimes connecting the answer and counter-subject with the re-introduction of the original subject (see Exs. 43 and 68).

(2) The counter-subject is primarily an accompaniment of the answer, and in a secondary sense, of the subject; but as such, must be according to the laws of strict counterpoint. It is usually written according to the laws of *double* counterpoint, in order that it may be used both above and below the subject or answer. Of course, the counter-subject may be in any species of counterpoint, but it most commonly is figurate, or florid, *e.g.* :

Ex. 30. MENDELSSOHN.

Subject.

Answer.

Counter subject.

But when the counter-subject is in simple counterpoint it generally happens that it is in notes of greater length than those of the subject in a rapid fugue, *e.g.*:

Ex. 31.　　　　　　　　　　　　　BACH.

Subject.

Answer.

Counter subject.

And *vice versâ*, shorter notes of counter-subject to those of the subject:

Ex. 32. Subject.　　Counter subject.　　J. S. BACH.

Answer.

But something more is required of the counter-subject than to be a mere accessory to the subject and answer; it is very often used as an episodal theme, either just as it stands, or in a slightly modified form. In the following example the counter-subject of Bach's beautiful E major fugue is given:

Ex. 33.　Subject.　　　　　Answer.

Counter subject.

Before the development of the Fugue has proceeded far, this (from *) is used as the subject of an episode, *e.g.*:

Ex. 34. *

&c.

If, therefore, the counter-subject is intended for separate use and treatment, it is necessary that it should be melodious in itself, as well as capable of forming good counterpoint in combination with the answer. In speaking of a tonal fugue it will be shown that the counter-subject sometimes has to undergo a change in order to suit both subject and answer.

The term counter-subject is often applied in a manner which leads to much confusion. If in a fugue with two subjects the second subject is given out at the same time as the first, thus forming an accompaniment to it, it is by some called the counter-subject, instead of the second subject, *e.g.*:

Ex. 35.　Subject or 1st Subject,　　MOZART.

&c.

Counter subject or 2nd Subject.

It were well if this use of the word counter-subject for second subject could be dispensed with, the former being limited to the signification of that counterpoint added to an answer or subject by a part which *has already gone through the subject or answer*. Nothing is gained by limiting the use of the words *second* and *third* subjects to such as are introduced separately.

(3) The answer of a fugue is one of the most important parts of its construction. If the subject be wrongly answered, the effect and success of the whole composition is marred. For not only does a wrong answer compel the construction of a false counter-subject, inasmuch as the counter-subject must be the accompaniment of the answer whether it be right or wrong, but also, it overthrows those episodes founded on the counter-subject, and not unfrequently the stretto too, as being founded on a close combination of subject and answer.

The large class of fugues called *tonal*, are so termed because the answer undergoes some slight modification in order to prevent a departure from the key-tonality of the subject. Roughly speaking, all answers are a fifth above or a fourth below the subject. If this relation of answer to subject were strictly carried out, a modulation in every answer would be inevitable. The answer is, however, often purposely made at strict intervals to the subject; in which case, the fugue is called strict or *real*. These two classes of fugues must be considered carefully.

First as to tonal fugues.

The idea which underlies all tonal treatment of answers is, that the scale is equally divided into two parts, namely, from the tonic up to the dominant, one part; from the dominant up to the octave-tonic, the other. But as a matter of fact the first half, tonic to dominant, contains five diatonic steps, while the second, dominant to tonic, only contains four. This is the source of the whole difficulty of making a correct answer to any given subject, *e.g.*:

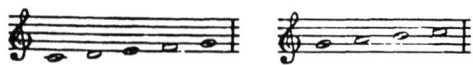

Now when the subject proceeds from tonic to dominant direct, the answer must proceed from dominant to tonic, *e.g.*:

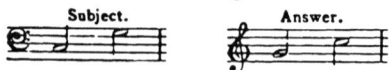

and *vice versa*, *e.g.*:

But if notes lying between the tonic and dominant are introduced, or if the subject exceeds the compass of a fifth, it is not easy to say that any uniform principle governs the relation of answer to subject, except that two notes must be represented by one, *e.g.*:

The following examples show how tonic is answered by dominant, and dominant by tonic:

Ex. 36.   Answer.   BACH.

Subject.   &c.

Ex. 37.   MENDELSSOHN.

Answer.

and, by the next it will be seen, that the *sub*-dominant also is answered by the tonic:

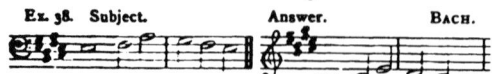

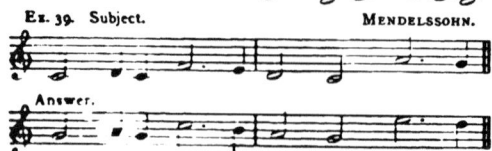

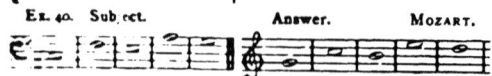

Ex. 38. Subject.   Answer.   BACH.

Ex. 39. Subject.   MENDELSSOHN.

Answer.

Ex. 40. Subject.   Answer.   MOZART.

The following illustrates the application of the same principle in a case where the subject

proceeds down to the dominant and then passes above the tonic:

Ex. 41. Subject.   BACH.

Answer.

The application of this principle to subjects in the minor key is much less easy than in the major. When, as formerly, fugues were often composed in the church modes, the position of the (so-called) *dominant* and *final* of the mode largely influenced the relation of answer to subject, but, although these complications do not lie in the path of the modern student, yet there is still much uncertainty and discrepancy as to the particular treatment of the *sub-tonic* of the minor. This arises from the fact that several sorts of minor scale are still in use, and the composer naturally frames his answer in accordance either to that kind of scale most congenial to him, or to that most capable of bringing into prominence the melodic form of his subject. Minor subjects are often too very chromatic, a fact which adds to the difficulty of forming a correct answer.

In its simple state, a minor subject is in effect answered by a modulation into the *minor* key a fifth above (or fourth below), *e.g.*:

Ex. 42. Subject. Key of F minor.

Answer. Key of C minor.

and the following shows the method of return to the original key, sometimes called a *codetta*:

Ex. 43.

Another instance is here given:

Ex. 44. Subject (C minor).

Answer.

Answer here modulates into G minor.

It is not an easy thing to connect two minor keys a fifth apart in a pleasing manner; it takes some little time to accustom the ear to the sound of the minor third of the new key; but the leading note of the old key must, of necessity, be discarded before the re-entry of the subject. In the fugue just quoted Bach inserts two bars between the close in G minor, as above, and the re-entry of the subject, namely :

Ex. 45. (Codetta.)

Re-entry of Subject.

As minor subjects naturally lead to a modulation in the answer, it happens, as might be expected, that the minor fugues are chiefly *real* ; for if a modulation must take place at all, it may as well include the whole of the subject as its closing portion, tonal alterations of the answer are therefore rendered to a certain extent unnecessary.

But in strictly *chromatic* fugues the tonal answer is very common, as the following examples will show, although it will be observed that, in some cases, the answer, before many notes are past, becomes a mere transcript at a fifth above or fourth below the original subject.

The next example is purely tonal :

Ex. 46. Subject. KIRNBERGER.

Answer.

The following is mixed, being partly tonal, partly at a strict interval :

Ex. 47. Subject (8ve. lower). HANDEL.

They loathed to drink.

Answer.

The tonal alteration of the answer to minor subjects often extends no further than the first note, *e.g.* :

Ex. 48. Subject. MENDELSSOHN.

Answer.

In major subjects this also happens, *e. g.* :

Ex. 49. Subject. BACH.

Answer.

This is more noticeable in short chromatic subjects, *e.g.* :

Ex. 50. Subject. Answer.

Ex. 51 Subject. Answer.

Enough has been said to show the general force of the laws of tonal answer. Study and experience are the only means of cultivating a true perception of this peculiar relation of subject to answer. Many writers have attempted to draw up a regular code of laws, but the exceptions which persistently come forward render them almost useless.

A real or strict fugue is one in which the answer is *throughout* at the interval of a fifth above or fourth below the subject, *e.g.* :

Ex. 52. Subject. BACH.

Answer.

Ex. 53. Subject. HANDEL.

Answer.

It is unnecessary to give more examples of this exact and constant distance between subject and answer.

The question naturally arises, How is it to be known when an answer ought to be tonal or real ? It is only possible to answer this in the most general way. If a subject has one or more direct melodic progressions from tonic to dominant or dominant to tonic it is difficult to make the answer *real* or *strict* without

* Made one octave lower to suit the compass of ordinary tenor voices.

giving an unpleasant effect of unnecessary change of key ; whereas, if the subject consist of a series of grades of the scale, it is difficult to make the answer *tonal*, without producing the effect of unnecessary alteration of melody (inasmuch as two notes have to do duty for one, and *vice versâ*). This is all that can be said, except that special prominence of the *sub-dominant* in the subject seems to demand a strict answer, *e.g.* :

Ex. 54. Subject.

Answer.

In cases where a fugue has more than one subject, if the second subject partakes of the tonality of the expected answer, and is introduced in the position ordinarily occupied by the answer, the answers of both first and second subjects may take place at the octave, sometimes without any alteration of the position of the parts, *e.g.* :

Ex. 55.   BACH.

The subjects are as often answered in the octave, but in *inverted positions*, *e.g.* :

Ex. 56.   SALA.

It has already been stated that the counter-subject is often written in double counterpoint, so that it may be used without grammatical error, both above and below the subject. What has been said of a counter-subject applies with equal force to a *second* subject, as the above example (56) shows.

But the first and second subject are given out very frequently, each at its own proper tonal distance, *e.g.* :

Ex. 57.   BEETHOVEN.

Et vi-tam

Sometimes the second subject appears after the first subject, but is not answered in the position expected, an answer to the *first* subject taking its place.

Ex 58.   HANDEL.

&c.

In other cases, the first subject is, after its first enunciation, set aside for a lengthy treatment of the second subject, the first being reintroduced when the development has been proceeded with.

The above examples of fugues with two subjects, have tonal answers ; but this is not always the case, as the following example of strict answer shows ;

Ex. 59.   CHERUBINI.

[musical notation: Ex. with &c.]

In fugues having three or more subjects, there seems to be no rule whatever as to the order or position of their entry. Sometimes they are enunciated in their order immediately after, or overlapping, each other; *e.g.* ;

Ex. 60.   3rd Sub, CHERUBINI.

[musical notation]
2nd Sub.
1st Sub.
Quam o-lim a - bra-hæ

1st Answer.

[musical notation]
2nd Ans.   3rd Ans.

They are not unfrequently introduced and developed separately, at long intervals of time, and only brought together towards the close of the work; in this case, of course, the answers are each true to the subject as delivered, and the fugue has the form of two or more separate developments which are capable of coalition; *e.g.* :

Ex. 61. 1st Subject,   BACH.
tr.

[musical notation]

Answer.   tr 30 bars.

[musical notation]

2nd Subject.

[musical notation]

In some cases the subjects are given out one by one, without any development being attempted till all have been heard, as in the well-known movement, "Let old Timotheus," from Handel's "Alexander's Feast," in which

the four following subjects are given out successively by solo voices :

Ex. 62.
1st Subject.   2nd Subject.

[musical notation]

3rd Subject.   4th Subject.

[musical notation]   &c.

Some fugues have what is called a *free* part; that is a part whose sole function it is to support or supplement those constructed in the prescribed fugue form. Such examples generally take the shape of a regularly constructed fugue, accompanied by and built upon a separate bass, or *basso continuo* :

Ex. 63.   BACH.

[musical notation]
Through Je - sus Christ
A
BASS.

[musical notation]

- men, A - men.

[musical notation]   &c.

[musical notation]   &c.

Other orchestral parts sometimes accompany a fugue, *e.g.* :

Ex. 64.
(TENORI.)   BACH.

[musical notation]
Ky -ri-e.
Oboi.

[musical notation]

(187)

(ALTI.)

Ky - ri - e

&c.

&c.

Tenors (8ve. lower).

Ky - ri - e.

&c.

From the two preceding examples, it will be seen that free accompaniment may take place, whether the fugue is tonal or real, or whether it has but one, or more than one, subject.

A chorale is not unfrequently introduced into a fugue as a free part, as the well known chorus, "But our Lord," in Mendelssohn's "St. Paul." There can be little doubt that the freedom of writing which distinguishes later fugues, was largely brought about by the habit of writing free parts on a ground-bass.

When the answer of a fugue is an inversion of the subject, the fugue is said to be *al rovescio*, e.g.:

Ex. 95. HANDEL.

To our great God.

To our great God.

To our great God.
To our great God.
To our great God. &c.

Fugues "by inversion," like all other kinds of fugues, are sometimes accompanied by free parts, *e.g.*:

Ex. 66. BACH.

Ky - ri - e.
Free Bass.

Episodes are passages introduced into a fugue, in which the actual development of the subject or subjects is for a time suspended in order to give some variety and relief to the ear. But it is important that episodes, while affording variety, should not disturb the character of the fugue of which they form part. To effect this object, they are generally made up of free or imitative treatments of a fragment of the subject, or of part of the countersubject, or of the coda connecting subject and answer, or of some new subject not dissimilar in style to one of these. An example (34) has already been given, of an episode formed on the countersubject. The following is an episode formed on a fragment of the *subject* given in Ex. 49:

Ex. 67. BACH.

&c.

The following is an example of an episode, founded on a *coda*:

Ex. 68. Subject. BACH.

Ans.

Coda connecting close of answer with re-entry of subject:

Episode founded on the figure of the above coda:

BACH.

Episodes founded on a theme not part of subject, countersubject, or coda, are very commonly met with; in the following example the theme is quite congruous with the subject:

Subject.

He trust-ed in God

Episodal subject.

let him de-liv-er him.

A fine example of episodes of a totally different character to the fugue into which they are introduced is to be found in Bach's organ-fugue:

Ex. 69. Subject.

tr

Episode.

The stretto is that part of a fugue in which the subject and answer are drawn or pressed closer together (Lat. *strictus* from *stringere*).

In nearly all carefully constructed fugues the entry of the subject and answer is brought closer together from time to time, as the development proceeds, but the word *stretto* is only applied to that special passage in which the whole of the parts, or as many as possible, take up the subject at as short an interval of time as possible. The simplest illustration of a stretto will be found in the treatment of some simple diatonic subject such as the following:

Ex. 70. Sub. Ans.

Stretto.

&c.

It not unfrequently happens that the subject and answer cannot be brought closer together than their original distance, owing to their harmonic inaptitude for such treatment. In such cases, an altered form of the subject, or a part of the coda, or part of the counter-subject, or even an entirely new subject, may form the theme of the stretto. In many fugues there is no one passage which can be pointed out as *the stretto*, but the interest of the development is sustained by various other contrapuntal devices, or modulations.

The *masterly stretto* (stretto maestrale) is formed in strict canon. If the subject is not capable of such treatment it may be slightly altered for the purpose.

It is not necessary that the same intervals should be observed between the parts forming a stretto as are absolutely necessary in the enunciation of subject and answer, *e.g.*:

Ex. 71.
Subject. BACH.

Stretto.

&c.

Strettos are often constructed on the pedal-point, an example of which will shortly be given.

Stretto, **by augmentation or diminution**, is when the subject, or subject and answer, are simultaneously introduced in notes of longer or shorter length, *e.g.*:

Ex. 72. Subject.   BACH.

Stretto.

A pedal-point is a long-sustained note, generally the dominant, on which imitation, subject and answer (simply or by augmentation and diminution), or even the stretto itself, are constructed. It is not always found as an essential part of a fugue, a vast number of fugues, especially for the pianoforte, are without it. But in vocal fugues with accompaniment, and in fugues for the organ, it can always be introduced with fine effect. Modern composers have not neglected this interesting element of the art of fugue, as the next example shows :

Ex. 73. Subject.   GOUNOD.

Et ip-se re-di-met Is-ra-el,.

Stretto on the pedal-point.

Sometimes the stretto precedes the pedal-point, sometimes it follows it. An episode introduced after the last close-imitation, or after the stretto, is called a *coda* to the fugue. It often is introduced on a tonic pedal, or worked into a prolonged plagal cadence.

A few general remarks are necessary. in conclusion. The whole structure of a fugue points out that it is a work intended to be of constantly increasing interest, from the first exposition of subject and answer to the final bar. Out of this fact grow all the common rules for its formation, such, for instance, as, " no perfect cadence shall be heard till the end." A perfect cadence in *any* key gives a certain feeling of repose, and this feeling is alien to the spirit of the work. The only exception to this rule is when a fugue, with more than one subject, is broadly divided into two parts, as in Schumann's fugue No. 6 on the name Bach. *Half-closes* are not uncommon under similar circumstances, as in " Egypt was glad " (Handel).

Again " contrapuntal devices should be introduced in the order of their interest or ingenuity, beginning with the simplest, and the most complicated being introduced last."

Enough modulation should be introduced into a fugue to make it pleasing, and to avoid the tame effect of one continuous key-tonality; but, on the other hand, too much modulation would lead the hearers to believe that the work was intended to be made interesting as a *specimen of modulation*, and so take away their attention from the treatment of subject and answer. Hence, fugue-modulation is in a general way limited to *related keys*. The same object is kept in view by the rule, " if there is a tonic pedal-point, it should never be heard *before* the dominant pedal-point." Of course a breach of this rule would entirely undo the wonderful effect which the massive imitations or stretto have, when heard over the dominant, for dominant harmony always causes a yearning for tonic-harmony, and when the tonic is at length reached, then it is time to add yet more to the delay by multiplying superposed tonic harmonies.

A glance at the subjects of fugues given in the examples will show that there is not much room for originality left to modern writers. The more the vast literature of fugues which has come down to us is studied, the more apparent does this fact become. It is indeed almost impossible to write a short diatonic subject, capable of easy handling, which shall be in any sense *original*. The true lesson to learn from this is, that the modern *treatment* of fugue subjects should at least be original, and the composer who now sets about writing a fugue, should feel himself compelled, as an artist, to make use of all the freshness and novelty which modern chords, key-relationship, and rhythm are capable of producing.

It may be objected, that such a modernized fugue ceases to be a fugue at all. But the history of fugue clears away such objections. Starting from the early time when fugue had barely commenced a separate existence from counterpoint, the word fugue meant nothing more than the *subject*, hence *fuga composita*, or *fuga recta* was, when the subject moved about by single degrees, or in conjunct motion ; and *fuga incomposita* was when the subject had skips in it, or proceeded by disjunct motion. Again, when the subject went upwards from the tonic it was called *fuga authentica ;* when it went downwards from the tonic it was called *fuga plagalis.* Such expressions point out a very elementary stage in the art of fugue. What would now be almost distressing to us, namely, a fugue without any episodes, one in which subject and answer never cease to be heard, was at one period considered the perfection of a fugue. It was called *fuga ricercata.* Again, it is easy to trace the gradual introduction of episodes, and modulation, and the discarding of the complicated laws which bound subjects and answers to the tonality of the ancient church modes.

Then, again, an extension both of the *compass* and *length* of subject gave new scope to composers, while " licences " in counterpoint became of more frequent occurrence. In short,

the fugue has gradually developed from an unartistic music-puzzle into a noble and splendid form, and it behoves modern composers to add their special share to its possible future development. It is quite true that a very large number of fugues, more or less in the old style, are at this time issued by so called scientific composers, and are considered clever, and favourably received by those who are not familiar with any music but that of the 19th century ; but, were it worth the labour, such modern-antique fugues, could be proved to be mere rescripts and collections of what has been written long ago, not only once or twice, but scores of times. Having carefully examined the various periods in the life and history of fugue, and having accustomed himself to treat with respect the rules which fence in its earlier rudimentary forms, the student who reads aright will unhesitatingly endeavour to make fugue-form the handmaid of modern music, and so avoid the too common error of wilfully casting aside all that accumulation of experience and progressive improvement, which we happily possess, and should learn how to use.

Fugue renversée (*Fr.*) An inverted fugue.

Führer (*Ger.*) (1) Subject of a fugue. (2) A leader, director.

Full anthem. An anthem in which there is neither solo nor verses. [Anthem.]

Full cadence. A perfect cadence. [Cadence.]

Full chord. (1) A chord, some of the essential notes of which are doubled. (2) A chord for the full power of an instrument, orchestra, or voices.

Full score. A score in which all the parts for voices and instruments are displayed. [Score.]

Full service. (1) A setting of the Canticles for voices in chorus, with or without organ accompaniment. (2) An Office in which music is used to the fullest extent allowed by the rubrics.

Füllstimmen. Additional chorus parts— *remplissage* (*Fr.*), *ripieni* (*It.*)—either of voices or instruments.

Full stop. (1) In lute playing, a full chord followed by a pause. (2) A chord in which all available fingers are occupied in stopping the strings.

Fundamental bass. [Harmony.]

Fundamental tones. The tones from which harmonics are generated. [Acoustics, § 10.]

Funèbre (*Fr.*) Funereal, mournful, in the
Funerale (*It.*) style of a dirge ; as, *marche funèbre*, a funeral march.

Fünffach (*Ger.*) Five-fold. When applied to a mixture stop of an organ—*having five ranks.*

Fünfstimmig (*Ger.*) In five parts.

Funzioni (*It.*) Functions, duty. The general title for services, oratorios, and other musical compositions performed in the Roman church.

Fuoco, con; fuocoso (*It.*) With fire, spirit, dash.

Furia, con; furibondo, furiosamente, furioso (*It.*) With fury, energy, vehemence.

Furlano (*It.*) A dance. [Forlana.]

Furniture. The name of one of the mixture stops in an organ.

Furore, con (*It.*) With fury, passion, enthusiasm.

Fusa (*Lat.*) A quaver, ♪

Fusée (*Fr.*) Rapid division, shake, or roulade.

Fusella (*Lat.*) A semiquaver, ♬

Fuss (*Ger.*) Foot. (1) The part of an organ pipe below the mouth. (2) The measure by which the pitch of organ stops is determined; as, 8 *füssig*, of 8 ft., or unison pitch.

Fz. Abbreviation for forzando.

G.

G. (1) The note Lichanos in Greek music. [Greek Music.]

(2) The first note of the church mode, called Eolian, the highest in pitch of the authentic modes.

(3) The lowest note of the grave hexachord; in the Guidonian system, *gamma ut*.

(4) The fifth note of the normal scale of C, called Sol.

(5) The lowest or fourth string of a violin, the third of the viola and violoncello.

(6) The key-note of the major scale, having one sharp in the signature.

(7) The letter-name of the treble clef.

G. *abb.* for *gauche (Fr.) Left;* as, *m.g.,* with the left hand.

Ga. The fourth syllable in the system of Bobibation.

Gabel *(Ger.)* A fork; *Stimmgabel,* a tuning-fork; *Gabelton,* the note A, as given for the pitch.

Gagliarda *(It.)* [Galliard.]

Gai *(Fr.) Gajo (It.)* Lively, merry, gay.

Gaillarde *(Fr.)* [Galliard.]

Gaiment *(Fr.) Gajamente (It.)* Gaily, cheerily, merrily.

Galantemente *(It.)* Gracefully, in good taste, bravely.

Galliard, Gaillard *(Fr.) Gagliarda (It.)* An ancient dance, so called because of its *gay* rhythm and motion. It is said by some to have been similar in character to the Cushion dance, and is described by Sir John Davis as:

—— " A swift and wandering dance,
With passages uncertain to and fro,
⁕   ⁕   ⁕   ⁕   ⁕
With lofty turns and caprioles in the air,
Which to the lusty tunes accordeth fair."

Like the minuet, of which it was probably the parent, the galliard was danced by a lady and gentleman. If more than one couple performed the dance, they did so independently of other dancers.

The tune was generally written in triple time. " Hence," says Butler (" Principles of Musick," 1636), " the triple is oft called galliard time ; and the duple, pavan time."

Brawls, corantos, and galliards were danced at court from the reign of Queen Elizabeth to that of Charles I., as country dances and minuets were in later time. Dowland's beautiful and well-known melody, " Now, O now," published, with words, in the " First Booke of Songes or Ayres, of foure parts," 1597, had been known before that date as a dance tune, under the name of the " Frog's Galliard." It is usually written in $\frac{6}{4}$ time ; but as it is of slow pace, the subsidiary accent might be made a primary one, and so bring it within the general character of the measure of the galliard.

The composers of the early part of the 17th century frequently employed the rhythm of the galliard as a vehicle for " fancies," with florid passages for the virginals. A good example of this form of writing may be seen in " Parthenia, or the Maydenhead of the first musick that ever was printed for the Virginalls," 1611. The following tune, by Girolamo Frescobaldi, 1637, will show the measure of the dance :

GAGLIARDA.

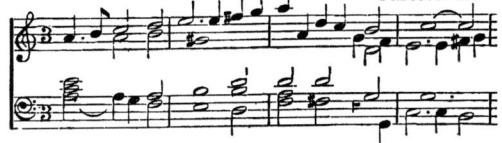

Sir John Hawkins says that "the tune for the galliard consists of five paces or bars in the first strain, and is therefore called *Cinque-pace*," but the existing galliards do not justify this description.

Some writers say that the dance came in fashion about the year 1540. It had a reign of popularity extending over a hundred years, after which time composers ceased to employ the title. [Country Dance.] [Pavan.]

Galop, galopade (*Fr.*) A lively dance in 2-4 time, originally a separate and independent dance, but now also forming a portion of a set of quadrilles.

Galoubet (*Fr.*) A small flute of a primitive character with three holes, similar to the Picco pipe.

Gamba, Viol da (*It.*) A stringed instrument of the viol sort, with six strings, weaker in tone and smaller in size than the violoncello, so called because it was held between the knees of the player. [Viola di Gamba.]

Gamba, or Viol di Gamba. An organ-stop, the pipes of which are, in continental organs, generally cylindrical, of small scale, and well cut up; but sometimes are conical in shape. Its tone is pungent and not unlike that of a violin or violoncello. In England the Bell Gamba is more commonly met with. [Bell Gamba.]

Gamme (*Fr.*) Gamut. [Notation.]

Ganz (*Ger.*) (1) Entire, whole; *Ganzton*, a whole tone; *Ganze Note*, a semibreve, &c. (2) Very, as *ganz langsam*, very slow.

Garbo, con (*It.*) With grace, politely.

Garlands. A general name for collections of ballads, and other inferior literature upon given subjects. [Ballad.]

Garrire (*It.*) To warble, to chirp, to chatter.

Gassatio. A word of varied meaning. Some writers use it to describe a street serenade, "hergeleitet von dem Herumspazieren auf den Gassen um die Jungfern ein Ständchen oder Hoferecht zu machen;" others say it is a "familiar expression for instrumental compositions generally, symphonies as well as quartetts." Others as-

suming that the word comes from the Italian *Cassatio* or *Cassazione*, describe it as meaning a farewell or final piece, whether in a programme or as part of a whole composition. The word *Gassaten* or *Cassatio* is often made to do duty in describing the whole thing of which it only forms part, and thus it is that Suites or Sonatas of the earlier composers are sometimes called *Cassazioni* when final movements ought only to be so called. [Suite.] [Serenata.]

Gassenhawer. (*Ger.*) The name given to one of the dance tunes in Wolf. Heckel's "Lautten Buch," Strasbourg, 1562, which contains many songs and pieces; "Auch vil faltige Newe Tentz, sampt mancherley Fantaseyen, Recercari, Pavana, Saltarelli, und Gassenhawer, &c." The word is collaterally related to *Passacaille*, which is from the Spanish *Passa calle* ("qui court les rues"). The subjoined is a translation into modern notation, from the Tablature in the book referred to above, of the melody of this dance, which it may be perceived is capable of bearing a ground bass, like the *chaconnes* or *passacailles*, to which class it unquestionably belongs.

WOLF. HECKEL's "Lautten Buch," 1562.

Gauche (*Fr.*) Left; as, *la main gauche*, the left hand.

Gavot, gavotte, or gavote (*Fr.*) *Gavotta* (*It.*) A dance tune of a lively yet dignified character, said to be of French origin, and to take its name from the Gavots, "Peuples montagnards du pays de Gap, ont donné le nom à cette danse que nous appellon gavote." The description of the dance, "a brisk round for as many as will," identifies it with the country dance, and the form of the tune supports this resemblance. The gavot seems to have been more popular as an instrumental piece than as a dance, and to have been a favourite movement in suites, lessons, and sonatas from the latter part of the 17th century, the time when the word appears to have been brought into use.

The descriptions of the measure and rhythm of the dance are many, and slightly different, one writer maintaining that it should begin "with two crotchets, or the half of a bar, with a rise of the hand in beating, ending also with two crotchets that begin the last bar." Another says, "It may begin with an odd quaver, as that in the 9th of Corelli's concerto does; or with a whole bar, as the same composer shows us in Sonata 1, Op. 2."

Hawkins says that the dance is in triple time, of two strains of four and eight bars respectively, the first ending in the key of the dominant; and quotes Walther, who states that the first strain should have its cadence in the third or fifth of the key; "for that if it be in the key-note itself, it is not a gavot, but a rondeau." It would be easy to produce numerous examples of gavots by well-known composers, in which the conditions mentioned above are not present. The following examples, selected originally with the intention of showing some early specimens of this dance, will also be interesting as bearing upon the question :

GAVOT IN GAMUT, BY DR. JOHN BLOW, 1700.

JEAN PHILLIPE RAMEAU, 1716.

FRANCOIS COUPERIN, b. 1668, d. 1733.

Corelli, Bach, Handel, and others who have written gavots, do not always adhere to the so-called rules of this form of composition, but display some remarkable deviations from it, which those interested in the subject may discover for themselves in the works of those writers. Like the galliard, the gavot, as an instrumental composition, had a limited period of popularity, for there are very few examples of later date than about the year 1760 to be found in the sonatas and suites. As a dance, the gavot was taught until a few years back, but the tune employed was different to those found in the compositions of the last century. Many of the old gavots are being restored to favour at the present time, and the composers of school-music are exercising their imitative powers in writing pieces after the manner of the old composers, to supply the demand made in consequence of the revived popularity of the melody and rhythm of this form of dance.

Gavotta (*It.*) *Gavotte* (*Fr.*) [Gavot.]

G clef. The character placed at the beginning of a stave, to indicate the pitch of the notes. [Clef.]

G dur (*Ger.*) The key of G major.

Gebrochene Akkorde (*Ger.*) Distributed harmony, or arpeggio. [Arpeggio.]

Gedackt (*Ger.*) Covered or closed. [Decke, § 2.]

Gefährte (*Ger.*) The answer to a fugue subject (Führer). [Fugue.]

Gefühl, mit (*Ger.*) With feeling, expression.

Gegenbewegung (*Ger.*) Contrary motion. [Motion.]

Gegengesang (*Ger.*) Antiphonal music.

Gegenpunkt (*Ger.*) Counterpoint.

Gegensatz (*Ger.*) Counter-subject.

Gehend (*Ger.*) *Andante* (*It.*) Lit., Going; at a moderate pace; *etwas gehend*, andantino.

Geige (*Ger.*) A violin. *Geigen-blatt*, the finger-board; *Geigen-bogen*, the bow; *Geigen-harz*, resin; *Geigen-saite*, fiddle-string; *Geigen-sattel*, the bridge; *Geigen-wirbel*, a peg.

Geist (*Ger.*) Spirit, genius, soul.

Gelassen (*Ger.*) Calm, tranquil.

Gemshorn (*Ger.*) (1) An instrument made of the horn of the chamois goat. (2) An organ stop, of conically-shaped pipes of tin, narrow at the open end, with ears at the broad end or mouth, to regulate the tuning. The tone is peculiar and pleasant. It is generally of 8-ft. tone, though sometimes of 4, and in the pedal organ of 16.

General-bass (*Ger.*) Thorough bass; *basso continuo* (*It.*)

Generator. A ground note, fundamental bass, root, derivative.

Genere (*It.*) *Genre* (*Fr.*) (1) Manner or style. (2) Kind or class (of scales); as, *diatonico, cromatico, enarmonico*.

Generoso (*It.*) Nobly, with dignity.

Gentile; gentilezza, con (*It.*) Noble, with dignity.

Genus (*Lat.*) Sort or class, especially used with reference to scales; as, the *diatonic, chromatic*, and *enharmonic* genera. [Greek Music.]

Gerade-bewegung (*Ger.*) Similar motion. [Motion.]

Gerade-taktart (*Ger.*) Common time.

German flute. [Flute.]

German sixth. [Extreme sixth, chord of.]

Ges (*Ger.*) The note G flat.

Gesang (*Ger.*) Singing, song, cantata, hymn, &c.

Geschwind (*Ger.*) Quick, rapid.

Ges dur (*Ger.*) The key of G flat major.

Gestossen (*Ger.*) Staccato.

Getern, Getron (*Old Eng.*) Guitar.

Ghazel (*Arab.*) A term used by Dr. Hiller to describe a piece in which a simple theme is constantly recurring. The name is suggested by those Eastern poems in which a word or sentence either forms the ending or commencement of the lines. The following is a short " ghazel," written by Dr. Hiller on the theme, G, A, B :

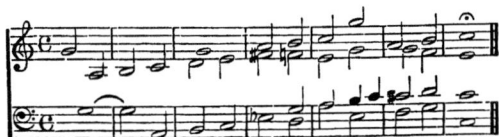

Ghiribizzi (*It.*) Fantastic devices.

Giga (*It.*) Jig.

Gigelira (*It.*) Giga vel lira. A name given to the strohfiedel (Xylophone).

Gingras. A small ancient flute, of Phenician origin, afterwards adopted by some European nations.

Gingrina (*Lat.*) [Gingras.]

Giochevole (*It.*) Merry, jocose.

Giocondamente (*It.*) Joyfully, merrily.

Giocondezza (*It.*) Mirth, jocundity.

Giocondato (*It.*) Happy, joyful.

Giocondo (*It.*) Jocund.

Giocosamente, giocoso (*It.*) Sportively, playfully.

Giojante, giojosamente, giojoso (*It.*) With mirth, joyfully.

Gioviale (*It.*) Jovial, pleasant.

Giovialità, con (*It.*) With jollity.

Giraffe. An ancient form of the spinnet. [Pianoforte.]

Gis (*Ger.*) The note G sharp.

Gis moll (*Ger.*) The key of G sharp minor.

Gittern. [Guitar.]

Gittith (*Heb.*) This word, which is found in the titles of Ps. viii., lxxxi., lxxxiv., is by some supposed to signify a musical instrument (perhaps as used at Gath); by others, a vintage-song, or well-known tune, to which the Psalm could be sung. Various other explanations have been offered, which it is unnecessary to give here.

Giubiloso (*It.*) Jubilant.

Giustamente (*It.*) Strictly, accurately.

Giusto (*It.*) Strict, correct, moderate ; *a tempo giusto*, at a moderate pace.

Glass. Musical instruments of this material are of two kinds, percussion and friction ; the first consists of a series of small plates of graduated sizes, supported on tapes secured in a wooden box, the several tones being regulated by the size of the glass : this is a mere toy. For a description of the best of the second class see Harmonica. Another form of a glass friction instrument is made of a number of tubes of various lengths, and as the tone is brought out by stroking the length of the several tubes with flannel or india-rubber, it is only capable of producing slow melodies.

Glee. A composition for voices in harmony, consisting of two or more contrasted movements, with the parts so contrived that they may be termed a series of interwoven melodies. It may be written for three or more voices, either equal or mixed ; but it is necessary that there should be only one voice to a part. It may be designed with or without instrumental accompaniment, and set to words in any style — amatory, bacchanalian, pastoral, didactic, comic, or serious. As a composition, the glee appears to have historically followed the catch, and to have had its origin at the time when part-singing began to be revived. But when musical skill was at a very low ebb, a satisfactory performance of existing vocal compositions for combined voices was neither possible nor desirable : not possible ; because the madrigal, to be effective, required many voices to a part ; and not desirable, because the words set to the catches, the other sort of secular part-music, were not of a character which fitted them for the ears of decent folk. The earliest glees, so called, were set to words of a pastoral character. One of the first, if not the very first, printed composition for voices to which the title was attached, was " Turn, Amaryllis, to thy swain," by Thomas Brewer, included in the second book of Hilton's " Catch that catch can," 1652. The most ancient collection in which glees are specially mentioned, was published by Playford. It is called, " The Musical Companion, in two books : the First Book containing Catches and Rounds for Three Voyces ; the Second Book containing Dialogues, Glees, Ayres, and Songs for two, three, and Four Voyces," 1673. The compositions contained in these books can only be regarded as exhibiting the qualities of preliminary attempts to fix and form the style, which afterwards became known as the " glee style." Many other species of musical works have grown to their present proportions by slow degrees ; but the glee seems to have started into existence in its modern form all at once, and not to have been the result of a series of developments. From the time when Playford's book was published until between the year 1760 and 1770, the specimens of part-writing to which the authors attached the word " glee," are somewhat rare, the terms " ode," or " three, four, or five-part song," being preferred for vocal compositions in harmony.

Sir John Hawkins does not mention the word once in his " History of Music," published 1776, although institutions for the encouragement of glee-writing were already established in his time.

The period of the existence of the glee, as we now understand it, was about seventy years, namely, from 1760 to 1830 ; the most successful of the glee-writers during that time were S. Webbe, Dr. Cooke, Dr. Callcott, R. J. S. Stevens, Reginald Spofforth, J. Stafford Smith, W. Horsley, Sir Henry Bishop, Charles Evans, and to this list must be added, Sir John Goss.

The compositions of these writers, with a few by their contemporaries, form the whole literature of this class. The so-called German glees are, for the most part, simply harmonised melodies, and belong to the order of part-songs rather than to that of glees. The application of the term to this class of composition is correct philologically, but not formally. The old word *glee* meant harmony or combination; and, therefore, all compositions for voices in harmony may be rightly designated by the term. But the word is understood to signify a special sort of vocal harmony, and if the pieces so called do not fulfil the conditions of the character, already described above, they ought not to be called by the term.

The glee, like the anthem, is of English growth, and has never been successfully imitated by foreign writers. The increase of musical taste has led to the formation of large choral societies, by whom the master-works of the great composers are given with effect; but it has also led to the neglect of private social musical gatherings, and, consequently, to the disuse of one of the most delightful musical pleasures, the performance of the glee. Glee-singing is almost a lost art in England. The tradition has not been properly maintained, and we are in the somewhat anomalous position of a people in the possession of a special literature, which we cannot rightly interpret or appreciate.

A few remarks upon the origin and meaning of the word Glee may not be considered uninteresting or out of place here. The word comes from the Anglo-Saxon " gle," meaning music, or the performance of music. For example, the " Story of Genesis," written about 1250, and reprinted by the Early English Text Society, has the following words :

" Jobal is broðer song and glew,
Wit of music well he knew."

Chaucer, in his " Troilus and Creseide," uses the word with a like meaning :

" For though that the best harpair upon live
Would on the beste sounid jolly harpe
That evir was with all his fingers five
Touch aie o string, or aie o warble harp
Were his nailis poincted nevir so sharpe,
It shuldè makin every wight to dull
To here his gle and of his strokis full."

In the " Promptorium Parvulorum" (1440), the same word, spelt *glu*, probably in accordance with the provincial pronunciation of the writer, is translated *armonia, minstrelsy.* Some modern writers suppose the word to

come from gligg, the Anglo-Saxon term for joy or merriment; or from *gleek*, which signifies to scoff, sneer, or banter. Neither of these derivations point to the musical use of the word; for the majority of glees are of a character too serious to be called merry, and too earnest to be called bantering.

The early writers of glees frequently used a qualifying term with the word, as " serious glee," " chearfull glee," &c., a practice which might be considered superfluous if the word only meant merriment. It may be, therefore, gathered, that they attached a meaning to the word similar to that found in the writings of the early poets and others, namely, combination. That glee meant consort or harmony is implied in the following extract from a poem by Robert Manning, of Lincolnshire, in the reign of Edward I., c. 1303 :

" Yn harpe and tabour and symphan gle
Worship God in trumpes ant sautre ;
Yn cordes, yn organes, and bells ringying,
Yn all these worship the hevene Kyng."

and in Davies poem, the Life of Alexander. [temp. Ed. II.]

" Orgues, chymbes, uche maner gle • • • • • •
Withouten the toums murey ; "
(Organs, chimes, all manner of harmony
Outside the town's wall).

[Catch.] [Madrigal.] [Part-song.]

Gleek. [Glee.]

Gli (*It.*) The; as *gli stromenti*, the instruments.

Glissando, glissato, glissicato, glissicando (*It.*) (1) Playing a rapid passage in pianoforte music, by sliding the tips of the fingers along the keys instead of striking each note with a separate finger. (2) A rapid slur in violin playing.

Glisser (*Fr.*) To slide. [Glissando,]

Glockenspiel (*Ger.*) An instrument made of bells tuned diatonically and struck with hammers, or by levers acted upon by a keyboard. It is occasionally employed in the orchestra, notably by Mozart in his opera, " The Magic Flute." [Bells.] [Carillon.]

Gloria (*Lat.*) A movement of the Mass. [Mass.]

Glottis. [Larynx.]

Glottis (*Gk.*, γλωττίς); *Lat., Lingula.* The reed used in some of the ancient flutes. These reeds were moveable, and were carried about in a little box called γλωσσοκομεῖον.

G moll (*Ger.*) The key of G minor.

Gnaccare (*It.*) [Castanets.]

Gong. An Eastern pulsatile instrument, composed of several metals mixed in proportions as yet unknown in this country. The gong has no distinct or appreciable note, but gives out a sound consisting of a combination of harmonics. It has been introduced with remarkable effect as an orchestral instrument by Meyerbeer, in his opera " Robert le Diable," and by Rossini in " Semiramide."

Gorgheggi, Gorgheggiare (*It.*) Trills, quaverings, warblings.

Gosba. An Arabian flute. There are two sorts of the gosba, the one with three holes in the lower extremity, producing four sounds which with their harmonics at the fifth complete the octave. The instrument is employed to guide the voice of a singer. The other gosba is larger and pierced with six holes, with a double hole at the back.

Grace notes. [Graces.]

Graces. A general term for ornamental notes or short passages, introduced as embellishments into vocal or instrumental music, not actually essential to its harmony or melody. In former times, in vocal music, the selection of graces was left to the judgment of the performer to a great extent, but in instrumental music numerous signs have from time to time been used, explanations of which will be found under their distinctive names. Harpsichord and lute music was always lavishly ornamented, and in lesson books for these instruments, much care and space is often given to a full explanation of their force and meaning. [Harpsichord.] Music for viols was also *graced* in various ways, but never to so great an extent as that above named. As all these instruments are now obsolete it is unnecessary to enter further into the subject. In our own time a reaction has taken place against the absurd embellishments indulged in by our forefathers, and it has become fashionable to sing and play music just as it is written. This is perhaps to be regretted, as those who are rendering music should carefully consider whether the writer wished ornaments to be excluded, or, omitted to write them under a belief that they would certainly be introduced in performance. [See Cadenza.] [Accompaniment.]

Gracieux (*Fr.*) Graceful; in a graceful style.

Gracile (*It.*) Small, thin; as, *voce gracile,* a thin voice.

Grad (*Ger.*) A degree or step of a scale.

Gradation (*Fr.*) Gradazione (*It.*) Gradation, by degrees of the scale.

Gradevole, gradevolmente (*It.*) Grateful, gratefully.

Graditissimo (*It.*) Most grateful.

Gradleiter (*Ger.*) A scale.

Grado (*It.*) Degree or step of a scale; as, *di grado,* by conjunct motion, as opposed to *di salto,* by a skip.

Graduale (*Lat.*) A gradual. A piece of music performed between the reading of the Epistle and Gospel in the Roman Church.

Graduellement (*Fr.*) By degrees.

Gradual modulation. A change of key by diatonic progression.

Graduate in music. One who has taken a degree in music at a university.

Gran cassa (*It.*) Grosse caisse (*Fr.*) The big drum.

Grand (*Fr.*) Grande (*It.*) Large, great, complete; as, *grand bourdon,* a double bourdon ; *à grande orchestre,* for a complete band.

Grand barré (*Fr.*) A position in guitar playing, the object being to alter the pitch of the instrument by making a temporary nut of the forefinger laid lengthwise across the strings. [Guitar.]

Grande mesure à deux temps (*Fr.*) Common measure of two beats.

Grandezza (*It.*) Grandeur.

Grandioso (*It.*) Grand, in a lofty manner.

Grandisonante (*It.*) Loud, sonorous.

Grand jeu (*Fr.*) The power obtained by the use of the whole of the stops in an organ, or by the employment of a stop so called in the harmonium which calls into use the whole of the available registers.

Gran gusto (*It.*) Elevated taste or expression.

Grande orgue (*Fr.*) (1) Full organ. (2) The great organ.

Grand pianoforte. [Pianoforte.]

Gran tamburo (*It.*) The big drum.

Grappa (*It.*) *Lit.*, a stem ; a brace which connects staves.

Grave (*Lat., It., Fr., Eng.*) (1) Deep in pitch ; as, *grave hexachord,* the lowest hexachord in the Guidonian system. (2) Slow in pace, solemnly.

Gravecembalum, gravicembalo (*It.*) [Harpsichord.]

Gravement (*Fr.*) Slow, and in a solemn style.

Gravita, con (*It.*) With dignity, weight, majesty.

Grazia, con (*It.*) With grace, elegance.

Graziosamente, grazioso (*It.*) Gracefully, elegantly.

Greater. Belonging to the major scale ; as, *a greater third,* a major third, as C to E ; *greater sixth,* a major sixth, as C to A. A piece of music, said by the old writers to be in any key with the *greater third,* was in the major mode ; with the *lesser third,* in the minor mode.

Great octave. The sounds lying between

and

represented, according to one system, by single capitals, C, D, E, &c. ; in another, by double capitals, as CC, DD, EE, &c. [Pitch.]

Great organ. [Organ.]

Greek Music (Systems of ancient).[*] From the time of Homer down to that of Terpander, who seems to have flourished some 300 years after Homer, the lyres of the Greeks had but four strings. At that early date the instrument could only have been used for the purposes of a pitch pipe, just as orators subsequently employed it to regulate the pitch of the voice. No tune could be drawn from four notes.

Terpander raised the number of strings from four to seven, for the service of the Gods. The following two lines, from one of his hymns, are preserved in the *Introductio Harmonica*, ascribed to, but evidently not written by, Euclid.[†]

"Ἡμεῖς τοὶ τετράγερυν ἀποστέρξαντες ἀοιδὴν,
Ἑπτατόνῳ φόρμιγγι νέους κελαδήσομεν ὕμνους."[‡]
—(p. 19, edit. Meibom.)

This scale of seven notes was formed by connecting the first tetrachord, or series of four notes, with a second series of four, by one sound common to both. To represent these sounds in modern notes, they would be as E, F, G, A, and A, B flat, C D united by the A in the middle, which was the key note to the two. The Greeks had the same number of perfect fourths in a scale that we have, but when they formed their scales by tetrachords, or fourths, they selected that position of the fourth, in which the semitone came between the lowest two strings—as E, F, G, A. The ORIGINAL SEVEN-STRINGED SYSTEM OF THE LYRE was then as follows :—

Upper Tetrachord.
d. NETE (shortest string, giving the highest sound).
c. PARANETE (beside Nete).
b flat. PARAMESE (beside Mese).
a. MESE (middle string and key note, connecting the two fourths).

Lower Tetrachord.
G. LICHANOS (forefinger string).
F. PARHYPATE (beside Hypate).
E. HYPATE (longest string, giving the lowest sound).

The above are names of the strings of the lyres, and not of notes of a fixed pitch. The

same names would have been retained if the lyre had been tuned one, two, or three notes higher. The longest string was called Hypate, although it gave the lowest sound. If pitch had counted for height instead of mere length of string, the order of Nete and Hypate would have been reversed.

The lower four strings of the lyre were played by the thumb and three fingers of the left hand, the string that fell under the forefinger being called *lichanos* (the licking-up finger), and the thumb upon the key note or *Mese*. The three treble strings were played upon by a plectrum, which was a piece of ivory, ebony, horn, or any hard wood. This was held in the right hand, and its use being only occasional, the right hand was in a measure left free for action in addressing the auditors.

The next improvement in Greek music is connected with the most important of all dates in Grecian History—that at which Egypt was thrown open to the Greeks by Psammetichus the First, King of Egypt. From that event sprang the rapid advances of the Greeks in science, in art, and in literature. Philosophers, law-givers, historians, astronomers, mathematicians, musicians, architects, physicians, and alchemists—indeed all who were intent upon the acquisition of learning—sought it in that world of ancient civilization. It was there that Thales learnt to measure the height of a temple or of a pyramid by the length of its shadow—there to divide the year into 365 days. It was there that one of the philosophical re-discoveries of the last and of the present century, viz., that sounds may be both too high and too low to reach the human ear, was known thousands of years ago.

Until the reign of Psammetichus the Greeks had been going on a wrong road to music. The seven strings could produce nothing worthy of the name of tune with such a scale as they had; at least so long as the middle string remained the key note of that scale. All the ancient fables of Orpheus and Amphion must rest upon their skill in poetical recitation, which was one branch of music in the Greek sense. As to Amphion, he, no doubt, sang in such lively rhythm as to expedite the builders in order to keep time to it, and hence the fable of his having raised the walls of Thebes by his lyre.

Psammetichus I. began his reign in 664, B.C.[§] He was the first of the Pharaohs who

---

[*] "The Systems of Ancient Greek Music compared with Modern Music," abbreviated from Chappell's History of Music.

[†] Two treatises on music are ascribed to Euclid, the *Introductio Harmonica* and the *Sectio Canonis*. The second is a mathematical treatise quoted by Porphyrius as Euclid's, but the first is an Aristoxenian or practical musician's treatise in a different school. (It is none the less valuable, whoever may have been its author.) With this reservation both will hereafter be quoted as Euclid's, to abbreviate references. Proclus says only that Euclid wrote on the elements of music. (Κατὰ μουσικὴν στοιχειώσεις.)

[‡] But we, loving no more the four-toned song,
Will sing aloud new hymns to a seven-toned lyre.

[§] In Dr. W. Smith's *Dictionary of Greek and Roman Biography*, the date of Psammetichus I. is given as 671, B.C., and to this is added a note that Boeckh dates his reign as 654, B.C. As Egyptian dates can be carried back with tolerable certainty from the conquest of Egypt by Cambyses, and the above is rather vague for a matter of such importance especially when early cultivated the friendship of the Greeks; he invited them as settlers, and engaged Carian and Greek mercenaries in his army. It was the change in Egyptian policy that enabled Pythagoras to go to Egypt, where he is said to have lived 22 years. He is the reputed discoverer of the octave system of music, which was certainly known in Egypt at least a thousand years before his visit.

The popular myth of the Egyptian Hermes and the lyre, is that, when walking by the banks of the Nile, he accidentally kicked the shell of a dried tortoise, in which there was nothing remaining but dried sinews, and that it emitted musical sounds, and thus suggested to him the idea of forming it into a musical instrument. The Egyptian name of the God was Thoth. The instrument was the Egyptian *nefer*, in hieroglyphics *nfr* (without the vowels), so sometimes translated *nofra* or *nefru*. This musical instrument is found in hieroglyphics at as early a date as the building of the second pyramid. The meaning expressed by the hieroglyphic is " good."

The difference between the Greek lyre and the Egyptian lute was that the former had no neck, against which the strings could be pressed. A lyre with an open back could give but one sound from each string, but when the same string was pressed against a finger-board it would produce notes in every variety, according as the vibrating part of the string was shorter or longer. The first lesson to be learnt from it was that the half of a string would produce the sound of the octave above the whole length; next, that, by stopping one-third of it, the remaining two-thirds would sound the musical interval of a fifth above the whole length; and that by stopping a fourth part, the remaining three-fourths would sound the interval of a fourth above the whole. In this way the Greeks learnt to produce every note of a scale, as well as the relation between geometrical proportions and musical sounds.

At the time of this discovery Greek lyres had only been made, on the Terpander model, to carry seven strings, so that, on learning the octave system, which required eight, they were obliged to leave out one of the notes.

authorities differ also by ten years in the length of his reign), the assistance of Samuel Birch, Esq., LL.D., F.S.A., keeper of the Antiquities in the British Museum, was sought for to decide between the discrepancies, and most kindly given in the following words :—" The highest monumental date known of Psammetichus I. is 54 years, according to the Apis tablets of the Sera-peium, which agrees with the statement of Herodotus. The date of 664, B.C., is the lowest probable date of the accession of Psammetichus, which *might* be a year or two higher, and Boeckh's date is inadmissible."

After new lyres had been made to carry eight strings the entire octave was included upon the instrument. The old system of tuning the lyre was then called *Synaphe* or Conjunction (συναφή),[*] and the new, or octave, system was called Harmonia (ἁρμονία), the " fitting in " system, because it fitted in the lesser consonances of the fourth and fifth into the greater consonance of the octave. (Verb. ἁρμόζειν, and the participle, used as an adjective, ἡρμοσμένος.) When the principle was fully established, harmonia became a synonym for music, in our sense of the word, for the Greek word, *Mousikè*, embraced all the arts and sciences over which the Muses presided.

The old dissonant seventh (from E to d) was made into an octave (from E to e) by the interposition of a tone between the two, previously conjoined fourths or tetrachords. This interposed tone was called the diazeuktic tone, or tone of disjunction (τόνος διαζευκτικός.)

The following is the scale for the seven, and for the eight stringed lyre upon THE EGYPTIAN OR OCTAVE SYSTEM. It is here printed in the Greek " common " musical scale—our A minor with a minor seventh :—

SEVEN STRINGED LYRE.

Upper Tetrachord.
- e. Nete.
- d. Paranete.
- c. (omitted.)
- b. Paramese or Trite.

Lower Tetrachord.
- a Mese (key note).
- G. Lichanos.
- F. Parhypate.
- E. Hypate

EIGHT STRINGED LYRE.

Upper Tetrachord.
- e. Nete.
- d. Paranete.
- c. Trite.
- b. Paramese.

The tone of Disjunction or Diazeuktic tone.

Lower Tetrachord.
- a. Mese (key note).
- g. Lichanos (or Diatonos).
- F. Parhypate.
- E. Hypate.

In the eight stringed lyre Paramese and Trite were no longer the same string. Paramese took its proper place, next to Mese, and Trite was third from the top, as its name indicates.

By this system the player had a fifth upwards from his key note and a fourth below it, so as to allow scope for recitation both above and below. He could then produce something more like to a tune than was possible upon the old scale. Before that time any Greek chant would have sounded to modern ears as never ending, for their key note would be to us as the third of the key, because we have a major scale (which the Greeks had not), and we could associate such recitations with the key of F major through the B flat. The scales of the Greeks were all in minor keys, and the nearest approach they had to a major scale was one of five tones, which might be extracted from the chromatic scale, of which hereafter.

The reason why Pythagoras preferred to omit C, which was a major third from the top on the seven stringed lyre, and a minor third above the key note (a), was because, at that time (but not after Didymus, Claudius Ptolemy, and other mathematicians had revised the scale) Greek thirds were not only esteemed as discords, but were so. They were so because, at first, the Greeks used only major tones in their scales, and there are less than six major tones in an octave. It is not proposed here to enter upon the mathematical divisions of scales, which, after the introduction of "equal temperament" (alias, equal putting out of tune), few, especially they who have their pianofortes tuned for them, seem to care about. But still a very easy experiment may be recommended to prove the case.

A major tone is the difference by which a fifth overlaps a fourth. Therefore, tune a perfect fourth from C down to G (or ask the tuner to do it), and then a perfect fifth up from G to D. There will be a major tone from C to D. Repeat the same, but beginning from D, a perfect fourth down to A, and a perfect fifth up to E. There will be another major tone from D to E, and the two will form an old Greek ditone, or third, from C to E. Try it by the ear, and it will be understood at once why the Greeks and the early writers upon church music (who had the worst of Greek divisions of a scale through the imperfect treatise of Boethius) for a long time treated thirds as discords.

Harmonia, which thus had primarily the meaning of "The Octave System of Music," came to signify "The Science of Music" and "Music" generally, because Pythagoras had limited the doctrines of the science to the sounds which are included in an octave,[*] so Harmonia and the later word Harmonica

($\dot{o}\rho\mu o\nu\iota\kappa\dot{\eta}$) had the same meaning. The Pythagorean writers on music were called Harmonici ($\dot{a}\rho\mu o\nu\iota\kappa o\dot{\iota}$),[†] and some of them, before the time of Aristoxenus, had given such exclusive preference to the seven-stringed system[‡] coupling with it the enharmonic division of the octave, and calling this enharmonic branch of the system "harmonia," that the word was not infrequently used, instead of enharmonia, for a long time after. This, however, was not the original meaning, as the following extract from Philolaos, who first published the Pythagorean doctrines, will show. It refers to the seven-stringed octave, so *Trite* is B, not C, which it became on the eight-stringed lyre.

§ Ἁρμονίας δὲ μέγεθός ἐντι συλλαβὰ καὶ δι᾿ὀξειᾶν · τὸ δὲ δι᾿ὀξειᾶν μεῖζον τᾶς συλλαβᾶς ἐπογδόῳ · ἔστι γὰρ ἀπὸ ὑπάτας ἐς μέσαν συλλαβὰ, ἀπὸ δὲ μέσας ποτὶ νεάταν δι᾿ὀξειᾶν · ἀπὸ δὲ νεάτας ἐς τρίταν συλλαβὰ · ἀπὸ δὲ τρίτασ ἐς ὑπάταν δι᾿ὀξειᾶν · τὸ δ᾿ἐν μέσῳ μέσας καὶ τρίτασ ἐπόγδοον. Ἀ δὲ συλλαβὰ ἐπίτριτον · τὸ δὲ δι᾿ὀξειᾶν ἡμιόλιον · τὸ διὰ πασᾶν δὲ διπλόον. Οὔτως ἁρμονία πέντε ἐπόγδοα καὶ δύο διέσιες, δι᾿ὀξειᾶν δὲ τρῖ᾿ἐπόγδοα καὶ δίεσις, συλλαβὰ δὲ δύ᾿ἐπόγδοα καὶ δίεσις.‖

In the above extract the distinction between Harmonia (the octave system) and Diapason (the octave) is clearly drawn. The use of the word *diesis* for the interval which Aristoxenians, or practical musicians, called a semitone, or rather hemitone ($\dot{\eta}\mu\iota\tau\dot{o}\nu\iota o\nu$), and Pythagoreans, or mathematical musicians, more accurately called a limma or remnant ($\lambda\epsilon\tilde{\iota}\mu\mu a$), proves that Philolaos refers to the diatonic scale, or scale of tones and semitones, and not to the enharmonic scale which had quarters of tones instead. When the enharmonic system came more into use the word "diesis" was transferred to its quarter tones, and to thirds of tones (when they were used) in one of the chromatic scales. The semitone was then no longer called diesis.

[*] Πυθαγορασ δ᾿ὁ σεμνὸς ... τῇ δ᾿ἀναλογικῇ ἁρμονίᾳ · αὐταρκὲς τ᾿ἐνόμιζε μέχρι τοῦ διὰ πασῶν στῆσαι τὴν τῆς μουσικῆς ἐπίγνωσιν.—Plutarch, De Musica. cap. 37.

[†] Οἱ καλούμενοι ἁρμονικοί, **says** Aristoxenus contemptuously, p. 40 and again p. 37.

[‡] ἀλλὰ περὶ αὐτῶν μόνον τῶν ἐπταχόρδων, ἃ ἐκάλουν ἁρμονίασ, τὴν ἐπίσκεψιν ἐποιοῦντο (p. 27.)

§ "The extent of the octave system is a fourth and a fifth; but the fifth is greater than the fourth by a tone of the proportion of 9 to 8; for [the interval] from the lowest [string E] to *Mese* [the key note A] is a fourth, but from *Mese* to *Nete* [the upper e] is a fifth; from *Nete* [down] to the third string is a fourth; from the third to the lowest is a fifth; between the key note and the third string is a tone of 9 to 8. The fourth is in the ratio of 4 to 3; the fifth in that of 3 to 2; and the octave [diapason] of 2 to 1. Thus the octave system, Harmonia [contains] five tones and two limmas [or semitones], the fifth [contains] three tones and a semitone, and the fourth two tones and a semitone.

‖ Philolaos, edit., Boeckh, p. 66, 8vo : Berlin, 1819.

Mese, which means middle, had also the office of key note at the time when it only connected the two fourths in the old seven-stringed system. It retained the name in the latter sense, as the centre and turning point of the system, when the lyre had eight or ten strings, and consequently no middle; for "eight has no middle," says Aristotle, referring to it.[*] "Systems without mutation," (ἀμετάβολα) says Aristides Quintilianus (in other words, "Systems in one key") are those with one Mese: Mutable systems (μεταβαλλόμενα) have several Meses."[†] No lyre could have several middle strings, so he can only mean key note. An endless number of quotations might be given to the same effect. Mese was not only the key note to all Greek scales; it is to this day the key note of our minor scales, which we derived wholly through the Greeks.

Although the Greeks had now arrived at the only true system of music, yet their old one was not allowed to die away. There were, no doubt, ancient hymns to the Gods upon that system, and so they continued to use it. Terpander, who first added a second tetrachord to the lyre, was a hymnologist, and more than 200 years after him, Ion of Chios, another hymnologist, added a third conjoined tetrachord, and so increased the number of strings from seven to ten. The following extract from one of Ion's hymns is preserved by Euclid :—[‡]

—Τὴν δεκαβάμονα τάξιν ἔχουσα
Τὰς συμφωνούσας ἁρμονίας τριόδους,
Πρὶν μὲν σ'ἑπτάτονον ψάλλον διὰ τέσσαρα πάντες
Ἕλληνες, σπανίαν μοῦσαν ἀειράμενοι.[§]

Ion produced his first tragedy (according to Suidas), B.C. 453, and died B.C. 421. It is clear that he here refers to the old system, and not to the new, by naming only three harmonies or concords (συμφωνίας) from ten strings, and from their meeting or conjunction; for the middle tetrachord of the conjunct system was united by its extremes to the other two. This system of Ion's was called Episynaphe, or Conjunction upon Conjunction [ἐπισυναφή].[||]

After the time of Ion, the original Greek scale received only one more string, the eleventh, which was added at the base to make an octave to Mese, thus borrowing from the octave system. It was a great improvement, for in this form it gave an octave of the Hypo-Dorian or common Greek scale (our A minor with a minor seventh) from A to a, and an octave of the Dorian scale (our D minor with a minor seventh) from D to d—the last through having the b flat in the upper part of the scale.

In this, its completed form, it became "The lesser perfect system" of the Greeks, until Claudius Ptolemy disputed the claim of such a scale to be called "perfect." The defect he saw in it was that it did not include the twelfth or fifteenth.

THE LESSER PERFECT SYSTEM.

The Synemmenōn Tetrachord (συνημμενων) or Conjunct Fourth.	d.	Nete	Synemmenōn.	
	c.	Paranete	id.	
	b♭.	Trite	id.	
The Mesōn Tetrachord (μέσων) or Middle Fourth.	a.	Mese		
	G.	Lichanos	Mesōn.	
	F.	Parhypate	id.	
	E.	Hyphate	id.	
The Hypatōn Tetrachord (ὑπατῶν) or Lowest Fourth (added by Ion).	D.	Lichanos	Hypatōn.	
	C.	Parhypate	id.	
	B.	Hypate	id.	
The acquired note not included in any Tetrachord.	A.	Proslambanomenos.		

The original seven strings had seven different names, but no new ones were given to those added by Ion, so it became necessary to distinguish between the new and the old by adding the name of the tetrachord, or fourth, to which they belonged. Thus the original Hypate (E) became Hypate-Meson (i.e. lowest of the middle tetrachord) and the

---

* Problems, 25 and 44 of Sect. 19.

† Arist. Quint., p. 17.   ‡ Euclid, Int. Harm., p. 19.

§ Having the ten-note scale
With three musical consonances conjoined

Till now with seven-stringed fourths all the
  Greeks hymned thee,
Upraising stinted song.

|| Bacchius, Senr., p. 21.

new Hypate (B) became Hypate-Hypaton, or lowest of the lowest tetrachord. And now, to quit the lesser perfect system and revert to the greater, and more important one.

Many have written of Greek music without distinguishing between the two systems, and as one instance, we may name Dr. Burney. He mixes the two into one as "the great, the perfect, the immutable system ... composed of *five* tetrachords" (p. 3), and then says: "after ascending regularly thus, up to D. by three conjoint tetrachords, the fourth in the great system is begun by *descending* a minor third to B natural ... Something of this *dodging* kind is to be found in the scale of Guido" (note to p. 5, vol. 1). This is altogether a mistake, there is no "dodging." The d, to which he refers, is the highest note of the lesser system, which was perfectly distinct from the greater.

Another difficulty of Dr. Burney's and of other writers, has been to understand Greek octaves. It was very natural to suppose that a Greek octave scale would begin and end like one of two octaves, viz., upon the key note; but it was not so. The Greek octave scale took from the middle of the two-octave scale, and began a fourth below the key note and ended a fifth above it. In other words, when the octave scale was increased to two octaves, it was by the addition of a new tetrachord or fourth at each extreme, and then joining on at the base, the "acquired tone" to make an octave to the key note, Mese. So that, whether they had a one octave or a two octave lyre, the key note was in or near the middle, and a Greek could recite or sing at least a few notes above, as well as a few notes below it.

The following is the "disjunct," two octave system complete.

THE GREATER PERFECT SYSTEM.

(συστήμα τελείον)

The extreme, or Hyperboleōn. (ὑπερβολαίων) Tetrachord.	a. Nete Hyperboleōn. g. Paranete id. f. Trite id.
The disjunct, or Diezeugmenōn (διεζευγμένων) Tetrachord.	e. Nete d. Paranete Diezeugmenōn. c. Trite id. b. Paramese id.
The tone of disjunction, or Diazeuktic tone (τόνος διαζευκτικός)	
The middle, or Mesōn (μέσων) Tetrachord.	a. Mese (key note). G. Lichanos (or Diatonos) Mesōn. F. Parhypate id.
The lowest, or Hypatōn (ὑπατῶν) Tetrachord.	E. Hypate id. D. Lichanos or (Diatonos) Hypatōn. C. Parhypate id. B. Hypate id.
The acquired tone not belonging to any Tetrachord.	A. Proslambanomenos.

This two-octave scale is at least as old as the fourth century B.C., and it was a sliding scale, to be taken to the extent of an octave higher. Aristoxenus speaks of the highest of the above tetrachords in one of his extant fragments, as well as of the art of writing down music (pp. 39, 40). He also enumerates the six different modes of tuning the lyre, viz., two diatonic, three chromatic, and one enharmonic (p. 50 *et seq.*). Of these hereafter.

When the Greeks changed from one genus, or kind of scale (γένος) to another, they never altered the tuning of more than the two inner strings of each tetrachord. The Lichanoses and Parhypates of the lower octave, and the Trites and Paranetes of the upper were alone moveable (κινουμένοι or φερομένοι). Of these it was only in the enharmonic genus that both second and third string of each tetrachord were tuned differently. In the Chromatic the third from the top (Trites or Parhypates) remained as they were. The extremes of tetrachords and the "acquired tone" (Proslambanomenos) were fixed sounds (ἑστῶτες). This did not prevent the re-tuning of the whole lyre to any other pitch.

A comparison of the greater with the lesser system will show that the lower octave is the same in both. It is only from the key note upwards that any change is made. In the lesser system, after a, it goes to b flat, c, d, and stops; while the greater system carries up a second octave of the same kind as the lower one.

The Greeks had in all fifteen Diatonic scales, viz., five Principal scales, Dorian, Iastian or Ionian, Phrygian, Æolian, and Lydian. Each of these had its attendant Hypo and Hyper, or Dominant and Sub-Dominant. The Hypos were a fourth below their principals (which gives the same scale as the fifth above) and the Hypers were a fourth above.

When they modulated from one key to another they did it as we do, by some sound common to both, and the greater the connection between the two scales, the better was the modulation esteemed.[*]

THE FIFTEEN SCALES OF ALYPIUS are:

PRINCIPALS.

(A.) Hypo-Dorian.	(D.) Dorian.	(G.) Hyper-Dorian or Mixo-Lydian.
(B♭.) Hypo-Ionian	(E♭.) Ionian.	(A♭.) Hyper-Ionian.
(B.) Hypo-Phrygian.	(E.) Phrygian.	(A.) Hyper-Phrygian.
(C.) Hypo-Æolian.	(F.) Æolian.	(B♭.) Hyper-Æolian.
(C♯.) Hypo-Lydian.	(F♯.) Lydian.	(B.) Hyper-Lydian.

It will be observed that the classical Lydian was F sharp, and not F, as in church scales. The true Lydian was a tone above the Phrygian.[†]

In Pindar's time the Hypo-Dorian scale was called Æolian; the above arrangement of intervals between scales is therefore less ancient than his date.

The Greeks had no fixed pitch—neither have we at this present time. The only directions about it are to tune the lyre from the lowest distinctly audible tone of the voice, and every man had a different voice. Instruments made to be played together would necessarily be at one pitch; but there was no fixed rule for them.

The Greeks had, in the fifteen scales, one beginning upon every semitone of the octave and two beginning beyond it. The five Hypos extended from A to C sharp, the five principals from D to F sharp, and the five Hypers from G to b.

The three highest Hypers were therefore the same scales as the three lowest Hypos, only taken an octave higher. These double names for the same keys were unnecessary, except in relation to their principals.

Dr. Burney says "That the ancients had no G sharp or E flat" (p. 26, vol. 1); but at p. 41 of the same volume he shows by a table of the modes that they had both. This

curious instance of self-contradiction remains in his second edition.

As all Greek scales were tuned with perfect fourth, fifth, and octave, and all (till about the birth of Christ) with major tones only, there could not possibly be any musical difference, other than that of relative pitch, between one scale and another, if the lyre was tuned for each scale. Differences of character between one key and another arise from one key being less perfectly in tune than another. But inasmuch as certain metres were associated with particular scales, and the character of the music would correspond with the spirit of the verse, there might be as much difference between them as between a hymn and a march. The difficulty is that Greek authors were not agreed upon the character of any scale but the Dorian. That was to be severe, grave, and manly. But as to Phrygian, while Plato esteemed it as smooth and fit for prayer, Aristotle speaks of it as enthusiastic and bacchic. These contradictory estimates have been collected by Boeckh in his Metres of Pindar (lib. iii. c. 8.)

The usual way of tuning the lyre was to the Dorian, the central scale of the seven, and esteemed as the true Greek system. This preference for the Dorian is proved by all the accounts of the Greek octaves. The seven principal scales are therefore presented in that form, showing what notes would come upon the octave lyre (within the cross lines) and upon the two-octave lyre.

---

[*] Euclid, p. 21.

[†] All Greek writers are agreed upon this; see, for instance, Bacchius, p. 12.

[‡] Gaudentius, p. 22, &c.

SCALES FOR THE LYRE.

Mixo-Lydian, or Hyper-Dorian. } G minor. — Octave Lyre. — Mese.

Lydian. F♯ minor. — Mese.

Phrygian. E minor. — Mese.

Dorian. D minor. — Mese.

Hypo-Lydian. C♯ minor. — Mese.

Hypo-Phrygian. B minor. — Mese.

Hypo-Dorian. A minor. — Mese.

In the above diagram the sharps and flats are marked to the notes (as well as at the signature) only for the purpose of showing to the eye, at a glance, which of the strings must be retuned to change from one key into another. The Dorian, being the centre scale, has its entire fifteen notes; but the three scales above it want one, two, or three of their upper notes, while the three below it want one, two, or three of their lower. The octave lyre has its series complete.

Supposing a Greek singer to begin in the Dorian, and to wish to take in the Hypo and Hyper (or Dominant and Sub-Dominant), he would require either to re-tune one string for each, or else to have a ten-stringed lyre. All the other strings serve for the three connected keys, and it would be the same in any other key. Thus, in the key of C we require but F sharp and B flat for its Dominant and Sub-Dominant. A ten-stringed lyre would include the principal and its two connected scales. Hence the importance of a ten-stringed lyre, or a ten-stringed psaltery, such as we read of in the psalms. It was not the mere addition of an upper note or two, which was a great objection, in the public eye; as likely to lead to extravagances in declamation. After the Greeks had once discovered the octave system, they might have added another octave with the same facility as another string.

The preceding (as well as the following) diagram will explain that most ancient puzzle, the Greek octaves. The root of the difficulty

has been this. Although the Greeks had different signs (σημεῖα) for writing down musical notes, and they wrote down music in the 4th century B.C., they had no fixed name for any note. Some readers may remember that there was an old plan of teaching singing in England (which has been partially revived), in which the key note was always called *Do*, and consequently every modulation or change of key made another *Do*. Just so with the Greeks, only instead of *Do* read *Mese*. Every string was tuned to Mese, and if a Greek knew the Mese he could tell the distance of any other note. So, when Euclid and others* say that the Mixo-Lydian octave begins upon Hypate Hypaton, they mean that it begins upon the lowest note but one of *its own* scale, just as it does in the preceding example. The key is G minor, with a minor seventh, and the octave lyre begins upon A. The great mistake has been to take the names of the strings for fixed sounds, and so to make a Mixo-Lydian octave in a Hypo-Dorian scale, instead of in its own scale. This error underlies all the old music called Gregorian (although in the time of S. Ambrose and S. Gregory there was no such peculiar music), and in consequence of this misapprehension "Gregorian tones or scales" have wrong key notes.

When Bacchius asks "What are the names of the three scales, if only three are used?" he answers for himself, commencing with the scale of highest pitch, "Lydian, Phrygian,

* Euclid, p. 15; Gaudentius, p. 19; Bacchius, p. 19; &c.

Dorian." And "when seven?" "Mixo-Lydian, Lydian, Phrygian, Dorian, Hypo-Lydian, Hypo-Phrygian, and Hypo-Dorian." These are the seven in the preceding example.

Claudius Ptolemy proposed to reduce the entire number of fifteen scales to the above seven, thinking them sufficient, and he proposed another very desirable change, viz., to transpose them all a fourth lower for the lyre, so as to bring them all within the reach of ordinary voices. Dr. Burney says that many persons imagined Ptolemy to have proposed to raise them a fifth higher (*History*, vol. I., p. 45, line 4). That would have made them impossible for men. They were decidedly very high for men at the ancient historical pitch.

Ptolemy gives precisely the same rule for transposing these scales that any musician would give to-day, and the following is the result:—

SCALES FOR THE LYRE TRANSPOSED A FOURTH LOWER, BY CLAUDIUS PTOLEMY.

It will be observed that the key notes occupy the same positions as before; therefore the succession of intervals must be the same, for, as with us, the key note determines the succession.

And now, quitting the diatonic scale which is by far the most important of all, and the only one which the Romans adopted, we turn to the CHROMATIC SCALE.

The Greeks had three kinds of Chromatic scale, of which only one was much used. Aristoxenus calls it the *Chroma tonaion* (χρῶμα τοναῖον). It ascended the tetrachord by semitone, semitone, and minor third, as below.

The outside notes of tetrachords are here marked in minims, and the inner notes in crotchets, only to be more readily distinguishable. Of the inner notes it is only the higher of each two that differs from the diatonic scale.

This chromatic scale is of interest in the history of music as being the first approach to a major scale among the ancients that has yet been discovered. It enabled them to play five tones in minor and to change them to five in major, but we have no proof that they ever made that use of the scale. There are the necessary F sharp and the C sharp for the key of A major, and, as the seventh of the scale is altogether omitted, the G sharp, which would be required in a complete scale, is not called into question. Five of the tones make a major scale, wanting the fourth and seventh of the key—in other words it is a scale of the five tones without the two semitones. If the major scale were played in the Lydian mode, beginning on F sharp, the succession of notes would be the same as the five short (and usually black) keys of the pianoforte. An enthusiastic Irishman or Scotchman

might think this sufficient evidence that the five-toned Irish and Scotch tunes (we might add English, for there are many of them) are to be traced back to ancient Egypt. Proof would be wanting, but imagination sometimes goes a long way as a substitute. Divide the scale into major and minor and it runs thus:

Key of A minor.

Key of A major.

There could not be a complete major scale among the Greeks, because they had a musical law that the seventh of the scale must be at least a tone below the key note. It might be more, but it could not be less.

This chromatic scale was of very simple formation on the lyre. It required but to lower the forefinger string (lichanos), and such others as occupied the like position in the upper tetrachords, half a tone; and so to make a skip of a minor third down, instead of only a tone, between it and the highest string of the tetrachord, as from A to F sharp instead of from A to G.

The ENHARMONIC SCALE was of the same kind as the chromatic, but made a skip down of a major third, as from A to F, instead of the minor third from A to F sharp, as in the chromatic. But the whole tetrachord only extended one semitone below F, viz. to E, and as there was a string already on E, and that a fixed sound, which could not be altered, the otherwise useless intermediate string was tuned to a quarter tone between E and F, and was occasionally used as a grace note. Such was the simple origin of quarter-tones in a Greek scale. They could not be harmonized.

Olympus, who seems to have flourished a short time after Terpander,* is said by Plutarch, on the authority of a lost work of Aristoxenus, to have discovered the enharmonic scale by merely passing over the lichanos, or forefinger string, in preluding— but that he did not use the quarter-tones. It was a later idea to utilize the unemployed string. The enharmonic of Olympus might have been played upon any lyre which had the ordinary tuning, for all the notes it re-

quired were common both to the Diatonic and to Chromatic scales.

The quarter tones were sometimes employed both in and before the time of Aristoxenus, for he says that a singer could neither sing them with certainty nor the hearer judge of them.† He also says that no one could sing three quarter-tones in succession.‡

OTHER SCALES BUT LITTLE USED.

Euclid, at the commencement of his treatise, (p. 3) names only the preceding principal scales, but afterwards recapitulates them together with others less used (p. 10). Although he gives but the tuning of one tetrachord of each he thereby explains the entire octave, because the octave (as we view it, i.e., beginning from the key note) was made up first by the diazeuktic tone, or tone of disjunction (next above the key note), and then of two conjoined tetrachords above it. It would have been the same if begun from Proslambanomenos, the octave below this diazeuktic tone. A tetrachord, or fourth, consists, in Aristoxenian phrase, or roughly speaking, of two tones and a semitone. To show the divisions of the tetrachord we adopt Claudius Ptolemy's plan of explaining them (lib. i. c. 13) in preference to that of Aristoxenus and of Euclid (p. 11 and 12).

Aristoxenus and Euclid represent the semitone by 6 and the tone by 12, making the whole tetrachord 30. Ptolemy counts a diesis or quarter-tone for 6, a semitone for 12, a tone for 24, and the entire tetrachord as 60. Thus he avoids fractions. The following is the COMPLETE LIST of Greek Scales:—

1. The Tonal Diatonic (already given)	διάτονον σύντονον	...	12, 24, 24 = 60.
2. The Soft Diatonic	διάτονον μαλακόν	...	12, 18, 30 = 60.
3. The Semitonic Chromatic (already given) ...	χρῶμα τοναῖον	...	12, 12, 36 = 60.
4. The Soft Chromatic	χρῶμα μαλακόν	...	8, 8, 44 = 60.
5. The Sesquialteral Chromatic	χρῶμα ἡμιόλιον	...	9, 9, 42 = 60.
6. The one and only Enharmonic (already given)		...	6, 6, 48 = 60.

* "Olympus must have flourished a short time after Terpander." Mueller's *Literature of Greece*, p. 202. M. Fétis most amusingly attributes this invention to an imaginary Olympus, who is said to have "lived about two centuries before the siege of Troy." The learned

writer is as liberal with his thousands of years for the Greeks as if they were but *mille francs*. (*Histoire Generale de la Musique*, I. 131, 8vo., 1869.)

† Aristox., p. 14, l. 20.
‡ Aristox., p. 28.

Aristides Quintilianus describes also six enharmonic modes which, according to him, are of "very ancient" origin.* These scales are not mentioned by any other writer on music, neither is there any kind of allusion to the use of any second description of enharmonic scale elsewhere. Even Aristides himself says that the enharmonic scale is indivisible (at p. 133), and it must have been indivisible because the quarter-tone was the smallest interval employed in Greek music. The only two moveable sounds were already quarter-tones. These "very ancient" scales can therefore be nothing more than mixed scales.

The version of them given by Meibomius, who first published the treatise of Aristides, has been hitherto accepted without question.† The text that Meibomius followed was undoubtedly very faulty, but, when he attempted to amend it, he patched it in the wrong places. Scales were a great trouble to him, and he even failed to give the conjunct scale of three tetrachords correctly.‡

The following are the scales as printed by Meibomius. The figures 1, 2, 3, relate to tones, and the ¼ to quarter-tones.

Lydian . . .	¼	2	1	¼	¼	2	¼ ...	
Dorian . . .	1	¼	¼	2	1	¼	¼	2
Phrygian . .	1	¼	¼	2	1	¼	¼	1
Iastian . . .	¼	¼	2	1½	1	...	...	
Mixo-Lydian .	¼	¼	1	1	¼	¼	3 ...	
Syntono-Lydian(*sic*)	¼	¼	2	1½	2	...	...	...

In the above, the key note of the Dorian is in its right place as the central scale, and, in that, it agrees with the manuscript. It has the diazeuktic tone next above it. The Phrygian, however, is in the wrong place. It ought to be a string above the Dorian. Meibomius has added a quarter-tone to this scale, to make it agree with the quantity stated in another line of the text; but he should have placed the added quarter-tone on the left instead of on the right of the key note. The figure 2 must be found wherever the key note or Mese is placed; but as it now stands, Dorian and Phrygian have their key note on the same string, which was impossible.

The scale above called "Mixo-Lydian" proves that these are mixed scales. There could be no interval of three tones without omitting both the key note and the diazeuktic tone—two fixed sounds—and there could not be a sequence of one tone after another in the enharmonic scale.

As to the scale here called Syntono-Lydian it is simply Hypo-Lydian, and nothing else. This is proved by its having its key note on the third string, and in that it accords with the manuscript. There was no such enharmonic scale as *Syntono*-Lydian, nor could such a prefix as Syntono be applied to any enharmonic scale whatever.§

The true positions of the key notes will be best exemplified by subjoining the enharmonic scales in their proper order on the octave lyre.

---

* Αἷς καὶ οἱ πάνυ παλαιότατοι πρὸς τὰς ἁρμονίας κέχρηνται (p. 21.)

† As by Boeckh in his Metres of Pindar, and by the late learned writer of the article "Musica" in the *Dictionary of Greek and Roman Antiquities*, edited by Wm. Smith, LL.D.

‡ See his notes upon Euclid, p, 63. He has omitted Hypate at the bottom of the lowest tetrachord (but Hypate was a standing sound, and could not be omitted), and commenced it upon Parhypate, which is one of the inner moveable sounds. All his tetrachords are therefore wrong. The origin of this mistake is that he has made Trite and Paramese into two strings, whereas in the conjunct scale they were never other than one, B flat. There should have been no Paramese in the scale, because it is the conjunct scale of Ion, and so dating more than 200 years after the octave system had been in use, Paramese then belonged only to the octave system. At some long previous time the names of Paramese and Trite had been indiscriminately applied to B flat in *that* system, but never as separate strings in the conjunct scale, but never as separate strings in that system. It is singular that an editor of the Greek writers upon music should not have been able to write out a scale, and perhaps equally singular that such errors should have passed for 200 years unobserved. It is desirable to draw attention to them because these are by no means solitary errors in Meibomius. One instance more: in his notes upon Aristides Quintilianus (p. 209, column 1, line 6) he says that the two most ancient tetrachords were joined together by a string common to both, and that that string was called *hypate meson*. This is an entire mistake; the string was Mese. It is singular that he did not know it, even by the position of the tone of disjunction. How strange that so eminent a man should have edited the Greek authors upon music and yet not have mastered the scale system.

§ συντεινω, to draw together. In the enharmonic scale the moveable sounds, instead of being drawn tight, were *relaxed* to the extreme. "Συντονωτάτη διάτονός ἐστιν," says Aristoxenus, p. 25, line 11, and again p. 26. Further he says, "καθόλου γὰρ βαρυτάται μὲν αἱ ἐναρμόνιοι λιχανοὶ ἦσαν, ἐχόμεναι δὲ αἱ χρωματικαί, συντονώταται δὲ αἱ διάτονοι," p. 24, lines 22 to 25. The enharmonic was πυκνότατον, and its lichanos βαρυτάτον the very opposite to συντονώτατον—πυκνὸν δ᾽ ἔσται τὸ ἐκ δύο διέσεων ἐναρμονίων καὶ χρωματικῶν ἐλαχίστων. Aristox. p. 24, lines 17 to 19.

THE GREEK ENHARMONIC SCALE.

			Mese						
Mixo-Lydian . .	1	$\frac{1}{4}$	$\frac{1}{4}$	2	$\frac{1}{4}$	$\frac{1}{4}$	2	1
Lydian	$\frac{1}{4}$	$\frac{1}{4}$	2	$\frac{1}{4}$	$\frac{1}{4}$	2	1	$\frac{1}{4}$
Phrygian . . .	$\frac{1}{4}$	2	$\frac{1}{4}$	$\frac{1}{4}$	2	1	$\frac{1}{4}$	$\frac{1}{4}$
Dorian	2	$\frac{1}{4}$	$\frac{1}{4}$	2	1	$\frac{1}{4}$	$\frac{1}{4}$	2
Hypo-Lydian . .	$\frac{1}{4}$	$\frac{1}{4}$	2	1	$\frac{1}{4}$	$\frac{1}{4}$	2	$\frac{1}{4}$
Hypo-Phrygian .	$\frac{1}{4}$	2	1	$\frac{1}{4}$	$\frac{1}{4}$	2	$\frac{1}{4}$	$\frac{1}{4}$
Hypo-Dorian . .	2	1	$\frac{1}{4}$	$\frac{1}{4}$	2	$\frac{1}{4}$	$\frac{1}{4}$	2

The diagonal line shows the key note of each scale with its tone of disjunction next above it. The other figures of 2 are the highest notes of other tetrachords. Iastian (or Ionian) has no place in these scales, because it would require the position of one of the above seven, and it was for such reasons Claudius Ptolemy proposed to reduce the number of scales to seven. As to the Syntono-Lydian of the manuscript, it is clearly a mistake for Hypo-Lydian. It may seem strange that I should have to correct a Greek writer, but this is an unmistakable case, and one in which he was only speaking of something "very ancient," of which he had no intimate knowledge. The date of the writer has been clearly over-rated, and the manuscript of his treatise is exceedingly corrupt. In order to make one line of the text agree with another, Meibomius twice changed the word "tone" into "ditone" in the Lydian scale; he added a diesis, or quarter-tone to the Phrygian, the same to the Mixo-Lydian, and the final ditone to what is called Syntono-Lydian. All these additions and alterations will be seen by comparing his Latin translation with the Greek text (p. 21), and they are admitted and justified in Meibomius's notes.

Meibomius was the first to publish the work of Aristides Quintilianus, and he seems to have been desirous of magnifying such an acquisition to literature, by ascribing to the author as remote a date as he could guess. Meibomius overlooks his having copied from Claudius Ptolemy (the numerical estimate of 60 for a tetrachord is taken from Ptolemy) and thinks that Martianus Capella (who lived about the end of the fifth century), copied from Aristides. The numberless petty differences between the two upon a common subject seem greatly to militate against the theory, and Meibomius's own notes afford the evidence. Aristides had evidently studied Latin, because he quotes Cicero; he passes judgment upon Spaniards, Celts, and Thracians. They are either wild, brutal, or drunken,

but Greeks are every thing that is good (pp. 72 and 73). Clearly he was a Greek. But even if he lived under the Roman empire, the Romans used no other scale than the one diatonic, so that all others were matters of history. We may meet in society a man of large general information, and yet if we ask him to define a "sackbut," he may fail; although he has probably seen one every time he went to opera or concert, and the name of the instrument was only changed in the last century. Or, we might even ask an accomplished musician to define a scale of Chaucer's time, and he might fail; so, likewise, may Aristides Quintilianus have failed. The corrections are supplied by his own ancestors. The passage referred to by Aristides is in the third book of the Republic of Plato.[*] The prefix of "Syntono" is usually unnecessary, because it means the *ordinary* Lydian, and therefore is rarely expressed, but Plato employs it, because he wishes to distinguish it from the Malakon (or laxly tuned) Lydian, to which also he adverts in the text.

Aristides Quintilianus is not the only Greek writer of comparatively late date, whose works require testing by those of his ancestors. The two Lexicographers, Hesychius and Suidas, explain musical terms indifferently, and the difficulties that have been found in translating certain passages of Plato and Aristotle, are in a measure due to reliance upon their imperfect definitions of technical words relating to the art.

Gregorianischer Gesang (*Ger.*) Gregorian chant. [Plain song.]

Gregorian. [Plain song.]

Griffbret (*Ger.*) Finger-board of a stringed instrument.

Groppo (*It.*) A bunch, or, group of notes.

Gros Fa. The square notation used in old church music.

Grosse (*Ger.*) (1) Major, applied to intervals. (2) Grand, or great; as *grosse Sonate*, grand sonata. (3) Double in pitch; as, *grosse Nazard*, a quint, an organ stop, an octave below the twelfth; *grosse Quinte*, a pedal stop of $10\frac{2}{3}$ ft. in length.

Grosse caisse (*Fr.*) The big drum.

Grosso (*It.*) Great, full, grand; as *concerti grossi*, grand concertos.

Gros tambour (*Fr.*) The big drum.

Grottesco (*It.*) Grotesque, comic, humorous.

Ground Bass. **Basse contrainte** (*Fr.*) *Basso ostinato* (*It.*) *Bassthema* (*Ger.*) A bass passage of four or eight bars in length, constantly repeated, each successive time

---

[*] Μιξολυδιστί, ἔφη, καὶ συντονολυδιστί. . . . . Τίνες οὖν μαλακαί τε καὶ σι μποτικαὶ τῶν ἁρμονιῶν; Ἰαστί, ἦν δ᾽ ὅς, καὶ λυδιστί. Lib. 3, p. 399a.

accompanied with a varied melody and harmony.

The idea of this peculiar form of composition was probably suggested by the practice of singing a varied descant upon a given plain song.

The old writers contemporary with, and immediately succeeding Palestrina, frequently made use of the church-tones as themes for counterpoint, but did not always give those themes to any one particular voice, but assigned them to all by turns. This form of writing was called by them "Falso-bordone." Monteverde in his opera "Orfeo," represented at Mantua 1607, has a Moresca, a dance written upon a sort of ground bass in a form that may be said to be the connecting link between one form of the falso-bordone and the basso ostinato. Strictly speaking, in this case, it is an imitated bass, as it appears each successive time in a new key, but the intervals are imitated throughout. It is repeated four times. The first time it is in G major, the second in C major, the third in A minor, the fourth time in D minor, each section ending with a major chord.

MONTEVERDE.

The employment of a ground bass as a regular musical device became more general later in the same century. In the works of the composers of that period, pieces with ground basses are frequently found, either strictly continued or with short digressions. They were employed for compositions in all styles, for the church, for the stage, or for the chamber; for movements in suites, arias, dance tunes, &c. Many famous musicians furnished "grounds" for the purpose of ex-

tempore performance. Well known "grounds" were often selected by composers for a species of writing called folias or follias. Thus Farinelli's or Fardinel's ground was used by Corelli, Vivaldi, and others.

Grounds by Purcell, Tollit, Moteley, Pepusch, and others, are often found as the bases of many compositions published, even so late as the latter part of the last century. The practice of performing upon a given ground bass gave rise to treatises professing to instruct the ambitious in the art. One of the most famous of these works, "Chelys Minutionem, or the Division Viol," by Christopher Simpson, 1665, gives, as far as possible, all the necessary rules, with many examples. His description of the method of performing "division on a ground," is interesting, and may not be out of place here. He says that "Diminution or division to a ground, is the breaking either of the bass, or of any higher part that is applicable thereto. The manner of expressing it is thus—a ground, subject, or bass, call it what you please, is prick'd down on two several papers; one for him who is to play the ground upon an organ, harpsichord, or whatever instrument may be fit for that purpose; the other for him that plays upon the viol, who, having the said ground before his eyes as a theme or subject, plays such variety of descant or division in accordance thereto as his skill and present invention do then suggest unto him." As the "grounds" given were very short, and the compass of the viol was in those days limited, this quaint sort of extempore descant was perhaps not difficult, neither could it have been very varied or interesting, except perhaps, to those immediately concerned.

The kind of ground bass given in the "Chelys" may be seen by the subjoined specimen:

There are also several "Divisions" on this ground given, which it is not necessary to quote.

The opera, "Dido and Eneas," written by Purcell in his 19th year, contains a very good example of a song written on a ground bass. The melody is beautiful and plaintive, and the harmonies rich and appropriate.

"Dido and Eneas," 1677.

When I am laid, am laid . . in . earth, may my

wrongs cre-ate no trou-ble, no trou-ble in thy

pp

breast, Re-member me, Re-

-mem-ber me, but ah! for-get my

fate, Re-member me but ah! . . for-get my

fate.

Chacones, and Passacailles or Passacaglios, were generally written on ground basses, and the ingenuity and skill displayed in many existing examples are both interesting and instructive. There are Passacailles and Chacones by Couperin and Rameau, Bach, Handel, and others, too long to quote here. Handel, whose sixty-two masterly variations on a ground bass in his famous Chacone are well known, has shown also how the like artifice may be effectively employed in choruses, as those in "Saul," "Susannah," and other works sufficiently prove.

Group. (1) A series of notes, of small time-value, grouped together; a division or run. (2) The method of setting out band parts in score.

Grundstimme (*Ger.*) The bass part.

Grundton (*Ger.*) (1) The bass note. (2) Fundamental bass.

Gruppetto, gruppo (*It.*) A series of notes grouped as a cadenza, division, or ornament. Playford (Introduction to the Skill of Musick) gives the name *Double relish* to the gruppo and the following directions for its performance:

Gruppo, or double Relish.

mi - - - - - - - - - a.

by which it would appear to have been similar to the grace now called a "shake." He writes the latter as follows:

Trill, or plain shake.

Cor - - - - - e.

G string. The name of the first string on the double bass, the third on the violoncello, viola, and guitar, and the fourth on the violin.

G Schlüssel (*Ger.*) The G or treble clef.

Guaracha. A lively Spanish dance in $\frac{3}{8}$ or $\frac{3}{4}$ time, usually accompanied on the guitar by the dancer himself.

Guddok (*Russ.*) A Russian fiddle. [Violin.]

Guerriero (*It.*) Warlike, martial.

Guet (*Fr.*) A flourish of trumpets.

Guida (*It.*) (1) A guide, a direct. (2) The subject of a fugue. [Fugue.] [Direct.]

Guide-main (*Fr.*) A hand-guide, a mechanical contrivance for regulating the position of the wrist in pianoforte playing, invented by Kalkbrenner.

Guidonian syllables. [Aretinian syllables.]

Guidonian system. [Notation.]

Guimbarde (*Fr.*) [Jew's Harp.]

Guitar. *Guitare* (*Fr.*) *Chitarra* (*It.*) *Guitarra* (*Sp.*) A stringed instrument, played by plucking or twitching the strings with the right hand while the left is engaged in forming the notes by "stopping" or pressing the strings against the frets on the finger board.

The modern, or Spanish guitar as it is called, has six strings, the three highest of gut, the three lowest of silk, covered with a fine wire. The *accordatura* is as follows:

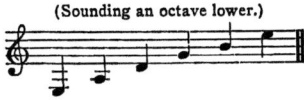

(Sounding an octave lower.)

The guitar is but little used now in England, though at one time it was very fashionable. Other nations who still employ it, call it by several names, most of which will be described hereafter. The guitar is rarely, if ever, employed as an orchestral instrument, but is very valuable as a portable means of accompaniment. The existence of frets upon the guitar limits the number of modulations capable of being performed in the normal tuning. When it is desired to make a complete change of key the *capo tasto* screwed over the finger-board alters the tuning at any desired point, or a temporary change is made by the *grande barré*, that is by laying the forefinger of the left hand completely over the strings, the remaining fingers being engaged in stopping a chord. In the classification of musical instruments it is convenient to speak of three general sorts, wind, string, and pulsatile. The guitar belongs to the second kind, and may be said to represent a very large family universally distributed, bearing a variety of names according to the tongue of the nation by which it is used. All instruments may be considered as belonging to the guitar family, which possess a resonance body or sound box, together with a finger-board, against which the strings with which they are furnished may be pressed or stopped.

Following the course of history, we find that instruments of the guitar kind are of great antiquity, as well as of general use by people of all nations.

The kinnor and nebel, mentioned in the Bible, were stringed instruments, of the guitar or harp family, but of their exact nature it must be confessed little is known, though much is conjectured.

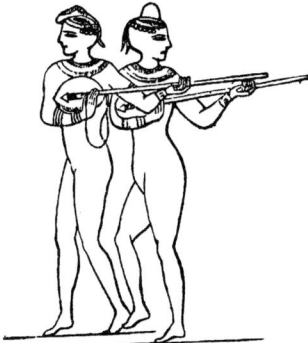

Egyptian Nefer.

The Egyptian frescoes and other paintings, valuable as showing the frequent use of musical instruments, include several specimens of the harp and guitar family. The Nefer, one of the latter class, had a neck, sometimes with a carved head, and was furnished with three strings, and had a resonance box. Upon the neck, or finger-board, frets were tied or fastened, as in the modern guitar. Each string is said to have been able to produce two octaves.

The three strings were supposed to correspond with the seasons of the Egyptian year.

Grecian writers, describing Egyptian instruments, do not afford much real information concerning them, and all attempts to reconcile their statements only lead to confusion; for conjecture is not conviction. Too much trust has been placed in the accuracy of sculptured and painted images, and various theories have been founded upon the character of musical instruments as deduced from their represented forms. As with ancient, so with modern musical instruments of far away countries, travellers' tales have too often been trusted, and their statements received as conclusive, when in the majority of instances they are confessedly ignorant of the subject upon which they give "authoritative judgment."

Philology does not, after all, furnish the best assistance towards determining relationships in this matter, and, as a rule, the picture of an instrument offers but a little help or guide in the matter. References to musical instruments by the poets of several ages offer no aid whatever, but on the contrary, often tend to mislead. If they were trustworthy, it might reasonably be assumed that no other instruments but the lyre and harp were ever employed to "assist the muse." But colloquial terms—often despised by classical poets—are of most value to the historian, and it is therefore found that the common names applied to a stringed instrument with a finger-board, kissar, cittern, zither, kitra, kithara, geytarah, guitar, point to a common origin.

There is no question but that the guitar was introduced into Europe after the Crusades. The name, purely Eastern, has been adopted with only such a variation in spelling as European use demands. The modern Egyptians call it "gytarah barbaryeh," the guitar of the Berbers, the people who are the direct descendants of the ancient race of the country; and as names and words in the East vary in the course of ages less than those in the West, it is likely that the word is of high antiquity.

This "gytarah," or kissar is of the following form :

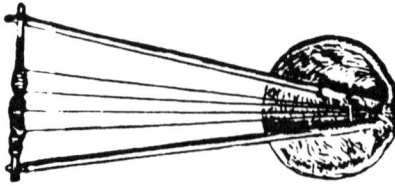

Nubian *Kissar*.

It is usually mounted with four strings tuned, according to Engel, as below :

Its form is not unlike some of the instruments represented on ancient Egyptian and Assyrian monuments, and although the name would imply some connection with the modern guitar, its shape would identify it rather as belonging to the lyre kind. But there are other stringed instruments used by Eastern people more in the form of the modern guitar.

The kitra or kuitra popular in Morocco sometimes has the resonance-box or body made of a tortoise shell, after the manner that Hermes is said to have constructed his lyre.

Tunisian Kitra.

Kitra or Gunibry.

The resonance-body of the Gunibry is made of a bottle-pumpkin cut longwise, and covered with sheep skin. Its two strings are of catgut.

The sitar, choutarah, or tamboura of Hindostan had originally but three strings of wire—as the name *sitar* implies—which were afterwards increased to four or five. The body is made of a gourd. the neck of cocoa wood furnished with pegs. The strings are played with a plectrum of twisted wire called by the name of *misrab*, worn on the forefinger of the right hand. There is another form of Hindoo guitar of a somewhat peculiar construction called Vina or Bina, which has a gourd at each end. [Bina].

Hindoo Guitar.

The Chinese, though a people of a different stock, have an instrument called Yue-kin or moon guitar, having four silken strings arranged in pairs, each pair being tuned in unison, and the two pairs a fifth apart. The instrument has been called by travellers following the method of pronouncing the name in Canton, *gut-kum*, which may or may not be philologically related to guitar. The *gut-kum, yue-kin*, or moon guitar, has inside its resonance box some pieces of loose metal which are occasionally shaken during performance.

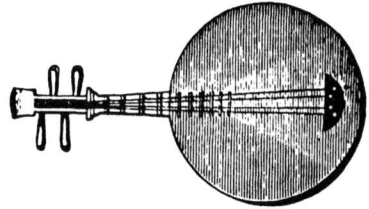

Chinese Yue-kin or Moon-guitar.

The lute, another member of this family, also comes from the East, the name is the European method of spelling its title "el 'ood." The pandore, bandore, pandoura, and mandoline are simply other names for a lute or guitar, arising from fancy or accident. The mandola or mandoline, for example, derives its title from the almond shape of the resonance-body. The Italian word for almond is mandola. Variety of names for the same thing, together with slight differences in form, often tend to confuse the enquirer. The method of performance, the shape, the mounting, the material of which they are constructed, and various other causes, are often taken into consideration in the naming of instruments. If these reasons are lost sight of, a certain amount of confusion naturally arises in the classification of musical names and titles ; and things are treated and spoken of as dissimilar, which are really closely connected. If, for example, we were five thousand years older, and no specimen of a pianoforte or of its musical literature existed, and we were left to judge of the form and use of the instruments called by the several names applied to it, we might say with good authority out of existing documents, that our ancient English ancestors were accustomed to listen for hours to a performance upon a broad wood, probably an extensive forest or a wide plank, as the acute future critic would say. Further, it might be inferred that our German contemporaries were enraptured with the skill of one who was able to produce similar effects from a flügel, the wing of a bird. The connection between a forest and a bird's wing might suggest some very ingenious comments. In cases where titles are given independently of those already applied to certain things, and detailed descriptions are wanting, the difference becomes apparently wider each successive age until all ends in chaos. If the ancient Eastern title *geytarah* had not been adopted with the instrument by the Spaniards, and by other nations following them; the changes in the form of the instrument might have been held as indicating many origins. There seems to be no connection between the words nefer, nebel, pandoura, lyre, and kithara, still it is not unlikely that they had a common start-point.

An instrument of a form like the Egyptian Nefer is found depicted upon Assyrian monuments, but strange to say there are no representations of a finger-board instrument among the Greek antiquities. That the Greeks knew of the pandoura is evident from the fact that it is mentioned by Nicomachus, and subsequent historians. The modern conclusion that they preferred their own instruments without necks, "although they adopted the system of the Egyptians for the subdivision and measurement of strings," is very doubtful, for the one could not have been done without the aid of the other. For if we are to believe that the strings of the Egyptian *Nefer* had a compass of two octaves each, those two octaves must have been obtained by means of a finger-board, and if the Greek instruments were without finger-boards, and the strings were open from end to end, without a backing along their lengths, how were they stopped, or how could a string be subdivided? It is therefore probable if Greek music was as perfect as it is said to have been, that finger-boards, fretted or otherwise, were known and used, and poets and sculptors, disdaining to employ common forms, gave fancy shapes to musical instruments.

The ancient Greek kithara (κιθάρα) is admitted to have been portable; and Mr. Chappell ("History of Music," p. 37) says, "the lower strings of the kithara were played by the fingers of the left hand, and the higher strings by the plectrum held in the right hand." And again, that the instrument "was held on the left side of the body, with the left arm behind the instrument, for the purpose of reaching the base strings which were furthest from the player." Now, the difficulty of performing upon an instrument of the lyre or harp kind under the conditions above set forth, must have been great. If the description be amended thus: "The lower *part of the* strings of the kithara were *stopped* by the fingers of the left, and the higher *part of the* strings *played* by the plectrum," &c., the whole matter becomes perfectly clear, and the kithara shows its relationship to the guitar, as well as its power of sounding octaves on each string like its Egyptian prototype.

When the drawings of ancient performers on stringed instruments are examined, it will be found that if, as they are represented in the majority of cases, a modern player were to hold his instrument in a similar fashion, he would be unable to support and play it at the same time. As the human form appears to have been pretty much the same in old time as it is at the present day, it is more than likely that the artists "evolved" the representations out of their "inner consciousness," and, therefore, that they are not to be confidently trusted.

Plato, quoted by Hawkins (p. 91, Novello's Ed.), "advises to train up children to use the right and left hand indifferently." In some things, says he, "we can do it very well; as when we use the lyre with the left hand, and the stick with the right." Unless some other occupation than that of merely holding the instrument were intended, such a piece of advice would be superfluous. The cithara is mentioned by Ovid, Horace, Virgil, and other Latin authors, with but little reference to the manner of performing upon it, other than that it was held in one hand, while the other struck the strings with a plectrum.

The number of strings upon the guitar has been varied from time to time in Europe; and since its introduction, the instrument has been more or less popular. By the name of gittern, gittron, gitteron, &c., it is spoken of by the mediæval poets; and as the lute, it was familiar during the 16th and 17th centuries.

In France, Spain, and Italy, the guitar is employed as an accompaniment for the dance as well as for the voice; and at one time, during the last century, it was so popular in England that the sale of pianofortes was interrupted, until an ingenious maker bethought him of a plan by which to weaken and ultimately to destroy its popularity. There is an extensive literature of guitar music, called into existence by the revival in favour of the instrument, brought about by the number of Spanish refugees resident in England during the Carlist rebellion of 1834-1839. But in the present day, the instrument is but little cultivated; in fact, it may be said to have become undeservedly neglected.

Gusto, con; **gustoso** (*It.*) With taste and expression.

Guttural. Tones produced in the throat.

H.

H. The note B natural in the German system of nomenclature, the letter B being used only for B flat.

Hackbrett (*Ger.*) [Dulcimer.]

Hadán or hadan (*Egyptian*). The call to prayer sung by the mueddins from the towers or minarets of the mosques, thus given by Lane:

Al - lá - hu ak-bar,   Al - lá - hu   ak-bar,

Al - lá - hu ak - bar,   Al - lá -

- - - - hu ak - bar.   Ash-hadu

an lá   i - lá - ha il-la-1 - láh,   Ash-hadu

an lá   i - lá - ha il-la-1 - lá - - - -

- - - - h.   Ash-hadu   an-na Mo-ham-ma-

- dar ra-soolu-1 - láh,   Ash-hadu an-na Mo-ham-ma-

- dar   ra-soolu-1 - lá - - - - h.

Hei-ya 'a-la-s - sa - láh,   Hei-ya 'a-la-s-sa - lá - - -

- - - h.   Hei-ya 'a-la-1-fe - láh,

Hei-ya 'a-la-1-fe - lá - - - - h.

Al - lá - hu ak - bar,   Al - lá - hu ak -

- bar.   Lá   i - lá - ha   i-1 - la-1 - láh.

which means :—God is most Great ! (repeated four times). I testify that there is not a deity but God! (twice). I testify that Mohammed is God's Apostle ! (twice). Come to prayer ! (twice). Come to security ! (twice). God is most great ! (twice). There is no deity but God !

Halbcadenz (*Ger.*) Half-cadence, or half-close. [Cadence.]

Halbnote (*Ger.*) A minim.

Halbtone (*Ger.*) A semitone.

Half cadence. [Cadence.]

Halfnote. (1) A minim. (2) A semitone.

Half shift. A position of the hand in playing on instruments of the violin family. It lies between the open position and the first shift. [Shift.]

Hallelujah. [Alleluia.]

Halling. A Norwegian dance, somewhat of the character of a country dance.

A HALLING.

Hals (*Ger.*) The neck of an instrument.

Hammer. (1) A piece of wood having a padded end or a nob, with which strings are struck. In the case of the dulcimer the hammers are held in the hand; in keyed instruments the hammer is acted upon by leverage from the end of the key. [Dulcimer.] [Pianoforte.] (2) The iron or wood striker of a bell. According to Denison, the weight of the hammer should be a fortieth part of a bell whose diameter is equal to twelve times the thickness of the sound bow. But the distance the hammer is made to rise for the blow must of course influence the weight of the hammer.

Handguide. [Guide-main.]

Hardiment (*Fr.*) Boldly, daringly.

Harfe (*Ger.*) [Harp.]

Harmonica. An instrument, the tones of which are produced by striking rods or plates of glass with hammers, either held in the hand or acted upon by keys. It has a compass of about two octaves from middle C or D upwards.

Harmonica. A name sometimes given to a mixture stop on foreign organs.

Harmonic Flute. [Harmonic stops.]

Harmonichord. An instrument played like a pianoforte, but sounding like a violin. The tone is produced by the pressure of the keys, which sets a revolving cylinder of wood, covered with leather, and charged with rosin, in action over the strings. It has also been called piano-violin, violin-piano, tetrachordon, &c.

Harmonici. The followers of the Pythagorean system of music as opposed to that taught by Aristoxenus. They were also called Musici. The Aristoxenians viewed music as an art governed by appeal to the ear; the Pythagoreans, as a science founded on physical laws.

Harmonicon. An instrument only used as a toy, which consists of free reeds enclosed in a box in such a way that inspiration produces one set of sounds, respiration another.

Harmoni-Cor. An instrument invented by Jaulin of Paris, consisting of a series of free reeds similar to those used in the Harmonium, placed in a tube shaped like a clarinet. The compass of the instrument is two octaves with intermediate semitones, the keys are arranged in a manner similar to those of a pianoforte, that is to say, all the notes of the normal scale are in one row and the chromatic notes in another. The wind is supplied by means of a mouth-piece.

Harmonics. The sounds produced by a vibrating string or column of air, when it is subdivided into its aliquot parts. [Acoustics, §10.]

Harmonic scale. The scale formed by a series of natural harmonics. [Acoustics, §10.]

Harmonic stops. Organ stops, both flute and reed, having tubes twice the normal length, but pierced with a small hole in the middle. Harmonic flute stops are of great purity and brilliancy, they are of 8 ft. or 4 ft. pitch. Harmonic piccolos are of 2 ft. pitch. Harmonic reed stops (tromba, tuba, trumpet, &c.,) are generally on a high pressure of wind, one of the great advantages of all harmonic stops being that they will take a very strong pressure of wind without overblowing. The fact is, that the harmonic-tube, having two synchronous vibrating columns of air, partakes of the nature of a pipe already overblown to its first harmonic, the octave.

Harmonie-musik (*Ger.*) Music for wind instruments.

Harmonique. (*Fr.*) Harmonic.

Harmonist. One who can sing or play in harmony.

Harmonium. A keyed wind instrument whose tones are produced by the forcing of air through free-reeds. The better class of harmoniums have several sets of vibrators of different pitch and of various qualities of tone. The stop called *expression* is a mechanical contrivance by which the waste-valve of the bellows is closed, so that the pressure of the foot has direct influence on the intensity of the sounds produced. A tremolo is produced by causing the wind to quaver as it passes through the reeds. The Vox Angelica gives a delicate undulating tone which is produced by two sets of vibrators to each note tuned slightly apart. [Reed.]

Harmony. In its earliest sense among the Greeks this word seems to have been a general term for music, a sense in which our own poets often use it. But from its meaning of "fitting together" it came to be applied to the proper arrangement of sounds in a scale, or, as we should say, to "systems of tuning." Whatever opinions may be held as to the antiquity of harmony in the sense of *symphony* or "sounds in combination," it is quite certain that among the ancients the art of harmony never advanced beyond the use of *accompanying chords*. Treatises on music, which we in these days call on "harmony," dealt (among the Greeks) with the following subjects:—The divisions of the monochord, the three genera, the sounds proper to the different modes, the shape and position of the letters representing musical sounds, and, to a limited extent, the art of tune-making, about which, however, but little is known. Boethius, who turned into the Latin tongue all the most important elements of Greek music, writes, on the rudiments such as sound, interval, consonance; on the ratios of intervals; on letter-notation; on the modes; on the discussions arising from the use of the monochord. When this work was written (in the early part of the sixth century) there had already been growing up for a considerable period a school of church music, probably started by Ambrose in the fourth century, whose function it was to form a practical school of music rather than scientific. But notwithstanding this fact, writers thought it either fashionable or necessary to found all their works on the then defunct Greek system. Even in the eleventh and following centuries, when the Hexachord system had rendered a study of the Greek scales practically useless, their discussion formed an important part of every treatise. Under the word Descant will be found a short description of the different stages through which early forms of harmony passed. But although a treatise on Descant and Counterpoint in one sense is a "treatise on harmony," yet a very different meaning is carried by the word in its more modern sense—it signifies, in fact, a statement of the system of forming chords with an account of their proper movement or progression according to key-relationship.

The authors of the earliest treatises upon harmony, in the sense just described, seem to have laboured to reconcile the old teaching with new discoveries, and though ostensibly treating with harmony, they began with ratios and proceeded into counterpoint, avoiding harmony in its proper sense altogether. In some cases the writers quietly and cleverly avoided the main question, giving apparently elaborate descriptions of the subject, which after all amounted to nothing. Thus Bateman, who in 1582 published an edition of Trevisa's translation of "Bartholomæus de proprietatibus rerum," gives to posterity the accepted signification of the word harmony in his own time, for although he is supposed only to have translated into more modern English the work of Trevisa, written in 1400, he actually altered and added to the text in such a fashion that his changes are as valuable as the original :

"DE ARMONYA.

"Armonya Rithmica is a sownynge melodye, and comyth of smything of stringes, and of tynklyng other ryngynge of metalle. And dyverse instrumentis seruyth to this manere armonye, as Tabour, and Tymbre, Harpe, and Sawtry, and Nakyres, and also Sistrum.
"And the melodye of musyk is nemdnyd and callyd by the names of the nombres. Dyatesseron, Dyapente, and Dyapason have names of the nombres whyche precedeth and gooth tofore the begynnynge of those sayd names. And the proporcion of theyr sownes is founde and had in those said nombres, and is not founde, nother had, in none other nombres."

One of the earliest books printed by its author on the subject of harmony was the "Theorica Musicæ" of Franchinus Gaffurius, Milan, 1480. The doctrines taught are essentially the same as those of Boethius, and as this has been described already nothing more need be said. It may here be noted, that the examples of harmony by Franchinus are more modern in style than those of other writers contemporary with or previous to him.

The next writer of any note among the scores of authors who wrote upon music was Andreas Ornithoparcus, whose "Micrologus," written in Latin and printed at Cologne in 1535. was translated into English by John Douland, and published in 1609. His chapters on harmony (concentus) show no advance of thought notwithstanding the fact that some modern writers claim a place for him in that

part of the Temple of Fame devoted to discoverers. The majority of the treatises of the 16th century were very learned and doubtless very clever, but they add nothing to literature not already known. Neither Salinas "De Musica," Salamanca, 1577; Calvisius "Melopeian," Erfurth, 1595; Zarlino, "Institutione Harmoniche," Venice, 1592; Valerio Bona, "Regole di Contrappunto," Milan, 1595; Zacconi, "Prattica di Musica," Venice, 1596; Bottrigari, "Il Melone," Ferrara, 1602; Cerone, "El Melopeia," Naples, 1613; nor the multitude of lesser writers of the period in which the above named authors existed, do anything but repeat the received theories, in a more or less wordy manner, rather increasing the confusion into which the knowledge of the science of harmony had fallen by their controversies and partisanships. While the writers of Italy, Spain, and Germany were adding to the "learned ignorance," our countryman, Thomas Morley, was not a whit more far-seeing than his contemporaries. If the state of music could be judged by the treatises alone, it might reasonably be considered that no new musical discovery had been made for centuries, and the constitution of music was such that new discoveries were impossible. But while the theorists sought to confine all music to certain "proportions and ratios," practical musicians were quietly finding out new and forbidden combinations of chords, to the utter confusion of the theorists, who gradually had the conviction forced upon them in such wise that they were compelled, reluctantly however, to confess that, "Il senso d'udito è stato e sarà sempre il solo legislatore dell' arte musica." The more daring musicians were supported by a large, and to a certain extent, an influential crowd of admirers who delighted in the unscientific pleasures the new music brought to the ear. We read of Claudio Monteverde, in the year 1600, being engaged in dispute with "some of the ablest musicians of his time," in consequence of his use of certain dissonances which were employed in an unprecedented manner. Also of Ludovico Viadana, about the same time, inventing or rather perfecting the system of musical shorthand now known as "thorough bass." And in later years Frescobaldi, following the path laid open by Monteverde, boldly introduced a series of progressions in his works, which were against all accepted rules. By this time—the first quarter of the 17th century—writers on theory silently abandoned the "proportions and ratios." Though it is easy to trace the effects of the old teaching, even when it is not expressed openly.

The principles of harmony or composition, as set forth by Dr. Thomas Campion, 1620,

and later by Christopher Simpson, 1678, treat of nothing more terrible than such common chords as could be formed out of the unaltered notes of the scale. Throughout the whole of the works by these authors the chord of the seventh on the dominant is introduced but sparingly, and when it is used, its "discordance is softened as much as possible." There is little, if anything, entirely new in these books, nothing at all to account for the new chords that musicians were occasionally introducing into their compositions. As Simpson's "Compendium" had a continued and steady sale, running through many editions, teaching the same old and worn-out principles, while Purcell was writing with all the hardihood of enthusiastic youth such chords and progressions as those found in the song quoted in the article "Ground Bass" *theory* running in a widely different direction from *practice*, did not hesitate to condemn these inventions; and, moreover, to wonder "how any judge of correct and pure harmony could tolerate such licences." It was probably owing to the fact of this diversity of opinion between the laws that were made for composers and those they made for themselves, that there are but few treatises on harmony belonging to the latter part of the 17th and the early part of the 18th centuries. The many editions of Simpson's "Compendium," Elway Bevin's "Briefe and Short Introduction," Morley's "Plaine and Easie Introduction," show how little improvement had been effected, and how rare a thing a new idea on the subject was. This state of things continued for some years more, when the publication of Rameau's "Traite D'Harmonie," Paris, 1722, turned all thinking minds into the direction suggested by that book. Looking at it by the improved light of the 19th century, it is difficult at first to trace the cause of the enormous popularity of the work, and its powerful influence on all classes of theorists. The plan is very simple but incomplete, accounting for a part, but not attempting to grapple with the whole science of harmony. The eagerness with which it was received and imitated, goes to prove how ripe men's minds were for the subject, and how willing they were to receive that which attempted to account for some, if not for all the intricacies of their art. The marrow of the whole work, the plot of the whole scheme proposed by Rameau, is comprised in the following words, according to the English edition of 1752:—
"All notes that carry the perfect or common chords may be deemed key-notes, and all notes that carry the chord of the seventh may be deemed governing notes, with this difference, that the governing note of the key must have a sharp third. These two are, as it were, the only chords in harmony."

The main principle of this book, the referring all harmony to a regular fundamental bass on which chords are constructed after the above plan, led its author into some errors, which were copied and increased by subsequent writers. In order to make the theory fit into and agree with practice, Rameau considered suspensions as essential chords, chords by *supposition* as he calls them. His desire to derive all the chords of modern harmony from a construction of third upon third was a praiseworthy one, and nearer the truth than many other theories. He avoids the chord of the ninth, calling it a secondary seventh, speaks of the fourth as an eleventh, admits that the judicious use of discords gives greater liberty to composers, states F and D to be the fundamental bass of the same chord, the chord now known by the name of the added sixth, and adds one or two other peculiar notions needless here to particularise.

The following is a figured bass passage with the fundamental bass, as given by Rameau:

Fundamental Bass.

The chords marked *, though really the same, are derived from different roots by Rameau. Godfrey Keller ("Rules for a Thorough Bass," London, 1731) proceeds upon a somewhat different plan to Rameau. He makes no mention of the fundamental bass, employs many new chords, including those now known by the names of the major and minor ninth, e.g.:

He allows that "the composer (especially in few parts) may compose as many sixes either ascending or descending by degrees as he thinks fit," but he does not lay claim to novelty in suggestion, though he might have done so safely.

The next writer on harmony, Roussier (" Traité des Accords," Paris, 1764), simply copies Rameau without acknowledgment. Following a rough chronological order, Marpurg next demands attention. In his "Handbuch bey dem General-Bass," Berlin, 1755, he professedly agrees with Rameau, but differs from him throughout by making the added thirds, which are to form chords by supposition, fundamental notes contrary to Rameau's teaching. Tartini, in his "Trattato di Musica," Padua, 1754, and "De' Principii dell'Armonia Musicale," Padua, 1767 ; Kirnberger, in his works, "Die wahren Grundsätze" and "Die Kunst des reinen Satzes," published in Berlin in 1773 and 1774, considered suspensions and all interruptions as no real part of a system, but, as the last named writer regarded them, "as clouds may be considered in astronomy, viz., as occasional occurrences, which must be tolerated when there, but which are passed by as if they had not been there at all." A very convenient, if not a satisfactory, method of getting over a difficulty. Twenty years later, Kollman (" Essay on Musical Harmony," London, 1796) endeavoured to found an entirely new system or theory ; the gist of his arguments is that " No interval, or chord, ought to be judged of or treated according to its individual appearance alone, but according to the proofs of a regular connection," which is almost the same idea as that propounded by Rameau seventy years before. Our own countryman, William Shield (" Introduction to Harmony," 1800), does not progress a single step in a new direction, but Weber ("Versuch einer geordneten Theorie der Tonsetzkunst," Mainz, 1817) does advance, for he says that " The harmonical truths are by no means (as many have thought, or affected to think), as in a philosophical science, deducible from one independent superior principle, and subordinate one to another, as it were in a tabular manner." and therefore every combination is explained according to its individual appearance.

Harp. *Harpe (Fr.), Arpa (It.), Harfe (Ger.)* A stringed instrument of triangular form, furnished with gut strings. It has a compass varying from three to six octaves and a half, according to the size of the instrument. There are several kinds of harps still in use :

(1) The triple or Welsh harp, with three rows of strings, two rows tuned diatonically in unisons or octaves, the third or inner row arranged to supply the accidentals, sharps or flats. The strings are thin, and the tone is consequently consonant with the character of the strings. " It is simply impossible to modulate upon this instrument farther than to touch an occasional accidental from among the inner row of strings." This harp is derived from, and is almost identical with, the Irish harp, of which more will be said presently.

(2) The double harp (*arpa doppia*) with two rows of strings is less inconvenient but equally imperfect ; all alterations of the pitch of the strings having to be made with the thumb.

(3) The single-action pedal harp, with one row of strings, containing a compass of nearly six octaves :

in the scale of E flat. There were seven pedals which altered the pitch of the note to which each pedal belonged, a semitone. The imperfection of the mechanism of the pedals involved the player in many difficulties, and rendered some keys perfectly useless.

(4) The double-action pedal harp, the invention of Erard. The compass of this instrument :

six octaves and a quarter, and the power of the pedals to change the pitch of each note two semitones, made it almost equal to the pianoforte in facility of modulation. This last-named harp is the one now generally employed for concert or orchestral purposes.

The invention of pedals to the harp has been variously attributed to Hochbrucker, of Donauwörth, in 1720, and to Paul Velter, of Nürnberg, in 1730. The harp in use before those times was generally tuned according to the key of the piece it was required in.

In the single harp passing modulations were made by stopping certain strings with the thumb, for continued change of key, all the notes in the new scale not in the ordinary tuning of the harp were made by turning the wrest pins during the progress of the music of all the notes required to be altered. Music for the harp is written on two staves. The instrument is capable of playing a melody with accompanying harmonies similar in character to pianoforte music. Successions of staccato chords have a fine effect upon the instrument, but broken chords (arpeggio) are better and more characteristic. The harp has been introduced into the orchestra with good effect, by several modern composers, Wagner and Gounod more especially. There is at present but little variety in the manner in which it has been used, arpeggios accompanied by violins playing on the high register *tremolo* with or without mutes, whenever angelic voices or exalted or heavenly ideas are intended to be presented.

The harp, like the guitar, may be traced to a very remote ancestry; it has, likewise, been subject to many vicissitudes of fortune. A favourite instrument with kings, it has also been the companion of beggars. Inspired strains have been sung to its strings, and it has accompanied verses neither pious nor inspired. By turns cultivated and neglected, it has never been wholly without a witness in the several ages of the history of music.

Engel, in "The Music of the Most Ancient Nations," says, that many Eastern nations have harps of different sorts, names and methods of stringing. The Burmese harp, called *saun*, has thirteen silken strings wound round a curved bar at one end in a way which admits of their being pushed up or down to be tuned. The harp is called *chang* in Persian, and *junk* in Arabic. The Negroes in Senegambia and Guinea call it *boulon* or *ombi*, and use strings made of fibre.

The harp in its primitive form is supposed to have been suggested by the warrior's bow. Many barbarous tribes preserve this form with some slight degree of variation. The "Nanga," or Negro harp is of this kind, as will be seen in the subjoined figure.

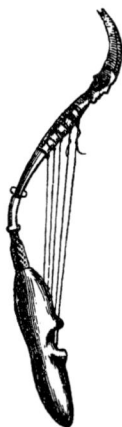

Nanga or Negro Harp.

It is said that some savage tribes still use their bows in times of peace as musical instruments. The harp of the Ossetes and Indo-Germanic tribe of the Central Caucasus have an instrument which supplies the connecting link between the form of the *Nanga* and the harps represented on ancient monuments. It is furnished with twelve strings of horse-hair, each string composed of six or eight hairs. It is about two feet in height, and has no forepillar. A specimen of this kind of harp is preserved in the South Kensington Museum.

The harp is mentioned in the authorised version of the Bible, Gen. iv. 21, "The father of all such as handle the harp and the organ." The word in the original, "*kinnor*," appears in thirty-six other places in the Old Testament: in every case it is translated "harp." But while there is reason for believing that the Hebrews were acquainted with the harp, it is not certain that the word *kinnor* really means harp. The form of the *kinnor* is a matter of much uncertainty.

Kalkbrenner, who is considered as an authority on the subject of Hebrew music, in his Histoire de la Musique, Paris, 1802, makes no attempt to describe it, but merely contents himself with a commonplace remark after quoting the early writers who speak of it. " Le *kinnor*, en grec *kinnyra*, qui d'après la description de Saint Jerome, avoit la figure d'un △ et qui étoit monté de 24 cordes; l'autre description hébraïque du livre Schilte Haggeborin, donne au kinnor 32 cordes, tandis que l'historien *Joseph* et beaucoup d'autres ne lui en attribuent que dix; quelles contradictions!" These contradictions may be reconciled by supposing that the *kinnor*, like the Egyptian *bounà* (both of which words are translated "harp"), was of various sizes, variously strung.

There are numerous representations of harps upon the Assyrian bas-reliefs, from which it would appear that the instrument consisted of a slightly curved frame acting as a resonance body and as a stay for the strings at one end, while at the other they were secured to a horizontal bar. There was apparently a sort of tassel, supposed to be made of the unstretched ends of the strings.

A slight difference of form may be seen in the various sculptures, but the general character of the Assyrian harp is the same as that shown above. It will be seen that there is no front pillar such as modern harps possess, by which it may be assumed that these harps were similar in construction to the Egyptian harp. The ancient Egyptian harps were of many sizes, and according to the representations preserved were strung with various numbers of strings, from three upwards. The player stood, knelt, or supported his instrument upon a stand while performing. Of the scale to which these harps were tuned, or of the manner in which they were kept in tune, no reasonable idea can be formed.

Egyptian Harp.

Egyptian Harp.

If they were kept in tension by the simple process of twisting with the finger and thumb round the horizontal bar, it is difficult to realise the idea that anything like a pre-arranged melody could be performed upon them. It is, moreover, probable that the greater part of the time of the performer was engaged in tightening the strings which his gripping had stretched. These views are grounded upon the assumption that the Egyptian and Babylonian artists have been as accurate in their delineations as they are said to be. But it was shown in the article "Guitar," that ancient artists are not always trustworthy as regards their pictures of lutes,

for the drawings and sculptures often delineate a performer actively engaged in playing upon an instrument in a position in which it cannot possibly be supported. But admitting them to be correct in form, and acknowledging that the artist may have omitted to show the means by which the performer steadied his instrument, it is doubtful whether the ancient harps had either power or sweetness; for the ornament which overloads many of the depicted musical instruments must have greatly interfered with the tone.

The Greeks, who borrowed all their musical instruments, and, as some say, even the very names from foreign nations, must have known the harp, but they do not appear to have chosen it as a subject for representation, either in their paintings, sculpture, or pottery. The famous vase now in the Munich museum, dating from the time of Alexander the Great, offers one of the few instances in which it is depicted. The instrument is in form like the Assyrian harp.

Grecian Harp.

The most favoured instrument in Grecian art was the lyre, which like the harp is described, in Greek literature, as having different numbers of strings, and to have been mounted occasionally on stands. The Pektis, the Simekion, and the Epigoneion, are supposed to have been actual harps. The first had only two strings, the others thirty-five and forty respectively. There was another instrument, the Phorminx, usually understood to be a lyre, which is sometimes translated harp.

The monuments of ancient Rome show very few examples of the harp in the forms familiar in those of Assyria and Egypt. The word "cithara," which is translated, harp, lyre, lute, guitar, &c., indifferently, offers no help in clearing away the cloud obscuring all knowledge of this matter. The claim of the Irish, asserted by Vincentis Galilei, in his "Dialogue Della Musica," 1581, to the invention of the harp cannot now be supported since the discovery of the Assyrian remains, but there is no doubt that they were acquainted with it at a very early period of the world's history. They had four kinds of harp—(1) the *clàr-seth*, *clar-scat*, or *clar-seach*; (2) the *Keir-nine*; (3) the *cionar-cruit*; (4) the *cream tine cruit*.

The first was brought to Ireland by the Celto-Phœnicians, the second was similar to the Eastern Kanun, and like it, was played with plectra. The third had ten strings stretched over a resonance-body; and the fourth was the same as the Crwth, had six strings, four of which passed over a finger board, and could be stopped at the will of the player, the two others formed a drone. The clar-seth, also called ᴄᴇᴀᴅʟᴏᴊꞃ pronounced Tealoin, or Telin, was the instrument adopted from the Irish by the Welsh. It received its new name from the fact that its adopters strung it with gut and hair, instead of the metal strings as used by the Irish.

Irish Harp.

Vincentino Galilei (p. 143 of his "Dialogo della Musica Antica e Moderna," Florence, 1602), speaking of ancient instruments, says: "Ci è prima mente l'Harpa, la quale non è altro che un' antica Cithara di molte corde; se bene di forma in alcuna cosa differente, non da altro cagionatagli dagli artefici di quei tempi, che dalla quantita di esse corde & dalla loro intensezza; contenendo l'estreme graui con l'estreme acute piu di tre ottaue. Su portato d'Irlanda a noi questo antichissimo strumento (commemorato da Dante) doue si lauorano in eccellenza & copiososamente; gli habitatori della quale isola si esercitano molti & molti secoli sono in essa, &c." By which it will be seen that the Welsh were not the only people who adopted the harp from the Irish. The old Italian harp had two rows of strings, arranged after the manner of the old Irish harp, from which it is supposed to be derived. An instrument of this sort, an "Arpa doppia" is mentioned as one of the accompanying instruments in Monteverde's "Orfeo," 1607.

The harp was a favourite instrument among the ancient Britons. The old laws of Wales, the Triads, if they are to be trusted, specify the use of the harp as one of the three things necessary to distinguish a freeman or gentleman from a slave. Pretenders were discovered by their unskilfulness in "playing of the harp." The same laws forbade a slave to touch a harp, either out of curiosity, or to acquire a knowledge of it, and none but the king, his musicians, and other gentlemen were permitted to possess one. The harp was exempt from seizure for debt, as it was presumed that he who had no harp lost his position, and was degraded to the condition of a slave.

The harp was a familiar instrument with the Anglo-Saxons, as many references in existing chronicles prove conclusively. The harp-player was respected for his skill, whether he was known or unknown. Harp in hand he might wander scot and scathe free even in the camp of an enemy. Colgrin, the son of Ella, when besieged in York, about 495, received assistance from his brother, who went through the camp of the besiegers disguised as a harper; an artifice also adopted by King Alfred four hundred years later.

Bede states that it was the custom at festive meetings to hand the harp round for each of the company to sing and play in turn, and mentions the fact that Caedmon, the poet, had so neglected his studies in this respect in the pursuit of more serious knowledge, that at an assembly where he was present, and the harp was sent round, he being unable to play, rose from the table in shame, and went home to his house. "Surgebat a medea cœna, et egressus, ad suam domum repedebat," or as King Alfred has rendered it into Saxon, "Thonne aras he for sceome fram tham symle, and ham yode to his huse."

Performers upon the harp of special skill were notable before the reign of William the First. The services rendered by Taillefer, the harper, on the battle field are well known matters of history, as also is the foundation of the priory and hospital of St. Bartholomew in Smithfield, by Rahere, harper to King Henry the First.

Musicians were courted and respected in olden times, the harp was a sure passport everywhere, and a warrant of welcome in every society from the highest to the lowest, among kings or churls, among friends or foes. Where other men failed, the minstrel succeeded; admission to a house or castle was granted to a "gleeman," which was denied to all else. The existence of this privilege is frequently taken advantage of by writers of the old ballads, romances, &c., who often describe a luckless lover or chivalrous adventurer, gaining access to some giant's fortress or enchanted castle, in the garb of a minstrel or harper:

> " Horn sette him abenche
> Is harpe he gan clenche
> He made Rymenild a lay."
>
> *The Romance of Horn and Rymenild.*

Well-known historians and poets, besides the anonymous ballad writers of mediæval times, make frequent mention of the harp, thus showing its continued popularity. The introduction of the guitar made the harp less cultivated by private people, and as lutes, viols, and other more easily portable instruments became known, the harp was more and more disused. That which the guitar and viol had begun, the clarichord, virginals, and harpsichord completed, and the harp became rarely seen and still more rarely used. It never became wholly silent, but was to be heard in rural districts played in the same style, strung in the same fashion, and tuned after the same mode, as when it belonged to a more remote generation. It was a sort of a Rip van Winkle among instruments, living through many changes, yet unconscious of them. Older than all of the existing members of the great family of musical instruments by which it was surrounded, but uninfluenced and untouched by the progress towards perfection which all else were making. Before Hochbrucker's invention, the harp had been unchanged for centuries, remaining in the condition it had been left by the ancestors of the various peoples with whom it was found. When Handel's oratorio " Esther " (written in 1720) was produced at the request of the Duke of Chandos, harp parts to one of the choruses, for two Welsh players of the name of Powell were inserted by the composer. The harp they used was the old Welsh harp already described. Even after Hochbrucker and Velter had made their improvements, and rendered the harp more available as an orchestral instrument, it was rarely employed as such, all harp effects being made by *pizzicato* playing on the violin.

Hoyle ("Dictionarium Musicæ," 1770) describes the harp as having, in his day, "three rows of strings, which in all make seventy-eight; the first row contains twenty-nine, which makes four octaves, the second row makes the half turn: the third is unison with the first row. It's musick is like that of a spinet, all the strings going by semitones, and is played on with both hands, by pinching them in the same manner together. Some give it the name of the inverted spinet." As this style of stringing is nearly the same as the Irish method of tuning in use ages before, it is difficult to believe Hoyle's statement that the "moderns have much improved" the harp. The name of "inverted spinet" is singular, as one of the names for the spinet was the "Couched harp." The harp was not popular in those days, it required closer application to master its difficulties than the musical young people of the time cared to devote to it. One instrument of the harp kind, called the "Bell-harp," was in constant use in the time that Hoyle wrote, and has not completely disappeared in the present day. No great skill is required to perform upon it, all that is necessary is prehensile power and strength of wrist. The instrument is a wooden box a little more than two feet long, all closed except over the wrest pins, and a space near the opposite end. It is strung with steel wire, with eight strings or more, tuned with the lowest notes outside:

Left thumb. Right thumb.

The fingers of each hand grasp the body of the box, leaving the thumbs free to strike the strings. The player swings the instrument as he strikes, producing the effect of the sound of a peal of bells borne on the wind.

To return to the main subject; when, in 1820, Erard improved the harp, it became suddenly and widely fashionable; nearly all the music published was "arranged for the pianoforte or harp." The instrument was as indispensable in the drawing-room of those calling themselves "musical," as the pianoforte is now. It was chiefly played by ladies, especially by those who possessed the advantages of a pretty hand and arm, not to mention a "neat foot," all these motive powers being well shown in harp playing. As the fair performers grew old, the charms of the harp decayed, and although the instrument is still played and taught, it is not cultivated to the extent which its merits might seem to warrant.

The derivation of the word is a matter of doubt, none of the earlier terms supplying the least etymological link. Du Cange, in his "Glossary," asserts that the harp takes its name from the Arpi, a people of Italy who were the first who invented it. In this he is not quite correct, as will be gathered from the foregoing account. Arpi was a very ancient city, without doubt, it was of a higher antiquity than Livy, who mentions it as an Apulian city. It is not at all improbable that the people of Arpi may have been the first to adopt the instrument upon its introduction into Italy, and as it is not at all unlikely that the Northern people adopted it from the Romans, the name may have been transmitted in its present form from the Arpi, the people whom the Romans may have believed to have been the inventors. That the word has a common origin, its similarity in most modern tongues may tend to prove. There is evidence enough in music to show that the name of a people may give a permanent title to a composition, and also to an instrument. There is no apparent connection between the words Kinnor, Bouni, Saun, Chang, Junk, Boulon, Ombi, Nanga, Pektis, Simikion, Epigonion, Phorminx, Cithara, Clar-seth, Telyn, and Harp, the names by which the instrument has been called by various peoples; but the words Earpe, Harp, Harpe, Harfe, and Arpa, point conclusively to one origin, and Du Cange may be right with regard to one part of his statement, for it is not at all unlikely that the harp, when brought by the conquering legions to, and adopted by the more northern nations, would be called by the title given to it by the people from whom it was most favourably received.

Harpe (*Fr.*) A harp.

Harpist (*Eng.* and *Ger.*) A player upon the harp.

Harpsecol. Harpsichord.

Harpsichord. *Clavicembalo, Cembalo (It.) Clavecin (Fr.) Flügel (Ger.)* A stringed instrument with a key-board, similar in form to a modern grand pianoforte. As the pressure of the fingers upon the keys, when heavy or light, made no difference in the quantity of tone produced, the harpsichord sometimes had two key-boards, one for the loud, the other for the soft tones. There were also stops in some instruments, by means of which the tone could be modified by connecting the mechanism with or detaching it from the three or even four strings with which each tone was furnished. The keys were attached to levers, which at their ends had slips of wood, called "jacks," furnished with plectra of crow-quill or hard leather; these struck or twanged the strings and produced the tone, which has been likened to "a scratch with a sound at the end of it." [Clarichord.] [Spinett.] [Pianoforte.]

Harpsichord graces. Certain turns and ornaments employed in playing upon the harpsichord, introduced for the most part as compensation for the lack of sustaining power in the instrument. They were called by the general term of *agrémens* in French, and *Manieren* in German. The chief of these ornaments were the following, other signs are explained according to alphabetical order.

Turn or *Doublé* (*Fr.*), *Doppelschlag* (*Ger.*)

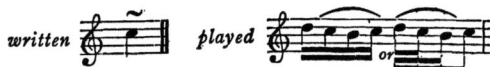

When the sign was placed upright it was understood to signify that the turn was to be commenced a note lower than the one over which it was written:

When the double was preceded by a small note or notes on the same line or space, the turn was to commence from that note:

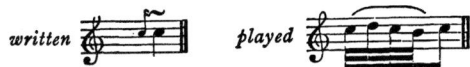

When the marked note was tied, the turn was to be commenced from the preceding note:

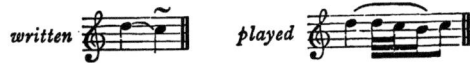

Battery, *Cadence* (*Fr.*), indicated by the sign +. When the cadence was written thus:

it was played:

and was called a full Cadence or *Cadence pleine;* when it was written:

it was played:

and was called *cadence brisée*, or broken cadence.

Sliding trill, *Flatté* (*Fr.*), *Schleifer* (*Ger.*):

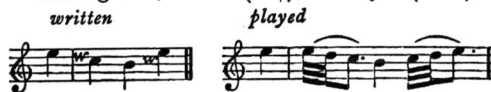

Or occasionally:

Trill; *Tremblement* (*Fr.*), *Pralltriller* (*Ger.*), expressed by the signs *tr*, ✔, ᠕ ᠕᠕. It was in effect a trill without the final turn, unless altered by other signs. There were six sorts of *tremblements;* namely, (1) the simple tremblement (*tremblement simple*):

(2) The doubled or turned trill (*tremblement doublé*):

(3) The detached trill (*tremblement détaché*), which was performed when the note which should begin the trill had a place in the melody preceding the marked note:

(4) The tied trill (*tremblement lié*) was almost the same at the preceding, only that the first two notes were tied:

(5) The prepared trill (*tremblement appuyé* or *préparé*) was when a slight pause was made before commencing the shake, and its speed gradually increased:

(6) A slided trill (*tremblement coulé*) when the shake was preceded by a slide:

Haupt (*Ger.*) Principal, chief, head; as *Hauptnote*, the essential note in a turn or shake, &c.

Hauptmanual (*Ger.*) The great organ.

Hauptnote (*Ger.*) An essential note.

Hauptperiode (*Ger.*) Principal subject.

Hauptsatz (*Ger.*) Principal theme or subject.

Hauptschluss (*Ger.*) A perfect cadence.

Hauptstimme (*Ger.*) Principal part.

Hauptwerk (*Ger.*) The great organ.

Hausse (*Fr.*) The nut of a violin bow.

Hausser (*Fr.*) To raise, lift, to sharpen.

Haut (*Fr.*) High; as, *haute contre*, the alto part; *haute dessus*, treble part; *haute taille*, first or high tenor.

Hautbois (*Fr.*) [Oboe.]

Hautbois d'amour (*Fr.*) A small species of oboe, now obsolete. Music written for it can be played on the ordinary instrument.

Hautboy. [Oboe.]

H dur. (*Ger.*) The key of B major.

Head. (1) The membrane stretched upon a drum. (2) That part of a violin or other stringed instrument in which the pegs are inserted. (3) The portion of a note which determines its position upon the stave, and to which the tail is annexed.

Head-stall. A head-band or *Capistrum*, q. v. The use of the word *stall* in the sense of *bandage* is still to be found in our word *finger-stall*.

Head-voice. [Voice.]

Heftig (*Ger.*) Boisterous, impetuous.

Heiss (*Ger.*) Hot, ardent.

Heiter (*Ger.*) Clear, calm. *Feierlich heiter*, solemn and calm.

Helicon (*Gk.*) ἑλικών. An instrument used by the Greeks in the calculation of musical ratios.

Hemidiapente. An imperfect fifth.

Hemiditone. The lesser or minor third.

Hemiolios (*Gk.*) ἡμιόλιος. (1) The ratio 3 to 2. The same as the *sesquialtera* in Latin treatises on music. (2) A kind of metre. A verse consisting of a foot and a half.

Hemiopus (*Gk.*) ἡμίοπος. Having a small number of holes. ἡμίοποι αὐλοί, small flutes with three ventages.

Hemitone. A semitone.

Heptachord. (1) A series of seven notes. A diatonic octave without the upper note. (2) An instrument with seven strings.

Herabstrich (*Ger.*) The down stroke of the bow in playing stringed instruments. A down-bow.

Herstrich. [Herabstrich.]

Hexachord. A series of six sounds. [Notation.]

Hey de Guise. A country dance.

" In our antique hey de guise we go beyond all nations."
Middleton.

[Country dance.]

Hidden Fifths, or Octaves. [Consecutives.]

Hinaufstrich } (*Ger.*) An up-bow.
Hinstrich

His (*Ger.*) The note B sharp.

Hissing. A manner of showing dissatisfaction. [Applause.] [Fiasco.]

H moll (*Ger.*) The key of B minor.

Hoboe. [Oboe.]

Hoboy. [Oboe.] [Waits.]

Hocket, Hoket, Ochetus. A species of part music, in which the voices seem to have had to keep a large number of rests, the notes being divided into several parts for the purpose. It was the same as *truncatio* (truncatio idem est quod hoket). The *truncatio* was certainly a division of a long note into many smaller ones with rests between (*pausatio*), and was founded either on an original theme (*tenorem excogitatum*), or a well-known tune (*certum cantum*) either popular (*vulgare*) or ecclesiastical (*latinum*). The application of the word to part-music seems to have been brought about by its Latin synonym *conductus*, for the Greek ὀχετός signifies also a *conduct* or *conduit*, and this name was commonly given in the 15th century to a kind of motet.

probably from the " bringing together" of the voices.

Hochzeitmarsch (*Ger.*) A wedding march.

Hohlflöte (*Ger.*) [Flute.]

Hold. An old English name for the sign of a pause ⌢.

Holding note. A note sustained in one part, while the others are in motion.

Homophony (*Gk.*) Unison of voices or instruments of the same character. ὁμόφωνος.

Hopper. [Pianoforte.]

Hopser or **Hops-tanz** (*Ger.*) A country dance.

Horæ Canonicæ. The canonical hours at which religious services are held. In time of persecution a night-service was held called *Nocturns*, which was, however, at a later period merged into *Lauds*—the thanksgiving for the dawn of day, and the whole was called Matins. But when Matins, or Nocturns, are retained they take place before *Lauds*. The following is the order of the Canonical hours: *Lauds*, at daybreak; *Prime*, or first hour, a later service; *Tierce*, or third hour, at nine a.m.; *Sext*, or sixth hour, at noon; *Nones*, or ninth hour, at three p.m.; *Vespers*, or evening service; *Compline*, or final service, at bed time. Each of these has fixed Psalms, except Vespers, which has certain Psalms read in course, and a Canticle. The Anglo-Saxon names of these services were, Uhtsang, Primesang, Undersang, Middaysang, Noonsang, Evensang, and Nightsang. The book for these Offices came to be called Breviary towards the end of the 11th century. It was sometimes called in England the Portifory.

Horn (Cor, *Fr.*; Corno, *It.*; Horn, *Ger.*) A metal wind instrument, formed of a continuous tube twisted into a curved shape for the convenience of holding. It is furnished with a mouthpiece and a bell. The mouthpiece is moveable, so as to allow additional pieces of tubing called crooks, to be added to its length in order to alter the pitch, and the bell is sufficiently wide to admit the hand of the player.

The horn sounds the harmonics of the fundamental note of its tube. That is to say, a horn in C, or sounding C as a generator has the following compass:

Notes written in the bass clef sound as they are written, those in the treble clef, an octave lower.

The notes in the section marked B are more difficult to produce than those in the section marked A.

The whole of the above notes are called the "open" notes; that is to say, they can be produced by simple blowing, and certain modifications of the form of the lips. There are other sounds called " closed," which are obtained by closing the bell in a certain manner with the hand.

The closed notes are less free in quality than the open notes, and they are therefore only employed when especial effects are required. Horns are generally employed in pairs, and the parts are usually written in the treble clef in the key of C. The most useful parts of the compass of the horn are those marked in section A. The " crooks"—alluded to above—serve to alter the pitch by lengthening the sounding tube, and the composer indicates the horn or horns required at the beginning of a piece of music thus: Corni in C; Corni in B flat; Corni in A, &c., though the parts are written as though they were to be played in C, the presumed normal key of the horn. All horns other than those in C are called transposing instruments, because the actual sounds produced are different to those represented on paper. And strictly speaking, the C horn is also a transposing instrument, because the notes are written an octave higher than they are played. Thus the passage:

would sound differently according to the horn employed:

If in D, it would be a seventh; in E flat a major sixth; in E a minor sixth; in F a fifth; in G a fourth; in A a minor third; in B flat alto a second; in B flat basso, a ninth lower than the notation.

In movements in a major key, in which four horns are used, two are generally in the key of the tonic, two in that of the dominant. Sometimes, two are in the tonic key, two in that of the mediant.

When horns are required for minor keys, one is set in the key of the relative major, the other in the tonic major. Thus in G minor, one horn would be in B flat, another in G. Composers, however, vary in their use of horns in minor keys, so that no definite rule can be laid down.

There are other kinds of horns used in the orchestra, which, by means of valves, pistons, or ventils, are capable of producing the "open" and "closed" sounds in a scale of semitones throughout the compass, of very nearly even quality, and with comparatively little difficulty to the player.

The horn, sometimes called the French horn, to distinguish it from the English horn (cor Anglais), which is altogether a different instrument, was introduced into the orchestra towards the end of the 17th century, and as it became very fashionable and popular in the early part of the 18th century, it is frequently found in the scores of orchestral compositions, and is also employed as an accompaniment to hunting songs. A horn-player, named Spandau, was one of the first who discovered the art of producing the closed or stuffed notes (*sons étouffés*) on the instrument. Sir John Hawkins makes a note in his "History of the performance of a Concerto in 1773," of this player, "part whereof was in the key of C with the minor third." The "improvement was effected by putting his right hand into the bottom or bell of the instrument, and attempering the sounds by the application of his fingers in the different parts of the tube;" by which means "the intervals seemed to be as perfect as in any wind-instrument."

The earliest attempts to make the scale of the horn perfect are attributed to Hampel, of Dresden, in 1748. Twelve years later Kölbel invented his amor-schall, which was a horn with *ventils*. Claggett, a Londoner, attempted further to improve these plans; but all these inventions were forgotten or laid aside, in favour of Müller's system of ventils, first proposed about the year 1830. These in time were superseded by the inventions of J. G. Saxe and others. Although the horn has been so far improved, that the difficulties of producing the tones intermediate to the harmonics have been considerably lessened, it cannot be said that any great improvement has been effected in the quality of the added sounds, and the old French horn, the plain tube, whose sounds are "attempered by the fingers of the player," is still unsurpassed in brilliancy of tone by any of the modern inventions.

Hörner. Horns. *Corni (It.),* as *Hörner in Es,* Horns in E flat.

Hornpipe. (1) The name of an old wind instrument of the *shawm* or *waits* character, receiving its name from the fact that the

"bell" or open end was sometimes made of horn. In Wales, Ireland, and Cornwall, in Brittany, it was called pib-corn. "Pib" or "piob," meaning pipe, and "corn," horn. Chaucer uses the word to describe an instrument of music in his translation of the "Romaunt of the Rose."

> "Controve he wolde, and foule fayle
> With hornepipes of Cornewaile."

The original (written in 1260) is :

> "Une hore dit lés et descors
> Et sonnez doux de controvaille
> As Estives de Cornoaille."

The word "controve" comes from the same root as that from which "Trovere" or "Troubadour" is derived, and means to invent, or compose, so that the passage translated into modern English would be :

> "He would compose and play songs (lés)
> To the accompaniment of the hornpipe."

That the hornpipe was harsh-sounding may be gathered from the context in Chaucer when he says in the preceding lines :

> "—— yit would he lye
> Discordaunt ever fro armonye
> And distoned from melodie."

In some editions of the "Romaunt of the Rose," the words "chalemeaux de Cornouaille," stand instead of "estives de Cornoaille." That the Waits or Shawms had reeds is well known, and that the hornpipe, its rustic relation, was not likely to have a softer tone may be assumed. Robert Bell supposes that Chaucer "wrote corn-pipes, which," says he, "would be the proper translation of Chalemeaux." Thus Virgil :

> "Musam meditaris avenâ."

And Shakespeare :

> "And shepherds pipe on oaten straws.'

Others imagine the word "estive" to come from Æstas, the hot season, whence our word *Estival* for summer, and the word "Chalameau" employed as a synonym for "estive" to be derived from "chaleur," heat. That the "estive," "Chalameau," or "horn-pipe," is "a shepherd's pipe made of corn which, growing in summer, furnishes the material for the instrument." These theories are, to say the least, ingenious. It is, however, much more in accordance with probability to infer that the word "Chalameau," or "Chalemeaux," comes from *Calamus,* a reed ; which is only similar to a straw in being hollow, and that the word "corn" has no connection with either reeds, straws, or oats. The word "corn" comes from "κέρας" through "cornu," and as the hard "c" is only one form of the guttural sound sometimes represented by the letter "h," the words "corn" and "horn" are the same when applied to a musical instrument. It may not necessarily be formed of horn or have horn in its composition, but may receive its name from being bent or curved as a horn.

The horn-pipe was probably the same kind of instrument as that now known as the "Cor Anglais" or English horn. The words corn, cornet, cornamusa, &c., are applied to different sorts of wooden wind instruments with reeds. The *hoboy, shalm, shawn, wait,* or *reed-pipe* were common instruments in days gone by, and often furnished the melodies to which dancing was performed. Therefore the supposition that the "hornpipe" gave the name to the dance so called may not be very far from the truth.

(2) A dance of English origin, so-called from the instrument which played the tune to which it was danced. The measure or rhythm of the Hornpipe is as varied as that of the tunes for country dances, therefore all descriptions of the dance, which are founded upon the supposition that there is only one form of rhythm, are misleading. One writer says, "It is in compound triple time of nine crotchets in a bar, six down and three up;" another says, "It is in triple time of six crotchets in a bar, four whereof are to be beat with a down, and two with an up hand;" another says, that it is in "common time of four crotchets played lively;" and another says, "It is always in double triple time of two parts of four and eight bars each with repeats." These descriptions tally with the character of the measure of the dance which was called hornpipe at the time the description was written. But the hornpipe is, and has been, often danced to tunes called by other names, such as Brawl, Coranto, Canaries, Fandango, Jig, Loure, Reel, Matelotte, &c., the steps being varied to suit the several measures. The hornpipe now-a-days is danced by a single performer, to a tune in duple measure. The performer generally stands still with arms folded during the time the first phrase of the melody is played, and then commences the dance by running round in a circular direction; and when dancing a hornpipe called by some special title, such as "The Sailor's," "The Jockeys," "The Countryman's," or "The Monkey's" hornpipe, generally introduces some gestures characteristic of the distinguishing title.

The following are some specimens of the various sorts of melodies of hornpipes:

HORNPIPE.

Mr. JERRY CLARK, 1700.

1st part a gaine.

End with ye 1st part.

RAVENSCROFT'S HORNPIPE (1730).

THE COLLEGE HORNPIPE.

MISS CATTLEY'S HORNPIPE.

PERFORMED AT SADDLER'S WELLS, 1780.

JACK AT GREENWICH.

C. DIBDIN, 1800.

Hosanna. [Mass.]
Huchet (Fr.) A postman's horn.
Hulfslinien (Ger.) Leger lines.
Hulfsnote (Ger.) An auxiliary note.

Hummelchen (Ger.) A kind of small bagpipe. A drone. The word *Hummel* is cognate with our *bumble;* see Bombaulius, a bagpiper.

Hunting Horn. *Cor de chasse* (Fr.) *Corno di caccia* (It.) *Hief horn* (Ger.) [Horn.]

Hunting. A term in change-ringing. There are two kinds, **hunting up,** and *hunting down.* The first is performed on any number of bells, " by pulling after the bell which pulled last after you ;" the second is accomplished by looking out for which bell strikes first of the set, and alter his number in the set at each change until he has gone through the full number of the bells, and then return to his original place. Thus, if he be first, he will next be second, then third, then fourth, fifth, sixth, and so on, according to the number of bells, and return backwards in counting sixth, fifth, fourth, &c.

Huntsup. A morning song, of a noisy boisterous character, afterwards applied to any unseemly clamour at any time of the day.

> " I never was yet
> At such a hunts up."
> MASSINGER, *The Duke of Milan.*

There is an old song of the time ot Henry VIII. called " The King's Hunts up," the tune of which is lively and spirited. The term "hunts up" may have been derived from the noise of horses, dogs, and men setting out on a hunting expedition. Butler, in his " Principles of Musick " (1636), defines a " *hunts up* " as morning music ; as does Cotgrave (1660), " Resveil, a hunts-up, a morning song for a new made wife." This last is an allusion to the custom of performing an *aubade* before a bride's window, thus mentioned by Gay :

> " Here rows of drummers stand in marshal file,
> And with their vellum thunder shake the pile,
> To greet the new made bride."

Hurdy gurdy. An instrument of ancient origin, popular among most of the European nations under the names of *Leyer* or *Bauernleyer.* It consists of a flat oblong sounding board, upon which are stretched four gut strings, two of which are tuned a fifth apart to form a drone bass, and placed where they cannot be acted upon by the ten or twelve keys fixed upon one side of the belly of the instrument ; the other two are tuned in unison, and are so arranged that they may be shortened by the pressure of the keys. The instrument is thus capable of sounding a scale of ten or twelve notes. The strings are set in vibration by the friction of a wooden wheel charged with rosin and turned by means of a handle at one end. The hurdy gurdy is only adapted to the production of melodies of the simplest character. The old name for the hurdy gurdy (vielle) has misled many authors with regard to the derivation and description of the instrument. Dr. Burney says, " That the instrument called a *rote*, so frequently mentioned by Chaucer, as well as by the old French poets, was the same as the modern *vielle*, and had its name from *rota*, the wheel with which its tones were produced."

The word *rota* is simply a Latinised form of the word *crwth*, *chrotta*, *rotta*, which was originally a sort of cithara or guitar, played by plucking the strings with the fingers.

In after time when an instrument of similar shape was played with a bow, it still retained the ancient name *crwth* or *crowd*.

Hurry. The technical, theatrical, or stage name for a tremolo passage on the violin, or a roll on the drum. The " hurry " is generally played as a preparation for the culminating point of a dramatic incident, the leading to a " picture," during stage struggles or like exciting actions.

Hurtig (*Ger.*) Nimble, quick, agile. *Allegro.*

Hydraulic organ. [Organ.]

Hymenaion, ὑμέναιος (*Gk.*) An epithalamium or marriage song.

Hymnology. The art of composing hymns.

Hymn tunes. The keen attention paid, in our time, to all forms of Church music, particularly to such as come under the term " Congregational," renders doubly interesting the distinction of style which can be traced in the " Corale," as we find it at different periods, and in the different churches of Christendom. We shall probably, from year to year, become better informed of the historical relations between sacred and secular music, especially as our method of translating into modern notation the neumas of the manuscripts of the 10th and 11th centuries becomes more certain and less open to doubt. There is in the library of the " Ecole de Medicine," of Montpelier, a MS. " Horace," in which the ode to Phillis is noted to the melody assigned by Guy d'Arezzo to the Hymn " Ut queant laxis." " Was the melody," asks a modern critic, " written for the ode, or for the hymn?" In close connection with the reply to this question is the inquiry of which it may be considered a part, " To what extent did the growth of musical measure or rhythm influence the manner in which the mediæval hymns were recited or sung?" It was the only part of the ancient church office in which this characteristic of " measure " was felt, and the form of such melodies as the following (both from the " Directory " of Guidetti) seems to point the " style of transition " from unmeasured Plain Song to measured music.

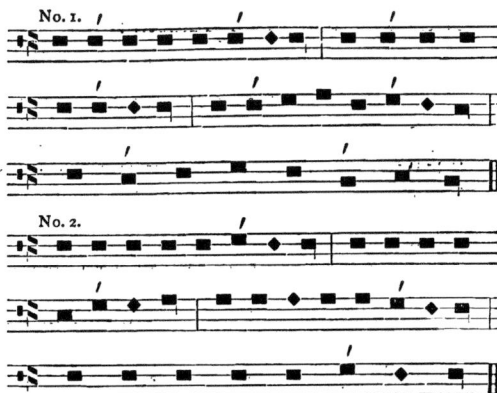

In No. 1 there is nothing but the " monotone " of the ancient chant in phrases 1 and 2, while every phrase of No. 2 commences with the same, and ends with the simplest inflection by way of melody. The strong " measure " or accent of both is noticeable—the latter would fall naturally into the following chant form :

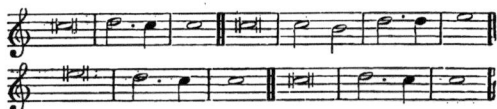

The Latin hymn tune, dating from about the 4th till the end of the 12th century, and as it appears in the office books in present use, must be considered as the first distinct " style " for the attention of the student. The distinctive characteristics of it are : 1. The scales to which its melodies belong—not the modern major or minor modes of the diatonic scale, but the so-called " modes " of the Church [Plain Song]. 2. The peculiarities of their rhythm, partly derived from the metrical flow of the verse itself, partly from the continually advancing sense of accent, or the alternation of " heavy and light."

It is matter of " pious belief," that in the great majority of cases the author of the hymn was the composer of the melody—a point which it will always be impossible to verify or to deny. It is certain that many of them are truly beautiful ; as *e.g.* the following, from the Salisbury Hymnal :

Je-su dul-cis me-mo-ri-a, Dans ve-ra cor-dis gau-di-a, Sed su-per mel et om-ni-a, E-jus dul-cis præ-sen-ti-a.

Or the following, from Guidetti :

E - ter -na Chris- ti mu - - - ne-ra. A-pos-to-lo-rum
Glo - ri - am, Lau - des ca - nen- tes de - bi - tas. . . .
Læ - tis ca - na - mus men - - ti - bus.

Others, on account of these two peculiarities, are probably wanting in that appeal to the popular sensibility which would make them "popular" in the vulgar sense.

The following authorities may be consulted on this part of the subject :

"Vesperale Romanum Mechliniæ," 8vo. F. J. Hanicq, 1848. This is one volume of a magnificent reprint of office books, carried out with great care and exactness, under the influence of Cardinal Sterkx, Archbishop of Mechlin.

"Manuel de L'Organiste ou Accompagnement diatonique des Chants Liturgiques les plus usuels (particularly as to accompaniment according to the laws of the Gregorian Modes), par P. G. C. Bogaerts et Edmond Duval. Malines, Dessain.

"Hymnal Noted." Rev. T. Helmore. Novello.

"Accompanying Harmonies to ditto."

The period of the Reformation was one of great musical activity. For some time previous a quiet and half unconscious preparation had been going on, in the circulation among the people of popular hymns and their tunes in the vernacular, and of course only sung in private ; and when Luther furnished his followers with metrical versions of the Creed, the Lord's Prayer, and other portions of the old Office Books, there were no bounds to the popularity of both hymns and tunes. Edition followed edition of books under the title of "Geistliche Lieder," &c., and in their multiplication many slight changes occurred in the original melodies ; even in some that by the popular voice are accredited to Luther himself, and even during his lifetime. As it has become the custom in Germany for each diocese to be provided, by authority, with its own "Gesang-Buch," the *variations* of these popular melodies have themselves become stereotyped, as it were, in different localities, so that the original is often difficult to trace. The great Sebastian Bach has often harmonized different forms of the same melody, and has even (so it seems) not hesitated to alter it, if it suited the counterpoint of his accompanying "parts" to do so. The place occupied to this day by these melodies of the 16th century in the heart of the German people is perhaps only just less in reverence than that due to Holy Writ. Some of them were intimately associated with the occur-rences of Luther's life—the following, for example, "Ein feste Burg ist unser Gott," which is probably his composition :

EIN FESTE BURG IST UNSER GOTT. *
M. LUTHER, 1529.

The following, "Nun danket alle Gott," has become the "National Hymn," and on occasions of popular rejoicing is often sung, in the open air, accompanied by all available force of military bands, and by the discharge of a cannon on each note of the melody. It was the composition of John Crüger, from 1622 to 1662 Music-Director in the St. Nicholas Church, Berlin.

NUN DANKET ALLE GOTT.
JOH. CRÜGER, 1649.

As an example of the alterations in melodies referred to, attention may be called to the various readings here given of the melody known in England as "Luther's Hymn ;" with the authorities for each.

* This is the melody treated so variously, and with such consummate mastership, in Meyerbeer's "Huguenots."

**VARIOUS READINGS OF THE MELODY KNOWN IN ENGLAND AS "LUTHER'S HYMN,"
WITH THE AUTHORITIES FOR EACH.**

19.

20.

21.

1. Is the original melody, ascribed to Luther, from the "Klug'schen Gesangbuch," 1535.

2. "Geistliche Lieder," Wittemberg, 1545 (Luther died 1546). "Geistliche Lieder," Leipzig, 1557. "Geistliche Lieder D. Martin Luther," Nuremberg, 1570. "Kern des Deutschen Kirchengesangs," Lairiz, Nördlingen, 1854. "Zion's Harpe," Kocker, 1855. Tucker, Stuttgart, 1854. D. W. Volkmar, Erfurt and Leipzig, 1853. Winterfeld's edition of "Luther's Corales," 1840.

3. "Geystliche Lieder," Nürmberg, 1558.

4. "Ein schon geistliche Gesangbuch, darinnen Kirchen Gesange und geistliche Lieder, D. M. Lutheri und anderer frommen Christen, so in den Christlichen Gemeynden zu singen gebrauchlich begriffen." Durch Melchiorem Vulpium, Cantorem in Weymar, 1609.

5. From Graun's Oratorio, "Der Tod Jesu." Followed by Sir Henry R. Bishop, in his "Twelve Corales," as performed from time to time under his direction at the "Ancient Concerts," dedicated to H. R. H. Prince Albert.

6, 7. From J. S. Bach's, 371 Vierstimmige Choralgesänge: Ed. C. F. Becker, Organist an der Petri Kirche, Leipzig, 1831. No. 6 is also to be found in his "Choralvorspiele," Griepenkerl's Ed., Peters, Leipzig, in the key of G (vol. vi., p. 36). See also J. S. Bach's "Choralgesänge und Geistliche Arien, herausgegeben von Ludwig Erk." Peters, 1850.

8. "Evangelische Gesang Buch," Elberfeld, 1843. "Chorale Book," Heinrich Wächter, organist in Wiburg; Halle, 1856. "Chorale Book," Adolphe Hesse, Breslau, 1840.

9. "Chorale Gesang Buch," C. H. Strube, of Wolfenbüttel. 1841. "Wirtemberg Choral Book," 1841. "Stutgart Choral Book," 1857.

10. "Chorale Book." John Augustus Bechel, Leipzig, 1847. "Sixty-one Choral Melodies to Paul Gerhard's Hymns;" Becker, Leipzig, 1851.

11. "Chorale Book," Adolphe Hesse, König. Preus. Musick-direktor und Ober-Organist, Op. 69; Breslau, 1851.

12. "Evangelische Chorale Buch." Adolph Bernard Marx, Dr. and Prof. in the University of Berlin. 1832. "Chorale Book," dedicated to the Queen of Prussia, D. H. Engel, Berlin, 1844.

13. "460 Choral-Melodien." C. Karow, of Bunzlaw-in-Schlesten; Dorpat, 1848. "Alte und newere Chorale-Melodien," C. G. Schramm, of Halle; Leipzig.

14. "Evangelische Choral Melodien Buch." A. G. Fischer, Musik-Direktor und Dom-Organist zu Merseburg; 1846-7.

15. From Martini's "Ecole d'Orgue," dedicated to the Empress Josephine; Paris, 1804. (?)

16. The modern form of the melody: supposed to have been introduced by the tenor singer Braham, who also interpolated an imitation of the trumpet of the "Dies Iræ." This form is also known in France (Chants Chrétiens; Paris, 1857, et ante).

17. From "Choral-Melodien for Hanover, Lüneburg and Hildesheim:" Heinrich Enckhausen: Adolph Nagel, Hanover (Modern).

18. Choral-buch,· von August Haupt, Organist der Parochial Kirche, in Berlin. Berlin: Schlesingerschen Buch und Musikhandlung: Robert Lienau.

19, 20. Both said to be of 1535, from Winterfeld's "Der Evangelische Kirchengesang," 3 vols. quarto; Leipzig, 1843—a work to which reference may be made on the whole subject of German Hymnody.

21. From the "Introduction" to the "Woman of Samaria," by Sir Sterndale Bennett. Here inserted as an example of the Melody, really in *Common Tune*, driven

against and in combination with a movement in *Triple Measure.*

Among the early labourers in this field should be mentioned two French composers, Claude Goudimel and Claude Le Jeune, of whom the former published " Les pseaumes mis en rime française, par Clement Marot et Théodore de Beze. Mis en Musique à quatre parties par Claude Goudimel." Without name of place, but with these words at the foot of frontispiece: " Par les heritiers de François Jaqui, 1565," 12mo. The melody is in the tenor (see below.) A second edition was published at Geneva, in the same year; a third at the same place in 1580; and another at Charenton, in 1607.

By the latter, 1. Do de ca corde contenant douze pseaumes de David, mis en musique selon les douze modes approuves des meilleurs autheurs anciens et modernes, à 2, 3, 4, 5, 6 et 7 voix, par Claude Le Jeune, compositeur de la Musique de la Chambre du roy. A La Rochelle par Hierome Haultin, 1598, 6 vol., in 4º obl. The words are from Clement Marot. The form of composition is that of the motets of the early Italian masters. Other editions of this work appeared at Paris in 1608 and in 1618. 2. Premier livre contenant cinquante Pseaumes de David, mis en Musique à 3 parties, par Claude Le Jeune, natif de Valenciennes, compositeur en Musique de la Chambre du roy, Paris, 1607, 3 vol., in 4º obl. The second and third books were published in 1608. No second edition of the work is known. 3. Les psaumes de Marot et de Théodore de Beze, mis en Musique a 4 et 5 parties, par Cl. Lejeune, natif de Valenciennes. La Rochelle 1608, 4º. Première edition, publiée par Cécile Lejeune, sœur du compositeur, et dediée au due de Bouillon, prince de Sedan. This edition is very rare. A second was published at Paris, 1613; a third at Geneva, in 1627; another at Amsterdam, in 1629; one at Paris, from which the Psalms in 5 parts had disappeared; one at Amsterdam, in 1633; and one at Leyden, in 1635. The music was also printed with a Dutch translation of the words at Schiedam, in 1664.

The first portion of the Church Service printed in the English language was the Litany, 1544; the celebrated letter of Cranmer to Henry VIII., in October of that year, mentions also his effort at translating the Hymn " Salve festa dies," to which he had " put the Latin note" as being " sober and distinct." (See Jenkyn's Cranmer, i. 315.) Within the next few years the custom of psalm-singing had become common enough to warrant the " Church Tunes" being referred to as "usual" or "wonted tunes." In 1562, the version of the Psalter, now known as the " old "

version, the joint production of Sternhold and Hopkins, was first printed with these melodies; and in the year after, under the editorship of John Day, " The whole Psalms, in foure partes, which may be sung to al musical instruments," &c., &c., in which Thomas, Tallis, William Parsons, Thomas Causton, Richard Edwards, and three others were the harmonizers. This was followed in 1579 by another publication by Day, the music arranged by William Damon, and in 1585 and 1591 other contributions of a like nature appeared; but inferior in their pretensions and interest to the collection published in 1592 by Thomas Est or Este, " the assigné of William Byrd, dwelling in Aldersgate Street, at the signe of the Black Horse." The arrangers of the tunes were Richard Allison, E. Blancks, Michael Cavendish, Wm. Cobbold, John Dowland, John Farmer, Giles Farnaby (Bac. Mus., Oxford, 1592), Edmund Hooper (Organist and Gentleman of the Chapel Royal), Edward Johnson (Mus. Bac., Cantab.), and George Kirbye. Of this work, a second edition appeared, in 1594, and a third, in 1604, and during the next twenty years more than twenty editions of the *old version* with Church tunes were published by the Company of Stationers, into whose hands the matter had fallen.

In 1621 appeared " The whole Book of Psalmes, with the hymnes evangelicall and songs spirituall, composed into 4 parts by sundry authors, to such severall tunes as have beene and are usually sung in England, Scotland, Wales, Germany, Italy, France, and the Netherlands, never as yet before in one vol. published," &c., &c. As it is also said to be " newly corrected and enlarged," by Thomas Ravenscroft, Bachelor of Musicke; it is possible this may not have been the original edition. Every Psalm of the old version is printed in full, with its tune, in four parts; some tunes, however, being several times repeated, so that the total number is ninety-eight, of which forty are new compositions.

Of these Psalters, two particulars should be noted: 1st, that many of the tunes, though not all, are distinguished by names—" Norwich," " Martyrs," &c., a custom which was English and Scotch exclusively; and 2nd, that the arrangement of voices places the tune in the *tenor part,* not in the treble, as is the modern custom. Though the vocal parts in Ravenscroft are much more difficult than in Este, it is doubtful whether either became a manual for use in Church, or whether it was ever intended to be so. If it were, the skill necessary for the correct execution of these parts must have been much greater then than is common in any but the *best* Church choirs now.

The following arrangement of the "Old Hundredth," by John Douland, is from Este, and will give a fair idea of his book:

1st TREBLE.

All peo - ple that on earth do dwell,

2nd TREBLE.

All peo - ple that on earth .. do dwell,

TENOR (the Tune).

All peo - ple that on earth do dwell,

BASS.

All peo - ple that on earth do dwell,

Sing to the Lord with cheer - ful voice;

Sing to the Lord with cheer - ful voice;

Sing to the Lord with cheer - ful voice;

Sing to the Lord with cheer - ful voice;

Him serve with fear, His praise forth tell,

Him serve with fear, His praise forth tell,

Him serve with fear, His praise forth tell,

Him serve with fear, His praise forth tell,

Come ye be - fore Him and re - - joice.

Come ye be - fore Him and re - - joice.

Come ye be - fore Him and re - - joice.

Come ye be - fore Him and re - - ioice.

The following is Ravenscroft's Harmony of the old 137th; the melody, as before, in the tenor. It is thought better for the general reader to reduce this to "short score." The

frequent occurrence of syncopation in the accompanying parts should be noticed; the correct execution of this harmony would not be easy, even for an accomplished church choir:

When as we sat in Ba - by - lon, The riv - ers

round a- bout, And in re - mem-brance of Si - on,

The tears for grief burst out. We hang'd our harps

and in - struments, The wil-low trees up - on:

For in that place men for their use.

Had planted ma - ny one.

In 1728, a professedly corrected edition of "Ravenscroft," edited by William Turner, was published by William Pearson; and another edition by J. Buckland in 1746. The "Harmonia Perfecta" of 1730, which professed to give the chief of Ravenscroft's tunes, avoided most of his syncopations, and spoiled many of his harmonies.

In 1615 appeared Andrew Hart's "Scotch Psalter; the cl. Psalms of David in prose and metre; with their usual notes and tunes, newly corrected and amended." Edinburgh, printed by Andrew Hart. In this edition the melody only appears, the harmonized edition being dated 1635. It contains a tune for each Psalm.

That the versifications of Tate and Brady, known as the "New Version" of the Psalms, had any beneficial influence on the culture of psalmody has never been pretended; but with the composition of hymns by Wesley and his followers came a new poetic material of which musicians were not slow to avail themselves. New compositions, in the new measures, and with the greater warmth of feeling suggested by the words, and differing entirely, both in melody and harmonization from the older school, follow naturally. The tune books and hymnals with which the press abounds, present every variety of these—from the very time of Wesley to the present—and these lie open before the student. In both melody and harmony they reflect not unhappily the style of the time in which they were written.

In the following example the employment of the voices is akin to that in a glee, and short passages are employed "a la fugue." It is from "Melodia Sacra; or, The Devout Psalmist's New Musical Companion," &c., &c. By William Tans'ur, Senior. "Musico Theorico," &c., London, G. Bigg, 1772. The method employed has long been acknowledged as utterly unsuited to any good purpose:

WESTERHAM. C.M.

As Ps. lxxxi. OLD OR NEW VERSION.

IN FOUR PARTS. W. T.

The following is from "Parochial Psalmody," dedicated to His Majesty George the Fourth, by Thomas Greatorex, Conductor of His Majesty's Concert of Ancient Music, and Organist of Westminster Abbey; London, 182 . . (?) Many good examples of this style of writing may be found in the works of composers of the same date:

WESTMINSTER. C.M.

Psalm cv. NEW VERSION. "Sing praise to God."

* A quotation from an older melody.

Remark in both the above (though separated by an interval of fifty years, and the latter about fifty years only from our own time), the frequent occurrence of the "tr," even on the four notes of the same chord.*

The following are examples of a style "to be avoided." They are reprinted without words, and in melody only, to show how unlike any accepted or acceptable form of music suited for Divine worship they are:

8.7.8.7. (DOUBLE.)

7.6.7.6. (TREBLE.)

Hyper, ὑπέρ (Gk.) Above. A prefix to the names of modes one fourth *above* the *authentic;* as, Hyper-Eolian, Hyper-Dorian, Hyper-Iastian or Ionian, Hyper-Lydian, Hyper-Phrygian. [Greek Music.]

Hyper-diapason. Super-octave.

Hypo, ὑπό (Gk.) Below. A prefix to the names of modes commencing one fourth *below* the authentic, otherwise called Plagal, as, Hypo-Dorian, Hypo-Eolian, Hypo-Iastian or Ionian, Hypo-Lydian, Hypo-Phrygian [Greek Music.] [Plain Song.]

Hyporchema (Gk.) ὑπόρχημα. A religious hymn and dance connected with the worship of Apollo from the earliest times.

* For some interesting remarks as to the *trillo* as an integral part of a composition, see Preface to Hullah's edition of Pergolesi's "Stabat Mater."

I.

Iambus. A metrical foot consisting of a short syllable and a long. [Metre.]

Hymns are roughly said to be *Iambic* when they consist of such feet, the music commencing on the upbeat, *e.g.*, "All praise to Thee, my God, this night."

Iastian. Ionic. [Greek Music.]

Idyll (*Gk.*) εἰδύλλιον. *Lit.*, a small form. Hence, a beautiful form. (1) A poem of elegant structure, frequently, though not always, on a pastoral subject. (2) Music set to a poem of this character.

Il doppio movimento (*It.*) Double time, twice as fast.

Il fine (*It.*) The end.

Il più (*It.*) *Lit.*, the most, as, *il più piano possibile*, as soft as possible, &c.

Imboccatura (*It.*), *Embouchure* (*Fr.*) *Birn* (*Ger.*) The mouth-piece of a wind-instrument.

Imitando (*It.*) Imitating, as, *imitando la voce*, imitating the voice part, &c.

Imitation. The repetition of a short subject by another part. The subject proposed is sometimes called the *antecedent*, and the passage which afterwards imitates it the *consequent*. If the consequent is at a fixed interval from the antecedent throughout, the imitation is said to be *strict*, *e.g.* :

If the consequent only roughly follows the antecedent, the imitation is said to be *free*, *e.g.* :

Imitation may be at any interval, and may be supported by any number of parts, and though it often forms an important element of fugue, it is unrestricted by the laws of subject and answer which are binding in that form of composition. The following are examples of imitation at the second :

This subject may be treated in three parts as follows, including imitation at the third and sixth :

Examples of imitation at various intervals and numbers of parts might be multiplied to any extent. Imitation *by augmentation* is when the consequent is in notes twice the length of those of the antecedent, *e.g.* :

Imitation *by diminution* is when the consequent is in notes half the length of those of the antecedent, *e.g.* :

Imitation *by inversion* is when the intervals of the antecedent are *inverted* in order to form the consequent :

Imitation is said to be *convertible* when antecedent and consequent are interchangeable. If strict imitation be continued for any length of time it is said to be *canonical*.

Immer (*Ger.*) Always, as, *immer langsam*, slow throughout.

Impaziente, impazientemente (*It.*) Impatient, impatiently.

Imperfect. Not perfect. (1) An imperfect interval is one which is a semitone less than perfect. (2) The imperfect consonances are the third and sixth, as opposed to the fourth and fifth. (3) An imperfect cadence is one which does not give complete rest in key. All cadences not having a dominant or subdominant penultimate are said to be imperfect. [Cadence.] (4) An imperfect stop on an organ is one, the pipes of which do not extend through the whole compass of the manual. A *short* stop. (5) Duple measure was formerly called imperfect, as opposed to *tempus perfectum*, triple time.

Imperioso (*It.*) With grandeur, dignity, imperiously.

Impeto, con (*It.*)
Impetuosamente (*It.*) } Impetuously.
Impetuoso (*It.*)

Implied discord. A discord, the actual percussion of which is not found unless other parts be added to the chord, *e.g.*:

The intervals forming the above chord are practically minor thirds, which are not in themselves discordant.

Implied intervals. Intervals not expressed in thorough bass figuring. [Figured bass.]

Imponente (*It.*) In an emphatic, pompous style.

Impresario (*It.*) A designer, conductor, or manager of a concert or opera party. This term is often applied to a man who trains singers, or obtains them for public performances.

Impromptu (*It.*) (1) A piece of music written or played without previous preparation of the subject. An *extempore* performance. [Extempore.] (2) A composition not in any set form, having the character of an extempore piece.

Improvvisamente (*It.*) Unprepared, unpremeditated, *extempore*.

Improvvisare (*It.*) To found an *extempore* piece upon a suddenly suggested subject.

Improvvisatore (*It.*) *Improvisateur* (*Fr.*) One who has the gift of improvising. [Extempore.]

Improviser (*Fr.*) To improvise.

In alt (*It.*) All notes in the first octave beyond the range of the treble stave. [Pitch.]

In altissimo (*It.*) All notes beyond the range of the first octave in alt. [Pitch.]

Incantation. The utterance of a charm or spell in a singing, monotonous tone.

Inchoatio (*Lat.*) The *Intonation* or introductory notes of a plain-song chant.

Indeciso (*It.*) Undetermined. In an undecided manner.

Indifferente
Indifferentemente } (*It.*) With indifference, or unconcern.
Indifferenza, con

Inferior. (*Lat.*) *Lit.*, lower. At an interval *below*, as, *Inversio in octavam inferiorem;* inversion at the octave below, &c.

Infinite Canon. [Canon.]

Inflexion. A departure from the Monotone in chanting. [Accent, § 4.]

In fretta (*It.*) In haste. Hurriedly.

Inganno (*It.*) *Lit.*, deception, as, *cadenza d'inganno*, a deceptive cadence.

Inner parts. Those portions of the harmony that are not at the top or bottom.

Inner pedal. A sustained note in one of the inner parts. [Sustained note.]

Inno (*It.*) A Hymn.

Innocentemente
Innocente } (*It.*) Innocently. In a child-like artless manner.
Innocenza, con

In nomine. (1) The name given to a *free* fugue as opposed to one constructed in strict accordance with the rules of fugue-form. (2) A piece in fugal style, that is, consisting largely of imitation and of contrapuntal devices, sometimes vocal, sometimes for instruments alone. When used in this sense the name has been by some traced to the words forming part of the Benedictus—*in nomine Domini*, and by others from the words of the Antiphon "in festo sanctissimi nominis Jesu," commencing "*in nomine* Jesu omne genu flectatur." Others again trace it to verse 5 of Psalm xx. "We will rejoice in Thy salvation, and triumph *in the name* (in nomine) of the Lord our God." The *in nomines* which exist are chiefly the production of composers of the 16th century.

Inquieto (*It.*) Restless, agitated.

Insensibile (*It.*)
Insensibilmente (*It.*) } Imperceptibly, by degrees.

Instrument à l'archet (*Fr.*) An instrument played with a bow.

Instrument à cordes (*Fr.*)
Instrumento a corda (*It.*) } A stringed instrument.

Instrument. Any mechanical contrivance for the production of sound : The musical instruments employed are divided into the following classes. Stringed, wind, and pulsatile. The stringed instruments are the pianoforte and older instruments of its kind which are played by means of a clavier or key-board; the guitar and others whose strings are struck or plucked by the fingers; and the violin class played with a bow. Wind instruments are of wood or metal; those that are of wood are the flute, piccolo, hautboy, cor anglais, clarionet, basset horn, and bassoon; those that are of metal are the horn, trumpet, cornet-à-pistons, trombone, ophicleide, saxhorn, bombardon, &c. The pulsatile or percussion instruments are the kettle-drums, great drum, side drum, triangle, cymbals, and tambourine. A description of each will be found under its proper head.

Instrumentation. The art of using several musical instruments in combination; also, the style or treatment of orchestral instruments with a view to the production of special effects. [Orchestra.]

Instrument à vent (*Fr.*) } A wind in-
Instrumento da fiato (*It.*) } strument.

Instrumentirung (*Ger.*) Instrumentation.

Intavolare (*It.*) To set in notes, to score, to copy.

In tempo (*It.*) or *a tempo*, in strict time. A direction to follow strict time after any passage in which has occurred a *rall.*, &c.

Interlude, interludium (*Lat.*) A piece of music either impromptu or prepared, played between the acts of a drama, the verses of a canticle or hymn, or between certain portions of a church service.

Intermède (*Fr.*) **Intermedio** (*It.*) An interlude.

Intermedietto (*It.*) A short interlude.

Intermezzo (*It.*) An interlude.

Interrupted Cadence. [Cadence.]

Interruzione, senza (*It.*) Without hindrance, without pause.

Interval. The distance between any two sounds. In discussing all subjects relating to melody, or to the construction of chords, it is necessary to find names for the various kinds of intervals. Hence, in the earliest treatises on music they are divided into classes. The old axiom that consonance depends on simplicity of ratio naturally led authors to draw a line at the point at which two sounds ceased to be consonant and became dissonant. Among the Greeks, the unison, octave, fifth, and fourth, were considered more perfect than the third and sixth and other intervals. In mediæval treatises an interesting division of intervals into perfect, medium, and imperfect is found; the unison and octave belonged to the first class, the fourth and fifth to the second, the third and sixth to the last. In later works appeared a division which is to this day followed by many writers, namely, into Perfect and Imperfect. This division runs thus:

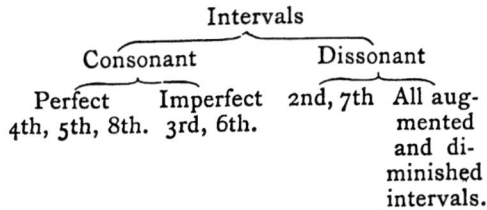

Intervals		
Consonant		Dissonant
Perfect	Imperfect	2nd, 7th All aug-
4th, 5th, 8th.	3rd, 6th.	mented and diminished intervals.

So far, this division seems plain enough. But modern music requires that intervals shall be designated according to their *scale* value.

Hence a perfect interval when accidentally flattened becomes imperfect, and a major interval minor. But the application of the word *imperfect* to a perfect interval made smaller led to serious confusion, because, an *imperfect fifth* came as a subdivision of perfect intervals, while *imperfect* intervals of themselves formed a separate class. To avoid this cross-division, theorists have in the last few years used the name *diminished* for perfect fifths reduced by one semitone. But it is important to note that by this change of name a new difficulty arises, for *diminished* has almost by universal consent been applied to certain intervals when made *less than minor*, for example, C♯ to B♭ is a diminished seventh because C♯ to B♯ is a major seventh, C♯ to B♮ a minor seventh, C♯ to B♭ one semitone less than minor. The word *diminished* when applied by these authors to a fourth or fifth signifies that it is reduced from its normal state *by one semitone*, but the same word "diminished" when applied to a seventh signifies that it is reduced *by two semitones*. That utter confusion should result from such an undigested system is absolutely inevitable; and it will be found that professors and teachers of music to this day are unable to talk intelligibly to each other on the simple subject of "Intervals." For many years a system has been taught in Germany which makes the whole matter perfectly plain. It is this:—

1. Intervals are reckoned upwards, inclusively, and by the number of *names* of notes they contain.

2. Intervals are in their normal state when reckoned from the first note of the major scale. The lowest note of the interval being considered for the time as a *tonic*.

3. Normal intervals are *major*. Thus, D to F♯ is a major third, because F♯ is the third degree of the scale of D; F to B♭ is a major fourth, because B♭ is the fourth of the scale of F; B to F♯ is a major fifth, because F♯ is the fifth of the scale of B; and so on. In other words, *all* the intervals of any major scale reckoning up from the tonic respectively are major.

4. Intervals one semitone less than major are *minor*. Thus, C to D♭ is a minor second

Q

because it is one semitone less than the normal D in the scale of C; B to F♯ is a minor fifth because one semitone less than the normal F♯ in the scale of B; and so on.

5. Intervals one semitone greater than major are *augmented*. Thus, C to D♯ is an augmented second, because it is one semitone greater than C to D, the normal interval; C to G♯, an augmented fifth; and so on.

6. Intervals one semitone less than minor are *diminished*. Thus, F♯ to E♭ is a diminished seventh; C♯ to G♭, a diminished fifth; C♯ to E♭, a diminished third; and so on.

The simplicity of this system is already apparent. The following diagram shows it at a glance:

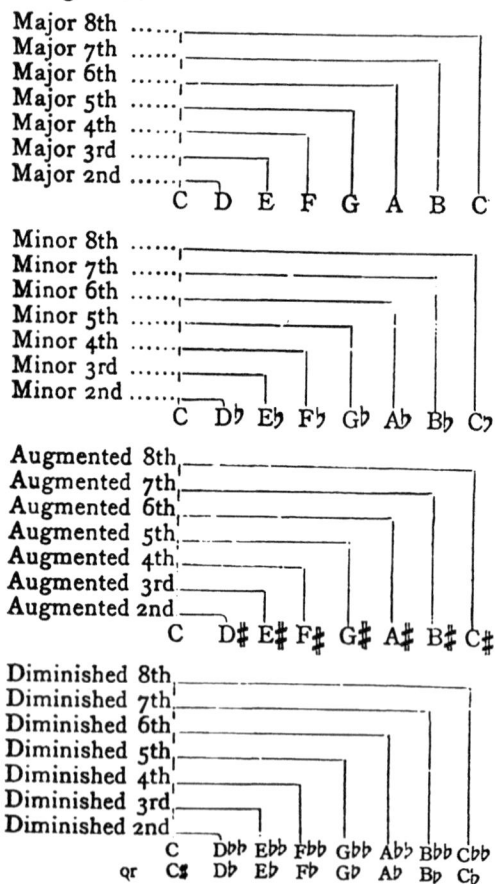

Major 8th ......
Major 7th ......
Major 6th ......
Major 5th ......
Major 4th ......
Major 3rd ......
Major 2nd ......

C D E F G A B C

Minor 8th ......
Minor 7th ......
Minor 6th ......
Minor 5th ......
Minor 4th ......
Minor 3rd ......
Minor 2nd ......

C D♭ E♭ F♭ G♭ A♭ B♭ C♭

Augmented 8th
Augmented 7th
Augmented 6th
Augmented 5th
Augmented 4th
Augmented 3rd
Augmented 2nd

C D♯ E♯ F♯ G♯ A♯ B♯ C♯

Diminished 8th
Diminished 7th
Diminished 6th
Diminished 5th
Diminished 4th
Diminished 3rd
Diminished 2nd

C   D♭♭ E♭♭ F♭♭ G♭♭ A♭♭ B♭♭ C♭♭
or C♯ D♭ E♭ F♭ G♭ A♭ B♭ C♭

It will be seen from this last that diminished intervals are produced in two ways—either by making the upper note of a minor interval flatter, or by making the lower note of a minor interval sharper. Hence it is that some intervals have to be calculated from notes not having a diatonic scale of their own; thus, B♯ to A♮. In such cases, the nature of the interval is readily found by temporarily reducing the lower note; thus,

B♯ to A♮ is a minor seventh, therefore B♯ to A♭, being a semitone less than minor, must be a *diminished* seventh.

The following is the simplest form of stating the rule for naming intervals according to this system. "When asked the nature of any interval, bear in mind the major scale of the lower note, then, if the upper note is higher by a semitone than it would be in the major scale of the lower note, it is *augmented*; if the upper note is actually a note of that major scale it is *major*; if it is less than major by one semitone it is minor; if it is less than minor by one semitone it is *diminished*. When the lower note is a sharpened note, which has no scale of its own, consider it as one semitone lower, when the interval can be easily determined, *e.g.*, C♯♯ to G♯ is a minor fifth, because the interval is one semitone less than C♯ to G♯, the normal fifth. When the lower note is a flattened note, which has no scale of its own, consider it as temporarily raised before determining the nature of the interval, thus C♭♭ to G♭ is an augmented fifth, because it is one semitone greater than the normal fifth C♭ to G♭."

The only obstacle to the general adoption of this excellent method of tabulating intervals is to be found in the pertinacity with which professors adhere to the expression *perfect* fifth and *perfect* fourth, and abhor the term *major* fifth and *major* fourth. This absurd prejudice, which arguments drawn from the history and science of music seem to have no power to remove, must be allowed to die of old age. If there is any real distinction between the perfection of a fifth and the imperfection of a third, it might even then be allowed to students to call fourths and fifths major, on the understanding that they also possessed a remarkable perfection which no other intervals possess.

It has been suggested that intervals should be called, instead of (1) minor, (2) major, and (3) augmented; (1) minor, (2) normal, and (3) major. This would certainly be a better system than any yet devised; but it is to be feared that it would be impossible to disturb the universally accepted meaning of the word major.

Intervals greater than major or normal have been termed (besides *augmented*) extreme, sharp, superfluous, pluperfect, &c.

Intimo (*It.*) With inward emotion.

Intonare (*It.*) To tune, to sing.

Intonation. (1) The method of producing sound from a voice or an instrument. (2) Correctness of pitch; *e.g., just intonation*, singing or playing in *perfect tune*. (3) The method of chanting certain portions of the church services. [Accent, § 4.] (4) The notes which precede the reciting-note in a Gregorian chant.

Intonator. A monochord, or single string stretched across a flat sound-board. Below the string is a diagram of the exact divisions of the monochord necessary for the production of the true musical scale. By means of a moveable bridge, the student is able to sound the notes represented on the diagram, and so, to educate his ear to a true sense of relative pitch.

Intonazione (*It.*) Intonation.

Intoning. The practice of chanting in the Anglican church service, which includes the delivery of the prayers in monotone, and the precenting or leading of the plain song of the Psalms, Credo, Canticles, &c.

Intrada (*It.*) (From *intra*, between). An interlude or *entr'acte.*

Intrepidamente	
Intrepidezza, con	(*It.*) Boldly, daringly, with courage.
Intrepido	

Introduction. A preparation for, or preamble of, a movement or series of movements. Introductions were formerly employed only before larger musical works such as oratorios and operas, but are now used as preparations to works of nearly every kind from a cantata to a waltz.

Introducimento (*It.*) An introduction.

Introduzione (*It.*) Introduction.

Introit. *Introito* (*It.*) *Introitus* (*Lat.* from intro-eo). An antiphon sung while the priest proceeds to the altar to celebrate mass. In the Anglican Church, a short anthem, psalm, or hymn, sung while the minister proceeds to the table to administer the Holy Communion. Formerly, in some English cathedrals, the Sanctus was sung as an Introit. This practice arose probably from the fact that the Communion Service soon after the Reformation ceased to be performed *chorally*, a proof of which is found in the fact that for nearly two centuries—namely, from 1660 to 1840—the Sanctus was never set to music except as an Introit, nor was the *Gloria in excelsis* set, but as an anthem. [Cathedral music.]

Invention. (1) The gift of finding new melodic phrases, or new combinations in harmony. The possessor of such a gift is frequently the founder of a school or style in music. (2) Suites des pièces. [Suite.] (3) The name of a piece of music of a fanciful character.

Invenzione (*It.*) Invention.

Inversion. The transposition of certain phrases having a common root. There are three kinds of inversions in music—(1) of chords; (2) of intervals; (3) of subjects.

(1) The inversion of a chord is effected by making one of the inner notes act as a bass note, and by this means as many inversions can be made, as there are actual notes in the chord, not counting the root. In such inversions the harmony remains the same, although the order of component parts is changed.

(2) Intervals are inverted by making that which was the upper note the lower, and the reverse. The inversion of an interval within the octave may readily be found in the difference between the figure 9 and the interval known; thus an interval of a second becomes a seventh by inversion, &c.

(3) The inversion of a subject is produced by inverting the intervals of which it consists. [Al rovescio.]

Invitatorium (*Lat.*) A sort of introductory sentence or antiphon immediately preceding one of the offices of the Church; such, for instance, as parts of the *Venite exultemus*, or other words inviting the presence or attention of the congregation.

Invitatory. [Invitatorium.]

Ionian mode. The Church mode commencing on the note C.

Ira, con	
Iratamente	(*It.*) Wrathfully, with anger.
Irato	

Irish bagpipe. [Bagpipe.]

Irish harp. [Harp.]

Irlandais (*Fr.*) In the Irish style.

Ironicamente	(*It.*) Ironically.
Ironico	

Irresoluto (*It.*) Uncertain, without settled purpose, in an undecided manner.

Isochronism. Periodical recurrence. [Acoustics.]

Ison (*Gk.*) In the music of the early Greek Church, the ison was the key-note or tonic of a chant. The ison was *moveable.*

Istesso (*It.*) The same; as, *l'istesso tempo,* at the same pace.

Istrumento. An old form of *stromento,* an instrument.

Italian sixth. The name of a chord containing a bass note accompanied by a major third and a sharp sixth.

[Extreme sixth.]

Italian strings. Catgut strings for violins and similar instruments, prepared in a peculiar manner, so that they are more transparent in appearance, and less liable to become false in use than ordinary strings. The majority of real Italian strings are made in Rome. [Catgut.]

Italienne, a l' (*Fr.*)	In the Italian style.
Italiano (*It.*)	

Ite missa est (*Lat.*) The concluding words of the Mass in the Romish Church, from whence the name of that service (Mass) is derived.

J.

Jack. The name of the hoppers attached to the keys of a harpsichord ; the end of the jack was furnished with a quill, as plectrum, to pluck the strings. [Pianoforte.]

Jäger-chor (*Ger.*) Hunting chorus.

Jaleo. *Zaleo* (*Sp.*) A national dance of Spain.

Janitscharen-musik (*Ger*). Janissary music, noisy music on instruments of percussion.

Jeu (*Fr.*) A stop on the organ, or harmonium. *Grand jeu*, the full power.

Jeu d'anche (*Fr.*) Reed stop.

Jeu d'ange (*Fr.*) The *vox angelica* stop.

Jeu de flûte (*Fr.*) Flute stop.

Jeu d'orgue (*Fr.*) An organ stop.

Jeux doux (*Fr.*) Sweet or soft stops.

Jeux forts (*Fr.*) Loud stops.

Jew's harp. *Jew's trump, tromp de béarn,* (*Fr.*), *Mundtrommel, Brummeisen* (*Ger.*) A simple musical instrument held between the lips, the musical sound coming from the vibrations of a tongue of metal, bent at a right angle, which is set in motion by being twitched with the forefinger. The sound is increased in intensity by the breath, and altered in pitch by the shape of the cavity of the mouth, which acts as a reflector. This name some derive from *jeu, play*, from the fact of its being a toy ; others find the derivation of the word in the manner in which the instrument is used, *Jaw's* trump ; the German word *Maultrommel* seems to confirm the latter derivation. Insignificant as the instrument seems, it is capable of producing the most beautiful and pleasing sounds of a melancholy character.

A common soldier, named Koch, who served in the army of Frederick the Great, first raised the Jew's harp from a toy to a solo instrument, and a M. Eulenstein gave concerts in London some fifty years ago, during which he performed upon sixteen instruments, by which means he obtained a compass of four octaves. The Jew's harp is an old invention, being mentioned under the name of Crembalum by Prætorius in his Organographia, in the year 1619. It is a favourite instrument with the Hottentots, at the Cape, who load the end of the elastic spring or vibrator with small portions of hard wax to deepen the tone. The inhabitants of the island of St.

Kilda were formerly great proficients upon this, which was their only instrument of music.

Jig. Gigue (*Fr*). Giga (*It.*) (1) A lively dance which may be performed by one or more dancers. It is popular among many nations, is distinguished by various titles, and has a certain amount of difference in the steps according to the habits and customs of the people by whom it is adopted. With some it is a sober, steady, jog-trot sort of a country dance, with others it is a wild, savage exercise, without point or meaning. With some it is made a means of displaying the agility of the lower limbs of a combined company of dancers ; with others it is a terpsichorean drama for two performers, in which all the emotions excited by love are represented by gestures and monosyllabic cries. The Hornpipe, La Matelotte, La Seguidilla, the Czardasch, the Reel, the Rant, are portions of the country dance ; the Bolero and the Chica are only jigs in various forms.

The term has been derived from the word chica, the name of a dance identical with the jig in some of its characteristics. But the similarity of the title of the instrument "Geige," a fiddle, with which the dance was usually accompanied, with the name of the dance, would seem to point to an origin similar to that of " hornpipe," where the character of the instrument gave the name to the tunes played upon it.

The *jig, gigue, gighe*, or *giga*, as it is variously spelt, was one of the instruments used by the musicians of the 12th and 13th centuries, and this is generally understood to have been a sort of fiddle.

The "Geige," or "jigg" may have received its name from the " up and down " motion with which it is played. A fiddlestick is still called in the west of England a "jigger," and there is a sort of pump used by brewers which has the same name. In the east of England a sieve is called a "jiggin," and there are many other words of cognate origin, which it would scarcely serve the present purpose to quote.

Songs sung by clowns in the interludes to the plays were called *jigs*, and any ambling rhyme was also called a "jig."

In the romance of "Gawaine and the Green Knight," the word Bauderyk is used. It is explained in the "Promptorium Parvulorum" as meaning "guige," a transverse strap, by which the shield was suspended round the neck. The use of the word with such a meaning may account for the fact that the *vielle* or *hurdy-gurdy* is called *geige*, *gigalira* or *giga-vel-lira* from having been slung round the body.

Jig-tunes or fiddle-tunes are frequently, found in old MS. and printed collections from the 16th century onwards. They are all of lively character though of no special or distinctive rhythm. Jigs, though now danced by one, or by two at the most, were formerly "round dances," in which many did indulge.

> —— "the mad lads
> And country lasses, every mother's child
> With nosegays and bridle-laces in their hats
> Dance all their country measures, rounds,
>   and jigs."
>   HEYWOOD "*A woman killed with kindness.*"

Mr. Chappell (Popular Music, p. 792), says that "the jig is now associated in the public mind with Ireland," but he further says that he has "not found one called Irish before the latter part of the 17th century." Scotch jigs were noticed before Irish jigs, as for example, by Shakespear in "Much Ado about Nothing," comparing "wooing, wedding, and repenting" with a Scotch jig, a measure and a cinque-pace; and this comparison implies that the Scotch jig was of a lively character.

(2) As a movement in a "suite," the jig is found in works produced towards the latter part of the 17th century, and onwards to the time of Haydn. At first the phrases were short, and of no more variety than was needed for the purposes of the dance, for the jig was occasionally one of the figures of the country dance. But later it was made the vehicle for display in harpsichord playing, and was lengthened and elaborated and became the origin of the last movement of the sonata. It was written in $\frac{3}{4}$, $\frac{3}{8}$, $\frac{6}{4}$, $\frac{6}{8}$, $\frac{9}{4}$, $\frac{9}{8}$, and $\frac{12}{8}$ time; the peculiarity of the rhythm of triplets was nearly always preserved if not insisted upon. Sir John Hawkins says that the characteristic of the jig "is duple time, thus marked $\frac{6}{8}$ or $\frac{12}{8}$," and "that the air consists of two strains, undetermined as to the number of bars;" others say it is "of compounds of threes in time," and many of the "gigues" belonging to the "suites" are written to show the prominence of the triplets. But the following "jigg" out of "Compositions for Broken and Whole Consorts of two, three, ffower, ffive and six parts, made by Matthew Locke, composer in ordinary to His Majesty Charles the II.," written in 1672, is an example of duple measure and unusual rhythm.

The subjoined specimens of jig tunes will give an idea of the progress in treatment from the earliest time when the dance was adopted as a harpsichord piece, until it began to be disused.

A JEGG.

BEN ROGERS, of Windsor, 1678.

JIG.*

Mr. ECCLES, c. 1690.

* A modification of this tune is still employed for the so-called Irish Jig.

GIGUE.

J. MATTHESON, 1681—1722.

Jingles. Discs of tin, brass, or bell metal, fastened at intervals round a tambourine. [Tambourine.]

Jobel (*Heb.*) A word applied in the Holy Scriptures to certain *trumpets* or *horns*. It is probably equal to the affix *jubilee*; but, *jubilee-horns* were used for other purposes besides that of proclaiming of jubilees.

Joculator. [Troubadour.]

Jodeln (*Ger.*) **Jodle, Jödl.** A peculiar method of singing adopted by the Swiss and Tyrolese, by the rapid alternation in melodic progressions, of the natural and falsetto voice.

The following is a specimen of a *jödl* at the close of a national Swiss song.

Jongleurs. [Confrérie de St. Julien.] [Troubadour.]

Jump. Another name for the dance called a dumpe. [Dump.]

Just intonation. The correct sounding of intervals in singing or playing. [Intonation.]

Juste (*Fr.*) *Lit.*, just. *In tune.*

Justesse (*Fr.*) Equality, purity, and correctness; as *justesse de la voix*, purity of intonation. *Justesse de l'oreille*, correctness of ear.

K.

Kabaro. A small drum used by the Egyptians and Abyssinians.

Kalamaika. A Hungarian dance.

Kammer (*Ger.*) Chamber, *e.g.*, *Kammer-concert*, chamber-concert; *Kammer-musik*, chamber-music (*q.v.*); *Kammer-ton*, concert pitch. [Chorton.]

Kandele or **Kantele.** The ancient minstrel's harp of the Finns. The name is also given to a species of dulcimer, having five strings, in use among the same people.

Kanon. [Canon.]

Kanonik. [Canon.]

Kanoon. A dulcimer. [Canun.]

Kapellmeister (*Ger.*) The leader or conductor of a band of music. [Capellmeister.]

Keckheit (*Ger.*) Boldness, audacity, vigour.

Keeners. Irish singing mourners, who, in olden times, were hired to howl at funerals, in perpetuation of a heathen custom derived from a Phœnician ancestry. The duty of professional keeners was undertaken by the females of the family, or acquaintance of the deceased. After the body had been dressed in grave-clothes, adorned with flowers, and placed upon a bier, the chief keener arranged his followers at the foot and head of the corpse, and recited at the first the *Caoinan*, in which were described the virtues and possessions of the departed. This eulogy sung softly, and accompanied upon the harp, was followed by a full chorus of all assembled; the *ullalu*, or *hubbaboo* as it was sometimes called, next followed, joined in by every one in a louder voice; and after this was ended, the *goul*, or lament, followed, in which the sounds were often raised to howls and yells. The process was repeated during the wake or vigil before the burial, the keeners sometimes following the corpse to the grave. When the body was laid down for the purpose of resting the bearers, or the procession came in sight of a wayside cross or chapel, the keening was suspended, and all present knelt to say in silence an *Ave* or a *Pater noster*, a practice which may be held to denote that keening was felt to be incongruous with Christian usage.

Kemangeh. An Arabian instrument of the fiddle class. [Violin.]

Kent Bugle. [Metal wind instruments.]

Keras (*Gk.*) Κερὰς, a horn. Originally, any instrument made out of the horn of an animal. *Lat., cornu.*

Kerana or **Kerrena.** The name of the Persian horn which is sounded at sunset and at midnight.

Keraulophon. An organ stop, invented by Gray and Davison. Its pipes are of small scale, and are surmounted by a moveable ring of metal. Its tone is soft, delicate, and reedy.

Keren. A Hebrew trumpet. The word is sometimes used in the Bible as synonymous with *shophar*, and to it is sometimes affixed *jobel*, rendered in the English version *rams'-horns*.

Kern (*Ger.*) The *language* of an organ-pipe.

Ketten-triller (*Ger.*) [Catena di trilli.]

Kettle-drums. Timbales (*Fr.*); Timpani (*It.*); Pauken (*Ger.*) Instruments formed of shells of copper or brass, over the top of which parchment is stretched. Parchment is considered best when most transparent.

There are two drums usually employed, the tuning of the larger being limited to the notes between

And of the smaller between

So that the two drums overlap each other in compass by a tone.

The tuning is effected by tightening or loosening the head or skin by means of a ring of metal moved by screws turned by a key. Several plans have been invented by which they may be tuned from one screw. Cornelius Ward's plan was by means of an endless cord passing into the interior of the drum. Potter's is by curved rods outside the shell and meeting in the centre at the bottom. Drums are usually tuned to the tonic and dominant of the piece in which they are employed, but other tunings are found in some scores, as, for example, in Mendelssohn's Rondo in B♮, in which the drums are in D and E. Beethoven, the first who elevated the drum from a mere noise-producing machine into an orchestral instrument, has his drums tuned in various ways in his scores, as a reference to his symphonies will show. In No. 7, 1st and 2nd movements, they are in fifths played as written; 3rd movement, in *sixths* as written. In No. 8, 1st and 3rd movements, in fifths played as written; 4th movement, in octaves. In No. 9, 1st movement, in fourths as written; 2nd movement, in octaves; 3rd movement, in fifths; 4th, in fourths.

Drums for all modern scores are of 8ft. tone, giving a definite and accurate note. When the drums are required simply for marking rhythmical measures, the 16ft. tone is best. For this reason modern writers add the long drum (grosse caisse, *Fr.*; gran cassa, *It.*; Trommel, *Ger.*) to their scores. The bass clef is usually employed in writing for the kettle-drums. Sometimes the notes required are written in their proper places on the stave, but the notes to which they are to be tuned is always stated, as:

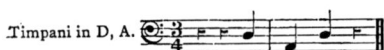

Timpani in D, A.

Neither sharps nor flats are ever written as signatures for the drums. If the sounds required are the tonic and dominant of the key, the drum part may be written in C. If other notes are needed, the rule is to write the actual notes, but without sharps or flats:

Timpani in B♭, F.

Drums were formerly used in combination with trumpets [Dettingen Te Deum, Mozart's No. 6 Symphony], Beethoven being the first to employ them as a means of gaining special solo effects (see his Symphony in F, No. 8, and Scherzo of No. 9).

Snare, or side-drums, are employed in the same manner that the long-drum is, that is to say for rhythmical, not for harmonic effects. [See Rossini's overture to " La Gazza ladra," and the " Benedizione de pugnali " scene in Meyerbeer's " Huguenots."]

The long-drum being played with one stick, the player is frequently called upon to perform upon the cymbals at the same time, not with the best effect with regard to the cymbals, for cymbals ought to be slided one over the other and not struck flat together.

The best sort of sticks for the kettle-drums are those having whalebone handles with a wooden button covered by a piece of sponge; by the use of these the finest gradations of tone may be gained.

A long roll upon the drum is thus indicated:

A short roll thus:

Kettle-drums are said to have been introduced into the orchestra by Handel, who employed a pair taken as part of the spoil at the battle of Dettingen, in the score of the Te Deum, written in celebration of that event; but the drum was first employed by Lully to strengthen the tutti parts of his overtures and choruses.

Among many remarkable passages for the drum may be noted that in A in the slow part of the overture to " Der Freischütz," also one note C *piano* when the first subject (syncopated) of the middle movement returns. Four notes in Violin Concerto, Beethoven. In Haydn's Mass No. 2, and of " Agnus Dei," on the words " Dona nobis pacem," some soft notes of the drum are introduced which at first seem inappropriate.

Key. (1) A mechanical contrivance for closing or opening ventages, as in flutes, clarinets, ophicleides, &c. By means of keys on such instruments, apertures too remote to be reached by the outstretched fingers are brought under control of the player. (2) A lever which brings the *pallets* of an organ under the control of the hand or foot of an organist. (3) A lever which controls the striking apparatus of a key-stringed instrument. In the harpsichord it acted on the *jack*, in the pianoforte it acts on the *hammer*. (4) The *wrest* or key used for tuning instruments having *metal* pegs. Its end is hollowed out, so as to fit over the four-sided end of the peg, and the crossbar with which it is surmounted gives leverage to the hand of the tuner, so that he is enabled to tighten or loosen a string, or (in the case of a drum) slacken or strain a parchment. (5) The sign placed at the commencement of the musical stave which shows the pitch of the notes, was originally called a *clavis* or *key*. This sign is called in modern music a *clef*. [Clef.] (6) *Key*, in its modern sense, is the starting point of the definite series of sounds which form the recognised scale. Different starting-points require the relative proportion of the steps of the scale to be maintained by means of sharps or flats in the signature. The key of C requires no flats or sharps for this purpose, hence it is called the *normal* key.

Key-board. *Clavier* (*Ger.*) The range of keys upon a pianoforte or organ. Keys played by the fingers are called *manuals;* those by the feet are called *pedals.*

Key-bugle. [Metal wind instruments.]

Key-chord. The common chord of the tonic, *e.g.* : C, E, G is the key-chord of C.

Key-note. The note which, according to the signature, forms the starting point of the scale. The tonic. The *doh.*

Key-trumpet. [Metal wind instruments.]

Khalil, Chalil, or **Halil** (*Heb.*) The flute of the Hebrews. As the word is traced to a root signifying *bored through,* it is quite possible that it may have been like the *aulus,* used to describe either a flute or an oboe.

Kin. A Chinese musical instrument, the *scholar's lute,* a sort of *dulcimer.*

King. A Chinese instrument of percussion, consisting of metal plates, which are struck with a hammer.

Kink. A twist in a catgut string from close laying, which, by uncoiling and weakening that part of the string in which it occurs, frequently makes it useless for the instrument for which it is intended.

Kinnor. One of the most ancient of the Hebrew string-instruments, being the first mentioned in the Bible ; Jubal " was the father of such as handle the harp (*kinnor*) and organ (*ugab*) " (Genesis iv. 21). The German version has it, " from him descended *fiddlers* (Geiger) and *pipers* " Pfeiffer). Several theories have been brought forward as to the nature of the kinnor. It has been variously described as a small harp, a lyre, and a guitar.

Kirche (*Ger.*) Church, as *Kirchencomponist,* church composer ; *Kirchenmusik,* church music; *Kirchenstyl,* church style, &c.

Kit. *Pochette* (*Fr.*) *Bretgeige* (*Ger.*) A small violin, about sixteen inches long, played with a bow of nearly the same length, used by dancing masters because of its convenience for carrying in the kit or pocket. It should be stated that some have derived the word from the Persian kitar, cithara, guitar. The Italian name of kit, *sordino,* is given to it because of its small *stifled* tone.

Klang (*Ger.*) Sound. Quality of sound, *timbre.* (*Fr.*)

Klangboden (*Ger.*) Sound board. Resonance box.

Klangfarbe (*Ger.*) *Lit., sound-colour.* Quality of sound, *timbre.* (*Fr.*)

Klanggeschlecht (*Ger.*) A kind or genus of sounds, as *diatonisches, chromatisches,* und *enharmonisches Klanggeschlecht,* the diatonic, chromatic, and enharmonic *genera.*

Klangleiter (*Ger.*) A scale. *Lit., soundladder.*

Klappe (*Ger.*) The key of any wind instrument. A valve.

Klappen-flügel-horn (*Ger.*) Keyed bugle.

Klappen-trompete (*Ger.*) Keyed trumpet.

Klein (*Ger.*) Small. (1) Minor, as *kleiner Halbton,* a minor semi-tone; *kleiner Nonenakkord,* the chord of the minor ninth, &c. (2) Small, as *Klein-bass,* or *kleine Bassgeige,* a violoncello; *klein gedackt,* a small stopped diapason, a stopped flute.

Klingel (*Ger.*) A small bell.

Knee stop. A mechanical contrivance on harmoniums, by which certain shutters are made to open gradually when the knees are pressed against levers conveniently placed for the purpose. A *crescendo* and *diminuendo* are thus produced.

Knell. A stroke upon a bell made at periodic intervals, at the time of a death or funeral.

" When thou dost hear a toll or knell,
Then think upon thy passing bell."
Old Proverb.

A single stroke is made for a child, two strokes for a woman, and three for a man.

Knicky-knackers. The common instrument of percussion known as *bones.*

" Then let our armies join and sing,"
And pit-a-pat make our knackers ring."
MIDDLETON. *The Gipsy Rout,* 1623.

Kniegeige (*Ger.*) A *Viola da gamba.*

Knoll. [Knell.]

Kopfstimme (*Ger.*) Head voice. *Voce di testa.* (*It.*)

Koppeln (*Ger.*) Couplers. [Organ.]

Kraft (*Ger.*) Energy, vigour. *Kräftig,* energetically.

Kreis-lieder (*Ger.*) A circle or series of songs.

Kreuz (*Ger.*) The sign for a sharp. *Doppelkreuz,* a double sharp.

Kriegslied, or **Kriegsgesang** (*Ger.*) A battle song.

Krome (*Ger.*) A quaver ♪ (*Lat. chroma*).

Krotalon. [Crotalum.]

Kroumatic. Instrumental. κρουματική μουσική (*Gk.*), instrumental music. Sounds produced by *striking.*

Krummhorn (*Ger.*) *Lit.,* crooked horn. *Cornetto curvo* (*It.*) *Corno storto* (*It.*) An organ stop, consisting of reed pipes. It is of 8ft. pitch. This name has been corrupted to *Cremona* on English organs.

Krustische instrumente (*Ger.*) Instruments of percussion (from Gk. κρούω, to strike). [Kroumatic].

Kuhhorn (*Ger.*) **Cor de vache** (*Fr.*) A cow horn. The common Alpine horn.

Kurz (*Ger.*) Short.

Kyrie eleison (*Gk.*) [Mass.]

L.

L. The letter employed as the abbreviation of the word *left* or *linke* (*Ger.*), as L. H. *left hand* or *linke Hand.*

La. (1) The solfeggio name for the sixth degree of the scale. (2) The key-note of the minor scale without a signature.

La bémol (*Fr.*) The note A flat.

La bémol majeur (*Fr.*) The key of A flat major.

La bémol mineur (*Fr.*) The key of A flat minor.

Labial. Organ pipes with lips. *Flue* pipes.

Labial-stimmen (*Ger.*) Stops belonging to the *flue* work.

Labium. The lip of an organ pipe.

Lacrimoso (*It.*) Mournfully.

Lade (*Ger.*) Wind-chest of an organ.

La destra (*It.*) The right hand.

La dièse (*Fr.*) The note A sharp.

Lagrimando (*It.*)⎱ Mournfully, sadly,
Lagrimoso (*It.*) ⎰ tearfully.

Lai (*Fr.*) A lay, song, *lied.*

Lament. The name given to some Scotch melodies of a mournful character, or to tunes set to words of a melancholy cast.

Lamentabile (*It.*)
Lamentabilmente (*It.*)
Lamentando (*It.*) ⎬ Mournfully,
Lamentevolmente (*It.*) plaintively.
Lamentevole (*It.*)
Lamentoso (*It.*)

Lampons (*Fr.*) Drinking songs, from the word *lamper*, to gulp down, whence, probably our word *lampoon*, a libellous ballad.

Lancers. The name of one of the arrangements of sets of country dances.

Ländler (*Ger.*) The name given to a dance popular among the Styrian peasants. The tune is of a lively, graceful character in $\frac{3}{4}$ or $\frac{3}{8}$ time. Many of the melodies proper to this dance are of a beautiful and simple style.

Langsam (*Ger.*) Slow; *etwas langsam*, rather slow; *ziemlich langsam*, moderately slow; *sehr langsam*, very slow.

Language of organ pipes. [Organ.]

Languemente (*It.*)
Languendo (*It.*) ⎬ In a languishing style.
Languente (*It.*)

Languettes (*Fr.*) (1) The vibrating tongues of brass or other metal attached to the reed-pipes of an organ or harmonium. (2) The keys or valves of wind instruments generally.

Languid. [Language.]

Lantum. A name of uncertain derivation given to a modern instrument in form not unlike the hurdy-gurdy, but larger, and having metallic reeds or tongues similar to those of the accordion, concertina, or harmonium. The air is supplied by a rotatory bellows, the handle of which is at the bottom of the instruments and the series of small square buttons or keys which are in front are played upon by the fingers.

Largamente (*It.*) Slowly, widely, freely, fully.

Large. A note formerly in use of the value of two longs, or four breves. [Nota.]

Largement (*Fr.*) [Largamente.]

Larghetto (*It.*) *Lit.*, rather broadly, widely. At a slow pace, but not so slow as *largo.*

Larghissimo (*It.*) Exceedingly slow, as slow as possible.

Largo (*It.*) Slow, broadly.

Largo assai (*It.*) Quite slow.

Largo di molto (*It.*) Very slow.

Largo ma non troppo (*It.*) Slow, but not too slow.

Larigot (*Fr.*) (1) An old name for the flageolet. (2) An organ stop of 16 inches pitch.

Larynx is the organ of voice ; the organ by means of which we produce vocal sounds. It is situated at the top of the trachea or wind-pipe, of which it forms a continuation, and its position is known popularly by that of the " Adam's apple," the prominence of one of the cartilages or masses of gristle which form it.

Fig. 1.

FRONT VIEW OF HYOID BONE, LARYNX, TRACHEA, AND BRONCHI IN THEIR MUTUAL RELATIONS.

h. Hyoid bone ; *e.* epiglottis ; *t.* thyroid cartilage ; *c.* cricoid cartilage ; *tr.* trachea ; *b.* right bronchus ; *b'.* left bronchus.

The essential parts are two semi-lunar membranes, placed with their flat sides next to one another, and called the " vocal cords," and the cartilages which support them. The accessory portions are certain other cartilages, the muscles which move these cartilages, and the nerves and blood-vessels by which the whole structure is nourished and furnished with sensation and motion.

The cartilages are nine in number, six paired, three unpaired. The unpaired cartilages are the thyroid, cricoid, and epiglottis ;

the paired are the two arytenoids, the two " cornicula laryngis " or cartilages of Santorini, and the cuneiform cartilages of Wrisberg.

Fig. 2.

BACK VIEW OF LARYNGEAL CARTILAGES.

1. Epiglottis. 2. Thyroid cartilage : *a.* attachment of epiglottis ; *b.* of false vocal chords ; *c.* of true vocal chords. 3. Cricoid cartilage : *a.* facet for arytenoid cartilage ; *b.* facet for lower bone of thyroid cartilage. 4. Arytenoid and accessory cartilages : *a.* arytenoid cartilages ; *b.* cornicula laryngis or cartilages of Santorini ; *c.* cuneiform cartilage or cartilage of Wrisberg.

The *cricoid* cartilage is ring-shaped, as its name (κρίκος, a ring) implies ; it is the base of the support of the other cartilages. It is not equally deep in all dimensions, but is much deeper, from above downwards, behind than in front. At the hindermost part are two small smooth elevations, and lower down are two other smooth surfaces. The former pair of these smooth surfaces serve as the articulations or joints for the arytenoid cartilages which are perched on them and work with great freedom ; the latter pair are the joints for part of the thyroid cartilages. The movements of the latter pair are not so free as those of the former, but are limited to a movement round an imaginary axis running across and through the cricoid cartilage, being thus a horizontal and transverse axis.

The *arytenoid cartilages* (ἀρύταινα, a pitcher) are perched on the two smooth elevations on the hinder part of the upper border of the cricoid cartilage. They are more or less pyramids of three sides in shape, but of the sides which form their base, two, viz., the posterior and internal, are at right angles to one another. The anterior tips are called the " processus vocales," or vocal processes, and to them are attached the vocal cords, of which we shall speak further on. On the summit of each of these pyramids are placed two other small cartilages, the " cornicula laryngis " (little horns of the larynx) or " cartilages of Santorini."

The *thyroid cartilage* (shield-like, from θυρεός, a shield) is the largest of the cartilages of the larynx. It is of a somewhat complicated shape. Take a thin book—a note-book will do very well—open it in the middle, place it upright, so that the two covers shall be at an angle somewhat more acute than a right angle; cut away the upper third of the back, or junction of the covers, so as to leave a notch above, and to each of the corners stick a piece of thin wood, such as a pencil, the two upper pencils pointing upwards, the lower downwards, and you will have a fair idea of the thyroid cartilage. The two lower horns articulate or join with the two lower smooth surfaces or "facets" on the cricoid cartilage; to the two upper horns, ligaments are attached, which suspend the thyroid cartilage to the hyoid bone, a horse-shoe shaped bone, with its convexity forward, forming the base of the tongue. The anterior part of the thyroid cartilage projects much more in adult men than in women or children, and the upper part of the anterior ridge, with the notch, form the projection known as the "pomum Adami," or Adam's apple, from an old tradition that the forbidden fruit stuck in his throat. The thyroid cartilage at the passage from youth to adult age grows very suddenly larger in men, and as suddenly but to a less degree in women. On this relative size and prominence of the thyroid cartilage depends the deepness of the voice, as will be hereafter mentioned.

Fig. 3.
BACK VIEW OF HYOID BONE, LARYNX, AND TRACHEA IN THEIR MUTUAL RELATIONS
(Only cartilages and bones shown).

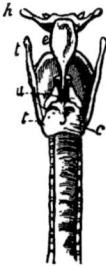

h. Hyoid bone; *e.* epiglottis; *t.* thyroid cartilage; *a.* arytenoid cartilages; *c.* cricoid cartilage.

The *epiglottis* (ἐπὶ on, and γλῶττα the tongue) is a soft cartilage situated at the back of the tongue. In shape it resembles what is called technically in botany an "ovate" or "obcordate" leaf, *i.e.*, it is oval above, and has a tail narrowing gradually from its lower end. This tail is prolonged by fibrous tissue and attached to the thyroid cartilage in the angle between its two sides, just below the notch. The front surface is free in its upper part, but below it is attached by an elastic ligament to the back of the hyoid bone. Its lateral or side borders are free at the uppermost part, but somewhat lower down a fold of mucous membrane (the skin lining any interior cavity is called by this name) runs backwards and joins the summit of the aryte-

noid cartilage of each side. This fold is called the glosso-epiglottidean fold. In these folds lie two small conical cartilages, the *cuneiform cartilages* or the "cartilages of Wrisberg." Below the level of the hyoid bone on the posterior surface is placed a pad of fat and mucous membrane called "the cushion of the epiglottis," functionally a very important structure.

Fig. 4.
INTERIOR OF LARYNX FROM BELOW.
(About life-size.)

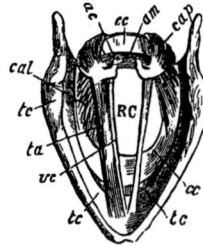

cc. Cricoid cartilage; *ac.* arytenoid cartilage; *tc.* thyroid cartilage; *am.* arytenoid muscle; *cap.* crico-arytenoideus posticus muscle; *vc.* vocal cord; *ta.* thyro-arytenoideus muscle; *cal.* crico-arytenoideus lateralis muscle.

The *true vocal cords*, otherwise called the "vocal cords," are two semi-lunar membranous folds which project on each side towards the middle line; they are attached behind to the tips of the "processus vocales" of the arytenoid cartilages, and in front, close together, to the angle between the two sides of the thyroid cartilage just below the notch. They are somewhat complex in structure, the basis of them is formed by two elastic bands near their edges, and both along these bands, the "inferior thyro-arytenoid ligaments," and more laterally, are muscles running in the same direction, which will be described later. The whole is covered by mucous membrane.

Fig. 5.
VERTICAL TRANSVERSE SECTION OF LARYNX.

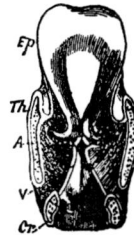

ep. Epiglottis; *th.* thyroid cartilage; *a.* ventricle of larynx; *v.* vocal cord and its free edge; *cr.* cricoid cartilage.

The *false vocal cords*, called also the "superior vocal cords" are two folds of mucous membrane of the same general shape and direction as the former; they are attached behind to the arytenoid cartilages above, and more laterally than the former, and in front to the thyroid cartilages just above the insertion of the true vocal cords. They enclose a ligament, the "superior thyro-arytenoid ligament." Their inner edges do not approach the middle line so nearly as the true vocal cords. Between the upper and lower vocal cord of each side is the opening to the saccule or ventricle of the larynx, a small saccule or cavity, as its name implies, containing some gland cells for secreting mucus. It only remains to say that all the structures are covered with mucous membrane.

Muscles. The larynx is covered with many muscles, but only those which are concerned in the production of the voice will here be mentioned.

Fig. 6.

SIDE VIEW OF LARYNX FROM RIGHT SIDE.

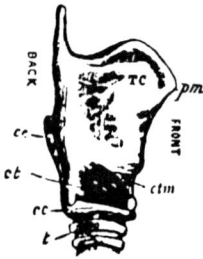

tc. Thyroid cartilage; *pm.* pomum Adami; *cc.* cricoid cartilage; *ct.* crico-thyroid muscle; *ctm.* crico-thyroid membrane; *t.* trachea.

The *crico-thyroid* rises from the fore part of the outside of the cricoid cartilage and running back, spreads itself on nearly the whole of the lower part of the thyroid cartilage.

The *posterior crico-arytenoid* rises from the back part of the outside of the cricoid cartilage and is inserted into the outer or lateral angle of the base of the arytenoid cartilage, sometimes called the "processus muscularis," it also extends some distance along the back part of the base of the arytenoid cartilage.

The *lateral crico-arytenoid* rises from the upper border of the side of the cricoid cartilage, and is inserted into the front side of the lateral projecting part of the base of the arytenoid cartilage nearly as far as the "processus vocalis."

The *arytenoid* is a single muscle, while all the other laryngeal muscles are paired; it runs across at the back of the arytenoid cartilages between them and joins them.

The *aryteno-epiglottidean* muscles rise from the lower and outer angles of the back of the arytenoid cartilages, run across to the upper and outer part of the base of the opposite arytenoid cartilages, crossing each other as they do so (like a pair of braces), and some fibres run no farther but are attached there; the rest pass forwards in the aryteno-epi-

glottidean fold and are inserted into the sides of the epiglottis.

The *thyro-epiglottideus* is composed of two parts, rising from the inner aspect of the fore part of the thyroid cartilage and having the following course, some (thyro-epiglottideus major) curve outside the saccule of the larynx and are inserted into the side of the epiglottis, others run straight up and are attached to the epiglottis on each side of the cushion and below the insertion of the larger muscle. This is called the "thyro-epiglottideus minor."

The *thyro-arytenoid* is likewise divided into two portions. Part of it (thyro-arytenoideus internus) runs just along the outer border of the true vocal cord. The other part (externus) runs from the arytenoid cartilage more externally, and before reaching the thyroid cartilage it surrounds the saccule of the larynx, it is therefore above as well as external to the former portion. Some of its fibres seem to lie in the false vocal cord.

The *nerves* of the larynx are two in number, called respectively the superior, and the inferior or recurrent laryngeal. Both of these are branches of the great vagus or pneumogastric nerve which rises from a special nucleus or mass of nerve cells in the medulla oblongata or upper portion of the spinal cord within the skull where this expands to form what is known as the "fourth ventricle." It leaves the cavity of the skull by the same opening as the internal jugular vein, which takes the greater part of the blood from the brain to the heart, and communicates with most of the large nerves in this situation. The pneumogastric nerve gives nerve-supply to the pharynx, gullet, stomach, liver, spleen, larynx, windpipe, lungs, and heart, and extends down as far as the middle of the abdomen.

The *superior laryngeal* nerve rises from the pneumogastric nerve just below the exit from the skull, and divides into two divisions called external and internal respectively. The *external laryngeal* nerve sends branches to some of the muscles which preside over swallowing, and ends in the crico-thyroid muscle. The *internal laryngeal nerve* gains the inside of the larynx above the thyroid cartilage, supplies the lining membrane of the larynx, and the arytenoid muscle, and sends a branch which joins the recurrent laryngeal nerve.

The *inferior or recurrent laryngeal nerve* has a most remarkable course. We have mentioned that the pneumogastric nerve supplies the lungs and heart; just after reaching the cavity of the chest, while on a level with, and in front of the large blood-vessels coming from the heart, it gives off on each side a large branch, the recurrent laryngeal nerve. This nerve dives underneath the arch of the aorta (the main blood-vessel rising from the heart) on the left side, and under the subclavian artery (supplying the arm) on the right side, and then runs upwards to the larynx. Thus the fibres of the recurrent laryngeal nerve, which come down in the pneumogastric nerve from the medulla oblongata (for each separate strand in the smallest nerve has a separate connection with its nervous centre, brain, spinal cord or ganglion, a nerve being like an electric cable, seemingly one rope, but really composed of innumerable insulated wires) curve back and run upwards again. Thus every separate movement of the muscles of the larynx is due to a nervous impression which travels from the medulla oblongata down into the chest and then up to the larynx again. This seemingly purposeless length of course will be explained when the development of the larynx is spoken of. On their way to the larynx, the recurrent laryngeal nerves give twigs to the gullet and wind-pipe, and when they have reached the larynx they supply all the muscles except the crico-thyroid.

Epithelium. The mucous membrane of the larynx is lined with a layer of small cells called epithelium (which is the name which it bears on all internal parts of the body; on the skin it is called epidermis). Each of these cells has a little hair-like filament which continually keeps lashing upwards, so as to drive any mucus towards the mouth. This kind of epithelium is found on the air-passages generally as well as in some other parts. Above the vocal cords it gradually loses these hair-like filaments from which its name, ciliated (provided with eyelashes), is derived. These filaments are absent over the true vocal cords, as if to indicate that their function is special (Quain, Vol. I. Fig. 245, p. 326).

Fig. 7.

CILIATED EPITHELIUM OF RESPIRATORY MUCOUS MEMBRANE.

A, vertical section of epithelial lining of human trachea magnified 350 times.

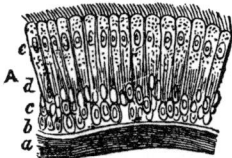

a. b. Subjacent membrane; *c.* lowest or spheroidal cells; *d.* middle or oval cells; *e.* superficial, elongated, and ciliated cells; B. separate columnar and ciliated cells.

Development. The larynx is essentially an apparatus for closing the wind-pipe, and in some of the lower animals has this function alone. The muscles, except the crico-thyroid and posterior crico-arytenoid, which lie outside of the calibre of the tube, are mere differentiations of a circle of muscular fibres called a "sphincter," such as surround, in some form or other, all the entrances and exits of the body. The cricoid and thyroid cartilages are probably developed in two separate halves.

Fig. 8.

DIAGRAM OF AORTIC OR BRONCHIAL VASCULAR ARCHES OF MAMMAL, ACCORDING TO RATHKE.

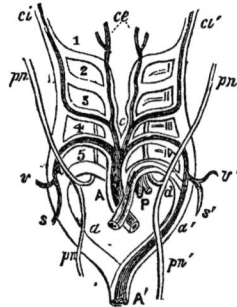

"A. P. primitive arterial stem or aortic bulb, now divided into A. the ascending part of the aortic arch, and P. the pulmonary; *a.* the right, *a'.* the left aortic root; A'. the descending aorta. On the right side 1, 2, 3, 4, 5, indicate the five bronchial primitive arterial arches; on the left side I.. II. III. IV., the four bronchial clefts, which for the sake of clearness have been omitted from the right side. It will be observed that while the 4th and 5th pairs of arches rise from the part of the aortic bulb or stem, which is at first undivided, the 1st and 2nd and 3rd pairs are branches above *c*, of a secondary stem on each side. The permanent systemic vessels are represented in deep shade, the pulmonary arteries lighter; the parts of the primitive arches which have only a temporary existence are drawn in outline only. *c.* Placed between the permanent common carotid arteries; *ce.* the external carotid arteries; *ci. ci'.* the right and left internal carotid arteries; *s.* the right subclavian rising from the right aortic root beyond the fifth arch; *v.* the right vertebral, rising from the same spot opposite the fourth arch; *v'. s'.* the left vertebral and subclavian arteries, rising together from the left or permanent aortic root opposite the fourth arch; P. the pulmonary arteries rising together from the left fifth arch; *d.* the outer or back part of the left fifth arch forming the ductus arteriosus; *pn, pn',* the right and left pneumogastric nerves descending in front of the aortic arches, with their recurrent branches represented diagrammatically as passing behind, with a view to illustrate the relations of these nerves respectively to the right subclavian artery, and the arch of the aorta and ductus arteriosus."

As to the recurrent laryngeal nerves, we must premise, that firstly the early embryo has no *neck*, the head abutting on the trunk, thus the heart is placed nearer the head; secondly, the arrangement of the blood-vessels corresponds strikingly with that which is permanent in fish. In them the heart sends off one large vessel which runs along the base of the gills and sends off branches on each side which run along the gills, and at the opposite extremity of them turn down and join in a common trunk which runs along the body and supplies it with blood, purified by having been aërated in passing through the gills. This is substantially the same in the human embryo, which possesses not true gills indeed, but slits in the neck just like the slits between the gills of a fish; along the bridges between these slits (five in all), corresponding to the gills, run the branches of the great blood-vessel. The further changes need not here be mentioned, but it will be sufficient to add that the last or hindmost of these arched blood-vessels of the branchial or gill-like bridges on the left side subsequently becomes the arch of the aorta, while the same arch on the right side is obliterated, the last but one becoming the subclavian artery. The larynx at the early stage is nearly or quite on a level with the lowest of these arches, the pneumogastric nerves run in front of them, and the recurrent laryngeal nerve, in its course to the larynx, runs directly, or nearly directly backwards, i.e., towards the spine. As the embryo grows, the head becomes further separated from the body, the larynx is drawn up with it, the neck appears, the slits are filled up; but in the upward movement of the larynx the recurrent laryngeal nerves are drawn up too, and as they are hooked round the lowest arch on each side they are drawn out to a prodigious extent round the arch of the lowest vessel on each side. But the lowest arch on the right side is obliterated and disappears, so the recurrent laryngeal nerve on the right side is caught, so to say, by the last arch but one, the right subclavian artery. The gradual growth of the neck takes place, not only in the development of the embryos of the higher animals, but we can trace it in the progress from the lowest to the highest animals. A fish has no neck, a frog hardly any, a reptile rather more, birds and mammals have well-developed necks.

Growth. During childhood the larynx hardly grows at all, and is of the same size in both sexes; both have equally high-pitched voices, and in neither is that prominence of the "Adam's apple" (which depends on the acuteness of the angle between the two halves of the thyroid cartilage, and on the absolute size of the whole cartilage) observable. At the age of puberty, the passage to adult life, a sudden growth takes place in both sexes, but much greater in males than females; the whole larynx grows much, and the two halves of the thyroid cartilage are set at an acute angle, forming the prominence of the "Adam's apple," the notch between them becoming

deeper. The larynx nearly doubles its size in males, becoming about one-third larger in females. It will readily be seen, that the growth of the thyroid cartilage, and especially its increase in prominence, implies a corresponding lengthening of the vocal cords, hence the increased deepness of voice at puberty which is always noticeable in males, sometimes in females—for a contralto voice in a child is a thing never heard; this is acquired at puberty. In old age a bone-like deposit is apt to form in all the cartilages of the larynx except the epiglottis, first or most often in the thyroid, next in the cricoid, then in the arytenoid. To this is due the cracked quality of the voice of old age, the quality of voice depending of course largely on the quality of the sounding bodies.

Physiology. The *crico-thyroid* muscles rotate the front of the thyroid cartilage on the cricoid, forwards and downwards. Since the pivots on which the thyroid works are below the attachment of the vocal cords, to the arytenoid, and therefore practically to the cricoid cartilage, any forward and downward movement of the thyroid will tend to lengthen the vocal cords. This will be evident from the diagram (Huxley's El. Phys. Fig. 50). If the finger be placed on the space in front, between the thyroid and cricoid cartilages, and a note and then a considerably higher one be sung, the space will be found to be considerably diminished; in other words, the crico-thyroid muscles will have pulled downwards and forwards the thyroid on the cricoid, and in so doing stretched the vocal cords, the increased tension producing the higher note. As before said, the external laryngeal nerve supplies the crico-thyroid muscles.

The *thyro-arytenoid* is the opponent of the crico-thyroid; it rotates the front of the thyroid cartilage upwards and forwards, and in so doing relaxes the vocal cords. Besides this action as a whole, the outer and upper part presses on the ventricle of the larynx, and tends to empty it of any contents; the inner portion, lying in the vocal cord (the thyro-arytenoideus internus) renders straight and tense the very edge of the vocal cord after the thyroid and arytenoid cartilages have been fixed by other muscles, and the length of the vocal cord thereby determined. By the contraction of its lower fibres, lying below the level of the vocal cord, the column of air might be narrowed, and the tone raised; for this is the result of such a narrowing of the column of air before reaching the resonant membrane. It is by this muscle that the peculiar quality of the notes of the "head-voice," as opposed to the "falsetto voice," is probably produced, the edge of the vocal cord being very tight and capable of very rapid vibrations; the comparative thinness of quality is owing to the smallness of the bulk of the vibrating body. The "crack" in the voice which sometimes occurs during the attempt to sing a high note, and is so annoying to performer and audience, is perhaps due to the sudden paralysis of this muscle, which strikes work when overstrained. But it may also be due to the vocal cords *touching* each other, nodes being instantly produced; this is more probable. This muscle is supplied by the recurrent laryngeal nerve.

The *arytenoid* muscle draws the arytenoid cartilages together, and also tends to prevent their rotation. It is supplied by the superior and recurrent laryngeal nerves.

The *aryteno-epiglottidean* muscles, since between them they embrace the whole orifice of the air-tube, act as a sphincter, and in so doing draw the arytenoid cartilages together and forward, the aryteno-epiglottidean folds together towards the middle line, and the epiglottis downwards and backwards.

The *thyro-epiglottidean muscles* depress the epiglottis, the greater and upper one the upper part, the smaller and lower one the "cushion"; by their action the epiglottis is pulled forcibly on to the top of the vocal cords, completely stopping the passage, as takes place in straining or in swallowing. They are supplied by the recurrent laryngeal nerve.

Before describing the action of the lateral and posterior crico-arytenoid muscles, we must premise, first, that the pivot on which the arytenoid cartilages move is a very loose joint, so that the arytenoid cartilages are able to be moved bodily in any direction *without* rotation.

The *posterior crico-arytenoid* muscles, acting alone, pull backwards and downwards the outer angles of the arytenoid cartilages. By so doing they rotate these cartilages (*aa* in following Figs.) on their pivots (*pp*) and separate the front angles, or "processus vocales," separating therefore the vocal cords. The dotted line represents their action.

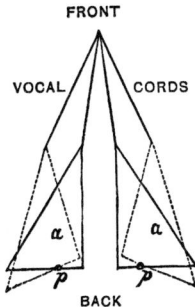

But if the posterior arytenoid acts with them it brings the hinder angles of the cartilages together and prevents them from being separated as they would be in rotation, so that the whole cartilages are moved bodily backward and the vocal cords are stretched.

The *lateral crico-arytenoid muscles* have an opposite effect. Acting alone, they pull forward the outer angles of the arytenoid cartilages. By so doing, they rotate these cartilages (*aa*) on their pivots (*pp*) and approximate the "processus vocales," bringing the vocal cords together. The dotted line represents their action:

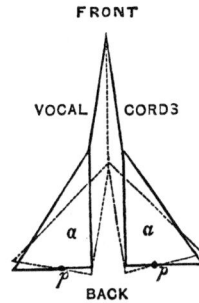

It will be seen that the posterior part of the glottis, between the cartilages, remains open, forming a triangular space with the apex forwards. This was formerly called the "glottis respiratoria" on the false idea that the position of the parts in this state was that of breathing. The space between the vocal cords in front was called the "glottis vocalis"; this name is correct, for it is only this part which assists in producing sound; but the "glottis respiratoria" is only an applicable name so far as it implies that this part is used in breathing, but not in producing sound. The *whole* glottis, however, is "glottis respiratoria" properly, as will be hereafter explained.

By the action of the arytenoid muscle this triangular space is obliterated. There are two other muscles which, though they do not properly belong to the larynx, yet assist in vocalization. These are the sterno-thyroid and the thyro-hyoid.

The *sterno-thyroid* muscles arise from the upper part of the sternum or breast-bone, and are inserted into the side of the thyroid cartilage. Their action is to pull down the thyroid cartilage, assisting the crico-thyroid muscles and helping to stretch the vocal cords. They are supplied by a nerve called "descendens noni," being a descending branch of the ninth or hypoglossal nerve which supplies the muscles of the tongue with motor power.

The *thyro-hyoid* arise from the hyoid bone,

Thus it will be seen that the "glottis" or aperture of the larynx takes a diamond-shape.

R

which forms the base of the tongue, and are inserted into the side of the thyroid cartilage. Their action is to pull upwards the thyroid cartilage, rotating it and helping the thyro-arytenoidei to relax the vocal cords. They are supplied by a branch of the ninth or hypo-glossal nerve.

The action of the sterno-thyroid muscle may be felt by placing a finger in the middle line of the neck just above the breast bone: in singing a high note, the muscles will be felt to contract.

TABLE OF MUSCLES.

Stretchers of vocal cords. Crico-thyroid, sterno-thyroid (posterior crico-arytenoid + posterior arytenoid), thyro-arytenoideus internus (stretches edge of vocal cords when arytenoid cartilages are fixed).

Relaxers of vocal cords. Thyro-arytenoid (when arytenoid cartilages are not fixed); thyro-hyoid. *Openers of glottis.* Posterior crico-arytenoid (alone). *Closers of glottis.* Lateral crico-arytenoid, posterior arytenoid.

Physiology of the voice. The following remarks are taken from Czermak's book, " Der Kehlkopf-spiegel," which contains the best observations that have been made with the laryngoscope.

During ordinary quiet breathing the epiglottis touches the back of the pharynx, so as only to leave one aperture behind and one at each side. Through the aperture behind and in the middle, a deeper view is obtained: one here sees the elevations of the cartilages of Santorini or cornicula laryngis, which surmount the tips of the arytenoid cartilages. In pronouncing the vowel ā as in "fate," the epiglottis raises itself and discloses the laryngeal cavity, even the front wall of the windpipe being visible. This is the best position in which to observe the preparations for making any vocal sound.

As soon as one prepares to make a sound with one's voice the arytenoid-cartilages rise and approach each other with surprising rapidity, the " processus vocales " are brought together and with them the vocal* cords by the lateral crico-arytenoid and arytenoid muscles. By practice this can be performed slowly, or even stopped half way, in which case one gets a position of the parts, as in Fig. 3.

It is impossible to actually observe the production of the lowest chest notes, for as

soon as we really sing such a note the arytenoid cartilages approach and touch each other, and bend under the edge of the overhanging epiglottis (Fig. 4), which gives us much the same appearance as in quiet breathing.

During the production of the higher chest-notes, especially when sung sforzando, and still more in using the head-voice, it is easy to see into the larynx. It is from these that we infer the position of the parts in the deepest chest notes.

In uttering a piercing cry a free view is afforded into the larynx (Fig. 5). In the middle are the vocal cords closely opposed; then on each side of these a slit, the opening of the ventricle or saccule of the larynx,† between the true and false vocal cords; still farther outside the false vocal cords. The whole arytenoid cartilages, " processus vocales " and all, are closely opposed; and these erected as they are, together with the epiglottis and the intervening aryteno-epiglottidean folds, in which are seen the prominences of the cartilages of Wrisberg, form a sort of additional tube on the top of the larynx, all the parts being (as one's sensations alone would tell one) in extreme tension. On the back of the epiglottis one sees the cushion which touches the insertion of the vocal cords.

On taking breath (Fig. 6) the " processus vocales " are turned outward (posterior crico-arytenoid alone) and we get the diamond-shaped glottis (diagram 1). Sometimes, however, we get the triangular " glottis respiratoria " with a second inverted triangular space in the " glottis vocalis " (perhaps from the action of the lateral crico-arytenoid muscles ; the posterior arytenoid and thyro-arytenoideus internus being much relaxed). Fig. 8. In these conditions all the parts are very relaxed.

It is seen that the upper opening of the larynx is formed by a fold of mucous membrane supported by seven cartilages, epiglottis, two cartilages of Wrisberg, two of Santorini, two arytenoid. (Fig. 2.)

In deeper quiet breathing the diamond-shaped glottis is exaggerated, as in Fig. 7.

During quiet breathing the parts of the larynx do not move, and in some cases the glottis is wide enough to admit a finger with ease.

During deep laboured breathing the arytenoid cartilages are brought somewhat together at each expiration, and are thrown into disorderly vibrations like the nostrils under

---

* It is plain that the glottis is smaller in singing than in breathing, and smaller in singing a high than a low note. This is easily proved by comparing the time taken to empty the lungs in each case. The larger the aperture, the shorter the time. No sound is produced when the vocal cords are more than one-tenth of an inch apart.

† Its function seems to be to ensure a free space for the vibration of the vocal cords, and to keep them lubricated.

similar circumstances; at each inspiration they are separated to their extreme limits.

It is possible, under favourable circumstances, to see as far down the wind-pipe as its division into the two bronchial tubes, that is as far into the chest as the third dorsal or rib-carrying vertebra. (Fig. 7.)

In the shrillest cries the cushion of the epiglottis appears to be pressed down on the front part of the vocal cords, and to shorten their vibrating portion just as a string is stopped by the fingers on the finger-board of a stringed-instrument.

In air-tight closure of the larynx, as in straining (which is best observed in passing from the position of Fig. 5, that of uttering a piercing cry): 1st, The arytenoid cartilages—"processus vocales" and all — are closely pressed together, and with them the vocal cords. 2nd, The false vocal cords apply themselves to each other and to the true vocal cords closely, so as to conceal the openings of the ventricles of the larynx. 3rd, The epiglottis presses its cushion tightly on the top of everything.

(It is curious that whereas these parts of the larynx resent being touched so strongly that the smallest touch of them produces at least a violent fit of coughing, they suffer being touched by one another and by the epiglottis quietly. Czermak asks whether this is due to the *kind* of touch which they suffer, or to the peculiarity of the nervous apparatus through which the reflex action, which a foreign body excites, is produced.)

These changes are partly simultaneous, partly so quickly following one another that we require the greatest watchfulness to observe them. For instance, the false vocal cords cannot be *seen* to touch one another, for the epiglottis bends down and hides them while they are still approaching each other; but it is inferred that they do so, for on suddenly opening the closed glottis they are seen to project as far towards the middle line as the true vocal cords which are known to be closely apposed to each other.

If we stop the closure of the larynx half way, we get the appearance presented in Fig. 9. In complete closure we get the appearance presented in Fig. 10. Later, however, the free edge of the epiglottis sinks, and we get the same appearance as in Fig. 4, the appearance during the production of the lowest chest-notes.

By this complex apparatus we can understand how the glottis can withstand the tremendous pressure put on it by the expiratory muscles in straining, &c. If these are put into action the whole of the parts closing the glottis are lifted up and become convex or dome-shaped upwards, resuming their position when the pressure is relaxed.

In clearing the throat the glottis is firmly closed, and then the expiratory muscles exerting their force, the parts closing the glottis are suddenly relaxed, the epiglottis being, so to say, blown violently up, and all the parts are thrown into violent disorderly vibrations so as to remove any foreign body or mucus.

In swallowing, the glottis is also closely shut. In increasing the strength of a note the cords are slightly relaxed to compensate for the increased pressure of wind which would otherwise raise the note.*

EXPLANATION OF CZERMAK'S FIG. (TAF. III.)

z. Root of tongue.	s. Cartilages of Santorini.
h.ph. Hinder wall of the pharynx.	p.v. Processus vocales.
œ. Opening of gullet.	u.st. True vocal cords.
e. Epiglottis.	o.st. False vocal cords.
a. Arytenoid cartilages.	v.m. Ventricles of the larynx.
e.w. Cushion of epiglottis.	
a.e. Aryteno-Epiglottidean fold.	v.t. Front wall of windpipe.
w. Cartilage of Wrisberg.	h.t. Hind wall of windpipe.
g.a. Elevation between cartilages of Santorini and Wrisberg.	b.d. Right bronchial tube.
	b.s. Left bronchial tube.

Fig. 1.*

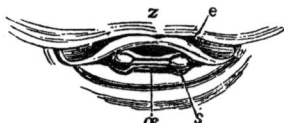

Quiet breathing. Wide glottis. Arytenoids apart and depressed. Epiglottis falling back so as to obscure the view into the larynx.

Fig. 2.*

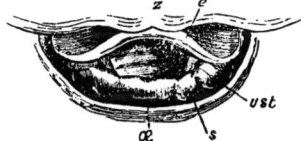

The same, but epiglottis raised by the pronunciation of ā as in "fate," or ee as in "green," but the actual sounding of the latter makes the tongue rise so high, as to obscure the view.

Fig. 3.*

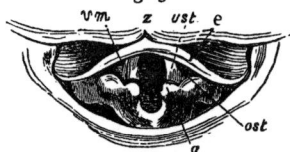

The preparations for sounding the voice after quiet breathing, the process stopped half-

* The parts to the right of the middle line of these figures, obtained by a mirror, necessarily correspond to those on the left side of the larynx, and *vice versa*. That which is situated above in the drawing in reality exists in front, that which is below is situated behind.

way. The arytenoids project and approach one another with free and rapid movements. The glottis is narrowed.

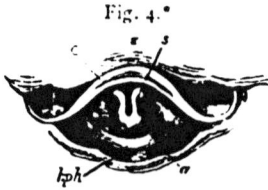

Position during a deep chest-note. The epiglottis lies back and obscures the view of the vocal cords.

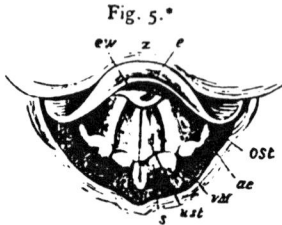

Fig. 5.*

Position during a very high note. Glottis very narrow, all the parts very tense, arytenoid cartilages, aryteno - epiglottidean folds, and epiglottis, forming a sort of additional tube above the floor of the larynx. In the highest possible notes, the epiglottis-cushion is pressed on the front insertion of the vocal cords, shortening their vibrating length.

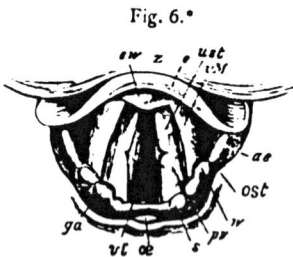

Fig. 6.*

Position of parts on taking a deep breath after singing a high note. All the parts are relaxed and appear thicker, the arytenoid cartilages move apart, the "processus vocales" are turned out, the glottis is larger and diamond shaped.

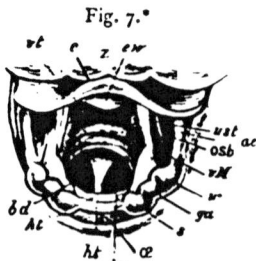

Fig. 7.*

Position in quiet breathing. The same as Fig. 6, but exaggerated. The glottis still

larger, large enough to easily admit a finger. The parts do not move during quiet breathing with inspiration or expiration.

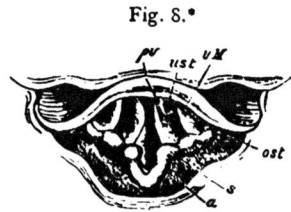

Fig. 8.*

Position during whispering. The arytenoids are seen near together, but not so near as the "processus vocales;" these last are however too far apart to cause a vocal sound. The "processus vocales," being closer together than the rest of the arytenoids, produces a form of glottis, the opposite of that shown in fig. 6, namely, one approaching to that of two isosceles triangles, with their apices apposed; the whisper becomes louder as the "processus vocales" approach one another, until at last all that remains is a triangular space (the hinder of the two triangles), between the arytenoids. In the louder hoarser whisper, the cushion of the epiglottis presses on the front part of the vocal cords and additionally prevents their being thrown into vibrations, though while any chink remains this cannot happen.

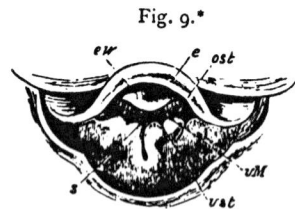

Fig. 9.*

Position in air-tight closure of the glottis; the process stopped half way. The arytenoids and the vocal cords are firmly apposed, the false vocal cords are being approximated, the epiglottis with its cushion is being pressed down on the glottis.

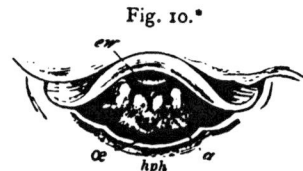

Fig. 10.*

The state of complete closure. The epiglottis pressed firmly on the glottis. The false vocal cords probably, the true vocal cords certainly, closely apposed. When the epiglottis is still further pressed back, we have a view similar to that during the sounding of a deep chest-note (fig. 4), except that a small space exists in the latter case, between the epiglottis and arytenoids, for the passage of the air.

Fig. 11.*

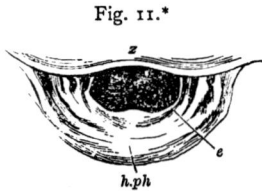

h.ph

Position at the commencement of the act of swallowing.

The laws governing the vibrations. It has been naturally attempted to identify the vocal cords with some type of sounding bodies, in order to examine the laws governing their vibrations. They have a considerable superficial resemblance to strings, the higher sounds are as in them produced (other things equal) by increased 'tension. But 1st. no string as short as the vocal cords could give out so low a note, 2nd. the number of vibrations does *not* (as in strings) vary directly as the square root of the tension. Therefore they are not strings.

The human vocal organs are not a flue-pipe, there is nothing to lead us to think that they are, and besides the sound written

requires an open pipe, nearly 6 feet long, and the case is clearly not one of a *stopped* pipe.

Is it a Reed instrument? The question is best answered by adducing some of the laws which govern them. 1st. The pitch of a reed may be lowered, but cannot be raised, by joining it to a tube, 2nd. it can never be lowered more than an octave, 3rd. after being thus lowered, the note is again raised by a further lengthening of the tube, and again lowered by a still further lengthening, 4th. the length of tube necessary to lower the pitch of the instrument to a given point, depends on the relation between the frequency of vibrations of the tongue of the reed, and those of the column of air taken separately. If a wind instrument depends for its note entirely on the length of its pipe, it must be a flue-pipe, if the range to which it can be altered depends only partly on the length of the tube, and if the range capable of being produced by lengthening the tube is never more than an octave, (the embouchure being constant,) it is a reed instrument.

This latter is the case with the larynx. The reed in the voice corresponds with the "free reeds," since it vibrates freely backwards and forwards, and does not "beat" against an aperture, but unlike those which are in use (Concertina, Harmonium, &c.,) it is formed *with* a tube.*

The reed of the voice differs from ordinary reeds in not being a stiff lamina fixed at one end, freely vibrating at another; it is a stretched membrane. Membranous tongues made elastic by tension may have three forms, 1st. a stretched band in an interval between two firm plates, leaving a chink on each side, 2nd. it may be stretched over part of the end of a tube, the other part being occupied by a solid plate, a narrow chink being left between the free edges, 3rd. two elastic membranes may be stretched over the mouth of a tube leaving a chink between them. The last is obviously the case in point. But if the membranes are prolonged in a direction parallel with the current of air, not their edges only, but their whole surfaces are thrown into vibrations. This resembles the larynx still more closely. An instrument on these principles has been constructed, and corresponds very closely in its behaviour with that of the larynx. In such an apparatus, pitch depends on the length, tension, and thickness of the membranes, and though their edges must be close together to produce sounds, the size of the chink has nothing to do with the pitch. A lower note is formed from a pair of such membranes than from one, their pitch is heightened by increasing the strength of the current of air, thus they differ from rigid reeds in which the note is lowered by a similar proceeding.

Their behaviour when furnished with pipes of various lengths, corresponds in the main with that of metallic reeds, but it is not so precisely determinable, as might be imagined. A certain length of pipe suits a certain tone best. A tube *prefixed* to the reed, has the power of altering the tone, but not so definitely as when *affixed*.

Thus the human vocal apparatus is a pair of membranous free reeds, with a prefixed tube and complex affixed resonance tube.

---

* Helmholtz in his book "Die Lehre von den Tonempfindungen," 1862, divides membranous reeds into two classes. (1) Those in which the aperture is *closed* by the shock of the air (German "einschlagend") —"beating" reeds; and (2) Those which are *opened* by the shock of the air (German "aufschlagend"—lit. "striking open")—"free" reeds. The beating reeds have the free edges of the limbs of the reed pointing *against* the current of air, the free reeds in the *direction* of the current. The beating reeds give a *lower* tone than they would do if vibrating freely, the free reeds a *higher* tone. The reeds of organ pipes and wooden wind instruments are beating reeds; the human lips in playing brass instruments are *opened* by striking, and are therefore free reeds (aufschlagend). They consequently give higher tones (apart from the question of the selection of a particular harmonic by the resonance tube of the instrument) than when vibrating alone. The Larynx is also a free reed, as will be seen by Fig. 5, v.

All the air-passages above the larynx, the pharynx, mouth, nose, and even the cells in the frontal bone, form part of this resonance tube. These tubes, forming the resonance tube, have an important part to play in vocalisation, though their complexity makes it difficult to determine that part accurately, still that they do play a part is evident from the following facts. In ascending from a low to a high note the whole larynx is lifted towards the skull, the thyroid cartilage being drawn up within the hyoid bone so as even to press on the epiglottis ; the space between the thyroid and cricoid cartilages is diminished, the soft palate is depressed and curved forward, the tonsils approach one another.

The aperture of the resonance tube is an important point, the smaller the aperture the lower the tone. In producing low notes the mouth is less open than in high notes. There is probably a certain length of both affixed and prefixed tubes and a certain size of the opening of the affixed tube which is most suitable for each given note, and these matters are partly managed automatically, and are partly the result of practice and education. In producing the lowest notes we retract and depress the tongue with the epiglottis so as to partly cover the lower aperture of the resonance tube.

The *head-voice* is probably produced by the vibration of the free edges of the vocal cords only. Helmholtz thinks this is produced by drawing aside the mucous coat below the cords, the edge of the cords being thus rendered sharper, the weight of the vibrating part less, the elasticity being constant.

The *falsetto voice* is a problem not yet cleared up. Many physiologists seem to have quite lost sight of the fact that it is different from the "head-voice." There are various theories on the subject.

Some believe that the vocal cords only vibrate in part of their length. We have seen this to be possible by means of the epiglottis-cushion. And it has thus much in its favour that some adventitious aid (if we may use the term) seems to be called in, for it is much easier to sing a very high note in the falsetto than in the chest register, the former depending on sheer muscular exertion as we know.

But on the other hand anyone can sing falsetto with his tongue out of his mouth, and consequently with the epiglottis-cushion far away from apposition with the vocal cords.

Others have said that the cords vibrate in segments and give harmonics instead of fundamental notes. This is possible, for some of the fibres of the thyro-arytenoideus internus muscle end at various points along the vocal cord and might favour such a splitting into segments.

Others say that the falsetto differs from the other registers in that only the edges of the vocal cords are thrown into vibration, instead of the whole of them. This is possible, the only objection being that the extreme tension of the very edge of the vocal cords seems to be an explanation involving far more labour than our sensations tell us is expended in the production of the falsetto voice. This seems much more likely to correspond with the production of the " head-voice."

In passing from the highest chest note to the lowest falsetto note, the space between the thyroid and cricoid cartilages in front which was closed suddenly opens, implying *relaxation* of the vocal cords. This is consistent with the hypothesis that they only vibrate in part of their length, for this would require less tension for a shorter membrane. In passing from the chest to the falsetto register, the larynx which was elevated descends and rises again as the falsetto voice rises.

Others have thought that the falsetto voice was the result of a flue-pipe arrangement, the glottis being the embouchure, the air passage the tubes. We have already dismissed the flue theory as untenable.

The person on whom most reliance is to be placed, M. Garcia, himself a singing-master, and the practical inventor of the laryngoscope gives a long account of the falsetto voice. He says that in the falsetto as in the chest register the lower tones are formed by the " processus vocales," as well as by the vocal cords, that these processes (which he calls the " apophyses") gradually approach one another in the middle line, that the vibrating length of the glottis is consequently diminished *pari passu*, that when the vibrating glottis is composed of the vocal cords and only the tips of the processus vocales, the weak uncomfortable tones well known to singers are formed, that when the processus vocales are so closely apposed throughout that only the vocal cords vibrate, the head voice is formed. " If we compare the two registers in these movements, we shall find some analogies in them ; the sides of the glottis, formed at first by the apophyses and their ligaments, become shorter by degrees, and end by consisting only of the ligaments. The chest register is divided into two parts, corresponding to these two states of the glottis. The register of falsetto-head presents a complete similarity, and in a still more striking manner. On other points, on the contrary, these same registers are very unlike. The length of the glottis necessary to form a falsetto note, always exceeds that which produces the unison of the chest. The movements which agitate the sides of the glottis are also augmented, and keep the vibrating orifice continually half opened, which naturally produces a great waste of air. A last trait of difference is in the increased extent of that elliptic surface (the glottis). All these circumstances show in the mechanism of the falsetto a state of relaxation which we do not find in the same degree in the chest register.

"When the external fibres of the lateral crico-arytenoid muscle remain inactive, we produce the falsetto. The lips of the glottis, stretched by the horizontal bundle of the thyro-arytenoid, come in contact by their edge alone, formed at once by the ligament and the apophyses, and offer little resistance to the air. Hence arises the great loss of this agent, and the general weakness of the sound produced here. During the chest register the vocal ligaments are stretched, and are in contact to an extent corresponding with the depth of the anterior apophyses of the arytenoid, whilst in the falsetto the edges alone of the ligaments are stretched and apposed."

Some have tried to show that the falsetto depends on the state of the parts below, others above, the larynx. There is nothing to say for these theories. Another theory again assigns to the false vocal cords a large share in producing the falsetto voice, and Garcia found that in producing high notes of the chest or falsetto register they were somewhat approximated.

In reviewing these various theories, we shall be assisted in arriving at some sort of an opinion by eliminating such of them as seem to us obviously untenable; such as the theory that the vocal apparatus is not used in the production of the falsetto voice as a reed instrument but as a flue-pipe, and that which states that the parts above or below the larynx (and not the larynx itself) are the necessary instruments for its production. The next theory to be discussed is that which states that only the edges as distinct from the whole of the vocal cords vibrate; this we shall put aside as accounting more satisfactorily for the "head voice," which is quite a different thing, especially when we remember the muscular effort necessary for producing a high head note as compared with the relative ease with which the same note can be produced in the falsetto voice, and also when we keep in view the fact above mentioned, that in passing from chest to falsetto register the crico-thyroid space enlarges, implying *relaxation* of the vocal cords. Let us now review the theory which sets forth that in producing the falsetto voice we

set the vocal cords vibrating not in one segment but in many segments or nodes. In the first place this is not inconceivable, but we must freely admit that we do not know the mechanism by which it would be produced. Garcia states that the length of the vocal cords necessary to form a given falsetto note always exceeds that which produces the unison of that note in the chest register, and adds that the falsetto note is accompanied by a *relaxed* state of the glottis; now if the length is increased while the cords are relaxed, we have two circumstances which would render the pitch *deeper* if the cords vibrated in their entirety, but both these factors would be favourable to vibration in *segments*. But there is another reason for supposing this, which seems to us worthy of consideration, though it does not depend on direct observation. When the voice "cracks" in singing a high note, it flies up not into the head but the falsetto register. Now we know that this "crack" is produced by the vocal cords coming into contact and splitting into "nodes," just as a violin string will sound harmonics if lightly touched with the finger (this crack is due to the fact that a high note requires that the vocal cords should be all but parallel to each other and all but touching, but either owing to a want of delicate muscular co-ordination or to their being swelled by a cold or other similar cause, they *touch* in some part of their length and nodes are at once formed). Thus we have two modes of production of the falsetto voice, one of which we know. Is it not likely that we produce the same effect (the falsetto voice) by a similar method in both cases (a splitting into vibrating segments or nodes)? We think, therefore, that it is most probable that the falsetto voice is produced by the vibration of the vocal cords not in their entirety but in nodes, though the mechanism by which this is brought about is unknown to us.

Timbre of voice depends partly on the conformation, partly on the quality of the structures composing the larynx. Garcia also says that the epiglottis plays a very important part, for every time that it lowers itself and nearly closes the orifice of the larynx, the voice gains in brilliancy; and when, on the other hand, it is drawn up, the voice immediately becomes veiled.

Range of voice in man. Garcia gives the following table of the full extent of the human voice:

He says, "Let us here observe, that three registers of voice are generally admitted—chest, falsetto, and head. The first begins lower in a man's voice than in a woman's; *the second extends equally in both voices;* the third reaches higher in the female voice." Part of this statement is remarkable, and would seem to imply some essential difference in the physiology of the voice in both sexes, a difference beyond mere dimensions. I must leave it to musicians to criticise his statement, which does not commend itself to me.

The whole of his paper is worth the careful study of every musician. It is found in "Proceedings of the Royal Society," Vol. VII., No. 13, pp. 399-410.

In speech the pitch seldom varies more than a fifth.

The *nasal tone* is produced by bringing the arches of the palate together, and bodily raising the larynx and also the tongue; thus the air is prevented from passing freely through the nostrils, that part of the "resonance tube" being cut off. Some have stated that the air is prevented by this means from passing freely through the mouth, and passes along the nose, the cavity of the nostrils alone vibrating freely; but this is seen to be incorrect when we remember that the nasal tone cannot be produced when the mouth is closed and all the air is driven through the nostrils, while it is produced when the nostrils are held closed, or when they are obstructed by mucus during a cold. Thus the expression "talking or singing through the nose," is physiologically quite incorrect.

The power of musical intonation depends on the power of accurate adaptation of the muscular parts concerned in the production of the voice to a state known to be capable of producing the desired sound. This state is at first recognised by the effect on the ear, and afterwards directly through the "muscular sensibility" of the muscles concerned. The previous experience has thus been acquired through the ear and also from the muscles, and an "idea" of the sound required precedes the production of the sound. Thus eventually an idea of the sound and of the necessary muscular state are presented simultaneously to the mind.

Let us enlarge somewhat on this. A sound is emitted and appreciated by the ear as having a certain relative number of vibrations, and this experience is stored up as a memory. Secondly, attempts are made to reproduce this sound: when the desired sound is produced, the ear recognises it as being the same as that before produced, by means of the memory: and at the same time the sensorium takes cognisance of the state of the muscles

of the larynx by means of "muscular sensibility," that sense by which we learn the state of our muscles, by which we know accurately the position of our limbs, &c., unassisted by our sight, and which is essential to a proper performance of any muscular action, especially of those beyond the regulating power of sight. Thus we have two memories stored up in intimate connection, viz., the memory of a definite sound and the memory of a definite state of muscles. This process is repeated for each note and fraction of a note, for each possible sound. By practice and frequent repetition of the process we get the phenomena reproduced in an inverted order, for whereas, in the first instance, hearing came first, muscular action with muscular sensibility second, we now have muscular action with muscular sensibility as the first executors or reproducers of a definite memory, continually checked, secondly, by the hearing. After a time this process becomes automatic, and is still more obviously so when a person is singing from notes, when we naturally have an additional factor or association, viz., that of a symbol with a definite musical sound.

Instrumental music can be expressed in precisely similar terms; it is true that at first muscular sensibility has less to do, for the guiding power of the eyes is possible, but this is only occasionally used as an additional sense when the performer becomes proficient. Again some instruments, viz., those in which the notes are already formed (all instruments but the stringed instruments and the trombone), require less guidance from the ear than those in which the production of each note, both in pitch and timbre, depends entirely on the performer. But these are only quantitative differences after all.

Thus we come back to what we said at first that all correct intonation, whether vocal or instrumental, is checked and regulated by two sensibilities, the acoustic and the muscular, in varying proportions. It is plain from what we have previously said, that musical intonation may be imperfect from various causes; of these the most serious is defect in the appreciation of sounds, since this is first in importance as in time,—a "bad ear" is irremediable; but a person may also play or sing out of tune from several other causes. First this may occur in the performance of a difficult passage. In this instance the muscular adaptability is deficient. Again a person may play or sing a single note out of tune from deficient muscular power, either the note is too high or too low or in other ways too difficult of production, or the performer may be tired with previous singing or playing. But when a person habitually plays or sings out of tune, or fails to keep in tune in performing an easy passage, we at once say correctly "he has no musical ear," that is, his sensorium is incapable of appreciating the delicate relations of musical sounds.

It may not be out of place here to venture a few remarks as to the reason why it is much more irritating to those with good musical ears to hear a person sing sharp than to hear him sing flat. One is, of course, as incorrect as the other, but there is something particularly exasperating in hearing sharp singing. First of all it would be interesting to know whether persons possessing good musical ears, without any knowledge of music, would find sharp singing more painful than flat singing; we should imagine that this would not be the case. On analysing our feelings when a person is singing sharp we fancy we detect in them a certain feeling of indignation at the singer doing something *unnecessary*. This is quite correct, he is using unnecessary muscular force, and we have a natural though not purely rational idea that if he took less pains, exerted himself less, he would sing in better tune—we feel he is committing a " presumptuous " musical sin. On the contrary, when a person sings flat, his muscular exertions are inadequate, and we feel a sort of pity mingled with our annoyance, we feel that he is doing his best, but is not strong enough to sing correctly; in both cases, however, it is generally not actual force which is deficient, but the " guiding sensation," the musical ear; but there is this much correctness in our feelings that a person with ever so good an ear may sing flat from sheer weariness, just as he may be too tired to perform any other muscular exercise properly, while there is not the same excuse for singing sharp.

Comparative Anatomy. — No invertebrate animal possesses a larynx. In *Fish* we have only one or two instances of a larynx, and in them it is connected with the entrance of the duct of the air bladder; these fish are otherwise remarkable, being the Polypterus and Lepidosiren. In the latter the glottis is supported by a sort of laryngeal cartilage. Another fish, named Trigla, is capable of emitting sounds.

In *Amphibia* we find a better developed larynx. In those which keep their gills through life it is extremely simple, as is the whole of the trachea and bronchi. The glottis is a simple slit each side, strengthened by a cartilage, which is sometimes subdivided. Below the glottis is a membranous chamber, the laryngeal cavity strengthened by cartilages, and from this chamber the lungs diverge either immediately or after a short trachea.

In the Frogs the larynx is well-developed, and is present in all but two frogs. The vocal cords are stretched transversely; above and below them is a pouch, and sometimes a cartilage between them. The muscles are briefly classified as constrictors or dilators of the glottis, and one stretches the vocal cords. In the Toad the vocal cords are thin elastic membranes, and consist of two pairs. In many frogs we find pouches attached to the larynx or the mouth, and these serve either as resounding sacs or as reservoirs of the wind supply. Since all Amphibia and Reptiles do not respire as we do, but *swallow* the air, this, which is a laborious process, is economised by an elastic sac, in which the air, having passed through the larynx, is retained, and which, in contracting again, by its elasticity drives the air easily back into the lungs; by this means a continuous croaking is produced.

Reptiles.—The Serpents have no vocal cords, and nothing beyond a hissing can be produced by the passage of the air through their simple glottis.

The Lizards have a better-developed larynx. Most have vocal cords, but in many of these they cannot be apposed or stretched.

In Turtles and Tortoises we first find the cartilages divided into cricoid, thyroid, and arytenoid. Some are capable of vocal sounds, some only of a hiss.

The Crocodiles have, again, only two cartilages, a crico-thyroid and two arytenoids; the vocal cords are capable of producing a sort of bellowing tone.

Birds.—Most Birds have *two* larynges, an upper and a lower. The upper larynx is situated as in us, at the top of the wind-pipe. There are several bony and cartilaginous supports, from two to ten in number. One of these represents the thyroid cartilage. The cricoid consists of three bony pieces, the two arytenoids are also bony. With respect to this, we may observe that many more parts are ossified in birds than in other animals. The glottis is simple, and composed of two rigid lips, which do not admit of being stretched, but only approximated. The principal action of the muscles is to close and open this glottis simply, which they can do with great accuracy. The function of this upper larynx is either simply to guard the opening of the windpipe, or at most to modify, and not in the first place to create the voice.

The lower larynx is placed at the bottom of the wind-pipe, where this divides into the two bronchial tubes, and is the true organ of voice. The purpose of its position here is probably to throw the weight which necessarily accompanies a complex apparatus of muscles and cartilages near the centre of gravity, instead of at the end of a long lever like the neck. In the same way the masticating apparatus of birds is not a set of teeth placed at the end of this lever, but a grinding machine, the gizzard, placed at the centre of gravity.

In singing birds the apparatus consists of a double glottis, produced by a bony bar called "pessulus" or "os transversale," which runs across the lower end of the wind-pipe from before backwards, and supports a thin membrane which projects into the calibre of the windpipe, and ends in a free concave edge; it is called the "Membrana Semilunaris."

The muscular apparatus is complex, and in some singing birds consists of five pairs of muscles. In some birds, as the Ostrich and the Vulture, the lower larynx is absent.

In some birds, as the Stork, Crane, Capercailzie and Wild Swan, the windpipe is several times folded on itself, being very long.

The Parrot tribe has a single glottis, with a vibrating membrane on each side, thus resembling ours. The adjacent sides of these are concave, and there are muscles which stretch, approximate or separate these vocal cords. It is perhaps due to this peculiarity, as well as to the fleshy tongue of the Parrots, that they are able to imitate human speech.

Mammals.—The larynx of Mammals in most particulars resembles that of man. In the Kangaroos the vocal cords are feebly developed, and incapable of being stretched. Most Marsupials have little or no voice.

Some Rodents have fairly developed vocal cords, as the Hare and Rabbit. Some, as the Porcupine, have no vocal cords, and it is only at the breeding season that they have any voice, when the male makes a low grunt. The Sloths have no false vocal cords, the Armadilios have no false vocal cords or voice.

In the Whales and Porpoises, as in many of the Marsupials, the upper opening of the windpipe is modified into a conical projection which rises up and is embraced by the muscles of the soft palate, so that a continuous air-tube is formed from the nose to the lungs, on each side of which fluid or solid food can continually pass to the gullet without getting into the wind-pipe. The purpose of this is obvious. In the Whales the large volume of water which they constantly receive into their wide open mouth, from which they extract their food, and which they eject through their blow-hole, is prevented from getting into their air-passages; in the young Marsupial while in the pouch the milk which it is constantly sucking is similarly prevented from going "the wrong way." Marsupials are born, as is well known, very immature, and while in the pouch are continually suckled; they are by this arrange-

ment saved from the necessity of constantly closing their glottis in the act of swallowing, as is the case with other animals. In those aquatic Mammals called the Sirenia (as the Dugong and Manatee, the herbivorous Whales) the glottis is very small, and T shaped, the transverse slit being above the longitudinal slit.

In the Ass the "bray" is produced by alternate inspirations and expirations, both producing sounds, and is assisted by two large air sacs between the vocal cords and the thyroid cartilage.

The Giraffe only has a voice at the breeding season. The male Deer's larynx enlarges greatly at each breeding season and this growth is associated with a large growth of a gland below it called the thyroid gland, the two producing that graceful prominence in the throat which one observes at that time.

The purring of the Cat is produced by the vibrations of the false vocal cords, which are well developed; the true vocal cords are small and have no membranous part.

Many animals have large air sacs in connection with the larynx, either opening into the sacculus laryngis or placed in front between the thyroid cartilage and epiglottis, and opening between the epiglottis and true vocal cords; or opening between the thyroid and cricoid cartilages. In one monkey—the Mycetes or howling monkey—there are a pair of pouches lodged in cavities in the cricoid cartilage, another pair similarly lodged in the thyroid and extending on each side between the thyroid bone and epiglottis, and into a huge sac in the thyroid bone, and another pair between the glottis and arytenoid cartilages, three pairs in all. Most of the Old World monkeys have a sac in the hyoid bone, but smaller than that of the howling monkey.

The Gibbon has a well-developed larynx, and alone of all the apes can sing a complete octave; moreover the quality of its notes is decidedly musical.

In the Ouran-outan the air sacs in the male extend down over the fore-part of the neck and upper part of the chest, being subdivided into several sacs.

Castration in all mammals which possess a definite voice arrests the sudden development which takes place at puberty. Compare the voice of the ox and of the bull.

W. C. Linnæus Martin, in his work, *A general introduction to the Natural History of Mammiferous Animals*, 1841., *p.* 431, says—

"*Hylobates agilis, Sumatra.*—The voice of this gibbon is extraordinary, not only for its power and volume, but for the succession of graduated tones in which its cry is uttered,

In a room, it is overpowering and deafening: it consists of a repetition of the syllables oo-ah, oo-ah, at first distinctly repeated, and ascending in the scale, but at last ending in a shake, consisting of a quick vibratory series of notes, during which the whole of the animal's frame quivers with the effort to produce them; after this, she appears to be greatly excited, and violently shakes the netting or branch to which she may be clinging; which action being finished she again traverses her cage, uttering the preliminary syllables oo-ah, oo-ah, till the shake again concludes the series. It is principally in the morning that the animal thus exerts this modulated cry, which is, probably, its natural call to its mate, and which, from its strength, is well calculated for resounding through the vast forests. The following observations on the voice of the animal were obligingly presented to the author by Mr. Waterhouse:—

" 'I should endeavour to give an idea of the whooping of the gibbon (as far as the music is concerned, but not as regards the quality of sound), by comparing it to the tuning of a harp; first beginning with an E string, and repeating it at short intervals; then being altogether silent for a little time, and then beginning again; next, two strings, as it were, are struck, E and E♯ (or F♮): the second string is then screwed up, by half-notes, until it reaches the octave; the E and F natural, E and F sharp, E and G natural, &c., being struck nearly together. It must be observed that before the upper note arrives at the octave, the animal amuses herself by occasionally descending a few semitones, then ascending again, and so on. But when the octave is once gained, and has been sounded a few times, we may imagine the upper string to be very rapidly let down by semitones; the lower note remaining the same as at first, and the two strings being always struck together. [*Note*: It appears, all through this rapid chromatic passage, as if the animal emitted two notes at a time, as in the music; but this is the effect of the rapid transition from the lower note to the upper.] The rapidity of the descending passage is equal to that of an extremely brilliant shake. The animal then remains quiet for a short time; after which follow two barks, each composed of the low and high E, sounded nearly together.

" 'It appeared to me that, in ascending and descending the scale, the intervals were always exactly half-tones; and I am sure that the highest note was the exact octave to the lowest. In this passage the lips were engaged, and rapidly vibrated during its execution.

" 'The quality of the notes is very musical; and I do not doubt that a good violinist would be able to give a correct idea of the gibbon's composition, excepting as regards it loudness. The gibbon's voice is certainly much more powerful than that of any singer I ever heard.

" 'One more fact I noticed, viz.: That the gibbon is usually a long time before she comes to the rapidly-descending passage; but when she has given it once she soon runs through the preliminary part of her composition, and again comes to the descending passage.'

To this we have only to add that the quality is like that of a very powerful male alto, and that the sounds are produced, alternately by inspiration and expiration—the high notes by the former. This alternation, of course, makes it possible for the animal to sing continuously what would otherwise be an impossible passage, exceeding any possible capacity of lungs.

Laryngoscope. *History of the Invention*—Taken principally from Dr. Morell Mackenzie's works.—The use of mirrors for examining the teeth is of exceedingly ancient date. Such mirrors were used by dentists in the Augustan age, and the tubular instrument for examining the various orifices of the body, called a speculum, is also a very old invention; one was found at Pompeii. The use of a mirror is obviously to reflect light into a dark cavity; the use of a speculum is to render patent a tube which is, under ordinary circumstances, collapsed, and to allow the entrance of light and, at the same time, unimpeded vision. Both these principles have been applied variously in the gradual development of the laryngoscope.

In 1743, M. Levret, a French accoucheur, invented a mirror as a means of illuminating the nostrils, throat, ears, &c., for the removal of growths from those parts, but he considered it only an accessory of his method of ligaturing these growths, and he did not value it as a means of diagnosing diseases of the larynx.

In 1804, Dr. Bozzini, of Frankfort-on-Main, invented an apparatus for examining the various orifices of the body. It consisted of a lantern and a number of specula; and the speculum intended for examining the throat was curved at a right angle and provided with a mirror in the angle. The speculum was divided by a vertical partition into two passages, one to convey the light to the larynx, another to convey the image from it. This division of the tube was, of course, quite unnecessary; but Bozzini appreciated the things necessary for a laryngoscopic examination, though he over-stated them. This invention was decried by the medical profession, while the public had an almost superstitious regard for it, imagining that it would render possible a direct examination not only of the orifices but also of the cavities of the body. This instrument was soon forgotten.

In 1825, M. Cagniard de Latour tried to examine the Larynx, with a small mirror in the Pharynx and another mirror to reflect the light on to the first, but failed.

In 1827, Dr. Senn made a similar unsuccessful attempt, but without trying any means of illumination.

In 1829, Dr. Benjamin Guy Babington invented an instrument closely resembling the present Laryngoscope. A small mirror on a stem at an angle of about 120° with the stem, was introduced into the Pharynx; to the stem was fastened a spatula (a sort of flat spoon) which depressed the tongue; this spatula he afterwards abandoned. A hand-mirror was used to throw light on to the Pharyngeal mirror. This instrument he called a "Glottiscope."

In 1832, Selligue, a mechanic in Paris who was himself suffering from disease of the Larynx, invented for his own case an apparatus like that of Bozzini, except that instead of employing one tube divided by a partition, he used two tubes. With this Dr. Bennati of Paris professed to be able to see the vocal cords.

In 1838, M. Baumês exhibited a mirror for examining the Larynx and posterior nares.

In 1840, Liston used a mirror on a stem for examining the throat, but apparently never thought of seeing as far as the vocal cords. He preferred the sense of touch to that of sight.

In 1844, Dr. Warden of Edinburgh, who had used a prism for seeing the Tympanum, thought of using one for seeing the Larynx. He used a powerful Argand lamp for illumination, with a second prism attached.

In 1844, also, Mr. Avery of London, tried to use a speculum and reflector for the same purpose; and besides, invented a circular mirror worn on the forehead and perforated in the centre; the mirror reflected the light into the mouth, and the observer looked at the same time through its central hole. The defects of this were that the small Pharyngeal mirror was in a speculum, instead of at the

end of a stem, and that a lamp (like Bozzini's) was attached to the mirror on the forehead, instead of being placed in any convenient position behind or at the side of the patient.

In 1854, M. Manuel Garcia, a singing-master still well known, thought of employing mirrors for studying the interior of the Larynx during singing. He made his observations on himself and succeeded admirably. He used a small mirror on a long stem suitably bent, and introduced this into the Pharynx. He directed the person experimented on to turn to the sun, so that the rays might be reflected into the Larynx, but adds that if the observer experiments on himself he should reflect the rays of the sun into his Pharynx with a second mirror, and, therefore, stand with his back to the sun. This second mirror served also for the person experimenting on himself to see the image of his own Larynx. Little notice was taken of Garcia's observations.

In 1857, Dr. Türck, of Vienna, who had read Garcia's paper, tried to use his mirror for clinical purposes. He used only one mirror, and employed no artificial light or second mirror for illumination. He did not succeed, and gave up his attempts after a few months.

Later, in 1857, Professor Czermak, of Pesth, borrowed from Dr. Türck the mirrors which he had discarded, and overcame all difficulties. He introduced artificial light, and the large circular perforated mirror worn on the forehead. He was the first to render the laryngoscope a practically useful instrument. He was favoured by nature for examining his own Larynx, since his Pharynx and Larynx were very large, his tonsils and uvula very small. His demonstrations of his own larynx convinced the world of the usefulness of the laryngoscope. Since this time no real improvement has been made, though the subject has been worked continually.

Fig. 1.

THE LARYNGOSCOPE

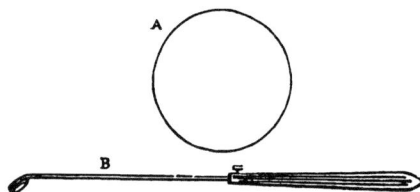

a Shape of mirror, b mirror and holder in profile much diminished in size.

The present apparatus consists of a mirror on a stem, bent at a suitable angle (about 120°), which is placed against the back of the pharynx; of a circular mirror, either flat or slightly concave, perforated at the centre, which is worn on the observer's forehead in some way so that his eye comes opposite the central hole, or it may be fixed to the illuminating lamp.

Fig. 2.

LAMP WITH CONVEX LENS FOR LIGHTING.

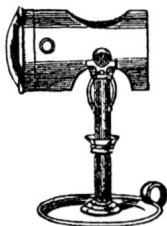

The third necessary part of the apparatus is a lamp, which may or may not be furnished with a double convex lens for concentrating the rays of light. The sunlight on a bright day may be used instead of a lamp. It is possible by casting a strong light on the neck from outside to illuminate the interior of the larynx, so that in this case the larynx is lighted *through* its walls.

The principles employed in making a laryngoscopic examination are the following; Dr. Morell Mackenzie thus well explains them :—

Fig. 3.

(TO ILLUSTRÁTE EQUALITY OF ANGLES OF INCIDENCE AND REFLECTION.)

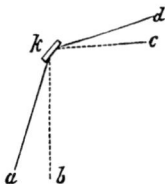

k. Mirror in profile, *ak.* is reflected as *kd., bk.* as *kc.,* and *vice versa.*

"When rays of light fall on a plane surface, the angle of reflection is equal to the angle of incidence. A small mirror is placed at the back of the throat, at such an inclination that luminous rays falling on it are projected into the cavity of the larynx; at the same time the image of the interior of the larynx (lighted up by the luminous rays) is formed on the mirror, and seen by the observer. The mirror is held obliquely, so that it forms an angle of rather more than 45° with the horizon. The plane of the laryngeal aperture (bounded by the epiglottis, the ary-epiglottidean folds, and the arytenoid cartilages) is also oblique, the epiglottis being higher than the apex of the arytenoid cartilages.

Fig. 4.

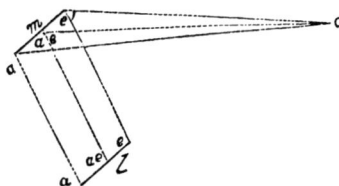

"The above diagram shows the position of the different parts, and explains their reflection. Let *m* represent the plane of the laryngeal mirror, *l* the plane of the upper opening of the larynx, and *o* the observer. In the plane of the larynx, *a* represents the arytenoid cartilages, *ae* the ary-epiglottidean folds, and *e* the epiglottis ; the rays from these parts impinge on the mirror, at *á*, *aé*, and *é*, and are thence reflected to the observer at *o*. Thus the epiglottis, which is really the highest in the throat, appears at the upper part of the mirror, the ary-epiglottidean folds appear rather lower and at each side of the mirror, while at the lowest part of the mirror are the arytenoid cartilages. These remarks apply to the vertical reflection. The only in-

Fig. 5.

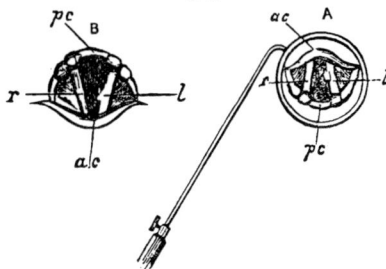

version which takes place in the formation of the image is in the antero-posterior direction ; the part which in reality is nearest to the observer, the anterior commissure of the vocal cords (ac. in B. fig. 5) becomes furthest in the image (ac. in A. fig. 5), and the posterior or inter-arytenoid commissure (pc. in B. fig. 5), which in reality is farthest from the observer, becomes nearest in the image (pc. in A. fig. 5). The symmetrical character of the image which makes it impossible to judge of right and left, and the antero-posterior inversion which actually takes place, often leads people to form erroneous opinions concerning the two sides of the larynx. The lateral relation of parts in the image must now be considered. The mirror being placed above and behind the laryngeal aperture, the rays of light proceeding from the larynx pass directly upwards and backwards, and the patient's right vocal cord is seen on the left side of the mirror, and the left vocal cord on the right side of the mirror (just as the patient's right hand is opposite the observer's left, and his left hand opposite the observer's right)."

Fig. 6.

A LARYNGOSCOPIC SITTING.

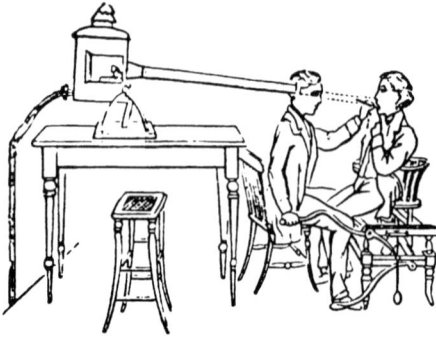

In making a laryngoscopic examination, "the patient should sit upright facing the observer, with his head inclined very slightly backwards. The observer's eyes should be about one foot distant from the patient's mouth; and a lamp burning with a strong clear light should be placed on a table at the side of the patient, the flame of the lamp being on a level with the patient's eyes. The observer now puts on the reflector, fixed generally on the forehead, and tries to throw a disk of light on to the fauces, so that the centre of the disk corresponds with the base of the uvula. He then passes the laryngeal mirror to the back of the throat, so that the posterior surface rests on the uvula, which should be pushed rather upwards and backwards towards the posterior nares. In this position the light is thrown from the mirror into the larynx, while the image of the larynx is observed on the mirror."

Auto - Laryngoscopy. The practice of Laryngoscopy in self-observation requires a second mirror to reflect the image from the laryngoscope to the observer. An ordinary toilet glass does very well.

Lateral Vibrations. [Acoustics, § 15.]

Laud (*Sp.*) Lute.

Laudi spirituali (*It.*) [Oratorio.]

Lauds. [Horæ canonicæ.]

Lauf (*Ger.*) (1) The peg-box in guitars or violins. (2) A run or division in singing or playing. A roulade.

Lauftanz (*Ger.*) *Lit.*, a running dance, a *coranto*.

Laut (*Ger.*) Loud, *forte*.

Laute (*Ger.*) [Lute.]

Lautenist (*Ger.*) A performer upon the lute.

Lavolta (*It.*) An old Italian dance, much practised in the days of Queen Elizabeth; many of the old dramatists allude to the dance, as Massinger in his play, "The Great Duke of Florence:"

" dance
A light lavolta with her."

It seems to have been the precursor of the modern waltz, as it is thus described in a poem by Sir John Davies, called "Orchestra," 1622:

" Yet there is one the most delightful kind
A lofty jumping or a leaping round,
Where arm in arm two dancers are entwined,
And whirl themselves with strict embracements bound,
And still their feet an anapæst do sound,
An anapæst in all their music's song,
Whose first two feet are short, the third is long."

Lay. A song (*Ger. Lied.*) (*Fr. lai.*) A ballad.

Lay vicars. *Lay clerks. Clerk vicars. Vicars choral. Secular clerks. Chanters. Songmen. Secular vicars. Secundarii.* The officers of a cathedral whose duty it is to sing that portion of the music of the services which can be performed by laymen or men in minor orders. In some of the old cathedrals they formed a corporation, often jointly with the priest vicars. In many cathedrals the vicars choral were formerly in priest's orders. With certain exceptions, in the new cathedrals lay vicars are not in holy orders and are merely stipendiary singers.

Lead. A point or short passage which has to be given out by one particular part. When the word is used as a direction, it calls attention to the importance of that point.

Leader. The name of the principal first violinist in an orchestra; of the chief clarinet-tist in a military band; and of the chief cornet-player in a brass band. Before the introduction of a separate conductor, the leader of an orchestra was its director, and gave the *tempo* with his fiddle-bow, a custom which has led to the use of a fiddle-bow as a bâton in France. [Conductor.]

Leading note. *Note sensible* (*Fr.*) *Characteristischer Ton* (*Ger.*) *Leit-ton* (*Ger.*) *Nota characteristica* (*Lat.*) *Subsemitonium modi* (*Lat.*) *Subtonic.* The seventh degree of the ascending major scale. It is called *leading* because of its tendency to rise or lead up to the tonic. It is called sensitive and characteristic, because it forms the essential difference between the modern scale and ancient modes. The Iastian or Ionic mode was the only church scale having a leading note. In consequence of the leading note forming part of the upper of the two tetrachords of which the modern scale is formed, that tetrachord is by some called *characteristic*.

Lebhaft (*Ger.*) Lively, *vivace* (*It.*)

Leçon (*Fr.*) A piece of music intended to develope the taste, skill and power of the performer. A study.

Ledger lines. [Leger lines.]

Legabile, legando (*It.*) Tied, connected, smoothly.

Legatissimo (*It.*) Exceedingly smooth, close, and connected.

Legato (*It.*) Bound, close, connected. A piece of music so marked is intended to be sung or played in an even, smooth, and gliding manner. It is opposed to *staccato*.

Legatura (*It.*) A bind, brace, or tie. *Accolade* (*Fr.*) *Bindungs-zeichen* (*Ger.*)

Leger or **ledger** lines. *Lit.*, light lines, *léger* (*Fr.*) Short lines drawn above or below the ordinary stave at the relative distances at which the whole lines would be placed.

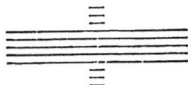

On and between these lines, notes belonging to passages beyond the extent of the stave are placed. The use of leger lines is comparatively modern in musical notation, for it was anciently supposed that the stave, with a certain clef prefixed, was sufficient for the compass of the voice or instrument using such clef. When the compass was extended, the clef was shifted so that the music might be still expressed within the limits of a stave. To avoid the frequent shifting of clefs, Frescobaldi, in his "Toccate d'Intavolatura di Cimbalo et Organo," Rome, 1637, employs two staves, comprising fourteen lines, as may be seen in the following fac-simile of the opening of the composition quoted in the article "Galliard."

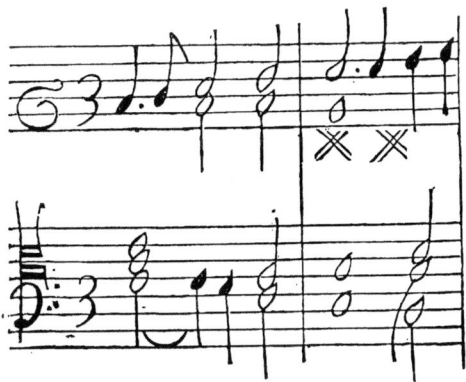

The name *ledger* is also given to account-books because of the light lines drawn in the margin of the pages.

Légèrement (*Fr.*) **Leggieramente** (*It.*) Lightly, easily, gracefully, rapidly.

Légèreté (*Fr.*) **Leggerezza** (*It.*) Lightness, rapidity.

Leggiadramente (*It.*) Beautifully, delightfully, charmingly.

Leggiadro (*It.*) Handsome, beautiful.

Leggiarezza, con (*It.*) With much lightness.

Leggiere (*It.*) Very lightly, rapidly.

Leggieramente (*It.*) Easily, lightly, swiftly.

Leggiero (*It.*) Light, easy, swift.

Leggierucolo (*It.*) Rather easily and lightly.

Legno, col (*It.*) With the wood. A direction to strike the strings of violins with the back of the bow.

Leicht (*Ger.*) Easy, light.

Leit-akkord (*Ger.*) A guiding chord. A chord which suggests an immediate resolution into another, as the chord of the dominant seventh, &c.

Leiter (*Ger.*) *Scala* (*It.*) *Lit.*, a ladder. The scale.

Leitereigene Akkorde (*Ger.*) Chords proper to the scale, that is, chords made up of the notes of any particular diatonic scale, as for instance, the triads on consecutive notes which are major on the fourth and fifth degrees, minor on the second, third, and sixth, and imperfect on the seventh. Also, chords of the seventh, and of the ninth similarly constructed on successive notes of the scale.

Leiterfremd (*Ger.*) Notes foreign to the scale.

Leno (*It.*) Faint, weak, dull, flexible, pliant.

Lent (*Fr.*) Slow, *lento*.

Lentamente (*It.*) Slowly.

Lentando (*It.*) Becoming slower by degrees; slackening the time.

Lentement (*Fr.*) Slowly.

Lento (*It.*) Slow.

Lenteur, avec (*Fr.*) **Lentezza, con** (*It.*) Slowly.

Lesser. Minor, as: *with the lesser third*, in the minor key; *lesser sixth*, a minor sixth.

Lesson. An assigned task, an exercise or tune for the voice or an instrument. The word formerly was applied to exercises (for the harpsichord or other instruments) of the character now known as Suites or Sonatas.

Lesto (*It.*) Light, lively, cheerful, gay.

License. Permission to break one of the rules or supposed rules of the art of music.

When the gradual growth of music in the church, and among wandering musicians, had proved that the loss of the art as practised by the Greeks was only temporary, attention seems to have been much more directed to the scientific side of music than to the artistic. No doubt the progress of music was considerably retarded by this, but the germ of harmony as found in crude diaphony was not to be stifled, and descant, counterpoint, canon, and fugue, came bit by bit into existence. But writers on music still continued to long for a perfect exactitude in the construction of music which should make mechanical skill of primary importance, and the inventive faculty of secondary value. At each stage, therefore, in its development, strong efforts were made by learned professors to build it up on a series of irrefragable laws, and fence it round with sundry warnings to the ignorant or unbelieving. The true artistic spirit can never submit to such restraint, and must ever be searching for new forms of the beautiful. Hence, these laws were from time to time broken, and as professors could but allow that the result was in many cases good, they satisfied their consciences by calling these breakings of the law " licenses," or in other words, they gave *dispensations*.

Any student fairly conversant with the history of music must have been convinced of this fact by the strongest evidence.

The rules of descant were framed as if any further growth of the art were not only impossible, but undesirable if conceivably possible. So too are the rules of counterpoint as first laid down.

In treatises of the fourteenth and fifteenth centuries, the novelties introduced by the then " moderni " are attacked with all the asperity and prejudice which some are directing at the present day against the so-called " music of the future."

A well-known living writer on harmony recommends the student to avoid certain counterpoints, " *although they have the sanction of great classical composers.*" The necessity of granting dispensations is thus made evident, for it is here admitted that *great classical composers* have practically repealed certain rules, yet, say the rule-makers, " the laws are true, so we will say they are broken *by license*." Examples of this obstructive tendency in most writers on musical subjects might be multiplied to any extent, but it will only be necessary to refer shortly to one more case. " Discords must be prepared " was a law which was enforced until public opinion asserted that many could be delightfully used without preparation. Then, and not till then, students were allowed to use certain dominant discords without preparation *by license*. This dispensation is happily not enforced in later treatises, and dominant discords "may be used without preparation." One author, more honest, though less logical, than his contemporaries, has said that fundamental discords (a name given for some unexplained cause to dominant discords) are called fundamental, " *because* they can be used without preparation."

Of course art *has* its laws, and every composer and painter writes and paints under the direction of innumerable rules gathered by him from broad generalization and experience. He feels their force and obeys them, but

whether they can ever be written down and codified is a question of great doubt. Even if music had now reached its climax of perfection, no power could succeed in converting it into an exact science, and rules should be sparingly made where "license" will certainly be craved in order to disregard them. Nor can it be said that there is any moral fault in breaking rules, for music is unlike morality, inasmuch as the artist should first do what his imagination prompts, and afterwards enquire whether it was right or wrong, and moreover, speaking generally, the end will justify the means. On the whole, the history of musical " license" is not very creditable to those to whom has been intrusted from time to time the training of enthusiastic musical youth; and even in these very days it would be well if critics and teachers could be made to understand that many innovations are legitimate growths, and not faults, pardonable only " by license."

Licensing (*musical and dramatic*). The laws relating to the licensing of musical and dramatic performances are so closely connected that it will be convenient to consider them in a single article. In early times there were no such laws, but in the time of Queen Elizabeth players were declared by statute to be rogues and vagabonds, unless they were acting as the servants of some baron or person of higher degree. The licensing laws, however, properly so called, take their origin from the revival of theatrical entertainments after the Restoration. At that period, the irregularities of the stage became so great, and continued, notwithstanding the efforts of the Lord Chamberlain and his subordinate officer, the Master of the Revels, so uncontrollable that it was at length thought expedient to include *all* common players of interludes in the Vagrant Act (12 Anne, stat. 2, c. 24). The evil, however, still prevailed, and was heightened by an attempt to enforce the law against a player who was a housekeeper. In 1735, the increased number of theatres (*six* in all!) in which the actors played without any legal authority, and the loose and scandalous nature of the performances, induced Sir John Barnard to bring in a bill " to restrain the number of houses for playing of interludes, for the better regulating of common players." But a clause being proposed to enlarge, or at least to confirm the power of the Lord Chamberlain in licensing plays, and it being understood that the Act could not pass without such addition, Sir John Barnard, who disapproved of the Lord Chamberlain's jurisdiction, abandoned the bill. Two years afterwards Sir Robert Walpole introduced and carried the statute 10 Geo. II., c. 28, to explain and amend the statute of Anne, imposing penalties for acting without patent from the king or licence from the Lord Chamberlain, requiring all new plays, &c., to be submitted to the Lord Chamberlain, and empowering him to forbid the performance of any dramatic entertainment. The fifth section, prohibiting the granting of a patent or licence to act elsewhere than in Westminster or where the king shall be resident, is said to have been inserted at the instigation of Sir John Barnard. It has been held that "tumbling" is not an entertainment of the stage within the meaning of this statute (see the case of R. v. Handy, 6, *Term Reports*, 286). The statute 28 Geo. III., c. 30, enables magistrates in sessions to license theatrical performances in places where they could not be authorized by the previous enactment. It was held, however, that a conviction under that statute for carrying on an unlicensed opera house, it was held that he could not recover money paid at the request of the defendant for carrying on such unlicensed house (see De Begnis v. Armistead, 10 *Bingham*, 107.)

By the Theatre Act, 1843 (6 & 7 Vict., c. 67) it is provided that all theatres for the public performance of stage plays must be licensed by justices, except in London, Westminster, Finsbury, Marylebone, the Tower Hamlets and Southwark, and such places as the Sovereign is in the habit of occasionally residing in. In those places the authority of the Lord Chamberlain is preserved. These licences are granted in special session of the justices, of which session seven days' notice must be given by their clerk. They must be under the hands and seals of four or more justices. The university towns of Oxford and Cambridge are the subject of special exceptions in favour of the authority of their respective chancellors or vice-chancellors. Performing stage-plays in unlicensed places subjects the offender to a penalty of not more than ten pounds per diem during the continuance of the offence. New plays, and additions to old ones, must be submitted for the approval of the Lord Chamberlain, and the maximum penalty for the performance of plays before they have been allowed, or that have been disallowed, is fifty pounds, the offender's licence also becoming void. The word *stage-play* includes every "tragedy, comedy, farce, opera, burletta, interlude, melodrama, pantomime or other entertainment of the stage, or any part thereof." It has been held, in the case of Thorne v. Colson

(3 *Law Times Reports*, New Series, 697), that a dramatic performance, which was in fact a duologue, was a stage-play within the meaning of this statute. A curious case was heard in the year 1865 (Day v. Simpson, 34 *Law Journal Reports, Magistrates' Cases*) in which it was proved that at a music hall, licensed for music and dancing, but not licensed as a theatre, a stage was erected with lights and other accessories, a performance was presented sustained by living persons with a dialogue between them and a regular plot, which was distinguished only from an ordinary stage-play by all the actors except two (the dialogue between whom was wholly subordinate to the plot of the piece) being not bodily on the stage, but represented merely by a reflection of their bodies on a mirror at the back of the stage. This ingenious contrivance was held to be a violation of the statute. It seems, that whether a certain performance be or be not a stage-play within the meaning of the act is a question of fact and not of law; and that a ballet out of which any regular story could be constructed would probably be held to be a stage-play requiring a licence. This point was argued in the Alhambra case (see Wigan v. Strange, 35 *Law Journal Reports, Magistrates' Cases*, 31), to which, and to the authorities cited therein, we must refer our readers for further information on this part of the subject.

The present law with reference to licences for music, dancing, or other public entertainment of the like kind is to be found in the statute 25 Geo. II., c. 36 (made perpetual by 28 Geo. II., c. 19). That act provided that all such places of entertainment, not licensed, were to be considered as disorderly houses, and persons keeping the same are liable to a penalty of £100, to such person as will sue, for the same within the space of six calendar months after the commission of the offence. Various other stringent provisions are made in the Act, but nothing therein contained applies to "such performances and public entertainments as are, or shall be, lawfully exercised or carried on under or by virtue of letters patent, a licence of the crown, or the licence of the Lord Chamberlain." A room in which musical performances are regularly exhibited, though it is not used solely for that purpose, is within this statute, and requires a licence (see the case of Bellis v. Beale, 2 *Espinasse's Reports*, 592); but a room kept by a dancing master for the instruction of his scholars and subscribers, and to which persons are not indiscriminately admitted is not (see Bellis v. Burghall, *ib.* p. 722). It seems to be doubtful whether the case is within the statute, where the musical entertainment is only the secondary object for which the place is open to the public, as where a supper room is so open and no charge made for admission (see Hale v. Green, 9 *Exchequer Reports*, 247).

From the above *resumé* the reader will be able to gain an outline of the law of dramatic and musical licensing. The statutes and decisions, however, above cited, should be consulted with care.

We conclude with the subject of *street music*, or the law regulating itinerant performers in the public thoroughfares of the metropolis. By § 1 of statute 27 & 28 Vict., c. 55, a previous enactment on the subject (§ 57 of 2 & 3 Vict., c. 47) is repealed, and in lieu thereof it is enacted that any householder within the metropolitan police district, personally or by his servant, or by any police constable, may require any street-musician or street-singer to depart from the neighbourhood of the house of such householder, on account of the illness, or on account of the interruption of the ordinary occupations or pursuits of any inmate of such house, or for other reasonable or sufficient cause. And every person who shall sound or play upon any musical instrument, or shall sing in any thoroughfare or public place near any such house after being so required to depart, shall be liable to a penalty of not more than forty shillings, or, in the discretion of the magistrate before whom he shall be convicted, may be imprisoned for any time not more than three days. And it is lawful for any metropolitan police constable to take into custody without warrant any person so offending. The offender must, however, be given into custody by the person making the charge, and the latter must accompany the prisoner to the station-house and there sign the charge-sheet kept for that purpose. Whenever any person charged with such an offence shall be brought to any station-house during the time when the police-court is shut, the constable in charge of the station-house may require the person making the charge to enter into a recognisance to appear to prosecute, and upon the refusal of such person to do so, the constable in charge may discharge the party from custody.

Lié (*Fr.*) Tied, bound.

Lieblich (*Ger.*) Lovely, sweet-toned, as *Lieblich gedackt*, lovely stopped diapason.

Lied (*Ger.*) The name for a composition of a simple character, which is complete in itself, a song. There are several kinds, but the chief are classed under the following heads. (1.) Sacred songs or chorales, secular songs, comprising national, people's songs (*Volkslieder*), drinking songs, and humorous songs. The French *chanson*, the English songs with their several peculiarities are described under their respec-

tive headings: it remains therefore, to speak of the German lied, the sacred lied or chorale being the earliest and most ancient form. Its music was founded upon the ecclesiastical modes and remained unchanged until the days of the Minnesingers, whose influence continued for a period of 400 years; though as a guild the Meistersingers existed so recently as the year 1839, yet the period of their power was from 1100 until 1500. The alterations and inventions of this body gave rise to the *Volkslieder*, a series of melodies of great beauty, rude in form and of a simplicity that vanished upon the application of contrapuntal treatment; thus, as the science of music became cultivated the *Volkslieder* began to fade and die, and to give rise to the " volksthümliche Lied," a sort of compromise between the volkslied proper and the " kunst lied," in which the spontaniety of the one was enriched with the scientific decoration of the other.

Liedertafel (*Ger.*) *Lit.*, song-table. A society meeting for the practice of part-songs for men's voices.

Ligaturæ (*Lat.*) Ligatures. An old system of connecting notes (notulæ) for purposes of singing. Notulæ, says Franchinus (lib. i., cap. ii.) are of three kinds, simplex, composita, mediocris. A " Notula simplex " is one which is not joined to another, and is shaped thus, ■, or with a stem (virgula) thus, ■. A " Notula composita " is one that is attached to another, and is of two kinds. If the ligature ascends, that is, if the second note is higher than the first, the first note has no stem, *e.g.* :

but if the ligature descends, the first note has a stem on its left hand side, *e.g.* :

A " notula mediocris " has the form of neither of the preceding, but appears like ordinary " mensurable " descending semibreves, of which there are not less than two in succession, *e.g.* :

The final notula of a ligature may be written in three ways, 1st, lower than the penultimate, thus :

2. Immediately over the penultimate, with a foursided body, thus :

3. Or over the penultimate, on the right

side, with a foursided body and a stem on the right side, thus :

It is wrong to write the ultimate of a ligature thus ꜩ , but two notes only may be written thus ; but an ascending oblique body may not be written upwards , at such a thing "usus perhorrescit."

To the middle notes of a ligature no special form is attached, they are either foursided, or oblique. Only one syllable is to be sung to all the notes included in one ligature.

Ligne (*Fr.*) A line.

Ligneum Psalterium (*Lat.*) A series of pieces of wood of graduated lengths, so arranged as to produce the various notes of a scale. These pieces are supported on two strings, running the length of the instrument, which is sometimes made in the shape of a boat. The tone is produced by striking. The instrument is very ancient and universal, modifications of its form being found in every country. It is also called Xylophone (*Gk.* wood-sound), *Strohfidel, Gigelira,* wooden-laughter, &c.

Lilt. An Irish dance accompanied with singing.

> "While the chanter with his merry pipes
> Struck up a lilt so gaily O."

[Ballad.]

Limma (*Gk.*) [Greek Music.]

Linea (*Lat.*) *Linie* (*Ger.*) A line.

Linien-system (*Ger.*) The stave of five lines.

Linke Hand (*Ger.*) Left hand

Lip, to. To adjust the lips so as to produce the proper tone of wind-instruments played by the mouth.

Lipping. [To lip.]

Lira (*It.*) A lyre. This word was formerly applied to many instruments of the viol class or others having a resonance-box, as, *lira da braccio,* a sort of large tenor-violin; *lira da gamba,* or *perfetta,* a sort of violoncello; *lira rustica* or *tedesca,* or *mendicorum,* a hurdy-gurdy (*Bauern-leyer*). *Lira barberina* was a bowed instrument, invented by John Baptist Doni, so named in honour of his patron, Cardinal Barberini.

Lire (*Fr.*) A lyre or harp.

Liressa (*It.*) An inferior lyre or harp.

Liscio (*It.*) Polished, smooth.

L'istesso (*It.*) The same, as *l'istesso movimento,* the same movement; *l'istesso tempo,* the same time.

Litany, λιτανεία (*Gk.*) A prayer, rogation, or supplication; in particular, that early form of prayer in which a minister recites a petition, and the people answer "Lord, have mercy." In the fourth century litanies were sung in solemn processions by the Eastern Church, but they were not employed by the Western Church till about a century later.

Until the time of Mamertus they were only used on special occasions, but he, at the close of the fifth century caused them to be recited on fixed days. *Kyrie eleison, Christe eleison, Kyrie eleison,* is called the Lesser Litany.

Lituus (*Lat.*) A crooked trumpet, used chiefly for giving military signals.

Liuto (*It.*) A lute.

Lo. (1) Abbreviation for *Loco.* (2) One of the syllables used in Bocedization.

Lobgesang (*Ger.*) A hymn of praise.

Loco (*It.*) In its proper place. A direction to return to the proper pitch after having played an octave higher:

Locrian (*Gk.*) A name sometimes applied to the Hypodorian mode.

Logeum (*Lat.*) λογεῖον (*Gk.*) [Pulpitum.]

Long. An ancient musical character equal to two breves.

Long Drum. [Drum.]

Longitudinal vibrations. [Acoustics, § 14.]

Lontano (*It.*) Far distant. *Tromba lontano,* a trumpet played in the distance.

Lo stesso tempo (*It.*) At the same pace.

Loure or **Louvre** (*Fr.*) A dance adapted to an air called "*L'aimable vainqueur*," said to have been a favourite of Louis XIV. Some authors, however, consider it to have been a kind of jig, or a waltz. The name is perhaps, derived from the word *lourer*, to bind notes together, to slide.

Lugubre (*Fr.*) Dismal, doleful, lugubrious.

Lu-lu (*Chinese*). The Chinese official collection of treatises on the art of music.

Lunga pausa (*It.*) A long pause.

Luogo (*It.*) [Loco.]

Lures. Ancient Scandinavian trumpets. Some specimens discovered in Denmark would, if straightened, have been six feet in length; in their curved form they were three and a-half feet long. Notwithstanding their great antiquity, they were considerably ornamented and in sufficiently good preservation to give out musical sounds.

Lusingando (*It.*)
Lusingante (*It.*) } Caressingly, in a
Lusinghevole (*It.*) } coaxing manner.
Lusinghevolmente (*It.*)

Lusinghiere (*It.*) } Caressing, coaxing.
Lusinghiero (*It.*) }

Lute. *Luth* (*Fr.*) *Laute* (*Ger.*) *Liuto* (*It.*) *Laud* (*Sp.*) An instrument of the Guitar family, formerly very popular in Europe. It was used for accompaniments and the performance of solos, duets, &c. It had five to six pairs of strings, each pair tuned in unisons or octaves. The *accordatura* was as follows :

The lower G was omitted on the five-stringed, and both G's on the four-stringed Lute.

The German lutenists called the six strings,

counting from the lowest, *Gross-brummer*, *Mittel-brummer*, *Klein-brummer*, *Grossangsaite*. *Kleinsang-saite*, and *Quintsangsaite*, or the five strings without the lower G, *Prime*, *Secund*, *Terz*, *Quart*, and *Quint*. In France, Italy, and Flanders, they were similarly named according to the language of the land, the upper string, upon which the melody was usually made being called *Soprano*, *il Canto*, *Chanterelle*, as well as *Quint*. In England the lowest string was called the *Bass*, the next the *Tenor*, the next the *Counter tenor*, the next the *Great mean*, the next the *Small mean*, and the highest the *Treble*. Gut strings were generally used, for covered strings were not known when the Lute was in common use. Thomas Mace ("Musicks Monument," 1676) describes the strings of his time in these words: "Be careful to get good strings which should be of three sorts, viz., minikins, Venice catlins, and Lyons (for basses).

Music for the Lute was written in Tablature *q.v.*

The word has been variously derived, from the Latin *ludere*, to play, from the Greek ἁλιευτικός, from the lyre which was a dessicated tortoise, and from the Saxon *hlud* or *lud*, sonorous, but it is most probably from the Arabic *el'ood*, as the instruments came into Europe from the Moors through the Spaniards, who still call it *laud*.

LUTE.

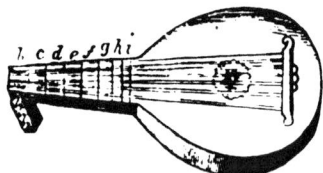

The several frets of the lute were distinguished by the letters of the alphabet, "one for each fret as many as there may be." The frets divided the strings into semitones.

The Orpharion Lute had a larger number of strings than the common lute, and its strings were of wire, instead of gut.

ORPHARION LUTE.

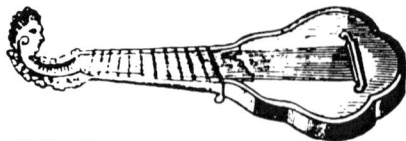

Luth (*Fr.*) A lute.

Luttuosamente (*It.*)} Mournfully, sadly.
Luttuoso (*It.*)

Lutenist. A performer upon the lute. The office of lutenist still exists in the Chapel Royal, but it has been a sinecure since the disuse of the instrument. The revival of the office was made in favour of Dr. Nares, in 1780.

Lychanos (*Gk.*) [Greek music.]

Lydian mode. [Greek Music.]

Lyon catlins. Thick spun strings for the basses of lutes or viols. [Lute.]

Lyra viol. An obsolete instrument, in form like the ordinary viol, having six strings and seven frets.

Lyra mendicorum (*Lat.*) [Hurdy-Gurdy.]

Lyre. One of the most ancient stringed instruments. The word lyre (λύρα) does not occur in Homer; he speaks only of the citharis (κίθαρις) and phorminx (φόρμιγξ). The distinction between a citharis (or *guitar*), and a lyre, is that the neck of the former runs behind the upper part of the strings, while the strings of the latter are free on both sides. A reference to the article "Guitar" will show the nature of the cithara. The following illustration of a Greek lyre exhibits the characteristic of the instrument just alluded to.

The lyre was also called *testudo* or chelys (χέλυς), because the back was of tortoiseshell, as shown in the next illustration.

The cross bar at the top was called the yoke ζύγον, Lat. *transtillum*, a little *transtrum* or cross-bar. The uprights were called the horns πήχεις.

The history of the progress of the lyre as a musical instrument, is the history of Greek music itself, and the reader is referred to the article on that subject for information. [Guitar], [Lute], [Greek Music.]

Lyric. Poetry or blank-verse intended to be set to music and sung.

Lyric Stage. A term applied to operatic representations.

M.

—◆—

M. Abbreviation of *mezzo, mano, main, manual.* M. M. stands for *Maelzel's metronome, q. v.*

Ma (*It.*) But; as, *vivace ma non troppo;* quick, but not too quick.

Machalath, or Mahalath (*Heb.*) This word occurs in the title of Psalms liii. and lxxxviii., the former is inscribed to the "chief musician upon Mahalath, the latter to the "chief musician upon Mahalath Leannoth." Mahalath is by some authors traced (like Machol), to a root meaning *pierced* or *bored,* hence it is thought these Psalms were accompanied by flutes. It is generally thought that the term *leannoth* refers to antiphonal singing. Other writers consider the titles of these and several other Psalms to be a reference to well known tunes to which they were to be sung.

Machine-head. An arrangement of rack and pinion for the purpose of tightening and keeping in tension the strings of the double-bass, and the guitar, as the ordinary pegs employed to stretch the strings are of unequal leverage.

Machicot (*Fr.*) An obsolete term for one of the *chori ministri minores* of a cathedral, who in singing, added passing-notes between intervals of the plain-song; or, according to others, added a part to the plain-song at an interval of a third or fourth, thus forming a sort of *organum* or *diaphony.* The music thus sung was called *machicotage.*

Machol, or Mahhol (*Heb.*) A word often found in the Old Testament, associated with "toph" (timbrel), and almost always rendered in the English version by *dances* or *dancing.* But some authorities trace the word to a root meaning *pierced* or *bored,* and therefore consider it to have been a flute. It is not improbable that *Machol* and *toph* may mean "pipe and tabor," but as these two instruments are often associated with dancing, our version, and others which follow it, cannot in any case be said to be incorrect.

Machwerk (*Ger.*) Composition, construction, the result of labour rather than spontaneity.

Madriale (*It.*) A word derived from madrigal, and as in the early operas madrigals were performed between the acts, without necessarily having any connection with them, the word came to be applied to any species of *intermezzo.*

Madrigal. In the doubt that has existed as to the origin of the word, many speculations have been advanced; Huet, Bishop of Avranches, supposed it to be a corruption of the word Martegaux, because he presumed that the inhabitants of that district in Provence, either invented or excelled in this peculiar style of composition, but as he produces no authority in support of his assertion, he gives occasion to Sir John Hawkins shrewdly to say, "had he known that there was a town in Spain called Madrigal, it is likely he would have deduced its origin from the Spaniards." The derivation of the word from the Italian *mandra,* because some of the madrigals are of a pastoral character, need not be entertained, because for every poem with such a theme, there is at least a score having other subjects of a widely different nature. The modern idea that the madrigal may have originally been a song to the Virgin Mary, is likewise based upon very doubtful authority, if upon any authority at all, for in the first place, it is necessary to prove that the word *madre* came to be exclusively applied to the Virgin, and in the second, that there should be some applicable meaning in the latter part of the word, for *gala* relates to gaiety in dress or ornament, and not to joyfulness in poetry or music, and finally, that the supporters of this idea should produce specimens of such songs in numbers sufficient to justify their ground in making the statement. The term may possibly be connected with the Spanish word *madrugada,* dawn of day, for many of the Spanish *cancioneros* or madrigals have the character of an "aubade." The word was applied to a poem of a popular character as early at least as the 14th century. The first madrigals on whatever subject they were written, were always in popular versification, and generally contained a well-known proverb, or the application of some commonplace wisdom. The words madrigal and *villancico,* or *villanella ballato* and *sonetto,* are frequently used to describe a popular song in popular language and versification.

The madrigal as a poem arose out of the

cancionero general, the invention of the Spanish poets of the early part of the 13th century. A theme or *moto* was selected, and the poet exercised his ingenuity in varying the motives, as a musician does a phrase.

The following poem or glose, by Don Jorge Manrique de MADRIGAL, will show the method of treatment:—

MOTE.

"*Sin vos, y sin Dios, y mi.*"
Yo soy quien libre me vi
Yo quien pudiera olvidaros
Yo so el que por amaros
Estoy des que os conoci
Sin Dios y sin vos y mi.

Sin Dios, porque en vos adoro
Sin vos, pues no me quereys
Pues *sin me* ya esto decoro
Que vos soys quien me teneys
Assi que triste naci
Pues que pudiera olvidaros
Yo soy el que por amaros
Esto desque os conoci
Sin Dios y sin vos y mi.

The early composers took the melodies of some of the popular madrigals and constructed counterpoint upon them, and further productions were called madrigals or motetts, either from their having a proposed theme, or from the character of the poem which furnished the theme. In Spain to this day the motetts sung at high mass on Christmas eve are called *villancicos*.

The word madrigal became a general term for secular compositions, of which there were three classes: (1.) The solo madrigal, or "Madrigale concertate con il basso continuo;" (2.) The madrigal in parts for voices unaccompanied, or "Madrigali di tavolino;" and (3.) The madrigal accompanied by several instruments, "apt for viols and voyces," or as they are described in Italian, "madrigali concertate con varie sorte di stromenti." It was the second class that obtained the greatest popularity in England after having been introduced by means of copies printed in Flanders in 1588, by an unknown gentleman who translated the words of some of the most famous Italian madrigals and adapted them to English verse for his own use. Immediately upon their introduction into England, the composers of the time produced works of a similar character which far exceeded in beauty of idea and construction all their prototypes, and so far exhausted the style that the Elizabethan madrigals have never been excelled for beauty and fancy in harmony and counterpoint, and the mere mention of the word madrigal calls into association such names as Morley, Wilbye, Ward, Benet, Dowland, Ford, and Gibbons.

The earliest compositions to madrigal words were similar in character to the hymn tunes or chorales now in use, the counterpoint being of the simplest form, note against note, each measure being similarly accented in all the parts, they were, in fact, harmonised melodies. The madrigal "Down in a flowery vale," by Constantius Festa (1517-1545), is a good example in this form. The original Italian words are in true madrigal style and rhythm. The ballets or fa las, printed at Venice in 1591, by Gastoldi, who is the reputed inventor of this form of madrigal, are of a like character. By degrees, as it was discovered that it was possible to arrange the parts so that they might become melodies interchangeable as to form and rhythm according to the plan now known as double counterpoint, a greater freedom was attained, and not only were madrigals improved, but the art of composition made a great advance. The motett and the madrigal, always side by side, always written in like style, benefitted by the improvement, the only difference in their construction being that as in the madrigal every improvement or "license" in harmony and melody was permitted, certain progressions were forbidden in the motett as being inconsistent with the solemn character of the words to which they were usually set. The motett was originally in madrigal form, that is to say, was arranged in short phrases to correspond with the versification of the madrigal, a matter of necessity when it is considered that the melodies of the well known and often profane madrigals were taken as the plain song upon which new and severe harmonies were based. Richard Edwardes, 1547; Phillipo Verdelot, 1549; Adrian Willaert, 1565; Vincenzo Ruffo, 1568; Thomas Tallis, 1575; Palestrina, 1588; and Claudio Merula, 1598; wrote sacred compositions in which the motett displays signs of this method of treatment. It may be needless to point out that what has been called "the conversational arrangement of short phrases," is essentially the character of the later madrigals, in which one part or more proposes a phrase which is replied to either in imitation or some such form by the other part or parts in turn, as in Converso's "When all alone my pretty love," 1580. In the longer madrigals a greater variety of phrasing is of course necessary, in order to avoid monotony of effect. "Shew" says Morley at page 180 of his "Plaine and Easie Introduction to Practicall Musicke," 1597, "to the very utmost your variety," and "the more variety you shew, the better you shall please." In course of time the original signification of the word was lost sight of and many compositions were styled madrigals without consideration of the primary meaning of the term, hence has arisen a certain amount of confusion with regard to this class of music.

The dates of the several productions so called do not always indicate the state of the mádrigal, some later writers using the earliest forms, as Dowland, Ford, and Gibbons, while the earlier writers in varying the accepted form of their time suggested improvements which were afterwards expanded. Existing madrigals may be divided into these groups:—

1. Madrigals with melody, harmonised note against note.
2. Those in which florid and double counterpoint is employed, but rarely consisting of more than one movement.
3. Those in which two or more movements are used, and every variety of counterpoint.

The Villanellas or Madrigals of Donati [1510-1590], the Ballets or Fa las of Gastoldi, already alluded to, and all like works belong to the first division; the Triumphs of Oriana, especially those by Weelkes and Morley, to the second; and all compositions like "Sweet honey-sucking bees" to the third class.

The characteristics a Madrigal should possess may be thus summed up :—

1. Themes suitable in character to the words.
2. Variety of rhythm.
3. Short melodic phrases.
4. Imitation and counterpoint.

There are many pieces called madrigals in which certain of these conditions are more present than others, indicating the advance in thought and treatment, afterwards developed in the Glee, such as Wilbye's "Thus saith my Chloris," Benet's "Flow, O my tears," and Gibbons's "Silver Swan" and "Oh that the learned poets." The two last named are specially held to be transitions or bridges between the madrigal and the glee.

Madrigale (*It.*) [Madrigal.]

Madrigaletto *or* **Madrialletto** (*It.*) A short madrigal.

Maestà, con.
Maestade, con.
Maestevole   (*It.*) With dignity,
Maestevolmente   majesty.
Maestoso

Maestrale (*It.*) or *magistrale*, a term sometimes applied to the Stretto of a Fugue. [Fugue.]

Maestri secolari (*It.*) Teachers of secular music.

Maestria (*It.*) Skill, address, authority.

Maestro del coro, or **di cappella** (*It.*) Choir master, leader, or conductor. [Capellmeister.]

Magadis (*Gk.*) μαγάδις. An instrument of twenty strings, on which music could be played in octaves.

Magadize, to (*Gk.*) μαγαδίζω. (1.) To play

upon the magadis. (2.) To play in octaves.

Magas (*Gk.*) μαγάς. (1.) The bridge (Lat. *pons*) of a cithara. (2.) A fret.

Maggiolata (*It.*) A May song. A song sung in celebration of the month of May.

Maggiore (*It.*) Major.

Maggot. One of the later names given to fancies, airs, and pieces of an impromptu character. The most celebrated of these fancies or *whimsical* airs was that by Moteley or Motley, which is subjoined.

From "A choice collection of lessons, being excellently sett for the harpsichord," 1705.

Magrepha. An organ mentioned in the Talmud as having been in existence in the second century. It had ten ventages, each of which communicated with ten pipes, and it was played upon by means of a clavier.

Main (*Fr.*) The hand, as *main droite*, the right hand; *main gauche*, the left hand, abbreviated thus, *m. d.* and *m. g.*

Maitre de chapelle (*Fr.*) Choir master. [Capellmeister.]

Majeur (*Fr.*) Major.

Major. Greater. A major third consists of four semitones, a minor third of three. A major tone is the whole tone having the ratio 8:9 ; a minor tone, that having the ratio 9:10. Intervals have had the term major applied to them in a conflicting manner. [See Interval.]

Major mode. The ordinary diatonic scale, having semitones between the third and fourth, and seventh and eighth degrees.

Major modus (*Lat.*) (Major mode.)

Malakat. [Ashantee trumpet.]

Malinconia, con ⎫
Malinconicamente ⎪ (*It.*) With sadness,
Malinconico ⎬ sorrow, or melan-
Malinconioso ⎪ choly.
Malinconoso ⎭

Mammets. Puppet-shows, usually accompanied with music on a dulcimer. [Dulcimer.)

Mancando (*It.*) Decreasing, dying away.

Manche (*Fr.*) The neck of a violin or guitar, &c.

Mandola (*It.*) ⎫ An Italian fretted
Mandoline (*Eng.*) ⎬ guitar, so called from
Mandolina (*It.*) ⎭ its almond shape.
There are several varieties, each with different tunings. The Neapolitan, considered the most perfect, has four strings tuned like the violin, *i.e.*, G, D, A, E. The Milanese, next in favour, has five double strings tuned G, C, A, D, E. A plectrum is used in the right hand, and the left is employed in stopping the strings. Mozart in Don Giovanni, wrote an accompaniment to "Deh Vieni" for this instrument.

Mandora (*It.*) A kind of guitar.

Manica (*It.*) Fingering.

Manichord. [Clarichord.]

Manico (*It.*) The neck of a violin or guitar, &c. *Manche* (*Fr.*)

Maniera (*It.*) Manner, style, method ; as, *maniera affettata*, an affected style, *maniera languida*, a languid, lifeless style.

Manière (*Fr.*) [Maniera.]

Manieren (*Ger.*) [Harpsichord graces.]

Männergesangverein (*Ger.*) A society formed for the performance of music for men's voices.

Mano (*It.*) Hand, as *mano destra, diritta*, right hand ; *mano sinistra*, left hand.

Manual. [Key-board.]

Manuductor. The man who beat time by striking the left hand with the right. Oyster-shells or bones were sometimes used as accessories.

Marcando (*It.*) Marking the time or expression.

Marcatissimo (*It.*) Very marked.

Marcato (*It.*) Marked, or emphasized.

March. A musical composition so arranged as to be suitable for accompanying troops in walking. There are quick and slow marches in duple and triple time, besides marches peculiar to certain nationalities.

Marche (*Fr.*) A sequence, as, *Marche des accords*, a sequence of chords.

Marche redoublée (*Fr.*) A double quick march.

Marche triomphale (*Fr.*) A triumphal march.

Marziale (*It.*) Martial, warlike.

Marimba. [Balafo.]

Marionette (*It.*) A puppet.

Marks of Expression. Certain words or signs used in music to regulate the degrees of accent, power, time, or tone, required by the composer to produce the proper effect of his composition. The employment of elaborate marks of expression is a practice of comparatively modern times, none of the earliest writers making use of any beyond the *time signs*, these being all that were then needed, as they suggested a certain pace generally understood. Most of the early printed music had no other directions than *soft* and *loud*, and these only sparingly. Thus, in Croft's "Musica Sacra or Select Anthems in score" 1724, the "First Essay of Publishing Church Musick in England," printed from engraved metal plates, all the directions are in English, as *loud, soft, fast, slow, grave, brisk* and *lively*, the only foreign words employed being *solo* and *ritornello*. The introduction of Italian music into this country in the eighteenth century necessitated a knowledge of the Italian terms of expression, which led to the gradual employment of a few of the terms so acquired, and Italian words or their abbreviations ultimately superseded the English words to such an extent that very few native terms for expression are to be found in music of modern times. The Italian words originally introduced were in their simplest forms, but as composers grew more fastidious and exacting, the phrases became complicated by the employment of diminutives, expansions, and compounds of terms, so that it became extremely difficult to determine the exact value of the many marks. The doubts that presented themselves to the minds of the performers as to *pace* necessitated the employment of a method by which the time of a piece should be taken, and a string divided into inches was at first used as a standard to regulate the time value of the notes in a bar. This gave rise to the invention of the metronome. [Expression.]

Marqué (*Fr.*) [Marcato.]

Marsch (*Ger.*) A march.

Marseillaise (*Fr.*) A song written by Rouget de Lisle, an officer of artillery in the garrison of Strasbourg in 1792. It received its title from having been sung by a party of the Marseillaise club as they entered Paris on the invitation of Madame Roland ; the song, though less sanguinary in sentiment than most of the songs of the revolution, was employed as accompaniment to many of the horrible deeds of that, and of later periods, and by association became dangerous enough to be included among the songs prohibited to be sung in France. The tune to which it is set by the author of the words, contains progressions so unusual in popular songs, that it is difficult to account for its general adoption.

Martelé (*Fr.*) }
Martellato (*It.*) } *Lit.*, hammered.

Martellare (*It.*) *Lit.*, to hammer. A term applied to *staccato* bowing on the violin, and to the strong percussion of notes of a pianoforte.

Masque. A species of dramatic entertainment in which originally the performers wore masks of peculiar forms suggestive of the allegorical characters assumed. In many instances the masque had no definite design or plot, but depended for its success upon the occasion for which it was written, the wit of the poet who furnished the words, the skill of the musician who supplied the music, and the ingenuity of the machinist and scene painter by whom the stage effects were produced. The early masques were simply acted pageants, but by degrees the genius of such writers as Fletcher and Ben Jonson furnished the poetical groundwork of many masques acted at Court by the children of His Majesty's Chapel Royal and St. Paul's Cathedral. The most beautiful work of this class is the "Comus" of Milton, acted at Ludlow in 1634, and although produced at a time when the taste for this class of entertainment had fallen off, it has always been held to be the most perfect specimen of a masque. [Ballet, Opera, Oratorio.]

Mass. Missa (*Lat.*) Messa (*It.*) Messe (*Fr.*) Messe (*Ger.*)

The portions of the Mass usually set to music, namely, the *Kyrie*, the *Gloria*, the *Credo*, the *Sanctus* and the *Agnus Dei*. An *Offertory* and *Benedictus* are sometimes added to these numbers. Masses are designated musically after the key in which they commence, as Beethoven in D ; and liturgically, according to the character and solemnity of the accompanying ceremonial,

as a "Low Mass" (Messa Bassa) in which the priest simply intones or reads the service ; a "Chanted Mass," in which certain tones with inflections are sung ; a "High Mass," in which the service is partly chanted by the priest, partly by the deacons who assist the priest, and partly sung by the choir to an elaborate musical setting with or without instrumental accompaniment.

It is only necessary here to speak of the various liturgical divisions of the service, so far as they are connected with the special form or character of their music.

In early times the ancient ecclesiastical plain song was alone employed as the music for the several sections of this service, and when musicians were possessed of inventive skill, they still retained the old character of the music by interweaving counterpoint, and new harmonies upon the old plain-song, either entirely unaltered, or with slight modifications such as those described in "Fa burden." Musicians afterwards took the tunes of popular hymns as well as the airs of vulgar songs, the latter ordinarily allied to words of questionable character, instead of the melodies of the plain-song, and the masses so composed were called after the name of the borrowed tunes. Thus Claude Merula calls his four "Missarum quinque vocum," Venice, 1573. (1.) "Missa *Benedicta es celorum Regina;*" (2.) "Missa *Susanne un giour;*" (3.) "Missa *Oncques Amour;*" and (4.) "Missa *Aspice Domine.*" Baini in his "Memorie storico-critiche della vita, e opere di Giovanni Pierluigi da Palestrina," Rome, 1828, gives what he calls a short list of some eighty secular tunes upon which masses had been composed and sung. If the language in which they are named indicate their origin, the majority were French songs, and if the titles are in any way suggestive of their character, they could not have been fit for church use. This custom of employing popular melodies in the construction of sacred music was not a distinctive characteristic of the 16th century, but it existed later, and was especially favoured by that class of religious formalists who prided themselves upon purity in thought and worship. Shakespeare alludes to the Puritan "who sings Psalms to hornpipes ;" the dissenting bodies of the last century showed by their collections of melodies sung during worship that they would not allow "the devil to have all the best tunes." The special hold obtained over the minds of the lower classes during the recent "revival" meetings was in a great measure due to the influence of the "hymns" which were almost invariably sung to well known song tunes, either entirely unaltered, or only slightly modified.

There is now a recognised treatment for every section of the mass to which music may be set, as well as a received canon for the style of composition in which most of the several subdivisions are composed. This arrangement is not set forth by written laws, but is the result of traditional use of a slow and gradual growth, as the appended short descriptions of certain representative masses from the latter part of the 16th century to the middle of the 18th will show. A short analysis of the manner in which the several movements have been treated is subjoined to help towards the formation of as correct a notion on the subject as can be obtained without a reference to and study of the works themselves. The majority of these are only preserved in the cabinets of the curious, for they are for the most part of an obsolete character, more interesting as musical monuments than valuable as being available at the present time for the service for which they were written.

There are many members of the church in which this form of musical composition is most employed who do not hesitate to say that a return to the older, and (as they say) *purer* forms of musical setting is desirable, for some musicians have taken advantage of the liberty allowed by non-interference with their designs, to introduce a style of composition utterly inconsistent with the character of the service it is intended to accompany. But modern writers have not only elaborated the various movements, they have also added music to certain parts of the service of the Mass which were left untouched in older times. The " Introit, Gradual, Offertory and Communio" were supposed to be given when sung to the ancient plain-song settings, and therefore these portions have been left alone by the earlier composers. Later writers have supplied music for these sections, and in the desire to be original have been tempted to write " sensuous settings " as well in these parts as in the others. The music preserved by Marbecke (1550) is simply an eking out of the old plain-song with phrases of his own invention in imitation of it. As there are no harmonies given, it is presumed that either they were not sung, or, if they were, some sort of "falso bordone " of a recognised character was intended to be used. Whether harmonised or plain, his " use " is very simple, and if it is, as some say, a mere transcription of that employed in his time, it is certain that no reasonable ground of complaint could be made against it, for it is not " overloaded with ornament nor spread abroad with superfluous syllabilisation." As only portions of Marbecke's settings can be traced to a remoter date than his own, he has

a claim to be considered among the composers of music to the mass. Next in order stands William Byrd, who, in a mass composed c. 1553, displays some degree of characteristic originality, together with a leaning towards old styles if not forms.

The " Kyrie " is simple and short, changing at the words " Christi eleison," and returning to the first subject and words, " Kyrie eleison." The " Gloria " is precented and is divided at the words " Domine Deus." The " Credo " is also precented and is divided at the words " qui propter nos homines," and also at " Et in spiritum sanctum." In the " Sanctus " there is a change of theme at the words " Pleni sunt." The " Benedictus " is a simple Motett-like setting, so also is the " Agnus Dei."

This arrangement was one generally followed by other writers of the period. The idea influencing all seemed to have been to make the setting solemn and not dramatic. Plain counterpoint, with little points of occasional imitation, and with rarely more than two notes to one syllable, was most favoured. The writers thus avoided the *pneumas*, upon which contempt had been thrown as the relic of a barbarous period, and as being incompatible with the more enlightened views then entertained. In the interlude of the " Four Elements " c. 1510 there is a dialogue between Humanity and Ignorance, in which the florid character of early conterpoint is thus satirized :

Hu.—Peace, man, prick-song may not be despised,
For therewith God is well pleased.
Honoured, praised, and served
In the Church oft-times among.

Ig.—Is God well pleased, trows't thou, thereby ?
Nay, nay ! for there is no reason why;
For is it not as good to say plainly
" Give me a spade,"
As " give me a spa-ve-va, ve-va-ve-vade ?"

In later times the " pneuma " was revived in the form of the " divisions," but these latter were made more acceptable by being introduced as an integral part of the composition in which they appeared, and not as a mere adjunct. In this improved state they are observed as early as the time of Carissimi, who in a mass in D minor for five voices has introduced short divisions, contrary to former custom. There is another point of importance in this mass. The first trace of a fugue to the words " Cum sancto spiritu " in the " Gloria " is met with, and also an attempt at dramatic expression at the words " Et incarnatus est."

In the " Missa ad imitationem Moduli *Dixit Joseph*," by Orlando di Lasso, Paris, 1607, we find in the setting of the " Kyrie " a few short simple chords note against note; a like arrangement in the "Gloria" to the "Domine Deus," at which point imitation is introduced, and another change at "Qui tollis" as well of time as character. The "Credo" changes style at "Et incarnatus est." The "Sanctus" like the "Kyrie" is simply set, and the arrangement of the "Benedictus" as a trio or tria upon a subject used in the "Kyrie" and "Sanctus," probably the "Dixit Joseph," completes the Mass.

In Colonnas'.""Messi Salmi, e Responsori per li Defonti," Bologna, 1685. The "Kyrie" is in imitation throughout. The "Sanctus," thirty-four bars long, is in eight part fugal writing. The "Benedictus" is short (fifteen bars), and in single counterpoint, the "Agnus Dei," like the "Kyrie," is in imitation, and is precented.

In a "Messe a quattro voci, concertato e stromenti," by Isabella Leonarda, Bologna, 1696, the "Kyrie" is set as a solo for alto at the words "Christe eleison." The plain setting of the "Gloria" changes at "Et in terra," and again at the words "Gratias agimus," an alteration of time rather than style at "Qui tollis," a return to the original form of the Kyrie at "Quoniam," and so on to the end. The "Credo" is divided at "Et incarnatus," "Et resurrexit," and at "Et iterum venturus est," the last movement having little points of imitation that must be called "Attacati," rather than fugal points.

Judging by the specimens existing, it must be confessed that composers did not think it worth while to devote their best energies to the service of the Church during the period of the first half of the eighteenth century. A comparison of the Mass of Leonarda, with one by Konigsperger produced nearly sixty years later, shows little if any progress. It is true that in the meantime Bach had written portions of his Mass in B minor, but as there is reason to believe that it is for the most part a *pasticcio*, and probably not much known at the time, its influence is altogether out of the question.

In the "Jubilatio Lyturgica" of Konigsperger, Augsburg, 1750, among much that might be called time-saving writing, there are one or two points worthy of observation for their early use. Thus the "Kyrie" is adapted to the "Dona nobis," which appears later. The "Osanna" is set to an elaborate division. The "Gloria" is divided at the words "Domine Deus," "Quoniam," and at "Cum Sancto Spiritu," this last movement appearing as a regular and well worked out, though short fugue. There is nothing in any of the other movements that calls for especial mention.

The Masses of Haydn, Mozart, Beethoven, Weber, Hummel, and Schubert, are sufficiently well known to render a detailed account here unnecessary.

Mass (*Ger.*) Measure, time.

Mässig (*Ger.*) Moderate, temperate. *Mässig langsam*, moderately slow.

Massima (*It.*) A semi-breve.

Masternote. An old term for the sensible or leading note.

Masure, Masurek, Masurka (*Ger.*) [Mazurka.]

Matelotte (*Fr.*) A sailors' dance. [Hornpipe.]

Matinée (*Fr.*) A morning concert.

Mattins. [Horæ Canonicæ.]

Maultrommel (*Ger.*) [Jew's-harp.]

Maxima (*Lat.*) A note equal to four breves.

Mazourk } (*Ger.*) [Mazurka.]
Mazurek }

Mazurka. A Polish dance of lively grotesque character, the music of which is in $\frac{3}{8}$ or $\frac{3}{4}$ time with a peculiar rhythm. It is generally performed by four or eight pairs of dancers, is popular in Germany as well as in Poland, and has been successfully introduced into England. The mazurka, like the waltz, has been treated in a classical manner, notably by Chopin.

M. D. Abbreviation of (1.) *Mano destra* or *main droite*, the right hand; (2.) Doctor of music.

Mean. The name formerly given to the *tenor* part as being the mean in pitch between the bass and treble. The middle strings of instruments were also called *mean*.

Mean clef. The C clef.

Measure. (1.) A general name for a slow and stately dance, supposed to be like the minuet—

> "But after then as men more civile grew
> He did more grave and solemn measures frame."
> *Davies' Orchestra.*

Reed says that "the measures were performed at court and at public entertainments of the societies of law and equity, at their balls on particular occasions. It was formerly not deemed inconsistent with propriety, even for the gravest persons to join in them ; and accordingly at the revels, which were celebrated at the Inns of Court, it has not been unusual for the first characters in the law to become performers in treading the measures." (2.) Time, pace. (3.) Rhythm. (4.) The contents of a bar.

Mechanism. (1.) That part of an instrument which forms the connection between the player and the sound-producing portion. (2) The physical power of performance, as distinguished from the intellect or taste which directs it.

Medesimo movimento (*It.*) The same movement.

Medesimo tempo. The same time.

Mediæval musical instruments. The

musical instruments known in the middle ages appear to have been flutes, flageolets, bugles, and trumpets among simple tubes; waits, cornets, bassoons, bagpipes, &c., among reed instruments; the harp, the guitar, the crowd, the violin or fiddle among stringed instruments; drums and tambourines, cymbals and bells among instruments of percussion, but all of these differ more or less from the instruments with the same names in use at the present day. There is a curious catalogue of musical instruments of the fourteenth century, which may be read with interest in reference to this subject, in a poem by Guillaume de Machault, entitled *Le Temps Pastour*. The description is headed *Comment l'amant fut au disner de sa dame* :—

> Mais qui veist, apres mangier
> Venér menestraux, sans dangier
> Pignez et miz en pure corps.
> Là feurent meints divers acors
> Car je vis là, tout en un cerne
> Viole, rubebe, guiterne
> L'enmovache, le mica mon
> Citole, et le psalterion
> Harpes, tabours, trompes, nacaires
> Orgues, cornes, plus de dix paires
> Cornemuse, flajos et chevrettes,
> Douceines, symboles, clochettes
> Tymberes, la flauste brehaingue
> Et le grand cornet d'Allemaingue
> Flajos de sans, fistule, pipe
> Muse d'Aussay, trompe petite,
> Buisines, èles, monocorde
> Ou il n'a quime seule corde
> Et muse de blet, tout ensemble
> Et certainement, il me semble
> Qu' oncques mais tele melodie
> Ne fut oncques veues ne oye
> Car Chascun d'eux, selon d'acort
> De son instrument, sans descort
> Viole, guiterne, citole
> Harpe, trompe, corne, flajole,
> Pipe, souffle, muse, naquaire,
> Tabour, et quanque ou put faire
> De dois, de pennes, et d'archet
> Oïs et vis en ce parchet.

If each name here mentioned represented a different and distinct instrument, it might be supposed that there was a far greater variety in use in the fourteenth century than in the present time, with all our increase of knowledge and improved skill in construction, but the truth is that many of the names are simply synonyms. For example the line :—

> "Cornemuse, flajos et chevrettes"

would seem to imply three sorts of music making machines, but the names refer to one and the same thing, neither more nor less than the bagpipes, and the "muse d'Aussay," "muse de blet," and "muse" simply, are varieties of the same instrument. The "viole and rubebe," refer to the fiddle, the "flajole pipe, souffle, and fistule," to the flageolets; "la flauste brehaingue" to the English flute; "le grand cornet d'Allemaingue, buisines,

douceines," were a species of bassoon; "tymberes, tabour, and naquaires," were drums; the "citole and psalterion," were dulcimers; "the guiterne" a guitar or cittern; "èles," signified harps, from their wing-like shapes; "L'enmovache," was also a harp of a larger kind; the "mica mon" is probably "maca man," a hand-drum or tambourine, and the rest are sufficiently obvious. Guillaume de Machault, the author of this poem, was probably not a practical musician, but simply made use of a list of instruments with whose use he was probably unacquainted, hence his repetition of synonyms. It is no uncommon thing to find a special ignorance of the use and qualities of musical instruments among modern poets, but when such a lack of knowledge is displayed by a poet writing in the palmy days of minstrelsy, it is not unfair to imagine that Guillaume de Machault was more of a *trouvère* than a *cantadour*. [Troubadour.]

Mediant. Mediante (*Fr.*) The third degree of any scale.

Mediation. That part of a chant which lies between the reciting-note and the next close. [Chant].

Medius (*Lat.*) The tenor part. [Mean.]

Mehrstimmig (*Ger.*) In many parts. Polyphonic.

Meisterfuge. (*Ger.*) A *fuga ricercata*, that is, a fugue without episodes, one in which the subject or answer is constantly heard.

Meistersinger. Meistersänger (*Ger.*) *Maître Chanteur* (*Fr.*) A title given to the most renowned musician of a township or district in Germany, during the middle ages.

When the Minnesingers or Troubadours, formed from among the ranks of the aristocracy, began to die away, the Meistersingers arose, and at the beginning of the fourteenth century formed themselves in the towns of Germany into guilds or trading companies, and agreed to uphold certain fanciful and arbitrary laws of rhythm.

Adepts in the poetic art, Master-singers, appear to have existed at the period when the Minnesingers were at their prime, and it is supposed that the title was only more universally and distinctively bestowed when the spirit of pedantry had become general and when the "Songschools" or "guilds" became in Germany what the "consistories" and "academies" were in other countries during the then general decay of art. Wandering orators in connection with the "Chambers of Rhetoric" who recited a miserable doggrell composed by themselves or others, afterwards formed themselves in Flanders and Brabant, into societies by the name of Chambers of Rhetoricians (Kamers der Rhetorÿkers or

Rederÿkers) and offered prizes for the most meritorious poems written according to their barbarous rules.

The ornaments and illustrations of this class of poetry were drawn from mean sources. Instead of princes, nobles, and knights, we have clerks, schoolmasters, and mechanics. Some of the poems, it is true, are not unworthy of notice and survive in one form or another to the present day; others have sunk into an oblivion not altogether undeserved.

The "Masters" were always anxious to clothe themselves with the ancient glory of the "Minnesingers." They were fond of tracing the origin of their school to a very remote antiquity; and the most celebrated names were placed by all sorts of anachronisms among the supposed united band of founders. Wherever the "hoch-deutsch" was spoken, there the Master-singers founded a colony and indulged the vulgar propensity of giving importance to bombast, parade, and external distinction to their hearts' content. A candidate was admitted into the school of the "Master-singers" with great form and ceremony. Four "Merker" sat behind a silken curtain to pass judgment upon his qualifications. One of these had to decide whether the diction of the novice was pure and his grammar accurate, the others attended to the rhyme and metre of the composition and the melody to which it was sung. If they united in declaring that the candidate had complied with the statutes and regulations, he was decorated with a silver chain and badge—the latter representing King David playing on the harp—and he was honourably admitted into the Society. The poems of the "Master-singers" were always lyrical and sung to music. The entire poem was called a "bar" and it was divided into five or more stanzas, or "Gesetze," and each "Satz" also fell into three portions, the first of which was a "Stole," the second an "Abgesang," and the third a "Stole" like the first. The rhymes were classed into "stumpfe Reime,","klingende Reime," "stumpfe Schlag-reime," and "klingende Schlag-reime," and other denominations needless to particularise. The poets, singers, and merkers counted the syllables on their fingers, and if there was the proper number it was of no consequence whether they were long or short. The length of the verse, the number of the lines, and the order of the rhymes in each "Stole" or "Abgesang" was variable and consequently the poems were susceptible of a great variety of forms, which were called tunes or "Weisen." The invention of a new "Weise" was considered the test of a Master-singer's abilities. There were some hundreds of these "Weisen," all named after their inventors; as Hans Tindeisen's rosemary Weise; Joseph Schmeirer's

flowery-paradise Weise; Hans Fogel's fresh Weise; Henry Frauenlob's yellow Weise; his blue Weise; his frog Weise, and his looking-glass Weise. The code of criticism to which the Master-singers were subjected was contained in the rules or "Tabulatur" of the societies, some of which rules were certainly severe. They were prohibited from employing "sentences which nobody could understand," or "words wherein no meaning could be discovered," interdictions which would completely disqualify many a so-called poet in the present day for membership.

Mélange *(Fr.)* A medley.

Melisma *(Gk.)* μέλισμα. (1) A song, tune, melody. In 1611, Ravenscroft published "Melismata; Musical Phansies fitting the Court, citie, and country humours." (2) A grace, roulade. *Fioritura.*

Melismatik. *(Ger.)* The art of florid vocalisation.

Melodia *(It.)* Melody.

Melodia *(Gk.)* μελῳδία. (1) The singing of an ode to a *melos*. (2) The tune to which lyric poetry was sung.

Melodicon. An instrument made of steel bars in different lengths tuned to the diatonic scale, struck with hammers held in the hand.

Melodico, melodicoso *(It.)* Melodiously, sweetly.

Mélodie *(Fr.)* Melody, tune.

Melodrama. A dramatic piece in which the interest is heightened by the character of the vocal or instrumental music accompanying certain situations. The melodrama is of French invention, and was introduced into England at the end of the last century; the subjects are generally of a romantic character, illustrated with picturesque costumes and scenery, and having serious and sensational incidents, and effective and striking tableaux. Although sometimes confounded with the opera, it differs from that higher class of work insomuch that the action is carried on in speaking and not in recitative and aria. [Opera.]

Melodrame *(Fr.)* **Melodramma** *(It.)* [Melodrama.]

Melody (*melos Gk.* μέλος). An agreeable succession of simple sounds, produced by a single voice or instrument, and so regulated as to give a pleasing effect, or to be expressive of some kind of sentiment. It is often founded on relative harmonies and yet is completely distinguished from harmony by not needing the addition of parts to make it perfect. The construction of melody is guided by certain rules in rhythm, and by the capabilities of the voice or instrument for which it is intended. Melos had a very general meaning among the Greeks, for it is said by

Plato to consist of "speech, music, and rhythm." In its more limited sense it signified any succession of musical sounds.

Melody Organ *or* **Harmonium.** A harmonium so constructed that the upper note of the chords played is louder than the rest of the sounds.

Melograph. An instrument invented for the purpose of writing down melodies when played upon a pianoforte. It has not yet been brought into use, as its action is imperfect.

Melopœïa (*Gk.*) μελοποιΐα. (1.) Music in general. (2.) The art or system of making a tune or *melos*. In this sense it is said, by Aristides Quintilianus, (Ed. Meibom. p. 28) to be of three kinds with reference to the pitch, namely, hypatoeides, mesoeides, and netoeides. He then divides Melopœïa into three parts, Sumptio (λῆψις), Mistio (μίξις), Usus (χρῆσις).

Sumptio, or the "taking," is the settlement of the pitch from which the "system" or scale is to be reckoned. Mistio, the mixing, is the co-ordinating or fitting together the sounds with regard to each other, or the modulations of the voice, or the key-systems. Usus, the use, is of three kinds, Ductus (ἀγωγή), Petteia (πεττεία), Nexus (πλοκή). Ductus is of three kinds, direct, reverse, circumcurrent (see Agoge). Petteia is the choosing of sounds that are suitable, and rejecting those that are unsuitable. Nexus is the interweaving of intervals or movements by skips. Quintilianus sums up by giving the following plain statement of the different kinds of melopœïa.

	Genus	Enharmonic.
		Chromatic.
		Diatonic.
Melopœïa	System	Hypatoid.
		Mesoid.
		Netoid.
is of different	Scale (tonos)	Dorian.
		Phrygian.
		Lydian.
kinds as to	Mode (tropos)	Gnomic.
		Dithyrambic.
		Tragic.
	Manner or character (ethos)	Systaltic. (Producing sadness.)
		Middle. (Producing calmness.)
		Diastaltic. (Producing excitement.)

Melopiano. An invention by which sustained sounds can be produced on a pianoforte. It consists of a series of small hammers set into very rapid vibration by the winding up of a spring. When a note is struck and held down, the constant repetition of the blows of the hammer causes a continuous vibration of the string which is of a most charming character. A beautiful crescendo is obtained by the ingenious device of

raising the hammers gradually further from the string, causing them to descend with more force. It was invented by **Caldara** of Turin in 1870.

Melos (*Ger.*) (μέλος). A succession of musical sounds as opposed to *noises*. A tune. A song. [Melody.]

Même mouvement (*Fr.*) The same movement. *L'istesso tempo* (*It.*)

Men, meno (*It.*) Less; as *meno forte*, not so loud; *meno piano*, not so soft; *meno presto*, less rapid; *meno vivo*, not so quick.

Menaaneim (*Heb*). This word occurs once in Holy Scriptures, in 2 Sam. vi. 5, where it is improperly translated *cymbals*. Its derivation points to a root meaning to swing to and fro, to vibrate. It is probable, therefore, that it was a *sistrum*. [Sistrum.]

Ménestrals (*Fr.*) [Troubadours] [Confrérie de St. Julien].

Meno (*It.*) [Men].

Menschen-stimme (*Ger.*) (1.) A man's voice. (2.) Vox humana.

Mensur (*Ger.*) (1.) The measurement of intervals on stringed instruments. (2.) The scale of organ pipes.

Mensurable Music. [Cantus mensurabilis.]

Mensuralgesang (*Ger.*) [Cantus mensurabilis.]

Mensuralnotenschrift (*Ger.*) Notation of Time measurement.

Menuet (*Fr.*) ⎫
Menuetto (*It.*) ⎬ [Minuet.]

Mescolanza (*It.*) Cacophony.

Mese (*Gk.*) [Greek Music.]

Messa (*It.*), *Messe* (*Fr.*) Mass.

Messa di Voce (*It.*) The swelling and diminishing of the sound of the voice upon a holding note.

Mesochorus (μεσόχορος.) [Coryphæus.]

Mesopycni (*Mediæval Lat., from Gk.* μέσος, *middle, and* πυκνὸς *close*.) Church modes having the close interval or semitone in the middle of their primary tetrachord, *e.g.*—

Dorian.   Hypodorian.

cf. Barupycni. Oxupycni.

Mesto, mestoso (*It.*) Sad, pensive.

Mesure (*Fr.*) Measure, time, as *mesure à deux temps* or *trois temps*. Duple or triple time.

Metallo (*It.*) *lit.* metal. The *ringing* quality of tone, as *bel metallo di voce.*

Metal pipes. [Organ.]

Metal plate of pianoforte. [Pianoforte.]

Metal wind instruments. Instruments formed of various lengths of brass tubing gradually enlarged towards one end called the "bell" and with a mouthpiece at the other end. The tubing is folded into a size convenient for carrying about, either into an oblong or circular form. A single length of tubing is capable of sounding the primary harmonics of its tonic with that note, in the following order, according to the power of lip possessed by the player, the key note being taken as C :—

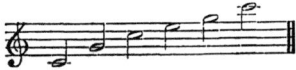

A double length of tubing enables the player to produce another octave with some additional harmonics, thus :—

and sometimes

as in the French Horn and Trumpet. These are called the open notes, the intermediate tones—

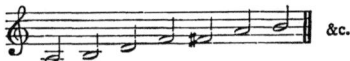

are made by inserting the hand in the "bell" of the Horn as well as the Trumpet, these are called closed notes and are less full and beautiful in character than the open tones, and being also difficult of production, are rarely written.

Upon the application of the slide to the trumpet, an application probably suggested by the trombone, the uncertainties of intonation were made somewhat less. The first instrument of the tube kind in which an improvement was sought to be effected was the Bugle, which was formerly without keys, like the horn and the trumpet. The bandmaster of an Irish regiment, named James Halliday, about the year 1814 or 1815, introduced a keyed bugle of his own contrivance which he called the Kent Bugle out of compliment to the Duke of Kent, the father of Her Majesty Queen Victoria, who was colonel of the regiment. The instrument became exceedingly popular, in consequence of the excellent performance of the elder Distin, who introduced it into the orchestra of Her Majesty's Theatre in 1830; and the French composer, Adolphe Adam, wrote several solos for it.

A bugle player named Macfarlane claims to have been the first who applied pistons or valves to the Cornopean. He called his contrivance "Russian valves," and he furnished his model with two of them, the first for the whole tone and the second for the half tone. As about that time (the year 1834) the celebrated player, Koenig, made his appearance from Paris with an instrument of similar make which he declared was by a French inventor, there was some controversy at the time, and as no one suspected the honesty of Macfarlane, it is possible that the same idea may have occurred simultaneously to the two claimants. The application of the third valve to the cornet or cornopean was claimed by a horn player named Kilback, but, on what grounds, it is difficult now to determine. Valves or pistons were employed in Germany before the introduction of the Russian valve (so-called) into England, these were the double cylinder and the rotatory valve, and the instruments played by Kalozdy's Hungarian band were on this latter principle.

The principle of the *Sax-valve* was a German invention, and was introduced to the public by a man named Stölzel. The *tuning slides* for the piston notes, and the improvement of Stölzel's valve are due to the maker whose name is connected with the invention. Since the time that the Sax-horns were introduced into England by the Distin family, many modifications and improvements have been effected, the object of each alteration being to obtain the easiest and most accurate means of lengthening and shortening the tube at will, so as to produce chromatic intonation.

The metal valved-instruments now in use may be thus classified :—

SOPRANO COMPASS.—Trumpet in F and E flat, both with slides and valves; soprano cornets in E flat and C, with 3 valves or pistons; soprano saxhorn in E flat, with 3 valves or pistons; soprano flügel horns in E flat and C, with 3 and 4 cylinder valves; bugle in C and B flat, with keys (rarely used now).

ALTO OR CONTRALTO COMPASS.—Cornet in B flat, with crooks for A, A flat, and G; alto saxhorn in B flat, with 3 valves; alto flügel horn in B flat, with 3 and 4 cylinder valves; alto trombone in E flat, both slide and valved.

TENOR COMPASS.—French horn, with and without valves, with 10 crooks; tenor saxhorn, with 3 valves; tenor flügel-horn, with 3 or 4 cylinder valves; tenor trombone, both slide and valved.

BARITON COMPASS.—Bariton sax-horn, with 3 valves; bariton flügel-horn, with 3 and 4 cylinder valves.

BASS COMPASS.—Trombone in F or G, both slide and valved; euphonium in C or B flat with 3 or 4 valves.

CONTRA-BASSO.—Bombardon in F or E flat, with 3 and 4 valves; bombardon, circular shaped; contra-bombardon in BB flat, with 3 pistons or valves; contra-bombardon, circular shaped.

Most metal wind instruments are formed from a sheet of brass cut into the proper size. The sheet of metal is turned in the shape of a pipe until the edges meet correctly. The edges are welded together in a brazing forge and the tube is "pickled" in a chemical bath to remove the traces of brazing. It is then made perfectly cylindrical by means of a "draw bench," and afterwards is bent into the required curve, the tube being filled with molten pitch, for slight curves, or with lead for "U" curves. As both pitch and lead will melt at a lower temperature than brass, there is no difficulty in removing the interior "filling" by heat, leaving the tube in the required form without breaking or flattening it. The "bell" is made by careful hammering on a "mandril" of the required size and form, and is fitted to the tube by means of solder and the blow pipe. Shanks, crooks and the other parts are then put together; the instrument is tested and polished, and is ready for use.

Méthode (*Fr.*) *Metodo* (*It.*) (1.) System of teaching, as, *Kalkbrenner's method, Crivelli's method,* &c. (2.) School or style of music, as, the *Italian method.*

Metre. A term used with various significations; (1.) A foot, as a subdivision of a bar or measure; (2.) The relation between two feet having the same subdivisions of time-units, but in a different order of succession; (3.) The proper grouping of a number of consecutive feet.

Authors who use the term in this last sense, consider it as equivalent to rhythm and divide it thus:

Metre (rhythm).
|
Measures (bars with accents).
|
Feet (groups of time-units).
|
Units of time (short and long).

But it will be seen further on that this division is not good; and also that the incorporation into music of the terms of prosody is not desirable. Before entering on this discussion, it is necessary to give a list of the names and nature of the most important feet.

Dissyllables have two units of time capable of a four-fold arrangement; *e.g.*,

Ex. 1.

– – Spondee.

Ex. 2.

◡ ◡ Pyrrhic.

Ex. 3.

MOZART. Symp. No. 1.

– ◡ Trochee.

Ex. 4.

BEETHOVEN. Symp. No. 1.

(or)

Ex. 5.

◡ – Iambic.

Ex. 6.

SCHUMANN

(or)

Trisyllables or feet consisting of three time-units are of eight kinds.

◡ ◡ ◡ Tribrach.

Ex. 7.

BEETHOVEN. Symphony No. 2.

♩. = 100.

◡ – – Bacchic.

Ex. 8.

SCHUMANN. "Paradise and the Peri."

◡ – ◡ Amphibrach.

Ex. 9.

BEETHOVEN. Symph. No. 6.

Ex. 10. MENDELSSOHN.

◡ ◡ — Anapæst.

&c.

Ex. 11.

MOZART.

&c.

— — — Molossus.

Ex. 12. Voices. WEBER. Mass in E♭.

_ ◡ ◡ Dactyl.

Ex. 13. F. C.

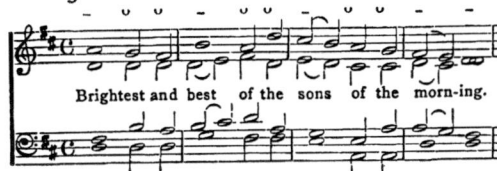

Brightest and best of the sons of the morn-ing.

Ex. 14. BEETHOVEN. Symph. No. 3.

_ ◡ _ Cretic.

&c.

— — ◡ Palimbacchic.

Ex. 15. BEETHOVEN. Ov. to Coriolan.

&c.

There are also tetrasyllables, sixteen in number, which, of course, consist of the possible positions of four syllables of different lengths.

◡	◡	◡	◡	Proseleusmatic (Double Pyrrhic).
◡	◡	◡	—	Third Pæon (Pyrrhic & Trochee).
◡	◡	◡	—	Fourth Pæon (Pyrrhic & Iambic).
◡	◡	—	—	Ionic a minore (Pyrrhic & Spondee).

◡	—	◡	—	Diambic (Double Iambic).
◡	—	◡	◡	Second Pæon (Iambic & Pyrrhic).
◡	—	—	◡	Antispast (Iambic & Trochee).
◡	—	—	—	First Epitrite (Iambic & Spondee).

—	—	—	—	Dispondee (Double Spondee).
—	—	◡	◡	Ionic a majore (Spondee & Pyrrhic).
—	—	◡	—	Third Epitrite (Spondee & Iambic).
—	—	◡	◡	Fourth Epitrite (Spondee & Trochee).

—	◡	—	◡	Dichoree (Double Trochee).
—	◡	◡	—	Choriambic (Trochee & Iambus).
—	◡	◡	◡	First Pæon (Trochee & Pyrrhic).
—	◡	—	—	Second Epitrite (Trochee & Spondee).

Feet of more than four "times" or syllables, are, strictly speaking, merely compounded of dissyllables and trisyllables. Musical examples of all the above could be easily given if space allowed.

On examination of the musical dissyllables and trisyllables (Exs. 1 to 15) many important questions present themselves.

1. It will be noticed that long syllables almost invariably fall on the accented part of a bar. Can we conceive of a long syllable in music as *quantity* without *stress?* This question has been discussed over and over again with reference to modern languages. Some authorities say that stress and non-stress have ejected *quantity* from our poetry, and bring forward such lines as the following in proof of their assertion:

"Th' infernal Serpent; he it was whose guile."

in which four out of the five syllables, short as regards *stress*, are by nature *long* in quantity.

Let us apply this to music, and ask whether we really reckon our feet by stress or quantity. If we reckon them by the latter then the following is correctly written:

Ex. 16.

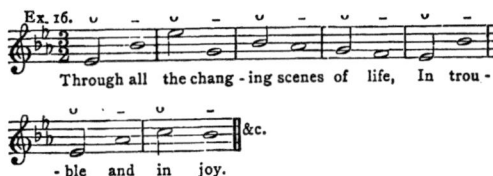

Through all the chang-ing scenes of life, In trou-

- ble and in joy.

Now this is *not* written correctly *musically,* because, although an iambus in poetry has only the relation of *short to long* in quantity, it has in music the relation *weak to strong* in emphasis. We therefore write it thus:

Ex. 17.

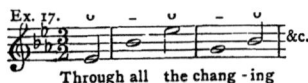

Through all the chang-ing

practically disposing of the first short syllable, and then presenting the succession of feet to the ear as *trochees;* for no one would venture to analyse this tune as consisting of the following groups:

Ex. 18.

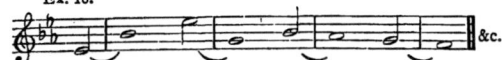

&c.

an analysis which is not only allowable but *necessary* if the analogy between poetry and music is to be sustained.

Again, in the following, the same *length* is given to the short syllables of the words as to the long:

Ex. 19.

All peo-ple that on earth do dwell,

Sing to the Lord with cheer-ful voice, &c.

One author, enthusiastic on the subject of quantity, actually proposes that the Old Hundredth Psalm should be thus sung:

Ex. 20.

All peo-ple that on earth do dwell,

Sing to the Lord with cheer-ful voice;

Him serve with fear, His praise forth tell,

Come ye be-fore Him and re-joice.

If musical feet were governed by quantity, and not by stress, the above would not only be correct but pleasant, whereas, we feel, that just in proportion as the words receive their due quantity, the true rhythm of the music is lost.

On the ground, then, that musical metre is governed more by stress than quantity, the analogy between ancient poetry and modern music cannot be maintained.

2. If the reader will refer to Ex. 4, which gives a musical trochee, he will observe that the short syllable is followed by a rest. This example was given, not because it was felt to be correct, but because similar examples are to be found elsewhere; but, as a matter of fact, *rests* in music form *part of rhythm*, and therefore, if two minims in a bar (being equal to each other in length) are considered as two long syllables, Ex. 4 is not a trochee but a spondee; and, what is more important still, iambics and trochaics can only be represented by *triple* time. Not only, then, is Ex. 19 incorrect, but *all* duple-measure psalm tunes set to hymns ordinarily spoken of as iambics are bad. On the ground, therefore, that when there are two notes of equal length in a bar we not only *may*, but *do* often consider the accented note long and the non-accented note short, we are again justified in saying that the analogy between poetical metre and musical rhythm does not hold good. With regard to the inclusion of silence or "rest" as a constituent part of rhythm, music diverges widely from poetry, and stands on a vantage ground peculiarly its own. It is true that *cæsura* in verse bears some similitude to a "rest" in music, in the effect it produces, but the likeness is only apparent, and the musician has the power of suggesting *length* in quantity, by a *short* note if it is a *stress-note, e.g.*:

Ex. 21. BEETHOVEN.
Ov. Men of Prometheus.

In the above example, each of the two bars is a trochee, the long syllable of which is represented by the chord and first rest, the short syllable by the final crotchet rest in each bar.

3. It will be seen that in Ex. 13, bars 3 and 4, two consecutive notes in each bar are grouped under one long syllable. This compression of two syllables into one foot, is a common occurrence both in ancient and modern poetry, as for example in the junction of consecutive vowels at the end of one word and commencement of another. In English poetry we have *mā ny a, glō rious*, &c., which exactly correspond to the musical junction of two notes under one metrical time-unit. This leads to the important question of the exact time relation of *short* and *long* in metrical feet. The general answer is that a long syllable occupies the time of two short syllables (—" Syllaba brevis unius est temporis, longa vero duorum "). But ancient writers relax this rule and say that all long syllables are not the same length, nor do they stand in the same relation to the short. Some allow that a short syllable may be a third of a long, or even less. How does this bear upon music? If we are to adopt the old system and names of metrical feet, are we only allowed to divide one long time-unit into two, three, four, or six parts? Our time table teaches that a semibreve is equal to thirty-two demisemiquavers, and this may be again multiplied by binding two stationary semibreves together into one "double" time-unit, in which case demisemiquavers will stand to it in the quantitative relation of sixty-four to one. The classical names of feet are therefore quite inadequate to represent the immense number of possible relations between the syllables of musical feet, and if we are to have musical metre on the model of classical metre, an entirely new system of nomenclature will be absolutely necessary.

After all, such names could only apply to

a single melody, or a simple harmonised tune, whereas, we know that one of the highest forms of modern music is harmony which consists of a combination of many melodies.

4. Lastly, is it of any practical use to adopt names and symbols of metre, if metre and musical rhythm are contradictory? That they may be so is shown by a comparison of Exs. 16 and 17, the former of which is perfectly correct metrically, perfectly ridiculous musically. Scholars explain this by saying that whereas metre depends on quantity alone, rhythm depends upon a combination of quantity and emphasis. Be it so, but in modern music, quantity without emphasis is inconceivable, therefore any nomenclature founded on quantity only is of no practical value.

It may be thought strange that so much space has been given to this subject of metre, solely for the purpose of depreciating its value and discouraging its use. But the classical names of feet are largely used as musical terms by certain writers, more perhaps from a desire to appear learned at a little cost, than from a knowledge of their real bearing on the art.

Metrometer. [Metronome.]

Metronome. An instrument said to have been invented in 1815 by Maelzel, for the purpose of measuring the relative duration of the notes in a piece of music. The machinery is of clockwork, and the various grades of time are measured on a balance-rod serving the purpose of a pendulum, the speed being regulated by a shifting or sliding weight. To be correct the metronome should beat seconds when set at 60.

Maelzel's claim to the invention rests on very doubtful authority, that is to say, only upon his own word; for in the "Journal für Deutschland" 1796 is a description of a time measurer in the form of a chronometer, J. S. Stoeckel, of Burg, claiming its invention; but this being of large and inconvenient size, Maelzel suggested to Winkel the desirability of a new contrivance, which Winkel succeeded in producing, Maelzel exhibited the instrument as his own invention, and his name is always associated with it, though all the part he really had in the matter was in dividing the balance-rod to agree with the varieties of musical *tempi*. The claim to this portion of the invention was allowed before the Dutch commission appointed to enquire into the subject at the request of Winkel, But neither of these has the right to be considered as the inventors of the machine, although Stoeckel and Winkel acted in good faith, and in ignorance probably of what had been done before them. A pendulum for measuring time, independent of clock-work machinery, was common in England before the metronome was introduced. This was a tape like that used by surveyors, and as the length was in actual inches, it was necessary to have so great a length that its general use was inconvenient. Many of the glees of Calcott, Horsley, Webbe, and some of the compositions of Crotch and other writers of the latter part of the last century have the time indicated by such a pendulum. Twelve years before the date of Stoeckel's invention, namely, in 1784, an amateur violinist and composer of Paris, Jean Baptiste D'Avaux, wrote to the "Journal Encyclopédique," describing a newly-invented pendulum for measuring time in music:—
" Lettre sur un instrument ou pendule nouveau qui à pour but de déterminer avec la plus grande exactitude les differentes degrés de vitesse, depuis le *prestissimo* jusqu'au *largo*, avec les nuances imperceptibles d'un degré à l'autre." This could hardly have been the invention of three-quarters of a century earlier, namely, in 1710, alluded to in the sixth edition of a work by Michel D'Affilard, published under the title of " Principes très-faciles, pour bien apprendre la musique, qui conduiront promptement ceux qui ont du naturel pour le chant jusqu'au point de chanter toute sorte de musique et à livre ouvert," in which the time of the exercises or airs is regulated by a "pendule." Taking the date into consideration, this instrument was probably the metronome or sonometer of Etienne Loulié, invented in 1696, described as a " chronometre ou instrument de nouvelle invention, par le moyen duquel les compositeurs de musique pourront desormais marquer le veritable mouvement de leurs compositions, et leurs ouvrages, marquez par rapport à cet instrument, se pourront, executer en leur absence s'ils en battaient eux-mémes la mesure." If this had been simply a cord or tape it would have indicated the time only while the motion lasted; but the contrivance was of clock-work, as " l'estampe représentant le chronometre" shows. In 1759 Henri, Louis Choquel also advocated the use of a chronometer, probably that of Loulié; and in 1807 Jeanne Etienne Despréaux published a chart or table of the different measures in music, under the title of " Chronomètre musical établi sur les bases du pendule astronomique," the machine employed being a modification of Loulié's invention. All that Maelzel did was to suggest the construction of an instrument more portable than any already in use, but the principle he worked upon was that which had been carried out nearly 100 years before he was born.

Mette (*Ger.*) Matins.

Metzilloth, Metzillthaim, Tzeltzelim (*Heb.*) These words are rendered in our version as *cymbals*, except in Zech. xiv. 20, where they are translated "*bells* of the horses," which is substantially correct, as little cymbals were formerly used in the trappings of horses. The cymbals used by the Hebrews were probably similar in form to those of the ancient Egyptians, some existing examples of which are here depicted. They were found in the tomb of a certain musician-priest named Ankhapê, lying close to his side. They are very small compared to modern instruments of the same class, being not more than five inches in diameter. [Cymbals.]

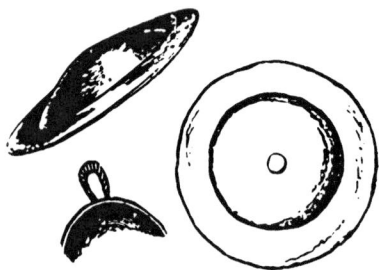

Mezzo, Mezza (*It.*) Half or medium, as, *mezza bravura*, semi bravura style; *mezza manica*, half shift; *mezza orchestra*, with half the orchestra; *mezza voce*, half the power of the voice; *mezzo carattere*, with a moderate degree of expression or execution; *mezzo forte*, moderately loud; *mezzo piano*, moderately soft; *mezzo soprano*, a voice lower in range than a soprano and higher than a contralto; *mezzo staccato*, slightly detached; *mezzo tenore*, a voice of tenor quality and baritone range; *mezzo tuono*, half the power of the voice; &c.

M. F. [Mezzo forte.]

M. G. Abbreviation of *main gauche* (*Fr.*), the left hand.

Mi. (1.) A syllable used to indicate E, the third note in the scale of C [Aretinian syllables]. (2.) In solmisation Mi always indicated the leading note. [Solfaing.]

Mi bémol (*Fr.*) The note E flat.

Mi bémol majeur or **mineur**. The key of E flat major or minor.

Mi contra fa. The name given by the old contrapuntists to the tritone, which was always to be avoided—"mi contra fa est diabolus." It is not as some suppose, the simultaneous sounding of the tonic with the leading note; but, as the notes of the scale of C in old solfaing were named—fa, sol, la, fa sol, la, mi, fa—the union or succession of the fa and mi would form the tritone, the leading note in the old scales always being called *mi*. [Solfaing.]

Middle C. The note standing on the first leger line above the bass stave, and the first leger line below the treble stave. [Stave.]

Mi dièse (*Fr.*) The note E sharp.

Militairement (*Fr.*), **Militarmente** (*It.*) In a military style.

Military Band. [Band, § 5.]

Minaccevole
Minaccevolmente
Minacciando ⎱ (*It.*) In a menacing, threatening manner.
Minacciosamente
Minaccioso

Mineur (*Fr.*) Minor.

Minikin. A small sort of gut string formerly used on the lute, viol, and other stringed instruments.

Minim. *Halbnote* (*Ger.*), *bianca* (*It.*), *blanche* (*Fr.*) A time character of the value of two crotchets. In modern music it is second in value to the semibreve now held to be the time standard, but in ancient music it was, as its name implies, of the shortest duration. Morley, in his "Introduction to Practical Musicke," 1601, ascribes the first use, if not the invention, of the minim to Philippo de Vitriaco, a musician of the 14th century, who is also credited with the invention of the crotchet. [Nomenclature.] [Notation.]

Minnesingers. The German name for poets of the Troubadour character, who devoted their talents to the production of love songs (Minnelieder). They enjoyed a certain amount of popularity in the higher grades of society for more than two hundred years (1138-1347), when they fell out of popular estimation, and were succeeded by the Meistersingers, *q. v.* [Troubadours.]

Minnim (*Heb.*) This word, which occurs in Ps. xlv. 8, and Ps. cl. 4, is probably a poetical allusion to stringed instruments generally. It is so rendered in the Bible and Prayer-book versions of the latter psalm. "Praise him with *stringed instruments* and organs." (*Bible.*) "Praise him upon the *strings* and pipe" (*Prayer-book*). In order to bring out its meaning in Ps. xlv. 8, it has been proposed to alter the text thus: "out of the ivory palaces, *stringed instruments* have made thee glad."

Minor (*Lat.*) Less, smaller. (1.) Intervals are said to be minor when they contain one semitone less than major. (2.) A scale is said to be in the minor mode when its third and sixth are minor. Formerly minor music was described as "with the lesser third." (3.) Flute minor, Klein flüte, a small flute-stop on the organ, of 4ft. or 2ft. pitch.

Minstrel. [Troubadour.]

Minuet (*Fr.*) The name of a graceful

dance said to have been invented in Poitou about the middle of the 17th century. The tunes for the first minuets are said to have been composed by Jean Baptiste Lully. A minuet was danced by Louis XIV. before his courtiers at Versailles. The Marquis de Flamarens introduced it into England in the reign of Charles II., who made the dance fashionable by having it frequently danced at Court. It continued to be popular as a court dance until the reign of George III.

The minuet form was used by many composers after Lully as a movement in sonatas, overtures, and the like, but composers made a few slight variations in the time and treatment in order to obtain as much originality as possible. The minuet with more or less success continued to be employed as a movement in instrumental music to the time of Beethoven, who abandoned it in favour of the Scherzo.

Independently of its use for dancing purposes the Minuet, almost immediately after its introduction, was adopted as part of a Suite, sometimes in the simple form as required for the dance and sometimes with a second minuet of a slightly different character and key appended. This second minuet was so arranged as to demand a return to the original key. The title of Trio for the second minuet is said to have been first suggested from the circumstance that only three parts or instruments were employed in the performance of that section; it is also stated that J. S. Bach is entitled to the credit of being the first so to call the second minuet. But the subjoined Round O (Rondo) minuet by Mr. Jerry Clark, c. 1700, shows an earlier division of the composition into three parts or strains, and the form itself suggests that the third part which takes the place of the trio in more modern minuets, is more likely to be called trio because of its third place than because it was written in three parts or for three instruments.

MINUET.

LULLY.

MINUET.

H. PURCELL. Chorus Lessons.

ROUND O MINUET.

1st Straine.

By Mr. JERRY CLARK.

2nd Straine.

Go to ye third straine ye second time.

3rd Straine.

1st Straine again.

End at ye 1st Straine.

Minuetto (*It.*) [Minuet.]

Miscella. A mixture stop of an organ.

Miserere. The 51st Psalm sung in the *Tenebræ* service in the Roman Catholic Church.

Mishrokitha, *or* **Masrakitha** (*Chaldaic*). This word occurs four times in the book of Daniel, and is probably rightly interpreted in the Septuagint by *Syrinx*.

Missa (*Lat.*) A mass, as, *missa pro defunctis,* a requiem mass ; *missa solemnis,* a solemn mass ; &c.

Misschallig (*Ger.*) Dissonant, discordant.

Missklang (*Ger.*) Discord, cacophony.

Misteriosamente, Misterioso (*It.*) Mysteriously. [Mass.]

Misura (*It.*) A measure, a bar.

Misurato (*It.*) Measured, in strict time.

Mit (*Ger.*) With, as *mit Begleitung,* with accompaniment ; *mit Bewegung,* con moto, &c.

Mitos (*Gk.*) μίτος. A thread, a term sometimes used for the string of a lyre.

Mittelcadenz (*Ger.*) An imperfect cadence, or half-close. [Cadence.]

Mittelstimmen (*Ger.*) Inner parts.

Mixed Cadence. An old name for a cadence, consisting of a subdominant followed by a dominant and tonic chord ; so called because the characteristic chords of the plagal and authentic cadences succeed each other.

Mixolydian. [Greek music.]

Mixture. An organ stop, consisting of several ranks of pipes to each note. It is only used in combination with the foundation and compound stops, as it consists of high harmonics of the ground tone. [Organ.]

Mode. (1) A scale [Greek music]. (2) A species of scale, as, *major mode, minor mode.*

Moderatamente
Moderato ⎫ (It.) Moderately.
Moderazione, con ⎭

Moderatissimo (It.) Very moderate.

Modificazione (It.) Modification, light and shade in expression.

Modinha. A Portuguese love song.

Modo (It.) A mode.

Modulation. (1.) Movement or graduation of sound; (2.) A change of key.

One of the chief characteristics of modern music is the constant change of key. In many of the recognized "Forms" it is absolutely necessary to introduce "second" subjects in a different, although a related key to the chief theme. Hence, in old Treatises on Music the subject is barely touched upon, whereas modern authors enlarge upon it. Modulation is of three kinds, Diatonic, Chromatic, and Enharmonic. The first of these is sometimes called natural; the last two, artificial.

A Diatonic modulation is the passing from one key to another by using chords from *relative keys*.

Ex. 1. BEETHOVEN, Symphony No. 1.

In the above (Ex. 1) a modulation is made from G minor to C, thus: G minor is a relative key of D minor, which is a relative key of A minor, which is the relative minor of C.

When a remote key is reached by relative keys, the modulation is by some said to be *extraneous*.

A chromatic modulation is the passing from one key to any other, by means of unrelated keys.

Ex. 2. BEETHOVEN, Symphony No. 3.

The above (Ex. 2) shows a chromatic modulation from the key of E♭ to that of F.

An Enharmonic Modulation is the passing from one key to another by the alteration of the *notation* of some of the over-lapping sounds, *e.g.*:

SCHUMANN, Song "Widmung."

It is not easy to distinguish between the use of the terms Modulation and Transition. It is generally understood that the former denotes an entry into a new key, with the intention of remaining for some time in it; the latter, the passing through a key rapidly, as for instance is often done in sequences. But by some, the word Transition is used for a *rapid modulation*. The Tonic Sol-faists call modulation in general, transition. Music-masters, who delight in technicalities, have, in addition to the above, divided modulation into (1) appropriate and digressive; (2) simple and compound; (3) partial and complete. (1) Appropriate modulation is when the sense of key is not disturbed by the movement of chords; digressive, when a complete change of key is made. (2) A simple modulation is a change of key into the next remove, that is, into a key having one more sharp or flat in the signature; a compound is the passing through relative keys into a remote key. (3) Partial modulation is a temporary change of key; complete, the establishment of a new key.

Moduliren (Ger.) To modulate.

Modus (Lat.) Mode. (1) A scale, as *Dorian mode*, &c. [Greek music.] (2) One of the three divisions of mensurable music [see Tempus and Prolatio]. Modus major was the division of a Maxim (*notula maxima*) into Longs. Modus minor the division of a Long into Breves. The "Modus major" was perfect when the Maxim contained three Longs, imperfect when it contained two. The "Modus minor" was perfect when the Long contained three Breves, imperfect when it contained two. The following (from Franchinus) exhibits the different kinds of Modus.

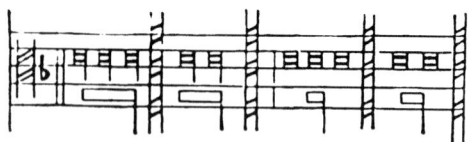

| Modus major perfectus. | Modus major imperfectus. | Modus minor perfectus. | Modus minor imperfectus. |

The division of Modus into "major" and "minor" was later in date than the division of mensurable music, into Modus, Tempus, Prolatio. Originally Modus (like Tempus and Prolatio) was only divided into Perfect and Imperfect. The former having the sign [..‾], the latter [.‾] This seems the more consistent, as then *Modus* is the division of Longs into Breves; *Tempus* the division of Breves into Semibreves; *Prolatio* the division of Semibreves into Minims. Each of these is *Perfect* when the division under it is trinary, *Imperfect* when binary.

(3) A Gregorian tone. This use of the word is not strictly correct, and has always been condemned.

Moll (*Ger.*) Minor.

Molle (*Lat.*) Soft. A term applied in mediæval music to B *flat*, as opposed to B natural which was called B *durum*. Hence, the term came to signify major and minor mode, as in the German, *e.g.*, A dur, the key of A major; A moll, the key of A minor. Hence too, the French formed the word *bémol*, a *flat*.

Mollemente (*It.*) Softly, sweetly.

Moll-tonart (*Ger.*) The minor mode.

Molto (*It.*) Much, very; as, *molto adagio*, very slow; *molto allegro*, very quick; *molto sostenuto*, much sustained.

Monaulos (*Gk.*) μόναυλος. A Greek single-pipe made of a reed. A flute à bec.

Monferina (*It.*) An Italian peasant dance.

Monochord. A single string stretched across a board or soundboard, under which a moveable bridge can be moved at pleasure. By placing under the string a diagram of the proportionate lengths of string required for the production of just intervals, the ear can be trained and experiments can be made. It was anciently called, or rather, the results obtained from experiments with it, the harmonic canon. [Acoustics.] [Temperament.]

Monocordo (*It.*) *Monocorde, à* (*Fr.*) On one string.

Monodia (*It.*) }
Monodie (*Fr.*) } A song for a single voice, generally of a plaintive character. The term was originally applied to vocal solos in the church service.
Monody. }

Monodrama. A dramatic piece for one performer only.

Monotone, to. To recite words on a single note without inflections.

Montant (*Fr.*) Ascending.

Monter in, ut, re, &c. (*Fr.*) To sing a scale of c, d, &c.

Montre. Mounted diapason. An organ stop whose pipes form part of the case or are placed away from the soundboard. One of the foundation stops is generally used for this purpose.

Morceau (*Fr.*) (1) A piece, a small composition of an unpretending character. (2) An excerpt.

Mordente (*It.*) *Beisser* (*Ger.*) A beat or turn or passing shake.

Written.

Played.

Morendo (*It.*) Dying away. A direction that the sounds of voices or instruments are to be gradually softened, and the pace slackened.

Morisca (*It.*) The Morris dance.

Morisco (*It.*) In the Moorish style.

Mormorando }
Mormorevole } (*It.*) In a gentle, murmuring, wishing manner.
Mormorosa }

Moriscoe, to. To dance the Morris dance.

Morris dance. *Morisca* (*It.*) A rustic dance performed in spring and summer time. There are many records extant to prove the universal popularity of this dance, both in the parish accounts of several dates and in the writings of poets of various periods. Douce in his illustrations to Shakespeare, supposes "that the Morris-dance derives its name from the Moors, among whom it originated, and that it is the same that gave rise to the Fandango. It was probably brought to England in the time of Edward III., when John of Gaunt returned from Spain. Few vestiges can be traced of it beyond the time of Henry VII., about which time, and later, the churchwardens' accounts show the dance to have been very popular at parochial festivals." Laneham, 1590, in his description of a Bride Ale, mentions "a lively Moris-dauns according to the auncient manner; six dauncers, Mawd-Marion and the fool."

The pipe and tabor were the ancient and are the present accompaniments to the dance, which is still occasionally performed at rural festivals. Tunes of various kinds were associated with it.

Morte (*Fr.*) The death note of any hunted animal sounded upon a bugle. "And whan the hare is take, and your houndes have ronne well to hym, ye shul the morte blowe oftirward, and ye shul yif to your houndes the halow." Twety in Rel. Ant., 1, 153, quoted in Furnivalle's reprint of the Percy MS.

> " And then to sigh, as't were
> The mort of the deer."
> SHAKESPEARE.

Mosso (*It.*) Moved, as *più mosso*, more moved or faster; *meno mosso*, less fast.

Mostra (*It.*) A direct √. A sign, suggested by Avison, for pointing out to a performer the entry of a particular point or subject.

Motett. A vocal composition in harmony, set to words generally selected from the Scriptures, or to paraphrases of the sacred writings. The motett was, at one time, a varied treatment of a given theme similar to the poem called in Spanish a "moto," referred to in the article Madrigal. Like the madrigal, the motett was at first set to words of a profane character, and there are ecclesiastical decrees extant forbidding its use in church. We read in Durandus "De modo generalis concillii celebrandi," cap. xix. "Videtur valde honestum esse quod cantus indevoti et inordinati motetorum et similium non fierent in ecclesia." And that the character of the motett was at one period the reverse of sacred, the following quotations from "Le Roman de la Rose," conjectured by Warton to belong to the 13th century, will show :

> " Qu'il faist rimes jolivettes
> Motes, fabliaux, et chansonettes
> Qu'il veuille à sa mie envoier."

And further :

> " Chantant en pardurableté
> Motes, gaudias, et chansonettes."

In the Constitut : Carmelit : Lib. III. :

"Neque motetos, neque uppaturam vel aliquam cantum magis ad lasciviam quam devotionem provocantem, aliquis decantare habeat, sub pœna gravioris culpæ."

And Du Cange quotes (verbo Motulus) a decree of Odo, Archbishop of Rouen, in which it is said :—"In festo S. Johannis et Innocentium nimia jocositate et scurrilibus cantibus utebantur utpote farsis, conductis, motulis ; præcepimus quod honestius et cum majori devotione alias se haberent."

The word motett was synonymous with *pulpitre* in the 15th century. In the account of the solémn entry of John of Burgundy, Bishop of Cambray in 1442, we read, "en

vidant de l'église, les enfants d'autels canterent le motet ou pulpitre, tournez le visage vers l'autel."

Morley, in his "Introduction to Musicke," imperfectly describes a motett as "a song made for the church, either upon some hymn or anthem, or such like ; and that name I take to have been given to that kinde of musicke in opposition to the other, which they called canto fermo, and we do commonlie call plainsong, for as nothing is more opposit to standing and firmness than motion, so did they give the motet that name of moving, because it is in a manner quight contrarie to the other, which after some sort, and in respect of the other, standeth still."

Probably for the reason above quoted, Du Cange suggests that the motett was originally of a gay and lively nature, and the similarity of style between the motett and madrigal of the 16th century would point to the conclusion that the titles were interchangeable until the character of the words of the madrigal fixed the title for this sort of writing, and the word motett remained to describe movements more especially intended for the church service.

Metrical psalms and hymns in which the several verses are sung to a varied setting are called motetts in the Roman Catholic Church. Many sacred cantatas of unconnected movements are also described as motetts. The early anthems took the place of the motett in the Anglican church, and many of the church compositions of the Elizabethan musicians are of the motett form. [Anthem.] [Madrigal.]

Motetto (*It.*) [Motett.]

Motion. (1) The movement of a single part with reference to intervals taken by it. *Conjunct motion* takes place when the sounds move by single degrees of the scale, *e.g.*, C, D, E, F ; *disjunct motion* is when they move by skips, *e.g.*, C, F, D, G. (2) The movement of two or more parts with relation to each other. *Similar* or *direct motion* is when parts move in the same direction either by single degrees or by skips ; *contrary motion* is when parts move in opposite directions ; *oblique motion* is when one part remains stationary while another moves.

Motivo (*It.*) *Motive*. (1) The sort of movement indicated by the opening notes of a sentence. (2) A subject proposed for development.

Moto (*It.*) (1) Motion, movement, as *con moto*, with spirited movement, keeping up the interest of the music. Hence *con moto* has become a time-sign, signifying *rather fast*. (2) *Moto continuo*, continuous motion, the constant repetition of a particular musical figure or group of figures. (3) *Moto con-*

trario, contrary motion ; *moto obbliquo*, oblique motion ; *moto retto*, direct or similar motion [Motion]. (4) *Moto precedente*, at the preceding pace ; *moto primo*, at the first pace.

Motteggiando (*It.*) In a bantering, jesting, jocose manner.

Motus (*Lat.*) Motion ; *contrarius*, contrary ; *obliquus*. oblique ; *rectus*, direct or similar. *Conjunctivus*, conjunct ; *disjunctivus*, disjunct. [Motion.]

Mounted cornet. [Cornet, § 3.]

Mouth. The speaking part of an organ pipe, as opposed to the *foot*, through which the wind enters.

Mouth organ. [Pan-pipes.]

Mouthpiece. *Embouchure* (*Fr.*) ; *Imboccatura* (*It.*) ; *Mundstück* (*Ger.*) That part of a wind instrument which is put into the mouth of the performer. In the case of brass instruments the end of the instrument is placed on the exterior of the lips, and in the case of reed instruments the reed itself is inserted in the mouth. The name *Kessel* is given by the Germans to the hollow or *cup* in the end of a brass instrument through which the air is forced, and *Schnabel* or *beak*, to the pointed end of oboes, clarinets, &c.

Movement. (1) Motion of melody, or of parts [Motion]. (2) A division, or definite portion of a work, as *first movement, slow movement*, &c., of a sonata or symphony, or other extended composition. (3) A portion of a musical piece separated from the rest by a complete change of time or key.

Mund (*Ger.*) Mouth of a pipe or musical instrument : *Mundstück*, mouthpiece.

Munter (*Ger.*) Lively, *allegro*.

Murky. A piece of harpsichord music, having a bass consisting of broken octaves, thus :

Musars. Ballad singers of the troubadour period.

Musette. (1) A small bagpipe (*corna musa*) formerly much used by the various people of Europe. (2) The name of a melody, of a soft and sweet character written in imitation of the bagpipe tunes. (3) Dance tunes and dances in the measure of those melodies. (4) A reed stop on the organ.

Musica (*It.*) Music. *Musica di camera*, chamber music ; *musica chiesa*, church music ; *musica da teatro*, operatic music.

Musical Box. A portable instrument the sounds of which are produced by a steel comb having teeth of graduated length. Projecting pegs or stops, in a metal barrel which is turned by clockwork set the teeth in vibration. They are chiefly made in Switzerland. Small specimens were formerly called musical snuff-boxes. A set of free reeds is now sometimes inserted for the purpose of sustaining a melody, in which case, the same mechanism which causes the barrel to revolve, also works a small bellows.

Musical Glasses. A series of goblets of graduated sizes fixed in a case. The tone is produced by the friction of the fingers of the player on the edge of the glass. The instrument has been recently revived under the name of Copophone. [Glass musical instruments.]

Musici. A name given to the followers of the Aristoxenian system. See Canonici.

Musico (*It.*) A musician, a term formerly applied to a Castrato (*q. v.*)

Muta (*It.*) A direction to a player on a horn, trumpet, &c., or on drums, to change the *key* of his instrument, as, *muta in A, B, &c.*

Mutation (*Fr.*) **Mutazione** (*It.*) Change.

Mute. A small instrument of brass, wood, or ivory, so made that it can be readily fixed upon the bridge of a violin or violoncello, to damp or deaden the sound. The direction for its use is written *con sordini* or *muta*, its discontinuance by *senza sordini*. A leather pad of a pear shape is employed as a mute for brass instruments, which, inserted in the bell, produces the effect of sound at a distance.

Mutiren (*Ger.*) The change of voice.

M. V. Abbreviation of *mezzo voce*.

N.

Nabla νάβλα (*Gk.*) [Nebel.]

Nablium (*Lat.*) [Nebel.]

Nacaire (*Fr.*) A large drum.

Naccare or Gnaccare (*It.*) [Castanets.]

Nacchera (*It.*) A military drum. [Nakeres.]

Naccherone (*It.*) A large military drum.

Nachahmung (*Ger.*) [Imitation.]

Nachdruck (*Ger.*) Emphasis, accent.

Nachspiel (*Ger.*) A postlude.

Nächstverwandte Töne (*Ger.*) The nearest Relative Keys, *q. v.*

Nacht-horn (*Ger.*) Literally "Night-horn," an organ stop consisting of stopped wood pipes of a moderately large scale, the tone of which is somewhat like that of a horn.

Nænia (*Lat.*) A funeral song of the Romans, mentioned in the laws of the twelve tables. "Honoratorum virorum laudes in concione memorantur; easque næniæ ad Tibicinem prosequuntor.

Nafiri. An Indian trumpet.

Nagaret or Nagareet. An Abyssinian drum; a kind of kettledrum. [Nakeres.]

Naguar. An Indian drum with one head only.

Naïf (*Fr.*) Simple, *naïvement*, artlessly, unaffectedly.

Nail Violin. [Eisen violine.]

Naked fifth. The interval of a fifth without a third.

Naked fourth. The interval of a fourth without the addition of any other interval.

Naker. A drum. [Nakeres.]

Nakeres (*Old Eng.*) The explanations of this word given by various authors are somewhat conflicting. Albert Way, in his edition of the "Promptorium Parvulorum," considers the word identical with the nagârah, or drum of the Arabs and Moors. Joinville speaks of the minstrels of the Soudan "qui avoient cors Sarrazinois, et tabours, et nacaires." Most probably nakeres were small metal drums, used in pairs. In the poem, "Sir Gawayn and the Grene Knyzt," (Early English Text Society,) the word occurs:

"Trumpez & nakerys
Much pypyng per repayres."

A genitive case "nakeryn" is found in the early English alliterative poems published by the same society. "Belshazzar's Feast."—(No. xiii.):

"& ay ðe nakeryn noyse, notes of pipes,
Tymbres & taborns, tulket among,
Symbales & sonetez swared ðe noyse."

Chaucer, too, makes mention of them in his knight's tale:

"Pipes, trompes, nakerers, and clariounes,
That in the bataille blowen blody sounes."

In Strutt's "Sports and Pastimes," a payment to Janino le Nakerer of sixty shillings as one of the minstrels of the King (Edward II.), is recorded.

Nanga. A negro harp. [Harp.]

Narrante (*It.*) As if narrating. A direction to a singer, implying that the music is to be subordinate, as it were, to the recitation of the words.

Nasard, Nazard or Nassat. An organ stop sounding a twelfth above the foundation stops. It will therefore be 2⅔ feet in length.

Nason Flute. A stop of 4ft. tone, sometimes found in old organs. It is of a soft and delicate quality of sound, and consists of stopped pipes.

Nassat. [Nasard.]

National Air, or National Music. Popular music, peculiar to, or characteristic of, a particular nation. It often happens, from the fact of a melody possessing the characteristics which render it generally popular, that it is passed rapidly *vivâ voce* from one person to another, with less consideration of the author than of the music he has composed: hence a tendency to lose the names of the composers of national music; but of course, music is none the less national because it has its author's name attached, and recent research has discovered the authorship of many a tune which was supposed to have this small claim to nationality.

It is impossible to describe a piece of music of any kind as national, until it has proved, by its continued existence, that it has those qualities which will enable it to live. Thousands of melodies, some of them unfortunately of the most worthless kind, from time to time take a firm hold of the common people of this and other countries; but the hold is not lasting, their popularity is but ephemeral, hence they are not truly national airs; and the airs which have become entitled to be called national, numerous though they are, are probably a mere fraction of the vast number which have had a short existence, and then sink into complete oblivion. Bearing these considerations in mind, it will not be difficult to give a definition of a "national air," as follows: an Air which, by its reflection or representation of a sentiment, taste, or habit of a nation, either through the music alone, or words and music combined, has become so commonly known and used by that nation, as to be inseparable from the idea of its special or characteristic music.

When the customs or tastes of nations are very similar, if their musical scale has also great similarity, we shall, of course, find many tunes common to all, and claimed by each. The more general the adhesion to the sentiment, or the greater the area over which the custom extends, or the more general the use of the scale from which it is formed, the more cosmopolitan will a piece of music become. The climate of a country, by acting upon the temperament of the inhabitants, influences indirectly the style of its music. It is incorrect to suppose that the minor mode is a universal characteristic of national music. From a statement drawn up in a tabular form by Carl Engel, in his important work, "An Introduction to the Study of National Music," it appears that in Sweden, Norway, Russia, Finland and Hungary, the minor mode predominates in the national music. In some countries, as for instance, in Moldavia, and Wallachia, and in Russia, the music seems to vacillate between the two modes, the tunes sometimes commencing in the major and ending in the minor. Sometimes also, tunes commence in the minor and end in the major. As might be expected, some melodies become altered in various ways in passing from generation to generation by oral tradition; our English Ballad literature, so ably collected and arranged by W. Chappell, abounds with examples. Some nations add profuse grace notes to a well known melody; this is the case with the Spaniards, but chiefly with the Arabs and Persians. The Welsh performance called *Pennillion* consists of varied accompaniments to the voice parts, and the tunes played on the violin by the Transylvanian gipsies abound in flourishes. As regards the scale in use in different countries, it does not happen, as might be expected, that a simple form of scale is used among nations of a low order of civilisation, and a more complicated form by a more civilised race. The contrary is often the case. The scale used by the Maories is

enharmonic, that is, contains intervals smaller than a semitone; while that of the Chinese is pentatonic, that is, consists of five sounds succeeding each other in a series similar to that which would be produced by playing only on the black keys of a pianoforte. The power of the ear to distinguish between sounds differing from each other by only a very small interval, varies considerably in different nations, some savage nations, the Maories for instance, having a perfect power of distinguishing between quarter-tones. The study of national music leads to the inevitable conclusion that all musical scales are purely conventional; the modern diatonic scale having no better claim to be founded on nature, or natural harmonics, than the complicated scales of the Arabs, Egyptians, or Hindus. Closely connected with the history of national music, is the history of national musical instruments, the two subjects throwing much valuable light on each other. The quality and pitch of that particular voice most common in any nation, will also much influence the style of the popular music. "Some Asiatic nations," says Engel, "sing in shrill notes by straining the voice to its highest pitch; others delight in a kind of vibration or *tremolando*. Some sing habitually in an undertone; others in a nasal tone. Others, again, cultivate with predilection the falsetto, and usually introduce it into their vocal performances." It is a fact generally known in this country that Russia abounds in deep Bass voices, and Italy in fine Tenor or Baritone voices. It is said that Hottentots are chiefly Tenors, and that the Chinese sing entirely in falsetto. A proverb current in the 14th and 15th centuries (see Chappell's Pop. Mus., p. IX., Vol. I.) says, "Galli cantant, Angli jubilant, Hispani plangunt, Germani ululant, Itali caprizant." The allusion to the English is undoubtedly meant for a compliment, they "sing cheerfully;" in "caprizant" is probably an allusion to the frequent use of the *tremolo*. It was commonly stated by English authors that England possessed no national music, but the researches of Chappell have brought together a collection of melodies of various kinds, which cannot be surpassed by any European nation. Unfortunately, our national songs are but little known in our large towns and cities; they are, however, handed down carefully in many rural districts where they may be heard in a more or less correct form.

Natural, ♮. A sign which restores a note to its place in the normal scale of C. It has the effect of sharpening a note previously flattened, or of flattening a note previously sharpened. It is an accidental, that is, it does not occur in the signature of a piece of music, unless at a sudden change of key, e.g.:

The earliest known use of the sign is found in Bonaffino's "Madrigali Concertati," 1623, a work in which also bars are employed as marking the correct divisions of time.

Natural harmonics. The sounds given off by any vibrating body over and above its original sound. Overtones. [Acoustics.]

Natural key. Key of C.

Natural modulation. Diatonic modulation, as opposed to Chromatic. [Modulation.]

Natural pitch. The pitch of a pipe before it is overblown.

Nay. A flute used in modern Egypt, but almost identical with the long flute anciently employed in that country. The most common *nay* is called the "Dervish flute," because with it those people accompany their songs at their zikrs or religious dances. Lane describes it as "a simple reed, about eighteen inches in length, seven-eighths of an inch in diameter at the upper extremity, and three-quarters of an inch at the lower. It is pierced with six holes in front, and generally with another hole at the back." It seems to have been played like our own flute, and like it to be capable of additional compass when blown hard.

Nazard. [Nasard.]

Neapolitan sixth. A name, apparently without much reason, given to a chord occurring on the subdominant of a minor key, and consisting of a minor third and minor sixth, e.g.:

It evidently can have nothing to do with the *key* of D♭ major in the position given above, although it appears at first sight to be the first inversion of the common chord of D♭. Nor can it be derived from the root G, inasmuch as a flattened fifth of a root is not admitted to exist by the best theorists. Some authors have explained the nature of the chord by calling the F A♭, notes derived from G, and the D♭ a note derived from C. This would make the chord a double-root chord (from G C) having the minor ninth of both roots, heard with the minor seventh and major third of the upper root. Another explanation found, is that it is derived from

the minor scale of the subdominant, in its modern form, e.g.:

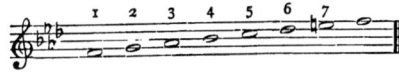

If we combine 1 3 6 of the above scale, we obtain the chord under examination. That it is so derived seems the more probable, inasmuch as it is often *preceded* by a common chord of that key-note, e.g.:

and sometimes *followed* by one, e.g.:

It is sometimes followed at once by a major tonic chord, e.g.:

Nebel (*Heb.*) One of the most important of the stringed-instruments of the ancient Hebrews. It was not as ancient as the kinnor, but was probably of more elaborate construction. It is almost always rendered, in our version of the Bible, by the word psaltery, two or three times by *viol*, once (Ps. lxxxi. 2) by the word psalm, "Take a *Psalm*, bring hither the tabret." This use of the word psaltery is most unfortunate, because it has by almost universal consent been the name of the ancient dulcimer, *psanterin, psalterion, psaltery, sautry*, &c. This has led to a double error, many theologians thinking that a psaltery is a *harp*, many musicians thinking that a nebel was a *dulcimer*. In all probability the nebel was a harp. It was portable because Saul met a company of prophets "coming down from the high place with a *nebel*." That it was used on secular occasions is proved by Isaiah's words (v. 12), "The harp, and the *nebel*, the tabret, and pipe are in their feasts." David was proficient on this instrument, and the list of his nebel-players is given in 1 Chron. xxv. 1, and elsewhere.

Nebendominant (*Ger.*) The dominant of the dominant, as D is in the key of C.

Nebengedanken (*Ger.*) Accessory ideas, or subordinate subjects.

Nebenstimmen (*Ger.*) (1.) Unessential parts, as for instance those notes which may be added to a triad, or those parts which are in unison with others. (2.) Accessory stops of an organ.

Nechiloth (*Heb.*) The generic name for wind-instruments.

Neck. That part of instruments of the violin and guitar class, which lies between the peg-box and the belly. To its upper surface is attached the finger-board or fret-board.

Nefer. An Egyptian guitar, called also Nofre. [Guitar.]

Neghinoth. [Nechiloth.]

Negligente, negligentemente, negligenza, con. (*It.*) In a negligent or careless manner.

Nel battere (*It.*) At the down stroke of the bar; on the beat.

Nel stilo antico (*It.*) In the old manner or style.

Nel tempo (*It.*) In time (after an *ad libitum*), or, in the previous time.

Nerves of hearing. [Ear.]

Nete (*Gk.*) [Greek music.]

Nettamente, netto (*It.*) Neatly, with precision.

Neumes. The musical notations employed from the eighth or ninth to the twelfth century. Their origin is doubtful; Kiesewetter considers them to be the ancient *nota Romana*, others believe them to have been of Asiatic origin. There can, however, be little doubt that the earliest system of musical notation was merely a series of directions as to the intonation (accentus) of the voice; the *acute* accent, directing the raising of the voice; the *grave*, the flattening of it; the *circumflex*, a movement up and down. These afterwards were modified into conventional cadences of various kinds, new signs being added from time to time to those already recognized, and the force and meaning of the old signs being amplified.

The progress of these signs from the acute, grave, and circumflex into *neumes* of different shapes can be traced with tolerable precision. The acute accent grew into the *virgula*, the grave accent into the *punctus*, the circumflex into the *clivus* and *podatus*. Hence, Coussemaker has, in his valuable " Historie de L'Harmonie au Moyen Age," divided neumes into *generators* and *derivatives*, separating the former into two kinds, " simple " (virgula and punctus) and " compound " (clivus and podatus); the latter class also into two kinds, " bound " and " conjoint." The following shews the accentual neumes as used in the eleventh century:—

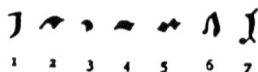

1 2 3 4 5 6 7

The names above are as follows:—1 Accentus acutus; 2 accentus gravis; 3 percussionalis brevis; 4 percussionalis longa; 5 inflatilis; 6 circumflexa; 7 muta.

The next illustration of neumes is part of an interesting list given in Gerbertus " De Cantu et Musica Sacra," Vol. II.:

It will be seen that the above shews the form of the scandicus, salicus, climacus, torculus, ancus, pentafon (spelt also pentaphone), strophicus, gnomo, porrectus, oriscus, virgula, cefalicus (cephalicus), clivus, quilisma, podatus. These are *dis*-arranged for the purpose of getting them into verse. But those who are curious on the subject will find two admirable explanatory tables in the work above alluded to, pp. 184, 185.

Neumes were originally written above the words to be sung to them. After the ninth century they began to assume graduated height and position, this was succeeded by the addition of lines and clefs. Neumes then grew into ligatures and into notes representing sounds of different lengths. The foundation of the modern system of musical notation was thus laid. [Notation.] The word neuma is probably connected with the Greek pneuma (πνεῦμα), a breath, and signified originally a group of sounds to be sung to a syllable; but later on this particular meaning seems to have merged into the more general one of *notes;* and *neumes* and *notes* are used almost as synonyms. When applied to the system of notation the word is spelt without the letter p (neuma); when applied to a series of notes to be sung to one syllable, the word seems generally to have retained its p (pneuma). The practice of singing pneumas has been at times carried to an almost ridiculous extent. They may be divided into two classes: first, the expansion of a melody in the middle of a word, as in modern runs or divisions; *e.g.*:

(*From the Compline Office on Holy Sunday.*)

This is not opposed to modern notions of musical form.

The second kind may be described as a sort of *coda*, or tail-piece to the final word of a sentence, and such pneumas were generally sung to the last syllable of the last word; *e. g.* :

Al - le - lu - ia . . . .

Neuvième (*Fr.*) The interval of the ninth.

Nexus (*Lat.*) One of three branches of Melopœïa—*Ductus, nexus, extensio.* Ductus was the movement up (*rectus*) or down (*revertens*) by single degrees. Nexus was movement by an interval, and was of three kinds; *rectus,* as *fa-gb-ac; revertens,* as *ca-bg-af; circumstans,* as *af-gb-af-ge.*

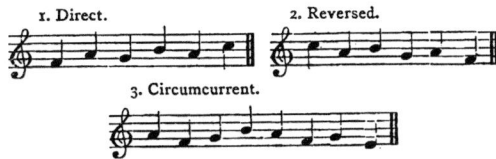

1. Direct.   2. Reversed.

3. Circumcurrent.

Extensio was the holding on of the same note. *See* Agoge.

Niederschlag (*Ger.*) The accented part of a bar.

Nineteenth. An organ stop. [Larigot.]

Ninna, nanna (*It.*) A cradle song.

Ninth, interval of a. A compound interval, equal to a second in the superior octave. It may be major, minor, or augmented, *e.g.* :

Major Ninth.   Minor Ninth.   Augmented Ninth.

Ninth, chord of the major. A chord formed by a combination of thirds starting with the dominant or fifth of the scale, called by some writers the " added ninth," because it consists of a chord of the dominant seventh, with the addition of the ninth; by others the " dominant' ninth," because it occurs on a dominant bass.

It is composed of five sounds, and, therefore has four inversions. Like all chords of the ninth, in its inversions the root or ground-note is seldom heard. They may be therefore written thus :

1st Inv.   2nd Inv.   3rd Inv.   4th Inv.

In the above, the ninth is made to resolve first, leaving the seventh to be resolved afterwards. In the following, both discordant notes are resolved in the next chord :

The fourth inversion, having the ninth in the bass, is not so commonly met with as the others. In the resolutions given above it will be seen that the third of the dominant, that is, the leading note, ascends to its tonic; the minor seventh descends; the major or added ninth descends also. The first inversion of this chord is sometimes termed the " chord of the seventh on the leading note," because the leading note of the scale is in the bass, and an interval of a seventh is found in the chord.

For similar reasons the second inversion is sometimes called the chord of $\frac{6}{5}$ on the supertonic, the third inversion that of $\frac{4}{3}$ on the sub-dominant, the fourth inversion that of $\frac{6}{4}{2}$ on the superdominant. This chord and its inversions (excepting the fourth) are often used without preparation.

Ninth, chord of the minor. One of the most important ingredients of modern music. Not only is it exceedingly beautiful to the ear, but from its peculiar form it gives the greatest possible facilities for modulation from key to key, whether closely related or not. It consists of a dominant, its major third, major (perfect) fifth, minor seventh, and minor ninth, *e.g.* :

In its inversions the dominant, that is, the root or ground-note, is nearly always omitted, *e.g.*:

In the above examples the ninth only has been resolved, leaving the seventh unresolved; but in resolving the seventh it will be found that the major or minor third of the succeeding chord may be used, thus :

Hence the chord is as often found in music in a major key, as in that in a minor. The beauty of the inversions no doubt arises from the fact that they consist practically of a combination of minor thirds, *e.g.* :

The alteration of the notation of the inversions of this chord gives scope for rapid enharmonic modulation. Take for example the second inversion :

No. 1 is derived from G, dominant of C
No. 2   ,,   E,   ,,   A
No. 3   ,,   C♯,   ,,   F♯
{ No. 4 ,,   B♭ } ,,   E♭ }
{ No. 5 ,,   A♯ } ,,   D♯ }

Nos. 4 and 5 are a complete change from a flat to a sharp key. Without altering the *sound* of the above chord it may be made to lead into any of the above keys or the keys related to them. Such a change of notation as this, without a change of sound, is termed an enharmonic modulation. It has already been shewn that the chord may resolve either into the major or minor mode ; therefore the tonic minors of the above notes, and also the keys related to them, may be reached with equal facility. On looking at the five changes given above, the reason why the ground-note or root is omitted from the chords becomes obvious, for not only would the symmetry of form produced by the conjunction of the minor thirds be destroyed, but also a definite resolution would become absolutely necessary, or, in other words, the invaluable property of "doubtfulness of key" belonging to such chords would be removed. One more fact should be noticed. If the list of the notes given above as the ground-notes of the five examples be read separately, thus : G, E, C♯, B♭, or, as Nos. 4 and 5 are convertible, G,

E, C♯, A♯, and their tonics, C, A, F♯, E♭, or C, A, F♯, D♯, we get the following :

which will be found to be identical with those derived from them when separated into ground-notes, both as to the nature of their construction and their capability for enharmonic modulation. The first inversion of this chord is often called the chord of the *diminished seventh*, because of the interval between the bass note and minor ninth of the root.

Ninth, chord of the suspended. A name given to the chord of the ninth on the tonic, as opposed to that of the ninth of the dominant, owing to the fact that the former is more often used as a *prepared* discord than the latter. The ninth may or may not be accompanied by the seventh (in this case the leading note). In the following examples the seventh is omitted :

The seventh is included in the following examples :

It will be seen that the note on which the suspension resolves· is not heard with the suspension, except in the original position of the chord ; also, that the third inversion is only to be obtained when the seventh is used. The ninth is not unfrequently resolved upwards, in which case some authors would not call it a "suspension," but a "retardation," *e.g.* :

The ninth and seventh are both used with the fourth, or, as it is more properly termed, the eleventh on the tonic ; under "Suspension," examples of their combination will be found.

The division of discords into discords of suspension, discords by retardation, discords by addition, and fundamental discords, is purely arbitrary, consequently hardly any two authors apply these names in the same way. It is highly desirable that a simple and consistent method of arranging chords should be generally adopted.

Nobile, nobilmente, con nobilità (*It.*) With grandeur, nobly.

Nocturns. Services of the church held during the night, for which certain portions of the Psalms are set aside, each of which is termed in the Breviary a nocturn. [Horæ Canonicæ.]

Nocturne (*Fr.*) [Notturno.]

Nodal line. [Acoustics, § 7.]

Node. [Acoustics, § 7.]

Nodus (*Lat.*) *Lit.* a knot. A Canon. So called because compositions of this class were sometimes given as enigmas, the meaning of which had to be unravelled. [Canon.]

Noël (*Fr.*) "Good news." *Old Eng.*: Nowell. A word used as a burden to Carols at Christmas. Hence, Carols are sometimes called noels, or nowells. [Carol.]

Nofre. [Nefer.]

Noire (*Fr.*) A crotchet ♩. The black note.

Noise (*Old Eng.*) Music, or a performance of music. As in Shakespeare's Henry IV., part II., Act 4, " See if thou canst find Sneak's *noise*." So also in Milton's " Ode on the morning of Christ's nativity : "

"When such music sweet
Their hearts and ears did greet,
As never was by mortal finger strook ;
Divinely warbled voice
Answering the stringed noise,
As all their souls in blissful rapture took."

The prayer-book version of the Psalms has " God is gone up with a merry *noise*." (" Ascendit Deus in jubilo." *Vulgate*.)

Nomenclature. In music the terms applied to the various signs employed to stand as the representatives of time, sounds, pitch, pace, and expression. Mr. Hullah, in a paper recently read before the Musical Association, says: " The signs relating to time are the breve, semibreve, minim, .crochet, quaver, semiquaver, and demisemiquaver. Of these names the first three have lost their significance ; the fourth is no longer appropriate ; the fifth, sixth, and seventh, are arbitrary.

" The Germans call these notes, beginning from our semibreve, the *whole note*, the *half note*, the *quarter note*, and so on. These appellations, so far as they express the proportion of the first note named to those which follow it, are convenient ; they form of themselves a time-table. But it is an imperfect one ; for they do *not* show, without further calculation, any intermediate proportion.

They show at once that eight quavers = one semibreve, but not at once that four quavers = one minim. But I have a much more serious charge to bring against them. They assume what, if not always false, is, as it seems to me, not always true—that the semibreve is, or that any form of note can be absolutely a 'whole note.' What is, or what should be regarded as a whole note? If I were sure that the word "phrase" represented to all of us the same idea as it does to me, I should answer unhesitatingly that a whole note was any note that could be divided into a phrase, or—to be a little more precise—any note divided or undivided, which would fill either an entire measure or require as many beats as would make one. This would give us practically four claimants to the title of *whole note ;*—the *breve*, the average whole note of the sixteenth century ; the semibreve, the average whole note of our own time ; the minim, and even the crotchet. For, that movements innumerable of four beats in a measure, each of which is a quaver, exist, I need not say, nor that the measure even of four semiquavers has been occasionally employed.

" It is certain that a sound lasting four beats may be expressed, and has been expressed by six different forms—the *maxim*, the *long*, the *breve*, the *semibreve*, the *minim*, and the *crotchet*. Perhaps some musician of the future may think proper to express such a note by a quaver.

" Let us now consider the names used by the French—a people possessing in high perfection the power of clear exposition of what they themselves see clearly. As usual, they leave or throw on one side whatever they regard as, uncertain, or equivocal, or not commonly accepted, and proceed to deal with the undisputed and indisputable facts or portions of facts before them. And what is there in respect to the forms which express the relative durations of sounds? First, that they are forms, and secondly, that they are different forms ;—that one is an oval or circle, that another is a circle with a stem, and another a circular spot also with a stem ; and that all other notes are opaque and have not only stems but hooks varying in number. They call these notes or forms as they find them,— *round, white, black, hooked, twice-hooked,* and *thrice-hooked.* I certainly prefer the German nomenclature, which, though raised on a false basis is consistent, to our own, which is inconsistent as well as false ; but I prefer the French to the German, because, not pretending to do so much, it does what it pretends to do perfectly.

" The nomenclature, not of sounds, but of the relations between them—the nomenclature of musical *intervals*, is a subject on which English theorists and practitioners are by no means agreed.

" I believe that the *seconds* and *thirds* and their inversions the *sevenths* and *sixths* found in the so-called 'natural' scale, and all scales made like it, are very generally called among us, *major* and *minor;* and that six of the *fourths* and their inversions the *fifths* are as generally called *perfect*. Here, however, agreement ends. For the one exceptional fourth and the one exceptional fifth rejoice each in as many aliases as a swindler finally run down by the police detective. To the exceptional fourth, which, according to the old theorists 'diabolus est,' I have heard and seen applied the name 'tritone,' and the epithets *sharp, superfluous, redundant* and *augmented;* to the exceptional fifth the epithets *flat, false, imperfect, diminished* and .*equivocal*. Others might possibly be added to this list. To the name *tritone* no objection is, I think, open; it expresses the contents of the interval— three tones; but it carries with it the disadvantage of there being no corresponding name for its inversion, the exceptional fifth. *Augmented* and *diminished* are no doubt antonyms; but both are epithets which, as I shall try to show, ought to be reserved exclusively for another class of intervals—the chromatic. *Superfluous* and *redundant* are, I think, clumsy epithets; but if either is to be applied to the exceptional fourth, its antonyms *scanty* or *insufficient* should be applied to the exceptional fifth. If this last interval is to be called *false*, its inversion (the tritone) should be called *true*. Only one of these epithets seems to me quite unobjectionable—*imperfect* as applied to the exceptional fifth. As an antonym to this I have long used the epithet *pluperfect*, which has been very largely adopted.

" I objected just now to the epithets *augmented* and *diminished* as applied to these particular intervals, the exceptional fourth and fifth. I think these should be reserved exclusively to chromatic intervals. I know of course that my objection involves a principle, or rather begs a question. What *is* a chromatic interval? This question, as often happens, throws us back on another. What is a chromatic *scale?* A chromatic scale I should define, with Dr. Crotch, to be a scale containing *more than two semitones*. The so-called 'natural' scale, and all other scales made like it, is not a chromatic scale, neither are any of the ancient scales formed from the arrangement of the same series of sounds in a different order. Of these last the 'natural' *minor* scale is one, and the only one familiar to the modern musician. Only however by means of a most serious alteration has it been

reconciled to modern tonality, which above all things demands, as the unequivocal sign, seal, or confirmation of a key, the combination known as the 'discord of the dominant seventh.' Such a combination on the 5th of the natural minor scale is only possible by an alteration or non-naturalization which at once brings it under Dr. Crotch's definition. In the series A, B, C, D, E, F♮, G♯, and A, we find three semitones, and one interval greater than a tone. Moreover, by skips from one note to another of a scale so constituted, we get three other intervals alien to the natural scale, the inversion of the altered second formed by F-G♯, the altered fifth formed by C-G♯, and its inversion. These intervals are, I conceive, augmentations or diminutions of intervals which would have remained unaltered, but for the artificial process needed to reconcile the minor key with modern tonality; they are therefore, I believe, generally called *augmented* and *diminished* accordingly. So all intervals, which the cultivated ear does not reject as cacophonous, formed by notes one or both of which are foreign to the key to which they are introduced, are but augmentations or diminutions of those that are natural to it. *Without change of key* we can augment certain of the unisons, seconds, fifths, and sixths; and diminish certain of the octaves, sevenths, fourths, and thirds. Now, as we have seen, in the unaltered or natural scale, major or minor, we find no examples of any one of these intervals; they are uniformly the result of artificial treatment. But, with the exceptional fourth and fifth the case is altogether different; they are not the results of artificial treatment, we find them ready to our hands; and they are as much constituent parts of the scale in which we find them as is the semitone between the third and fourth sounds. How then can the interval F-B in the scale of C, be augmented or B-F diminished? Of what are they augmentations or diminutions? Of F-B♭, or of F♯-B? Are B♭ or F♯ constituents of the scale —I do not say the key—of C? If they are, our modern tonality must be reconstructed *de fond en comble*, and every scale must be allowed three dominants instead of one. Again, we find that the intervals of the natural scale which bear augmentation are the largest of their kind in it, and those which will bear diminution the smallest. Of the seconds we can augment only the *major;* of the thirds we can diminish only the *minor*. Can we augment the tritone, the largest fourth in the scale, or diminish its inversion, the smallest fifth? Both have reached their utmost limits, and resist and defy all attempts to put them further asunder or bring them nearer together. If it be answered that they are already augmented and diminished, I ask again what was their original condition ? The tritone and its inversion are, I repeat, constituents of the diatonic scale ; and they are diatonic intervals accordingly. For the latter an epithet, *imperfect*, is already largely accepted ; I submit to you, in the absence of a better, the epithet *pluperfect* for its inversion.

" Before quitting this second division of my subject—pitch—I will ask you to give me your attention for a few moments longer. It seems to me that musicians have much cause to complain of the way in which not merely general *littérateurs* but even scientific writers employ words to which, since music has been an art, musical artists have agreed in attaching certain definite significations. Perhaps the most glaring instance of this, and it is the only one which I shall give, is the employment of the word ' tone ' to express the thing or sensation which we and they also sometimes call ' sound.' A *tone* with us is not a sound, but the relation or difference between one sound and another. This acceptation of the word would seem to be, if not as old as the musical art itself, at least of great antiquity, as is shewn in the co-existence of two such words as *tetrachord* and *tritone ;* the one, observe, representing a passage of four *sounds*, or strings which produce them. The other, an interval which, though it includes four sounds, is named after the three intervals— *tones*—which separate them. We hear now of *over-tones*, or the acute sounds resulting from spontaneous vibration ; and of *under-tones*, meaning grave sounds resulting from the combination of others. Some of us have occasionally been at a good deal of pains to explain that a major third consists of or includes *two* tones : if a tone be a sound, a major third must consist of three or even of five tones—or of both three and five. The most recent and extravagant employment of this word, in this sense, is in its application to great composers. Beethoven especially we often hear of as a great ' tone-poet.' I should say that if this terminology is to be accepted at all, it should be graduated or made more precise ; so as to express the rank of the poet to whom it is applied. If Beethoven be a *tone* poet, some of our contemporaries should be authorized to call J. S. Bach an *augmented* tone poet, and, *e converso*, Rossini a *semitone* poet. What designation should be applied to the vast crowd of less successful aspirants to musical fame I know not. Perhaps they might be put off with some of those minute intervals the excess or insufficiency of which disturbs the minds of those who still generously devote themselves to the search after that philosopher's stone of our art—Perfect intonation.

"I pass on now to the consideration of *expres-*

sion, under which term we may class words or signs indicative of *pace, intensity*, and *style*.

"A growing disposition has been observable of late among the different musical peoples of Europe to use their own languages as vehicles for these indications. I think this is to be regretted : (1) as inconvenient to foreigners among whom their music is likely to go. It seems hard on an English, French, Italian, Hungarian, or Bohemian musician, that to understand a piece of music by any eminent modern German master, he must not only be a musician, but a linguist ; that he should not merely be able to appreciate the musical sound of the notes in the score before him, but have also a vocabulary, practically unlimited, of German words. He opens, say, Schumann's Overture to ' Genoveva.' He sees by the position of the stave, headed by the C clef and designated ' *Bratsche*,' what is the meaning of that word ; he need not have much doubt about the stave similarly headed and holding three parts, against which is written *Posaunen ;* by the shapes of the passages intended for them, he may construe *Ventilhorn* in Es, *Waldhorn*, and *Pauken ;* and by the help of the metronome mark he may come at the meaning of *langsam*. But a little further on he encounters *leidenschaft-lich bewegt*, which is harder upon him ; and a little further still, *sehr frisch*, which is really too bad. This example has lately found imitators among the Scandinavians, who expound their musical intentions in words which a German of philological tastes and pursuits could doubtless make out, but which to the average German must be as unintelligible as to the average Englishman. Strange to say, the French, who take it for granted that everybody understands their language, or ought to, have not sinned in this way so much as the Germans. It is true that the scores of their operas are covered with phrases like ' avec chaleur,' ' très-simplement,' ' à demi-voix,' ' avec ironie,' but these may be regarded as ' stage directions ' addressed to, and inevitably intelligible to those who are to play the parts as well as sing the music to which they refer. Otherwise French composers limit themselves in their scores to a few native words such as *détaché, douce-ment*, and the like. As for ourselves, our modern musical publications would indicate, what certainly is the reverse of true, that we are the greatest linguists on earth. It is needless to present examples of what everybody is familiar with ; we have all seen, and see daily, title-pages, for instance, in which two, three, and even four languages are employed. (2) Irrespective of its practical inconvenience, which I do not wish to overrate, this practice takes from music its noblest characteristic—its catholicity. We musicians are able to discourse in a language touching to the hearts, if not always clear to the intelligences, of every people on the face of the globe ; and we are furnished with an alphabet in which to write this language, which is not the invention of a single mind, but of a thousand minds—a thing which has marched on to its present perfection *pari passu* beside music itself ; an alphabet so clear, to him who knows how to read it, that a musical composition, no matter of what intricacy, composed, let us say at Moscow, can, without any serious violation of the intentions of its author, and without his personal assistance, be performed within a few days, weeks, or months, in London, Paris, New York, or Melbourne—wherever there are artists to interpret it. Let us cherish this precious possession, and do what we can to prevent its acquiring a sectarian, provincial, or even national character, through the introduction of any peculiarities whatever. The directions of which I have spoken were, up to a comparatively recent time, made all the world over in one language — Italian. And even to this hour, the most Teutonic of musical composers are still obliged to resort to that language. In the score of which I have just spoken, Schumann's 'Genoveva,' there are as many Italian words or abbreviations of Italian words as there are measures, very often more. The words *dolce, sempre, basso, soli, divisi*, and the like, are of frequent occurrence ; and as for the contraction of *piano, forte, crescendo, diminuendo, sforzato*, and the like, they may be counted by hundreds. Granted that Italy has not been observant of Andrew Marvel's caution—

> "The same arts that did attain
> A power, must it maintain :"

granted that she has not held her own against such competitors as Germany during the last hundred years has brought into the field, are we to lose all veneration for the people whom the slightest acquaintance with musical history will show to have been the musical teachers of all the world ? Are we to kick down the ladder by which we have risen to our present superiority—to turn a cold shoulder on old friends because we have become better off, and it may be wiser than they ? Not, however, to throw more sentiment round this matter than it will bear, it does seem unwise to subject ourselves to the inconveniences of which I have spoken, when they can be avoided by the simple process of using only *one* vocabulary, and that not a new or unaccustomed one, but one with which every musical people is at least partially familiar."

Nomos. νόμος (*Gk.*) A song. νόμοι πολεμικοί, war-songs.

Nona (*It.*) A ninth.

Nonenakkord (*Ger.*) The chord of the ninth.

Nonetto (*It.*) A piece of music for nine voices or instruments.

Nonny, or "Hey nonny." A common burden to old English ballads, as " fa, la, la," was to madrigals.

Nonuplet. A collection of nine notes to be played in the time of eight, or six.

Normal Pitch. [Pitch.]

Normalton (*Ger.*) The standard sound. [A. § 5.]

Normaltonart (*Ger.*) The normal scale, C major and its relative minor A.

Nota (*It.*) A note, as, *nota buona*, an accented note ; *nota cambiata*, in counterpoint, the proceeding from a discord to a concord by a skip, *e.g.* :

nota caratteristica, a leading or characteristic note ; *nota cattiva*, an unaccented note ; *nota d'abellimento*, a grace note, note of transition ; *nota di passaggio*, a passing note ; *nota sensibile*, the leading note or subtonic.

Nota, or **Figura** (*Lat.*) (1) In general, any musical sign. (2) In particular, the signs placed upon the stave which shewed by their shape and position the duration and pitch of sound. They constitute the essence of *mensurable music* (cantus mensurabilis) as opposed to mere " signs of *intonation*," such as were the neumes. The first division of notes was, as might be expected, into long and short (breve or brief), "mensurabilis musica est cantus longis brevibusque mensuratus." (Johannes de Moravia.) The long was a four-sided note with a tail (No. 2); the breve a four-sided note without a tail (No. 3); the semibreve a diamond note (No. 4).

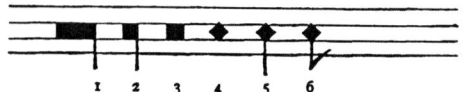

These notes varied in length (1) according to the time-signature, (2) according to the notes which preceded or followed them. (1) In *duple* measure each was equal to *two* of the next order ; in *triple* measure each was equal to three. Thus, an imperfect (duple) long was equal to two breves ; a perfect (triple) long to three breves, and so on. (2) A long was perfect when placed before another long ; imperfect when preceded or followed by a breve, &c. The double long or *maxim* or *large* is shewn in No. 1. It was in form like a long, but had an extended head.

The introduction of the *dot* (punctus) fortunately relieved musicians of the complications above mentioned, by adding half its value to a note regardless of its position or the time-signature. In course of time six musical figures were admitted, as shown above: 1, double long; 2, long; 3, breve; 4, semibreve; 5, minim; 6, semiminim.

In the fifteenth century an extraordinary movement to create novelties in notation seems to have arisen, and treatises of that date abound with rules as to the position of the *tails* of notes; for their absolute length or proportion to each other was made to depend on this. A breve was allowed a tail to the left, a long to the right. Also, notes with tails up and down ♦ were invented, called *dragme* or *fuiscée*, and notes with two tails in the same direction ⋎

Then, again, open notes (evacuatæ) were used, and when the head was black they were one-third less in value. These, and other similar complicated systems, never appear to have been generally received.

On the disuse of the double long (No. 1) the note No. 2 seems to have been made into the breve, No 3 into the semibreve, and No. 4 into the minim. The note No. 5 then became a *semiminima* (crotchet), and No. 6 the fusa or *unca* (hooked-note or quaver).

The notes Nos. 2, 3 and 4 were adopted by Marbecke, 1550, as his breve, semibreve, and minim, and are so named in one of the latest and best treatises on Church-song, "Les vrais principes du chant Grégorien" (Malines, 1845). But it should be remarked that in the "Traité théorique et pratique du plain-chant" (Paris, 1750). No. 2 is called the long, and No. 4 the breve. Other authorities might be cited to show that uniformity of nomenclature has never existed with regard to this subject. In the majority of modern works on Plain Song, No. 2 is the breve, No. 3 the semibreve, No. 4 the minim.

Notation, Early Systems of Musical, down to the invention of Notes.—The most ancient system known to us of expressing musical sounds upon paper, or other material employed for that purpose, is that of Alypius for the music of ancient Greece. This treatise supplies a complete method of representing the notes by letters of the Greek alphabet, the letters being sometimes upright, sometimes on their sides, and sometimes upside down, or broken in half. Unluckily, there are but three extant specimens of Greek music, in the genuineness of which any reliance can be placed, to which this system can be applied. The three are Greek hymns, of uncertain date, which were first published by Galilei in 1580, and by successive writers down to Dr.

Burney; but there are evidently mistakes, as well as omissions, in the manuscripts from which the printed copies were derived, and the results are therefore unsatisfactory. The system of Alypius does not supply an adequate clue to the scales that are included in the later Greek treatise of Aristides Quintilianus. Scales are a sure test as to whether a clue be right or wrong, especially where the accompanying text gives an explanation of the intervals that should occur, as in that case. The system of Alypius has therefore become, for practical purposes, useless. It may suffice then to say, that it may be referred to in the collection of Greek writers upon music published by Meibomius at Amsterdam in 1652. If any further specimens of Greek music should be discovered, it seems more probable that the later system of musical notation included in the treatise of Aristides Quintilianus will be of avail than that of Alypius. Aristides begins with the double *omega* for *gamma*—the *g* on the lowest line of the bass clef—and carries up the scale to the extent of three octaves and a third, viz. to *b*, including every intervening semitone as well as tone. This notation will be found on the lower half of p. 27 of his treatise, which is also included in Meibomius's collection of the Greek Authors on Music. The notation may be described as a later form of that employed by Alypius. Variations between the manuscripts used by Meibomius and others are noted at pp. 243 to 245 of the same work.

One other Greek system remains to us of uncertain date. This is the ecclesiastical notation of the Greek Church. It is supposed to have originated in Greek accents, and to have been gradually enlarged into a complicated system of signs for chanting. These were written over the words without lines or spaces. Specimens of this kind of writings of various ages, may be seen in Gerbert's *De Cantu et Musica Ecclesiæ* (vol. ii. p. 56 *et seq.*), and the signs are explained by Chrysante de Madyte, Archbishop of Durazzo in Illyria, in the third chapter of his Introduction to the theory and practice of ecclesiastical music,* published in Paris in 1821.

The Chinese have a good diatonic scale, but have now degenerated into a state of musical barbarism, and do not know how to use it. The Chinese system of musical notation is explained by Morrison in his Dictionary of the Chinese language. Chinese musicians use principally the five tones of the scale without the semitones, but they occasionally use semitones also, as is proved by the song, "Nien lai yun chue koo woo e,"

---

* Εἰσαγωγὴ εἰς τὸ θεωρητικὸν καὶ πρακτικὸν τῆς ἐκκλησιαστικῆς μουσικῆς (8vo.) Paris, 1821.

and by some others, printed in China about 1790. In these cases, supposing the interval between E and F to be a semitone as in our tonal system, it is to be found in passages both ascending and descending. As the fact of the use of semitones by the Chinese is denied by M. Fétis, it is well to give the title of the work from which this opposite conclusion is drawn. It is "Sin ting kew kung ta ching nan tsze kung poo," and is compiled by Chow Tseang-yüh and others. The music and the words of the song were kindly transcribed for the writer by Mr. Robert K. Douglas, of the British Museum, who adopted Morrison's interpretation of the musical notes.

We next come to the Romans, who derived both their system of music and of musical notation by letters of the alphabet, from the Greeks. The Romans adopted only one of the Greek divisions of the scale, viz., the diatonic, consisting of tones and semitones, as in modern music. They had therefore a sufficient number of characters in their alphabet without breaking the letters into parts, and without turning them round about, like the Greeks.

We have no extant specimen of the music of classical Rome, and there remains but one Roman treatise on music that has any claim to completeness, and yet it is far from being complete. This is by the "ultimus Romanorum" Boethius, who was put to death by Theodoric the Goth in 525. It is entirely copied from the Greeks by a philosopher who had read Greek treatises, but who seems to have had no practical knowledge of music, and in many cases to have mistaken the meaning of Greek musical terms, even of those which express the lowest and the highest sounds.

In later ages, Boethius was claimed as a Christian, and as he wrote in Latin, instead of Greek, there was a double reason why his work should be chiefly followed by writers on Church music.*

Nevertheless, the seven letters of the alphabet, A to G, which were used as names for the seven notes of the scale, were referred back by them to Virgil, as the "septem discrimina vocum," alluded to in the Æneid (vi. 645).

In the treatise of Boethius the letters run beyond G, and up to O and P,† for the second octave, but they are intended as demonstrations of the diagrams in the fourth book, rather than as musical notes. This is proved by A being there marked to the note that would be C in music, and by the same sys-

tem of illustration by letters being adopted throughout his treatise.

The mediæval system of musical notation was sometimes by letters of the alphabet, from A to G for the lowest seven notes, and from H to O for the second seven; but it was far more generally by marks or signs over the words called *neumes*, or *pneumata*, breathings for sounds. These names were taken from the Greek words, πνεῦμα and its plural πνεύματα. There are cases, but they are rare, in which the two systems of letters and neumes are combined, the letters giving greater certainty to the neumes. An early instance of this combination is found in a collection of Latin hymns, anciently used at St. Augustine's, Canterbury. The writing is of the tenth century, and the hymn is addressed to the Saint Augustin of the English (Austin the Monk). It begins: "Gemma sacerdotum! rutilans lux alma piorum Anglorum."

The compass of this hymn is nine notes, from bass C to tenor D, and the letters go up to L. (Cotton MSS., Brit. Mus. Vesp. D., vi. fol. 77.) A book was printed in facsimile in Brussels, a few years ago, entitled *Antiphonaire de Saint Grégoire*, supposed at first to be from a contemporary manuscript, and afterwards from a copy made about the year 790. The facsimile shows writing not older than the tenth century, and Father Schubiger conclusively disproves the assumed age and character of the manuscript by identifying one of the sequences included in it, "Laus tibi, Christe" (p. 62) as written by Notker, Abbot of the Monastery of Saint Gall. There is little reason for believing that the chants in any antiphonary of the time of Gregory the Great would be intelligible now, or indeed that they ever were legible without living help, for Saint Isidore, Bishop of Seville, who was a junior friend of Gregory's, and one who had long outlived him, says in the third book of his *Origines*, or Etymologies, that "unless sounds are retained in the memory, they perish, because they cannot be written."‡ This Saint Isidore wrote at the beginning of the seventh century. It seems to argue that the letters of the Roman alphabet were not in use for noting down Church music at that early date.

Neumes which had neither lines nor letters added to them were but marks or signs over the words, to serve as rough guides to the eye, whether the voice should rise or fall. They could only serve to remind the singer of chants which he had first learnt by ear. He could not tell exactly how far to ascend or to descend, and whether by tone or semitone, nor the note to begin upon. There was no

---

* This had an unfortunate effect upon Church music, and we propose to show elsewhere that at least one of its defects may be traced back to this cause.
† Our i and j count but as one letter.

‡ "Nisi enim ab homine memoria teneantur, soni pereunt, quia scribi non possunt."

precise measure of time in them. The earlier neumes were but an expansion of the system of accents and stops. At a later date, the flourish at the end of a chant, or of an *alleluia* was called *the neume*. These had no words to them, and were to be sung in one breath.

The next system was one without neumes, but with a ladder of letters placed one above the other at the beginning of the chants. The syllables of the words were then disconnected in order to place each syllable on a level with the letter which represented the note to which it was to be sung.

This system seems to have been invented in Flanders, by Hucbald, a monk of Saint Amand, who died at an advanced age in 930 or 932. Instead of using seven letters, he employed but four (on the Greek tetrachord system), viz., D, E, F, and G. He turned these four into four different positions, to make four disjoined tetrachords or fourths. The twisting about of the letters was probably borrowed from the Greek notation of Alypius. They were first in their ordinary position, then faced the reverse way, and then turned upside down, and faced to the left and to the right. By this means he obtained a scale of sixteen notes, and, for the seventeenth and eighteenth, to complete his number, he turned the first and second letters jacent on their faces.

It must be noted that Hucbald's scale was not what the ecclesiastical, or "Gregorian" scale is commonly supposed, and said, to have been. He made all his fourths to have the semitone between the second and third notes, as in D, E, F, G. This has been overlooked by all who have written about his notation, and Kiesewetter, in his *History of Music*, has translated Hucbald's examples without marking a single sharp or flat. Yet Hucbald's text is clear enough to any one not prepossessed with the immutability of "Gregorian" music, for he says repeatedly that his tetrachords have the same succession of intervals whether taken up or down.*

It is a mistake to suppose that what is called "Gregorian music" is of the age of Saint Gregory. The word means nothing more than the "use of Rome." "Nos Gregoriani

et nos Ambrosiani"—"We who follow the use of Rome, and we who follow the use of Milan." As another proof that the music is changed since the tenth century, a second writer of the same age may be cited. Notker says in his *De Octo Tonis*, that *every* chant of the first and second tones ends in B; of the third and fourth in C; of the fifth and sixth in D; and of the seventh and eighth in E.† This differs much from the law of later times.

The "Gregorian" tones have been changed by altering the positions of the semitones in the scales. The first and second of later dates end on D; the third and fourth on E; the fifth and sixth on F; and the seventh and eighth on G. The music cannot be the same, because the intervals follow in a different succession. It is not surprising that the music should have been changed since the tenth century, the only wonder would be, if it had not.

Hucbald's tetrachord, with its semitone in the middle, became the parent of the hexachord system, or six-note scale. It consisted of a tetrachord of the same kind as Hucbald's in the middle, and a tone added at each end. It had quite the same object—that of bringing the semitone into the middle (between *mi* and *fa*) so as to make the succession of intervals the same whether the scale were taken up or down.

Hucbald's scale was as follows: Γ (gamma) A, B♭, C,—D, E, F, G,—a, b♮, c, d,—e, f♯, g, a,—b, c♯. His letters were placed in spaces formed between lines, which lines were designed to represent strings. In the following example, our ordinary letters are used, instead of Hucbald's oddly shaped antiquities, because they are more readily intelligible to general readers.

A		a		
G		da	te	num
F	Lau		mi	de
E			do	e
D				cœlis.

The words are: "Laudate Dominum de cœlis."

One great objection to this system was the dislocation of syllables; and another was, that it rendered necessary the doubling and trebling of the vowels when there were two or three notes to one syllable. Lastly, Hucbald's musical scale was not ruled by musical

---

* See Hucbald's *Musica Enchiriadis*, in Gerbert's *Scriptores de Musica Ecclesiæ*, v. 1, p. 152. In col. 1, lines 17 and 18, "ut semper quatuor et quatuor ejusdem conditionis sese consequantur." In col. 2, lines 2 and 3, "Secundus deuteros, tono distans a proto; tertius tritos, semitonio distans a deutero." At p. 156, lines 1 to 4, "Sed dum forte in sono aliquo dubitatur qualis sit, tum, a semitoniis quibus constat semper deuterum tritumque disjungi; toni in ordine rimentur." P. 152, col. 2, "Sive sursum sive jusum sonos in ordine ducas." If it is to be the same up or down, the semitone must always be in the middle.

† "Ex septem bis quatuor sunt, nempe B, C, D, E, in quas omnis cantus desinit: qui primi et secundi toni est, desinit in B; qui tertii et quarti in C; qui quinti et sexti in D; qui septimi et octavi in E." Gerbert's *Scriptores*, I. 96. There were two Notkers at St. Gall, and this treatise is attributed by Gerbert to Notker Labeo (large lipped), but both were of the tenth century. The first was the abbot, and the second a monk of St. Gall.

laws. He had b♮, f♯, and c♯ as octaves to B♭. F. and c. Surely then some licence must have been taken by the singer. for no man with ears about him could sing such octaves. These were indeed the dark ages of music. Hucbald's harmony is equally barbarous.

In all countries which were in communion with the Church of Rome. the system of writing down the music of the chants, either by neumes or by letters, endured for several centuries. The great preponderance was by neumes; indeed. the use of letters was comparatively rare. The neumes were written over the words, without either lines or spaces to fix them to any pitch, or to distinguish tone from semitone. The earliest improvements upon this general practice are to be found in the Prosæ et Sequentiæ (Hymns of Praise) which each country produced for itself.

The earliest use of four lines and spaces is to be found in England. There are extant hymns with the neumes written upon alternate line and space, and with an index letter at the signature to fix the position of all, and these in a manuscript of the reign of Ethelred II, who is prayed for by name in the Third Litany as " our King" (regem nostrum), and whose reign was from 978 to 1016. The manuscript was then in use at Winchester Cathedral, and is now in the Bodleian Library at Oxford (MSS. Bodley, No. 775). The difference between this early English notation and that of later general use is neither great nor important. It consists only in the English use of any letter of the octave at the signature, instead of confining it to F, C, or G. Yet this is a sufficiently distinctive mark.

Only the new hymns are upon four lines and spaces. The prayers and the psalms have the old indefinite neumes.

The English continued to use any one of the seven letters at the signature down to the first half of the thirteenth century. At that time notes had been invented, and neumes were being gradually changed into the forms of notes.

Although early English service books are exceedingly scarce, owing to the wholesale destruction of them enforced by the severest penalties for having any in possession in the reign of Henry VIII., yet there are a few still extant. Among these are the Saint Alban's Gradual in the British Museum (MSS. Reg. 2 B. iv.), and an equally beautiful manuscript in the Cotton Collection (Caligula A. 14). These contain some of the same hymns which are included in the Winchester manuscript. and to the same music. An examination of the foreign collections of hymns, enumerated by Daniel, Mone, and G. Morel, does not reveal any of the same as having been in

use abroad, neither does the use seem to have extended beyond the southern half of England, all yet discovered belonging to the province of Canterbury.

Early English advances in music are to be traced to the same cause as the early proficiency in other arts and sciences, and in Greek and Latin. It was the fortune of England, about seventy years after the conversion of the southern part of the kingdom by Saint Augustine, to have a very learned Greek as Archbishop of Canterbury, and he came to England, accompanied by an almost equally learned African, who became Abbot of Saint Peter's, afterwards called Saint Augustine's, at Canterbury.

Pope Vitalian had offered the Archbishopric to Hadrian, but Hadrian pleaded his youth and unworthiness, and recommended Theodore in his place. The Pope was doubtful whether Theodore might not introduce some of the usages peculiar to the Eastern Church, and therefore sent Hadrian to accompany him, and to keep an eye over him in that respect. Theodore remained in England till his death, viz., from 669 to 690, and Hadrian survived him till 709. These two taught the arts and sciences as well as the languages of Greece and Rome, and the gain to the nation was soon apparent through the many learned men that England speedily produced.

The venerable Bede says that some of their scholars were living in his own time, who were as well versed in Greek and Latin as in their native tongue.* Aldhelm, who was one of Hadrian's pupils, was also one of the first Englishmen who became celebrated for his skill in music, in poetry, and in other liberal arts. It is clear that the organ was introduced into England about the time of, and probably by, Theodore, from Aldhelm's full description of it in his Laus Virginitatis.

It was a great advantage for us to have a Greek master, for the Romans, from Boethius downwards, knew very little about music. Boethius seems only to have known, or taught, the antiquated Pythagorean division of a scale, with all major tones in it, and so false thirds. The celebrity of Greek teachers endured at least till the 11th century, for Guido d'Arezzo, in his letter De ignoto Cantu, thus alludes to them : " I have seen many very acute philosophers who, for the study of this art of music, have not only sought Italian, French and German masters, but even the very Greeks themselves.† Neither did the cultivation of music, once introduced, die away in England, for, in the time of St. Dunstan, who was himself an organ-builder, the Winchester organ

---

* Bede's *Ecclesiastical History*, Book 4, cap. 2.
† " Ipsos que etiam Græcos quæsivere magistros."

had 400 pipes. The large number of men necessary to blow this organ (which was to be heard all over Winchester), seems to prove the bellows to have been on the Greek construction. Wolstan (or rather Wulstan) of Winchester, who describes this great organ in his metrical life of Saint Swithun, was the author of a treatise on harmony (*De Tonorum Harmonia*); which continued in use in the 13th century. William of Malmesbury describes it as a most useful book (*valde utile*), nearly a hundred and fifty years after it had been written, while St. Dunstan was the author of a still extant "Kyrie," a creditable specimen for the age, in good Greek Dorian or D minor.

Some of the Anglo-Latin hymns, written upon lines and spaces, are of a very florid character. (See, for instance, Cotton MSS., Julius A., vi. fols. 18 and 19.)

The next musical system in order of date was that of the hexachord. This endured for many centuries, and yet it seems impossible to find any thing in it to commend. It is Hucbald's system applied to the later church-scale, and with extra complexity.

The one argument in its favour adduced by old writers is the ultra-perfection of the number 6. This admirable quality is discovered through its containing within itself all its aliquot parts, viz., 3, 2, and 1, and "such perfect numbers are rare."[*] To all this, it might have been answered that the hexachord does not contain six equal parts; but, in any case, its perfections will weigh lightly in modern estimation against the far more ancient, the one and only true system of the octave. Eventually the hexachord system was combined with that of the octave.

The hexachord required not only the alphabetical name for the note (which sufficed by itself in the octave system) but also to tag on two or three other names. Wherever the interval between two notes was but a semitone, there was placed a *mi* for the one, and a *fa* for the other; and as there was a b flat in use, as well as a b natural in the *acute* and *super-acute* parts of the scale, so there must be a separate hexachord for each of the two, and at the interval of only one tone, the first hexachord beginning on F, and the second on G. The addition of the tone below Hucbald's tetrachord seems, by accident rather than by design, to have changed the hexachord from minor into part of a major scale, by moving the position of the semitone to the interval of one tone higher. If any one had designed such a reason for the change, there would have been some sense in the system, although it was still but an imperfect attempt to return to the octave. As it was,

it may have been an accidental stepping-stone to the use of the major scale, by placing C below Hucbald's D, and thus making the intervals in that position, C, D, E, F, G, A, but this order of notes already existed in the scale. The ancient Greek scale was wholly minor, and beginning and ending on the third note of a minor scale must make a "relative" major. The sharp seventh is a comparatively modern addition to minor scales.

The following is the Hexachord system included in the octave scale:

	e†	la		
	d	la	sol	
Super-acute.	*c*	sol	fa	
	b♮		mi	
	b♭	fa		
	a	la	mi	re
	g	sol	re	ut
	f	fa	ut	
	e	la	mi	
Acute.	*d*	la	sol	re
	c	sol	fa	ut
	b♮		mi	
	b♭	fa		
	a	la	mi	re
	G	sol	re	ut
	F	fa	ut	
	E	la	mi	
Grave octave.	D	sol	re	
	C	fa	ut	
	B	mi		
	A	re		
	Γ	ut		

All this surplusage of names does not suffice to distinguish the notes of one octave from another. There are two E-la-mis, two F-fa-uts, two G-sol-re-uts, two A-la-mi-res, two b-fas, and three b-mis. The only notes distinguished are C and D, so there could hardly be a more complicated and useless system of nomenclature. It was taken from the initial syllables of a hymn to Saint John the Baptist, which is too short to be omitted.

Ut queant laxis   *Solve* polluti
Resonare fibris,   *Labia* reati,
Mira gestorum   *Sancte* Johannes.
Famuli tuorum:

Here was a *sa* for the seventh note of the scale; but, on account of the perfection of the number 6, it was not employed. In later use, in order to mark another semitone by the vowel i (as in *mi*) *sa* was turned into *si*. *Ut* was also changed to *Do* (France excepted) for the sake of openness of the vowel, although it was already included in *sol*.

Guido Aretino, or d'Arezzo, had for a long time the credit, or discredit, as some may think it, of having invented the hexachord system. He makes no claim to it in any of his works, and as M. Fétis has justly re-

* Walter Odington, *apud* De Coussemaker's *Scriptorum*, I. 215.

-† This "*e*" in the super-acute part of the scale is an addition made in the 14th century.

marked. Guido's fame has rested far more upon what has been attributed to him, than upon what he really did. His reputation as a teacher was well deserved, for he directed his pupils to sing intervals without always referring to the monochord, but, instead of it, to think of similar intervals in some well-known hymns, such as this "Ut queant laxis." It appears from John of Cotton,* who wrote soon after Guido, and who was one of his great admirers, that this had been long the practice with French, Germans, and English, and even upon this particular hymn, but it was unknown to Cotton that the Italians had ever employed it for that purpose before Guido's time.†

A second system, which has been attributed to Guido, is that of the red and yellow lines for F and C. In his *Micrologus* Guido says: "In order that sounds may be discerned with certainty, we mark some lines with various colours, so that the eye may immediately distinguish a note, in whatever place it may be. For the third of the scale [C] a bright saffron line. The sixth [F], adjacent to C, is of bright vermilion, and the proximity of others to these colours will be an index to the whole. If there were neither letter nor coloured line to the neumes, it would be like having a well without a rope—the water plentiful, but of no use to those who see it."‡ This exactly describes the state of all music with neumes only, and it sufficiently accounts for all the changes that have occurred in the traditions of several centuries. Of the fact of change there can be no reasonable doubt. Much of the Gregorian

music is now just as deficient in tonality as the Chinese ; but a skilful organist can, by the use of anti-Gregorian harmonies, bring some of it into shape.

It will be observed that Guido does not claim to have invented the use of the red or yellow line, but to have employed them. There are specimens of both colours, among the fragments printed in Martini's *Storia della Musica*, which have been judged to be decidedly older than Guido's time, and M. Fétis (in his memoir of Guido) states that he has in his own library some more ancient still. The superior antiquity of the red line seems to be beyond question. This system was undoubtedly an improvement upon the oldest—that of having neither line nor letter to the neumes—but it was not one that would lead up to the use of alternate line and space, because the lower C, the third of the scale, was below F, the sixth, and there could be no line between them, unless lines only, and not lines and spaces, were employed. D and E only intervened between C and F, and so a single line with its space on each side would have been too much.§

Guido himself makes claim but to one invention, which he describes as "most useful" and "hitherto unheard."|| John of Cotton gives him the credit for the same.¶ It is but a modified copy from Hucbald, utilising the spaces without employing the lines. Instead of twisting round the four letters, as Hucbald did, Guido placed the five vowels, a, e, i, o, u at the ends of the spaces ; and when more notes than five were wanted, then the a, e, i, o and u were repeated. The system is shown in the following example :

Ma	a,				ma		ra	a
F	ri		ri		lis	u	be	e
		ve			ter,			i
				so			os	o
						tu	u	u

The words are: "Maria, veri solis mater, ubera tuos." This system will hardly be judged as an improvement upon that of Hucbald. The vowels were not even distinguished by capital and small letters, so that a, e, and i, each represented three different notes, and o and u two ; unless there were a double line of a, e, i, o, u's, as with the mi fas. A, for instance,

---

* This author is largely quoted by foreign writers, and always as Johannes Anglicus, but his precise birthplace is not known. There are four places named Cotton in England (besides Cotton Abbots and Cotton Edmunds). They are in Suffolk, Yorkshire, Cheshire, and Shropshire. It may be conjectured that he was one of the monks driven from England in the time of William I., for, if he had remained here, his excellent treatise would surely have been quoted by some English writers, such as Odington, and he could hardly have escaped notice by Bale and others. Cotton dedicates his treatise "Domino et patri suo venerabili antistite Fulgentio"—not "*Anglorum* antistite," as printed by Gerbert. There is an imperfect copy of his treatise, written in the 12th century, in the Cotton Collection (*Vespasian*, A., xi. fol. 131). It is to be inferred that he went from one of the northern counties, in the province of York, as he does not seem to have known Canterbury use.

† Cap. i. *apud* Gerbert's *Scriptores*, 2, 232.

‡ Regulæ Musicæ Rythmicæ, apud Gerbert, ii. 30-31.
"Ut proprietas sonorum discernatur clarius,
Quasdam lineas signamus variis coloribus ;
Ut quo loco quis sit tonus mox discernat oculus.
Ordine tertiæ vocis splendens crocus radiat,
Sexta ejus, sed affinis, flavo rubet minio ;
Et affinitas colorum reliquis indicio.
At si littera vel color neumis non intererit,
Tale erit quasi funem dum non habet puteus.
Cujus aquæ. quamvis multæ, nil prosunt videntibus."

§ Some years ago the writer exhibited several specimens of this musical notation with the red and yellow lines to the Musical Society of London. The parchments had been cut up to line the covers of old books. The chants were plagals, so the C line was always below F.

|| "utilissimum usui, licet hactenus inauditum," *Micrologus*, Cap. 17.

¶ "Adhuc et aliam modulandi monstramus viam, pulcram sane, sed ante Guidonem inusitatam." Cap. xx., Gerbert's *Scriptores*, II. 256.

might be either gamma, the lowest note of the scale, the E above it, or the c above E.

Guido's invention was dying out of use about 1220, when Walter Odington wrote his treatise.* Odington does not in any way notice the red and yellow line system, which, if it was ever adopted by English scribes (and that seems doubtful), must soon have passed away. His own examples are upon the English plan of employing any one of the seven letters as a clef note, and of utilising four lines, and spaces, changing the clef (*clavis*) when the compass extended beyond them.†

There are some difficulties in fixing the exact date of Guido Aretino, or d'Arezzo. The one fact which ought to be beyond question is the evidence of Guido's cotemporary, Adam of Bremen, who says that, about 1067, Hermann, Archbishop of Bremen, called Guido, the musician, to Bremen, to correct the music, as well as the monastic discipline of his See.‡ At the other extreme of date stands the prose version of the *Micrologus*, which is dedicated to Theobald, Bishop of Arezzo, who, according to Ughelli, died in 1037. There seems but little doubt that Cardinal Baronius (writing in the 16th century) was wrong in placing Guido the musician, under the year 1022. The very quotation that he copies supplies a sufficient correction. It is from a manuscript of the *Micrologus*, ending: "Explicit Micrologus Guidonis, suæ ætatis anno *trigesimo* quarto,§ Johanne *Vigesimo* Romanam gubernante ecclesiam, sub quo ejusdem Guidonis librorum editio facta est." The Cardinal adds of Pope John XX.: "Successit hic Benedicto," and again: "ex cujus numeratione pariter

intelligimus Joannem Benedicto successorem, *Vigesimum* ordine nuncupatum ejus nominis Romanum Pontificem." (*Annales Ecclesiæ*, anno 1022.) As Benedict VIII. was Pope in 1022, that date could not be right for either of the Johns. John XIX. succeeded Benedict VIII. in 1024, and John XX. followed Benedict IX. in 1044, and was deposed by the Council of Sutri in 1046, after which Benedict IX. was restored.‖ The short reign of John XX., his speedy deposition, and the restoration of Benedict, have caused John to be overlooked by some chronologers, and there is a gap in the list of Johns which they supply variously. M. Fétis has adopted John XIX. as Guido's John XX., and it has seemingly been the cause that induced him to question, if not wholly to reject, the most reliable of all the evidence—that of Adam of Bremen—because Guido might be supposed to be too old to be sent for in 1067. But the date of John XX., 1044 to 1046, would restore the probability, and Baronius's error of 1022 may be accounted for by a confusion between Guido Aretino the musician, and another Guido Aretino, who became prior of the convent of Santa Cruce at Avellano in 1029. The latter has often been mistaken for Guido the musician, and M. Fétis has enumerated some of the cases.¶

Having touched upon the date of Guido, it is of more importance to our present subject to point out some anachronisms in the copy of the *Micrologus*, printed by the Abbé Gerbert. A manuscript of the earliest date should have been selected for publication, for, in so popular a work, it might have been expected that the notation of the examples would be adapted by the copyist to the use of his own age. Those at pages 10 and 12 of Gerbert's edition have been thus modernised. They are printed on lines and spaces, which Guido did not use together, and a comparison of the whole text with that of one of the manuscripts in the British Museum,** proves that large additions have been interpolated to Guido's text in Gerbert's edition, not only in the *Micrologus*, but also more largely in the *De ignoto Cantu*.

The transition from neumes to notes was an easy one. It was called "quadrating"

---

* "Sed talis modus componendi jam evanescit." See Coussemaker's *Scriptorum*, I. 217.

† See "De Clavibus," p. 214. "Unam dictarum clavium semper una linearum lineatur, aliter spaciatur; linearis pro eo quod lineæ applicatur; spatialis pro eo quod spatium occupat, ut hic." This most useful treatise has been recently printed by M. E. de Coussemaker, in his *Scriptorum de Musica medii Ævi nova Series a Gerbertina alterum*. The only writer unquestionably English in Gerbert's Series is John of Cotton. M. de Coussemaker has added John Hothby (called Ottebi by Italians), Walter Odington, John of Garland, John of Tewkesbury, Simon Tunstede, Robert de Handlo, John Hanboys, Theinred of Dover, and the works of some anonymous writers, together with a greatly increased number of good foreign authors. The limited number of copies printed makes the speedy acquisition of this collection desirable to all those who are interested in the subject.

‡ "Musicum Guidonem Hermannus, Archiepiscopus, Bremam adduxit, cujus industria melodiam et claustralem disciplinam correxit." *Historia Ecclesiarum Hamburgensis et Bremensis*, &c., *ab anno 788 ad 1072*, lib. 2, cap. 102, p. 30.

§ M. Fétis has printed it 24 instead of 34 in his Memoir of Guido. *Biographie Universelle des Musiciens*, v. 4, p. 147, col. 1.

‖ "Silvestre III., antipape, étoit évêque de Sabine, lorsqu'après avoir chassé Benoit IX., en 1044, les Romains le mirent à sa place. Trois mois après, Benoit fut retabli par sa famille : son rival forcé de céder, vendit sa dignité à un prêtre, qu'il sacra sous le nom de Jean XX., mais resta lui-même à Rome, et conserva ses partisans. Le conseil de Sutri, 1046, les déclara tous les deux usurpateurs—Voyez Benoit IX. et Gregoire VI." (*Dictionnaire Général de Biographie et d'Histoire*, par Ch. Dezobry et Th. Bachelet, Paris, 8vo, 1857.)

¶ *Biographie Universelle*, v. 4, p. 148, col. 2.

** Addit. MSS., No. 10,335, eleventh century,

them, *i.e.*, squaring them like the old shape of the natural B. They thus filled the spaces between the lines. But although such changes were easy, they were practically slow, because old habits and prepossessions worked against them.

The best explanation of neumes is that of M. de Coussemaker, in his *Histoire de l'Harmonie au Moyen Age*, where two tables of neumes with their interpretations, will be found at p. 184. Whoever shall desire to modernise neumes will do well to consider first the country and the age in which the manuscript was made. For instance, the *Quilisma* may be either a mark for a tremulous expression without altering the note,* and it may be a sign of graduated ascent of two or three notes.† The first is the earlier use (and just what its form would seem to have been invented to express) and the second is the later use, when neumes were soon to be altered into notes. The reader will find many pages of facsimiles of neumes in M. de Coussemaker's great work, and some in Gerbert's *De Cantu et Musica Ecclesiæ*, v. 2, about and after p. 60. A third source for the student is at the end of the so-called *Antiphonaire de Saint Gregoire*,

* [Quilsima est] "unisonum quia not habet arsim et thesim" [*i.e.* neither rise nor fall] "nec, per consequens, intervallum vel distanciam, sed est *vox tremula :* sicut est sonus flatus tibiæ vel cornu, et designatur per neumam quæ vocatur Quilisma" (B. Engelbertus, per Gerbert, *De Cantu*, v. 2. p. 60).

† "Hæ Antiphonæ, licet a finali incipiant, tamen, quia per Quilismata, quæ nos *gradatas neumas* dicimus, magis gutturis." (Bernonis Augiensis *Tonarius*, Gerb. *Scrip.* v. 2, p. 80.)

which he should bear in mind to be only a facsimile of a manuscript of the tenth century. The names of the neumes transformed into notes will be found in Walter Odington's treatise (p. 213). and in some other treatises in M. de Coussemaker's collection.

Notazione musicale (*It.*) The system of musical notation.

Note. A sign of a sound made of various shapes to denote relative duration. Hence, the term is used generally for the sounds of which notes are signs, as when we say of a singer that his high *notes* are good, or that a player plays wrong *notes*. [Nota.]

Note (*Fr.*) A note, as, *note dièsée*, a sharpened note; *note d'agrément*, a grace note, note of transition ; *note de passage*, a passing-note ; *note sensible*, the leading note or sub-tonic ; *notes de goût*, (Fr.) notes of embellishment.

Notturno (*It.*) Originally, a kind of serenade ; now a piece of music of a gentle and quiet character.

Notula (*Lat.*) The notes used in writing ligatures. [Ligature.]

Noursingh. An Indian horn or trumpet, formed of a straight metallic tube. It is supported in a horizontal position by means of a long stick.

Novemole. [Nonuplet.]

Nuances (*Fr.*) Shades of musical expression.

Nuovo, di (*It.*) Again.

Nut. The fixed bridge formed by a slight prominence or ridge at the upper end of the strings of instruments of the violin and guitar family.

O.

O. A circle, formerly the sign of Tempus perfectum, as the incomplete circle C was of Tempus imperfectum. [See Tempus, Modus and Prolatio.]

O (*It.*) Or, as *flauto o violine*, flute or violin.

Oaten-pipe. The simplest form of a reed pipe, a straw with a strip cut to form the reed, at the end closed by the knot.

Ob. Abb: of *Oboe*, also of *obbligato*.

Obbligato. An instrumental part or accompaniment of such importance that it cannot be dispensed with.

Ober (*Ger.*) Over or upper, as, *Ober-manual*, or *Oberwerk*, the upper manual; *Oberstimme*, and *Obertheil*, upper part.

Obligé (*Fr.*) [Obbligato.]

Oblique motion. When one part moves and the other remains stationary. [Motion.]

Oboe. One of the most ancient, as also one of the most charming instruments of music. In some of the Egyptian pipes in the British Museum were found pieces of thin wood or straw inserted into the tubes in such a manner as to suggest at once the similarity between them and the oboe. In all probability the Greeks used instruments of this class, although they called them by the general name of "flute." That the reeds used were very small, and of more perishable material than the tubes into which they were inserted, is quite sufficient to account for the fact that we have not discovered a pipe with a reed fixed in it ready for use, among Greek antiquities. Moreover, it must be remembered that musicians do and always did carry their reeds and mouthpieces about, separated from the instrument. The word γλωσσόκομον proves that Greek players were not exceptions to this rule. Almost all European nations have some form or other of the oboe in use, though the different kinds vary much in their merits as musical instruments, some being in the simplest form of a reed-pipe played by mountaineers, as the *chalumeau* (from *calamus*, a reed), which is still played by the peasantry in the Tyrol, and the *piffero pastorale* of the Italians, a similar instrument to the *chalumeau*, called *Schal·ney* by the Germans, and formerly *shalm* or *shawm* in England. The immediate forerunner of the modern oboe was the bombardino, or little bombardo, called by the Italians *bombardo piccolo*, a kind of *chalumeau*. The date of the introduction of the oboe is about 1720, but from the mention in Bach's Passion-music of two kinds of oboe, the oboe d'amore and oboe da caccia, it is evident that well-known varieties were in use in his time. The oboe d'amore, which was also called *oboe luonga*, produced a delicate and sweet tone, while the *oboe da caccia* corresponded to the tenoroon oboe, or corno inglese. The latter, though not in common use, is occasionally introduced into the scores of modern operas, as in Halévy's *Jewess*, Meyerbeer's *Huguenots*, &c.

The oboe now in use owes its large compass, like many other wind instruments, to the overblowing of the player, which brings into existence a set of *overtones*. The overtones of the oboe are similar to those of an open pipe, that is, they are represented by the numbers 1, 2, 3, 4, &c., while on the other hand, the overtones of a clarinet correspond to those of a stopped pipe as represented by 1, 3, 5, 7, &c. The notes lying just between the sounds produced by the natural length of the pipe (as shortened also by finger-holes and keys), and those produced by an altered pressure of wind from the player's mouth, always present difficulties of execution when required to be played in rapid succession. The clarinet has a single reed; the oboe, a double one. The extreme compass of the oboe now in use is two octaves and one fifth, namely:

with the intermediate semitones, subject to certain limitations in their use. Some instruments have the low B♭

but it is not yet commonly met with. The compass given above should be very much curtailed for general use, the four or five lower notes being weak and thin, the two or three upper notes harsh and shrill. The latter, however, are not objectionable in *fortissimo* passages in *tutti* parts. The following shakes, lying between intervals played with difficulty, are given by Berlioz (Instrumentation) as difficult :

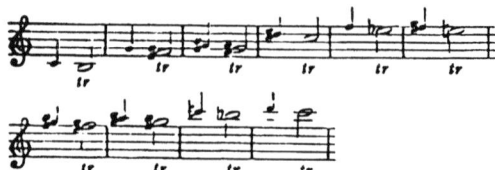

The following are impossible (and all tonal or semitonal shakes above this):

The oboe is more effective, because more easily played, in simple keys, than in keys with many sharps or flats; and in simple passages, than such as are complicated or rapid. As an instrument of a pastoral character it can be cheerful or plaintive; it possesses also in its peculiar quality of tone, the wail of grief or agitation, but it has also the power of soothing and calming the mind after disturbing influences.

Oboe. An organ stop consisting of reed pipes slightly conical and surmounted by a bell and cap, of 8ft. pitch. The tone is thin and soft. An *orchestral* oboe is an organ stop intended as a more perfect imitation of the orchestral instrument than that ordinarily made.

Oboe da caccia. The "hunting" oboe, a large kind of oboe. [Oboe.]

Oboe d'amore. The oboe "of love." A small oboe. [Oboe.]

Oboist. A player on the oboe.

Oboista (*It.*) An oboist.

Ocarine (*It.*) A series of seven musical instruments made of terra cotta pierced with small holes, invented by a company of performers calling themselves the Mountaineers of the Apennines. With these instruments, which are of a soft and sweet, yet "travelling" quality of tone, operatic melodies with simply harmonised accompaniments were given.

Octave. (1) The interval of an eighth. It may be major, minor, or augmented, *e.g.* :

It was the *diapason* of the Greek system. (2) The first note of the harmonic scale. (3) An organ stop of 4ft. pitch on the manuals, or

8ft. on the pedals. (4) The eight days following a great festival of the Church.

Octiphonium. [Ottetto.]

Octochord. An instrument with eight strings.

Octuor. [Ottetto.]

Octuplet. A group of eight notes which are to be played in the time of six.

Odeon. ωδεῖον (*Gk.*) A building in which odes or other compositions could be performed for public approval or private rivalry.

Odeum (*Lat.*) [Odeon.]

Œuvre (*Fr.*). Opus or work, as, *œuvre première*, Opus 1 ; *chef d'œuvre*, a masterpiece.

Offen (*Ger.*) Open ; as, *Offenflöte*, open flute. [Flute.]

Offertoire (*Fr.*) **Offertorio** (*It.*) **Offertorium** (*Lat.*) [Offertory.]

Offertory. (1) The collection of alms during the celebration of Holy Communion. (2) A piece of music performed during the Offertory.

Oficleida (*It.*) [Ophicleide.]

Ohne (*Ger.*) as, *ohne Ped.* without Pedals. *Ohne Begleitungen,* without accompaniments.

Oioueae. The vowels of "World without end, Amen," an imitation of the *Evovae*, the vowels of " seculorum amen," used to designate the ending of a mode. [Evovae.]

Oliphant. The name of an obsolete species of Horn, so-called because it was made of ivory (olifaunt, olivant, olyfaunce, being old forms of the word elephant). Three specimens of this instrument are in Kensington Museum, two of the eleventh century, one of the fifteenth.

Ombi. A harp used by negroes in Western Africa, the strings of which are made of fibrous root or creepers. It bears a strong resemblance to the Oriental harp.

Omnes, omnia (*Lat.*) Chorus or Tutti.

Omquäd. The name of the refrain of some old Danish ballads, called the " Kämpe Viser."

Onágon. A Chippawa drum.

Ondeggiamento, ondeggiante (*It.*) With an undulating, or quivering sound; making a tremolo.

Onduliren (*Ger.*) To make a tremolo, or produce an undulating tone.

Ondulé (*Fr.*) Undulating. [Ondeggiamento.]

'Ood or Oud. An Egyptian instrument of a similar character to the guitar, *q. v.* It is flat on the upper surface and convex at the back. The neck is like that of the guitar but without frets, and there are seven pairs of strings, each pair tuned in unison. The player uses a plectrum formed of a strip of vulture's quill. [Lute.]

Open Diapason. The name in England of the chief open foundation stop of an organ, called by Germans "Principal" or "Prestant," and by French "Principal," or if in front, "Montre." On the manuals it is of metal, on the pedal organ of metal or wood. The metal pipes of this stop are cylindrical, and of the best material. A great number of foreign organs, and a few in England, contain open diapasons made of pure tin (Organ, § 13). It is, however, more commonly made of spotted metal, or of an equal mixture of tin and lead. If two or more open diapasons are allotted to one row of keys, they are made of different scales, in order that they may not destroy each other. One is then sometimes called large, another small. This stop is of 8ft. length on the manuals, and 16ft. on the pedals, unless stated to the contrary on the register.

Open Harmony. Chords formed by as equidistant a disposition of the parts as possible, e.g. :

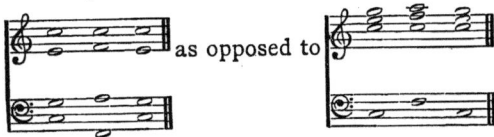

as opposed to

Open Notes. Of stringed instruments, —the notes of the open strings (q. v.) Of wind instruments, such as the horn, trumpet, &c., the series of natural harmonies which can be produced by the lip of the performer without the assistance of a slide, key, or piston.

Open Pipe. A pipe open at the top, as opposed to one closed at the top. The pitch of a closed pipe is approximately one octave lower than that of an open pipe of the same length. [Organ, § 14.]

Open Score. When each part has a separate line assigned to it, music is said to be in open score. When more than one part is written in each line, in close or short score.

Open Strings. Strings producing the sounds assigned to them according to the "accordatura," or system of tuning belonging to the particular instrument. Strings are said to be stopped when their pitch is altered by the pressure of the finger.

Opera (It.) A dramatic entertainment, in which music forms an essential and not merely an accessory part. Rousseau declares that Opera does not mean so much a musical work, as a musical, poetical, and spectacular work all at once, and the same definition is insisted upon by Wagner. This, scarcely the exact or true meaning of the term even now, was still less true in the days in which it was first written, as many works well known at the time, Rousseau's among the number, do not answer this description. The various titles given to works included in the general term Opera, also argue against Rousseau's definition, for if opera meant all he declares it does, there would scarcely be any need to speak of operas as scenica, tragica, sacra, regia, comica, esemplare, regia ed esemplare, etc. Algarotti calls his work on the opera "Saggio sopra l'Opera in musica," a title he could scarcely have given with propriety if the word Opera implied even music, much less if it included all the terms used by Rousseau. The opera, as we now understand it, is composed of solos, recitatives, duets, trios, quartetts or other pieces for single voices; choruses and finales; accompanied throughout with instruments variously combined to produce certain desired effects. Overtures or introductions precede the whole work or its several acts in nearly every case. The dramatic effect is aided by the accessories of costumes and scenery, but they are not absolutely indispensable portions of an Opera. The libretto or book of words, rarely possesses any claim to literary merit, but serves as a mere framework for the purposes of the composer.

Recitative is a species of musical declamation, not necessarily in rhythmical form, but so arranged or designed as to assimilate musical sounds as near as possible to ordinary speech.

In many of the German and French operas of a lighter character, spoken dialogue is introduced in the place of recitative, and the same practice is often observed in English opera, so called.

There are many varieties of opera, but the chief are: the grand opera or opera seria, the romantic opera, or opera drammatica; and the comic opera, or opera buffa. There are of course many works which partake of more than one of the styles indicated by the above divisions, but as a rule, these three classes are sufficiently distinct.

The opera is of Italian origin, and of comparatively modern date, and is the immediate successor of the miracle-plays with music, as the Oratorio is of the ancient mysteries. The consideration of the important part played by music in the performance of the ancient Greek drama, has given probability to the idea of a high antiquity for opera; and Menestrier (c. 1670) whose ingenuity has made him a favourite authority in musical history, considers the song of Solomon as the earliest opera extant. The first composition in any way resembling the lyric opera of later date, is said to be a work by Adam de la Hale, called "Le gieus de Robin et de Marian," produced some time in the 13th century. But as few trustworthy particulars have descended to us, there is nothing but the mere statement to rely upon. The title of this early opera implies, however, that it had some degree of connection with the ancient secular plays sometimes performed as a relief to the mysteries. The deeds or " gests " of " Robin Hood and Maid Marian," form the subject of more than one early play. Sir John Hawkins, in his " History of the Science and Practice of Music," declares that " the invention of the musical drama or opera is due to Emilio del Cavaliere, who in the year 1590 exhibited in the palace of the Grand Duke of Florence, *Il Satiro* and *La Disperazione di Fileno*, two dramas of the pastoral kind set to music." Others state that Ottavio Rinuccini is the inventor, and that the first opera (performed privately) was called *Dafne*, and that this was followed by the production of *Eurydice*, in the year 1600, the music to both works being furnished by Jacopo Peri, one of the inventors of recitative. But there is evidence to show that a musical drama by Claudio Merulo was performed in 1574 at Venice, when Henry III. passed on his way from Poland to France to claim the crown. Claudio Monteverde, a member of a society called the Florentine Academy, who also set to music Rinuccini's *Dafne*, introduced an improvement by giving great importance to the accompaniments. One of Monteverde's operas, *L'Orfeo*, was the first of the kind printed with the music. The *dramatis personæ* and the instruments used in performance are worth quoting.

PERSONAGGI.	STROMENTI.
La Musica Prologo......	Duoi Gravicembani (Clavicembali.)
Orfeo......	Duoi Contrabassi de Viola.
Eurydice	Dieci Viole di Brazzo.
Choro di Ninfe e Pastori	Un Arpa doppio
Speranza	Duoi Violini piccoli alla Francese.
Caronte....................	Duoi Chittaroni
Choro di spiriti inferni	Duoi organi di legno.
Proserpina	Tre bassi di gamba
Plutone	Quattro tromboni.
Apollo	Un Regale.
Choro di pastori che fecero la Moresca nel fine	Duoi Cornetti. Un Flautina alla Vigesima seconda. Un Clarino con tre trombe sordine.

There was scarcely any difference between the church music of the period and the operas, inasmuch as both were in the same conventional forms, and with little attempt at religious or dramatic expression. The choruses in the early operas were written in what is called the Madrigal style, and were seldom essential parts of the work ; there were instrumental preludes to each of the acts, and the artifice of accompanying a certain voice with a special instrument was occasionally employed. As the study of music progressed, and the capabilities of the instruments forming the orchestra came to be better understood, the lyric drama began to assume its present character. Of the vast number of Italian operas produced up to the middle of the last century, only one, Cimarosa's *Matrimonio Segreto*, retains its place upon the stage. Though not absolutely the founder of the modern Italian school, Cherubini may be said to have inaugurated it. After the production of his first operas at Milan, he settled in France, leaving the direction of the opera to the illustrious Rossini. The versatility of Rossini's genius is well shown in those of his operas that keep their places upon the lyric stage, for although *Semiramide, Il Barbiere, Otello, La Gazza Ladra*, and *Guillaume Tell*, contain much that is bad and unworthy, among some noble thoughts nobly expressed, yet each opera is distinct in style and treatment. As a melodist Bellini ranks next in order of merit, as he does in point of time, and his operas *Norma, I Puritani*, and *La Sonnambula* give greater pleasure through the beauty of their melodies, than they do by their dramatic force. The same power of melody is the chief attraction in Donizetti's operas, but this last named composer has shown in *Lucrezia Borgia, La Favorita*, and in *Lucia di Lammermoor*, that he was also gifted with the spirit of conveying dramatic expression, though scarcely in so great a degree as his successor Verdi. Rossini who found Italian opera weak from inanity, by the efforts of his genius, made it strong and powerful, but the charm of melody with which he graced the revived form had greater fascinations for his followers than dramatic vigour, the real life and soul of opera. Italian opera has quietly subsided into the lifeless state in which it was found by Rossini, for there is no representative composer worthy or willing to develop and perpetuate that which is considered as the true Italian school, the characteristics of which are wealth of melody, sentiment without pathos, and little regard for instrumental effect. Rossini, by the infusion of a foreign element, departed in some degree from the standard models, for until his time German music was held in the greatest contempt in Italy, but he laid the foundation for a taste among his countrymen for the despised music by quietly introducing in his works many of the characteristics held to be essentially Teutonic, and at variance with the established orthodox style of operatic music. Verdi, the next great composer after Rossini, shows in his compositions the result of the grafting of German ideas upon an Italian stock.

His works, while possessing many points peculiar to Italian music, really belong to the German school of art, as much because of the freedom displayed in the instrumentation, as the evident and often successful attempt to impart the expression of passion by means of pure declamation. Therefore, as Verdi is accepted as the modern exponent of Italian opera, it may be safely said that Italian opera proper has almost ceased to exist.

The introduction of the opera into France is said to have been the work of Lully, but it is stated upon better authority, that the credit rests with Cardinal Mazarin ; for there exists the record of the performance in Paris of an opera in Italian in 1645, a time when Lully was only in his twelfth year. It is also affirmed that the first opera performed in Paris was the composition of an Italian, named Baltzarini, also called Beaujoyeux, who came to France in the year 1580, and was afterwards made *valet de chambre* to the queen of Louis XIII. In the year 1669 the Abbé Perrin obtained a patent from Louis XIV. to establish an academy of music, the former privilege granted by Charles IX. to Antoine le Baïf having become valueless. Under the rule of the Abbé the first opera in French delighted the ears of the Parisians. Notwithstanding the popularity of Lully and his successors, and the influence of court patronage—which may be said, in passing, to be not always of the best advantage to art—the French have failed to establish a school of grand opera peculiar to themselves, and it was not until the time of Auber that they were able to claim any individuality in opera at all.

The support of the French court dying with Louis XIV., opera in France suffered many vicissitudes, until new life was infused into operatic taste at the beginning of the present century, from which time opera has been steadily encouraged, many of the best works of modern time having been first produced in Paris.

The encouragement given to the production of grand opera in Paris, does not establish a right for the French to lay claim to the works so brought out as belonging to their school of art, a mistake which they and others seem inclined to make.

The greatest triumphs of musical art in France were first gained by Gluck, and there is no doubt but that such individuality as the French composers have been able to gain for themselves, is due to the example set by him. This individuality, if such it may be called, is to be found in the writings of Gretry, Mehul, Boieldieu, Halévy, Auber, and Gounod, which upon examination will be found to be of a composite character, as much Italian as German, and more Italian and German than French.

The history of attempts to establish a school of national opera in England would be a mere record of rash and unfortunate speculations. The example set by Purcell has never been successfully followed, and while he has been proudly pointed to as the founder of the English school of opera, two centuries have passed, and scholars are still wanting to the school.

Purcell's operas, judged by the ordinary standard, and not by the three-fold characteristics demanded in our own days, have especial claims to consideration. The happy union of words and music in them was far in advance of anything that had been produced before. The delicacy of expression with which his compositions abound has not been surpassed by any subsequent English opera composer. His occasional " barbarisms," as they have been called, may be considered as " unavoidable compliances with the false taste of the age in which he lived."

After Purcell's death there was no attempt made to continue English opera. Works in Italian alone occupied the attention of the public, until burlesqued and driven out of fashion by the " Beggars' Opera." The " Beggars' Opera," which keeps a certain place upon the stage, is a mere pasticcio of old tunes, popular for that reason, but valueless as a representative of English opera. With the exception of " Artaxerxes," by Dr. Arne, the majority of the operas of the last century were composed of old fragments by various writers, borrowed either with or without acknowledgment.

The pioneer of modern English opera was Sir Henry Bishop, who deserves to be honourably named, some of his concerted works being remarkable for originality and vigour, and others for beauty of melody and form, so that the ungrateful neglect into which his music has fallen is inexplicable. It is true that he quoted thoughts from other writers, when he found those ideas better suited to his purpose than his own inventions, but it has yet to be determined how far in music such a license is damaging to general originality. In literature quotations are frequently considered to enhance the force of the subject treated of, and the writer is praised as the possessor of extensive knowledge, as a scholar and as a man of taste ; but in music, as there are no means to make extracts distinguishable, all such introductions are stigmatised by the ugly name of plagiarisms. Bishop's writings were received with great favour in their day, and are not without value as contributions to art. Considering this, and noting the success attained by the productions of Balfe, Wallace, Macfarren, and others, in recent times, some hope is inspired that an English opera is possible in the future, more especially when it is called to mind how immense are the disadvantages under which Englishmen labour in their endeavours to obtain a just recognition of their unquestionable musical merit.

The first important step necessary towards the founding of a good and permanent school of English operatic music, must be the discovery of a poet-musician or musician-poet, one who has perfect command over and familiar acquaintance with his language, an exact sense of the requirements of the musician, and the power of writing sensible, effective and useful combinations of words in vigorous and telling English.

Italian opera was introduced into England in 1706, when *Arsinoë* was performed at Drury Lane theatre, but to English words. The first opera performed in Italian was *Almahide*, by a company of Italian singers (ridiculed by Addison in the *Spectator* when still smarting under the failure of his *Rosamund*); this was succeeded by others, and ended in the establishment of Italian opera in England. Handel did much towards securing this end, and was himself the composer of 44 operas, all of which are now forgotten. The operas of the period were not of the complicated character of the modern opera, but consisted of a few songs, with or without recitative, and but slight instrumental accompaniments, the harpsichord supplying all deficiencies. For the later progress of Italian opera in England see *History of the Opera* (1862) by Sutherland Edwards, *Memoirs of the Musical Drama* (1851) by George Hogarth, and Eber's *Seven years of the King's theatre.*

For some years past there have been two companies performing Italian opera in London, and it is not an uncommon occurrence to find excellent representations in the more important provincial towns. In addition to a large staff of principal singers of both sexes, an opera company consists of from 60 to 80 chorus singers, male and female, about 10 first violin players and 10 seconds, 8 violas, 8 violoncellos, 8 double basses, 2 flutes, 2 hautboys, 2 bassoons, 2 clarinets, 4 horns, 2 trumpets or cornets, 3 trombones, 1 pair of kettle-drums, 1 great drum and cymbals, with a military band occasionally appearing in the costume supposed to be proper upon the stage, a conductor, a prompter, *maestro al piano*, and chorus master. When the score requires the use of the cor anglais, bass clarinet, and other rarely used instruments the players upon instruments of like character in the orchestra perform on those instruments. The works are produced in Italian in London, independently of the language in which they may have been originally written, and the patronage bestowed is great and encouraging, though without being subsidised by Government, as is the case in most foreign cities. The opera is resorted to less now as a matter of fashion, than as the result of a real taste for this species of entertainment. Many of the operas are placed upon the stage in the most magnificent style, with scenery that is in many instances beautiful as artistic work, and with costumes and other accessories remarkable for their historical accuracy. This excellence is not confined to operas produced in Paris or London, but is extended to other continental cities, so that without admitting the definition of Rousseau as a necessity, opera is frequently found to combine the several characteristics spoken of by him.

It is in Germany that the highest forms of development have been made, the expression of passion, the perfection of instrumental accompaniments, orchestral colouring and scientific writing, being especially due to German invention and influence.

Gluck, the founder of the French school of opera, was a German, and as already intimated, to a fellow-countryman of his, George Frederic Handel, the establishment of Italian opera as an entertainment in England is due. That which Monteverde began, Gluck revived, Mozart continued, and subsequent composers have expanded and extended, and the instrumental accompaniments to an opera are becoming equally as important as the vocal portion, in illustrating the emotions aroused by the story upon which the general subject is based. In Mozart's operas, *Idomeneo, Le Nozze di Figaro, Zauberflöte*, and *Don Giovanni*, the construction is such that, while they delight the educated musician by the ingenuity with which the resources are managed, they also give the highest pleasure to the unscientific lover of music; and by this means, the widest and most lasting popularity is secured. Following Mozart, the greatest operas are *Fidelio* by Beethoven, *Oberon, Euryanthe*, and *Der Freischütz* by Weber, *Faust* by Spohr, *Les Huguenots, Robert le Diable, L'Étoile du Nord*, and *Le Prophète* by Meyerbeer. It was Mozart's music that dealt the first serious blow to the supremacy of Italian music in Europe—a blow which it has not yet recovered.

The further extension of musical expedients has been attempted by Wagner, with large and growing success. In his early operas, *Rienzi* and *Der Fliegende Holländer*, Wagner has few of the advanced thoughts upon which later he founded his claim to originality. In his volume of essays, "Oper und das Drama," he sets forth his ideas upon the composition of opera. He maintains that "opera consists of music, poetry, and dramatic effect, and these should not be made separate objects, but should mutually combine and aid each other." In taking credit to himself for having reformed the opera by effecting this combination for the first time he is wrong, for the same union was attempted by Meyerbeer in his operas ; he is in error also in believing that the contrivance of announcing or accompanying certain characters by the use of special instruments is his own idea, for Monteverde, and nearly all the early opera composers, with very limited resources at their disposal, had adopted the like plan. The innovations for which he deserves most credit are those which he does not insist upon as novelties, yet for which his name will be remembered by posterity as the pioneer of a new path. The first is in not marring his situation by the introduction of symmetrical and wearisome melodies, and the second and more important is the restoration of tonic harmonies in place of the well used and almost worn out dominant harmonies. He may also claim credit for being possessed of the faculty of writing his own libretti. The words of his later operas are adapted to a declamatory style of recitative, without what is known as "airs," and accompanied by harmonies and instrumentation according to the spirit of the situation. Wagner's eccentricities, his impatience of adverse opinions among others, have been, and still are, the self-imposed bars to his being accepted as the founder of an advanced school; but his firm stand against musical conventionalities has set many clever musicians thinking in his train, with a result that cannot possibly be without good influence over coming generations.

Operist (*Ger.*) An opera singer.

Ophicleide. A keyed serpent. (ὄφις and κλείς). A brass instrument of large compass and great power, but having so peculiar a quality of tone as to necessitate careful treatment by a composer. There are two sorts of ophicleides, alto and bass. The bass instrument has a compass of three octaves and one note, from

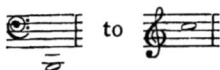

with all the intermediate semitones. Bass ophicleides in B♭ produce, of course, sounds one whole tone below those written, and those in A♭, sounds a major third below those written. The ophicleide is capable of a great deal of execution, if not too chromatic and too low in its compass. The alto ophicleide has a compass similar in extent to that of the bass instrument, but starting from a note one octave higher, that is from

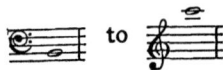

But as the alto ophicleide is in F or E♭, the real sounds produced will be a major fifth or major sixth lower than the notes written. Three or four of the lowest notes and two or three of the highest notes should be avoided. This instrument is not so satisfactory as its bass fellow, and is therefore but rarely heard. The quality of the tone is not unpleasant, but it does not combine well with that of other members of the orchestra. This unpleasant prominence of character tends to limit the use of the instrument.

Opus (*Lat.*) A work. Composers number their works for purposes of distinction and reference.

Opusculum (*Lat.*) A short work.

Oratorio (*Ital.*) A composition for voices and instruments illustrating some subject taken directly from scripture or paraphrased upon some theme in sacred history. The music consists of symphonies or overtures, airs, recitatives, duets, trios, choruses, &c., with accompaniments for orchestra or organ.

The origin and growth of oratorio is almost coeval with that of opera, both being developments of the early forms of drama, or, to speak more clearly, oratorio may be said to be the successor of the mediæval Mystery play, as was the opera of the Morality. In both cases the poetical description of the subjects chosen is accompanied with music, but with this difference, that whereas the opera requires also scenery and dramatic action in its representation, oratorio is now performed without either.

The soldiers and pilgrims of the first crusade, in their attempts to delineate dramatically the Passion of our Lord, and other incidents of sacred history, together with the legends of the deeds and endurance of saints and martyrs, imitated the practice observed in the performance of secular plays by the introduction of music at these representations. It is probable that more than one of the hymns written by St. Bernard of Morlaix and others living about the time were contributed for this purpose, and that the audience joined in the singing. As many of the first oratorios were mystical expositions of doctrine such as that described in many of the early hymns, some colour is given to the supposition that musical exposition and teaching in the form known as oratorio may be as old as the time of the Crusades. It was not until five centuries later that it was made a recognised and distinct medium of instruction and pleasure. St. Philip Neri, in the endeavour to establish firmly the institution he had founded in Rome, and also moved by a desire to win the people to the observance of religious duties, relied upon the universal love for music to gain his object. With this intention he engaged Giovanni Animuccia, a Florentine, as his Maestro di Cappella, who during his connection with the oratory produced several musical pieces, consisting of motetts, psalms, and songs of praise set to Latin and Italian words, known by the general title of "Laudi Spirituali." Animuccia published his first collection at Rome in 1563. The character of these compositions is similar to that known as the madrigal style, and these "laudi" have been taken as the origin of that class of composition. Animuccia was afterwards appointed choirmaster to the Vatican, a post he held until his death in 1571, when he was succeeded by Palestrina.

The experiment succeeded so well that not only was a new form of composition originated, but what was probably more to the purpose of the founder, the congregation of the Fathers of the Oratory was placed upon so firm a basis that it exists to the present day. These musical performances were divided into two parts, a short form of prayer preceding the first, a sermon the second, the whole being concluded with religious exercises. By this plan those who came for the main purpose of the music were constrained to take part in the devotional observances, and doubtless, obtained much spiritual advantage. If in the performance of oratorio at the annual festivals in some of our English cathedrals the same or a similar arrangement were adopted, much of the scandal now accruing might be unquestionably avoided if not totally suppressed.

By degrees, the psalms and spiritual songs gave place to sacred stories or events in scripture written in verse, sometimes in dialogue, and set to music. The subjects most popular in early times were — *The Good Samaritan, The Prodigal Son, Tobit with the Angel, The Sacrifice of Abraham*, and others, and the name of the place where these were first heard was given to the class of music performed. The first work in any way corresponding to the more modern form of oratorio, with solos, recitatives, choruses, and orchestral accompaniments was called *La Rappresentazione di Anima e di Corpo*, composed by Emilio del Cavaliere, performed in the oratory of the Church of Santa Maria della Vallicella at Rome in 1600. Ten years previously Cavaliere had produced two pastoral dramas at Florence, and he has, therefore, claim to the honour of being considered

as one of the first writers, if not the inventor of opera. Cavaliere's oratorio was represented in action on a stage erected in the church, with scenery and costumes; dances were also introduced. The recitatives in both his operas or oratorios were furnished by Jacopo Peri, and it was supposed that in the introduction of recitative the ancient use of the Greeks and Romans was recovered. In the preface to Cavaliere's oratorio each singer is required " to have a fine voice, perfectly in tune, and free from all defects in the delivery of it, with a pathetic expression, the power of swelling and diminishing the tones," and is enjoined to be " particularly attentive to the articulation and expression of the words, and to have an equal respect for the composer as for the poet." The instruments, consisting of a double lyre, double guitar, a harpsichord, and two flutes, accompanied this oratorio behind the scenes. The choruses served as the music for the dancers, and madrigals commenced and concluded the performance. The violin was only sparingly used in the early oratorios, one of the first writers who wrote freely for that instrument being Domenico Mazzochi, and for this reason his name deserves mention among the early composers; beyond this fact there is nothing remarkable in any of the works produced until the time of Stradella, 1670, for the only noticeable points in most of these compositions are the curious mixtures of piety and profanity. Stradella's best oratorio was on the subject of *St. John the Baptist*, and, judging from the specimens printed in Martini's " Exemplare di contrappunto fugato," is remarkable for beauty and sublimity; the scoring also shows some progress in musical thought, but the work is little known, as it still remains in manuscript. The next writer of importance was Carissimi; his compositions are marked by sweetness of melody, clever modulations, and skilful harmony; his most noted oratorios are the *Judgment of Solomon*, and *Jephtha*. One of the choruses in the latter work, " Plorate filiæ Israel," was appropriated by Handel, and introduced into *Samson* to the words " Hear Jacob's God." The chorus " Exululantes filii Ammon " also forms the conclusion of " With thunder armed " in *Samson*. " Et clangebant tubæ " is imitated in the symphony of " We come in bright array " in *Judas Maccabæus*, and the recitative in *Alexander's Feast*, " He chose a mournful muse " is note for note identical with " Heu mihi, filia mea," from Carissimi's *Jephtha*. Many other instances might be cited of Handel's obligations to this musician, the most striking and important being that all his recitatives were formed upon the improved model furnished by Carissimi, who, in addition to other advancements in music, gave great importance to the use of stringed instruments in his accompaniments, made the basses of his compositions move more freely than former masters permitted, and first recommended the introduction of the cantata upon the stage. He died in 1675 at a great age. Dean Aldrich, who was an enthusiastic admirer of his works, made a large collection of them, which he placed in the library of Christ Church, Oxford, where it still remains. After Carissimi, Scarlatti deserves the next place of honour, not only as a prolific, but as a thoughtful composer; his works are rarely heard now, except when some of the choruses with Handel's name attached are performed. The device of accompanying recitatives with a string quartett was first tried by Scarlatti, and this plan was followed by Leonardo Leo, whose contrapuntal writing, similar in character to Handel's in sublimity and massiveness, forms the chief beauty of his oratorios and sacred pieces. As a master of counterpoint Caldara is worthy of mention, while as melodists Hasse and Pergolesi are best known; the beauty and grace of melody in these two composers is also to be found in a certain degree in the writings of Jomelli, who was the last of the oratorio writers of the Italian school.

Like the opera, oratorio arose and was nourished in Italy, to be developed to its highest form by German writers, and, although it was permitted to be used in the offices of the Roman church, and was to some extent abused by Italian writers, yet the value of oratorio was recognised by the German reformers of the sixteenth century, who encouraged its introduction into their churches with a result that ultimately led to its most complete forms. It was formerly the custom in the German Lutheran church to have oratorios performed with instrumental accompaniments on solemn occasions; the congregation was encouraged to join at intervals in the chorales or Psalm tunes which were introduced for this purpose. *The Passion, according to St. Matthew*, by John Sebastian Bach, is an excellent example of this kind of work. [Passion music.] Bach, one of the most original, versatile, and prolific writers that the world has yet seen, was born at Eisenach in 1685, and died at Leipsic in 1750. The study of his music has influenced the thoughts and writings of most composers of importance since his time, his organ compositions have created a new school of players, and the comparatively recent knowledge of his oratorios and vocal music has shown the extraordinary power and value of his genius, which, unknown or not understood in his own time, is now thoroughly

appreciated. It is quite reasonable to assume that, had his vocal works been earlier known, a greater advance in oratorio music would have been made than has been made. The *Passion Music* alluded to above is written for two choirs and two orchestras. The choruses and chorales are exquisitely harmonised, the airs are remarkable for tender pathos and truth of expression, and the recitatives are notable for the admirable force with which the meaning and intention of the text is conveyed. Bach's oratorios were written for the service of the church, and were never intended for any other purpose, the introduction of the oratorio into secular places being a later idea. The subjects are partly in narrative and partly deductions from the incidents, after the manner of the old Greek chorus. This is the true form of oratorio as adapted to worship; but as the oratorio was disused as an aid to devotion, and employed in the theatre and concert room, the narrative form was the one most favoured for the purpose, and it is in this form that the majority of Handel's oratorios are written.

Handel, who is allowed to be the representative composer of oratorio, produced his first work, *La Resurrezione*, while he resided in Italy, before he was twenty years of age. Fifteen years later, while he was organist to the Duke of Chandos, *Esther*, the first oratorio written by him in England, was brought forward privately; it was, however, not until 1732 that it was produced in public, having been laid aside for twelve years. In the advertisement announcing this performance it was considered necessary to give the following explanation of the plan, as oratorios were then a novelty in England: "By His Majesty's command, at the King's Theatre in the Haymarket, on Tuesday, the 2nd May, will be performed the sacred story of *Esther*, an oratorio in English, composed by Mr. Handel, and to be performed by a great number of voices and instruments. N.B. There will be no acting on the stage, but the house will be fitted up in a decent manner for the audience." This explanation was probably made in deference to the objection popularly entertained at the time against any performance savouring of Popery and profanity, and was needful because of the prevalent prejudice against the dramatic performance of sacred subjects. After the production of *Esther* Handel was engaged in the production of operas and other secular works, and in the establishment of his short-lived academy of music—this entailed a loss of health and of much money. After the advanced age of 53, and in defiance of prejudice and failure, he gave to the world those immortal productions with which his name is now familiarly associated. The majority of these works were performed at the "theatre in the Haymarket," *Deborah* being first given in 1733, *Athaliah* in 1734, *Israel in Egypt* in 1738, *The Messiah* in 1741, *Samson* in 1742, *Judas Maccabæus* in 1746, *Joshua* in 1747, *Solomon* in 1749, and *Jephtha* in 1751. The greatest works in this list are *Israel in Egypt* and *The Messiah*. In all these, with the exception of the last-named, Handel availed himself freely of the license of appropriating other men's works and incorporating them in his own. It has been said that he has always improved and invigorated all pieces so borrowed, but it is hard to believe that the mere adaptation of words different to those originally set can be considered an improvement. Notwithstanding this pillage there is enough originality in Handel to constitute him a great composer, especially when it is considered that the work by which he is most popularly and extensively known, *The Messiah*, is for the most part his own. It is in broad choral writing that Handel's great strength exists, for he only sparingly employed instrumental effects, for the orchestra was only imperfectly developed in his time, and he generally employed his instruments more for the sake of supporting the voices than for any peculiar effects of colouring to be obtained from their use. There are some exceptions to this plan, but they are very few; the scantiness of Handel's effects, and the more extensive means employed for the performance of his works, gave rise to the additional parts which have been made for instruments either only partly known in his time, or of subsequent invention. The first of these additional accompaniments was furnished by Mozart to *The Messiah;* Mendelssohn, Macfarren, Perry, Costa, and Sullivan have supplied parts to the other of the more frequently performed works with more or less success.

The example set by Handel was followed by such writers as Stanley, Dr. Arne, Dr. Worgan, Dr. Arnold, but little encouragement was offered to their efforts, so that no new oratorio of importance was heard in London until Haydn's *Creation* was performed.

Haydn was the author of but few oratorios, *The Return of Tobias, The Seasons, The Seven Last Words,* and *The Creation,* being all his compositions that can be in any way classed under this head. *The Seven Last Words* is more in accordance with the character of the Lutheran oratorios, being intended to follow as many short sermons on the last words of our Lord. *The Seasons* is somewhat secular in character; and the same sweetness of melody prevalent in this is found in Haydn's best known work, *The*

Creation, produced in 1798. **The special** qualities of this oratorio, besides those already alluded to, are found in the brightness of the choruses and the interest of the instrumentation. In general design *The Creation* is inadequate to the subject treated of, and while the ear is pleased by the sparkling and varied treatment, the heart is never moved by emotions which the grandeur of the theme should have inspired.

Beethoven's *The Mount of Olives* is a drama rather than an oratorio, full of sublime and noble thoughts, but ineffective without the aid of scenery and accessories.

Spohr's oratorios, *The Crucifixion, The Last Judgment,* and the *Fall of Babylon,* contain many grand and surprising thoughts, much beauty of melody and clever harmonies; the restless modulations employed by him cease to excite wonder after a time, and so, to a certain extent, their end is defeated. In the peculiarity of enharmonic changes on a dominant harmony, Spohr so far exhausted the possible combinations, that composers in imitating his style simply reproduce his thoughts. The most successful composer in this manner of modern date was Mendelssohn, and his *Elijah* and *St. Paul* served to revive the drooping taste for oratorio. *Elijah* was produced at Birmingham in 1846, and *St. Paul* ten years previously at Düsseldorf, and both works have since held high rank as well in the estimation as in the affections of musicians. Of the two, *St. Paul* more completely fulfils the conditions of oratorio proper, in the happy arrangement of its narrative and didactic portions. The production of this form is due to the assiduous study of the works of its great perfecter, John Sebastian Bach, and for this reason, and for its intrinsic merit, *St. Paul* is held to be Mendelssohn's best oratorio. *Elijah* is more dramatic in constitution, and if the prejudice should ever be sufficiently overcome to permit of its performance on the stage, with proper scenery and action, it will attain even greater importance than that it at present enjoys.

Of the more recent contributions to oratorio music, there are few worthy to be particularised, as they are for most part feeble filterings of an almost exhausted stream.

Oratorio has ever been more patronised in England than on the Continent, but until the establishment of the Sacred Harmonic Society in 1832 the opportunity for hearing it was of rare occurrence, being confined almost to the annual meetings of the three choirs of Gloucester, Hereford, and Worcester in the provinces, and to the Lenten performances in London. The example set by this Society has been imitated with success, not only in London, but in the country, and oratorio performances are now frequent, and upon a scale of grandeur, magnificence, precision, and perfection hitherto unattained and completely unknown elsewhere.

Orchesis (*Gk.* ὄρχησις). **Orchestik** (*Ger.*) The art of rhythmical dancing as it existed in the Greek Theatre.

Orchester (*Ger.*) Orchestra.

Orchestra (*Gk.*) (1) The ὀρχήστρα or "dancing-place" in the Greek theatre was that circular space, immediately below the lowest seats of the semicircular part or κοῖλον, which was given up to the chorus. The level of the orchestra was twelve feet below that of the lowest seat, and twelve feet below that of the proscenium (προσκήνιος), but between the orchestra and the proscenium was a platform six feet higher than the orchestra, called the thymele (θυμέλη). If, therefore, the part-circle formed by the front of the lowest row of seats were supposed to be completed, it would be found that the orchestra would contain an area about one-third of the circle in that part farthest from the stage. (2) The place where the band, or band and chorus, are placed in modern concert-rooms, theatres, &c. (3) The collection of instruments of varied compass and quality of tone which constitutes a *full band*. There are no orchestral scores earlier than the latter part of the sixteenth century, so all statements as to concerted instrumental music before that time are wholly conjectural.

Many of the early poets speak of harmony in a manner that shows that their construction of the term was the same as our own. It is well known that harmony was not a sudden discovery, but the result of slow growth, and it is reasonable to suppose that one who could sing part-music according to a recognised system, and also play upon an instrument, would be led to select one as much in accordance with the compass of his own voice as possible, and so would *play* the part he was accustomed to *sing*. Accidental circumstances might suggest combinations which were afterwards made permanent, and from small beginnings the adjustment of tone considered necessary in a modern orchestra might be gradually arrived at.

One of the first authentic attempts to gain special effects may be traced in the disposition of the instruments accompanying the first operas. The score of Monteverde's *Orfeo* performed in 1608, contains indications of a purpose in the employment of what appears in the present as a somewhat strange arrangement of accompanying instruments. Orpheus sings to the accompaniment of the basses, Apollo to the organ, Pluto to the trombones, Eurydice to the violas, and Charon to the lutes or guitars. The use of particular in-struments to accompany the music sung by special characters was revived by Hoffman in his opera *Undine*, and introduced by Wagner as a new invention; but the idea belongs to Monteverde, as the directions in the score quoted above prove. Information regarding this branch of musical history is to be obtained only by reference to scores of various dates, by which it will be seen that composers, for a long time subsequent to Monteverde, did not follow out the hints he had given. They made some omissions in the number and arrangement of the instruments, and in most cases simply contented themselves with violins, and sometimes added an organ for the accompaniment of everything but recitative, for which the harpsichord or lute was employed. The lute was used at the opera-house so late as 1790, the harpsichord much longer; the musician who sat at the latter instrument was called the conductor, and it was his business to give the time of the several pieces to the leader of the band. It is only within the present century that an independent time-beater, one not playing an instrument, has been fully recognised, and his position in the orchestra established. The story of Dr. Philip Hayes standing up to beat time for a band which Cramer was leading, and the refusal of the latter to play until " de fat man was sit down," shows that the practice of " conducting " was not general at the latter part of the last century.

In addition to violins, wind instruments were used, sparingly at first, but afterwards with great liberality. In Handel's time the proportion of treble reed wind instruments to the violins were as two to three, that is to say, for every six fiddles four oboes were employed. This is a matter which should not be lost sight of in calculating Handel's orchestral effects, for there is every reason to believe, however strange the combination might be to modern ears, that a restoration of the proportions of the orchestra for which Handel wrote would place his music in a far different light from that in which it is viewed at present, not that it would lose, but perhaps would rather gain in grandeur. It can scarcely be said that Handel did much towards developing the resources of the orchestra; he seemed to be mainly content with treating it as an accompanying body, for even in his concertos, he was contented with the performance of a phrase by the full body, which had been given out by a single instrument to a part. In a few cases he seems to have made a happy choice of an accompanying instrument, but even then it is considered so doubtful as to whether he meant what is called an " orchestral effect " or not, that many composers, following the example of Mozart, consider themselves justified in adding instrumental parts to Handel's scores, not always with the laudable desire of exhibiting an improved knowledge of instrumental quality, not always with correct taste or judgment. Mozart himself declared to Attwood that his sole reason for adding parts to the scores of Handel's works was to make his countrymen think as highly of the compositions as he himself did; so that all the stories about his undertaking the task at the request of a noble patron, against his own inclination, are pure inventions. Mozart's additions to the *Messiah* are specimens of noble orchestral colouring, and give so much beauty to the score that a performance of the work without them would seem tame and uninteresting to ears that have grown accustomed to them.

The composer in whose works the first consistent and concentrated efforts in the direction of improvement of the orchestra are to be traced is Gluck. All his biographers agree in declaring that his sole aim in orchestral writing was "expression." He disregarded the usages of fashion and custom, and thought for himself, and like every independent thinker founded a school of his own, to become in time the conventionality of a future age.

In the introduction of new instruments by which fresh combinations and effects can be obtained, a difficulty will be always present, in that skilful players are not readily found, and musicians do not care to study an instrument that is rarely employed, and therefore of little profit to them professionally. This is the one reason why trumpet playing is comparatively a lost art. There is no remedy against this drawback, and therefore many instruments of unquestionable value in an orchestra are neglected and disused.

Meyerbeer did much towards obtaining a recognition for certain disregarded instruments, and although he was fortunate enough to find players with sufficient enthusiasm or interest in the matter to take them up and study them, he could not secure a succession, and, consequently, in the performance of his operas, such passages as are written in the score for obsolete instruments have to be performed by those in general use.

The introduction of new effects is always a work of time, and the development of some degree of daring. Lully wrote parts for drums to some of his choruses to strengthen the deep tones; Beethoven wrote solos for the same instrument. The prominence given by a composer to a certain instrument is to be accounted for in more than one way. He may have had a special training in that particular instrument, a partiality for its tone,

or he may have in his orchestra players of exceptional ability. Thus Weber writes so wonderfully for the horns, because he was a player; Spohr for the violin, an instrument on which he was a master; Spontini loved the tone of the trombone, and wrote often for it; Handel had Valentine Snow to play his trumpet parts, and Snow had a special gift for trumpet playing; and many other instances may be quoted if it were needful.

Haydn has been considered the father of modern orchestral writing; and in the utilization of accepted materials his genius as a composer is best shown. In charm of orchestral shading Mozart's are perfect studies; while for nobility of effect Beethoven has never been surpassed.

The tendency of the present order of writers for the orchestra is to seek to obtain a fictitious grandeur by the liberal use of "Janitscharen-musik," cymbals, bells, big drum, &c. This is all very well when it is desirable to conceal the defective playing of the strings and wind, but when an orchestra comprises performers of excellent skill, having familiar knowledge of the capabilities of their several instruments, such noise is not only needless, but offers a great temptation to carelessness in playing on the more delicate instruments.

Ordinario (*It.*) Ordinary, as *a tempo ordinario*, in the usual time, or, at a moderate pace.

Orecchia musicale (*It.*) An ear for music, or musical ear.

Oreille musicale (*Fr.*) [Orecchia.]

Organ (from the *Gk.* ὄργανον). This word originally signified an *implement, instrument,* or *piece of mechanism* for any purpose. Hence, it came to be applied to any *musical* instrument, and later still to the compound wind-instrument now known as the organ, which, no doubt, grew out of the *ugab* of the Hebrews and the *syrinx* of the Greeks (*Pan's-pipes*), when combined with the wind-chest, as naturally suggested by the leathern reservoir of the *bagpipe*. Only, it must be remembered, that the pipes of Pan had, each separately, to be made into a sort of *flûte à bec*, having a foot to convey the air to the block and lips; also, that under each pipe a little slide had to be placed in order to prevent all the pipes from speaking at once. This early slide, which permitted particular pipes to speak at the will of the performer, has now developed into the *pallet* and the *key-action;* and we now apply the word *slide* or *slider* only to that strip of wood which, passing under a row of pipes from right to left, admits the air to a particular *row of pipes* or stops. Neither of these two arrangements—the *key*-slide and *stop*-slide— required any special mechanical skill, and it may safely be said that they were used at a much earlier date than is commonly supposed.

The real difficulty of ancient organ-builders was *inequality* of the pressure of wind. It is needless to observe that the leathern reservoir of a bagpipe could never be so equally pressed all round as to produce an uniform current of air. Nor could the simple forms of bellows as used by blacksmiths to this day produce an equal pressure, because, when they are being filled, the air is under too great compression, and as the top sinks the pressure becomes less and less. There can be but little doubt that the so-called *hydraulic* organ owed its utility and consequent fame to the fact, that in it water was used in such a manner as to counterbalance the hitherto variable pressure. The ignorant, no doubt, thought that the water went near to, or even entered, the pipes, but this was palpably not the case. Those who are interested in the supposed details of the hydraulic organ will find information in the "Bible Educator" (Parts 8 and 10, Vol. II.), in Rimbault and Hopkins on the Organ, and in Chappell's "History of Music" (p. 325). The ordinary organ in which no water was used came to be called the *pneumatic* or *wind-organ*. In order to keep up a due supply of wind, while bellows were being refilled, organ builders multiplied their number. The modern inventions of the double-action feeder, &c., fully explained further on, made this system of blowing unnecessary. If the account given of the Magrepha (*q.v.*) be true, it must have really been an organ. It will be unnecessary to trouble the reader with long untrustworthy quotations from old writers in explanation of, or in praise of, the wonders of organs. It will suffice to state where and when some of the oldest known instruments were built, and note the progress in their construction. Julian, the Apostate (who died A.D. 363), mentions an organ in a Greek epigram, but in such a manner as to make it doubtful whether it had *keys*. Aldhelm, (who died A.D. 709), mentions an organ which had *gilt pipes*. An organ having leaden pipes was placed in the Church of S. Corneille, at Compiegne, in the middle of the eighth century. The story of St. Dunstan's organ with its brass pipes is well known. One of the most interesting of the mediæval organs was that built for Winchester Cathedral at the close of the tenth century. According to the account given by the Monk Wulston it had *thirteen pairs of bellows* and *four hundred pipes* distributed so that forty pipes were under the control of each key. By pressing down the key belonging to any one set of pipes, they all sounded together after the manner of the mixture; the separation of the wind-chest by means of slides was apparently not attempted in this case.

The large pipes of every key of the oldest organs stood in front; the whole instrument sounded and shrieked in a harsh and loud manner. The key-board had 11, 12, even 13 keys in diatonic succession without semitones. It was impossible to get anything else than a choral melody for one voice only, on such an organ.

By degrees the keys and pipes in organs increased in number, but no alteration was made in the register of the pipe-work; the chromatic intervals, too, were added. The pedals were devised in 1470 by Bernhard the German, a skilful musician at Venice, and so quickly came into fashion that in Germany few organs were built without them. Originally they had only eight keys—♮B, C, D, E, F, G, A, ♮B, which were attached to the valves of the pipes with cord. As time went on the key-boards of the manuals became increased to three. This was the case in the large organ (built in 1361) at Halberstadt, described by Prætorius after its renovation in 1495, in "Syntagma Musicum" (1619). It had three key-boards and pedals, the latter, however, being added at the time the organ was restored. The Præstant, or row of pipes standing in front (the Principal or open diapason), was separated from the other portion of the pipe-work, which was almost detached, and was called Hintersatz. A difference of tone could thus at least be obtained by using the principal alone, or by coupling it with the whole hintersatz and pedals. The highest row of keys, called "Discant," had a compass from B♮ C, C♯ chromatic to G, A, and served for the full organ principal and hintersatz coupled. The second key-board of the same compass, and also called Discant, served for the principal alone without the hintersatz. The third row of keys was a bass key-board, contained a large bass principal in side-towers, with a compass from C to C, and was used with the left hand as principal in the second row of keys. The pedals extended from C to B♭.

It must not be thought that the manner of playing these old organs was anything like that now-a-days: the breadth of a key-board containing nine keys extended to three-quarters the length of a yard, that of the single key amounted to three inches (Bedos de Celles speaks of organ keys even from five to six inches). The keys were of a peculiar shape, *e.g.*:

The valves of the keys and the whole mechanism being clumsy, playing with the finger was not to be thought of, but the keys were obliged to be struck with the clenched fist, and the organist was often called "pulsator organorum." It was consequently impossible to play chords with one hand, but a kind of duet or trio could be produced with the assistance of the pedals. The early organs were often a tone or a tone and a half above the choral pitch [v. Chorton], and lower than the kammerton by about a tone.

But when the organ had once attained a certain degree of perfection, it proceeded quickly towards further improvement. The keys were made gradually smaller, so that the Fifth had a width of a span, something similar to our octave, as in the old organ at Braunschweig. In the keys of the organs in the monastery at Bamberg (enlarged 1493), in the church of the Barefooted Friars at Nuremberg (1475), in the cathedral at Erfurt (1483), in that of St. Blasius at Braunschweig (1499), the width of the span of the octave amounted only to about one key more than at the present time, but the action was still clumsy. The compass of the manuals, mostly beginning at B flat, had extended to EE and FF, but the pedals were still limited in compass from A or B flat to B flat or B natural.

But the most considerable stride in improvement was the division of the Hintersatz into separate registers, which could now be used singly through the invention of the spring-box. Prætorius, about 1619, describes the slide-box as being quite common, and further states that it had already been in use for two hundred years, so that it must have been invented at the end of the fourteenth or the beginning of the fifteenth century, but was a long time gaining recognition. In the beginning of 1500 the pipe-work itself had also begun to be perfected in different ways. Hitherto it had the scale of the principal throughout. Pipes began to be covered probably about 1530. In later times reed-pipes and pointed flutes came into vogue, and by degrees bellows of very thin board were put in the place of the old bellows, which were constructed in folds, and the portable chamber-organ [Regals], since grown out of use. introduced. About the year 1677, Christian Förmer (born 1610) invented the anemometer.

The mistaken zeal of the Puritans caused a wanton destruction of organs and the discouragement of organ-building, so that when a revival of interest in the instrument took place. it was found that England had lost her ancient supremacy. and there was no longer a sufficient number of builders in the country. Foreign organ-builders were invited to England. and the most celebrated of these—Bern-

hard Schmidt (generally called Father Smith) with his nephew and Renatus Harris, established themselves in this country. Their immediate successors were Christopher Schroeder, Snetzler, and Byfield. These were followed by Avery and Green, and from them sprung the present generation of organ-builders, whose skill and ingenuity have done much to restore the ancient supremacy of organ-building in England.

Organ Construction. (§ 1.) A complete organ may be said to consist of five parts: choir organ, great organ, swell organ, solo organ, and pedal organ. These are all, however, in reality constructed on the same principle, that is to say, the manner of connection between the keys and the pallets, which admit a current of air to the pipes, is similar in principle in all. A large organ therefore consists of a number of small organs differing in quality of tone, and so arranged as to be under the control of one performer.

(§ 2.) Before explaining the connection between a key and a pipe, it will be necessary to explain the construction of the bellows, a receptacle which encloses atmospheric air and forces it through passages called "wind-trunks" to the sound-boards over which the pipes are arranged. The construction of modern bellows, termed horizontal to distinguish them from the old diagonal bellows (q.v.), and for the invention of which organists are probably indebted to an Englishman, Samuel Green, who is known to have furnished two organs with them in 1787 and 1788, may be best explained by the following figure:

Fig. 1.

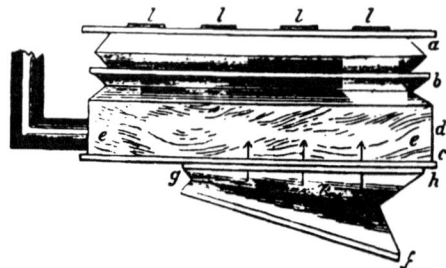

The top board a is substantially and strongly made of pine, ledgered at each end, or in large bellows panelled; some of the panels being moveable allow easy access to the interior for repairs. The middle frame b is merely a surrounding frame of wood to which is attached the lower edge of the upper ribs and the upper edge of the lower ribs. The middle board c is slightly larger than the top-board, and on it rests a strong ridge d called the trunk-band or lining, to which the wind trunks can be at any point joined, as at *e*. The bottom board *f* is the bottom of the feeder *f g h*, and is sometimes nearly as large as the top board. In large bellows provision is made for the due support of the weight of the top board by placing posts inside, or a ridge of wood extending the whole length of the middle board, of such a height that when *a* and *b* are at the position rest, *a* is touching the top of the posts or ridge. On the bottom of the middle board are a number of holes for the admission of air from the feeder, covered by leather valves or suckers, which fall and prevent the exit of the air by the way it came. The valves being hinged at one end only, rise for the entry of the air from the feeder, and then fall by their own weight. The bottom of the feeder *f* is supplied with a similar set of suckers, or valves, so that the operation of "blowing" is as follows: To the end of *f* are attached, in any way most convenient, the levers connected with the bellows handle, so that by its stroke *f* is raised towards *c*. The atmospheric contents of the feeder are then forced through the interior valves † † † and the top board rises. When *f* has reached its nearest point to *c*, and begins to return to its position in the figure, the leather valves fall over the openings † † †, and the air is forced by the heavy top board and its incumbent weights *l l l l* to depart by the only way open to it, namely, by the wind trunk *e*. It will be noticed that one set of ribs is turned inwards, the other outwards. This ingenious though simple arrangement, which was first suggested by a clock-maker named Cummins, and immediately adopted by Flight, the organ-builder, entirely removes the inequality of pressure spoken of in the article on "diagonal bellows." But as the feeder *f* is descending, no air can of course be supplied to the bellows. The simplest means of obtaining a constant supply of wind is to have two feeders, or, as it is termed, a double-feeder, which may, according to circumstances, be placed either under the side or end of the bellows.

Fig. 2.

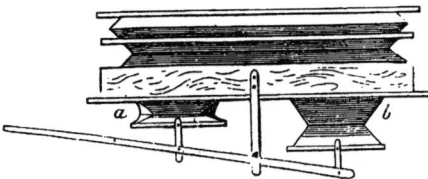

As one feeder *a* is descending, the other *b* is ascending. A like result is produced by the use of the *cuckoo feeder*, so-called because it is constructed on the same principle as the little bellows of the cuckoo toy.

Fig. 3.

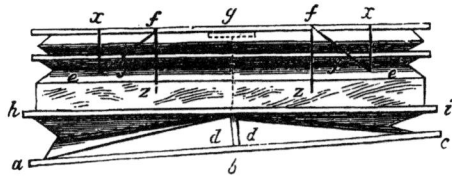

The bottom board *a c* is hinged at *b*, so that when *a* ascends, *c* descends, both *a* and *c* being, of course, provided with the ordinary valves. The under lining *d d* is sometimes exactly reversed in position, being attached to the middle board instead of the bottom board. Before leaving the subject of bellows, the *counter-balances* must be explained. Their object is to make both sets of ribs expand or contract equally, and prevent the swinging to and fro of the top of the bellows. They consist of three flat pieces of iron, and are fixed to the upper board at *x* (Fig. 3), the middle board at *y*, and the trunk lining at *z*; and being moveable at every joint but *x* and *z*, as *x* rises, *e f* impart a proportionate rise to *y*. In order to prevent an undue rising of the bellows when more wind is supplied than used, a *waste-pallet* is placed in every bellows. It consists of a valve (*g* Fig. 3) pressed under an opening in the top board by a spring, having attached to its under-side a piece of cord (dotted line) which is fixed to the bottom board *h i*. When the top board rises higher than the length of the cord, the valve is of course pulled downwards, and the superfluous air escapes. If any part of the middle board is not over a feeder, the pallet may be placed inside the middle board, and the cord fixed to the top board, in which case the pallet will be pulled up when the top board, by its rising, pulls the cord.

(§ 3.) But notwithstanding all these improvements in feeders and bellows, it was found that an unsteadiness of wind was caused, if many of the larger pipes were suddenly made to speak, or as suddenly, to cease speaking. In the former case so large a supply of atmosphere was taken from the wind chest that the air remaining expanded by its own elasticity; in the latter, the supply of air did not cease with the demand. Both these defects are remedied by the clever invention by Mr. Bishop, the organ-builder, of the concussion-bellows, which are a reservoir hinged at one end and therefore wedge-shaped, which is attached to the side of the wind-trunk, with a spring tending to force the moveable board towards the trunk.

Fig. 4.

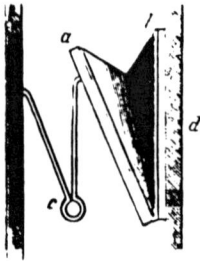

When there is no air being forced through the trunk *d*, *a* reaches its nearest point to *b*. When the trunk is filled with compressed air the spring *c* just counterbalances it. When a sudden demand is made upon the contents of the trunk *d* the spring forces *a* nearer to *b*; when the air in the trunk is more than usually compressed, the spring allows *a* to recede from *b*.

(§ 4.) The wind-trunk is made of an oblong form, and is shaped so as to carry the air by the most convenient route, to the wind-chest, which is immediately under the sound-board. It will be perhaps better before entering into details to give at once a general idea of the wind-chest and sound-board.

Fig. 5.

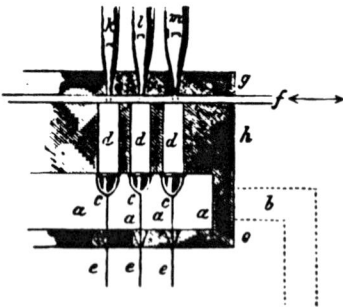

The above figure (Fig. 5) represents a section of a sound-board and wind-chest viewed from front. *a* is the wind-chest into which compressed atmospheric air has been introduced either through the side or bottom, from the end of the wind-trunk *b*. The pallets *c c c* are held tightly against the openings *d d d*, leading from the wind-chest to the mouth of the pipes by springs underneath them, thus:

Fig. 6.

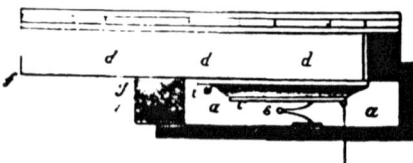

The spring *s* keeps the pallet *c* against the opening into *d*. The wires called *pull-downs* (*e e e* Fig. 5), which pass through small holes in the bottom of the wind-chest and are in connection with the key-board, are attached to a loop of wire called the *pallet-eye*, fastened to the moveable end of the pallet. A piece of wire is placed on each side of every pallet to steady it and keep it in the perpendicular during its ascent and descent, and every pallet is covered at top with soft leather, to make it fit closely and work quietly. When *e* is pulled down (Fig. 5) the pallet *c* descends, and air from the wind-chest *a a a* rushes through *d* into the pipe over it. But the slider *f* is a narrow strip of wood, so placed between the woodwork *g* and *h* that it may be moved backwards and forwards from right to left, and is pierced with holes corresponding throughout to those just under the pipes. If the apertures in the slider are under the pipes (as represented by dotted lines in Fig. 5), the opening of a pallet will make a pipe speak; if, however, the slider has been moved so that the apertures do not correspond (as shewn in Fig. 7 by dotted lines), even if the pallet be opened and the chest full of air from the trunks, no sound will be produced.

Fig. 7.

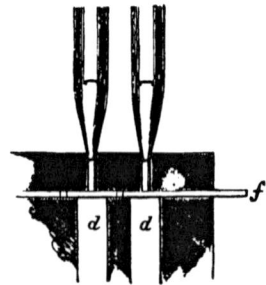

When the apertures in the slider are under those below the pipe, the "stop," the handle of which controls the position of the slider, is said to be *out*, or *drawn*. When the apertures do not correspond, the stop is said to be *in*. Thus it is that when no stops are drawn no sound is produced, even although the wind-chest be full of air from the wind-trunk. Looking at Fig. 5 again, it will be observed that if another row of pipes (or a "stop") were placed immediately behind *k*, *l*, *m*, with another slider under them, the same openings *d* could supply both sets of pipes, subject to the control of the sliders. The only limit to the number of rows of pipes will therefore be the depth of the air passage *d* over which the pipes stand. But, inasmuch as *one* pallet under the control of *one* key will admit air to all the pipes placed over any one air-passage *d*, it is evident that only those pipes must be placed over *d* which belong to one particular note on the key-board. The air passage *d* is technically termed a *groove*, the wood which separates one groove from another is technically termed a sound-board *bar*. Every row of keys on an organ will therefore have in connection with it a sound-board, having as many grooves and pallets as there are notes in its compass; and as many sliders as it has stops. Having made a slight digression in order to give a general idea of the construction of this important part of the instrument, it is now time to enter more into detail, and first, it will naturally follow that large pipes will require a larger groove and pallet than those that are smaller, hence the grooves vary in size throughout the whole sound-board.

(§ 5.) The usual arrangement of pipes on a sound-board is to have the largest on the outside, say on the right and left sides, and then to proceed by degrees to the smallest which thus come nearest to the middle of the sound-board. But the arrangement of pipes must be spoken of again hereafter. If a greater supply of wind than usual is required for the due speaking of any large pipe, two grooves may be allotted to that note. These *double-grooves*, as they are termed, are said to have been first introduced by England, the organ-builder. By reference to Fig. 6, it will be seen that the groove *d* runs much farther back than the wind-chest *a, a, a*. This is, of course, necessary where a large number of stops has to be placed over it. The width and depth of the grooves varies according to the number of the stops, and the size of the pipes. A sound-board is made by taking a strong piece of wood of the required size, turning it over and then glueing the sound-board bars to it, placing between the ends of the bars pieces of wood called *fillings in*, the width of the groove; then the ends of the bars and the fillings in which form the front and back (called the *cheeks*) are planed down and covered firmly with a strong piece of mahogany or other hard wood. Then the wind-chest, pallets, &c., cover over part of the grooves, and the remainder (*f, g*. Fig. 6), the openings of which have hitherto been exposed to view, are covered by parchment or leather. This, of course, becomes the underside of the sound-board when it is turned over into its proper position. The wood to which the grooves are glued now becomes the *table*, and is bored to admit air to the pipes. On the table are arranged the sliders, over the sliders are the upper-boards, into the holes of which the ends (*noses*) of the pipe enter, above the upper-boards are the pipe-racks, simple frame-

works of wood which keep the pipes in a perpendicular position.

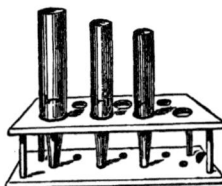

As the amount of room which an organ occupies is generally a matter of some importance, the pipes in the sound-board are rarely arranged in a straight line thus,

but are placed slightly zig-zag, thus:

but as the grooves run in the direction indicated by the plain lines, and the sliders as indicated by the dotted lines, it is evident that such an arrangement only affects the piercing of the table, slider, and upper boards. The sliders might, if their edges touched one another, disturb each other's position when pulled in and out; to prevent this, between each slider and that next to it is placed a *bearer* or immoveable strip of wood, which receives the weight of the upper-boards, and to which the upper-boards are screwed. There should of course be no pressure on the sliders, otherwise their free movement will be hindered.

(§ 6.) Having thus given some account of the progress of the wind from the time it enters the bellows until the drawing down of the pallet, and the position of the slider has permitted it to enter into the pipes and make them speak, it remains to show, first, by what means the key is enabled to pull down the pallet; next, by what method the stop-handle or register acts upon the slider. But before the former can be explained it will be necessary to say a few words as to the arrangement of the pipes on a sound-board, for on this will depend to a great extent the kind of connection between key and pallet. The simplest arrangement will of course be to place the smallest pipe on the right-hand side of the sound-board and to proceed thence by gradation to the largest pipe on the left-hand side. This would be naturally suggested by the order in which the keys are placed, the highest note, produced by the smallest pipe, being on the right; the lowest note, produced by the largest pipe, on the left. This arrangement is known as Vogler's system, because that learned musician and organist brought it prominently before the public. But it has some great disadvantages, the chief of which are as follows: first, as the lowest notes are produced by the largest pipes, all the largest pipes, and in consequence the greater part of the *weight* of an organ, rests on one side of the sound-board; secondly, the largest pipes occupy by far the greatest space, hence, the left-hand side of a sound-board must be proportionately roomy in length and depth: thirdly, one end only of the wind-chest is taxed with the supply of all the big pipes; lastly, if it is found necessary to *convey* wind from the grooves to ornamental pipes standing in the front, the distance is extremely great. In order to explain this last objection it must be here stated that if a pipe does not stand in its proper place on the sound-board, either because there is not room for it, or because it is placed at a distance in the front of the organ, a roughly made pipe of light metal is glued at one end into the proper hole and carried by any course most convenient, forming sometimes the most fantastic shapes, to the base of the new position of the pipe, the other end is then firmly glued into a small hollow immediately under the pipe. Therefore, if *conveyances* (as these supplementary tubes are called) are very long, the pipe does not speak very readily, the compressed air when the pallet is opened, having to travel from the place where the pipe ought to be, to the spot where it may happen to be. The third objection above stated may be surmounted by making larger wind-trunks and wider grooves. But even if there be no case to an organ, the Vogler system has its disadvantages, for the outline formed by an unbroken succession of pipes from 16ft. to a few inches in length, standing side by side, in the short space of a sound-board, can hardly be rendered pleasing to the eye. The second system of arranging pipes has already been alluded to, namely, that of placing the largest pipes alternately on the outside, proceeding by degrees until the smallest are in the centre, and the outline formed by the tops of the pipes nearly assumes the shape of a slightly flattened V. The third system is the reverse of the above, the large pipes being placed in the middle and the small ones at the sides, the outline of the pipes will be therefore not unlike Λ.

The fourth system is a compromise between the first and second, most of the pipes being arranged semitonally, but some of the larger pipes being placed on either side. The outline of the pipes will, therefore, be of this kind. These four are the chief arrangements

of pipes in vogue, but of course exceptional positions for an organ necessitate exceptional dispositions of the pipes.

(§ 7.) Before explaining the means which connect keys with pallets, it must be pointed out that there are two kinds of keyboards or *claviers*, one of which is played by the hands, called the manual-clavier or *manual*; the other played by the feet, called the pedal-clavier or *pedals*. The long keys of a manual are generally made of lime-tree wood covered with ivory, and the short keys of ebony, or some other wood stained black. Both long and short keys are balanced on a ledge of wood called the *pin-rail*, because metal pins, fixed into it and entering into punctures in the keys, steady them perpendicularly whilst allowing them to move on them, as on pivots. A similar rail passes immediately under the front of the keys, with another set of pins, to produce steadiness of movement, only these punctures do not go completely through the key as in the previous case. The pieces of wood on each side of the manual, to which the pin-rails are firmly fixed, are called *key-checks*. To prevent an undue rising of the key when the finger is suddenly removed, a piece of board covered on the underside with baize, and loaded with lead, called the *thumping-board*, lies on the keys transversely immediately behind the part which is used by the fingers. The pedal keys are made of oak, mahogany, or any hard wood, and work on centres at the heel end, being steadied at the toe end. A spring under each key holds it in position subject to the pressure of the foot.

(§ 8.) On pressing down a manual key, the back of one key rises, and raises a *sticker*, a thin piece of wood, round or square, and of length varying from a few inches to a couple of feet, provided with a pin of wire firmly fixed in the upper end, which passes into the end of the *back-fall*, a horizontal lever, to which is attached a tracker, a strip of light wood provided with a tap wire and leather button at the end, passing through the back-fall, and with a hook of copper at the end connected with the pull-down, thus—

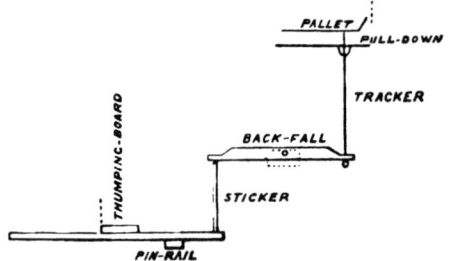

If, then, the arrangement of the pipes be according to the first plan given (largest on the left hand side, smallest on the right), the back-falls are arranged thus, on the back-fall frame,

so that the end of the back-fall may come under the pull-down. This kind of movement is, from its appearance, called the *fan-frame* movement.

But if the pipes are arranged according to the second plan given, a piece of mechanism called the roller-board comes between the end of the back-fall and the puller down. It is a series of rollers so arranged on a flat board standing upright, that whilst one end of the roller is under the pull-down, to which it is attached by a second tracker, the other end is over the corresponding back-fall, the back-falls, in this case, lying parallel to each other. Thus, by means of the roller board, the finger is enabled to communicate with pipes on either side of the sound-board. The system employed must, however, depend greatly on the position of the sound-board with relation to the keys.

Where corners intercept action, or where it is necessary to carry action at right angles, either horizontally or perpendicularly, *squares* are largely used. The square is of this shape, and generally in two pieces, dove-tailed, so that no strain may cause one arm to snap off. The arms are generally about 3 inches in length. The block in which the squares work is termed the *square-frame*. Of course the length of stickers, trackers, and back-falls must entirely depend on the space to be occupied by an instrument, or the position in which it is placed. Long stickers or trackers are steadied by being made to pass through holes in a flat piece of wood called a register.

The connection between pedal-keys and pedal-pipes does not differ in principle from that between manual-keys and manual-pipes, but from the usual position of the pedal organ squares have frequently to be used.

(§ 9.) The draw-stop handle acts upon the slider by means of a series of levers, the position of which varies greatly in different instruments. The most common system is called the wooden-trundle draw-stop action.

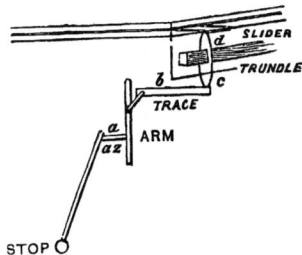

When the stop is pulled out, the arms *a a* draw the trace *b* from right to left, the end of the trundle *c* being attached to the trace is moved in a similar direction, whilst the other end of the trundle *d* moves in an opposite direction, and draws out the slider. When metal trundles are used, this action is simplified. Sliders are sometimes made to move by means of small bellows placed under them, which, upon being filled with compressed air, suddenly expand, and as they expand draw the slider. A large organ, it will be now understood, is practically several distinct instruments, not differing in the principles of their construction so much as in quality of tone. But if this were all, the interior of an organ would appear very simple—there are still to be considered those contrivances which enable a performer to play upon more than one set of keys simultaneously.

(§ 10.) The draw stops producing combinations of manuals or of manuals to pedals are termed couplers. Suppose an organ to consist of four manuals and pedals, *viz.:* solo organ, swell organ, great organ, choir organ, and pedal organ, the couplers assigned to it would probably be "Solo to Great," "Swell to Great," "Swell to Choir," "Choir to Great," "Solo to Pedals," "Swell to Pedals," "Great to Pedals," "Choir to Pedals." To these are sometimes added couplers combining the super-octave or sub-octave of the swell with the great, or similar intervals of the swell organ on itself.

The construction of unison manual-couplers is generally of the following kind. A rod passes between the back of two sets of manual keys, which is pierced with a series of holes in which are placed little stickers of this shape. The length of the sticker is the distance between the two sets of keys to be combined, so that when the lower one is pressed down by the finger the sticker is pushed up by the back of the key and raises the back of the key lying above it. When not required for use the coupler-stop leaves the stickers standing in a hollow purposely made in the keys, thus:—

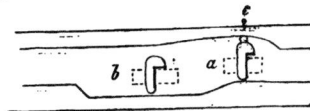

a representing the coupler when ready for use, or "drawn," *b* when not required, and *c* the regulating button. The *tumbler* coupler is now almost obsolete. It consisted of a rod containing stickers, which were turned at an angle when not required for use thus: but it will be seen that if a coupler of this kind is "drawn" while the fingers are on the lower row of keys, the fingers will have to withstand a sudden pressure. This evil is avoided in the modern coupler. Octave couplers, coupling the octave either above or below, are of the backfall description. As the pedal-keys occupy more space than the manual-keys a roller-board is used, made on the same principle and practically for the same purpose as that already described. One end of the roller is over the pedal-key and the other under the manual-key desired to be affected. A sticker rests on the end of the backfall, when the pedal-coupler is " out," but is thrown out of the perpendicular when the coupler-stop is " in." A coupler attaching the great to the swell organ, termed a sforzando coupler, capable of being used for a single chord if required, is formed by a double backfall thus,

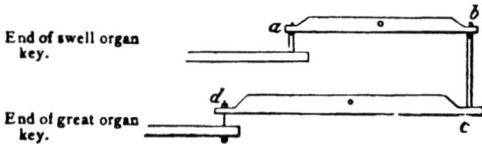

End of swell organ key.

End of great organ key.

so that when *a* rises *b* is depressed and forces down *c* which in turn raises *d*.

(§ 11.) To enable a performer to make rapid changes of stops, short iron pedals are placed over the pedal-clavier, called composition-pedals or combination-pedals, whose office it is to produce certain definite arrangements of the registers when pressed down with the foot. A single-action composition pedal is one that draws out a certain number of stops, but does not alter the arrangement of the other stops on the same manual during the operation. A double-action composition pedal is one that has the power of drawing *in* any stops not belonging to its prescribed combination which may happen to be *out;* for example, supposing the trumpet and sesquialtera on the great organ are drawn out, and the foot is then placed on the composition pedal which draws out the diapasons, if the action of the pedal be *single* the trumpet and sesquialtera will remain out as the diapasons are drawn ; if the action be *double*, as the diapasons are being drawn out, the trumpet and sesquialtera will be *drawn in*.

Composition pedals act by leverage either on the back of the draw stop handles or on the ends of the sliders, but it would exceed the due limits of this article to explain even a few of the many systems of connection between composition pedals and sliders which are in use among organ builders. Pneumatic bellows are not unfrequently employed for purposes of combining registers, and are often set in motion by small pegs or nobs projecting between the manuals, instead of iron pedals. In cases where several sound-boards are attached to one manual, containing

each of them part of the stops, changes of combination are sometimes obtained by pedals or pegs, called *ventils*, which admit the wind to, or cut the wind off from, the separate sound-boards.

(§ 12.) The pneumatic action is a contrivance for lightening the touch of manual or pedal keys by placing near each key a small bellows, having two openings on the under side, one of which is a pallet in a chest of compressed air, the other a waste-valve. The following diagrams will explain this :—

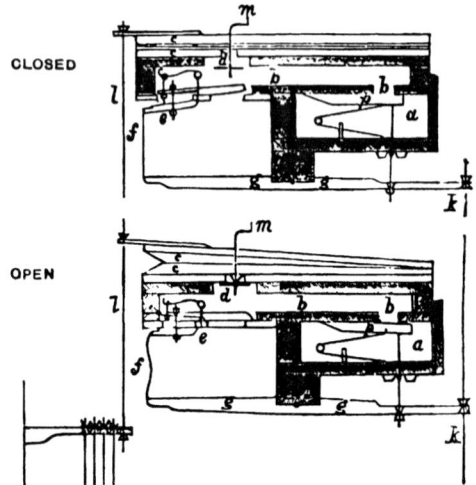

When either the finger or foot is pressed upon a key connected with *k*, the outer end of the back-fall *gg* is pulled down, which opens the pallet *p*. The compressed air in *a* then rushes through the groove *bb* into the bellows *cc*, which rises and lifts with it all the action attached to it by *l*. As the top of the bellows *cc* rises, it lifts up the throttle-valve *d* (regulated by the wire *m*) which prevents the ingress by any more compressed air by *bb*. But the action of the key on *gg*, which opened the pallet *p* also allowed the double-acting waste-valve *e* to close, and the tape *f* hangs loose. The compressed air, therefore, as it is admitted through *bb* cannot escape, but on the other hand when the key releases the outer end of *g*, and lets it rise up again, the tape *f* becomes tightened and opens the waste-valve, the bellows *cc* then drops into its closed position.

The principle of this invaluable invention was introduced by Mr. Hamilton of Edinburgh, or Mr. Barker. The latter gentleman succeeded in making its importance understood by some leading French organ-builders, by whom it was at once adopted, and whence it found its way back to this country. English organ-builders have, however, altered very much the original form of the pneumatic lever. The diagrams given above represent the lever as improved by the eminent organ-builder, Henry Willis, to whose talent organists are also indebted for the compressed-air action instead of trackers, for long distances—a simple and safe communication between two sides of a church. The organ in St. Paul's Cathedral which is divided into three portions on this principle, the Pedal-organ being under one of the arches of the chancel, the great and solo organs on the north-side, and the choir and swell on the south-side, deserves to be called a masterpiece of mechanical skill.

(§ 13.) Organ pipes are divided, with reference to their material, into metal or wood; with reference to their manner of producing tone, into reed and flue. Of the metals used in making organ pipes tin is the best, lead the worst. A mixture of tin and lead in equal proportions is technically termed "metal." An excess in the relative quantity of lead renders "metal" of proportionately less value. Zinc is used sometimes for large pipes, where cheapness is an object. Antimony may be used, but not in too great quantities, its brittleness being a serious drawback to its durability. Spotted metal is so called because of the mottled appearance of its surface. The spots are considered a guarantee of a fairly good material, as they do not rise unless there is one third of tin in the metal. Metal is prepared for use by being, when melted, poured into a wooden trough with a slit in the back, and passed rapidly along a bench faced with tick. The thickness of the sheet of metal depends, of course, on the size of the slit in the trough. It is afterwards planed down carefully to an uniform surface.

Deal, pine, and cedar, are the woods most commonly used for pipes; more rarely, oak, mahogany, maple, &c.; the harder woods being generally chosen for pipes to be used in hot countries.

The tone of a flue-pipe is produced by the resonance of a column of air, which is set in vibration by a current of compressed air forced through a slit, over which is placed a sharp edge. The pitch is therefore dependent on the length of the pipe. The tone of a reed-pipe is produced by a thin strip of metal which is placed over the entrance of a tube, in such a manner that the compressed air, in trying to force its way into the tube sets the strip of metal into vibration. The pitch of the reed-pipe is, therefore, dependent on the number of vibrations of the reed (strip of metal), *not necessarily on the length of the tube.*

(§ 14.) Flue pipes are of two kinds, open or closed. The tone of a closed pipe is, in its pitch, an octave below that of an open pipe

of the same length, the cause of which is, that in an open pipe the vibrating column of air is divided by a node (or point of rest) at its centre, whereas in a closed pipe the column of air is undivided. An open metal flue pipe consists of *foot*, and *language*, and *body*. The foot is that on which it stands, and into which the compressed air enters.

FOOT.   LANGUAGE.

The language is a flat piece of metal fastened by its edge to the top of the foot, and which by its shape, only permits the air to leave the foot in one direction. The whole of the pipe above the foot and language is termed the body. The lower edge of the body is indented in front thus, the indentation is called the *leaf.* The lower edge of the leaf forms the *upper lip* and the corresponding edge of the foot which is also indented is termed the *lower lip.* The space between the lips is termed the *mouth.* A wooden flue-pipe consists of a *foot, cap, block,* and *body.* The foot is a hollow wooden tube on which the pipe stands, and through which the air enters into it.

The air on entering is arrested in its upward course by the *block.*

It, therefore, comes out towards the front through the *throat*, as the opening in the block is termed, and passes along the cap by which it is forced through the small opening between the top of the cap (the *under-lip*) and the top of the block, called the *wind-way.* The four boards used in making the pipe form the *body.* The *upper-lip* of a wooden pipe is generally made by bevelling off that part of the body of the pipe just over the upper edge of the cap,

but the mouths are sometimes inverted thus :

Occasionally also the block is superseded by a wooden " language," similar in its position and office to that in a metal pipe, thus :

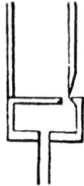

The block is sometimes bevelled off on its underside, while the cap remains straight, thus :

The following section of a flue-pipe will probably make its construction clear :—t is the foot through which air enters; c the space between the block and cap; $d e$ the slit through which the air is directed to strike against the lip. $a b$; and r is inside of the pipe, which acts as a resonance-box.

(§ 15.) A reed-pipe consists of a *boot, block, reed, tongue, wedge, tuning wire,* and *tube.*

The *boot* is a metal case corresponding somewhat in its office to the *foot* of a flue-pipe, inasmuch as the weight of the pipe rests upon it, and through it the air passes upwards. The *block* is a round piece of metal fitting into the boot, pierced in two places, one to contain the reed, the other to admit the tuning wire. It would appear thus in section. Into the larger orifice the reed is forced, through the smaller the tuning wire is passed. The rim prevents it from being forced into the boot by the superincumbent weight of tube.

The *reed* is a brass tube rather wider at the bottom than the top, and closed at the bottom, having a narrow orifice over which lies the *tongue,* a thin elastic piece of brass large enough to cover the orifice and its edges.

It is kept in its position by a small **wedge** of wood which is forced into the orifice in the block with the reed. The lower end of the tongue is therefore perfectly free. The *tuning-wire* is a piece of common wire bent in such a manner that a flat part of it lies across the *tongue.* By moving the wire from the outside, more or less of the tongue is allowed to vibrate, and thus the pitch is regulated. The upper end stands just in front of the *tube* of wood or metal, into which the air passes when leaving the reed, and which adds so materially to the tone of a reed-pipe. In small pipes the tube is generally of metal, but in large pipes often of wood ; it is conical in shape if a full tone is required ; if not, circular or circular with a bell-top ; and is either soldered to the top of the block, as is the case in small pipes, or is dropped into a small socket on the top of the block. Though, as before stated, the tube is not essential for the regulation of the pitch, its length and shape greatly influence the quality of sound produced. The *closed reed* is a reed which admits a much smaller quantity of wind than the open or common reed.

(§ 16.) The free or common harmonium reed is a reed the tongue of which does not lie over the edge of the aperture, but is able to pass freely backwards and forwards. Hence its name *free,* in opposition to the kind of reeds above described which are termed " percussion reeds." They are not commonly used in organs, but are more often met with in continental than in English organs.

(§ 17.) The swell organ is the successor of the old echo organ, a portion of a few stops enclosed in a wooden box in order to produce a subdued tone, or the effect of distance. In 1712, Abraham Jordan invented the " Nag's-head swell," as it was afterwards termed. It consisted of an echo organ, having, instead of a fixed front, a moveable shutter working up and down in a window sash. A pedal on the right hand side of the performer raised and closed the shutter at will, thus producing a *crescendo* and *diminuendo.* But the mechanism of this old " swelling organ " was most unsatisfactory. A very heavy pressure on the pedal was required before the shutter would stir, but once in motion it would often run up to its extreme limit against the wish of the performer, coming down to its closed position again when the pedal was released with a loud "bang." After half a century, England, and Avery, and afterwards Green, made use of the Venetian Swell, which consists of a series of shutters from six to ten inches in breadth, and from a half to two and a half inches in thickness, each hung on an axis one-third from the top of its breadth. The edges of each shutter are bevelled away at an angle of about forty-five degrees, so that each two contiguous boards overlap each other, and also are covered with felt in order to fit close, shut quietly, and shut in the sound thoroughly. The inside of the whole box may be lined with thick brown paper, glued on to the wood-work; this prevents the escape of sound, and does not injure the reverberation when the shutters are open. The Venetian Swell is so named because of the similarity of the appearance of the shutters to that of a common Venetian blind. The shutters sometimes are placed perpendicularly instead of horizontally, and occasionally open at the sides or back, as well as in the front.

(§ 18.) The quality of tone, and to some extent the pitch of pipes, whether they are wood or metal, reed or flue, depends upon their shape or outline, their scale, and the pressure of the wind to which they are subject. Metal pipes are in shape either cylindrical, conical, or inverted-conical, or surmounted by a bell whether cylindrical or conical. Wood pipes are four-sided, the opposite sides being equal in width, or pyramidal, or inverted-pyramidal.

(§ 19.) By Scale is meant the relation between the width and length of a pipe. If a pipe is wide in proportion to its length it is said to be of a large scale; if narrow in proportion to its length of a small scale. Inasmuch as scale affects to some degree the pitch of a pipe, it necessitates a proportionate alteration in its length, thus a pipe of a small scale must be made somewhat longer than a pipe of a large scale sounding the same note.

(§ 20.) The amount of the pressure or weight of wind is regulated by the weights placed on the bellows. It is found, by using a wind-gauge or Anemometer, a bent glass tube, which is fixed into a socket, and into which a little water is poured. On placing the socket on one of the holes in the upper board of a sound-board, and admitting the air from the bellows, the water is forced up the tube, and the difference between the level of the two surfaces of water is measured in inches. The usual weight of wind on the swell, great, and choir organs of a church organ, is from two and a half to three inches, the pedal organ (where a separate bellows makes it feasible) receiving rather a higher pressure. The fourth manual or solo organ is nearly always voiced to a very high pressure, as very fine effects are in this way obtained both from reed and flue pipes. Organs in concert rooms and public buildings are often voiced throughout to a higher pressure than those in churches. The average amount of surface weight on the bellows required to produce a three-inch wind is nine pounds and three quarters per superficial foot.

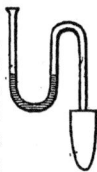

(§ 21.) As regards the disposition of the various qualities of tone between the manuals,— the choir organ, being as its name implies, intended for the accompaniment of voices, generally receives stops of a delicate and subdued quality of tone, such as the Spitzflöte, Gemshorn, Viol di Gamba, Dulciana, Keraulophon, &c. The great organ being required for grand effects, has allotted to it the large scale Diapasons, together with a complete set of octave, twelfth, super-octave, mixture stops, and a proportionate number of large scale reed-stops. The swell organ has a larger proportion of reeds than any other manual, chiefly because of the fine effects they produce during the opening and closing of the shutters of the swell box. The reed-stops are generally placed in the front of the swell sound-board, just inside the box, not only because in that position the effect of a *crescendo* is increased, but also because they are more easily within the reach of a tuner. The Pedal Organ, as an independent organ, cannot be said to have been known in England for more than the last half century, although apparently always a constituent part of a good German instrument. The deepest tones (32 feet) are consigned to the Pedal Organ, as also a large number of 16 feet stops, to serve as a bass to the manuals, which have rarely more than one or two of that pitch, on any separate manual.

(§ 22.) An organ is tuned by means of hollow cones and reed-knives. The former are used for tuning metal flue-pipes, and are used in this manner. If a pipe is too sharp, the apex of the cone is inserted into the top of the pipe, and the cone being forced in enlarges the orifice and flattens the pitch. If a pipe is too flat, a cone whose base is so broad that it will admit the top of the pipe,

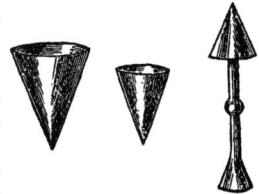

is placed on the pipe and squeezed down until the orifice is reduced in size, and the pitch is sufficiently raised. Cones are made of metal or wood, more often the latter, because of its comparative lightness. Wooden flue-pipes are tuned, if stopped, by moving the stopper up or down ; if open, by a piece of lead placed on the back of the top of the pipe for the purpose.

Large open wood pipes are tuned by cutting off part of the top if too sharp, and by raising a piece of wood screwed for the purpose near the top if too flat.

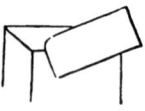

The largest metal-pipes have generally an opening at the back of the top, which can be opened or closed as it is necessary to make them flatter or sharper.

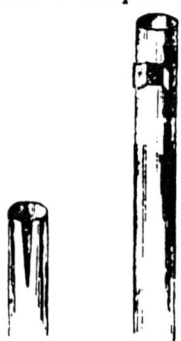

Metal pipes, with soldered covers, with or without chimneys, are tuned by altering the position of the ears, which are made specially long.

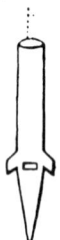

(§ 23.) The reed-knife is a long piece of common iron or steel in this shape, hence its name.

The tuning wire is provided at its upper extremity with a hook or projection by which the edge of the knife is able, by gentle taps, to gradually raise it. The wire is pushed in by being struck on the top. By referring to the account of the tuning wire given in §15, it will be understood that raising the wire flattens the note, depressing it sharpens it.

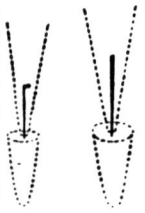

Organetto (*It.*) A little organ.

Organic Music. A mediæval name for instrumental music.

Organo (*It.*) Organ. *Organo pleno*, the full organ.

Organochordium. An instrument having pipes and strings, invented by Vogler.

Organo di legno. A claque bois. [Xylophon.]

Organophonic. The name assumed by a band of Polish performers, who imitated the sounds made by various instruments with their mouths.

Organo portabile (*It.*) A *portative* organ. A small organ capable of being easily carried about.

Organ-point. [Fugue.]

Organum. (1) An early form of harmony, called also *diaphony* [Descant.] (2) An organ.

Organum hydraulicum (*Lat.*) Hydraulic organ.

Organum pneumaticum (*Lat.*) The common organ.

Orgel (*Ger.*) [Organ.]

Orgelgehäuse (*Ger.*) An organ case.

Orgel-punkt (*Ger.*) A pedal point. [Fugue.]

Orgue (*Fr.*) Organ or harmonium.

Orgue expressif (*Fr.*) Harmonium.

Orgue portatif (*Fr.*) A portable organ.

Orificium (*Lat.*) The mouth of an organ-pipe.

Original position. A chord is said to be in its original position when the ground-note is in the bass ; in other words, before it has undergone inversion : or, when its upper notes are in the order 3, 5, 8.

Ornamenti (*It.*) Grace-notes and other embellishments.

Ornatamente, Ornato (*It.*) With embellishments.

Orpharion. A kind of lute, having *wire* strings. [Lute.]

Osservanza, con (*It.*) With exactness.

Ossia (*It.*) Or else, as *ossia più facile*, or else in this more easy way.

Ostinato (*It.*) *Lit.* obstinate, used in the sense of "frequently repeated," as *basso ostinato*, a ground-bass, q.v.

Oton. An Indian wind instrument producing only a single sound, employed during the dancing of the Bayadères. The player holds the oton in his left hand while with his right he beats a tambourine fastened to his belt. [Tabor.]

Ottava (*It.*) An octave, as *ottava alta* (to be played), an octave higher, *ottava bassa*, an octave lower.

Ottavina (*It.*) The little or higher octave.

Ottavino flauto (*It.*) [Flute.]

Ottemole. [Octuplet.]

Ottetto (*It.*) A composition in eight parts.

Ouïe (*Fr.*) The hearing.

Ouvert (*Fr.*) Open, as *à livre ouvert*, at sight.

Ouverture (*Fr.*) [Overture.]

Overblow. A pipe is said to be overblown when the pressure of air forces it to speak an over-tone, instead of its fundamental note.

Overtura di ballo (*It.*) An overture in the style of dance-music.

Overture. Overtura (*It.*) **Ouverture** (*Fr.*) An introductory symphony for instruments. It is usual to say that there are four kinds of overtures, two in the ancient, and two in the modern style. This may be true with regard to the limit placed upon the ancient overtures, but it is not entirely so with respect to the modern ones, for they are as various as the fancies of composers, and defy all attempts to reduce them to classification.

Old overtures may be arranged into two classes, the French and the Italian, or to describe them by the names of their reputed inventors into the Lully and Scarlatti overtures. The Lully overture usually opened with a slow and stately movement, by way of introduction. The succeeding theme was treated in imitation in the old Canzona style; if divided into sections, the first section ended in the key of the dominant if it began in a major key, and in the relative major if it began in the minor. All kinds of free imitation were allowed in the next section. After this a "grave" was repeated, and a minuet, or some lively movement concluded the overture. This form is employed by Handel, Bach, Keiser, Telemann, Hasse, Graun, and other composers of the early part of the 18th century, with more or less alterations according to fancy. When Sonata Form began to be understood, overtures in the form described above were more rarely written, but the style was not wholly disused until the commencement of the present century.

The Scarlatti form of overture consisted of three movements or sections; the first and third were quick or lively, and the second was slow. In the slow movement, a change of pace, and also of accent or rhythm was used, and fewer instruments were employed, so that the scoring might afford a strong contrast to the other portions. A near approach to the arrangement of the Sonata and Symphony was thus made, and the Italian overture or "Sinfonia" may be called the immediate precursor of the symphony as it now stands.

The modern overture dates from the latter part of the 18th century, and may be described in a few words as a composition in the form of the first movement of a sonata, concerto, or symphony, with the exception that the sections are not always marked for repetition. It has occasionally a short introduction in a slow *tempo*, of a marked and stately character. Its principal themes are often taken from the work it precedes. Sometimes the "free fugue" style is chosen, and occasionally the sonata and fugue form are happily united, as in Mozart's overture "Die Zauberflöte."

Many modern overtures consist almost entirely of a series of clever contrasts independent of form. These should be described as *medley* overtures, though the medley overture proper includes portions of the chief melodies in an opera. One of the most effective works of this class is the overture to "Guy Mannering" by Sir H. R. Bishop. The invention of the medley overture is attributed to Richard Charke, the son-in-law of Colley Cibber.

Overtures not connected with, or part of a larger work, are known as "Concert Overtures!" but it does not follow that overtures originally written as preludes to a special work, may not be treated as "Concert" pieces, even if the work to which they were attached has ceased to be known.

Oxupycni (Med. *Lat.* from *Gk.* ὀξὺς, acute, and πυκνὸς, close.) Church Modes having a pycnon or semitone high in the tetrachord *e.g.* :

Oxybaphon (*Gk.*) ὀξυβάφον. *Lit.* a vinegar jar. Hence (like the acetabulum) an earthenware vessel used for experiments as to sound.

P.

P. Abbreviation of *piano*, soft.

Paduana, Padouana. [Pavan.]

Pæan, παιάν. The ancient choral song addressed to Apollo, named after its burden, ἰώ παιάν. It was sung sometimes before battle, and sometimes after a victory. Donaldson thinks it probable that it was at first accompanied on the phorminx, which, however, was afterwards superseded by the flute. From the ancient Pæan sprang the gymnopœdic, pyrrhic, and hyporchematic dances.

Pæon. A foot consisting of one long syllable and three short. The position of the long syllable can be varied in four ways, hence the Pæon is said to be primus, secundus, tertius, or quartus. [Metre.]

Pair of Organs. The word pair simply means a *set*, and it is used in this sense in the expression a " pair of stairs," or a " pair of scissors." It was formerly in more general use than now, and " pair of cards," and " pair of beads," are met with in the old poets. A " pair of organs " means, then, an organ having a complete set of pipes.

Palalaika. [Balalaika.]

Palco (*It.*) The stage of a theatre, &c.

Palilia. The rustic dance at the Festival of Pales, in which the shepherds leapt round and over burning straw. It may have been to some extent the origin of the May-pole dance.

Pallet. [Organ, § 4.]

Palmula (*Lat.*) Manual of an organ.

Pambe. A small Indian drum.

Pandean-pipes. [Pan's-pipes.]

Pandora. [Bandore.]

Pan's-pipes, or **mouth-organ.** The earliest form of a compound wind instrument, undoubtedly the precursor of the organ. It was the σύριγξ of the Greeks, *fistula* of the Romans, and probably the *ugab* of the Hebrews. It was formed of seven, eight, or nine short hollow reeds, fixed together by wax, and cut in graduated lengths, so as to produce a musical scale. The lower ends of the reeds were closed and the upper open and on a level, so that the mouth could easily pass from one pipe to another.

Pantaleone. An instrument invented by Hebenstreit in 1705. It was a sort of dulcimer, but strung with catgut and metal strings in two series.

Pantalon (*Fr.*) One of the movements of a quadrille.

Parallelbewegung. [Parallel motion.]

Parallelen (*Ger.*) Consecutives.

Parallel motion. The movement of two or more parts at fixed intervals, as thirds, sixths. Parallel fifths are under certain limitations forbidden. [Consecutives.]

Paramese (*Gk.*) παραμέση. [Greek music.]

Paranete (*Gk.*) παρανήτη. [Greek music.]

Parhypate (*Gk.*) παρυπάτη. [Greek music.]

Parlando, Parlante (*It.*) In a declamatory manner, as if speaking.

Parlante (*It.*) *Lit.* speaking. (1) In the style of a recitative ; (2) played in the style of vocal recitation.

Paroles (*Fr.*) Words ; as, *Sans paroles*, without words.

Part. (1) So much of a piece of music, or work, as is performed by any one voice or instrument ; (2) Division of a work.

Parte (*It.*) Part. *Parte cantante*, vocal part. *Partie* (*Fr.*)

Partial tones. Those simple sounds which in combination form an ordinary sound and cause its special quality of tone. [Acoustics.]

Partimenti (*It.*) Figured basses, used as exercises.

Partition (*Fr.*) **Partitur** (*Ger.*) [Score.]

Partitura, Partizione (*It.*) [Score.]

Part-Music. Music in two or more parts, performed by more than one person.

Part-Song. A vocal composition, having a striking melody harmonized by other parts more or less freely, but from which counterpoint is for the most part excluded. The Part-song owes its origin to the habit prevalent among the Germans of adding simple harmonies to their " Volksgesänge." On the model of these harmonized airs, fresh compositions have from time to time been produced, sometimes with a little more elaboration in their construction than their models, in such numbers, that there is now an extensive literature of this kind of music. Almost every town in Germany has its " Singverein," " Liedertafel," or " Männergesangverein," all of which largely encourage this special class of composition. From Germany Part-songs have been imported into England, and our native composers have produced a large number, many of which are of great merit. The Part-song holds now the position which the glee held in this country from the middle of the last century to the beginning of this, and which the madrigal held from the middle of the sixteenth to the middle of the seventeenth century. The simplest form of Part-song is that in which the same music (*tutti*) is repeated for each verse of the words; the most elaborate that in which soli parts occur, or a separate solo accompanied by the other parts, either *pianissimo* or *con boccha chiusa*. Part-songs may be for soprani, contralti, tenori, and bassi, or for men's voices only. In the latter case, the upper part is in Germany sung by high tenors, but in England, where the alto voice is still cultivated by alti, the score includes an alto, two tenor parts, and a bass part, instead of the ordinary two tenor and two bass parts of those by German authors. A Part-song differs from a madrigal in its exclusion of contrapuntal devices; from a glee, in its being sung by many voices instead of by one only to each part. The treatment of the chords and the harmonical progressions sufficiently stamp the madrigalian style, while the peculiar melodiousness of the inner parts of a glee, coupled with its special adaptability for chamber use, mark its character distinctly; and on the other hand, the Part-song by its strong outlines and modern harmonization can easily be distinguished from a glee.

Pas (*Fr.*) A dance, as *pas seul*, *pas de deux*, a dance by one or two performers. A step, as *pas redoublé*, a quick step, or march.

Paspy. The English name for the dance *Passepied*, called also *Passamezzo* by the Italian and *Paspie* by the Spanish writers. It was a precursor of the minuet, some of the tunes called by the title Paspy resembling the minuet in rhythm and measure. Hawkins says it "is said to have been invented in Bretagne, and it is in effect a quick minuet." The old English writers call it passa-measure, passy-measure, passing-measure, or simply measure. It was a favourite dance in the time of Queen Elizabeth, and from the fact that examples exist by writers as late as Purcell and Croft, it could not have been out of fashion in their time.

PASPY.   H. PURCELL.

THE ENGLISH PASPY.

CROFT, c. 1700.

Passacaglio, passacaglia (*It.*); *Passe-caille, passe-rue* (*Fr.*); *Passacalle* (*Sp.*); *Gassenhawer* (*Ger.*) A dance in triple measure, constructed on a ground bass. Bach has used this form for one of his grandest compositions for the organ. [Gassenhawer.] [Chaconne.]

Passage. (1) A phrase of music. (2) A figure. (3) A run.

Passage (*Fr.*) [Passage.]

Passage-boards. Boards placed in different parts of an organ, on which the tuner can walk, and from whence he can reach pipes or mechanism.

Passaggio (*It.*) A passage or phrase, as *passaggio cromatico*, a chromatic passage. Also a run, or rapid succession of notes.

Passa mezzo (*It.*) [Paspy.]

Passe-pied. [Paspy.]

Passing discord. [Passing note.]

Passing note. A note not essential to harmony, forming an unprepared discord, which is not objectionable because it is a fragment of a scale. It is a necessary characteristic of a passing-note, that it should have a degree of the scale on each side of it. Passing-notes having degrees of a diatonic scale on each side are said to be *diatonic ;* those having degrees of a chromatic scale on each side, are said to be *chromatic.*

Diatonic passing notes.

Chromatic passing notes.

Passing notes generally occur on unaccented parts of a bar. When unessential notes occur on accented parts of a bar, they are generally called *auxiliary notes, e.g.* :

Passionatamente, passionate, passionato, con passione (*It.*) In an impassioned manner.

Passione (*It.*) A cantata founded on the incidents of the Passion, or on the seven last words.

Passion Music. Music set to the narrative of our Lord's Passion in the Gospels. Dramatic representations of the subject date from a very early period, there being still extant a play ascribed, though somewhat doubtfully, to Gregory Nazianzen, Bishop of Antioch. It is in 4th century Greek, and is entitled "χριστός πασχών." This, like many of the religious plays of a subsequent date, was designed only to be spoken as in ordinary dramatic representations, and is independent of musical aid. For, although music was occasionally employed to add to the attraction of the performance of these Mysteries or Miracle plays in early times, it was only in a secondary manner, and not so connected with or inseparable from the action as in still later times, or in the form now known. Passion plays are still occasionally performed in remote continental places, with music as an accessory.

The dramatic performance of the Passion arose in imitation of the ancient custom, still observed in the Roman Catholic Church of dividing the recital of the Gospel of the Passion in Holy Week between two, three, or more readers, assigning those parts which reproduce the words of the people (turbæ) to

the congregation or choir. To one priest was assigned the part of Jesus, to others those of Pilate, Judas, the High Priest, &c., and the connecting portions of the narrative by a narrator. All these parts were recited according to the rules of the *accentus ecclesiasticus,* while the turbæ or people's part was delivered in monotone.

When the Passion was played at other times than during the course of the service, it is supposed that the words were spoken without the aid of music. So popular did these plays become that as early as 1264 a company of monks was formed for the express purpose of performing the " Sufferings of Christ." Bayle, Burney, and others give a series of dates of several notable mediæval performances of the Passion, for example, at Padua in 1243, at Friuli in 1298, at Civita Vecchia in the same year, at Paris before Philip le Bel, and our own Edward II. in 1313, at St. Maur near Paris in 1404, at Constance during the Council in 1417, by the English fathers, at Paris, on the entrance of the Kings of England and France into that capital in 1420, in the same city in 1424, in 1431 on the occasion of the entry of Henry VI. of England, as King of France, and at Poitiers with great magnificence in 1486. In the Imperial library at Paris is preserved a copy of " Le Mystère de la Passion Jesus Christ," printed on vellum by Antoine Verard, 1490, in which a MS. note describes the performance of this play at Metz and at Veximiel, with some curious details respecting the representation at the latter place. In Rymer's " View of Tragedy," there is a quotation from the Register of the Parliament at Paris in which the Procureur General du Roi lays a complaint against four laymen for having undertaken to perform *Christ's Passion* and the *Acts of the Apostles,* " with a company of illiterate and incompetent men ; that they had moreover introduced apocryphal matters, and interlarded their plays with drolls and farces, so as to spin out the play and make it last six or seven months ; that they had played for lucre, and made their performance so attractive that nobody went to church, charity grew cold, and immoral excesses were occasioned." Their proceedings were stopped during the King's pleasure, and they were condemned to pay a fine of 800 livres out of their profits.

The reformation witnessed, among the many important changes to which it gave rise, the modification of the representation of the Passion. Luther encouraged the continuance of the practice, and a development of the ancient custom by which the several incidents told in the gospels were recited by different individuals, gave opportunities to the composers of the period to set music of their own to the story, in the place of the traditional church tones, and by this means the story was told, not only at the times commanded by the ritual of the church, but at other periods, in other places, and on other occasions. One of the first versions of the text of these improvements was printed at Wittenberg in 1573, with the music for the recitative and the choruses for the turbæ in four-part harmony. The author of this interesting specimen of composition is unknown, though some writers attribute it to Antonio Scandell. Fifteen years later, namely, in 1588, Bartholomæus Güse, or Gese, produced a more elaborate composition, in which the expressions uttered by the priests, people, or disciples, were called by the general name "Turbæ." These were set in harmony or plain-song and sung in chorus. The words of our Lord, of Peter, Pilate, Judas, the High Priest, &c., were usually sung by separate solo voices; but in the work of Bartholomæus Gese, a different practice is resorted to. The words of the maid-servant are set for *two* voices, those of Peter and Pilate for *three*, those of the Saviour for *four*. In this work, the words of Holy Scripture alone are used as the text.

There was little attempt to vary the old plain-song in the early settings of the Passion, until Heinrich Schütz, or as he sometimes styled himself in accordance with the fanciful custom of his time, Henricus Sagittarius, introduced a new feature into the Passion music; that of the reflective chorus, as supposed to be sung by the "Christian community,"—and while the greater part of his harmonies are based upon the old church modes, there is a noteworthy attempt in his recitatives to free himself from the *accentus ecclesiasticus*, and to make them more independent. The design thus suggested was carried out by Johann Sebastiani, who was organist and Kapellmeister at Brandenburgh, in 1672, to whom also the introduction of orchestral, in the place of an organ accompaniment, is due. A still further deviation from the ancient plan was made by Reinhard Keiser at the beginning of the 18th century. Taking, instead of the gospel narratives of the Passion, original poems on the subject as his libretto, he made his "Passion Music" of like character with his many operas. In one of these works, "Der Blutige und Sterbende Jesus," the libretto by Menantes, he employs the term "soliloquia" to describe the reflective or interjaculatory passages set in "arioso recitative," so frequently employed later by John Sebastian Bach.

The words of Reinhard Keiser's "Passion" were written by Brockes, a Hamburg poet, who added to the Bible narrative, soliloquia, or reflections for the "Daughter of Sion," and "The Believing Soul." Telemann, Mattheson, and Handel set Brockes' poem to music, and traces of the influence of the poem are to be found in Bach's Matthew "Passion." A statement is made by Rietz that in the MS. score in Bach's handwriting certain solos, and solos with chorus, are marked as though they were to be sung by the Daughter of Zion, or Zion, or the Faithful. As there are several pieces in both the existing works on the Passion by Bach (the St. Matthew and the St. John), similar, if not identical with Brockes' soliloquia, there is a reasonable ground for believing the statement of Rietz. The credit of the introduction of the chorale has been assigned to Bach, but although he employed it freely, Telemann, Mattheson, and Handel, also used chorales in their works on the Passion. The earlier writers, Gese, Schütz, Keiser, and Sebastiani did not use the chorale as Bach probably did, with the design of enlisting the voices as well as the sympathies of the congregation. Bach selected from among a wealthy store of well known hymn-tunes those which had the greatest influence over the minds of German worshippers, tunes set to various words inseparably associated with the sentiments, affections, life, and citizenship of the people.

Passy-measure (*Old Eng.*) A corruption of the word *passa mezzo.* [Paspy.]

Pastete (*Ger.*) [Pasticcio.]

Pasticcio (*It.*) *Lit.* a pie, or pasty. *Pastiche* (*Fr.*), *Pastete* (*Ger.*) An opera, cantata, or other work, the separate numbers of which are gleaned from the compositions of various authors, or from several disconnected works of one author.

Pastiche (*Fr.*) [Pasticcio.]

Pastoral. (1) A simple melody in six-eight time in a rustic style. (2) A cantata, the words of which are founded on pastoral incidents. (3) A complete symphony, wherein a series of pastoral scenes is depicted by sound-painting, without the aid of words.

Pastorale (*It.*) [Pastoral.]

Pastorella (*It.*) A short pastoral.

Pastorelle (*Fr.*) [Pastorella.]

Pastorita. A shepherd's pipe. *Fistula pastoricia* (*Lat.*) An organ stop, the Nachthorn.

Pastourelle (*Fr.*) One of the movements of a quadrille.

Pateticamente, Patetico (*It.*) In a pathetic manner.

Pathétique, Pathétiquement (*Fr.*) In a pathetic manner.

Patimento (*It.*) Suffering, as *con espressione di patimento*, with an expression of suffering.

Pauken (*Ger.*) [Kettle-drums.]

Pausa (*Lat.*) A sign for silence. A rest. Ancient authors allowed four kinds of rests: the long rest being a perpendicular stroke drawn from a line to the second line below; the breve rest, a similar stroke from line to line: the semibreve rest, a stroke commencing from any line, and descending half way between the lines; the minim rest, the reverse of the semibreve, that is, a stroke ascending half way between the two lines; the semiminima rest (crochet), a line equal to half the distance between the lines, but bent to the left. These are, of course, practically the same as modern rests, but the way in which they were written was far from preventing confusion. There were also varieties of form or position to indicate rests in triple or common time.

Pausa (*It.*) A rest or pause. *Pausa generale*, a rest or pause for all the performers.

Pause (*Fr.*) (1) A rest or pause; (2) a bar's rest.

Pavan. A dance tune of a stately character, deriving its title from Padua, where it is said to have been invented. Others find the origin of the word in " Pavo," a peacock, because it was danced with " such circumstance of dignity and stateliness."

Morley's " Introduction to Practicall Musicke," speaks of it in these terms :—

" The next in grauitee and goodness vnto this is called a pauan, a kinde of staide musicke, ordained for graue dauncing, and most commonly made of three straines, whereof euerie strain is plaid or song twice. A straine they make to contain 8, 12, or 16, semi-briefs, as they list, yet fewer than eight I haue not seen in any pauan.

"After every pauan we vsualy set a galliard. The Italians make their galliards (which they tearm salta relly) plain, and frame ditties to them, which in their *mascaradoes* they sing and dance."

By this it would appear that the galliard and the pavan, when played upon the virginals, harpsichord, or spinet, formed a primitive sort of suite or sonata.

That the pavan was not used entirely for the dance may be gathered from the title of a work published by John Dowland, "Lachrymæ or Seaven Teares, figured in Seaven passionate Pavans, with divers other Pavans, Galliards, and Almands."

The pavan, when in duple time, is not unfrequently spoken of as a " quadron or quodran pavan." The " saltarello " or " salta relly," as Morley calls it, was in triple measure. When the pavan was played faster it was called a passamezzo.

PAVAN, TRANSLATED FROM TABLATURE IN WOLF HECKEL'S "LAUTTEN BUCH," 1562.

Pavana (*It.*) [Pavan.]
Pavane (*Fr.*) [Pavan.]
Paventato, Paventoso (*It.*) With an expression of fear.

Pavillon (*Fr.*) The bell of a horn, or other instrument of a like kind. *Flûte à Pavillon* (*Fr.*) an organ stop, the pipes of which are surmounted by a bell. *Pavillon chinois*, an instrument consisting of little bells attached to a staff.

Pectis. A Greek instrument of the lute or dulcimer kind.

Ped: Abb. (1) of pedal. In pianoforte music a direction to press down the pedal which raises the dampers. (2) Of pedals. In organ music a direction that the lowest part is to be played by the feet.

Pedal. Any projecting piece of metal or wood which is to be pressed down by the foot. (1) On the pianoforte there are usually two pedals, one of which enables the performer to play only on one string (*una corda*); the other, to remove the dampers (*sordini*). (2) On the organ there are combination pedals, which alter the arrangement of the registers, and a pedal clavier or keyboard, on which the feet play. (3) On the harp there are pedals, each of which has the power of flattening, sharpening, or making natural, one note throughout the whole compass of the instrument.

Pedal-claviatur (*Ger.*) The pedal keyboard of an organ.

Pedal coupler. An accessory stop of an organ, by means of which the pedal keys are enabled to draw down the keys of a manual.

Pedale (*It.*) (1) A pedal key of an organ. (2) A pedal note, or pedal point. [Fugue.] (3) The pedal of a pianoforte, which raises the dampers.

Pedalflügel (*Ger.*) A pianoforte, to which a set of pedal keys is attached.

Pedaliera (*It.*) The pedal keys of an organ.

Pedalion. A set of pedals acting upon strings, producing notes of a deep pitch, so constructed as to be capable of being used with a pianoforte.

Pedal-pipes. The name given to the one stop which was often, in former times, in this country the sole representative of an independent pedal organ. It generally consisted of open wooden pipes of a large scale.

Pedal Sound-board. The sound-board containing the pipes belonging to the pedal organ.

Pedicula, Scabella, or Scabilla (*Lat.*) [κρούπεζα.] [Croupeza.]

Pedarii, Podarii, and Pedicularii. The beaters of time in the performance of Greek music. It was done with the foot, which was furnished with wooden or iron sandals for the purpose. [Croupeza.]

Peg of an Instrument. A small round piece of wood or metal, placed in a hole, or two holes, so as to be capable of being turned round, and pierced to receive that end of a string or wire which is not fixed. It is prevented from slipping round under the influence of the tension of the string or wire, either by being made slightly tapering in form, and then forced into its hole as in a violin; or by being made with serrated edges, as in a pianoforte. The outer end of the peg expands into a broad flat surface which can be easily turned round between the thumb and forefinger, or has a four-sided head on to which a key can be fixed.

Penillion singing. A Welsh custom of singing improvised verses on a given theme to a melody either well-known or then and there learnt from the harper who accompanies the Penillion. There is a similar custom among the Hungarian gipsies called the "Verbunges." [Dutch concert.]

Penorcon. An obsolete instrument of the guitar family, somewhat broader and shorter than the Pandora, with a very broad neck over which passed nine brass strings, which were played upon by the fingers.

Pentatone. An interval of five whole tones, an augmented sixth.

Pentatonic scale. The name given by Carl Engel to the ancient musical scale which is easiest described, as that formed by the black keys of the pianoforte. It consists of the 1st, 2nd, 3rd, 5th, and 6th degrees of a modern diatonic scale, *e.g.*:

Per (*Lat.*), by, as *per diminutionem*, by diminution; *per inversionem*, by inversion.

Per (*It.*), by or for; as, *per il violino*, for the violin.

Percussion. An ingenious contrivance whereby a hammer strikes the tongue of a reed and sets it in motion simultaneously with the admission of air from the windchest, thus securing the rapid speech of the reed. Were it not for the percussion, the reed would be only gradually set in motion by the admission of the current of air, and the sound would not instantly follow the striking of the key. It is commonly used in harmoniums, but has also been applied to the largest reeds of an organ.

Percussion of a discord. The striking of a discord, which takes place after its preparation, and which is followed by its resolution.

Percussione (*It.*) The striking of a chord.

Perd. Perden. *Abbreviations of*

Perdendo, Perdendosi (*It.*) Losing time and power, implying both *dim.* and *rall.*

Perfect. Complete. (1) Perfect cadence, an authentic or plagal cadence. [Cadence.] (2) Perfect concord, a common chord in its original position. (3) Perfect consonance, the consonance produced by the intervals fourth, fifth, or octave. (4) Perfect interval, one of the divisions of intervals. [Interval.] (5) Perfect time. An old name for triple time.

Perfetto (*It.*) Perfect (of intervals, &c.)

Perijourdine. A song-dance, a ballad, named after the district in which it was used.

CHANSON À DANSER DE SARLAT EN PERIGORD.

Period, *Periode* (*Fr.*), *Periodo* (*It.*) A complete musical sentence. [Form.]

Periodenbau (*Ger.*) The construction of musical periods.

Periodic Vibration. [Acoustics, § 9.]

Period of Vibration. [Acoustics, § 3.]

Perlé (*Fr.*) *Lit.*, pearled. *Cadence perlée*, a brilliant cadence. A *pearly touch* is an expression of our own for a delicate and bright touch in playing the pianoforte.

Perpetual canon. A canon so constructed that it may be repeated constantly without a break in the time or rhythm. [Canon.]

Per recte et retro. A species of imitation in which the antecedent is repeated at the unison, reading the notes backwards. The following chant by Dr. Crotch is a simple example. The numbers over the bars will show the retrogressive movement.

Pesante (*It.*) With weight, or importance. Impressively.

Petite flûte (*Fr.*) Kleine Flöte (*Ger.*) Piccolo. [Flute.]

Petite mesure à deux tems (*Fr.*) Two-four time.

Petteia (*Gk.*) A term of Greek "Melopœia." Perhaps the same as *extensio*, the holding out of a sound, or its frequent repetition to different words or syllables.

Petto (*It.*) The chest. *Voce di petto*, the chest voice.

Peu à peu (*Fr.*) Little by little, gradually.

Pezzi (*It.*) Pieces, as *pezzi concertanti*, concert pieces or *concerti ; pezzi di bravura*, pieces for the display of rapid execution and manual dexterity.

P.f., abb. of (1) Pianoforte. (2) *Piano, forte*, soft then loud. (3) *Più forte*, louder.

Pfeife (*Ger.*) Pipe, fife, little flute.

Pfeifenwerk (*Ger.*) The pipe work (of an organ), including both reed and flue pipes.

Phantasie (*Ger.*) [Fantasia.]

Phantasy, pl. **Phantasies** (*Old Eng.*) [Fancy.]

Phonascus (*Lat.*, from *Gk.* φωνασκός). A master who trained the voices of those who were preparing themselves for orators, singers, &c.

Phonometer. An instrument for ascertaining the number of vibrations of a given sound.

Phorminx (*Gk.*), φόρμιγξ. The ancient lyre or cithara, which had probably not more than seven strings. [Lyre.]

Phrasing. The proper rendering of music with reference to its melodic form. A performer who brings into due prominence the grouping of sounds into figures, sentences, &c., is said to *phrase* well. Formerly the phrasing of music was left to be discovered by the intelligence and taste of the performer. Modern writers use various signs as indications of their wishes, such as, the *slur, sf*, &c. [Expression.]

Piacere, a (*It.*) At pleasure (the time be modified at the performer's pleasure).

Piacevole, Piacevolezza con, Piacevolmente (*It.*) In a playful or light style. Pleasantly.

Piacimento (*It.*) [Piacere.]

Piangendo, Piangevole, Piangevolmente (*It.*) As if weeping. In a plaintive manner.

Pianette (*Fr.*) A small pianoforte.

Pianino (*It.*) [Pianette.]

Pianissimo (*It.*) As softly as possible, abbd. *pp*.

Piano (*It.*) Softly, abbd. *p*.

Piano à queue (*Fr.*) A grand pianoforte.

Piano carré (*Fr.*) A square pianoforte.

Piano droit (*Fr.*) An upright pianoforte.

Pianoforte, Forte-piano (*It.*) Hammerclavier, Flügel (*Ger.*) (1) A stringed instrument with a key-board. The name *soft-loud* was given to it because the gradations of sound are under the control of the performer.

(2) It is a development of the harpsichord, which in itself was an improvement upon the clarichord and spinet, but it differs from each in the manner in which the tone is produced and the strings set in vibration. In the earlier instruments this was effected by the scratching of quills or hard leather, acting as *plectra*. In the pianoforte the strings are struck by means of hammers. The dulcimer is undoubtedly the origin of the pianoforte; in fact, the pianoforte is nothing but a keyed dulcimer. The possession of "keys" and other mechanism often assisted the makers in finding titles for the early instruments. Thus we find keyboard instruments called *clavicytherium*, or keyed cithara; *clavichord*, or string struck by means of a key; *virginells* or *virginal*, from the rods attached to the keys; *spinet*, from the quills which struck the strings, and *clavicymbalum*, from *cembalo* one of the Italian titles for a dulcimer.

(3) The clavicytherium, *clavierharpe*, *claviercither* (*Ger.*) is supposed to be the oldest of the stringed instruments with a key-board. It was at one time arranged in an upright position, but was afterwards placed in a horizontal position similar to the grand pianoforte of the present day. The earliest representation of the instrument is to be found in the "Musurgia seu praxis musicæ" of Luscinius, Strasbourg, 1536; but the picture, as well as the accompanying description, is very vague, and it is therefore difficult to gain a correct idea of its construction. According to the picture and description, the clavicytherium must have been an oblong box with a lid, having a number of catgut strings arranged in triangular form. When the keys were pressed the strings were set in vibration by *plectra* of hard leather.

(4) The clavichord, *clavicordo* (*It.*), *Clavier* (*Ger.*) had strings of wire instead of gut. In other respects it was at first identical with the clavicytherium. The "action was simply a brass wedge or *tangent*, which was placed vertically at a point where it could be struck or pressed against its proper string; this wedge could be held against the string as long as required by the firm pressure of the finger. It thus formed the wrest-pin for the string, which vibrated only while the key was held down." The shorter length of the string had a cloth or list damper which checked the vibration of the whole length of the string when the finger was raised from the key, allowing the *tangent* to return to its place. The tangents struck and "stopped" the strings like a violin player's finger, so that

more than one sound could be produced from the same string. Forkel says that "Bach delighted in the instrument as he considered it best for study, and, in general, for private musical entertainment. He found it most convenient for the expression of his thoughts, and he did not consider it possible to produce such a variety in the gradations of tone from any harpsichord or pianoforte as from the clavichord."

The names clarichord, manichord and monochord were also applied to the clavichord.

The clavicymbalum, mentioned above, differed from the clavicytherium and clarichord in having strings of steel wire, which were set in vibration by means of quill plectra.

The clavichord is frequently mentioned by writers of the sixteenth and seventeenth centuries in such a manner as to show that the instrument was in general use at that period.

Clavichords were made in Germany as late as the middle of the eighteenth century. The last maker of any note, according to Dr. Rimbault, was Krämer of Göttingen, "some of whose instruments may still occasionally be met with in the old baronial residences with which that romantic country abounds."

(5) The virginal, or spinet, used a long time during the same period, gradually superseded the clavichord in England and elsewhere. It was an improvement upon the clavicytherium, having brass instead of gut-strings. The plectrum was of quill, attached to the tongue of a piece of wood called "a jack." When the key was struck the jack rose up, forced the quill past the string, and set it in vibration. The quill remained above the string so long as the key was held down. As soon as the finger was moved from the key, the jack returned to its place, when a small cloth damper on its top checked the vibrations of the string.

VIRGINAL AND

HARPSICHORD JACK.

In "Musick's hand-maid, new lessons and instructions for the virginals or harpsichord,"

c. 1660, it is said, that "the virginals, according to the ancient standard, were made to contain 29 keys (with the half notes 48 keys), but of later times they add to that number both above and below." It was usually placed upon a table or stand when performed upon. The instrument was a favourite one in the time of Queen Elizabeth, and continued to be popular until the commencement of the eighteenth century.

The virginals or spinets were sometimes highly ornamented with inlaid work of different woods, and sometimes with mother-of-pearl and precious stones. It is needless to say that these ornaments did not improve the tone.

A "PAIR OF VIRGINALS."

(6) The Spinet, absorbing the title of the Virginal, the instrument next in historical order, differed from the older Virginals in that it was always of a triangular shape.

SPINET, OR COUCHED HARP.

It had the wires carried over a bent bridge, which modified their sounds. Like the Virginal it was furnished with one string to each note, which string was set in vibration by means of the jack before described.

The following is a diagram of the Spinet or Clavichord action.

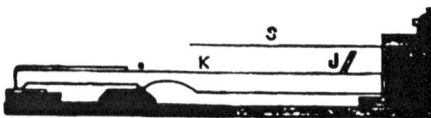

K Key, J Jack, and S String.

(7) The Harpsichord, or horizontal Harp, had sometimes two rows of quills and jacks, and there was a contrivance by means of which one set of jacks could be moved out of reach of the strings if the player desired a soft effect. If power was required the mechanism was moved so that both rows of jacks could act upon the string at once. Additional rows of jacks and additional key-boards were added to the Harpsichord until it became a very intricate piece of mechanism. The effects produced were pleasing but very weak. Some Harpsichords had three and even four strings to each note, so arranged that, upon using certain "stops," the octave above or below the strings could be sounded. It was difficult to keep such an instrument in tune. The quills in a well-used instrument required constant renewal; and, as the process of "quilling" took some hours, tortoiseshell, ivory, and leather plectra were sometimes substituted for quills, but not with any permanent success.

The general appearance of the Harpsichord may be imagined from the subjoined drawing of Handel's Harpsichord, presented by Messrs. Broadwood and Sons to the South Kensington Museum.

HANDEL'S HARPSICHORD.

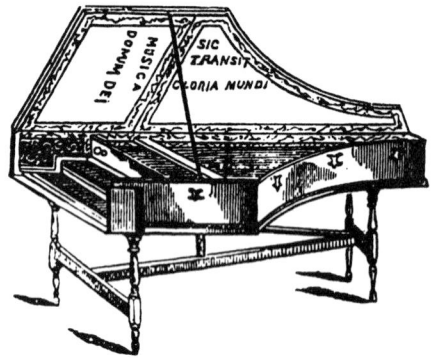

The action of the Harpsichord may be seen upon reference to the following diagram.

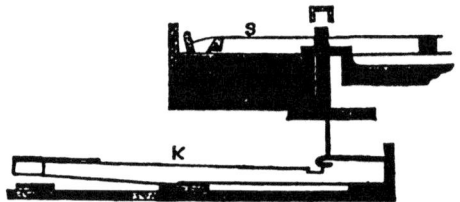

K Key, J Jack, S String.

Harpsichord makers made many attempts to improve their mechanism so that the performer might gain expression in playing.

Fétis, in his "Sketch of the History of the Pianoforte," says that "Harpsichords were constructed with more than twenty different modifications, to imitate the sound of the harp, the lute, the mandoline, the bassoon, the flageolet, the oboe, the violin, and other instruments. In order to produce these different effects new rows of jacks were added, which were furnished with various materials for dampers; and yet, with all the complications of stops, springs, extra rows of keys, and Venetian swells over the strings, the grand secret—the real *shading* of the *piano* and *forte*—was still wanting."

Godfrey Silbermann of Freyburg, about the middle of the eighteenth century made several improvements in the harpsichord, by lightening the touch, and extending the keyboard. He also advanced one step towards the invention of the pianoforte by constructing his *clavecin d'amour* in such a manner that the *tangent*, which he restored, struck the string in the middle, leaving each half to vibrate freely.

The compass of the harpsichord, originally only three octaves, was gradually extended to five. Many of the Italian and Dutch harpsichords were ornamented with elaborate paintings inside the lids, often the work of famous artists.

The most famous of the harpsichord makers of England in the last century were Kirkman, Schudi, and Broadwood.

(8) It is difficult to determine now who was the original inventor of the pianoforte, as it appears, by the evidence brought forward, to have been conceived by three persons, very nearly, if not actually at one and the same time: a German organist named Schröter, a French harpsichord maker named Marius, and an Italian named Bartolomeo Cristofali. In 1717 Schröter, when only eighteen years of age, constructed the model of a "Clavier," with hammers upon which one could play loudly or softly, which model was exhibited at the Court of Dresden, and received the approval of the Elector of Saxony. His invention was copied by Silbermann of Strasbourg, Stein of Augsburg, and Spätt of Dresden, without acknowledgment or profit to the author. Silbermann submitted two of his instruments to the judgment of Bach, who praised the mechanism, but found fault with the tone. Silbermann ultimately conquered this defect, and produced an instrument which Bach pronounced faultless.

Marius is said to have "submitted two *clavecins à maillets* to the examination of the Académie des Sciences, in February, 1716." The mechanism was very imperfect; a piece of wood covered with sheepskin fastened at the end of each key formed the hammers.

Cristofali's invention was earlier by five years. It was made known in 1711, and there is little doubt, from the description of the instrument existing, that, of the above-named makers, Cristofali has the strongest claim to the invention of the pianoforte. The description, which is too long to quote here, is printed in Rimbault's "History of the Pianoforte." It was originally inserted in the "Giornale de Litterati d'Italia," Venezia, 1711, and its title runs thus: "Nuova invenzione d'un gravicembalo, col *piano* e *forte*; aggiunte alcune considerazioni sopra gli strumenti musicali." By this account it is shown that Cristofali made improvements in every part of the instrument. The invention is also claimed for Father Wood, an English monk at Rome, who made a pianoforte in 1711, and sold it to Samuel Crisp, who re-sold it to Fulke Greville. It admitted of much greater expression than the existing harpsichords, but it was incapable of rapid execution. This particular instrument became very celebrated, and was known as "Mr. Greville's pianoforte."

In 1760 some German makers settled in London, and gave an impetus to the new instrument. A succession of improvements were made from time to time by such makers as Broadwood, Erard, Stodart, Clementi, Collard, Wornum, Hopkinson, Brinsmead and others, and the instrument has arrived at a wonderful degree of perfection, chiefly through the labours and thoughtfulness of Englishmen.

The compass of the instrument, originally five octaves, has been gradually increased to seven. The mechanism, however varied it may be by the several makers, is as ingenious as it is effective.

(9) There are four chief parts of a pianoforte: the back or framework, the sounding-board, the mechanism or action, and the case. The construction of the framework is of great importance, for as it has to bear the enormous tension of the strings, a tension amounting, in a full-sized grand piano, to sixteen tons, it is necessary that it should be strong and durable. The method of "framing," though varied in details by several makers, is upon the same broad plan. "The strings are fastened to pins upon a wrought iron string-plate, which is curved to follow the hollow side of the instrument. From this plate, and fastened to it, metallic bars or tubes are extended parallel to and above the strings, their ends being so connected with the string-plate at one end, and the wrest-plank at the other, as to take upon themselves the whole tension of the strings. At the same time the string-plate, being screwed down firmly upon the wooden bracings or framing below, the whole forms one combined trussing

to which both wood and iron contribute to the strength. The reason for the use of so great a quantity of metal in the grand piano is, that the wood framing under the strings is necessarily severed completely across the opening through which the hammers rise to strike the under part of the strings." The bracing or "back-making" is simpler in upright pianofortes. There is no opening through the framing for the hammers to pass, and there is less strain to be resisted. The "sounding-board," usually made from the best Swiss fir, is carefully selected and prepared, and its edges attached to the framing so as to leave the central part to vibrate freely under the strings when they are struck.

The "mechanism" or "action," that is, the keys, hammers, and dampers, when inserted in the instrument, leaves it ready for the finisher and tuner.

There are differences of detail in the action as constructed by different makers. Some are more complicated than others, but all are upon the same broad plan, only modified in shape and arrangement. The following diagram will show the action in use as early as 1777, called the horizontal or common grand.

COMMON ACTION TO GRAND PIANOFORTES.

K Key, H Hammer, E Escapement, J Jack, D Damper, S String.

In the "first patent for pianofortes," the above is the drawing as given in the specification, but no claim is made by any one maker to its invention.

VIENNA PIANOFORTE ACTION.

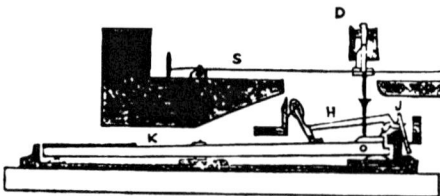

K Key, H Hammer, D Damper, J Jack, S String.

The invention of the Vienna action is generally attributed to an organ builder of Augsburg. Its principle of action was adopted by almost all the makers in Germany.

(10) The first pianofortes had the mechanism so arranged that the hammers were raised from below by buttons attached to upright wires fixed at the back ends of the keys. The motion given to the hammers when the keys were pressed caused them to strike the strings, after which they immediately fell back on to their buttons, leaving the struck strings free to vibrate. This was called the "single action." As the hammer, when resting on the button with the key pressed down, was necessarily at a little distance from the string, the effectual working of this action required that a certain impetus should be communicated to the hammer to enable it to touch the string. Hence it was next to impossible to play very *piano*. This defect was remedied by the invention of the "Hopper," a jointed upright piece attached to the back end of the key in place of the wire and button. To prevent the hammer rebounding on the string, a projection called the "check" was fixed on to the end of the key. This caught the edge of the hammer as it fell, and prevented it from rising. In this mechanism it was impossible to repeat a note until time had been allowed for the full rise of the key. This was remedied in "repeating or repetition actions," which hold up the hammers while the key is returning.

The upright action was invented for the purpose of constructing pianofortes whose mechanism might be confined within a limited space. By means of this invention a pianoforte can be made which will occupy a space about a fourth of the depth of the "grand." The names given to such instruments are many and sometimes fanciful, though most of them indicate the object for which they were contrived. Many of these upright actions are very ingeniously arranged, as the following diagrams will show.

BROADWOOD'S UPRIGHT ACTION.—PLAIN COTTAGE.

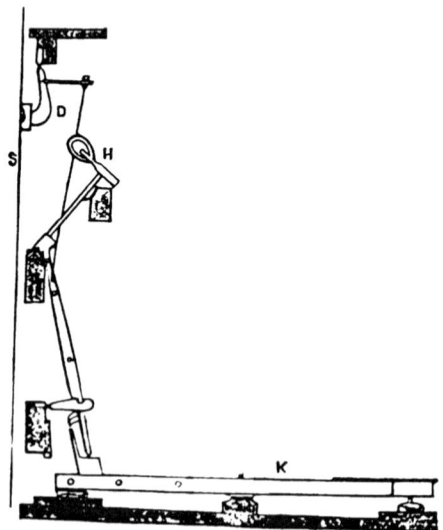

K Key, H Hammer, D Damper, S String.

BROADWOOD'S UPRIGHT CHECK ACTION.

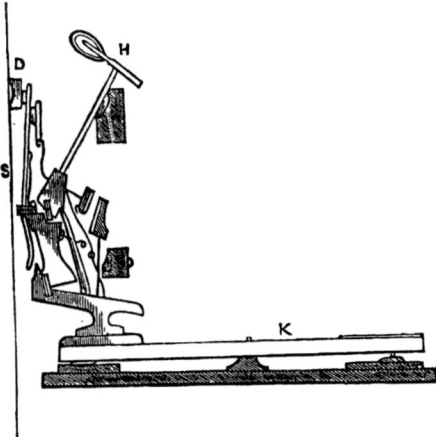

K Key, H Hammer, D Damper, S String.

BROADWOOD'S GRAND ACTION.

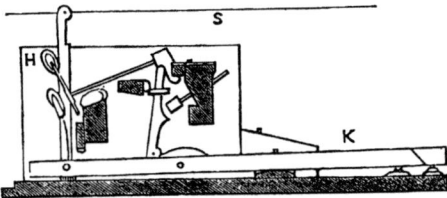

K Key, H Hammer, S String.

The following is a diagram of Erard's action :—

PATENT REPETITION ACTION FOR HORIZONTAL PIANOFORTES.

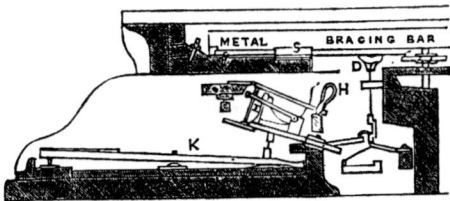

K Key, H Hammer, D Damper, S String.

(11) The strings of the pianoforte are of varying thickness and strength. The bass strings are covered with a fine copper wire to give depth of tone without any very great increase of diameter. When the loud pedal is used it raises the dampers, when the soft pedal is pressed down it either shifts the hammers sideways so as to allow them to strike one or two strings at a time, or else the strings are covered with a strip of cloth which deadens the sound.

(12) Pianofortes have been named (1) from their shape or supposed resemblance to well known objects. Thus, the grand pianoforte has been called *Schweinskopf* from its likeness to the profile of a pig's head, and *Flügel*, because it is like a bird's wing. Upright pianos have been called *giraffes* from their tall appearance, and horizontal ones have been called *couched harp*, or *square pianoforte;* the latter should more correctly be *oblong;* (2) the number of strings used for each note for a considerable part of the compass also serves to describe pianos of some sort, as *bi-chord*, *tri-chord*, &c. ; (3) the purpose for which pianos have been made, whether for the *cottage*, *boudoir*, *drawing-room*, or *concert-room*, and (4) the size, as *piccolo*, *semi-grand*, and *full grand*.

Pianoforte score. A score of a vocal or instrumental composition, under which is written in two lines a condensed form of the harmonies for the use of a pianoforte.

Pianograph. An ingenious machine, which on being attached to a pianoforte, inscribed what is played. Invented by M. Guérin.

Piatti (*It.*) [Cymbals.]

Pibroch. The wild, irregular martial music of the Scottish Highlanders played on the bagpipe. The term is also figuratively employed for the instrument itself.

> " Cast your plaids, draw your blades
> Forward each man set ;
> Pibroch of Donuil Dhu
> Knell for the onset."—*Scott.*

The pibroch style of music is irregular in rhythm, and, according to Sir Walter Scott, those learned in the matter affect to discover in it a well-composed representation of the sounds of a march, attack, flight, pursuit, and all the conflict of a " heady fight." The pibroch has so peculiar a connection with the bagpipe that it could scarcely have preceded the use of that instrument, therefore, the pibroch called the " Battle of Harlaw," and supposed to have been written at the time of the struggle [1411], is probably of later date, as the old chroniclers and the ballad descriptive of the scene mention only trumpets and horns as being there used. [Bagpipe.]

Picciolo (*It.*) Small ; as, *violino picciolo*, a small-sized fiddle.

Piccolo. An organ stop of 2 ft. length—the pipes are of wood, the tone bright and piercing.

Piccolo flute, or piccolo. A small flute, having the same compass as the ordinary orchestral flute, but whose sounds are one octave higher than the notes as they are written. Its compass may be said to be from

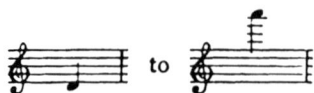

or even one note higher, but the lowest octave is so weak as to be far more effective when played by the higher octave of the common flute, and the upper notes are so shrill as to be only available in *fortissimo tutti* passages, or for peculiar and striking effects. Both Gluck and Beethoven use it in representing a storm, the former in his "Iphigenia in Tauris," the latter in his "Pastoral Symphony." Spontini combines the short piercing scream of the piccolo with the crash of cymbals in his "Danaïdes." The tendency of modern orchestral writers is to use the piccolo too often, and in inappropriate passages. It should be reserved for rare and special effects.

Picco pipe. A small pipe having two ventages above and one below. It is blown by means of a mouthpiece like a *flûte à bec* or whistle; and in playing, the little finger is used for varying the pitch by being inserted in the end. The player, Picco, after whom it was named, produced a compass of three octaves from this primitive instrument.

Piccorn. *Lit.*, horn-pipe. [Horn-pipe.]

Pièce (Fr.) A piece, as *suites des pièces*, sets of pieces. [Suite.]

Pieds (Fr.) The feet, as, *avec les pieds*, with the feet, *con pedale*.

Pieno, Piena (It.) Full; as, *à piena orchestra,* for a full band.

Pietosamente, Pietoso (It.) With pity, tenderly.

Piffaro, or Piffero (It.) The old form of the oboe, still in use in some districts of Italy and the Tyrol, formerly called the schalmy. [Oboe.]

Piffarari, or Pifferari (It.) Players on the piffaro.

Pifferino (It.) A little piffero.

Piffero (It.) [Piffaro.]

Pileata (Lat.) Capped (of an organ pipe). Stopped. *Pileata major.* 16 feet stopped. *Pileata minor.* 4 feet stopped. *Pileata diapente.* Stopped quint.

Pincé (Fr.) Pinched. (1) A direction in French music equivalent to pizzicato, *q.v.* (2) The name of an ornament in harpsi-

chord playing, indicated by the signs here shown :

The first was called *pincé simple*, the second *pincé double*. The note of ornament of the pincé was below the note written, while the added note in the *tremblement* was above. A pincé or trill with a flattened note.

Pincé bemolisé (Fr.) An ornament in harpsichord playing

Pincé dièsé (Fr.) A pincé or trill with a sharpened note

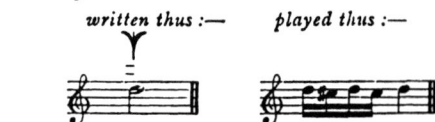

Pincement (Fr.) [Pincé.]

Piqué (Fr.) On string-instruments a kind of bowing, by which a *staccato* is produced by allowing the bow to lie perfectly still on the string between each separate note. It is written with dots and a slur, thus :

It is also called *spiccato*.

Piquiren (Ger.) To play *piqué*.

Pitch. (1) The position of a sound with reference to the number of vibrations which produce it. The relative height of a sound.

It is much to be regretted that one standard of pitch has not been universally adopted.

The following Table selected from that given in the "Journal of the Society of Arts" (June 6, 1860), and from other sources, will show some of the variations. The number of vibrations in each case represent the note

	No. of Vibs.
Paris Grand Opera, 1699	404
Ditto 1858	448.
French " Diapason Normal " (generally adopted)	435
Handel's tuning fork (c. 1740)	416
Sir George Smart's " Philharmonic " fork (early in this century)	433
Italian Opera (London), 1859	455
Scheibler's pitch (recommended by the Society of Arts)	440

It will be seen from the above that the tendency to raise the pitch has been arrested in France, and to a great extent in this country also. The chief obstacle to the introduction of a lower pitch at our Operas seems to be the *wind-instruments*. An attempt to use the French pitch, lately made at Her Majesty's Opera, had only the unfortunate result of putting everybody thoroughly out of tune. For valuable information on this subject, the reader is referred to Mr. Ellis's XIX. Appendix to his translation of Helmholtz.

(2) The method, now generally adopted, of showing the particular *octave* in which a sound occurs, is as follows :—

C D E F G A B   c d e f g a b
(Great octave.)   (Small octave.)

c' d' e' f' g' a' b'   c'' d'' e'' f'' g'' a'' b'' &c.
(Once-accented octave.)   (Twice-accented octave.)

Sounds in the octave next below the *great octave* C, D, and so on. Sounds above the *twice-accented octave* c''' d''' and so on.

The pitch of organ pipes is, however, still named after the old system, as follows :—

CCC (8ve lower.)
(or) 16ft C
(or) Three C's

CC
8ft C
Double C

C
4ft C
Tenor C.

c
2ft C
Middle C

cc
1ft C
Treble C

6 inches C''
C in alt

The octave below CCC being CCCC, and that above c in alt, c in altissimo.

Pitch-pipe. A wooden-pipe having a moveable stopper or *tampion* with marks, showing where it should be placed for the production of different notes of the scale. This form of pipe has been almost entirely superseded by an ingenious invention known as " Eardsley's Patent." It consists of a free reed capable of being lengthened or shortened by a graduated curve, on which are registered the notes of the scale.

Più (*It.*) More, as *più allegro*, faster ; *più forte*, louder ; *più lento*, slower ; *più piano*, softer ; *più presto*, more rapid ; *più stretto*, more urged or closer ; *più tosto allegro*, rather quick.

Piva (*It.*) A bagpipe.

Pizz. Abbreviation of *pizzicato*.

Pizzicato (*It.*), **Pincé** (*Fr.*), **Gekneipt** (*Ger.*) *Lit.* pinched. A direction to violinists to produce the tone by plucking the string with the finger instead of using the bow. The place at which the use of the bow is to be resumed, is pointed out by the words *coll' arco*, or simply *arco*.

Placidamente, Placido (*It.*) Quietly, peacefully, placidly.

Plagal. The name given to those Church modes which were formed from the four older or authentic modes by taking the fourth below as the new key-note, and proceeding thence to the fifth above, *e.g.* :

Authentic.   Plagal.

The plagal modes were distinguished by the addition of ὑπὸ, *e.g.* : Doric, an authentic mode ; Hypodoric, a plagal mode formed from the Doric. [Plain Song.]

Plagal cadence. The cadence formed when a subdominant chord immediately precedes the final tonic chord, *e.g.* :

The plagal cadence of the old church writers corresponded more to the modern half-close, which is formed when the final chord is dominant, and is preceded by a tonic chord, *e.g.* :

Plagiaulus (*Gk.*) πλαγίαυλος, (*Lat.*) *Tibia*

obliqua. The cross-flute, or *flauto traverso.* [Flute.]

Plain-Chant. [Plain Song.]

Plain Song. The kind of music used from time immemorial in the worship of the ancient Jewish or Israelitish Church, as well as among all the churches of Christendom throughout the world.

The first principles of all music being found in nature, and its various forms having been gradually evolved by scientific and artistic industry and research from those principles, there must necessarily be found much of co-incidence, and similarity, if not an actual identity, in the practical results of such inquiries and experiments. Hence it is not strange to find some Greek Music traced to the Hebrew, nor that of the early Christian Church to both. In fact, so far as in any country the natural development of the musical art has grown up healthily, according to its inner principle of life, there can be little doubt that, in all essential particulars (allowing, of course, a certain amount of characteristic individuality) there will be so much of resemblance to that of other countries as to lead historians (rather too fondly) to trace a parentage and derivation, where, be the fact as it may, neither are necessary to account for the likeness. The Plain Song of the Christian Church is a well known, and universally practised form of musical accent, recitation, and simple melody, written records of which are extant dating from the eighth century; and these are themselves records of Christian Plain Song of still earlier times, of which some, it is not unreasonable to believe, are the very melodies sung by Our Lord Jesus Christ and His Apostles, and of Templar origin.

The music of the Christian Church, like the gospel itself, was doubtless propagated orally, and by tradition, in the first years of its history; and as in the New Testament traces are discoverable of a primitive liturgy and hymnody, so we also find in early writers indications of certain efforts to fix and rule the vocal performance of these, by an appointed choral arrangement, with somewhat of a scientific connection.

One point of primary importance in this respect would naturally be the pitch most convenient for the singing of the various parts of Divine Psalms, Hymns, and Spiritual Songs; the relation in which the several parts of the service, musically considered, were to stand to each other; as also the interchanges to be made as to singing, either by course in alternate choirs, or by the clergy and people, in solo or in chorus.

The writings of the New Testament and of the early Fathers are not without various interesting indications, both of the important functions discharged by vocal music in Christian worship, and also of various ritual *uses;* in such wise, moreover, as excited *then,* as they do *now,* the approval and admiration of some, the indignation and blame of others.

Thus, " Sabellius and Marcellus took occasion to incense the Church of Neocesarea (A.D. 363), against their Bishop S. Basil, as being an author of new devices in the service of God," when he introduced the antiphonal chanting after the custom of Antioch, where it had been taught by S. Ignatius, a contemporary and disciple of the Apostles, specially of S. John. S. Ambrose, Bishop of Milan, was a great admirer of S. Basil, and introduced the same kind of chanting into his church as had originally prevailed in the East, as we learn from S. Basil's refutation of the heretics' charge of novelty and singularity, alleging the example, not only of the Church at Antioch, but also " of the Churches of Egypt, Lybia, Thebes, Palestine, the Arabians, Phœnicians, Syrians, Mesopotamians, and of *all that reverenced the custom of singing Psalms together.*"

Here, it would seem, we have ample grounds for the very general belief that in setting the music at first traditionally sung to various Psalms and Hymns, and the portions specially vocal in their Liturgies, the characters then used in noting music would be taken advantage of, to fix and perpetuate the arrangements of the early Christian music to the words. But the notation of the most artistic music then known was the Greek, which, like other refinements, was also at first used by the Romans, and subsequently improved by the use of the Roman letters, instead of the more complicated Greek characters. But with the Greek notation would, to a great extent, be adopted Greek modes of arrangement, and Greek notions as to the construction of the scales in which any chant, antiphon, or hymn tune might most fitly be said to stand. If its general character, *e.g.,* were major or minor, a similar mode or scale of the Greek music would be selected, and to this it would be assigned, just as in the present day a modern musician's arrangement of any ancient melody would, in the absence of any other system to which he might be able to assign it, necessarily be in the modern major or minor scale. But in our inquiries as to the ancient Plain Song, we must always remember that both it and the Greek modes were founded simply on *melodic,* and not on *harmonic* considerations, in our present meaning of those terms. With their usual acumen, the Greeks, in their *diatonic, chromatic,* and *enharmonic* genera, analyzed all the tone modulations of the human voice, with a discrimination most admirable, and effects most wonderful, as all are ready to admit who have studied their theoretic treatises, and the accounts recorded of the practical results of their performances; results, it may be suggested, such as poetic, oratorical, and musical recitation can even now occasionally produce in the case of sing--rs of rare eloquence and sympathetic voices, on an appreciating and impressible audience. Sentiment and feeling, the soul and spirit of all true music, are not confined to any set of outward appliances, however vast, as in the present orchestra; but may be felt in the impassioned delivery of a Simple Plain Song, or the thrilling notes of an unaccompanied solo instrument. It is probable that the first kind of musical notes used by the Christian Church, called pneums (from the Greek πνεῦμα, *breath*) were derived from the Greek characters, after the fashion of the Hebrew accents for reading. The diatonic genus of the Greek music most nearly resembled (if it was not, in some modes, identical with it) the tonality of the Christian Plain Song and the ancient Hebrew music, of which it was, in part undoubtedly, the traditional record and sacred depository after the dispersion of the Jews and the consequent disuse by them of their Temple music, which, in their state of humiliation, they deemed it unlawful any more to sing. What music they now practice in their synagogues is still, however, eminently of the same character as the ancient Plain Song of the Christians. The fact above stated forestalls any objection that might be made from the modern Jews not now using them, to the belief that the well-known Ecclesiastical Psalm Tones have descended, through the "ages all along," the thirty centuries from the days of King David, the sweet singer of Israel, in an unbroken tradition, to our own day.

The sources of information as to the history of Plain Song, in addition to the various references scattered throughout the early writers and Fathers of the Church, may be found in the voluminous pages of *Burney* and *Hawkins* in English, and of *Gerbertus* in Latin; as also in the original authors quoted by them, specially the *Septem Scriptores Antiqui* of Meibomius; in the French *Histoire de L'Harmonie au Moyen Age,* by E. De Coussemaker; in the XXIXth Vol. of the *Nouvelle Encyclopédie Théologique,* edited by M. L'Abbé Migne, being a *Dictionnaire de Plain Chant, et de Musique Religieuse;* in the pages of Alfieri, La Feillé, Clement, Janssen, Lambil-

lotte, Alix, and in English in the various editions of Latin service and instruction books by Lambert, Benz, Chas. Child Spencer, and the prefaces to the Rev. T. Helmore's Accompanying Harmonies to the Psalter Noted and Hymnal Noted; more satisfactorily still in the MS. and printed books of Plain Song in various libraries at home and abroad. The subject is very wide, and cannot easily be studied without a large acquaintance with the numerous books of Ritual music, both of the present time, and of all the centuries backwards, till the very first in which any written remains of Plain Song can be discovered. A sketch of what may be gathered as the result of such an investigation is all that can be here attempted.

PLAIN SONG, then, it may be stated, is a definite, well known system of Church Song, which all Catholic musicians are obliged by their duties to study, and from which all the great composers, down to our own times, have more or less tinctured their highest and best compositions.

It has already been stated that the ancient church modes of the Plain Song or Gregorian music had their prototypes, if not their very birth, from the Diatonic genus of the Greeks. Perhaps it would be more true, and in accordance with the notions before expressed, to say that the Greek Diatonic genus was identical with the ancient Hebrew music, and with that of the Christian Church which perpetuated it. Here, then, is a digest of what can be gathered from ancient writers as to the Greek Diatonic scale.

It embraces fifteen sounds, which practically might be produced by the strings of a harp, fifteen in number; or by the voice of any man of ordinary medium vocal power.

It is divided into tetrachords, or divisions of four sounds each,—beginning, not on the first of the system, which (as its name implies) was originally an extra note added below, but on the second, or B. In the lower nine sounds the second and third tetrachords are reckoned to begin, each upon the fourth sound of the foregoing; and are therefore styled *conjoined tetrachords.* The first pair of tetrachords is also succeeded by a tetrachord, an octave above the first, beginning on the sound next to the fourth of the second tetrachord, and consequently denominated the *disjoined* tetrachord. Then a fifth tetrachord occupied the highest part of the system; all which will be better seen and understood by Diagram I., in which the Greek names for the various sounds (written in English letters) are given, with a translation of their characteristic nomenclature.

DIAGRAM I.

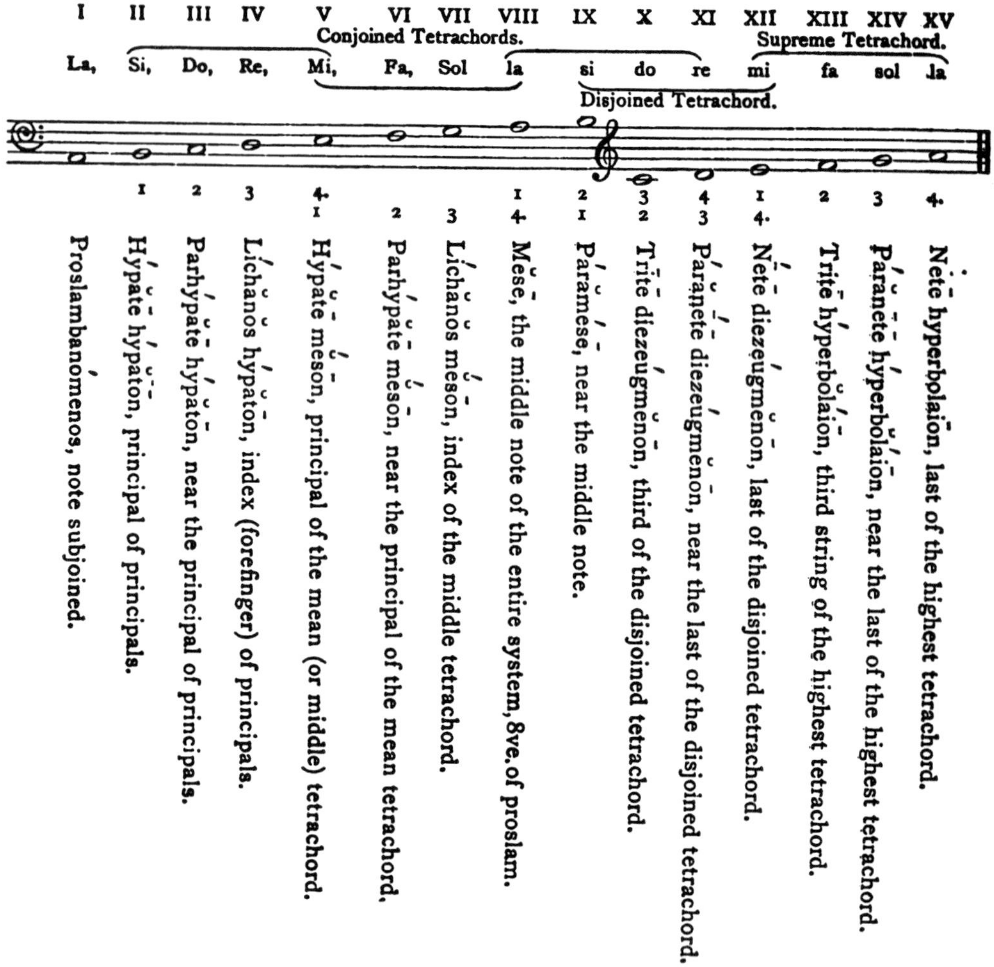

I	II	III	IV	V	VI	VII	VIII	IX	X	XI	XII	XIII	XIV	XV

Conjoined Tetrachords.
Supreme Tetrachord.

La,	Si,	Do,	Re,	Mi,	Fa,	Sol	la	si	do	re	mi	fa	sol	la

Disjoined Tetrachord.

Vertical note names (read top to bottom of the diagram):

- Proslambanomenos, note subjoined.
- Hýpate hypaton, principal of principals.
- Parhýpate hypaton, near the principal of principals.
- Líchanos hypaton, index (forefinger) of principals.
- Hýpate meson, principal of the mean (or middle) tetrachord.
- Parhýpate meson, near the principal of the mean tetrachord.
- Líchanos meson, index of the middle tetrachord.
- Mese, the middle note of the entire system, 8ve. of proslam.
- Paramese, near the middle note.
- Trite diezeugmenon, third of the disjoined tetrachord.
- Paranete diezeugmenon, near the last of the disjoined tetrachord.
- Nete diezeugmenon, last of the disjoined tetrachord.
- Trite hyperbolaion, third string of the highest tetrachord.
- Paranete hyperbolaion, near the last of the highest tetrachord.
- Nete hyperbolaion, last of the highest tetrachord.

N.B.—The accents and prosodaic marks are here used simply for the English reader. They are not Greek.

It will soon be seen that these same fifteen natural notes are those from which the Church modes are all constructed. The musical theorists who, about the eighth century, disputed as to the number of modes or scales to be recognized in Church music, seem to have laid down the principle that a scale or mode must consist of the combination of a perfect fifth (diapente) with a perfect fourth (diatessaron). The division of a scale into these two component parts might be made so as to have either a diapente or a diatessaron in the lower position. The division which had the fifth in the lower and the fourth in the higher place was called *Harmonic*, as being that which music naturally suggests; and the other division of the eight notes of a scale where the fourth was in the lower, and the

fifth in the upper portion was called *arithmetical*, because, in the science of numbers, the greater numbers take precedence of the less, and are counted their superiors. This fanciful nomenclature is mild in comparison with many other conceits and far-fetched analogies of ancient theorists.

The Church modes, then, are formed of the seven natural notes of the scale and their octaves, beginning upon any one of the seven, and extending to its octave, subject to the rule just stated that the fifths and fourths of which any scale was composed must be perfect.

Now the Church melodies were generally contained within the compass of an octave or a little more. Some had a much less range from the highest to the lowest notes. When the melody ascended to the fifth above the *final* and the fourth above the fifth, and did not descend below the final, it was said to be *authentic;* when it extended to a fifth above the final and a fourth *below it,* it was called plagal. The sounds of which these two sorts of melodies consisted being set down in orderly succession from the lowest to the highest, naturally arranged themselves into two corresponding classes; and the ecclesiastical modes are therefore matched, or (as mediæval writers have termed it) wedded to one another in pairs, authentic and plagal, in which male and female characteristics are respectively developed.

Now, taking the notes before given as the Greek Diapason, and supposing any Antiphon or other piece of Plain Song to descend to the lowest note A, and, after ascending by various intervals to the A an octave above it, to settle down and close on D, we should, accordingly, by arranging these sounds in an orderly sequence from the lowest to the highest, have a scale whose final or closing note is D, and its range of notes from A to A, and this, as before explained, would be the lower, collateral, and plagal scale or mode of another beginning on D, the final, and rising to its octave, which would be its own proper authentic, or ruling and authoritative mode. Such, in fact, are the first two modes of the Gregorian Plain Song, and the pair, as husband and wife, have reciprocal functions, and though two, are yet one by participation of one common bond of union, viz., the diapente D, E, F, G, A.

In Diagram II. we see, then, the 11 notes of the Dorian Modes, Authentic and Plagal, called the 1st and 2nd.

The 1st is authentic, and ranges from the 4th to the 11th note, having a perfect fifth from D to A, which same fifth is the upper part of the plagal mode. From A the 8th to D the 11th is a perfect fourth, and thus fulfils the requirements before mentioned as essentials of a Church mode; while the same law is obeyed in the case of the 2nd or plagal mode, as from A the 1st to D the 4th is the required perfect diatessaron.

The terms *hyper* (*above*), and *hypo* (*below*), are used to distinguish the two, though the *hyper* is often omitted as unnecessary; and besides, it seems to have been used in another way by some of the Greek writers.

We are told that in Charlemagne's reign (about A.D. 768) a great dispute arose as to the allowable number of the modes, and that the Emperor at first decided in favour of the first eight alone; but that on the remonstrance of the malcontents, the 9th, 10th, 11th, and 12th, were also allowed. The ritual books of the church have, however, been generally arranged for the eight tones only, and those portions of the Plain Song which formerly were assigned to the 9th, 10th, 11th, and 12th modes were so re-arranged by a transposition, as to *appear* to have been composed in some one or other of the first eight; though a careful inspection of these transpositions will serve to show that the means at command were not (while no other change of sound was allowable than the B flat) sufficient to effect a *perfect* transposition. This will appear in the subsequent examples.

DIAGRAM II.

1st AND 2nd MODES.
Dorian or Hyper-Dorian, and Hypo-Dorian.

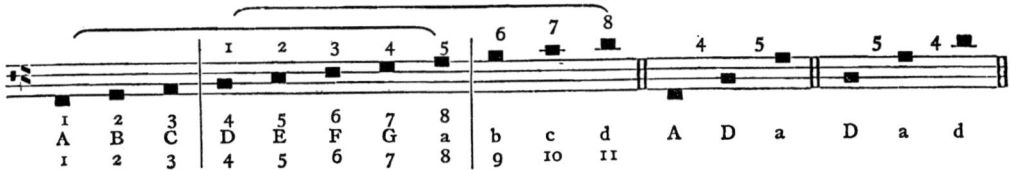

I	2	3	4	5	6	7	8				4	5		5	4	
I	2	3	4	5	6	7	8									
A	B	C	D	E	F	G	a	b	c	d	A	D	a	D	a	d
I	2	3	4	5	6	7	8	9	10	11						

3rd AND 4th MODES.
The next pair is the Phrygian, thus :—Phrygian or Hyper-Phrygian, and Hypo-Phrygian. Final E.

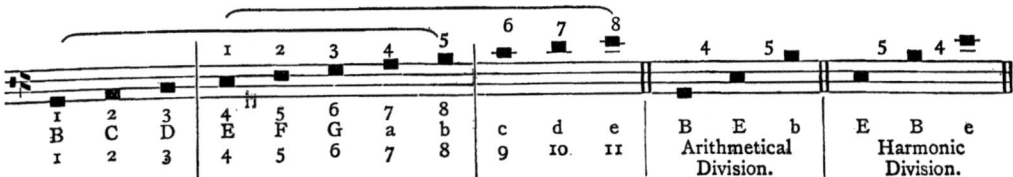

I	2	3	4	5	6	7	8				4	5		5	4	
B	C	D	E	F	G	a	b	c	d	e	B	E	b	E	B	e
I	2	3	4	5	6	7	8	9	10	11	Arithmetical Division.			Harmonic Division.		

5th AND 6th MODES.

These are the Lydian or Hyper-Lydian, and Hypo-Lydian. Final F.

									C	F	c		F	c	f
C	D	E	F	G	A	B	c	d	e	f	Arithmetical		Harmonic		
			1	2	3	4	5	6	7	8	Division.		Division.		
1	2	3	4	5	6	7	8	9	10	11					

7th AND 8th MODES.

The Mixo-Lydian or Hyper-Mixo-Lydian, and the Hypo-Mixo-Lydian. Final G.

									D	G	d		G	d	g
			1	2	3	4	5	6	7	8	Arithmetical		Harmonic		
D	E	F	G	A	B	C	d	e	f	g	Division.		Division.		
1	2	3	4	5	6	7	8	9	10	11					

9th AND 10th MODES.

The Æolian or Hyper-Æolian, and Hypo-Æolian. Final A.

									E	A	e		A	e	a
E	F	G	A	B	C	D	e	f	g	a	Arithmetical		Harmonic		
			1	2	3	4	5	6	7	8	Division.		Division.		
1	2	3	4	5	6	7	8	9	10	11					

B cannot become the final of a mode as the 4th below it is F, and the interval a pluperfect 4th, and the 5th above it is also F, and the interval an imperfect 5th.

11th AND 12th MODES.

The Ionian (or Iastian) or Hyper-Ionian (or Hyper-Iastian), and Hypo-Ionian (or Hypo-Iastian). Final C.

									G	C	g		C	g	c
G	A	B	C	D	E	F	g	a	b	c	Arithmetical		Harmonic		
			1	2	3	4	5	6	7	8	Division.		Division.		

Thus it will be seen that the ancient system of scales took every one of the six natural notes on which the union of the perfect diatessaron and perfect diapente can be effected as the final of a pair of modes, thus placing the diatonic intervals of tone and semitone in every possible position with respect to the two tetrachords of each, and of the final of each pair.

There was yet another method of securing to each mode its own characteristic features, by which it is clearly to be discerned from all the rest. In each there is a note higher than the final which assumes the next importance to it, from being another point of sound about which the melodies principally, as it were, revolved, and on which the voice more frequently and (in the case of the recitation of any psalm, antiphon, or canticle) most continuously dwelt. From thus predominating over the other sounds of each scale it is called the DOMINANT. But it must not be confounded with what in general is now understood by that term, nor with the harmonic associations which it suggests to the mind of a modern musician.

In every authentic mode the dominant is the 5th above the final, except in the third mode, where B, the fifth, being a changeable note, i.e., sometimes natural and sometimes flat, and also standing, unlike any other note in the scales, at the forbidden interval of a tritone, or pluperfect fourth from the F below it, and of an imperfect fifth from the F above it, is rejected, and C, the nearest sound to it, is the dominant, being a minor 6th above the final E.

In the six plagal modes the dominant is the third note in the scale below the dominant of each relative authentic mode, except in the 8th, where B, the 3rd below D, is also on the same grounds discarded for C.

DIAGRAM III.

Finals.

1. Authentic, Hyper-Dorian				d	e	f	g	a (Dom.)	b	$\bar{c}$	$\bar{d}$
2. Plagal, Hypo-Dorian	A	B	c	d	e	f (Dom.)	g	a	—	—	—
3. Authentic, Hyper-Phrygian			e	f	g	a (Dom.)	b	$\bar{c}$	$\bar{d}$	$\bar{e}$
4. Plagal, Hypo-Phrygian	B	c	d	e	f	g	a (Dom.)	b	—	—	—
5. Authentic, Hyper-Lydian			f	g	a	b (Dom.)	c	$\bar{d}$	$\bar{e}$	$\bar{f}$
6. Plagal, Hypo-Lydian	c	d	e	f	g	a (Dom.)	b	$\bar{c}$	—	—	—
7. Authentic, Hyper-Mixo-Lydian			g	a	b	$\bar{c}$ (Dom.)	$\bar{d}$	$\bar{e}$	$\bar{f}$	$\bar{g}$
8. Plagal, Hypo-Mixo-Lydian	d	e	f	g	a	b (Dom.)	$\bar{c}$	$\bar{d}$	—	—	—
9. Authentic, Hyper-Æolian			a	b	$\bar{c}$ (Dom.)	$\bar{d}$	$\bar{e}$	$\bar{f}$	$\bar{g}$	$\bar{a}$
10. Plagal, Hypo-Æolian	e	f	g	a	b (Dom.)	$\bar{c}$	$\bar{d}$	$\bar{e}$	—	—	—
11. Authentic, Hyper-Ionian or Iastian			$\bar{c}$	$\bar{d}$	$\bar{e}$	$\bar{f}$ (Dom.)	$\bar{g}$	$\bar{a}$	$\bar{b}$	$\bar{\bar{c}}$
12. Plagal, Hypo-Ionian or Iastian	g	a	b	$\bar{c}$	$\bar{d}$ (Dom.)	$\bar{e}$	$\bar{f}$	$\bar{g}$	—	—	—

Thus A is the Final of the 9th and 10th, and Dominant of the 1st, 4th, and 6th.

"	C	"	11th	"	12th	"	"	3rd, 5th, 8th, and 10th.
"	D	"	1st	"	2nd	"	"	7th.
"	E	"	3rd	"	4th	"	"	9th and 12th.
"	F	"	5th	"	6th	"	"	2nd.
"	G	"	7th	"	8th	"	"	11th.

The following formula committed to memory will be of immense use in grasping the otherwise troublesome varieties of the Church modes.

Finals	D	D,	E	E,	F	F,	G	G,	A	A,	C,	C.
Dominants	A	f	c	a	c	a	d	c	e	c	g	e
Mode No.	1	2	3	4	5	6	7	8	9	10	11	12

[N.B.—The dominants spell the mnemonic word Afcăcăd[é]cĕcgĕ.]

Of this ancient system the German Professor of Music at the University of Berlin, Dr. Adolph Bernhard Marx, justly remarks that its "profound ideality is undeniable," and while thoroughly imbued with the notions and feelings of a modern, confesses that in many points it displays nicer distinctions and more striking characteristics than our own. Whatever view, however, may be true with regard to the discoveries and improvements of the musical art in our day, it is certain that for sacred music generally, and for Church music in particular, the study of Plain Song as it has come down to us, with all the hallowed associations of a definite history of twelve centuries and with an indefinite period of great extent before them, together constituting a sequence of near upon three thousand years' use in the highest acts of human concern, cannot be neglected without much injury to the sentiment and feeling of composers, and a secularising of Church music, both in its composition and in the style of its execution, highly to be deprecated by every true lover of Sacred Art, and of the Christian Church throughout the world.

It remains to say a few words on the time, accent, rhythm, and metre of Plain Song, all of which have unfortunately suffered much in the opinion of mankind by being misunderstood in theory, and dreadfully distorted in practice.

It is the opinion of those who, like Coussemaker, have most deeply studied the subject, that there was by no means that monotonous equality in the length of the notes, which we have found practised and thought right since the Plain Song of the Church has been so generally neglected for more strictly mensurable modern compositions.

A manifest tendency has long existed to lengthen the short notes of ancient MSS., in order probably that the accompanying organists may give (as they intend) a greater dignity to the solemn march of their harmonies, and get rid of the charming varieties of what may be styled the *bars*, speaking after the fashion of modern music. Two striking instances of this will explain what is meant better than further description.

There is in the British Museum, among the Lansdown MSS. (No. 463), a fine well-written copy of the ancient *Sarum Antiphonary;* and in the Bodleian Library, Oxford, there is a corresponding MS. most splendidly written, which formerly belonged to Archbishop Laud; in both of these the writer of this article has found very many notes short (*i.e.*, the ◆ ◆ diamond shaped semibreve) where in the printed folio (c 35 l., Paris, 1519. 20 B. M.), they are changed into breves thus ▬ ▬. The difference thus made in the music may be compared to an alteration of all the quavers in " God save the Queen " into crotchets !

Another instance of the same perverse treatment may be seen in the version of the melody "Veni, veni, Emmanuel," set to the words "O come, O come, Emmanuel," in *Hymns Ancient and Modern* (No. 36, first tune), where all the short notes, originally printed (in the *Hymnal Noted*) correctly from the MS. copied by the late J. M. Neale from a French Missal in the National Library, Lisbon, are deliberately, and of set purpose, turned into long ones, seemingly to avoid the interspersion of a triple bar, in several places, among the duple or quadruple measures. See *Hymnal Noted*, "Veni, veni, Emmanuel," 65 Ac. Har., p. 213, " Draw nigh, draw nigh, Emmanuel."

The time or rhythm of the Plain Song, where best understood and properly rendered, is a most entire and definite flow of melody in accordance with the accents of the words and the construction of the musical phrase combined. The fullest development of this is perhaps in the Ancient Metrical Hymns,

in which the varied prosodaic metres are always complied with by the Plain Song, the accents of which correspond to those of the words ; and the notes fall into what we should now call *bars*, sometimes regular in their formation, and of one time, but often in duple and triple forms mixed.

There is, to the lovers of Plain Song who have caught the spirit and intention of its various phrases, a charming variety and freedom from stiffness in these changes of measure, somewhat akin to the pleasure we derive in verse from similar departures from one stereotyped succession of accents or quantities. For example, after the regular iambics of this couplet—

" Thro' life's long day and death's dark night, Ŏ gentle Jesŭs, be our light—"

how pleasing is the introduction of the *trochee* in the beginning of the next verse :

" Labour is sweet for thou hast toiled."

Something of the same kind seems to occur, in such a phrase as this, put into measured time, as it should be sung from the usual notes of the Gregorian Plain Song.

Thou the an - oint - ing spi - rit art,

Who doest . . thy seven - fold gifts impart.

In conclusion, it may be remarked that the more highly people are educated in all that concerns the employment of art in the Service of the Church, and the more deeply they enter into the *rationale* of the use of music as the handmaid of religion, the better will they appreciate the value of Plain Song, the better will they execute it, and the better too will they know and feel what other music is fittest, and really the best, to stand side by side with it in the Lord's House, as the offering of the first-fruits of man's highest art and most exquisite skill, to Him from whom all skill and all talent are derived, and who will be worshipped by each according to that he hath, be it little or much. The Plain Song of the Church gives all who can sing the best means of discharging this sacred duty.

Plainte (*Fr.*) An elegy, or lament.

Plaisanterie, or Pleasantrie. A kind of concerto for a solo instrument, in which various cheerful tunes or dance melodies were introduced.

Planxties, or Laments. Certain melodies were so called by Irish and Welsh harpers. They were not always of the doleful character their name would seem to imply.

Plaqué (*Fr.*) Struck at once. A direction that a chord is not to be played *arpeggio*.

Play-house Tunes. Musical compositions performed between the acts of the tragedies or comedies in the old theatres of London.

After the Restoration, music became more general as a relief to the performers and the performances in theatres; compositions, called Playhouse or Act Tunes, were written and played in concert, and not in unison as formerly, and the theatre music was of a superior character. "Insomuch," says Sir John Hawkins, "that to say of a performer on any instrument that he was a playhouse musician, or of a song that it was a playhouse song, or a playhouse tune, was to speak of each respectively in terms of the highest commendation." The most popular were the "Genius of England," Madame Subligny's "Minuet," the "Louvre" (or "Loure,") and many others. The principal composers of this kind of music were Mr. John Reading, John Bannister, Godfrey Fringer, Matthew Lock, Henry and John Eccles, Raphael Courteville, &c. A coranto written by Bulstrode Whitelock, one of the Lords Commissioners of Charles II., in conjunction with Henry Lawes, was played at the theatres for more than thirty years regularly "by the Blackfriars musicians, esteemed the best in London."

Plectrum (*Lat.*) πλῆκτρον. A little staff made of ivory, horn, quill, or metal, with which (having it in his right hand) the player on a lyra or cithara, set the strings in vibration. It cannot yet be said to be obsolete, inasmuch as one is used by the performer on a modern mandolin and zither. From the method of using a plectrum to the cithara, the more perfect instrument, the dulcimer (Hackbrett), probably took its origin; and from the dulcimer came the spinet, harpsichord, and eventually the pianoforte. But it should be remembered that while the quill of a harpsichord plucks, as it were, a string, just as a plectrum would, the hammer of a pianoforte *strikes* the string. The plectrum was not invariably used by the ancients, for some of the paintings discovered at Herculaneum depict citharists using the ends of their fingers.

Plein jeu (*Fr.*) With the full power.

Plica (*Lat.*) A term used by the old writers on mensurable music, the exact meaning of which it is difficult to discover. Franco of Cologne (Gerbertus, Script. iii. 6) says, "Plica est nota divisionis ejusdem toni in gravem et acutam" (Plica is a sign of the division of the same note into a higher and lower sound). This would seem to describe it as an ornament or grace. Joannes de Muris says, "Plica dicitur a plicando, et continet notas duas, unam superiorem et aliam inferiorem" (Plica is so called from *plicando*, folding, and it contains two notes, one higher, the other lower). This would make *plica* a part of the system of ligatures. At other times the word seems used by old authors as synonymous with *cauda* or *virgula*, a stem.

Ploke (*Gk.*), πλοκή. [Melopœia.]

Plures ex una (*Lat.*) Many parts from one. The old name of a canon because originally written only on one line.

Plus (*Fr.*) More, as; *plus animé*, more animated, with greater spirit.

Pneuma. [Neuma.]

Pneumatic bellows. [Organ, § 12.]

Pneumatic Organ. Organum pneumaticum. The ordinary organ as opposed to the ancient hydraulic organ, or organum hydraulicum, in which water was used, not as was popularly supposed at the time, for the purpose of entering the sound-boards or pipes, but to act as a regulator of the pressure of air. [Organ.]

Pocetta (*It.*) [Poche.]

Poche, Pochette (*Fr.*) A little fiddle used by dancing-masters. [Kit.]

Pochettino, Pochetto (*It.*) A little, as, *ritard un pochettino*, making a slight *rallentando*.

Poco (*It.*) A little, as *poco a poco*, little by little; *poco animato*, rather animated; *poco lento*, rather slow; *mosso poco meno*, rather less quick; *poco piano*, rather soft; *poco più allegro*, rather faster; *poco presto*, somewhat rapid.

Poggiato (*It.*) Leant upon, dwelt upon.

Poi (*It.*) Then, as *piano poi forte*, soft then loud. *Poi segue*, then follows.

Point (*Fr.*) A dot.

Point d'orgue (*Fr.*) A pedal-point. [Fugue.]

Point de repos (*Fr.*) A pause.

Pointé (*Fr.*) Dotted.

Polacca (*It.*) Polish. A title applied to melodies written in imitation of Polish dance tunes. It is synonymous with the French word polonoise, or polonaise. It is a term of modern introduction, as neither Brossard, Grassineau, nor Rousseau, have the word in their dictionaries. Kollmann on "Style and National Music," describes it as "a particular characteristic piece in $\frac{3}{4}$ time, and its movement like a majestic but fluent andante or andantino. It deviates from the general rule respecting simple measure in making every rhythmical cæsure, not on the first, but on the last time or crotchet in the bar."

In No. 3 of Handel's twelve grand concertos is a polonaise or polacca, of a slightly different rhythm, and there are other polaccas which differ still more from the model described above.

Polka. A dance of world-wide popularity, the music to which is in $\frac{2}{4}$ time, with the third quaver accented. There are three steps in each bar, the fourth beat is always a rest, the three steps are performed on the three first beats of every bar.

It is stated that Anna Slezak, a farm servant at Elbeteinitz, near Prague, invented the polka about 1830. The room in which she was accustomed to dance being of small dimensions, the movements of her feet were short, and so the dance was called the "Pulka" dance, that is the "half" dance. The title was changed when it was introduced into France, as were also the steps and the character of the dance. In Bohemia, where it is said to have originated, it is danced with a peculiar alternative of hurrying and halting steps to which the music has to be accommodated.

It was brought into England about the year 1843, and was received with an extraordinary enthusiasm by all classes. It effected a revolution in the style of dancing which had prevailed up to that period. Country-dances and quadrilles were even performed with livelier steps than hitherto, for the polka was so popular that it absorbed every other dance for a time. Articles of food, of clothing, and of ornament, were named after it. Comic songs and farces were written on the *polka-mania*, as it was called. To such a height did this absurd fancy reach, that public-houses were called the "Polka Arms," and newly-built streets "Polka" terraces or crescents. When the mania subsided these names were altered to titles less suggestive of a passing folly.

Polonaise *or* **Polonoise** (*Fr.*) [Polacca.]

Polychord. An instrument invented by Fried. Hillmer of Leipzig, in 1799. It was strung with ten strings. In shape it was not unlike a double bass without a neck. It was never generally used.

Polycephalus. One of the neumes. [Neumes.]

Polymorphous. Of many shapes, a term applied to compositions, the parts of which are capable of inversion, as in double counter-point : or of augmentation, diminution, *per thesin et arsin*, and other devices, as in Canon.

Pommer. [Bombardo.]

Pomposamente, Pomposo (*It.*) Pompously.

Ponderoso (*It.*) With weight, impressively.

Ponticello (*It.*) *Lit.*, a little bridge. (1) The bridge of a violin or other instrument. (2) The break in the voice. [Break.]

Pont-neuf (*Fr.*) A common ballad, such as was formerly sold on the Pont-neuf, Paris.

Poogye. The nose-flute of the Hindoos. Probably blown by the nose instead of the mouth, in order to avoid possible defilement of caste.

Portamento (*It.*) A lifting of the voice, or gliding from one note to another.

Portando la voce (*It.*) Sustaining the voice, or gliding.

Portative organ. A little organ which could be carried about, as opposed to a *positive* organ which was fixed. Many consider the portative organ to have been identical with regals ; they were certainly of the same class. A portative organ was often carried in processions, on a man's shoulder, who, when it was required, placed it on a stool and worked the bellows.

Portato (*It.*) Lengthened, sustained.

Port de voix (*Fr.*) A kind of appoggiatura combined with the Pincé, *q.v.*, written in old harpsichord music thus :

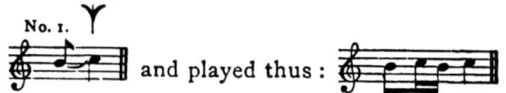

No. 1.

and played thus :

or, No. 2.

and played thus :

No. 1 is the *Port de voix simple*, and No. 2 the *Port de voix double*.

Portée (*Fr.*) Stave.

Porter la voix (*Fr.*) [Portando.]

Portunal-flute. An organ stop, the pipes of which are of wood, and are open, and larger at the top than at the mouth.

Posato (*It.*) Quietly.

Posaune (*Ger.*) [Trombone.]

Posaune. A reed-stop on the organ, of a rich and powerful tone. Its pipes are of a very large scale. It is of 8 ft. on the manuals, and of 16 ft. or 32 ft. (*contra-posaune*) on the pedals. The tubes of the manual stop are generally of metal, sometimes of tin ; those of the pedal stop, sometimes of metal, often of zinc or wood.

Posément (*Fr.*) Gravely, sedately.

Position. (1) A chord is said to be in its *original position* when the groundnote is in the bass, in other *positions* when the relative arrangement of the component notes is changed. (2) The position of a chord is the same as the *disposition* of its parts. A close position is *close harmony ;* an open position *open harmony*. (3) A *position*, on a violin or other string instrument, is to use the fingers otherwise than in their normal place. [Shift.]

Position (*Fr.*) [Position 3.]

Positive Organ. An old name for the

choir organ. Originally a positive organ was a fixed organ. [Portative organ.]

Positif (*Fr.*) A chamber organ. A choir organ.

Positiv (*Ger.*) A chamber organ. A choir organ. [Portative organ.]

Possibile (*It.*) Possible, as, *il più forte possibile*, as loud as possible.

Post-Horn. (1) A wind instrument consisting of a simple metal tube, without valves or pistons, blown by postmen. It can hardly be termed a musical instrument. (2) A piece of music suitable to, or in imitation of the notes or passages of a post-horn. [Bugle.]

Postludium (*Lat.*) *Nachspiel* (*Ger.*) A concluding voluntary. A piece played at the end of service.

Potpourri (*Fr.*) A medley; a collection of various tunes linked together; a capriccio or fantasia on popular melodies.

Poule, la (*Fr.*) One of the movements of a quadrille.

Poussé (*Fr.*) [Up bow.]

PP. abb. of *pianissimo*.

Pralltriller (*Ger.*) A transient shake, signified by *w*.

Preambulum, Preludium. *Vorspiel* (*Ger.*) An introductory voluntary.

Precentor, Præcentor, Cantor, Caput Scholæ (*Lat.*), **Capiscol, Cabischol, Armarius, Primicerio** (*Sp.*), **Préchantre** (*Fr.*), **Grand Chantre** (*Fr.*), **Vorsänger** (*Ger.*) An officer in a cathedral, who in dignity ranks next to the dean. His stall is on the opposite side of the choir, and that side is called cantoris side, the side of the *cantor*, as the other is called decani, the side of the *dean*. The office of the Precentor was an important one in olden times, and the duties are variously defined. The Rev. Mackenzie Walcott, Precentor of Chichester, in his valuable book " Cathedralia," thus speaks of the Precentor and his duties : " The primicerius, the first named on the waxen tablets or roll of singers, or precentor, was the bishop's vicar, who governed the inferior clergy, presided at the canonical hours, directed the lectures by the clerks, and controlled the order and mode of singing by the choir. From a mere office the precentorship in cathedrals became a dignity. He only sang on the greater feasts. In some places he had authority over all the city and diocesan schools, and was known as *caput scholæ, magister scholæ*, being also *scholasticus*. No one could open a song-school without his leave. He saw that all were attentive in the choir and observant of the statutes, he corrected faults and chastised offenders. In England the office of precentor was instituted at an early period—at Exeter, c. 1080; at Salisbury in 1091; at Chichester, 1115; at

Wells, c. 1135; at St. David's, 1224; at Hereford, c. 1195; at Lichfield, 1130; Lincoln, 1097; York, 1090; and at St. Paul's in the reign of King John. The duties of the Precentor were generally alike, but differed only in a few local or diocesan peculiarities. A summary of his duties as laid down in the statutes of the several places may be briefly told. He had to direct the divine offices as regards the chant ; to select candidates to supply vacancies ; to provide and keep the choir-books in good condition ; to table the weekly rota, or list of officers, with their duties ; to choose and present a succentor when necessary ; to instal the dean and canons, and to assign stalls to the prebends ; to superintend the training of the choristers, not only as regards food and clothing, but also their morals and choral instruction. On great feasts he ' ruled the choir,' when two canons, robed in the red sontane (cassock) were the chanters, whom he followed up and down the choir, regulating the offices, and overseeing the service in rochet and cope, holding a staff in his hand, which was gloved and ornamented with a ring. He further observed that all the choir sang with proper modulation, and that various and proper chants, according to the day and festival, were used. He gave the note to the canon celebrant at the altar, distributed the copes in the choir, and having presented offenders to the dean and chapter, left correction to them."

In most cathedrals, the revenues of the office have been taken away and its dignity and status lowered, but nevertheless, during the last few years there has been a general attempt to revive the *musical* responsibilities of the holder.

Precipitamente, Precipitato, Precipitazione, con ; Precipitoso (*It.*) With precipitation, impetuously, hurriedly.

Precipité (*Fr.*) [Precipitamente.]

Precisione, con (*It.*) With exactitude or precision.

Prefectus Chori. Director of the choir. Precentor.

Prelude. A movement played before, or an introduction to, a musical work or performance.

Preludio (*It.*) A prelude, introduction, or introductory voluntary.

Preludium (*Lat.*) [Preludio.]

Première (*Fr.*) First, as *première fois*, the first time, *prima volta* (*It.*) ; *première dessus*, first treble, *canto primo*.

Preparation. The causing a discord to be heard as a concord immediately before its percussion. It must take place in the same part as that which has the discord.

Preparazione (*It.*) [Preparation.]

Presa (*It.*) *Lit.* taken, caught. A character or mark used generally in continuous fugues or canons to mark the point of entry for the voices or instruments. A lead.

Pressante (*It.*) Pressing on, hurrying the time.

Pressiren (*Ger.*) To hurry the time.

Prestamente, Prestezza, con. Hurriedly, with rapidity.

Prestant. The open diapason of an organ, sometimes of 16 feet, sometimes of 8 feet in length.

Prestissimamente (*It.*) As rapidly as possible.

Prestissimo (*It.*) Very fast indeed.

Presto (*It.*) Fast. *Presto assai.* Very fast.

Prick-Song. Written music, as opposed to extempore descant.

Prima (*It.*) First (fem.), as *prima buffa*, chief comic actress or singer; *prima donna*, chief female singer in the opera; *prima viola*, first viola; *prima vista*, at first sight; *prima volta*, the first time, *i.e.*, before repeating.

Prime. (1) Tonic or generator. (2) The lowest note of any two notes forming an interval. (3) The first partial-tone.

Primicerius (*Lat.*) Prior scholæ cantorum. In cathedrals the precentor, succentor or cantor.

Primo (*It.*) First (masc.), as *tempo primo*, at the original pace or time; *violino primo*, first fiddle; *primo buffo*, chief comic actor or singer; *primo musico* and *primo uomo*, principal male singer in the opera.

Principal (*Old Eng.*) The subject of a fugue, the answer being termed the Reply.

Principal (*Ger. and Fr.*) An organ stop. [Open diapason.]

Principal. On English organs the chief open metal stop, one octave higher in pitch than the open diapason. On the manual 4 feet, on the pedal 8 feet in length.

Principal. Chief, as *principal violin*, the leader; *principal vocalists*, those to whom the solos are allotted.

Principal. The name given by Handel to the third trumpet in the "Dettingen Te Deum."

Principale (*It.*) [Principal 4.]

Principalis mediarum (*Lat.*) [Hypate meson.]

Principalis principalium (*Lat.*) [Hypate hypaton.]

Principalis extenta (*Lat.*) [Lichanos hypaton.]

Principal Subject or Theme. One of the chief subjects of a movement in sonata form, as opposed to a subordinate theme.

Printing of Music. Music is printed in various ways: from plates, from lithographic stones, or from moveable type.

The plates for music are generally of pewter, and the notes and characters are stamped with punches of the shape and character required. Corrections are made by beating up the back of the plate, so that the surface may be as equal as possible for making the alterations. The music is either printed direct from the plate, or an impression is transferred to a lithographic stone, and so printed. This latter plan is the most usual when large impressions are needed, or when it is desirable to preserve the plates.

In the earliest engraved music copperplates were used, and every note was made with the *graver*. Both words and notes were formed in imitation of the writing of the time. "Parthenia,"—"the first musicke that was ever printed for the Virginals,"—in which there are compositions by Byrd, Bull, and Gibbons, was "engraven on copper," in 1611, and the character employed is very like writing. This style prevailed in France and Italy, as well as in England, until the commencement of the eighteenth century, when stamping musical notes on plates became more general for this class of work. The process of stamping, which has been more or less improved according to the skill of the stamper, has always been called "engraving," though, strictly speaking, it ought to be called "punching."

The invention of moveable music type is claimed for Ottaviano Petrucci, who established a printing press at Venice, and was working as early as 1503, the year in which he published some Masses by De La Rue. Petrucci, removing to Fossombrone in 1513, obtained a patent from Leo X. for his invention of moveable types, for the sole printing of *Cantus Figuratus* and *Organorum Intabulaturæ*, for a term of twenty years. There is, therefore, good reason for believing his claim to be supported by trustworthy contemporary evidence. The very first known example of printed music is in the Milan edition of Franchinus. The notes there printed are not, however, music types, but engraved wood blocks, like the musical characters in Higden's "Polychronicon," translated by Trevisa, and printed by Wynkin de Worde in Westminster in 1495.

Dyapason. Dyapente. Dyatessaron. Duplex Dyapason.

These characters were improved in a book published by **Grafton** in 1550, entitled "The

Booke of Common Praier Noted," by John Marbecke, Organist of Windsor.

The printer thought it necessary to prefix an explanation of the types he employed, which he does in the following words: "In this booke is conteyned so much of the order of Common Praier as is to be song in Churches, wherein are used only these iiij. sortes of notes:—

The first note is a strene note and is a breue, the second note is a square note and is a semybreue, the iij. a prycke and is a mynymne. And when there is a prycke by the square note, that prycke is half as muche as the note that goeth before it. The iiij. is a close, and is vsed at only yᵉ end of a verse."

John Day, who in 1560 printed the Church Service in three and four parts, and in 1562 the "Whole Booke of Psalmes," by Sternhold and Hopkins, used music types, as did also many of the printers who immediately succeeded him.

1575. Thomas Vautrollier, in Blackfriars, printed, among other works, Tallis and Byrd's "Cantiones," under a patent to the authors. The patent allowed them the monopoly of "ruling" paper, and as music was printed on ruled lines they managed to include it in their patent.

It would form an interesting episode in the history of printing if special attention were to be given to the progress of the art of printing music from types in Europe, so that detailed accounts of the chief works produced by the several "Fathers of the Chapel" from time to time might be given. Such a list would be entirely beyond the limits of the present article. It has therefore been thought advisable only to include a few of the chief and, to antiquarians, well-known works of the early printers before Playford.

After Vautrollier in chronological order comes Thomas Este, the assigne of William Byrd, living and working by Paul's Wharf. The chief of his productions were the following:—

1588. Byrd's Psalmes, Sonets and Songs; Younge's Musica Transalpina.

1589. Byrd's Songs of sundrie natures. Black Horse, Aldersgate Street.

1590. Watson's Italian Madrigalls Englished.

1591. Farmer's Divers and Sundry ways of two parts in one, to the number of 40 upon one playn song.

1593. Morley's Canzonets, 3 voices.

1594. Mundy's Songs and Psalmes. Morley's Madrigals, 4 voices.

1595. Morley's Ballets, 5 voices; Morley's Canzonets, 2 voices.

1597. Weelkes' Madrigals, 3, 4, 5, and 6 voices; Yonge's Musica Transalpina, 2nd Book; Morley's Canzonets, 4 voices; Kirbye's Madrigals.

1598. Wilbye's Madrigals, 1st Set. Morley's Madrigals, 5 voices; Weelkes' Ballets and Madrigals, 5 voices.

1600. Weelkes' Madrigals of 5 and 6 parts, as assigne of Thomas Morley; Weelkes' Madrigals of 6 parts; Dowland's Songs or Ayres of 4 parts, Book II.

1601. Triumphs of Oriana; Jones's First Book of Ayres.

1603. Robinson's Scoole of Musicke. [In tablature.]

1604. M. Este's Madrigals; Bateson's 1st Set of Madrigals.

1605. Pilkington's Songs or Ayres of 4 parts.

1606. Danyel's Songs.

1608. Youll's Canzonets; Croce's Musica Sacra, Englished.

1609. Wilbye's 2nd Set of Madrigals;* Rosseter's Lessons for Consort;* Ferrabosco's Ayres.

1610. M. Este's 3rd Set of Madrigals; Campian's Two Books of Ayres.

1611. Byrd's Psalmes, Songs, and Sonnets; Morley's Consort Lessons; Maynard's XII. Wonders of the World.

1612. Gibbons's Madrigals; Campian's 3rd and 4th Books of Ayres; Corkine's 2nd Book of Ayres; Dowland's Pilgrim's Solace.

1613. Ward's Madrigals; Pilkington's Madrigals.

1614. Lichfild's Madrigals.

1615. Robert Tailour's Sacred Hymnes.

1618. Bateson's 2nd Set of Madrigals; M. Este's 4th and 5th Set of Madrigals; Ravenscroft's Pammelia; Mason and Earsden's Ayres in the King's Entertainment.

1619. Vautor's first Set of Ayres.

1620. Martin Pearson's Private Musicke.

1621. Adson's Courtly Masquing Ayres.

1622. Thomas Tomkins's Songs of 3 and more parts; Attey's Ayres.

1624. M. Este's 6th Book (Anthems); Pilkington's 2nd Set of Madrigals.

Contemporary with him was Peter Short, at "The Starre, on Bread Street Hill." He produced—

1597. Morley's Introduction to Practical Musicke; Dowland's Songes or Ayres of 4 parts, Book I.; Morley's Canzonets, 5 and 6 voices; Holborne's Cittharn Schoole.

1598. Farnaby's Canzonets, 4 voices.

1599. Cavendish's Ayres for 4 voices.

---

* On the title-pages he calls himself Thomas Este, *alias* Snodham. He subsequently used the latter name only.

1601. Rosseter's Ayres; Jones's Second Book of Ayres.

1603. Dowland's Third Book of Songs or Ayres.

And William Barley, the assigne of Thomas Morley, in Little St. Helen's, and sold at his shop in Gratious Street.

1596. Booke of Tabliture.

1599. Farmer's Madrigals; Bennet's Madrigals.

1608. Weelkes' Ayeres or Phantasticke Spirites.

1609. Ravenscroft's Pammelia.

In later years Edward Allde printed—

1614. Ravenscroft's Brief Discourse.

1615. Amner's Sacred Hymnes.

Following next on the list was Humphrey Lownes, who produced in 1608 Morley's Introduction; and in 1627 Hilton's Ayres or Fa las.

John Leggatt, London, was the printer in 1637 of "Sandys's Paraphrase on the Psalmes of David, with tunes by Henry Lawes."

Edward Griffin in 1641 printed Barnard's "Selected Church Music," a book of which no complete copy is known.

John Haviland, London, printed in 1636 Charles Butler's "Principles of Musik," a book remarkable for its quaint diction; and William Turner, Oxford, in 1634, the same writer's "Feminine Monarchie."

James Young, London—

1648. Henry and William Lawes's Choice Psalmes.

William Godbid—

1656. Matthew Locke's Little Consort.

1657. Walter Porter's Mottets. (No place of printing mentioned.) Gamble's Ayres and Dialogues.

1659. Gamble's Ayres and Dialogues, 2nd Book; Select Ayres and Dialogues.

1662. Dering's Cantica Sacra (Inner Temple); Courtly Masquing Ayres, various authors.

1668. Tompkins's Musica Deo Sacra (Little Britain).

1669. Henry Lawes's Ayres, Third Book.

1674. Dering and others, Cantica Sacra. (No place.)

William Hall, Oxford—

1661. Lowe's Directions for performance of Cathedral Service.

1664. Ditto, 2nd edition.

1668. William King's Songs and Ayres.

J. Heptinstall, London—

1690. Purcell's Songs in Dryden's Amphitryon.

1694. Purcell, &c. Don Quixote. Parts I. and II.

1696. Blow's Ode on the death of Dryden.

1697. Purcell's Ten Sonatas in 4 parts; Purcell's Ayres for the Theatre; Purcell's Te Deum and Jubilate for S. Cecilia's Day, 1694.

Some writers declare that the Germans invented moveable music types, but this is not the case. It is certain that they were employed in Germany for books at a very early period. One of the first, if not actually the first book printed in Germany with music was entitled:—" Musicæ activæ micrologus, libris quatuor digestus, omnibus musicæ studiosis non tam utilis quam necessarius." Leipsic, 1517. Andreas Ornithoparcus. It was translated into English by Dowland in 1609.

When type was employed all musical notes were printed separately; quavers and semiquavers, no matter how many there were in succession, were all distinct. In or about the year 1660 John Playford invented what he called the "new tyed note," that is to say, he used a common stroke or strokes to connect a series of quavers or semiquavers. This improvement, which made music neater to the eye and easier to read, was soon adopted by other nations, the Dutch first, the French next, and after them the Germans. The Italians did not adopt it until many years later, for Marcello's Psalms, printed in 1734, had the old disjointed notes. To continue the record of improvements made in type music-printing, mention must next be made of William Pearson, who with John Heptinstall mentioned above, was employed by Henry Playford, the son of old John. In 1699, Playford published "Twelve New Songs, with a Thorow Bass to each Song, Figur'd for the Organ, Harpsichord or Theorbo, chiefly to encourage William Pearson's New London Character." This improvement of William Pearson's consisted in *matrices* for music type, so cut that the several pieces cast in them could be better "ranged" than formerly.

The commencement of the eighteenth century brought with it a change concerning music printing. Music types were considered ugly, and the pages they formed inelegant, and so a strong tide in favour of engraved music set in. In order to make the present sketch to a certain extent complete, and to show the state of music printing in its several branches, it will not be considered superfluous if we turn back to speak of engraved music, and of its progress up to the period at which we have traced type music.

Frescobaldi's "Toccate d'Intavolatura di Cimbalo et Organo, partite di diverse Arie e Corrente, Balletti, Ciacone, Passaghali," Rome, 1637, was one of the earliest books printed in Italy from copper plates; a facsimile specimen of the character of the engraving may be seen in the article "Legerlines." Hawkins implies that the English adopted the practice from the Italians, in company with the Germans and the French.

"The English," says he, in speaking of Frescobaldi's publications, "also gave into it, as appears by a collection of lessons by Dr. Bull, Byrd, and others, entitled 'Parthenia,' already alluded to;" but this work was produced in 1611, twenty-six years before Frescobaldi's books, and it is not easy to see how a previous work can be indebted to a later one.

Type, however, was most generally used for printing music in England as well as abroad. In fact, there was only one engraver of music in London at the beginning of the eighteenth century, one Thomas Cross. The great labour of engraving music, the cost of the plates, and other incidental expenses, made music type preferable to the pocket of the producer, although it was inferior in appearance and elegance. Some Dutch printers are said to have discovered a means of softening copper so as to make it " susceptible of an impression from the stroke of a hammer or a punch, the point whereof had the form of a musical note." There were many works produced by this process, and for more than a quarter of a century, from the year 1700, the Dutch printers had the monopoly of work. Sir John Hawkins further states that " the difficulty of getting music from abroad, and the high duty on the importation of it, were motives to an attempt of a somewhat similar kind in England." The attempt included the use of pewter for copper, as the former material was more workable with punches than the latter. The enterprising publishers who carried this plan to a successful end were John Walsh, of the " Harp and Hoboy," in Catherine Street in the Strand, and John Hare, of the " Viol" in St. Paul's Churchyard. The first book printed from their plates was issued in 1710. The method of stamping which they introduced has been continued with scarcely any improvement in England to the present time. The Germans are more accomplished in this branch of the art of music printing than other European nations. Their punches are of more elegant shapes, and they can produce their work at a less cost than other folk. It is, therefore, not a matter for wonder when it is found that a great many English works are engraved and even printed in Germany in the present day.

Many of the books of Walsh and Hare were clumsily and inelegantly sent forth, but still these men kept the trade in their own hands, and outlived all attempts to beat them off the ground. Richard Mears attempted to rival them, but ruined himself. Walsh's son produced better works than his father, and with almost the same materials published much neater music. Better punches were cut by a Welshman named Phillips, who,

with his wife and son, " improved the practice of stamping to so great a degree that music is scarce anywhere so well printed as in England " in his time. A native of Lapland, named Fougt, obtained about the year 1764, in England, a patent for printing with moveable types of his own cutting and founding, but he was undersold by the pewter plate music engravers, and compelled to leave the country.

The French engravers exhibited more taste and elegance than any others. A reference to any work printed in Paris about the years 1710—20 will show this. Their work was expensive, as music was cultivated only as a luxury in France. When it began to be popular it became necessary to produce cheaper work, but the artistic excellence which the engravers had attained in former times did not desert them, and their cheap work was less clumsy in appearance than that issued in England. When the French printed from music types they employed English founts, for they were the best in Europe, as they had been for a century and a half before, and are still to the present day. Any one who has leisure, will, and opportunity, may see by comparison that books printed in Venice, in Holland, and even in Spain, were set up from the same founts of type with which English books were printed at the beginning and nearly all through the seventeenth and eighteenth centuries.

A vast improvement in music type took place at the commencement of the present century. A series of oratorios in folio size, published by Jones and Lackington, at the "Temple of the Muses," Finsbury Square, were printed in beautiful, legible, and sharp outlined characters. It is not necessary to trace the art of music printing beyond that point, or to say more than that it has arrived at a pitch of elegance and usefulness probably undreamed of by the early and enthusiastic printers.

Proasma. An introduction, or a short symphony.

Probe (*Ger.*) A rehearsal.

Proceleusmaticus. A foot consisting of four short syllables, or of two Pyrrhics. [Metre.]

Program, *or* **Programme.** A list of the names of the pieces of music to be performed at a concert or other musical entertainment.

Progression. There are two kinds of progression, melodic and harmonic. Speaking in general terms, the former is a " succession of sounds forming a tune or melody," but the term is also applied to an " imitative succession of melodic phrases," that is to a melodic sequence. Harmonic progression is " the movement of one chord to another," and is diatonic or chromatic. The term is also sometimes used as synonymous with sequence.

Progressionsschweller (*Ger.*) A contrivance of Vogler for gradually drawing out, and then in, the stops of an organ in their harmonic order, thus producing a crescendo, forte, and diminuendo.

Prolatio (*Lat.*) Prolation, one of the three divisions of mensurable music is, according to Franchinus, "essentialis quantitas semibrevibus ascripta." Prolatio is perfect or imperfect; perfect when the semibreve is divided into three minims, imperfect when divided into two. The perfect, or ternary division of the semibreve is called by some "prolatio major;" the imperfect, or binary division, "prolatio minor." The presence of a dot (punctus) in the time-signature (in temporali signo) shews that the prolation is perfect; the absence of the dot shows that it is imperfect, unless rests are added in the place of the dot. Perfect and imperfect prolation may each occur in perfect or imperfect time, that is, in time having three semibreves equal to the breve, or two.

Prolatio is the subdivision of a semibreve into minims, as Tempus is of a breve into semibreves, and as Modus is of a long into breves, or of a maxim into longs.

Promptement (*Fr.*) Quickly.

Prontamente, pronto (*It.*) Readily, quickly.

Prope media (*Lat.*) [Paramese.]

Proper-chant. An old name for the key of C major which had its *mi in B*, that is which had B for its leading note.

Proportio (*Lat.*) "Duorum numerorum ad invicem habitudo." The ratio of two numbers to each other. The discussion of the ratios of intervals formed one of the chief parts of mediæval treatises on music. Proportio is of three kinds: (1) Multiplex. (2) Superparticularis. (3) Superpartiens. *Proportio multiplex*, is when the larger number contains the smaller so many times without a remainder, as 2:1 (dupla), 3:1 (tripla), 4:1 (quadrupla). *Proportio superparticularis* is when the larger number exceeds the smaller by one only, as 3:2 (sesquialtera), 4:3 (sesquitertia), 5:4 (sesquiquarta). *Proportio superpartiens* is when the larger number exceeds the smaller by more than one, as, 5:3 (superbipartienstertias), 7:4 (supertripartiensquartas), 9:5 (superquadripartiensquintas). The following tables from Boethius, explain fully the kinds of proportio:

Thus, it will be understood, that instead of giving simply the ratio between two numbers, early writers on arithmetic and geometry, as well as music, coined a single word to express that ratio; for example, 17:5 was said to be *Triplasuperbipartiensquintas*, *i.e.*, that the larger number contained the smaller number three times (tripla) with two remainder (bipartiens). Again, *Triplasupertripartiensquartas* proportio, signified that the larger contained the smaller three times and three over, as 15:4, 27:8, &c., the last part of the compound word always pointing out the smaller of the numbers compared, or an exact multiple of it. Lastly, the addition of *sub* showed that the smaller number was compared to the larger, *e.g.*, 4:15 would be called *Subtriplasupertripartiensquartas* proportio. This system of proportion was used not only with reference to intervals but also to the comparative length of notes.

Proposta (*It.*) The subject of the fugue.

Prosa (*Lat.*); *Prose* (*Fr.*); *a prose.* A hymn sung after the gradual and before the gospel in the Roman Church. Some authors believe them to be of high antiquity and to have had their origin in popular hymns, sometimes metrical and written in the vulgar tongue. S. Cyprian uses the word in this sense in his life of S. Cæsar of Arles. "Adjecit et compulit ut laicorum popularitas psalmos and hymnos pararet, altaque et modulata voce instar clericorum alii Græce, alii Latine, *prosas* antiphonasque cantarent."

Other authors say that the prose was the result of setting words to the long neumes of alleluias, a specimen of which will be seen under the head Neume. From this cause a prose came to be called *Suite de l'alleluia*, or an *alleluiatic sequence*, or in short, a *sequence* (*sequentia*). Notker, a monk of S. Gall in the 9th or 10th century, is said to have introduced this custom of setting words to the "notæ pneumaticæ."

Their use spread with great rapidity, and about the twelfth century they began to assume the form of rhythmical and rhyming poetry set to a well defined melody. They then threw off the former rule that the prose should be if possible in the *mode* of the alleluia, and the result is that the music of the proses (a large number of which are in triple time) are some of the most beautiful melodies handed down to us.

Their use was limited by Pius V. to Easter-day ("Victimæ paschali laudes"), Whit-sunday ("Veni Creator Spiritus"), Holy Sacrament ("Lauda Sion"), and Commemoration of the Dead ("Dies Iræ"). But a vast literature of proses exists, and the term has often been somewhat loosely applied to hymns of various kinds, amongst which is the " Stabat Mater."

Prosæ Sequentiæ (*Lat.*) [Prosa.]

Prosarium (*Lat.*)   A book of proses.

Proscenium. (1) The quadrangular space behind the *logeum* or stage. (2) The stage front ; all that part of the stage between the footlights and the curtain.

Proslambanomenos. (*Gk.*) προσλαμ-βανόμενος. [Greek Music.]

Prosody. [Metre.]

Prova (*It.*) **Probe** (*Ger.*) A rehearsal.

Provençales. Troubadours of Provence, in which country the rhymers and minstrels of mediæval times seem to have had their origin. So little of their music has been handed down that it is difficult to form a just opinion on its merits. It is certain, however, that they paid little regard to the laws of music as laid down by their contemporaries, but constructed rhythmical melodies, in whatever scale was pleasing to the popular ear. The date of the rise of provençal poetry is by some stated to have been as early as the tenth century, but was more probably the twelfth.

Psallettes. *Maîtrises* (*Fr.*) Schools in which, at the time of, Franco of Cologne, descant was taught.

Psalm Melodicon. An instrument invented in 1828 by Schuhmacher Weinrich. It was a wind instrument with keys and ventages, imitating the tone of several orchestral instruments. In 1832 it was improved by Leo Schmidt, and named the Apollo-Lyra.

Psalmody. [Hymn tunes.]

Psalmistæ. An order of clergy instituted about the time of the introduction of the Cantus Ambrosianus ; for the special duty of singing from the Ambo, such music as would have been marred by the singing of the congregation. At the council of Laodicea, held between the years 360 and 370, it was ordered that no one but the canonical singing-men should presume to sing in the church ; and by a canon of the fourth council of Carthage the following form of words was prescribed for their ordination. " Vide ut quod ore cantas corde credis, et quod corde credis operibus comprobes."

Psalterium (*Lat.*) (1) A *Psalter*, generally with musical notation above the words. (2) A Psaltery. [Nebel.]

Psaltery. [Nebel.]

Psaltriæ (*Lat.*) Female musicians who sang and played during a banquet.

Pulpitum (*Lat.*) (1) The λογεῖον, or stage of the Greek Theatre. A wide but shallow space in the shape of a parallelogram, in the middle of which the chief actors usually spoke. Behind it was another quadrangular space termed the *proscenium*, not so wide as the *logeum*. The remainder of the *logeum*, right and left of the *proscenium*, had at the back a wall rising as high as the uppermost tier of spectators ; at the front, a way down to the orchestra, or space set aside for the chorus. (2) A motett. *Pulpitre* (*Old Fr.*) [Motett.]

Pulsatile. A term applied to instruments of percussion, such as the drum, gong, cymbals, &c.

Pulsator organorum. An organ-player, at the time when the keys were very large and had to be struck sharply. [Organ.]

Punctus (*Lat.*) A point or dot. A punctus was of various kinds. The *punctus additionis*, or *augmentationis*, added to a note one half of its value, as does the modern dot, making an *imperfect* note (or binary), into a *perfect* (or ternary). The *punctus divisionis* formed thus ✓, performed the office of a modern bar. The *punctus perfectionis*, similar in shape to the former, was in effect the same as a *punctus additionis*. The *punctus prolationis* was the dot inserted in the circle or half circle ⊙ ⊂ which distinguished *prolatio perfecta* from *prolatio imperfecta*.

Punkt (*Ger.*) Dot. *Punktirte Noten.* Dotted notes.

Punta (*It.*) The point, as *colla punta dell'arco*, with the point or tip of the bow.

Puntato (*It.*) Pointed, detached, made staccato.

Pupitre (*Fr.*) [Pulpitum § 2.]

Pyknon (πυκνόν). The close note. (1) A name given to those half or quarter tones which came together in the chromatic and enharmonic genera of the Greeks. (2) In mediæval music, a semi-tone.

Pyramidon. An organ stop of 16 ft. or 32 ft. tone, the pipes of which are closed at the top, and pyramidical in shape, the top being more than four times the width of the mouth. From a pipe only 2 ft. 9 in. in length, 2 ft. 3 in. square at the top, and 8 inches at the block, the note C C C is produced.

Pyrophone. An instrument invented by Kastner, the sounds of which are produced by jets of gas burning under glass tubes. It has three manuals.

Pyrrhic. (1) A dance among the Greeks, danced by boys in armour, accompanied on the lyre or flute. In it was much warlike gesticulation and rapid movement. (2) A foot consisting of two short syllables. [Metre.]

Pythagoreans. The followers of the system of Pythagoras, in which the consonance or dissonance of an interval was judged by the ratio of the vibrations without appeal to the ear. The Aristoxenians, on the other hand, held that the ear should be the sole judge of right or wrong in music. The former were called Canonici, because they appealed to the monochord or harmonic canon for their laws, the latter Musici, because they made the ear and practice their guide.

Q.

◆

Quadrate (or B quadratum). The sign ♮, used originally to raise B rotundum ♭, one semitone. Hence arose its general use for the raising of all flattened notes, as exemplified in its modern form of a natural, ♮.

Quadratum (*Lat.*) A breve, |⊟|.

Quadrible. [Quatrible].

Quadricinium *or* **Quatricinium.** A composition in four parts.

Quadrille. A well-known dance, consisting of five movements ; Le Pantalon, La Poule, L'Eté, La Trenise (or la Pastourelle), La Finale. [Dancing.]

Quadruple Counterpoint. Counterpoint of four parts, so constructed that all the parts may be transposed among themselves without transgressing the laws of progression. A perfect piece of this kind of counterpoint will be capable of twenty-four different dispositions of the parts. It is only feasible at the interval of the octave. [Counterpoint.]

Quadruple Croche (*Fr.*) A hemi-demi-semiquaver, ♬

Quart. The interval of a fourth.

Quarta. (*It.*) The interval of a fourth.

Quarta (*Lat.*) An interval of a fourth, as *major, minor, abundans* (superflua), a major, minor, or augmented fourth. *Quarta modi, Quarta toni,* the fourth of the scale, the modern subdominant.

Quart de mesure (*Fr.*) A crotchet rest.

Quart de soupir (*Fr.*) A semiquaver rest.

Quarte de nazard (*Fr.*) An organ stop of 2 ft. length, so called because it is a fourth above the nazard or twelfth.

Quarte du ton (*Fr.*) The subdominant.

Quarter note. A crotchet, ♩.

Quarter tones. A general name of intervals less than a semitone, introduced into enharmonic instruments.

Quartet. (1) A composition in four parts, or for four performers. (2) Part of a movement sung by four voices *soli* as opposed to *coro.* (3) A composition for four instruments,

in complete symphony-form, consisting of an introduction (occasionally), (1) allegro, (2) andante or adagio, (3) minuet and trio, or scherzo, (4) finale. Each of these movements has its form. [Sonata form.] By far the largest number of instrumental quartets are composed for two violins, a viola, and a violoncello, not only on account of the smoothness and evenness of their individual and collective tone, but also because of the compass of each instrument allowing an ever-varying disposition of the harmony. The complete quartet, quintet, or sestet, is to chamber music what the symphony is to concert music. Both are, in their way, the highest production of which instrumental music, apart from vocal, is capable. Attempts at a separation of instrumental and vocal music were made in this country as early as the beginning of the seventeenth century, by John Jenkins (b. 1592), one of whose three-part *Fancies* has been reprinted by Hullah, in his "Transition Period of Musical History," p. 194. Allegri, who died in 1652, composed a quartet for two violins, a viola, and basso di viola. But the string-quartet did not reach its prime until the time of Haydn and Mozart, simultaneously with the settlement of the form of the symphony.

Quartetto (*It.*) [Quartet.]

Quartfagott (*Ger.*) A kind of bassoon, a fourth lower than that commonly in use.

Quartflöte (*Ger.*) A small flute, a fourth higher in pitch than the common flute.

Quartgeige (*Ger.*) A small sized fiddle. *Violino piccolo.*

Quarto d'aspetto (*It.*) A semiquaver rest, ⅂.

Quasi (*It.*) As if, or in the style of. Used to qualify certain terms, as, *quasi allegretto,* somewhat allegretto ; *quasi sonata,* a composition very similar to a sonata, but in which sonata form is not strictly adhered to ; *quasi fantasia,* a piece in which form is displaced by the style of a fantasia.

Quatre mains, à (*Fr.*) For four hands.

Quatrible (*Old Eng.*) To descant by singing fourths on a plain song (see Quinible).

Quatricinium. [Quadricinium.]

Quatricroma (*It.*) [Quadruple croche (*Fr.*)]

Quattro mani, à (*It.*) For four hands.

Quatuor. [Quartet.]

Quaver. The eighth part of a semibreve, ♪ *Achtel-note* (*Ger.*) *Croche* (*Fr.*)

Querflöte (*Ger.*) Flauto traverso (*It.*) The flute played sideways, as opposed to the flute which was blown at one end, and held straight in front of the performer. [Flute.]

Querpfeife (*Ger.*), **Fiffaro, Fifre.** The Swiss fife; a small kind of flute, with six holes, but no keys. It has an incomplete compass of two octaves.

Querstand (*Ger.*) [False Relation.]

Queue (*Fr.*) (1) The tailpiece of a violin or other instrument. (2) The tail of a note.

Quick Step. A quick march.

Quinible. (*Old Eng.*) To descant by singing fifths on a plain song (see Quatrible). In Chaucer's "Miller's Tale," it is said of Absolon:

> "In twenty manere coud he trip and dance,
> (After the scole of Oxenforde tho)
> And with his legges casten to and fro ;
> And playen songes on a smal ribible ;
> Thereto he song sometime a loud quinible."

Quindecima. [Quinta decima.]

Quint. (1) The interval of a fifth. (2) An organ stop, sounding a fifth above the foundation stops, of $5\frac{1}{3}$ ft. length on the manuals, $10\frac{2}{3}$ ft. on the pedal. It should not be used without a double diapason, to which it forms the second natural harmonic, or twelfth. It is sometimes used on the pedal organ without a double diapason (32 ft.), but with questionable effect.

Quintabsatz (*Ger.*) A half close. The imperfect cadence, the penultimate chord of which is a tonic triad; the final chord, a dominant triad. [Cadence.]

Quinta decima (*Lat.*) (1) The interval of a double octave. (2) An organ stop, sounding the double octave of the foundation stops, fifteenth.

Quinta modi (*Lat.*) The fifth of the scale. The modern dominant.

Quintaton (*Ger*). An organ stop consisting of closed metal pipes, of a small scale, so voiced that the twelfth is heard with the ground-tone.

Quinta toni (*Lat.*) [Quinta modi.]

Quinte, Quintsaite (*Ger.*) *Chanterelle* (*Fr.*) The E string of a violin. The lowest string of violoncello and viola being C, A is their fourth string, hence the higher string of the violin came to be called the Quinte, or Quintsaite.

Quinterna, or Chiterna. A species of guitar not unlike a violin in shape, having three, or four, or five pairs of catgut strings, and sometimes two single strings covered with wire in addition, played with the fingers, not with a plectrum. About two centuries ago it was commonly used in Italy by the lower orders of musicians and comedians.

Quintet. (1) A composition in five parts, or for five performers. (2) Part of a movement sung by five voices *soli*, opposed to *coro*. (3) A composition for two violins, two tenors, and a violoncello; or two violins, a tenor, and two violoncellos; or two violins, a tenor, a violoncello, and double bass, having the same form as a sonata.

Quintfagott (*Ger.*) [Basson quinte.]

Quintfuge (*Ger.*) A fugue, the subject of which is answered at the interval of a fifth.

Quintole. A group of five notes to be played in the time of four—

Quinton (*Fr.*) The five-stringed viol.

Quintoyer (*Old Fr.*) to descant at the fifth; to quinible.

Quintuor. [Quintet.]

Quintviola. An organ stop of the gamba species, but of the pitch of a quint, or of a twelfth.

Quire (*Old Eng.*) The collective title of the body of trained and authorized singers in a church.

Quirister. A member of a Quire, whether man or boy. [Chorister.]

Quodlibet. (1) A sort of Fantasia; (2) a pot-pourri. (3) A Dutch concert. At the annual re-unions of the members of the Bach family singing or improvising *quodlibets* was one of the amusements indulged in.

R.

R, abb. for right, as R.H., with the right hand.

Rabanna, *or* **Rabani.** A kind of Indian drum, of a small size, beaten by the hand.

Rabbia, con (*It.*) With fury.

Rackett, Rankett. (1) An obsolete wind-instrument of the double bassoon kind, it had ventages but not keys. It was not of an extended compass, being incapable of producing harmonics. It was a double-reed instrument, the reed being at the end of a tube through which the player blew. The tone was nasal and produced with difficulty. The rackett was improved by Denner at the beginning of the last century, but was not able to hold its own against the then much superior *bassoon.* (2) An organ stop of 16 ft. or 8 ft. pitch now obsolete.

Raddolcendo, Raddolcente (*It.*) With gradual softness and sweetness.

Raddoppiamento, Raddoppiato (*It.*) The doubling of an interval or part.

Radical bass. The fundamental bass, ground note, or root of a chord.

Ragoke. A small Russian horn.

Rags, Raginees. Certain Hindoo melodies founded on fixed scales. They were of three kinds, *sumpoornu,* or those comprising seven notes in a determined succession; *khadoo,* or such as comprised six notes; *oodoo,* or those comprising only five notes.

Rall., abb. for rallentando.

Rallentamento (*It.*) At a slower pace.

Rallentando, Rallentato (*It.*) Getting gradually slower.

Rank of pipes. A row of pipes (of an organ) belonging to one stop. A stop is said to be of two, three, four, or five *ranks,* according to the number of rows of pipes under the control of its one register.

Rant. An old dance; a sort of country dance. This name is often attached to tunes to which country dances were performed. It is perhaps a corruption of the word *coranto.*

Ranz des vaches (*Fr.*), *Kuhreihen* (*Ger.*) The tunes or flourishes blown by Swiss shep-herds on their cow-horns or Alpine-horns (long tubes of fir-wood), as signals to the animals under their charge, such as the following :—

The notes marked F♯ are not properly thus represented, they being the natural harmonic lying between E and G, consequently a sound between F and F♯.

Rapidamente, Rapidità, con, Rapido (*It.*) With rapidity.

Rasgado (*Sp.*) To *sweep* the strings of a guitar with the thumb, for the purpose of producing a full chord, *arpeggio.*

Rastral. [Rastrum.]

Rastrum (*Lat.*) (*Ger.* Harke.) A rake. The name given to the five-pointed instrument for ruling the stave.

Räthselcanon (*Ger.*) A riddle-canon. *Canon ænigmaticus,* one part and the number of parts being given, the student to write it out in full.

Ratio (*Lat.*) Relation or proportion. [Acoustics.] [Proportio.]

Rattenendo, Rattenuto (*It.*) Restraining or holding back the time.

Rauscher. A passage of repeated notes.

Rauschpfeif, Rauschquint, Rauschwerk, Rauschflöte, Ruszpipe. A stop in old organs of two ranks of pipes, consisting of a twelfth and fifteenth, or a fifteenth and octave twelfth.

Ravanastron. A stringed instrument played with a bow in use among the Buddhists. [Violin.]

Ravvivando (*It.*) Becoming again animated. *Ravvivando il tempo,* quickening the time.

Re. The name of the second note of the scales, in the system of hexachords, and of the fixed sound D, in modern solmization. [See Notation, early systems of.]

Real Fugue. A strict fugue. The term is now used in opposition to a *tonal* fugue. The answer in a real fugue being a fifth higher or a fourth lower than the subject, note for note; that in a tonal fugue being so far altered that dominant answers tonic and *vice versâ*. So that in a tonal fugue, a subject occupying a compass of five notes, namely from a tonic to its dominant, has to be answered in a compass of four notes, namely from the dominant to the tonic lying above it. [Fugue, § 3.]

Rebab. [Rebec.]

Rebec, *or* **Rebeck.** The English name of a three-stringed instrument played with a bow. It was of Arabian or Turkish origin and was introduced into Spain by the Moors, under the name *rabel* or *rebel*. It found its way thence, in the ninth or tenth century, into Italy under the name of *rebica*, and into England under the name *rebec*. In other European countries it was variously called rebeb, or *rebebe, reberbe, rebesbe, rubebe*, or *erbeb;* in Egypt and Asia, *rebab*. In its earliest form it probably had a long neck and small round body, made of cocoa-nut shell, or some such material, over which parchment was stretched to form the sound-board. After its introduction into Europe, the third string was added, for although the Persians have now a three-stringed *rebab*, the older form was probably only two-stringed. After its introduction into England, the rebec gradually assumed the form of a viol, of which instrument it was the precursor. [Violin.]

Re bémol *(Fr.)* The note D♭. *Re bémol majeur*, the key of D♭ major.

Rebibe, Rebible *(Old Eng.)* A small rebec or three-stringed viol. [Rebec.]

Recheat. A hunting signal, which recalls the hounds.

Recht *(Ger.)* Right, as *rechte Hand*, the right hand.

Recitando, Recitante *(It.)* In the manner of a recitative. As if reciting.

Recitatif *(Fr.)* [Recitative.]

Recitative. Musical declamation. An art lost to Europe in the destruction of Greek music, and not revived till the early part of the seventeenth century. It grew out of the *aria-parlante* or *monody*, which was an attempt on the part of certain Florentine *dilettanti* to restore the ancient recitation of poetry. The names associated in this work, which exercised such a wonderful influence over the art of music, were Vecchi, Galilei, Caccini, Peri, Cavaliere, and Montiverde. It is impossible to point to any one of these as the actual inventor of *recitative*, because the style cannot be said to have been perfected until it had received the free handling of

Carissimi and Scarlatti, but their names deserve to be held in reverence. Recitatives were for a considerable period accompanied, at performances both of oratorios and operas, on a harpsichord with a double bass supporting the *basso continuo*. On the removal of harpsichords from our theatres and concert-rooms, which took place at the close of the last century, *an arpeggio chord* on the violoncello was substituted for the harpsichord-part, a double-bass (as before) sustaining the lowest note of each chord. If a band did not possess a very excellent violoncellist these arpeggio chords were often cruelly out of tune. Hence modern composers had no choice but to use soft chords in four-parts played by the whole string-band. This has been gradually followed by the use of the full band in recitatives, and as a natural result, pure *declamation* is to some extent merging into a semi-strict *arioso*. It is quite possible that this is what the authors of *aria parlante* were aiming at in their early efforts. [Opera.]

Recitativo *(It.)* [Recitative.] *Alla recit.*, in the style of a recitative.

Recit. accomp. Recitative with accompaniment.

Recit. secco. A recitative supported only by a chord from a violoncello or double bass, or by a cembalo. [Recitative.]

Recit. stromentato. Recitative accompanied by a band.

Record, to, Recorders *(Old Eng.)* The verb *to record* is used with reference to the singing of birds, as in Shakspeare (Pericles, Act IV.)

> . . . . "or when to the lute
> She sung, and made the night-bird mute
> That still *records* with moan;" . . . .

The instrument "Recorder" was originally a *flageolet* or *tibia minor*, but the name was afterwards used as synonymous with *flute*.

Recte et retro. [Per recte et retro.]

Re dièse *(Fr.)* The note D♯.

Redita *(It.)* A return. A repeat.

Redondillas *(Sp.)* Roundelays.

Redoublement *(Fr.)* *Raddoppiamento* *(It.)* A doubling of an interval or part.

Redowa, Redowak, Redowazka. A Bohemian dance, originally in ¾ and ¾ time alternately. The time was afterwards altered, and the dance was made into a sort of polka.

Reductio modi *(Lat.)* (1) The bringing back a transposed mode to its original pitch. (2) The conversion of an old mode into its corresponding modern scale.

Reed. A thin strip of metal or cane set in vibration by a current of air; the vibrations so caused, at the same time, dividing the current of air into rapid discontinuous puffs which produce a musical sound. The reed itself does not produce the sound, but is only a means of obtaining the sound from the current of air directed against it. "It is constructive, not generative" (Tyndall on Sound, p. 192). Reeds are of two kinds, *striking* and *free*. A *striking* reed is rather larger than the aperture, and is placed on that side of it against which the air is directed, being slightly bent upwards at its unattached end. As the current of air attempts to pass by it, the reed is forced against the sides of the aperture, and the progress of the air is suddenly checked, but the elasticity of the reed causes it immediately to recover its former position, when the current of air again rushes through, and so on. A *free reed* is of such size that it will freely pass in and out the aperture. The current of air forces it upwards, and its own elasticity restores it to its place again, and so on.

The *striking* reed is that commonly used in an organ, the *free reed* in a harmonium.

The tone of reeds is greatly intensified by the addition of a pipe or tube, care being taken that the tube should contain a column of air whose vibrations synchronise with the note produced by the reed, or with one of its overtones. In instruments of the horn or trumpet class, the lips perform the function of the reed, the notes produced being the fundamental note of the tube and its harmonics or overtones. The human voice is a reed instrument. [Larynx.]

Reed instruments of an orchestra. Oboes, clarinets and bassoons, with others of their class.

Reed of harmonium. [Reed.]

Reed of organ. [Reed] and [Organ, § 15.]

Reed-stops [Organ, § 15.]

Reel (*Old Eng.*) *Kreol.* A lively rustic dance, popularly supposed to be Scotch, but probably of Scandinavian origin. The Danish *kreols* are very similar to the reel. [Country dance.]

Refrain [Burden.] [Chorus.] [Ballad.]

Regals, Rigals, Rigoles. These terms seem to be synonymous with "Portative Organs," although distinguished by some authors. The word regal is supposed to have come from *rigabello*, mentioned in the following passage: "In Æde Sancti Raphaelis Venetiis, instrumenti musici cujusdam forma extat, ei nomen *rigabello;* cujus in ecclessiis usus fuerit ante organa illa pneumatica quæ hodie usurpantur. *Rigabello* successit aliud quod *turcello* dictum est, cujus Venetias usum induxit homo Germanus." Regals had generally only one row of pipes, and were probably used to support the treble voices. In an inventory of the musical instruments of Henry VIII., taken after his death (Sir Henry Ellis's original letters. Second series. Vol. I., p. 272), we read of "thirteen pair of single

regalls," and "five pair of double regalls." Double regals had two rows of pipes.

Bernard Gates in 1767 received a salary as "tuner of regalls" in the Royal Chapel, but in 1770 he is called "tuner of organs." Snetzler the great organ builder could remember the regals in use in Germany.

Regales de bois (*Fr.*) [Claque-bois.]

Regel der Octav. [Rule of the octave.]

Register. An organ stop (1) in a limited sense; "the handle on which is written the name of the stop;" (2) in a general sense—a stop or "the pipes belonging to, and acted upon by, one slider."

Register (of an organ.) A frame through which long trackers pass. [Organ, § 8.]

Register (of a voice.) Compass.

Régle de l'octave (*Fr.*) [Rule of the octave.]

Regular form. A work is said to be "not in regular form," if its subjects and their disposition depart from the plan or form conventionally considered most suitable to a composition of its kind.

Regular fugue. A *strict*, as opposed to a *free* fugue, or one in which the laws are not strictly obeyed. [Fugue.]

Regular motion. Similar motion. [Motion.]

Regulation (of a keyed instrument). The adjustment of the touch; in the pianoforte, by means of the regulating-pin; in the organ by means of leather buttons on a tap-wire, which when turned round shorten or lengthen parts of the action.

Rehearsal. *Probe* (*Ger.*), *Prova* (*It.*) A general practice before a performance. *Full Rehearsal*, a rehearsal at which soloists, band and chorus are present. *Public rehearsal*, a rehearsal to which the public are admitted.

Relatio non harmonica (*Lat.*) [False relation.]

Relative chord. A common chord made up of notes taken from the scale, *e.g.* :

The chords of D minor, E minor, F major, G major and A minor are therefore relative to the chord or scale of C, these being the only common chords which can be made from the scale of C.

Relative key. A key whose tonic chord is a relative chord; that is to say, a key whose first, third, and fifth degrees form a common chord made up of notes of the key to which it is related. Thus D minor, E minor, F major, G major, and A minor are relative keys of C. The first, third, and fifth of each of these scales forming one of the relative chords of C.

Religiosamente, Religioso (*It.*) In a religious or devotional manner.

Remplissage (*Fr.*) A filling up. Intermediate part.

Renversement (*Fr.*) Inversion.

Renvoi (*Fr.*) A repeat.

Repeat. *Wiederholungszeichen* (*Ger.*) A sign that a movement or part of a movement is to be twice performed. That which is to be repeated is generally included within the sign of two or four dots in the spaces, thus,

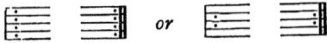

When the performer does not, on repeating, go so far as the last dot-sign, but finishes at a previous cadence, it is usual to write over the repeat, Da Capo, placing a pause and *fine* over the chord at which the performer is to stop. If the signs of the repeat do not coincide with a well-defined portion of a movement the sign ⅋ is sometimes added thus,

A few bars are sometimes marked *bis*,

but this sign is only used over a very short phrase.

Répétition (*Fr.*) A rehearsal.

Repetizione (*It.*) Repetition, as *senza repetizione*, without repeating.

Replica (*It.*) Repetition, as *senza replica*, without repeating; *con replica*, with repetition.

Replicato (*It.*) Repeated.

Reply. The answer in a fugue, the subject being called *principal*.

Réponse (*Fr.*) The answer in a fugue.

Repos (*Fr.*) A pause.

Reprise (*Fr.*) (1) Burden of a song. (2) *Reprise d'un opera*, the reproduction of an opera.

Requiem (*Lat.*) A name given to the "Missa pro defunctis," because the words "requiem eternam dona eis," occur in it.

Research. An extemporaneous performance on the organ or pianoforte in which the leading themes or subjects in the piece to which it serves as prelude are suggested and employed.

Resin, *or* **Rosin.** A gum, the viscid exudation of certain trees, chiefly of the fir tribe, which is obtained in large quantities by cutting away part of the bark, a vessel being placed below to catch the gum as it exudes. When purified and prepared it is used to rub over the hair of a bow, the surface of which it renders rough and so enables it to "grip" the string. [Colophony.]

Resolution. (1) The moving of a discordant note to another which produces a satisfactory effect. This is done sometimes by taking the discord downwards one degree, as,

sometimes by taking it upwards, as

Resonance. [Acoustics, § 21.]

Resonance-body, **Resonance-box,** *Resonanzboden* (*Ger.*) The hollow part of a stringed instrument which reinforces the sound of the vibrating strings. Its shape is of the utmost importance, and, in the case of the violin has only been definitely fixed after great practical and scientific research. The resonance-box has certain openings to admit of the escape of the reinforcing vibrations.

Respiro (*It.*) A semiquaver rest.

Response. (1) The answer to a versicle in the Church Service. The following are the signs for these words, ℣, ℟.

Responsorium. A response-book ; a choir-book containing the music of the versicles and responses.

Rests. Signs enjoining the silence of a performer for a given length of time. Each note has its corresponding rest, *e.g.* :

There is, unfortunately, no distinctive sign for a bar's rest. If the bar contain less than a semibreve, as in $\frac{3}{4}$, $\frac{6}{8}$ times, &c., a semibreve rest denotes a bar's rest ; but, of course, rest for part of a bar is denoted by its proper signs, thus :—

If the bar contain more than a semibreve, a bar's rest is usually denoted by the sign of a *breve rest*, but this is not universally adhered to, as some authors use a semibreve rest for a bar's rest in $\frac{3}{2}$ time.

Dots may be affixed to rests and have the same effects upon them as upon notes, *e.g.* : is equal to a three-quavers' rest ; , equal to a seven-semiquavers' rest. For an account of earlier forms of rest see *Pausa.*

Resultant Tones. [Acoustics, § 19.]

Retardation. (1) A gradual slackening of pace in the performance of a passage. (2) The holding on of a concordant note into the succeeding chord, in such a manner that it becomes a discord, which is resolved *up-wards*. A discord of retardation is thus opposed to a discord of suspension, the latter being resolved downwards, *e.g.* :

Retardation.   Suspension.

Retardation of two parts.   Suspension of two parts.
(or a double Retardation.)   (or a double Suspension.)

Three or more parts may be retarded or suspended, and retardations and suspensions may occur in the same chord.

Retro. [Per recte et retro.]

Retrogrado (*It.*) [Retrogradus.]

Retrogradus (*Lat.*). *Motus retrogradus*, reading music backwards. *Imitatio retrograda*, imitation *per recte et retro*, *q.v. Contrapunctus retrogradus*, counterpoint *per recte et retro*.

Retto (*It.*) Direct, as *moto retto*, direct or similar motion.

Reveil, Revelly (*Old Eng.*) Music which wakens from sleep. A signal given by drum to soldiers at dawn (from *Lat.* revigilare).

Reveille (*Fr.*) [Reveil.]

Reverse motion *or* **movement.** Movement by inversion of intervals.

Rf., *abb. of* Rinforzando.

Rhapsodes (ῥαψῳδοί). Wandering minstrels in ancient Greece, of the Ionian race, who formerly recited epics in public places, holding in their hands a staff (ῥάβδος) as a sign of their calling. It is doubtful whether the rhapsode had always a musical accompaniment to his recitation, as one of his hands would be occupied by his staff. Rhapsodical recitation must be regarded as the forerunner of stage-acting, and as forming when conjoined with the Bacchic chorus, the complete Greek drama.

Rhapsodie (*Fr.*) (*Ger.*) [Rhapsody.]

Rhapsody. A composition of irregular form, and in the style of an improvisation.

Rhythm. [Metre.]

Rhythmopœia (*Gk.*) The due arrangement of *arsis* and *thesis* in metre. [Metre.]

Ribattuta, Ribattitura (*It.*) A beat (𝓌) or passing note.

Ricercari (*It.*) (1) Difficult passages or flourishes. (2) Exercises.

Ricercata (*It.*) (1) A sort of fantasia or toccata. (2) *Fuga ricercata*. A fugue containing nothing but various treatments of the subject. A fugue without episodes. [Fugue.]

Ridotto (*It.*) Reduced, arranged from a full score.

Rifacimento (*It.*) A reconstruction or restoration of a work.

Rifiorimenti (*It.*) Extemporaneous embellishments.

Rigabellum (*Lat.*); *Rigabello* (*It.*) [Regals.]

Rigadoon. An old lively dance performed by a man and a woman, as the jig is danced in some places. It is said to have been invented in Provence by one Rigand, and from him to have taken its title, but as there are more examples of melodies by English composers than by French, it is not unlikely that the word is English, coming from the same root as " Rig," which means wanton, lively. The character of the rigadoon would justify this derivation.

The two dances without authors' names are from a work entitled " The newest Minuets, Rigadoons, and French Dances, perform'd at Court and Publick Entertainments. London, 1716."

Rigadoon. Mr. H. Purcell. Choice Lesson, 1705.

Rigadoon, 1716.

Rigadoon, 1716.

Rigols. [Regals.]

Rigore (*It.*) Strictness, as, *al rigore di tempo*, in strict time ; *con rigore*, with exactness.

Rigoroso (*It.*) [Con rigore.]

Rikk. A small tambourine of modern Egypt.

Rilasciando (*It.*) Relaxing the time.

Rilch, Rilka. A Russian lute.

Rinf., *abb.* of Rinforzando.

Rinforzando, Rinforzare, Rinforzato (*It.*) Reinforcing, or strengthening the power and emphasis of a musical sentence.

Ringelpauke (*Ger.*) A sistrum having rings on bars, which rattled when the instrument was shaken. [Sistrum.]

Ripienist. A performer who only assists in the *ripieno* parts.

Ripieno (*It.*) (1) An additional or *filling-up* part. Any part which is only occasionally required for the purpose of adding to the force of a *tutti*, is said to be *ripieno*. (2) A mixture stop on Italian organs ; as, *ripieno di due, tre, quattro, cinque*, &c. A mixture stop of two, three, four, five ranks, &c.

Ripresa (*It.*) (1) A reprise or burden. (2) A repeat.

Risentito (*It.*) With expressive energy.

Risolutamente, Risoluto, Risoluzione, con (*It.*) With resolution. *Risolutissimo*, very resolutely.

Risonanza (*It.*) [Resonance.]

Risposta (*It.*) A reply or answer to a fugue-subject.

Ristretto (*It.*) Stretto. [Fugue.]

Risvegliare (*It.*) To rouse up, awaken, re-animate ; *risvegliato*, in an animated manner.

Rit., abb. of *Ritardando*.

Ritardando, Ritardato (*It*). With gradually increasing slowness of pace.

Ritardo (*It.*) [Retardation.]

Riten., abb. for Ritenendo.

Ritenendo, Ritenente, Ritenuto (*It.*) Holding back the pace.

Ritmo di tre battute (*It.*) In the rhythm of three beats, or triple measure. An expression used when the group of accents is formed by three bars in rapid time, *e.g.* :

The above passage is marked by Beethoven (Choral Symphony) *ritmo di tre battute*, but,

is in *ritmo di quattro battute*. The former is practically in compound triple time, the latter in compound common time.

Ritornello. [Interlude.]

Riverso. [Rovescio.]

Rivolgimento (*It.*) The inversion or transposition of the parts in double counter-point.

Rivoltato (*It.*) Inverted or transposed as in double counterpoint.

Rivolto (*It.*) [Rivolgimento.]

Roccoco, Rococo (*It.*) Old fashioned, queer.

Rock harmonicon. An instrument, the sounds of which are produced by striking graduated lengths of rock-crystal with a hammer.

Rohr (*Ger.*) A reed.

Rohrflöte (*Ger.*) Reed-flute. An organ stop consisting of closed pipes, the tone of which is slightly reedy in quality, but very sweet.

Rohrwerk (*Ger.*) Reedwork, the collective name of the stops consisting of reed-pipes, as opposed to flue-work or stops consisting of flue-pipes. [Reed.] [Flute.] [Organ.]

Rôle (*Fr.*) The extract from a drama which an actor has to commit to memory. From *Lat. rotula.* The part assigned to an actor.

Roll. The regular and rapid beating of a drum by two sticks so as to make the sound as far as possible *continuous.* It is commonly expressed thus :

In the case of a tambourine, the *roll* is produced by a rapid succession of blows from the knuckles, as the hand is swung backwards and forwards.

Rolle (*Ger.*) A *run*, a group or series of groups of short notes. In vocal music they are mostly sung to one syllable of a word, *e.g.* :

Rollo, Rollando (*It.*) Roll of a drum or tambourine. [Roll.]

Romance (*Eng., Fr., Sp.*), **Romanza** (*It.*), **Romaunt** (*Old Eng.*) The dialect spoken in the south of France, in parts of Spain and of Italy, and elsewhere in the south of Europe during the middle ages ; so called, because it was founded on the *Roman* or Latin language. In the Romance dialect the greater portion of Troubadour poetry was recited, hence the term " Romance " came to be applied to any touching love-story, and in music is now frequently given to any simple rhythmical melody which is suggestive of such a story. [Troubadour.]

Romanesca (*It.*) An Italian dance, a galliard.

Romanesque (*Fr.*) A galliard.

Roman-strings. Fiddle-strings made of the intestines of lambs, although commonly called " cat-gut." Italy still supplies the finest quality of strings, hence called *Roman.*

Romantique (*Fr.*) In the style of a romance, imaginatively.

Romera. A Turkish dance.

Römischer Gesang (*Ger.*) Catholic Plain Song. Not correctly called *Roman*, because common to the whole church. England had its own old-established *uses*, before any Roman Plain Song had entered the country. [Plain Song.]

Romanzesco (*It.*) [Romantique.]

Ronde (*Fr.*) The round note, *i.e.*, *a semibreve.* [Nomenclature.]

Rondeau (*Fr.*) [Rondo.]

Rondiletta, Rondinetta, Rondino, Rondoletta (*It.*) A short rondo.

Rondo. [Form.]

Root, called also *fundamental note*, generator, and ground-note. (1) A note which, besides its own sound, gives over-tones or harmonics. (2) That note from amongst whose over-tones any chord may be selected, *e.g.* :

is produced from the vibration of the lowest note C, therefore C is said to be the *root* of this chord. An attempt to reduce chords to their *roots* forms the chief part of many treatises on harmony, but almost insuperable difficulties are met with in consequence of certain over-tones being omitted in our scale and other sounds being introduced which can only be obtained by a minute sub-division of the monochord. The flat seventh and the eleventh of nature are unused, and various notes are arbitrarily inserted in the modern scale in order to obtain more or less of temperament (*q.v.*) Some authors derive all their chords, or rather all those called *fundamental* (which constitute but a very small number of the chords actually in use), from *three* roots—the tonic, sub-dominant, and dominant. Others, again, insist on only *two* roots, the tonic and dominant. Not a few modern musicians use the word *root* without reference to any mathematical laws, and only as describing a note on which, when either expressed or implied, a chord is built up.

Rosalia (*It.*) The repetition of a phrase or passage, raising the pitch one note at each repetition. Ex. 1 is from Beethoven's *Symphonia Eroica*, Ex. 2 is from a Litany by Mozart. In the first the passage mounts by semitones, in the second by tones.

Rosin. [Resin.]

Rota (*Lat.*) A Round, but the word is sometimes applied to anything with frequent repeats, as for instance a Hymn tune.

Rote (*Old Eng.*) [Hurdy Gurdy.]

Rotondo (*It.*) Round or full, with reference to quality of tone.

Rotruenges. Roundelays of the minstrels.

Rotulæ (*Lat.*) *lit.* little rounds. A term applied to Christmas Songs or Carols.

Roulade (*Fr.*) An embellishment, a flourish, ornamental passage of runs.

Round. A composition in which several voices starting at stated distances of time from each other, sing each the same music, the combination of all the parts producing correct harmony. It differs from a Canon therefore in that it *can only* be sung at the unison or octave. It differs from a Catch, which is like it in construction, only in the character of the words. The catch should be amusing, the round may be even sacred. A round may be written out in the form of a canon, if it is of an elaborate construction, or has an independent accompaniment. When sung at the unison, a Round is said to be for *equal voices.*

TRAVERS.

Roundel. A dance in which all joined hands in a ring. It was sometimes called a Round and a Roundelay. Minshew explains the latter word to mean "Shepheards' daunce."

"When that Arcite had romed all his fill,
And songen all the roundel lustily,
Into a studie he fell sodenly."
CHAUCER, *Knight's Tale.*

"And arm in arm
Tread we softly in a Round."
BEAUMONT & FLETCHER, *The faithful Shepherdess.*

Roundelay. (1) A poem, certain lines of which are repeated at intervals. (2) The tune to which a Roundelay was sung.

Round O. A Rondo. [Minuet.]

Rovesciamento. [Rovescio.]

Rovescio, *al rovescio, alla riverso* (*It.*), *motus contrarius* (*Lat.*) By inversion. The contrary motion between two parts, caused when one ascends the exact diatonic intervals which the other descends, *e.g.* :

The above, the commencement of the chorus "Egypt was glad at their departing," (*Israel in Egypt,*) is said to be a subject answered *al rovescio.* Imitation *al rovescio* is when the converse of the intervals is not rigidly adhered to. Fugue subjects when treated by inversion are still often amenable to the laws which regulate the use of the plagal and authentic portions of the scale. A Canon *by inversion* is formed when the answer is in *contrary motion* to the subject *throughout the movement.* Perhaps the most ingenious specimen of this difficult construction is by Purcell, in the Gloria to his "Deus Misereatur" in B♭.

Ruana. A Hindoo instrument of the violin class.

Rubato (*It.*) *lit. stolen* or *robbed. Tempo rubato* represents the alteration made in the time, when some notes are held for more, and others for less than their strict duration.

Rückung (*Ger.*) [Syncopation.]

Rückfall (*Ger.*) A back-fall, a kind of grace note, *e.g.* :

Rückpositiv (*Ger.*) A back choir organ, *i.e.,* a choir organ which is behind the player, the connecting mechanism of which passes under his feet.

Ruhepunkt, Ruhezeichen (*Ger.*) A point of rest, *i.e.,* a pause.

Ruhig (*Ger.*) Quiet, tranquil, calm.

Rule (*Old Eng.*) A line of the stave, *e.g.* : "There standeth the F fa ut cliefe on the fourth *rule* from below." (Morley's Introduction.) "And so distinguish the *cleffs* and *notes* as they stand in *rule* or *space;* for knowing the *notes'* places, their names are easily known." (Playford, Introduction to the skill of musick.)

Rule of the Octave. A name given to a system of adding harmonies to the diatonic scale, using it as the lowest part. From the nature and relation of the chords added, many laws as to progression and modulation were deduced; in fact it was formerly taught as a formula for the assistance of students, who committed to memory the harmony or harmonies which each degree was capable of bearing.

The above shows the simple form of these harmonies, to which great importance was once attached.

Rullante (*It.*) Rolling, as, *tamburo rullante*, the small military drum, the side drum.

Run. A rapid succession of notes. In vocal music usually sung to one syllable, hence called in the German "Silbendehnung." Except for the purpose of training the voice, *runs* may be said to be out of fashion in this half-century. In writing the words under a run in vocal music, it is usual now to place under the first note as much of the word as will show what the whole consists of. This was not formerly the custom, and in one of the songs in Blow's "Amphion Anglicus," the words under a lengthy run are thus divided, "*th* - - - - - - *us fl* - - - - - - - *y*," an absurd division, as the combination of letters to which the run is supposed to be sung closes the mouth effectually. The word *run* being English, is avoided in fashionable critiques and *roulade* is generally adopted.

Running. The improper sounding of an organ pipe or pipes from a defect in the sound-board, or other causes. A running is not heard until keys are held down. The most common way of testing the workmanship of a sound-board is to put in *all* the registers, and hold down full chords. If there is any fault in its construction, a *running* will then be immediately heard.

Ruollo (*It.*) *Lit.* a roll; according to some an Italian dance, a waltz, from which the expression used by children "rowly powly" is derived. (*Fr. rouler*, to roll, and *poulie*, anything which rolls round, a *pulley*.)

Russian horn-band. A band of players whose instruments are so designed that each produces a single note only. For the performance of a simple theme at least twenty horns are required, but the complete band numbers thirty-seven, comprising a compass of three octaves, the tones and semitones, in their relative degrees, being gained by the use of instruments of various lengths, the longest being more than twelve feet, and the smallest nine inches. The effect of the music played is said by those who have heard it to be extremely fine and of pure tone. As each player can give no more than his one note, his attention is fully engaged during the performance. The effort of mind needful being purely mechanical, similar to that required for hand-bell ringing, the players are not necessarily men of a high intellectual order. The invention of this horn music is assigned to J. A. Maresch, a Bohemian in the service of Prince Narischkin in 1751, who being permitted for the purposes of his experiments to employ serfs, did not scruple to use severity in order to make them perform with accuracy, rapidity, and distinctness. Having drilled his forces for four years, Maresch conducted the first performance in the presence of the Imperial Court in 1755, and the tradition he then established has been, or was until recently, strictly maintained. A Russian horn-band visited England in the year 1834.

Rusticano, Rustico (*It.*) In a simple, rustic manner.

Rutscher (*Ger.*) *Lit.* the slider, the galopade.

Rymour (*Old Eng.*) A bard or minstrel.

S.

—◆—

S. Abb. of *sinistra*, left; *subito*, suddenly; *segno*, sign; *solo*, &c.; as M.S., *manu sinistra*, with the left hand; V.S., *volti subito*, turn over quickly; D.S., *dal segno*, to the sign; V.S., *voce solo*, voice alone, &c.; also Abb. for (1) *scriptus*, written, as MS., manuscript, hand-written; (2) *senza*, as S. *Ped.*, without the pedal or pedals, S. *Sordini*, without the dampers, or without mutes.

𝄋 A sign used to point the extent of a repeat, as *al segno* (𝄋) go back *to the sign* 𝄋, *dal segno* (𝄋), repeat *from the sign* 𝄋. The word *fine* (*It.*) is generally placed over the last chord of a movement repeated by the above directions.

Sabeca. One of the musical instruments mentioned in Dan. iii. 5, 7, 10, 15. It is generally supposed to have been identical with *sambuka*, a large species of harp, perhaps the large Egyptian harp. In the authorised version it is unfortunately rendered *sackbut*, an utterly unwarranted translation.

Saccade (*Fr.*) Strong pressure of a violin bow against the strings, which by forcing them to a level enables the player to produce three or four notes simultaneously.

Sackbut. (1) One of the Babylonian musical instruments mentioned by Daniel in chap. iii. v. 5, 7, 10, 15. It is the translation in the English version of the Bible of the word *sabeca*. Some authors identify it with the sambuka (σαμβύκη) of the Greeks and Romans, a kind of harp. [Sambuka.] (2) The old English sackbut or sagbut was a bass trumpet, with a slide like the trombone. "As he that plaies upon a sagbut by pulling it up and down alters his tones and tunes."— *Burton's "Anatomy of Melancholy."*

Sackpfeife (*Ger.*) [Bagpipe.]

Sacring bell. [Sanctus bell.]

Sailours. A word used in Chaucer which has given some trouble to commentators,

> "There was many a timbestere,
> And *sailours*, that I dare well swere
> Yeothe ther craft full parfitly."
> *Romaunt of the Rose.*

It probably signifies *dancers;* and is derived from the *Fr. saillir, Lat. salio.*

Saite (*Ger.*) [String.]

Saitenhalter (*Ger.*) [Tail-piece.]

Salamanie. An oriental flute.

Salicional, Salicet, Salcional, Sol- cionell. A term derived from the Latin *salix* (a willow). An organ stop of soft and delicate quality, supposed to be similar in character with the *salicis fistula*, or *withy-pipe*. It is generally placed in the choir organ, but sometimes in the swell, in either case taking the place of the dulciana, to which it bears a strong resemblance.

Salii. Priests of Mars Gradivus, twelve in number, who had the care of the twelve Ancilia, and who, during the feast of that God, were accustomed to go through the city carrying the Ancilia, singing and *dancing,* whence their name.

Salpinx. An ancient Greek trumpet.

Saltarello (*It.*) (1) A dance in which leaping steps are introduced, similar to the Siciliano and Forlana of Italy, and the Jig of England. It is triple in time, with a triplet always at the commencement of each phrase. Saltarelli are frequently found as movements or separate pieces in harpsichord and pianoforte music. (2) A harpsichord jack, so-called because it jumps when the note is struck. (3) Counterpoint is said by old authors to be "in Saltarello," when six quavers of the accompaniment are given to each minim of the Canto fermo, *e.g.*:

GERLACH.

Canto Fermo.

&c.

Salterio | (*It.*) The Psalter, or book of
Saltero | psalms.

Salto (*It.*) (1) A dance in which there is much leaping and skipping. (2) A leap, or skip from one note to another beyond the octave.

(3) Counterpoint is said to be *di salto* when the part added moves in skips.

Sambucistria (*Lat.*) A player on the sambuka.

Sambuka (*Gk.*) σαμβύκη. This word, though applied sometimes to several musical instruments of different kinds, such as a lyre, a dulcimer, a triangular harp or trigon, and a large Asiatic harp, seems to have been chiefly used as a term for the last-named instrument. By some authors it has been identified with the large Egyptian harp, illustrations of which are so familiar to all of us as to render one unnecessary here. It is generally thought that the *sabeca* mentioned in the book of Daniel, iii. 5, 7, 10, 15, and which is improperly rendered *sackbut* in our version, was a *sambuka* or large harp. It has been suggested that "sambuka" was used as a general term for instruments made of elderwood (*sambucus*); but the best authorities will not allow any relationship between the two words.

Sampogna, Zampugna. [Bag-pipe.]

Sancho. A negro instrument of the guitar species, made of hollowed wood and furnished with a long neck. It is strung with the tough fibres of a creeping plant. It is tuned by means of sliding rings.

Sanctus (*Lat.*) *Ter Sanctus*, or, *Trisagion* (*Gk.*) *Holy, Holy, Holy, &c.* A part of the Communion Service in the Church of England, and a part of the Mass in the Church of Rome. In many cathedrals where it is not usual to celebrate the Holy Eucharist chorally, the Sanctus is used as an Introit, a custom which cannot be too strongly condemned. [Cathedral Music.]

Sanctus bell, Saints' bell. A small bell which is rung in order to mark the progress of the office of the mass. In some churches bells of this kind are placed outside the church, so that those unable to be present inside may be reminded of important parts of the service.

Sanft (*Ger.*) Soft. *Mit sanften Stimmen*, with soft stops.

Sans (*Fr.*) Without; as, *sans pédales*, without the pedals.

Santoral (*Sp.*) Church choir book.

Saquebute (*Fr.*) [Sackbut.]

Saraband, Sarabanda, Zarabanda (*Sp.*)
Sarabande (*Fr.*) A Spanish dance of Moorish origin, for a single performer, who accompanies himself with the castanets. The tune is in $\frac{3}{4}$ time, but slow and stately, and with a strong accent on the second beat in the bar. This peculiarity would identify it with the Moresca. In olden times it was accompanied with singing the *coplas* or *canciones*, poetry of a trivial sort. Jenkins, Purcell, Blow, Bach, Handel and Scarlatti, in their *suites* for the harpsichord or clavichord, frequently employed the saraband as a movement.

There is a Spanish proverb with reference to weak verses, that "they are not worth as much as the couplets of the saraband." "No vale las coplas de la sarabanda."

Saraband. (From E. ROGER's Virginal book.)

Saraband. H. PURCELL.

Saroh. Indian instruments played with a bow.

Sattel (*Ger.*) [Nut.]

Satz (*Ger.*) A theme, a subject, a composition; a piece.

Saut (*Fr.*) [Salto.]

Sautereau (*Fr.*) The old name for the jack of a spinet.

Sauterie (*Old Eng.*) A psaltery.

Sax-horns. Cylinder horns invented by Antoine (usually called Adolph) Sax. They have 3, 4 or 5 cylinders, so that each horn is capable of playing all the notes of its scale without difficulty. A sax-horn band comprises seven instruments, a small high horn, a soprano, an alto, a tenor, a baritone, a bass, and a double-bass. [Metal wind instruments.]

Saxophones. Brass wind instruments, the invention of M. Sax. They are played with a single reed and a clarinet mouth-piece. The quality of tone is soft, yet telling and expressive. They are six in number, the high, soprano, alto, tenor, baritone and bass.

Saxtrombas. Brass cylinder wind instruments with wide mouth-pieces, of a shrill and piercing tone, a combination of the trumpet and the bugle quality. The complete set is six, divided as the saxophones.

Saxtuba. Deep-toned brass bass instruments of similar character to the saxtrombas.

Saynetes (*Sp.*) Interludes or *entremeses*, introduced between the prologue and the principal comedy in the Spanish drama, in which music and dancing form prominent features. Saynetes are generally of a burlesque or humorous character.

Sbalzo (*It.*) A leap, a skip.

Sbarra (*It.*) A bar. *Sbarra doppia.* Double bar.

Scala (*It.*) A scale or gamut.

Scald. [Skald.]

Scale. The graduated series of sounds used in music.

To give a history of the scale would be to give a history of music itself; it must suffice, therefore, to say a few words on the growth of the scale to its present shape. Nothing is known with certainty of the nature of the scales of any of the most ancient nations. If it be admitted that the Greeks obtained their notions of music from the Egyptians, it may be hazarded, merely as a supposition, that the Egyptian scale was tetrachordal, that is, consisting of groups of four notes.

In the article Greek Music the reader will find a full explanation of the manner in which the *octave system* became practically a part of the ancient tetrachordal system, which it was destined afterwards to supersede entirely. Although our modern scale was unquestionably a development of the diatonic scale of the Greeks, yet, for several centuries, a hexachordal system was in use, a full account of which will be found under the head "Notation." The Church modes were probably the connecting link between the ancient Greek music and the modern diatonic scale. [Plain Song.] The division of the octave into twelve parts, called semitones, each of which can be used as a key-note, became only feasible when keyed instruments were tuned on the system known as *equal temperament*. [Temperament.] This gives to the chromatic notes of our scale a far greater value than the chromatic or enharmonic notes of the ancients, as it is probable they were never used but as passing or auxiliary notes. The whole system of music hangs upon the relationship of the sounds used to a *tonic*, which, in modern music, is always the first note of whatever octave system (key) is chosen, but in Greek music and early Church-song was a note at or near the *middle* of the scale.

The old Church mode corresponding to the modern scale was the Ionic or Iastian, but when this was finally adopted as the normal scale, a still older form was retained for use with it, founded on the Dorian and Hypo-Dorian modes, to which, now slightly modified, we give the name *minor mode*, and by starting from any one note in the semitonal scale, we can have twelve minor modes. As a minor mode largely consists of the notes of the major scale beginning on its third degree, it is said to be *relative* to that scale. The form of the minor mode has varied from time to time, and even now cannot be said to be definitely settled.

Ex. 1.

Normal Scale.

Ex. 2.

Oldest form of minor mode.

Ex. 3.

Form of minor mode sometimes used melodically.

Ex. 4.

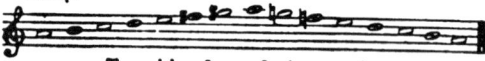

Transition form of minor mode.

Ex. 5.

Modern minor mode.

The scale shewn in Ex. 2 is by no means obsolete. The revival of old Church-song has caused many composers to study its forms, and their works are, perhaps insensibly, tinctured with its influence. The somewhat odd *descent* of the scale in Ex. 3 is to be met with in Handel, Bach, and other writers. When this *descending* scale is harmonized, it is generally founded on the following bass :—

A	E	B	E	G♯	A	E	A
5	5	♯5	5	6	5	5	5
3				5	3		3

It will thus be seen that the descending F♯ of the scale is made part of a chord of B major, a sort of new dominant to E, the dominant of A minor.

The form of Ex. 4 is familiar to all, and has not yet been entirely superseded by that of Ex. 5, which always presents both harmonic and melodic difficulty in its augmented second from F♮ to G♯. There seems to be no reason why one particular form of the minor scale should be used to the exclusion of another; all are at times useful and beautiful. Perhaps the great importance of the form given in Ex. 5 arises from the fact that it is the veritable source of the chord of the diminished seventh—

F
D
B
G♯

The musical scales of extra-European countries are so varied in character that it is impossible to draw any reliable conclusions from their form. The Arabs, Indians, and many uncultured tribes in all quarters of the globe have more than twelve divisions in the octave, that is, use *enharmonic* scales. The Chinese have the old five-note scale, called by Engel, Pentatonic.

This scale is associated also with Scotch and other Celtic melodies.

In some nations the natural harmonic, known as the sharp eleventh, which we discard, is in use, probably because it is produced upon their simple tube instruments.

The degrees of the ascending scale are distinguished in harmony by the following names.

First	...	...	Tonic.
Second	...	...	Supertonic.
Third	...	...	Mediant.
Fourth	...	...	Subdominant.
Fifth	...	...	Dominant.
Sixth	...	...	Superdominant.
Seventh		...	{ Subtonic or leading note.

Scagnello (*It.*) The bridge of a stringed instrument.

Scemando (*It.*) An equivalent to *diminuendo*, gradually decreasing in power.

Scena (*It.*) (1) A scene. (2) A solo for a single voice, in which various dramatic emotions are displayed.

Scenario (*It.*) The plot or main incidents of an opera or drama.

Scenici (*Lat.*) Games instituted, according to Livy, B.C. 364. They were the germ of the Roman play.

Schäferlied, Schäferspiel (*Ger.*) A pastoral.

Schallbecken (*Ger.*) Cymbals. *Lit.* *Sound-cups.* [Cymbals.]

Schallhorn } (*Ger.*) Bell of a horn, cornet,
Schallstück } trumpet, &c.

Schalmey. [Chalameau.]

Scharf (*Ger.*) *Lit.* Sharp. A mixture stop of an organ, formed of a combination of acute harmonics.

Scherz (*Ger.*) Drollery, fun.

Scherzando, Scherzandissimo, Scherzante, Scherzevole, Scherzevolmente, Scherzoso (*It.*) (1) Playful, lively, jokingly, merry. (2) A movement of a lively and droll character.

Scherzhaft (*Ger.*) Droll, funny.

Scherzo (*It.*) A term, meaning literally a *jest*, applied to a movement in a Sonata or Symphony of a sportive, playful character. Beethoven introduced it in the place of the minuet, and sometimes in addition to it, and it has been supposed that the credit of its invention is due to him. But Haydn had previously done a similar thing in his quartetts, and J. S. Bach had also called one of the pieces in a suite, by the name. Other writers had directed certain movements to be played " Scherzando," but only in connection with some other word descriptive of the general character of the movement. Thus Schobert, 1724-1768, marked the second movement of his Sixth Sonata, " Badinage Scherzando." In 1734 George Philip Telemann published at Hamburg " Scherzi melodichi, per divertimento di coloro che prendono l'acque minerali in Pirmonte, con ariette semplici e facili, a violono, viola e fondamento," and nearly 130 years before, Monteverde issued at Venice " Scherzi musicale a tre voci." These were similar in style to the " Cantici " or humorous songs in parts, the predecessors of the Catch. Though they cannot fairly be considered as belonging to the class of composition included under the general term *Scherzo*, yet they serve to show that Monteverde believed music to have a merry as well as a serious side. The Scherzo of Bach, alluded to above, is here added :

Scherzo.   J. S. BACH.

Schiettamente (*It.*) Pure, simple, neat.

Schietto (*It.*) Pure, neat.

Schisma (*Gk.*) σχίσμα. An approximate half of a Pythagorean comma, that is, half of the difference between twelve-fifths and seven octaves.

Schlag (*Ger.*) A stroke or beat, (1) of time, (2) of a vibrating reed, (3) of an instrument of percussion.

Schlagfeder (*Ger.*) [Plectrum.]

Schleifbogen, } (*Ger.*) *Lit. Slide-bow.*
Schleifezeichen } A slur. The sign ⁀.

Schleifen (*Ger.*) To slide, to glide.

Schleifer (*Ger.*) Slurred note.

Schluss (*Ger.*) The conclusion, finale. *Schlusschor*, final chorus.

Schlüssel (*Ger.*) A clef.

Schlussfall (*Ger.*) Cadence.

Schlussreim (*Ger.*) The burden or refrain of a song.

Schluss-stück (*Ger.*) Finale.

Schmelzend (*Ger.*) *Lit.* Melting away. Dying away, diminishing.

Schmerz (*Ger.*) Grief. *Schmerzhaft*, sorrowful, dolorous.

Schnabel (*Ger.*) The mouth-piece of the clarinet, flûte à bec, and instruments blown in like manner.

Schnarrpfeifen, Schnarrwerk (*Ger.*) Reed pipes or stops in an organ.

Schnell (*Ger.*) Quick. *Nach und nach schneller*, quicker and quicker. *Etwas bewegter schnell*, a little quicker.

Schneller *or* **Schnelzer** (*Ger.*) A trill.

Schophar *or* **Shophar**. A Hebrew trumpet.

Schottische (*Ger.*), **Ecossaise** (*Fr.*) *Lit.* The Scotch dance. A slow dance of modern introduction, written in ⅔ time.

School. (1) A method or system of teaching; as, Rink's *organ school*, Crivelli's *vocal school*, Spohr's *violin school*, &c. (2) Style; as, the *madrigal school*, *ecclesiastical school*, *operatic school*, &c. (3) The manner or characteristics of a composer, or performer; as, Handel's *school*, Rossini's *school*. (4) A group of composers whose works mark an epoch in the history of music. Such a school is generally named after the place where such composers resided; as, the *Venetian school*, the *Neapolitan school*, &c.

Schreibart (*Ger.*) Style.

Schrittmässig (*Ger.*) Slowly. *Andante.*

Schultergeige (*Ger.*) The shoulder-fiddle, or common violin, as opposed to the *Kniegeige*, or *viola da gamba*, the viol played between the legs.

Schusterfleck (*Ger.*) A facetious name for a Rosalia.

Schwach (*Ger.*) Weak, feeble, soft.

Schwärmer (*Ger.*) *Bombo.* An old name given to four or more notes repeated rapidly on the same degree of the scale.

Schweigezeichen (*Ger.*) A rest.

Schweinskopf (*Ger.*) *Lit.* Pig's head. A name given to pianofortes because of their outline, as viewed from the side of the instrument.

Schweizerpfeife, Schweizerflöte, Feldpfeife. The name given in Germany to the old *flauto traverso* or *Querpfeife*, which, when introduced into this country, was known as the *German flute*.

Schweller (*Ger.*) The swell organ.

Schwermuthig (*Ger.*) Sad, pensive.

Schwingungen (*Ger.*) Vibrations. [Acoustics.]

Scioltamente, Scioltezza, con, Sciolto (*It.*) Freely, with agility, easily. *Fuga Sciolta*, a free fugue.

Scolia. Short songs of the Greeks. They were distinct from the religious hymns, as they were frequently sung during feasts or banquets. Though at first they were like the Pæans sung by the whole company assembled, they were afterwards performed by each guest alone, holding in his hand a myrtle branch, which, at the conclusion, he passed to his neighbour, and so on in turn. Sometimes they were sung to an accompaniment.

Scolia were of three kinds: (1) Moral songs, like some of those preserved by Athenæus. (2) Mythological hymns and historical songs. (3) Miscellaneous songs, chiefly on love and wine.

Scordato (*It.*) Out of tune.

Scordatura (*It.*) The mis-tuning of an instrument. When a violinist alters the *accordatura* of his instrument for a special purpose, he is sometimes said to make a *scordatura*. [Accordatura.]

Score. *Partitur* (*Ger.*), *Partition* (*Fr.*), *Partizione, Partitura, Sparta, a partito* (*It.*) A copy of a musical work in which all the component parts are shewn, either fully, or in a compressed form. (1) A *short* or compressed score is when all the parts are arranged or transcribed so that they shall appear in two staves. Such scores are commonly used for hymn tunes, and also (especially in Germany) for part-songs. When counterpoint is introduced into vocal music, or when the parts frequently cross, short-scores become too complicated for general use. But in simple vocal music, more or less note against note, they effect a great saving of space. In transcribing four-part music into short score, the two upper parts are arranged in the treble stave; the two lowest in the bass, the tails to the notes of the first and third parts being invariably turned *up*, those of the second and fourth parts *down*. (2) A pianoforte or organ score is one in which the voice-parts are written out in full on separate lines, and the instrumental accompaniment is arranged in two lines, treble and bass, for performance on a pianoforte or organ. (3) A vocal score is (or was formerly understood to be) one in which the voice-parts are written out in full, and the accompaniment (if any) is indicated by a figured bass. (4) A full score is one in which each part is written on a separate line one over the other, subject, however, to the modification that the parts to be played by two wind instruments of the same name and compass may be included on one line. For example, the parts of the two oboes, two flutes, two clarinets, &c., and, sometimes, of the alto and tenor trombones are written on one line;

the tails of the notes to be played by the first instrument being uniformly turned upwards; those to be played by the second, downwards. The first and second violin parts are never written on the same line unless they are to play in unison; but the violoncello and double-bass parts are usually written on one line. The parts of similar instruments are not *necessarily* written on the same line, unless it is desirable to economise space. The order in which the instrumental parts are arranged in a score has from time to time varied considerably, the only point of uniformity being that voice parts are nearly always placed immediately above the line or lines set aside for the violoncello and double-bass part.

The following are a few examples of the manner of grouping instruments and voices:

Ex. 1.	Flauti
Trombe	Oboi
Tympani	Fagotti
Corni	Violino 1mo.
Flauti	Violino 2do.
Oboi	Viola
Fagotti	(Violoncelli (e)
Violino 1mo.	(Bassi
Violino 2do.	
Viola	Ex. 5.

(1
(2 Voci
(3
(4
(Violoncello
(e Basso
Organo

Ex. 2.
Violino 1mo.
Violino 2do.
Viola
Fagotti
Oboi

(1
(2 Voci
(3
(4
(Organo e
(tutti Bassi

Ex. 3.
(Violino 1mo.
(Violino 2do.
  (in unison and on
  one line.)
Oboe
Viola
Basso

Ex. 4.
Tympani
Trombe (or) Clarini
Corni
Clarinetti

Ex. 5.
Pauken
Trompeten
Hörner
Flöten
Hoboen
Clarinetten
Fagotte
Posaunen } Alt und Tenor } Bass
Violine, 1ste
Violine, 2te
Bratsche
Violoncell
Contrabass

Ex. 6.
Flutes
Oboes
Clarinets
Bassoons
Horns
Trumpets
Trombones
Drums
Violins, 1
Violins, 2
Violas
(1
(2 Voices
(3
(4
Violoncellos and
  Basses
Organ

Exs. 1, 2, and 3 illustrate a disposition often followed by Handel; Ex. 4 the arrangement often found in the works of Mozart, Haydn, and others. Ex. 5 shows the arrangement sometimes followed by Schumann, which is peculiar as separating the trombones (Posaunen) from the trumpets. The above examples (1 to 6) show only a few of the many arrangements sometimes found. The disposition of the parts now most generally followed is shown in Ex. 6.

Where more than the usual number of instruments are employed, this last disposition may be indefinitely extended, if only the instruments are grouped into classes, as follows:

1. Wood wind instruments.
2. Soft-toned brass instruments.
3. Loud brass instruments.
4. Instruments of percussion.
5. String instruments (excepting the bass part).
6. Voices.
7. Bass string instruments.
8. Organ or pianoforte.

Modern scores owe much of their apparent intricacy to the individual existence which is now given to almost every separate instrument in an orchestra, for the purpose of obtaining constant change of "colour," as it has been called. In the scores prior to the commencement of this century, it is no uncommon thing for the first oboe to be directed to play throughout a whole movement with the first violins, the second oboe with the second violins, the bassoons with the violoncellos. It is still more remarkable that the *viola* should often have been made to play the *bass* part in unison, or (when below its compass) at the octave; for the power and beauty of the "string-quartet" was thus wantonly destroyed.

Printers of music use the word score to denote any lines (two or more) united by one *brace*.

Scorrendo (*It.*) Gliding from one sound to another. [Glissando.]

Scorrevole (*It.*) Running, flowing, gliding.

Scotch Scale. [Pentatonic Scale.]

Scotch Snap. A peculiarity of the comparatively modern Scotch melodies in which a short note precedes a long one:

It is the characteristic of Strathspey tunes. Reels and jigs are distinguished from the Strathspey by the absence of the snap. The best informed among the Scotch writers on music declare it to be the mark of imitations of Scotch melodies, such as, "Within a Mile of Edinboro' Town" and the *Scherzo* in

"Mendelssohn's Scotch Symphony," as none of the ancient tunes contain any examples of its use. It has been conjectured that its introduction into Scotland is due to the Hungarian gipsies, as the snap is characteristic of their tunes.

Scozzese (*It.*) Scotch, as, *alla scozzese*, in the Scotch style.

Scriva (*It.*) Written. *Si scriva*, as written.

Sdegno, con ; Sdegnosamente, Sdegnoso (*It.*) Scornfully, disdainfully.

Sdrucciolando (*It.*) Sliding.

Sdrucciolare (*It.*) (1) To slide, by pressing down the keys of a pianoforte in rapid succession and lightly, with the finger nails. Scales upon the harpsichord were frequently played thus.

Se (*It.*) As, if; *se bisogno*, if required.

Sec (*Fr.*), **Secco** (*It.*) Dry, unadorned, plain, as, *recitativo secco*, plain recitative, that is, without band accompaniments. [A table sec.]

Seccarara (*It.*) A Neapolitan dance.

Sechsachteltakt (*Ger.*) Six-eight time, $\frac{6}{8}$. *Sechsvierteltakt*, $\frac{6}{4}$ time.

Sechssaitig (*Ger.*) Six stringed.

Sechstheilig (*Ger.*) In six parts.

Sechszehnfüssig (*Ger.*) Of sixteen feet. The unison pitch of the pedal organ.

Sechszehntheilnote (*Ger.*) A semiquaver. The sixteenth part of a semibreve.

Second, Chord of the. An old abbreviation of the chord $\frac{6}{4}$ [Figured Bass.]

Second, Interval of a. [Interval.]

Second (*Fr.*) Second ; as, *second dessus*, the second treble ; *seconde fois*, the second time.

Secondo (*It.*) Second ; as, *violino secondo*, second violin ; *seconda parte*, the second part ; *seconda volta*, the second time.

Secund (*Ger.*) The interval of a second. *Die kleine Secund*, the minor second ; *übermässige Secund*, an augmented second.

Secundakkord (*Ger.*) [Second, chord of the.]

Sedecima (*Lat.*) A sixteenth. A name formerly given improperly to the *fifteenth stop* of an organ.

Seg : Abb. of segue ; also, of segno.

Segno (*It.*) The sign $\mathbf{X}$ [Al segno.]

Segue (*It.*) Follows, succeeds, comes after ; as, *segue il coro*, the chorus follows ; *segue il aria*, the aria follows.

Seguendo, Seguente (*It.*) Following, as, *attacca subito il seguente*, begin the following at once.

Seguenza (*It.*) A sequence.

Seguidilla (*Sp.*) A lively Spanish dance, similar to the country dance ; the tune is in $\frac{3}{4}$ or $\frac{3}{8}$ time.

SEGUIDILLA.

Seguite (*It.*) [Segue.]

Sehnsucht (*Ger.*) Ardour, desire, fervour, longing.

Sehr (*Ger.*) Very, much, extremely; as. *sehr lebhaft*, very lively; *sehr langsam*, very slow.

Sei (*It.*) Six; as, *sei stromenti*, six instruments.

Seitenbewegung (*Ger.*) Oblique motion. [Motion.]

Seizième de soupir (*Fr.*) A semiquaver rest.

Semeia (*Gk.*) σημεῖα. The musical characters.

Semibreve. [Nota.]

Semichorus. A direction that the passage so marked is to be sung by half the chorus, or a selected portion of it.

Semicroma. A semiquaver ♪.

Semidemisemiquaver. A half demisemiquaver, the 64th part of a semibreve.

Semi-diapason (*Lat.*) An imperfect octave. *Octava deficiens.*

Semi-diapente (*Lat.*) An imperfect or diminished fifth. *Quinta deficiens.*

Semi-diatessaron (*Lat.*) An imperfect or diminished fourth. *Quarta deficiens.*

Semi-ditonus (*Lat.*) A minor third. *Semi-ditonus cum diapente.* A minor seventh.

Semifusa (*Lat.*) A semiquaver.

Semiminima (*Lat.*) A crotchet.

Semiquaver. The 16th part of a semibreve.

Semiquaver rest. The sign ⁊ representing silence for the length of a semiquaver.

Semisuspirium (*Lat.*) A quaver rest.

Semitone. A half a tone, or an approximate half of a tone. [Temperament.]

Semitonium (*Lat.*) A semitone. *Semitonium modi.* The leading note, sensible, master note, or major seventh, called also *subsemitonium modi.*

Semituono (*It.*) A semitone.

Semplice (*It.*) Pure, plain, simple, unadorned.

Semplicemente (*It.*) Purely, plainly, simply, without ornament.

Semplicità, con (*It.*) With simplicity, unaffectedly.

Sempre (*It.*) Always, ever, continually; as, *sempre forte*, loud throughout; *sempre legato*, smooth throughout; *sempre piano*, always soft; *sempre più affrettando il tempo*, continually hastening the time; *sempre più forte*, continually increasing in loudness; *sempre ritardando*, continually slackening the time; *sempre staccato*, staccato throughout.

Sennet, Synnet, Signet, Synet. (1) A word chiefly occurring in the stage directions of the old plays, indicating the sounding of a note seven times:

(2) A *flourish* consisting of a phrase made of the open notes of a trumpet or other tube-instrument.

Sensible (*It.*) Expressive.

Sensibilità (*It.*) Sensibility, feeling.

Sensibile (*Fr.*) The leading note of a scale, the major seventh, *note sensible.*

Sentie (*Fr.*) Expressed; *mélodie bien sentie*, the melody well expressed or marked.

Sentimental. A term applied to all songs having words that are not positively humorous, comic, or bacchanalian, whether they express a special sentiment or not.

Senza (*It.*) Without; as, *senza accompagnamento*, without accompaniment; *senza bassi*, without the basses; *senza fiori*, without ornaments, plainly, simply; *senza interruzione*, without interruption, go on without stopping; *senza oboe*, without the oboe; *senza organo*, without organ; *senza ornamenti*, without embellishments or ornaments; *senza pedale,* without the pedal; *senza repetizione, senza replica*, without repetition; *senza rigore,* not in strict time; *senza sordini*, without the dampers in pianoforte playing; *senza sordino,* without the mute of a violin; *senza stromenti*, without instruments; *senza tempo*, without time, in no definite or exactly marked time.

Separation. An old name for a grace or passing note "not reckoned in the measure or time, put between two real notes rising a third, and only designed to give a variety to the melody."

Se piace (*It.*) At will, as it pleases the performer.

Septet, Septetto (*It.*), Septuor (*Fr.*) (1) A composition for seven voices or instruments. (2) A piece in seven parts.

Septième (*Fr.*), Septime (*Ger.*) The interval of a seventh.

Septimenakkord (*Ger.*) The chord of the seventh.

Septimole. A group of seven notes to be played in the time of four or six.

Sequence. The recurrence of a harmonic progression or melodic figure at a different pitch or in a different key to that in which it was first given. Ex. 1 shows the repetition (five times) of the progression from a minor common chord to the major common chord of the third below:

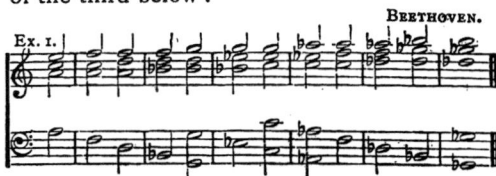

BEETHOVEN.

Ex. 1.

In Ex. 2 will be found the recurrence of a short phrase at the interval of one note higher:

Ex. 2. BACH. &c.

In modern music a striking effect is often obtained by the repetition of a phrase or theme at the interval of one semitone, (Ex. 3):

Ex. 3. WAGNER.
Orch.
Voice.
Accpt.
&c.

Sometimes a striking melodic figure and a harmonic progression are combined in the formation of a sequence:

Ex. 4. BEETHOVEN.
&c.

Some authors divide sequences into *tonal* and *real;* others make a like division but term them *diatonic* and *chromatic.* A tonal or diatonic sequence is when no modulation takes place (see also Exs. 1 to 4 of Suspensions). A chromatic or real sequence takes place when the recurrence of a phrase at an exact interval causes a change of key, as Exs. 1, 2, 3 above.

Seraphine. An instrument introduced in the early part of this century, the sounds of which were produced by free-reeds, but being very coarse and unpleasant in tone, it rapidly disappeared on the introduction of the harmonium.

Serenade. Originally a vocal or instrumental composition for use in the open air at night, generally of a quiet, soothing character. The term in its Italian form, *serenata*, came to be applied afterwards to a cantata having a pastoral subject, and in our own days has been applied to a work of large proportions in the form, to some extent, of a symphony. Serenades were sometimes called Ständchen (*Ger.*)

Serena (*It.*) An evening song; an *Abendlied.*

Sereno (*It.*) Calm, serene, tranquil.

Seria (*It.*) Serious, grave, tragic, as, *Opera seria*, a tragic opera.

Serinette (*Fr.*) A bird-organ.

Serioso (*It.*) In a serious, thoughtful manner.

Serpent. Serpente (*It.*) A bass instrument of a powerful character. It is of wood, twisted into a curved form, and covered with leather, with a mouth-piece like a horn or trombone, with keys for the several notes to be produced. It was invented by a French priest at Auxerre in 1590, and is frequently used in the orchestra to strengthen the bass part; but it requires to be very skilfully blown, as it is capable of producing a quarter tone above or below the note intended, and there are three notes in its compass

of greater power than the rest of its scale, which ranges from

to

with every intermediate tone and semitone. The serpent is a transposing instrument, being in B flat, and the part it is to take is therefore written a note higher than its real sound. [Ophicleide.]

Serpentono (*It.*) [Serpent.]

Serrata (*It.*) A concluding performance.

Service. As a term used in church music, this word signifies a musical setting of those portions of the offices which are sung by the choir, such as the Canticles, Sanctus, Gloria in excelsis, &c. A " Burial Service " is a setting of those portions of the Office for the

Burial of the Dead which may be sung by a choir.

Servi Symphoniaci, *or* **Pueri Symphoniaci.** The band of musicians kept by persons of rank among the Romans.

Sesquialtera. (1) Numbers in the proportion 3 : 2. [Proportio.] (2) An organ stop consisting of several ranks of pipes, sounding high harmonics for the purpose of strengthening the ground tone. [Organ.]

Sesta, Sesto (*It.*) A sixth.

Sestet, Sestetto (*It.*) A composition for six voices or instruments.

Settima, Settimo (*It.*) The interval of a seventh.

Setzkunst (*Ger.*) The art of musical composition.

Seventh. [Interval.]

Seventh, Chords of the. Chords are named on two principles: (1) by the largest interval contained in their component notes; (2) by the largest interval they contain when referred to their supposed fundamental-bass or root.

On the former of these principles sevenths have been divided into *primary* and *secondary;* primary being those which have the tonic or dominant for their bass note; secondary, those which have the second, third, fourth, sixth, and seventh of the scale for their bass, *e.g.* :

Primary chords Secondary chords of the seventh.
of the seventh.

(1) The inversions of No. 1 are

and its most common resolutions, as follows :

From the above it will be seen that the seventh from the tonic sometimes ascends, sometimes descends. In the former case (Exs. 1, 3, 5, 7), it is called the suspended leading-note or sub-tonic; in the latter, the chord of the tonic seventh.

(2) The next primary seventh

is called the chord of the dominant seventh, or minor seventh, and, by some, the fundamental seventh. It has three inversions, namely :

It is only possible to give a few of its many possible resolutions :

These resolutions have been divided into diatonic, chromatic, and enharmonic; also, into simple and compound; and into related and extraneous, &c., &c.

(3) The secondary sevenths are generally

named after the degree of scale on which they occur; thus, chord No. 3 (Ex. 25) is called the "seventh on the supertonic;" No. 4 (Ex. 26) "seventh on the mediant;" No. 5 (Ex. 27) " seventh on the subdominant;" No. 6 (Ex. 28) "seventh on the submediant;" No. 7 (Ex. 29) "seventh on the leading-note."

Ex. 25.
(Chord No. 3.)   1st Inv.   2nd Inv.   3rd Inv.

Ex. 26.
(Chord No. 4.)   1st Inv.   2nd Inv.   3rd Inv.

Ex. 27.
(Chord No. 5.)   1st Inv.   2nd Inv.   3rd Inv.

Ex. 28.
(Chord No. 6.)   1st Inv.   2nd Inv.   3rd Inv.

Ex. 29.
(Chord No. 7.)   1st Inv.   2nd Inv.   3rd Inv.

The following are the most common resolutions of chord No. 3, the seventh on the supertonic:

Ex. 30.   •   Ex. 31.   •

7   6
     5

Ex. 32.   •   Ex. 33.   •

6   6
4   4
3   2

The first inversion of the supertonic seventh (Ex. 31) is also known as the chord of the added sixth. q.v. By some authors, the chord No. 3 (Ex. 25) is said to be derived from G, it becomes therefore the chord of the 11, 9, 7, 5, of that fundamental bass. On this principle, the chord • (Ex. 30) is the second inversion of the chord of the eleventh on G: the chord • (Ex. 31) the third inversion of the same chord, and so on.

(4) The resolutions of chord No. 4 (Ex. 26) are commonly as follow:

Ex. 34.   Ex. 35.

Ex. 36.   Ex. 37.

Most authors treat this as part of the chord of the ninth on C; namely, C, E, G, B, D, with the C omitted. [Ninth, chord of.]

(5) The resolutions of chord No. 5 (Ex. 27) are generally as follow:

Ex. 34.   •   Ex. 35.   •

Ex. 36.   •   Ex. 37.   •

Many authors call the above the third (Ex. 34), fourth (Ex. 35), fifth (Ex. 36), and sixth inversions of the chord of the dominant thirteenth of G, of which fundamental bass they form the intervals of the 7th, 9th, 11th, and 13th.

(6) The following are common resolutions of chord No. 6 (Ex. 28):

Ex. 38.   •   Ex. 39.   •

Ex. 40.   •   Ex. 41.   •

This chord is by some authors considered as a derivative of the subdominant F. From this point of view the chords * (Exs. 38, 39, 40, 41) become the first, second, third, and fourth inversions respectively of a fundamental F. Others look upon this chord as a thirteenth from G, and as analogous to that described in No. 5.

(7) The following are the common resolutions of chord No. 7 (Ex. 29), known as the "seventh on the leading-note."

Ex. 42. Ex. 43. Ex. 44. Ex. 45.

This chord is attributed by almost universal consent to the fundamental note G, and is called the chord of the "dominant ninth," or "added ninth," or "fundamental ninth," or "major ninth."

Chords of the seventh are also called four-fold chords, because in their full form they are made up of four sounds.

The chord of the diminished seventh will be found described under the chord of the minor ninth.

Severamente (*It.*) Severely, strictly, exactly.

Severità (*It.*) Severity, strictness, exactness.

Sexquialtera (*Lat.*) [Sesqualtera.]

Sext (*Ger.*) (1) A sixth. (2) The name of an organ stop of two ranks, having the interval of a sixth between them, namely, a twelfth and tierce.

Sextetto. [Sestetto.]

Sextolet. *or* **Sextuplet.** A double triplet, six notes to be performed in the time of four.

Sextuor. A composition in six parts.

Sf. *or* **Sfz.** Abb. of *Sforzando* or *Sforzato*.

Sforzando (*It.*) [Sforzato.]

Sforzato (*It.*) Forced. A term signifying that the note or notes pointed out by the sign *sf.* are to be emphasised more strongly than they would otherwise be in the course of the rhythm.

Sfz. p. Abb. for *Sforzato piano*, a sudden forte followed by a *diminuendo* or *piano*. Also indicated by the sign ⬐.

Sfuggito (*It.*) Avoided, shunned, as *Cadenza sfuggita*, an interrupted cadence.

Shading of pipes. The placing of anything so near the top of an organ pipe as to affect the vibrating column of air which it contains.

Shake. *Trillo* (*It.*), *Pralltriller* (*Ger.*) An ornament produced by the rapid alternations of two notes, either a tone or semitone apart, as the case may be. The sign of a

shake is *tr.* (the first two letters of the word *trillo*) placed over the chief note:

Written. *Performed.*

an indefinite number of times according to the fancy of the performer or the duration of the note. A shake, preceded by an appoggiatura is generally finished with a turn:

Written.

Performed.

Written. *Performed.*

A succession of shakes is called a chain, *Catena di trilli.* A shake which commences with a *turn* is called a *prepared shake.* In harpsichord music a shake was written thus:

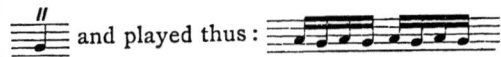

a plain note and shake, written thus:

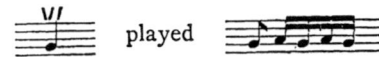

a turned shake written thus:

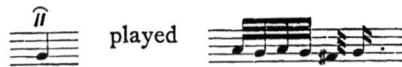

Sharp. (1) The sign which raises a note one semitone above the normal or *natural* scale. A note so affected is restored to its normal pitch by the use of a natural. In old music sharps were often used to raise notes which had been previously flattened, for which purpose a natural is always now used. (2) An augmented interval is said by some to be *sharp.* In old writers a major third is called a *sharp* third. (3) Out of tune, by being higher in pitch than is just. (4) Shrill or acute, as *sharp mixture*, an organ stop.

Shawm. [Chalameau.]

Shift. A change of the position of the hand in violin playing, by which the first finger of the player has to temporarily become the nut. Shifts are complete changes of four notes; thus, the first shift on the violin is when the first finger is on A of the first string; the second shift, when it is on D above. The intermediate points on which the first finger can be placed are called *positions*; thus, the *first position* (called also the *half shift*) is when the first finger is on G; the second position is the first shift; the third position is when the first finger is on B;

the fourth when it is on C ; the fifth position becomes the second shift, &c.

Short octaves. In old organs, in order to avoid the expense of large pipes which were not frequently used, only the most important notes between *c c* and *g g g* were employed. The following was a common system of arranging the four lowest sounds in English organs :—

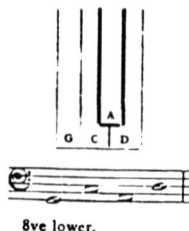

8ve lower.

The keys as above *appeared*, of course, to be B, C, C♯, D.

Si. The name of the seventh degree of the scale of Do. It was first suggested as a solfeggio syllable by Ericius Puteanus, of Dodrecht, in 1580, and again by Lemaire, of Paris, about the year 1690. In the scale as divided into hexachords by Guido, the seventh note as the first was called Ut ; but the use of solmisation rendered a seventh name necessary. Za and Sa were both suggested at different times, the latter because it was a portion of the first syllable of the word *sancte*, one of the concluding words of the verse of the hymn which gave the names to the other notes. [Aretinian syllables.]

Andreas Lorente, in a part of his book, " El porque de la musica," 1673, suggested the syllable Bi for the leading note of the scale, but the syllable adopted by Puteanus and Lemaire took firmer hold of the musical mind of the public, from a supposed notion that the sibilant sound indicated to some extent the peculiarity of the tone.

Si bémol (*Fr.*) The note B♭.

Siciliana, Siciliano (*It.*) A graceful dance of the Sicilian peasantry, set to a melody in $\frac{6}{8}$ or $\frac{12}{8}$ time, of a simple pastoral character. Compositions or movements of like character are so named.

Side-drum. A small military drum frequently used in the orchestra. It is suspended at the side of the player and beaten with two wooden sticks on the upper head or surface, the lower having catgut strings called snares, stretched across to check the reverberation. Rossini was the first to employ the side-drum as an orchestral instrument. See the score of the overture to La Gazza Ladra. [Drum.]

Siebenklang (*Ger.*) (1) A chord of the seventh. (2) A heptachord or scale of seven notes.

Siebenpfeife des Pan. [Pan's pipes.]

Siegeslied (*Ger.*) A song of triumph.

Siegue. [Segue.]

Sifflöte, Sufflöte (*Ger.*) [Flute.]

Signa. (1) An old name for large Church bells. (2) Characters and signs in mediæval music.

Signalist (*Ger.*) A military trumpet player.

Signatur (*Ger.*) [Signature.]

Signature. The signs placed at the commencement of a piece of music. There are two kinds of signature, the time-signature and the key-signature, the latter requiring a clef to show the pitch. (1) The key signatures, including the clefs, are usually written on every stave ; the time-signature only at the commencement of the first line and where changes occur. It would be more proper to call the time-signature the *measure-sign*, as it shows the contents of a bar but not the *pace* at which the music should be performed.

The signatures of minor keys are the same as those of their relative majors. This leads to some inconvenience, as it is often necessary to look into a piece before determining whether it is in the major or minor. Various remedies have been proposed for this, the most important of which is to mark the raised leading-note and minor sixth in the signature, *e.g.* :

A minor. E minor. B minor. F♯ minor. C♯ minor. G♯ minor.

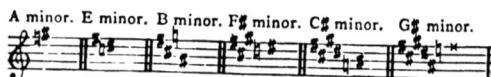

D♯ minor. A♯ minor.

D minor. G minor. C minor. F minor. B♭ minor. E♭ minor. A♭ minor.

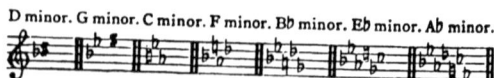

It is remarkable that writers before the middle of the eighteenth century frequently placed one sharp less in the signature than was absolutely necessary, and consequently were obliged to use an accidental at every recurrence of the leading-note. It seems difficult to account for this custom, unless such writers thought it wrong to acknowledge that the force of the leading-note overthrew the old church modes. Some writers consider that it was done in order not to disturb the proper position of the *mi* and *fa* in sol-faing. [Sol-faing.]

(2) Time-signatures are expressed by fractional parts of a semibreve. But the signs C and ¢ are, it is to be regretted, still much in vogue in common time. The former is a corruption of the semicircle C, which was used to denote duple or *imperfect* measure,

the whole circle O being used to denote *perfect* or triple measure. The stroke through the sign ₵ has two distinct meanings, namely, (1) a halving of the *contents* of the bar; (2) a halving of the *pace* of the music. Thus, C formerly denoted *four minims* in a bar; and ₵ *two minims* in a bar, that is, half-measure.

But in modern music ₵ generally indicates four minims in a bar, *allegro*, that is half the pace. There is not the smallest necessity for the use of either of these signs, as will be seen by the following excellent tables, drawn up by the Rev. J. Troutbeck, M.A. (Troutbeck and Dale, *Music Primer.*)

	DUPLE.				TRIPLE.			QUADRUPLE.			
Simple.	₵ or $\frac{2}{2}$ 𝅝 𝅝			$\frac{3}{2}$ 𝅝 𝅝 𝅝			₵ or $\frac{4}{2}$ 𝅝 𝅝 𝅝 𝅝				
	$\frac{2}{4}$ ♩ ♩			$\frac{3}{4}$ ♩ ♩ ♩			C or $\frac{4}{4}$ ♩ ♩ ♩ ♩				
	$\frac{2}{8}$ ♪ ♪			$\frac{3}{8}$ ♪ ♪ ♪			$\frac{4}{8}$ ♪ ♪ ♪ ♪				
Compound.	$\frac{6}{4}$ 𝅝. 𝅝.			$\frac{9}{4}$ 𝅝. 𝅝. 𝅝.			$\frac{12}{4}$ 𝅝. 𝅝. 𝅝. 𝅝.				
	$\frac{6}{8}$ ♩. ♩.			$\frac{9}{8}$ ♩. ♩. ♩.			$\frac{12}{8}$ ♩. ♩. ♩. ♩.				
	$\frac{6}{16}$ ♪. ♪.			$\frac{9}{16}$ ♪. ♪. ♪.			$\frac{12}{16}$ ♪. ♪. ♪. ♪.				

An excellent suggestion is thrown out by the above writer, the adoption of which would point out where the *accent* falls in compound times. He proposes to say $\frac{2}{2}$. (two dotted minims) instead of $\frac{6}{4}$, and $\frac{2}{4}$. (two dotted

crotchets) instead of $\frac{6}{8}$, and so on. Not only are the number of beats, and consequently, the position of accents in this way shewn, but a simple and uniform table can be drawn up thus (*Music Primer*, p. 41):

	DUPLE.				TRIPLE.			QUADRUPLE.			
Simple.	$\frac{2}{2}$ 𝅝 𝅝			$\frac{3}{2}$ 𝅝 𝅝 𝅝			$\frac{4}{2}$ 𝅝 𝅝 𝅝 𝅝				
	$\frac{2}{4}$ ♩ ♩			$\frac{3}{4}$ ♩ ♩ ♩			$\frac{4}{4}$ ♩ ♩ ♩ ♩				
	$\frac{2}{8}$ ♪ ♪			$\frac{3}{8}$ ♪ ♪ ♪			$\frac{4}{8}$ ♪ ♪ ♪ ♪				
Compound.	$\frac{2}{2}$. 𝅝. 𝅝.			$\frac{3}{2}$. 𝅝. 𝅝. 𝅝.			$\frac{4}{2}$. 𝅝. 𝅝. 𝅝. 𝅝.				
	$\frac{2}{4}$. ♩. ♩.			$\frac{3}{4}$. ♩. ♩. ♩.			$\frac{4}{4}$. ♩. ♩. ♩. ♩.				
	$\frac{2}{8}$. ♪. ♪.			$\frac{3}{8}$. ♪. ♪. ♪.			$\frac{4}{8}$. ♪. ♪. ♪. ♪.				

In ancient music, when the semibreve was really a short note, a duple measure of 2 (◯ ◯); a triple measure of 3 (◯ ◯ ◯); a quadruple measure of 4 (◯ ◯ ◯ ◯); with compound measures $\frac{6}{2}$ (◯ • ◯ •) and $\frac{9}{2}$ (◯ • ◯ • ◯ •); are to be found.

Sign. A note or character employed in music.

Signe (*Fr.*) The sign 𝄋. [Segno.]
Siguidilla. [Seguidilla.]
Silence (*Fr.*) **Silenzio** (*It.*) A rest.
Si leva il sordino (*It.*) A direction that the mute (sordino) is to be taken off.
Silver strings. The covered strings used on violins, tenors, violoncellos, guitars, &c. [String.]
Sim. Abb. of *simile.*

Simicion *or* Simicon (*Gk.*), σιμίκιον. A harp with thirty-five strings, known to, and occasionally used by the Greeks.

Similar motion. [Motion.]

Simile (*It.*) Like; in the same manner. A direction that a method of performance previously ordered is to be adhered to in all similar passages.

Simpla (*low Lat.*) *Semiminima.* A crotchet.

Simple. (1) Not florid; as, *simple counterpoint.* (2) Not developed; as, *simple imitation.* (3) Not exceeding an octave; as, *simple interval.* (4) Containing only one group of notes; as, *simple measure, simple time.* (5) Without valves or pistons; as, a *simple tube.* (6) That which cannot be resolved into constituents; as, *a simple tone.*

Sin' al fine (*It.*) To the end.

Sinfonia (*It.*) **Sinfonie** (*Fr.*) [Symphony.]

Singakademie, Singschule (*Ger.*) An academy or school for singing.

Singend (*Ger.*) [Cantabile.]

Singetänze (*Ger.*) Song-dances. Ballads.

Singhiozzando (*It.*) In a sobbing style.

Single action. [Pianoforte.] [Harp.]

Single chant. [Chant.]

Single fugue. A composition in which only one subject is employed. [Fugue.]

Single relish. An old ornament in harpsichord music, violin playing, or singing. It was also called a *cadent.*

Written.

Played.

Singschule (*Ger.*) A school for teaching vocal music. A song-school.

Singspiel (*Ger.*) [Opera.]

Singstimme (*Ger.*) A vocal part.

Sinistra (*It.*) The left hand.

Sinkapace. [Paspy.]

Si piace (*It.*) At pleasure, *ad libitum.*

Si replica (*It.*) To be repeated.

Si scriva (*It.*) As written, without impromptu embellishment or alteration.

Si segue (*It.*) As follows, go on.

Sister (*Ger.*) An old German guitar having seven gut strings, the three lowest covered. It was tuned to G c f g c' e' g'.

Sistro (*It.*) A triangle.

Sistrum (*Gk.*), σεῖστρον (from σείω to shake). A rattle used by the ancient Egyptians, the Greeks, and Romans. It is not improbable sistrums were known also to the Hebrews, if the word *menaancim* is correctly traced to a root signifying to "rattle." Its common form was that of a handle surmounted by a loop of metal having cross-bars on which rings were sometimes placed. (Fig. 1.)

Fig. 1.

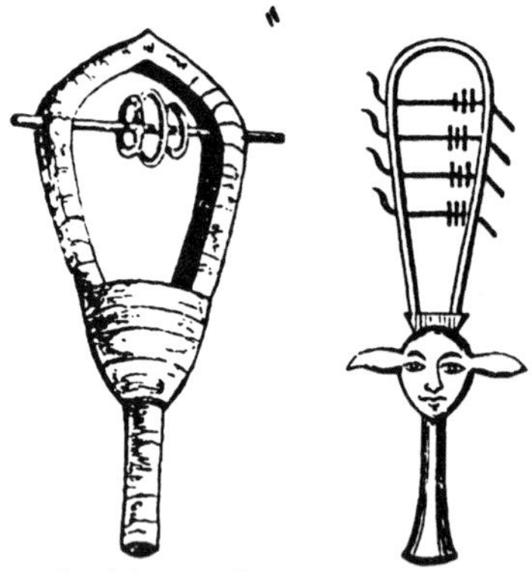

Others had bars of unequal length without rings, a fact which has led some writers to suppose that they were struck with a piece of metal held in the other hand. (Fig. 2.)

Fig. 2.

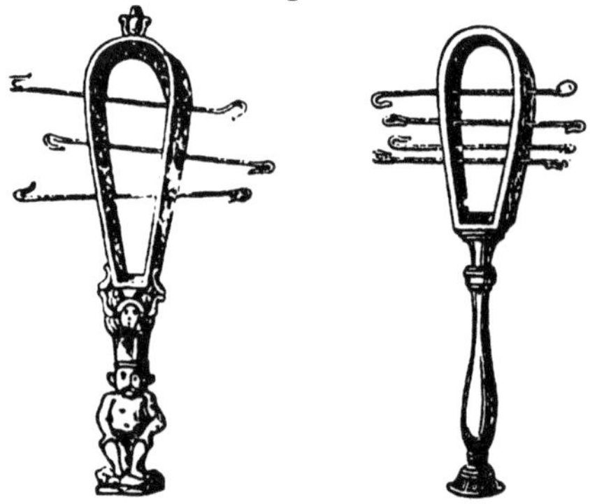

Fig. 3 shows Egyptian ladies rattling sistrums at a religious ceremony.

Fig. 3.

Sitole. [Citole.]

Si tace (*It.*) Be silent.

Si volta (*It.*) Turn over.

Sixième (*Fr.*) The interval of a sixth.

Six pour quatre (*Fr.*) A sextuplet, *q.v.*

Sixte (*Fr.*) The interval of a sixth.

Sixteen feet. The length of the open pipe which gives the unison of the pedal organ and the double of the manuals.

Sixteenth note. A semiquaver, the sixteenth part of a semibreve.

Sixth, added. [Added sixth.]

Sixth, chord of the. The first inversion of the common chord; it consists of a note with its minor third and minor sixth.

Sixth, chord of the French, German, Italian. [Extreme Sixth.]

Sixth, Neapolitan. [Neapolitan Sixth.]

Skald *or* **Scalld.** A Gothic poet, priest, or bard. According to Percy the word denotes "smoothers and polishers of language," but others derive it from *gala* to sing, whence *galld*, enchantment, and *sgalld*, *skalld*, an enchanter. The root "gala" appears in the termination *gall* in the word nightingale. The name was especially applied to those who, in addition to natural gifts, possessed some degree of education, that is to say, a knowledge of versification, mythical imagery, and the traditions of their country. Skaldic poetry had for its object the celebration of the deeds of living warriors or their ancestors. The Skalds were attached to the courts of the Scandinavian princes, it being accounted honourable to be possessed of the most skilful of these poets. There are few complete poems of the Skalds extant, but a large number of fragments are preserved, partly by the younger Edda, partly in the Sagas and the Heimskringla. The Eddas are songs as old as the 6th century, the Sagas are historical and legendary tales. The Heimskringla, or Mythic ring of the world, records the history of the kings of Norway from the earliest times to the year 1177, the year in which the historian Snorri Sturleson was born.

Skip. A movement from any one note to another which is at a greater interval than one degree. [Disjunct motion.]

Skitzen (*Ger.*) Sketches. Short pieces, sometimes suggestive of some particular subject, not in any prescribed form.

Slancio, con (*It.*) With eagerness, impetuosity; from *slanciare*, to rush upon.

Slargando, Slargandosi (*It.*) Widening, opening, extending. Used as an equivalent for *rallentando*.

Slentando (*It.*) Slackening the time, becoming slower by degrees.

Slide. (1) An arrangement in the trumpet and trombone, by means of which the tube can be lengthened so as to generate a new series of harmonics. (2) To slide is to pass from one note to another without any cessation of sound, or distinction between the intervals. (3) A slider of an organ.

Slider. [Organ.]

Sliding relish, *Coulé* (*Fr.*) A grace in old harpsichord music,

Slur. A curved line placed over notes directing that they are to be played legato. [Bind.] A slur is often used in modern music to shew the phrasing. In violin music a slur directs that the notes under it are to be played with one bow. [Bowing.]

Small Octave. The name given by the Germans to the notes,

and their intermediate semitones. It is also called the lesser octave, and is described by the small letters c, d, e. [Pitch.] [Tablature.]

Smaniante, Smaniare, Smanioso (*It.*) Furious, frantic, with rage.

Smanicare (*It.*) To shift. [Shift.]

Sminuendo, Sminuito, Smorendo (*It.*) Diminishing, decreasing gradually, lessening the time and tone.

Smorfioso (*It.*) Affected, coquettish.

Smorzando, Smorzato (*It.*) Gradually fading away.

Snap. [Scotch Snap.]

Snare Drum. [Side Drum.]

Soave, Soavemente (*It.*) Agreeably, delicately, gently, softly, sweetly.

Sobb. An old word for *damping* in lute playing. "Cause them (the strings) to sobb, by slacking your stopping hand so soon as they are struck; yet not to unstop them, but only so much as may dead the sound on a sudden. This gives great pleasure in such cases." Mace, 1676.

Soggetto (*It.*) Subject, theme, motive, proportion of a fugue.

Sol. The note G. [Sol-faing.]

Sol-bémol (*Fr.*) The note G flat. *Sol-bémol majeur*, the key of G flat major. *Sol-bémol mineur*, the key of G flat minor. *Sol-dièse*, the note G sharp.

Solennemente (*It.*) Solemnly.

Solennità (*It.*) Solemnity, pomp.

Sol-fa (*It.*) A general name for the notes in music. [Sol-faing, Solfeggi, Tonic Sol-fa.]

Sol-faing. A system of singing; a composition in which the names of the notes are employed instead of the words to which it may be set. Formerly only four of the seven names of the notes—Ut, Re, Mi, Fa, Sol, La, Si, were used, namely, Mi, Fa, Sol, La. These were applied to every note in the scale, on the principle that it is naturally divided into two halves of similar proportions.

Thus, from 1 to 2 is a tone, from 2 to 3 is also a tone, and from 3 to 4 a semitone, whether the upper or lower series be the first reckoned. So, as in the scale of C, from Fa to Sol and from Sol to La are each a tone apart, and from Mi to Fa only a semitone; *all* tones in the scale were distinguished by these names for the purpose of Sol-faing.

Mi was always used for the leading, or master note. This series, repeated to any extent, was supposed to express all the different orders of tones and semitones in the diatonic scale. "Above Mi will stand Fa, Sol, La, and below it the same inverted La, Sol, Fa, and one Mi is always distant from another an octave, which cannot be said of any other of them, because after Mi ascending come always Fa, Sol, La, Fa, which are repeated invertedly, descending."

The old rules for remembering Mi in all keys were thus set forth, the positions of the notes being called by the seven letters of the alphabet in use then as now;

If that no flat is set in B,
Then in that place standeth yᵣ Mi:

But if your B alone is flat,
Then É is Mi, be sure of that:

If both be flat, your B and E,
Then A is Mi, here you may see:

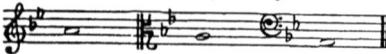

If these be flat, E, A and B,
Then Mi alone doth stand in D:

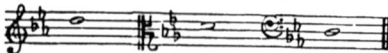

If all be flat, E, A, B, D,
Then surely Mi will stand in G:

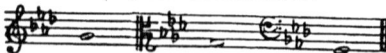

Learn this, and learn it well by rote,
That Mi is aye the last sharped note
For if a sharp on F be set,
To call that Mi, do not forget:

And if another on C be found,
Remember there your Mi to sound:

And if one more be set on G,
Then in that place will stand your Mi:

If all be sharp, F, C, G, D,
Then Mi alone will stand in D:

In the modern method of Sol-faing no distinction is made between tones and semitones by the use of a fixed nomenclature for the proportions of the scale, but the notes in any key are called by the names they bear in the key of Do or C.

Thus, a piece in E or E flat would be Sol-faed by calling the scale notes—Mi, Fa, Sol, La, Si, Do, Re, Mi, whether they were sharp, flat, or natural. The Tonic Sol-fa method calls all scales starting from any one of the twelve semitones by the same names as it gives to the notes of the scale of C, namely, Doh, Ray, Me, Fah, Soh, Lah, Te, Doh.

Solfége (*Fr.*) A vocal exercise in which the notes are called by the several names Do, Re, Mi, Fa, Sol, La, Si. [Sol-faing.]

Solfeggiamenti (*It.*) Solfeggi.

Solfeggiare (*It.*) To practice solfeggi.

Solfeggio. [Solfége.]

Solist. [Soloist.]

Solito (*It.*) Usual, used, accustomed. In the ordinary manner.

Sollecito (*It.*) Careful; a word directing a careful and attentive manner of performance.

Solmisare (*It.*), **Solmizare** (*It.*), **Solmisiren** (*Ger.*) To Sol-fa. [Sol-faing. Solfeggio.]

Solmisation. [Sol-faing.]

Solo (*It.*) Alone. *Soprano solo*, the soprano alone; *voci soli*, voices alone, &c.

Soloist. One who sings or performs alone, with or without the aid of accompaniment.

Solo pitch. The tuning of an instrument a little higher than the ordinary pitch in order to obtain brilliancy of tone with a certain amount of ease to the player. [Accordatura.]

Solospieler (*Ger.*) A solo player.

Solostimme (*Ger.*) A solo part.

Son (*Fr.*) Sound, tone.

Sonabile (*It.*) Sounding, resonant.

Sonare (*It.*) To sound, to play upon. *Sonare alla mente* to play extempore. *Sonare il violino* (*It.*) To play upon the violin.

Sonata. The word Sonata is supposed by some to be derived from the Italian word *sonare*, to sound, but by others from *sonetto*, a sonnet.

The term Sonata or Suonata, as applied to a musical composition, was first used about the beginning of the 17th century. Those of that time so called, had but one movement; they were in fact, simply *airs* arranged in parts, for an instrument or instruments. But the title of *airs* was given to some Sonatas as late as 1770, for in Hoyle's " Dictionarium musicæ" of that date, *voce* "Suonata," we read " of Corelli's Musick, the first and third operas are Church Sonatas, and the second and fourth, Chamber Sonatas ; though the common distinction among us is made by the name of *airs*."

Other terms were occasionally used to describe Sonatas, such as Consorts, Ayres, Lessons, Fantasies or Fancies, " so made as they must be plaid and not sung," and "Ayerie Fancies that may be as well sung as plaid."

Sir John Hawkins, in his " History of Music," says these titles were disused about the middle of the 17th century, when new forms of concerted pieces of a more elegant character came into vogue; these were called " the Sonata di Chiesa and the Sonata di Camera." The first of these, as being adapted to Church Service, was grave and solemn, consisting of slow movements, intermixed with fugues; the other admitted of a variety of airs to regular measures, such as the Allemande, the Courant, the Sarabande, &c.

The slow movements "intermixed with fugues," arose from the introduction of the Canzona, and Sir John Hawkins in mentioning this as a characteristic of the Sonata, unconsciously proves that the influence of the Canzona style had not weakened or faded at the time he wrote.

The connection of the Canzona with the Sonata is to a certain extent indicated in the pieces by Frescobaldi, published at Venice (1634). " Canzone da Sonare a una, due, tre, et quattro, con il basso continuo," which are exactly similar in style to the compositions recorded in early times as Sonatas. When in subsequent compositions of this kind two or more movements were employed, those most favoured were a Canzona or something in Canzona style, and a dance tune, such as a Pavan, an Allemande, or a Coranto. The Canzona was probably selected by the composer as a vehicle for the display of art and skill, and the dance tune was offered as a conciliation to the taste of his hearers. Long after the form was fixed, compositions bearing the name of Sonatas, constructed on the principles and according to the models of older times, were published, some as late as the end of the last century, as intimated above.

Frescobaldi's Canzone consist of only one movement, with various changes of time. A short analysis of the whole piece from which the illustration to the word Canzona is taken, will give an idea of the character of these early Sonatas. The first phrase of 19 bars is in fugal style, then follow 12 bars in $\frac{6}{4}$, after which are 27 bars in duple time in which free imitation is employed, then $9\frac{1}{2}$ bars in $\frac{6}{4}$ again, the music of a different character to that in the former movement, of the same pulse measure, then 2 bars by way of a coda or conclusion, in common time. No portion is marked for repetition, but the whole thing goes straight on from the first note to the last.

The earliest compositions to which the title of Sonata or Suonata was attached, were written by Bonifacio Graziani (1609-1672), Marc Antonio Cesti (1624-1675), and Paolo Colonna (1630-1690), among others. It is presumed that some of the works of these musicians were those brought to England by John Jenkins (1592-1680), who afterwards, upon the models so suggested, published in 1660 in London "Twelve Sonatas for two violins and a bass, with a thorough bass for the organ." These were the first compositions of the kind by an Englishman. Jenkins was already well known as an agreeable writer of "fancies for viols," and his Sonatas show a certain amount of artistic progress in the arrangement of contrasted movements. Most writers on musical history declare that Francis Henry Biber (1648-1698), was the first who published a work with the title of a Sonata, but his compositions did not appear until 1681, more than twenty years after those by Jenkins with the same title ; and there were also the still earlier Italian writers named above, from whom Jenkins confessedly obtained the idea. Considering the variety of the German tongue, and the unwillingness of the German people to use a foreign term when a native equivalent can be found, it is scarcely likely that the term Sonata would be first attached to a German composition by a German composer ; therefore it is reasonable to assume that the word would have been adopted by the musicians of the country to which it belongs. Graziani, Cesti, and Colonna, who died before the time Biber published his Sonatas, used the term to describe certain of their compositions ; but supposing the honour of first using it belonged to a German, then Johann Rosenmüller, who published at Venice " XII. sonate a camera, a 5 stromenti," in 1667, has a prior claim to Biber.

Henry Purcell (1658-1695), who was one of the earliest English writers of Sonatas, has almost as strong a claim to an early use of the word as Biber. Purcell composed Sonatas which were published in 1683, with the title of " Twelve sonatas of three parts, two violins and a base, to the organ or harpsychord." These were issued in separate parts, and in the sixth Sonata of this set is the melody whose character has given rise to the erroneous statement that Purcell composed the air upon which "God save the King" is founded. Furthermore, some writers declare that there is evidence in the construction of this set of Sonatas, that Purcell was indebted to Corelli for his ideas. If there is a sufficient similarity of style to warrant the assertion, there still remains the doubt whether Purcell could have seen the work of his Italian contemporary before his own was published, as both sets were issued in the same year, and communication, especially with a foreign country, was not so rapid then as now.

In the preface to this book of Sonatas, Purcell states that " he has faithfully endeavoured a just imitation of the most famed Italian masters, principally to bring the seriousness and gravity of that sort of musick into vogue and reputation among our countrymen, whose humour 'tis time now should begin to loath the levity and balladry of our neighbours." He further states, " He is not ashamed to own his unskilfulness in the Italian language, but that is the unhappiness of his education, which cannot justly be counted his fault; however, he thinks he may warrantably affirm he is not mistaken in the power of the Italian notes, or elegancy of their compositions." If Purcell benefited by the writings of any Italian musician, it could hardly have been by those of Corelli.

Purcell also composed a second set about the same time, but they were not printed until after his death. Among this second set was one well-known by the name of the "Golden Sonata," and as it is a very fair example of Purcell's compositions of this kind, and indeed of most others of the period, a short description may not be out of place here. It is written in three parts, for two violins and a figured bass. The key is F, and the first movement, only twenty-six bars in length, is a *largo* in common time of four crotchets. The subject, proposed by the bass and imitated by the trebles, is repeated in the key of the dominant at the 8th bar, but by the bass only, the trebles having a second subject. At the 12th bar the subject is inverted in the bass and answered according to the inversion by the other parts in fugal form, modulating into the key of the relative minor, in which key the subject re-appears, having for counterpoint an inversion of the first and second subjects; and with an imitation of the first episode as coda the movement ends.

There are altogether five movements, a *largo* of great beauty of melody, the second an *adagio* in $\frac{3}{4}$ time, with all the notes not in the key of F major written as accidentals, the third called *canzona allegro* is in F major (duple time), the fourth a *grave* in D minor (duple time), and the fifth is an *allegro* in F major $\frac{3}{8}$. No portion of any one movement is marked for repetition. The movements are each short, the last being the longest, and there is but little indication of that which is known as Sonata form in any, though each is written in a form regular enough in itself. Every device of imitation, inversion, and augmentation of the subjects proposed is employed freely, though not to a great extent. Lully [1634-1687], Pachelbel [1653-1706], Buononcini [1658-1702], the great Arcangelo Corelli, and Kühnau [1667-1722], may be mentioned as Sonata writers contemporary with Purcell. Kühnau being, perhaps, next to Corelli, the most remarkable. His early Sonatas were in three movements, an *allegro*, *andante*, and *allegro*, and for this reason his claim to merit as the suggestor of the modern form has been made out. One of these Sonatas or suites (No. 3) in E minor, may be taken as an example not only of the rest of his works, but of the form the Sonata had assumed in his day. Commencing with a Præludium of 22 bars in which sentences given out by the right hand are imitated in the left, there follows an Allemande with the half close in B minor, a Courante and a Sarabande with the first sections ending in B major; in none are the subjects developed, but the Gigue with which the suite concludes contains the nearest approach to modern form, in that the second section commences with the subject first proposed, though by inversion, and oddly enough the second half of the Gigue contains two bars less than the first, a very unusual circumstance—as in nearly all other instances the latter portion of a Gigue is the longer. There is not any attempt in either movement to introduce a subject of sufficiently marked character to justify its being called a second or distinctive theme.

The yearning after a fixed form, and the suggestion of the treatment which became expanded into the Sonata form may certainly be traced in Kühnau's "Frische Clavierfrüchte," seven Sonatas, published in 1703 (not in 1696, as some say). In melodic treatment and expansion of subject these show a decided advance. That which in Frescobaldi appeared to be a mere capricious change of *tempo*, in Kühnau became developed into movements of respectable length, but still without any remarkable development of chosen themes. Kühnau often makes the first subject of some of his movements heard in the dominant (whether the suite is in a major or a minor key) in the middle of a movement, but does not call, as it were, special attention to the fact by means of a double bar or a repeat. Johann Mattheson (1681-1722) frequently imitates his first subject in the second movement by inversion, and occasionally shows that he contributed something towards the settlement of form by the manner in which he treats his "Gigues," as may be seen in the example quoted *sub voce* "jig." His Sonata, published in 1713, and dedicated "to the person who shall best perform it" is in one movement only, and is capriccio-like in treatment. It may be here mentioned as an interesting fact that in the majority of the suites a Gigue is chosen as the concluding movement, and in its lively character as well as in the style of its construction is more in accordance with modern Sonata form than any other portion; this was the method often employed by Bach, Handel, and others to a later time. The thirty Sonatas of Alessandro Scarlatti (1659-1725), the next writer of importance after Mattheson, have each two movements, in which may be discerned a still further attempt to fix the style, and to impart some degree of unity.

Contemporary with Scarlatti was Tomaso Albinoni [1674-1745], whose Sonatas were at one time so popular in England, that the common fiddlers were able to play movements from them; but there is little indication of Sonata form in any one of his compositions. Domenico Alberti [1705-1739], whose name is associated with the arpeggio bass, said to have been invented by him, was one among the first, if not the very first who employed the nearest approach to modern Sonata form that had as yet been made. In his "VIII. Sonate per Cembalo" (1737), each one has two movements, and nearly each movement two well-defined subjects, properly introduced. With the exception of an occasional opening or closing chord, the whole of these movements are written in two-part harmony, and they are pleasingly effective. C, F, G major and minor, and A are the keys selected in obedience to the usual custom of the time of avoiding extreme keys, but Alberti employs accidentals freely for his bold and advanced modulations.

In the works of these earlier writers an advance towards the Sonata form may be traced, for in more than one there is a close upon the dominant in the first section, and the original subject is announced in the key of the dominant at the commencement of the second section; but there is little indication, if any at all, of what might be called a second or subsidiary theme.

In five out of eight of the Sonatas of Domenico Alberti, the Sonata form is nearly observed in the first movement, and often in the second, and there are few compositions of better construction, either for voices or instruments, of earlier date than his "Sonata in stilo nuovo" (1737).

Alberti's Sonatas are in two movements only, like those of many of those of his contemporaries and immediate successors, particularly those by Dr. Croft (1679-1727), Nicolo Porpora (1685-1767), Dr. Boyce (1710-1779), Fedeli (1715-1762), Carlo Tessarini (1715-1765), Frederic Theodor Schumann (1729-1760), Valentin Roeser (1740-1787), &c. Francesco Durante (1684-1755), who, as a teacher, enjoyed a high and honourable reputation, as a writer of Sonatas displays a refined and correct taste, but very little originality of conception, many of his thoughts being based upon the ideas of Scarlatti his master. The Sonatas and clavecin compositions of Domenico Scarlatti (1683-1757), were, according to Burney, "the wonder and delight of every hearer who had a spark of enthusiasm about him, and could feel new and bold effects, intrepidly produced by the breach of almost all the old and established rules of composition," but they contribute little towards a settlement of form.

It is probable that Handel noted the growth of the form, and occasionally employed it, some of the movements in his "Suites" having the orthodox first and second subject, while others have only a single subject in each section. Some of the songs in his Italian operas are almost in Sonata form, wanting only the observance of certain details.

Some of the Sonatas of Christopher Wagenseil (1688-1779) are in correct form, though the second subject is timidly introduced and employed. The lingering fondness for the same tonality, which is the characteristic of the Suites, and the earliest Sonatas, is to be found in Wagenseil; one of his Sonatas in the key of F, a fair specimen of his work in this style, has an *allegro assai* as the first movement, an *andante grazioso* as the second, and a *minuet* as the third. The first and last movements are in F major, and the *andante* in F minor. The collection in which this Sonata is to be found was published between 1740 and 1750.

The changes of *tempo* in the earliest compositions of this kind, probably suggested a division into separate movements. Inherent musical feeling would doubtless prompt the composer to make the several movements offer as much contrast as possible, and the variety thus introduced would be accepted as the first canon of this class of composition.

The arrangement of the earliest "Suites des pièces" may be studied with advantage in reference to this point. In the "Pièces de Clavecin" by François Couperin, 1713, there is a set in C minor, consisting of an Allemande, followed by a first and second Courante, then a Sarabande, a Gavotte, and finally a Minuet, each movement varying in *tempo* as well as in character, though not in key. The number of movements in a Suite alternated between five and seven for many years, but by degrees they became lessened in number. Although the names of dance tunes ceased to be attached to the several movements, it was easy to see that much of their character was retained; for as composers began to feel that the measure of the dance tune had a tendency to cramp their musical thoughts, their models were altered or abandoned, and they expanded their movements at pleasure, without reference to the needs of the dance. Later, when three movements were adopted, the dance tune was restored, a preference being given to the Minuet or something in its kind, and this, with a slow and a quick movement, for a long time made up the recognised constitution of a Sonata. Beethoven added a fourth movement, the Scherzo, which he used sometimes instead of, sometimes in addition to, the Minuet; but he was not, as some say, the inventor of that movement, as Haydn in his quartets, and Bach in his Suites had previously employed a movement called *Scherzo*.

The "Clavier-Uebung," of J. S. Bach, published singly between 1726 and 1730, marked in Hoffmeister's edition as Œuvre I., No. 1, containing six Suites in various keys, offers a very remarkable series of studies, inasmuch as they show the master mind yielding to the custom of his time in the order and style of the arrangements of his suites or Sonatas, but as free from conventionality as possible, and pointing in the direction so worthily followed by later writers. In the first number there are six movements, all in the key of B flat, namely, a *prelude*, an *allemande*, a *courante*, a *sarabande*, a *minuet* and *gigue*. Each, with the exception of the Prelude, is, as near as possible, in Sonata form, though the second subject is not always treated in the tonic in the second section. As usual, there is a second Minuet in the place now occupied by the trio, of which more presently. The second Suite is in C minor, and commences with a *symphony* or overture of two contrasted movements, but free in form: the next movement is an *allemande*, the first section closing on the dominant (G major); the third movement a *courante*, similarly written; the fourth a *sarabande*, with the first close in the relative major: the fifth is a *rondeau*, in the form proper to such pieces; the last is a *caprice*, the second

section having the first subject inverted. The third Suite, in A minor, opens with a *fantasia*, followed by an *allemande*, which is succeeded by a *courante*, more or less free in treatment. The next piece is a *sarabande* in good form, then a *burlesca*, next a *scherzo* in duple time (given as an illustration to the article "Scherzo"), lastly a *gigue* in fantasia style. The fourth Suite, in D major, begins with an *overture* of some length; then comes a *courante* not in form, then an *allemande*, then an *aria*, then a *sarabande*, the three last named obeying the rules of form; then there is a short *minuet* of two movements, and the last is a *gigue*. The fifth Suite, in G major, opens with what he calls a *preamble*, after which an *allemande*, a *courante*, a *sarabande*, a *tempo di minuetto*, a *passepied* and a *gigue*, the saraband only of all these movements answering to any extent the requirements of form. The sixth Suite, in E minor, the most remarkable and difficult of the whole set, begins with a long and beautiful *toccata*, having next an *allemande* with the close of the first section on the dominant B major, next a *courante*, treated in like fashion, then an air in rondo form, then a *gavotte* in Sonata form, a *sarabande*, written in fantasia style, and a *gigue* in the somewhat unusual *tempo* "alla breve," the first bar of which is quoted under the head "alla breve." In the third book of the second set, "Zweiter Theil der Clavier-übung," there is a minuet in B minor which, instead of a second minuet in the relative major, according to custom, has a "trio" in B minor; this is noteworthy, as it is probably the earliest instance of this use of the word. The construction and arrangement of this second set is so similar to the first, that with the exception just now pointed out, there is little or no point of difference to call for special remark.

The "Sechs leichte Clavier-Sonaten," of C. Philipp Emanuel Bach (1711-1788), published at Leipsic, 1766, contain each the orthodox three movements, a moderate, a slow and a quick; and the first, and sometimes the last movement of each is written in Sonata form, with the exception of No. 6, which begins with a movement in rondo form. Not one has the name of a dance tune attached, though there are several which would answer all needs, were they so named. Many of the Sonatas of his brother Wilhelm Friedemann Bach (1710-1784) though, cleverly and ably written, show a less regard for the symmetrical form so characteristic of the works of Philipp Emanuel. More than one of Friedemann's Sonatas, like those of the older writer, consist of a continuous movement with a frequent change of time, rhythm and tonality. Some portions fulfil all the requirements of form, but they are not marked for repetition. There are no separate and distinct movements, and the form chosen might be called, if not a caprice, at all events an original idea of the rondo, for after many and varied contrasts of time and subject, the Sonata often concludes with the phrase originally given out.

Schobert's Sonatas, published in 1741, are especially remarkable, because the second subjects are introduced in proper keys, after due preparation, although they are not so fully developed as those by later writers. There is an evident design in expanding the subjects to a greater extent than that which had been the custom before his time. So many of the Sonatas by E. Bach and Schobert are constructed according to Sonata form as now accepted, that the honour of having fixed the form may fairly be divided between these two composers.

Schobert's works were at one time the most popular of any performed in England, Dr. Burney having introduced them here in 1766. This writer makes a mistake when he says that Schobert published nothing until 1764, for he was already well known as a composer when he was invited to become " Musician to the Prince de Conti " in 1760, and copies of his Sonatas were in the hands of every harpsichord player before that time. Emanuel Bach knew Schobert's value as a musician, for Dr. Burney states that " his (Bach's) party allowed Schobert to be a man of genius, but spoiled by his affectation of a new and extraordinary style. They further accused him of frequently copying himself." His writing is perfectly individual, is fresh and novel, and more like an anticipation of Haydn and Mozart than Bach, from whom all the musicians of the time were wont to copy.

It is scarcely necessary to pursue the question further, or to enter into any elaborate argument in support of the claim of any particular musician to the invention of that to which probably all have contributed more or less. For at the period of time to which our inquiries have now led, the Sonatas of Haydn and Mozart became the recognised form of this species of composition, and they are happily so well known that a particular description is unnecessary. But, notwithstanding the existence of such noble models, not every composer of a Sonata cared to use the recognised or Sonata form ; even Cherubini, with his love for form, sometimes wrote Sonatas not in true form.

It is unnecessary, perhaps, to say that the Sonata was brought to its present perfection by Beethoven. The works of Clementi, the father of pianoforte - playing, Dussek,

Hummel, Weber, Field, Onslow, Moscheles, and Schubert show no further advance in progress in development.

A modern Sonata is generally constructed upon the following plan:—

The *first movement* is an *allegro*, sometimes with an introduction, but more frequently without one; the *second movement*, ordinarily called "the slow movement," is set in any time, between *adagio* and *andante;* and the *final movement* is an *allegro*, written either in Sonata or in rondo form. If there is a *fourth movement*, it is usually placed after the slow movement, and is either a scherzo or minuet and trio. This is the broad outline; the details require a little more particular description.

The first movement should have two themes, unlike each other in character ; for example, one vigorous and spirited, the other tender and expressive ; and each should be capable of varied treatment. After the first subject has been well announced, a modulation into the key of the dominant, if the subject starts in the major, and into the relative major if the subject commences in the minor, should be made. In either case the second subject must be heard in the changed key before the half close or perfect cadence concludes the first part of the *allegro*. In the second portion of the *allegro*, a greater amount of license is permitted, this section often partaking of the nature of a free fantasia. The two principal themes are subjected to all kinds of treatment, and are introduced in various keys at the will of the composer. Having exhausted all chosen devices, the first subject must now enter in its entirety, then the second subject should be heard, this time in the tonic or key in which the movement is written, if that mode be major ; or it may appear in the key of the tonic major, if the mode be minor ; but the episode and cadence which are to usher in the conclusion of this section, must be in the tonic key. Sometimes a coda, formed of a portion of the first subject, is added, and the movement ends in the key first proposed. This method of treatment is called the " Sonata " or " Binary " form.

The second movement may be written in several different ways, that is to say, treated like the first movement with two principal themes, or with only one principal theme.

Whatever be the precise form selected, the style of the music should afford a great contrast to that of the *allegro*.

The style of the last movement should afford a still greater contrast by its character, whatever be the form selected ; if it is a Rondo, it should be lighter than the first or second movements. Many instances could be quoted in which the final movement is made the vehicle for the expression of quaint musical humour.

Sonata da chiesa (*It.*) A church sonata, an organ sonata.

Sonate (*Fr.*) [Sonata.]

Sonatina (*It.*), **Sonatine** (*Fr.*) A short sonata. One in which the subjects are not developed at length.

Sonatore (*It.*) An instrumental performer.

Sonevole (*It.*) Sonorous, sounding, resonant.

Song. (1) A short poem intended for music. (2) A musical setting of a short poem or portion of prose. The word is generally applied to solos, but sometimes also to compositions for two or more voices. (3) The second subject of a sonata is sometimes called the "Song." [Air.] [Ballad.] [Lied.]

Sonometer. An instrument for measuring the vibrations of sounds.

Sonoramente (*It.*) Sonorously.

Sonore (*Fr.*), **Sonoro** (*It.*) Sonorous, resonant, harmonious.

Sonorità (*It.*) Harmony, resonance, sonorousness.

Sonorophone. A metal wind instrument of the Bombardon class.

Sons (*Fr.*) The name given by the Provençal poets to their lyrical productions.

Sons étouffés (*Fr.*) Stifled, veiled, or muffled tones. Sounds produced by a muted instrument.

Sons harmoniques (*Fr.*) Harmonic tones or sounds.

Sons pleins (*Fr.*) Full tones, applied to the production of full round tones by a voice or instrument.

Sonus (*Lat.*) Sound.

Sopra (*It.*) Above, before, over, upon, upper, as *Di sopra*, as above; *Come sopra*, as above or before; *Nella parte di sopra*, in the upper or higher part; *Contrappunto sopra il soggetto*, counterpoint over the subject.

Sopran (*Ger.*), **Soprano** (*It.*) The highest kind of female or boy's voice. Also the singer possessing that voice.

Soprana corda (*It.*) The highest string on the fiddle, *chanterelle.*

Soprano clef. The C clef upon the first line of the stave. [Clef.]

Sorda (*It.*) Muffled, veiled, muted, damped.

Sordamente (*It.*) Softly, gently, silently.

Sordini (*It.*) (1) Mutes. Small instruments of metal, bone, or wood made to fix upon the bridge of a violin to damp or deaden the sound, by intercepting the vibrations. Mutes of wood covered with leather, of a pear shape, are sometimes used to check the sound of horns, trumpets, cornets, clarinets and oboes, the mute being inserted in the bell. (2) When mutes are required during a performance, the direction *con sordini* is placed above the part so to be played, the contrary direction being *senza sordini.*

Sordino (*It.*) A small pocket fiddle, a *pochette* or *kit*, formerly used for the purpose of giving the pitch, &c., at music parties.

Sordo, sorda (*It.*) Damped with a mute; as, *clarinetto sordo, tromba sorda*, &c. [Sordini.]

Sordun, Sordono (*It.*) (1) An old form of wood wind instrument, having a double reed, with twelve ventages and two keys. (2) A sort of mute for a trumpet. (3) An organ reed stop of 16 ft. pitch.

Sortisatio (*Lat.*) Counterpoint *alla mente.* [Alla mente.] [Chant sur livre.]

Sortita (*It.*) (1) A word applied to the first piece sung by any one character in an opera. Thus, "Come per me" is the *aria sortita, aria d'entrata*, or entrance air for Amina in *La Sonnambula.* (2) A concluding voluntary, played as the congregation leaves the church.

Sospensivamente (*It.*) Doubtfully, irresolutely, waveringly.

Sospirando, Sospirante, Sospirevole, Sospiroso (*It.*) Sighing, subdued, wretched, doleful.

Sospiro (*It.*) A crotchet rest. In old music a minim rest.

Sost. Abb. of *Sostenuto.*

Sostenendo, Sostenuto (*It.*) Sustaining. Maintaining the tone for the full duration of the notes written.

Sotto (*It.*) Below, under; as, *sotto voce*, in an undertone; *sotto il soggetto*, below the subject.

Soubasse (*Fr.*) Sub-bass. A stop in the organ, of 32 ft. pitch.

Soubrette (*Fr.*) A serving maid. A female singer in a minor part of a comic opera.

Souchantre (*Fr.*) Succentor.

Souffárah (*Persian.*) The general name among the Persians and Arabs for wind instruments without reeds.

Soufflérie (*Fr.*) The apparatus connected with the bellows of an organ. [Organ.]

Souffleur (*Fr.*) (1) A prompter in a theatre. (2) An organ blower.

Soum. A Burmese harp.

Sound. [Acoustics.]

Sound-waves. [Acoustics § 3.]

Sound-board. (1) A piece of fir or other resonant wood placed behind the strings of a pianoforte for the purpose of increasing the power of the sounds. [Pianoforte.] (2) In an organ, the sound-board is that chamber of air into which the feet of the pipes are placed. [Organ.] (3) A wood screen placed behind a pulpit for the purpose of "reflecting" the preacher's voice; or over it, to prevent the sound from ascending into a lantern-tower, or a dome.

Sound-body. Sound-box. [Body.] [Resonance Box.]

Soupir (*Fr.*) A crotchet rest ℾ.

Soupir de croche (*Fr.*) A quaver rest ⅂.

Soupir de double croche (*Fr.*) A semiquaver rest ⅃.

Soupir de triple croche (*Fr.*) A demisemiquaver rest ⅄.

Sourdeline (*Fr.*) A small kind of bagpipe, or musette. [Bagpipe.]

Sourdine (*Fr.*) (1) A mute (Sordino.) (2) A stop on the harmonium, which by limiting the supply of wind to the lower half of the instrument, enables the performer to play full chords *piano*.

Sous (*Fr.*) Under; as, *Sous-dominante*, the sub-dominant or fourth of the scale. *Sous-mediante*, the sub-mediant, or sixth of the scale. *Sous-tonique*, the sub-tonic or seventh of the scale; the leading or *note sensible*.

Spaces. The intervals between the lines of the stave. The stave consists of five lines and includes four spaces, but notes in spaces between leger lines above and below the stave, are employed. [Stave.]

Spagnoletta (*It.*) A dance in the Spanish style.

Spanisches-Kreuz (*Ger.*) The Spanish cross, the sign of a double sharp, 𝄪.

Spanish guitar. [Guitar.]

Spart. [Sparto.]

Sparto (*It.*) Scattered, distributed; hence, *a Score*, as the parts are arranged on several lines. [Score.]

Spartito (*It.*) Scored.

Spassapensiere (*It.*) Jew's harp.

Spatium (*Lat.*) } (1) A space on the stave,
Spazio (*It.*) } (2) an interval.

Spianto (*It.*) Smooth, level, even.

Spiccatamente (*It.*) Brightly, brilliantly.

Spiccato (*It.*) Distinct, detached, pointed. The direction for this is by *dots* over notes. [Bowing.]

Spielart (*Ger.*) Manner of playing, method of performance.

Spielen (*Ger.*) To play upon an instrument.

Spieler (*Ger.*) A player.

Spielmanieren (*Ger.*) Ornaments, graces, *broderies*.

Spinæ (*Lat.*) *Lit.*, thorns. A name given to the quills and jacks of a spinet, and sometimes to the instrument itself.

Spinet. Couched harp. *Spinett* (*Ger.*) *Spinetta* (*It.*) *Épinette* (*Fr.*) An ancient keyed instrument similar in construction to, but smaller in size than, the Harpsichord. The strings, which were placed at an angle

with the keys, were sounded by means of leather or quill plectra (Spinæ.) [Clarichord.] [Harpsichord.] [Pianoforte.] [Virginals.]

Spirito, con, } (*It.*) In a spirited,
Spiritosamente } lively, animated, brisk
Spiritoso } manner.

Spirituale (*It.*) Sacred, spiritual.

Spirituel (*Fr.*) Ideal, pure, ethereal.

Spissa (*Lat.*) Close. (1) Intervals in the enharmonic and chromatic genus were said to be *spissa*, (πυκνά.) (2) In mediæval music a *pycnon* (πυκνόν) or *spissum* was a *semitone*.

Spitzflöte, Spindelflöte (*Ger.*) *Cuspida, flauto cuspido* (*It.*) An organ stop of 8 ft. or 4 ft. pitch, consisting of open flue-pipes, of a conical shape. Its tone is thin and reedy. *Spitzquint*, a quint-stop or twelfth of conical pipes.

Spondalium, *or* **Spondaulium** (*Lat.*) A Hymn sung during a sacrifice, accompanied by a flute.

Spondee (*Lat.*) A musical foot consisting of two long syllables. [Metre.]

Sprung (*Ger.*) A skip.

Square-piano. [Pianoforte.]

Squillante (*It.*) Ringing, sounding, bell-like in tone, from *squilla*, a little bell.

Sroutis. The name of the twenty-two parts into which the Hindu scale is divided.

Sta (*It.*) As it stands; to be performed as written.

Stabat Mater. A well-known Latin Hymn on the crucifixion, sung during Passion week in the Roman Catholic Church. Jacopone, a Franciscan who lived in the thirteenth century, is supposed to have been the author of the words. In addition to the ancient setting, probably contemporary with the words, many composers have written music to the Stabat Mater, but the compositions which are best known are those by Palestrina, Pergolesi, the last effort of his life, and Rossini. The first of these three is a noble work, the second is full of pathos and expression, and the last is a quaint unison of operatic effects and florid vocal writing.

Stabile (*It.*) Firm, steady.

Stacc. Abb. of Staccato.

Staccare (*It.*) To make *staccato*.

Staccatissimo (*It.*) As *staccato* as possible.

Staccato (*It.*) Detached, taken off, separated. In music the word signifies a detached, abrupt method of singing or playing certain notes, by making them of less duration than they otherwise would be. A small dash over a note signifies that it is to be played *staccato*.

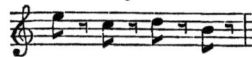
Written.   *Played.*

Sometimes a dot over a note is called a

staccato mark, but it is more properly the sign of a *spiccato*. Staccato notes are played shorter than those marked *spiccato*.

Stadtmusikanten, Stadtpfeiffer, Stadt-zinkenisten, Kunstpfeiffer, Hausleute (*Ger.*) Town musicians. [Waits.]

Staff. [Stave.]

Stammakkord (*Ger.*) A key-chord or fundamental chord.

Stampita (*It.*) A sonata, an air, a song.

Standard pitch. [Pitch.]

Ständchen (*Ger.*) A serenade.

Standhaft (*Ger.*) Firm, steady, steadfast.

Stanghetta (*It.*) A bar-line. The vertical line placed on the stave to mark the division of bars.

Stanza (*It.*) *Lit.*, A station or resting place. (1) A series of metrical lines forming a verse or subdivision of a poem. (2) A strophe.

Stark (*Ger.*) Strong, loud; as, *mit starken Stimmen*, with loud stops.

Stave. Linien-system (*Ger.*) Portée (*Fr.*) (1) A term applied to the five horizontal and parallel lines in music, upon which the notes or rests are supported.

(2) Kircher describes a Greek manuscript which he found in the Jesuits' library of S. Salvator at Messina, the age of which he declared to be more than seven hundred years, in which hymns are set to music, written on staves of eight lines, no use being made of the intermediate spaces. Guido d'Arezzo, to whom the invention of the stave is usually assigned, may only have reduced the number of the lines, by making use of the spaces as steps in representing diatonic degrees. In the thirteenth century the number of lines was further reduced to four, a number still found sufficient for the purposes of the Plain Song.

Staves of various numbers, from three to six lines, are found in mediæval music, and in fact it was not until the invention of printing that the number of lines was settled at five. It is by no means an unusual thing to find six lines ruled in manuscript music books of the seventeenth and early part of the eighteenth centuries, and in some of the early printed books a variable number of lines is occasionally found. Frescobaldi in his "Tocate, canzone versi d'Hinni Magnificat, Gagliardi, Correnti, et Altri Partite di Cimbalo et organo," which was printed from copper plates in 1637, employs a stave of eight lines.

The stave of eleven lines, called also the "grand stave," has been in use for many generations; the following from, "L'Armonica pratico el Cimbalo di Francesco Gaspa-

rini," Venice, 1729, shows the form with the clefs then in use in Italy.

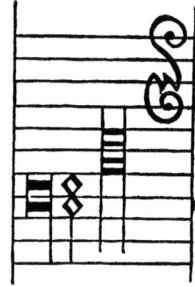

Sir John Hawkins, in his "History of the Science and Practice of Music," quotes a canzona from Frescobaldi's collection, but he has modernised the stave. Although five is now the general number of lines employed as the stave for all voices and instruments, yet it is by no means an unfrequent thing to find a stave of one line only for pulsatile instruments with a single unvarying tone, as cymbals, gongs, triangle, great drum, &c.

(3) In modern music the position of the clef upon the stave gives a special title to the stave; the G clef upon the second line, the C clef upon the first, second, third or fourth lines, and the F clef upon the fourth line, cause the stave to be known as the treble, soprano, mezzo-soprano, alto, tenor or bass staves respectively. A double stave, with the G and F clefs connected by a brace, is used for pianoforte and organ music, &c.

(4) A stanza, a portion of a song. A verse.

Steg (*Ger.*) The bridge of a violin, &c. *Ponticello* (*It.*), *Chevalet* (*Fr.*)

Stem. *Cauda* (*Lat.*), *Virgula* (*Lat.*) The line attached to the head of a note. All notes but the semibreve, or whole-note, have stems; quavers and their subdivisions have stems and hooks. In writing a " single part" for a voice or instrument, it is usual to turn the stems of notes lying below the middle line of the stave *upwards*, of notes lying above the middle line *downwards*. Notes on the middle line have their stems up or down as seems best, *e.g.* :

When two parts are written on one line, the tails of the upper part are *always* turned upwards, those of the lower part downwards. When both parts play the same note the stem is drawn both up and down, and if it is a semibreve, two notes intersect each other, *e.g.* :

In *short* score, or a compression of four parts into two lines, the tails of notes in the treble part are always turned up, those of the alto down, those of the tenor up, those of the bass down ; the treble and alto parts being confined to the upper stave, the tenor and bass to the lower, *e.g.* :

In groups of notes falling between the upper and lower stave the stems are sometimes partly up and partly down for convenience, *e.g.* :

Up to the middle of the seventeenth century each note having a stem and hook was printed separately, instead of being bound together as in the above groups of semiquavers. [Printing of Music.] In mediæval music, for a short period, the position of the stem, up or down, affected the length of the note.

Stentando (*It.*) Delaying, retarding.

Stentato (*It.*) Forced, emphasised.

Steso (*It.*) Extended, spread, diffused. *Steso moto*, slow movement.

Stesso (*It.*) The same. *L'istesso tempo*, the same time.

Sthenochire. A hand strengthener. A machine for imparting strength and flexibility to the fingers for pianoforte-playing.

Sticcado *or* **Sticcato.** An instrument composed of pieces of wood of graduated lengths, flat at the bottom and rounded at the top, resting on the edges of an open box, and tuned to a diatonic scale. The tone is produced by striking the pieces of wood with small hard balls at the end of a flexible stick. A similar instrument made of glass or metal is called a Harmonicon. [Gigelira.]

Stiefel (*Ger.*) Boot of a reed-pipe in an organ. [Organ.]

Stift (*Ger.*) The jack of a spinet or harpsichord. [Jack.]

Stil (*Ger.*) Style.

Stile (*It.*) Style. [Stilus.]

Still-gedact (*Ger.*) An organ stop of soft tone.

Stilus (*Lat.*) Style, as, *stilus choraicus* (*stilo coraico*, *It.*) the dance style ; *stilus ecclesiasticus* (*stile ecclesiastico*, *It.*) the church style ; *stilus familiaris* (*stile familiare*, *It.*) the simple style, note against note ; *stilus*

hyporchematicus, the theatrical style ; *stilus madrigalescus*, the madrigal style ; *stilus melismaticus*, the florid style ; *stilus motecticus*, the motet style ; *stilus phantasticus* (*stile fantastico*, *It.*) the fantasia style ; *stilus recitativus* (*stile rappresentativo* or *drammatico*, *It.*) the dramatic style ; *stilus syllabicus*, the syllabic style, in which not more than one note is given to each syllable ; *stilus symphoniacus* (*stile sinfonico*, *It.*) the instrumental style.

Stimme (*Ger.*) (1) The voice. (2) Sound. (3) The sound-post of a violin or violoncello. (4) A part in vocal or instrumental music. (5) An organ stop, or rank of pipes.

Stimmgabel (*Ger.*) Tuning-fork.

Stimmhölzchen (*Ger.*) Sound-post of a fiddle, &c.

Stimmhorn (*Ger.*) Tuning cone. [Organ.]

Stimmpfeife (*Ger.*) A pitch-pipe.

Stimmschlüssel, Stimmhammer (*Ger.*) A tuning key.

Stimmstock (*Ger.*) The sound-post of a violin or violoncello.

Stinguendo (*It.*) Fading away, dying away.

Stiracchiato, Stirato (*It.*) Widening, enlarging, retarding the time.

Stockfagott. [Rackett.]

Stonante (*It.*) Discordant, untuneful.

Stop. (1) The pressure by the fingers of the strings upon the fingerboard of a stringed instrument. (2) A fret upon a guitar or similar instrument. (3) A collection, register, or row of pipes in an organ.

Stopped diapason. [Organ.]

Stopper. The plug inserted in the top of an organ pipe, in order to " close " it.

Stopples. Plugs inserted in some of the ventages of the flute in order to accommodate its scale to some particular mode.

Storto, Storta (*It.*) A name formerly given to the horn, serpent, &c., because of their twisted form.

Strain. A musical subject forming part of, and having relation to, a general whole. At one time every subordinate portion of a composition either marking rhythmical pauses or completed sentences was distinguished by a double bar, and therefore the double bar was held to mark the strain, a practice which is still observed in writing chants and hymn tunes, where the double bar marks a strain, but not a completed phrase or subject.

Strascicando (*It.*) Dragging or drawling.

Strascicato (*It.*) Dragged, drawled.

Strascinando (*It.*) [Strascicando.]

Strascinando l'arco (*It.*) Drawing or dragging the bow over the strings so as to bind the notes together.

Strascino (*It.*) A drag or slur ; a term applied to a slurring movement from sound down to sound, the pace at the same time being slightly slackened.

Strathspey. A Scotch dance in duple time, invented about the beginning of the 18th century, and first danced in Strathspey, from whence it derives its name. The " Scotch Snap " is one of the peculiarities of the tunes for this dance.

Stravagante (*It.*) Extravagant, capricious, fantastical.

Stravaganza (*It.*) Extravagance, eccentricity.

Streichinstrument (*Ger.*) A stringed instrument played by the *stroke* of a bow.

Streichquartett (*Ger.*) String quartet.

Streichzither (*Ger.*) A zither played with a bow.

Strene. The name given by Marbecke to a breve.

Two explanations have been given of the meaning of the word *strene;* the first is, that it is a note which may be *stretched* or *strained* for the purpose of recitation ; the second is that is bounded or *constrained* by two lines. Marbecke's use of the note certainly does not justify the first of these meanings.

Streng (*Ger.*) Strict, severe, rigid. *Streng gebunden,* strictly, tied or legato, exceedingly smooth. *Streng in tempo,* strictly in time. *Strenge Fuge,* a strict fugue.

Strepito (*It.*) Noise.

Strepitosamente (*It.*) Noisily.

Strepitoso (*It.*) Noisy, impetuous.

Stretta (*It.*) A coda, a final passage taken in quicker time than the preceding movements. The conclusion of the chorus in Haydn's *Creation,* " The heavens are telling," is a *stretta.*

Stretto (*It.*) Contracted, close. A stretto in a fugue is the bringing closely together the subject and its answer. [Fugue.]

Striking-reed. A percussion reed. [Reed.]

String. Abb. of *stringendo.*

String. Prepared wire or catgut, plain or covered, used for musical instruments. Strings of steel or brass wire are used for all instruments which are struck with hammers or plectra, as dulcimers, zithers, mandolines, and pianofortes, and strings of catgut for instruments played with the unprotected fingers, or with a bow, as guitars, harps, violins, violas, violoncellos, and double-basses. Violin strings are made of catgut, each string being of a different thickness according to the tone and tension required, the fourth string being covered with a fine wire either of silver or white metal; hence it is called the silver string. Violas and violoncellos have each two silver strings, the object in using covered strings being to ensure a sufficient gravity of tone without having too clumsy a material. The covered strings on the guitar

are upon a basis of silk instead of catgut, and the double bass strings are of thick gut uncovered. A large quantity of catgut strings for musical instruments is made in England, but the best are imported from Italy, which has, from time immemorial, been famous in this branch of industry. Rome, Venice, Pistoja, Lyons, were mentioned by Thomas Mace, 1676, as the most famous places from whence strings were brought in his day.

Silk has been sometimes used as the material of first violin strings, but with questionable success.

Among uncivilised people strings are made of the hair of animals, the fibres of creeping plants, of fibrous roots of trees, of cane, and of thongs of leather.

Stringendo (*It.*) Pressing, hastening on the time.

String-gauge. A small instrument for measuring the thickness of strings for violins, guitars, &c., consisting of a disc or an oblong piece of metal, with a graduated slit and engraved table.

String Organ. A new musical instrument, the sounds of which are produced by the association of a free reed and wire string in the following manner : " Near the extremity of a free reed is attached a small rod or pin, which is in turn fastened to a point near the middle of a steel pianoforte wire properly stretched above it in the same linear direction, and the reed is then excited by a harmonium bellows." The tone produced is very sweet and pure, and by graduating the size of the reed, and thickness and tension of the string, a very extensive compass can be obtained. Mr. John Farmer, of Harrow, some years ago made experiments on this method of obtaining musical sounds, and so interested his pupil, Mr. J. Baillie Hamilton, that he has since that time devoted himself enthusiastically to the development of its resources, with every prospect of success.

String quartet. (1) A composition in four parts ; for two violins, viola and violoncello. (2) The group of stringed instruments in a band.

Strisciando (*It.*) Creeping, gliding, slurring smoothly from one note to another.

Strofa (*It.*) A strophe. [Stanza.]

Strohfiedel (*Ger.*) [Gigelira.]

Stroke of the bow. [Bowing.]

Strombettare (*It.*) To sound a trumpet.

Strombettiere (*It.*) A trumpet-player.

Stromentato (*It.*) Instrumented, scored for an orchestra.

Stromento (*It.*) An instrument. *Stromento di fiato* or *di vento,* a wind instrument. *Stromento di corda,* a stringed instrument.

Strophe (*Gk.*) στροφή. *Lit.,* A turning. The turning of the Greek Chorus towards a particular part of the orchestra in dancing; as *antistrophe* (ἀντιστροφή) was their *returning.* Hence, the term came to be applied to the portions of the poem sung during these movements.

Stubenorgel (*Ger.*) A chamber organ.

Stück (*Ger.*) A piece, air, tune, composition.

Study. A term applied to an exercise for the pianoforte or other instrument.

Stufe (*Ger.*) A step, a degree. *Stufe der Tonleiter,* a degree of the scale.

Stürmisch (*Ger.*) Boisterously, furiously, impetuously.

Style. Character, form, or temperament of music with reference to, (1) the result of individual influence; as, *Handel's style, Spohr's style;* (2) the conformity of music to the purpose for which it was written, as the *Church style,* the *Glee style;* (3) the conventional or national method of performance; as, the *Italian style,* the *Scotch style;* (4) its construction; as, the *Chromatic style,* the *Fugue style.*

Suabe flute. [Flute.]

Suave (*It.*) Sweet, agreeable, pleasant.

Suavemente, Suavità, con (*It.*) Sweetly, with delicacy.

Sub-bass, Sub-bourdon. A pedal register in the organ of 32 ft. tone. [Organ.]

Sub-chanter. Succentor.

Subdiapente, Subdominant. The fifth below or the fourth above any key note.

Subduple proportion. [Proportio.]

Subitamente, Subito (*It.*) Suddenly, without pause. *Volti subito,* turn quickly.

Subject. The theme or principal phrase of any movement, from which all the subordinate ideas spring or are developed. In sonata form there should be two chief subjects, called first and second; in rondo form, one is sufficient. In a fugue the subject is called also the exposition, dux, proposition. [Fugue.] [Sonata.]

Submediant. The sixth of the scale.

Suboctave. A coupler in the organ which pulls down keys one octave below those which are struck.

Subprincipal. An organ stop consisting of open pipes, of 32 ft. pitch on the pedals, and of 16 ft. pitch on the manuals.

Subsemifusa (*Lat.*) A demisemiquaver.

Subsemitone. [Leading note.]

Subsemitonium modi (*Lat.*) The leading note.

Subtonic. The leading note. *Note sensible* (*Fr.*) Master-note, the semitone below the tonic.

Succentor, Sub-chanter, Sou-chantre (*Fr.*) An officer of the choir, the deputy of the Præcentor, appointed by the Dean and Chapter of a cathedral. In "Cathedralia" we find that :—" The succentor originally led the antiphonal chant on the side opposite the Præcentor, as S. Augustine includes under *cantores* the præcentor ' qui vocem præmittit in cantu;' and the succentor ' qui subsequenter canendo respondet.' The succentor major of canons was first instituted at Wells A.D. 1130-74. At Hereford the succentor or præcentor presented absent Vicars. The sub-chanter at York directed the minor canons, and the succentor, as in other cathedrals, was the præcentor's vicar, with regard to vicars-choral and songmen, and delated offenders to the Saturday chapter. At Chichester and Exeter he tabled the duties of the vicars in the week. At Salisbury and York he ranked next to the archdeacons. He supplied the præcentor's place during absence, and ruled the song-school by his officer. At Wells and Lichfield he wrote out all chants not in the table, arranged the method and order of the processions, enjoined the lections on greater doubles and in masses, and after Benedicite on Saturday in chapter arranged the table of services for the ensuing week. At St. Paul's he acts in the præcentor's absence, as regards the regulation of the service, and in olden times had to be obeyed by major canons, minor canons, and all other ministers. At Chichester his duty was to give stripes, seven or fourteen in his discretion, to the boys, if they behaved badly in the choir, and at Hereford his duty was to bear the ' burden' of the psalmody and chant, to distribute copes on the greater festivals, to order processions, to punish clerks of the first form who were not of the family of a canon, and suspend others offending. He delated offenders to the chapter, he took care that the singing was reverently conducted, and appointed five boys of clerks of the first form, removeable at his will, to sing the antiphons, and to carry tapers and thuribles. An honest robe, shoes, and stockings were provided for these boys out of the allowances of the succentor."

Succession. (1) The order in which the notes of a melody proceed. There are two sorts of succession, regular or conjoint, and disjunct. A regular or conjoint succession is that in which the notes succeed each other in the order of the scale to which they belong, either ascending or descending. In a disjunct succession the melody is formed of intervals greater than a second.

(2) A sequence is sometimes spoken of as a succession, and passages of similar chords or progressions are described as a succession of thirds, fourths, fifths, sixths, sevenths or octaves, as the case may be.

Sudden modulation. [Modulation.]

Sufflöte, Sifflöte (*Ger.*) [Flute.]

Suite (*Fr.*) A set, series, or succession of movements in music. The term was applied at an early period to collections of dance tunes of contrasted character but similar tonality. Galliards and Pavins chiefly formed the Suites composed until the middle of the seventeenth century. After which, almains, or allemands, corantos, grounds (passecailles), sarabands, jigs, minuets, passepieds, gavots, &c., were more favoured; and in the middle of the eighteenth century the titles of all the dances were dropped with the exception of the minuet, which was retained. Then the Suite became a Sonata, and the word Sonata, instead of being loosely applied to "Suits of Lessons for the Harpsichord," became employed to describe a composition of definite form and arrangement.

Suivez (*Fr.*) Follow. A direction to an accompanist to watch the singer or soloist, and accommodate the accompaniment to his singing or playing.

Sujet (*Fr.*) A subject, melody, phrase or theme.

Sul, Sull', Sulla (*It.*) On, upon, by. *Sulla soprano corda*, upon the first string; *sul ponticello*, by or near the bridge, in violin playing; *sulla tastiera*, upon the key-board.

Sultana. A violin with strings of wire in pairs, like the cither or cittern. It was similar to the *Streichzither*.

Summation tones. [Acoustics, § 19.]

Suo loco (*It.*) In its own place, in the register as written.

Suonata (*It.*) A sonata. *Suonata di camera*, a chamber sonata, a secular piece. *Suonata di chiesa*, sonata for the organ, piece for church use.

Super (*Lat.*) Above, over. *Superdominant*, the note next above the dominant. The sixth of the scale. *Supertonic*, the second of the scale.

Superfluous intervals. Those intervals greater by a semitone than major or perfect. [Interval.]

Superius (*Lat.*) A name given to the upper part in a composition by the writers of the sixteenth century.

Superoctave. (1) An organ stop tuned two octaves above the diapasons. (2) A coupler pulling down keys one octave above those struck.

Supersus. A term formerly applied to high treble parts.

Supertonique (*Fr.*) Supertonic.

Supplichevole (*It.*), **Supplichevolmente** (*It.*) In an imploring, supplicating manner.

Supposed bass. A term applied to any bass note forming one of the inversions of a chord, in contradistinction to the real bass or generator.

E is the supposed, C the real bass.

Sur (*Fr.*) Upon, on, over. *Sur la quatrième corde*, upon the fourth string; *sur une corde*, on one string.

Suspended cadence. An interrupted cadence. [Cadence.]

Suspension. The holding or prolongation of a note in any chord into the chord which follows, thereby often producing a discord. The first appearance of the note to be suspended is called its preparation; its presence as a discord, its percussion; its removal to a note of *rest in key*, or some legitimate sound of a sequence, its resolution. Suspensions are named after the interval of the note forming the discord. Two suspended notes form a *double* suspension; three a *triple* suspension, and so on. The intervals most commonly suspended are the fourth, sixth, seventh, and ninth.

The percussion of a discord of suspension is generally on the strong accent of a bar.

The above (Ex. 1) shows the suspension 4 3 on every note of the scale. It cannot legitimately appear on the subtonic, owing to the imperfection of the fifth.

The next (Ex. 2) shows suspended sixths on every degree of the scale but the seventh, on which it is not considered a genuine suspension.

The next (Ex. 3) shows that suspended

sevenths can occur on every degree of the scale.

Ex. 3.

7 6 7 6 7 6 7 6

7 6 7 6 7 6

In the following (Ex. 4) a ninth is suspended on every degree of the scale. The chord marked * is rarely met with, and probably would not be tolerated unless as part of sequence such as that in which it occurs.

Ex. 4.

9 8   9 8   9 8   9 8

9 8   9 8   9 8

In Ex. 5, at *a* will be found the double suspension $\frac{9}{4}\frac{8}{3}$; at *b* the double suspension $\frac{9}{7}\frac{8}{6}$; at *c* the triple suspension $\frac{9}{6}\frac{8}{5}$; at *d* the triple suspension $\frac{9}{7}\frac{8}{4}$; at *e* the quadruple suspension $\frac{9}{7}\frac{8}{5}\frac{.}{3}$.
$\frac{6}{4}$

a   b   c

Ex. 5.

9 8   9 8   9 8
4 3   7 6   6 5
              4 3

d   e

9 8   9 8
7 6   7 5
4 3   6 3
          4

An exhaustive list of suspensions has never yet been attempted. The constant use of chromatic progressions in modern music has led to the formation of a vast number of *chromatic* suspensions which early writers on

harmony never could have anticipated, and which modern theorists make no attempt to explain.

Süss (*Ger.*) Sweet.

Sussurando, Sussurante (*It.*) Whispering, murmuring.

Sustained note. A name given to prolonged notes which partake of the character of a pedal-point by their immunity from ordinary harmonic rules, but which cannot with propriety be called pedal-points owing to their occurrence in the middle or upper part, *e.g.* :

Soprani.   Beethoven's Mass in C.

Svegliato (*It.*) Awakened, brisk, lively.
Svelto (*It.*) Swift, light, quick, free, easy.
Swell. [Organ.]
Symphonion. A combination of the pianoforte and harmonium, invented by Kauffman of Dresden.

Symphony, Symphonie (*Fr.*), **Sinfonia** (*It.*) (1) A composition for an orchestra, similar in construction to the sonata, which is usually for a single instrument. A symphony has several varied movements, generally four, never less than three. The first, an allegro ; the second, a largo, or andante ; the third, a scherzo, or minuet and trio ; and the fourth, an allegro. The form of the first and last movement is usually that of the sonata. The scherzo, or the minuet, in some symphonies is placed before instead of after the slow movement.

The arrangement of the symphony after this order is due to Haydn. About the same period Gossec composed a symphony, the twenty-first out of twenty-nine of which he was the author, which was a decided advance in musical form, not only upon his own previous compositions, but also upon those of others. Gossec's symphonies are of varied character, and according to the short description given by Fétis, belong chiefly to the class of concerto rather than to that of symphony, as they are for the most part for certain obbligati instruments. The "Symphonie en ré," written for the "Concert des Amateurs," gave the first impulse towards the perfection of instrumentation in France. It was written for two violins, viola, violoncello, contrabass, two oboes, two clarinets, a flute, two bassoons, two horns, two trumpets, and drums. " L'effet en fut très remarquable." It is, however, to Haydn that the perfecting of the symphony is due. For he possessed an extensive acquaintance with the character and resources of every known orchestral instrument. " If any doubts arose during composition, his situation at Eisenstadt gave him the power of resolving them into certainties immediately. He rang the bell for a rehearsal, the performers appeared, he caused them to execute the doubtful passages two or three various ways, and making his choice of one of them, dismissed the orchestra, and returned to his labours." [Sonata.]

(2) Formerly overtures were called symphonies; in the Dublin MS. of the " Messiah," the property of Sir Frederick Ouseley, Handel has called the overture " Sinfonica," and it was a common practice in his time to name any long instrumental piece after this manner.

(3) The introductory, intermediate, and concluding instrumental parts of a song or other vocal piece are also called symphonies.

(4) In the seventeenth century the virginal was sometimes spoken of as a symphony.

(5) A bagpipe has also been called a symphony, perhaps a corruption of the word *sampogna.*

Symposiac. A term applied to cheerful and convivial compositions for voices, as glees, catches, rounds, &c.

Synaphe (*Gk.*) The conjunction of two tetrachords. [Greek Music.]

Synaulia (*Gk.*) A concert of flute players performing alternately.

Syncopation, Syncopatio (*Lat.*), **Syncope** (*Fr.*) Suspension or alteration of rhythm by driving the accent to that part of a bar not usually accented. Syncopation may be completed in a bar :

Or it may be carried by sequence through several bars :

Or it may be so that more than one bar is involved in the syncopation :

Syncopated counterpoint is the fourth species of counterpoint.

Syncopiren (*Ger.*) To syncopate. [Syncopation.]

Synnemenon. [Greek Music.]

Syren. [Acoustics.]

Syrinx. [Pan's Pipes.]

Szopelka (*Russ.*) A kind of oboe, about fifteen inches in length, made of elder wood, having a brass mouth-piece and eight large and seven small finger holes. It is a popular instrument in Southern Russia, and is the Western representative of the Eastern *Zourna.*

T.

T. Abb. of tasto, *t.s.*, *tasto solo*, manuals only; also of *tenor*, and *tutti*.

Ta, te, tee, to. (τα, τε, τη, τω) (*Gk.*) Syllables used by the Greeks for purposes of solmization.

Taballo (*It.*) Kettle-drum.

Tabarde, *or* Tabarte (*Old Eng.*) Tabor.

Tabl. An Egyptian drum formed from a hollowed block of wood, or made of earthenware, with a skin stretched over one end.

Tablature (*Fr.*) Intavolatura (*It.*) Tablatur (*Ger.*) (1) A general name for all the signs and characters used in music. Those who were well acquainted with these signs were said to sing by the Tablature. (2) A peculiar system of notation employed for instruments of the lute class, for viols, and certain wind instruments. The earliest systems of notation, like the music of Asiatic nations to this day, were different sorts of Tablature of the character shown in the following example from Fétis:—

NOTES OF A PIPE IN TABLATURE.

TABLATURE NOTES TRANSLATED BY FÉTIS.

That which may be called the modern Tablature was invented not earlier than the sixteenth century. The general character of the tablature employed was nearly the same in England, France, Spain, and Italy, though each country made variations in it according to fancy, and sometimes the several professors who taught in those countries had little peculiarities of their own in which they differed from their brother professors. These differences doubtless contributed towards making the general system as perfect as it could be in the end. Sir John Hawkins, quoting Mersennus, says that several skilful men had laboured to improve the Tablature, but they affected to make a mystery of it, and this gave rise to a diversity of notation between them. It is therefore probable that systems of writing in Tablature were in existence long before the publication of treatises on the subject. Adrien le Roy, a bookseller in Paris, published about 1570 a book with the title of " Briefve et

facile Instruction pour apprendre la Tablature, à bien accorder, conduire, et disposer la main sur la Guiterne;" the popularity of this work was so great that it was translated into sundry languages as soon as possible after publication. An English translation, the basis of all subsequent systems published in England, was made by one signing himself with the initials F. K., and published by John Kingston in 1574.

The tuning of the lute according to Adrien le Roy was as follows:—

so that, with the use of the frets, usually eight, and lettered from *a*, the open string, to *i*, each string was capable of giving a minor sixth from its open tone. The letters refer to the frets which were on the finger-board, each fret representing a semitone, the letter *a* always standing for the open string. The horizontal lines stand for the strings, and the letters, the points at which they are to be stopped, so forming the notes of the composition. The signs for time were

 Semibreve.

 Minim.

 Crotchet.

 Quaver.

 Semiquaver.

placed over the stave, and were intended to correspond with the semibreve, minim, crotchet, &c., respectively. It was to be understood that the sign after the bar represented the value of all the notes in that bar unless otherwise contradicted.

which being translated into ordinary notation would read:—

It is a remarkable fact that while in music the ordinary notation bars were either entirely omitted, or used as guides to the eye rather than as exact divisions of the notes into measurable bars, in Tablature the bars were more often properly divided according to the value of the time signature than not. An earlier publication than that of Adrien le Roy is the *Lautten Buch* of Wolf Heckel, a writer concerning whom nothing is known, beyond the fact of the production of this book, copies of which are extremely rare; one is preserved among the treasures of the Sacred Harmonic Society's library. It bears date Strasbourg, 1562, and its title runs thus, " Lautten Buch, von mancherley schönen und lieblichen stucken, mit zweyten lautten zusammen zuschlagen, und auch sonst das mehrer theyl allein für sich selbst. Gute Teutsche, Lateinsche, Frantzösische, Italienische Stuck oder lieder. Auch vilfaltige Newe Tentz, sampt mancherley Fantaseyen, Recercari, Pavani, Saltarelli, und Gassenhawer, &c." The book is an oblong quarto, printed in a bold type, and the Tablature is entirely different to that employed by the English, French, or Italian writers for the lute, as the following example will show, when compared with the other specimens.

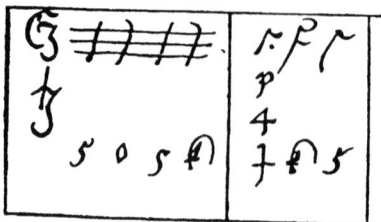

The above cut shows the first two bars of the Tablature of the dance tune given under " Gassenhawer."

The Italian and Spanish writers employed figures instead of letters to indicate the particular fret to be used, as in " Il Fronimo, Dialogo sopra l'arte del ben intavolare e rettamente suonare la Musica," Venezia 1583, by Vincentio Galilei—the father of the famous mathematician. In the " Nobilta di Dame," Venice, 1605, the tunes are set in " l'Intavolatura del Liuto " as well as in the ordinary notation. The Italian Tablature was used in England for MS. lute music, as shown in the subjoined specimen from a book written about the end of the sixteenth or beginning of the seventeenth century.

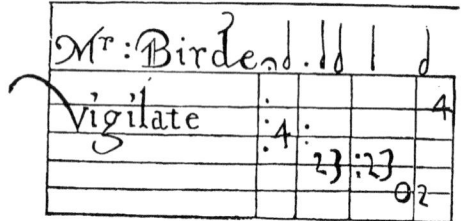

Guitar music was written in " an Alphabet."

The above specimen is taken from Kapsperger's " Libro Primo di Villanelle à 1, 2 et 3 voci accommodate per qual si vogliæ strumento con l'intavolatura del Chitarone et *alfabeto* per la Chitarra Spagnuola," Rome, 1610. The Tablature for the arch-lute (Chitarone) is after the ordinary Italian manner, while the alphabet for the guitar is placed over the usual notation, implying, however, the employment of a single note at a time only, and answering the purpose of figures for fingering, as in elementary pianoforte music of the present day, unless the letters refer to a system of chords. The precise value of this "Alfabeto" is not now clear.

In England Tablature was employed for all stringed instruments, and as those most in use at the end of the sixteenth century were those plucked by the fingers, the greater number of the early specimens existing refer to this class of instrument. The following portion of an "Almaine for the Lute"

is to be found in "A new Booke of Tablature, containing sundry easie and familiar Instructions, shewing howe to attaine to the knowledge to guide and dispose thy hand to play on sundrie Instruments, as the Lute, Orpharion, and Bandora: Together with divers new Lessons to each of these Instruments. Whereunto is added an Introduction to Pricke-Song, and certain familliar rules of Descant, with other necessary Tables plainely shewing the true vse of the Scale or Gamut, and also how to set any Lesson higher or lower at your pleasure. Collected together out of the best Authors professing the practise of these Instruments." London, 1596.

A like form of Tablature was employed for viols, as in John Dowland's second book of Songs or Ayres, printed in 1600, in which is a lesson in this peculiar notation for the bass viol, entitled "Dowland's Adeu for Master Oliver Cromwell;" and the "Schoole of Musicke," by Thomas Robinson, lutenist, has a song for the viol in Tablature.

The number of lines employed in Tablature was regulated by the number of strings the instrument possessed. The following portion of a "Pavin" is for the cittern, which had four strings :—

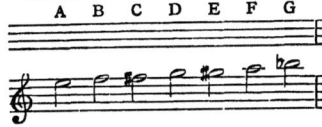

Outhernes Pauin.

From Philip Rossetor's "Lessons for Consort," London, 1609.

To show a little variation in the Tablature in use in these and similar books, the opening notes of a "Coranto," from "Musick's Recreation on the Lyra Viol. Being a choice collection of New and Excellent Lessons for the Lyra Viol, both easie and delightfull for yong Practitioners," c. 1656; are here added :—

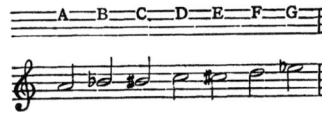

Oranto.

So late as the year 1682 Playford published his "Apollo's Banquet, containing instructions and variety of new tunes Ayres and Jiggs, for the treble violin (fretted)," in which Tablature is employed, with the compass of the four strings thus set forth— the upper line indicating the frets to be used :—

The First or Treble.
A B C D E F G

The Second or Small Mean.
A—B—C—D—E—F—G

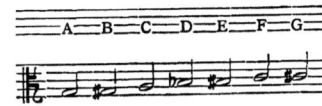

The Third or Great Mean.
A—B—C—D—E—F—G

The Fourth String or Base.
A—B—C—D—E—F—G

TUNING OF THE LUTE.

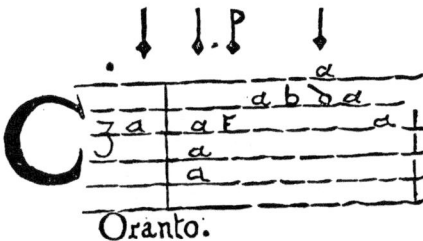

By unisons.   By octavions.

Music for viols was written sometimes in the ordinary notation, or *gamut-way;* but lute music was always written in Tablature or *Lyra-way*.

Tablature for wind instruments was expressed by dots on a stave of six, seven, or eight lines, according to the number of holes in the instrument, the number of dots signifying the number of holes to be stopped by the fingers. This method, employed for the German flute, hautboy and flageolet, is shown in the following example, taken from "The Pleasant Companion; or New Lessons and Instructions for the Flagelet," by Thomas Greeting, gent. London, 1680.

A Jigg or Horne Pipe

To use the author's own words :—"All tunes or lessons for the Flagelet are prick'd upon six lines, answering to the six holes in the instrument, by certain characters called dots. These dots direct what holes are to be stopt, there being so many, and the same holes to be stopt on the Flagelet each breath, as there are dots placed perpendicularly on the six lines." The time was marked in a manner similar to that in lute Tablature.

Another system of Tablature will be best explained by the following diagram (altered from that given by Koch in his Lexicon)

which shows the sounds, proceeding by semitones, by the side of their letter signs. It will be seen that the strings are called by the old names fifth-string or quint, small fifth-string, great fifth-string, small prummer,* middle prummer, great prummer. Capital letters are reserved for the deepest string, but the alphabetical system is carried out by the small letters beginning from the *a* of the mittelprummer working upwards to the letter *e* of the quint; then from the mittelprummer *f* up to *k*, and so on.

5	Quintsait	ε (b♭)	ʜ (b♮)	ɢ (c)	ϭ (c♯)	9 (d)	ε ε (d♯)	ʜ ʜ (e)	ɪɪ (f)
4	Clainsancksait	b (f)	i (f♯)	o (g)	t (g♯)	x (a)	♭♭ (b♭)	i i (b♮)	
3	Grossancksait	ε (c)	♭ (c♯)	π (d)	s (d♯)	ʒ (e)	ε ε (f)	♭♭ (f♯)	
2	Clainprummer	b (g♯)	g (a)	m (b♭)	x (b♮)	ʀ (c)	♭♭ (c♯)	g g (d)	
1	Mittelprummer	x (d♯)	f (e)	l (f)	q (f♯)	ʀ (g)	x x (g♯)	f f (a)	
1	Grossprummer	ʒ (b♭)	♪ (b♮)	ʒ (c)	Q (c♯)	ʒ (d)	ʒ x (d♯)	♪ i (e)	

Organ Tablature was a system of writing the notes without the stave by means of letters. Thus the several octaves were called great, little, one and two-line octaves, according to the style of letter employed to indicate them.

Fig. 1.

C D E F G A B c d e f g a b
c d e f g a b c d e f g a b

This system is liable to be confused with another of a similar character, which was adopted at the commencement of the sixteenth century, for organs which only went down to F.

f g a b c d e f g a b
c d e f g a b cc dd ee ff gg

In these systems sharpened notes were indicated by a downward curved line at the side, a‿, c‿ (a♯, c♯) and flattened notes by an upward curved line a', B', c' (a♭, B♭, c♭).

The duration of notes and rests was expressed by the following signs—

Notes.	Rests.	Value

When several notes were employed together, the tails were united thus: ▦ or when rapidly written ▦ as they appear in the fac-simile from Wolf Heckel's Lautten Buch, given above.

Figured bass has also been called Tablature.

The latest publication in which this peculiar form of notation was employed was in "The New Flute Master," printed in 1704. The dot notation for wind instruments survived the Tablature for the lute from which it was derived by a few years only. With the disuse of the lute, arising from the trouble and expense of keeping it in order, the employ-

* The word *Prummer* or *Brummer* means literally a *growler* or *grumbler*, and its use with reference to deep-toned strings is still kept up in this country by rustics, who call the violoncello a *grumbo*, as the Germans call it *brumm*.

ment of Tablature faded away, and as it was found that the common notation was equally available for all kinds of voices and instruments, the employment of a special notation for individual instruments was completely dispensed with.

Tabl el musahhir. Also called the Baz, a drum used by Egyptian criers during the Ramadan or annual fast, to accompany the religious and congratulatory sentences, uttered before the houses of the wealthy. The Baz or Tabl is also employed by the Dervishes in their religious dances called zikrs.

Tabl Shamee. An Egyptian drum, suspended from the neck and beaten with two small sticks.

Table d'harmonie (*Fr.*) (1) A table or diagram of chords, &c. (2) A sounding-board.

Table d'instrument (*Fr.*) The belly of an instrument of the violin or guitar classes. The upper plate.

Table music. (1) Compositions intended to be sung by several persons sitting at a table. Many of the early printed music books of madrigals, psalm tunes, &c., had the parts so arranged on one page that two or more persons sitting opposite each other at a table could sing from the same book. The following duet, by Dr. Rogers, is given that readers may try for themselves how far this is a convenient system:

TREBLE.

In the mer-ry month of May, In a morn by break of day, Forth I walkt the wood so wide, When as May was in her pride, There I spi-ed all a-lone Phil-li-da and Co-ri-don.

The ingenuity of composers was sometimes exercised to produce pieces apparently in one part but really in two, like the subjoined, which may be performed by two players sitting opposite to each other, each beginning at the top of the page relatively to him:

Allegro Moderato. Duet for two violins, composed by NICOLO MESTRINO, 1720-1790.

(2) German part-songs (from the word *Liedertafel*).

Tabor. This instrument, under the name *toph* (Arabian, *aduf*), is several times mentioned in the Bible. It is probable that it only differed from the tambourine by being without jingles in the hoop. It is often associated with a word which some translators give as *pipe*, but which in the authorized version of the Bible is rendered *dancing* or *dances*.

(419)

The old English tabor was hung round the neck and beaten with a stick held in the right hand, while the left hand was occupied in fingering a pipe. The pipe and tabor were the ordinary accompaniment of the morris-dance.

Taboret, Tabouret, Tabourin (*Fr.*) Tabor.

Tabret. [Tabor.] [Tambourine.]

Tacet (*Lat.*), **Tace** (*It.*), **Taciasi** (*It.*) Be silent. *C.B. tacet*, let the contrabasso be silent, a direction that the violoncelli only are to play the bass part.

Tact (*Ger.*) Takt.

Tactus (*Lat.*) The stroke of the hand or *bâton* in beating time. In mediæval music the time stroke was called *tactus major* when the time consisted of a breve in a bar, and *tactus minor* when it was a semibreve.

Tafelmusik (*Ger.*) [Table music.]

Tail. [Stem.]

Taille (*Fr.*) (1) The tenor voice or tenor part. (2) The tenor violin, the viola.

Tail-piece. That part of an instrument of the violin kind to which the strings are fastened at the lower end. The tail piece is usually of ebony.

Takt (*Ger.*) Time, measure, bar; as *Taktart*, the sort of time, whether duple or triple; *taktfest*, steady in keeping time; *Taktführer*, conductor; *takthalten*, to keep time; *taktmässig*, according to the time; *Taktmesser*, a metronome; *Taktnote*, a semibreve; *Taktpause*, a bar-rest; *taktschlagen*, to beat time; *Taktstock*, a *bâton*, or stick for beating time; *Taktstrich*, a bar-line; *Takttheil*, a division of time; *Taktzeichen*, a time-sign.

Takigoti, or Takigoto. A species of dulcimer in use among the Japanese, provided with moveable bridges, to alter and regulate the pitch. It is played with the fingers and with plectra.

Talabalacco. A Moorish drum.

Talon (*Fr.*) The heel of a bow. [Bow.]

Tambour (*Fr.*) Drum, the great drum.

Tamboura. An instrument of the guitar species, with strings of wire struck with a plectrum. The neck is long, and the body, of gourd-shape, is often beautifully ornamented. The Tamboura is found in Persia, Turkey, Egypt, and Hindustan, and it was known to the Assyrians and Egyptians under various names. The Egyptians called it *nofre* or *nefer*, a term said to be synonymous with *nebel*, the Hebrew word for a stringed instrument. [Guitar.]

Tambour de Basque (*Fr.*) A tabor with jingles, a tambourine. [Tambourine.]

Tambourin (*Fr.*) (1) A stage dance formerly popular in France. It was of a lively measure, and accompanied with a pedal bass in imitation of the drone caused by rubbing the thumb over the skin of a tambourine.

(2) A movement in a suite, of which the following is a specimen:

TAMBOURIN D'ALCIMADURE.

From "Premier Recueil de Menuets, Allemandes, &c., Entremelés D'airs agréables à Chanter, avec leurs accompagnements, arrangés exprès pour Le Cythre òu Guitthare Allem^de. Par Mr. L'Abbe Carpentier." Paris, c. 1760.

Tambourine, Tambour de Basque, Timbrel. An ancient pulsatile instrument of the drum class, popular among all European people, but particularly those of the South. The Biscayan and Italian peasantry employed it on every festal occasion. It is formed of a hoop of wood, sometimes of metal, over which is stretched a piece of parchment or skin; the sides of the hoop are pierced with holes, in which are inserted pieces of metal in pairs, called jingles. Small bells are sometimes fastened on to the outer edge of the hoop. It is sounded by being struck with the knuckles, or by drawing the fingers or thumb over the skin, which produces what is called "the roll," a peculiar drone mingled with the jingle of the bells or pieces of metal. In a book of instruction for the Tambourine the names of the several effects and the manner of writing for them, and of producing them, are thus set forth:—

"'Flamps' are made with the knuckles near the centre of the *skin* of the instrument; they are thus indicated:

'Semi-flamps' are struck nearer the *rim*; you make them where you see the music written thus:

To make the 'Travale'

draw your wetted thumb in a circular direction over the skin. The 'double-travale'

is twice as quick. Use the 'jingles' where the music is marked thus :

and the 'Roll' when the tails of the notes are waved :

The 'Roll' is performed by shaking the instrument.

"N.B.—There are no sharps or flats in tambourine playing."

Tambourineur (*Fr.*) Drummer, tambourine player.

Tambour major (*Fr.*) Drum major.

Tamburino (*It.*) A drummer.

Tamburo (*It.*) A drum.

Tamburone (*It.*) The great drum.

Tam-tam (*It.*) [Gong.]

Tändelnd (*Ger.*) In a playful style.

Tangent (*Ger.*) The striking pin of a clarichord.

Tanto (*It.*) So much; *Allegro non tanto*, not so fast; *a tanto possibile*, as much as possible.

Tanz (*Ger.*) A dance. *Tanzkunst*, the art of dancing.

Tarantella (*It.*) A rapid Neapolitan dance in triplets, so called because it was popularly thought to be a remedy against the supposed poisonous bite of the Tarantula spider. Older specimens of the dance are not in triplets.

TARANTELLA, 1654.
Primo modus.

Secondo modus.

Antidotum tarantulæ.

Tardamente (*It.*) Slowly.

Tardando (*It.*) Retarding the time.

Tardo (*It.*) Slow, dragging.

Tartini's tones. [Acoustics, § 19.]

Tastame (*It.*), **Tastatur, Tastenbrett** (*Ger.*), **Tastatura** (*It.*), **Tastiera** (*It.*), **Tastenleiter** (*Ger.*) The key-board of a pianoforte or organ. A hand-guide, *guidemain*. *Tastenschwanz* (*Ger.*), the extremity of the keys. *Tastenwerk* (*Ger.*), a keyed instrument.

Tasto (*It.*) (1) A key of a pianoforte. (2) The touch of a pianoforte or organ.

Tasto solo (*It.*) One key alone. A direction to play the part without accompanying chords; in unison.

Tatto (*It.*) The touch.

Tattoo, *or* **Taptoo.** The beat of the drum at night to call soldiers to their quarters; the morning beat is called Reveille or Revelly.

Tche *or* **Tsang.** A Chinese instrument strung with wire, tuned by means of pegs and moveable bridges, and played with the fingers like a guitar.

Teatro (*It.*) A theatre.

Technik (*Ger.*) A general name for the systems, devices, and resources of musical art.

Tedesca, alla (*It.*) In the German style.

Tell-tale. A moveable piece of metal or bone attached by a cord to the bellows of an organ, which gives notice to the blower or the performer of the quantity of wind in the wind-chest. [Organ.]

Tema (*It.*) A theme, or subject; a melody.

Temperament. The division of the octave. After discussing this, an appendix on the calculation of intervals and beats shall be given.

The problem is, to divide the octave into *Nature of Problem.* a number of intervals such, that the notes which separate them shall be suitable in number and arrangement for the purposes of practical harmony. We *Notation required.* must provide ourselves with a notation and means of expression suited to the subject before we can discuss the treatment it has received.

The simplest form of temperament is that *Intervals expressed in eq. temp. semitones.* in common use, which divides the octave into twelve equal semitones. It is most convenient to express all intervals in terms of these semitones. The perfect fifth contains 7.019550008654 semitones; the perfect third 3.863137138649 semitones. Five places are enough for all practical purposes.

In all harmonious music the fifth to any given note may be required at any time. Hence all systems provide series of fifths of *Series of fifths.* a more or less complete character. We shall found on this remark a notation suitable for general discussion.

If a series of perfect fifths be constructed starting from *c*, octaves being disregarded, it will not return exactly to *c* again. Taking the fifth to be 7.01955 semitones, each note in the series lies further than the last from the equal temperament note of the same name ; and this *departure* increases by .01955 for each step in the series, the equal temperament fifth being seven semitones. Thus the *c* to which we return after twelve fifths is higher than that from which we started by 12 × .01955 = .23460 of a semitone. This interval is called the comma of Pythagoras.

We employ the following notation to repre-
Notation for series of fifths. sent this *departure*. We take the series of fifths,

$$f\sharp—c\sharp—a\flat—e\flat—b\flat—f—c—g—d—a—e—b,$$

for a standard series. On passing to the next $f\sharp$ we denote that it is higher than the first one by prefixing to it a mark of elevation $(\prime f\sharp)$; thus $b—\prime f\sharp$ is a perfect fifth. We proceed to form another series like the first, to all of which the mark $(\prime)$ is prefixed; so that $\prime c$ is the note to which we return on completing the circle of twelve fifths from *c*. We may extend this indefinitely. Thus we have a succession of notes, as $c—\prime c—\prime\prime c—\prime\prime\prime c \ldots$, each additional $(\prime)$ representing the change of pitch caused by rising twelve fifths in the series, *i.e.* the Pythagorean comma. Similarly we may extend the series in the other direction : thus the fifth below $f\sharp$ is $\backslash b—f\sharp$, where $(\backslash)$ is a mark of depression, and we have such notes as $\backslash c—\backslash\backslash c \ldots$, each $(\backslash)$ representing the depression of a Pythagorean comma caused by traversing a circle of twelve-fifths downwards in the series. In these series such distinctions as that between $a\sharp$ and $b\flat$ are not observed. The place in the series is entirely determined by the prefix. The use of this notation may be extended to fifths which are not perfect.

Theorem. If from any note (c) eight perfect fifths be tuned downwards, a note $(\backslash e)$
Thirds formed by eight fifths down. is determined which forms an approximately perfect third to (c). This theorem is the foundation of Helmholtz's system. For if we tune $c—f—b\flat$ $e\flat—a\flat—d\flat—g\flat—\backslash b—\backslash e$, we depress the pitch 8 × .01955 = .15640 below equal temperament. But the perfect third is 3.86314 semitones, *i.e.* .13686 below equal temperament, which differs from the preceding value of $(\backslash e)$ by about $\frac{1}{74}$ of a semitone. In the practical application of this, it is generally attempted to distribute the error over the eight fifths; but for all ordinary approximate purposes it does not matter where the error lies. We note here that the notes b, e, a, d have their major thirds in the same series, as $d—f\sharp$; all other notes in the series below, as $c—\backslash e$.

The following definitions will now be received without difficulty :—

Regular systems consist of notes which
Definitions. form a continuous series of
Regular System. fifths, *e.g.* the system of perfect fifths.

Regular cyclical systems consist of notes
Regular Cyclical System. which form a continuous series of fifths, and divide the octave into a certain number of equal intervals.
Order of Systems. Primary regular cyclical systems are those in which the departure of twelve of the approximate fifths of the system from the starting point is equal to one unit of the system. Secondary systems are those in which the departure of twelve fifths from the starting-point is two units, and so on.
Positive and Negative systems. Positive systems have fifths sharper than equal temperament fifths; *negative* systems have fifths flatter than equal temperament fifths.

The division of the octave into 53 equal intervals furnishes an important primary positive system ; into 118, a secondary positive system ; into 31, a primary negative system ; into 50, a secondary negative system.

HISTORICAL.

The earliest systematic division of the octave on record is known as the Pythagorean system ; it consists of a series of perfect fifths. The third employed was that
Pythagorean system. formed by four fifths up, which still bears the name of the Pythagorean or dissonant third. Thus where $c—g—d—a—e$ are perfect fifths, $c—e$ is the Pythagorean or dissonant third. The true third is said to have been discovered by Archytas.

The Greeks were acquainted with the prin-
Monochord. ciple of the monochord, and with
Vibration of strings. the numerical ratios obtainable
Vibration numbers. from that instrument ; a short ac-
Vibration ratios. count of these is necessary to our subject. We shall include vibration numbers and ratios.

The number of vibrations per second given by a string of varying length, tension and weight of string per unit of length being the same, varies inversely as the length. Thus half the string vibrates twice as fast as the whole string.

If two vibrating strings have the same tension and weight per unit of length, but lengths differing in a given ratio, they will always sound notes which include the same interval; and hence :—

If two sounds have different vibration numbers, the interval between them is always the same when the ratio of the vibration numbers is the same. Thus if the lengths are as 1:2, the vibration numbers are as 2:1, and the interval is an octave; if the lengths are as 1:3, the vibration numbers are as 3:1, and the interval is a twelfth, and so on. The notes thus produced by fractions of the length of a string are called harmonics. The order of a harmonic is the denominator of the corresponding fraction. The following table exhibits the vibration, ratios, and intervals of the first sixteen harmonics, the intervals being taken to three places of decimals :—

Harmonics.

Table of Harmonics :—distance from fundamental = n equal temperament semitones.
order of Harmonic = denominator of string fraction ;—
= number of vibrations relatively to number of fundamental ;—
= x.

FIRST OCTAVE.		SECOND OCTAVE.		THIRD OCTAVE.		FOURTH OCTAVE.	
x	n	x	n	x	n	x	n
1 (Fundamental)	0·000	2 (Octave)	12·000	4 (Fifteenth)	24·000	8	36·000
						9	38·039
				5 (Tierce)	27·863	10 (Octave Tierce)	39·863
						11	41·513
		3 (Twelfth)	19·020	6 (8ve. Twelfth)	31·020	12	43·020
						13	44·405
				7 (Seventh Harmonic)	33·688	14	45·688
						15	46·883
2 (Octave)	12·000	4 (Fifteenth)	24·000	8	36·000	16	48·000

Mersenne's work on Harmony was published in 1636. Amongst other things he treats particularly of intervals. The following table contains a list of the principal intervals discussed by theorists. The last two columns show the number of units of the division of the octave into 53 equal parts which represents each interval most closely, with the equivalent of this representation in equal temperament semitones. This arrangement forms a classification of the various intervals in question, which will much assist the mind in the comprehension of their relations. The system of 53 is the most important primary positive system. One or two of the intervals are from Kircher, who wrote soon after Mersenne.

Mersenne.

Intervals.

MERSENNE and KIRCHER.	DIFFERENCE OF.	Ratio.	Equal Temperament Semitones.	$\frac{1}{53}$rds of Octave.	$\frac{1}{53}$rds in Eq. Temp. Semitones.
Octave	....	2 : 1	12·00000	53	12·00000
Fifth	....	3 : 2	7·01955	31	7·01902
Fourth	Fifth and Octave	4 : 3	4·98045	22	4·98045
Major Third	....	5 : 4	3·86314	17	3·84914
Minor Third	Major Third and Fifth.........	6 : 5	3·15641	14	3·16988
Major Tone	Fourth and Fifth	9 : 8	2·03910	9	2·03778
Minor Tone	Major Tone and Major Third......	10 : 9	1·82404	8	1·81136
				7	1·58494
Semitone Maximus	Major Tone and Minor Semitone	27 : 25	1·33237	6	1·35852
Major Semitone	Fourth and Major Third.........	16 : 15	1·11731	} 5	1·13210
Apotomè Pythagorica ...	Seven Fifths up, Four Octaves down..	2187 : 2048	1·13685		
Semitone Medius, or Chromatic Semitone...	Major Tone and Major Semitone	135 : 128	·92179	} 4	·90568
Pythagorean Semitone...	Fourth and 2 Major Tones or 5 Fifths down and 3 Octaves up	256 : 243	·90225		
Minor Semitone .... Semitone Minimus ...... Chromatic Diesis	} Major and Minor Third or Minor Tone and Major Semitone	25 : 24	·70673	3	·67926
Enharmonic Diesis	Major Semitone and Minor Semitone (Chromatic Diesis)	128 : 125	·41058	2	·45284
Comma (Major)	Major and Minor Tone or 2 Major Tones and Perfect Thirds..............	81 : 80	·21506		
Comma of Pythagoras...	Twelve Fifths either way and 7 Octaves the reverse		·23460	} 1	·22642
Diaschisma	Half Enharmonic Diesis		·20529		
Comma (Minor)	Enharmonic Diesis and Major Comma	10240 : 10125	·19552		
Schisma	Fraction of Comma				

Mersenne's Systema Perfectum in F. Mersenne gives numerous systems of scales which admit of the construction of perfect concords. We will give one as an example. It is a scale of the key of F, with 18 intervals in the octave; the division is irregular, but can be represented as follows by means of a broken series of fifths :—

$$\text{ⵡ}b—\backslash f\sharp—\backslash c\sharp—\backslash g\sharp; \quad \backslash g—\backslash d—\backslash a—\backslash e—\backslash b;$$
$$e\flat—b\flat—f—c—g; \quad \text{ı}g\flat—\text{ı}d\flat—\text{ı}a\flat—\text{ı}e\flat.$$

The resources of this system are very limited. We have :—

Major chords of $c—f—b\flat—e\flat$

———— $\backslash e—\backslash a—\backslash d—\backslash g$ thirds to the above :

———— $\text{ı}a\flat—\text{ı}d\flat—\text{ı}g\flat$ to which the first given three notes are thirds.

Minor chords of $—c—f—b\flat—e\flat$;

———— $\backslash e—\backslash a—\backslash d—\backslash g$, thirds to the above:

———— $\text{ⵡ}b—\backslash f\sharp—\backslash c\sharp$, thirds of the chords of $\backslash g—\backslash d—\backslash a$.

The minor chord of $\backslash g$ gives the perfect chord of the sixth on the subdominant in the key of F, i.e., $(b\flat, \backslash d, \backslash g)$, thus requiring two different keys $(g, \backslash g)$ to represent the second of the key of F. A key-board for the system is delineated in Mersenne, in which the double G key appears. This double second has always been a characteristic of the more intelligent attempts at systems of pure intonation. Several other key-boards for more complex systems are drawn in Mersenne.

Huyghens. In a tract, "Cyclus Harmonicus," (1698) Huyghens first described correctly the properties of the division of the octave into 31 equal intervals, which was previously known to be of interest. It is the most important primary negative system.

Smith. Smith's Harmonics, 1759. Three systems are principally discussed, one called equal harmony, which has very flat fifths and flat thirds; it is negative, and resembles the system of 50, as Smith points out: the mean tone or old unequal temperament, which resembles the system of 31, and has flat fifths and perfect thirds: and a system in which the thirds are just as sharp as the fifths are flat.

Woolhouse. An important tract is Woolhouse's Essay on Musical Intervals (1835). He performs a part of his reckoning with the notation of equal temperament semitones.

In the solution of the problem of temperament, Woolhouse adopts as basis the division of the octave into 50 equal intervals; this is a secondary negative system. But instead of treating it as a regular system, he selects from it notes sufficient to form a certain limited number of scales. This treatment

we regard as imperfect. He distinguishes between such notes as $c\sharp$ and $d\flat$. We shall see later that this distinction is true and sufficient in negative systems only.

Woolhouse also gives scales based on the system of 31. The same remarks apply.

De Morgan. A paper by De Morgan (Cam. Phil. Trans. X. 129) "On the beats of imperfect consonances," contains some details on the calculation of intervals. The treatment of the problem of beats is fundamentally erroneous, as are all accounts of this subject before that of Helmholtz. De Morgan employs equal temperament semitones as the measures of intervals, and gives rules for calculation nearly identical with those used independently by the writer. See Appendix.

Herschel. A paper by Herschel (Quarterly Journal of Science, V. 338) contains proposals for systems of temperament. The character of these will be sufficiently illustrated by one example. In the table at top of p. 348, we have substantially a Pythagorean system, with twelve notes in the octave; the break is made at $d—\backslash a$; this fifth is a Pythagorean comma out of tune. Such a fifth cannot be used in music; and this system would exclude from use the keys of G, D, and A, both major and minor. The Pythagorean system is also defended by name.

Thompson. Poole. Two important practical attempts are those of Gen. T. P. Thompson and Mr. H. W. Poole (Silliman's American Journal, Vol. xliv.) The limits of this article forbid more than a concise reference to the former. Gen. T. P. Thompson in his Enharmonic organ, arranged three key-boards, each starting from a key of the ordinary board in perfect tune, and admitting of performance in related keys by means of auxiliary notes; there were 40 notes in the octave. Looking at the material of notes from our point of view, it may be regarded as constituting a series of approximately perfect fifths extending from $\text{ⵡ}c\sharp$ to $\text{ı}c$, with the omission of two single notes $\text{ⵡ}d$ and b. These omissions, and the distribution between different key-boards, greatly diminished the resources of the instrument, which were, however, far greater than those of any instrument previously constructed. We cannot omit to notice Gen. Thompson's method of using the monochord. He varied the weight by which the string was stretched, as well as the length. We judge that his form of the instrument is probably the most perfect that has been constructed.

Helmholtz. The subject of temperament owes much to Helmholtz. The principal conclusions which we shall require to borrow from him, are :—The approximate formation of a perfect third by eight fifths turned downwards; and the theories of harmonics, and of difference tones (subharmonics or Tartini tones) so far as we require them for the calculation of beats. We must also note his definition of dissonance, now universally received by physicists; viz., the intermittent excitation of the ear by a sound. Thus consonant and dissonant properties of chords depend on the beats they furnish. Such combinations as fourths and harmonic sevenths, which give no beats, may be distinguished as *unsatisfied combinations*.

Harmonics.
Beats.
The theory of harmonics;—Musical notes consist of combinations of harmonics with their fundamentals (*i.e.* every note contains 8ve, 12th, &c., in very considerable strength). The ear analyses this complex note by receiving it on a resonant instrument, which may be roughly compared to a harp. The tones of different parts of the scale are thus so far separated that no direct interference can take place between tones more than a minor third apart.

The beats of imperfect consonances arise: (1) From the interference of pairs of harmonics nearly coinciding in pitch (*e.g.* imperfect fifth, by interference of 12th of C with octave of G).

(2) From the interference of difference tones (Tartini tones) with each other or with harmonics, in pairs nearly coinciding in pitch. For Ex. see Appendix.

Difference
Tones.
(Tartini
Tones.)
Difference tones (Tartini tones) are such that their vibration number is the difference of the vibration numbers of their primaries. Ex., if $c''-d''$ be a major tone (8 : 9) [nine] its difference tone is (1) [one] *i.e.* C, the lowest note of the organ key-board. If $c''-d'$ be sounded on a clarabella or harmonic flute, the difference tone will be distinctly heard, in the equal temperament of course not exactly in tune. For the somewhat abstruse theory of difference tones we must refer to Helmholtz. The old theory, in which their origin was ascribed to beats, is no longer received by physicists.

Rule for Beats.
The number of beats per second made by two notes nearly coinciding in pitch, is the difference of the vibration numbers of the two notes.

The above principles are required for numerical calculation, see Appendix.

Distinction
between
(c♯ d♭)
when admissible.
The remark already made, that in positive systems the distinction between say (c♯ d♭) fails, while in negative systems it is true and essential, is the generalization of an observation of Helmoltz's. As this is very important we will shortly explain the reason.

Not in positive
systems.
The perfect third is below the equal temperament third in pitch. Hence in positive systems, which have larger fifths than the equal temperament, a third formed by downward fifths will approximate to the true third. That is to say the thirds of these systems will be formed by eight fifths down (see Th. p. 3); according to this, the major third to *a* would be the note commonly called d♭. But it must be written c♯; so in order to be clear, we cease to recognise any distinction between these two expressions, and denote the position in the series of fifths by the notation before described.

But in negative.
But in negative systems, where the fifths are less than equal temperament fifths, fifths up depress the pitch; so that the third formed by four fifths up is the representative of the perfect third, and the distinction between c♯ d♭ becomes true and essential.

Ellis.
A paper by Mr. A. Ellis, F.R.S., (Proceedings of Royal Society, 1864,) contains much information and copious references on the subject of temperament.

GENERAL THEORY OF REGULAR CYCLICAL SYSTEMS.

Importance of
Regular
Systems.
The importance of Regular Systems arises from the symmetry subsisting between the various scales to which they give rise. No idea in the present day is more connected with progress in music than that of the similarity of all keys.

Regular
Cyclical
Systems.
The importance of regular *cyclical* systems arises from the infinite freedom of modulation which is possible in properly arranged systems of this class. In non-cyclical systems, modulation is apt to bring us to the end of our material.

We shall consider the theory of regular cyclical systems in its simplest form.

Seven-fifths
Semitone.
Definitions. The interval formed by tuning seven fifths *up* (disregarding octaves), is called a seven-fifths semitone, and it lies above the starting point.

Five-fifths
Semitone.
The interval formed by tuning five fifths *down* is called a five-fifths semitone, and lies above the starting point.

The seven-fifths semitone is the Apotomè Pythagorica, (Table of Intervals) when the fifths are perfect. The five-fifths semitone is the Pythagorean semitone when the fifths are perfect.

Theorem on
Semitones
in Octave.
Theorem. In any regular system, five seven-fifths semitones and seven five-fifths semitones make up an exact octave.

For the departures from equal temperament of five seven-fifths semitones are due to thirty-five fifths taken upwards, and the departures of seven five-fifths semitones are due to thirty-five fifths taken downwards; so that the departures destroy one another, and leave the twelve semitones of the equal temperament, which give an exact octave.

Theorem. In positive systems of the first Theorem on difference of the semitones. order (primary), the seven-fifths semitone is greater than the five-fifths semitone by one unit; in positive systems of the second order (secondary), by two units; and so on. In negative systems less.

For, in regular systems, the seven-fifths semitone has the departure from equal temperament due to seven-fifths up. (*Ex. gr.*, $c-g-d-a-e-b-1f\sharp-1c\sharp$.) The five-fifths semitone, taken downwards, has the departure due to five more fifths taken up. (*Ex. gr.*, $1c\sharp-1a\flat-1e\flat-1b\flat-1f-1c$.) Hence, in positive systems, the seven-fifths semitone exceeds the five-fifths semitone by the departure of twelve fifths from the starting point ($c-1c$). But this is one unit in primary systems, two in secondary, and so on. (Definition.) And in negative systems (in which the fifths are less than equal temperament fifths, and twelve fifths fall short of the octave), the seven-fifths semitone is less than the five-fifths semitone by the departure of the twelve fifths, which is one unit in primary systems, two in secondary, and so on.

These two theorems permit us to construct positive or negative cyclical systems of any order. Those few alone which present some points of interest are entered in the following scheme:—

Scheme of Regular Cyclical Systems.

PRIMARY POSITIVE.

Seven-fifths Semitone, $= s$ units.	Five-fifths Semitone, $= f$ units.	Octave (Th. p. 12), $= 5s + 7f$.
2	1	17
3	2	29
4	3	41
5	4	53
6	5	65

SECONDARY POSITIVE.

11	9	118

PRIMARY NEGATIVE.

1	2	19
2	3	31
3	4	43

SECONDARY NEGATIVE.

3	5	50

PROPERTIES OF INTERVALS OF THE ABOVE SYSTEMS.

Departure, means displacement from equal temperament. *Error*, from the perfect interval.

Units in Octave, $= n$.	Value of Unit in Semitones, $= \frac{12}{n}$.	Departure of 12-fifths.	Error of Single Fifth.	Departure of Thirds.	Error of Thirds.
17	·70588	·70588	·03927 Sharp.	·47059	·33373 Flat.
29	·41379	·41379	·01493 Sharp.	·27586	·13900 Flat.
41	·29268	·29268	·00484 Sharp.	·19512	·05826 Flat.
53	·22642	·22642	·00068 Flat.	·15640	·01954 Flat.
65	·18462	·18462	·00416 Flat.	·12308	·01378 Sharp.
118	·10169	·20339	·00260 Flat.	·13559	·00127 Sharp.
19	·63158	·63158	·07218 Flat.	·21053	·07367 Flat.
31	·38710	·38710	·05181 Flat.	·12903	·00783 Sharp.
43	·29707	·29706	·04432 Flat.	·09902	·03784 Sharp.
50	·24000	·48000	·05955 Flat.	·16000	·02314 Flat.

Selection of systems. On inspecting the columns of errors, we at once see that the system of 118 affords the greatest combined perfection of fifths and thirds; and next to it comes the system of 53, which we prefer in practice as more manageable. The system of 31 has fifths $\frac{1}{20}$ of a semitone flat; and this is enough to be disagreeable with sharp qualities of tone, but its thirds are very good. This system forms very nearly a cyclical form of the mesotonic system, which, in an imperfect condition, was the old unequal temperament. The rule of that system was simply that all the fifths of the continuous series were made so flat as to bring down the third made by four fifths up to a perfect third.

We cannot here enter on the subject of sevenths, except to remark that the systems of 53 and 31 both afford good approximations to the harmonic seventh.

PRACTICAL EMPLOYMENT OF THE SYSTEM OF 53.

System of 53. We will now point out shortly the arrangement which has been adopted for the practical treatment of the system of 53; it is applicable to all regular systems.

Position relations of general key-board. A key-board is arranged according to position in a series of fifths. There are twelve vertical divisions in the octave; in the c division there are notes such as $\backslash\backslash c — \backslash c — c — \imath c — \imath\imath c$; these are placed in ascending and receding order. The vertical displacement $c — \imath c$ is divided equally amongst the 12 intermediate fifths. Thus the whole tones of two-fifths each form diagonal lines, and six whole tones lead from c' to $\imath c''$. The following scheme shows the relative positions of a portion of this arrangement, with the characteristic numbers of the system of 53.

[SCHEME.]

```
″c₆                                    ″f₂₈              ″bb₅₀                    ″c₆
                        ″eb₁₉                     ″ab₄₁                 ′b₁
        ″c♯₁₀                              ″f♯₃₂              ′a₄₅
                    ′d₁₄      ′e₂₃                    ′g₃₆          ′bb₄₉
′c₅                              ′f₂₇                                          ′c₅
                        ′eb₁₈                      ′ab₄₀
        ′c♯₉                           ′f♯₃₁                          b₅₃
                    d₁₃      e₂₂                    g₃₅          a₄₄
c₄                          f₂₆              g₃₅    ab₃₉    bb₄₈              c₄
                    eb₁₇                f♯₃₀
        c♯₈                    e₂₁               g₃₄                  ‵b₅₂
                ‵d₁₂                ‵f₂₅                   ‵bb₄₇
‵c₃                                      ‵g₃₄        ‵a₄₃                  ‵c₃
                    ‵eb₁₆                      ‵ab₃₈
        ‵c♯₇                    ‵f♯₂₉                              ‵b₅₁
                ‵d₁₁           ‵e₂₀        ‵g₃₃              ‵a₄₂
‶c₂                        ‶f₂₄               ‶g₃₃      ‶bb₄₆              ‶c₂
                ‶eb₁₅                    ‶ab₃₇
        ‶c♯₆                    ‶f♯₂₈                          ‶b₅₀
            ‶d₁₀        ‶e₁₉                    ‶g₃₂  ‶a₄₁
‶c₁                                ‶g₃₂                                  ‶c₁
```

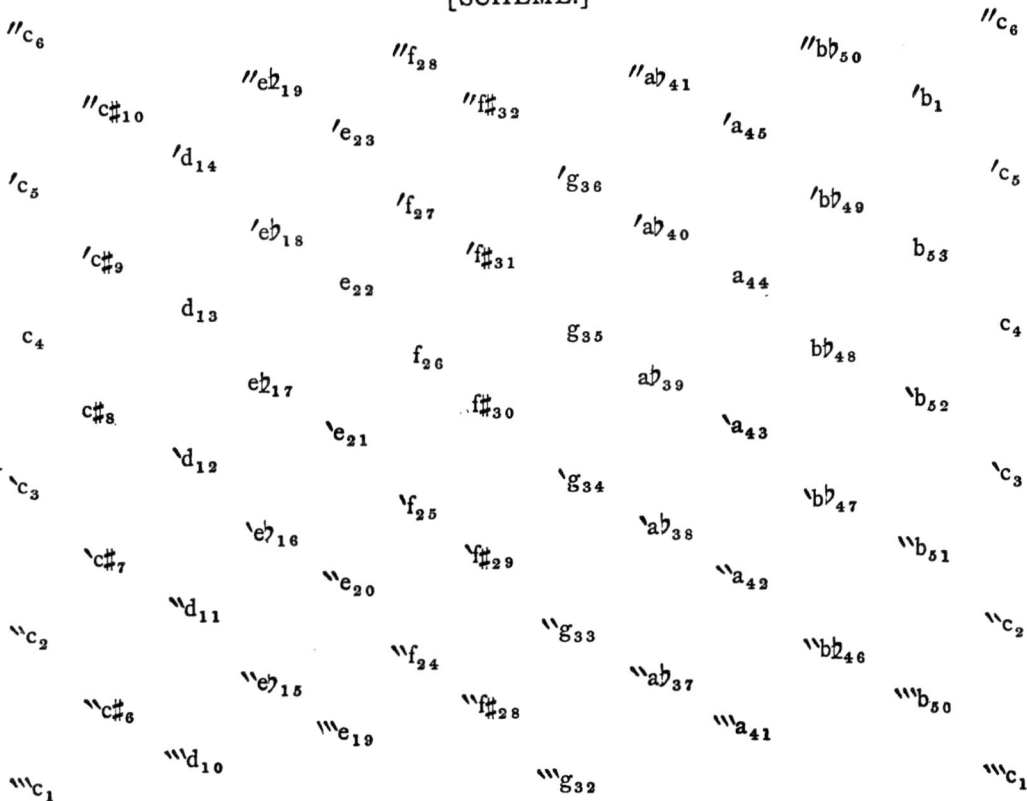

It is to be noted that, by the symmetry of the principle of arrangement, the scales on a keyboard constructed on this principle are the same in all keys, as far as form and fingering go.

According to the formation of the system of 53, we see that the seven-fifths semitones exhibit differences of 5 units, the five-fifths semitones of 4—*Ex. gr.* c_4—$\imath c♯_9$; and c_4—$c♯_8$.

A harmonium has been constructed with
Enharmonic harmonium. a key-board of 84 keys to the octave, the position relations of a portion of which are shown by the preceding scheme. Some notes at the top are identical with adjoining notes at the bottom, on the right. Thus infinite freedom of movement is secured, and any one of the 53 notes can be used as key-note in exactly the same manner, and with the same facility. The rule for identifications is as follows: "A note near the top of one division is identical with one near the bottom of the adjoining division on the right, when the lower division is white (♮), if the sum of the marks is 4, and when the lower division is black (♯ or ♭), if the sum of the marks is 5."

$$E.g.: \quad \shortmid\shortmid c_6 = \backslash\backslash c\sharp_6.$$
$$\shortmid\shortmid c\sharp_{10} = \backslash\backslash\backslash d_{10}.$$

We have altogether four position marks in the first pair, five in the second.

A few examples are subjoined, to illustrate the practical employment of the notation.

(1) Common major chord of C.

(2) Common minor chord of C.

(3) Common chord of dominant, with first form of second.

(4) Chord of sixth on sub-dominant, with second form of second.

(5)

Example of the successive use of the two forms of the second; the (o) is used to nullify the preceding mark of depression (\).

(6) Approximate harmonic seventh.

Hence the theorem : if the harmonic seventh be used on the dominant, it must not be suspended to form a fourth with the tonic. For if we suspend the \f in the above, we obtain the fourth c—\f, a comma flat, which is unbearable.

(7)

The passing note illustrates the combination formed by the division of the octave into three major thirds. The major third being

$\frac{17}{53}$ of an octave, three major thirds fall $\frac{2}{53}$ short. We may distribute this error in a variety of ways. The example shows the case in which two of the thirds, c—\e—\g♯, are made perfect. The remaining third, \g♯—c is $\frac{19}{53}$, instead of $\frac{17}{53}$. Noticing that $\frac{18}{53}$ is the ordinary dissonant third, we may call \g♯—c, a super-dissonant third. If we employ g♯ as the passing note, we should have two ordinary dissonant thirds. In the equal temperament, the error of nearly half a semitone is divided equally among the three intervals. The most favourable distribution is judged by the writer to be that given in the example. Another common instance of the same combination is the following :

(8)

Here \b— ιe♭ is a super-dissonant third.

The application of this arrangement to the systems of 118 and 31 presents considerable interest, but our limits preclude the discussion.

If the above scheme be considered without
Non-cyclical regular systems. the characteristic numbers of the system of 53, we have the form of application to any non-cyclical regular system. The only difference then is that, there being no identifications, continuous modulation, upwards or downwards, on the scheme would soon bring us to the end of the material of notes provided. This displacement takes place, in positive systems, most rapidly by modulation between major and minor keys ; e.g. :

(9)

&c.

The a♭ at the beginning of the second bar, and ιd in the last, are derived from inversions of chords into which harmonic sevenths enter.

The defects of the equal temperament may
Defects of equal temperament. be estimated physically by means of Helmholtz's definition of dissonance. Beats begin to be disagreeable when their number exceeds 3 or 4 in the second, attain the maximum of dissonance when about 33 in the second, and remain audible as beats up to considerably beyond 100 per second, when produced by interference of tones of sufficient strength. The application of this remark to the results calculated in the Appendix serves for the estimation of the dissonances of the equal temperament. An ear accustomed to pure chords recognizes these dissonances immediately, even in the organ and in the full-toned

modern pianoforte ; but especially in the harmonium.

In cases where difference tones are strongly formed, as with wide-scaled organ-pipes, or with two treble voices singing duets, errors in small intervals displace the difference tone by many times their own amount; and to educated ears this displacement, though not always involving beats, is very offensive. Helmholtz, who has written much on this subject, regards this as the most offensive characteristic of the equal temperament. *E.g.*: The difference tone of e'—g' should be C (8 ft.). In the equal temperament it bears to that note the ratio $\frac{21}{22}$ very nearly, which is roughly about $\frac{3}{4}$ of a semitone.

Melodic sequences. The question of melodic progressions, as affecting the excellence of temperaments, is too extensive for our limits. We believe that it is a matter entirely of custom and education, and that the ear can accustom itself to any melodic sequences whatever.

The writer has accustomed his ear to such sequences as the following, which are new in music, whatever may be the opinion as to their effect :—

(10)

(The o nullifies the elevation and depression marks.)

The following example illustrates an instance in which a direct depression of pitch by a comma (\ ) has proved to have a good effect.

The second chord contains a depression of the tonic *g*. It may be regarded as derived from a passing dominant harmony on *a*, containing \g as harmonic seventh.

APPENDIX.

On the Calculation of Intervals, and of Beats.

(1) To find the equivalent of a given vibration ratio in equal temperament semitones.

RULE.—Take the common logarithm of the ratio ; subtract $\frac{1}{300}$ of itself, and call this the first improved value. From the original logarithm subtract $\frac{1}{300}$ of the first improved value, and $\frac{1}{10,000}$ of the first improved value. Multiply the remainder by 40. The result is the required equivalent. If we take logs. to seven places, five will generally be correct in the result.

Example.—To find the equivalent of a perfect fifth, whose ratio is $\frac{3}{2}$.

$$\log. 3 = \cdot 4771213 \qquad \log. \tfrac{3}{2} = \cdot 1760913$$
$$\log. 2 = \cdot 3010300 \qquad \qquad \cdot 0005850$$

$$\log. \tfrac{3}{2} = \cdot 1760913 \qquad \cdot 1755063$$
$$\tfrac{1}{300} = \cdot 0005870 \qquad \qquad 1755$$

First improved value. $\}$ $\cdot 1755043 \qquad \cdot 17548875$
$$\qquad\qquad\qquad\qquad 40$$

$$\tfrac{1}{300} \quad \cdot 0005850 \qquad 7 \cdot 01955 | 00$$

In this case the whole seven places are correct, but this is accidental.

(2) To find the vibrations ratio of an interval given in equal temperament semitones.

To the given number add $\frac{1}{300}$ of itself and $\frac{1}{10,000}$ of itself; divide by 40. The result is the logarithm of the ratio required. We must not take more than six places ; then as many as we take will be correct in the answer.

Example.—To find the vibrations ratio of the equal temperament third, consisting of 4 semitones.

$$\qquad\qquad 4 \cdot 000000$$
$$\tfrac{1}{300} = \cdot 013333$$
$$\tfrac{1}{10,000} = \cdot 000400$$

$$40 \,)\, 4 \cdot 013733$$

$$\cdot 1003433 = \log. 1 \cdot 259921$$

The ratio of the perfect third is $1 \cdot 250000$, so that the ratio of the equal temperament third to the perfect third is very nearly $\frac{126}{125}$.

The calculation of beats is essential to the accurate construction of systems of tuning. The principles to be applied have been already enunciated.

Ex. 1.—To determine the number of beats per second in the equal temperament fifth c'—g' ($c' = 256$).

The twelfth of c' is $g'' = 768$. This interferes with the octave of g'; and this is $\cdot 0195500$ flat, since a perfect fifth contains $7 \cdot 0195500$ semitones.

To find the vibration number of the note $\cdot 0195500$ below $g'' = 768$.

Proceeding by Rule 2 we have—

$$\cdot 0195500$$
$$\cdot 0000652 = \tfrac{1}{300}$$
$$19 = \tfrac{1}{10,000}$$

$$40 \,)\, \cdot 0196171$$
$$\cdot 0004904 = \log. \text{ ratio of note to } g''$$

Again—$\log. 768 = 2 \cdot 8853613$
$$\log. \text{ ratio} = \quad \cdot 0004904$$

$$\log. \text{ tempered } g'' = 2 \cdot 8848709$$
$$= \log. 767 \cdot 133$$

The number of beats per second is the difference of the vibration numbers.

$$768 \cdot 000$$
$$767 \cdot 133$$

$$\cdot 867 = \text{no. of beats per second.}$$
$$60$$

$$52 \cdot 02 = \text{no. of beats per minute.}$$

Ex. 2.—To determine the number of beats per second in the equal temperament third c'—e', caused by the interference of the tierce c' with the double octave of e'.

From p. 25—log. ratio $\dfrac{e'}{c'}$ $= \cdot 1003433$

$$\log. \ c''' = \log. \ 1024 = 3 \cdot 0103000$$

$$\log. \text{ tempered } e''' = 3 \cdot 1106433$$
$$= \log. \ 1290 \cdot 16$$
$$\text{and } e''' = 5 \times 256 = \quad 1280 \cdot 00$$

$$10 \cdot 16$$

or 10 per second very nearly.

These beats are, then, rapid enough to be offensive in the higher parts of the scale, where the notes used contain the harmonics of the 4th and 5th order in sufficient strength.

Beats of difference tones (Tartini Tones).

Ex.—To find the number of beats per second produced by the difference tones of c'—e', e'—g', in the equal temperament triad. From the above examples we have—

$$c' = 256 \quad g', = 767 \cdot 133$$
$$\overline{\qquad\qquad} = 383 \cdot 566$$
$$2$$

$$e' = 1290 \cdot 16$$
$$\overline{\qquad\qquad} = 322 \cdot 54$$
$$4$$

whence

$$322 \cdot 54 \qquad 383 \cdot 56$$
$$256 \cdot \qquad 322 \cdot 54$$

diff. of e'—$c' = 66 \cdot 54 \quad 61 \cdot 02 = $ diff. of g'—e'

These are the vibration numbers of the two difference tones ; and we have—

$$66 \cdot 54$$
$$61 \cdot 02$$

$$5 \cdot 52$$

or $5\frac{1}{2}$ beats per second nearly.

Application to the construction of systems.

For this purpose it is necessary to know the absolute pitch, as all the numbers in question vary with it. The following method can be carried out with a few organ pipes or harmonium reeds :—

RULE.—To the note (c) to be determined tune a perfect fifth (c—g), and to this (g) a

perfect fourth down (g—d). Then (c—d) is a major tone.

Interpolate between these two notes so many others that the beats between each pair are just slow enough to admit of counting. Count the number of beats given by each of the pairs in two minutes : add, and divide the sum by 15. The result is the number of vibrations of (c) in one second.

Ex.—A harmonium reed sounded a note near tenor c ; d was made a major tone to it as above : four notes (I., II., III., IV.) were arranged so as to give countable beats. The numbers observed in a quarter of a minute were :—

$$c— \ \text{I.} = 58$$
$$\text{I.}— \ \text{II.} = 44 \cdot 5$$
$$\text{II.}—\text{III.} = 70$$
$$\text{III.}—\text{IV.} = 49$$
$$\text{IV.}— \ d = 40$$

$$261 \cdot 5$$

Multiply by 8 we have the number for two minutes $= 2092$; and dividing by 15 we get $139 \cdot 5$ for the vibration number of the given note.

When we have the vibration number of the starting-point, we can proceed to obtain numbers of beats for guidance in tuning.

E.g.—To tune the equal temperament by fifths.

The following are the beats per minute when $c_i = 264$:—

c' —g'	53·4
$c'\sharp$—$g'\sharp$	57·
d' —a'	60·3
$e'\flat$—$b'\flat$	64·2
e' —b'	67·5
f' —c''	71·6
$f'\sharp$—$c''\sharp$	75·6
g' —d''	80.4
$a'\flat$—$e''\flat$	85·2
a' —e''	90·
$b'\flat$—f''	95·4
b' —$f''\sharp$	101·4

The methods indicated in the foregoing brief sketch are sufficient for the solution of problems in tuning. Our limits preclude further discussion on the subject.

Tempestosamente (*It.*) Impetuously, furiously.

Tempestoso (*It.*) Tempestuous, moved, agitated.

Tempête (*Fr.*) A dance invented in Paris about twenty-five years ago. The dancers are arranged as in a quadrille, in parties of four couples. Two couples stand side by side facing their respective *vis-à-vis*, so that as there are no side couples as many sets can be arranged as the ball-room will accommodate. " The step is the same as the quadrille, varied sometimes by the introduction of the galop step, when the couples cross to each others' places, or advance to the lines of the next set." La Tempête is danced to quick music in $\frac{2}{4}$ time.

Tempo (*It.*) Time or measure. *Tempo comodo*, convenient, easy, moderate time; *Tempo di Ballo*, dance time; *Tempo di Cappella*, in the time of Church music [A Cappella]; *Tempo di Gavotta*, in the time of a gavot [Gavot]; *Tempo di Marcia*, in marching time; *Tempo di Menuetto*, in the time of a minuet [Minuet]; *Tempo di Polacca*, in the time of a polacca [Polacca]; *Tempo di prima parte*, in the time of the first part, or original movement; *Tempo di Valse*, in waltz time [Waltz]; *Tempo frettevole* or *frettoloso*, in quick, hastened, hurried time; *Tempo giusto*. [A tempo giusto]; *Tempo ordinario*, in ordinary or usual time; an ordinary walking pace, an *andante*. *Tempo perduto*, lost, interrupted, broken, and irregular time. *Tempo primo*, first or original time; a direction to resume the pace with which the movement started after an alteration. *Tempo reggiato*, regulated time. A direction to accommodate the pace to the solo performer. *Tempo rubato*, robbed or stolen time. Time occasionally slackened or hastened for the purposes of expression.

Tempo wie vorher (*Ger.*) The time as before.

Temps, or Tems (*Fr.*) (1) Time; (2) the parts or divisions of a bar. *Temps faible*, (1) weak time; (2) the unaccented parts of a bar. *Temps fort*, (1) strong time; (2) the accented parts of a bar. *Temps frappé*, the down beats in a bar [Down beat]. *Temps levé*, the up beats in a bar [Up beat].

Tempus (*Lat.*) Time, one of the three early divisions of mensurable music, which were—(1) Mode; (2) Time; (3) Prolation. *Modus* was the division of a maxim into longs, or of a long into breves; *Tempus*, the division of a breve into semibreves; *Prolatio*, the division of a semibreve into minims. Tempus was of two kinds, "perfectum" and "imperfectum;" in the former, the breve was divided into three semibreves; in the latter, into two semibreves. The sign of the former is a complete circle, ○; that of the latter, an incomplete circle, ℂ. It is from this latter sign, in all probability, we derive our mark for common time now usually written as a ℂ.

Ten., abb. of *tenuto*.

Tendrement (*Fr.*) Tenderly, delicately.

Tenebræ (*Lat.*) An office celebrated on the afternoons of Maundy Thursday and Good Friday, and on other special days in the Roman Catholic Church, to commemorate the darkness over the earth at the time of the Crucifixion.

Tenendo il canto (*It.*) Sustaining the melody.

Teneramente (*It.*) Delicately, tenderly.

Tenerezza, con (*It.*) With tenderness, softness, delicacy.

Tenero (*It.*) Tender, soft, delicate, sensible, careful.

Tenete (*It.*) Keep, hold, sustain.

Tenor, Tenore (*It.*), **Taille** (*Fr.*) (1) The third of the four kinds of voices arranged with regard to their compass. It is the highest of male chest voices, and its extent lies between tenor C and treble A.

(2) The tenor voice is sometimes called by way of distinction "the human voice," from an idea that it is the quality and compass of voice most common to man. The Plain Song of the Church was formerly given as a tenor part, the harmonies being constructed above and below it; the supposed derivation of the word tenor from *teneo*, I hold, is supported by the fact that the *cantus firmus* was known and sung by the congregation or greater body of singers. Many of the hymn tunes employed up to the first quarter of the eighteenth century, as well as many of the arrangements of the responses used in the Church Service, were written with the melody in the tenor part.

(3) In old music the tenor voice was divided into three classes—*altus*, *medius*, and *bassus*—high, mean, and low tenor.

(4) The larger violin of low pitch is called the tenor, viola, bratsche, and sometimes alto violin. [Viola.]

(5) The principal bell in a peal, or set, is distinguished by the name of tenor bell.

Tenor C. (1) The lowest C in the tenor voice.

(2) The lowest string of the tenor violin.

Tenor clef. The C clef placed upon the fourth line of the stave.

It is used for the tenor voice, tenor trombone, the higher register of the bassoon and violoncello, &c. The treble clef is sometimes employed for the tenor voice, but the notes are then expressed an octave above their true sound. The late Thomas Oliphant suggested that two treble clefs conjoined should be the sign of the tenor G clef.

Tenore (*It.*) (1) Tenor voice. (2) A tenor singer; *Tenore buffo*, a tenor singer to whom is assigned a comic part in an opera ; *Tenore leggiero*, a tenor singer with a voice of light, small quality ; *Tenore robusto*, a tenor singer with a full, strong, sonorous voice.

Tenorist. One who sings the tenor part, or plays the tenor violin.

Tenoroon. (1) The name of an old tenor oboe with a compass extending downwards to tenor C. (2) A word affixed to an organ stop to denote that it does not proceed below tenor C, as, *tenoroon hautboy*. A *tenoroon diapason* is a double diapason which does not extend below tenor C.

Tenor posaune (*Ger.*) Tenor trombone. [Trombone.]

Tenor schlüssel (*Ger.*) Tenor clef.

Tenor trombone. A trombone with a compass of two octaves and a fifth

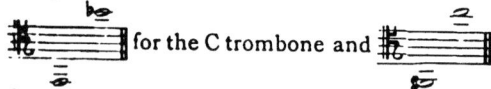

for the C trombone and

for the B flat trombone. [Trombone.]

Tenor violin. The viola. [Viola.]

Tenorzeichen (*Ger.*) The tenor clef. [Clef.]

Tenth. (1) A compound interval comprising an octave and a third, nine conjoint degrees, or ten sounds. The tenth is the octave of the third, and may be major or minor, diminished or augmented. [Intervals.] (2) An organ stop, tuned a tenth above the diapasons, called also *double tierce* or *decima*. [Organ.]

Tenuto (*It.*), **Tenu** (*Fr.*) Held on, sustained, kept down for the full time.

Teorbo (*It*) [Theorbo.]

Teoria (*It.*) Theory. *Teoria del Canto*, the theory of singing; *Teoria d'armonia*, the theory of harmony.

Tepidamente (*It.*) In a lukewarm manner. with indifference.

Tepidità (*It.*) Coldness, indifference.

Ter (*Lat.*) Thrice.

Tercet (*Fr.*) A triplet. [Triplet.]

Ternary form. Rondo form. [Form.]

Ternary measure. Triple time. Perfect time. [Signature § 2.]

Terpodion. An instrument invented by David Buschmann of Hamburg, in 1816, resembling in appearance the pianoforte, but the tone was produced from blocks of wood struck with hammers. It contained also a contrivance by which the sound might be increased or diminished at pleasure.

Tertia (*Lat.*) [Tierce.]

Tertian. An organ stop composed of two ranks of pipes, sounding a major third and fifth of the foundation pipes, in the third octave above; a *Tierce* and *Larigot* on one slider.

Ter unca (*Lat.*) Thrice hooked. A demi-semiquaver

Terz (*Ger.*) [Tierce.]

Terza (*It.*) (1) The third. *Opera terza*, the third work; *Violino terzo*, the third violin. (2) [Tierce.]

Terzdecime. An interval of a thirteenth, the octave of the sixth.

Terzdecimole. A group of thirteen notes to be performed in the time of eight, or of twelve.

Terzetto (*It.*) A little composition for three performers.

Terzflöte (*Ger.*) (1) A flute sounding a third above the notes written. (2) An organ stop. [Tierce.]

Terzina (*It.*) A triplet.

Terzo mano (*It.*) *Lit.* a third hand. An octave coupler on Italian organs.

Terzquartakkord (*Ger.*) The $\frac{4}{3}$ or $\frac{6}{4}{3}$ chord. The second inversion of the chord of the dominant seventh.

Terzquartsextakkord (*Ger.*) [Terzquartakkord.]

Terzquintsextakkord (*Ger.*) The $\frac{6}{3}$ chord. The first inversion of the chord of the dominant seventh, figured $\frac{6}{5}$.

Testo (*It.*) (1) The text, theme, subject of a composition. (2) The libretto of an opera, or the words of a song.

Testudo (*Lat.*) A name for the lyre, because the sounding part or hollow was made of the shell of the sea tortoise or turtle. [Lyre.]

Tetrachord. A scale-series of *four* notes. The word in its modern sense signifies a half of the octave scale, *e.g.*:

First Tetrachord.   Second Tetrachord.

It will be seen that the position of the tones and semitones is similar in both tetrachords. A third tetrachord placed above these two would lead into the key of G., *e.g.*:

and another into the key of D,

and so on through all the sharp keys. Similarly, tetrachords placed below the first lead into flat keys, *e.g.*:

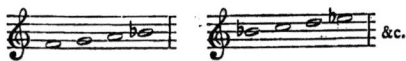
&c.

Tetrachords which overlap are said to be *conjunct*; those having a degree between them, *disjunct*.

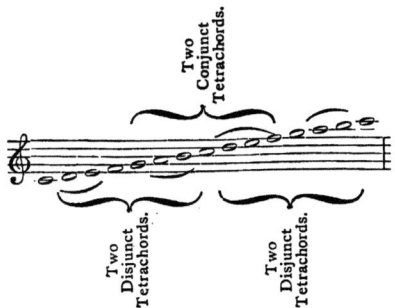

Similar disjunct tetrachords necessarily pass through the whole key-series, and a combination of conjunct and disjunct tetrachords is required to form a diatonic scale of more than one octave in compass. [Greek music.]

Tetrachordal system. The early form of the system now known as *Tonic Sol-fa*. [Tonic Sol-fa.]

Tetrachordon. An instrument similar in appearance to a cottage pianoforte, and like it played by finger-board, but the tone, instead of being produced by striking, is obtained by means of a cylinder of india-rubber charged with rosin, kept in motion by a pedal, variety of tone being gained by the depth of pressure on the keys by the fingers. It is called the tetrachordon from an idea that its sounds are similar to those produced by a string quartet. The instrument is constructed also with self-acting machinery. [Bogen-clavier.] [Xänorphika.] [Hurdy Gurdy.]

Theil (*Ger.*) (1) A part or division of a bar. (2) A phrase, strain, or part of a piece. (3) A piece, composition, work.

Thema (*Ger.*) [Theme.]

Thême (*Fr.*) [Theme.]

Theme. (1) One of the divisions of a subject, in the development of sonata-form. [Form.] (2) The *cantus firmus* on which counterpoint is built. (3) The subject of a fugue. (4) A simple tune on which variations are made.

Théorbe (*Fr.*) [Theorbo.]

Theorbo, Tiorba (*It.*); **Théorbe** (*Fr.*); **Basslaute** (*Ger.*) (1) An old stringed instrument resembling the lute in form or tone. It had two necks, to the longest of which the bass strings were attached. It was employed for accompanying voices, and was in great favour during the seventeenth century. Mace describes it as "no other than that which we call'd the old English lute." It differed from the lute in the possession of its two necks, from whence it is sometimes called cithara bijuga.

The strings were usually single in the Theorbo, and when double, or tuned in octaves or unison with the bass or treble notes, the instrument was called the arch-lute, or chittarone.

(2) Its invention has been variously assigned to an Italian, Signor Tiorba, from whom it is said to have derived its name; to one called Bardella about the year 1600; and to Hotteman, a German, living in France in 1650.

Sir John Hawkins attributes the invention to a nameless Neapolitan, who called it Tiorba from its resemblance to an instrument used for pounding perfumes so called. Johannes Kapsberger, a German of noble birth, who died about 1630, was a skilful performer on the instrument, and wrote a large quantity of music in tablature for it.

(3) The Theorbo was used as an instrument in the orchestra as late as the year 1708 by Francesco Conti. It was also employed in the performance of sonatas in the place of the cembalo, from its power of rendering a figured or thorough bass. Corelli's third set of sonatas, published in Bologna in 1690, contains a part for the Theorbo or violone.

Theoretiker (*Ger.*) A theorist.

Théoricien (*Fr.*) A theorist.

Theorist. One who studies the nature of sound or the principles of musical art.

Theory of music. The science of music. The speculations arising from a knowledge of the principles of sound. The rules for composition and arrangement of music for voices and instruments in rhythm, melody, harmony, counterpoint, and instrumentation.

Thesis (*Gk.*) The downward wave of the hand to denote the absence of accent. [Accent, § 5.] [Arsis.] [Metre.]

Thin. (1) Meagre and scanty harmony. (2) A poor quality of tone in a voice or on an instrument.

Third. [Interval.]

Third flute. [Terzflöte.]

Third stave. A name given to the stave upon which pedal music is written for the organ.

Thirteenth, chord of the. A chord called by some a suspension; by others, a secondary seventh (*see* Seventh, Exs. 34—41). It consists generally of the 3rd, 7th, and 13th of the dominant, and is used both in the major and minor modes. The following are its most common forms.

(Without 7th.)

(With 7th.)

Thirty - second note. A demisemi-quaver.

Thorough bass, Basso continuo (*It.*), **Basse contrainte**(*Fr.*) A species of musical shorthand, reduced to a system by Ludovico Viadani, about the year 1605, which has remained substantially unimproved since his day. It consists of a bass part with the accompanying harmonies indicated by figures. Henri Dumont was the earliest musician in France who made use of thorough bass, about 1640, and the first treatise on thorough bass, published in England, was the work of Matthew Lock, issued under the title of "Melothesia; or, Certain General Rules for Playing upon a Continued Bass, with a choice collection of Lessons for the Harpsichord and Organ of all sorts," London, 1673. Francis de la Fond in 1725, suggested a new method of figuring a bass by calling the notes of the chromatic scale by the numbers one up to thirteen. [Figured Bass.]

Threnody. An elegy, or funeral song, from the Greek θρηνῳδία.

Thrice - marked - octave (*Dreigestrichen octav*). The name given in Germany to all the notes of the octave above C in alt. [Pitch.]

Thrum. (1) To play without skill upon a stringed instrument. (2) The sound so made.

Thürner(*Ger.*) A town musician. [Waits.]

Tibia (*Lat.*) [Flute.]

Tibiæ pares (*Lat.*) [Flute.]

Tibiæ utriculariæ. [Bagpipe.]

Tibia major. An organ flute-stop of 16ft. pitch. [Flute.]

Tibicen (*Lat.*) (From *tibia* and *cano*.) A flute-player; *tibicina*, a female flautist; *tibicinium*, a piping; *tibicino*, to pipe.

Tie. (1) A curved line placed over two or more notes in the same position on the stave:

The tie is also called a *bind*, and the curved line, when used over notes representing different sounds, is called a *slur*. [Bind.] [Slur.] (2) When two or more quavers, semiquavers, &c., are united, instead of being written with separate tails, they are said to be *tied*. [Stem.] [Printing of Music.]

Tief (*er.*) Deep, low.

Tierce (*Fr.*) (1) A third. (2) An organ stop tuned a seventeenth above the diapason. [Organ.] (3) The service which took place at the third hour of the day, the undersang of the Anglo Saxons. [Horæ Canonicæ.] (4) The natural harmonic produced by ⅕ of a vibrating string. [Acoustics.]

Tierce de Picardie (*Fr.*) The sharpened third in the concluding chord of a composition in the minor mode.

Tierce coulée (*Fr.*) A slurred third. In old harpsichord music the *tierce coulée* was expressed by a dash through the notes of the third, in a diagonal direction, thus:

when it was called the rising slurred third, *tierce coulée en montant*, and was played:

A stroke in the opposite direction

was called the falling slurred third, *tierce coulée en descendant*, and was played:

Timb. Abb. for Timballes. [Kettle-drums.]

Timbale (*Fr.*) [Kettle-drum.]

Timballo (*It.*) [Kettle-drum.]

Timbre (*Fr.*) Quality of tone or sound. *Klang* or *Klangfarbe* (*Ger.*) [Acoustics, § 16.]

Timbrel. [Tabor.] [Tambourine.]

Time. (1) The division of musical phrases into certain regulated portions measured with regard to the value of the notes with respect to the semibreve, which, in modern music, is held to be the standard of time. There are two sorts of time, duple with two, four, or eight beats in a bar, and triple with three beats in a bar. There is also compound time, or time formed of the union of triple with duple, and triple with triple, each having a distinctive time signature. [Signature, § 2.]

(2) The pace at which a movement is performed is called its *time*.

Timorosamente (*It.*) Timidly, hesitatingly, with fear.

Timoroso (*It.*) Timorous, with hesitation.

Timp. Abb. of Timpani.

Timpani (*It.*) Kettle-drums.

Timpanista (*It.*) A drummer.

Tintement (*Fr.*) The tinkling of a bell.

Tintinno (*It.*) [Tintement.]

Tintinnabulum (*Lat.*) A rattle (*Gk.* πλαταγή) formed either of small bells or little plates of metal.

Tiorbo (*It.*) [Theorbo.]

Tipping. [Double tongueing.]

Tirade. The filling up of an interval between two notes with a run, in vocal or instrumental music, *e.g.*:

Tirante (*Sp.*) The brace of a drum.

Tirasse (*Fr.*) The pedals of an organ which act on the keys or manuals.

Tirato (*It.*) (1) A down bow. [Bowing.] (2) A scale passage in notes of equal length.

Tira tutto (*It.*) A pedal commanding the full power of the organ. (*Fr.*) *Grand jeu.*

Tiré (*Fr.*) (1) Drawn, pulled. (2) A down bow. [Bowing.] (3) The drawing out of an accordion.

Titty, tziti, toutari. An Indian bagpipe. [Bagpipe.]

Toccata (*It.*) (1) A prelude or overture. The overture to Rinuccini's opera "Orfeo," 1609, is called a *toccata*, and is directed to be performed three times, "Avanti il lever de la tela," "before the rising of the curtain." (2) Compositions written as exercises. (3) A fantasia. (4) A suite.

Toccatina (*It.*) A short toccata.

Todtenmarsch (*Ger.*) A funeral march.

Tombestere *or* **Tymbestere** (*old Eng.*)

A female dancer, who accompanied herself upon a tambourine, occasionally throwing her instrument in the air and catching it.

"There was many a tymbestere,
Couthe her crafte full parfytly."—*Chaucer.*

Tom-tom. A gong.

Ton. (*Fr.* and *Ger.*) (1) Tone, sound. (2) The interval of a second.

Tonabstand (*Ger.*) An interval.

Tonada (*Sp.*) A tune, air, or melody.

Tonadilla (*Sp.*) A short tune, an interlude, ritornello, symphony to a song.

Tonal Fugue. [Fugue.]

Tonarion *or* **Tonarium.** A pitch-pipe (according to Quintilian) used by the Latin orators for the purpose of regulating the pitch of their speaking voice, called also *fistula eburneola.* Dionysius limits the compass of the oratorical voice to *five notes.* When this compass was exceeded, an attendant blew the *tonarion* to enable the orator to recover his proper pitch.

Tonart (*Ger.*) Mode, tune, key, scale-system, *tonality.*

Tonausweichung (*Ger.*) Modulation.

Ton bas (*Fr.*) A deep, low tone.

Tondichter (*Ger.*) A composer. A poet *in sounds*, as a painter may be described as a poet *in colours.* This word has been badly rendered "tone-poet."

Tondichtung (*Ger.*) A musical composition. A sound-poem.

Tone. (1) Sound. (2) Quality of tone. [Acoustics, § 16.] (3) The interval of a second. [Interval.] (4) A Gregorian chant. [Plain Song.]

Tonfall (*Ger.*) A cadence.

Tonfolge (*Ger.*) A succession of sounds. A melody.

Tonführung (*Ger.*) (1) A melodic succession. (2) [Modulation.]

Tonfuss (*Ger.*) A foot. [Metre.]

Tongang (*Ger.*) [Tonführung.]

Ton-générateur (*Fr.*) [Root.]

Tongeschlecht (*Ger.*) The character of the modes. There are two *Tongeschlechter*—major and minor. [Scale.] [Mode.]

Ton haut (*Fr.*) An acute sound.

Tonic, Tonica (*It.*), **Tonique** (*Fr.*) (1) The key-note of any scale. The ground-tone or basis of a scale or key. (2) The key-chord in which a piece is written, and with which it concludes.

Tonic Sol-fa. A letter-system of notation. Many attempts have from time to time been made to produce a simpler notation than the stave, clefs, signature, &c., of the so-called "Old Notation."

As early as the year 1672, Thomas Salmon wrote a book entitled, "An essay to the advancement of music, by casting away the perplexities of different cliffs, and uniting all sorts of music, lute, viol, violins, organ, harpsichord, voice, &c., in one universal character." In this he proposed to write all music on a stave of four lines, which should give the notes the names of the first seven letters of the alphabet, octaves above or below being marked with the name of the octave to which they belong. The proposition was violently opposed by Matthew Lock, but other musicians treated it with contempt, and Salmon's book and proposition now exist only among the literary curiosities of music. Jean Jacques Rousseau suggested a notation whereby the notes of the scale were indicated by the numbers 1 to 7. This, or rather an improved form of it, is still largely used in France. Miss Sarah A. Glover, of Norwich, about thirty years ago projected and taught successfully a system which she called the tetrachordal system, which was the Tonic Sol-fa notation in its original form ; but it has since received such important modifications and additions from the hands of the Rev. J. Curwen, that it is now justly associated with his name.

Its chief *raison d'être* is that the ordinary notation, just in the degree that it accommodates itself to the keyboard and the theory founded more or less thereon, is not fitted as a notation for the greatest of all instruments, the human voice. Tonic Sol-faists nevertheless maintain that their notation may be used in all branches of the art, and pupils are taught to play instruments, to study harmony, musical form, and composition, entirely from the syllables. The leading features of the notation are as follows : Of the two relationships of musical sounds, those of pitch and key, the latter is of transcendent importance. It is argued, therefore, that it is of the first consideration that this supremely important fact should be prominently shown. The keynote of a piece is, therefore, always called *doh*, the second of the scale *ray*, and so on, *me, fah, soh, lah, te*. The reason for this departure from the ordinary spelling is, that the above is considered easier for English people to pronounce. In printing music, the initial letter indicates the scale note. *Si* and *soh* having the same initial, the former is altered to *te*. Higher or lower octaves are shown by figures placed by the side of the notes, *d¹, d², m¹*. and *s₁, m₂, d₂*. The first part of the National Anthem is written in tune thus, *d d r t, d r m m f m r d r d t, d*. The particular pitch of the key-sound is shown by the statement at the beginning of the piece, key G, key E♭, key A, &c. The minor mode is regarded as derived from the relative major, the tonic being called *lah*. It is maintained that to call the tonic of the minor scale *doh*, would lead to extraordinary practical diffi-

culties, besides being false in theory. Changes of key in the course of a piece are met by what are called *bridge tones*. The note of the key quitted is placed side by side with the note of the same pitch in the key approached, and the pupil is taught to think and sing the sound of the first note, and to call it by the name of the second. Thus, *d r m f ¹d t, d* would show a transition, say from key C to key G. By this means changes of the most complex nature are simply represented by Tonic Sol-faists, and they assert that the music has yet to be quoted which cannot be expressed in their notation. The chromatic scale is named by adding the vowel *e* to the initial of sharpened notes, and *a* (pronounced *aw*) to notes to be flattened. Thus *de, re, fe, se*, are respectively *d, r, f, s*, sharp, and *ma, la, ta*, are *m, l, t*, flat. The sharp sixth of the minor scale is called *bah* to distinguish it from *fe* the sharp fourth of the major. Time and accent are indicated by measurement across the page thus :

| : | : | : |

the space between one sign and the next, representing the pulse or beat ; the line showing the stronger beat or accent, and the colon the weaker. For short divisions a dot | . : in the centre of the pulse divides it into halves, and commas | , . , : are used to divide into quarters, and other divisions are similarly shown. A stroke — through a pulse means that a previous note is to be continued. Sol-faists believe that their fixed standard of a pulse or beat gives them considerable advantage over the ever-shifting standard of the ordinary notation. " Rule Britannia " is thus written :

.s,|d   :d |d,r.m,f:s .d | r   :r .m,f|m .etc.

No account of the Tonic Sol-fa Notation would be complete without reference to its indispensable adjunct the Tonic Sol-fa Method, *i.e.*, the distinctive plan of teaching the musical facts indicated by the notation. This method is the outcome of years of laborious enquiry by Mr. Curwen, and of the collated experience of all the best teachers of the system. Great stress is given to the doctrine of *mental effect*, by which is meant the various impressions or colours of the notes of the scale when sung slowly. Thus *doh*, is considered firm ; *te*, sharp and piercing ; *lah*, sorrowful ; *fah*, gloomy ; *soh*, bright and clear, &c., &c. Teaching by pattern is also insisted on ; the scale is taught in the following order, first the notes of the tonic chord *d m s* and their replicates, next the dominant chord *s t r*, then the sub-dominant chord *f l d*. In developing the scale, large use is made of what has been justly called the backbone of the system, the MODULATOR, without a proper use of which, it is not too much to say, the method cannot be fairly taught or learned.

```
r'  s  d'      f'
          t  —  m'  — l   r'  s
d'  f
t  m  l  =  r'  —  s   d'  f
                          t  m
l   r  s  —DOH'— f
           TE  — m  l   r
s  d  f   ta    le
   t,  m —LAH = r   s  d
f         la    se         t,
m  l,  r —SOH— d  f
          ba    fe   t,  m  l,
r  s,  d  — FAH
    t,  — ME  — l,  r  s,
d  f,     ma    re
t,  m, l, = RAY — s,  d  f,
           de          t,  m,
l,  r,  s,  — DOH — f,
     t,  — m,  l,  r,
s,  d,  f,
   t,  m, —  l,  = r,  s,  d,
f,                          t,
m,  l,  r, —  s,  — d,  f,
                    t,  m, l,
r,  s,  d,  —  f,
    t,  —  m,  — l,  r,  s,
```

This Modulator is a sort of map of musical sounds. It represents pictorially in an upright position the relative places of the notes of a scale, its minor mode, its chromatics, and its more closely related scales. By frequent and systematic handling of this sheet, the upward or downward motion of the notes printed all on one level, is adequately realised by the pupil. The Modulator is manipulated with great effect by the best teachers of the system. In teaching Time an adaptation of the time-names used in the French Cheve system' has lately been more or less adopted by Sol-faists. Syllables are used to show the length of notes just as they are to show the relation of sounds. Thus *taa* is the name of a pulse, *taa-tai* of half pulses, and *tafatefe* of quarter pulses. Continuations of any kind are met by dropping the consonant. It is thought that the finer accents of divided pulses, as well as the broader accents of the measure, can be better taught by the use of this language of duration than on any other plan.

Tonkunst (*Ger.*) The art and science of music.

Tonkünstler (*Ger.*) A musician. A musical artist.

Tonleiter (*Ger.*) A scale. [Scale.]

Ton majeur (*Fr.*) Major key or mode.

Tonmalerei (*Ger.*) Composition, invention, sound-painting.

Tonmessung (*Ger.*) Tone-measuring, metre, rhythm.

Ton mineur (*Fr.*) Minor key or mode.

Tonos (*Gk.*) τόνος. [Tone.]

Tonsatz (*Ger.*) A musical composition.

Tonschluss (*Ger.*) A cadence.

Tonschlüssel (*Ger.*) [Key.]

Tonschrift (*Ger.*) (1) Written music. (2) Musical notes or characters.

Tons de la trompette (*Fr.*) Crooks used to alter the pitch of a trumpet. [Crook.]

Tons de l'église (*Fr.*) Church modes or tones. [Plain Song.]

Tonsetzer (*Ger.*) (1) A composer. (2) (In a sarcastic sense) a music-maker.

Tonsetzkunst (*Ger.*) The art of musical composition.

Tonsetzung (*Ger.*) A musical composition.

Tonspieler (*Ger.*) A performer.

Tonsprache (*Ger.*) The art of expressing thoughts and feelings in music.

Tonstück (*Ger.*) A piece of music, a composition.

Tonstufe (*Ger.*) A step or degree of a scale.

Tonsystem (*Ger.*) (1) The systematic arrangement of sounds according to the rules of melody, harmony, and rhythm. (2) A scale.

Tonverhalt (*Ger.*) Rhythm.

Tonzeichen (*Ger.*) (1) A note or other character used in music. (2) Accent.

Toomourah. An Indian tambourine.

Toorooree. A trumpet used by the Brahmins in their religious processions.

Toph (*Heb.*) A drum. [Tabor.] [Tambourine.]

Torcelli. A name anciently given to organs in Italy.

Tosto (*It.*) Quick, swift, rapid. *Più tosto,* more rapid; *Tostamente,* quickly, rapidly; *Tostissamamente, Tostissimo,* very quickly, with great rapidity.

Touch. (1) The resistance made to the fingers by the keys of a pianoforte or organ. Thus the touch of the keyboard may be hard or light accordingly as the resistance is great or little. (2) The peculiar manner in which a player presses the keyboard, whether light, pearly, heavy, clumsy, firm, &c.

Touches (*Fr.*) The keys of a pianoforte, organ, harmonium, and concertina.

Touquet (*Fr.*) [Toccato.] [Tucket.]

Tours de force (*Fr.*) (1) Roulades, runs, or divisions for the voice. (2) Passages of rapid execution upon an instrument.

Toys. An old English name for dance tunes and light and trifling pieces of music. "Pavens, Galiards, Almaines, Toies, Jiggs, Thumpes, and such like." Ford's "Musicke of sundre kindes," 1607.

Trachea. [Larynx.]

Trackers. [Organ.]

Tractur (*Ger.*) [Trackers.]

Tractus (*Lat.*) A melody sung in the Roman Catholic Church during Lent instead of the Alleluia.

Tradotto (*It.*) Transposed, arranged, translated. [Arrangement.]

Trainé (*Fr.*) Slurred, bound, dragged.

Trait (*Fr.*) (1) A run, or division; *trait de chant*, a melodious vocal phrase. (2) A special passage, or phrase for body of instruments of the same class. Like the *trait des violons* in Cherubini's overture to "Anacreon," or the passage for strings in Beethoven's No. 3, "Leonora." (3) A sequence in harmony, *trait d'harmonie*. (4) *Trait d'octave*, rule of the octave.

Traité (*Fr.*) A treatise on the theory or practice of music.

Tranquillamente (*It.*) Tranquilly, calmly, quietly.

Tranquillità, con (*It.*) With tranquillity, calmness.

Transcription. The arrangement or modification of a composition for some instrument or voice other than that for which it was originally written.

Transient Modulation. The temporary introduction of chords or progressions from an unrelated key. [Modulation.]

Transitio (*Lat.*) Change of key.

Transitus (*Lat.*) Progression by passing notes; *transitus regularis*, diatonic progression, the passing notes on the unaccented portions of the bar; *transitus irregularis*, progression in which some of the notes of the scale are omitted; passing notes on the accented part of the bar.

Transition. (1) A modulation. [Modulation.] (2) A passing note. [Passing Note.]

Transponiren (*Ger.*) Alteration of the original key. [Transposition.]

Transponirende Instrumente (*Ger.*) [Transposing Instruments.]

Transpose. To alter the key in which a piece is set, by changing it into a higher or lower scale.

Transposing Instruments. A general name for all instruments which do not produce the exact sounds written on paper for them.

Thus, a B♭ clarinet is so called because the *written* note C, when sounded, is B♭; its part, therefore, is written one note higher than the actual sounds required. Similarly, the A clarinet is so called because the *written* note C, when sounded, is A; its part, therefore, is written a minor third higher than the sounds actually required. The C clarinet is so called because it plays *as written*. The Cor Anglais and Corno di bassetto produce sounds a major fifth below those written.

A C horn produces sounds one octave below those actually written; a D horn, a minor seventh below; an E horn, a minor sixth below, and so on. A B♭ *alto* horn produces sounds a whole tone below that written; a B♭ *basso* horn, a ninth below.

Similarly, a trumpet in B♭ produces sounds one note below those actually written, and a D trumpet sounds *one note above*. Drum parts are usually written as if always in the key of C, directions being given as to the tuning, at the commencement of each movement.

The only transposing string-instrument is the double bass, which produces sounds an octave below those written, as far as its compass will permit. Flutes, oboes, bassoons, and trombones, are not transposing instruments; but the *piccolo* flute produces sounds one octave higher than those written, and the *double bassoon* sounds one octave lower.

Transposing Piano. A pianoforte so constructed that its key-board may be moved to admit of its giving sounds, other than those which the scale used would seem to imply. The key-frame is made in duplicate, and on it is screwed, by means of ordinary thumb-screws, the action, making it perfectly rigid. At each extreme end of the keys the block of wood, called the "key-block," is also attached to the key-frame, and thus rendered moveable. These blocks are pierced with holes exactly a semitone apart, in which small pegs of wood are inserted. When it is required to alter the piano to a higher or lower pitch the pegs are taken out, and the key-board can then be moved up or down the scale.

Transposition. (1) A change of key. [Transpose.] (2) An inversion of parts in counterpoint.

Trascinando (*It.*) Dragging, delaying the time.

Trascritto (*It.*) Transcribed, copied.

Trattato (*It.*) A treatise.

Traversière (*Fr.*) Across. *Flûte traversière.* The flute held crossways, as is now usual; the *flûte à bec* being blown with a mouthpiece like the oboe. [Flute.]

Traverso (*It.*) [Traversière.]

Tre (*It.*) Three. *A tre voci*, for three voices; or, in three parts.

Treble. (1) The highest vocal or instrumental part, sung by women or boys, or played by violins, flutes, oboes, clarinets, or other instruments of acute tone. (2) The treble or soprano voice is the most flexible of all vocal registers, its ordinary compass is from middle C upwards to the extent of a twelfth, its exceptional range a fifteenth, or even beyond this. [Triplex.]

Treble Clef. The G clef on the second line of the stave, used for treble voices and instruments of high and medium pitch, such as flutes, oboes, clarinets, horns, violins, and trumpets. [Stave.] [Clef.]

Trem. Abb. of *tremando* and *tremolando*.

Tremolando (*It.*) Trembling, wavering. (1) A chord or note played or bowed with great rapidity so as to produce a quavering effect. (2) Vibration of the voice in singing, arising from nervousness, or a bad production; or used for the purpose of producing a special effect. [Vibrato.]

Tremolant, or Tremulant. An organ and harmonium stop which causes the air as it proceeds to the pipes or reeds to pass through a valve having a moveable top, to which a spring and weight are attached. The up and down movement of the top of the valve gives a vibratory movement to the air which similarly affects the sound produced. On American organs, a fan-wheel by rotating in front of the wind chest causes a *tremolando*.

Tremore (*It.*) [Tremolando.]

Tremoroso (*It.*) [Tremolando.]

Trenchmore. An old English country dance, or Hey-de-guy. It was of a lively character. Dr. Barton in his "Anatomy of Melancholy," 1621, says: "There is no remedy; we must dance Trenchmore over tables, chairs, and stools;" and Selden in his "Table-Talk" speaks of the dance as an "Omnium Gatherum, tolly polly, hoite cum toite." It is mentioned by several of the dramatic writers of the time of Queen Elizabeth.

TRENCHMORE.

Trenise (*Fr.*) The fourth figure in a quadrille.

Très (*Fr.*) Very. *Très animé*, very animated; *très vif*, very lively.

Triad. (1) A chord of three notes. (2) A common chord. Triads are said to be major, *e.g.*

; minor,

; augmented,

; diminished,

Triangle. An instrument of steel bent into a three-sided form. It is usually held by a string in the left hand and struck with a small bar of iron or steel with the right. It is employed with effect occasionally as an orchestral instrument.

Trias deficiens (*Lat.*) Imperfect triad. [Triad.]

Trias harmonica (*Lat.*) Perfect or major triad. [Triad.]

Tribrach. A foot consisting of three short syllables. [Metre.]

Tricinium (*Lat.*) A composition in three parts.

Trill. A shake.

Trill. Abb. of *trillando*.

Trillando (*It.*) Shaking. A lengthened vocal or instrumental shake.

Trille (*Fr.*), **Triller** (*Ger.*), **Trillo** (*It.*) A shake. In a tract entitled "A brief discourse of the Italian manner of singing, wherein is set down the use of those graces in singing, as the trill and gruppo, used in Italy, and now in England; written some years since by an English gentleman who had lived long in Italy, and, being returned, taught the same here," published by Playford about 1683; the trill is described as a shake upon one note only; it would therefore be similar to the effect called now the *vibrato*, while the gruppo was the *shake* as now practised.

Trillerkette (*Ger.*) A chain or succession of shakes. *Catena di trilli.*

Trillo caprino (*It.*) A goat-like shake.

Trinklied (*Ger.*) A song in praise of drinking.

Trio. (1) A composition for three voices or instruments. (2) A part of a minuet, march, &c. [Form.] [Minuet.]

Triole, Triolet (*Fr.*) A triplet. Three notes played in the time of two of the same name.

Triomphale, Triomphant (*Fr.*) **Trionfale, Trionfante** (*It.*) Triumphant.

Tripedisono. A *capo tasto*.

Tripeltakt (*Ger.*) Triple time.

Triphonisch (*Ger.*) Having three sounds.

Triple croche (*Fr.*) A demisemiquaver.

Triple counterpoint. A counterpoint in three parts, so contrived that each part will serve for bass, middle, or upper part as required. [Counterpoint.]

Triplet. A group of three notes performed in the time of two. The triplet is always indicated by a slur and the figure 3:

Triple time. Time of three beats, or three times three beats in a bar. [Signature § 2.]

Triplex, Triplum (*Lat.*) The name originally given to a third part when added to two other parts, one of which was a *canto fermo*, the other a *counterpoint*. This additional part was generally the *upper part*, hence the word *treble* or *triplex* came to be applied to the *canto primo*. (2) A motet or other composition in three parts.

Trisagion (*Gk.*) Thrice holy. *Ter Sanctus* (*Lat.*) The opening words of the Sanctus.

Trite. [Greek music.]

Tritone, Triton (*Fr.*), **Tritono** (*It.*), **Tritonus** (*Lat.*) An augmented fourth, containing three whole tones.

The use of the tritone was anciently forbidden in harmony or counterpoint, as it was regarded in the light of what is called a *false relation*. It was not permitted to be employed in the upper note of one chord and the lower note of the following, as in the subjoined examples:

In each case it was called *mi contra fa*, the leading or sensitive note being known as *mi*, and according to the old rules, *mi contra fa diabolus est*.

Tritt (*Ger.*) Tread, treadle, step.

Trittschuh (*Ger.*) A place for the foot on the bellows of old organs.

Trochee. A foot consisting of one long and one short syllable – ◡. [Metre.]

Troll. To take part in a catch or round, the voices succeeding each other at regulated intervals with the same melody.

Tromb. Abb. for *tromba*, trumpet, and trombone.

Tromba (*It.*) (1) A trumpet. (2) An organ reed stop of 8 ft. pitch.

Tromba bassa (*It.*) A bass trumpet.

Tromba cromatica (*It.*) A keyed trumpet capable of producing intermediate semitones. [Trumpet.]

Tromba marina (*It.*) [Trumpet marine.]

Tromba sorda (*It.*) A trumpet whose sound is stifled by the insertion of a mute in the bell.

Tromba spezzata (*It.*) An obsolete name for the bass trumpet.

Trombetta (*It.*) A small trumpet.

Trombone. (1) A large, deep and loud toned instrument of the trumpet species, the name being an augmentative of *tromba*. It consists of two tubes, so constructed that one may slide in and out of the other, and thus form one tube that can be lengthened at will and made of varying pitch. There are three kinds of trombones, called after their compass the alto, tenor, and bass trombones. Soprano trombones have also been made, but they are rarely used. The general compass of the trombone is a little more than two octaves, the pitch of the instrument varying with the length of the tube. Thus an alto trombone, the part for which is written sometimes in the alto clef, sometimes in the tenor clef, can play all notes between

a tenor trombone all between

and a bass trombone all between

including every intermediate semitone. Each instrument can also sound the note an octave below the first note shown as the commencement of the compass, besides other notes outside the notes indicated above, but as they are difficult and uncertain they are very rarely written. The trombone when judiciously used has a very fine effect, but the modern custom of forcing its tone, and playing in short sharp barks, is much to be regretted. The value of the instrument was well understood by Gluck, (who was probably the first who employed it in the orchestra), as well as by Mozart, Beethoven, Spontini and Weber, as a reference to the scores of Alceste, Die Zauberflöte, Fidelio, La Vestale, and Der Freischütz will prove. (2) A powerful reed stop in the organ of 8 ft. or 16 ft. scale on the manuals and 16 ft. or 32 ft. on the pedals.

Trommel (*Ger.*) Military drum.

Trommelklöpfel, or Trommelschlägel (*Ger.*) Drumstick.

Trommelschläger (*Ger.*) A drummer.

Trompe (*Fr.*) (1) A trumpet. (2) A hunting horn.

Trompe de Bearn (*Fr.*) [Jew's-harp.]

Trompete (*Ger.*) A trumpet.

Trompetenzug (*Ger.*) Trumpet stop or register in an organ.

Trompette (*Fr.*) (1) A trumpet. (2) A trumpeter. (3) A reed stop in the organ.

Trompette à clefs (*Fr.*) A keyed trumpet.

Trompette à pistons (*Fr.*) A valve trumpet.

Troop. (1) A march in quick time.

"When the drums and fifes sounding a troop
Off they briskly set."—DEFOE.

(2) The second beat of the drum as the signal for marching.

Troparia (*Gk.*) τροπάρια. Hymns which probably had their origin in the ancient custom of inserting ejaculations in the Psalms, especially when used as introits. "Tanto opere enim christiani primis sæculis medii ævi psalmorum cantui, patrum institutis quasi consecrato, favebant, ut nova cantica integra comprobare non auderent, sed *in brevibus strophis psalmorum versibus intexendis vel adfigendis acquiescerent.*" But in time the Christian poets *did* dare to write complete new poems which grew out of the ancient *troparium* just as the later prose or sequence grew out of the early attempts to set words to *pneumas.* [Sequence.] It is an interesting fact that in the early Greek Church a troparium for a great festival was called an ἀκολουθία, which, of course, is actually synonymous with *sequentia.*

Troparion. An office-book of the Greek Church containing the sequences or chants sung after the lessons. An ancient troparion with the musical notes is preserved in the Bodleian library at Oxford.

Troppo (*It.*) Too much. *Troppo caricata,* too much loaded, overloaded with ornaments or accompaniment. *Non troppo allegro,* not too quick.

Troubadour. A polished poet, who, unlike the jongleur, did not wander about the country singing for hire. In the days when all classes of the community were equally unrefined, there was no such distinction, every verse-maker was called a troubadour, a word derived probably from the Provençal *trobar,* to invent or find; and ultimately the term came to be confined to kings, princes, and nobles, who practised poetry for pleasure, or out of chivalrous gallantry. The minstrels or jongleurs only recited or chanted poems, but did not write or invent them; or perhaps accompanied on some instrument the troubadour who sang his own compositions. It was not an unusual thing for a troubadour to have several minstrels or jongleurs in his service; the word minstrel meant probably a minister or servant.

The minstrels in later times formed a separate guild, uniting for the purposes of mutual protection and support; but the troubadours were always independent, and this independence gives a character to their individual productions, unfettered as they are by the trammels of any particular school of thought. The same free spirit gives a colour to the rude outline of their history, so that the practice of their art is to be traced, not so much by its expansion and development in classes as in individuals. Troubadours frequently attached themselves to the courts of kings and nobles, whom they praised or censured in their songs; but it was a rule that some lady was selected as the "dame de du cœur," and to her, under some general or fanciful title, love songs, complaints, and other poems were addressed. The "love service" of the troubadours was often nothing more than a mere artificial gallantry, but there are instances on record where it became something more earnest.

Contests, competitions, or verse battles were sometimes entered into, generally on questions of gallantry suggested by the ladies who presided as judges over a tribunal called the Court of Love, and awarded prizes to the victors. The poems of the troubadours were not always confined to subjects of gallantry, sometimes they treated of the conditions of society, the evils of the times, the degeneracy of the clergy and other subjects.

There is reason for supposing that the art of the troubadours, generally called the *gay science,* was derived from the East, coming into Europe through the Spaniards, and the troubadours of Provençe learning from their neighbours of Spain. Troubadour poetry was cultivated in Provençe, Toulouse, Dauphiné, and other parts of France south of the Loire, as well as in Catalania, Arragon, and Valencia in Spain, and in the north of Italy. Its duration was about 200 years (1090-1290), the period when Eastern customs were giving a tone to those of Western Europe, and while chivalry began to redeem men from barbarism. Warton (History of English Poetry) rightly estimates the value of the poems of the troubadours, when he says:—"The Provençal writers established a common dialect, and their examples convinced other nations that the modern languages were no less adapted to composition than those of antiquity. They introduced a love of reading, and diffused a general and popular taste for poetry by writing in a language intelligible to ladies and the people. Their verses, being conveyed in a familiar tongue, became the chief amusement of princes and feudal lords, whose courts had now began to assume a greater brilliancy; a circumstance which necessarily gave great encouragement to their profession, and by rendering those arts of ingenious entertainments universally fashionable, imperceptibly laid the foundation of polite literature. From these beginnings it were easy to trace the progress of poetry to its perfection through John de Meum in France, Dante in Italy, and Chaucer in England."

Trouveur, Trouverre, *or* **Rymour.** According to Ritson, one who composed *Romants, Contes, Fabliaux, Chansons,* and

Lais, whilst those who devoted themselves to the composition of *Contes* and *Fabliaux* were called *Contours, Conteurs,* or *Fabliers.* [Troubadour.]

Trugschluss *or* **Trugcadenz** (*Ger.*) An interrupted or deceptive cadence.

Trumbscheit (*Ger.*) [Trumpet marine.]

Trummel (*Ger.*) [Trommel.]

Trump. A poetical name for the trumpet.

Trumpet, Tromba (*It.*), **Trompette** (*Fr.*), **Trompete** (*Ger.*) A metal wind instrument of bright and penetrating tone, formed of a single tube curved into a convenient shape, with a mouthpiece at one end, the other having a bell. Its part is usually written in the key of C with the treble clef, though by means of crooks or lengthening pieces the sounds produced may be in various keys. The trumpet required for a piece is indicated at the commencement; as, trumpet in C, D, E flat, E, F, or G.

The scale of the instrument is formed of the harmonics of an ordinary open pipe.

By means of the slide, the B flat shown above, which is a little flat, may be sounded in tune, and certain intermediate semitones obtained.

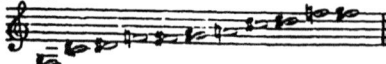

In addition to the notes shown above, the trumpet is capable of producing,

but the higher tones are very difficult to obtain. Handel and other writers of the last century frequently wrote them, but trumpeters of the present day omit them.

In old scores the trumpet was often coupled with the drums, the notes of the one corresponding to the beats on the other.

Gluck and Handel were among the earliest writers to discover the effect of long-holding notes, and the power of the softer tones of the trumpet.

Trumpets with pistons or valves capable of producing every chromatic sound within their compass are sometimes used, but the tone is by no means to be compared with the true trumpet tone.

Trumpet marine. An instrument formed of a triangular chest, over one side of which is stretched a thick gut string, passing over a bridge slightly uneven on its feet, one side being fastened and the other free. When the string is set in vibration by means of a bow, the rapid impact of the loose foot of the bridge on the belly slightly checks the vibration and causes the sound to resemble that of the trumpet. The fingers of the left hand of the player, being passed lightly over the strings, the ordinary harmonics of an open string are produced.

Tuba (*Lat.*) (1) A trumpet. (2) A powerful reed stop in the organ.

Tuba major, *or* **Tuba mirabilis.** A stop invented by William Hill, consisting of an 8 ft. reed on a high pressure of wind.

Tucket, Touquet (*Fr.*) A flourish on a trumpet. Mr. Staunton, in his notes on Shakspeare, conjectures it to be derived from the Italian *toccata,* or the Spanish *tocar; tocar trompeta,* to sound a trumpet.

Tumultuoso (*It.*) Tumultuous, agitated.

Tune. (1) A melody or air. [Air.] (2) Just intonation.

Tuning Fork. An instrument of steel with two prongs, which when set in vibration gives out a musical sound varying in pitch according to the thickness of the metal or the length or width apart of the prongs. It was invented by John Shore, sergeant trumpeter to George I. There is a considerable variety in the pitch of tuning forks, arising from the absence of any recognised standard of tonality. [Pitch.] The ordinary fork gives out a single note only, but one has been introduced from Germany which has a slider on each prong which can be moved up or down so as to alter the pitch.

Tuning. The adjustment of the sounds naturally produced by any instrument to some standard pitch and to their proper relation to each other. Wind instruments played by the mouth are tuned by adjusting the length of the tube to one particular note; and after that the just intonation to a great extent depends upon the construction of the instrument, subject of course to certain artificial alterations made by varying the pressure of wind, or altering the length of the vibrating column of air by the insertion of the hand, &c.

String instruments of the violin, guitar, and pianoforte class are tuned by altering the tension of the strings at the end where they are carried round a moveable peg. In the first of these three instruments, after the strings or open notes have been tuned, true intonation depends on the correct *ear* and mechanical skill of the former; in the second class the position of the *frets* determine the pitch throughout. In the pianoforte and the organ, the intonation is entirely out of the control of the player, and owing to the large number of octaves in their compass certain notes are first tuned to the system of temperament adopted, and from these the whole instrument is tuned. These sounds first adjusted are called *bearings.* But the whole subject of tuning these two instruments is so intimately connected with Temperament that the reader is referred to that article.

Bells are tuned by paring off a portion of the inner side of the sound-bow, thus altering the relation of diameter to thickness.

Musical glasses can be altered in pitch by pouring a liquid into them. Drums are tuned by tightening or relaxing their parchments.

Reeds in an organ or harmonium can be tuned by altering the length of the part allowed to vibrate, also by varying their thickness or breadth.

Organ flue-pipes are tuned by opening or closing the orifice, a process which has practically the same effect as shortening or lengthening the column of vibrating air.

Tuning hammer. An instrument employed for tuning pianofortes or harps. It is in shape like a common hammer, but has a head of wood instead of iron and a shank of iron instead of wood. In the bottom end of the shank is a square or oblong hole made to fit the tops of the pegs round which the strings of the instrument are twisted; these pegs being turned to the right or left, tighten or loosen the strings as needed. The old name for the tuning hammer was *wrest*.

Tuono (*It.*) (1) Body of tone, sound. (2) A tune.

Tuono ecclesiastico (*It.*) [Accentus ecclesiasticus.]

Turbæ (*Lat.*) The chorus part or voice of the multitude in a Passion-Music.

Turca (*It.*) Turkish; *alla turca*, in the Turkish style.

Turkish Music, *or* **Janitscharenmusik.** Noisy music produced solely by instruments of percussion such as cymbals, gongs, &c.

Turn. An ornament in music formed by taking the adjoining notes above or below the principal note, according to the position of that note in the diatonic scale. The turn indicated by the sign ~ must be performed in the time the note it alters would occupy without it. Thus the common turn, which takes a *higher* note first in the change:

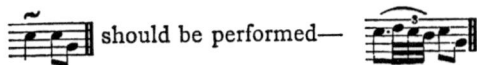

should be performed—

The back-turn taking a lower note first in the change:

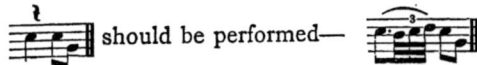

should be performed—

When the turn appears over a note followed by a rising or a falling interval:

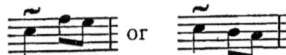

or

The turn should consist of four notes besides the principal:

or in the case of the back-turn, written thus:

it should be performed:

If it is desired to alter the note above or below a turn, that is to say, to change the character as it appears in the scale, the following signs are used. The position of a sharp or flat underneath the sign of the turn shows whether the note above or below is to be sharpened or flattened; the dash through the turn always signifying a sharpened note.

Performed:

A turn over a note in the unaccented part of the bar is usually performed with the changed note first.

Written.   Played.

Turr. A Burmese violin with three strings.

Tutta (*It.*) All, the whole; *tutta forza*, the full power or force; *tutto arco*, the whole length of the bow.

Tutte corde (*It.*) Without the use of the dampers in pianoforte-playing.

Tutti (*It.*) All. Every performer to take part in the execution of the passage or movement.

Tuyau d'orgue (*Fr.*) An organ pipe.

Tuyaux à anche (*Fr.*) Reed pipes.

Tuyaux à bouche (*Fr.*) Open pipes.

Twelfth. (1) An interval of twelve diatonic degrees, the replicate of the fifth. (2) An organ stop tuned twelve notes above the diapasons.

Tympani. [Timpani.]

Tympanon. A dulcimer.

Tyro. A learner or beginner in music or any other science.

Tyrolienne. (1) A song accompanied with dancing. Rossini's "Toi que l'oiseau," in the third act of *Guillaume Tell*, is the earliest specimen of a Tyrolienne other than the popular *Volkslieder*. (2) Popular songs or melodies in which the jodl, *q.v.*, is freely used.

Tzetze. An Abyssinian instrument of the guitar kind, formed of a long carved neck attached to a gourd. It has frets and one string usually made of the tough fibre of a palm-tree.

U.

U.C. Abb. of *una corda*. [A una corda.]

Uebelklang
Uebellaut } (*Ger.*) Discord, cacophony.

Uebereinstimmung (*Ger.*) Consonance, harmony.

Uebergang (*Ger.*) Passage, transition.

Uebermässig (*Ger.*) Augmented.

Uebung (*Ger.*) An exercise.

Ugab, Huggab, Agub (*Heb.*) The first wind instrument mentioned in the Bible, rendered *organ* in the authorized version, "such as handle the harp and the organ" (Gen. iv., 21.) In the Septuagint it is sometimes translated by *cithara*, sometimes by *psalm*, sometimes by *organ*. It is probable that in its earliest form the *ugab* was nothing more than pans-pipes or a syrinx, but that it gradually developed into a more important instrument. In Psalm cl. it may be possibly used in a poetical sense of all wind instruments, as *minnim* is of string instruments. "Praise Him upon the strings (minnim) and pipe (ugab)."

Uguale (*It.*) Equal, like, similar, *Canone a tre voci uguali*, a canon for three equal voices.

Ugualmente (*It.*) Equally, alike, similarly.

Umana,
Umano } (*It.*) Human; as, *voce umana*, the human voice.

Umfang (*Ger.*) Compass, extent; as *Umfang der Stimme*, compass of the voice.

Umkehrung (*Ger.*) Inversion.

Unharmonischer Querstand (*Ger.*) [False relation.]

Un
Una
Uno } (*It.*) One; as, *Una corda*, one string; *Una volta*, once, &c.

Unca (*Lat.*) A quaver.

Uncoupled. A direction that the manual or pedal is to be detached from the row to which it was coupled. [Organ.]

Unda maris. Lit. *Wave of the sea.* A name given to the "Vox Angelica" Organ-stop, because of its wavy undulating tone. [Vox Angelica.]

Undecima (*Lat.*) An eleventh.

Undecimole. A group of eleven notes to be played in the time of eight of the same name.

Undersong. [Burden.]

Undertones. [Acoustics, § 19.]

Undulazione (*It.*) The tremulous sound produced by violinists by the vibratory pressure of the finger upon the strings.

Unequal Temperament. [Temperament.] [Wolf.]

Unequal Voices. Voices of mixed qualities, those of women combined with those of men. [Equal Voices.]

Unessentials. Notes not forming a necessary part of the harmony. Passing, auxiliary, or ornamental notes.

Ungerader Takt (*Ger.*) Triple time.

Unison. (1) Having the same number of vibrations; homophonous. (2) Music *in octaves* for mixed voices or instruments.

Unisoni (*It.*) Unisons; two or more parts playing in unison with each other, or at the octave, according to the character of the instrument or voice.

Unisono (*It.*)
Unisonous (*Eng.*) } In unison, or in octaves.
Unisonus (*Lat.*)

Unitamente (*It.*) Together, unitedly.

Uno a uno (*It.*) One by one, severally.

Un peu plus lent (*Fr.*) A little more slow.

Un pochettino,
Un pochino } (*It.*) A little, a very little; as, *Un pochino più mosso*, a very little more lively.

Un poco (*It.*) A little; as, *Un poco allegro*, rather quick; *un poco più*, a little more; *un poco ritenuto*, held back a little, slightly retarded.

Unterbass (*Ger.*) A double-bass.

Unterdominant (*Ger.*) Subdominant. *Unterdominant-akkord*, the chord of the subdominant.

Unterhalbton (*Ger.*) The leading note.

Unterleitton (*Ger.*) The dominant seventh.

Untersatz (*Ger.*) Sub-bass.

Unterstimme (*Ger.*) An under-part.

Upbeat. The beat of a bar at which the hand is raised. An unaccented beat. [Accent.] [Arsis.] [Metre.]

Upbow. [Bowing.]

Uppatura (*Med. Lat.*) A song of a profane character, forbidden to be sung in church by the Constitution of the Carmelite order. [Motet.]

Urh-heen. The Chinese fiddle. [Violin.]

Ut. [Aretinian syllables.] [Notation.]

Ut bémol (*Fr.*) The note C flat.

Ut dièse (*Fr.*) The note C sharp. *Ut dièse mineur*. The key of C sharp minor.

Utriculariæ. Tibiæ utriculariæ. [Bagpipe.]

Ut supra (*Lat.*) As above, as before. *Gloria Patri ut supra*. The Gloria as before.

Uvula. [Larynx.]

V.

V. Abb. of *verte, violino, violini, voce, voci, volta, volti, &c.*

Va. Abb. of *viola.*

Va (*It.*) Go on; as *va crescendo*, go on increasing the power; *va rallentando*, go on dragging the time.

Vacillando (*It.*) Wavering, uncertain as regards the time or tone.

Vago (*It.*) With a vague, indefinite expression.

Valce (*It.*), **Valse** (*Fr.*) Waltz.

Valeur (*Fr.*), **Valore** (*It.*) The value, worth, or length of a note.

Valse à deux temps (*Fr.*) A form of waltz, now most commonly danced, in which two steps are made to each measure of three beats.

Vamp. To improvise an accompaniment.

Variamente (*It.*) In a varied manner.

Variations, Variationen (*Ger.*) **Variazioni** (*It.*) Certain modifications with regard to the time, tune, and harmony of a theme proposed originally in a simple form. At one period it was considered indispensable that the subject chosen should be heard unchanged through all the variations, that no alteration should be made either in the relation, length, or melodic progression of the sounds. This only permitted the employment of the several species of counterpoint as variations. Afterwards a ground bass was selected, or written, in which more freedom and variety was attainable. Subsequently composers altered their melodies by the addition of florid passages, but not to such an extent as to make the subject not easily recognisable. There are many instances in the works of most of the classical writers in which this artifice is successfully employed. The old composers called their variations " Doubles." Modern transcriptions are often nothing more than elaborate variations of a theme.

Variato (*It.*), **Varié** (*Fr.*) Varied, changed, altered, with variations.

Vaudeville (*Fr.*) A term originally applied to a country song of like kind with those written by Oliver Basselin, of the valleys of Vaux de Vire in Normandy, in the fifteenth century. These songs, which were satirical, had for their subjects love, drinking, and passing events. They became very popular, and were spread all over France under the name of *Lais des Vaux de Vire.* The peculiarity of their character lived after their origin was forgotten, and plays, interspersed with songs of this description, came to be called Vaudevilles, and occasionally *Virelais.* The songs in Vaudevilles should form an integral portion of the plot or subject.

The following melody of a Vaudeville is from the " Second livre de Pièces de Viole avec la Basse continue. Composé par Mons. De Caix D'Hervelois." Paris, c. 1719.

VAUDEVILLE GAVOTTE.

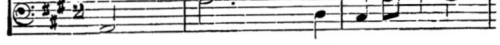

Veemente (*It.*) Vehement, forcible.

Veemenza, con (*It.*) With vehemence, force.

Velato, Velata (*It.*) Veiled, as *voce velata*, a voice the tone of which is not clear.

Vellutata, Vellutato (*It.*) From *velluta*, velvet. In a soft, smooth, velvety manner.

Veloce (*It.*) Rapid, swift.

Velocissimamente (*It.*) Very swiftly

Velocissimente (*It.*) Swiftly.

Velocità, con (*It.*) With swiftness, rapidity.

Velocity of sound. [Acoustics § 5.]

Ventil (*Ger.*), **Ventile** (*It.*) (1) A valve, by means of which brass tubes may be made to sound the semitones and tones between the natural open harmonics. [Metal wind instruments.] (2) A mechanical contrivance on an organ for the purpose of cutting off the wind from a particular sound-board.

Venusto (*It.*) Beautiful, graceful, fine.

Veränderungen (*Ger.*) (1) Variations. (2) The mechanical arrangement by which "stops" on a harpsichord were moved in and out.

Verbindung (*Ger.*) Combination, union, connection, binding.

Vergnügt (*Ger.*) Pleasantly.

Verhallend (*Ger.*) Dying away, *decrescendo.*

Verhältniss (*Ger.*) Proportion ; *ratio.*

Verilay (*Fr.*) [Vaudeville.]

Vermindert (*Ger.*) Diminished ; as *Verminderter dreiklang,* diminished triad.

Verschiebung (*Ger.*) The soft pedal of a pianoforte ; *mit Verschiebung, Una corda.*

Verse. (1) Those portions of an anthem or service intended to be sung by a single voice to a part. [Anthem.] (2) A separate stanza of a song or a ballad. (3) A verse anthem is one which begins with soli portions as opposed to a full anthem, which commences with a chorus.

Versette (*Ger.*) Short pieces for the organ intended as preludes or voluntaries.

Versetzen (*Ger.*) To transpose.

Versetzungszeichen (*Ger.*) Accidentals.

Verspätung (*Ger.*) Retardation, delay.

Verstimmt (*Ger.*) Out of tune.

Versus Fescennini (*Lat.*) Nuptial songs, so-called because they were first used by the people of Fescennia in Etruria. From this kind of poetry arose the Epithalamium, a needful refinement upon the Fescenninian verses.

Vertatur, Verte (*Lat.*) Turn over.

Verwandt (*Ger.*) Related, as *Verwandte tonarten,* related keys.

Verwechselung (*Ger.*) Changing, altering. as to tone, time, key.

Verweilend (*Ger.*) Delaying, *rallentando.*

Verwerfung (*Ger.*) Transposing.

Verzierungen (*Ger.*) Ornaments, decorations, embellishments.

Verzögerung (*Ger.*) Retardation.

Vezzosamente (*It.*) Tenderly, softly, gracefully.

Vezzoso (*It.*) Tender, sweet, graceful.

Vibrante (*It.*) Vibrating, tremulous.

Vibrato (*It.*) A tremulous quality of tone, as opposed to a pure equal production.

Vibration. [Acoustics § 3.]

Vicar choral. [Lay vicar.]

Vide (*Fr.*), **Vido** (*It.*) Open. [Vuide.]

Viel (*Ger.*) Much ; as, *Mit vielem Tone,* with much tone.

Vielle (*Fr.*) The hurdy-gurdy.

Vielstimmig (*Ger.*) For many voices.

Vierfach (*Ger.*) Four-fold ; having four ranks of pipes. [Organ.]

Viergesang (*Ger.*) Song for four parts.

Vierspiel (*Ger.*) A composition in four parts. Quartet.

Vierstimmig (*Ger.*) For four voices of instruments, or in four parts.

Vierstück (*Ger.*) A piece for four players, a quartet.

Viertelnote (*Ger.*) Quarter note, a crotchet, the fourth part of a semibreve.

Viertheilston (*Ger.*) A quarter tone, half a semitone.

Viervierteltakt (*Ger.*) Duple time of four crotchets in a bar.

Vierzweiteltakt (*Ger.*) Duple time of four minims in a bar.

Vif (*Fr.*) Lively, brisk, quick.

Vigorosamente (*It.*) Vigorously.

Vigoroso (*It.*) Vigorous, bold, forcible.

Vihuela (*Sp.*) A simple kind of guitar.

Villancico (*Sp.*) A species of song of two or more stanzas, each containing seven lines, belonging to the poetry of the 15th century, which, like the madrigal, is of an epigrammatic form—formerly very popular in Spain. The composers of that country employed the tunes of many of these songs as themes for counterpoint in church motets. Those motets which are sung during high mass on Christmas-eve are always called Villancicos.

Villanella (*It.*) A rustic dance accompanied with singing. The melody was usually lively and the rhythm well marked. The words, when any were used, were commonplace epigrams, and were also called madrigals and ballets. The villanella or villotte, and villancico were the precursors of the madrigal. When the title *villanella* began to be used to describe compositions in rustic style, not intended for voices, those compositions were embellished with variations upon the original subject.

Villotte (*It.*) The name given to the first secular pieces in harmony after the rules of counterpoint were fixed. Every so-called " license " in harmony was used in this kind of composition ; whereas church music could only be written according to strict rules; therefore, secular pieces were called *vile* or *rustic,* as being more fitted for clownish than for courtiers' ears. Morley, speaking of the villanella says, " many perfect chords of one kind, nay, even disallowances may be taken at pleasure, uniting a clownish music to a clownish matter." [Villanella, Villancico, Madrigal.]

Vina. [Bina.]

Viol. A stringed instrument, a little larger in shape than the violin; it was furnished in England with five or six strings, had a fretted finger-board and was played with a bow. The viol was called in mediæval Latin, vitula, and is found depicted in MSS. as early as the 11th century. In France, Germany, and Italy the number of the strings varied between three and six. It is supposed that they were tuned in fourths and thirds. A chest of viols consisted of six instruments of various sizes, the smaller ones were called in England, *treble*, the next *mean*, and the larger *bass* viols. In Germany the names were Bratsche, Schultergeige, and Bassgeige, and in Italy viol di braccio and viol da gamba were the names given to distinguish the several sizes.

Viola (*It.*) *Bratsche* (*Ger.*) The tenor violin. It has four strings, tuned thus:

The two lowest are covered strings. Music for this instrument is written in the *alto* clef, whence it is sometimes called *alto viola*.

Viola di Bardone (*It.*) An instrument of the violin kind, strung with six or seven catgut strings tuned in the following manner:

Beneath the gut were metal strings, varying in number from sixteen to as many as forty-four, arranged in a diatonic order from

as the lowest tone. The sympathetic strings were occasionally plucked with the left hand in playing. The instrument is now obsolete, but was in use in the time of Haydn, who at the request of Prince Esterhazy composed upwards of sixty pieces for it. It is also called *viola di fagotto*, and *baryton*.

Viola Pomposa (*It.*) A species of *viol da gamba*, invented by John Sebastian Bach. It had five strings, the four lower strings were tuned like the violoncello, in fifths, and the fifth string was tuned to E, by means of which greater facility in the execution of extended passages was possible. Improved skill on the part of violoncello players made the *viola pomposa* unnecessary.

Viol da Gamba (*It.*) One of the larger instruments among a chest of viols. It received its name from being held within the knees of the performer. It had a fretted finger-board and six strings, tuned thus:

It was particularly adapted to the performance of broken harmony and extended chords.

Viol d'amore (*It.*) An obsolete instrument of the violin family. In addition to catgut strings, metal strings were placed under the finger-board, which, by the production of sympathetic sound, gave a peculiar quality of tone to the instrument.

The tuning varied according to the piece to be played, the "accordatura" being often indicated at the commencement of the copy which was played from, but the most usual method of tuning was the following:

Meyerbeer has written an obbligato part for this instrument in the first act of the "Huguenots."

Violetta. A little viol.

Violetta Marina (*It.*) A stringed instrument similar in tone to the viol d'amour. It was called *violetta piccola*, and by the French *Haute-contre*.

Violin. Discantgeige (*Ger.*) Violon (*Fr.*) Fiddle (*Eng.*) The most familiar of all stringed instruments played with a bow. It is somewhat smaller than the old viol, as its name implies, violin being a diminutive of viol. Like the rest of the family it represents, it consists of a wooden chest of peculiar form, made of two curved surfaces, called the back and the belly, united by sides, and with a hollow half-way in the length. A neck at one end has a finger-board, over which the four strings pass, being fastened at one end of the chest or body to a tail-piece, and kept in tune and position by a series of pegs at the end of the neck. The strings are raised above the belly by the bridge. In the belly are two holes, called the *f* holes from their similarity to the shape of that letter. The sound is produced by drawing a bow of horse-hair charged with rosin across the strings, which are tuned in fifths:—

the changes of pitch being gained by "stopping" the strings with the fingers of the left hand against the finger-board, thus shortening the vibrating portion of the string. The harmonics of the violin are very telling in quality, and are produced by touching the strings lightly instead of pressing them upon the finger-board. The *sordino* or *mute*, placed upon the bridge, produces a peculiar modification of tone, and a good effect is gained by plucking the strings, as in playing a guitar. [Pizzicato.]

The compass of the violin ranges between :—

with every intermediate shade of sound. The extreme high notes are rarely used, as they are harsh and shrill. The violin is capable of producing a limited harmony by means of double stops and bowing in "arpeggio," while as to power of expression and execution there is no other instrument which can be compared to it. It has a wide range of sounds, to which any degree of loudness or softness, *staccato* or *legato*, can be given. This variety of tone, added to the capability of being played a great length of time with less fatigue than any other orchestral instrument, renders it invaluable, either for solos or combinations. The violin or string quartet, as it is called, that is to say, 1st and 2nd violins, viola, and violoncello, form an indispensable portion of a score; while the same combination, used for quartets, is productive of the highest pleasure when well and skilfully managed.

Stringed instruments played with a bow are in use among many Eastern nations, the form of the instrument so played varying considerably. The number of strings and the form of the bow also differ. The *Urh-heen*, or

CHINESE URH-HEEN.

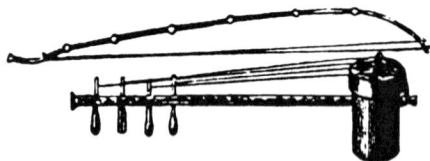

Chinese fiddle, has no finger-board. There are usually only two strings, but some specimens have as many as four. The bow is twisted under the strings, and it is said that the Chinese fiddlers have to practise assiduously in order to produce the tone properly from strings so placed. The resonance body of the Urh-heen is covered with snake-skin.

The "Burmese Thro, Theyaou, or Tarau," has three strings of silk, and although the tone is nasal, it is not of unpleasant quality.

BURMESE THRO OR TARAU.

The "Kermangeh," another bowed instrument, is in use among Mohammedan nations.

It is usually furnished with three strings of gut, and there are two sound-holes beside the bridge. The *Kermangeh* is made in several sizes, like the European violin family. The larger instruments are supported on an iron peg.

KERMANGEH.

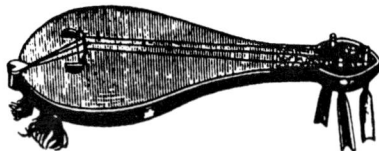

The Hindu "Chikarah" is supposed by some to be the modern representative of the ancient *Ravanastron*, the oldest form of fiddle.

CHIKARAH.

The "Rebab" of Egypt has one string of horse-hair stretched over a resonance-body of skin. In Egypt it is used to accompany the recitations of the storytellers and the motions of the dancers.

REBAB.

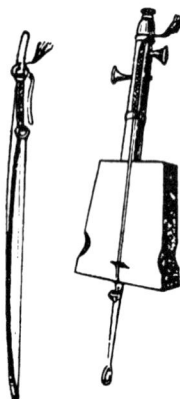

It is sometimes made in shape like the "Kermangeh," and furnished with three or even more strings. Whatever the form may be, it is a favourite with the country-people who use it. It is also called *rabel* or *arrabel*. When it was introduced into Europe it retained its Eastern name, with certain modifications; *rebebe, reberbe, rubebe, rubeck, rebec; but it was altered in shape.* The old English *jig, jegg,* or *gig,* as it is variously spelt, was also called *rebec,* the " jocund rebeck " mentioned by Milton and other poets; it had three strings like its Eastern prototype, the rebab.

Modern writers find the origin of the violin in the above-mentioned Indian *Ravanastron*, an instrument still existing, and used by the poor Buddhist begging monks. From the Ravanastron descends the rebab, kermangeh, whence comes the Scandinavian guddok, the ancestor of the Welch and Anglo-Saxon crwth. From the crwth, the fithele, vitula, or viol descended, and from the viol the violin, the whole progress representing a period of nearly 5,000 years in history. The violin has not altered its form since the 16th century, many instruments of that time being still in actual use. One of the earliest makers of violins was Gaspar di Salo, in Lombardy, 1560-1610.

In Cremona, during the 17th century, the Amati family, Andrew, his sons Jerome and Antonio, and Nicolo the son of the latter, were famous makers of violins. Antonio Straduarius, also of Cremona, pupil of Nicolo Amati, surpassed, if possible, the productions of the Amatis, and the reputation of Cremona for violins was maintained by Guarnérius and Rugerio. The Tyrolese makers, Jacobus Stainer and Matthew Klotz (and his sons) became as famous as the Italians for violin-making. Villáume, of Paris, is the most celebrated modern maker.

Violin clef. The G clef placed upon the first line of the stave.

In this position it is known as the *French violin clef.*

Violino principale (*It.*) Solo violin, or leader. *Violino primo*, first violin. *Violino secondo*, second violin. *Violino ripieno*, a violin part required only to fill in and strengthen the *tutti*.

Violin-steg (*Ger.*) The bridge of a violin.

Violon (*Fr.*) The violin; in Germany the same word is used for the double bass.

Violoncello (*It.*) The little *violone*. When the violoncello supplanted the bass viol or the viol di gamba in the early part of the eighteenth century, many of the other instruments were so altered by having the number of strings reduced, as to make them playable like the violoncello. Excepting occasionally, when the exigences of an old score demand the use of a viol di gamba, no other small bass stringed instrument is employed in the orchestra, as the variety of tone it is capable of—almost equal in resource to the violin—renders the use of others unnecessary. The violoncello is strung with four gut strings, the lower two covered with silver wire; all are tuned a fifth apart.

The compass usually employed extends between

though soloists play an octave higher, with all the intermediate semitones. Music for it is written in the bass clef up to

but the C clef, or sometimes the G clef, is employed for the higher notes of the scale.

The tone of the violoncello is peculiarly sympathetic, almost tearful in the higher register, and these notes are frequently employed with great effect as well in solos as in orchestral music. In the band the violoncello is coupled with the double-bass, and the union of the tones of the two instruments is wonderfully telling and solid. Mendelssohn has used the double-bass without the violoncello in *Elijah*, and the effect is stormy and uncertain, while the violoncello without the double-bass is light and expressive of unrest. The violoncello is capable of giving rapid passages with more clearness than the double-bass, and so it is frequently found that composers give essential notes to the larger, and intermediate notes to the smaller of the two orchestral basses.

The division of the two parts in this fashion was at one time a matter of necessity, as double-bass players were not sufficiently skilful to be able to perform such passages, but at the present time there is scarcely a double-bass player who is not able to take such divisions with ease.

In addition to the single notes of its scale the violoncello can give double notes, seconds, thirds, fifths, sixths, sevenths, and octaves in nearly every key between the two notes

Seconds, thirds, and fourths can be made when the upper note is an open string, as

Fifths, sixths, and sevenths when the lower note is stationary:

Violone (*It.*) The double bass.

Virelay (*Fr.*) [Vaudeville.]

Virginal. A stringed instrument played by means of a keyboard, like the modern pianoforte. It was in form like a box, or desk of wood without legs or supports, and was usually placed upon a table or stand. The strings were of metal, one for each note, and the sound was made by means of pieces of quill, whalebone, leather, or occasionally elastic metal, attached to slips of wood called "jacks," which were provided with metal springs. The compass was about three octaves. This title has been by some supposed to have originated as a compliment to Queen Elizabeth, who was an expert performer upon the instrument; but as the word was in use before her birth this supposition is not valuable. Others say that the name was applied because of the smallness and delicacy of its tone, as it was and is considered proper for a woman "to speak small." It is more likely to have received its name from the word "virgæ." The virginal, also called spinet, from the quills with which the string was sounded, was the precursor of the harpsichord, now superseded by the pianoforte. [Dulcimer, Spinet, Pianoforte.]

Virgula (*Lat.*) (1) The stem or tail of a note. (2) A neume.

Virtuoso (*It.*), **Virtuose** (*Ger.*) A skilled performer on some particular instrument, specially the violin. The term was formerly applied to an amateur, "one who feels delight in, and possesses a taste for, the musical science."

Vista (*It.*) Sight; as, *a prima vista*, at first sight.

Vistamente, Vitamente (*It.*) Briskly, quickly, rapidly, with life.

Vivace, Vivacemente (*It.*) Lively, quickly, sprightly.

Vivacetto (*It.*) Rather lively.

Vivacezza, Vivacità (*It.*) Liveliness, vivacity.

Vivacissimo (*It.*) Very lively.

Vivamente (*It.*) Lively, briskly.

Vive (*Fr.*) Brisk, quick, lively.

Vivente (*It.*) Animated, lively.

Vivezza, con (*It.*) With life, liveliness.

Vivido (*It.*) Brisk, lively.

Vivo (*It.*) Alive, brisk, lively, animated.

Vocal. (1) For, or by the voice; music intended to be sung. (2) Compositions so written as to be easy and effective for the voice. (3) The "singing" quality of tone obtained from an instrument.

Vocale (*It.*) Belonging to the voice.

Vocalezzo (*It.*) An exercise for the voice.

Vocalisation. (1) Control of the voice and vocal sounds. (2) Method of producing and phrasing notes with the voice.

Vocalizzi (*It.*) Vocal exercises, solfeggi.

Vocal Score. [Score.]

Voce (*It.*) The voice; as, *Voce di camera*, literally, a voice for the chamber, applied to a voice of small quality, better fitted to the limited area of a private room than for a public concert room. *Voce di gola*, a guttural or throaty voice; *Voce di petto*, the chest voice, the lower register of the voice; *Voce di testa*, the head voice, the upper range of the voice; sometimes the falsetto is so termed. *Voce sola*, the voice alone, unaccompanied.

Vogelflöte (*Ger.*) A bird-call, flageolet, or whistle. Mozart employs one in the score of the *Zauberflöte*.

Vogelpfeife (*Ger.*) [Vogelflöte.]

Vogelgesang (*Ger.*) A musical instrument composed of a series of small pipes standing in water, through which the wind had to pass. A *merula*.

Voglia (*It.*) Ardour, desire, longing.

Voice. Voices may be arranged in six orders or classes, according to gravity or acuteness, viz.:—The bass, baritone, tenor, alto, or contralto, mezzo-soprano and soprano. The first three are the natural voices of men and the second three those of women. The compass or range of notes is different in each voice, but it is not compass alone which determines the class to which any voice may belong, as very frequently a baritone quality of voice is limited to the range of a bass, and a tenor quality to the compass of a baritone. It is almost impossible to describe in words the general character of the several voices, it must be sufficient to give the number of notes they are capable of using.

The part for the bass voice is written in the F clef and its most effective notes are those indicated in the following by crotchets, though for solo purposes the notes shown by the minims are often used.

The baritone voice has a compass between

its quality and character best fit it for solo singing. Its part is now written in the bass or F clef, on the fourth line, though there are instances, as, for example, in Dr. Cooke's setting of Collins' "Ode to the Passions," where the baritone clef, that is to say, the F clef on the third line, is used for the voice.

The compass of the tenor voice is between

The most serviceable notes being those between the two crotchets. Its part is written in the C clef upon the fourth line. The alto voice is an artificial and not a real voice. It is made by cultivating the falsetto notes instead of the true chest voice. The C clef is also used for this voice, but it is placed upon the third line, and the compass employed is between the notes:

All the tones between the two crotchets are produced from the chest, the D generally dividing the two qualities of chest and falsetto, the point of junction being known as "the break."

The contralto voice is of the lowest tone in female voices, and nearly corresponds in range to the bass voice in men, only, the sounds produced are an octave higher. Music is written for it in both the alto and treble clefs, more frequently the latter. Its range is between

The mezzo-soprano, often confounded with the contralto voice, has a compass of an octave and a fifth or sixth.

It is more flexible than the contralto, though less brilliant in tone than the soprano voice,

which latter has effective and useful notes between

and even beyond these limits, in exceptional cases.

Voicing. The regulation of the tone and power of an organ-pipe. [Organ.]

Voix (*Fr.*) The voice.

Voix céleste (*Fr.*) [Vox Angelica.]

Volante (*It.*) Flying, applied to the execution of a rapid series of notes, either in singing or playing.

Volata (*It.*) A run, or division; a light and rapid series of notes.

Volkslied (*Ger.*) A popular song. [Lied.]

Voll (*Ger.*) Full; as, *Vollgesang*, with the full chorus; *mit vollem Werk*, with the full power.

Vollstimmig (*Ger.*) Full-voiced, full-toned.

Vollstimmigkeit (*Ger.*) Fulness of tone.

Volonté (*Fr.*) Will, pleasure, *à volonté*, at will.

Volta (*It.*) Turn, or time; as, *Una volta*, once; *due volte*, twice; *prima volta*, first time; *seconda volta*, second time.

Volta (*It.* and *Fr.*) An old dance. [Lavolta.]

Volteggiando (*It.*) Crossing the hands in pianoforte-playing.

Volteggiare (*It.*) To cross the hands.

Volti (*It.*) Turn; as, *Volti subito*, or abbreviated, *v.s.*; turn quickly.

Volume. A term applied to the power and quality of the tone of a voice or instrument, or of a combination of sounds.

Voluntary. An organ solo played before, during, or after any office of the Church; hence, called respectively introductory, middle, or concluding. Such solos were formerly, and are often now unpremeditated, or improvisations, as the name *Voluntary* seems to imply. Towards the end of the last century the style of the music performed had greatly degenerated; the ordinary voluntary consisted of running passages played by the right hand on a cornet-stop or flute-stop, while the left hand sustained a few soft chords by way of accompaniment. The protests of clergy and sound musicians against such performances had not such a powerful influence in eradicating them as the general introduction into this country of complete sets of pedal-keys, and the consequent study of John Sebastian Bach's compositions for the organ. Arrangements from instrumental and orchestral works are at the present time largely used as voluntaries, and although it must be said in their favour that they bring the themes of great masters under the notice of many who would not otherwise hear them, yet it is to be feared that they tend to discourage the composition of genuine organ-music, and foster the mischievous notion that the organ is intended to be an imitation of a full band.

The custom of performing voluntaries and interludes in Church was at one time carried to an absurd extent. Not only was the Psalm-tune introduced with a "very pretty flourish," but interludes were played between each line of the tune, whether the sense was complete or not. A specimen of the style of these performances may be seen in the following, from "The Psalmes set full for the Organ or Harpsicord as they are Plaid in Churches and Chappels in the maner given out, as also with their Interludes of great variety," by D. Purcell, c. 1700.

VOLUNTARY.
St. David's Tune given out.

Vorausnahme (*Ger.*) (1) Anticipation, *e.g.*:

(2) Preparation of a discord.

Vorbereitung (*Ger.*) Preparation of discords.

Vorgeiger (*Ger.*) Leader. First fiddle.

Vorgreifung, Vorgriff (*Ger.*) Anticipation.

Vorhalt (*Ger.*) (1) Syncopation. (2) Suspension.

Vorschlag (*Ger.*) Appoggiatura, beat.

Vorspiel (*Ger.*) Prelude, introductory movement, overture.

Vorspieler (*Ger.*) A leader or principal performer upon any instrument.

Vortänzer (*Ger.*) Leader of a dance.

Vorzeichnung (*Ger.*) Signature, *q.v.*

Vox (*Lat.*) (1) A voice; as *vox humana*, the human voice. (2) A part; as *tres voces*, three parts. (3) A sound; as, *inter aliquam vocem et octavam a se*, between any sound and its octave. (4) A key. [Acutæ claves.] (5) A theme; as, *vox antecedens*, the subject of a fugue.

Vox Angelica (*Lat.*) An organ stop consisting of two ranks of pipes of small scale and delicate quality of tone, one of which is tuned slightly sharp, in order to produce a wavy and tremulous sound. Called also *Voix céleste, unda maris*, &c.

Vox humana (*Lat.*) A reed stop in the organ intended to imitate the sounds of the human voice, consisting of a large reed and short tube; called *voce umana* in Italian, *voix humaine* in French, and also *anthropoglossa*.

V.S. Abb. for *volti subito*, and for *violino secondo*.

Vuide (*Fr.*) Open, as *corde vuide*, open string on the violin or violoncello.

W.

———◆———

Waits, _or_ Wayghtes. Originally certain minstrels or musical watchmen attached to the households of kings and other great persons, who paraded an assigned district sounding the hours at night. Until very recently, the Waits of the City of Westminster were regularly sworn before the "Court of Burgesses." In the "Liber niger domus regis" quoted in Rymer's "Fœdera," in an account of the musicians of the household of Edward IV., mention is made of " A Wayte, that nightely from Mychelmas, to Shreve Thorsdaye, pipe the watche within this courte fowere tymes ; in the somer nightes iij tymes, and makyth Bon Gayte at every chamber, doare, and offyce, as well for feare of pyckeres and pillers." Many cities and towns, both English and foreign, encouraged and licensed their " waits," Exeter among other places having a regular company as early as the year 1400.

In the "Coxcomb," by Beaumont and Fletcher, we find this allusion to a neglect of duty on the part of the watchmen.

" Where were the Watch the while? Good sober gentlemen
They were like careful members of the City,
Drawing in diligent ale and singing Catches."

The word was sometimes used to describe those who acted as the town musicians but who did not do duty as watchmen. It was also given to any company of performers when employed as serenaders.

The instruments used were a species of hautboys, called also shawms, and from their use " waits."

Dr. Busby in his Musical Dictionary [1800] says " The noun formerly signified hautboys, and (which is remarkable) has no singular number. From the instruments, its signification was, after a time, transferred to the performers themselves."

In _The famous history of Dr. Faustus_, the word is in a list of musical instruments. " Lastly was heard by Faustus all manner of instruments of music—as organs, clarigolds, lutes, viols, citterns, _Waits_, hornpipes, anomes, harps, and all manner of other instruments of music." Butler in his " Principles of Musick in singing and setting, with the two-fold use thereof [Ecclesiastical and Civil]" published in 1636, identifies waits

with the hautboy ; and Mr. H. Coleridge adds his testimony founded upon a passage in the romance of _Kynge Alysander and Sir Eglamore,_ that the waits were wind instruments.

A writer in the " Gentleman's Magazine," in 1756, describing the method of constituting freemen at Alnwick, says :—" They (the proposed freemen) are generally met by women dressed up with ribbons, bells, and garlands, who welcome them with dancing and singing, and are called _timber-waits,_ probably a corruption of _timbrel waits,_ players on timbrels."

At the present day the waits are detached bodies of impromptu musicians who make night hideous for three weeks before Christmas, with wretched performances of indifferent melodies. The waits or town musicians in Germany were called _Zinkenisten_— players of the _Zink,_ a coarse reed instrument.

Waldflute, Waldflöte, Waldpfeife (_Ger._) Forest flute. An organ stop of 4 ft. pitch consisting of open wood pipes. [Flute.] Waldquinte or Waldflötenquinte is a similar stop one fifth higher in pitch.

Waldhorn (_Ger._) A hunting horn.

Walnika, _or_ Walynka (_Russ._) A simple kind of bagpipe used among the Russian peasantry.

Waltz, Valse (_Fr._), **Valce** (_It._), **Walzer** (_Ger._) A dance said to have originated in Bohemia, now of almost universal adoption. The time is of triple measure in crotchets or quavers, and consists of eight or sixteen bar phrases. Modern waltz writers frequently add to the original dance-form an introduction and coda. The " Vienna " waltz is characterised by a rapid movement and strict unbroken time. Ländler are slower and more dignified than the waltz.

" Classical waltzes " are compositions in waltz-form intended for set pieces, not for dance tunes. In them, greater scope is given to the composer and performer than is compatible with the rhythm of the dance.

Walze (_Ger._) A roll. A symmetrical run or division, _e.g._ :

Wasserorgel (*Ger.*) Hydraulic organ.

Waves of sound. [Acoustics § 3.]

Wayghtes. [Waits.]

Wechselgesang (*Ger.*) Responsive or antiphonal song.

Wechselnote (*Ger.*) *Nota cambiata* (*It.*) In counterpoint, proceeding from a discord by a skip, *e.g.*:

Weich (*Ger.*) Minor.

Weight of wind. [Wind gauge.]

Weissenote (*Ger.*) White note; *nota bianca* (*It.*), a minim.

Weiteharmonie (*Ger.*) Dispersed harmony.

Welsh harp. [Harp.]

Wenig (*Ger.*) Little, as *ein Wenig stark*, rather loud.

Wesentlich (*Ger.*) Essential; as *wesentliche Septime*. Essential, or dominant seventh.

Wheel. The refrain or burden of a ballad.

"You must sing, *Down, a-down, an you call him a-downa.*

O, how the *wheel* becomes it!"—SHAKSPEARE.

Whiffler. A wand-bearer to head a procession. A fifer. "Whifflers originally headed armies or processions as fifers or pipers; in process of time the word *whifflers*, which had always been used in the sense of a *fifer*, came to signify any person who went before in a procession." Douce's "Illustrations of Shakspeare."

Whistle. (1) To make a musical sound with the lips and breath without using the vocal cords; the hollow of the mouth forming a resonance-box. The pitch of whistling is an octave higher than is generally supposed.

Whistle, *tin whistle, penny whistle.* The common wood or tin *flûte à bec* having six ventages. Its scale is:

when softly blown, which may of course be considerably extended upwards by increasing the pressure of wind, as in other flutes.

Whole note. A semibreve.

Wiederholung (*Ger.*) Repetition.

Wind band. (1) A military band. (2) The wind instruments of an orchestra.

Wind chest. Windlade (*Ger.*) [Organ.]

Wind gauge. [Organ, § 20.]

Wind trunk. [Organ.]

Wind instrument. A musical instrument whose sounds are produced by the breath of the player, or by means of a pair of bellows.

Wirbel (*Ger.*) (1) A peg of a violin, &c. (2) The stopper of a closed organ pipe. (3) *Wirbelstock*, a sound-board into which pegs are fixed. (4) *Wirbeltanz*, a whirling or circular dance.

Wolf. (1) The bad effect produced when playing in certain keys on an organ tuned to "unequal temperament." It is well known that tempered thirds are more distressing to the ear when heard from instruments of continuous-tone like the organ and harmonium than from pianofortes, &c. To obviate this difficulty, tuners of organs formerly made certain of their thirds untempered, that is, true to nature, in the ratio 4:5. Thus C♯ was made a true third above A; E♭ a true third below G; F♯ a true third to D; G♯ a true third to E; B♭ a true third below D, *e.g.*:

The common chords, therefore, of C, D, E♭, E, F, G, A, were perfectly in tune. But as will be seen from the above, the following would be heard for the chord of some remoter keys:

The divergence of these intervals from just pitch was painfully apparent. Modern organs are almost without exception tuned to equal temperament. [Temperament.]

(2) Some particular note often found on a violin, violoncello, or other stringed instrument, the intonation of which is not true.

Wood wind, *or* **Wood wind-band.** The flutes, oboes, clarinets, bassoons, and instruments of their nature, in an orchestra.

Wood stops. Organ stops, the pipes of which are of wood.

Wrist guide. [Chiroplast.]

Würde (*Ger.*) Dignity. *Mit Einfalt und Würde*, with simplicity and dignity.

X——Y——Z.

Xänorphica. A key-violin. An instrument somewhat like the tetrachordon, invented by Röllig (1761-1804), the sounds of which were produced by bows set in motion by a pedal, and acted upon by keys.

Xyloharmonica, Xylosistrum. An harmonicon consisting of graduated blocks of wood, struck with hammers acted upon by keys. Instruments of this class were made by Röllig (1761-1804), and by Uthe (1810).

Xylophone. [Gigelira.]

Xylorganum. [Gigelira.]

Yang Kin. A Chinese instrument furnished with brass strings, which are struck with two small hammers, like a dulcimer.

Yo. An Indian flute.

Yu. An interval of the Chinese scale. The ancient Chinese divided the octave into twelve equal parts, like the semitones of our chromatic scale, which were called *lu*. Their scale, as commonly used, consisted, however, of only five notes, which were called koung, chang, kio, tché, and yu, and which corresponded to our F, G, A, C, D; koung or F being considered to be the normal key.

Yue Kin. A guitar called by the Chinese, "Moon Guitar," [Guitar.]

Za. Formerly a *solfeggio* name for B♭.

Zambomba (*Sp.*) A common toy instrument in Spain, formed of an earthen pot tightly covered at its open end with a parchment, into which is inserted the stem of a reed. When the reed is rubbed up and down with rough or moist fingers, the vibrations are transferred to the air enclosed in the vessel, and a hollow rumbling sound is produced.

Zampogna (*It.*) A bagpipe in use among Italian peasants. The name is supposed to be a corruption of *Symphonia*. [Bagpipe.] A rough-toned reed instrument without a bag is also called Zampogna or Zampugna.

Zaner. [Zummarah.]

Zanze. A negro instrument. Known also by the names of mambira, ambira, marimba, ibeka, vissandschi, in different parts of Africa. It consists of a wooden box, on which a number of sonorous slips of wood or tongues of iron are fixed, in such a position as to admit of their being made to vibrate by pressing them down with the thumb or with a stick. The compass of two such instruments is given in Engel's "Music of the most ancient nations," pp. 12, 13.

Zapatadeo (*Sp.*) A dance in which the heel is struck violently on the ground to mark the rhythm.

Zarabanda. [Saraband.]

Zarge (*Ger.*) The sides of instruments like the violin or guitar.

Zart (*Ger.*) Soft, delicate; as, *mit zarten Stimmen*, with soft stops.

Zartflöte (*Ger.*) A delicate-toned flute.

Zärtlich (*Ger.*) Softly, delicately.

Zarzuelas (*Sp.*) A sort of drama, said to have been first produced at Zarzuela in the time of Philip IV.

Zeichen (*Ger.*) A musical sign, note, or character.

Zeitmass (*Ger.*) Time, measure.

Zèle (*Fr.*), Zelo (*It.*) Zeal, energy.

Zelosamente (*It.*) Zealously, ardently, earnestly.

Zeloso (*It.*) Zealous, energetic.

Zergliederung (*Ger.*) *Lit.* dissection. The reduction of a subject to its component figures in order to expand it by their repetition.

Zerstreut (*Ger.*) Dispersed, spread, open, as *Zerstreute Harmonie*, dispersed or open harmony.

Ziemlich (*Ger.*) Moderately, as *ziemlich langsam*, moderately slow.

Ziffern (*Ger.*) To cypher.

Ziganka. A dance popular among the Russian peasantry, similar in its figures to the English country-dance. The tune is lively, and the accompaniment is usually a "burden," or "bag-pipe bass," as shown in the following example:

ZIGANKA.

Zikrs. Religious dances of the dervishes in Egypt.

Zingaresca. A gipsy song or dance.

Zinke (*Ger.*) Cornetto curvo (*It.*) [Cornet, § 1.]

Zither (*Ger.*) Cither. A flat stringed instrument, placed upon a table or on the knees, having brass strings played with the thumb of the right hand, while the melody is brought more prominently out by the use of a plectrum.

Zögernd (*Ger.*) *Ritardando.*

Zoppa (*It.*) [Alla zoppa.]

Zufällige (*Ger.*) Accidentals.

Zufolo (*It.*) A flageolet or whistle.

Zug (*Ger.*) (1) A drawstop in an organ. (2) A pedal of a pianoforte. *Zugwerk*, the mechanical appliances of an instrument.

Zuklang (*Ger.*) Unison, consonance.

Zummarah. An Egyptian wind instrument. [Bassoon.]

Zunge (*Ger.*) (1) The tongue of a reed-pipe. (2) The metal tongue in the reed of a harmonium.

Zurna. A Turkish wind instrument, similar in character to the oboe.

Zurückhaltung (*Ger.*) Retardation.

Zusammengesetzt (*Ger.*) Compound. *Zusammengesetztakt*, compound time.

Zusammenklang, Zusammenlaut (*Ger.*) Harmony, consonance.

Zweifache (*Ger.*) (1) Two-fold. (2) Having two ranks of organ pipes. (3) Com-pound intervals. (4) A dance having alternate triple and duple time. It is also called *Zweifacher* and "*Grad und Ungrad.*"

ZWEIFACHER.

Played four times.

Zweigestrichen (*Ger.*) Having two strokes. [Pitch.] [Tablature.]

Zweiunddreissigtheilnote (*Ger.*) A demisemiquaver.

Zweivierteltakt (*Ger.*) Two-four time. $\frac{2}{4}$.

Zweizweiteltakt (*Ger.*) Two-two time. $\frac{2}{2}$.

Zwerchflöte (*Ger.*) The German flute. *Flauto traverso* (*It.*)

Zwerchpfeife (*Ger.*) The piccolo flute, or fife.

Zwischengesang (*Ger.*) An interpolated song.

Zwischenräume (*Ger.*) The spaces of the stave.

Zwischensatz (*Ger.*) An episode.

Zwischenspiel (*Ger.*) An interlude played between the verses of a hymn or choral.

Zwölfachteltakt (*Ger.*) Twelve-eight time.

Zymbel (*Ger.*) [Cymbal.]

Lightning Source UK Ltd.
Milton Keynes UK
27 December 2009

147928UK00001B/2/P

9 781108 000918